Happy Birthday, Aileen
Hope you'll enjoy this
with the wee ones on
wet days at the Cabin.
Much love
Yours aye,
Moira
X

BIRD

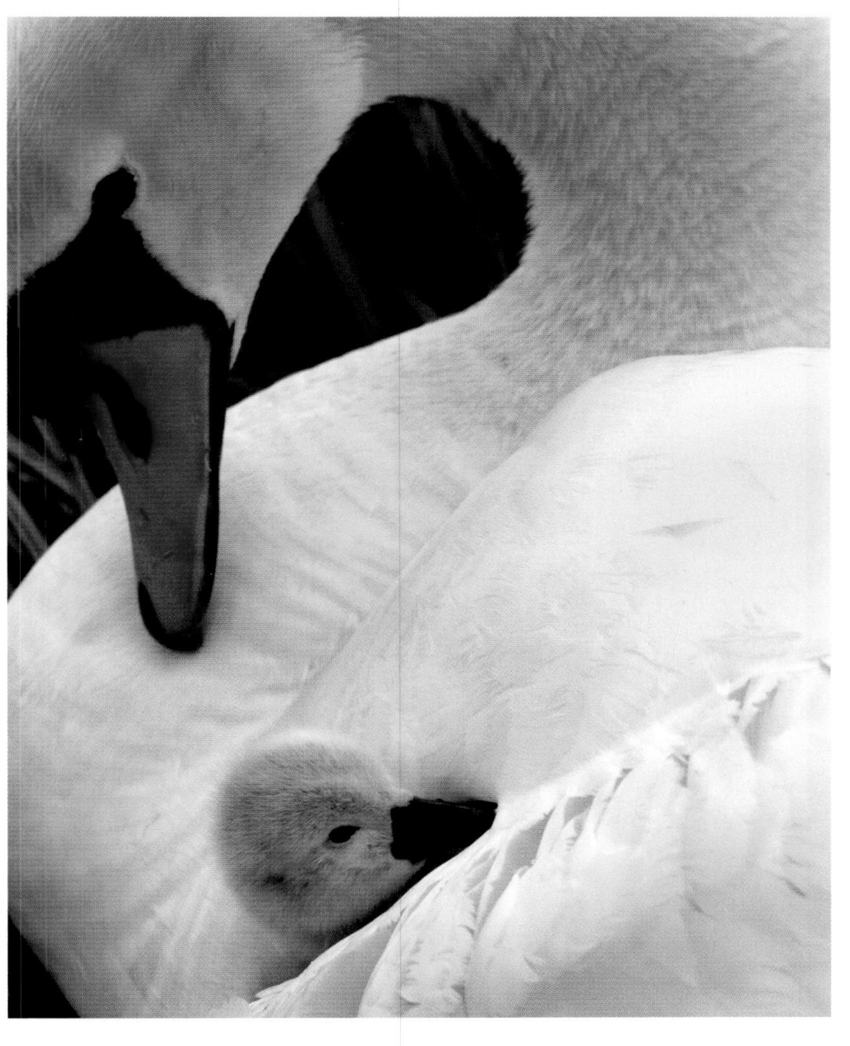

February 2009

BIRD

THE DEFINITIVE VISUAL GUIDE

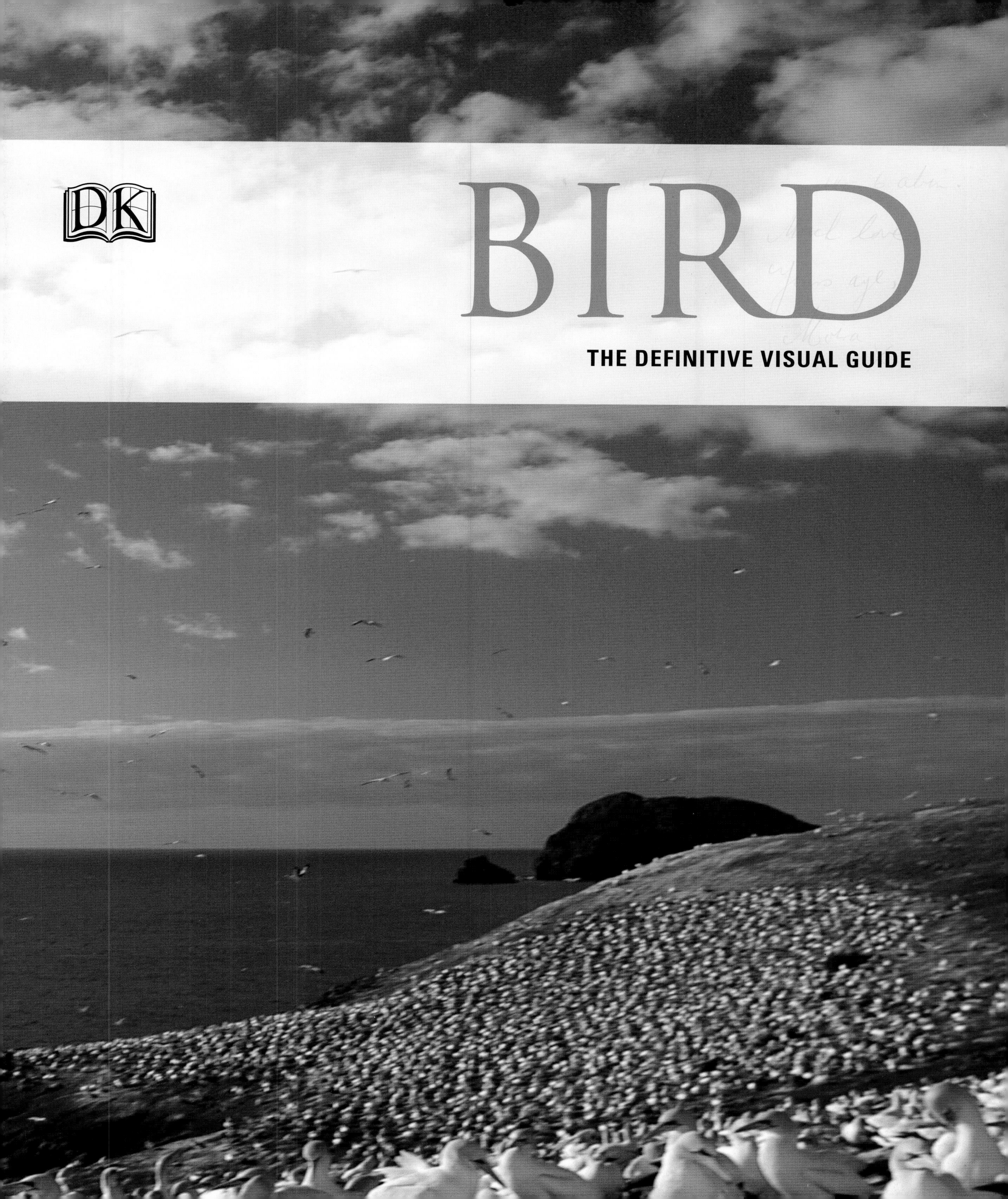

LONDON, NEW YORK, MELBOURNE, MUNICH AND DELHI

SENIOR EDITOR Peter Frances
MANAGING ART EDITOR Louise Dick
MANAGING EDITOR Sarah Larter
SENIOR MANAGING ART EDITOR Phil Ormerod
PRODUCTION CONTROLLERS Melanie Dowland, Shane Higgins
JACKET DESIGNER Duncan Turner
REFERENCE PUBLISHER Jonathan Metcalf
ART DIRECTOR Bryn Walls

SCHERMULY DESIGN COMPANY

PROJECT EDITOR Cathy Meeus
ART DIRECTOR Hugh Schermuly
EDITORS Gill Edden, Jo Godfrey Wood, Ben Hoare
DESIGNERS Steve Woosnam-Savage, Lee Riches

DK DELHI

DTP COORDINATORS Balwant Singh, Sunil Sharma
DTP DESIGNER Govind Mittal
EDITORS Saloni Talwar, Alicia Ingty, Aditi Ray, Ankush Saikia, Rohan Sinha, Pankhoori Sinha, Aakriti Singhal
DESIGNERS Mini Dhawan, Romi Chakraborty, Tannishtha Chakraborty
ART DIRECTOR Shefali Upadhyay
EDITORIAL MANAGERS Dipali Singh, Glenda Fernandes
HEAD OF PUBLISHING Aparna Sharma

BIRDLIFE INTERNATIONAL

PROJECT CO-ORDINATOR Adrian Long
SPECIES DISTRIBUTION MAPPING Mark Balman, Gill Bunting, Ian Fisher, Simon Mahood, Dan Omolo, Louisa Richmond-Coggan, Andy Symes

AUDUBON

PROJECT CO-ORDINATOR Sandy Pinto
EDITORIAL CONSULTANT Sally Conyne

INDEXER Sue Butterworth

PICTURE RESEARCHERS Neil Fletcher, Will Jones

ILLUSTRATOR John Woodcock

First published in Great Britain in 2007 by Dorling Kindersley Limited 80 Strand, London WC2R 0RL

A Penguin Company

2 4 6 8 10 9 7 5 3

A CIP catalogue record for this book is available from the British Library

ISBN 978 1 4053 0633 1

Colour reproduction by Colourscan, Singapore
Printed and bound in Singapore by Star Standard Ltd

See our complete catalogue at www.dk.com

CONTENTS

BIRD SPECIES

ABOUT THIS BOOK

THIS BOOK IS DIVIDED INTO THREE CHAPTERS. An overview of the physiology and behaviour of birds is given in the INTRODUCTION; the chapter on HABITATS looks at the distribution of birds throughout the world, both in terms of geography and types of habitat; and BIRD SPECIES, provides detailed information on orders, families, and individual species of bird.

INTRODUCTION

This opening chapter provides information on the phyical characteristics of birds, focusing on the aspects of their physiology that differentiate birds from the rest of the animal kingdom. Bird behaviour is also examined, from different feeding preferences and methods to systems of communication, courtship rituals, and breeding and parenting. There is also coverage of migration behaviour and routes. Threats to birds and steps being undertaken to protect them through conservation efforts are also discussed in the closing pages of this chapter.

◀ ANATOMY AND PHYSIOLOGY
These pages include detailed descriptions of the physical characteristics of birds and the ways in which these have evolved to serve the needs of different types of bird in a variety of environments.

BIRD FLIGHT ▶
This key aspect of bird behaviour is examined in detail, including aerodynamics, different types and patterns of flight of a variety of bird species.

◀ BIRD BEHAVIOUR
Covering topics such as social behaviour, courtship, nesting, breeding, and migration, this section addresses all aspects of how birds behave.

BIRD CONSERVATION ▶
The final part of this chapter examines how birds are adapting to conditions in the modern world. As well as looking at the threats, it also describes the positive steps that being taken to conserve bird species.

CONTRIBUTORS

David Burnie Introduction, Habitats, introductions to bird orders

Ben Hoare Great Sites, introductions to passerine families, Glossary

Joseph DiCostanzo Introductions to passerine families

BirdLife International provided the text and maps for the species profiles in this book. The species texts were written by the following contributors:

Phil Benstead Gamebirds, Waterfowl, Pelicans, Waders, Gulls, and Auks, Cuckoos and Turacos, Passerines

Chris Harbard Penguins, Birds of Prey, Kingfishers, Passerines

Guy Kirwan Rheas, Cassowaries and Emus, Penguins, Divers, Albatrosses and Petrels, Pelicans, Cranes, Pigeons and Doves, Parrots, Swifts and Hummingbirds, Mousebirds, Trogons, Kingfishers, Woodpeckers and Toucans, Passerines (species and families)

Krys Kazmierczak Grebes, Storks and Herons, Cranes, Waders, Gulls, and Auks, Passerines

James Lowen Tinamous, Ostriches, Waterfowl, Gamebirds, Flamingos, Owls, Kingfishers, Woodpeckers and Toucans, Passerines

Nick Langley Kiwis, Gamebirds, Storks and Herons, Birds of Prey, Cranes and Relatives, Waders, Gulls, and Auks, Owls, Nightjars and Frogmouths, Passerines (species and families)

Ed Parnell Storks and Herons, Birds of Prey, Cranes, Waders, Gulls, and Auks, Parrots, Owls, Woodpeckers and Toucans, passerine families

Ian Peters Gamebirds, Birds of Prey, Waders, Gulls, and Auks, Parrots, Cuckoos and Turacos, Swifts and Hummingbirds, Kingfishers, Woodpeckers and Toucans, Passerines

Craig Robson Waterfowl, Birds of Prey, Waders, Gulls, and Auks, Sandgrouse, Pigeons and Doves, Passerines

Andy Symes and Richard Thomas Additional editorial support.

HABITATS

This chapter opens with an overview of the biogeographical realms in which birds are distributed throughout the world, and the ways in which different groups of birds have evolved in different regions over millions of years. An overview of the variety of environments - or biomes - in which bird life exists is followed by a detailed description of each main type of habitat, from polar regions to deserts and urban environments. These accounts include information about the bird species that are adapted to these conditions and their lifestyle, including diet, nesting, and migration.

a map indicates the main areas of the world in which the habitat exists

HABITATS ▲
Pages such as the ones shown here describe different habitats and a selection of the typical bird species that are found in that habitat.

BIRD SPECIES

This final chapter is devoted to a detailed look at over 1,200 bird species. It opens with an overview of the different ways in which birds are classified. The rest of the chapter is organized according to taxonomic order, with the non-passerine orders being covered first, followed by the passerines. Introductory sections describing the different bird orders and, in the passerine section, bird families are followed by profiles of individual species within that group. In most cases each species profile includes a photograph of the bird, a map showing where it is found, summary data detailing its size, migration status, and preferred habitat. For the most threatened species, information is also given on status according to the IUCN Red List. The chapter is interspersed with illustrated accounts of great bird-watching sites around the world.

DISTRIBUTION MAPS
Each profile includes a map showing the natural range of that species, sometimes including well-established introduced populations. Different colours are used to indicate whether the bird is an all-year resident, or inhabits the area only during breeding or non-breeding phases.

Non-breeding. Also used to indicate ranges for seabirds.

Resident. Areas inhabited by non-migrant birds.

Breeding. Areas in which a migrant species breeds.

scientific name of the profiled species

Todirhamphus sanctus

Sacred Kingfisher

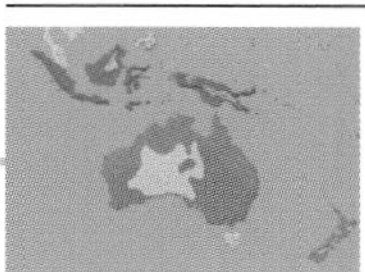

LENGTH
50–65cm (19½–26in)

WEIGHT
1.4–3.9kg (3–8½lb)

MIGRATION
Non-migrant

HABITAT Sub-tropical to temperate forests and shrub, plantations, and farmland

widely accepted common name of the profiled species

length and weight figures are for adult birds, with ranges encompassing males and females

description of types of habitat in which species is found

RED LIST CATEGORY
If the profiled bird species is judged to be Critically Endangered, Endangered, or Vulnerable according the Red List of the IUCN (International Union for the Conservation of Nature) (see p.67), this information is given under a separate heading following the habitat description.

SPECIES PROFILES ►
Pages such as the ones shown here contain descriptions of individual species of bird. All species profiles contain a text description and a distribution map, and in most cases a photograph of the featured bird.

panel shows position of group being described (indicated with white line) in the classification hierarchy

ORDER	Pelicaniformes
FAMILY	8
SPECIES	64

coloured panels provide additional information on the physiology or behaviour of the species, places where it is found, or on its relationship with humans

◄ INTRODUCTIONS TO BIRD ORDERS AND FAMILIES
All bird orders, as well as families within the passerine order, are described in overviews such as these. These introductions cover the common physical and behavioural features of the group.

description of the site's location

map providing a visual indication of the location of the area

selected birds typical of the species that can be seen at the site are pictured

GREAT SITES ►
Throughout the world there are places that are famous for their bird life – either in terms of its rich variety or the sheer numbers of certain species that congregate there. These pages focus on a representative selection of these places from around the world. Other sites are described in panels within species profiles.

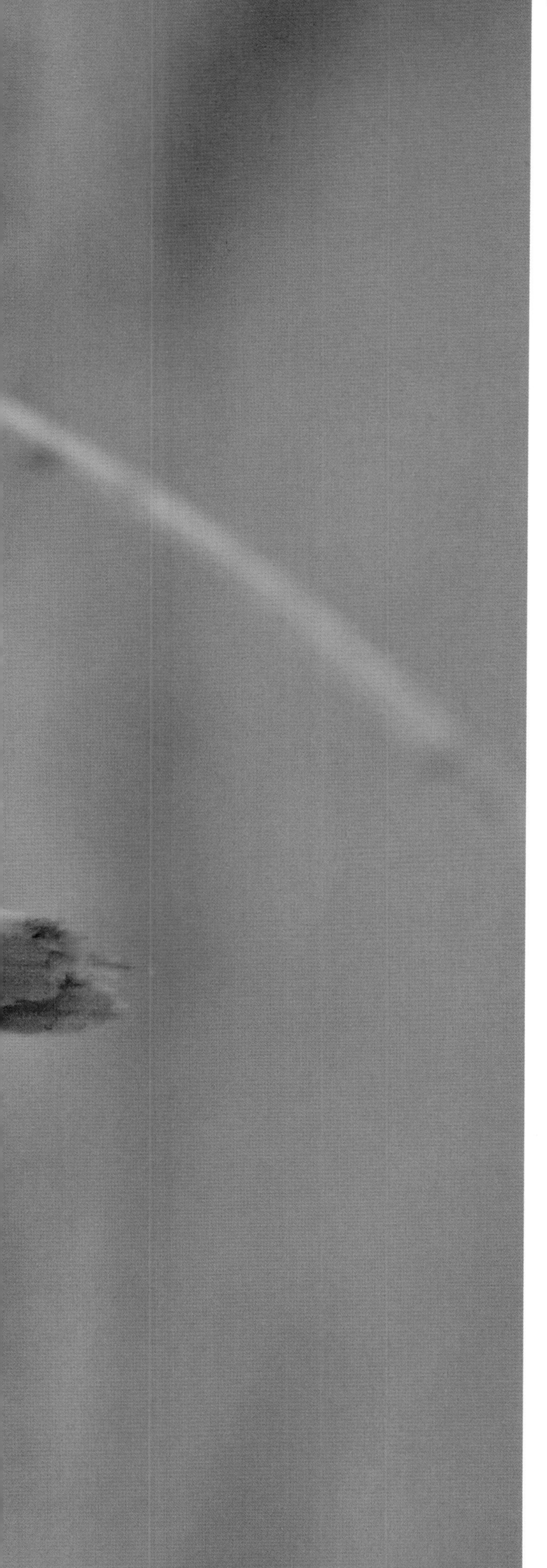

FOREWORD

Birds are no more extraordinary than any other living organisms. Yet it is their greater familiarity with people that can make them seem so special. They fly, they sing, they are rich in colour and pattern, they are animated, and they are almost everywhere, almost always. No other group of animals can say as much of themselves, however interesting they are.

Bird superbly illustrates what astonishing diversity there is among birds. The male Great Bustard (page 207) holds the record for being the heaviest of all flying birds weighing in at 1,800g (40lb). At the other end of the scale are the hummingbirds – some of them so small that they can easily be mistaken for insects and the smallest of which bears an insect's name, the Bee Hummingbird (page 298), that weighs less than 2g (1/16oz).

The familiarity of Birds has lead them to be a great source of inspiration to people throughout our shared history. They have a powerful place in our cultures as symbols of freedom and wisdom as well as spirituality. And the future of the world's 10,000 species of birds is inextricably linked to the welfare and livelihoods of people. One in eight bird species is threatened with extinction; the loss of even one diminishes us all. I hope that this beautifully produced encyclopedia will not only serve as a celebration of birds but also strongly encourage greater efforts to conserve them before it is too late.

DR MICHAEL RANDS, CHIEF EXECUTIVE, BIRDLIFE INTERNATIONAL

SOUND AND COLOUR
The Bearded Reedling (also known as the Bearded Tit) is a beautifully coloured inhabitant of wetlands. It usually gives its presence away with a ping-like call.

DAYLIGHT HUNTER
Like other birds of prey, owls are accomplished predators. Most are active at night, but the Great Grey Owl also hunts by day. It uses its exceptional hearing to find prey, which it can locate even beneath deep snow.

MOVING AROUND
Some birds rely on their legs and feet as much as their wings to move around. Jacanas have extremely long toes that allow them to walk on floating plants.

ORNAMENTED TOOLS
Birds have evolved bills in a vast array of shapes, mainly to exploit different food sources, but those of hornbills are also adorned with impressive ornaments.

HOLDING ON
The Coal Tit belongs to the huge group of birds called the passerines or perching birds. A unique foot design enables these birds to clasp even slender twigs.

BATTLE OF WITS
Eating a diet of other animals provides birds with energy and protein, but it often also demands ingenuity. For example, to avoid being stung by their prey, bee-eaters rub or thrash bees against a branch until the sting is discharged. They will often use the same favoured perch to both watch for prey and later disarm it.

KEEPING OUT THE COLD
Birds have adapted to life in all of the Earth's climate zones. Emperor Penguins are famed for the lengths to which they will go to protect their eggs and young from the harsh Antarctic conditions. This chick is sitting on an adult's feet to reduce heat loss to the ice beneath.

SHIFTING POPULATIONS
At any given time, great numbers of birds are migrating long distances to find food. These Whooper Swans are wintering in Japan; they breed elsewhere in Asia.

INTRODUCTION

BIRD ANATOMY

SOME GROUPS OF ANIMALS are easily confused, but there are no such problems with birds. They are the only animals that have feathers, and the only living vertebrates – apart from bats – that have evolved wings and powered flight. Internally, they have a range of special features, including hollow bones, powerful flight muscles, and a breathing system that extracts the maximum amount of oxygen from air. Thanks to these adaptations, some birds soar as high as passenger planes, while others spend years on the wing before finally landing to breed.

INTERNAL ORGANS
Birds have similar body systems to mammals, but their organs differ. Most have a crop and a gizzard in the digestive system, and a single opening called the cloaca for excretion and reproduction.

SKELETON AND MUSCLES

All birds have evolved from the same distant ancestors and, as a result, they share the same underlying body plan. Their skeletons contain fewer bones than a mammal's, and they have bills rather than teeth and jaws. Their wing bones are light and hollow, and end in a three-fingered "hand", while their legs have a Z-like shape, with a raised ankle joint that looks like a backward-pointing knee. In most birds, the ribcage is compact, but the breastbone has a large vertical flap, called a keel, which acts as an anchor point for the muscles that power the wings. In fast or powerful fliers, such as pigeons and doves, flight muscles can make up 40 per cent of the body's total weight. These muscles generate a large amount of heat, helping birds to maintain their high body temperature, which averages 40–42°C (104–107°F).

SKELETON
Birds often have long and highly flexible necks, but the rest of the backbone is much more rigid. The keel projects forwards from the breastbone. Immediately above it, the furcula, or wishbone – formed by a fusion of the collar bones – functions like a spring when the wings beat up and down.

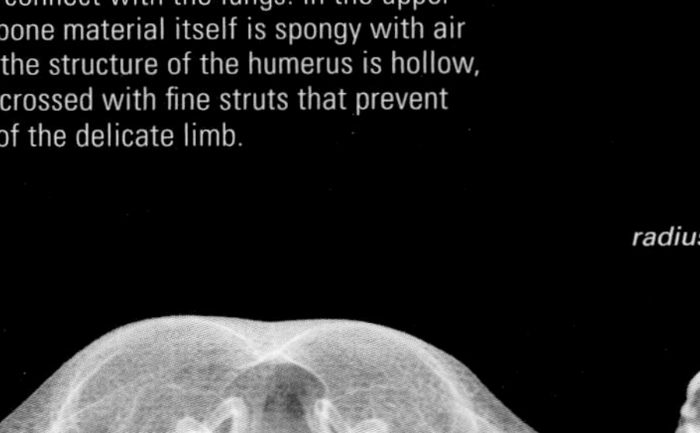

AIR-FILLED BONES
To save weight, many of a bird's bones are pneumatized, or filled with air. These air spaces develop early in life, and are extensions of air sacs that connect with the lungs. In the upper arm, the bone material itself is spongy with air sacs and the structure of the humerus is hollow, but criss-crossed with fine struts that prevent collapse of the delicate limb.

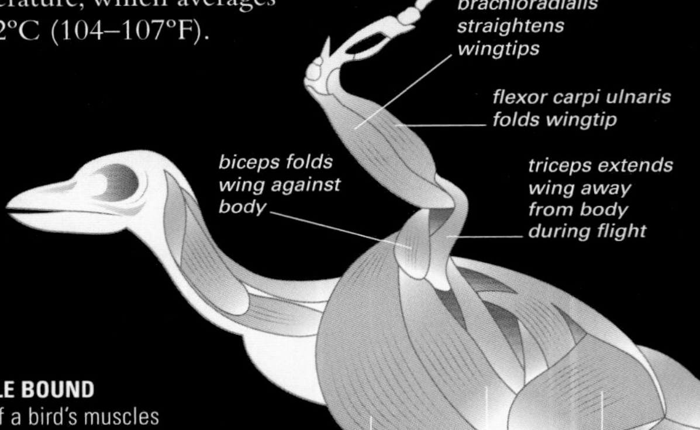

MUSCLE BOUND
Most of a bird's muscles are packed close to its body, giving it a streamlined shape. In flying birds, the largest muscle is the pectoralis major – this produces most of the power needed for flapping flight.

NERVOUS SYSTEM

To fly, birds need fast reactions, and an ability to process rapidly changing information, particularly from their eyes. Their brains are well developed and, in small birds, they can be twice as big as in mammals of a similar size. As well as flying, birds carry out many kinds of complex behaviour, from courtship rituals to long-distance navigation. Most of this behaviour is "hard-wired" into their nervous systems, which means that it does not have to be learned. However, birds do learn new forms of behaviour as they grow up, and some of their instinctive skills – such as nest building – improve with experience.

BRAIN AND SPINAL CORD
A large part of a bird's forebrain is devoted to vision. The large cerebellum deals with movement and balance.

THE SKULL
Bird skulls are strong, although often paper-thin. Seen from above, this scan of a bird skull shows the circle of bony plates, called the sclerotic ring, which supports each eye.

DIGESTIVE SYSTEM

Some birds – such as crows and gulls – eat anything edible that they find, but most have specialized diets and digestive systems that have evolved to deal with particular foods. Because birds do not have teeth, the majority swallow their food whole. As it goes through the digestive system, food is stored in the crop before passing through a two-chambered stomach. The first chamber, the glandular stomach, secretes acidic digestive juices. The second chamber, the gizzard, has muscular walls which contract to grind up food. After this, nutrients are absorbed and waste expelled. Digestive systems are modified in different ways. Seed-eaters have large crops, so that they can eat rapidly and move on. Many seabirds also have large crops, to allow them to carry food back to their young. The Hoatzin's crop is enormous, and functions like a microbial fermentation tank, breaking down large quantities of leaves. Glandular stomachs are largest in birds of prey, vultures, and fish-eaters. The big Lammergeier Vulture produces such powerful stomach acids that it can digest bones thicker than a human wrist. The gizzard is largest in birds that eat seeds and nuts: many of these swallow grit and stones that become lodged in their gizzards, helping to grind the food.

DOWN IN ONE
Birds often have a surprisingly large swallow. This Double-crested Cormorant is tackling a large fish – several minutes' work.

femur
ilium
ischium
tail vertebrae
pygostyle
ribs
pubis
fibula
external digits (fused together)
tarsometatarsus
tarsus

LUNGS AND BREATHING

When a mammal breathes, air flows into its lungs and back out again. Bird lungs work differently: air flows straight through the lungs, via a system of air sacs, before being exhaled. This one-way flow allows air and blood to move in opposite directions, known as countercurrent. As a result, bird lungs are more efficient at transferring oxygen and carbon dioxide than those of mammals, so that some birds can fly at over 10,000m (33,000ft) – an altitude where a mammal would lose consciousness. Most flying birds have nine air sacs, which connect with air spaces in major bones. Diving birds have poorly developed air spaces, but in some land birds – such as hornbills – they reach as far as the toes.

trachea
cervical air sacs
interclavicular air sac
anterior thoracic air sacs
lung
abdominal air sacs
posterior thoracic air sacs

LUNGS AND AIR SACS
A bird's lungs take up less space than those of a mammal, but they are much more efficient. Air sacs act as reservoirs. Unlike the lungs, they do not absorb oxygen.

BREATHING CYCLE

Unlike mammals, birds take two complete breathing cycles to move a single breath in through the trachea, through the lungs, and back out of the body. When Şying, their breathing rate can speed up by 20 times to power the extra energy required.

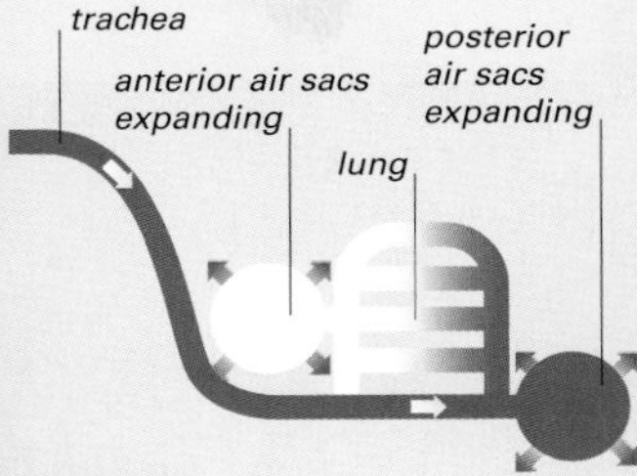

INHALATION 1
At the start of the cycle, the forward and rear air sacs expand. Inhaled air travels through the bird's trachea and into the rear air sacs.

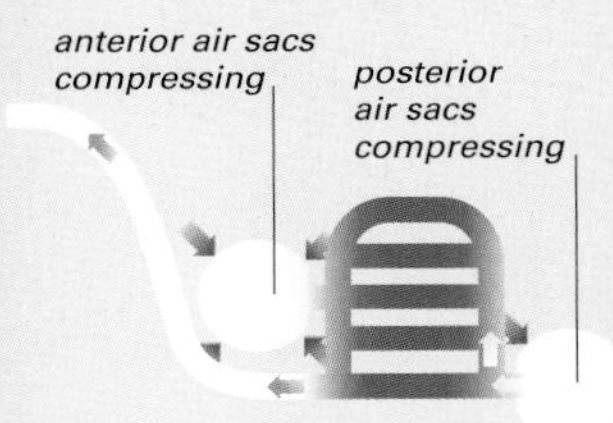

EXHALATION 1
Both sets of air sacs are now compressed, so that air is squeezed out of the rear air sacs and into the lungs.

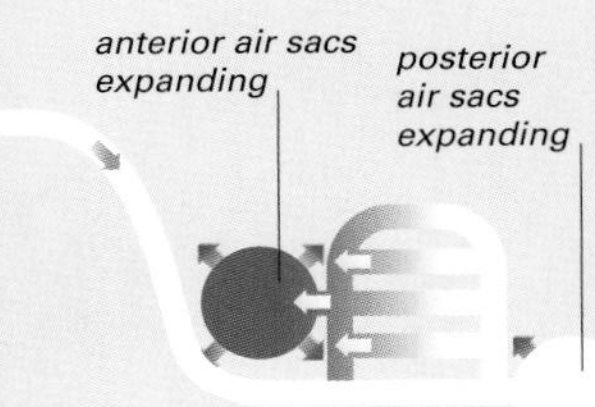

INHALATION 2
The air sacs expand again, drawing more air in through the trachea. Meanwhile, air already in the lungs moves into the forward air sacs.

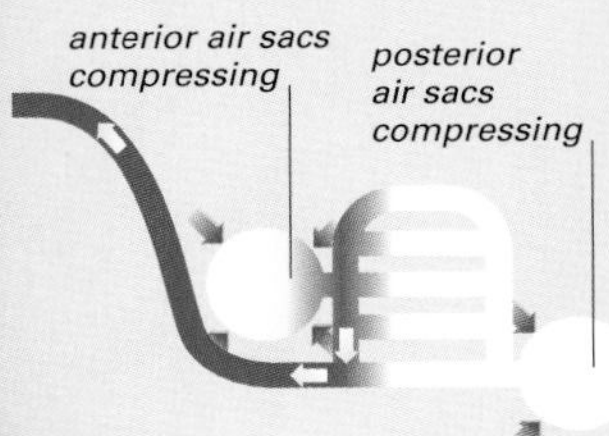

EXHALATION 2
To finish the double cycle, the air sacs are compressed, driving the air in the forward air sacs back out through the trachea.

REPRODUCTIVE SYSTEM

All birds reproduce by laying eggs. Apart from mound-builders, or megapodes, all of them incubate their eggs by sitting on them, and play some part in caring for their young. In many birds, the reproductive system follows an annual rhythm, switching on at the beginning of the breeding season, and then shrinking again when its work is done. Female birds usually have a single ovary, which produces eggs like units on a production line. Eggs contain all the nutrients that a developing embryo needs, but they do not start to develop until the eggs are laid, and incubation begins.

MATING BEE-EATERS
In birds, as in mammals, eggs are fertilized inside the female's body. In some species, the female can store the male's sperm for several weeks.

SENSES

FROM THE MOMENT A BIRD starts life, it depends on its senses to survive. For all birds, vision is the key external sense, and one that uses up a large proportion of the brain's processing power. Hearing is also important, but for most bird species – apart from notable exceptions such as kiwis – smell and taste are not nearly as significant as they are for us. Specialized navigational senses, on the other hand, are vital tools for migrant species, while the sense of balance is essential for all birds, particularly when they are in the air.

KEEPING TRACK
Compared to humans, birds have very large eyes, but theirs are not as mobile as ours. To follow a moving object, an owl has to turn its head – highly mobile vertebrae allow its neck to turn through 180 degrees.

VISION

Birds have excellent colour vision, and they can be up to three times better at picking out detail than humans. Their eyes often take up a large amount of space in the head, but they differ widely in their shape and positioning. Some bird eyes are spherical, but others are tubular, or even conical, flaring out inside the skull. In many birds they face sideways, but in owls and birds of prey they face forwards, giving a relatively large field of binocular vision. In birds, visual perception differs from our own. Birds are particularly good at spotting movement, but even in the open, they can fail to register motionless predators or prey.

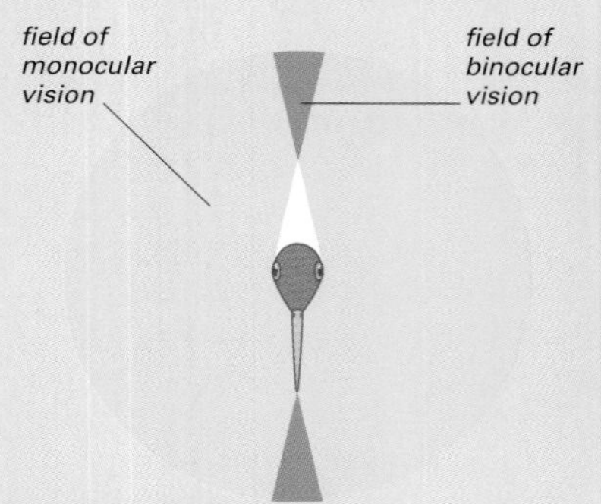

MONOCULAR VISION
A wader's sideways-facing eyes give it a 360 degree field of view. Most of this field is monocular, with little sense of depth.

ALL-ROUND VISION
Sitting on its eggs, a Eurasian Oystercatcher has a complete view of its surroundings, so it is hard for predators to attack by surprise. This kind of vision is found in many birds.

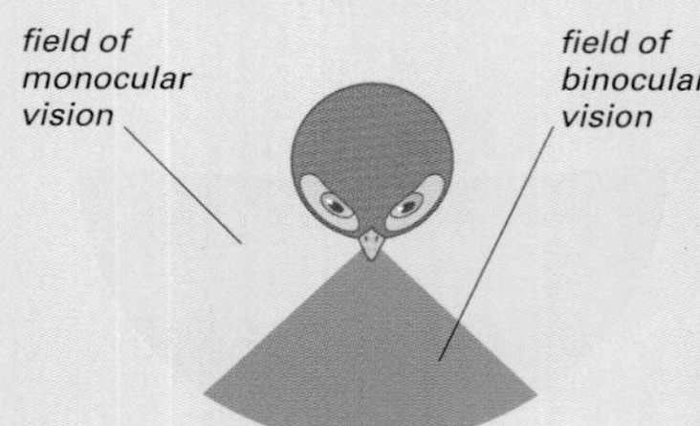

BINOCULAR VISION
An owl's eyes face forwards, so their fields of view partially overlap. This overlap allows owls to judge distances very accurately, an important aptitude for a night hunter.

FORWARD FOCUS
Like all birds, this Northern Goshawk has a sensitive area, called a fovea, at the centre of each retina. Some birds of prey have two foveae, while terns and swallows have three.

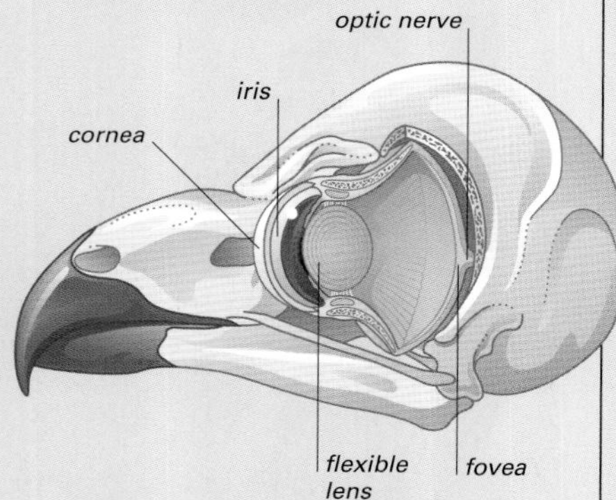

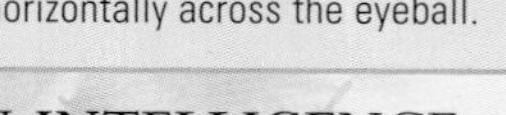

AVIAN EYES
Bird eyes have an adjustable iris, and a flexible lens that focuses light on the retina. The most sensitive part of the retina is the fovea – a central area packed with light receptors. Day-active birds have spherical or flattened eyes, but owl eyes are tubular, opening out inside the head. The surface of the eye is cleaned by the nictitating membrane, or "third eyelid", which flicks horizontally across the eyeball.

AVIAN INTELLIGENCE

Birds are far from stupid, although much of their behaviour is instinctive rather than learned. In captivity, several species – notably crows and parrots – demonstrate good problem-solving skills. Birds also have a good spatial memory, which is particularly well developed in nutcrackers and jays, which store food in hidden "caches" for later use.

INTELLIGENCE TESTS
Laboratory tests show that many birds quickly learn to relate particular colours or shapes with the promise of food.

HEARING

Like their reptilian ancestors, birds lack external ears; some owls have feathery ear tufts, but these have little or nothing to do with hearing. A bird's ear openings are typically funnel-shaped, and are hidden beneath its plumage, behind and below each eye. In general, bird hearing is not much more acute than our own, but some birds have special abilities linked to the way they live. Barn owls, for example, are unusually sensitive to high frequencies, allowing them to home in on rustling sounds produced by small mammals after dark. Birds are also extraordinarily good at sound recognition. Even when dozens of different species are singing, songbirds can instantly pick out the calls of their own kind. Birds that nest in large colonies – such as gannets and shearwaters – show even greater discrimination. They often pinpoint their partners solely by their calls, although thousands of other birds may be calling at the same time.

HUNTING BY HEARING
A Barn Owl's heart-shaped face helps to channel sound to its ears. Asymmetrical ear openings help the owl to pinpoint the source of the sound with accuracy.

BALANCING ACT
Standing on one leg is a simple matter for this flamingo, even when fast asleep. Like mammals, birds maintain their balance using fluid-filled cavities of the inner ear.

A NOSE FOR FOOD
With long tubular nostrils, the Southern Giant Petrel can locate food by day or by night while out at sea. Tubenoses are particularly attracted by the smell of floating animal fats.

SMELL AND TASTE

For many birds, the chemical senses – smell and taste – play a relatively minor part in daily life. Most terrestrial birds have a poor sense of smell, and birds generally judge food by its appearance, rather than by its taste. They also have remarkably few taste buds: parrots have about 350, and blue tits just 24, compared with about 10,000 in humans. However, as with hearing, smell and taste are much better developed in some groups of birds than others. New World vultures can locate dead remains by their smell, and tubenoses (albatrosses and their relatives) use smell to track down food on the open sea. Kiwis also sniff out their food, using nostrils at the tips of their bills. Honeyguides can smell beeswax – an ability that helps them to track down the bees' nests that supply their food.

SUBTERRANEAN SCENT
Kiwis are the only birds that have nostrils at the tips of their bills. They also have highly developed olfactory bulbs – the part of the brain that manages the sense of smell.

NAVIGATIONAL SENSES

Birds have a remarkable ability to find their way – whether they are close to home, or on long-distance migrations. On home ground, most birds find their way by sight, but a handful of cave-nesting birds use echolocation to navigate in total darkness. Like bats and dolphins, they emit short bursts of sound, and then listen for the echoes that bounce back. Migrating birds use a wide variety of sensory cues to find their way to their destination. One of these is the direction and strength of the Earth's magnetic field. This sense is still poorly understood, but it seems to involve specialized proteins in a bird's eyes, and tiny specks of the mineral magnetite, which are found in a bird's cranial nerves (see also Migration, p.58).

ECHOLOCATION
Oilbirds roost and nest deep in caves in Central and South America. Using echolocation, an Oilbird can navigate its way through 500m (1,650ft) of winding stone passages between its nest and the cave mouth.

SECRET SENSES
During their migration flights, geese, such as these Barnacle Geese, make use of a constant stream of sensory data to navigate. Vision, hearing, and even smell may play a part, together with their ability to sense the Earth's magnetic field.

FEATHERS

FEATHERS ARE THE MOST versatile body covering in the animal world. Even in the coldest habitats, they keep birds dry and warm, and, significantly, they enable birds to fly. Individual birds can have up to 25,000 feathers, but to stay airworthy, the majority of species replace most of their plumage at least once a year.

STRUCTURE AND TYPES OF FEATHER

Feathers are made of keratin, the same protein found in human fingernails. The most important part of a feather is the hollow shaft, which is anchored in the skin. The base of the shaft is bare, forming the feather's quill, but in most feathers, the rest of the shaft has two rows of parallel branches, or barbs, arranged on either side. In down feathers, the shaft is often short, and barbs are loose and fluffy, creating a layer of insulation next to the bird's skin. In contour feathers, the barbs are stiffer, and they are locked together by microscopic hooks, creating a smooth surface known as a vane. Most of a bird's contour feathers are arranged like roof tiles, giving its body a streamlined shape. However, on the wings and tail, some are specially developed, with extra-large vanes. These are a bird's flight feathers – the unique feature that separates birds from their reptilian ancestors, and which enables them to fly.

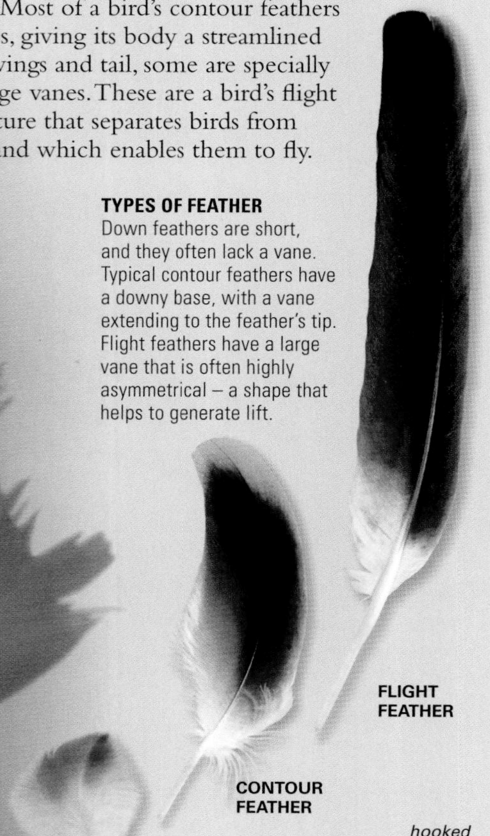

TYPES OF FEATHER
Down feathers are short, and they often lack a vane. Typical contour feathers have a downy base, with a vane extending to the feather's tip. Flight feathers have a large vane that is often highly asymmetrical – a shape that helps to generate lift.

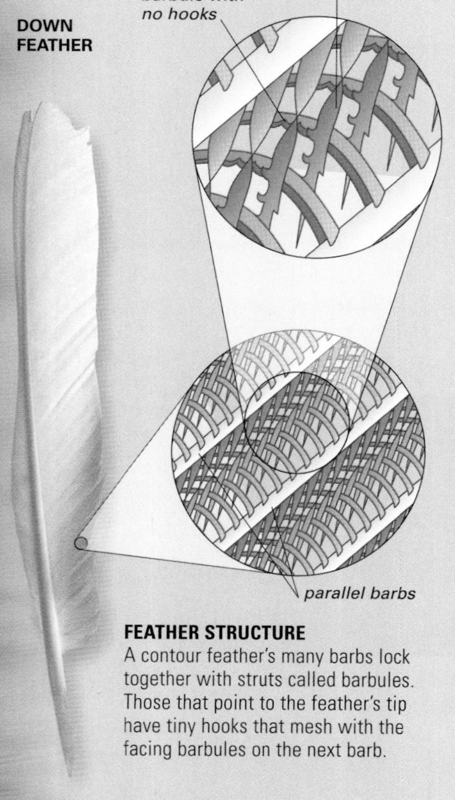

FLIGHT FEATHER

CONTOUR FEATHER

DOWN FEATHER

hooked barbule

barbule with no hooks

parallel barbs

FEATHER STRUCTURE
A contour feather's many barbs lock together with struts called barbules. Those that point to the feather's tip have tiny hooks that mesh with the facing barbules on the next barb.

WHOOPER SWAN PREENING
Feathers are one of the most prominent features of a bird's anatomy. Through the processes of moulting or preening, feathers can change a bird's colour and markings, and even its apparent size.

FEATHER FUNCTIONS

A bird's feathers are vital to conserve body heat, particularly in small species that endure cold winters. For example, Boreal Chickadees have a body temperature of about 42°C (107°F), and they manage to keep it at this level even when the winter air plummets to -35°C (-31°F), which is an amazing achievement for a bird that weighs less than 10g (1/3oz). Feathers also help to keep birds dry. Contour feathers are naturally water-repellent, but many swimming birds go one step further and make them fully waterproof by coating them with oil from their preen glands.

Feathers can also function as camouflage, or as visual signals, helping to attract a mate. Moulting and feather wear enable the same bird to look strikingly different at different times of year. A bird's plumage is also highly sensitive to touch: in many species, this sense is accentuated by hair-like feathers called filoplumes, which are thought to detect movement of the other feathers around them. Some birds have stiff, vaneless feathers resembling bristles. Nightjars use these to sweep flying insects into their mouths, while in ostriches and hornbills, they function like eyelashes.

KEEPING WARM
By fluffing out its feathers, a bird can improve its own insulation. This female Red-winged Blackbird has its feathers fully fluffed, giving it a plump outline.

BREEDING DISPLAYS
In many bird species, the males grow highly elaborate feathers for use in courtship rituals. This male Great Egret is showing off the long, extremely fine plumes that normally lie flat on its back.

TREE SWALLOW NESTLINGS
These chicks are starting to grow their feathers. Like most birds, their plumage grows in defined areas called feather tracts, separated by bare skin.

MOULTING PENGUIN
Halfway through its first moult, this young King Penguin looks distinctly unkempt. Its brown juvenile down is replaced by waterproof adult plumage.

PLUMAGE DEVELOPMENT

As a bird grows up, it goes through a series of plumage changes. Altricial birds (see p.54) often hatch naked, but rapidly grow a complete set of down and contour feathers. Precocial birds are better developed on hatching, and are usually covered in down, which is later replaced by the adult plumage. In most birds, the adult plumage is grown and replaced on an annual cycle. Many adult birds replace their plumage in a "prenuptial moult", which is the point when male birds adopt their bright courtship colours. When the breeding season is over, they moult a second time, and the male plumage becomes more subdued.

HOW FEATHERS GROW

Feathers develop from follicles – small outgrowths in a bird's skin. Each one develops from the base upwards, forming barbs and barbules as it grows. When the feather reaches full size, growth comes to a halt. By this stage, the feather is largely dead, but it stays attached to the skin until moulted, when its working life comes to an end.

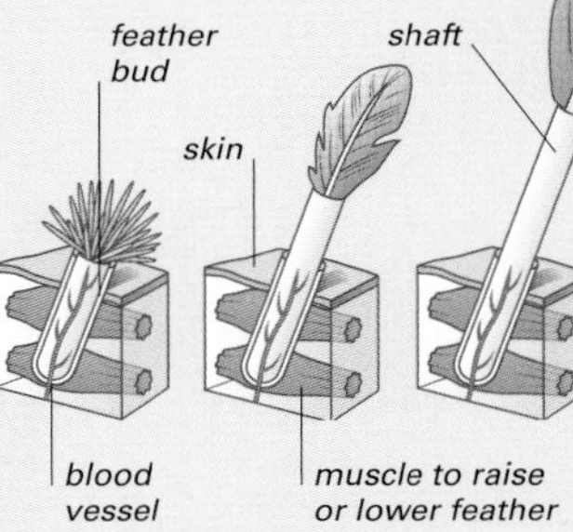

DEVELOPMENT OF A FLIGHT FEATHER
In early stages of development, flight feathers are protected by cylindrical sheaths. These fall away as the feathers take shape.

CARE AND RENEWAL

Feathers need constant cleaning and maintenance to keep them in good condition. Many birds regularly bathe in fresh water, although species that live in dry habitats often bathe in dust or sand instead. Throughout the day – but particularly after bathing – a bird will preen its feathers, arranging them correctly and wiping them with waterproof oil from a gland near the base of the tail. Birds that do not have preen glands, such as hawks and parrots, keep their plumage in good condition with specialized feathers called powder down, which release a fine dust that works like talc. When birds moult, they usually shed their flight feathers in a set pattern, which varies from one species to another. Most shed their wing feathers in symmetrical pairs, so that they can stay airborne as moulting progresses. However, many waterbirds moult all their primary flight feathers at once. For several weeks, they are unable to fly.

DUST BATHING
With all of its feathers fluffed out, a male Golden Pheasant gives itself a vigorous dusting. Gamebirds frequently bathe in dust, but never in water.

MISSING FEATHERS
This Black Kite is in mid-moult, so has gaps in its wings where some of its flight feathers have been shed. Replacement feathers are already growing in their place.

MOULTING PATTERN
Most songbirds shed their primary and secondary flight feathers in two sequences, which occur simultaneously to minimize the impact on their flight.

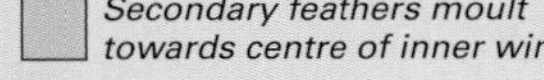

WINGS

BIRD WINGS DEVELOPED from five-fingered limbs, but over millions of years, evolution has completely transformed them for flight. They are light and flexible, with an infinitely variable geometry, which gives the best performance over a wide range of different speeds. They can fold away when not in use, and their feathers replace themselves to make up for wear and tear. Bird wings vary hugely in size and shape, but stripped of their feathers, they are all constructed on the same plan.

STRUCTURE

Bird wings have an internal framework of hollow bones, anchored to the body at the shoulder – often the biggest joint in the skeleton. Apart from the shoulder, wings have two other main joints: one is equivalent to the human elbow, while one nearer the wingtip is equivalent to the wrist. These joints allow the wing to open and close, and also to swivel – crucial for flight. The muscles that power the wings are mainly in the chest, rather than in the wing itself. Several sets of tendons connect the muscles to the wing bones, moving like a system of cables. When a bird is in the air, its wings are constantly adjusted, fine-tuning the amount of lift produced. In most birds, these adjustments control height and speed; steering is carried out mainly by the tail. Swifts are an exception: they can twist and turn in the air by beating each wing at a different speed.

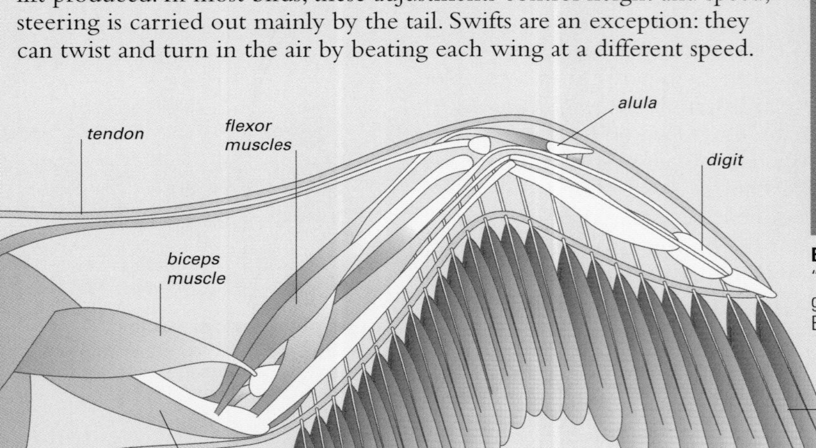

ANATOMY OF THE WING
A bird's wings are powered by the large pectoral muscles in the chest. The biceps muscle in the wing folds up the inner part of the wing, while the triceps spreads it out. Smaller muscles control the outer part of the wing.

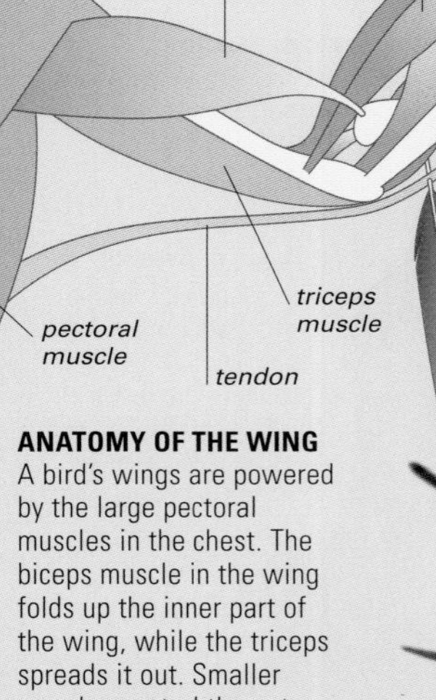

FOLDED WINGS
A Western Yellow Wagtail splays its tail while perching on a rock. Like most birds, its wings fold into a Z-like shape when not in use, so that they can be held flat against the body. In non-flying birds, such as penguins and ostriches, wings are less flexible, and rarely fold.

SIZE AND SHAPE

In the bird world there are many different wing shapes, which deliver a very different performance in terms of endurance, manoeuvrability, and speed. Gliding birds have long, narrow wings with only a slight bend at the "elbow" – a shape that combines strength and maximum lift. Birds that soar on thermals have broad wings, often with splayed flight feathers resembling extended fingers. Fast fliers, such as swifts, have backswept wings ending in a narrow point – a shape that reduces turbulence and therefore the energy needed to stay in the air. Most songbirds have short wings with a rounded rear edge, which gives excellent manoeuvrability.

LONG AND NARROW
The Black-browed Albatross has extremely long wings that it holds out stiffly, enabling it to soar and glide over the sea for hours.

POINTED AND BACKSWEPT
The Common Swift's elbow joints are very close to its body, and its extra-long, curving flight feathers give narrow, pointed wingtips.

BROAD WITH SPLAYED TIPS
"Slotted" flight feathers, separated by visible gaps, generate extra lift in the White-tailed Eagle and other large soaring birds.

SHORT AND ROUNDED
Songbirds such as the European Greenfinch have short, rounded wings for a rapid take-off and plenty of manoeuvrability in mid-air.

REDUCED TURBULENCE
Alulas – small feathery flaps attached to each "wrist" – are visible in this young European Honey Buzzard. When raised like this, the alula helps to reduce turbulence.

LONG WINGS
Wandering Albatrosses, shown here performing a greeting display, are supremely elegant fliers at sea, where their remarkable wingspan enables them to glide with barely a wingbeat.

WINGSPAN

The largest flying bird ever was an extinct species called *Argentavis magnificens*, which lived 12–5 million years ago and had a wingspan of up to 8m (26ft). Today, the absolute record is held by the Wandering Albatross, which has a wingspan of up to 3m (10ft). On land, the title is held jointly by the Andean Condor and Marabou Stork, which share a maximum wingspan of just below 3m (10ft). At the other end of the scale, the Bee Hummingbird of Cuba has a tiny wingspan of just 3cm (1⅕in) – far smaller than many insects.

SHORT WINGS
The Ruby-throated Hummingbird has tiny wings that give superb agility and flexibility.

SPECIES	WING LOADING (g/cm²)
Leach's Petrel	0.11
Barn Swallow	0.14
Barn Owl	0.29
Golden Eagle	0.71
Mute Swan (below)	1.66

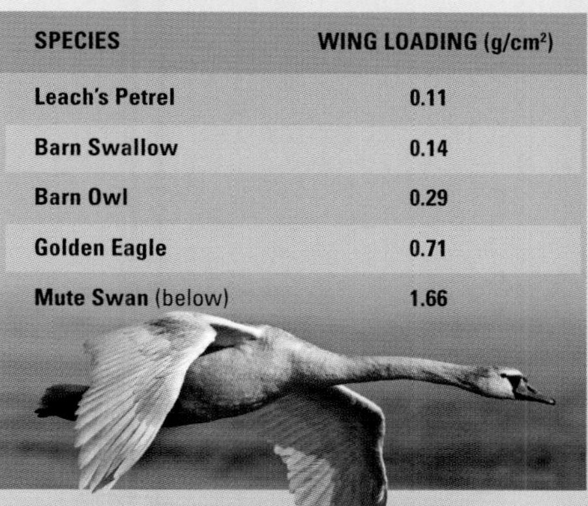

WING LOADING
The table above shows the wing loading for different birds of varying weight. Mute Swans weigh up to 15kg (33lb) and are among the heaviest of all flying birds. They need a long "runway" to become airborne.

WING LOADING

Although larger birds have larger wings, wing area and body weight do not increase in step. Instead, large birds typically have a greater wing loading, meaning that each unit area of wing has to carry more weight. Wing loading affects a bird's manoeuvrability and the amount of energy it requires to fly. The greater the wing loading, the harder birds have to work, unless they soar or glide. In the most extreme cases, including swans, bustards, and turkeys, taking off is a real struggle and the birds flap hard for several seconds to get into the air.

FLIGHTLESS BIRDS

If flight is no longer a great advantage to a bird, evolution can gradually make wings smaller, until flight is no longer possible. At least 13 bird orders, including ostriches, kiwis, grebes, penguins, auks, pigeons, and even parrots, contain species that have become flightless. In penguins and auks, the wings are well developed and are used like flippers for propulsion in water. By contrast, the wings of kiwis are so tiny that they are invisible under their plumage and have no function. Flightlessness is most common among birds that live on oceanic islands, where there are no mammalian predators. In the rail family, over a quarter of island species cannot fly. One of them, the Inaccessible Island Rail, is the world's smallest flightless bird, weighing just 30g (1oz). Many similar species have become extinct following the introduction of cats and other predators.

MULTI-PURPOSE WINGS
Although ostriches cannot fly, they use their well-developed wings for displaying, and for temperature control, exposing or covering up the bare skin on their legs.

FLYING UNDERWATER
Penguins have stiff, compact wings that are highly effective flippers, allowing these Gentoo Penguins to reach speeds of over 25kph (16mph) under water.

FLIGHT

THE POWER OF FLIGHT GIVES ANIMALS huge advantages, particularly in the search for food. Over millions of years, it has evolved independently in several different groups of animals, including flying reptiles called pterosaurs, whose leathery wings were up to 12m (40ft) across. Today, the animal kingdom includes many species that can glide, but only three kinds of animal – birds, bats, and insects – can stay airborne by flapping their wings. Of these, insects are by far the most numerous, but birds lead the field in speed, endurance, load-carrying capacity, and total distance flown.

AIRLIFT
Birds have a strict "baggage allowance" that limits their own body weight, and also the weight of anything they carry into the air. The strongest lifters are birds of prey, which carry their victims in their claws. The large, fully grown trout that this Osprey is carrying may equal half its body weight.

FLIGHT FORCES

Flapping flight is a highly complex form of movement, which is still not fully understood. However, the basic principles behind bird flight are well known. Like aircraft, birds have to generate two forces to fly. The first, known as lift, counteracts the downward pull of Earth's gravity. The second force, called thrust, counteracts air resistance or drag, and pushes the bird forwards. In both birds and aircraft, lift is produced by the stream of air moving over the curved surfaces of the wings, while in most birds thrust is produced by flapping. However, bird wings are highly flexible, and so flapping flight can involve many other factors as well. For example, pigeons generate extra lift by bringing their wings together on the upstroke, while hummingbirds can generate a constant downdraught by making each wing trace a path like a figure 8. Gliding birds (see p.34) are quite different: they exploit the air currents around them, saving much of the energy required in flapping flight.

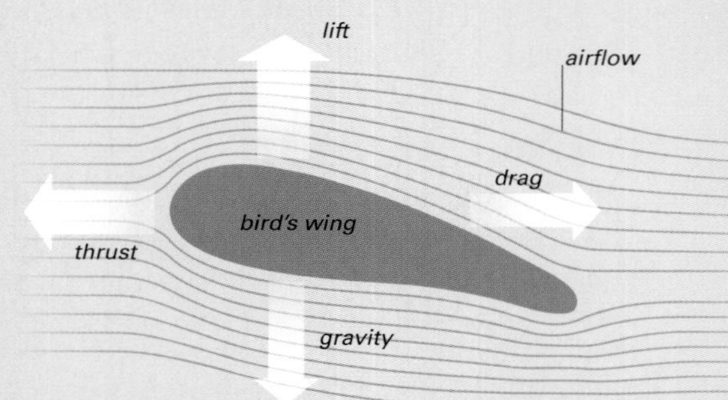

WING AERODYNAMICS
Seen in cross-section, a bird's wing forms a shape called an aerofoil. Air moves over the upper surface faster than the lower one, causing a reduction in pressure that results in lift. If lift is greater than the pull of gravity, the bird rises, and if thrust exceeds drag, it accelerates forwards. But if each pair of forces is balanced, the bird stays at the same height and speed.

TAKE-OFF AND LANDING

Body weight has a far-reaching effect on the way birds take off and land. Small songbirds can take off in a split-second with just a kick of their legs, but heavily built birds take much longer to get into the air. Pheasants and other gamebirds are a notable exception to this rule: powerful flight muscles give them an explosive take-off to escape from danger. Taking off can be hard work, and in heavy birds, the wing's geometry changes to maximize lift and minimize energy-wasting turbulence. These changes are reversed once the bird is in the air.

Landing requires careful coordination, and also plenty of space in the case of heavy birds such as bustards and swans. When birds land, they increase the angle of their wings, like an aeroplane lowering its flaps. The bird then swings its legs forwards, and if all goes to plan, it lands on them without toppling over. But for a heavy bird, such as a swan, it is very difficult to lose so much momentum in a short time. Instead, swans land on water, using their large webbed feet as brakes.

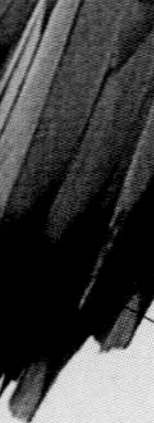

LIFTING OFF
When birds take off, their wings work in complex ways. Instead of pushing downwards and backwards like a pair of oars, a pigeon's wings twist at the bottom of the downstroke, helping to pull the bird through the air like a pair of propellers. To reduce turbulence, the primary flight feathers are spread apart and the alula, a small feathered flap that protrudes from the "wrist" of each wing, is temporarily raised.

LANDING
To land, a songbird drops its airspeed until it is just about to stall. With its wings and tail both acting as brakes, it drops onto its perch. Small birds such as this European Robin weigh little, so come to a standstill quickly.

FLIGHT SPEEDS

The speed of a flying bird is difficult to measure, so many records from the early years of ornithology are now thought to be unreliable. Birds are also experts at taking advantage of prevailing winds, and wind-assisted flight can make some long-distance speed records misleading. However, there is little doubt that the Peregrine Falcon holds the absolute record for speed in the air. When it is diving, it probably exceeds 200kph (124mph). The fastest birds in level flight are ducks, geese, and swifts. Some of these can reach an airspeed of nearly 80kph (50mph). In general, birds rarely fly faster than 30kph (18mph). The slowest birds of all – woodcocks – can fly at a leisurely 8kph (5mph) without stalling, which is not much faster than a brisk walk.

POWER DIVE
With its wings partly folded, a Peregrine Falcon dives, or stoops, towards its airborne prey hundreds of metres below.

LEISURELY FLIGHT
At dusk a male Eurasian Woodcock carries out its courtship flight. This is the slowest bird flight not to involve gliding or hovering.

widely spread flight feathers increase wing's surface area

alula is raised during take-off

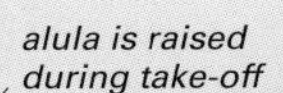

wings almost meet at top of upstroke

feet are stowed away close to body

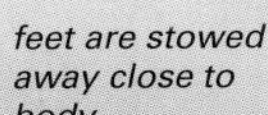

FLIGHT PATTERNS

Birds often have characteristic flight patterns, which can help to identify them when they are on the wing. Some follow a level flight path, flapping their wings at a steady rate, varying from about 200 beats a minute for pigeons, to a much more leisurely 25 beats a minute for large birds such as herons. Many other birds intersperse flapping with short bursts of gliding, but some species dip up and down, flapping their wings in short bursts, and then holding them against their sides. This is common in finches, which have an undulating or "bouncy" flight path, and it is even more pronounced in woodpeckers and toucans.

FAST FLAPPING
Pigeons and ducks both have a fast, direct flight – a characteristic shared by auks and cormorants as they speed over the sea.

SLOW FLAPPING
A wide variety of birds, including harriers, gulls, and Barn Owls, flap their wings slowly so that they can scan the ground for food.

INTERMITTENT FLAPPING
This flight style produces an undulating path, and the longer the intervals between flapping, the more noticeable the undulations.

RANDOM FLAPPING
This flight pattern is typical of aerial insect-eaters, such as swifts and swallows, and also of some larger birds, including kites.

HOVERING
Only hummingbirds, kingfishers, and kestrels routinely hover for extended periods. Feeding at a flower, this Mangrove Hummingbird may beat its wings 50 times a second.

GLIDING AND SOARING

COMPARED TO FLAPPING FLIGHT, gliding and soaring are highly efficient ways of moving through the air. Gliding birds slowly coast towards the ground, but the largest soaring species – such as birds of prey and vultures – can climb to a height of several kilometres with barely a beat of their enormous wings. Many birds mix gliding, soaring, and flapping flight. The most aerial, including terns and swifts, can stay airborne for several years before they finally land to breed.

SOARING ON THERMALS

When the ground is warmed by the sun, the air above it warms as well. This creates columns of warm air called thermals, which rise through the cooler and denser air around them. Soaring birds seek out these natural elevators, and spiral around inside them to climb high into the sky. The commonest soaring birds are raptors, such as eagles, buzzards, and vultures, together with many larger storks. All of these birds have broad wings with "slotted" primary flight feathers – something that is particularly noticeable when they are seen from below. Most birds use soaring as an effortless way of locating food, but some species – such as the White Stork – also save energy on their migrations by soaring, creating a dramatic spectacle as thousands of them spiral into the sky at the start of their journey.

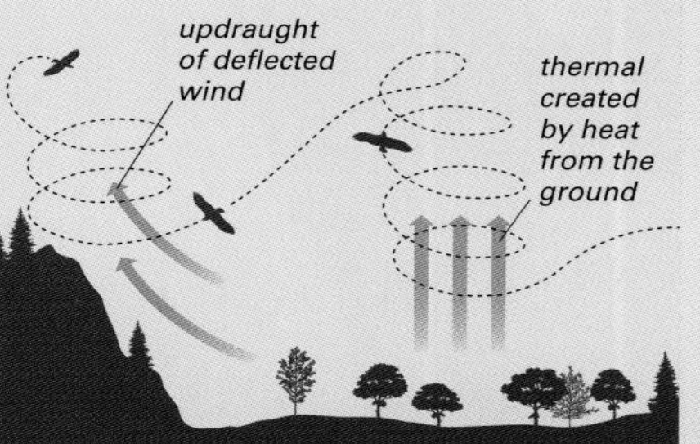

THERMALS AND UPDRAUGHTS
Once a bird is inside a thermal, it can rise at speeds of up to 5m (16ft) a second. Having reached the top of one thermal, it glides down to locate another. Slope-soaring birds use updraughts created by mountainous terrain.

THERMAL RIDER
White Storks ride thermals to start their migration between Africa and Europe. At narrow crossings – such as the Straits of Gibraltar– they climb as high as possible before heading out across the water.

DELAYED TAKE-OFF

Before thermals can form, the ground first has to heat up. This heat then has to be transferred to pockets of air, which are thus given enough energy to rise through the air around them. All this takes time, particularly in desert and mountain regions, where night-time temperatures often fall below freezing. As a result, heavy soaring birds, such as eagles, vultures, and buzzards, rarely get off to a prompt start at dawn. Instead, they are grounded until the sunshine gathers strength. To give themselves a headstart, they often roost on cliffs, trees, or other tall plants for an easier launch. This perch may also be a vantage point for spotting prey.

GREETING THE DAWN
Perched on a tall cactus, a Turkey Vulture spreads its wings in the early morning sunshine. It warms itself up while waiting for the day's thermals to form.

EASY RIDE
A young Andean Condor soars above steep slopes in Colca Canyon, Peru. At this latitude, the sun is strong, allowing condors to soar on thermals as well as updraughts.

SLOPE-SOARING

Cliffs and mountain ranges deflect the wind upwards, allowing birds to soar high above rough terrain. Unlike thermals, these updraughts often blow for months at a time, and they are present even when the weather is cold. This allows soaring birds to operate far away from the warmth of the tropics. The Andean Condor, for example, soars along the entire length of the Andes chain, from western Venezuela to Tierra del Fuego, while sea eagles soar over mountainous coasts in Scandinavia and Siberia. As well as eagles and vultures, slope-soarers also include a variety of smaller birds. Gulls and fulmars soar over coastal cliffs, while choughs and jackdaws often soar over cliffs and mountainsides inland. Choughs perform spectacular aerial displays during their breeding season in spring, with a characteristic tumbling flight.

AERIAL ACROBAT
With its wings and tail splayed, an Alpine Chough rides on the mountain wind. Choughs are superbly acrobatic birds.

DYNAMIC SOARING IN ACTION
An albatross rises and falls as it moves across the sea. Depending on the strength of the wind, it can rise to about 50m (160ft) before dropping close to the waves.

LONG-DISTANCE SOARING
The Wandering Albatross, the largest of all seabirds, may cover 10,000–20,000km (6,000–12,000 miles) in 10–20 days with its dynamic soaring flight, journeying right round the Earth in its search for food..

DYNAMIC SOARING

Dynamic soaring is a special form of flight used by albatrosses and their relatives. Instead of riding on thermals – which are rare above the open ocean – they exploit the strong winds that blow across the water's surface. Dynamic soaring works because the wind's speed is slowest near the surface and faster higher up. An albatross uses this difference in a cycle of movements, tracking its way across the sea. The cycle begins when the bird glides down towards the surface, gathering momentum. Just as it nears the surface, it suddenly turns into the wind, and the increased effect of the wind makes it climb sharply. By the time it has returned to its original height, it may have moved several hundred metres farther on. By repeating this cycle, albatrosses can travel immense distances with very little effort.

MIXED FLIGHT

Instead of using a single kind of flight, many birds use a mixture of flapping flight and gliding or soaring. This is particularly common in aerial insect-eaters, such as swifts and swallows. Flapping gives them the manoeuvrability they need to catch their food, while gliding helps them to save energy – an important capability for birds that spend much of their time in the air. Mixed flight is also common in seabirds. Gannets and Brown Pelicans, for example, characteristically mix bursts of flapping with long glides. Frigatebirds – among the most accomplished of all soaring birds – are quick to switch to flapping flight with their long, slender wings, when they are chasing other birds and trying to steal their food.

FLYING IN FORMATION
Despite their size, Brown Pelicans are supremely graceful in the air. On their way to feeding grounds, they often fly in lines, just skimming the sea.

ENDURANCE RECORDS

Energy-efficient flight allows some birds to spend an extraordinary amount of time in the air. The world's most aerial bird is thought to be the Sooty Tern. It feeds by snatching prey from the sea, rarely if ever settling on the surface. It may spend its first 8–9 years in the air, before setting foot on land to breed. On land, the record is held by the Common Swift. It remains airborne for 2–4 years, eating, sleeping, moulting, and even mating on the wing.

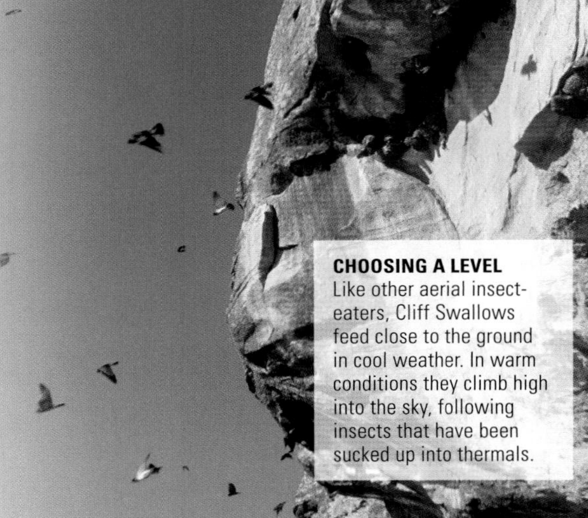

CHOOSING A LEVEL
Like other aerial insect-eaters, Cliff Swallows feed close to the ground in cool weather. In warm conditions they climb high into the sky, following insects that have been sucked up into thermals.

LEGS AND FEET

BIRDS ALL SHARE the same leg bones, but evolution has made the legs of different species even more varied than their wings. Some birds – such as swifts – have such tiny legs that they can barely use them to move on land, while some flying birds can run at over 30kph (18mph) and even a week-old duckling can swim as fast as a human can walk. This huge range of size and function enables birds to exploit many different habitats and sources of food.

ANATOMY

Compared to human legs, bird legs look as if they have backward-bending knees. However, the "knee" is actually the bird's ankle joint; its true knee is usually hidden by plumage. The leg muscles are close to the body, near the centre of gravity. The lower leg, containing bones and tendons, is covered in scales and has little muscle, which is why birds' legs often look pencil-thin. No bird has more than four toes, and some species have only two. The toes can be free and flexible, for perching, or they can be equipped with lobes or webs, for swimming or diving.

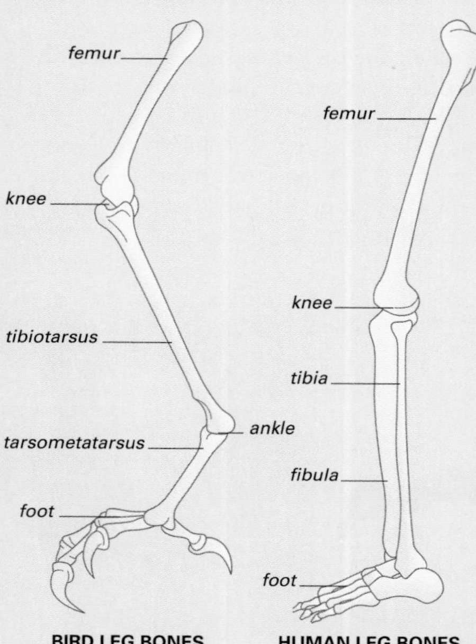

COMPARING LEGS
Unlike human legs, most bird legs are shorter above the knee than below it. Birds also have far fewer bones in their ankle joint. Several of these bones are fused, creating the tarsometatarsus – a compound bone that works as part of the leg, instead of part of the foot.

GRIPPING AND HOLDING

Because birds have wings, their legs carry out many of the tasks normally handled by front limbs. These include feather care – particularly in places where a beak cannot reach – and gripping perches, nesting materials, and food. Apart from ostriches, all birds have feet with opposable toes. Most have three toes facing forwards, and a single one that closes against them. Parrots and woodpeckers have two toes pointing in each direction, giving an unusually firm and stable grip, while Ospreys and owls can swivel their outer toe in either direction. Many birds grip food with their feet; raptors are armed with sharp talons enabling their feet to kill. Like humans, birds are right- or left-handed. In African Grey parrots (left), there are roughly equal numbers of each, but in other species, "left-handers" outnumber "right-handers" by three to one.

GRIPPING FOOD
Parrots are examples of birds that grasp food with one foot, lifting it up and then biting off pieces. Their toes are short and fleshy, but unusually strong and flexible.

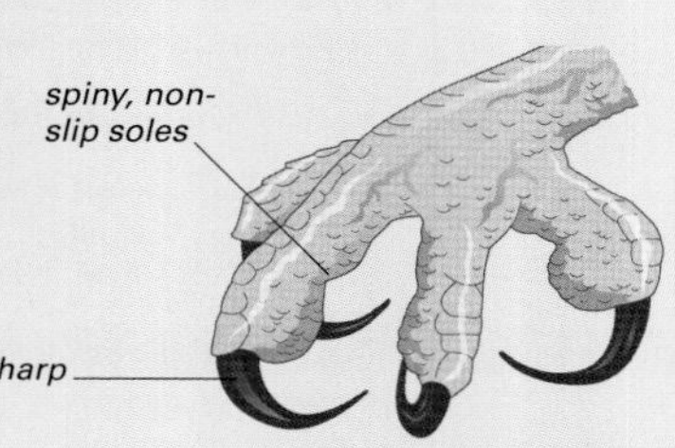

ANTI-SLIP FEET
Ospreys feed on fish, and the soles of their feet have short, stiff spines that stop fish from wriggling out of their grasp. They also use their claws to pick up nesting material.

PERCHING

On land, most birds can perch. Even long-legged species, such as herons and storks, take to trees when they nest or roost. But the true experts at perching are the passerines – an enormous group of over 5,000 species, known simply as "perching birds" (see pp.330-33). Passerines are usually small, and their feet have four highly flexible toes – three facing forwards and one behind. When a passerine lands on a perch, the bird's weight puts pressure on tendons in its legs, and its toes automatically close. The bird's ankle and toe joints are extremely mobile, which allows passerines to perch on the slenderest twigs, even on telephone lines. When perching birds fly, they draw in their legs to keep themselves streamlined – like a plane pulling in its undercarriage. Long-legged birds cannot do this. Instead, their legs fold back and trail behind them.

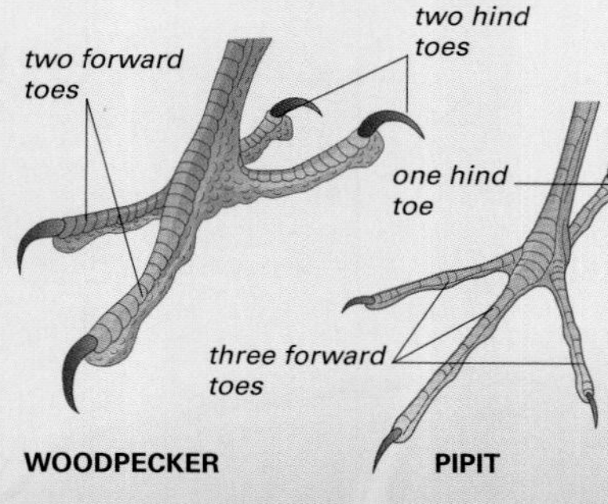

CLINGING AND PERCHING
A woodpecker's feet give a firm grip on bark. Pipits have typical passerine feet, with slender and highly flexible toes.

STAYING BALANCED
A good sense of balance is essential for staying on a perch. Even asleep, these Sun Parakeets automatically monitor their own posture.

TENACIOUS GRIP
Blue Tits and other small songbirds have a remarkably strong grip and are able to hang upside down to feed – they can do this by one leg if the other is injured.

SWIMMING FOR LIFE
A duckling's webbed feet help it to escape trouble by fast swimming. This is useful, as duck mothers are famously careless of their young.

SWIMMING

Under threat, ducklings swim so quickly that they almost run over the surface of the water. This kind of speed is possible only with webbed feet. Webbing is a feature shared by many groups of waterbirds, and it can join the full length of the toes, or just part. In most species, the three forward-facing toes are webbed, but cormorants and their relatives have four webbed toes, leaving distinctive tracks when they walk across soft mud. Three groups of birds – coots, grebes, and finfoots – have rounded flaps attached to each toe, instead of webbing.

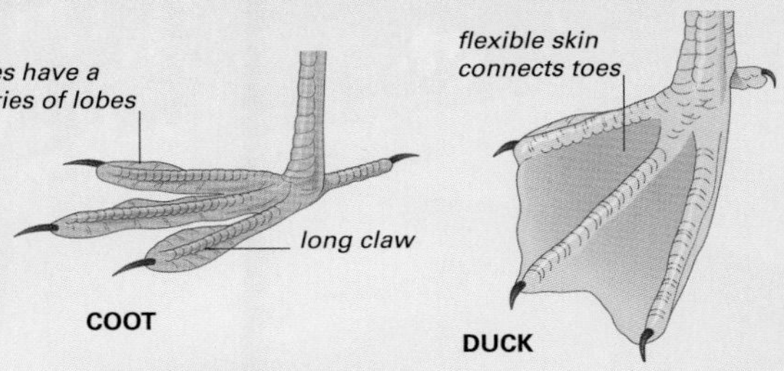

SWIMMING STYLES
Coots' toes have wide lobes that open when they kick backwards. Ducks have webbing linking the three forward-facing toes. Webbing gives faster propulsion, but lobes are better for walking on wet mud.

KEEPING WARM

Birds are widespread in cold habitats, and some – such as the Emperor Penguin – can spend weeks standing on ice. However, few apart from ptarmigans have insulated legs and feet. Instead, blood entering their legs flows through a "countercurrent" system, which removes most of its heat. As a result, a bird's legs and feet have less heat to lose.

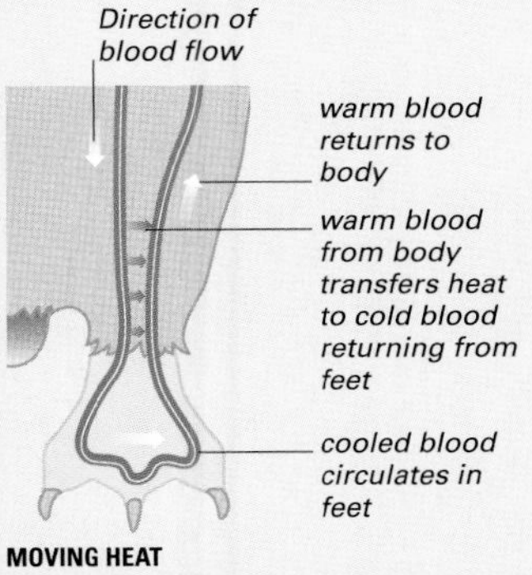

MOVING HEAT
High in a penguin's leg, a countercurrent reduces the temperature of blood flowing to the foot. Captured heat is kept within the body.

WALKING AND RUNNING

Most small birds hop, but above a certain weight, this becomes an inefficient way of moving on the ground. Instead, heavier land birds walk or run. Walking birds, such as ground hornbills and pheasants, have strong feet with short toes, which they often use to scratch up the ground. However, in the fastest runners – such as rheas and ostriches – evolution has reduced the size of the feet to minimize friction with the ground. Rheas have three toes, but an ostrich has just two. Its feet are the nearest thing to hooves among birds. At the other extreme, jacanas have four extraordinarily long and slender toes, spreading their weight as they walk across waterlily leaves.

OSTRICHES ON THE RUN
Long, powerfully muscled legs and compact, hoof-like feet enable ostriches to hit record speeds when running across firm ground. Above the ankle joint are the powerful leg muscles that form a giant "drumstick". Bare skin on this part of the leg helps to prevent overheating when an ostrich is running at speed.

WALKING ON WATER
An adult African Jacana weighs less than 250g (9oz), so its huge toe span can support its weight on floating lily leaves. Males are nearly 50 per cent lighter than females, making them even less likely to sink.

FEET FOR WALKING AND RUNNING
A jacana's long, thin toes spread its weight over delicate surfaces. The feet of a rhea or ostrich do exactly the opposite; they have fewer and shorter toes, with short, thickened claws for efficient walking and running.

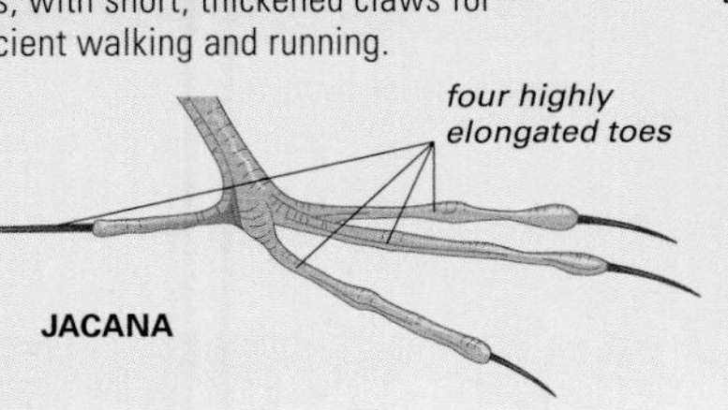

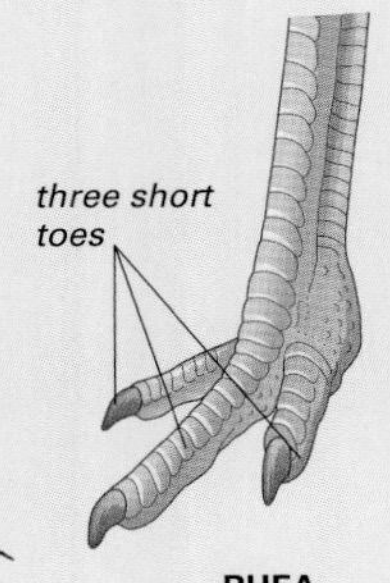

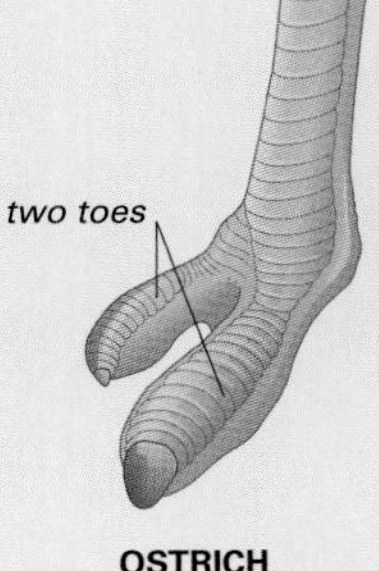

BILLS

A BILL IS A MULTI-PURPOSE TOOL, used foremost for feeding, but also for preening, for building nests, and for keeping enemies at bay. Unlike mammals' jaws, bills do not contain teeth, but they do have a living outer covering, which grows constantly to make up for wear and tear. Bills have an extraordinary variety of sizes and shapes, and some are so distinctive that the birds can be recognized by their bills alone.

BILLS AND SKULLS

A bird's bill is an extension of its skull. The bill's upper and lower halves, known as the maxilla and the mandible respectively, have an underlying framework of bone, covered by a thin layer of nerves, blood vessels, and rapidly dividing cells. These cells produce keratin, the hard protein that makes up the outer part of the bill. Unlike the bony part of the bill, this hard covering – known as the rhamphotheca – grows throughout a bird's life. The growth compensates for the considerable amount of wear it endures, in the same way as growth compensates for wear on a bird's claws. When a mammal opens its mouth, only the lower jaw actually moves. But in many birds, both halves of the bill are hinged, allowing the upper half to open as well, widening the gape significantly.

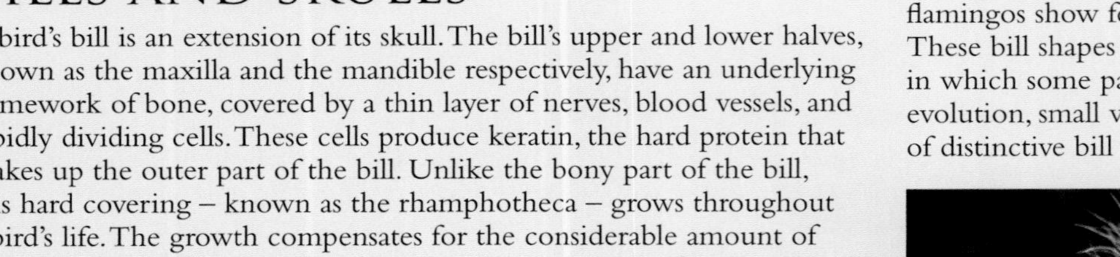

KERATIN AND BONE
In this crow's skull, the bill's dark outer covering, made of keratin, contrasts with the regions made of bone. The keratin is thickest at the hard-wearing tip of the bill.

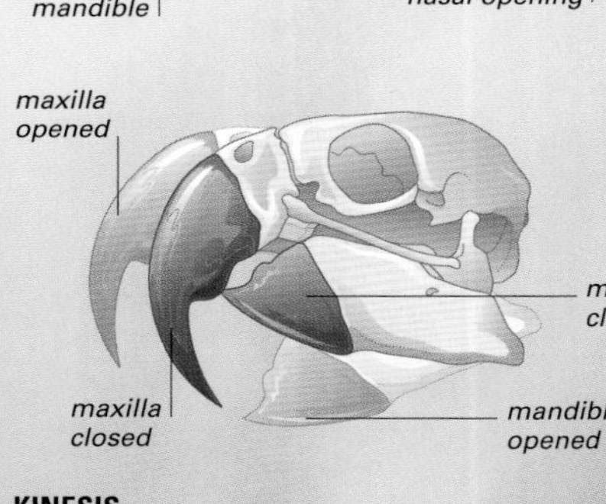

KINESIS
Many birds can raise the upper half of their bill – something known as kinesis. This diagram shows how kinesis widens a parrot's gape, enabling it to grasp and crack open large nuts.

BILL DEVELOPMENT

When young birds hatch, their bills often look quite different from the adult form of the same species. Young songbirds typically have bills with a wide gape and brightly coloured margins – two adaptations that encourage the parent birds to cram them with food. Young herons hatch with short bills, while newly hatched flamingos show few signs of the adult's bent bill or "roman nose". These bill shapes develop by allometric growth – a form of growth in which some parts of the bill grow faster than others. During bird evolution, small variations in allometry have created the wide range of distinctive bill shapes that exist in some groups of birds.

RIGHT ON TARGET
A young Gouldian Finch opens its bill to reveal metallic spots – known as "reflection pearls" – that aid accurate food delivery.

NESTLING BEAK
When it hatches, an egret has a short bill with a funnel-like gape – useless for fishing, but ideal for receiving food deliveries.

ADULT BEAK
An adult egret's bill is long and slender – an ideal implement for spearing fish and catching frogs.

MARK OF DISTINCTION
A toucan's huge, flamboyant bill doubles as a feeding device and a visual signal, enabling each species of toucan to recognize its own kind.

TYPES OF BILL

Bill shapes have evolved hand-in-hand with different diets. General feeders, such as starlings, typically have straight, symmetrical, pointed bills, but the most specialized feeders, such as flamingos, have highly individual bills tailored to one specific diet. Birds like these are often unable to switch to any other type of food and are therefore very vulnerable to habitat change. In most birds, the bill follows the body's midline, and the upper part of the bill is equal in length to, or longer than, the lower part. However, there are two interesting exceptions to these rules: skimmers have a shortened upper part, or maxilla, while in adult wrybills, the tip of the bill curves to the right.

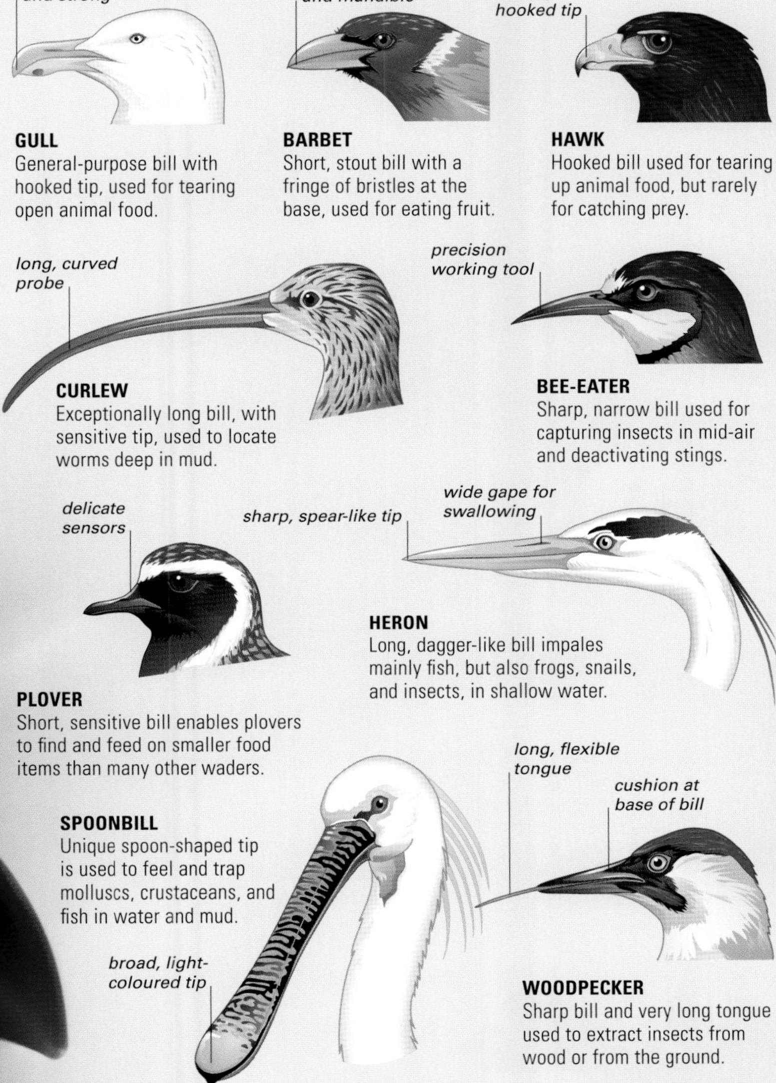

GULL
General-purpose bill with hooked tip, used for tearing open animal food.

BARBET
Short, stout bill with a fringe of bristles at the base, used for eating fruit.

HAWK
Hooked bill used for tearing up animal food, but rarely for catching prey.

CURLEW
Exceptionally long bill, with sensitive tip, used to locate worms deep in mud.

BEE-EATER
Sharp, narrow bill used for capturing insects in mid-air and deactivating stings.

PLOVER
Short, sensitive bill enables plovers to find and feed on smaller food items than many other waders.

HERON
Long, dagger-like bill impales mainly fish, but also frogs, snails, and insects, in shallow water.

SPOONBILL
Unique spoon-shaped tip is used to feel and trap molluscs, crustaceans, and fish in water and mud.

WOODPECKER
Sharp bill and very long tongue used to extract insects from wood or from the ground.

BILL USES

Apart from their primary role in feeding, birds use their bills in many other aspects of daily life. One of the most important is preening (see p.29), or routine feather care. During preening, birds use their bills like a combination between a comb and a pair of tweezers, smoothing out their feather barbs so that they link up in the correct way. Waterbirds also use their bills to apply the oil that keeps their plumage waterproof. During the breeding season, many birds use their bills to build their nests. For penguins and grebes, this often involves little more than picking up a few dozen stones or some floating waterweed. At the other extreme, tailorbirds use their bills like needles, piercing large leaves and then sewing their edges together using plant fibres or the silk from spiders' webs.

Bills also play an important role in communication; either visual – for example, in toucans – or audible, in species that clatter their bills or drum them on hard surfaces. Just like plumage, bill coloration is often most pronounced at the beginning of the courtship season. Puffins, for example, sport splendidly coloured bills in early spring, but look much more drab six months later, when the outer, brightly coloured layers of the bill have flaked off. During courtship, some pairs of birds may caress each others' bills or feed each other, to help form and strengthen their relationship.

BALANCING ACT
The Sword-billed Hummingbird has the longest bill in relation to its body. To stay balanced, it holds its bill at a steep angle both when feeding and when perched.

EATING ACCESSORY
The Bald Eagle's bill acts like a piece of cutlery, rather than a weapon. Once it has landed a fish with its talons, it uses the hooked tip to tear up its food. Most other fishing birds swallow prey whole.

RECORD BREAKER
Pelicans have the largest bills in the bird world, up to 47cm (18½in) in length. The sides of the mandible are strong but springy, allowing them to bulge outwards when the pouch fills with water.

SENSITIVITY

Birds use their bills with great precision, thanks to nerve endings that make them sensitive to touch. This sensitivity is present from the moment that they hatch. Young songbirds, for example, often have fleshy "lips" around their bills: these are highly sensitive to touch, and make the bill spring open the moment the parent bird brushes it with food. In adult life, sensitive bills are particularly important for wading birds, which feed in muddy water or damp soil where it is difficult to see the prey. Their bills have nerve endings concentrated in the tip, while dabbling ducks have many along the sides. Using these nerves, a duck can sense things that move, and it can even feel the difference between seeds and inedible pieces of grit or mud.

RAPID REACTIONS
Avocets scythe their bills through the water to catch small animals. Their reaction time, if they touch anything edible, can be as short as 1⁄60th of a second.

FEEDING ON ANIMALS

COMPARED TO MANY OTHER ANIMALS, birds have high-energy lifestyles, and so they need a large intake of food. For more than two-thirds of the world's birds, this consists mainly of animals. Animal food is high in energy and in protein, but it has one major drawback: it takes skill and time to catch.

MEAT-EATERS

Two unrelated groups of birds – birds of prey and owls – hunt by catching prey with their talons, either on the ground, in water, or in mid-air. Known as raptors, they all have hooked bills, and use them to tear up prey that is too large to be swallowed whole. Raptors feed mainly on vertebrates, but the smallest species, such as falconets and the Elf Owl, catch dragonflies, beetles, and moths. Most raptors are solitary hunters, but a few, such as Harris's Hawk, cooperate to make kills.

Some meat-eating birds are scavengers. This lifestyle requires long periods spent searching for dead animals, or carrion, but it avoids the energy-draining effort of more active hunting. Vultures rely entirely on scavenging, but many other scavengers eat both carrion and live food. They include several storks, including the Marabou and the Greater and Lesser Adjutants.

CARRION-EATERS
Hunched over the remains of a wildebeest, two Marabou Storks digest a recent meal. By soaring, they can scan huge areas for carrion, in much the same way as vultures.

CARRYING PREY
Gripping a fish in its talons, a White-tailed Eagle heads back towards the shore. Unlike diving birds, which swallow their prey straight away, birds of prey and owls almost always return to a perch before eating their catch.

KLEPTOPARASITES

Rather than catch their own prey, some birds specialize in stealing food that other birds have caught. They are known as kleptoparasites, which literally means "thief parasites", and are most common in coastal habitats, where they chase other birds for fish. Kleptoparasites include skuas, jaegers, and frigatebirds.

NEST ROBBER
In subantarctic waters, skuas rob food from penguins, and also steal their eggs. Here, a Gentoo Penguin is trying to fight back.

FISH-EATERS

Birds that fish for a living can be found almost wherever there is water, from ponds, rivers, and lakes to the furthest reaches of the open ocean. Many search for fish on the wing, and attack from the air. Terns and kingfishers often hover before they dive, but gannets and boobies slam into shoals of fish like a salvo of arrows, giving their prey little chance of escape. Diving birds chase fish underwater, and to help them swim faster have adaptations to reduce their buoyancy. Anhingas and cormorants have "wettable" feathers, a feature that drives out pockets of air from their soaked plumage, and penguins have unusually dense bones compared to the lightweight skeletons of other birds.

SPEARING FISH
Anhingas use their bills like daggers, impaling fish rather than gripping them. Having made a catch, they toss the fish into the air, then swallow it headfirst.

INSECT-EATERS

Invertebrates are by far the most numerous animals on land, which explains why so many birds use adult insects and insect grubs as their main source of food. In temperate regions, most insect-eaters are migrants, but in the warmth of the tropics, birds can survive on insects all year round. Many insect-eating birds feed on little else – apart from other small animals such as spiders – but plant-feeding birds often catch insects as well, particularly when they are raising a family. They do this because insects provide the protein young birds need for growth. Insects are also a vital supplement for nectar-feeders such as hummingbirds, because although sugary nectar is high in energy, it lacks necessary protein.

The majority of insect-eaters search for food on foliage or on the ground. The smallest of them are so sharp-eyed that they can spot individual insect eggs, or pick up aphids one by one. Larger birds often specialize: North America's Black-billed Cuckoo eats hairy caterpillars, for example, and several species of woodpecker target ants. Insect-eaters also include aerobatic hunters such as swifts, swallows, bee-eaters, and nightjars. Swifts, and their night-time equivalents the nightjars, hoover up the small flying insects that make up clouds of "aerial plankton".

VENOMOUS PREY
Bee-eaters are expert at feeding on stinging insects. Before it swallows the bee, this Little Bee-eater will thrash it against the branch to squeeze out the insect's venom.

MID-AIR FEEDING
Many small falcons catch insects on the wing. This Eurasian Hobby has just caught a dragonfly, and has transferred it from its talons to its bill to dismember in mid-air.

WADERS AND FILTER-FEEDERS

Apart from fish, water contains a wide variety of other animals eaten by birds. This is particularly true in the shallows and on tidal mudflats – habitats that attract large flocks of waders (or shorebirds). Many waders search for buried worms and molluscs, which they locate mainly by touch. A wader's bill is far more versatile than a simple pair of pincers: it functions as a highly sensitive probe, and at its tip the two mandibles can often separate while the rest of the bill is closed, enabling the bird to grip buried animals without getting a mouthful of sticky mud or sand. Another common system for finding food in water is filter-feeding. Instead of catching animals one at a time, filter-feeders sieve them in bulk from the water. Some ducks use a simple form of filter-feeding when they sift small animals from mud, while prions also filter animals at sea. However, the most specialized filter-feeders are flamingos, which live in fresh water, salt lakes, and brackish lagoons. Flamingos use their bills and bristle-edged tongues to filter out a range of small organisms, from crustaceans and insect larvae to microscopic algae called diatoms.

SWEEPING UP FOOD
Avocets (such as these Pied Avocets) are unlike most waders in that they filter feed by rhythmically sweeping their fine, upturned bill from side to side to sift tiny shrimps out of shallow water.

SMASH AND GRAB
The Eurasian Oystercatcher feeds mostly on molluscs such as mussels and limpets. It hammers the shellfish open on rocks, or deftly cuts the muscle that holds the shell closed, then stabs the soft animal inside.

USING TOOLS

Relatively few species of bird use tools, and when they do it is almost always to get at animal food. The most renowned avian tool-user is the Woodpecker Finch of the Galapagos Islands, which snaps off a cactus spine to help it prise hidden insects out of wood. Egyptian Vultures throw stones to crack open ostrich shells, while Song Thrushes batter snails against a stone "anvil" to break them apart. The Green Heron has one of the most remarkable tool-using techniques: it crouches by the water's edge, then throws bait onto the surface to attract minnows. Its commonly used bait includes earthworms, insects, and feathers.

Tool-using behaviour was once thought to be "hard-wired" into birds' brains – in other words, it did not have to be learned. But now most ornithologists think the true situation is more complex than this. In captivity, Galapagos ground finches have learned how to use cactus spines by watching Woodpecker Finches, and in Egyptian Vultures, stone-throwing also seems to be a cultural trait (as opposed to an inherited trait) that is passed on when one bird imitates another.

BREAKING EGGS
Using a stone, a young Egyptian Vulture tries to break into an ostrich egg. During the learning process, it will often throw the stone in the wrong direction, missing the egg.

TWEEZERING GRUBS
By holding a cactus spine, the Woodpecker Finch can overcome the disadvantage of having a short bill and winkle insect grubs out of crevices in tree bark.

FEEDING ON PLANTS

UNLIKE MAMMALS, FEW BIRDS EAT LEAVES, but many rely on other types of plant food. The most important vegetarian foods for birds are seeds and fruit, and in warm parts of the world many species feed on nectar and pollen. Plant food is often seasonal, which means that birds tend to use a series of different food sources throughout the year. Some birds are omnivorous – they eat more or less whatever they can swallow and digest, which makes them successful colonizers in towns and cities.

FEEDING AT FLOWERS

More than 1,500 species of bird feed mainly or entirely on flower nectar and pollen. The majority live in the tropics, but they also include migrants such as the Rufous Hummingbird, which has a summer range that extends north to within a few hundred kilometres of the Arctic Circle. Australia also has a large number of flower-feeders, many of which pollinate its trees and shrubs. Most of the birds that feed at flowers, such as hummingbirds, honeyeaters, and sunbirds, have long bills and tongues for reaching into blooms to suck up nectar. Lorikeets have a different technique. These parrots crush flowers in their bill, then lap up the nectar and pollen using their brush-tipped tongues.

SIPPING NECTAR
Clinging tightly with its feet, a Malachite Sunbird sips nectar from the flowers of an aloe plant in southern Africa.

VITAMIN SUPPLEMENT
For many plant-eating birds, such as this Ashy-headed Goose from Patagonia, flowers are a source of extra vitamins, not a staple food.

SEED-EATERS

Seeds are packed with nutrients, and they are easy to digest – two factors that explain why more birds eat them than any other plant-based food. Seed-eaters include a vast range of small songbirds, such as finches, weavers, and sparrows, as well as larger birds such as nutcrackers and jays. Most seed-eaters have short, heavy bills. In finches, the upper half has a grooved edge, and the bird rolls the seed inside it to crack away the outer husk. Nuthatches use a more forceful technique, wedging seeds in crevices and then pecking them apart. Many small seed-eaters feed in flocks, and some species are so abundant that they can be major agricultural pests. Unlike fruit or leaves, seeds remain edible for a long time if they are stored, and in regions with cold winters birds often bury seeds so that they can retrieve them when food is in short supply. This behaviour, known as caching, is particularly widespread in crows, jays, and nutcrackers. Clark's Nutcracker, from western North America, can store over 30,000 seeds in a single year and relocate its caches under several centimetres of snow.

SEED FEAST
The European Goldfinch has a fine, sharply tipped bill with which it dextrously extracts seeds from the dozens of tiny holes in flower heads.

STORING NUTS
In western North America, Acorn Woodpeckers store food in "granary trees". They collect masses of acorns and force each one into a hole drilled in the wood or bark.

CRACKING OPEN FRUIT
Thanks to their massive bills, macaws can feed on hard-shelled fruit, splitting it to reach the nutritious kernels inside. These Hyacinth Macaws are eating the fruit of the Acuri Palm in Brazil's Pantanal wetland.

FRUIT-EATERS

In temperate regions, insect-eating birds often develop a taste for fruit during the autumn and early winter. Many thrushes, including the Eurasian Blackbird and American Robin, make the most of this seasonal harvest until the supply finally runs out. But in the tropics and subtropics, different trees come into fruit at various times throughout the year, and so many birds there feed on fruit all year round. They include birds such as toucans, trogons, and turacos, a large number of parrots, and also many pigeons and doves. In rainforests, a large fruiting tree soon attracts flocks of these birds, which rapidly strip the tree, often in the company of squirrels and monkeys. One unusual fruit-eater in the tropics – the Oilbird of South America – feeds at night and finds ripe fruit by smell alone. Most fruit-eaters swallow their food whole. Once a bird has digested the flesh, it scatters the seeds in its droppings, helping its food plants to spread. Small berries are easy for birds to tackle, but in the tropics, some pigeons gulp down wild figs and palm fruit measuring up to 5cm (2in) across.

MIGRATION FUEL
Fruit can be an important food for migratory birds. White-winged Doves time their journey through North America's Sonoran Desert for when the Saguaro Cactus bears ripe fruit.

DIGESTING PLANT FOOD

Birds do not have teeth, so they cannot chew their food. Instead, most of them swallow it whole. The food's first stop is often a sac-like elastic chamber called the crop, just in front of the bird's furcula or wishbone. The crop is a temporary store that enables birds to feed in a hurry, reducing their chances of being spotted and attacked; once swallowed, food reaches the crop very quickly and it can be digested later when the bird is in a safe place. In carnivorous birds, the food then travels into the upper part of the stomach, called the proventriculus, where it is broken down by powerful acids. But in plant-eaters, this simply softens up the food, and the real task of breaking it down is carried out by the lower part of the stomach, a chamber called the gizzard. This has thick muscular walls, and it crushes the food, gradually reducing it to a pulp. To help this process, seed-eating birds often swallow grit or small stones that lodge in their gizzard. These hard fragments form an abrasive paste that aids digestion. Ostriches carry up to 1kg (2¼lb) of gizzard stones, and may even swallow metal objects such as keys, which their gizzard is strong enough to bend. In predatory birds, the gizzard has a different role. It collects indigestible remains, such as fur, feathers, or beetle wing-cases, and squeezes them into slippery pellets. The bird brings the pellets back up, showing exactly what it has been eating. For some rare forest owls, pellets retrieved from the ground are the only source of information about their diet.

DIGESTION AID
This female Grey-headed Bullfinch from China is gathering grit on the ground. Grit is particularly important for seed-eating birds such as this, because without a regular supply their digestive system does not work at peak efficiency.

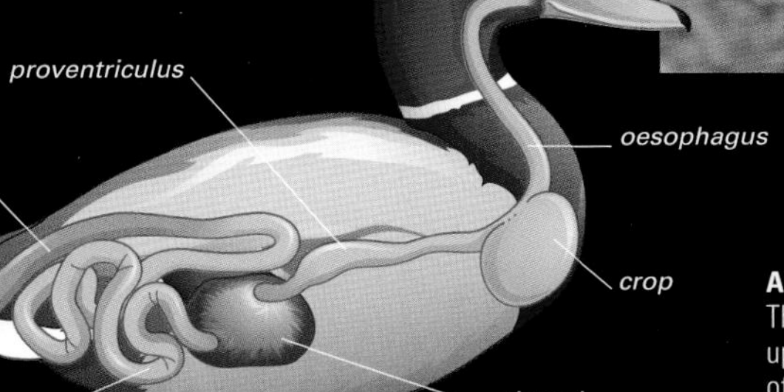

ANATOMY OF A BIRD'S DIGESTIVE SYSTEM
The digestive systems of all birds are made up from the same parts, but the relative size of each structure varies between species according to its diet. The Mallard duck, shown here, is omnivorous and has a well developed crop and gizzard.

OMNIVORES

The Common Starling is a classic example of an omnivorous bird. Bold and aggressive, it eats whatever it can find, from seeds and insect grubs to scraps of leftover food. This versatility helps to explain its rapid spread across North America, and other parts of the world where it has been introduced. Many other urban birds, such as crows and gulls, show the same kind of behaviour, although not all omnivores are this bold. In freshwater habitats, ducks often eat a mixture of seeds, aquatic plants, and small animals, which they obtain from the water or wet mud. On land, some of the most widespread omnivores are gamebirds, which often scratch up their food with their feet. Domestic chickens share this typical gamebird trait: when left to range freely, they eat seeds, flowers, insects, earthworms, and even slugs – one of the widest diets in the bird world.

STARLINGS FLOCKING
Some omnivorous birds have benefited hugely from human changes to the natural world. For example, open pasture, playing fields, and airfields are ideal feeding grounds for Common Starlings. They also thrive in urban areas and in winter often gather in large flocks to roost.

COMMUNICATION

IN THE BIRD WORLD – just as in the human one – the main methods of communication are sight and sound. Birds use visual signals to recognize each other, attract potential mates, and keep rivals at bay. The same is true of their calls and songs, but this kind of communication has one crucial advantage: the message stills gets across when a bird is hidden or some distance away.

SPECTACULAR TRANSFORMATION
Most of the time, the male Superb Lyrebird keeps its tail closed and is hard to spot. But it is impossible to miss during its noisy courtship display, as it rotates on the spot with its lacy tail plumes held up high.

VISUAL COMMUNICATION

Birds cannot produce facial expressions, and they have limited scope for gesturing in other ways. Instead, their feathers play a key role in visual communication. Brightly coloured plumage works like an identity badge, and in some species, such as lyrebirds and birds of paradise, the males seem to transform themselves completely when they carry out displays. Less eye-catching, but just as important, are the many subtle signals that birds send out at close quarters. For example, many songbirds convey aggression or excitement by raising their head feathers, or by spreading their tails. These movements may last for just a fraction of a second, but this is long enough for other birds to notice and respond.

PATTERNS AND COLOURS

Birds have superbly detailed, full-colour vision (see p.26), which is why plumage colours are often a key feature that enable birds to identify their own kind. In European Robins, the sight of an intruding male's breast will often trigger a resident male to stage an attack. This instinct is so strong that robins will even attack a red sponge fixed to a stick. Young European Robins have brown breasts, and so until they moult into adult plumage are safe because they do not provoke the same belligerent response. Another illustration of birds' instinctive reaction to bright coloration is provided by parent songbirds. Their nestlings have red or orange mouth linings, which stimulate the adults to push more food into them.

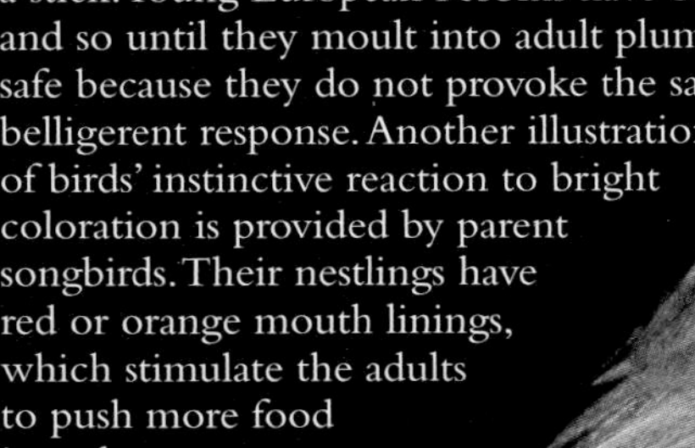

MALES FIGHTING
When male European Robins come this close, a fierce skirmish is sure to follow. Females have exactly the same coloration, but males can tell they are potential mates, rather than rivals, by the way they behave.

SPRING SOUNDS
Passerines, such as this Golden-winged Warbler, sing energetically in spring to establish a territory, especially on sunny days, but seldom in winter.

CALLS AND SONG

Bird sounds range from simple calls to songs of extraordinary beauty and complexity. The loudest songs – a deep booming produced by large species of bittern – can be heard up to 5km (3 miles) away. But, for their size, small songbirds are even more impressive. The Winter Wren, for example, weighs as little as 10g ($^1/_3$oz), but its explosive song is often audible from hundreds of metres. In general, birds produce two kinds of sound. Alarm calls and contact calls are made by both sexes, to signal danger or to ensure that birds remain in a group, and are normally short and simple. By contrast, songs are usually produced only by male birds, although females may join in to form a duet. Songs are often far more elaborate than calls, and are used to claim territories and attract mates.

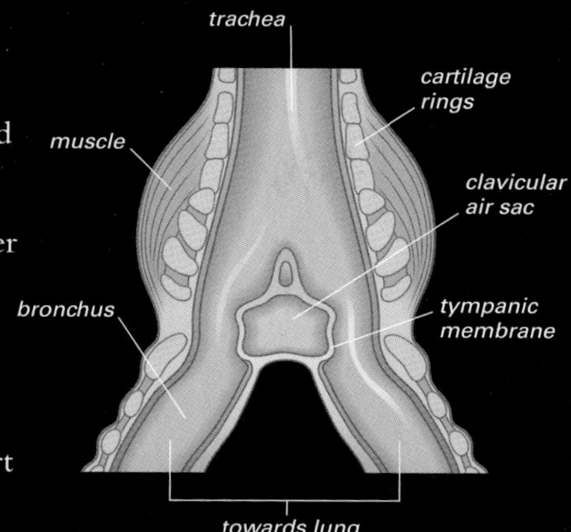

SYRINX
Bird calls and songs are produced by the syrinx. This is usually positioned at the top of the chest, where the trachea or windpipe divides into two bronchial tubes on its way to the lungs. As a bird exhales air, the tympanic membranes in its syrinx vibrate, producing the tone of the call or song. The pitch is controlled by rings of cartilage, which tighten or relax to change the air pressure inside the clavicular air sac in the centre of the syrinx.

SONG DEVELOPMENT

Birds hatch with the instinct to sing, and in some species, such as pigeons and doves, little or no learning is needed. But in most songbirds, fledglings inherit only the basics of the song. As they grow up, they refine their singing technique by listening to adults around them. The spectrograms below show how a Common Chaffinch's song develops as it grows up. At first, the song is unstructured and erratic, but the adult bird's song has clear phrases repeated each time it sings.

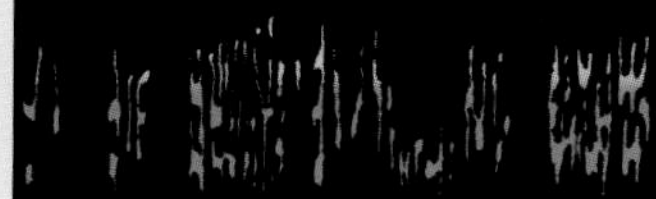

EARLY JUVENILE

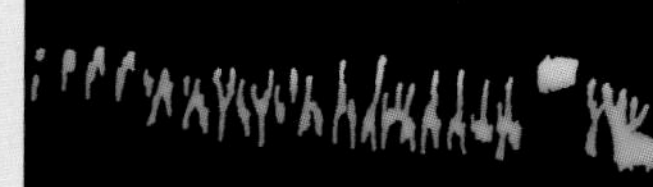

LATE JUVENILE

ADULT

COMPETITION FOR MATES
Male Three-wattled Bellbirds perform their song from a high perch – often a broken-off branch. Rival bellbirds use their metallic, powerfully resonant song as a form of sonic combat, to vie for the attention of the listening greenish-yellow females.

GREY PARROT
In captivity, this parrot can pick up a vocabulary of more than 100 words. It seems to be able to communicate simple ideas.

NORTHERN MOCKINGBIRD
This North American mimic can copy the calls and songs of up to 30 species of bird, building them into a melody of its own.

COMMON HILL MYNA
A popular cage-bird, the Hill Myna belongs to the starling family – a group known for their loud and often expert mimicry.

MIMICRY

Parrots and mynas are famous for their ability to mimic human speech, but mimicry does not only occur in captive birds. A wide variety of wild songbirds, from Marsh Warblers to mockingbirds, incorporate mimicked sounds in their calls or songs. Male Marsh Warblers have been known to imitate up to 80 other species of bird – some from their breeding range in Europe, and others from their winter range in Africa. Birds also mimic all kinds of background sounds, from machinery to mobile phones. Until recently, mimicry was thought to involve nothing more than simple copying by rote. However, research shows that Grey Parrots can learn to communicate through human speech, and they may have linguistic skills as advanced as those of a Chimpanzee.

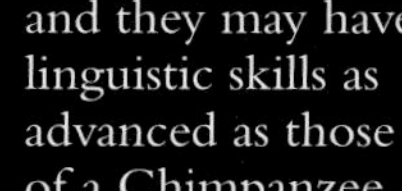

MECHANICAL SOUNDS

Bird sounds are not restricted to calls and songs – many birds can also make non-vocal sounds, which they use for communication. One of the simplest is wing-clapping – a signalling technique used by many birds, including pigeons and doves. Male woodpeckers make loud drumming sounds by hammering with their bills, while courting grouse often stamp with their strong feet. But some of the most extraordinary sounds are made by birds that have specially modified feathers. The Common Snipe makes loud bleating sounds with its outer tail feathers as it dives through the air, and some hummingbirds whistle with their wings. Male manakins can produce bizarre snapping and buzzing sounds, by rubbing together their inner wing feathers, which have thickened shafts.

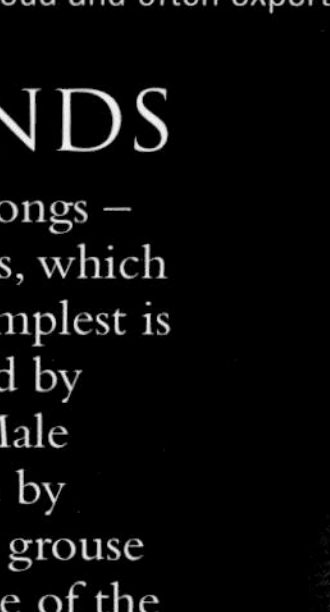

BILL CLATTERING
With their heads raised, a pair of White Storks clatter their bills in a greeting ceremony at their nest. Such displays can be seen throughout the breeding season.

DEFENCE

BIRDS ARE CONSTANTLY IN DANGER from predators, yet only a handful have effective weapons. For this reason, most birds take flight or run to cover at the least sign of trouble. In the breeding season, they stand their ground with much more determination. Many breeding birds are weaker and smaller than their enemies, but they have some fascinating ways of protecting their nests and putting predators off the track.

EMERGENCY ESCAPES

For all birds, survival depends on perpetual vigilance and readiness to flee. Ground-feeding birds have a limited view of their surroundings, and so they spend much time nervously looking up – in a flock of grazing geese, for example, there are always several alert birds acting as sentries. When threatened, most birds immediately fly or run away, but gamebirds often sit tight before bursting into the air at the last moment.

Birds that feed above the ground have a better view, so are harder to catch by surprise. However, after dark they turn into easy targets because they are reluctant to fly. Many predators, including tree snakes, owls, and martens, exploit this weakness by hunting roosting birds at night.

DISTRACTION DISPLAYS

A few songbirds fight back if their nests are threatened, but most abandon their eggs or young rather than risk their lives. It makes more sense to start again and raise another brood than to die for a hopeless cause. However, many ground-nesting birds try to lure predators away from their nests with special distraction displays. For example, waders often limp from their nest, holding out a fluttering wing as if it is broken. With luck, a predator will follow the "injured" parent and can be led away from the eggs.

CONFUSING PREDATORS
This Eurasian Dotterel is carrying out a distraction display. The aim of this high-risk strategy is to divert the attention of a potential predator, so that it leaves the bird's nest alone.

NEST DEFENCE
Splashing furiously, a Eurasian Coot tries to protect its nest from a Grey Heron. Coots are naturally aggressive, and this one stands a good chance of driving off the intruder.

FIGHTING BACK

Among the handful of birds able to inflict serious damage on their enemies is the flightless Southern Cassowary, which can deliver slashing wounds with the long, sharp claw on its innermost toe. Terns are notoriously aggressive if their nests are threatened, and take off to dive-bomb any intruders, including people, who stray too close. They may make contact with their sharply pointed bill, often drawing blood. Birds without such a formidable weapon must adopt different defensive tactics. Some ground-nesting birds protect their vulnerable eggs by appearing more dangerous than they actually are – usually by rearing up with outstretched wings. This display is enough to prevent cattle trampling the nest, but is less successful with carnivorous mammals. Songbirds and gulls rely on strength in numbers to harass predatory birds such as hawks, owls, or ravens, by swooping around them in a gang until they eventually leave the area. This form of collective defence is known as mobbing.

MOBBING
A pair of Hooded Crows mob a passing Eurasian Sparrowhawk. Eventually, the relentless harassment by the crows will drive the bird of prey elsewhere.

HUMAN IMPACT

RECOGNIZING DANGER

Birds start life with an instinctive ability to recognize predators. Nestlings can often identify birds of prey, while many birds have a fear of snakes. However, these instinctive recognition systems are not foolproof. In the past, many seabird colonies were decimated by hunters, because the birds did not perceive people as a threat.

SITTING TIGHT
These Laysan Albatrosses are nesting on a golf course on Midway Island, Hawaii. They have no instinctive fear of humans.

CAMOUFLAGE

Compared to mammals, many birds are brightly coloured, which makes camouflage seem like an unlikely kind of defence. In reality, even some of the world's most eyecatching birds, such as trogons, cotingas, and fruit pigeons, can be remarkably difficult to see in their natural habitat. Their vivid colours make them extremely conspicuous in the open, but they seem to disappear altogether against a background of sun-dappled leaves. However, camouflage is best developed in birds that feed at night and roost by day. Owls, nightjars, and potoos all use it to help them blend in with trees or open ground while sleeping during the day, and bitterns and rails use their camouflage to hide among reeds. Male songbirds are often colourful, while females have more muted plumage in shades of grey or brown. This difference has evolved because – in most cases – the female is the sole or chief incubator. Sitting on her nest for hours at a time, she relies on camouflage to avoid being seen. The male, on the other hand, can fly away from danger, which offsets the risk of being easy for predators to see.

VANISHING ACT
When a Eurasian Bittern senses danger, it stretches upwards with its bill pointing skywards, to emphasize the reed-like streaks in its superbly camouflaged plumage.

EVADING PURSUIT

For birds, even the air is unsafe, because some predators specialize in catching birds on the wing. Small songbirds are the most frequent victims, and so they are particularly aware of this danger. If they spot a bird-eating hawk or falcon, they disappear into cover almost instantly, often giving a hurried alarm call to alert other birds nearby. They remain completely still and silent until the hawk has moved on. In the open air, flocking birds such as waders and Common Starlings bunch together if a bird of prey appears, twisting and turning in a tight aerial formation – an amazing display of timing and coordination. This behaviour makes it much more difficult for the predator to select a target bird from the confusing mass of moving bodies in the group.

DOUBLE DEFENCE
Snipe have a two-track strategy for dealing with danger. Initially, they crouch down and rely on their camouflage to escape detection – sometimes until almost trodden on. If a snipe is flushed from cover, it flies away in a zig-zag path (left) to shrug off its pursuer.

BREEDING

REPRODUCTION IS THE MOST important task in a bird's life. It is a challenging process with many stages, from setting up a territory and attracting a mate, to making a nest, incubating the eggs, and finding enough food for the young. Sometimes these tasks are shared fairly equally, but bird breeding systems are very varied. In some species, the male participates fully, and in others the female raises her family alone. During the breeding season, timing is critical, particularly in the far north and south where the window of opportunity may be just a few weeks long.

RIVALS IN THE COLONY
Like many seabirds, Mediterranean Gulls nest close together, but each breeding pair claims its own territory within the colony. Parents have to be on their guard because their neighbours may try to eat unattended eggs or chicks. Noisy squabbles are a frequent occurrence.

TOGETHER OR APART

The manner in which birds breed is often affected by the availability of nesting sites. Seabirds typically nest at very high densities in large colonies, partly because suitable sites may be few and far between. Every year, the birds return to the same location, often meeting up with the same mate from the year before. Their loyalty to the site can be extraordinarily strong. For example, Juan Fernandez Petrels wander over most of the west and central Pacific, but all of them come together to breed on Robinson Crusoe Island – a remote outcrop of volcanic rock 675km (420 miles) west of Chile. Site faithfulness also stretches far back in time. Frozen Adelie Penguins, found entombed in Antarctic ice, prove that some of this species' breeding sites have been in use for at least 600 years.

Birds that live on land face fewer restrictions when looking for a home, and so many species breed in individual territories, setting up a new one each year. But for some land birds, nesting sites are not always easy to find. Hole-nesters require a suitably sized cavity in a tree, cliff, or building, and these are in limited supply. Often there is such strong competition that if a resident bird is absent – even for a few minutes – another may take over and move in.

BREEDING SEASONS

On and near to the equator, many species of bird breed more or less all year round. But in the rest of the world, particularly in temperate and polar regions, the breeding seasons of birds are often sharply defined. They are triggered mainly by changes in day length, although rising temperatures also play a part. If all goes well, the outcome is that birds raise their young when the food supply is at its peak. Most birds are not simply reluctant to breed at other times – they are physically incapable of doing so. This is because their reproductive system shuts down and shrinks, an adaptation that helps flying birds to save weight. The main exception to this rule are nomadic desert species, such as Zebra Finches and Budgerigars. These can "switch on" their breeding cycle within days of rain to make the most of the sudden breeding opportunity.

When the breeding season is in progress, different species divide it up in different ways. Most seabirds raise a single brood, often consisting of one offspring. In warm regions, however, songbirds may raise several families in a few months. In an exceptionally good year, a pair of House Sparrows can raise five successive broods – a marathon reproductive effort.

EARLY START
Dusted with snow, a Southern Giant Petrel incubates its single egg. Like most polar birds, it begins to breed before winter is over because its offspring takes a long time – up to 130 days – to leave the nest.

EXCAVATED NEST SITES
Southern Carmine Bee-eaters need sandy river banks to dig their nesting burrows, and where conditions are ideal dozens of birds breed in close proximity.

TERRITORIES

When a male bird is ready to breed, it starts by establishing a territory – a piece of ground that it defends from its rivals. For species that nest in groups, territories can be less than 90 square cm (144 square in), but for large eagles they may be several kilometres across. Territories serve as mating grounds, and often – but not always – as places for nesting and gathering food. A good territory helps to attract females, and if they are impressed enough, they mate and move in. Because territories belong to individual birds, they change with time. The most extreme form of this occurs in species whose males display to females in communal leks (see p.50). Here, territories are reduced to symbolic patches of ground, and the owner of a desirable patch may hold it for as little as half an hour.

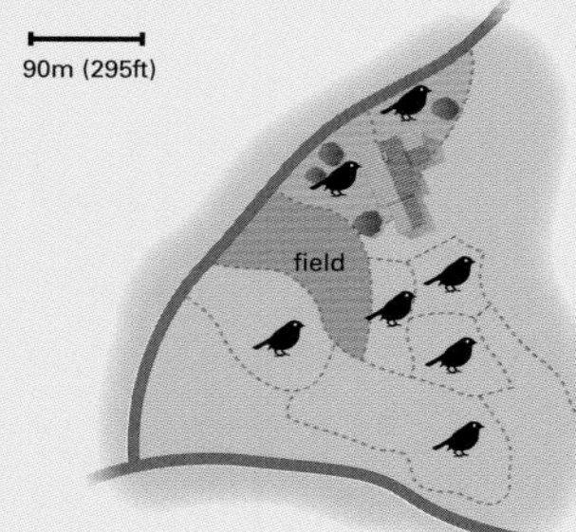

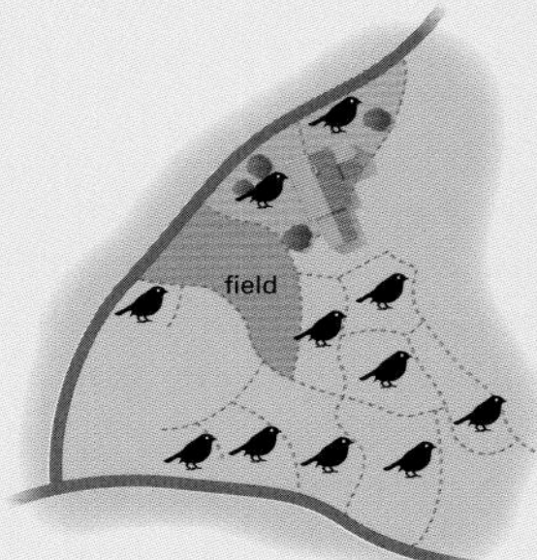

SMALL TERRITORIES
When crammed together on a sea cliff to breed, guillemots have some of the smallest territories of any bird. They lay their eggs directly on the rock, and each pair "owns" a section of cliff just a few centimetres across.

ROBIN TERRITORIES IN SPRING
A study of European Robins shows how territories change through the year. There are fewer territories in early spring because many birds die in the winter; some territories are quite large.

ROBIN TERRITORIES IN WINTER
Nine months later, young robins have swelled the population and so there are more birds competing for the same amount of ground. As a result, several new territories have been set up, mostly carved out of existing ones.

BREEDING SYSTEMS

Around 90 per cent of all species of bird are usually monogamous: they have one partner. The pair bond lasts for a single nesting, or more often, for two or more broods over the course of an entire breeding season. In a few monogamous species, such as storks, swans, eagles, and albatrosses, the pair bond lasts for life, although couples may "divorce" if they fail to breed. Polygamous birds have several partners in a single breeding season. They include bowerbirds and grouse, in which the males concentrate on mating with as many females as they can. Most species that are normally monogamous may also take part in extra matings outside their pair bond.

MONOGAMOUS BIRDS
White Storks mate for life, and often perform greeting displays to reaffirm their pair bond. Each pair of storks also returns to the same nest year after year. The species is traditionally associated with longevity and fidelity throughout its Eurasian breeding range.

COOPERATIVE REARING
Once parent birds have successfully raised their young, the juveniles normally take up life on their own. However, in at least 300 species of bird – including these Laughing Kookaburras – young birds remain with their parents after they have left the nest, to act as helpers with their next brood. Parent kookaburras can raise twice as many young when they have this kind of assistance.

POLYGAMOUS BIRD
A Winter Wren sings from a tree stump to attract partners. Male Winter Wrens are often polygamous, building several nests in their territory, one for each of their mates. But they can only do this if food is plentiful because they usually help to feed the young – to raise several broods, a male has to be able to find food quickly.

COURTSHIP

FEW ASPECTS OF ANIMAL BEHAVIOUR are as eye-catching as the courtship displays of birds. These remarkable rituals enable birds to attract partners and form a pair bond – the essential prelude to mating. Courtship ensures that birds choose partners of the same species, and it defuses the instinctive aggression between birds. Most courtship rituals are private affairs with just two participants, but some species gather in groups at traditional display grounds called leks.

FLAMBOYANT DISPLAY
Male Indian Peafowl contribute nothing to breeding, apart from the act of mating. All of their energy is devoted to staging unbeatable courtship displays, using a fan made from highly modified tail coverts.

MALE DISPLAYS

During courtship, it is usually the female that chooses the male. In many species, her choice is based on a combination of factors. These include the male's physical appearance, his talent as a singer, and also a range of more practical assets, such as his territory and nest-building skills. In polygamous species (see p.49), the male often plays no part in family life, so the female's choice is not based on practical qualities. Instead, her decision is based entirely on appearance and courtship display. Over countless generations, this has made the males more flamboyant, and their courtship displays ever more complex. Ruffs, birds-of-paradise, and peafowl are examples of birds that have evolved in this way.

LEKS

Some birds do not display in separate territories but assemble at collective courtship grounds, or leks. The males travel to the lek from the surrounding area, usually in the early morning or occasionally in the evening, and once there begin to carry out elaborate displays. Closely watched by the females, they vie with each other to claim a territory nearest the lek's central point. Males nearest the centre will mate with the most females, while those at the edge often do not mate at all. Lekking is common in gamebirds, but it has also evolved in a variety of other species that have polygamous males. Among them are Ruffs and various snipes, which display on the ground, and cotingas, manakins, and hummingbirds, which display on branches or in mid-air.

MALES AT THE LEK
During the breeding season, male Ruffs congregate at a lek to display. Each bird has a unique courtship plumage and a differently coloured face and bill, and the same lek site may be used for years.

PREENING AND FEEDING

Normally preening is an activity that birds carry out on their own. However, during courtship potential partners sometimes preen each other – an activity that can continue long after the pair bond has formed. Known as allopreening, this is common in birds such as parrots (see p.252) and waxbills (see p.458), which seem to enjoy physical contact and often perch close together. Courtship feeding is another behaviour that often occurs when a pair bond has formed. In terns, either sex may feed the other, but courtship feeding is usually triggered by the female, which imitates a noisy begging chick.

PREENING RITUAL
A Red-browed Finch, from Australia, preens its partner's plumage. This ritual helps to defuse the aggression that is often triggered if another bird comes close.

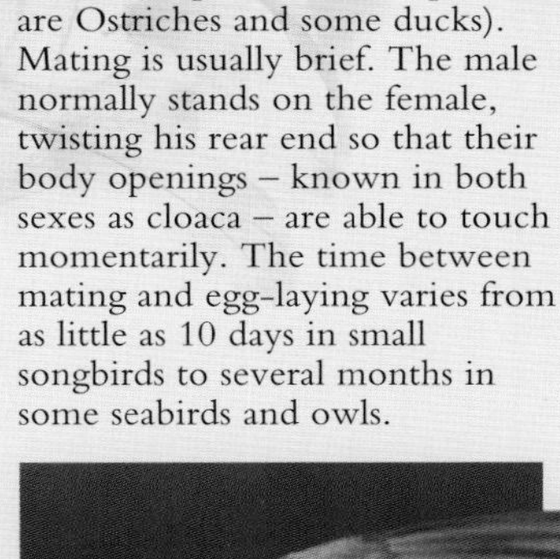

FOOD GIFT
Taking care to stay out of pecking range, a male Common Kingfisher offers a fish to his partner. In kingfishers and some other birds courtship feeding is immediately followed by mating, although the male may have to make several offerings before he is successful.

COURTSHIP DANCES

When a male has attracted a female, the stage is set for pair formation to begin. In some species, the female simply watches the male's performance, but in many, the prospective partners join in ritualized dances that help to cement their bond. These dances can last for a few seconds, or be played out over many hours. Grebes have some of the most elaborate courtship rituals of all birds. Their ritual is divided into several separate dances, each with its own carefully choreographed steps. If either partner carries out one of the dances incorrectly, the performance ends; if the ritual does not come together after repeated attempts, the pair bond is likely to fail. Different species of grebe have different dances, so following the correct steps prevents cross-breeding.

RUSHING DISPLAY
The courtship rituals of Great Crested Grebes include furious paddling and splashing, brief "confrontations", and equally rapid retreats.

THE "PENGUIN DANCE"
Paddling hard, the two grebes rise up in the water to present a billful of weed to their partner – a ritual called the penguin dance.

HEAD-SHAKING CEREMONY
During this dance, the two birds come face to face with their necks fully extended, and flick their heads from side to side.

MATING

Unlike mammals, male birds do not have a penis (the exceptions are Ostriches and some ducks). Mating is usually brief. The male normally stands on the female, twisting his rear end so that their body openings – known in both sexes as cloaca – are able to touch momentarily. The time between mating and egg-laying varies from as little as 10 days in small songbirds to several months in some seabirds and owls.

COPULATION
While he mates, a male European Turtle Dove flutters his wings to balance on the female's back. The male's sperm fertilizes the female's egg cells while they are at an early stage of development, before their shells have formed.

BOWERS

In New Guinea and Australia, bowerbirds have evolved some of the strangest courtship behaviour in the bird world. The males are polygamous, but unlike other males with multiple partners, their plumage is usually subdued. Instead, they attract females by building extraordinary structures, called bowers, on the forest floor. Bowers are made of sticks and stalks, and their shapes vary between species. Some are like avenues, but the largest kinds – built by "gardener" bowerbirds – look like thatched cottages with pointed roofs and can be over 1.5m (5ft) high. When a bower is complete, the owner decorates it with bright objects, such as pebbles, fruit, or flowers, and waits for females to inspect his work. After mating, the females fly away to build a nest alone elsewhere.

FEMALE INSPECTING A BOWER
Satin Bowerbirds decorate their bowers with all kinds of blue objects, including plastic litter. Unusually for their family, the males are brightly coloured; females are dull green.

NESTS AND EGGS

UNLIKE MAMMALS, ADULT BIRDS rarely make homes for themselves. Instead, most of their nests are used solely for raising young. Some birds lay their eggs directly on the ground or in a tree hollow, but many make elaborate structures from an immense range of building materials, including twigs, leaves, mud, spiders' webs, saliva, and even rotting seaweed. A nest helps to conceal vulnerable hatchlings, and it also insulates them – a crucial feature if they have no insulation of their own.

BUILDING WITH MUD
Safely beyond the reach of most predators, these Cliff Swallow nests are made of mud mixed with saliva – a material that becomes rock-hard as it dries, and lasts for years.

NESTING OFF THE GROUND

Songbirds are usually blind and featherless when they hatch, so a robust nest is essential for their survival. The majority of species nest off the ground, chiefly in trees and bushes, but songbirds also nest on rocks, in caves, and even behind waterfalls. Their nests are typically cup-shaped, but evolution has produced all kinds of refinements to this basic design. One of the commonest is the domed nest with an entrance at one side. Even more effective, in security terms, are nests that hang from the ends of slender branches. Weavers often build nests like these, but the largest are made by oropendolas in tall tropical trees. Shaped like an extended pouch, their nests can be up to 2m (6½ft) long, with the living quarters hanging up to 50m (160ft) above the ground. However, songbirds are not the only tree-nesters: this behaviour is widespread in many other birds. Ovenbirds, which also belong to the passerine order – build some of the most complex nests of all. Shaped like an old-fashioned clay oven, the nests have a slit-like entrance and a curving corridor leading to the nest chamber inside. Non-passerines typically make crude platform nests from sticks. Even elaborate nests are built quickly. A structure that requires thousands of billfuls of moss or leaves can be complete in a couple of days.

WEAVER AT WORK
Nest-building is controlled by instinct, but requires enormous skill. Using strips of grass, male Southern Masked Weavers build ball-shaped nests that hang from the tips of branches. Once the nest is complete, the male hangs upside down beneath it, and flutters his wings to attract passing females.

CAVITY NESTERS

Tree-holes and other natural cavities are used as nests by a wide range of birds. At one extreme, these include small songbirds such as tits; at the other are 1m- (3ft-) long hornbills, and macaws. Woodpeckers excavate holes themselves, but many other birds take them over once the original owners have moved on. Hornbills have a particularly unusual form of cavity nesting behaviour. Having found a suitable nest hole, the female moves in. The male then seals the entrance with a wall of mud, leaving a small hole so he can supply his mate with food. Cavity nesters also include birds that burrow into the ground, or into riverbanks, or sandy cliffs. Most use their beaks to peck their way through the earth, although the North American Burrowing Owl excavates with its feet. Bank-nesters, such as kingfishers, often give their tunnels a slight upward slope to prevent them from becoming flooded.

STARTING FROM SCRATCH
Woodpeckers can chisel holes in healthy, living wood. Once the hole has been opened up, the wood eventually begins to rot, allowing other birds to expand the nest in subsequent years. A Eurasian Three-toed Woodpecker is pictured.

PERMANENT NESTS

Songbirds usually abandon their nests when their young have fledged, and build new ones next time they breed. This sounds wasteful, but it is a good way of avoiding the attention of predators and reducing parasite infestation. Birds of prey are different: they frequently return to the same nest year after year. With each breeding season, they add more sticks, increasing the size of the nesting platform. Because these birds are long-lived, the largest species – such as Bald Eagles – can end up owning nests of a colossal size. White Storks also reuse their nests, but the most remarkable permanent nests are made by the African Hamerkop. Although only about 30cm (12in) high, this marshland bird builds an immense spherical nest out of sticks, up to 2m (6½ft) across. The Hamerkop's nest is multi-chambered, and is so strong that it can support the weight of an adult man.

ANCESTRAL PILE
A Bald Eagle looks out from its nest high in a pine tree. Bald Eagles make the world's biggest nests – the largest one ever measured was nearly 3m (10ft) wide and over 6m (19½ft) deep. These giant nests are often built by several generations of birds.

COMMUNAL NESTS

Many birds nest in groups, but a few species build nests that are physically attached to each other. The result is a giant communal nest, like a building with lots of self-contained apartments. In Africa, Sociable Weavers make communal nests out of grass; in South America, Monk Parakeets use sticks.

SHARED ACCOMMODATION
The communal nests of Sociable Weavers are usually built in isolated trees. They can contain up to 300 separate nesting chambers, each with its own downward-pointing entrance.

GROUND NESTERS

A large number of birds – particularly in open habitats – lay their eggs on the ground. Many use no nesting material, relying instead on camouflage or out-of-the-way nest sites to protect their eggs and young. These birds include many seabirds and waders, as well as nightjars, some vultures, and large flightless birds, such as ostriches and emus. Some excavate a shallow depression called a scrape, but guillemots and razorbills do not have this option. They breed on cliff ledges, and lay a single egg directly on the bare rock.

In addition to these "non-builders", ground-nesting birds include many species that have at least some construction skills. Penguins often breed on rocky shores, gathering small piles of stones or sticks. Waterfowl and gamebirds show greater expertise, building bowl-shaped nests from plants. The largest structures are built by megapodes: their mound-shaped nests can be over 10m (33ft) across and up to 5m (17ft) high, containing several tonnes of leaves.

MALE IN CHARGE
Ostriches lay their eggs directly on the ground. Several females contribute to the clutch, which is guarded by a single male. Eventually, the nest may contain over 50 eggs. Only half of them are incubated – the ones at the edge do not hatch.

HOME SECURITY
Standing by its nest, this Gentoo Penguin is not only guarding its egg, but also its nesting materials. Neighbours are quick to help themselves if materials are in short supply.

EGGS

A bird's egg is a single giant cell, protected by watertight membranes and a porous shell. The embryo starts to take shape during incubation, when the original cell divides repeatedly, creating the tissues and organs of a developing bird. Seabirds often produce a single egg, while gamebirds lay the largest clutches: some species, such as quails and partridges, can produce over 20 eggs each time they breed. There is no straightforward connection between a bird's size and the size of its eggs. The Bee Hummingbird produces the smallest eggs – as little as 7mm (¼in) long – while the Ostrich's are the largest, weighing up to 1.5kg (3⅓lb). However, the Kiwi's solitary egg is the biggest in relative terms, measuring about a quarter of the female's weight. The eggs of cavity nesters are often white, while those of ground-nesters are usually camouflaged.

INSIDE AN EGG
An egg is lined with a series of membranes that help to keep water in, but which let oxygen and carbon dioxide pass through the shell. As the embryo grows, the yolk (which provides nourishment) shrinks, and the air space enlarges. The shell thins, as its calcium is used for the embryo's skeleton.

SHAPE AND COLOUR
Some eggs are almost round; guillemot eggs have a sharp point, to stop them rolling off cliffs. The shell has a basic colour, with markings added just before laying.

PARENTAL CARE

THE ONLY BIRDS ABLE TO fend for themselves from the moment they hatch are the Australasian brush turkeys, or mound-builders (see p.108). In all other species, young birds depend on parental care to survive. This care starts with incubation, and it continues after the young have hatched, until they are fully self-reliant. The amount of time that parents devote to these duties varies enormously, from as little as three weeks in small songbirds to almost a year in the largest albatrosses. However, brood parasites avoid this work entirely by laying their eggs in other birds' nests.

INCUBATION

The process of incubation keeps eggs at a steady warm temperature, so that development can take place. It does not necessarily start as soon as the first egg has been laid – in many species of bird, the parents wait until their clutch is complete (see Hatching Intervals, right). However, once incubation is underway, it must continue around the clock, or the developing embryos will die. During the breeding season, many parent birds develop bare areas on their breasts. These are called brood patches and make it easier for the parents' body heat to be transferred to the eggs. Some seabirds, such as gannets and boobies, lack brood patches and incubate their eggs by wrapping their webbed feet around them, but the Emperor Penguin is the only bird to incubate its egg on top of its feet, under a fold of skin. In most birds, incubation is carried out by both parents, or by the female alone. In a small minority, including the Emperor Penguin, Emu, and rheas, the male incubates on his own.

INCUBATION PERIODS
When incubation has started, it follows a precise timetable that varies between species. Woodpeckers have some of the shortest incubation periods, while the longest belong to albatrosses, which can sit on their eggs for over 2½ months.

SPECIES	INCUBATION PERIOD
Great Spotted Woodpecker	10 days
Domestic chicken	21 days
Great Crested Grebe	28 days
Golden Eagle	44 days
Wandering Albatross (below)	82 days

EGG TURNING
Incubating birds periodically turn their eggs to ensure that they are equally warmed. Here, a Great Crested Grebe stands up on its floating nest to carry out this essential task.

JUVENILE DEVELOPMENT

Birds hatch at very different stages of development. In general, the shorter their incubation time, the less developed the young are when they break out of their shells. Altricial species, which include most songbirds, hatch at a very early stage. Naked, blind, and helpless, they depend on their parents for food and warmth until they are ready to leave the nest. Precocial young are quite different: they hatch with functioning eyes and a covering of fluffy down. Within minutes of hatching, they are on the move, and soon can feed themselves. This type of young are produced by ground-nesting birds such as waders, ostriches, waterfowl, and gamebirds. Between these two extremes are intermediate species that do not fit either category. For example, gulls and terns hatch with a covering of down and are able to walk, but stay at the nest to be fed by their parents.

ALTRICIAL BIRD
Like most songbirds, Winter Wrens depend on frequent food deliveries by their parents while they complete their development.

PRECOCIAL BIRD
Ostrich chicks are insulated by down feathers, and have fully functioning eyes and leg muscles, so they are ready to leave the nest soon after they hatch. They follow their parents around but find food themselves.

HATCHING INTERVALS

The timetable birds use to incubate their eggs can have far-reaching effects on the way in which their families develop. Nesting songbirds (see Passerines, p.330) instinctively know when the female has produced her last egg, and only then do they begin incubating. As a result, all of the eggs in the clutch develop in step. The entire brood will hatch within the space of a few hours – a system known as synchronous hatching – and the young will all be ready to leave the nest at the same time.

A wide variety of other birds, including pelicans, owls, and birds of prey, use a different system, called staggered hatching. The adults start incubating as the first egg is laid, and the eggs hatch in a sequence to produce young of different ages and sizes. The first egg to be laid hatches first, producing the oldest, largest chick, the second egg hatches next, producing a slightly smaller chick, and so on. Although it seems cruel, the oldest chick is able to bully its younger, weaker siblings, and the parents seldom do anything about it. If food is scarce, the oldest chick gets most or all of it, while the youngest are left to go hungry and often die.

AGE DIFFERENCE
This Snowy Owl has produced three chicks, which vary in age and in size. If the food supply is good, all three will thrive. If not, the older chicks may kill their youngest sibling (centre) – a harsh strategy that means they are more likely to survive.

FEEDING EFFORT
The Wood Thrush of North America feeds its helpless young for 12 days in the nest, and in this time each parent makes several thousand feeding trips.

FEEDING THE YOUNG

After their young have hatched, adult birds face a monumental task to keep their growing family fed. Every day, a pair of thrushes may make several hundred return flights with billfuls of food, while smaller birds, such as tits or chickadees, can make two thousand or more trips daily. However, this feeding technique – widespread among songbirds – only works if food is easy to find and is available close to the nest. Birds that find food further afield cannot afford to shuttle backwards and forwards in this way. For example, birds of prey make fewer journeys to and from the nest, but depending on their size, they can usually carry larger prey in their talons. Seabirds often swallow their food, making it easier to transport on the long flight back to the nest. During this journey the food is partly digested, so the parent feeds its young by regurgitating the remains. Pigeons have a unique solution: they produce a fatty secretion called crop milk, which their young drink by reaching into their throats.

FOOD DELIVERY
A Young Brown Pelican reaches into its parent's throat pouch for a meal of partly digested fish. This efficient way of delivering food is widespread in birds that fish at sea.

CRECHES

Young precocial birds sometimes form large groups for defence by joining together with the young of other families. These groups, known as creches, are supervised by one or more adults. Creches are common among flamingos, pelicans, and penguins, and also among flightless land birds such as ostriches and rheas.

OSTRICH CRECHE
When ostrich families meet, the chicks all rush towards each other, forming a creche that adult males compete to control.

BROOD PARASITES

For any bird, reproduction involves a large amount of time and energy. This is sometimes also true of brood parasites, which lay their eggs in other birds' nests, tricking the unwitting foster parents into taking care of the incubation and feeding of their young. In brood parasites, the "work" can involve searching the area for suitable host nests, and then waiting for the chance to sneak in and lay their egg. Around one per cent of the world's bird species rely partly or fully on this breeding technique. They include cowbirds, whydahs, indigobirds, some ducks, and many Old World cuckoos.

OUTSIZED OFFSPRING
An adult European Reed Warbler feeds a Common Cuckoo chick, oblivious to their huge disparity in size. Female cuckoos can lay their eggs in seconds when a nest is unguarded.

LIVING TOGETHER

ACCORDING TO THE FAMOUS PROVERB, birds of a feather flock together. But why should some birds live together when others seem to survive equally well on their own? The answer is that, for birds, being sociable depends on a balance of different factors. Some favour flock formation, while others encourage birds to live apart. Only a small number of species, such as weavers, form flocks all year long. The majority of species flock together at certain times of the year, or even particular times of day – for example, when sleeping.

FLOCKS

Bird flocks can be enormous. The largest, formed by Red-billed Queleas in Africa, may contain over a million birds. In the past, the now-extinct Passenger Pigeon travelled across North America in even larger flocks, sometimes of over a billion birds – a large proportion of the entire species. At the other extreme, many flocks consist of only a dozen or so birds, which stay in a loose group as they search for food. Most birds form flocks for two reasons: flocking makes it harder for predators to attack by surprise; and it helps birds to exploit large supplies of food. However, flocking is not suitable for catching prey by stealth. It also encourages food theft, particularly in species that eat food in sizeable pieces, which their neighbours can snatch and carry away. Taken together, these factors explain why flocking is common in seed-eaters, flamingos, and waders, but much rarer in birds of prey.

CHAIN REACTION
Alarmed by a disturbance, Red Knots burst into the air. In flocks, some kinds of behaviour are highly contagious, so the reactions of a single bird can make a whole flock follow suit.

PERSONAL SPACE

Parrots are happy to rub shoulders with their neighbours, and so are some other flock-formers, such as bee-eaters and finches. But for most birds, this kind of behaviour would trigger retaliation, because it would infringe their personal space. Personal space varies from species to species, and is often directly related to how far a bird can peck. However, it is not entirely fixed. It often increases as birds grow older, but decreases when a flock is under attack. In all birds, breeding also involves a temporary relaxation of the "rules", so that partners can get used to physical contact.

SPACE TO LAND
This Glaucous-winged Gull has found a vacant slot on a roof, out of pecking range, so can safely land.

ROOSTING

With the exception of polar species during the perpetual daylight of summer, very few birds are busy around the clock. During their "time off", birds seek a safe place to roost. Most birds roost off the ground, and they can be remarkably effective at hiding. Many species roost in groups, especially in winter. Starlings often roost in city centres, gulls head for offshore islands and reservoirs, and many other birds roost in reeds. In cold weather, small birds such as wrens huddle together to keep warm.

NIGHT ROOST
Silhouetted by the setting sun, more Brewer's Blackbirds arrive to join those already settled down for the night in the branches of a tree. These American blackbirds can form huge roosting flocks that contain tens of thousands of birds.

DAYTIME ROOST
Black-crowned Night Herons hunt after dark, and roost together by day. This group has birds of different ages – the adults are black and grey, and the young birds are brown.

PECKING ORDER

For generations, poultry farmers have noticed the way chickens organize themselves in flocks. Young chicks relate to each other on equal terms, but adults develop a strict "pecking order". One bird dominates the flock, while the least fortunate chicken is pecked at by all the rest. As time goes by, the order of rank gradually changes, as the oldest birds gradually weaken and die, and younger ones move up in the ranking to take their place.

Pecking orders, also known as dominance hierarchies, are found in many birds that form flocks, and they have evolved as a way of stabilizing life in social groups. Where there is no pecking order, birds waste a lot of time and energy fighting. Once a pecking order is established, however, disputes are avoided and the birds can spend more time searching for food.

AGGRESSIVE POSTURING
Two Great Black-backed Gulls fight to assert their dominant position. Gulls have relatively weak pecking orders, and often squabble over status and food.

COOPERATIVE FEEDING
These American White Pelicans have spread out in a line to catch fish. After the line has formed, the pelicans paddle towards the shore together. This drives all the fish into shallow water, where they are easy to catch.

FEEDING IN A GROUP

Although birds often flock together to feed, they rarely cooperate in any structured way. Within a flock, each bird looks after itself, even if that means stealing food from its nearest neighbours. However, there are several exceptions. Some pelicans cooperate to catch fish, and cooperative hunting is also found in Harris's Hawk, and perhaps also some other birds of prey. These hawks operate in small flocks, with some of the birds flushing prey from cover so that the "catchers" can move in to make the kill. A few birds, such as Acorn Woodpeckers, team up to create and defend communal food stores.

MIGRATION

OVER HALF THE WORLD'S BIRD SPECIES carry out long-range movements or migrations. Travelling alone or in flocks, they navigate with precision, dividing their lives between places that are far apart. Unlike many other animals, birds need abundant food all the year round. Migration allows them to exploit seasonal changes, and to breed where the food supply is best.

WHITE STORK

RED-BILLED TOUCAN

RESIDENTS AND MIGRANTS

Wherever they live, birds can be divided broadly into two categories: resident species and migrants. A resident species lives in a particular region all year round. A migrant species breeds in one region, but spends its non-breeding period somewhere else, often thousands of kilometres away. Near the equator, most birds are resident, because there is a reliable food supply all year round. At higher latitudes, where seasons are more clearly differentiated, the proportion of migrants increases, with the largest percentage being found near the poles. However, not all species follow this clear-cut split. Partial migrants, such as the Eurasian Robin, are migratory in some parts of their range, but resident in others. This variation reflects differences in local climate. In Finland, for example, most robins migrate south to escape the severe winter. But in the British Isles, where winters are milder, most robins stay all year round.

TRAVELLERS AND STAY-AT-HOMES
The White Stork breeds in Europe and parts of Asia, wintering in Africa, Pakistan, and India. The Red-billed Toucan is a resident species, confined to northern South America; seasonal movements are small-scale and vary from year to year.

COSTS AND BENEFITS

Migration is an arduous and dangerous undertaking. Every year, millions of migrating birds are blown off course, and many more die of starvation. Migrants also risk being attacked by falcons and other predators, which gather along migration routes. The combined effect of these losses is staggering. With small songbirds, such as the Barn Swallow, up to three-quarters of the current year's young may fail to make the return journey to their birthplace. However, this enormous toll is offset by the fact that migration pays big dividends, particularly for species that breed at high latitudes. Here, migrants can exploit the huge surge of food that comes with the long days of spring and early summer, often in less crowded conditions than they would experience in the tropics. This explains why migration has evolved in many bird species, despite the high price that individual migrants pay.

EMERGENCY LANDING
This migrating Honey Buzzard has touched down, exhausted, on a beach in Mauritania – an alien and unwelcoming environment.

TIMING

Migrating birds instinctively know when the time has arrived to set off. In the weeks leading up to their departure, most migrants store extra body fat – high-energy fuel that powers their flight. They become increasingly restless, and some species form excitable flocks that may make several "false starts" before their journey actually begins. A late brood of chicks may have to set off almost as soon as they leave the nest. In most species, "pre-migration" behaviour is triggered by an internal biological clock, which is kept in step by changes in day length. However, birds do not rely on day length alone. If the weather is poor, they wait for better conditions, and if it is unusually warm, they may set off early. Variability has become particularly noticeable in recent years, as birds respond to the effects of global warming.

READY TO GO
Clustered together, Tree Swallows prepare for their autumn flight from Canada to Central America. Parents gather their newly hatched young to wait.

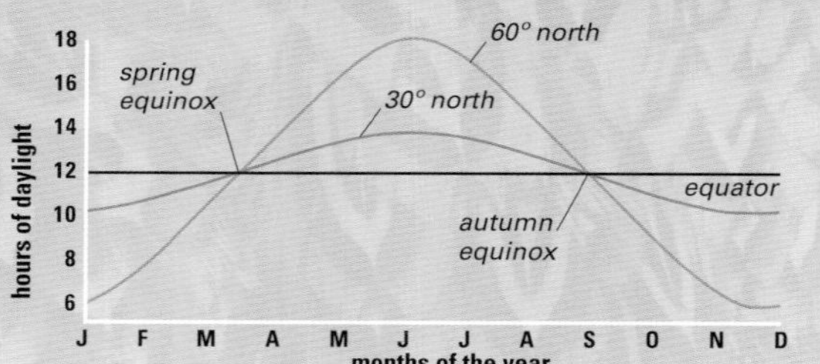

RIGHT ON TIME
Changes in day length follow a predictable pattern. Day length barely alters on the equator, but at a latitude of 60°, the rate of change reaches nearly five minutes a day during spring and autumn equinoxes.

PURPOSEFUL FORMATIONS
By forming in a V-shaped skein, migrants can reduce the energy spent in migration. Here, a skein of ducks is about to make an overnight stop.

NOMADIC BIRDS

Not every long journey qualifies as true migration. Some birds from high latitudes – such as Snowy Owls and waxwings – spread far beyond their normal range when their food is scarce. These events, known as irruptions, often occur in cycles of between four and ten years. Unlike true migration, irruptions are sporadic, and once they are over, the birds do not necessarily return to their point of departure. In dry habitats, such as deserts and scrubland, some birds have an even more marked tendency to wander. Instead of having a fixed "home", they keep on the move, travelling constantly between places where rare rainstorms produce a flush of food. Many nomads are small seed-eaters but, in Australia, they include even pelicans and swans affected by the changing water levels in rivers.

NO FIXED HOME
Australia is particularly rich in nomadic species. Wild Budgerigars fly hundreds of kilometres in search of seeds.

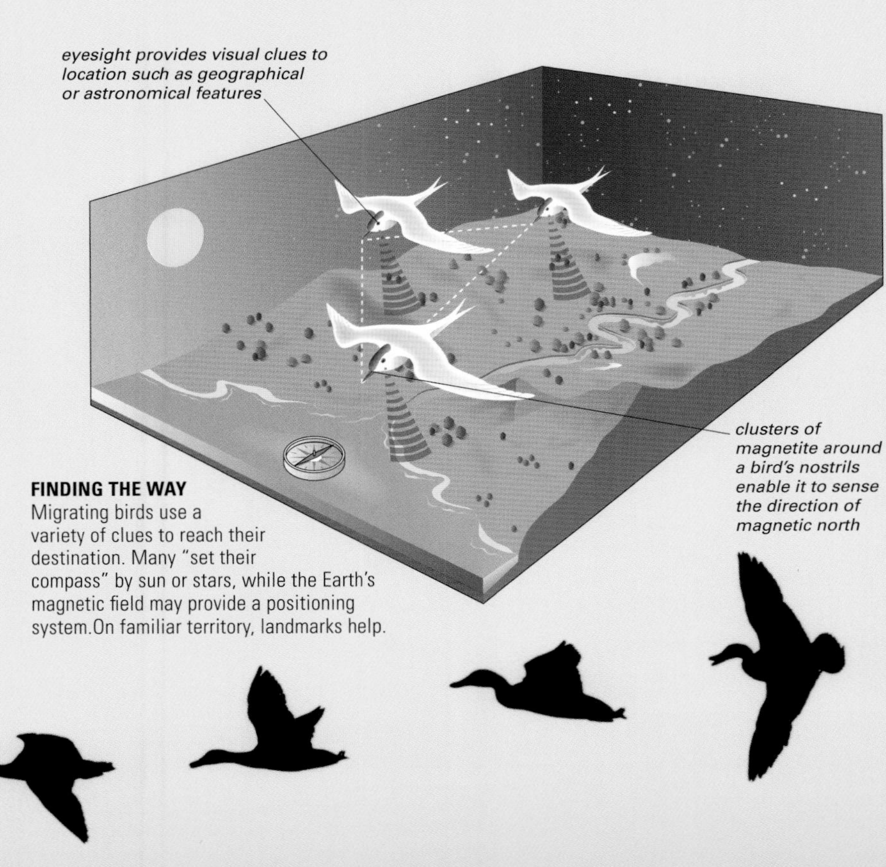

FINDING THE WAY
Migrating birds use a variety of clues to reach their destination. Many "set their compass" by sun or stars, while the Earth's magnetic field may provide a positioning system. On familiar territory, landmarks help.

DIRECTION FINDING

Young birds often fly with their parents, but some species, such as cuckoos, migrate entirely alone and find their way to places they have never visited before. To find its way, a bird needs two skills. Firstly, it must be able to orient itself, or point in the correct direction. Secondly, it needs to be able to navigate, or judge its position, while on the wing. In many birds, orientation is quite well understood, and is based on the sun or stars. Navigation over open ocean is much harder to explain. Homing birds, such as shearwaters and pigeons, seem to navigate by sensing the Earth's magnetic field, and it seems likely that this sense is important in migratory birds.

NIGHT FLIGHT
Many birds migrate at night, when there is less risk of attack by predators. Here a flock of migrating Barnacle Geese is picked out against the full moon.

HOMING INSTINCT

In 1953, a Manx Shearwater was taken from its nest off the coast of Wales and carried by plane to Boston, Massachusetts, on the opposite side of the Atlantic Ocean. Just 12 days later, it was back in its nest, having Şown 5,470km (3,400 miles) over unfamiliar water. On its way east, it overtook the letter sent from Boston announcing its release. All species of shearwater have an unusually strong attachment to their nest sites.

MIGRATION ROUTES

MIGRATION ROUTES HAVE EVOLVED over millions of years. Few are the shortest paths from A to B. Instead, migration routes are shaped by factors which vary from one species to another. Some birds migrate non-stop, flying straight over deserts and other obstacles. Others follow landmarks such as rivers and coasts, and need frequent refuelling breaks. Seabirds roam the ocean, but their routes are influenced by currents and wind direction. All these differences create a complex web of migration routes that stretches across the globe.

FLYWAYS

Major migration routes over land – known as flyways – are typically oriented in a north–south direction. Some of them follow coasts or large river valleys, such as the Mississippi or the Nile. As the journey progresses, birds are often funnelled into narrow corridors that avoid long and dangerous sea crossings. In the Americas, the busiest by far is the Isthmus of Panama. Here, millions of land birds travel over a neck of land that is only about 60km (40 miles) wide. In Europe, huge numbers of birds converge on the Strait of Gibraltar, cutting out a long journey across the Mediterranean. Oceanic birds also travel huge distances – sometimes literally circling the globe. Many of these journeys are similar to migration over land, because they follow recognizable routes. However, many seabirds spread out over a wide area once they have finished breeding. This behaviour, known as dispersal, can last for several years, until a bird eventually returns to the site where it hatched.

The majority of birds breed in the northern hemisphere, principally because this contains most of the world's land. An exception is the Short-tailed Shearwater; this is one of many migratory seabirds that nest on islands scattered across the globe. The migration distances shown in the bird profiles are maximum values for a complete round trip. They are not exact because migrants set off from widely scattered departure points, and arrive at different destinations.

VAGRANT SPECIES

Some birds – known as vagrants – get blown far off course, and end up thousands of kilometres outside their normal range. This happens particularly during fierce winter storms or other unusual weather conditions. Sometimes the individual will rest and then continue its journey, slowly finding its way back on to its normal route. Occasionally an individual may remain where it is to die, or to live among groups of other species; these individuals are, of course, unable to breed. If several vagrants are blown off course into the same area, this may lead to a new colony of breeding birds.

BLOWN OFF COURSE
The Killdeer originates in North America but vagrants are occasionally seen in winter on meadows or sandy shores in the British Isles.

RUFOUS HUMMINGBIRD
Selasphorus rufus

BREEDING RANGE Northwestern North America
NON-BREEDING RANGE Southeastern USA, Mexico
MIGRATION DISTANCE 6,000km (3,700 miles)

This tiny migrant, only 9cm (3½in) long and weighing less than 3.5g (⅛oz), has the longest migration route and breeds further north than any other American hummingbird. Its summer range extends as far as Alaska's Kenai Peninsula, just 750km (470 miles) from the Arctic Circle. During the northward migration, the males arrive first, setting up their feeding territories.

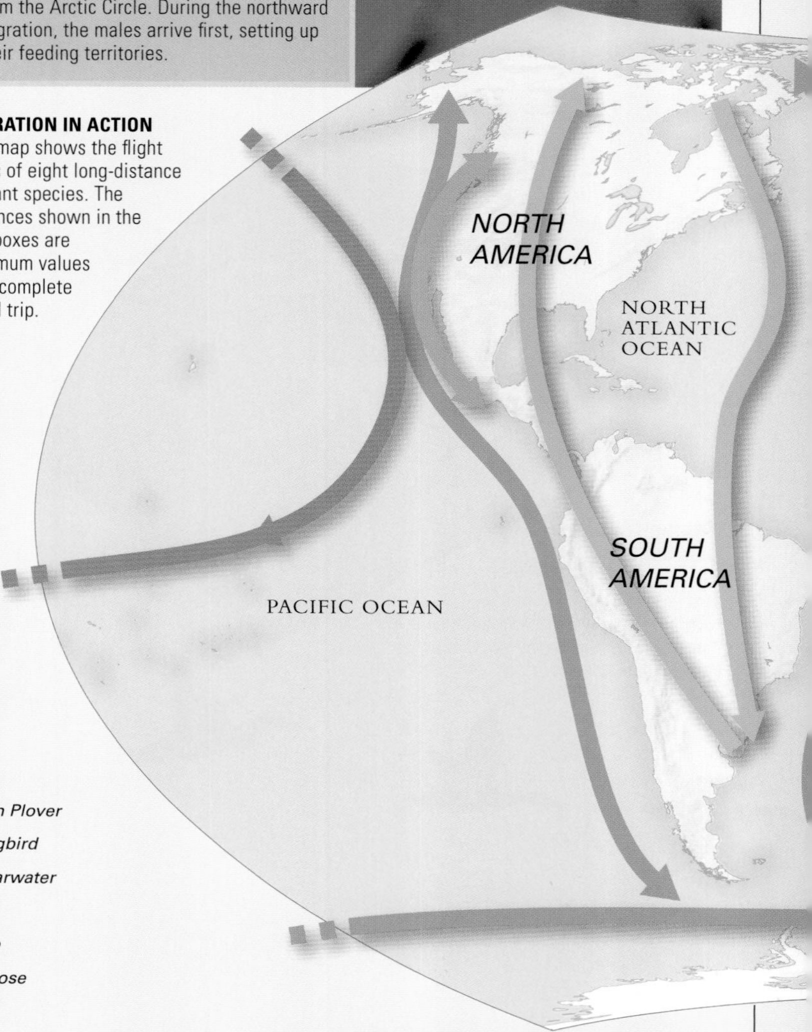

MIGRATION IN ACTION
This map shows the flight paths of eight long-distance migrant species. The distances shown in the text boxes are maximum values for a complete round trip.

NORTH AMERICA
NORTH ATLANTIC OCEAN
SOUTH AMERICA
PACIFIC OCEAN

KEY TO ROUTES
- *American Golden Plover*
- *Rufous Hummingbird*
- *Short-tailed Shearwater*
- *Arctic Tern*
- *Common Cuckoo*
- *Red-breasted Goose*
- *Eastern Curlew*
- *Eleonora's Falcon*

SHORT-TAILED SHEARWATER
Puffinus tenuirostris

BREEDING RANGE Tasmania and islands in Bass Strait
NON-BREEDING RANGE Circumpacific
MIGRATION DISTANCE 32,000km (19,000 miles)

Like most shearwaters, this species breeds on islands (in burrows), and spends the rest of its life at sea. With an adult wingspan of approximately 1m (3½ ft), and a body weight of only 500g (1lb), this is a spectacular flier. Its migration route follows a huge figure-of-eight, taking it northwards from Tasmania towards Japan, and then around the entire perimeter of the northern Pacific, before crossing the ocean and heading home. Youngsters fly with the breeding flock soon after leaving the burrow, but first breed at five years old.

AMERICAN GOLDEN PLOVER
Pluvialis dominica

BREEDING RANGE North American Arctic
NON-BREEDING RANGE Uruguay, eastern Argentina
MIGRATION DISTANCE 20,000km (12,500 miles)

Many American Golden Plovers carry out a loop migration, with different routes north and south. On the flight north, they fly overland, feeding on the way. On the flight south, when food is scarcer, they head out over the Atlantic, making their landfall on the northern coast of Brazil. This is one of the longest migratory routes of any land-based bird.

COMMON CUCKOO
Cuculus canorus

BREEDING RANGE Europe, temperate Asia
NON-BREEDING RANGE Southern Africa, Southeast Asia
MIGRATION DISTANCE 10,000km (6,200 miles)

The Common Cuckoo breeds in Europe and temperate areas of Asia, including China and Japan, and winters in equatorial regions of Asia and in southern Africa. On migration, the parents leave first, followed later by their young (which fly alone). This species is very rarely seen on migration, suggesting that it perhaps crosses the Mediterranean Sea and the Sahara Desert in a single non-stop flight.

ARCTIC OCEAN
EUROPE
ASIA
AFRICA
PACIFIC OCEAN
INDIAN OCEAN
AUSTRALASIA
SOUTH ATLANTIC OCEAN
SOUTHERN OCEAN
ANTARCTICA

RED-BREASTED GOOSE
Branta ruficollis

BREEDING RANGE Russian Arctic
NON-BREEDING RANGE Eastern Europe and Caspian Sea
MIGRATION DISTANCE 10,000km (6,200 miles)

Compared to most geese, this species has a highly restricted migration range. It breeds in the arctic tundra of the Taymyr Peninsula of northern Siberia, in northeast central Russia, and overwinters near the shores of the Caspian and Black Seas. Migrating via Bulgaria, Romania, or Kazakhstan, occasionally it may be seen as far south as Greece. Like other migrants with narrow ranges, it is highly vulnerable to habitat change caused by shifts in agricultural practices and by climate change.

EASTERN CURLEW
Numenius madagascariensis

BREEDING RANGE Eastern Siberia
NON-BREEDING RANGE Southeast Asia, Australasia
MIGRATION DISTANCE 20,000km (12,500 miles)

Curlews are all long-distance travellers, often migrating along coastlines where there are plenty of opportunities to stop and feed on the shore and wetlands. The Eastern is the largest species of curlew. It breeds inland in the freshwater marshes of the far east of Russia, but its non-breeding range reaches southwards as far as the estuaries and salt marshes of New Zealand, with most individuals wintering in Australia. Flying in large flocks, often in V formation, groups of calling curlews are an attractive and welcome sight.

ARCTIC TERN
Sterna paradisaea

BREEDING RANGE Arctic and adjoining regions
NON-BREEDING RANGE Southern Ocean
MIGRATION DISTANCE 40,000km (25,000 miles)

Flying non-stop for eight months of each year, the Arctic Tern migrates farther than any other bird. It divides its time between the northern and southern polar regions, making maximum use of summer and daylight hours around the globe. While on migration, it usually travels over shallow coastal waters, feeding as it goes, and can rest on the sea. Breeding in colonies in the rocky Arctic, adults continue to feed their young with fish as the migration begins; this helps the young birds on the first leg of their extensive migrations.

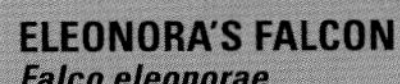

ELEONORA'S FALCON
Falco eleonorae

BREEDING RANGE Mediterranean region
NON-BREEDING RANGE Coastal East Africa and Madagascar
MIGRATION DISTANCE 9,500km (6,000 miles)

This lightly built, agile falcon specializes in attacking songbirds on migration. Unusually, it breeds in late summer, so that its chicks hatch when European songbirds are beginning their migration south. This breeding strategy ensures that the parents are able to catch the maximum amount of food – in fact they often catch more birds than are needed and store the surplus for later use. During its own migration, and in its winter quarters, the Eleonora's Falcon feeds mainly on insects.

BIRDS UNDER THREAT

RECENT ESTIMATES PLACE 12 per cent of the world's birds – over 1,200 species – at threat of extinction. This is catastrophic, and not only for birds themselves, because their changing fortunes mirror the health of the global environment. Birds are threatened in many ways, but most current problems have the same root cause: human-induced changes to the natural world.

RHINOCEROS HORNBILL
Hornbills are threatened by a wave of deforestation that is sweeping southeast Asia.

HARPY EAGLE
Fragmented habitat threatens large birds of prey throughout Central America.

RED-HEADED PICATHARTES
Forest fragmentation in Africa now endangers both species in this small family.

HABITAT LOSS

The destruction of natural habitats is the biggest threat that birds face today. Farming and forestry are the main driving forces, followed by the growth of cities, and development of coasts. Most birds are adapted to a particular habitat and cannot survive elsewhere. As a result, widespread birds become more localized, while those that were localized to begin with risk becoming extinct.

Habitat destruction is not new – it dates back to the start of farming, about 10,000 years ago. However, it has never taken place on the scale seen today. Deforestation in the tropics hits the centre of bird diversity, while the growth in cities and infrastructure takes its toll on bird life all around the world. When cities spring up on what used to be forest or wetlands, the environmental damage is clear to see. But habitat destruction also occurs in less visible ways. For example, oil palms or fast-growing conifers are often grown on land where the natural forest cover has been cleared. These plantations may look green and lush, but their bird life is only a faint echo of the richness in natural forest habitats.

INTENSIVE AGRICULTURE

With over 6 billion people to support now, and over 9 billion expected by the middle of this century, food production has never been more important. Increasingly, food is supplied by intensive farming – a form of agriculture that depends on the routine use of artificial fertilizers and pesticides. Intensive farming produces high yields, but this comes at a high price to the environment. With wild plants and insects kept at very low levels, birds soon run short of food. As a result, species that were once a common sight in rural areas are in rapid decline. In Europe, intensive agriculture has had a particularly damaging effect on ground-nesting species such as the Eurasian Skylark and Northern Lapwing, and similar declines have affected farmland birds in many other regions.

CLEAN SWEEP
Modern combine harvesters are highly efficient, and leave little or no waste grain for birds to glean. Intensive farming also compacts the soil, reducing the supply of earthworms and small animals.

ON DANGEROUS GROUND
In intensively farmed areas, larks such as this Eurasian Skylark face a double threat to survival. Food is hard to find, and as ground-nesters, they also risk having their eggs or nestlings destroyed by tractors.

TOTAL DESTRUCTION
Deforestation affects birds worldwide. Charred stumps are all that remain of these eucalypt trees cut for timber in the Central Highlands of Victoria, Australia.

EXPLOITING BIRDS

Throughout the world, birds are exploited for food, for sport, and for the cage-bird trade. Hunting can be particularly damaging, because the targets are often birds on migration, which are easy to pick off where they cross mountains or coasts. Even in countries where the hunting season is controlled, regulations designed to protect migrants are often ignored. The cage-bird trade affects some bird families far more than others. For example, over 50 species of parrot – out of a total of 352 – are in serious danger. Some other commercial activities, particularly fishing, also have damaging effects. Some birds, such as gulls, thrive on fishing waste, but the picture is very different for diving birds, such as guillemots and puffins, which face increased competition for food. Albatrosses are in a steep decline, following the growth of long-line fishing. Every year, many thousands of albatrosses drown after taking long-line baits and becoming hooked.

HUNTING FOR SPORT
On a hillside facing the Mediterranean, two Maltese hunters pick off migrating birds. Often defended on the grounds of tradition, this destructive "sport" has been attacked by conservation organizations, leading to a tightening of regulations in recent years.

UNCERTAIN CATCH
Albatrosses and gannets swoop around a trawler off the coast of South Africa. The huge growth in fish catches has had damaging effects on birds' food supply.

INTRODUCED SPECIES

Over the centuries, humans have accidentally or deliberately introduced alien species to far-flung parts of the world. For birds, this mixing up of the world's biodiversity has had extraordinarily damaging results. Since 1500, about 150 species of bird have become extinct, and in half these cases, introduced species have been the chief cause. In some cases, these undesirable aliens are predators that have a direct and deadly effect on local birds. Cats and rats are often the culprits, particularly when they arrive on remote islands that have no native mammals of their own. Both are highly efficient predators, not only of adult birds, but also of nestlings. More subtle, but no less dangerous, is the effect of introduced grazing and browsing animals, such as goats. These can strip islands of their native vegetation, which removes the cover that many birds need to breed. Finally, introduced species may bring disease. In the Hawaiian Islands, for example, introduced mosquitoes brought with them avian malaria and avian pox. At low altitudes, where mosquitoes are abundant, many of the islands' native birds have disappeared.

ORGANIC POLLUTANTS
Pesticides and other organic pollutants are a major threat to the world's birds. In southern Asia, vultures have declined by up to 95 per cent in less than a decade – a side-effect of the veterinary drug Diclofenac finding its way into dead remains.

VULNERABLE GOOSE
Like many migrants, the Red-breasted Goose has a sharply defined distribution, which has evolved over many thousands of years. Its main breeding area lies in the remote Taymyr Peninsula in northern Siberia, a region that is currently experiencing rapid climate change.

CLIMATE CHANGE

In the coming decades, climate change threatens to become the biggest challenge facing the world's birds. As climate patterns change, natural habitats are likely to shrink or shift, making it harder for birds to find food and to breed. The outcome of this is hard to predict – all that can be said with any certainty is that birds with highly specific ecological needs are likely to be the hardest hit. These needs can take many forms. For example, the Red-breasted Goose breeds in tundra in one part of northern Siberia, and relies on this habitat for its survival. If the region continues to warm at its present rate, this goose's breeding habitat will shrink dramatically, making its population plummet. Many other species will be affected by changes in vegetation, or by shortages of food at the time when they normally breed. At sea, gradual warming is likely to disrupt normal patterns of plankton growth. As a result, fish supplies will become less reliable, creating food shortages for seabirds. The outcome, for birds, is a world where there are some winners, but far more losers. In the long run, a substantial proportion of these risk becoming extinct.

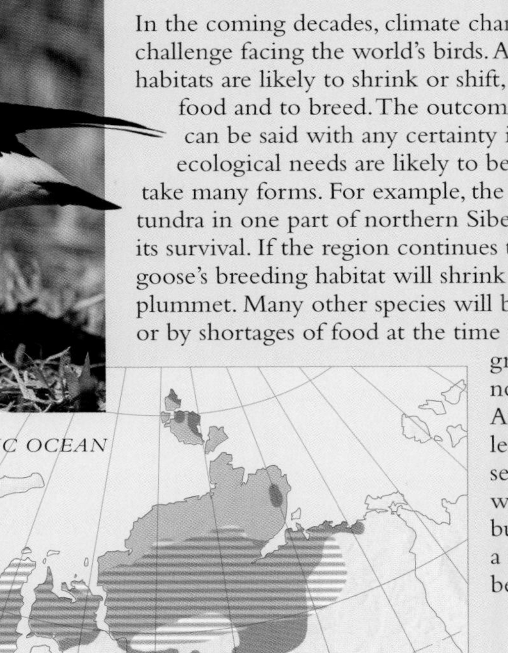

A SHRINKING HABITAT
This map shows projected changes in the tundra of northern Siberia, assuming that the current warming trend continues. By the year 2070, up to three-quarters of the area of the Red-breasted Goose's nesting grounds are likely to be invaded by trees, thereby preventing it from breeding.

CONSERVATION

WITH SO MANY SPECIES currently under threat, bird conservation is more important than ever. On every continent, work is under way to save threatened species, and – just as importantly – to improve the state of the environment for birds as a whole. Already, there have been some remarkable success stories, with critically endangered species brought back from the brink of extinction. However, much more remains to be done.

PROTECTING AND MANAGING HABITATS

By far the most effective way to protect birds is to protect the habitats on which they depend. At a national level, key bird habitats are often protected by nature reserves and national parks. On a global level, several international agreements – such as the Ramsar Convention on Wetlands – help to safeguard key bird areas. To protect birds, habitats may also have to be actively managed – for example, by eradicating introduced animals or plants. On island habitats, this work frequently involves getting rid of rats, but introduced predators also include much more appealing animals, such as hedgehogs, foxes, or cats. Wherever it is carried out, this kind of conservation causes controversy. However, when mammalian predators are removed, the result is usually a spectacular recovery in the numbers of indigenous birds.

CAUGHT ON CAMERA
Red Foxes are a major problem for ground-nesting birds. In Australia, foxes have been successfully excluded from the Peron Peninsula.

EMERGENCY INTERVENTION

For some critically endangered species, direct intervention is the only way of reversing the imminent threat of extinction. In some cases, the remaining birds may be relocated to a safer area, or captured and used as breeding stock. These measures have saved a number of species, such as the California Condor, the Nene (Hawaiian Goose), and New Zealand's Kakapo – the world's only flightless parrot. The Black Robin, endemic to the Chatham Islands, was successfully rescued after its total population dropped to just five birds. For species that are further from the brink, successful conservation starts with research to identify the causes of the decline. Once these have been established, often quite simple steps can be taken to remedy the situation.

READY FOR RELEASE
Fitted with a tag and a radio transmitter, this captive-bred California Condor is preparing to taste life in the wild. Birds bred in captivity often have to be trained how to find food, so that they can survive when released.

KEEPING TRACK
In southern California, a researcher uses a tracking device to follow the movements of captive-bred condors that have been released into the wild.

PROTECTED AREAS
On Aldabra Atoll, a remote World Heritage Site island in the Seychelles, visitors come face to face with protected nesting birds and giant tortoises.

PROTECTING MIGRANTS

Migratory birds are particularly vulnerable to hunting and habitat change. To protect them, international agreements regulate hunting and give special protection to key feeding or refuelling grounds. In North America, one of the earliest bilateral agreements was signed between the US and Canada in 1916. On a global level, the most important is the Convention on the Conservation of Migratory Species of Wild Animals – known as the Bonn Convention – a UN treaty that came into effect in 1983. Since it was drawn up, it has been signed by over 100 countries. Treaties like these vary in their effectiveness but, nevertheless, migratory birds now have better legal protection than ever before. In 1995, that protection was further strengthened by the African-Eurasian Waterbird Agreement, which safeguards 235 species of waterbird that migrate between Africa, Europe, and Asia. Many of these birds now have protected status right across their range, from wintering grounds in southern Africa to breeding sites in the Arctic tundra.

STOP-OFF POINT
In North America, the Platte River is a vital stopover point for migrating Whooper Cranes. Water flows on the river are to be managed to help a surviving migratory flock of only about 230 birds.

HUMAN IMPACT

SPECIES RECOVERY PLANS

Popular as a cage-bird, the Gouldian Finch has declined rapidly in the savanna grassland of northern Australia. The Gouldian Finch Recovery Project is a major conservation effort. Updates posted on the internet show the finch's current status.

GOULDIAN FINCH
This tropical finch has a remarkable variety of distinctive colour forms – something that used to encourage trapping for the cage-bird trade.

HAZARD REDUCTION

Today's birds face many hazards that were unknown a century ago. Low-flying birds, such as the Barn Owl, are often hit by cars, and for ground-dwelling species the situation is worse. Traffic noise is also a problem. Research has shown that busy roads can reduce the level of bird life up to 3km (2 miles) away. With traffic on the rise, these risks are difficult to reduce, but where other hazards are concerned, small technical changes can sometimes lead to enormous improvements in bird survival. Electricity pylons can be lethal to large birds, but devices can be installed to reduce the risk of electrocution. Wind turbines are another cause for concern. Here, careful siting of wind farms can do much to reduce potential problems. At sea, simple changes to fishing methods can lead to a huge drop in bird deaths from long-line fishing. Tests of an advanced "bird-scaring line", carried by a Norwegian fishing boat, showed that bird deaths dropped to almost zero, and fish catch actually went up.

ENDANGERED EAGLE
With a wingspan of over 2m (6½ft), the Spanish Imperial Eagle is at risk from power lines. In Spain, over 14,000 pylons have been modified to reduce the danger of electrocution.

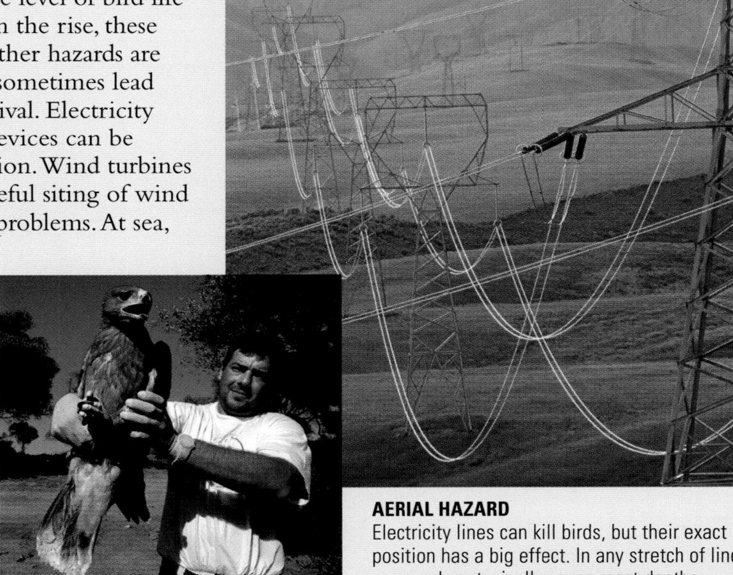

AERIAL HAZARD
Electricity lines can kill birds, but their exact position has a big effect. In any stretch of line, some pylons typically cause most deaths .

PROMOTING CONSERVATION

One of the oldest bird conservation movements – Britain's Royal Society for the Protection of Birds – began life in 1889, in a wave of anger about the use of grebe skins in fashionable clothing. In America, the Audubon Society was founded in 1905, with the mission of protecting birds, as well as other animals and their habitats. Today, conservation organizations represent a powerful force worldwide, and are responsible for keeping wildlife and its welfare at the top of the political agenda. BirdLife International forms an umbrella group for conservation organizations in over 100 countries, helping to maintain habitats and biodiversity. An important part of this work is the Important Bird Areas programme, which identifies and protects key locations for birds all over the globe. To date, over 7,500 locations are on the BirdLife list.

MINDO CLOUDFOREST
The Masked Trogon, and many other birds, are found only in the Mindo Cloudforest of northwest Ecuador. Local landowners are working to preserve this key bird habitat.

EXTINCT BIRDS

EXTINCTION IS A NATURAL PART of evolution, because success for some species inevitably means failure for others. Since birds first appeared on planet Earth, over 180 million years ago, thousands of species have evolved, flourished, and then disappeared. However, in recent history, the rate of bird extinction has soared, and today birds are dying out far faster than ever before. This wave of extinction has been triggered by human activity, and research shows that it is most pronounced in remote habitats, where birds have evolved in isolation from the rest of the world.

EXTINCT GIANTS

Many extinct birds survived until relatively recently, but died out before they could be studied scientiŞcally. These include a large number of Şightless giants. Elephant birds of Madagascar were the heaviest birds ever to have existed, weighing over half a tonne. Moas (left), in New Zealand, stood 3m (10ft) tall, with no trace of wings. Over a dozen species were alive when the Şrst human settlers arrived in New Zealand, about a thousand years ago. Eyewitness accounts suggest that the last species of moa may have clung on until the early 1800s.

PASSAGE TO OBLIVION

Extinction usually happens in stages, and a species can be destined to die out long before the final few individuals disappear. The first stage is local extinction, which splits a species into fragmented groups. As the groups shrink, they become increasingly isolated, inbred, and at greater risk from threats of all kinds – from food shortages to habitat change. This is the situation facing many endangered birds today. The Northern Bald Ibis, for example, was once widespread in the European Alps, North Africa, and the Middle East, but is now restricted to a handful of widely scattered locations, with a total population in the wild of about 400 birds. Once a species has declined this far, it risks dropping below its minimum viable population – the number of birds needed for any chance of long-term survival. Minimum viable populations vary from one species to another, because they are influenced by factors including the stability of the bird's habitat, and its reproductive behaviour. Some birds breed successfully as separate pairs, but colonial species – such as the extinct Passenger Pigeon – breed successfully only in groups. For these species, extinction can be inevitable even when thousands of birds are still left in the wild.

NORTHERN BALD IBIS
After a precipitous drop in numbers during the 20th century, the Northern Bald Ibis faces a struggle for survival in the wild. The only significant numbers are found on the Atlantic coast of Morocco, with a few dozen birds in Turkey, and a handful in other parts of North Africa and the Middle East.

MAURITIUS KESTREL
One of the greatest success stories in bird conservation, the Mauritius Kestrel had the closest brush with extinction ever recorded in birds, but its forest habitat continues to be threatened.

RESCUED FROM THE BRINK

Emergency action has saved a number of birds from extinction. One of the most remarkable examples involved the Mauritius Kestrel, a distinctive bird of prey from the Indian Ocean. Found only on the island of Mauritius, it was affected by deforestation and introduced species. By 1974, its population dropped to just four individuals, making it the rarest bird in the world. However, following a successful captive breeding programme, its population has now climbed to over 800 – more than enough to rescue the species, and to repopulate the remaining areas of its natural habitat. If a species does disappear, there is always a chance that some birds remain hidden in the wild. Sightings of "extinct" birds are made every year, generating great excitement, but most turn out to be erroneous. However, there are examples of birds on the extinct list coming back to life. One is New Zealand's flightless Takahé, which was presumed extinct, and then rediscovered in a remote mountain range in 1948. Since then, a breeding programme has increased its numbers to about 130 birds.

TAKAHE
Threats facing this giant rail came from introduced mammals. Stoats feed on its eggs and young; red deer browse the mountain tussac grass that is its main source of food.

EXTINCTIONS SINCE 1500

The year 1500 is often taken as a dividing line in the rate of bird extinctions, because it marked the start of scientific collection and record keeping, and of global exploration at sea. Since that time, nearly 130 species are known to have become extinct, and about 20 further species are probably extinct, although these extinctions have yet to be confirmed. Between 1500 and 1900, the vast majority of these extinctions involved species that lived on remote islands. Almost all of these died out following the introduction of alien mammals, such as cats and rats. Since 1900, the rate of extinction on islands has dropped, almost certainly because the most vulnerable species have now disappeared. By contrast, the extinction rate on continents has climbed – a result of worldwide changes in natural habitats.

number of extinctions
70
60
50
40
30
20
10
0
1500s 1600s 1700s 1800s 1900s

AN UPWARD CURVE
Since the 1500s, the rate of bird extinctions has risen sharply. The 21st century has not begun well; the last wild Spix's Macaw disappeared in the year 2000, and the last surviving Hawaiian Crows vanished in 2002.

HUMAN IMPACT

IUCN RED LIST CATEGORIES

For over 40 years, the World Conservation Union or the IUCN (International Union for the Conservation of Nature and Natural Resources), has published a Red List of threatened species. Like all listed species, threatened birds are assigned categories that show how much danger they face. The principal categories are shown here. A further category, Least Concern, includes species that are not under threat. BirdLife International is responsible for providing the Red List evaluations for the IUCN.

EXTINCT
Definition Species for which there is no reasonable doubt that last individual has died.
Number of birds in this category About 150 (since 1500)

EXTINCT IN THE WILD
Definition Species that have died out in the wild, but which still exist in captivity.
Number of birds in this category 4

CRITICALLY ENDANGERED
Definition Species that face an extremely high risk of extinction in the wild.
Number of birds in this category 181

ENDANGERED
Definition Species that face a very high risk of extinction in the wild.
Number of birds in this category 351

VULNERABLE
Definition Species that face a high risk of extinction in the wild.
Number of birds in this category 674

NEAR THREATENED
Definition Species that are close to qualifying as above or likely to qualify in the near future.
Number of birds in this category 795

BIRDS OF THE PAST

Despite recent advances in gene technology, extinct species cannot be brought back to life. As a result, knowledge of them is based on contemporary accounts, and also on stuffed specimens, bones, and other remains. The most famous of them – the Dodo – has become a byword for extinction. A giant flightless pigeon, it was a classic example of a flightless island bird that fell victim to hunters and introduced predators. The Great Auk was also flightless, but its demise was brought about by hunters and egg collectors, rather than by habitat change. The Passenger Pigeon was also a victim of hunting, carried out on an unprecedented scale. At one time, it was probably the most abundant bird in the world, with a population of about 5 billion. Its disappearance was the steepest decline ever recorded in bird extinction.

PASSENGER PIGEON
This North American pigeon was a highly social bird, feeding and nesting in vast flocks. The birds were hunted with firearms, traps, and nets, and by the mid-1800s, tens of millions of birds were killed every year. The population collapsed, and the last survivor – named Martha – died in a zoo in 1914.

DODO
The ground-nesting Dodo lived on the island of Mauritius, where it fed on fruit. Discovered by visiting Dutch sailors in 1598, it became extinct in the late 1600s. The Dodo is often portrayed as portly and dull-witted, but this is probably based on overweight birds that were kept in captivity.

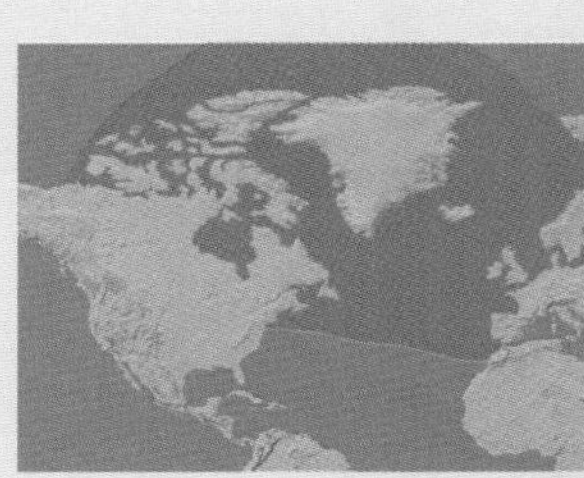

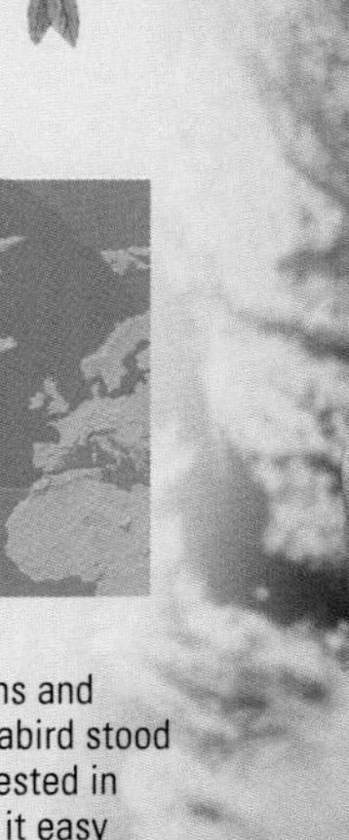

GREAT AUK
A flightless relative of puffins and guillemots, this northern seabird stood about 75cm (30in) high. It nested in large colonies, which made it easy for people to hunt for its meat and its eggs. The last breeding pair was killed on the island of Eldey, off Iceland, in 1844. A number of stuffed Great Auk specimens exist in museums.

HABITATS

BIRD GEOGRAPHY

BIRDS ARE THE MOST MOBILE ANIMALS on Earth. They can cross continents and oceans, and some routinely fly tens of thousands of kilometres during their annual migration. But, paradoxically, few birds are found all over the globe. Instead, the majority of species are restricted to particular regions; some are confined to tiny specks on the map, such as remote oceanic islands. This patchiness is a key feature of bird geography. It has come about over millions of years, as birds have evolved and adapted to a changing world.

GLOBAL SPECIES
The Barn Owl and the Osprey are among the few birds whose natural range includes every continent except Antarctica. Some coastal birds, such as the Ruddy Turnstone, are almost as widespread. The House Sparrow and the Common Starling are found across the globe, but largely as a result of human intervention.

BIOGEOGRAPHICAL REALMS

The world's wildlife can be divided between eight regions known as biogeographical realms. Realms may share similar habitats, such as forest or grassland, but each has its characteristic wildlife. This distinctiveness results from factors including climate, topography, and – over the much longer term – the rearrangement of Earth's landmasses by continental drift. The totals given for each realm include both endemic families and species (see below) and those shared with neighbouring realms.

DIVIDED WORLD
Biogeography dates back to the mid-19th century, when naturalists began to recognize striking differences in the bird life of different regions of the world. The boundaries between realms are not fixed precisely, but indicate transition zones where marked changes in bird life occur.

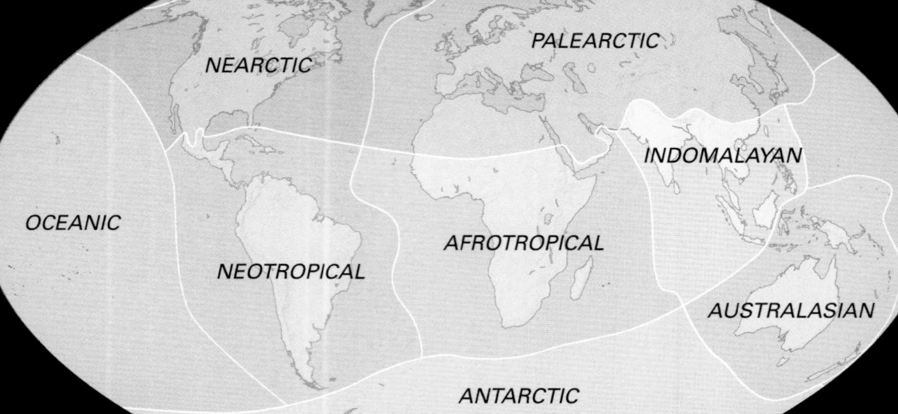

PALEARCTIC
FAMILIES: 69
SPECIES: 937
Despite being the largest realm, the Palearctic has just one endemic family – the accentors. It has a large number of insect-eaters, including Old World warblers, the biggest single family in this region. The majority of birds are migrants.

NEARCTIC
FAMILIES: 61
SPECIES: 732
Low in bird diversity, the Nearctic has no endemic families. Its bird life has strong links with the Palearctic realm, but includes hummingbirds and tanagers originating in South America. Most birds are migratory, reflecting a cold winter climate.

INDOMALAYAN
FAMILIES: 69
SPECIES: 1,700
Only four families – the leafbirds, bluebirds, ioras, and bristleheads – are endemic to this region, but its bird life is rich and varied. The climate is almost entirely tropical, and its birds include many species that feed on fruit and seeds.

OCEANIC
FAMILIES: c.35
SPECIES: c.200
For their size, islands in the Oceanic realm are home to an exceptionally rich variety of birds, but only 2 per cent of the global total. As well as marine species, such as albatrosses and tropicbirds, they include many endemics, such as flightless rails.

ANTARCTIC
FAMILIES: 12
SPECIES: 85
Antarctica's tiny species total masks a great abundance of bird life. The overwhelming majority of its species are marine. Penguins remain within its borders all year, but most seabirds – including skuas and terns – are summer migrants.

NEOTROPICAL
FAMILIES: 95
SPECIES: 3,370
This realm has more bird species than any other. A third of families are endemic, including tinamous, curassows, puffbirds, toucans, and several families of primitive passerines. Neotropicals include many fruit and nectar feeders.

AFROTROPICAL
FAMILIES: 73
SPECIES: 1,950
With large expanses of desert and grassland, this realm is rich in terrestrial birds and seed-eaters. Endemic families include ostriches, mousebirds, and turacos. There are strong links with families in the Indomalayan realm.

AUSTRALASIAN
FAMILIES: 64
SPECIES: 1,590
There are 13 endemic families here, including cassowaries, emus, lyrebirds, birds-of-paradise, and honeyeaters, plus large numbers of terrestrial and nomadic species, and nectar-feeders. Kingfishers, parrots, and doves are abundant.

PINK PIGEON
Endemic to the island of Mauritius, the Pink Pigeon came close to extinction in 1990, with only 10 birds left in the wild. Thanks to captive breeding, the population now stands at several hundred.

ENDEMICS

An endemic family or species is one that is restricted to a particular locality. Bird families are often endemic to individual realms – for example, toucans are found only in the Neotropical realm, while cassowaries are found only in the Australasian realm. Families can be spread across wide areas, but the range of endemic species can be extraordinarily small. One of the most restricted is the Floreana Mockingbird, which lives on two tiny islands in the Galapagos, with a combined area of less than 1 square km (0.4 square mile). Many endemics are island species, but endemic species can also be found in isolated locations on land. For example, the Scissor-tailed Hummingbird is found only in forest in the Paria Peninsula of northeast Venezuela, a mountainous spine of land only about 20km (12.5 miles) wide.

CONTINENTAL DRIFT

Over millions of years, continental drift has slowly reshaped the Earth's surface. Although these changes are extremely slow, they seem to have played a significant part in the way birds are distributed today. In the Triassic Period, before birds first appeared, all of today's continents were united in a single landmass, called Pangea. By the late Jurassic Period, when the primitive bird *Archaeopteryx* was alive, the continents were beginning to split apart, carrying their plants and animal life with them. This process helps to explain some intriguing peculiarities in bird geography. For example, there is some evidence that ratite birds – such as ostriches, rheas, and emus – are descendants of a group of birds that lived in the southern supercontinent, Gondwanaland. After this split up, they became widely separated. Continental drift has also brought distinct bird faunas close together. One example of this occurred when Australasia moved northwards and came into contact with southeast Asia. However, today – millions of years later – the region's bird life still changes abruptly at a biological frontier known as Wallace's Line.

ON THE RIGHT SIDE
Cockatoos are found only on the Australasian side of Wallace's Line. The Sulphur-crested Cockatoo – shown here – lives in northern and eastern Australia, and in New Guinea, but not in Indonesia.

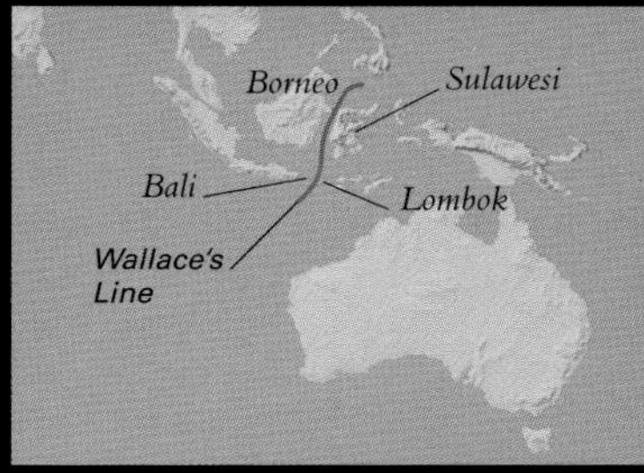

WALLACE'S LINE
Nineteenth-century pioneering biogeographer Alfred Russel Wallace identified this frontier between Indomalayan birds, to the west, and Australasian birds, to the east. In Indonesia, the line runs between Bali and Lombok.

BORNE ON THE WIND
Albatrosses occasionally manage to cross the equator, soaring on unusually strong winds. These conditions are infrequent, however, so they have only a very small chance of making the return trip.

BARRIERS AND STEPPING STONES

Despite being able to fly, birds are often "kept in place" by physical or biological barriers. Southern hemisphere albatrosses are one example: they can circle the Earth in the Southern Ocean, but they hardly ever manage to cross the doldrums – a zone of slack winds around the equator – that separates them from the albatrosses of the northern Pacific. At the other extreme, some land birds are reluctant to go anywhere near the sea. In Europe, for example, the Black Woodpecker is found throughout the continent, but it has never managed the short flight across the sea to reach the British Isles. For some birds, islands can act like stepping stones, helping them to spread. One of the best examples of this is in the western Pacific, where atolls and islands are scattered far out to sea. Some land birds, such as lorikeets, have successfully travelled from island to island, slowly extending their range.

CLEAR WATER BIRDS
Brown Pelicans fish by spotting prey from the air. They are common along the Atlantic and Pacific coasts of the Americas, but absent from estuaries where water is heavily laden with silt.

MOUNTAIN CORRIDORS
Instead of acting as barriers, mountains can form corridors for soaring birds. Andean Condors are found along the whole of western South America, but they never venture into the low-lying ground further east.

BIRD HABITATS

A BIRD'S HABITAT PROVIDES it with food, somewhere to breed, and everything else that it needs to survive. A small number of birds live in a wide range of habitats. However, most non-migratory birds are restricted to just one habitat, while migrants typically live in two similar habitats at different times of the year.

MOUNTAINS
Mountains have a huge range of climatic conditions. Peregrine Falcons are found across many mountain ranges, but endemic species can be restricted to individual ranges, or even isolated peaks.

HABITATS OF THE WORLD

Strictly speaking, a habitat is the environment occupied by a single species, whether it is a bird or any other living thing. However, the term is commonly used in a much broader sense, to mean a distinctive type of living environment, or biome. There are many ways of classifying biomes. Some kinds, such as coasts, have sharply defined boundaries. Others, such as scrubland and grassland, often merge with each other, creating transitional zones with their own characteristic mix of wildlife. In terms of bird species, the richest land habitats are tropical forests, followed by scrublands and grasslands. Colder habitats generally have fewer species, but during the breeding season some birds can be present in enormous numbers. The map on these two pages shows the natural spread of the world's major habitats. Many of them – particularly forests and grasslands – have been transformed by agriculture and development, leaving them much more fragmented than they originally were, and accordingly presenting problems to their bird populations.

TEMPERATE FOREST
Most temperate trees are deciduous, encouraging an enormous influx of insect-eating birds when buds burst in spring. Most year-round residents, such as this Great Spotted Woodpecker, feed on insect grubs or seeds.

SEAS AND OCEANS
Fewer than 200 species of bird roam the seas and oceans, returning to land only to breed. However, many of these birds have huge populations, and some – such as the Northern Gannet – form enormous colonies when they nest.

CONIFEROUS FOREST
Coniferous forest covers vast areas of the northern hemisphere. It is low in bird species, but owls and birds of prey are common, as are seed-eaters such as crossbills, which extract food from cones.

TROPICAL FOREST
More bird species live in tropical forests than in all other terrestrial habitats combined. Few species are migratory and the Keel-billed Toucan, with many others, has evolved a specialized lifestyle and thus a restricted distribution.

WETLANDS
A combination of lush vegetation and abundant food makes freshwater habitats prime places for birds. Where winters are cold, many wetland birds migrate to waters nearer coasts. The Great Crested Grebe is familiar on reed-fringed lakes.

COASTS
The teeming bird life of coasts is dominated by a single bird order, the charadriiformes. This group includes waders like the Eurasian Oystercatcher, as well as gulls, skuas, terns, and auks.

DESERTS
Being able to fly makes it easier to find water, but, even so, most desert birds apart from raptors feed on the ground. They include sandgrouse, pigeons, drought-adapted waders, finches, sparrows, and larks such as this Greater Hoopoe-Lark.

SCRUBLAND AND HEATH
In these two related habitats, a patchwork of trees, shrubs, and open vegetation creates ideal conditions for birds that nest in cover, but which feed in the open. Ground-feeding species such as the Eurasian Hoopoe feed alongside flycatchers and other aerial feeding birds.

FARMLAND AND CITIES
Covering an increasing amount of the planet's surface, farmland and cities offer mixed opportunities for birds. For some species – such as the Common Pigeon – close association with humans has proved to be a passport to success.

POLAR REGIONS
During the summer months, the Arctic attracts huge numbers of migrant waders and wildfowl. Antarctica is visited by many seabirds, but few, apart from these Emperor Penguins, breed on the ice.

GRASSLAND
Ostriches, and most of the world's large flightless birds, live in grassland. This habitat is also rich in seed-eaters such as finches, which typically feed and breed in flocks. When they enter farmland, the same birds can become major agricultural pests.

GRASSLANDS

WITH THEIR SWEEPING LANDSCAPES and open horizons, grasslands are a distinctive habitat. They form where there is enough rain to keep grass alive, but not enough for woodland or forest to grow. Most grasslands are in the interior of large continents, away from rain-bearing winds, but grasslands also exist in areas where mountains block moisture coming from the sea. Bird life in grasslands consists mainly of seed- and insect-eaters, together with birds of prey. But in some types of grassland – particularly in the tropics – grasses and woody plants intermingle, providing a home to a much richer variety of birds.

TEMPERATE GRASSLAND

The temperate world once held vast swathes of natural grassland, including pampas and prairies in the Americas, and the steppes of eastern Europe and central Asia. Today, much of this land is farmed, but remaining areas of grassland still have their own characteristic birds. Some of the commonest are seed-eating songbirds, such as finches, sparrows, and larks, but temperate grassland is also the natural habitat of many gamebirds, such as partridges, quail, and grouse. Grassland birds also include some waders, such as coursers and dotterels; unlike most of their relatives, these species are adapted for survival in dry surroundings. In the northern hemisphere, the largest birds in this habitat are bustards and cranes, while in the southern hemisphere the flightless rheas and Emu take first place in terms of size.

For birds of prey, temperate grasslands make good hunting grounds, but most species are resident only where trees and rocky outcrops provide suitable nest sites. The few exceptions include harriers, which unlike most birds of prey nest directly on the ground.

DEMOISELLE CRANE
Unlike other cranes, which have declined as a result of habitat change, the Demoiselle Crane is faring well. It breeds in marshy ground in central Asia, migrating southwards to southern Asia and Africa to spend the winter in dry grassland.

EURASIAN SKYLARK
Often heard before it is seen, the male sings during its display flight high in the air. Like many grassland songbirds, the species feeds mainly on seeds, but it supplements its diet with insects during the breeding season.

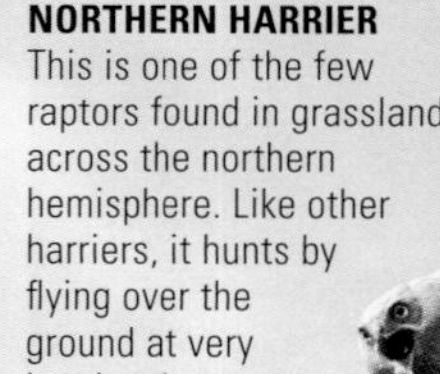

NORTHERN HARRIER
This is one of the few raptors found in grasslands across the northern hemisphere. Like other harriers, it hunts by flying over the ground at very low level.

temperate grasslands   tropical grasslands

GRASSLAND DISTRIBUTION
Most temperate grassland is found on low-lying plains or high steppes in the centre of large landmasses, far away from the influence of coasts and moist air. Tropical grassland also lies in the interior of continents, but in places it occurs closer to the sea.

WESTERN MEADOWLARK
Using their sharp bills, the various species of meadowlark probe grass and soft ground for insects and other small animals.

GREAT BUSTARD
Once common throughout central Asia and Europe, the Great Bustard has declined as a result of hunting and the conversion of grassland to farmland.

TROPICAL GRASSLAND

Pure open grassland is rarer in the tropics than in the temperate world. Instead, its place is often taken by savanna – a habitat that mixes areas of grassland with thickets and scattered trees, particularly acacias and baobabs in Africa, eucalypts (gum trees) in Australia, and palms in South America. Trees can make a big difference to birds, because they enable species that nest off the ground to colonize the habitat. These include a host of seed-eating songbirds, including weavers and waxbills, and many birds with broader diets, from starlings to shrikes. Even when trees are dead, they provide vital living quarters for cavity-nesters, such as parrots, hornbills, and owls.

In subtropical grassland, rainfall can be heavy, but it is usually concentrated in a rainy season, while the rest of the year is dry. During the long drought, the grass dies back and often burns off in wild fires. Although the blackened land appears devastated, fires do not do lasting harm to the grassland itself because the grass roots stay alive underground. However, the flames send insects, lizards, and other small animals fleeing for their lives, and this gives birds a welcome feast. They flock to the flame front to grab the refugees, attracted from far afield by the smoke. In Africa's tropical grasslands, these opportunists include hornbills and bee-eaters.

Tropical grasslands are home to a wide variety of birds of prey, from small insect-eating falcons to one of the world's largest eagles – the Martial Eagle of sub-Saharan Africa. A variety of vultures scan the land for dead remains. They are joined at carcasses by storks, including the huge Jabiru in South America and Africa's equally large Marabou Stork. Savanna also supports a handful of unusual ground-based predators, such as the long-legged Secretary Bird – a specialist snake-killer.

WITHOUT TREES

A variety of birds with tree-nesting ancestors have adapted to treeless conditions. They include owls, pigeons, and a handful of highly unusual woodpeckers. The latter excavate nesting holes in banks of earth – behaviour more typical of kingfishers. In the 19th century, Charles Darwin studied these atypical ground woodpeckers on his travels across the pampas of South America. He later used their behaviour to support his theory of evolution.

GROUND WOODPECKER
This grassland woodpecker from southern Africa digs its nest burrow in exposed banks. The burrow has an upward slant to stop rain flooding it.

BUDGERIGAR
The wild Budgerigar is a seed-eating parrot from the grasslands of Australia. It nests in tree-holes – if necessary even in logs lying on the ground – and will breed whenever and wherever there is an adequate supply of grass seeds.

SOUTHERN RED BISHOP
The Southern Red Bishop is found in grasslands across much of Africa. A member of the weaver family, it typically feeds in flocks, and is one of several weaver species that plunder grain from fields. The bird pictured is is a male in its bright breeding plumage.

MARABOU STORK
The Marabou Stork has a scavenging lifestyle very similar to that of vultures, with which it is often seen. It soars over the African savanna on huge wings, rapidly dropping to the ground when it spots a carcass.

COMMON OSTRICH
With their exceptional height and keen vision, ostriches are quick to spot danger. Most of the world's large flightless birds live in open habitats, using vigilance and speed to evade predators.

SUPERB STARLING
Starlings are some of the most common omnivorous birds of East African grasslands. Naturally inquisitive, the Superb Starling searches the grass for seeds and insects, and also makes a good living by begging for food at campsites.

DESERTS

AT LEAST A QUARTER of the planet's land surface consists of desert. For many birds, deserts are dangerous, inhospitable places, or barriers that complicate migratory journeys. But for drought-adapted birds, the huge size of deserts and the shortage of competing species make up for the hostile climate and erratic food supply. Desert bird life varies across the world, but in deserts everywhere its richness depends on one crucial factor – rain.

TRUE DESERT

The driest deserts receive less than 25cm (10in) of rain a year. Not only is rain scarce, it is also highly unpredictable, often falling in sudden downpours separated by months of drought. Vegetation is very sparse, and the wind can be strong and relentless.

Some desert birds, such as seed-eating finches, are able to get all the water they need from their food, but for most, survival depends on a permanent water source. Adult birds can fly great distances to reach water, but their range is limited once they start to breed. As a result, desert birds often nest close to pools and irrigated land, dispersing once their young have fledged. Some sandgrouse have evolved an unusual solution to this problem. At daybreak, the males fly off to waterholes, which can be up to 50km (30 miles) away. Here, they wade in up to their chests, using their breast feathers to soak up water like a sponge. They then deliver this water to their chicks. This daily airlift enables sandgrouse to colonize areas that are inaccessible to many other breeding birds.

In arid regions, the largest birds are often raptors, which cruise on thermals (see Gliding and Soaring, p.34) generated by the sun-baked ground. However, the most abundant birds are usually small songbirds such as larks and chats, gleaners of seeds and small insects. Many are nomadic, breeding after rain and moving on when drought returns.

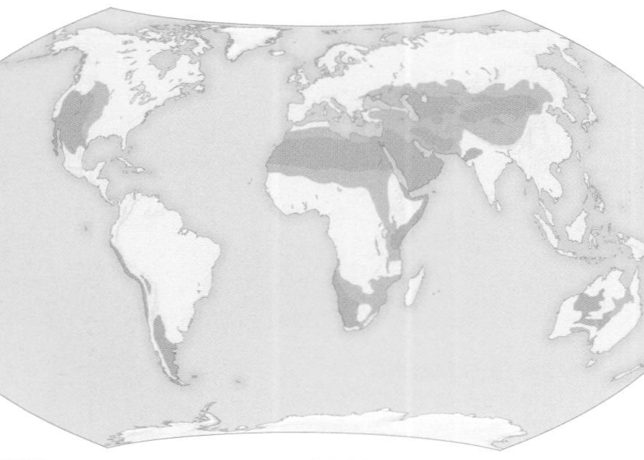

DESERT AND SEMI-DESERT DISTRIBUTION
Outside the poles, deserts are found mainly in mid-latitudes, where high pressure systems dominate the climate, blocking the flow of rain-bearing winds. On their margins, where rainfall is higher, are areas of semi-desert that often grade into grassland and shrubland.

LAPPET-FACED VULTURE
This powerful scavenger is able to force its way past smaller species, including other vultures, when it lands to feed.

DESERT WHEATEAR
Found in arid habitats from Africa to central Asia, this insect-eater migrates in the east of its range, where winter temperatures can fall far below freezing.

NAMAQUA DOVE
Africa's small, slender-bodied Namaqua Dove ranges from thorny scrubland to true desert, where its plumage provides excellent camouflage.

GREATER HOOPOE-LARK
Rather than flying from danger, this long-legged lark often runs instead, seeming to vanish among the rocks and stones. Males have a distinctive song flight.

CROWNED SANDGROUSE
Sandgrouse are found in arid habitats in southern Europe, Africa, and Asia. This species lives across the Sahara, where it collects water at pools and oases.

SEMI-DESERT

Compared to true desert, semi-desert is a much richer habitat for both animals and plants. Plants provide birds with cover and, directly or indirectly, such vegetation is also the ultimate source of all their food. In this habitat, many birds have broad-ranging diets, but semi-desert is also home to birds with much more specific needs. Most specialized of all are nectar-feeders, which visit desert flowers. In North America's arid zones, hummingbirds feed on nectar from cacti, and from shrubs such as ocotillos. In Africa, sunbirds have a very similar lifestyle.

Semi-desert is an important habitat for seed-eaters, particularly finches, larks, and ground-feeding doves. In South America, this habitat is also home to seedsnipes – unusual short-legged waders that have evolved a vegetarian diet. But some of the most conspicuous semi-desert birds feed on insects, either darting out to catch them in mid-air, in the case of flycatchers, or swooping down from a perch – the tactic used by shrikes. In the deserts of the southwest USA, these insect-eaters also include the Gila Woodpecker, which pecks nest holes in the thick stems of large cacti. Once its nests have been abandoned, they are often taken over by Elf Owls – a classic example of one bird creating opportunities for another.

Semi-desert is particularly rich in reptiles, and birds are their most important predators. Gamebirds, such as Africa's guineafowl, often eat small lizards as well as seeds and insects, while in North America roadrunners chase this kind of prey on the ground. But for reptiles generally, the greatest danger is overhead, in the form of birds of prey. Scanning the ground as they soar overhead, they swoop down on snakes and lizards basking in the sun. In Africa and Asia, the snake eagles specialize in this kind of food, but reptile-eating raptors are also common in the Americas.

HARRIS'S HAWK
Often kept in captivity, this raptor lives in the semi-deserts of the Americas. It often hunts by swooping from a tree or cactus.

ELF OWL
This tiny owl, from the southwestern USA and Mexico, is nocturnal. It takes insects in mid-air or on the ground.

CACTUS WREN
Spines are no deterrent for this bird – one of North America's largest wrens. It builds large domed nests in cacti, relying on their spines to keep predators at bay.

ANNA'S HUMMINGBIRD
Hummingbirds are common migrants in arid regions, but this is one of the few species that can be seen in North American semi-deserts all year.

GREATER ROADRUNNER
Famous for its speed and agility, this terrestrial member of the cuckoo family can run at up to 20kph (12mph).

BREEDING AFTER RAIN

Instead of having a fixed breeding season, some desert birds start to nest after sporadic periods of heavy rain. The Gibberbird, from central Australia, is a typical example. It normally breeds between July and November, but rain outside this period switches on its reproductive behaviour. "Gibber" is the Australian term for desert covered with a broken pavement of wind-scoured stones. This kind of desert has no soil and almost no shade, making it one of the world's most extreme habitats used by birds.

GIBBERBIRD
Clutching an insect in its beak, a Gibberbird prepares to fly back to its nest. In common with some waders, Gibberbirds use a "broken wing" display to distract predators from their eggs and young.

TROPICAL FOREST

MORE BIRD SPECIES OCCUR in tropical forest than any other habitat, despite the ravages of deforestation. Some species are well known for their vivid colours, but there are many less conspicuous birds that also live in this habitat. The bird life is strongly influenced by climate, and there are major differences between the birds of the Old and New World tropics.

AMERICAN RAINFOREST

Central and South America remain unequalled in the richness of their birds. Many bird families are restricted to the Americas, and for the overwhelming majority, rainforests are by far the most important habitat. These families range from toucans and cotingas – some of the most flamboyant and vocal of all forest birds – to antbirds and tapaculos, whose drab colours form highly effective camouflage. Other American rainforest species include tyrant flycatchers, hummingbirds, and American blackbirds and orioles.

Fruit-eating birds, such as toucans and quetzals, play a key role in tropical forests because they help to spread seeds. Many other forest birds actually feed on seeds and nuts. In the Americas, the most conspicuous among them are macaws – the world's largest parrots – which are found only in this region. Generally speaking, tropical forests are difficult habitats for scavengers and birds of prey, since the dense cover makes it hard to find food. However, the American tropics are home to several spectacular examples, including the King Vulture and Harpy Eagle.

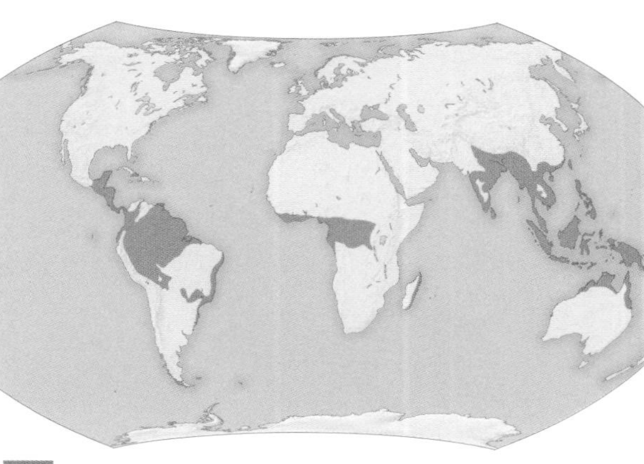

tropical forest

TROPICAL FOREST DISTRIBUTION
Rainforest is found worldwide on and near the equator, where intense sunshine produces almost daily downpours of rain. Towards the edges of the tropics, the climate is much more seasonal. Here, evergreen forest gives way to monsoon forest, which is dry for much of the year.

SCARLET MACAW
Like many other forest parrots, the Scarlet Macaw flies over the canopy in noisy flocks to and from its night-time roosts. It is one of the most abundant macaws.

KING VULTURE
This is the largest vulture found in American tropical forests – and by far the most colourful. It locates food by smell and its diet includes dead mammals in the forest itself, as well as dead fish washed up on riverbanks.

KEEL-BILLED TOUCAN
Fruit and a variety of small animals feature on the Keel-billed Toucan's menu. The species is widespread in America's lowland rainforests.

FORK-TAILED WOODNYMPH
In the Americas, hummingbirds are important pollinators of forest flowers. Despite their small size, the males can be pugnacious, attacking each other in mid-air to defend patches of flowers.

AFRICA AND ASIA

Thanks to their long geological links (see Bird Geography. p. 70), Africa and Asia's tropical forests share many families of birds. Among the most impressive are the hornbills, which are the Old World counterpart of toucans. Hornbills live in a variety of habitats, but the largest species are found in the forests of southeast Asia. Old World tropical forests are also an important habitat for bulbuls – medium-sized songbirds that often have crests. Dozens of species live in tropical forests, and although many are secretive, some visit gardens near forested land. Flower-visitors include sunbirds, which probe deep into blooms with their long curved bills, and white-eyes. Compared to most nectar-feeders, white-eyes have short bills, and they often reach their food by pecking holes in the base of flowers.

In temperate regions, pigeons are typically drab-looking birds that feed in the open. But in the Old World tropics, dozens of species of sumptuously coloured pigeons and fruit-doves live and feed in forests. Some species are widespread, while others are localized, particularly in the islands of southeast Asia and the western Pacific. Despite their brilliant colours, fruit-doves can be difficult to see. Parrots are different: their bright plumage and noisy habits often make them a conspicuous part of the forest fauna. Some of the most colourful kinds, such as lorikeets, feed mainly at flowers, lapping up pollen and nectar with their brush-tipped tongues. Australasian tropical forests are home to two highly distinctive families found nowhere else: the cassowaries and birds of paradise.

MONSOON FOREST

Unlike tropical rainforest, monsoon forest has a sharply defined wet season, followed by months of drought. Many monsoon forest trees are deciduous, losing their leaves during the dry season, and they sometimes flower while their branches are still bare. The largest area of this habitat is found in southern Asia. Here, forest birds include hornbills, parrots, and many species of babbler. There are also a wide variety of gamebirds, including the Indian Peafowl and the Red Junglefowl – the wild ancestor of the farmyard chicken. Like most gamebirds, they feed on the ground but roost in trees.

PHILIPPINE EAGLE
This enormous eagle hunts up in the forest canopy, where it is a predator of monkeys and colugos (flying lemurs).

LONG-BILLED SPIDERHUNTER
Spiderhunters are named for their habit of plucking spiders from their webs, but also (as here) feed on nectar. They belong to the sunbird family, and like other sunbirds build hanging, pouch-shaped nests.

GREEN IMPERIAL PIGEON
This Asian forest pigeon feeds mainly on soft fruit, digesting the flesh but scattering the seeds in its droppings.

GREAT BLUE TURACO
Also known as the Blue Plantain-eater, this large forest bird occurs throughout much of equatorial Africa. Pairs or small family groups can be seen feeding on fruit, flowers, and leaves in the tops of tall trees.

OLIVE SUNBIRD
The Olive Sunbird from tropical Africa is a highly active species that flits between forest flowers like a hummingbird.

MALABAR PIED HORNBILL
Resident in southern Asia from India to Sri Lanka and Borneo, this hornbill prefers open forest, often near human habitation.

TEMPERATE FOREST

FEW HABITATS MATCH the amazing surge in bird life that occurs each spring in temperate woodland. This huge influx occurs mainly in deciduous woods, when trees are coming into leaf, and insect food is abundant. In warm parts of the temperate world, woodland is often evergreen. This habitat usually supports fewer insect-eating birds, but more that feed on reptiles or at flowers.

DECIDUOUS WOODLAND

Across the northern hemisphere – and in places as far south as Chilean Patagonia – deciduous woodland changes dramatically through the seasons, as trees grow and then shed their leaves. Birds echo these changes, reaching peak numbers in spring as migrants flood in, and then declining again in autumn as the leaves start to fall. The earliest arrivals are often warblers, which probe bursting buds for newly hatched caterpillars, followed by larger insect-eaters, such as vireos, and also by flycatchers, which catch insects in mid-air. Spring also sees the arrival of migratory raptors, and in Europe and Asia, the Common Cuckoo. At this time of year, the dawn chorus rivals anything that can be heard in the tropics.

In autumn the pattern is reversed, as the migrants leave, together with their young. Of the songbirds that remain during the winter, most feed on seeds and nuts, or on invertebrates gleaned from cracks in bark or on the ground. They include jays and thrushes, as well as titmice and chickadees, nuthatches, treecreepers, and wrens. All these species are potential food for predators such as hawks and owls.

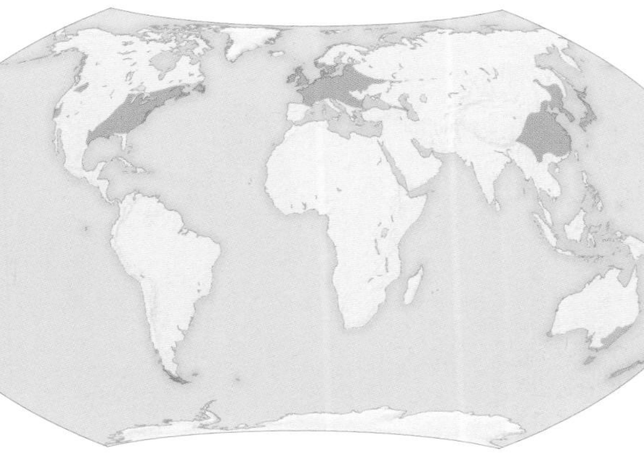

TEMPERATE FOREST DISTRIBUTION
Deciduous woodland is found in the northern hemisphere, particularly in eastern North America, western Europe, and the Far East. The main areas of temperate evergreen woodland are in South America, Australia, New Zealand, and the Mediterranean and Caucasus region.

BROAD-WINGED HAWK
A summer visitor to woods and forests in eastern North America, this hawk rarely hunts on the wing. Instead, it watches for prey from a low branch.

TAWNY OWL
Named for its plumage, the Tawny Owl can be very difficult to see, but is in fact one of the most common owls in European woodland.

GREAT SPOTTED WOODPECKER
This widespread Eurasian woodpecker eats mainly insects and seeds. In spring it also pecks into nest-holes to reach the nestlings of other birds. The male (left) drums loudly on a dead tree to establish a territory.

BLACK-AND-WHITE WARBLER
Most warblers feed among the foliage, but this one creeps along branches like a tiny woodpecker.

COMMON CUCKOO
The cuckoo is a brood parasite that lays its eggs in the nests of other birds; open woodland and clearings provide it with many suitable songbird hosts.

GREY GOSHAWK
There are two colour forms of this raptor: pure white (left) and grey-backed. It lives in the forests of northern and eastern Australia.

GREY CURRAWONG
Despite their crow-like appearance, currawongs belong to a distinct family of birds unique to Australasia. They occur in a wide variety of wooded habitats.

NOISY FRIARBIRD
The friarbird is a common visitor to fruiting trees and flowers in dry eucalypt woodland. As its name implies, this member of the honeyeater family is highly vocal.

RAINBOW LORIKEET
All kinds of wooded country suit this vividly coloured nectar- and fruit-eating parrot, which ranges from temperate Tasmania northwards to Indonesia.

LAUGHING KOOKABURRA
The kookaburra is an aggressive and omnivorous predator that swoops to the forest floor to snatch its prey.

OLD AND NEW WORLD WARBLERS

Throughout the northern hemisphere, warblers are the most abundant insect-eaters in broad-leaved woodland. Warblers of the Old and New World often behave in similar ways. Most feed by picking insects from leaves and twigs, they usually have distinctive and complex songs, and the majority are migratory. Despite these similarities, however, these birds belong to two unrelated families: the Old World warblers (family Sylviidae); and the New World or wood warblers (family Parulidae). Their similarities are the result of a process known as parallel evolution.

COMMON CHIFFCHAFF
The Common Chiffchaff is one of the earliest warblers to arrive back in the woodlands of northwest Europe each spring.

NORTHERN PARULA
Measuring only 11cm (4½in) long, this tiny wood warbler is a summer visitor to eastern North America and winters in Central America.

TEMPERATE EVERGREEN WOODLAND

In parts of the world with cold winters, conifers are often the only evergreen trees, but where the climate is warmer, many broad-leaved trees also keep their leaves. In Portugal and Spain, cork oak woodland creates an evergreen habitat for Azure-winged Magpies, and on the opposite side of the Atlantic, California's live oaks provide food for jays and Acorn Woodpeckers. One continent – Australia – follows a different pattern. Here, there are large areas of temperate woodland, but almost all of it consists of evergreen eucalyptus trees.

Unlike deciduous trees, eucalypts or gum trees have slender branches and drooping foliage, and they create a patchwork of dappled shade. This provides ideal conditions for birds such as kookaburras, which perch on low branches and drop down onto animals below the trees. Kookaburras feed on a wide range of small animals, especially lizards, which often bask on the sun-warmed ground. Woodland reptiles are also hunted by birds of prey, such as the Grey Goshawk.

Eucalypt leaves are full of aromatic oils, which makes them difficult for insects to eat. As a result, further up the food chain, relatively few birds survive entirely on insect food in eucalypt woodland. Instead, this habitat abounds in birds such as honeyeaters, which feed at the nectar-rich eucalypt flowers. Honeyeaters are found all over Australia, but dozens of species live south of the Tropic of Capricorn, with a few reaching as far as Tasmania. These birds often share the treetops with lorikeets – distinctive parrots that have slender bodies, graduated tails, and long, brush-tipped tongues. Like honeyeaters, lorikeets move in noisy flocks, and help to pollinate flowers as they move from tree to tree.

CONIFEROUS FOREST

THIS HABITAT IS HOME TO a narrower range of birds than broad-leaved forest, but what it lacks in variety it more than makes up in scale. The vast coniferous forests that stretch across the far north, called boreal forest, form the largest wooded area left on Earth. Conifers also grow in warm regions and are important for many mountain birds.

BOREAL FOREST

Circling the Arctic across three continents, boreal forest covers about 15 million square km (6 million square miles). It is also known as taiga and is a remarkably even, unbroken habitat, in which immense stretches of forest are dominated by only a handful of different types of tree. Winters are long and severe, with the short winter days of northern latitudes making it even harder for birds to survive. Given these harsh conditions, most of the small insect-eaters – such as kinglets, tits, and warblers – are migrants that spend the winter in forests further south. In the summer, they feed mainly out of sight high up in the canopy, so the forest can seem strangely devoid of birds.

By contrast, the seed-eaters of boreal forest tend to be year-round residents, because their food supply may actually increase during the winter months. The most specialized seed-eaters are the crossbills, which use their cross-tipped beaks to lever open cones, before extracting the seeds. Other common seed-eaters include jays and nutcrackers – birds that have a strong instinct for storing surplus food. In North America, the Grey Jay remains in boreal forest even when the temperature plunges far below zero, while the Eurasian Nutcracker does the same. Energy-rich conifer seeds and an extra-thick, insulating plumage are all that these species need for survival.

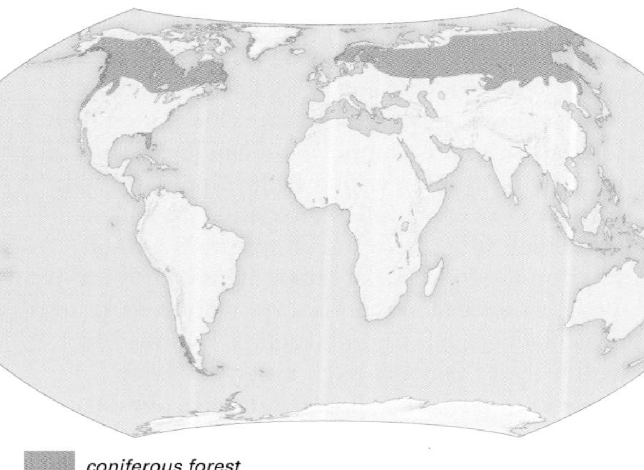

CONIFEROUS FOREST DISTRIBUTION
Conifers grow all over the world, but the largest coniferous forests form a band across the far north of Eurasia and North America, where the climate is too severe for most broad-leaved trees. In the southern hemisphere, the biggest area of coniferous forest is in southern Chile.

RUBY-CROWNED KINGLET
Weighing as little as 5g (¼oz), this tiny insect-eater breeds in the boreal forest of North America, and in mountains further south. Only males have crests.

EURASIAN SISKIN
This small, seed-eating finch often feeds in clearings and nests high up in conifers. The male (left) has a smart black crown in the breeding season.

NORTHERN GOSHAWK
Like many boreal forest species, the Northern Goshawk ranges right around the Arctic. It preys on birds and squirrels.

EURASIAN WOODCOCK
High, sideways-facing eyes give this wader an all-round view of danger as it feeds on the forest floor.

WESTERN CAPERCAILLIE
Male capercaillies like this one gather at communal display grounds, or leks, in late winter and early spring.

HABITATS

NATURAL FOREST AND PLANTATIONS

When conifers are planted close together, the ground soon becomes smothered with a thick carpet of fallen needles. For birds, finding food here is difficult, since there are few small animals apart from ants. But where coniferous forest is more open, far more plants and animals can thrive. This richness – a characteristic feature of natural forest, and one that is absent from plantations – creates more opportunities for ground-feeding birds, and for predators such as hawks.

Across the northern hemisphere, several species of grouse live in open coniferous forest, and on its margins. They include the Black Grouse and Western Capercaillie in Europe, and the Spruce Grouse and Ruffed Grouse in North America. During the summer, these birds eat buds, seeds, and many other kinds of plant food, but in winter they often rely on needle-shaped conifer leaves. Few other birds can digest this tough food, but grouse have powerful gizzards that break it down. Damp clearings are also an important habitat for snipe and woodcock – superbly camouflaged waders that probe the ground with their pencil-like bills. During the breeding season, male snipe perform remarkable display flights, using specialized tail feathers to produce drumming or fluttering sounds as they dive headlong.

Woodpeckers are common in coniferous forest, both in the Arctic and warmer climes. The smallest species are not much bigger than a European Starling, but the largest kinds, such as the Black Woodpecker of Europe and Russia, can be nearly 50cm (20in) long. The Black Woodpecker's nest holes are as wide as a clenched fist, and the ground below is often piled with wood flakes the size of clothes pegs. Once abandoned, the holes are ideal homes for owls.

NORTHERN HAWK-OWL
With its long tail and pointed wings, this forest owl has a distinctly hawk-like shape. Like most northern owls, it hunts partly by day during the summer months.

MAGNOLIA WARBLER
The Magnolia Warbler winters in the tropics and in spring migrates north to its breeding grounds in the coniferous forests of Canada and the northern USA.

RED CROSSBILL
Young crossbills hatch with straight bills, but after they fledge the tips cross over to produce the species' tweezer-shaped bill, as seen in this adult male.

BLACK WOODPECKER
Twice the size of most other Eurasian woodpeckers, this impressive bird feeds mainly on insects, but also attacks other birds' nests to steal eggs and chicks.

SOUTHERN SEED-EATERS

Conifers grow from the fringes of the Arctic tundra south to Australia and South America. In the southern hemisphere, they include araucarias – eye-catching trees with prickly foliage, large cones, and nutritious seeds, of which the most familiar species is the distinctive Monkey-puzzle Tree. Araucaria seeds are an important food for many birds, and also for native peoples. In Australia, cockatoos feast on the seeds of the Bunya Pine – an araucaria with enormous cones up to 30cm (12in) wide. In southern Brazil, the fast-growing Parana Pine, another araucaria, relies on the beautiful Azure Jay (below) to spread its seeds.

AZURE JAY
This colourful member of the crow family lives in southeast Brazil and northeast Argentina – the natural habitat of the Parana Pine. It is declining as a result of deforestation.

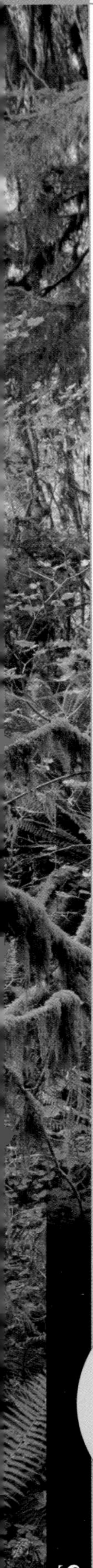

SCRUBLAND AND HEATH

OFTEN DISMISSED AS WASTE GROUND, scrubland can be exactly the opposite for birds. It is found in places where local conditions limit the growth of trees, and its patchy mix of open space and dense cover provides many opportunities for feeding, nesting, and hiding from predators. Heath is similar to scrubland, but instead of being a natural habitat, it is often created by human activity.

SCRUBLAND

Natural scrubland is a feature of regions that have mild, wet winters and long, dry summers. This type of climate is typical of the Mediterranean and parts of southern Africa and Australia. There are also large expanses of scrubland at similar latitudes across the world, including California and the interior of South America and Africa, where it is too dry for woodland and grassland but not dry enough for desert. Many scrubland plants are low-growing and woody, and they can regenerate from ground level if scorched by wild fires during the parched summer months.

For humans, dense scrubland can be inhospitable terrain, because the vegetation often bristles with thorns. But for insects, it is a rich habitat, and this is mirrored in the profusion of insect-eating birds. Apart from songbirds, scrubland birds include rollers and hoopoes – brightly coloured relatives of kingfishers that eat not only insects, but also lizards and snails. Small birds of prey are common in scrubland, and it is also a prime habitat for nightjars and owls. California's scrubland, called chaparral, is favoured by hummingbirds, attracted by flowers, which they help to pollinate. Many are migrants, with just a few species remaining in this habitat all year round. Many scrubland plants in the southern hemisphere depend entirely on birds for pollination.

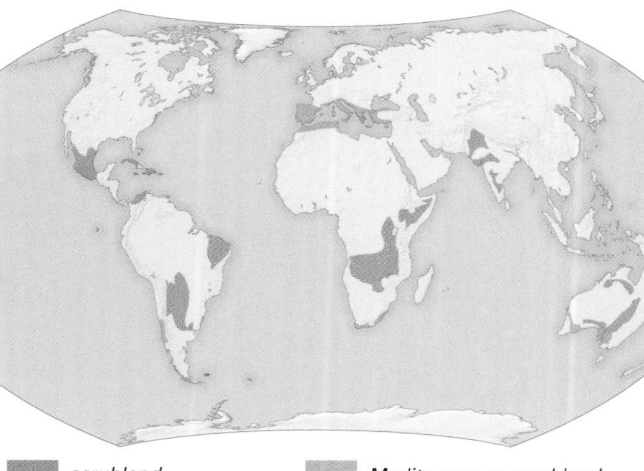

SCRUBLAND DISTRIBUTION
Most scrubland occurs in warm temperate regions, dry parts of the tropics, and on the fringes of deserts. Mediterranean scrubland is characteristic of southern Europe, North Africa, and other areas with a similar climate, such as southern Africa and Australia.

EURASIAN HOOPOE
With their bold markings and large crest (folded in this individual), hoopoes are conspicuous summer visitors to southern Europe's scrubland. They feed on the ground.

NEW HOLLAND HONEYEATER
Australia's scrubland is home to many species of honeyeater, including this one from southern and eastern coasts. Like most honeyeaters, it is non-migratory, although it wanders in search of food.

WHITE-FACED SCOPS OWL
Many scops owls live in the heath and scrub of Africa and southern Eurasia, where they hunt the abundant insects and spiders. The strikingly marked species pictured (left) has a large range in Africa south of the Sahara Desert.

CAPE SUGARBIRD
This long-tailed nectar-feeder lives only in *fynbos* – the low-growing evergreen shrubland unique to the Cape region of South Africa. Sugarbirds often feed at protea flowers, as here, although they also catch passing insects.

EURASIAN HOBBY
This falcon is a summer visitor to the heathlands of Europe. It is one of the last migratory birds to breed. Its young hatch in midsummer when the songbirds on which it preys are plentiful.

WOODLARK
Like most larks, the Woodlark thrives in open habitats, especially heath. Due to the lack of trees, it sings in mid-air to attract a mate and nests on the ground.

EUROPEAN BEE-EATER
Sun-warmed scrub and heath provide this insect-eater with a good supply of bees, wasps, and hornets. It is the only member of its family found in Europe.

GREAT GREY SHRIKE
Shrikes often nest in thorny bushes, which also provide spikes for impaling prey. The Great Grey Shrike inhabits Europe's heathland and forest edge.

EUROPEAN NIGHTJAR
In the north of its range, this nightjar depends on pine-studded heathland. It is a ground nester, relying on camouflaged plumage to protect itself and its young.

HEATH

Unlike scrubland, heath is more open, with wide expanses of low-growing vegetation studded with isolated shrubs and trees. This kind of habitat develops naturally in places with sandy, nutrient-poor soils, and close to coasts, where salt spray makes it difficult for trees to grow. But in some parts of the world, such as northwestern Europe, heath is often an artificial habitat, produced by deforestation. This may be recent, or it may date from prehistoric times.

For birdwatchers, man-made heath holds lots of interest, because its bird life is distinctive. European heathland is a major habitat for the Eurasian Hobby, a small and remarkably agile falcon that catches other birds on the wing. It usually preys on small songbirds, but it may sometimes be seen chasing swallows in a breathtaking aerial chase. Other heathland birds of prey include kestrels and harriers, which search the ground for rodents and young birds. Like scrubland, heath is rich in insects, particularly where boggy pools allow damselflies and dragonflies to breed. In the heaths of southern Europe, insect-eating birds include the European Bee-eater and various species of shrike, which impale surplus food or half-eaten victims on thorns to create a grisly larder.

After dark, nocturnal insect-eaters take to the air. Nightjars and their relatives are a feature of heath in many parts of the world. During the day, their mottled brown and grey plumage makes them almost invisible as they roost motionless on the ground, but at dusk they can often be seen in silhouette, flying in leisurely circles on sharply pointed wings. Like many insect-eating heathland birds, nightjars are usually migrants in temperate regions, and spend the winter in warmer climates where there is a reliable source of food. As a result, throughout the winter months heathland can seem empty and quiet, with small songbirds in particular being very scarce.

FEEDING AT FLOWERS

Nectar- and pollen-eating birds are common in the tropics, but much rarer in other parts of the world. Australia is a major exception to this rule. Even in the scrubland on its stormy southern coast, honeyeaters and parrots forage among wind-pruned shrubs, searching out banksias and other flowers. Here, birds and shrubs have a very long history of co-evolution, with each adapting to the other. Honeyeaters have long bills for probing deep into tubular flowers, while many of the shrubs have long flowering periods, with different species blooming in a staggered sequence. As a result, nectar-eating birds can find food all year.

WESTERN SPINEBILL
Confined to the southwest corner of Australia, this species of honeyeater gets most of its food from column-shaped *Banksia* flowers.

MOUNTAINS

MOUNTAINS CAN BE a very tough environment for birds, but are extremely rich in different species because of their wide climatic variation and range of habitats. Individual peaks may have many vegetation zones, each with their own distinctive bird life. Today, the world's uplands provide a last refuge for hundreds of endangered bird species due to habitat destruction in lowlands.

LOWER SLOPES

Many of the birds found in the foothills of mountain ranges also live in neighbouring lowland areas. However, steep hillsides and narrow valleys or inaccessible gorges often have more undisturbed habitat than the flatter, fertile lowlands, because the terrain is more difficult to clear for farming or settlement. As a result, the lower slopes of mountains frequently support a greater number and variety of birds than lowland plains. Many rare birds, especially tropical forest species, have their last remaining strongholds in mountainous regions. Montane forests are home to many fruit- and seed-eaters, such as pigeons, pheasants, and parrots, with crossbills, siskins, and nutcrackers specialized for life in coniferous forests (see pp.82–83).

MID-ALTITUDES

Higher up mountainsides, a new selection of habitats and species takes over. Here, typical habitats include scrub, alpine meadows, bamboo thickets, rocky outcrops, cliffs, and scree slopes. The type of forest changes, too, with different trees suited to the normally wetter, cooler climate. Dense cloudforest is found at mid-altitudes in the tropics and is shrouded in mist for much of the day. It is one of the world's

mountain ranges

MOUNTAIN DISTRIBUTION
In the temperate zone, the highest, most extensive mountain ranges lie in Eurasia, North America, and southern South America. The Andes are by far the largest mountain chain within the tropics, but there are isolated ranges in Central America, East Africa, and southeast Asia.

ANDEAN CONDOR
Due to its huge size the Andean Condor has difficulty in getting airborne – to get aloft it relies on powerful updraughts from cliffs and steep-sided canyons, which also provide it with inaccessible ledges to roost and nest. The condor soars up to 5,500m (18,000ft) high.

TORRENT DUCK
Unusually for a species of waterfowl, this duck from the Andes is adapted to the rapids of mountain rivers and streams. A female is pictured (left); males are mostly black and white with red bills.

KEA
The Kea's viciously hooked bill is a clue to its diet, which uniquely for a parrot includes sheep carrion and scraps scavenged from car parks and campsites.

RUFOUS-TAILED ROCK THRUSH
This rock thrush breeds on insect-rich, sun-warmed slopes from southern Europe east to China, but winters in the savanna of sub-Saharan Africa to avoid the cool northern winter when such food becomes scarce.

SEASONAL PLUMAGE

A few mountain birds moult to match the changing appearance of their upland habitat through the seasons. They include several species of grouse, such as the Rock Ptarmigan. This gamebird spends its entire life on the ground, often on open treeless slopes, so it relies on camouflage for protection. In winter (below left), the Rock Ptarmigan is white apart from a narrow black mask, and vanishes against the snow. During the summer (below right), it is greyish-brown with fine black bars and mottling, to blend in with grass, heather, and rocks. In spring and autumn, the ptarmigan has an intermediate plumage.

ROCK PTARMIGAN
Emboldened by its seasonally camouflaged plumage, the Rock Ptarmigan is usually very fearless. It freezes when a predator approaches, only running away or taking flight at the last moment.

PEREGRINE FALCON
Mountains are a major habitat for birds of prey, such as the fast-flying Peregrine Falcon. Its cliff-side nest sites, called eyries, may be used by the same pair year after year.

SNOW BUNTING
In the south of its circumpolar range the Snow Bunting lives in high mountains. Here, it is threatened by global warming because the higher temperatures destroy the sparse alpine vegetation.

CITRIL FINCH
Many finches and sparrows around the world are mountain specialists, including this native of southern Europe. It often moves downhill in severe weather.

GOLDEN EAGLE
Probably the most numerous raptor of its size in the world, the Golden Eagle takes prey as big as hares or grouse. A pair of eagles often hunt together to help trap and catch their prey.

richest bird habitats – some cloudforests in Central and South America have an astonishing 400 species of bird, including quetzals and cotingas. Sometimes species are so well adapted to the conditions at a particular altitude that they occur within a vertical band as narrow as 500m (1,650ft); in the tropics, where species diversity is highest, ornithologists carry altitude-calculating GPS devices to help identify similar species found in adjacent altitude zones.

HIGH PEAKS

Alpine slopes and plateaux support the smallest variety of species, but many of these birds do not occur anywhere else. Among the high-altitude residents are seedsnipes, which live on windswept bogs and meadows in the Andes, and snowcocks – large, turkey-like gamebirds of central Asia and the Himalayas. At these altitudes, most small birds, such as snow finches and accentors, feed on seeds and insects, while the Wallcreeper probes crevices for insects on barren scree slopes and sheer rock faces up to the snow line. The Red-billed Chough, a species of crow, has been seen at the summit of Mount Everest – the highest that any animal has ever been recorded.

Supplies of food are often scarce or seasonal on mountaintops, so birds here roam larger areas. Birds of prey, in particular, travel huge distances to make a kill or locate carrion. The difficulties of survival at altitude has also driven some birds to develop unusual diets; for example, the Kea of New Zealand is the world's only meat-eating parrot. Another problem facing high-altitude species is the extreme climate, including strong winds and very low temperatures at night. One survival strategy is simply to move lower down the mountains in harsh weather. But in the Andes a few hummingbird species survive the bitterly cold nights by becoming torpid – a form of night-time hibernation that saves precious energy.

POLAR REGIONS

WITH THEIR SUPERB INSULATION, birds are well equipped to cope with the extreme cold near the poles. Some birds remain in the far north or south all year round, but the majority are migrants, often from far afield. Antarctica's visitors are all seabirds, whereas those in the Arctic include vast numbers of waterfowl and waders, which flood northwards in spring to breed in the tundra zone.

SNOWY OWL
Found throughout the far north, this large ghostly owl hunts in broad daylight during the polar summer. The owl nests on the ground, choosing a raised site to ensure that its chicks stay dry.

LITTLE AUK
The Little Auk is abundant in the Arctic and feeds mainly on animal plankton, storing the food in a throat pouch ready for the return trip to its nest.

ARCTIC TUNDRA

Despite the changes caused by global warming, the Arctic Ocean remains largely frozen for most of the year. Relatively few birds, such as the Ivory Gull, venture far over unbroken ice. Instead, the majority are found either close to the coast, over open water, or in the bleak and treeless tundra. Compared to the tropics, the number of bird species in the Arctic is low, although it is still far higher than in the Antarctic. However, during the breeding season, some Arctic birds congregate in extraordinary numbers. In northwest Greenland, an estimated 30 million Little Auks nest on coastal cliffs and among fallen rocks, and throughout the Arctic millions of terns lay their eggs on shingle banks and shores. Plovers, sandpipers, and many other waders nest on the open tundra, sharing their habitat with geese and swans. Geese graze on vegetation, which grows rapidly during the lengthening days in late spring, but most of the waders eat the invertebrates that thrive in the boggy ground. These large concentrations of birds attract plenty of airborne predators and scavengers. Snowy Owls prey mainly on small mammals, but also take the young of ptarmigans. Skuas specialize in robbing seabirds of their catch, and loiter in nesting colonies to steal any unattended eggs or chicks.

LONG-TAILED JAEGER
With its long, pointed wings and tail streamers, this aerial pirate is a more elegant bird than most skuas and uses its flying skills to harass gulls and terns.

RED KNOT
The globetrotting Red Knot is one of the commonest breeding waders in Arctic tundra, but winters as far south as South Africa and New Zealand.

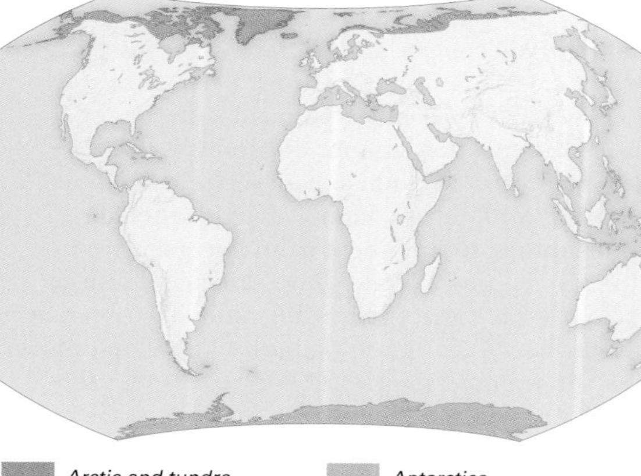

POLAR REGIONS
Geographically, the polar regions lie inside the two polar circles – the areas around the North and South Poles where the Midnight Sun can be seen once a year. However, the biological boundaries of the polar regions depend more on the prevailing ocean currents and climate.

KING EIDER
Vivid facial markings make male King Eiders (above) easy to identify. These coastal seaducks dive for molluscs, and stay in the far north all year round.

SUBANTARCTIC SKUA
Skuas are as widespread in the Antarctic as in the Arctic. This one breeds on subantarctic islands such as South Georgia, and on the northernmost part of the Antarctic Peninsula.

SNOWY SHEATHBILL
Confined to the extreme south, the sheathbill is a dumpy, chicken-like bird that lives mainly on the shore. It eats anything from eggs and chicks to rotting remains washed up by the tide.

SOUTH GEORGIA PIPIT
This is the world's most southerly songbird. It nests in tussac grass – a dense plant that offers shelter from the fierce wind – and manages to survive on the scarce supply of insects and seeds.

EMPEROR PENGUIN
At sea, Emperor Penguins chase fish and squid at depths of up to 250m (820ft). Adults take turns to go fishing, returning with a regurgitated meal for their chick.

ANTARCTIC COAST

In the whole of the far south, only two species of bird are entirely based on land. One is a pipit, and the other is a duck – the Yellow-billed Pintail. Both are found on the island of South Georgia (pp.146–147), which lies north of the Antarctic Circle. On outlying islands such as this, "tubenoses" and cormorants are the most abundant seabirds, and huge numbers can be seen during the summer months. Cormorants rarely travel far when collecting food for their chicks, but albatrosses – the largest tubenoses – can fly thousands of kilometres before returning to their nests. This remarkable breeding strategy is only possible because the adults swallow their catch, then regurgitate a soup-like slurry when at their nests.

Mainland Antarctica is home to only 11 species of breeding bird, and directly or indirectly, all of them depend on food from the sea. Penguins are famous emblems of the continent's bird life, but of the 17 species in the penguin family, only five actually set foot on Antarctic shores. Penguins spend the winter far out to sea, but during the polar summer gather at breeding sites on coasts. Most of these colonies are on rocky ground, and some have been in constant use for thousands of years. The Emperor Penguin is exceptional in breeding on Antarctic ice, and in following a breeding cycle that starts in the autumn, rather than in spring. The males, which carry out incubation, experience the lowest temperatures of any bird in the world. Only petrels breed further south than this. One species – the Snow Petrel – has been found nesting over 250km (155 miles) inland, on ice-free cliffs in Antarctica's mountains.

Throughout Antarctica and its outlying islands, a selection of avian pirates and scavengers eat food that has been brought ashore. Skuas often attack other birds, just as they do in the Arctic, but Southern Giant Petrels and Snowy Sheathbills also tackle more substantial fare, including seal and whale carcasses.

FROM POLE TO POLE

Despite its name, the Arctic Tern is a migrant that travels between both of the polar regions – a round-trip of at least 40,000km (25,000 miles). It is the only bird to do so, and this immense journey requires a large amount of energy. Unlike some migrants, the Arctic Tern is an unhurried traveller, and feeds constantly on the way. Most Arctic Terns travel off westerly coastlines on their way north and south. Once they reach the far north, they breed around the shores of the Arctic Ocean. After breeding, they set off for the Southern Ocean, where they arrive a few months later and disperse to feed. Some skuas travel almost as far – species that nest in the Arctic sometimes overwinter as far south as the Antarctic Circle, while the South Polar Skua can reach Alaska in the northern summer.

ARCTIC TERN
During an average lifespan of about 20 years, the Arctic Tern can migrate nearly 1 million km (620,000 miles).

WETLANDS

WHEREVER THEY ARE, freshwater wetlands act like magnets for birds. From Arctic lakes to luxuriant tropical marshes, they support a wide range of species, often concentrated in a way that few other habitats can match. The most successful wetland species include some of the most widely distributed birds in the world. In temperate regions, ponds and lakes can freeze over in winter, forcing many of their birds to move to larger bodies of water or to coasts. In the tropics, freezing is not a problem, but lakes and rivers often rise and fall with the seasons, sometimes drying up entirely before rain returns.

TEMPERATE WETLANDS

Having fallen as rain or snow, fresh water returns to the sea as part of the planet's water cycle, creating many different habitats on the way. In temperate regions, relatively few birds live in the first of these habitats – fast-flowing mountain streams. Dippers are a remarkable exception: the world's only aquatic songbirds, they feed below the surface, using their wings to stay submerged as they walk upstream. Some unusual ducks also live in whitewater, such as the Blue Duck from New Zealand and the Torrent Duck of South America. However, birds become much more numerous where rivers widen and the current slows. Here, waterfowl, moorhens, and coots all use the thick waterside vegetation to conceal their nests, while kingfishers dig nest tunnels in exposed banks of earth.

The bird life of lakes varies according to location, and also with depth. Deep northern lakes are the breeding habitat of divers, while lakes further south are often fished by grebes. Cormorants and herons are also frequent visitors to lakes, particularly ones that are artificially stocked with fish. But reedbeds are the richest freshwater habitat of all. Often found near to the coast, they are home to rails, crakes, bitterns, waterfowl, and waders.

WATER RAIL
A narrow, laterally flattened body enables the Water Rail to slip easily between reeds. Normally very shy, it reveals itself by its loud call – a startling series of pig-like grunts and squeals.

EURASIAN BITTERN
Camouflaged by its plumage, this large bittern hunts among reeds. Unlike other members of the heron family, it is rarely glimpsed out in the open as seen in this photograph.

TUFTED DUCK
The Tufted Duck is named for its droopy crest, just visible in this photograph. It is a bird of deep lakes, and dives from the surface to feed. Like most ducks, it takes off explosively at the first sign of danger.

EURASIAN REED WARBLER
A summer visitor across most of Europe, this warbler builds a cup-shaped nest supported by reed stems. Common Cuckoos often use it as a foster parent for their young.

temperate wetlands *tropical wetlands*

WETLAND DISTRIBUTION
Apart from major rivers, the world's largest freshwater wetlands are found in the tundra zone. Major tropical wetlands include the Amazon flood plain and Pantanal swampland in South America, inland deltas and flood plains in Africa, and parts of northern Australia.

GREAT CRESTED GREBE
Grebes are streamlined fish-eaters that spend their entire lives on water. They build floating nesting platforms, often among reeds.

GREAT NORTHERN DIVER
Also known as loons, divers are clumsy on land but very agile underwater. They nest beside lakes in the far north, usually moving to coasts in winter.

TROPICAL WETLANDS

Due to their combination of water, nutrients, and warmth, tropical wetlands are powerhouses of biological activity. Waterfowl are common, but tropical lakes and rivers have some much more statuesque birds, such as the huge Goliath Heron and the bizarre Shoebill, or Whale-headed Stork, both from Africa, and the Jabiru of Central and South America. Tropical waterways also attract many aerial hunters. More than 90 per cent of the world's kingfishers are found in the tropics – particularly in Southeast Asia – and tropical wetlands are also home to several species of fish eagle, as well as the Snail Kite. After dusk, night herons and small bitterns stalk food at the water's edge, while fish owls snatch prey from the surface. In some parts of the tropics, low rainfall coupled with rapid evaporation creates extensive soda lakes. Their highly saline water is toxic to most freshwater life, apart from some crustaceans and algae. This food is exploited by flamingos, which can form flocks containing hundreds of thousands of birds. High in the Andes and in East Africa's Rift Valley (see p.157), huge flocks of flamingos make some of the most breathtaking bird spectacles anywhere on Earth.

TEMPORARY WETLANDS

On the equator, torrential downpours ensure that wetlands rarely run dry, but towards the edges of the tropics rain is more seasonal. As a result, wetlands expand and shrink on an annual cycle. In arid regions, these changes are more extreme and wetlands are often temporary features, appearing after sudden storms, then drying out altogether weeks or months later. Wetland birds adapt to this by adopting a nomadic lifestyle. In Africa, for example, Blacksmith Plovers are remarkably successful at tracking down temporary pools. In Australia, pelicans and Black Swans will fly very long distances to visit temporary lakes caused by heavy rain.

AUSTRALIAN PELICAN
Despite being dependent on water, Australia's only native pelican can be encountered in the continent's dry interior. A great wanderer, it seeks out isolated temporary lakes.

PIED KINGFISHER
This noisy species is widespread in Africa and Asia, and often hovers above the water's surface before diving in to catch its prey.

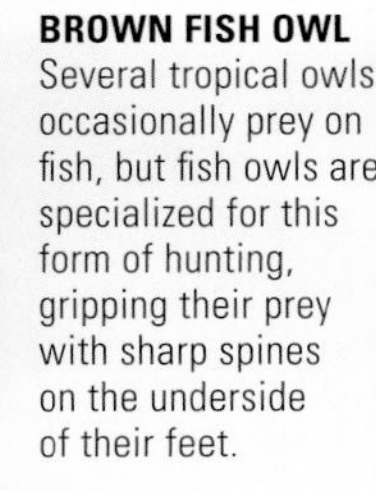

SNAIL KITE
Uniquely for a raptor, the Snail Kite feeds only on molluscs. It uses its fine-tipped bill to pull water snails from their shells.

BROWN FISH OWL
Several tropical owls occasionally prey on fish, but fish owls are specialized for this form of hunting, gripping their prey with sharp spines on the underside of their feet.

SHOEBILL
This massive-billed stork haunts the swamps of tropical Africa and eats all kinds of animal food, including turtles and young crocodiles.

AFRICAN PYGMY GOOSE
Despite its name, this bird is Africa's smallest duck. Like nearly all waterfowl in the tropics, it is non-migratory, but it may be nomadic during droughts.

BRONZE-WINGED JACANA
Extraordinarily long toes enable jacanas to walk on waterlily leaves. Jacanas are found throughout the tropics – this species lives in south and southeast Asia.

COASTS

ALMOST EVERY COASTLINE is home to birds, even on small remote islands and in polar regions. Coasts provide a vast and varied supply of food and birds tackle virtually all of it, from worms and molluscs hidden in coastal mud to remains washed up by the tide. Some coastal birds, such as turnstones, live only in this habitat, but they are a minority. Gulls and waders often wander far inland, while oceanic birds, such as gannets, petrels, and auks, live at sea and visit coasts only to breed. Ultimately, the bird life of coasts is shaped by geology – whether the shore is rocky, muddy, or sandy, and flat or raised into cliffs.

ROCKY SHORES

Some birds of rocky shores have no direct connection with the sea. For Red-billed Choughs, Common Pigeons, and Peregrine Falcons, coastal cliffs are simply the seaside equivalent of the habitat they use inland. But for true seabirds, cliffs are vital nesting sites that provide safety from predatory mammals. During the breeding season, cliffs in the northern hemisphere can be crowded with murres, razorbills, puffins, and kittiwakes, creating an impressive chorus of noisy calls – and often a powerful smell (see Breeding p.48). In the North Atlantic, and off southern Africa and Australia, gannets breed on bare rocky islands, with thousands of pairs spaced just pecking distance apart. Rocky turf-covered islands are used by shearwaters, which lay their eggs in burrows. By day, their nesting colonies seem deserted, but the adults return with food as soon as it is dark. Rocky shores are also home to seaducks, such as eiders, and to many birds that feed on animals exposed by the tide, including 10 species of oystercatcher.

GREAT BLACK-BACKED GULL
This huge North Atlantic gull is a formidable predator. It often preys on other seabirds and their young, and is able to kill mammals up to the size of a rabbit.

WHITE-TAILED EAGLE
Like the Bald Eagle of North America, this Eurasian bird of prey tackles a wide range of food. Its diet includes fish (caught alive or scavenged) as well as other birds.

BLACK SKIMMER
In calm conditions, skimmers fly low over lagoons and estuaries. They slice through the water's surface with an open bill, and scoop up fish by means of their projecting lower mandible, a unique adaptation.

MAGELLANIC OYSTERCATCHER
Despite differences in plumage, oystercatchers are remarkably alike in their feeding habits. This species lives on the wild coasts of southern Chile and Argentina.

GREAT CORMORANT
The Great Cormorant is equally at home in fresh water and on coasts. Like all cormorants, it swims low in the water, peering under to look for fish.

RUDDY TURNSTONE
This short-billed wader patrols the tideline, flicking seaweed aside to catch sandhoppers and other small animals. One of the most widely distributed coastal birds, it lives on every continent except Antarctica.

MUDFLATS AND ESTUARIES

On low-lying shores, tides play an important part in the life of birds. For many, the busiest time is when the tide recedes, revealing banks of sand or mud. Sand contains relatively little animal life, but mud teems with it, and this food is exploited by huge numbers of waders all around the globe. Low-lying coasts are also home to birds that feed in the brackish water of estuaries and lagoons. Among them are avocets, stilts, spoonbills, and skimmers. Low-lying coasts are major summer nesting habitats for terns. But in temperate regions, the bird life of muddy and sandy shores is richest in winter. At this time of year, big flocks of waders arrive from their distant breeding grounds, and many freshwater birds, such as grebes and waterfowl, fly in to avoid cold weather inland.

MANGROVES

In temperate parts of the world, flat muddy coastlines are often backed by a salt-marsh zone. But in the tropics, the same kind of low-lying coast is fringed by mangroves – specialized evergreen trees able to grow in coastal mud, with tangled prop-like roots that can survive being flooded by salty water. Wherever they grow, mangroves are important roosting and nesting sites for birds. These include ibises, spoonbills, and egrets, which sometimes breed in large mixed colonies, and also birds of prey such as the Osprey and Brahminy Kite. Mangrove forests are also a good place to see kingfishers. The Mangrove Kingfisher, from Southeast Asia and Australia, makes its nest holes in rotten mangrove trunks or in abandoned termite nests slung from mangrove branches. Seasonal visitors to mangroves include a few land birds, such as the lorikeets and honeyeaters that visit the mangroves of northern Australia to drink nectar from flowers.

HUMAN IMPACT

MANGROVE DESTRUCTION

In recent decades huge areas of mangroves have been destroyed to make way for building projects or shrimp farming, especially in Central America and Southeast Asia. Many of the surviving trees are dying off due to pollution, including sewage and the waste water from shrimp ponds. As a result, birds unique to mangroves are under increasing pressure.

DEAD MANGROVES, COLOMBIA
The mangrove forests on the Caribbean coast of north Colombia are vanishing due to urban sprawl. They are the only home of the critically endangered Sapphire-bellied Hummingbird.

GREY HERON
Herons are often seen on coasts. Some species are true shoreline birds, but the Grey Heron, from Eurasia and Africa, usually breeds by fresh water and visits coasts during the winter.

EURASIAN CURLEW
Like many waders, curlews breed on wetlands inland but are more obvious in winter when they move to coasts. The Eurasian Curlew winters as far south as southern Africa and Indonesia.

SANDERLING
Resembling small clockwork toys, Sanderlings scuttle along sandy beaches on fast-moving legs. They stay near the water's edge to snap up small animals exposed by the waves. The bird shown is in summer plumage.

COMMON SHELDUCK
The Common Shelduck inhabits low-lying coasts, estuaries, and salt lakes, where it methodically sifts wet mud for food. Its young often form crèches, supervised by several adults.

COMMON GUILLEMOT
Guillemots, also called murres, lay a single egg on narrow ledges high on sea cliffs. The egg has a strongly oval shape to help stop it rolling off the ledge.

OCEANS AND SEAS

NO BIRD SPENDS its entire life at sea, but several come very close. The Sooty Tern roams tropical oceans for up to eight years before it returns to land to breed, and many other species – such as gannets and boobies – remain at sea until they are four or five years old. Some oceanic birds land on the water to feed, but others stay in the air round the clock, snatching their food from the surface, or from other birds.

TEMPERATE SEAS

On land, warm regions often have the most wildlife, but in oceans the situation is usually reversed. Cold water contains much more dissolved oxygen than warm water, and is often richer in nutrients. As a result, large numbers of pelagic (ocean-going) birds live in temperate seas, or in regions where cold currents flow into the tropics. Some species are astoundingly abundant. For example, Wilson's Storm-petrel – a pelagic bird about the size of a sparrow – is estimated to have a population running into tens of millions, making it one of the world's most numerous birds. Shearwaters and petrels are almost as common, and their larger size makes them easier to see as they speed just above the waves. Many of these birds breed in temperate waters and disperse into the tropics when they leave their nests.

In temperate seas, by far the largest pelagic birds are albatrosses. These depend on strong winds to soar – something that largely excludes them from the tropics, because tropical seas are often calm. Gannets follow albatrosses in size, but they fly strongly whatever the conditions on distinctive, sharply pointed wings. At a distance, gannets may be mistaken for gulls, but no gull can match their skill at dive-bombing fish.

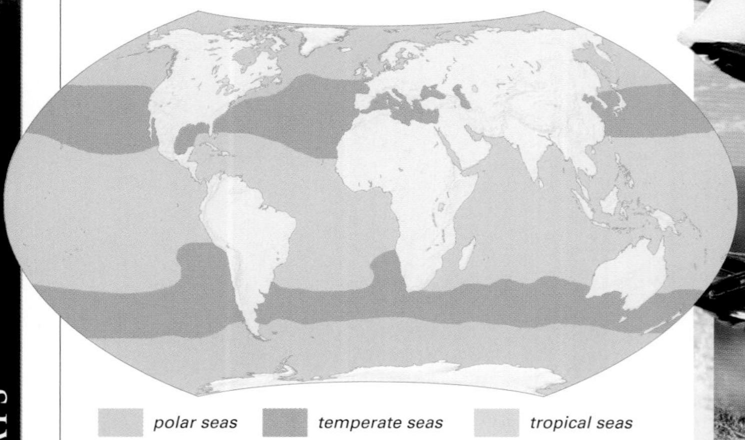

THE OCEANS
Seabirds live in all the world's oceans, but the highest densities occur in temperate and polar seas. Most seabirds live on continental shelves – shallow, gently sloping coastal areas that flank deeper water – or in regions with upwelling currents, such as South America's west coast.

BLACK-FOOTED ALBATROSS
This species is one of three albatross species found in the North Pacific, and it is occasionally seen on migration off the west coast of the USA.

WILSON'S STORM-PETREL
Storm-petrels feed by fluttering close to the water, and often patter the surface with their feet to help keep their balance as they pick up items of food.

BLACK-LEGGED KITTIWAKE
Kittiwakes are small ocean-going gulls that peck food from the water's surface. After breeding, this species disperses throughout northern oceans and seas.

NORTHERN GANNET
When a gannet dives headlong into the sea for fish, the splash can be seen from afar. Air sacs under the skin of its breast help cushion the impact.

GREAT SKUA
The North Atlantic's largest skua, this predator and scavenger often follows fishing boats out to sea. It is strong enough to rob gannets of their catch.

TROPICAL SEAS

GREAT FRIGATEBIRD
Found only in the tropics, frigatebirds soar far out to sea, using their long tails as rudders. In flight, they have an angular silhouette with rakish wings.

In the tropics, ocean-going birds tend to be thinly spread and some fly great distances to search for food. Frigatebirds, for instance, travel by soaring high overhead on massive outstretched wings. They obtain almost all their food from the sea, often by stealing it from other birds, but seldom settle on the surface as they lack waterproof plumage and cannot swim. Unlike true pelagic birds, they head back to islands and coasts at the day's end, spending the night perched in bushes and trees. By contrast, the Fairy Tern is fully oceanic. It is a tireless flier, often being spotted from ships hundreds of kilometres from the nearest land. Tropicbirds are almost as wide-ranging, but Sooty Terns and Brown Noddies have the widest distribution of all: both nest right around the globe, on atolls and other remote islands.

Some tropical seabirds, including Fairy Terns and tropicbirds, are solitary at sea, whereas Sooty Terns can be encountered in huge flocks that look like smoke against the sky. Boobies also feed in flocks, although on a smaller scale. Tropical relatives of gannets, they plunge into the water like a volley of arrows whenever they spot shoals of fish. Most range far over the oceans when they have finished breeding.

Of all the birds found in tropical seas, the ones that perhaps might have been least expected to occur there are a pair of freshwater waders – the Grey and Red-necked Phalaropes. These elegant species change habitat entirely after breeding. They nest on bogs and pools in the tundra of the extreme north, but migrate south to spend the winter far from the coast in tropical waters.

RED-BILLED TROPICBIRD
Tropicbirds feed by shallow plunge-diving, a technique also used by many terns. Graceful in flight, they are easily recognized by their long tail streamers.

FAIRY TERN
The Fairy Tern is a familiar bird to sailors in tropical seas because of its inquisitive nature. It often appears from nowhere to examine passing ships, before flying on.

RED-NECKED PHALAROPE
Seen here in its more colourful breeding plumage, the Red-necked Phalarope migrates to tropical seas for the winter months.

OCEANIC ISLANDS

Remote islands are important nesting sites for pelagic birds, particularly if they are free of egg-eating mammals such as rodents or foxes, which can wreak havoc in seabird colonies. Shearwaters dig nesting burrows, but many other pelagic birds, such as gannets, terns, and albatrosses, nest out in the open, using little or no nesting material. In places with a hot, dry climate, thick deposits of fossilized droppings, called guano, show that some sites have been in continual use for thousands of years. However, dependence on limited sites also makes seabirds vulnerable. If predators are deliberately or accidentally introduced, nesting colonies can be wiped out in a matter of a few years. Several species have been pushed to the brink in this way, including the Bermuda Petrel or Cahow, which almost died out due to predation by introduced rats, cats, and dogs.

MASKED BOOBY
The largest of the world's six species of booby, this powerful plunge-diver fishes in deep water throughout the tropics, except for the eastern Atlantic.

SOOTY TERN NESTING COLONY
Sooty Terns breed in very large colonies on islands – the colony shown here, on Midway Atoll, Hawaii, is used by 50,000 pairs. The birds lay their eggs directly on the ground.

FARMLAND AND CITIES

OVER A THIRD OF the Earth's land surface is currently used for farming, and around 3 per cent is occupied by cities or towns. Together, this adds up to a huge area – one that continues to grow as the human population expands. For birds as a whole, this transformation of the natural world has had all kinds of negative effects, but some species have benefited from the change.

TURKEY VULTURE
This widespread American scavenger is a frequent sight in cattle- and sheep-ranching country. It scans highways for roadkill – a source of food that has soared with the growth in traffic.

FARMLAND

In farmland, one of the surest signs of success is to be ranked as a pest. Several dozen species of bird can claim this status, and for obvious reasons, most are seed-eaters. In the tropics, they include the Red-billed Quelea – a finch that causes huge crop losses in Africa – and the brightly coloured Java Sparrow, which plunders rice fields in southeast Asia. North American crops are attacked by the Bobolink and Red-winged Blackbird, but in temperate regions, the worst damage is often caused by birds that eat seeds before they have sprouted. These include a wide variety of omnivores such as gulls and crows, which descend on fields when the soil is ploughed and drilled, while pigeons feed on the young plants.

By contrast, insect-eaters are generally welcome visitors, and the expansion of farming originally helped many of them to thrive. Cattle Egrets are a common sight in pasture in many parts of the world, and aerial feeders, such as the Barn Swallow, also benefit from the insect life above meadows. But due to changes in agriculture, intensively farmed land is now bird-free for much of the year. Insecticides and herbicides deplete the birds' food supplies, and heavy machinery destroys the eggs of ground-nesting birds.

BARN SWALLOW
Swallows thrive in regions with damp pasture, because this type of landscape is an ideal breeding ground for insects. The Barn Swallow has a virtually global distribution, but its numbers fluctuate with the changing food supply.

CATTLE EGRET
Originally found alongside wild grazing mammals, the Cattle Egret has moved into farmland. It feeds on insects and other small prey flushed out by cattle.

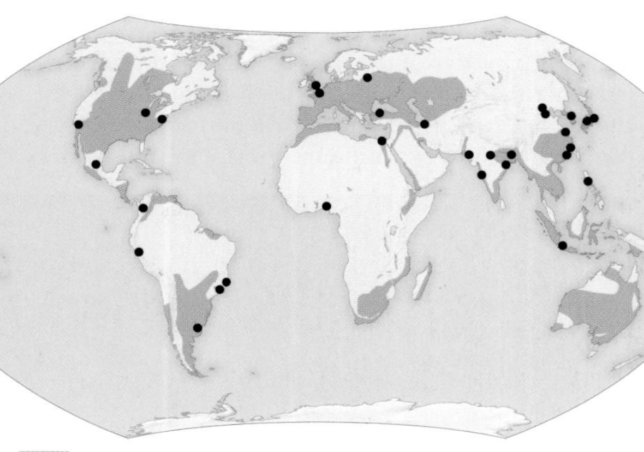

FARMLAND AND URBAN AREAS DISTRIBUTION
Humans began farming around 10,000 years ago, and so farmland is a very new addition to the world's list of habitats. Cities are an even more recent habitat in ecological terms. Both habitats are increasing in size – the planet's proportion of urban land is set to double by 2025.

RED-WINGED BLACKBIRD
When it forms huge flocks, this songbird can devastate entire fields of grain. But the gradual disappearance of suitable nesting habitat means that the species is not as damaging as it was in the past.

CITIES

No accurate figures exist for the world's urban bird population, but it almost certainly exceeds the human one. In most of the world's cities, birds manage to flourish, although the number of species is often low. So what makes a successful urban bird? The answer is several key features. Among them are a wide-ranging diet, a readiness to try new foods, and an ability to feed and breed in busy, built-up surroundings.

Probably the oldest-established urban bird is the House Sparrow. Its natural range includes the Middle East – the region where urbanization first began. Today, House Sparrows are found all over the world, and their ability to get inside buildings is unrivalled. They are often seen in supermarkets and subway systems, and have even been spotted on the 80th floor of the Empire State Building in New York. Although House Sparrows are primarily seed-eaters, they are also ready to feed on all kinds of edible scraps.

House Sparrows moved into towns and cities without any human help, but several top urban birds – including the Common Pigeon and Common Starling – have a more complicated history. The ancestors of the former species nested on cliffs and rocky ground, and were domesticated several millennia ago as a source of food. Over the centuries, many of these birds escaped and began breeding in towns. Rooftops and windowsills mimic their natural habitat perfectly, and some cities now have a pigeon population running into millions.

Originally from Europe, the Common Starling was introduced into North America in the 1890s, when about 100 birds were released in New York's Central Park. It spread rapidly and is now a common sight on city streets, and an aggressive competitor to many of the continent's native birds. It has had similar success in eastern Australia and New Zealand, with equally damaging results for the local bird life.

COMMON PIGEON
Descended from domesticated birds, these pigeons are so at home in urban areas that they are often considered a pest.

GALAH
A rare success story in the parrot family, the Galah has become an abundant bird throughout Australia's wheat-growing belt, and in some of its cities too, such as Melbourne and Perth.

COMMON STARLING
Buildings make ideal nest sites for this starling. In winter, starlings often gather at mass roosts in towns, performing spectacular aerial manoeuvres before landing.

HOUSE SPARROW
The chirping of male House Sparrows (above) is a familiar sound in urban areas across the world. They nest in holes or among foliage, often in groups.

COMMON NIGHTHAWK
This nocturnal species is now a common urban bird in the USA, where it nests on gravel-covered flat roofs. At night the artificial lighting attracts its insect prey.

NESTING SPACE

The urbanization of the countryside has generally been good news for swifts, swallows, and martins, because it has created new nesting opportunities. These birds are all aerial insect-eaters and originally nested in crevices or among rocks, but today they often use artificial structures. Barn Swallows and Common House Martins breed in farms or villages, so that they can fetch mud from the surrounding countryside to build their nests, whereas Common Swifts avoid open country, and instead nest in cities. They mould their nests from saliva and feathers.

COMMON HOUSE MARTIN
House Martins nest under eaves. The nests look precarious, but the mud and saliva building mixture bonds to hard surfaces like glue.

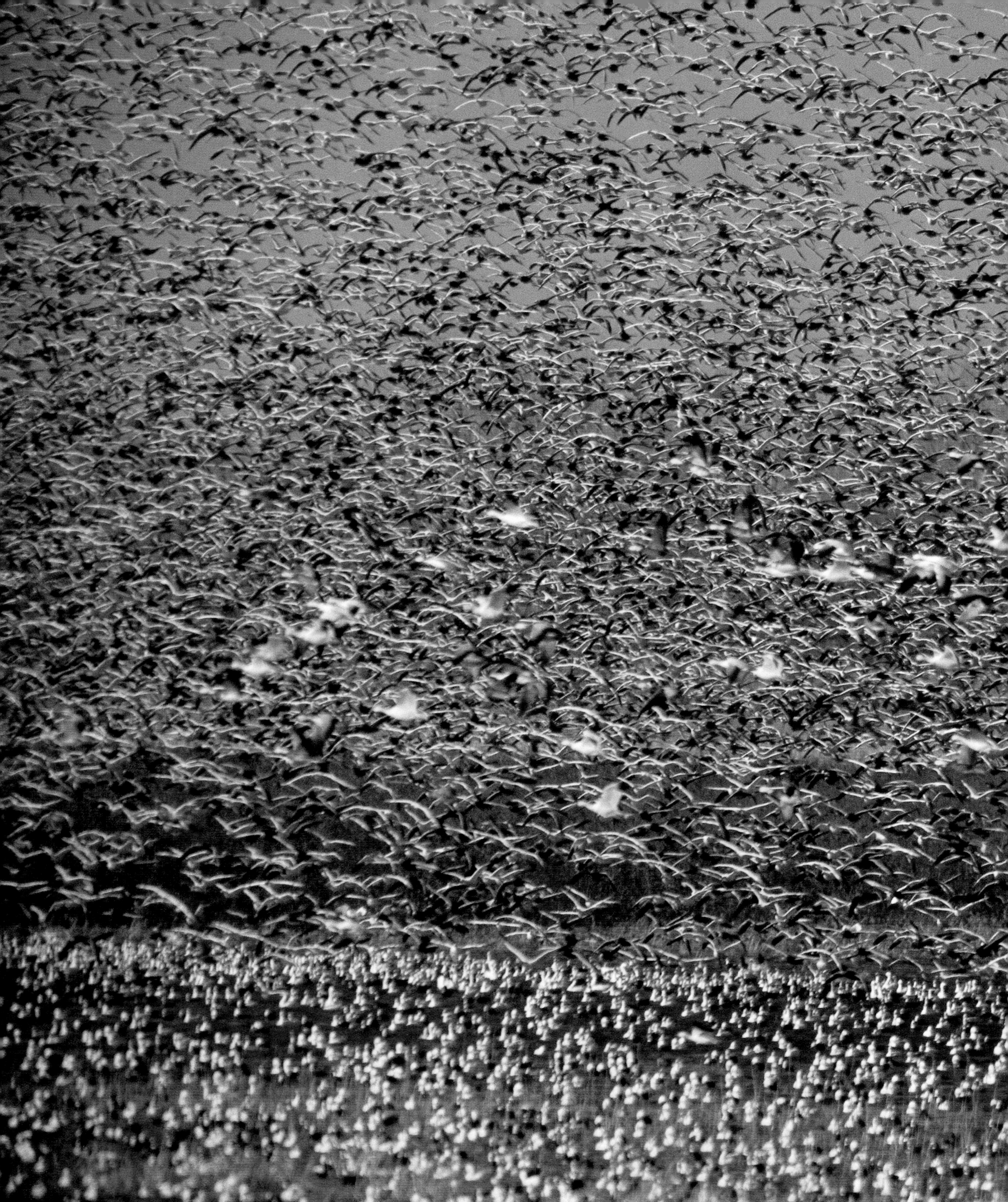

BIRD SPECIES

CLASSIFICATION

CLASSIFICATION IS THE SCIENCE of identifying and categorizing living things and, among ornithologists, few topics generate as much debate. This is because classification involves much more than simply giving birds scientific names. Instead, it delves deep into their evolutionary history, as scientists try to establish how all the world's birds are related. Traditionally, classification is based on physical features, and on other inherited characteristics, such as internal processes or behaviour. But in recent years, the advances in molecular biology have allowed ornithologists to go to the very source of bird evolution, by studying DNA itself.

RUBY-THROATED HUMMINGBIRD

A SHARED PAST
Despite their extraordinary range in shape and size, hummingbirds and penguins – together with all other birds – have evolved from a single ancestor that lived in the distant past. In classification terms, they and their direct forebears make up a clade: a single branch of life's evolutionary tree. Since the branch started growing, it has divided many times, leading to the variety of species that exist today.

HUMBOLDT PENGUIN

CLASSIFICATION GROUPS

In biological classification, the most fundamental unit is the species. This is a group of living things that share the same features, and that breed with each other. To distinguish species from each other, each one is given a unique two-part scientific name. Unlike a common name, this is recognized worldwide. Once classified, each species fits into groups of increasing size, from genera and families, which contain a species' closest living relatives, through orders, classes, and phyla to the Animal kingdom – one of the fundamental divisions of life on Earth.

CLASSIFICATION IN ACTION

The major classification levels are listed here, using the Common Starling as an example. Below species level, distinct variants are classed as subspecies.

KINGDOM Animalia
Includes multicellular organisms that obtain energy by eating food. Most have nerves, which enable them to sense their surroundings. Many are able to move.

PHYLUM Chordata
Animals that have a strengthening rod, or notochord, running the length of their bodies. In some chordates it may be present only during the embryo stage.

CLASS Aves
Contains all the world's birds. Birds are, like mammals, warm-blooded, but they are the only living chordates that have feathers. Most of them can fly.

ORDER Passeriformes
The largest order of birds, containing over 5,200 species. All its members have specialized feet for gripping slender perches. Many have complex songs.

FAMILY Sturnidae
This family contains all the world's starlings – over 100 species. Starlings have straight beaks and an omnivorous diet, and they are often gregarious.

GENUS *Sturnus*
This genus contains a group of 15 species of Asian and European starlings. The most noticeable difference between species is their coloration.

SPECIES *Sturnus vulgaris*
The Common Starling has dark plumage with iridescent spots, which become pronounced in the breeding season. It often roosts in large flocks.

PROBLEM OF VARIATION

Traditional classification suffers from some major problems. One of the biggest is that some species show marked variations in different parts of their range. The Carrion Crow, for example, has six regional variants, spread across Europe, North Africa, and Asia. The Collared Kingfisher has about 50, many restricted to tiny islands. In cases like these, classification is often a matter of opinion, with experts differing on whether variants are full species or not. As a result, there is no agreed figure for the total number of bird species. Most ornithologists estimate there are between 8,500 and 10,000, but as more subspecies are "promoted" to full species, the total continues to rise.

HOODED CROW
Classified as *Corvus corone coronix,* this Carrion Crow is found in northern and eastern Europe. It may breed with the all-black form.

CARRION CROW
This all-black form of the Carrion Crow is the subspecies found in most of western Europe. It is classified as *Corvus corone corone.*

CLASSIFICATION TECHNIQUES

In evolution, some physical features can change much more rapidly than others, so this has to be taken into account when species are compared. "Conservative" features, such as the arrangement of muscles and bones, evolve very slowly, while "derived" features, such as songs, can evolve much more rapidly. Taken together, these can show which birds share distant ancestors, and which ones are more recently related. Anatomical evidence is often clouded by convergent evolution. In this process, unrelated birds can become deceptively similar, by adapting to similar ways of life.

In the 1980s bird classification was revolutionized by the analysis of DNA samples taken from the world's bird species, which showed their relationships. This confirmed many of the groups that had been determined by studying bird anatomy, but it also revealed some previous mistakes in classification.

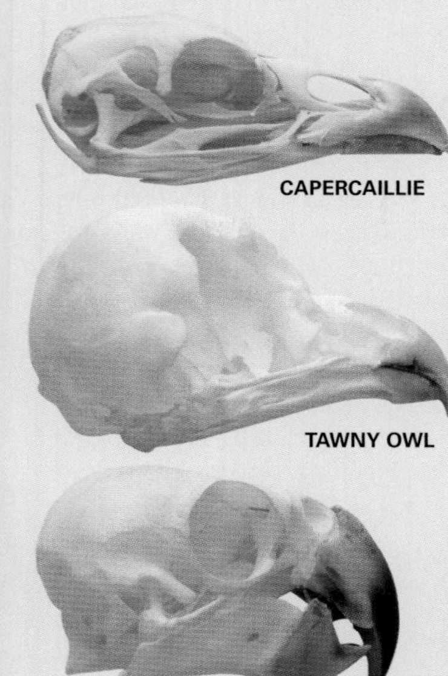

HARD EVIDENCE
Skull anatomy is important for the study of bird evolution. Bill shapes can evolve fairly rapidly, but the arrangement of skull bones is consistent over millions of years.

SUPERB FAIRYWREN
Australian songbirds – such as fairywrens – were originally thought to have evolved from songbirds that arrived from Eurasia. DNA analysis has shown that this is probably not true and that Australia's songbirds form a separate "home-grown" group.

MOLECULAR MATCH
When strands of DNA from different species are compared, the closer the match, the more closely the two species are related. DNA evidence has shown, for example, that flamingos and grebes are each other's closest living relatives.

UNSOLVED QUESTIONS

With some groups it remains hard to trace the path of evolution. One of these problem groups is the ratites – flightless birds such as ostriches and emus, which do not have a keel on their breastbone. This unusual feature, and several others, suggest that the ratites share the same ancestor. They are assumed to have evolved in the ancient continent of Gondwanaland, before it divided. However, DNA evidence suggests that they diverged much more recently, which throws this theory into doubt. Similar puzzles exist with several other groups.

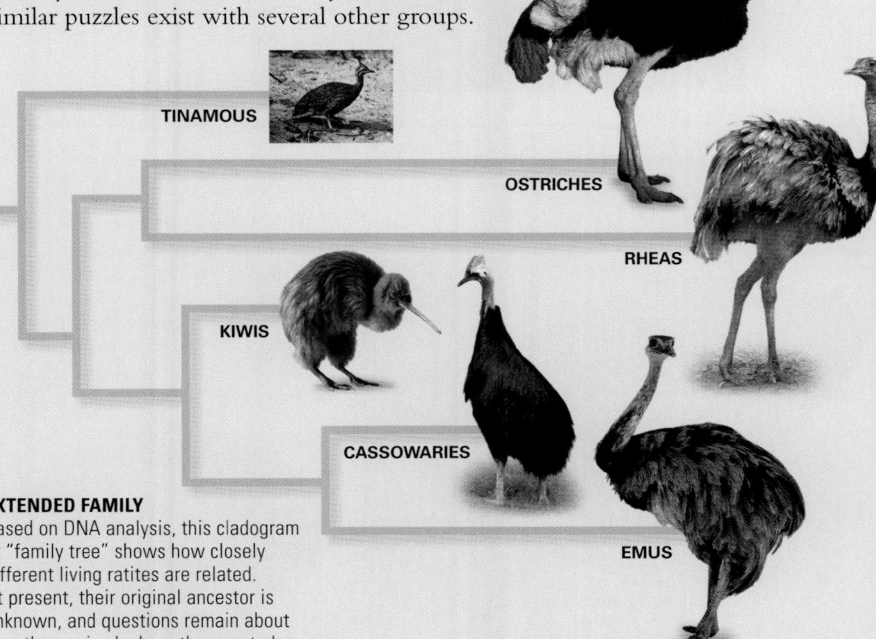

EXTENDED FAMILY
Based on DNA analysis, this cladogram or "family tree" shows how closely different living ratites are related. At present, their original ancestor is unknown, and questions remain about how they arrived where they are today.

BIRD ORDERS

This section of the book follows the names and classification sequence used in *The Howard and Moore Complete Checklist of Birds of the World* (2003) – one of the most comprehensive and authoritative sources in bird classification. In this sequence, a total of 9,721 bird species are recognized, belonging to a total of 204 families. In this book, these families have been grouped into the following 29 orders.

Group	Order	Families	Species
TINAMOUS	Tinamiformes	1	46
OSTRICHES	Struthioniformes	1	1
RHEAS	Rheiformes	1	2
CASSOWARIES AND EMUS	Casuariiformes	2	4
KIWIS	Dinornithiformes	1	3–6
GAMEBIRDS	Galliformes	5	289
WATERFOWL	Anseriformes	3	157
PENGUINS	Sphenisciformes	1	17
DIVERS	Gaviiformes	1	5
ALBATROSSES AND PETRELS	Procellariiformes	4	107
GREBES	Podicipediformes	1	22
FLAMINGOS	Phoenicopteriformes	1	5
STORKS AND HERONS	Ciconiiformes	3	115
PELICANS AND RELATIVES	Pelicaniformes	8	64
BIRDS OF PREY	Falconiformes	3	304
CRANES AND RELATIVES	Gruiformes	11	199
WADERS, GULLS, AND AUKS	Charadriiformes	16	344
SANDGROUSE	Pteroclidiformes	1	16
PIGEONS AND DOVES	Columbiformes	1	298
PARROTS	Psiitaciformes	1	352
CUCKOOS AND TURACOS	Cuculiformes	3	161
OWLS	Strigiformes	2	194
NIGHTJARS AND FROGMOUTHS	Caprimulgiformes	5	115
SWIFTS AND HUMMINGBIRDS	Apodiformes	3	429
MOUSEBIRDS	Coliiformes	2	6
TROGONS	Trogoniformes	1	39
KINGFISHERS AND RELATIVES	Coraciiformes	11	208
WOODPECKERS AND TOUCANS	Piciformes	5	396
PASSERINES	Passeriformes	92	5,200

TINAMOUS

ORDER	Tinamiformes
FAMILY	1
SPECIES	46

FOUND ONLY IN Central and South America, tinamous superficially resemble gamebirds (see p.107), with small heads, plump bodies, and short legs. However, although they can fly, their skeletons show that they are more closely related to the flightless ratites, which include rheas and ostriches. Tinamous live in woodland and open grassland, including the Andean Altiplano. They feed on the ground, eating seeds and berries, as well as insects, and small animals. They can fly rapidly over short distances on small, fast-beating wings but, if threatened, their first instinct is to run away.

BREEDING

Tinamous nest on the ground, laying up to a dozen eggs. Their eggs are remarkable, with a bright background colour and glossy sheen. The male is responsible for building the nest and for incubation, which lasts for about three weeks. The chicks are well developed when they hatch, running after their parents within hours.

MALE ON NEST
A male Highland Tinamou incubates a clutch of eggs, with a recently hatched chick by his side.

Tinamus major

Great Tinamou

LENGTH 42cm (16½in)
WEIGHT 1kg (2¼lb)
MIGRATION Non-migrant

HABITAT Primary and secondary rainforest, with an open forest floor

ADULT GREAT TINAMOU

The haunting song of the Great Tinamou, consisting of up to seven tremulous, whistled notes, is one of the most evocative of Neotropical bird sounds, cutting through the forest before dawn and around dusk. It is a large, brown bird that wanders on the forest floor, eating insects, frogs, berries, fruit, and seeds.

Crypturellus soui

Little Tinamou

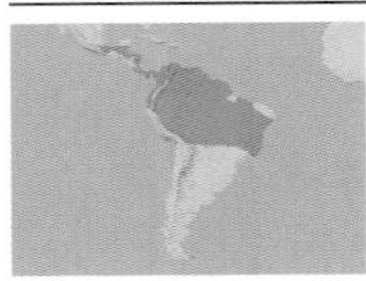

LENGTH 23cm (9in)
WEIGHT 225g (8oz)
MIGRATION Non-migrant

HABITAT Tropical and lower subtropical forest, especially in dense undergrowth on forest edges

In common with other members of its genus, the Little Tinamou is found in the forest undergrowth. It has a black crown, nape, and head sides that contrast with its base plumage, which varies from olive-brown to ochre. The female has a brighter plumage than the male.

The call of this species is a series of clear, tremulous whistles, rising in pitch and volume before stopping abruptly. It is a shy bird, usually remaining in dense thickets, which makes it well camouflaged. If surprised in the open, it will either freeze or, more usually, scurry away. The Little Tinamou is omnivorous. While its main diet consists of fruit, berries, tubers, and seeds, it also eats insects and frogs. Like some other tinamous, it swallows small pebbles to aid digestion. It lays two eggs, which are incubated by just the male.

Nothoprocta pentlandii

Andean Tinamou

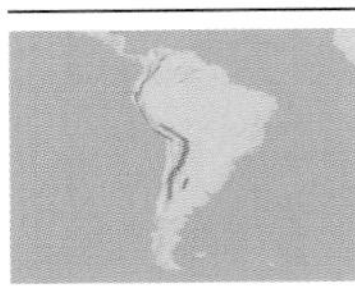

LENGTH 27cm (10½in)
WEIGHT 275g (10oz)
MIGRATION Non-migrant

HABITAT Steep slopes at high altitude, including forest edges, steppes, and vegetation along streams

The Andean Tinamou occurs in semi-open habitats, and is most often glimpsed crossing a road. Its most distinctive feature is its slender decurved bill, which is black above and pink below. Its iris is yellow to pale brown. The upperparts are brown with white streaking, grey mottling, and rufous barring. The underparts are pale buff colour. The wings are heavily barred buff, and its legs are pale yellow.

The Andean Tinamou is a shy bird and has a tendency to hide under rocks and vegetation, staying very still. When disturbed, it flies off with strong wingbeats. It feeds on seeds, shoots, buds, fleshy fruit, crops such as potato and barley, and insect larvae.

The call of the Andean Tinamou is a high-pitched, abrupt whistle, usually at long intervals. The male builds the nest in the breeding season and mates with different females, who lay about 14 eggs each. It is the male who incubates the eggs and cares for the brood. The chicks are able to feed themselves a few hours after hatching.

ADULT ANDEAN TINAMOU

Eudromia elegans

Elegant Crested Tinamou

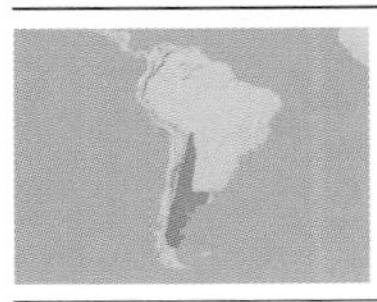

LENGTH 39cm (15½in)
WEIGHT 675–750g (24–27oz)
MIGRATION Non-migrant

HABITAT Arid and semi-arid grassland, dry savanna, open woodland, steppes, and sandy areas

A large terrestrial inhabitant of arid Patagonia, the most spectacular feature of the Elegant Crested Tinamou is its long, thin, upcurled crest. Its plumage is basically dark brown, with darker markings. There is a prominent white stripe leading from the eye to the base of the neck and a parallel white stripe starting from the bill. The bill itself is short and decurved and its wings are spotted white. Unlike most tinamous, it has only three toes, lacking a vestigial hind toe.

The Elegant Crested Tinamou is remarkable in its breeding behaviour – either sex may have several mates, and the species is often found in these unusual groupings. The Elegant Crested Tinamou is sedentary, but groups move over large areas in response to food shortages.

ADULT ELEGANT CRESTED TINAMOU

SHINY EGGS

Tinamou eggs are among the most beautiful in the world and look as if they are made of porcelain. Such an egg would appear to attract predators. However, this is not the case as most tinamou predators are nocturnal, relying on scent rather than sight.

OSTRICHES

ORDER	Struthioniformes
FAMILY	1
SPECIES	1

FOUND ONLY IN AFRICA, the ostrich is the world's largest living bird. It has held this title for the last five centuries, since the extinction of the elephant birds of Madagascar. Its wings are large, but too weak to be used for flight. To escape danger, it runs at high speed on its hoof-like, two-toed feet. The ostrich belongs to the ratite group of birds, which includes rheas, emus, cassowaries, and kiwis. All have a flat breastbone, with no keel.

BEHAVIOUR

Ostriches live in open habitats, and are usually seen in groups of 10–25 birds. They feed on small animals and seeds, often mingling with grazing mammals to catch insects stirred up by their feet. Ostrich social life differs from that of many birds, because the male takes a leading part in raising the young. His partner, known as the major hen, scrapes out a nest on the ground and lays up to 12 eggs. Several other females lay in the same nest, creating a shallow pile of up to 50 eggs, each weighing over 1kg (2¼lb). Once the clutch is complete, the major hen incubates by day, with the male taking over at night. The chicks hatch after about 40 days, and immediately follow the male to find food. When two males meet, their chicks instinctively congregate to form a crèche. One male guards the crèche, until the young are able to fend for themselves. Ostriches have a dangerous kick if cornered, but are docile in captivity. At one time, they were much in demand for their feathers, but today they are farmed as a source of meat.

MOVING OUT
With their commanding height, ostriches are quick to spot danger. Here a group of ostriches run for safety in southern Africa's Kalahari Desert.

FIGHTING RIVALS
During the breeding season, male ostriches fight with their feet as they build up harems of hens. However, once the chicks are hatched, they co-operate.

MALE AND FEMALE
The feathers of the adult male are mostly black, with white wing feathers. It also has a white neck band and tail. The female is greyish brown with no white feathers.

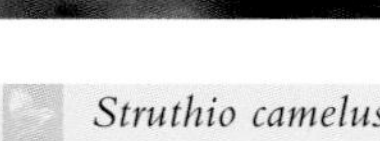

Struthio camelus

Common Ostrich

LENGTH 1.8–2.8m (6–9¼ft)

WEIGHT 100kg (220lb)

MIGRATION Non-migrant

HABITAT Variety of open semi-arid plains (from desert to savanna) and open woodland

The single species of Ostrich is placed in a separate order to all other birds. A creature of superlatives, it is the tallest and heaviest of all birds. The Ostrich is flightless but is better adapted to running than any other bird, aided by its powerful, two-toed feet. It can reach speeds of 70kph (45mph), and has remarkable stamina, "cruising" at 50kph (30mph) for 30 minutes – an important adaptation for fleeing predators and foraging over large, barren areas.

The Common Ostrich's eye measures 5cm (2in) in diameter – the largest of any terrestrial vertebrate. It has 16 primary feathers (an unusual number), which help to create an impressive display. The male is one of the few birds to have a penis, which it displays during courtship. The male chooses the breeding site and mates with three or more females. The eggs are the largest of any bird, and about 2–11 of them are laid in a communal nest. Incubation takes 42 days, the dominant female sitting on the eggs during the day, while the male takes his turn at night. The resulting offspring form large crèches, tended by one or more adults. The diet of the Common Ostrich is varied, including plant matter, carrion, lizards, and even small tortoises.

DEFENCE OF CHICKS
The adult shelters its chicks under its wings to protect them from sun, rain, and predators. It uses its powerful kicks to drive away predators.

RHEAS

ORDER	Rheiformes
FAMILIES	1
SPECIES	2

OFTEN COMPARED TO OSTRICHES, rheas are smaller and much more lightly built birds that live in the grasslands of South America, and the foothills of the Andes. They live in flocks of several dozen birds but, even in the open, their grey-brown plumage can make them difficult to see. As with ostriches, male rheas mate with several females, and take charge of raising the young after they have hatched. Several centuries ago, rheas were extremely common birds, but they have been badly affected by hunting and by the spread of farming.

DARWIN'S RHEA
In typical hunched posture, Darwin's Rhea searches for food in dry grass. Adult rheas feed mainly on plants; the young often eat insects.

ANATOMY

Like ostriches and other ratites (large flightless birds), rheas have flat breastbones without a keel. Without this attachment point, their flight muscles are far too weak for them to fly. However, rhea wings are large, with long loose feathers, while the neck and legs are covered with shorter, denser feathers that help to keep them warm. Rheas have three toes on each foot and a single claw on each wing, which they use if cornered by predators. During the breeding season, incubating males can be remarkably aggressive, even to their own kind. They chase away females, and have even been known to attack cars and people on horseback.

Rhea americana

Greater Rhea

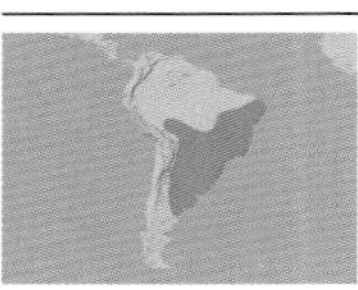

LENGTH
1.2–1.4m (4–4½ft)

WEIGHT
20–40kg (44–88lb)

MIGRATION
Non-migrant

HABITAT Grassland and ranchland, often at edges of lightly wooded areas

Known as the "ostrich of South America", the Greater Rhea is long-legged and flightless. It is grey to brown and white in colour, which helps to camouflage it. Like other ratites, there is little difference between the male and female Greater Rhea, except that the male has a dark collar in the breeding season and the female is smaller and paler in colour. The juvenile has more grey in its plumage and is marked with dark stripes that disappear about six months after hatching.

The species commences its breeding cycle in very early spring, engaging in elaborate displays, during which rival males may bite one another viciously and utter booming calls reminiscent of a bellowing animal. The male mates with about seven females, each of which may mate with more than one male. Occasionally, two males occupy the same nest, but one is dominant. The young are able to leave the nest within a few hours of hatching, under the supervision of the male. Populations of the bird are declining due to the loss and fragmentation of its native grassland habitats, mainly because of clearance of land for soyabean monocultures.

MALE ON THE MOVE
The Greater Rhea's docile-looking face belies a fierce nature and swift turn of foot when alarmed.

CLUTCH OF EGGS
A number of females lay their eggs in the same nest. Up to 30 eggs may be laid to be incubated solely by the male.

Pterocnemia pennata

Darwin's Rhea

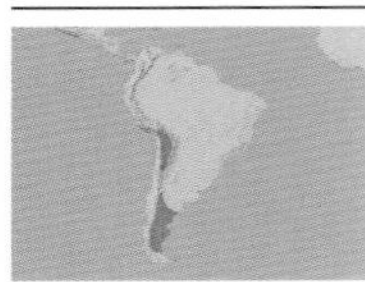

LENGTH
90–100cm (35–39in)

WEIGHT
15–20kg (33–44lb)

MIGRATION
Non-migrant

HABITAT Open country in lowland, steppes, deserts, and puna (cold, arid mountain tops)

Smaller than the Greater Rhea (left), Darwin's Rhea has a shorter bill and slightly longer legs. It has uniformly grey plumage, with white tips to the upperpart feathers, white underparts, and three toes, with sharp claws. The head and the back of the neck are covered with dense feathers. The male has a booming call, but the female is not vocal.

Like the Greater Rhea, Darwin's Rhea principally feeds on leaves, fruit, seeds of various grasses, herbs, and insects. The species is sociable, living in groups, usually in flocks of 5–30, which, when disturbed, tend to flee from danger by running in zigzags. Although a fast runner, this rhea uses other tactics to escape from predators – it suddenly squats under a bush and flattens its body against the ground to avoid detection. It does not fly, but is a strong swimmer and can cross large lakes to reach abundant feeding areas.

This species commences breeding in late winter, when the male displays vigorously during courtship to attract several females, all of which lay eggs in the same nest. The male incubates the eggs for about five weeks.

ADULT DARWIN'S RHEA

CASSOWARIES AND EMUS

ORDER	Casuariiformes
FAMILY	2
SPECIES	4

LARGE FLIGHTLESS BIRDS with vestigial wings, cassowaries and emus live in Australia and New Guinea. One species – the Southern Cassowary – is found in both, a relic of the time when Australia and New Guinea were linked by dry land. Unlike ostriches and rheas, these birds have finely divided plumage, which often looks like coarse hair. Cassowaries live in forest, but emus are birds of scrub and grassland, often travelling over long distances to find their food.

COMMITTED PARENT
During the 8-week incubation period, the male emu neither eats nor drinks. The male stays with the chicks for over a year.

ANATOMY

Cassowaries and emus look quite different, but they all have tiny wings concealed under their plumage, and feet with three toes. In cassowaries, the inner toe carries a long claw, which can inflict lethal wounds on an enemy. Emus are the tallest birds in this order, but the Southern Cassowary is the heaviest, being more thickset. All four species have areas of bare skin on their necks. A cassowary also has a brightly coloured wattle hanging in a loose fold from the neck, and a conspicuous casque that projects impressively from the top of the head. The casque is most obvious in adults, and it continues to grow throughout life.

CASSOWARY CASQUES
Cassowaries use their casques to push through vegetation, but the casque may also play a part in asserting dominance when breeding.

CASSOWARY FOOT
Cassowaries have wide-spreading feet, and the inner toe – seen here on the left – carries a sharp claw up to 10cm (4in) long.

BEHAVIOUR

Emus normally live in small groups, but huge flocks congregate where food supply is abundant. Cassowaries are shy and solitary, vanishing at first signs of intrusion, but attack fiercely if unable to escape. Emus live on seeds and berries; cassowaries feed on fallen fruit, helping to disperse the seeds of forest trees. In the breeding season, the male takes sole charge of the clutch once the female has laid her eggs. Females often mate with several partners in a season, unlike ostriches and rheas. Deforestation threatens cassowaries but, with the spread of agriculture, emus have benefited from easy access to grain.

Casuarius casuarius

Southern Cassowary

LENGTH 1.3–1.7m ($4^{1}/_{4}$–$5^{1}/_{2}$ft)

WEIGHT 30–60kg (66–130lb)

MIGRATION Non-migrant

HABITAT Dense tropical rainforest and, more rarely, eucalyptus and palm forest

Also known as the Double-wattled Cassowary, the powerfully built Southern Cassowary has red wattles that vary in length, hanging from the front of the neck. Most of the head and neck are covered by bright blue, bare, wrinkled skin. Adult birds have a large grey casque (helmet). It is threatened by hunting in New Guinea and, to a lesser extent, by logging in Australia, although the Australian population appears to be stable.

JUVENILE SOUTHERN CASSOWARY

HUMAN IMPACT

ROAD HAZARD

Road signs, such as the one above, are needed in Queensland's Mission Beach, which supports a sizeable population of cassowaries, because the birds are in danger of being run over by cars between the beach and the sloping hinterland.

ADULT DWARF CASSOWARY

Casuarius bennetti

Dwarf Cassowary

LENGTH 1m ($3^{1}/_{4}$ft)

WEIGHT 17–26kg (37–57lb)

MIGRATION Non-migrant

HABITAT Forest and secondary growth, usually in hills and mountains as high as the tree line

The smallest of the cassowaries, the Dwarf Cassowary differs from the Southern Cassowary (left) in that it lacks the dangling neck wattles and has a flattened triangular black casque on top of the head. It has an orange foreneck and its plumage is black. The female is generally larger than the male, usually with brighter red and blue bare skin on the head and neck, and has a longer casque. The Dwarf Cassowary is usually observed alone or in small family groups, feeding on fruit, insects, and small animals. It forms pairs only in the breeding season.

Dromaius novaehollandiae

Emu

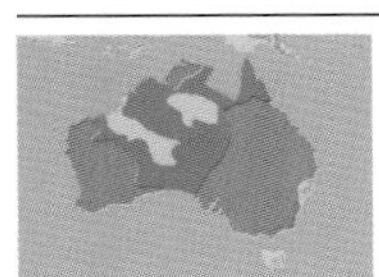

LENGTH 1.4–1.7m ($4^{1}/_{2}$–$5^{1}/_{2}$ft)

WEIGHT 18–48kg (40–105lb)

MIGRATION Non-migrant

HABITAT Open country, preferring areas developed as pastoral land and shunning very arid zones

The flightless Emu is the sole representative of a family of birds that is confined to mainland Australia. It has a long neck and legs, but a short bill and tiny wings that are rarely noticeable amid its greyish brown to almost black, shaggy plumage. It can travel great distances at a fast trot and, if necessary, can sprint as well. The male incubates the eggs and tends to the young.

ADULT EMU

KIWIS

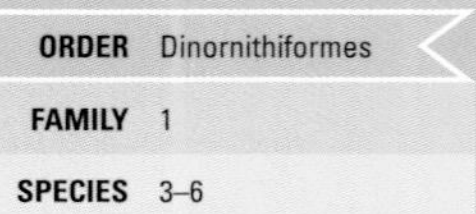

ORDER Dinornithiformes
FAMILY 1
SPECIES 3–6

WITH HUMPBACKED BODIES AND LONG, decurved bills, kiwis are unmistakable, and recognized the world over as New Zealand's national bird. There is disagreement about how many species exist, but the differences between the species are small. All kiwis are flightless, with tiny vestigial wings and brown plumage that looks like coarse fur. They have an excellent sense of smell, with nostrils positioned at the tip of the bill. They live in forests, and are strictly nocturnal, emerging at night to probe damp vegetation for earthworms and other small animals.

HUMAN IMPACT

CONSERVATION

Like many of New Zealand's native birds, kiwis have been decimated by introduced mammals. A nationwide conservation programme is aimed at reversing a decline of up to 5 per cent a year. Conservation measures include setting traps (right) for rats and stoats, which prey on kiwi chicks.

BEHAVIOUR

Kiwis are monogamous and, despite their harmless appearance, will attack rivals with their claws, sometimes inflicting severe wounds. However, confrontations like this are rare, because territory holders advertise their presence with loud calls. During the day, kiwis hide, either in a burrow, or in thick vegetation. They sleep with their heads tucked incongruously under a wing just 5cm (2in) long. The female lays her eggs in a nesting burrow and, in most kiwis, the male incubates the egg, which takes about 70 days to hatch. Initially, the young bird is nourished by the remains of the yolk sac, which is still attached to its body, but by the end of the first week, it ventures out of the burrow to feed. Many kiwis fall victim to predatory mammals at this stage, before they are large enough to defend themselves.

GIANT EGGS
Kiwi eggs are about 12cm (5in) long, and contain unusually large amounts of yolk. Females lay only one or two eggs each time they breed.

Apteryx australis

Brown Kiwi

LENGTH 50–65cm (19½–26in)
WEIGHT 1.4–3.9kg (3–8½lb)
MIGRATION Non-migrant

HABITAT Subtropical to temperate forests and shrub, plantations, and farmland

RED LIST CATEGORY Endangered

The Brown Kiwi is typical of the kiwis, being a flightless ground-dweller. As its name suggests, it has brown feathers. It has a long, ivory-coloured bill. The shrill whistles of the male Brown Kiwi can be heard up to 1.5km (1 mile) away. Calling begins soon after sunset, when these nocturnal birds become active. The chicks, which hatch fully feathered, are able to leave the nest unaccompanied a week after they have hatched, but around half are killed by introduced predators such as stoats.

ADULT BROWN KIWI

GREAT SITES

STEWART ISLAND

Brown Kiwis are relatively common on New Zealand's Stewart Island. The island is rich in other bird species including the Yellow-eyed Penguin (the world's rarest penguin). Predator-free islands around Stewart are home to some of the world's rarest birds, such as the Kakapo.

Apteryx owenii

Little Spotted Kiwi

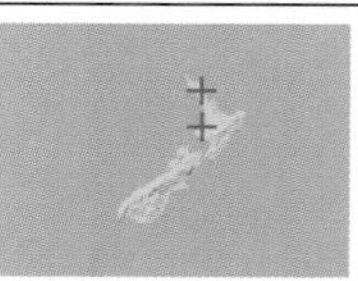

LENGTH 34–45cm (13½–17½in)
WEIGHT 880–1,950g (2–4½lb)
MIGRATION Non-migrant

HABITAT Evergreen and deciduous forest with dense undergrowth.

RED LIST CATEGORY Vulnerable

The Little Spotted Kiwi is the smallest kiwi, with irregular bands of brown, giving it a mottled appearance. The call of the male is an ascending, high-pitched whistle. Before European settlement, the Little Spotted Kiwi was found in forested areas throughout New Zealand. It is now extinct on the main islands, and survives only in introduced populations on five offshore islands. The most successful population is on Kapiti Island. Kiwis are long-lived birds. The oldest known wild Little Spotted Kiwi reached 17 years of age. They do not reach breeding maturity until their third year. Little Spotted Kiwis remain faithful to the same territory year after year, and pair bonds are similarly long-lasting.

ADULT LITTLE SPOTTED KIWI

GAMEBIRDS

ORDER	Galliformes
FAMILY	5
SPECIES	289

THIS ORDER OF GROUND-DWELLING birds includes species renowned for their beauty, such as peafowl and pheasants, and one that plays a key part in human nutrition: the chicken, or domestic fowl. Most gamebirds feed on the ground, but have strong wing muscles, and rely on an explosive take-off to escape danger. Their feet are well developed; many use them to scratch the ground in search of food. Gamebirds are found in a variety of habitats, from tropical forests to Arctic tundra.

ANATOMY

Typical gamebirds have plump bodies, small heads, and short, rounded wings. They range in size from quail weighing as little as 50g (2oz), to wild turkeys weighing up to 10kg (22lb). Gamebirds rarely fly far – the chief exception being migratory species, such as quails – but well developed pectoral muscles allow many to take off almost vertically when threatened with danger. Their bills are short and slightly curved, a shape that allows them to eat a wide mixture of plant and animal food, most of it small items pecked up one by one. Gamebirds have strong legs, and in some species – including pheasants – males have sharp spurs on the ankles, which they use when fighting with rivals. At night, many gamebirds roost in trees. Guans and currasows are entirely arboreal, feeding and nesting off the ground.

COMPARE AND CONTRAST
Common Pheasants typify the sexual dimorphism shown by many gamebirds. The female, here on the left, has camouflaged coloration that conceals her on the nest, while the male is highly ornamented. He retains coloured plumage throughout the year.

PLUMAGE

In some gamebirds, the sexes look alike, but this order includes some of the most extreme examples of sexual dimorphism in the bird world. This reaches its height among pheasants and peacocks, whose males have sumptuous and often iridescent plumage, and extraordinarily flamboyant tails. Many of these male birds also have colourful wattles – in some species, they can be inflated to increase their allure during courtship displays. These sex differences also extend to size: in turkeys and grouse, the males can be twice the weight of the females. In the far north, ptarmigans moult their plumage up to three times a year to blend in with the bare tundra in summer, and snow in winter. They are unique among birds in having completely feathered toes.

BREEDING

Except for guans and currasows, gamebirds nest on the ground. They are prolific parents, producing large numbers of eggs. Bobwhite Quails lay up to 28 eggs, while Grey Partridges produce an average of 16. If eggs are removed as they are laid, many gamebirds will keep replacing them – a trait exploited in domestic chickens. Gamebird chicks are well developed when they hatch, and are soon ready to follow their parents. The young of megapodes – such as Mallee Fowl – are the only birds that receive no parental care. Incubated in nests that heat up like compost heaps, they are quickly able to fly.

LIFT OFF
Wings widespread, a male Black Grouse bursts into the air. Gamebird flight muscles produce good bursts of power, but in non-migrating species they quickly fatigue.

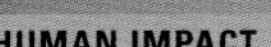

HIDDEN CLUTCH
Grouse lay camouflaged eggs in a hollow lined with grass. Once the young have hatched, they are particularly vulnerable to birds of prey, and only a small proportion survive to reach adulthood.

HUMAN IMPACT

DOMESTICATION

The first bird to be domesticated, probably at least 5,000 years ago, was the Jungle Fowl of southeast Asia – the ancestor of the farmyard hen. Today, there are approximately 16 billion chickens, making them by far the world's most common bird. Domesticated species also include turkeys, originally from Central America, and guineafowl, from Africa. All are flock-forming birds that are easy to keep in captivity.

Alectura lathami

Australian Brushturkey

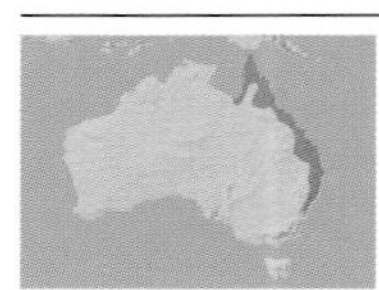

LENGTH 60–70cm (23½–28in)

WEIGHT 2–2.5kg (4½–5½lb)

MIGRATION Non-migrant

HABITAT Tropical and warm, temperate forest and dry woodland

The Australian Brushturkey is the largest of the megapodes (large-footed birds) of Australia. Both sexes are mainly black in colour, with a red or pink head, yellow throat wattles, and a broad, flat tail. The male tends to be larger and brighter, especially in the breeding season, when its neck pouch becomes bright yellow. The diet of the Australian Brushturkey consists of plant materials and termites. In the breeding season, this bird constructs mounds of vegetation to incubate the eggs. The female is capable of laying between 15–27 eggs in a season, and the mound, which is kept at a constant temperature by the heat released by decaying vegetation and direct sunlight, is protected by the male. A mound often contains eggs from more than one female, and the male has been known to protect two mounds at the same time. The eggs hatch after 47–52 days, and the young birds develop rapidly.

The population of this species is not globally threatened, but clearance of forests has reduced the range and fragmented the habitat in some areas.

MALE AUSTRALIAN BRUSHTURKEY
The male is distinguished by the red head and yellow neck, which becomes brighter in the breeding season.

LEAVING THE NEST
A juvenile Australian Brushturkey digs its way out of its nest of leaf litter. It is capable of flying within hours of leaving the mound.

Leipoa ocellata

Malleefowl

LENGTH 60cm (23½in)

WEIGHT 1.5–2kg (3¼–4½lb)

MIGRATION Non-migrant

HABITAT Woodland and scrub, typically in semi-arid areas

The Malleefowl is one of the most distinctive of the megapode family, with a variegated brown, white, and black back, upper tail, and wings. The head and neck are grey, with broken black markings down the front of the throat. Both the sexes are alike, although the females tend to be slightly smaller. It is thought to be omnivorous, with the most important elements of its diet being various seeds. Two distinct populations are found in south Australia and western Australia.

ADULT MALLEEFOWL

INCUBATION MOUND

Malleefowl lay their eggs in a giant heap of leaves, sticks, and bark, which rises to about 0.6m (2ft) above ground level. As this organic litter decomposes, it gives off heat, which helps incubate the eggs. The entire process takes about 11 weeks.

Macrocephalon maleo

Maleo

LENGTH 55cm (21½in)

WEIGHT 1.5kg (3¼lb)

MIGRATION Non-migrant

HABITAT Lowland and hill forest up to 1,200m (3,900ft)

RED LIST CATEGORY Endangered

Confined to the Indonesian island of Sulawesi, the Maleo can be identified by its prominent bony casque. The sexes are similar, with bare yellow facial skin, the black head, back, wings, and tail, and a pink wash on the breast and belly. Little information is available about its diet, although the bird is known to feed on fallen fruit. It is usually a silent bird, but its calls include a loud, braying sound and quacking, rather like a duck. The Maleo lays its eggs in burrows, which are often communal, although it is known to be monogamous. The species is classified as endangered and is declining over much of its range as a result of egg-collecting and illegal encroachment into protected areas.

ADULT MALEO

MALEO EGG

The Maleo egg is large, about five times the size of a domestic chicken's egg. Each egg is laid in a separate hole, up to 1m (3¼ft) deep, and left to incubate by heat from the sun or volcanic activity. The eggs hatch after 60–80 days and the young make their own way back to the forest.

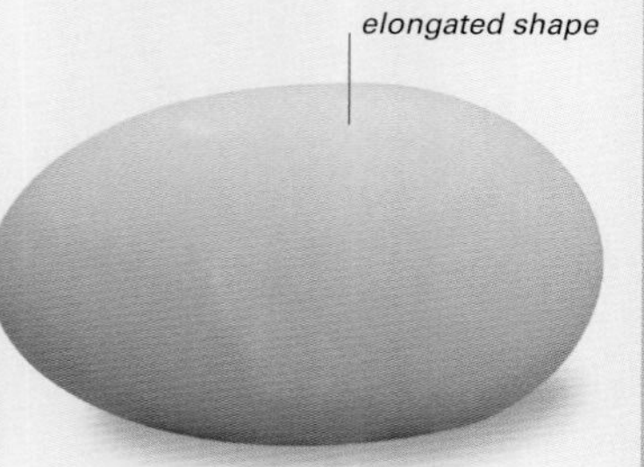

Ortalis vetula

Plain Chachalaca

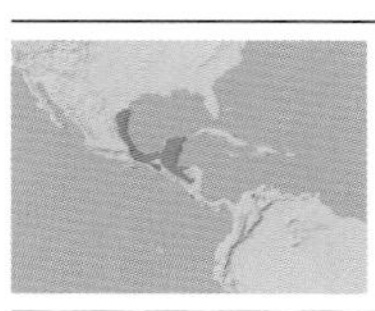

LENGTH 48–58cm (19–23in)

WEIGHT 425–800g (15–29oz)

MIGRATION Non-migrant

HABITAT Dense scrub and secondary growth

The Plain Chachalaca has a dark brown back, paler brown underparts, a long green-tinged tail, and a red throat patch. The male and female are similar. Its diet consists mostly of fruit, which is collected from the ground by groups of up to 15 birds. It also eats leaves, seeds, buds, and insects. The nest is a fragile platform of sticks, grass, and leaves, lined with a few green leaves. The average clutch size is three and the incubation period lasts for 22–27 days. The Plain Chachalaca is known to breed at one year of age, although most birds mature at two years. The species has two distinct subspecies. Its range is almost entirely confined to Central America and Texas, USA. The population of the Plain Chachalaca is not globally threatened, but has declined due to human activity: hunting and agriculture.

ADULT PLAIN CHACHALACA

Oreophasis derbianus

Horned Guan

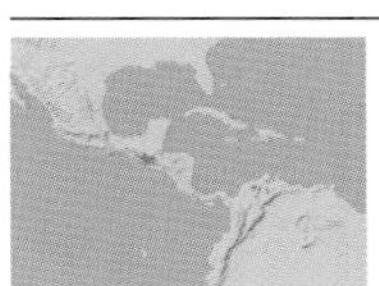

LENGTH 75–85cm (30–33in)

WEIGHT Not recorded

MIGRATION Non-migrant

HABITAT Humid montane forest

RED LIST CATEGORY Vulnerable

Named for the unusual red horn on its head, this bird has black plumage with a blue-green sheen and white foreneck and breast. It mostly feeds on vegetable matter, with fruit being an important part of its diet. It nests high up in trees and generally in areas where there is running water. The Horned Guan is classified as vulnerable due to the serious decline in its numbers owing to the high level of hunting as well as trapping for the illegal bird trade.

ADULT HORNED GUAN

Crax daubentoni

Yellow-knobbed Curassow

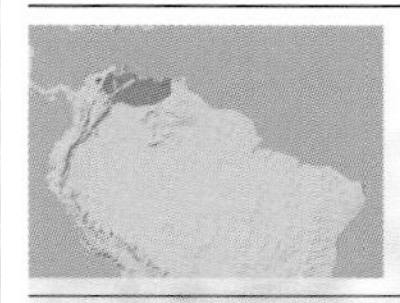

LENGTH 84–92cm (33–36in)

WEIGHT 2.5–3kg (5½–6½lb)

MIGRATION Non-migrant

HABITAT Gallery forest at low altitude between 100–500m (330–1,600ft)

The male Yellow-knobbed Curassow has a yellow bill, with a knobbed structure on it that gives the species its name. It has a crest with curling feathers. Both sexes are entirely black, except for a white belly and tip to the tail. It eats fruit, seeds, and small animals.

MALE YELLOW-KNOBBED CURASSOW

ADULT CRESTED GUAN

Penelope purpurascens

Crested Guan

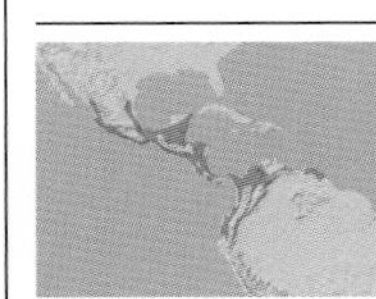

LENGTH 72–91cm (28–36in)

WEIGHT 1.5–2.5kg (3¼–5½lb)

MIGRATION Non-migrant

HABITAT Humid forest or forest edges, up to an altitude of 2300m (7,500ft)

The largest of the guans, the Crested Guan is a dark bird with a white crest and a prominent red throat pouch. It has a black face and chestnut-brown underparts. Its diet mostly consists of fruit and sometimes insects, for which it forages singly or in pairs or small groups. Breeding takes place in the rainy season, when a bulky nest is built from twigs and branches. There are normally two eggs in each clutch, although three eggs have been recorded in some nests. Although not migratory, this species makes seasonal movements in mountainous parts of its range. It is common over much of the range, despite being heavily hunted.

Penelope obscura

Dusky-legged Guan

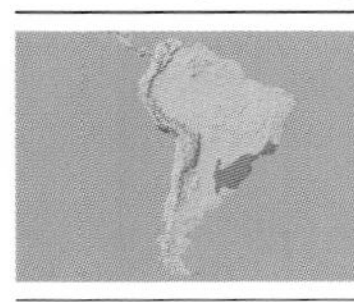

LENGTH 68–75cm (27–30in)

WEIGHT 950–1,200g (34–43oz)

MIGRATION Non-migrant

HABITAT Mature and secondary forest up to an altitude of 2,200m (7,200ft)

Similar to the Crested Guan (left), but with a more elongated appearance, the Dusky-legged Guan is distinguished by the dark legs that give the bird its common name. Research suggests that its diet is almost entirely made up of fruit, although some birds have been observed feeding on corn. It forages on the ground singly, in pairs, or in groups of up to six birds, with larger groups of 30 being recorded on rare occasions. Its nest is bowl-shaped and built from twigs in a dense cover. Three distinct populations of the species exist within its range. The Dusky-legged Guan is heavily hunted and, for this reason, its numbers are under threat, especially in Argentina.

ADULT DUSKY-LEGGED GUAN

Numida meleagris

Helmeted Guineafowl

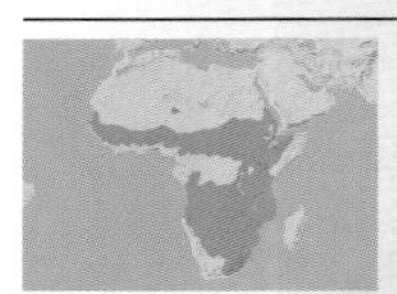

LENGTH 53–63cm (21–25in)

WEIGHT 1.3kg (3¼lb)

MIGRATION Non-migrant

HABITAT Bush, savanna, and grassland, often near cultivation

Like other guineafowl, the Helmeted Guineafowl is a highly sociable bird, which walks rather than flies. It has a large body and relatively tiny head, made to look larger by its "helmet" (also known as a casque). Its plumage is dark and spotted in white. The Helmeted Guineafowl is now classified as a single species, but at least four separate species were formerly recognized across the huge sub-Saharan range. Individuals vary in size, the shape of their helmets, and the form and colour of their wattles.

During the breeding season, Helmeted Guineafowl separate into pairs or small groups, but in winter and the dry season, flocks of 20 to 25 are common, and hundreds or even thousands, have been reported at water holes. They wander widely on foot over their home territory and roost in trees. An unfussy feeder on roots, seeds, insects, and snails, the Helmeted Guineafowl is easily domesticated. The species has been introduced with varying success elsewhere in Africa and the rest of the world. Flocks seen outside the normal range may be farmed or feral birds.

ADULT HELMETED GUINEAFOWL

HELMET AND WATTLES

Crowned with a golden orange bony casque (helmet) covered with horny cartilage, the Helmeted Guineafowl also has bright blue facial skin. These features, along with the red-tipped blue wattles on each side of its red, upper bill, make for its extravagantly colourful appearance.

Acryllium vulturinum

Vulturine Guineafowl

LENGTH 61–71cm (24–28in)

WEIGHT 1.3kg (3¼lb)

MIGRATION Non-migrant

HABITAT Savanna and semi-arid grassland with scrub; also riverside thickets

The largest and most spectacular guineafowl, the Vulturine Guineafowl sports an elegant cape of silver and blue, the word "vulturine" referring to its bald head and scrawny neck. The cape is made up of iridescent, elongated feathers, which combines with the bird's red eyes, blue-tinted head, and brown side-whiskers to make this guineafowl easily recognizable. Unlike other types of guineafowl, it has a long, drooping tail. Vulturine Guineafowl walk or run rather than fly, even from predators. They move in flocks of up to 30 birds, but in the breeding season the adults form pairs. The female lays 4–6 eggs in a scrape on the ground and incubates them for 30 days.

MALE VULTURINE GUINEAFOWL

GREAT SITES

TSAVO NATIONAL PARK

More than 400 species of birds have been recorded in Tsavo National Park, Kenya's largest national park, where the Vulturine Guineafowl thrives. The park offers a range of ecosystems, from semi-desert, savanna, and open plains, to acacia woodland, palm thickets, mountain forest, riverine vegetation, and swamps.

Callipepla californica

California Quail

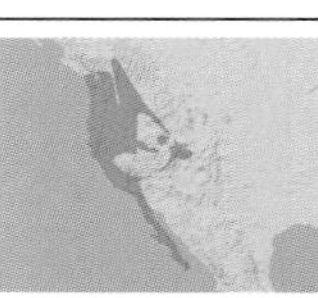

LENGTH 23–27cm (9–10½in)

WEIGHT 150–175g (5–6oz)

MIGRATION Non-migrant

HABITAT Grassland and scrub, farmland, open woodland, and chaparral

ADULT CALIFORNIA QUAIL

Its forward-drooping, teardrop-shaped crest immediately distinguishes the California Quail, although it resembles the closely related Gambel's Quail (*C. gambelii*), which also has a black face with a white bridle pattern. The California Quail tends to be loyal to its small home ranges, rarely moving far, even outside the breeding season.

Colinus virginianus

Northern Bobwhite

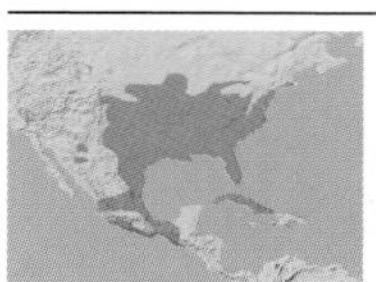

LENGTH 24–28cm (9½–11in)

WEIGHT 175g (6oz)

MIGRATION Non-migrant

HABITAT Grassland, scrub, and open woodland; avoids dense forest

Named after its whistling call, often rendered "bob-white" or "bob-bob-white", the Northern Bobwhite is a shy bird, more often heard than seen. Like many other gamebirds, this bird tends to sit quietly when approached, before bursting up and scattering almost from under the intruder's feet. The Northern Bobwhite varies greatly in size and colour, with many subspecies recognized, 16 of which are found in Mexico alone. The Northern Bobwhite feeds on seeds, insects, worms, and spiders.

ADULT NORTHERN BOBWHITE

Meleagris gallopavo

Wild Turkey

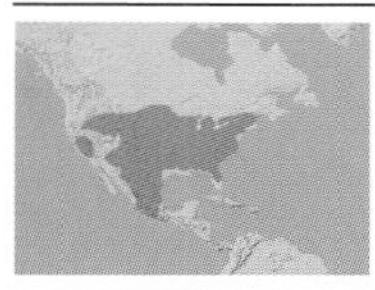

LENGTH 1–1.5m (3¼–5ft)

WEIGHT 4.3–8kg (10–18lb)

MIGRATION Non-migrant

HABITAT Open woodland, forest with clearings, scrub, and farmland

The male Wild Turkey is readily identified by the familiar gobbling call that is shared by the farmyard turkey, which is descended from it. The male of the wild species also has a bald blue head and naked red wattle (or snood), which hangs down from between its eyes to one side of its beak. The female is duller in colour, but both sexes have a long body and athletic legs.

FEMALE WILD TURKEY

MALE RUFFED GROUSE

Bonasa umbellus

Ruffed Grouse

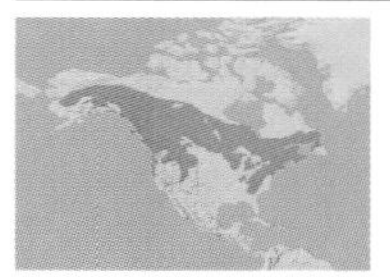

LENGTH 43–48cm (17–19in)

WEIGHT 500–575g (18–21oz)

MIGRATION Non-migrant

HABITAT Dense forest, always including deciduous trees, especially aspen

In spring, the forests of Canada and northern USA resound to the drumming of the male Ruffed Grouse. However, drumming can occur at any time of year. When drumming, the bird leans back against its tail and beats its wings strongly, with gathering speed. The Ruffed Grouse has a small crest on its head, brown or grey upperparts with heavy white spotting, and brown or grey barred underparts.

Cyrtonyx montezumae

Montezuma Quail

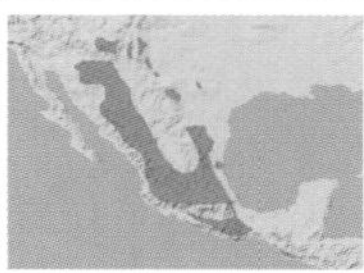

LENGTH 21–23cm (8½–9in)

WEIGHT 175–200g (6–7oz)

MIGRATION Non-migrant

HABITAT Oak and pine-oak woodland; grassland with bushes and trees

Also known as the Harlequin Quail for the clown-like black and white face pattern of the male, the Montezuma Quail has a relatively large head, which appears even larger and rounder because of its crest. The female has a smaller crest and a fainter version of the male's face pattern. This quail is found in coveys of up to 20 birds. When roosting on the ground, coveys form a circle facing outwards. The Montezuma Quail feeds on bulbs and tubers, seeds, and fruit.

Falcipennis canadensis

Spruce Grouse

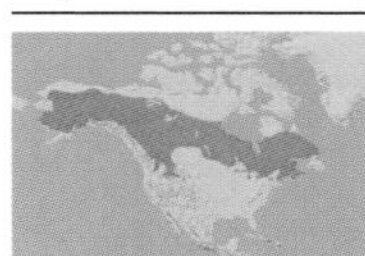

LENGTH 38–43cm (15–17in)

WEIGHT 450–500g (16–18oz)

MIGRATION Non-migrant

HABITAT Young coniferous forest with dense undergrowth

DISPLAYING MALE SPRUCE GROUSE

The displaying male Spruce Grouse is easy to identify when it fluffs its feathers and fans its tail. Unlike the Ruffed Grouse (above), it is a very quiet bird, and when it does drum or call, the sound does not carry far. It is most often seen at the edge of forest clearings or beside forest roads. It is easy to hunt because of its trusting nature, but habitat damage is a bigger threat to it than hunting.

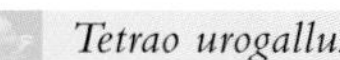

Tetrao urogallus

Western Capercaillie

LENGTH 60–87cm (23½–34in)

WEIGHT 1.8–4.1kg (4½–8¾lb)

MIGRATION Non-migrant

HABITAT Mostly coniferous forest, sometimes mixed forest with conifers or other evergreens

A dark grouse the size of a turkey, the Western Capercaillie is easily recognized. Despite its huge size, it is light on its feet and flies easily – and powerfully – among trees when disturbed. The male has blackish grey plumage, a white spot on its shoulder, and a broad white-speckled tail, while the female has an orange chest and dark bars on its orange-brown back. The species feeds on pine needles and berries.

Tree felling and human disturbance over much of its range have driven the Western Capercaillie to remote mountain areas, although it can still be found in lowland forest, such as the Siberian taiga, where human populations are small. Numbers are continuing to fall over much of its range, and the species is extinct in many European countries.

NESTING IN SPRING
The Western Capercaillie breeds from March to July; the female (above) makes a scrape in undergrowth or at the foot of a tree and lays 5–8 eggs.

LEKKING
The male Western Capercaillie shows off its beard-like throat tufts and fans its tail as it performs a courtship dance.

Centrocercus urophasianus

Sage Grouse

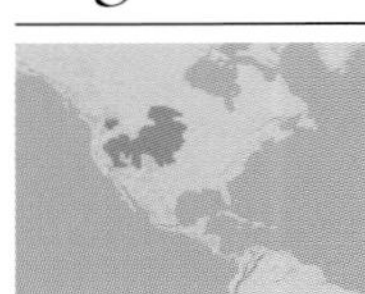

LENGTH 48–76cm (19–30in)

WEIGHT 1.5–3kg ($3^1/_4$–$6^1/_2$lb)

MIGRATION Non-migrant

HABITAT Arid grassland containing sagebrush

With its contrasting black, mottled grey-brown and white plumage, the male Sage Grouse is a spectacular bird. When courting, it displays at a lek by raising the feathers of its white collar and arching its spikey tail above its back. The female is smaller and plainer and lacks the male's eyecombs and black bib. Males that are successful at the lek may breed with several females. The nest is a shallow depression, lined with grass and sagebrush leaves. The common name of the Sage Grouse comes from its diet of sagebrush, which makes up most of its food intake.

DISPLAYING MALE

Lagopus lagopus

Willow Ptarmigan

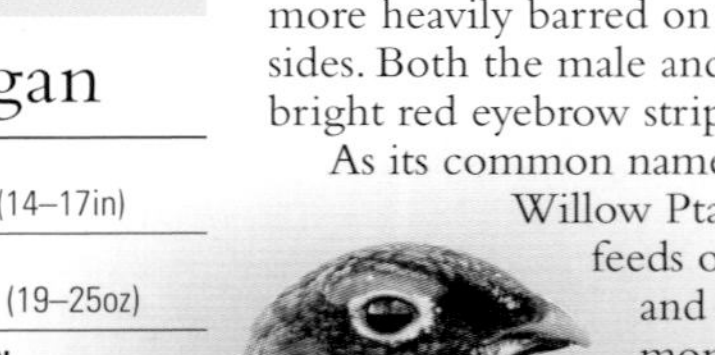

LENGTH 36–43cm (14–17in)

WEIGHT 525–700g (19–25oz)

MIGRATION Partial migrant

HABITAT Arctic tundra and open areas of woodland

Widespread across Arctic and subarctic regions, except for Greenland, the Willow Ptarmigan is a hardy gamebird, well adapted to the cold. It has reddish brown plumage, which turns white in winter (see panel, below). The male is slightly larger than the female and has a chestnut head and breast, while the female is more heavily barred on the breast and sides. Both the male and female have bright red eyebrow stripes.

As its common name suggests, the Willow Ptarmigan mainly feeds on willow twigs and buds. It is monogamous, with the male guarding a single incubating female throughout the nesting period. There are about 20 subspecies, most of which are sedentary, although there is some migratory movement in the northern parts of its range.

ADULT WILLOW PTARMIGAN

WINTER PLUMAGE

In winter, the plumage of the Willow Ptarmigan changes to white, helping to camouflage it as it nestles in snow and keeping it safe from predators. White feathers also grow to cover its feet in winter. When the birds moult in summer, they appear brown and white. However, some subspecies do not have a complete plumage change, with only patchy areas turning white.

Lagopus muta

Rock Ptarmigan

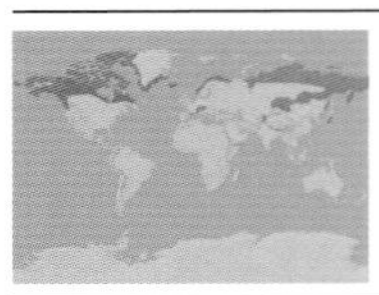

LENGTH 33–38cm (13–15in)

WEIGHT 425–750g (15–27oz)

MIGRATION Non-migrant

HABITAT Rocky tundra with sparse vegetation, also on high peaks above 2,000m (6,500ft)

The Rock Ptarmigan is similar to the Willow Ptarmigan (below left) but is more slender and has a longer tail. However, the females of the two species can be difficult to distinguish at a distance. The male has small red combs over the eyes, mottled brown plumage, and a black tail. In the breeding season, it displays its swollen red combs. The plumage in winter is white. The diet of the Rock Ptarmigan varies throughout the year, but it mainly feeds on low-growing plants such as dwarf birch and in winter finds food such as twigs and buds.

MALE ROCK PTARMIGAN

ADULT HIMALAYAN SNOWCOCK

Tetrogallus himalayensis

Himalayan Snowcock

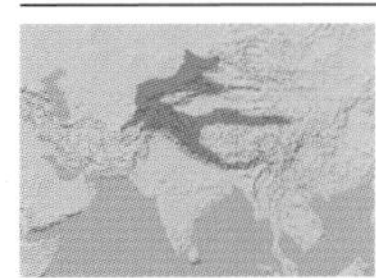

LENGTH 54–72cm ($21^1/_2$–28in)

WEIGHT 2–3.5kg ($4^1/_2$–$7^3/_4$lb)

MIGRATION Non-migrant

HABITAT Open mountain slopes to the snow line

Mainly grey and white in colour, which helps to camouflage it, the Himalayan Snowcock is a large bird, although the female is slightly smaller than the male. Its diet consists of roots and tubers, with the birds moving uphill during the day while feeding. They are not migratory, but are often found at a higher altitude when the snow line retreats in summer.

MALE GREATER PRAIRIE CHICKEN

Tympanuchus cupido

Greater Prairie Chicken

LENGTH 41–47cm (16–$18^1/_2$in)

WEIGHT 775–1,000g (28–36oz)

MIGRATION Non-migrant

HABITAT Open prairies or prairies enclosed by farmland and scrub oak

RED LIST CATEGORY Vulnerable

Both the male and female Greater Prairie Chicken have elongated black neck feathers and brown upperparts with brown, buff, and white barring. The male's display, in a territory called the "booming ground", is dramatic. It raises its neck feathers and lowers its head to display its ornamental fleshy yellow-orange eyecombs as it inflates its golden neck sacs, creating the characteristic booming sound. The tail is upright during the display. The male reaches sexual maturity at one year of age, but does not usually breed successfully until the second year of life, when it mates with several females. The nest of the Greater Prairie Chicken is a shallow bowl lined with feathers, leaves, and grass and is built by the female, who also incubates the eggs. The diet of this species includes insects, rosehips, leaves, shoots, and a range of cultivated grains.

Alectoris chukar

Chukar Partridge

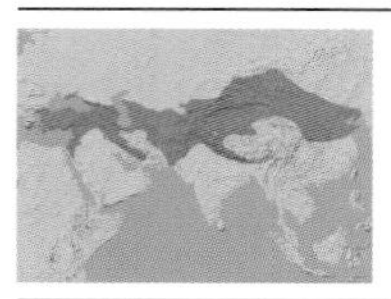

LENGTH 32–39cm ($12\frac{1}{2}$–$15\frac{1}{2}$in)
WEIGHT 450–800g (16–29oz)
MIGRATION Non-migrant

HABITAT Bare areas from low arid plains to 3,000m (10,000ft)

The Chukar Partridge has a grey back, upper breast, wings, and tail, with alternate black and white stripes on its flanks and a black stripe framing the lower face and white throat. It also has a prominent red bill and eye-ring. The male and female are alike, but there is much variation in the geographical subspecies. Although native to Asia, it has been released in North America as a gamebird and is established in arid, rocky areas of the West. The main food is vegetable matter, especially seeds, roots, and cheatgrass. The juvenile takes some invertebrates, although this makes up less than half of its total diet. The birds are resident breeders and are mostly monogamous, with pairs forming in mid-March.

ADULT CHUKAR PARTRIDGE

CAPE SPURFOWL DRINKING

Pternistis capensis

Cape Spurfowl

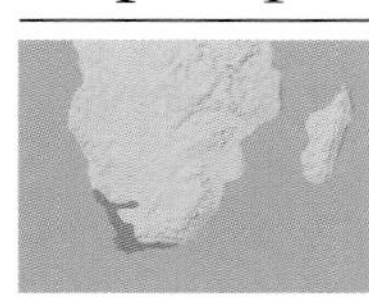

LENGTH 40–43cm ($15\frac{1}{2}$–17in)
WEIGHT 450–900g (16–32oz)
MIGRATION Non-migrant

HABITAT Scrub of various types; rarely, in gardens

The Cape Spurfowl, also known as the Cape Francolin, is uniformly dark in colour, with a distinct pattern of white streaks. The sexes are alike although the female is usually smaller. The male has leg spurs that it uses during fights with other males.

This species feeds on a wide range of plant material, especially roots and shoots, and also takes molluscs, termites, and various other insects. The breeding period varies according to local climate and can be any time between July and February. Although its breeding behaviour has not been described in detail, it is thought to be monogamous. Its nest is a hollow lined with grass and the clutch generally consists of 6–8 eggs. These birds rarely fly, and run when escaping from danger. The range of the species is limited to the area around the Cape peninsula of South Africa, with no overlap of related species. The Cape Spurfowl has been placed in different groups; it was formerly placed in the genus *Francolinus*. The Cape Spurfowl is not globally threatened and can be locally common, but its limited range is a potential concern.

Perdix perdix

Grey Partridge

LENGTH 29–31cm ($11\frac{1}{2}$–12in)
WEIGHT 300–450g (11–16oz)
MIGRATION Non-migrant

HABITAT Grassland, steppes, and open arable land

The Grey Partridge can have a dull appearance in the field although the birds are colourful in good light. The predominant colour is grey, but both sexes have a red facial pattern, and the male (and rarely, the female) has a chestnut-coloured patch on the belly. Much of the diet of this species consists of seeds, cereals, and weeds. Changes in the diet have been noted at various times of the year, with grass becoming more important in autumn. The juvenile also relies on insects for the first two weeks after hatching. The species was introduced in North America and has become established in the prairies.

The Grey Partridge does not defend a breeding territory, despite the fact it is monogamous. A bond between a male and female is often formed well ahead of breeding, but there is often a change of partners before the pair is finally established. The species is sometimes seen in small groups outside the mating season. It is not currently under threat, but declines have been noted over its range as a result of intense farming and hunting.

GREY PARTRIDGES IN SNOW

Perdicula asiatica

Jungle Bush-Quail

LENGTH 15–18cm (6–7in)

WEIGHT 55–80g (2–3oz)

MIGRATION Non-migrant

HABITAT Dry scrub and brush up to 1,200m (4,000ft)

Very different from the female, the male Jungle Bush-Quail has a white moustache, heavily barred white underparts, and variegated wings. The female has a uniform, rich chestnut breast and belly. However, both the male and the female have red and white streaks on the head. The diet of the Jungle Bush-Quail consists mainly of seeds, particularly of grasses, although it also takes insects. Breeding takes place after the rains and lasts until the onset of colder weather, with the precise period varying across the range; 5 or 6 eggs are produced and incubation takes between 16 and 18 days. The species is not globally threatened as it has an extensive range and tends to avoid agricultural areas. The population in Sri Lanka has contracted since the 1950s, but is thought to be widespread and common elsewhere in the range. The Jungle Bush-Quail is largely sedentary, although the birds in Nepal are thought to migrate in winter.

ADULT FEMALE JUNGLE BUSH-QUAIL

Arborophila torqueola

Hill Partridge

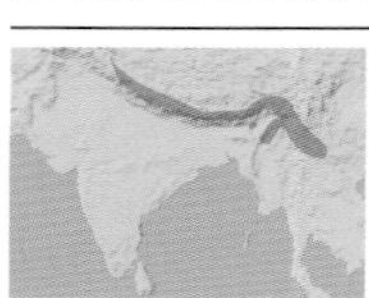

LENGTH 29cm (11½in)

WEIGHT 225–425g (8–15oz)

MIGRATION Non-migrant

HABITAT Evergreen forest or scrub up to 1,500–2,700m (5,000–8,850ft)

With its combination of an orange crown and face set against a black head and streaked throat, the Hill Partridge is an attractive species. The female lacks the head markings but shares the variegated wings and grey streaked underparts of the male. Four subspecies have been identified on the basis of differences in the head markings of the male. The food of this species comprises seeds and various invertebrates, which it collects by scratching in leaf litter. The birds are mostly seen in pairs or small coveys of up to 10 individuals that may be made up of family groups. The Hill Partridge has a hen-like contact call that is constantly uttered when it is feeding. Indian populations breed between April and June, although earlier breeding has been recorded at lower altitudes. The average clutch size is 3–5 eggs but up to nine eggs have also been observed. Incubation time is not recorded in wild birds but is reported to be 24 days in captive birds. The nest is shaped like a bowl, with a dome of grass when it is placed in a bank. The range spans over a narrow band from the western Himalayas to north Vietnam. The species is not globally threatened and is common in most parts of its range.

ADULT HILL PARTRIDGE

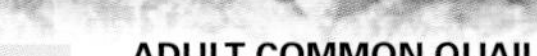

ADULT COMMON QUAIL

Coturnix coturnix

Common Quail

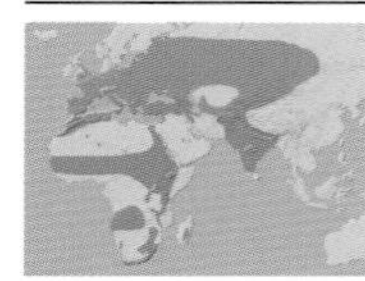

LENGTH 16–18cm (6½–7in)

WEIGHT 70–150g (2½–5oz)

MIGRATION Migrant

HABITAT Open areas, including agricultural land

A small gamebird, the Common Quail has a pale belly and black and buff streaks on its flanks. The sexes are similar, although the female tends to be duller, with darker markings on the head than the male. The diet of this bird is varied, ranging from seeds of over 100 plant species to invertebrates taken from the ground. Its call is a repeated "whit wit-wit", the male and female establishing contact by calling during the breeding season.

A widespread species, this quail is found through much of Europe and central Asia as a breeding bird. Resident populations also exist in north Africa, east southern Africa, southern Europe, and northern India, while wintering birds migrate long distances to India and Africa.

Rollulus roulroul

Crested Partridge

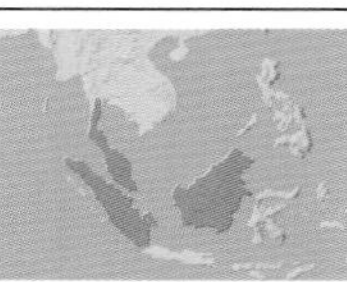

LENGTH 26cm (10in)

WEIGHT 200–225g (7–8oz)

MIGRATION Non-migrant

HABITAT Evergreen forest mostly on plains, but also up to 1,200m (4,000ft)

RED LIST CATEGORY Vulnerable

Named for its spectacular orange or red crest, the male Crested Partridge is a stunning bird. It has a bright red eye-stripe and its plumage is dark green, with black wings. The female lacks the crest and is paler, with chestnut wings. The sexes are similar in length but the male is often slightly heavier. The diet of this partridge mostly consists of seeds and fruit, with some invertebrates taken on the ground. Breeding occurs throughout the year, although there are peaks in activity at various places within the range. The nest is a simple depression made in dried leaves on the ground and 5 or 6 eggs are laid. The female incubates them for about 18 days. The range of the species is southeast Asia, including inshore islands around Sumatra. Habitat loss due to logging is leading to declines in some areas.

ADULT MALE CRESTED PARTRIDGE

BIRD SPECIES

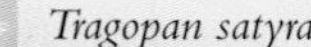

Tragopan blythii

Blyth's Tragopan

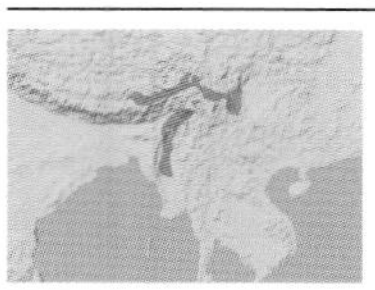

LENGTH 58–70cm (23–28in)

WEIGHT 2kg (4½lb)

MIGRATION Non-migrant

HABITAT Wooded valleys and hills up to 3,300m (11,500ft) in summer; moves lower down in winter

A colourful gamebird, Blyth's Tragopan has a bright yellow facial skin with a deep orange-red head, neck, and upper breast. The male has a black crown and cheeks, a red neck and breast, a pale grey belly, black and white upperparts with brown spots, and white-spotted flanks. The female has brown spots on its plumage. Little information exists on the diet of this species, but is thought to include shoots, invertebrates, and even frogs. It feeds in small groups, moving in undergrowth on steep slopes. The calls of this gamebird include a loud "ouwaa" and "gock gock". Two subspecies are known, with the total range confined to northeast India and Bhutan – the population in India is classified as endangered due to habitat loss and hunting. Its population may never have been high but fragmentation of remaining areas of its range is adding to the dangers facing the species.

Tragopan temminckii

Temminck's Tragopan

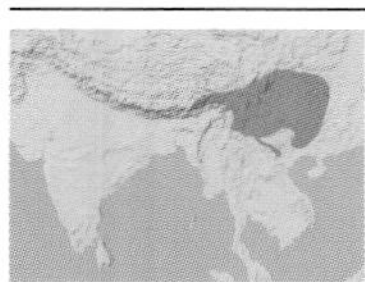

LENGTH 58–64cm (23–25in)

WEIGHT 1–1.5kg (2¼–3¼lb)

MIGRATION Non-migrant

HABITAT Dense evergreen or mixed forest over 2,500m (8,000ft) in Burma

The male Temminck's Tragopan is a striking bird with orange plumage around the neck. It has blue facial skin which can be expanded into an enormous lappet with red markings during courtship. The back and wings are darker, with white spots. It has an orange breast and belly, with large white spots outlined in black. The female is smaller and plainer, with a variegated brown plumage. It feeds on plant stems, ferns, berries, seeds, and insects.

Tragopan satyra

Satyr Tragopan

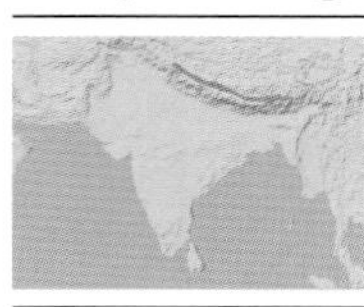

LENGTH 60–70cm (23½–28in)

WEIGHT 1–2.1kg (2¼–4½lb)

MIGRATION Non-migrant

HABITAT Bamboo and rhododendron growth in valleys up to 2,400–4,250m (8,000–14,000ft)

The male Satyr Tragopan is distinguished by its bright blue facial skin, black head, and deep red neck and breast. The plumage resembles Blyth's Tragopan (left) whose head is distinctively paler, even when viewed from a distance. It has brown upperparts with black and white spots, white-spotted red underparts, and a dark brown rump and tail. Its grey and red wings are spotted with white. The female has brown and rufous plumage with paler spots and bars.

The Satyr Tragopan feeds on the ground, its main diet consists of leaves and buds. However, it is known to have a wider and more omnivorous diet that includes various insects, such as cockroaches. Unlike many similar species, it seems to forage selectively rather than randomly. Details of its nesting behaviour have only been observed in captive birds and have not been widely described. However, the breeding season is thought to occur during May and June. The nest may be in a tree or on the ground and contains 2 or 3 eggs, which are incubated for about 28 days.

The species is not migratory, but seasonal movements have been recorded, sometimes at distances as great as 1,000-2,000m (3,300–6,600ft). Its daily movement is usually 100-200m (330–660ft), depending on the topography.

MALE SATYR TRAGOPAN

ADULT BLOOD PHEASANT

Ithaginis cruentus

Blood Pheasant

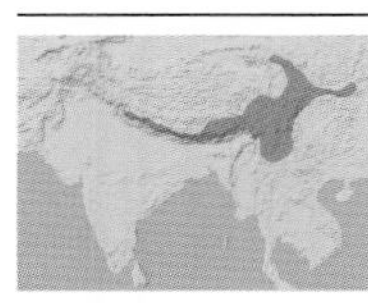

LENGTH 40–48cm (15½–19in)

WEIGHT 400–650g (14–23oz)

MIGRATION Non-migrant

HABITAT Rhododendron and other scrub up to 2,700–4,500m (8,850–14,500ft)

Named for the red plumage on the male's head, the Blood Pheasant is relatively plain compared to other pheasants. The male is slightly larger than the female and has a generally greyer appearance, the female being largely brown. The diet of this gamebird consists mainly of vegetable matter and some invertebrates. It collects most of its food by scratching on the ground, but has also been known to feed in trees. It lays its eggs between April and June in a simple depression on the ground, lined with grass. It is not a migratory bird, but some altitudinal movement is known to occur in response to changing levels of the snow line.

MALE HIMALAYAN MONAL
With its long wiry crest and metallic blue, purple, yellow, and red plumage, the male Himalayan Monal is a spectacular bird.

FEMALE HIMALAYAN MONAL
The female, with its white throat and mottled brown plumage, is plainer than the male.

Lophophorus impejanus

Himalayan Monal

LENGTH 63–72cm (25–28in)

WEIGHT 1.5-2.5kg (3¼–5½lb)

MIGRATION Non-migrant

HABITAT Open coniferous or mixed forest up to 2,100–4,500m (6,500–14,500ft)

A colourful bird, the male Himalayan Monal has a crested head, black breast and underparts, and a chestnut-brown tail. The female is smaller, with a short crest, and has black, buff, and white streaks on its plumage. Both the male and the female have a turquoise-blue patch around the eye. The diet of this species varies with its location, but mainly consists of berries, seeds, and insect larvae that are dug from the ground, sometimes to a depth of 25cm (10in). In April to June, 3–5 eggs are laid in a scrape in the ground, usually under a bush or other cover. Incubation lasts for about 27 days and is undertaken by the female.

MALE GREAT ARGUS

Argusianus argus

Great Argus

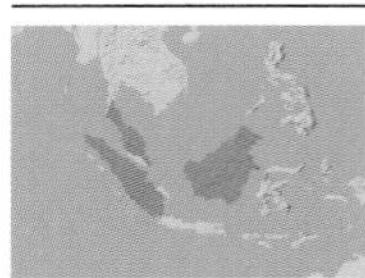

LENGTH 0.7–2m (2¼–6½ft)

WEIGHT 1.5–2.5kg (3¼–5½lb)

MIGRATION Non-migrant

HABITAT Tall, dry lowland; primary and logged forest up to 1,300m (4,300ft)

A large pheasant, the male Great Argus has a conspicuous naked blue head and neck and a short black crest. The upperparts are warm brown above with fine white spotting, but its most striking features are the elongated inner flight feathers and very long tail. The female is similar, but lacks the male's ornamentation and long tail and is, therefore, shorter.

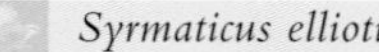

Syrmaticus ellioti

Elliot's Pheasant

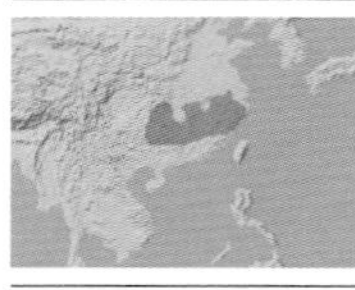

LENGTH 45–80cm (17½–31in)

WEIGHT 875–1150g (31–41oz)

MIGRATION Non-migrant

HABITAT Sub-tropical forest and scrub

RED LIST CATEGORY Vulnerable

Elliot's Pheasant is restricted to the forests of southeastern China. The male is a stunning, boldly patterned, mainly brown bird with a white head and nape, white shoulder and wing bars, and an elongated brown and a white, evenly barred, tail. The black throat and breast contrast strongly with the white belly. The female is a more greyish brown, lacks the white wing and shoulder bars, and has a shorter tail with indistinct bars. Elliot's Pheasant is considered to be vulnerable because of the decline in the extent of its habitat.

MALE ELLIOT'S PHEASANT

Gallus gallus

Red Junglefowl

LENGTH 41–78cm (16–31in)

WEIGHT 450–850g (16–30oz)

MIGRATION Non-migrant

HABITAT Forest edges, open woodland, scrub, and grassland

The Red Junglefowl is the wild ancestor of the domestic chicken. When breeding, the male is very colourful, with red and gold hackles or neck feathers, drooping crimson shoulder feathers and sides, a white rump patch, and glossy dark green wing feathers and tail. During the breeding season, the bright red comb, facial skin, and hanging wattles are engorged with blood, but quickly shrivel afterwards. The colourful hackles and showy tail also disappear.

MALE RED JUNGLEFOWL

Phasianus colchicus

Common Pheasant

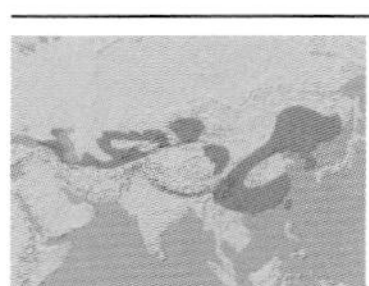

LENGTH 53–89cm (21–35in)

WEIGHT 0.7–1.5kg (1½–3¼lb)

MIGRATION Non-migrant

HABITAT Open woodland, scrub, low vegetation, and agricultural areas

Much larger and with a longer tail than the female, the male Common Pheasant is a colourful and beautifully marked bird with iridescent plumage. Predominantly brown above, its underparts are more chestnut in colour. Its dark head has a purple and green gloss, and its facial wattles are red. Many males also have a white neck ring and a maroon breast. The female is drab, with pale brown plumage and dark mottling, especially on the back and wings.

The inconspicuous plumage of the female Common Pheasant makes it hard to spot and provides excellent camouflage when it is incubating eggs, since the nest is usually a scrape on the ground. During the breeding season, the male's presence can always be detected because of its repeated, far-carrying, sudden, and explosive crowing. It also whirs its wings very loudly, a sound that can be heard up to 1.5km (1 mile) away in suitable conditions. The male is polygamous, gathering a harem of females on its display territory and defending the females against rival males.

In autumn, the species is gregarious, but in winter the sexes tend to segregate. The Common Pheasant is an opportunistic feeder, usually foraging on the ground, feeding on a variety of seeds, grain, and fruit as well as insects and other and small animals. This is one reason why it has adapted so well to habitats such as agricultural land. It roosts in trees at night.

With more than 30 subspecies, this pheasant is a biological success story and is a familiar bird in its huge natural range, which takes in large parts of mainland Asia. In addition, its popularity as a gamebird has seen successful introductions of the species throughout Europe, Australia, New Zealand, Hawaii, and North America.

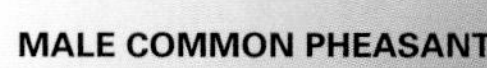

MALE COMMON PHEASANT

MALE GOLDEN PHEASANTS

Chrysolophus pictus

Golden Pheasant

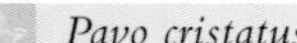

LENGTH 60–110cm (23½–43in)

WEIGHT 550–700g (20–25oz)

MIGRATION Non-migrant

HABITAT Dense upland scrub

A spectacular bird, the Golden Pheasant is a resident of the mountains of central China, where it is very hard to locate in its dense scrub habitat. The male has a golden domed crown created by the elongated head and nape feathers and it has a resplendent long tail. The barred cape on its neck is used during the breeding display, when it is flicked forward like an inverted fan, producing a pattern of orange and black concentric rings.

Pavo cristatus

Indian Peafowl

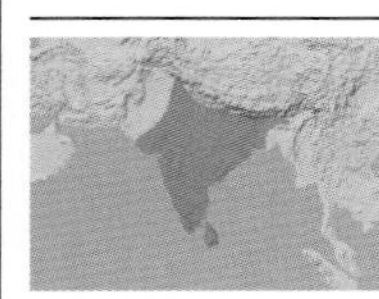

LENGTH 0.9–2.2m (3–7¼ft)

WEIGHT 3.5–5kg (7¾–11lb)

MIGRATION Non-migrant

HABITAT Deciduous forest, farmland, and cultivation

Although native to the Indian subcontinent, the Indian or Blue Peafowl has been domesticated around the globe as an ornamental bird. The male is stunningly beautiful with a blue neck and breast and a very long, glossy green train of elongated uppertail feathers. These feathers are adorned with iridescent blue-centred, green and copper eyespots, or ocelli. A single displaying adult male fanning its tail at a female creates a dramatic effect. In India, where the bulk of the wild population can be found, the Indian Peafowl is held in high esteem and goes about undisturbed, so much so that it has become very tame. It is not unusual to see it in villages and even nesting on buildings, but truly wild birds are shy.

MALE INDIAN PEAFOWL

ADULT MALE

Polyplectron napoleonis

Palawan Peacock-Pheasant

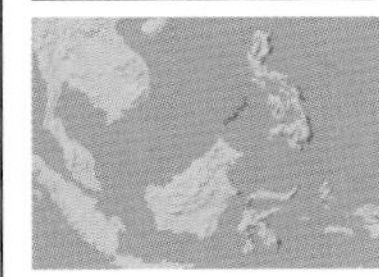

LENGTH 45–51cm (17½–20in)

WEIGHT 325–450g (12–16oz)

MIGRATION Non-migrant

HABITAT Forest and secondary woodland

RED LIST CATEGORY Vulnerable

The superb Palawan Peacock-Pheasant is endemic to the island of Palawan in the Philippines. Like other members of this Asian genus, the male has a uniformly grey plumage that is relieved by occasional bursts of iridescence in the velvety black upperparts. Its white face is split by a black eye-stripe and red eye-ring and it has a green crest. The most prominent features are the violet blue-green "blind" ocelli, or eyespots, in the metallic blue-green tail feathers and modified uppertail coverts. They are considered "blind" because, unlike those of the Indian Peafowl (above), the ocelli lack a central "eye". This ostentatious ornamentation plays a vital role in display and a male's breeding success depends on its finery.

The Palawan Peacock-Pheasant can be very hard to observe in the wild as it is shy and often slips quietly away when it sees an intruder. It is best located by its call, a loud and persistent "angk".

Afropavo congensis

Congo Peafowl

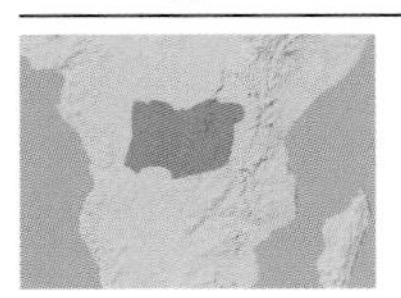

LENGTH 60–70cm (23½–28in)

WEIGHT 1–1.5kg (2¼–3¼lb)

MIGRATION Non-migrant

HABITAT Primary rainforest

RED LIST CATEGORY Vulnerable

FEMALE CONGO PEAFOWL

This shy inhabitant of the forest understorey is a striking bird. The male Congo Peafowl has a bare, red throat, a black and white crest, dark bronze-green upperparts, and black underparts. The female (shown here) is a smaller brown bird with glossy green upperparts.

This threatened gamebird is a poorly known species that is only found in the dense forest of the Democratic Republic of Congo. Due to the turbulent recent history of the country, it is very hard to be certain of its exact current range and population levels. The Congo Peafowl is listed as vulnerable because it has a small and fragmented population that is inevitably declining in the face of habitat loss and hunting. Fortunately, important populations exist in several protected areas.

INDIAN PEAFOWL
The male Indian Peafowl has a long train of tail feathers. To create its familiar display fan, the bird lifts its tail, pushing the feathers upwards and forwards.

WATERFOWL

ORDER	Anseriformes
FAMILY	3
SPECIES	157

WATERFOWL HAVE a long history of domestication, and of being hunted in the wild. Found on every continent except Antarctica, they include ducks, geese, swans, and screamers in South America. All are swimming birds with waterproof feathers, webbed feet, and typically a broad, flattened bill. Most waterfowl are found on freshwater wetlands, rivers, and ponds, but a number live on coasts or farther out to sea. Ducks and swans usually feed afloat, but some species – particularly geese – graze on land. Waterfowl are powerful fliers, and many migrate long distances to breed.

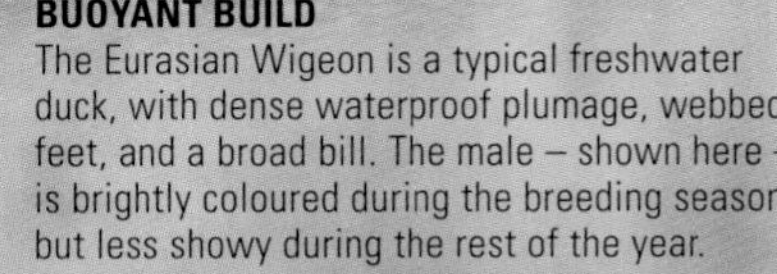

BUOYANT BUILD
The Eurasian Wigeon is a typical freshwater duck, with dense waterproof plumage, webbed feet, and a broad bill. The male – shown here – is brightly coloured during the breeding season, but less showy during the rest of the year.

ANATOMY

Waterfowl typically have plump bodies, powerful wings, and short legs ending in webbed feet. Most also have the classic "duck bill", although in fish-eating species, such as mergansers, the bill is narrow, and has toothed edges like a saw. In general, ducks have short necks, while the necks of swans and geese are longer, and also more muscular. If they are alarmed, many ducks have an almost vertical take-off, but swans and geese often have to run over the surface of the water to become airborne. Once they are on the wing, their flight is fast and direct. Compared to many other aquatic birds, waterfowl are also good at moving about on land. Geese will often spend all day grazing on their feet, while female Mallards sometimes escort their ducklings a kilometre (1/2 mile) or more to find a suitable stretch of water. Screamers walk over mats of floating vegetation, and rarely swim.

PLUMAGE AND MOULTING

Waterfowl keep their plumage waterproof by covering it with oil from a preen gland positioned near the tail. This oil is so effective that water literally rolls off a duck's back; even when ducks dive, their insulating down feathers do not get wet. In geese and swans, the males and females often look identical, but most ducks show striking differences between the sexes. During the breeding season, many male ducks, or drakes, have eyecatching colours – the reason why they are often kept as ornamental birds. By contrast, the females tend to be drab, helping to conceal them while they incubate their eggs. Immediately after breeding, ducks, geese, and swans moult all their flight feathers, which leaves them unable to fly for up to four weeks.

MALE BREEDING PLUMAGE
During the breeding season, the male Red-breasted Merganser moults into a more colourful plumage, which contrasts with the female's subdued feather tones.

MALE ECLIPSE PLUMAGE
In early summer, male Red-breasted Mergansers lose their breeding plumage, and acquire an "eclipse" plumage much more like the female's.

FEMALE PLUMAGE
The female Red-breasted Merganser shows much less seasonal variation. Although it moults, it has a similar pattern and colour scheme all year round. During the breeding season, this helps to hide it while it is on the nest.

FEEDING

Most waterfowl feed on aquatic plants and animals. Geese are an exception: most are vegetarian, grazing on land near fresh water and coasts, or gleaning leftover seeds in fields. A goose grazes by gripping plants in its bill, then tugging with its powerful neck. A large goose – such as a Greylag – can eat over 1kg (2.2lb) grass a day. Swans also graze, but spend more time feeding in water, where they eat small animals as well as plants. By up-ending, the largest swans can reach the bottom in water nearly 1.5m (5ft) deep. Ducks have a variety of feeding methods, which they use in water and on land. Shelducks walk over mudflats and through shallow water, sweeping the sediment with their bills and sifting out small animals. On the water itself, dabbling ducks, such as Mallard, feed by sweeping up floating weed from the surface, and by up-ending to collect food farther down. The South American Torrent Duck plunges into mountain streams, gripping boulders with its sharp claws. True diving ducks, such as the Canvasback and Tufted Duck, dive under water to collect small animals and waterplants. Sawbill ducks, such as the Goosander, are even better at diving. They chase fish, gripping them in serrated bills. At sea, most marine ducks dive for food.

SIFTING THE SHALLOWS
Shelduck use side-to-side movements of their bills to collect small molluscs from water or tidal mud. On exposed mud, this leaves a characteristic zig-zag trail.

EXTENDED REACH
Up-ending allows swans to reach food buried in sediment. Like dabbling ducks, swans feel for food with sensitive bills, rather than using eyesight.

UNDERWATER PURSUIT
Propelling itself with its feet, a Goosander successfully catches a fish. Sawbill ducks, including the Goosander, are similar to cormorants in the way that they feed.

FAMILY ON THE MOVE
Like all young waterfowl, these Common Goldeneye chicks instinctively follow their mother into the water. Hatching is almost simultaneous, so the young are all ready to leave the nest at the same time.

NESTING AND PARENTAL CARE

Swans and geese pair up for life, but in ducks the pair bond usually lasts for a single breeding season only. With some notable exceptions – such as Wood Ducks – waterfowl nest on the ground, making their nests from waterside plants, such as grass and reeds. Many species line their nests with their own down, creating a warm lining. On average, swans lay about five eggs, but ducks can lay over a dozen, with the female taking sole charge of incubation. Waterfowl are well developed when they hatch, and soon leave the nest to follow their parents to water. Young Magpie Geese are fed by their parents, but the young of all other waterfowl are able to feed themselves.

MIGRATION

Many species of waterfowl undertake long seasonal migrations. Geese and swans typically fly in V formation, travelling between breeding grounds at high latitudes and wintering grounds in milder regions, often close to coasts. The farthest travellers, such as the Brent Goose, can make round trips of over 12,000km (7,500 miles), with several rest and feeding stops en route. In their wintering grounds, flocks of wildfowl can be spectacular. Snow Geese, for example, gather in tens of thousands in some parts of southern USA. Waterfowl have been hunted for millennia, and migrating birds often find themselves in the firing line. However, for many migrants, habitat change in their wintering grounds is now an equally important threat. Many geese also overwinter in areas that are farmed, creating difficulties when they eat seeds and germinating crops.

TRAVELLING SOUTH
Greater White-fronted Geese migrate from the far north, and overwinter in temperate regions from Mexico to the Nile Delta and southern Japan. There are a number of different subspecies, and each one has its own breeding and wintering grounds.

Chauna torquata

Southern Screamer

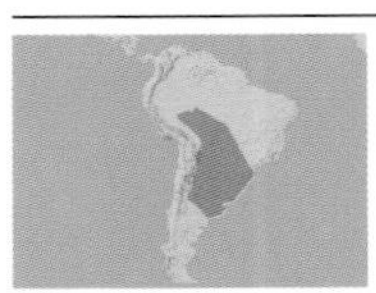

LENGTH 80–95cm (31–37in)

WEIGHT 4.4kg (10lb)

MIGRATION Non-migrant

HABITAT Wetlands and wet grassland, usually with scattered trees

The calls of pairs of the Southern (or Crested) Screamer – from tree perches or while flying – carry for up to 3km (1.8 miles). This crested, long-legged bird, with a short, decurved bill, frequently soars across the landscape as it moves between wetland areas. Non-breeding birds flock together throughout the year, wandering in search of food and water. These birds are often domesticated and make excellent guards.

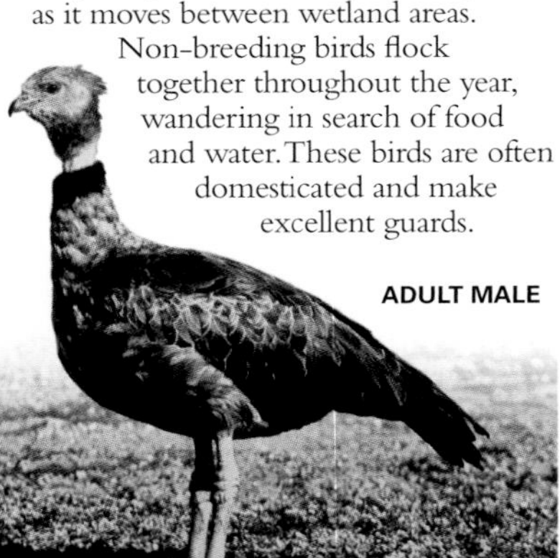

ADULT MALE

Anhima cornuta

Horned Screamer

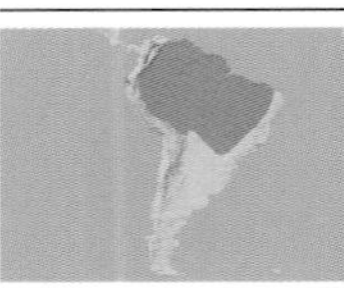

LENGTH 80–94cm (31–37in)

WEIGHT 3.1kg (6½lb)

MIGRATION Non-migrant

HABITAT Moist tropical forest, swampy wetlands, and lowland

The Horned Screamer gets its name from the "horn" on its forehead, which is actually a feather shaft. This horn resembles an antenna and may be straight or curved back or forward. Probably used for display purposes, it can almost reach the bill tip and may touch the ground when the bird is feeding. Black and white in colour, the Horned Screamer has a bulky body. Its other distinctive features include a narrow bill and long legs ending in partially webbed feet.

Certain anatomical differences, such as lightweight, hollow bones, and air sacs under the skin, make screamers distinct from the turkey family. They tend to mate for life, with pairs forming long-lasting bonds, and may breed at any time of the year. The female nests on the ground, laying 4–6 olive-brown eggs, which take six weeks to hatch. This species feeds on land rather than in water.

Anseranus semipalmata

Magpie Goose

LENGTH 75–85cm (30–33in)

WEIGHT 2–2.7kg (4½–5½lb)

MIGRATION Partial migrant

HABITAT Tropical floodplains, swamps, and damp grassland, within 80km (50 miles) of the coast

A primitive, aberrant (atypical) goose that provides the evolutionary link between wildfowl and screamers, the Magpie Goose has unusual features such as partially webbed feet and a long hind toe. Both the male and female are highly vocal. Some males mate with two females, which lay eggs in the same nest. The pair or trio usually bond for life.

ADULT MALE

Anser cygnoides

Swan Goose

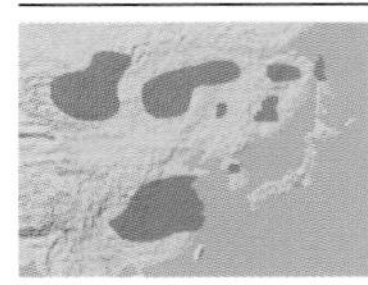

LENGTH 81–94cm (32–37in)

WEIGHT 3.5kg (7¾lb)

MIGRATION Migrant

HABITAT Lowland lakeside marshes, rice fields, and estuaries

RED LIST CATEGORY Endangered

Despite having been domesticated 3,000 years ago, the Swan Goose, also called the Chinese Goose, is one of the northern hemisphere's most poorly known wildfowl. Its population is declining rapidly as a result of habitat loss and hunting. With its long bill, small head, and slim neck, this distinctive goose has a slightly top-heavy appearance. It has a brown cap and orange legs. The species breeds on steppe marshes and lakesides, usually in ground nests.

Dendrocygna viduata

White-faced Whistling Duck

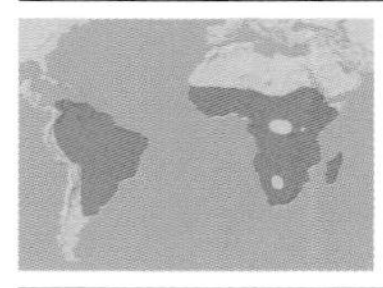

LENGTH 44cm (17½in)

WEIGHT 700g (25oz)

MIGRATION Partial migrant

HABITAT Bodies of fresh water, often with some emergent vegetation

Named after its striking call, a three-syllable whistle, the White-faced Whistling Duck has dark plumage and a white head, which makes the adult easy to identify. The juvenile is trickier to spot, being hard to distinguish from the juvenile Fulvous Whistling Duck (*D. bicolor*), with which it overlaps in range. This species is unusual in that it is widespread over two continents: Africa and South America. Surprisingly, there are no plumage differences between the two populations.

GREGARIOUS SPECIES

The White-faced Whistling Duck is both aquatic and land-based and lives in large flocks on bodies of open water. Unlike some other whistling ducks, which are also known as Tree-Ducks, it rarely perches. Most feeding occurs at night, and takes the form of both dabbling and up-ending. The species may undertake extensive seasonal movements – up to 500km (310 miles) – in response to the availability of water and food.

Anser albifrons

Greater White-fronted Goose

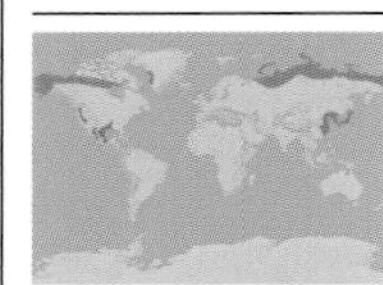

LENGTH 64–78cm (25–31in)

WEIGHT 2–3kg (4½–6½lb)

MIGRATION Migrant

HABITAT Breeds on lowland tundra, often by lakes and rivers; winters on open steppes and grassland

The distinctive white face of the Greater White-fronted Goose is most apparent when viewed head on and, like the broad, black bars across the belly, varies in extent between individuals. This species has orange-yellow legs and feet. In flight, the brown plumage and U-shaped rump patch are clearly visible. Four subspecies breed in the northern tundra from Russia to Greenland, and large flocks winter in specific areas of the USA, Mexico, Europe, and the Middle East.

ADULT MALE

Anser anser

Greylag Goose

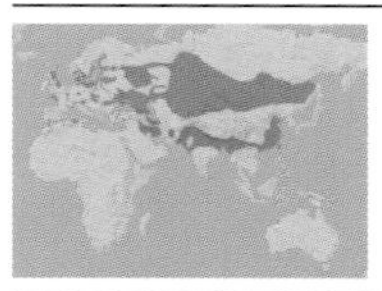

LENGTH
74–84cm (29–33in)

WEIGHT
3.1–3.5kg (6½–7¾lb)

MIGRATION
Partial migrant

HABITAT Mainly in open country, often wintering in lowland farmland

The Greylag Goose is the wild ancestor of many breeds of domestic geese. It breeds further south than all the other grey geese (such as the Greater White-fronted Goose, opposite), and its European and Asian ranges have been fragmented by hunting. The largest and bulkiest of the grey geese, it has a large head, thick neck, and a heavy bill adapted to probing in marshy lands and pulling out roots. Most breeding populations are migratory. This is the only European grey goose to be seen in large numbers during the summer.

ADULT GREYLAG GOOSE

HIGH-ALTITUDE MIGRANT

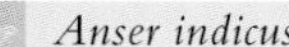

Anser indicus

Bar-headed Goose

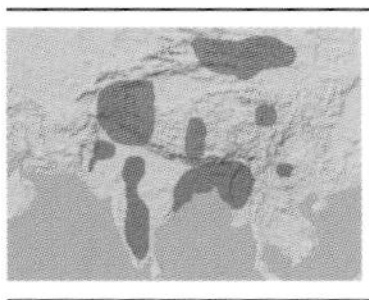

LENGTH
71–76cm (28–30in)

WEIGHT
1.9–2.4kg (4½–5½lb)

MIGRATION
Migrant

HABITAT Breeds by high-altitude lakes in boggy open country; winters by marshes, lakes, and rivers

Distinguished by the double dark brown crown-bands on its white head, the Bar-headed Goose is pale grey in colour. It breeds in colonies on the high plateaus of central Asia. The world's highest-altitude migrant, this sociable bird undertakes remarkable migrations in spring, crossing the Himalayas – to winter in large flocks in the marshy lowlands of north India.

ON THE WING
Flying in flocks that make broad V-formations, Snow Geese have a strong, direct flight with moderate wingbeats; in winter they fly south to the Gulf of Mexico.

Anser caerulescens

Snow Goose

LENGTH
65–75cm (26–30in)

WEIGHT
2.4–3.4kg (5¼–7¾lb)

MIGRATION
Migrant

HABITAT Breeds in low tundra, winters on cultivated land

The Snow Goose has two colour forms (see panel, right). The white form is brilliant white, with a thick red bill, a grey patch adjacent to bold black wing-tips, and deep pink legs. Two subspecies are also recognized. The Lesser Snow Goose (*A. c. caerulescens*) is the more widespread and common; its blue form predominates. The Greater Snow Goose (*A. c. atlanticus*) has a limited breeding range and winters along the Atlantic seaboard; its blue form is rare. As their names suggest, the subspecies differ mainly in size. Highly gregarious throughout the year, this goose breeds in closely packed colonies across Arctic North America and winters in flocks of tens of thousands.

large bill with "grinning patch"

black wing-tips

SOCIABLE BIRDS
Family groups stay together throughout the year; a mixed family of blue and white forms is pictured here.

COLOUR FORMS

The Snow Goose occurs in two colour types: one white (see left) and the other dark (called the "Blue Goose" because of its grey-blue wings). Breeding adults tend to mate with their own colour form – mixed pairings usually produce dark juveniles (pictured above).

GREAT SITES

KAKADU NATIONAL PARK

LOCATION On the northernmost coast of Australia's Northern Territory, around 250km (150 miles) east of Darwin.

Australia is the driest inhabited continent on Earth, but for a brief period the tropical belt that stretches across the northern third of the country is awash with fresh water – and spectacular concentrations of birds. In December, midsummer storms begin to sweep inland from the Indian Ocean, and over the next few months rivers burst their banks, flooding the low-lying land and creating enormous wetlands. Kakadu National Park lies on the coast in the extreme north of this tropical wet-dry zone. It is among the best places to watch birds in Australia, with more than 280 species being listed. Although the rainforests of the northeast support a more varied bird life, few other areas offer such good bird-viewing opportunities.

TRANSIENT WETLAND

The wet season in Kakadu usually lasts until April, by which time much of the park is under water and its extensive stands of Paperbark trees have turned into a flooded woodland accessible only by boat. Huge numbers of water birds flock to the area, sometimes travelling great distances across Australia's arid interior to feed or breed in this temporary swampland. They include whistling ducks, shelducks, and vast numbers of Magpie Geese, which graze on the green carpet of sprouting wild rice plants. Endemic to Australia and New Guinea, these noisy waterfowl are polygamous breeders – each male mates with two or three females, which share the same nest. Egrets, herons, and storks wade through the shallows to hunt fish, while flotillas of Australian Pelicans patrol the more open areas. In May and June Kakadu's wetlands slowly start to shrink, and both fish and the birds that eat them become concentrated in isolated pools, or billabongs. By August–September, these waterholes offer impressive birdwatching.

Best known for its waterbirds, Kakadu is also home to a rich selection of land-based species, including birds of prey, pittas, honeyeaters, pigeons, and parrots. The rare Gouldian Finch and Red Goshawk are among its residents. In 1981, Kakadu was listed as a World Heritage Site.

GATHERING OF GEESE
During the wet season, floodwaters pour into the flat lowlands of Kakadu National Park. For a few months these lush wetlands attract a wealth of water birds, including flocks of Magpie Geese.

WHAT TO SPOT

COMB-CRESTED JACANA
Irediparra gallinacea

MAGPIE GOOSE
Anseranas semipalmata
(see p.122)

RED GOSHAWK
Erythrotriorchis radiatus

GOULDIAN FINCH
Erythrura gouldiae
(see p.461)

Branta sandvicensis

Nene

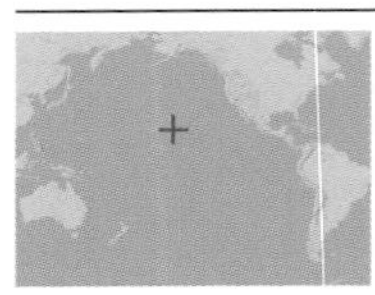

LENGTH 56–71cm (22–28in)

WEIGHT 2kg (4½lb)

MIGRATION Non-migrant

HABITAT Barren volcanic slopes with sparse vegetation on some Hawaiian islands and pastures

RED LIST CATEGORY Vulnerable

A small, brown goose with a black head and bill, distinct feather grooves on its neck, and partially webbed black feet – the Nene is one of conservation's success stories. A reintroduction programme contributed to its recovery from just 30 birds in the early 1900s to 1,000 today. Hawaii's only goose, it is also known as the Hawaiian Goose. The name "Néné" is derived from its low, moaning call.

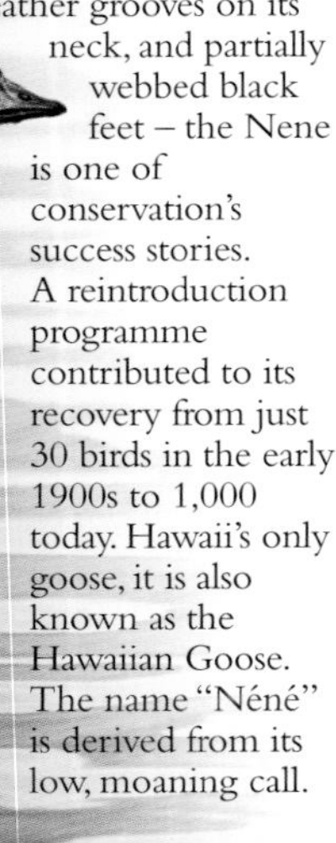

ADULT NENE

CANADA GEESE IN FLIGHT

Branta canadensis

Canada Goose

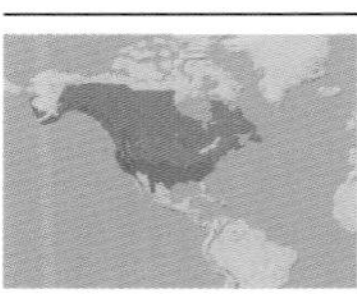

LENGTH 0.6–1.1m (2–3½ft)

WEIGHT 1.2–4.8kg (2¼–11lb)

MIGRATION Partial migrant

HABITAT Various lowland habitats, from tundra and wetlands to reservoirs and farmland

The size variation between the different subspecies of the Canada Goose is more extreme than for any other bird: the largest subspecies is seven times heavier than the smallest. In fact, some scientists have grouped several of the subspecies into a separate species, named the Cackling Goose (*B. hutchinsii*). The plumage of all Canada Geese, however, is basically similar and the combination of a black head and neck, with a white chinstrap and brown body, is easy to spot. The call of the smaller subspecies is a rapid cackle, while larger subspecies make deep honking sounds. The Canada Goose is a dabbler and a grazer; it walks well on land, and feeds on a variety of aquatic and terrestrial plants.

The natural range of this gregarious species is North America south to Mexico, but populations introduced into Europe and New Zealand since the 17th century are now abundant. The total population is estimated to be around three million. Some populations are migratory, while others are sedentary. A dispersal of flocks to traditional moulting grounds often takes place after breeding, some geese flying distances of up to 1,500km (900 miles) to moult.

Branta ruficollis

Red-breasted Goose

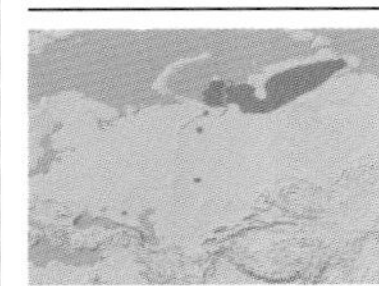

LENGTH 53–55cm (21–21½in)

WEIGHT 1.1–1.4kg (2¼–3¼lb)

MIGRATION Migrant

HABITAT Breeds by tundra close to rivers; winters in open steppes among pasture and crops

RED LIST CATEGORY Vulnerable

PATTERNED GOOSE

While strikingly patterned, the chestnut head and neck of this unmistakable goose are inconspicuous at long range, when the species appears simply black and white. The Red-breasted Goose breeds in northern Russia and winters almost entirely at five sites in Bulgaria and Romania. Its range continues to decline due to climate and land-use change.

Cygnus atratus

Black Swan

LENGTH 1.1–1.4m (3½–4½ft)

WEIGHT 5–6kg (11–13lb)

MIGRATION Partial migrant

HABITAT Large, shallow lakes, flooded agricultural land, coastal lagoons, and sheltered coastal bays

Unique to Australasia, the adult of this species is sooty-black, with white flight feathers that are hidden at rest, and a bill that is bright red. The juvenile is greyer than the adult. The Black Swan is highly gregarious, with flocks of tens of thousands on some lakes. Breeding colonies are densely packed, and the breeding season varies with the climate across Australia.

ADULT BLACK SWAN

Cygnus olor

Mute Swan

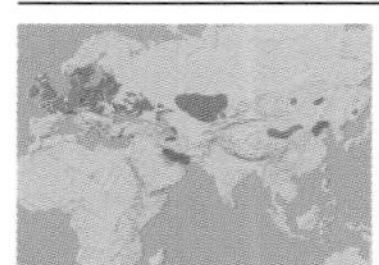

LENGTH 1.2–1.6m (4–5¼ft)

WEIGHT 9.5–12kg (21–26lb)

MIGRATION Partial migrant

HABITAT Lowland bodies of fresh water, especially manmade; sheltered coastal areas

The Mute Swan is most familiar as an inhabitant of lakes in urban areas of Europe as well as northeastern North America, but it is actually a bird from the Central Asian steppes. This is due to its long history of domestication in Europe. In its indigenous Asian range, it is wary and unapproachable and is possibly still threatened by habitat destruction. The adult is distinguished by its orange bill with a black basal knob, pure white plumage, long pointed tail, and its habit of swimming with arched wings and neck held in a gentle S-shape. While most cygnets are brownish grey, some are all white, in a colour form called the Polish Swan (*C. immutabilis*). The Mute Swan's common name is a partial misnomer – although it is certainly the least vocal of the swans, it is by no means silent. It has a variety of distinctive calls, notably a snake-like hiss when threatened. In flight, the wings make a loud "singing" sound.

ADULT MUTE SWANS

extensive yellow area on bill

distinctive long neck

Cygnus cygnus

Whooper Swan

LENGTH
1.4–1.7m (4½–5½ft)

WEIGHT
9.5kg (21lb)

MIGRATION
Migrant

HABITAT Breeds by open water, often in taiga forest; winters in lowland farmland and floodplains

The Whooper Swan is best known for its loud, clear trumpet-like call, which is responsible for the species' common name. This sound is produced by well-developed structures in the throat that resonate strongly. The second largest swan in the world, the Whooper Swan is superficially similar to the Tundra Swan (below), differing in its larger size, more angular head shape, and wedge-shaped bill. The yellow on the bill is also more extensive than that of the Tundra Swan.

The Whooper Swan is a Eurasian species, breeding across the north of the continental mass and wintering in coastal lowlands, particularly around the North, Black, and Caspian Seas (European birds); and Japan, Korea, and coastal China (Asian breeders). On breeding grounds, pairs of these swans are territorial and nesting sites are well spaced. In wintering grounds, Whooper Swans are gregarious, with congregations numbering up to 3,000 birds. Migrating parties fly in lines or in V-shaped formations, arriving on the grounds in October or November, and departing between March and May.

ADULT WHOOPER SWAN

FLOCK ON WATER

Cygnus columbianus

Tundra Swan

LENGTH
1.1–1.5m (3½–5ft)

WEIGHT
6.5–7kg (14–15lb)

MIGRATION
Migrant

HABITAT Breeds in tundra near bodies of fresh water; winters in lowland marshes, wet pastures, cropland

The Tundra Swan comprises two distinct subspecies: the Whistling Swan (*C. c. columbianus*) of North America and Bewick's Swan (*C. c. bewickii*) of Europe and Asia. They differ in the colour of their bills: the Whistling Swan is entirely black, whereas the Bewick's swan has varying amounts of yellow. The exact pattern of yellow is unique to an individual, making it possible to track specific birds when flocks arrive on wintering grounds on the Atlantic and Pacific coasts. The Tundra Swan feeds on aquatic vegetation and roots of submerged plants, which it digs up by dipping its long neck and head under water. Known to be a solitary nester, it is a monogamous bird that finds a mate and then pairs for life. It departs from its breeding grounds in September or early October. These birds migrate in family flocks along well-established routes, sometimes pausing at the usual stopover sites until forced to move onwards by colder weather.

ADULT BLUE DUCK

Tachyeres pteneres

Fuegian Steamer Duck

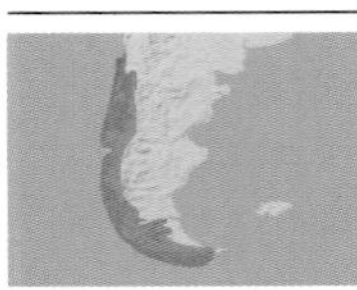

LENGTH 74–84cm (29–33in)

WEIGHT 4.2–5.5kg ($8^{3}/_{4}$–12lb)

MIGRATION Non-migrant

HABITAT Rocky coasts with sheltered bays and kelp beds

The flightless Fuegian Steamer Duck is the largest of a group of coastal southern South American ducks, all but one of which are incapable of flying. The sexes of this sturdy duck are similar, with predominantly grey plumage and a bright orange-yellow bill and legs. It finds its food by diving among beds of kelp and spends its time loafing around on rocks. It is not flock-forming and lives in pairs or family groups.

Plectropterus gambensis

Spur-winged Goose

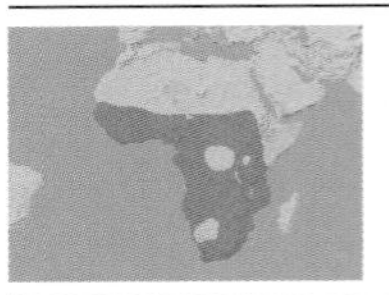

LENGTH 75–100cm (30–39in)

WEIGHT 3.9kg ($8^{3}/_{4}$lb)

MIGRATION Non-migrant

HABITAT Freshwater lakes, pools, and rivers in open grassy lowland areas; swamps and river deltas

Named for the spur on the bend of its wing, which is used by this goose to defend its territory during the breeding season, the large Spur-winged Goose has a long neck, white face, red skin around the eyes, and long legs. It lives in flocks around tropical African wetlands and grazes on waterside vegetation and aquatic plants. It often takes over abandoned nests of other large birds or places its nest in cavities in trees and rocks.

ADULT MALE

Hymenolaimus malacorhynchos

Blue Duck

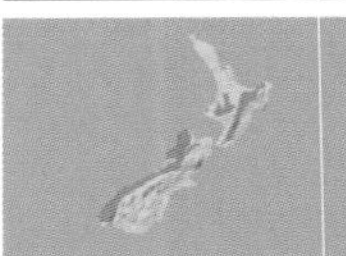

LENGTH 50–57cm ($19^{1}/_{2}$–$22^{1}/_{2}$in)

WEIGHT 775–900g (28–32oz)

MIGRATION Non-migrant

HABITAT Clear, fast-flowing mountain rivers and streams in wooded regions

RED LIST CATEGORY Endangered

As its name suggests, the Blue Duck is mainly blue-grey in colour, and has a dark-rimmed pale pink bill with flaps at the sides. It feeds by swimming and diving in the rapids of fast-flowing mountain rivers. When it is not feeding, it likes to rest on boulders in the mid-stream and only rarely flies. The highly territorial male will drive away any intruder along its stretch of river. Unfortunately, this New Zealand duck is declining in numbers and faces threats from introduced species as well as the construction of dams.

ADULT FEMALE WITH CHICKS

Alopochen aegyptiaca

Egyptian Goose

LENGTH 63–73cm (25–29in)

WEIGHT 1.9kg ($4^{1}/_{4}$lb)

MIGRATION Non-migrant

HABITAT Inland wetlands in tropical Africa; parkland, meadows, and pastures where introduced in Europe

The Egyptian Goose is mainly a bird of tropical Africa, but is widely kept in captivity and now occurs in a feral state in parts of western Europe, particularly the UK. It has two colour forms: one with grey-brown on the upperparts, the other with red-brown. The species is found in pairs, but flocks together when not breeding. Although it can swim well and dive, it feeds mainly on land, where it grazes on grass or leaves and also raids certain crops. It has a noisy display in the breeding season when its wings are opened out and its neck is stretched forwards. Egyptian Geese nest in a variety of places, from tree-cavities and cliff-ledges to abandoned nests of other birds. The female Egyptian Goose lays 5–8 eggs, which hatch after four weeks. The downy chicks are fed and cared for by both parents.

Neochen jubata

Orinoco Goose

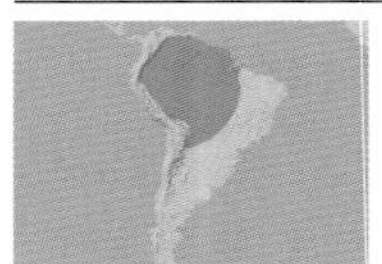

LENGTH 61–76cm (24–30in)

WEIGHT 1.3kg (3lb)

MIGRATION Non-migrant

HABITAT Banks of rivers in lowland tropical forest; various wetlands in more open forest and savanna

A pale head and neck, dark bill, chestnut flanks, dark upperparts, and black wings with a white patch distinguish this goose. The male and female are similar in appearance. Although it spends most of its time on the ground, it readily perches in trees. It mainly grazes on grass, but will also eat molluscs, worms, larvae, and aquatic insects. It usually nests in tree-hollows. The male has a high-pitched whistling call, and the female cackles like the related Egyptian Goose (above right).

Chloephaga melanoptera

Andean Goose

LENGTH 70–80cm (28–31in)

WEIGHT 2kg ($4^{1}/_{2}$lb)

MIGRATION Non-migrant

HABITAT Lakes and marshes in high-altitude Andean grassland, moving to lower levels during winter

A hardy species that lives at very high altitudes – usually well above 3,000m (10,000ft) – in the Andes of South America, the Andean Goose is a striking black and white bird, with a black-tipped pink bill and pinkish orange legs. The female is similar to the male, but is smaller.

This species feeds almost entirely by grazing in short grassland. Although usually found in pairs or small family groups, larger gatherings can be seen after the breeding season. Despite being classified as a waterbird, it avoids water and will swim only in an emergency. The male can be very aggressive when defending its territory in the breeding season. Pairs apparently stay together for life and breed from November to January, making a simple, feather-lined nest on bare ground, usually on slopes overlooking a lake or pool. The female lays 6–10 eggs and the young become independent about three months after hatching.

BREEDING MALE DISPLAYING TO FEMALE

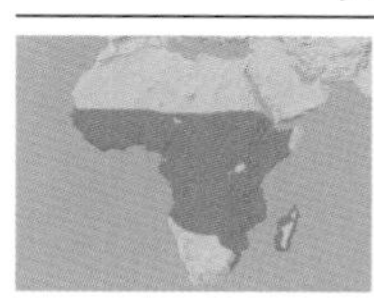

Nettapus auritus

African Pygmy Goose

LENGTH 28–33cm (11–13in)

WEIGHT 275g (10oz)

MIGRATION Non-migrant

HABITAT Freshwater lakes and pools, particularly those that are deep and well-vegetated

This very striking small waterbird is the smallest species of waterfowl in Africa, and is usually found swimming and feeding in groups among floating wetland vegetation.

The male African Pygmy Goose has a conspicuous head-pattern, with black, white, and green markings, as well as a bright orange-yellow, black-tipped bill. The female has a duller, mostly white face with a broken dark eye-stripe. Like other Pygmy Geese, the African Pygmy Goose prefers to nest in tree-holes above the ground. When the young birds hatch, they have to leap down to get to the water or the ground. Sexually mature at two years, these birds have been known to live for up to 15 years in captivity. Large gatherings of non-breeding birds are found in the Okavango delta in Botswana.

MALE AFRICAN PYGMY GOOSE

PAIR OF COMMON SHELDUCKS

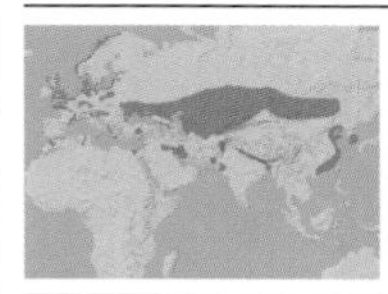

Tadorna tadorna

Common Shelduck

LENGTH 58–67cm (23–26in)

WEIGHT 1kg (2¼lb)

MIGRATION Migrant

HABITAT Sea coasts, estuaries, and larger inland lakes (particularly saline ones); gravel- and sand-pits

The Common Shelduck is one of the most distinctive ducks of western European coasts. The sexes are similar, but the female is somewhat smaller and duller than the male, with white facial markings and a broken chest-band. The red bulge on the bill of the male is absent in the female. Juveniles are browner, with a white face, foreneck, and chest. During late winter and spring, pairs become quite vocal. The male utters low whistling calls, but the female's call is quite different, being a rapid chattering "gag-ag-ag-ag-ag".

Common Shelducks often nest in rabbit burrows in sandy places, as well as tree-hollows and even haystacks. The female typically lays 8–10 eggs and incubates them for about four weeks. Soon after the young have left the nest, the adults leave for their annual moult (see panel, below). Broods of juveniles are then left in the care of one or more adult "attendants", thought to be failed breeders or non-breeders. If approached, these adults take to the wing, uttering warning quacks to the juveniles, who dive with skill to avoid danger.

GREAT SITES

WADDEN SEA

The adult Common Shelducks that breed along the coasts of northwestern Europe move to the Wadden Sea (Waddenzee) on the north coast of Germany in late summer and early autumn for their annual post-breeding moult, forming large congregations.

WILDLIFE-RICH SALT MARSH
The Wadden Sea is an extensive area of tidal mud flats and salt marshes. It is home to a wide variety of animal life.

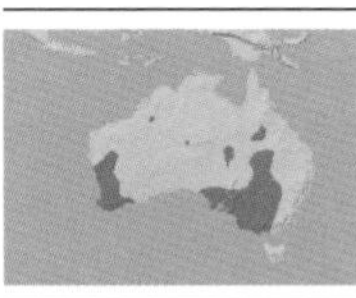

Malacorhynchus membranaceus

Pink-eared Duck

LENGTH 36–45cm (14–17½in)

WEIGHT 350–400g (13–14oz)

MIGRATION Partial migrant

HABITAT Shallow inland wetlands, temporary pools; occasionally coastal inlets and mangrove swamps

This Australian duck is most closely related to shelducks, despite the difference in their appearance. The black head-pattern, with a pink spot behind the eye patch, and barred body make this bird unmistakable. It has a large, square-tipped bill designed to help it feed on the plankton (including algae), crustaceans, molluscs, and insects it is dependent on, the pliable flaps of the bill acting as a sieve to filter algae and plankton from the water.

PAIR OF ADULT PINK-EARED DUCKS

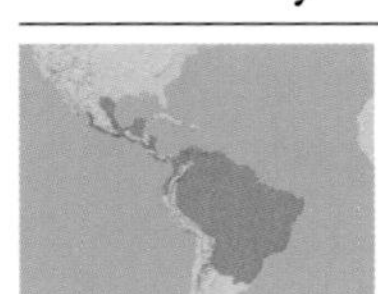

Cairina moschata

Muscovy Duck

LENGTH 66–84cm (26–33in)

WEIGHT 2–3kg (4½–6½lb)

MIGRATION Non-migrant

HABITAT Lowland lakes, lagoons, marshes, and rivers in forested areas; brackish coastal wetland

This large duck had probably been domesticated for centuries by indigenous South American people before the arrival of European colonists. Selective breeding in captivity has produced larger domestic Muscovy Ducks with unusual and highly individual colour markings. Wild birds are black all over, apart from their white wing-coverts. The naked skin on their faces is mostly dark, with only a small amount of red, and they have a domed crest on top of the head.

The male is larger than the female and has a prominent knob on top of its bill. Muscovy Ducks do not form stable pairs, and forced sexual intercourse can occur. The female lays 8–10 white eggs, usually in a tree-hole or hollow. The diet of this species consists of leaves and seeds of various plants, obtained by grazing or dabbling in shallow water, and includes small invertebrates and insects. Muscovy Ducks roost in small groups in trees.

DOMESTIC MUSCOVY DUCK

Aix sponsa

Wood Duck

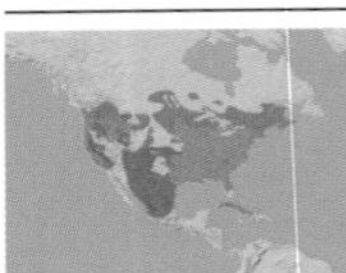

LENGTH 43–51cm (17–20in)

WEIGHT 625–675g (22–24oz)

MIGRATION Partial migrant

HABITAT Freshwater ponds, lakes, and slow-flowing rivers in well-wooded places; open areas in winter

DRAKE WOOD DUCK PREENING

A close relative of the Mandarin Duck (right), the North American Wood Duck is often kept in captivity. A black and white patterned head, crowned by a shiny green, floppy crest, distinguishes the male, while the female resembles the Mandarin Duck but has darker cheeks, a more contrasting white throat, and much more white around the eye.

When swimming, Wood Ducks bob their heads backwards and forwards in a jerking motion. The male's call is a rising whistle, while the female gives a whistled "whoo-eek" if startled. Like the Mandarin Duck, this species usually nests in a tree-cavity, and will also take advantage of specially made nest-boxes in suitable habitats. If nest-boxes are placed too close together, the female may lay eggs in the nest of a neighbour, resulting in clutches of as many as 40 eggs and unsuccessful incubation. The Wood Duck prefers nesting over water so that the ducklings can swim and find their food as soon as they leave the nest.

Aix galericulata

Mandarin Duck

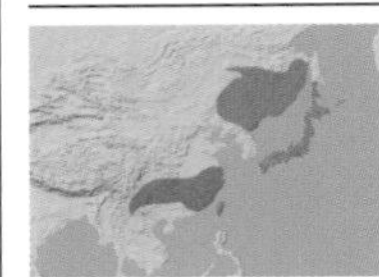

LENGTH 41–49cm (16–19½in)

WEIGHT 500–625g (18–22oz)

MIGRATION Partial migrant

HABITAT Lakes, pools, and rivers in well-wooded places; also more open areas in winter

The beautifully ornate plumage of the male Mandarin Duck has made it one of the world's most familiar ducks in captivity. The male's coloration is very showy, with a red bill, broad white eyebrow, an orange fan of neck hackles, orange wing sails, and two white bands on the black breast. The female is more subtly coloured, with a grey head, white "spectacles" and throat, and dark greenish brown upperparts. It has a white belly centre and dark brown breast and flanks covered with heavy white mottling.

TREE-HOLE NESTS

Mandarin Ducks choose to nest in tree-cavities 6–7m (20–23ft) above the ground, where they are safe from most predators, and often several hundred metres from the nearest body of water. They line the nest with rotten wood and bits of vegetation. Soon after hatching, the ducklings make their way to the edge of the nest-hole, before leaping down to the water or ground below.

The Mandarin Duck feeds by dabbling or walking on land where it eats plants, seeds, nuts, and insects. During courtship, several males compete for the attention of a female. In traditional Chinese lore, the Mandarin Duck symbolizes wedded bliss and fidelity, but in reality, it finds a new partner each year. The species was once widespread in eastern Asia, but it is now threatened due to the destruction of its forest habitat. The populations in eastern Russia and in China are both probably well below 1,000 pairs, although Japan may have about 5,000 pairs.

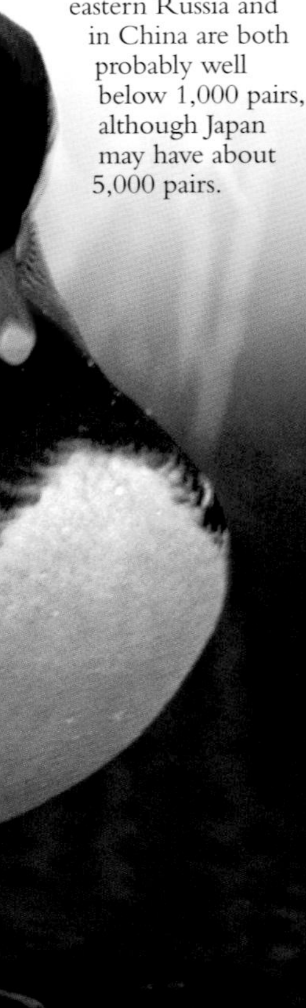

PAIR OF MANDARIN DUCKS

Anas strepera

Gadwall

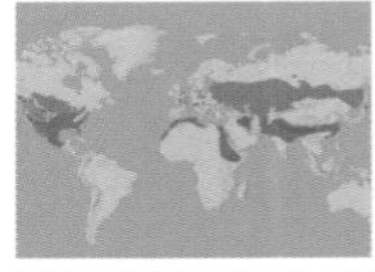

LENGTH 46–55cm (18–21½in)

WEIGHT 875–975g (31–35oz)

MIGRATION Migrant

HABITAT Freshwater lakes and marshes in lowland areas; also coastal wetlands

The Gadwall is one of the more widespread dabbling ducks. The male is mostly grey with black tail coverts, but shows a prominent white wing patch in flight. The female resembles a female Mallard (opposite) but shares the white wing patch of the male Gadwall and has an orange-sided bill.

This species is less gregarious than many other dabbling ducks and forms relatively small flocks outside the breeding season. It nests on the ground, often some distance from the water, and the ducklings start life on a diet of insects.

MALE GADWALL

Anas americana

American Wigeon

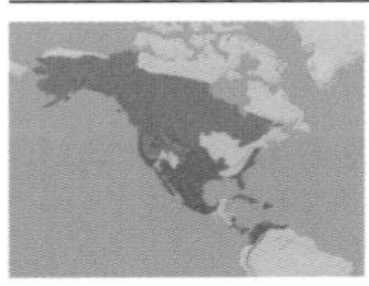

LENGTH 45–56cm (17½–22in)

WEIGHT 725–800g (25–29oz)

MIGRATION Migrant

HABITAT Lakes and marshes in open wooded areas; winters mainly in coastal marshes and estuaries

With a grey hood, dark eye patch, and brown to chestnut breast and flanks, the female American Wigeon is plainer than the male, which has a conspicuous white forehead and crown. The male utters a clear, three-note whistle "whoee-whoe-whoe", while the female's call is a low, growling "qua-ack".

MALE IN BREEDING PLUMAGE

These dabbling ducks are highly gregarious and gather in large flocks during the winter months to graze on coastal marshlands. They are strongly migratory, and a few individuals fly across the Atlantic Ocean each year to western Europe.

MALE IN FLIGHT
The male Mallard's white collar and white-bordered blue speculum on its wings are clearly visible in flight.

Anas platyrhynchos

Mallard

LENGTH 50–65cm (19½–26in)

WEIGHT 1.2kg (2½lb)

MIGRATION Migrant

HABITAT All kinds of freshwater wetland, as well as coastal habitats

The familiar Mallard is the ancestor of most domestic ducks, apart from those that have descended from the Muscovy Duck (see p.129). The breeding male has a glossy green head, white collar, grey-brown back, and rufous breast. However, the non-breeding male is similar to the female, which is mottled brown, buff, and white. The male's call is a low "kwek-kwek-kwek", while the female's is a loud series of quacks.

The Mallard is a strongly migratory and gregarious species outside the breeding season and is found in the wild right across the northern hemisphere. It is classified as a dabbling duck because it feeds on the surface and does not dive. It mostly eats aquatic vegetation, but also grazes on grasses and takes some invertebrates. It nests on the ground, usually in dense vegetation near water. The male Mallard only forms a pair until the female lays eggs, and then goes its separate way. The clutch of 8–13 eggs is incubated for about 28 days. The ducklings can swim and feed themselves on insects as soon as they hatch, although they stay with the female for 7–8 weeks until they fledge.

SHELTERED FROM THE SUN
On clear summer days, the female Mallard may stand over the ducklings to protect them from the bright sunlight.

ADULT MALE

Anas clypeata

Northern Shoveler

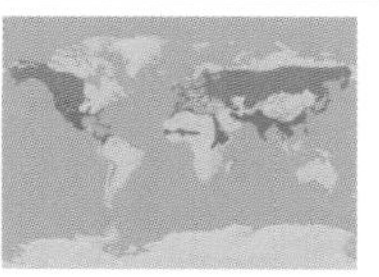

LENGTH 44–52cm (17½–20½in)

WEIGHT 600–650g (21–23oz)

MIGRATION Migrant

HABITAT Various kinds of wetland, particularly shallow freshwater lakes and pools, and marshes

Spoon-shaped and long, the large bill of the Northern Shoveler sets it apart from other ducks. The male has a black head with a green sheen and rich chestnut sides, while the female resembles the female Mallard. It feeds by dabbling for plant food, often swinging its bill from side to side; it also eats molluscs and insects in the nesting season. The nest, a shallow depression on the ground, is filled with grasses and lined with down.

Anas aucklandica

Brown Teal

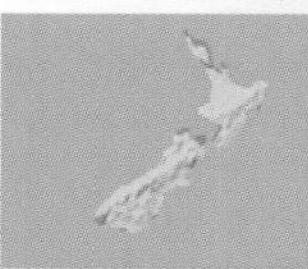

LENGTH 36–46cm (14–18in)

WEIGHT 400–500g (14–18oz)

MIGRATION Non-migrant

HABITAT Swampy pools and streams with some cover of bushes and trees; coastal bays and estuaries

RED LIST CATEGORY Vulnerable

This small brown duck, with a chestnut breast and white-ringed eyes, is only found in New Zealand. However, it has not been able to cope with the changes brought about by human settlement and is now one of the rarest waterbirds in the world. It has evolved over the centuries into three subspecies: *A. a. chlorotis* on the mainland and offshore islands, and the flightless *A. a. nesiotis* and *A. a. aucklandica* (which have virtually been exterminated by cats, rats, and stoats) on subantarctic islands in the Campbell and Auckland groups.

ADULT MALE

MALE IN BREEDING PLUMAGE

Anas acuta

Northern Pintail

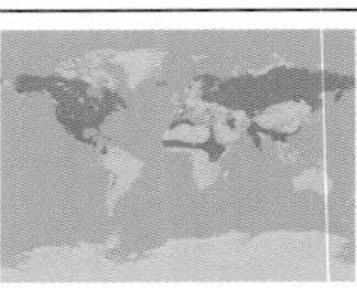

LENGTH 51–66cm (20–26in)

WEIGHT 750–850g (27–30oz)

MIGRATION Migrant

HABITAT Open, marshy wetlands in breeding season; also found in coastal habitats in winter

The male Northern Pintail has a long, slender neck and an elegant, pointed tail that is 10cm (4in) longer than the female's. The breeding male has a pale grey body, white breast and lateral neck stripe, and dark brown head. This species is one of the dabbling ducks, a group that feeds by sieving food from the water's surface with its bill or by upending in shallow water. Like many wildfowl, this bird mostly feeds during the evening and at night.

Anas crecca

Common Teal

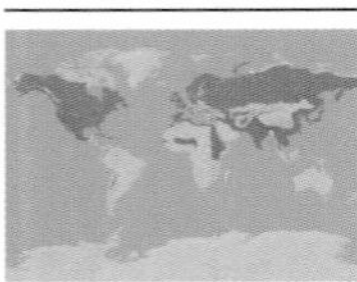

LENGTH 34–38cm (13½–15in)

WEIGHT 350g (13oz)

MIGRATION Migrant

HABITAT Marshy freshwater pools and lakes in breeding season; wider range of wetlands in winter

The diminutive Common Teal is found throughout the northern hemisphere. The male in breeding plumage, with its chestnut head and metallic green eye-patches outlined with cream stripes, is easy to identify. As with many ducks, the female is much drabber. Two distinct forms of the species occur in Eurasia and North America that differ slightly in their plumage. The North American subspecies is sometimes considered a separate species, *A. carolinensis*.

MALE COMMON TEAL

PAIR OF MARBLED DUCKS

Marmaronetta angustirostris

Marbled Duck

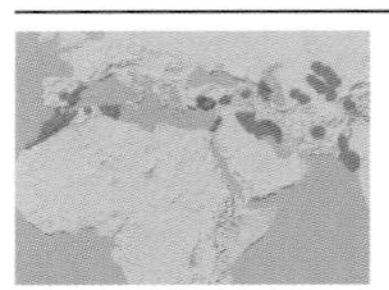

LENGTH 39–42cm (15½–16½in)

WEIGHT 450–600g (16–21oz)

MIGRATION Migrant

HABITAT Temporary or permanent shallow freshwater and brackish wetlands with emergent vegetation

RED LIST CATEGORY Vulnerable

Identifiable by its mottled grey-brown plumage and distinctive dark mask, the Marbled Duck has a small tuft at its nape and pale spots on its flanks. It has a dark bill, but the back and tail are pale. In flight, the darker tips of the wings can be seen. The male and female Marbled Ducks are similar, while the juvenile has more spots than the adult.

Since the Marbled Duck feeds mainly by dabbling, it was earlier classified with the dabbling ducks. However, it is currently considered to be an unusual diving duck because of the similarities in courtship displays and because it lacks the coloured wing patch or speculum that is a noticeable feature of the dabbling ducks.

Unobtrusive but gregarious, these ducks remain in flocks for most of the year, although they form pairs in winter. During breeding, they form small colonies, with their nests no more than (3ft) apart.

The Marbled Duck is considered to be a threatened species. Wide-scale destruction of its preferred wetland habitat has caused a rapid decline in its population and a patchy, fragmented distribution within its range.

ADULT MALE

Aythya ferina

Common Pochard

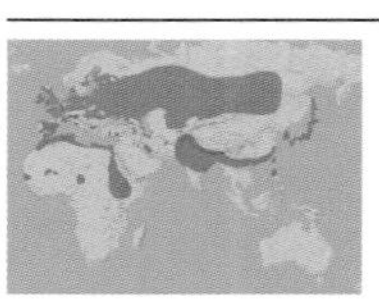

LENGTH 42–49cm (16½–19½in)

WEIGHT 850–950g (30–34oz)

MIGRATION Migrant

HABITAT Shallow to relatively deep, open bodies of fresh water; occasional in coastal habitats

A typical diving duck, the compact Common Pochard is boldly marked, with a big head. Diving ducks, as the name suggests, feed by diving and taking food from the bottom. The Common Pochard prefers to feed in water about 1–2.5m (3¼–8¼ft) deep. This species has benefited from forest clearance for agriculture in Europe, and as a result its range has expanded into western Europe.

Aythya fuligula

Tufted Duck

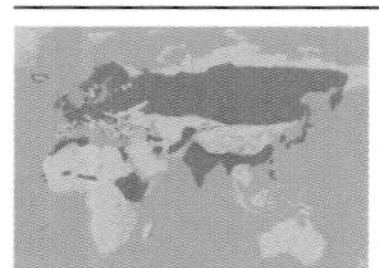

LENGTH 40–47cm (15½–18½in)

WEIGHT 0.5–1kg (1–2¼lb)

MIGRATION Migrant

HABITAT Temperate, lowland bodies of fresh water; occasional in sheltered marine habitats in winter

The male Tufted Duck has a neat appearance, with an attractive plumage in contrasting black and white, a long, drooping crest, and a black-tipped, blue-grey bill. The female is largely brown, with a short crest on the nape, and both sexes show a broad, white wing stripe in flight. This species feeds during lengthy dives to depths of 3–14m (9¾–46ft). This behaviour allows it to use a range of manmade pits and reservoirs that are not always suitable for other wildfowl. Its diet includes both plant and animal matter, collected mostly from the bottom. The distribution of the Tufted Duck has increased in the west of its range, mainly due to the construction of bodies of deep water by the sand and gravel extraction industry.

MALE TUFTED DUCK

ADULT MALE

Aythya marila

Greater Scaup

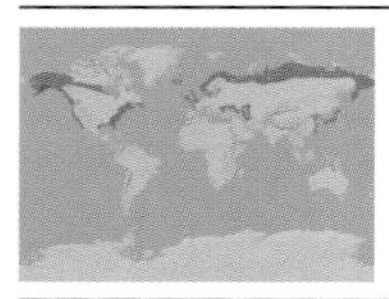

LENGTH 42–51cm (16½–20in)

WEIGHT 0.7–1.3kg (1½–3¼lb)

MIGRATION Migrant

HABITAT Breeds in tundra wetlands; winters in food-rich marine habitats

Although similar to the Tufted Duck (left), the Greater Scaup lacks an obvious crest and the upperparts are grey, not black. The Greater Scaup breeds in the northern hemisphere at very high latitudes in a variety of tundra wetlands. During the winter, the species further demonstrates its hardiness by feeding almost exclusively at sea, often gathering in huge flocks in food-rich areas, such as mussel beds and sewage outflows.

Somateria spectabilis

King Eider

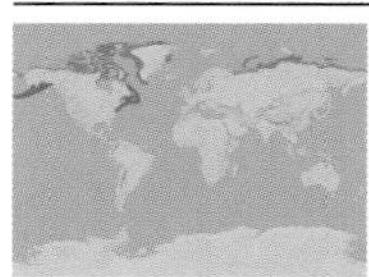

LENGTH 47–63cm (18½–25in)

WEIGHT 1.5–2kg (3¼–4½lb)

MIGRATION Partial migrant

HABITAT Breeds on coastal and inland tundra wetlands; winters at sea, mostly north of Arctic Circle

Pastel shades of grey, green, and salmon-pink on the head and neck of the male King Eider contrast with its bright red bill, enormous yellow-orange frontal shield outlined in black, and the starker black and white plumage of its body. The body is further ornamented by unusual raised inner feathers on the back that form two "sails". The female is drab and brown (as is usual for ducks), differing only in minor plumage and anatomical details from the females of other eider species.

The King Eider often flies in big flocks, abreast, not behind each other. It dives to depths of 55m (180ft) to feed on molluscs and crustaceans. A true Arctic species, it breeds in the tundra at high latitudes and most winter at sea north of the Arctic Circle. The species is common throughout its range and may be the most abundant eider species in the world, with a total population possibly exceeding three million birds.

SPECTACULAR PLUMAGE
Named "king" for its large blue-grey crown, the male King Eider displays vivid plumage in the breeding season.

GREGARIOUS WATERFOWL
Large flocks of King Eiders gather to feed in the coastal waters of the Arctic Ocean, migrating in even larger flocks during spring.

SOLITARY NESTER

Forming individual pairs, King Eiders arrive at their nesting ponds in June. The female scrapes a shallow depression on raised, dry ground near the water and lines it with plant material and large amounts of down. It lays 4 or 5 eggs, after which the male returns to sea, leaving the female alone to incubate the eggs for the next 27–30 days. The female King Eider tends to the young until they leave their nest to find their own food.

Histrionicus histrionicus

Harlequin Duck

LENGTH 38–45cm (15–17½in)

WEIGHT 525–675g (19–24oz)

MIGRATION Migrant

HABITAT Breeds in fast-flowing upland watercourses; winters along rocky shorelines

No other wildfowl species sports the striking combination of dark blue-grey and rich chestnut that is a distinctive feature of the Harlequin Duck. Another noticeable feature is the unique head pattern of the male, with its white facial crescent, cheek spot, neck stripes, and stunning chestnut eye-stripe. It has a small, blue-black bill, several white lines on the body, and a long, pointed black tail. However, the female is a drab brown, with two spots in front of the eye and a white cheek patch.

This is a tough species, quite at home in icy cold, rough water, both at sea and on the fast-flowing rocky rivers where it breeds. Though usually silent, it is a noisy breeder, its calls characterized by high-pitched squeals and whistles – a common vocal adaptation among birds breeding in turbulent water. Wintering birds always select coastal areas with rugged shorelines, such as exposed headlands and cliffs. Harlequin Ducks feed almost exclusively on animal matter, diving to remove food items from rocks with their small bills.

MALE HARLEQUIN DUCK

MALE BLACK SCOTER

Melanitta nigra

Black Scoter

LENGTH 44–54cm (17½–21½in)

WEIGHT 1kg (2¼lb)

MIGRATION Migrant

HABITAT Breeds in freshwater wetlands; winters mainly in shallow coastal waters

Otherwise uniformly plumaged, the Black Scoter shows a silvery grey sheen in flight. The species is divided into two subspecies, each of which are considered by many authorities to represent distinct species on their own.

The Black Scoter (*M.n. nigra*, shown above) belongs to the subspecies that occurs in Europe and western Asia and can be identified by the distinct knob on its bill and the restricted area of yellow below it. The subspecies (*M.n. americana*), found in eastern Asia and North America, has a yellower bill.

The species is most often seen in dense wintering flocks in shallow coastal areas, where it feeds by diving for molluscs and crustaceans. Although considered a sea duck, this species actually breeds across the subarctic region in a variety of freshwater habitats.

Clangula hyemalis

Long-tailed Duck

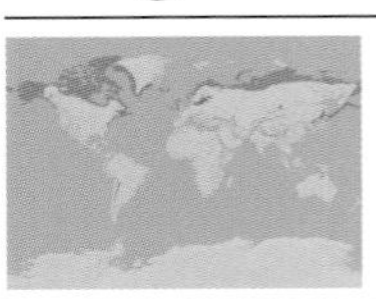

LENGTH 36–60cm (14–23½in)

WEIGHT 800–950g (29–34oz)

MIGRATION Migrant

HABITAT Breeds in a variety of Arctic aquatic environments, such as fjords; winters coastally

The Long-tailed Duck is named after the adult male's elongated pair of central tail feathers, which are 13cm (5in) longer than the female's tail. In flight, this species is easily identified, as it is the only duck in its range with a white body and all-dark wings. Its flight is rapid, with shallow, stiff wingbeats, during which it swings from side to side, showing alternating black and white as first the upperparts and then the underparts can be seen.

In winter, Long-tailed Ducks gather together in large flocks over shallow coastal feeding areas, where they jump-dive for prey, especially small crustaceans and molluscs. Such large congregations make this species vulnerable to oil pollution.

Males and females pair up when they move northwards in late winter and spring, as well as on the Arctic breeding grounds. The male's courtship display involves "head-tossing" and presenting its rear end, emphasizing the long tail to good effect. Nests are placed on the ground, close to tundra pools and small lakes. In behaviour typical of ducks, the male abandons the female soon after she starts to incubate the eggs and joins other males gathered on a lake to moult.

all-dark underwing

brownish black patches

MALE LONG-TAILED DUCK

Bucephala clangula

Common Goldeneye

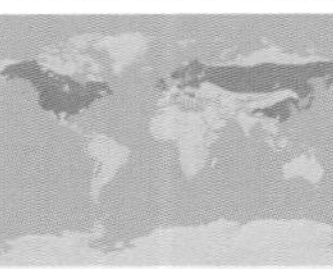

LENGTH 42–50cm (16½–19½in)

WEIGHT 0.8–1.1kg (1¾–2¼lb)

MIGRATION Migrant

HABITAT Breeds on forest lakes and rivers; winters on large lakes and shallow coastal habitats

A chunky, muscular diving duck, the Common Goldeneye has a curious large, triangular head and striking black and white plumage. Energetic and restless, it rises easily from the water. In flight, the wings make a distinctive whistling noise, which is especially pronounced in the male.

The Common Goldeneye breeds throughout the Arctic-Alpine forest zone and is heavily dependent on the availability of tree-holes for nesting.

Nest sites are often high above the ground and after hatching, the flightless ducklings often have to leap down to the female so that they can accompany her to a suitable feeding area. Fledging takes 8–9 weeks, after which the juveniles join the adults wintering further south in small flocks on freshwater lakes and shallow coastal areas. Here they dive to about 4m (13ft) in the water, searching for snails, shrimps, and insect larvae.

MALE COMMON GOLDENEYE

MALE SMEW

Mergellus albellus

Smew

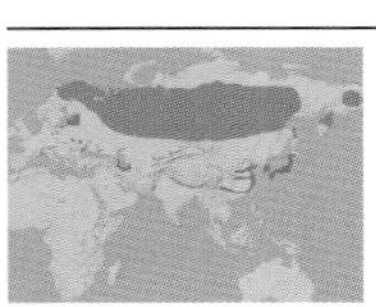

LENGTH 38–44cm (15–17½in)

WEIGHT 550–650g (20–23oz)

MIGRATION Migrant

HABITAT Breeds near forested freshwater wetlands, especially rivers; winters on lakes and estuaries

The male Smew has a striking pied plumage, which is largely white with decorative black markings and includes goggle-like eye patches. The female has a rufous head, conspicuous white cheeks, and browner plumage. The juvenile also has a rufous head. This small diving duck has a breeding habitat similar to that of the Common Goldeneye (left), but prefers well-forested, lowland river basins.

Mergus merganser

Common Goosander

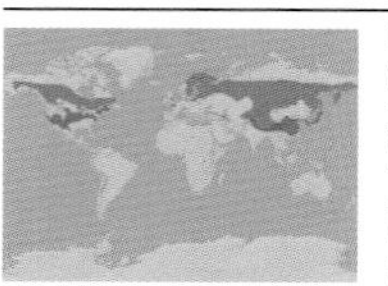

LENGTH 58–66cm (23–26in)

WEIGHT 1.2–1.7kg ($2^1/_4$–$3^1/_4$lb)

MIGRATION Migrant

HABITAT Breeds on upland rivers and lakes; winters on large bodies of water, mostly fresh water

A heavily-built duck, the Common Goosander, or Merganser, is the largest of the fish-eating goosanders. The male has a dark green head, while the female's head is reddish brown in colour. The male Common Goosander's mostly white body, dark head, and red bill sets it apart from other goosanders, making it easy to spot at a distance or in flight.

The diet of this species consists almost entirely of fish, as reflected in the structure of its long, thin beak, which is very different from the typical duck's bill. It submerges its head while searching for food and captures fish by diving. An expert diver, it uses only its webbed feet (which are towards its rear end) to propel itself forwards during pursuit.

A DUCK WITH TEETH

Goosanders are sometimes referred to as "sawbills" because of a unique adaptation that allows them to control slippery fish when hunting. The cutting edges of both the upper and lower mandibles are lined with backward-projecting spines or "teeth". This design helps give it a firm grip on its catch, ensuring that the captured fish is unable to escape on its route to the bird's stomach.

FEMALE COMMON GOOSANDER WITH CHICKS

Heteronetta atricapilla

Black-headed Duck

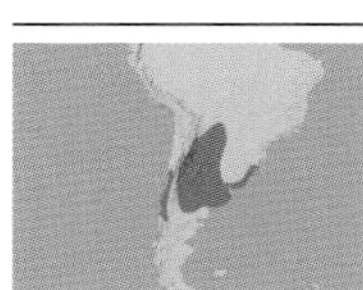

LENGTH 35–38cm (14–15in)

WEIGHT 500–575g (18–21oz)

MIGRATION Partial migrant

HABITAT Swampy freshwater habitats

Rather peculiar in appearance, with its long body coupled with short wings and tail, the small Black-headed Duck is drably coloured. The male has a black head and mantle, and paler flanks and belly, while the female is pale brown all over.

This species practises a parasitic way of rearing its young that is unique among wildfowl. Rather like a cuckoo, it lays its eggs in the nests of other wetland birds such as ducks, coots, gulls, and even birds of prey. Unlike the cuckoos (see p.274–75), however, this breeding practice does no damage to the host species. Once the chick has freed itself from the confines of the egg, it is independent and leaves the nest to fend for itself.

Oxyura jamaicensis

Ruddy Duck

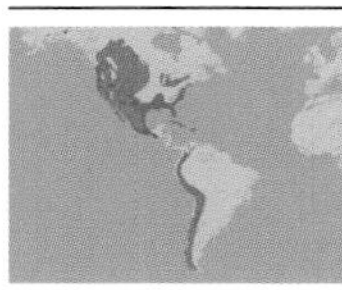

LENGTH 35–43cm (14–17in)

WEIGHT 575–625g (21–22oz)

MIGRATION Partial migrant

HABITAT Freshwater lakes with abundant marginal emergent vegetation

With its often upright tail, the Ruddy Duck is an excellent example of a small group of ducks called "stiff-tails". The male breeding display is extraordinary, being accompanied by an array of sounds that do not come from its vocal chords. These include a rattling noise produced by the open bill, "ticks" or croaks (that can be heard when the duck taps its inflated throat with its bill), and a rapid series of notes produced when it beats its wings on the water.

MALE RUDDY DUCK

Biziura lobata

Musk Duck

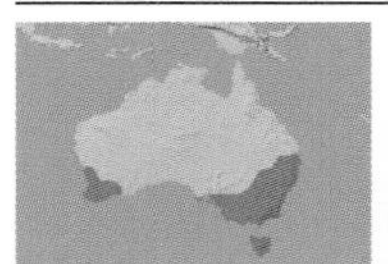

LENGTH 55–66cm ($21^1/_2$–26in)

WEIGHT 1.5–2.4kg ($3^1/_4$–$5^1/_2$lb)

MIGRATION Partial migrant

HABITAT Freshwater wetlands, estuaries, and sheltered coastal areas

The Musk Duck of Australia is a heavy and unusual-looking member of the "stiff-tail" duck group. Its large, webbed feet are situated well back on its body and the fanned tail is distinctive. The most striking feature is the huge lobe hanging beneath the bill of the mature male. Another oddity is that during the breeding season, the plumage of the male is usually oily and exudes a pungent musky odour – hence its common name. This oil can even be observed on the surface of the water during the strenuous and noisy displays as the male tries to attract a coterie of females.

MALE MUSK DUCK

PENGUINS

ORDER	Sphenisciformes
FAMILY	1
SPECIES	17

FAMILIAR WORLDWIDE AS EMBLEMS of the Antarctic, penguins are found only in the southern hemisphere. They lost the ability to fly millions of years ago, and instead use their flipper-like wings to swim. Thanks to their streamlined, bullet-shaped bodies, and unusually dense bones, they are the fastest birds underwater, and the deepest divers. Their legs are short and set far back, giving them an upright stance and characteristic "penguin waddle" when they move on land.

ANATOMY

Penguins are the most marine of all birds, typically spending much more time at sea than they do on land. All have thickset but highly streamlined bodies, with sharp bills, short tails, and large, webbed feet with well-developed claws. The classic penguin colour scheme, with a white front and a dark back, helps to camouflage them at sea, both from above and from below. Penguin wings are narrow and stiff, and move only at the shoulder joint – something that distinguishes them from the wings of all other birds. Unusually for non-flying birds, they have powerful wing muscles attached to a well developed keel. In adults, penguin plumage is short and dense, with a texture like a hard-wearing carpet. Beneath the skin, a layer of insulating fat, or blubber, helps to retain body heat, even in temperatures far below freezing.

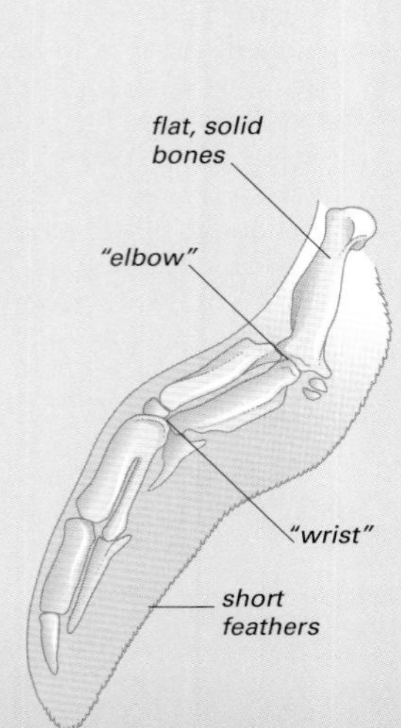

PENGUIN WING
With its stiff elbow and wrist joints, and narrow elliptical shape, a penguin's wing makes a highly effective paddle.

PENGUIN ANATOMY
With legs set close to the tail, a penguin has a vertical posture on land. Many penguin species, including this Rockhopper, have characteristic head markings or crests, with the feet the only naked parts of their bodies.

HABITAT

Although often photographed on land or ice, penguins spend much of their lives at sea. When they do come ashore, it is in order to breed or to moult. Five species breed in Antarctica, while the remainder nest on subantarctic islands, or on cold-water coasts in South America, South Africa, Australia, and New Zealand. The northernmost species is the Galapagos Penguin, which lives on the equator, at the northern limit of the cold Humboldt current. Seawater is never colder than about -2°C (28°F) because below this temperature it freezes. However, on land or on ice, penguins experience a huge range of temperatures, from -60°C (-76°F) during the winter in Antarctica, to +30°C (86°F) or more in breeding colonies on the coast of Argentina.

HUMAN IMPACT

MARINE POLLUTION

At one time, penguins were heavily exploited for their meat, skins, and oil. Today, they are protected, but still face many threats, including marine pollution and climate change. Oil spills are a problem for the Jackass Penguin, which lives close to a major shipping lane off southwest Africa.

OIL SPILL VICTIM
In 2000, thousands of Jackass Penguins became oiled after a tanker sank off Cape Town, South Africa. A rescue operation saved many of them.

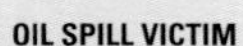

ADELIE PENGUINS ON ICE
The Adelie is one of just two species of penguin that winters in Antarctica. It breeds in enormous colonies containing hundreds of thousands of birds.

PENGUINS AT SEA

Although awkward on land, penguins are superb swimmers, using their wings as underwater flippers. When resting, they float low on the surface, with heads and tails raised, but when hunting they dive. Dives typically last less than a minute but, in the case of Emperor Penguins, they may last for 10 minutes. Emperors can dive to depths of 500m (1,650ft) although they usually hunt closer to the surface. To move at speed, many larger penguins periodically leap clear of the surface – behaviour known as porpoising. This covers their plumage with a layer of friction-reducing bubbles, allowing them to reach speeds of over 25kph (16mph). Adelie Penguins also make spectacular leaps from the water to land on ice or rocks.

SWIFT SWIMMER
Head horizontal, a King Penguin speeds through water, propelled by its wings, with webbed feet acting as rudders. Heavy bones help reduce buoyancy.

FEEDING

In the wild, penguins never feed on land – instead, all their food is caught live at sea. Their eyes work better underwater than in the air, allowing them to pursue their prey by sight. The largest penguins feed on fish and squid, while smaller ones take shrimps and krill. All penguins have spiny tongues, which help them to grip their catch. The food intake of large colonies is enormous: at the height of the breeding season, Adelie Penguins in the South Orkneys are estimated to eat 9,000 tonnes of small fish and krill a day. However, compared to other birds, penguins can go for long periods without eating. Most penguins are forced to fast when they moult, and some also fast during incubation. During this time, they live off their body fat.

DIVING FOR FOOD
Group hunting in shallow water, Galapagos Penguins burst through a shoal of fish. Despite their plump shape, penguins are agile underwater, banking and swerving as they chase their prey.

BREEDING

Penguins are highly social birds, and many species gather in large colonies to breed. These colonies tend to be at fixed sites and archaeological evidence shows that, in some cases, the same sites have been used for thousands of years. The largest colonies are formed by Adelie Penguins: one of the biggest, at Cape Adare in Eastern Antarctica, contains about a million birds. Adelies nest on rocky shores, and gather stones to make rudimentary nests. However, a number of other species nest in burrows. Penguins in the genus *Spheniscus*, such as the Magellanic and Jackass Penguins, occupy their burrows during the breeding season only, but Fairy Penguins live in theirs all year round, coming back to shore only after dark. Emperor and King Penguins make no nest at all. Instead, the single egg is incubated on a parent's feet, and kept warm by a fold of skin. The majority of penguins lay their eggs in late spring or early summer, so that their chicks are fledged and ready to go to sea before the winter begins. However, with Emperor and King Penguins, the incubation and fledging period is too long for this to work. Instead, Emperors incubate their eggs throughout the winter, while King Penguins have one of the strangest breeding cycles in the bird world. They have two egg-laying periods, and they alternate between them, producing two young every three years.

NESTING IN BURROWS
Magellanic Penguins and their relatives nest in burrows on isolated coasts. They lay two eggs, but often only one chick survives.

PENGUIN CRECHES
Seen in summer, this colony of King Penguins consists of adults, and fully grown chicks still with their brown natal down. Chicks remain in creches until they have moulted and grown adult plumage.

Aptenodytes forsteri

Emperor Penguin

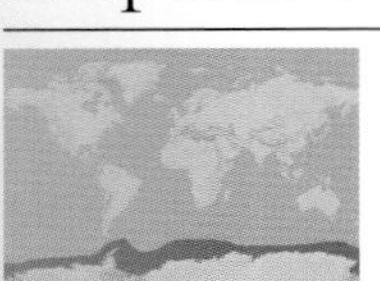

LENGTH 1.1m (3½ft)

WEIGHT 30–40kg (66–88lb)

MIGRATION Migrant

HABITAT Antarctic ice and sea

The largest penguin, the Emperor Penguin endures the harshest conditions, facing temperatures as low as -62°C (-80°F). Its head and wings are black, contrasting with its white front, its black bill has a yellow-orange streak, and there are two yellow patches on the sides of its neck.

Breeding begins in March or April, when these penguins return to their icy breeding grounds, some walking more than 150km (95 miles) from the sea. As winter closes in, the males huddle together to keep warm. During their time in the breeding colony, they do not eat, but survive on fat stored in their bodies over the summer, many losing up to half their body weight. The female lays a single egg, leaving the male to incubate it for 62–67 days while she returns to the sea to feed. He covers the egg with a fold of warm skin and rests it on his feet. On hatching, the chick is fed on fat-rich milk regurgitated by the male. When the female returns, she takes over the feeding and the male makes his way back to the sea to have his first food in nearly four months. As the ice shelf recedes and the sea becomes closer, both parents are able to feed the chick. An Emperor Penguin feeds largely on fish or krill, diving to depths of more than 500m (1,600ft) and remaining underwater for up to 20 minutes.

MALE EMPEROR PENGUINS

PAIR OF KING PENGUINS

Aptenodytes patagonicus

King Penguin

LENGTH 90cm (35in)

WEIGHT 11–13kg (24–29lb)

MIGRATION Migrant

HABITAT Subantarctic islands, free from ice; breeds on sloping beaches

Smaller than the Emperor Penguin (above), the King Penguin has a silver-grey back, black head, and bright orange ear patches. Its streamlined shape and powerful flippers enable it to pursue fish and it may dive more than 100 times a day to feed.

The species lives in large colonies, some numbering tens of thousands of pairs. It has the longest breeding cycle of any penguin. Adults rear only two chicks every three years. The single egg is incubated by both parents in turn until it hatches after about 55 days. This chick remains with its parents for over a year and chicks of very different ages can be found at the same colony.

Pygoscelis papua

Gentoo Penguin

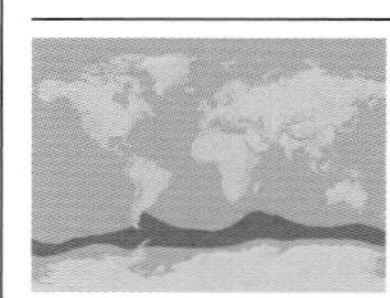

LENGTH 82cm (32in)

WEIGHT 6kg (13lb)

MIGRATION Non-migrant

HABITAT Subantarctic islands and ice-free areas on the Antarctic Peninsula

The Gentoo Penguin has a distinctive orange bill and white head patch. It has long, stiff tail feathers, which are prominent when it walks or swims. Gregarious at sea, these penguins move in groups of up to several hundred birds to catch prey and are the fastest underwater swimming penguins. They feed largely on krill, and some small fish, catching them close to the breeding colony. They live in small colonies, building circular nests of pebbles, twigs, or seaweed. The male gathers nest material, often taking it from other nests. The female lays two eggs and both parents incubate and feed the chicks. The young chicks gather with others into groups or crèches, which helps to keep them warm and protects them from predators. When an adult returns from feeding, it calls to its young, who recognize the call and reply.

Pygoscelis adeliae

Adelie Penguin

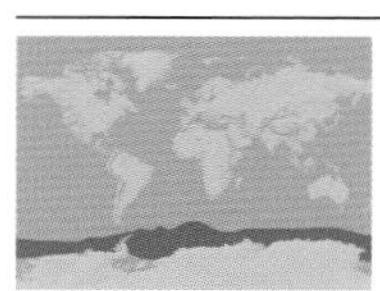

LENGTH 70cm (28in)

WEIGHT 5kg (11lb)

MIGRATION Migrant

HABITAT Ice-free Antarctic shores with sandy beaches and accessible rocky areas

The smallest of the Antarctic penguins, the Adelie Penguin has a black back and head and white-ringed eyes. When it swims fast, it breaks the water surface and shoots through the air to dive and then surface again, rather like a porpoise. It is among the most southerly breeding of bird species. After the breeding season, it leaves its colony and disperses northwards, up to 600km (375 miles) away, returning in spring. The noisy colonies are filled with the birds' raucous calls. The parents incubate their two eggs in shifts of 11–17 days so that one of them is free to feed.

JUMPING ONTO ICE

Adelie Penguins frequently jump onto ice floes in groups. They swim very fast up to the edge of the floe and leave the water in a leap that can take them about 1m (3¼ft) into the air, making them look as if they are flying.

GROUP OF ADELIE PENGUINS

ADULT ROCKHOPPER PENGUIN

Eudyptes chrysocome

Rockhopper Penguin

LENGTH 50cm (19½in)

WEIGHT 2.5kg (5½lb)

MIGRATION Migrant

HABITAT Caves and crevices; breeds on rocky slopes among clumps of tussock grass

RED LIST CATEGORY Vulnerable

This penguin has a black and yellow crest, an orange bill, and pink, webbed feet. The Rockhopper Penguin lives up to its name, arriving at its breeding slopes by jumping from rock to rock, often reaching the top of very high cliffs. The noisy breeding colonies are often close to other seabirds and the unoccupied nests of albatrosses or cormorants are sometimes used. The female lays two eggs.

Eudyptes chrysolophus

Macaroni Penguin

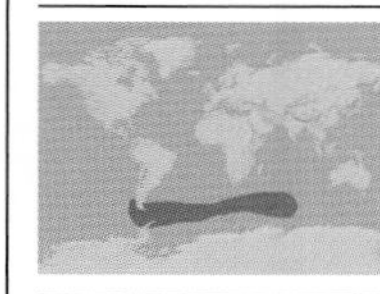

LENGTH 71cm (28in)

WEIGHT 4.5kg (10lb)

MIGRATION Migrant

HABITAT Subantarctic islands with rocky slopes and beaches

RED LIST CATEGORY Vulnerable

Distinguished by its crest of yellow plumes and its large, orange-brown bill, the Macaroni Penguin is the world's most common penguin, with at least nine million pairs, but in the last 36 years its population has reduced by at least 30 per cent. It breeds in large colonies, and a few small groups have been established on the Antarctic Peninsula, usually within colonies of other penguin species. Larger than its relative, the Rockhopper Penguin (left), the Macaroni Penguin walks rather than hops. The female lays two eggs, but usually only the larger second one hatches successfully. Adults take turns in looking after the eggs or chicks in shifts.

ADULT MACARONI PENGUIN

GENTOO PENGUINS AT THE WATER'S EDGE

Megadyptes antipodes

Yellow-eyed Penguin

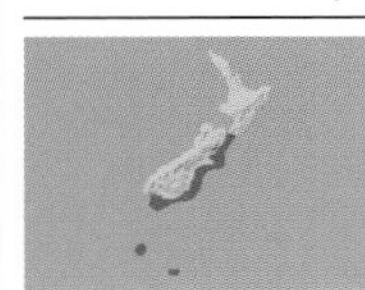

LENGTH 66cm (26in)

WEIGHT 5.5kg (12lb)

MIGRATION Non-migrant

HABITAT Dunes and coastal forests

RED LIST CATEGORY Endangered

Named for its bright yellow eyes, this penguin has a yellow band stretching from its eyes to the back of its head and a stout reddish purple bill. The world's rarest penguin, numbering as few as 5,000 birds, it is found only in New Zealand. Its population has been declining due to habitat loss and natural predators. It is the most retiring of the penguins, each pair nesting well away from other birds. Unlike some other northern penguins, it does not breed in burrows, but uses the cover of forests and other dense vegetation to keep out of the sun. Young females only lay one egg, while older birds lay two.

ADULT YELLOW-EYED PENGUIN

KING PENGUIN
Penguins move with far more ease and grace in water than on land. Diving in search of fish and squid, King Penguins occasionally reach depths of 200m (650ft).

Eudyptula minor

Fairy Penguin

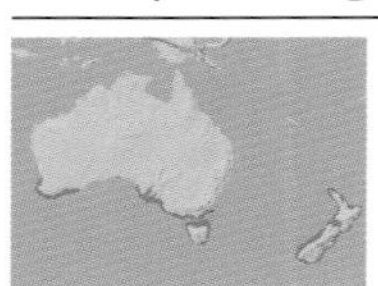

LENGTH 40–45cm (15½–17½in)

WEIGHT 0.5–2kg (1–4½lb)

MIGRATION Non-migrant

HABITAT Coasts and offshore islands; breeds in burrows in dunes and vegetated slopes

The smallest of the penguins, the Fairy Penguin has dark blue-grey upperparts and white underparts. It is further distinguished in being the only penguin that can lay two clutches of eggs a year, incubating them for just over a month. The chicks remain in their nest burrows for about two months, with both adults bringing food. When the chicks are almost ready to fledge, the adults visit the burrow only at night. The young do not breed until they are two years old, and like adults, they remain in close proximity to the sea.

The Fairy Penguin is found on the southern coast of Australia, New Zealand, and the Chatham Islands. Its population appears to be stable, although known threats include human disturbances and predation by introduced animals.

Spheniscus demersus

Jackass Penguin

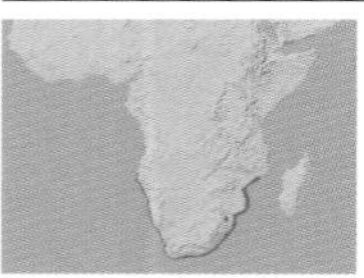

LENGTH 60–70cm (23½–28in)

WEIGHT 2.1–3.7kg (4½–7¾)

MIGRATION Non-migrant

HABITAT Onshore islands; breeds colonially in burrows on rocky ground on the African mainland and islands

RED LIST CATEGORY Vulnerable

A medium-sized penguin, the Jackass, or African, Penguin has a patch of bare pink skin in front of and around the eye, all-black upperparts, and a narrow black band across the otherwise white underside. The male and female have similar plumage, but the female is smaller with a shorter bill. This is the only species of penguin to breed in Africa. In early August, the bird comes ashore to nest in burrows that are not densely packed like those of many Antarctic penguins, but lie at some distance from one another. Most females lay two eggs, which are incubated by both parents, and hatch in about 5 or 6 weeks. The adults feed the young, which take 2–4 months to fledge, bringing anchovies and other schooling fish to the burrow. As a result of food shortages, oil spillages, and environmental changes, their numbers have declined significantly, though some colonies are increasing.

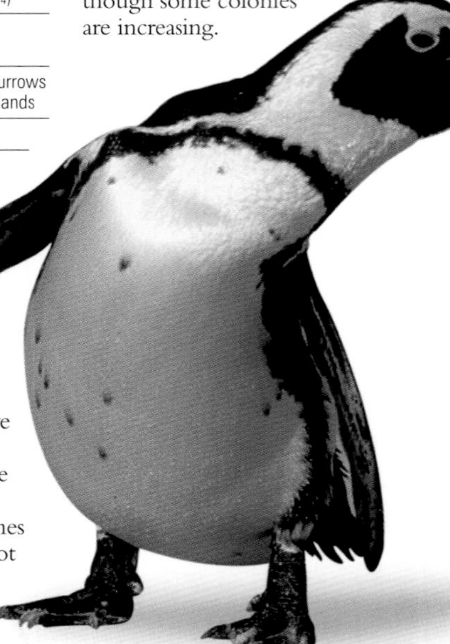

ADULT JACKASS PENGUIN

GREAT SITES

BOULDERS BEACH

Initially chosen by just a single pair of Jackass Penguins, the Boulders Beach penguin colony (one of only two in mainland South Africa), near the Cape of Good Hope, South Africa, has grown to include over 900 pairs. It is a recent phenomenon, as these penguins did not nest in the area before 1985. The birds suffer no predation as they nest close to the suburban dwellings of Simon's Town and there is no large-scale commercial fishing in the area.

Spheniscus magellanicus

Magellanic Penguin

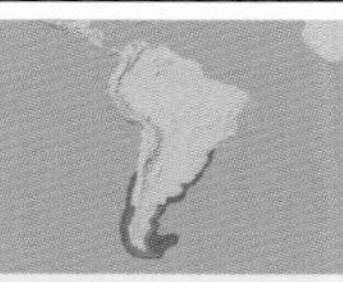

LENGTH 70cm (28in)

WEIGHT 2.3–8kg (5½–18lb)

MIGRATION Partial migrant

HABITAT Cold, temperate water; breeds on the mainland or islands, in burrows on slopes

The Magellanic Penguin has pink skin around the eye that reaches down to the bill and two dark breast-bands. It has a black to brown back and a white chest with black spots. The Magellanic Penguin principally feeds on small crustaceans and fish, which are caught underwater. Since it takes in sea water as well, along with its prey, it has a salt-excreting gland which has evolved to filter out the salt. Appearing ungainly and comical on land, in the water it is an extremely capable swimmer and can swim for long distances. It uses its wings like paddles to propel itself.

Like all penguins, it is gregarious and monogamous. Breeding commences in early spring, when adults come to the shore to nest in loose colonies. Although the species has not (yet) been recorded in Africa, vagrants have reached as far as Australia. Some birds have been known to migrate as far north as Brazil in winter.

GROUP OF ADULTS

Spheniscus mendiculus

Galapagos Penguin

LENGTH 53cm (21in)

WEIGHT 1.7–2.1kg (3¼–4½lb)

MIGRATION Non-migrant

HABITAT Tropical water; breeds in loose colonies in burrows and crevices on islands

RED LIST CATEGORY Endangered

A thin white stripe from the eye to the chin and a black band around its chest distinguish the Galapagos Penguin from other penguins. The only one of the world's penguins to breed in the tropics, the Galapagos Penguin defies the common perception of penguins as creatures of snow and ice. It is not migratory and stays in coastal water, feeding on small tropical fish, such as sardines and crustaceans.

ADULT GALAPAGOS PENGUIN

DIVERS

ORDER	Gaviiformes
FAMILY	1
SPECIES	5

RENOWNED FOR THEIR FAR-CARRYING CRIES, this is a small order of fish-eating birds of the northern hemisphere. They breed in remote lakes scattered across the northern forests and Arctic tundra. They have sleek, streamlined bodies, with dagger-like bills and, during the breeding season, all but one species have striking black and white markings across their backs. These are agile on and in water, and fly well, despite having the smallest wing to weight ratio of any flying bird. With feet set far back towards their tails, they are ungainly on land.

HEAD UP
In its breeding plumage, a Black-throated Diver shows the striking markings typical of this group of birds. Males and females look identical.

ANATOMY

Even from a distance, divers are easy to recognize, as they have a characteristically low profile in the water, and often hold their bills with an upward slant. They have long bodies with thick necks, and they propel themselves with their large webbed feet. These are positioned almost at the end of the body, like propellers on a ship's stern. Uniquely among birds, only their ankles and feet protrude from the body, which gives them a slow, shuffling gait on land. These birds can adjust their buoyancy by altering the amount of air trapped in their plumage. They also have heavy bones, which makes it easier for them to dive.

BEHAVIOUR

Divers are migratory, breeding on freshwater and wintering on coasts. They feed mainly on fish, and dive for several minutes at a time to depths of 50m (160ft) or more. In winter, they feed in groups, close to the shore, but they become highly territorial during the breeding season, forming long-lasting monogamous pairs.

Pairs may return to the same lake each year. After elaborate courtship rituals, they nest by the water's edge, often on small islands where they are more secure. Their young are well developed on hatching, and immediately take to the water, where the parents feed them for several weeks.

PARENTAL PROTECTION
A young Red-throated Diver swims alongside a parent. The young peck at insects and other animals near the surface, but it takes many weeks to develop diving skills.

Gavia arctica

Black-throated Diver

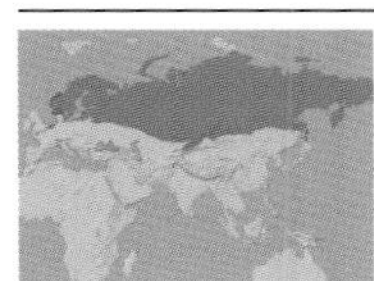

LENGTH 63–75cm (25–30in)
WEIGHT 2.5–3.5kg (5½–7¾lb)
MIGRATION Non-migrant

HABITAT Breeds on islands in freshwater lakes; winters at sea

The summer plumage of the Black-throated Diver (or Loon) is distinguished by its black throat and grey head. It has delicate white spotting on the back and inner wings and narrow black and white vertical stripes on the neck. It lacks the distinctive dark collar of the breeding-plumaged Great Northern Diver (right). In winter, the bird is principally grey above and white below. It utters desolate but evocative cries during the spring courtship period, shortly after returning to its breeding lake, but is silent for the rest of the year. It mainly feeds on fish, such as herring, and can remain submerged for a long time, reappearing some distance from where it initially dived. Its nest is a low mound of aquatic vegetation next to the water.

ADULT IN SUMMER PLUMAGE

ADULT IN BREEDING PLUMAGE

Gavia stellata

Red-throated Diver

LENGTH 55–67cm (21½–26in)
WEIGHT 1.5kg (3¼lb)
MIGRATION Migrant

HABITAT Breeds on small lakes, even pools, in tundra regions; winters at sea

This is one of the most northerly of all aquatic birds. The smallest of its family, the Red-throated Diver (or Loon) has a distinctive breeding plumage, with a grey head, red throat, and white underparts. In winter, it moults to a dowdy grey and white garb. It has red eyes, and its bill is narrower than those of other divers and is usually tilted slightly upwards. It is a fish-eater, diving to 7.5m (25ft) to catch its prey.

Gavia immer

Great Northern Diver

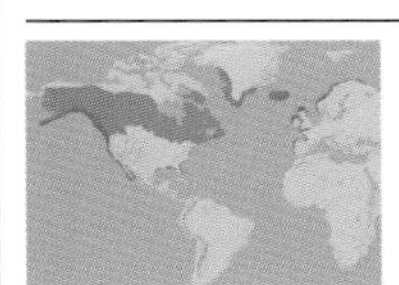

LENGTH 73–88cm (29–35in)
WEIGHT 4.5–5.5kg (10–12lb)
MIGRATION Migrant

HABITAT Breeds on islands in deep lakes and coastal bays within treeless tundra; winters at sea

One of the largest divers, the Great Northern Diver is a large, heavy-billed bird, much heavier than the Black-throated and Red-throated Divers (left), which helps distinguish the species in their grey winter plumage, when all three divers look similar. When breeding, the adult has a black head, white underparts, and black and white horizontal patterns on its mantle. The species arrives on the breeding grounds from the sea already in pairs, and little courtship or display is observed near the nest site.

BREEDING ADULT

ALBATROSSES AND PETRELS

ORDER	Procellariiformes
FAMILY	4
SPECIES	107

OFTEN FOUND FAR OUT TO SEA, and capable of staying on the wing for months at a time, albatrosses and their relatives are the most far-roaming of the world's seabirds. The largest albatrosses have the biggest wingspans of all birds, but this order also includes shearwaters and storm petrels, some of which are not much bigger than sparrows. A key feature that unites all these birds is their large, tubular, external nostrils – a sign of their unusually good sense of smell. Collectively known as "tubenoses", they typically pluck their food from the surface of the water, travelling enormous distances to feed and to breed.

TUBENOSES
This Southern Giant Petrel clearly shows the long tubular nostrils that are typical of albatrosses and their ocean-wandering relatives.

ANATOMY

Albatrosses are unmistakable birds with large bills and long narrow wings. Instead of beating their wings, they hold them out stiffly and fly by dynamic soaring – a form of flight that exploits strong winds blowing close to the surface of the sea. Other members of this group – particularly shearwaters and petrels – are much smaller, but have the same stiff-winged flight. Completely in their element at sea, tubenoses are often clumsy once they land. Albatrosses and large petrels stand upright on webbed feet, but shearwaters and storm petrels cannot raise their ankles off the ground. As a result, they shuffle rather than walk. This makes them vulnerable to predators, but they can defend themselves by ejecting a strong-smelling stomach oil, which can travel 1m (3ft) or more. As well as having long nostrils, tubenoses have sharp, hook-tipped bills – an adaptation that helps them to snatch up slippery food. In anatomy and behaviour, diving petrels differ from the rest of the group. They have smaller wings and use them to swim underwater, sometimes flying straight through the waves.

WIDESPREAD WINGS
Often mistaken for gulls, Northern Fulmars fly with wings held out stiffly – a characteristic shared by other tubenoses. Unlike gulls, they rarely wander inland.

BEHAVIOUR

Most tubenoses feed at sea, guided by their excellent sense of smell. Their diet includes fish, jellyfish, and small crustaceans, but albatrosses and fulmars are also dedicated ship-followers, scavenging waste that is thrown overboard. This scavenging lifestyle is even more marked in giant petrels, which feed on the dead remains of marine mammals, as well as preying on other seabirds and their chicks. Storm petrels also follow ships, but their method of feeding is unique: instead of snatching food while in flight, they patter over the sea's surface with their feet, pecking while fluttering their wings. All tubenosed birds are great travellers, often dispersing thousands of kilometres from their nesting sites after breeding. Some species – including the Wandering Albatross – roam over vast areas of the ocean, wherever favourable winds and food happen to coincide. Albatrosses take many years to become adult and, before they land to breed, those that live in the Southern Ocean may circle the Earth several times. By contrast, many smaller tubenoses have more clear-cut annual migration routes. Manx Shearwaters breed in the North Atlantic, but spend the winter as far south as the seas off Argentina. The Short-tailed Shearwater flies even farther, leaving its breeding grounds near Tasmania and circling the entire North Pacific before heading home – a journey of at least 32,000km (20,000 miles).

SURFACE FEEDING
An Elliot's Storm Petrel appears to walk on the water as it feeds, although it is actually supported by the flutter of its wings.

BREEDING

Tubenoses are long-lived, and reproduce more slowly than other seabirds of their size. They breed in colonies on remote cliffs and islands and typically lay a single egg a year, although Wandering Albatrosses breed only one year in two. Albatrosses and fulmars nest in the open, but many of the smaller tubenoses nest in burrows, often in vast numbers, and do not come ashore until after dark. Incoming birds find their burrows by listening for their partners' calls, and the air is filled with a bizarre chorus from underground. Tubenose chicks are usually fed by both parents, and often become heavier than the adults on their diet of oily fish. In many species, the adults finally abandon the chick, leaving it to make its own way to the sea.

REUNITED
A Black-browed Albatross tends a solitary chick. The young may be left for days at a time while parents search the Southern Ocean for food.

Phoebetria fusca

Sooty Albatross

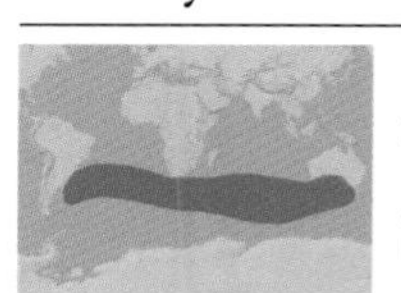

LENGTH 84–89cm (33–35in)

WEIGHT 1.8–3kg (4½–6½lb)

MIGRATION Migrant

HABITAT Open ocean or sea; breeds only on cliffs and slopes on remote islands

Evenly dark brown in colour, the plumage of the Sooty Albatross is relieved only by white shafts at the tips of the wings. It has long, broad wings, a long, diamond-shaped tail, and grey feet. It has more solitary nesting habits than other members of its family. As with most albatrosses, the male and female form a life-long bond, and a pair breeds every two years. In the breeding season, a cone-shaped nest is made and a single egg is laid. Both the male and female undertake incubation and bring food for the young. This species now faces the twin threats of longline fisheries and introduced predators.

Thalassarche melanophrys

Black-browed Albatross

LENGTH 80–96cm (31–38in)

WEIGHT 2.9–4.6kg (6½–10lb)

MIGRATION Migrant

HABITAT Open ocean or sea; breeds only on bare rocky areas and slopes on islands

RED LIST CATEGORY Endangered

The Black-browed Albatross takes its name from the tiny dusky mark running through the eye. It is mostly white with grey highlights. It has yellowish orange webbed feet and an orange bill, tipped darker orange. It flies for hours over the sea, looking for fish, krill, cephalopods, salps, and jellyfish. Unlike many albatrosses, it breeds annually. It nests on terraces on top of coastal cliffs or steep slopes up to 300m (985m) above sea level. Once, one of the most common and widespread of the smaller species of albatrosses (collectively known as mollymawks), this species has declined dramatically in recent years due to overfishing and longline fisheries.

ADULT BLACK-BROWED ALBATROSS

Diomedea immutabilis

Laysan Albatross

LENGTH 81cm (32in)

WEIGHT 2.4–3.8kg (5½–8¾lb)

MIGRATION Migrant

HABITAT Open ocean or sea; breeds only on low coral or sandy islands

RED LIST CATEGORY Vulnerable

An albatross that is almost entirely restricted to the Hawaiian islands during its breeding season, the Laysan Albatross was discovered as recently as the 1890s. Locally known as a "gooney" in Hawaii, it has a white head, neck, and underparts, while its mantle and upperwings are black. It feeds mainly on squid.

A monogamous bird, the Laysan Albatross breeds in October, when it makes a nest of grass and shrubbery piled into a large mound; only a single egg is laid. The Laysan Albatross faces various threats, including rats on land and Tiger Sharks that feed on fledglings in its breeding lagoons.

ADULT LAYSAN ALBATROSS

Diomedea epomophora

Royal Albatross

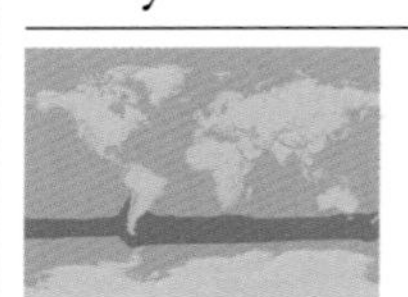

LENGTH 1–1.2m (3¼–4ft)

WEIGHT 6.5–10kg (14–22lb)

MIGRATION Migrant

HABITAT Open ocean or sea; breeds on islands and mainland

RED LIST CATEGORY Vulnerable

Mainly white in colour, with black wing-tips, the magnificent Royal Albatross breeds every two years on islands in the New Zealand subantarctic region, with half the population returning to the colony in any given year. When not breeding, these birds fly over the sea as far afield as the south Atlantic and southern Chile. Until recently, Royal Albatrosses were considered as a single species, but some ornithologists now treat them as two: the northern and southern species.

ADULTS IN COURTSHIP DISPLAY

Diomedea exulans

Wandering Albatross

LENGTH 1.1–1.4m (3½–4½ft)

WEIGHT 6.5–11.5kg (14–25lb)

MIGRATION Migrant

HABITAT Open ocean or sea; breeds only on bare ground in valleys and plains on islands

RED LIST CATEGORY Vulnerable

The majestic Wandering Albatross appears equally at home in gigantic seas and fierce storms and in calm conditions. The adult male is mostly white, with black-tipped wings and tail, and a pink bill and feet. The female is slightly browner. The juvenile is chocolate-brown with a white face mask and underwing, but it becomes whiter with age. Pairs mate for life and breed every two years. The nest is a mound of mud and vegetation, and is placed on an exposed ridge near the sea. Capable of flying huge distances in search of food for its young, the Wandering Albatross is the largest flying bird in the world, with a wingspan stretching to 3m (9¾ft).

It feeds mainly on the surface of water, primarily on squid. It also congregates in large numbers to follow trawlers and snatch scraps in their wake.

ADULT WANDERING ALBATROSS

HUMAN IMPACT

THREAT FROM LONGLINE FISHING

Long lines with hundreds of baited hooks are used by fisheries to catch tuna and Patagonian toothfish. These also attract large numbers of seabirds, including albatrosses, which drown after becoming ensnared on the hooks. The Wandering Albatross is facing extinction because of this method of fishing.

GREAT SITES

SOUTH GEORGIA

LOCATION South Atlantic Ocean, approximately 1,390km (860 miles) southeast of the Falkland Islands.

One of the bleakest and most isolated wildernesses on Earth, this small and mountainous group of islands lies where the south Atlantic meets the often stormy Southern Ocean. The archipelago is a haven for an extraordinary density of wildlife, including around 30 million breeding birds. South Georgia attracts such magnificent gatherings of seabirds for two reasons. First, there are plenty of safe nesting sites: wide beaches, sea cliffs, steep slopes covered with hummocks of coarse tussac grass, and rocky offshore islets. Second, the archipelago is surrounded by cold waters rich in fish, krill (tiny crustaceans), and other forms of marine life, which provide an abundant supply of food for the adult birds and their chicks.

WHAT TO SPOT

ANTARCTIC TERN
Sterna vittata
(see p.238)

BLACK-BROWED ALBATROSS
Thalassarche melanophris
(see p.145)

SUBANTARCTIC SKUA
Stercorarius antarcticus

SOUTHERN GIANT PETREL
Macronectes giganteus
(see p.148)

BIRD-RICH WILDERNESS

South Georgia is largely uninhabited. The island's only visitors are the crews of passing fishing vessels and the tourists who arrive by sea, mostly between December and March during the southern summer, when the seabird breeding season is well under way.

Probably the most impressive seabird seen at South Georgia is the Wandering Albatross, which has the largest wingspan of any bird. Up to 4,000 pairs nest here – 15 per cent of the world population. There are also 100,000 breeding pairs of Black-browed Albatrosses and 80,000 pairs of Grey-headed Albatrosses. Many of these species of albatross are in decline, so South Georgia is vitally important to their conservation.

A wide variety of smaller "tubenoses" breed on South Georgia, including petrels, storm petrels, diving petrels, and prions. Cape Petrels nest on high rock ledges on the coast. Antarctic Terns make their nesting scrapes among rocks or on beaches. South Georgia is also home to vast colonies of penguins, particularly King, Macaroni, and Gentoo Penguins. A single hillside on Bird Island (off the main island of South Georgia) is the breeding ground for 35,000 of the archipelago's two million pairs of Macaroni Penguins.

Only few land birds can survive on South Georgia's rugged terrain. They include Yellow-billed Pintail and the island's only endemic species – the South Georgia Pipit, which is under threat from introduced rats.

CLIFF-TOP NURSERY
The precipitous, tussac-grass-covered sections of coastline on South Georgia and neighbouring Bird Island provide popular nest sites for the Grey-headed Albatross.

Macronectes giganteus

Southern Giant Petrel

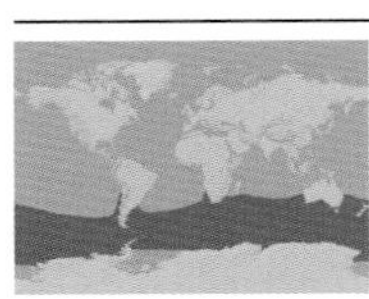

LENGTH 85–100cm (33–39in)

WEIGHT 3.8–5kg (8¾–11lb)

MIGRATION Migrant

HABITAT Open ocean and sea; breeds on exposed beaches, gravel areas, and tussock grass

RED LIST CATEGORY Vulnerable

The Southern Giant Petrel occurs in two forms: one is largely dark brown with a white head and neck, and the other, which is less common, is completely white, except for a few scattered dark feathers. Large and aggressive, this bird is a scavenger, detecting food by smell, and feeding on penguin and seal carcasses. It also kills live birds and often gathers near trawlers and sewage outfalls. Like many albatrosses, its decline may be linked to longline fishing.

ADULT SOUTHERN GIANT PETREL

Thalassoica antarctica

Antarctic Petrel

LENGTH 40–46cm (15½–18in)

WEIGHT 675g (24oz)

MIGRATION Migrant

HABITAT Open ocean and sea; breeds on snow-free surfaces on steep slopes and cliffs

The beautiful white and grey-brown Antarctic Petrel is one of the few birds restricted to the Antarctic continent in the breeding season. Its colonies, inhospitable to others, provide one of its main safeguards. It is highly gregarious, both at sea and on land, sometimes congregating in large numbers around trawlers and feeding with whales and dolphins.

ADULT BIRD

NORTHERN FULMARS FEEDING

Fulmarus glacialis

Northern Fulmar

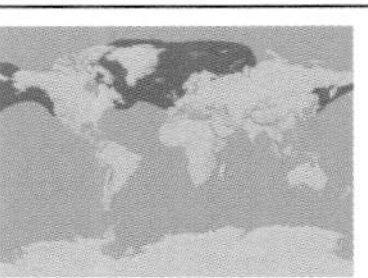

LENGTH 43–52cm (17–20½in)

WEIGHT 575–650g (21–23oz)

MIGRATION Migrant

HABITAT Open ocean and sea; breeds in burrows and cliff ledges, on headlands, islands, and buildings

The Northern Fulmar is distinguished by its tubular bill, with its large, raised nasal tubes, its thick neck, and a large head. There are two colour forms: the more southerly light-coloured form has a yellowish white head and breast, and grey back and wings. In the north of the range, the species has blue upperparts.

It feeds mainly on fish offal from trawlers – large numbers follow fishing fleets – as well as small fish, jellyfish, and squid. Unlike many tubenose seabirds, this bird does not make long migrations and is among the first species to return to its breeding colony. The Northern Fulmar generally prefers flatter ground for its nest site than many other species in this family.

This species is a conservation success story, in that it has colonized new sites, even nesting in buildings, and the population is increasing.

Pagodroma nivea

Snow Petrel

LENGTH 30–40cm (12–15½in)

WEIGHT 200–600g (7–21oz)

MIGRATION Migrant

HABITAT Open ocean and sea; breeds on cliffs and slopes, in crevices and under boulders

Popularly known as the "angel of Antarctica" for its beauty, the Snow Petrel has pure white plumage and contrasting black eyes and bill. It feeds mainly on krill, staying close to the sea to search for food. Often seen in flocks on icebergs, it ranges north in the Southern Ocean outside the breeding season and is partly nocturnal. An unusual habit is that the young of the Snow Petrel do not return to breed in their original colony.

NESTING IN ANTARCTICA

Breeding farther from the sea than any other bird in Antarctica, up to 300km (185 miles) inland, the Snow Petrel arrives at its nesting colony from October onwards and lays a single egg, which is incubated for about 50 days. However, breeding is affected by snowfall. These birds are unable to breed if their nest-sites are frozen.

ADULT SNOW PETREL

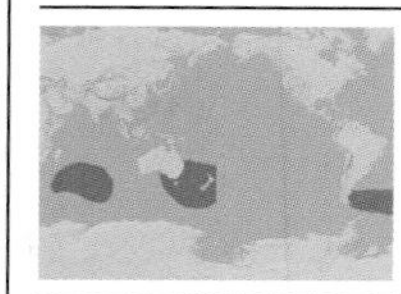

Pachyptila turtur

Fairy Prion

LENGTH 23–28cm (9–11in)

WEIGHT 90–175g (3¼–6oz)

MIGRATION Migrant

HABITAT Open ocean and sea; breeds only in rocky crevices and burrows on islands

The six to seven species of prion are all found in the Southern Ocean, but are rarely identifiable at sea. The Fairy Prion is small, with a short bill, a grey crown, an indistinct face pattern, and a broad tail-band. It has richer blue upperparts than most other prions. Like all prions, it is gregarious both on land and at sea, and is highly colonial. It only returns to its colony at night and is very vocal. The Fairy Prion feeds mainly on small crustaceans and small fish, which it catches by patting the water with its feet and then seizing the prey with its bill. It usually feeds at night.

FAIRY PRION PATTING THE WATER

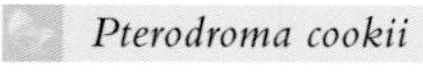

Pterodroma cookii

Cook's Petrel

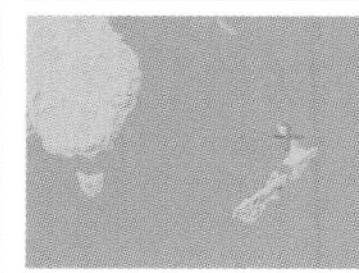

LENGTH 25–30cm (10–12in)

WEIGHT 150–200g (5–7oz)

MIGRATION Migrant

HABITAT Open ocean and sea; breeds only in burrows on forested islands

RED LIST CATEGORY Endangered

One of several similar-looking species, Cook's Petrel is consequently hard to identify. Relatively small in size with an acrobatic flight, it is one of the so-called "gadfly" petrels. It has a thin bill, a pale grey crown, white underparts, and pale grey upperparts. It is a solitary species at sea, but forms large colonies on shore. Cook's Petrel is also one of the rarest seabirds, its breeding grounds being confined to a few small islands off the south and north ends of New Zealand.

ADULT COOK'S PETREL

Pachyptila desolata

Antarctic Prion

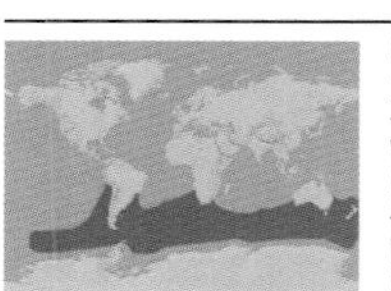

LENGTH 25–27cm (10–10½in)

WEIGHT 95–225g (3⅜–8oz)

MIGRATION Migrant

HABITAT Open ocean and sea; breeding only in burrows on islands

One of the rarest of the prions, with a population estimated at fewer than 100,000 pairs, the Antarctic Prion is under threat from predators, such as rats, cats, and even rabbits, and large-scale harvesting of krill, its main food. The species has blue-grey upperparts, white underparts, and black markings on its wings and tail. The adult nests in burrows, which it excavates itself and the single egg is incubated by both the male and female.

ADULT ANTARCTIC PRION

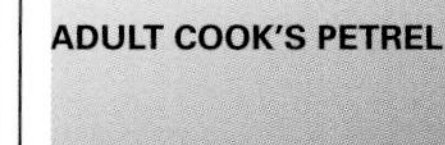

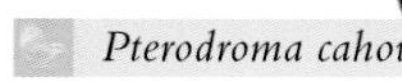

Pterodroma cahow

Cahow

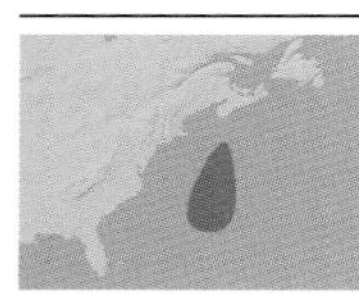

LENGTH 38cm (15in)

WEIGHT 250g (9oz)

MIGRATION Migrant

HABITAT Open ocean and sea; breeds in burrows on islets

RED LIST CATEGORY Endangered

One of the "gadfly" petrels (named after their remarkably acrobatic flight), the Cahow, or Bermuda Petrel, was feared extinct for over 300 years, prior to its rediscovery in 1935. The world population currently numbers about 200 birds. This continues to increase slowly on Bermuda's Nonsuch Island due to a strong local protection scheme that closely monitors the birds' breeding success. The Cahow has a dark head, mostly greyish brown upperparts and white underparts, and a pale band at the base of the tail.

Daption capense

Cape Petrel

LENGTH 35–42cm (14–16½in)

WEIGHT 425–450g (15–16oz)

MIGRATION Migrant

HABITAT Open sea and ocean; breeds on cliff ledges and rocky and gravel areas on islands and mainland

Also known as the Cape Pigeon, the Cape Petrel has a largely black head, boldly patterned black and white upperparts, a bright white belly, and a white tail marked with black speckles and a black band. The Cape Petrel often follows ships and is regularly drawn to feeding flocks of other seabirds that gather at trawlers. It also hunts crustaceans and small fish along with whales and dolphins, and will even feed on mammal carcasses. The birds are apparently reliant on smell to locate food. This petrel nests in colonies and mainly breeds in Antarctica, but during the rest of the year may occur almost as far north as the equator.

ADULT CAPE PETREL

Calonectris diomedea

Cory's Shearwater

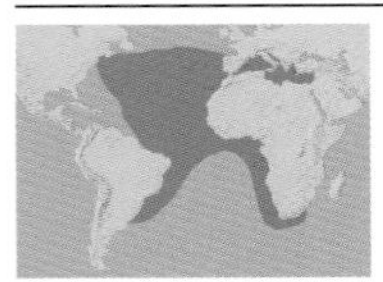

LENGTH 45–56cm (17½–22in)

WEIGHT 600–1,000g (21–36oz)

MIGRATION Migrant

HABITAT Open sea and ocean; breeds in burrows or crevices, usually on islands

Cory's Shearwater has a large, pale yellow bill and brown upperparts that blend with its white underparts. It flies with long glides, with the wings angled back, and skims the surface of the ocean with slow wingbeats. A gregarious species, Cory's Shearwaters gather in large flocks, which number in the hundreds or thousands, to feed on fish, large squid, and crustaceans from the water surface. They breed in dense colonies in nest burrows.

ADULT CORY'S SHEARWATER

Puffinus griseus

Sooty Shearwater

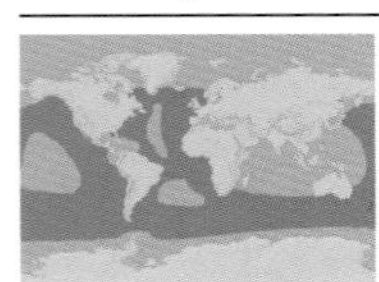

LENGTH 40–46cm (15½–18in)

WEIGHT 650–950g (23–34oz)

MIGRATION Migrant

HABITAT Open sea and ocean; breeds in self-excavated burrows on islands and the mainland

With a population of over 20 million pairs worldwide, the Sooty Shearwater is one of the most numerous and gregarious of the tubenose petrels. It is stocky and short-necked, with dark brown plumage. It has long, slender, dark wings with silvery grey underwing feathers (some may have a white underwing lining). Its colonies are tightly packed, visited only at night to avoid predators, and characterized by a cacophony of sound at the height of the breeding season. It is highly social, both at sea (when feeding or on migration) and on land. Both adults and the young learn to distinguish calls in order to locate one another in the dark.

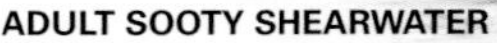

ADULT SOOTY SHEARWATER

Like most petrels, the Sooty Shearwater is not territorial, except in the immediate vicinity of its burrow. The nest burrow is at least partially concealed by vegetation and sparsely lined. A single egg is laid, which is not replaced if taken by a predator, and both male and female share incubation and feeding the young. The chick takes 130–160 days to fledge.

Puffinus tenuirostris

Short-tailed Shearwater

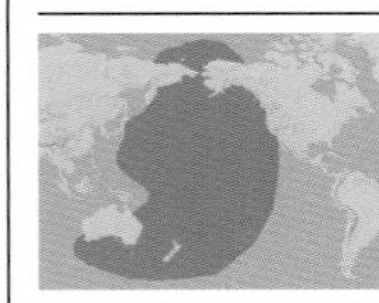

LENGTH 40–45cm (15½–17½in)

WEIGHT 500–800g (18–29oz)

MIGRATION Migrant

HABITAT Open sea and ocean; breeds in self-excavated burrows in vegetated areas on islands

This large, dark-toned shearwater is similar to the Sooty Shearwater (above), but has a different wing pattern, with flecks of white in the centre of the underwing. A sociable species, it gathers in flocks to feed on krill, small fish, and squid and breeds in large, densely packed colonies. Like most tubenoses, it lays just one egg, which is incubated by both sexes.

ADULT SHORT-TAILED SHEARWATER

ADULT MANX SHEARWATER

Puffinus puffinus

Manx Shearwater

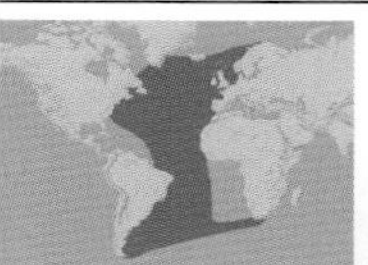

LENGTH 30–35cm (12–14in)

WEIGHT 425–500g (15–18oz)

MIGRATION Migrant

HABITAT Open sea and ocean; breeds in burrows and under rocks on islands

The Manx Shearwater can be identified by its sooty-black upperparts, with white underparts, including the undertail feathers. The remarkable navigational ability of this species was proved by experiments in the 1950s on its ability to find its way. It is well known for its long-distance migrations, which can take even the young birds, fresh out of the nesting burrow, from their colonies in the north Atlantic to winter off the coasts of southern South America. A young Manx Shearwater, like a great many seabirds, is generally faithful to the colony in which it is born, but does not necessarily return to breed until it is seven years old. Like most tubenoses, Manx Shearwaters have relatively low breeding yields, but this is countered by adult longevity.

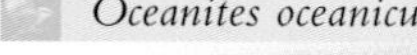

Oceanites oceanicus

Wilson's Storm Petrel

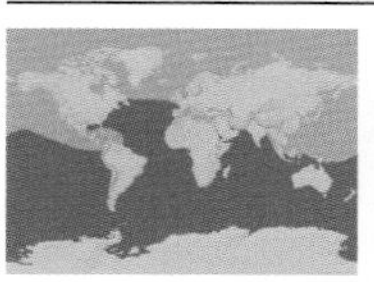

LENGTH 15–19cm (6–$7^{1}/_{2}$in)

WEIGHT 30–50g ($1^{1}/_{16}$–$1^{3}/_{4}$oz)

MIGRATION Migrant

HABITAT Open sea and ocean; nests in crevices and burrows on islands

Named after the famous Antarctic explorer and naturalist Edward Wilson, this tiny bird performs one of the longest migrations of all the petrels. It has short, rounded wings, a large white U-shaped rump patch, and a short squared tail. It nests at subantarctic and Antarctic latitudes and moves north in the post-breeding season as far as the north Atlantic and Pacific. This species breeds from November to February.

ADULT WILSON'S STORM PETREL

Hydrobates pelagicus

European Storm Petrel

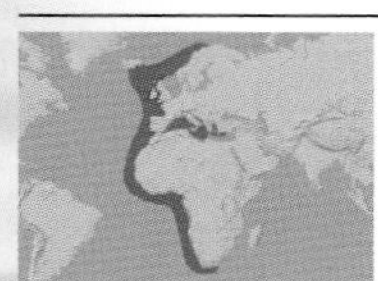

LENGTH 15cm (6in)

WEIGHT 20–35g ($^{11}/_{16}$–$1^{1}/_{4}$oz)

MIGRATION Migrant

HABITAT Open sea and ocean; breeds in burrows, crevices, and even stone walls, mainly on islands

This sooty-black storm petrel recalls the generally similar Wilson's Storm Petrel (above), but is smaller, usually with a variable white band on the underwing and a less obvious pale panel on the upperwing. Its flight is weak and low, and its feet do not project beyond the end of its tail. When feeding, it holds its wings midway above the back and patters on the water's surface with its feet. Most of the population leaves the north Atlantic colonies at the end of the breeding season to winter south of the equator, and the young may remain there until they are two years old.

Pelecanoides urinatrix

Common Diving Petrel

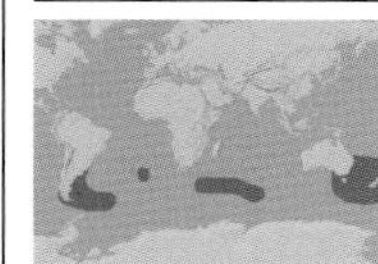

LENGTH 20–25cm (8–10in)

WEIGHT 95–175g ($3^{3}/_{8}$–6oz)

MIGRATION Non-migrant

HABITAT Open sea and ocean; breeds in burrows and rocky crevices on islands

There are four species of diving petrel, all of which have a small bill and are black or dark above, with white underparts. The wings are short and rounded. This petrel comes to land only to nest and breeds in huge coastal colonies. It lays a single egg in a burrow but, unlike many tubenose petrels, replaces it if it is taken by a predator.

Fregetta tropica

Black-bellied Petrel

LENGTH 20cm (8in)

WEIGHT 45–65g ($1^{5}/_{8}$–$2^{3}/_{8}$oz)

MIGRATION Migrant

HABITAT Open sea and ocean; breeds among rocks, in depressions on scree and burrows on islands

Essentially dark above, the Black-bellied Petrel has a black head, variable dark markings on the underparts that appear as a black line down the entire belly, white under the wing, and a broad white rump patch. Most of its feeding is nocturnal, and it takes plankton, small fish, and crustaceans by pattering the water surface and then seizing the prey in its bill. Like other petrels in the family, this species visits its colony only at night.

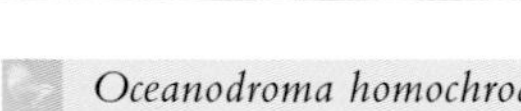

Oceanodroma homochroa

Ashy Storm Petrel

LENGTH 25–27cm (10–$10^{1}/_{2}$in)

WEIGHT 35–40g ($1^{1}/_{4}$–$1^{7}/_{16}$oz)

MIGRATION Partial migrant

HABITAT Open sea and ocean; breeds only in crevices and rocky cavities on islands

RED LIST CATEGORY Endangered

This storm petrel is medium-sized, with dark brown plumage, a pale bar on the upperwing, and a noticeably forked tail. Its short wings give it a stout appearance, and this, coupled with its normally slow fluttering flight and shallow wingbeats, helps to distinguish it from other dark storm petrels.

The Ashy Storm Petrel appears to remain in the vicinity of its colonies virtually all year, although it visits land only at night and is apparently most abundant between February and October. It feeds mostly at night. The bird utters rasping calls from within the burrow and in flight, enabling pairs to establish each other's whereabouts. Most breed on islands off the California coast. Incubation takes about 45 days, and the young remain in the nest for about 84 days, the incubation and feeding of the young being undertaken by both the male and female. This bird is gregarious, and the entire population spends the summer in Monterey Bay. Its range is restricted, and it is a rare species – the total population is thought to number only about 10,000 birds, at less than 20 colonies, and is threatened by predators, such as gulls and owls, and by oil pollution at sea.

ADULT ASHY STORM PETREL

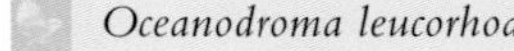

Oceanodroma leucorhoa

Leach's Storm Petrel

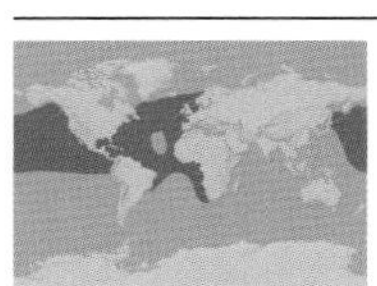

LENGTH 18–21cm (7–$8^{1}/_{2}$in)

WEIGHT 30–55g ($1^{1}/_{16}$–2oz)

MIGRATION Migrant

HABITAT Open sea and ocean; breeds in crevices and burrows on islands, in grassy or wooded areas

Named after a mollusc expert, Leach's Storm Petrel is a large storm petrel, with long and angled wings, a broad pale bar on the upperwing, a white rump broken by a grey-brown stripe, and a well-forked tail. Like most other species of storm petrel, its plumage is predominantly dark. It feeds on small squid, crustaceans, and fish on the water surface and nests in colonies. It is strictly nocturnal at the breeding sites to avoid predation by gulls and skuas.

GREBES

ORDER Podicipediformes
FAMILIES 1
SPECIES 22

SITTING HIGH IN THE WATER, with long necks and sharply pointed bills, grebes are distinctive, elegant freshwater birds. Found throughout the world on inshore waters, they are renowned for elaborate courtship displays. Grebes dive to catch fish and small animals, propelled with long lobed toes.

HABITAT

Grebes breed on sheltered lakes and freshwater wetlands, but in cold climates they winter on coasts. A few species are very localized and vulnerable to habitat change. In the American tropics, two species have recently become extinct, and the Titicaca Flightless Grebe is endangered.

ANATOMY

Grebes are sleek and streamlined, with sharply pointed bills, long bodies, but almost no trace of a tail. Their legs are set far back, and their feet have lobed toes instead of webbing. Unusually flexible joints allow them to swivel their feet and toes, so they can be used for steering as well propulsion. Their plumage is thick and lustrous, and works like an adjustable float, allowing grebes to sink out of sight if threatened. Grebes have small, slender wings. Once airborne, most fly rapidly, but some cannot fly at all.

REPRODUCTION

The grebe breeding season opens with intricate courtship dances, which involve the female as much as the male. In larger grebes, the dances often include the ritual collecting of underwater weed and an extraordinary "grand finale", in which the pair speed almost upright across the water. Once the pair bond has been formed, both help to build a mat-like nest of wet vegetation by the water's edge. The female lays up to 10 eggs; the young are well developed when they hatch.

SAFE PASSAGE
Grebes are attentive parents, with both male and female taking care of the young. Young Clark's Grebes ride on their parent's back. They stay aboard even when the adult dives.

ASSISTED TAKE-OFF
Running across the water, a Horned Grebe takes to the air. When airborne, grebes tend to trail their feet.

Tachybaptus ruficollis

Little Grebe

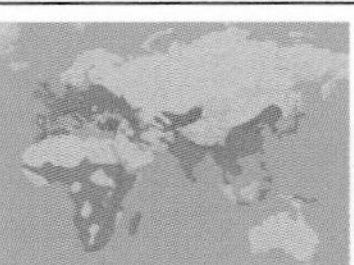

LENGTH 25–29cm (10–11½in)
WEIGHT 125–225g (4–8oz)
MIGRATION Partial migrant

HABITAT Mainly freshwater ponds, vegetated lakes, and reservoirs; also on coastal waters in winter

Also known as the Dabchick, this species is one of the smallest of the grebe family. It is widespread in its range, although often quite unobtrusive. Its presence is often revealed by its call, a high-pitched, whinnying trill. The bird's fluffy rear end and short, stumpy tail give it a characteristic dumpy, round shape. In winter, the Little Grebe's plumage is drab and inconspicuous, but in the breeding season, its cheeks and neck turn a rich chestnut colour and a pale patch at the base of the bill becomes yellow.

The Little Grebe feeds mainly on insects and their larvae and is a skilful diver, staying under water for up to half a minute or more. Many of these birds are sedentary, but some may move to coastal areas in winter.

ADULT LITTLE GREBE

Tachybaptus novaehollandiae

Australasian Grebe

LENGTH 23–27cm (9–10½in)
WEIGHT 225g (8oz)
MIGRATION Partial migrant

HABITAT All kinds of freshwater habitats

The Australasian Grebe is closely related to the Little Grebe (left). In the breeding season, both the male and female are dark brown above the bill, with yellow eyes, a striking chestnut facial stripe, and a prominent pale yellow face spot below. Both are duller, with no chestnut stripe outside the breeding season. The legs of the Australasian Grebe are set well back on its body, and its toes have lobes that open and close against the water, giving a thrust to its backstroke. This enables it to swim and dive powerfully.

ADULT AUSTRALASIAN GREBE

ADULT IN BREEDING PLUMAGE

Rollandia rolland

White-tufted Grebe

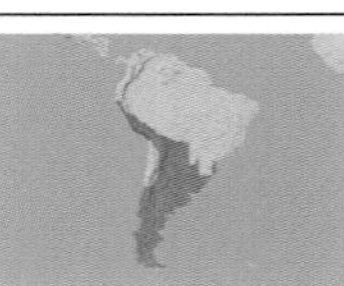

LENGTH 24–36cm (9½–14in)
WEIGHT 250–425g (9–15oz)
MIGRATION Partial migrant

HABITAT Well-vegetated ponds, lakes, and slow-moving waterways

The White-tufted Grebe is the only member of its family with a tuft of white feathers at each side of its head. The tufts are a feature of the bird's otherwise black and chestnut breeding plumage. In the breeding season, it builds a floating nest anchored to water-margin vegetation during September and October and lays 1–3 eggs. The White-tufted Grebe occurs in lowland areas and at altitudes up to 4,500m (15,000ft).

Poliocephalus poliocephalus

Hoary-headed Grebe

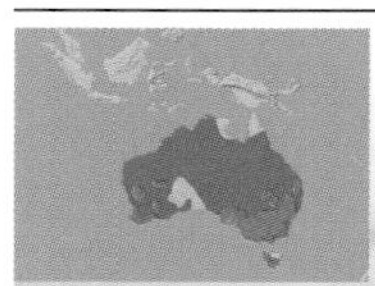

LENGTH 27–30cm (10½–12in)

WEIGHT 225–250g (8–9oz)

MIGRATION Partial migrant

HABITAT Prefers large, open freshwater lakes, but also found on coastal waters in winter

ADULT HOARY-HEADED GREBE

Like all other members of its family, the Hoary-headed Grebe spends most of its time in water, only leaving the water to nest or, occasionally, to rest on dry land. Supremely adapted to its aquatic lifestyle, it has water-repellent and very dense plumage, with more than 20,000 individual feathers. The legs are set well to the rear of the body so that the bird walks in an almost upright, awkward fashion. Both the male and female have dark bills with a pale tip, but the male has a longer bill.

Podiceps grisegena

Red-necked Grebe

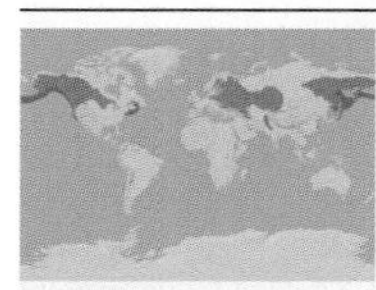

LENGTH 40–50cm (15½–19½in)

WEIGHT 1kg (2¼lb)

MIGRATION Migrant

HABITAT Breeds in shallow, well-vegetated ponds and lakes; winters near coastal waters

The Red-necked Grebe has a thick, chestnut neck, a grey and white face, and a black cap that reaches below the eyes. Its stout, dagger-like bill has a yellow base. An adept swimmer, this grebe cannot walk on land and awkwardly shuffles to leave its semi-floating, waterweed nest. The sexes are alike, but the male is slightly bigger and more boldly coloured (as shown in the photograph below, where the bird on the left is the male). Although courtship generally takes place in the water, the actual mating is usually performed on dry land or on the nest.

This grebe has a variety of calls – its vocabulary includes an assortment of whinnies, cackles, honks, grunts, rattles, hisses, and squealing sounds which fulfil a range of functions. During the breeding season, it may call during courtship. The calls of the Red-necked Grebe may be used to advertise its presence, to warn off intruders, to proclaim territory, or to keep contact with its family. The juvenile has a typical call when it is hungry.

MALE AND FEMALE CALLING TO EACH OTHER

ADULT CLARK'S GREBE

Aechmophorus clarkii

Clark's Grebe

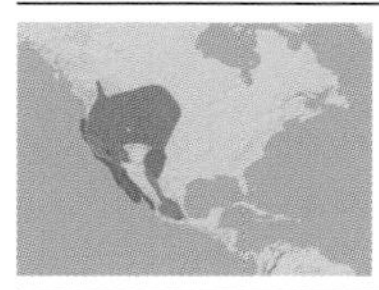

LENGTH 51–74cm (20–29in)

WEIGHT 0.9–1.3kg (2–3¼lb)

MIGRATION Partial migrant

HABITAT Breeds on bodies of freshwater and brackish water; prefers coastal waters in winter

This species is distinguished by its black cap, white face, and bright yellow bill. Its scientific name – derived from *aikhme,* the Greek word for "spear" and *phorus*, which means "thrower" – refers to the way it catches small fish by lunging at them with its long, spear-like bill. It is, however, an opportunistic feeder and will often also take small amphibians, crustaceans, and aquatic insects.

Podiceps cristatus

Great Crested Grebe

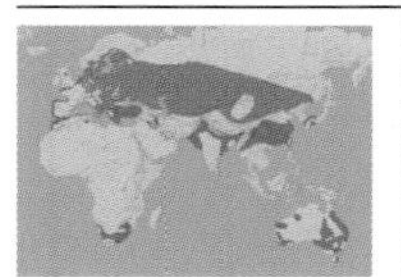

LENGTH 46–51cm (18–20in)

WEIGHT 600–750g (21–27oz)

MIGRATION Migrant

HABITAT Large, open freshwater lakes fringed with vegetation; disperses to coastal waters in winter

A dagger-like bill, an upright, slender neck, and black head plumes are characteristic of this species. It constructs its nest as a floating platform of water weeds with a depression in the middle, usually anchored to aquatic plants away from the bank of the lake. This distance from the shore offers some protection against nest-robbing mammals. When the parent leaves the nest, it covers the eggs with loose nesting material in order to hide them. The female normally lays 3–5 eggs, although as many as nine have been recorded in one nest. Great Crested Grebes dive under water, staying there for long periods in search of fish and aquatic invertebrates.

ADULT ON NEST

COURTSHIP DANCE

In an elaborate and ritualized courtship display in water, both members of the Great Crested Grebe pair dive together under the surface to bring up a piece of decorative pond-weed in their bills. Face-to-face, with crests raised and frills inflated, they shake their heads from side to side. At times, they may lean against each other breast to breast and, by paddling very fast, rise right out of the water, waggling their heads constantly.

FLAMINGOS

ORDER	Phoenicopteriformes
FAMILY	6
SPECIES	5

DESPITE MANY YEARS OF RESEARCH there are many unsolved questions about how flamingos evolved. However, recent DNA work indicates that the closest living relatives to flamingos are grebes. There is no doubt that they form an ancient and highly unusual group of birds. Their extraordinary shape is matched by an equally remarkable lifestyle, which involves filtering tiny organisms out of water using a highly specialized bill. Unlike any other bird, a flamingo feeds with its bill upside down, often for many hours a day. Flamingos are social birds, travelling and feeding in large flocks, and their habitat varies from coastal lagoons to desolate salt and soda lakes.

ONE OF A CROWD
An adult Greater Flamingo inspects its single egg. The flamingo's brilliant colour is derived from its food. Captive flamingos may fade unless given dietary supplements.

ANATOMY

Relative to their bodies, flamingos have some of the longest necks and legs of all birds. Their wings are long and pointed, and they have feet with three webbed toes. Despite their unwieldy proportions, they fly remarkably well. They can also swim, although they rarely do so once they are adult. A flamingo's bill works like a sieve, with water being pumped through it by the tongue. It is small and straight in newly hatched birds, but slowly develops its characteristic bent shape in the first few months of life. Both halves of the flamingo's bill are fringed with fibrous plates. With the bill held slightly open, they mesh together to form a sieve that traps food.

BREEDING

Flamingos form monogamous lifelong pairs, and all species have similar breeding habits. The male and female work together to build a volcano-shaped nest made of mud, which stands about 30cm (1ft) high. The female lays a single egg, and incubates it for about 30 days. After the chick has hatched, the parents feed it on "milk" made in their crops – flamingos being the only birds apart from pigeons to produce liquid food in this way. After several days in the nest, chicks congregate in thousands to form crèches; their parents continue to feed them, locating them by their calls. The young feed themselves from the age of 6–11 weeks.

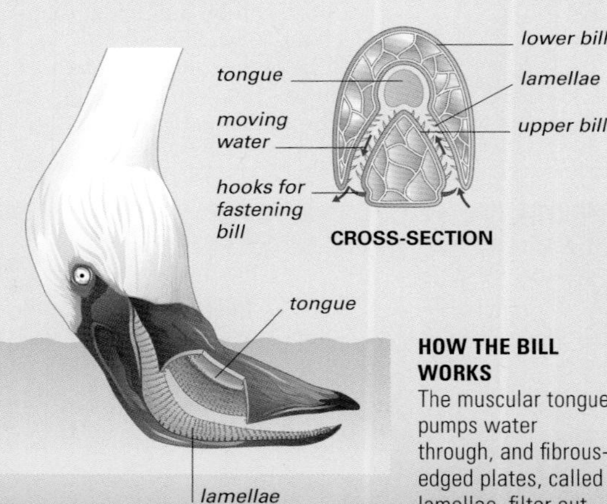

HOW THE BILL WORKS
The muscular tongue pumps water through, and fibrous-edged plates, called lamellae, filter out the food.

UNMISTAKABLE SILHOUETTE
Flamingos fly with legs and necks outstretched. For their length, they are light birds with a low wing loading that enables them to travel long distances.

BEHAVIOUR

Flamingos rarely do anything alone. They feed, breed, and travel en masse, sometimes in groups containing hundreds of thousands of birds. Much of their behaviour – such as noisy head-flagging and courtship displays – seems to have an infectious quality, spreading through a flock until enormous numbers of birds are taking part. Flamingos move on when food becomes scarce, in long, straggling lines. Some are migratory: Greater Flamingos travel from the Mediterranean to tropical Africa, to feed in the Rift Valley salt lakes.

ON THE LOOKOUT
Standing nearly 1.5m (5ft) high, flamingos are quick to spot predators approaching their feeding grounds. If threatened, they produce a noisy chorus of alarm calls.

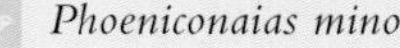

Phoenicopterus roseus

Greater Flamingo

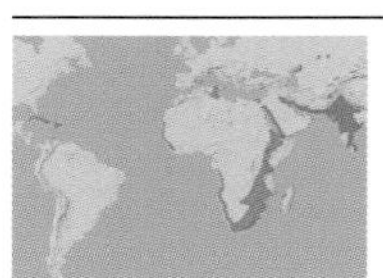

LENGTH 1.2–1.5m (4–5ft)

WEIGHT 2.5–3.5kg (5½–7¾lb)

MIGRATION Partial migrant

HABITAT Salt-pans, saline lagoons, large shallow inland lakes, mudflats, and sandbanks

The Greater Flamingo is the largest member of its family. Both the male and female have bright pink plumage, with splashes of red on their wings that are visible when they are at rest or in flight. The female is smaller than the male and has shorter legs. Like other flamingos, the Greater Flamingo's long legs enable it to wade in deep water, while its exceptionally long, slender neck makes it possible for it to sift for aquatic invertebrates from the lake bottom, probing for prey with its blunt, angled bill. This bird normally feeds with its head completely under water. Its diet varies from insects and worms to algae and pieces of vegetation.

The Greater Flamingo is long-lived: the oldest-known wild bird lived for 33 years and the oldest captive bird recorded was 44 years old. Highly gregarious, the species breeds in colonies of up to 200,000 pairs, and its nests are flattened cones of mud. Both parents incubate the single egg.

ADULT GREATER FLAMINGO

Phoeniconaias minor

Lesser Flamingo

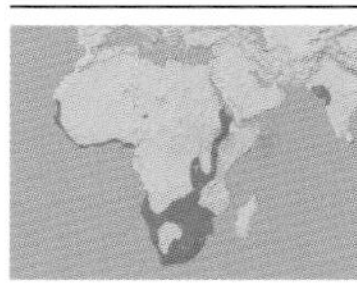

LENGTH 80–90cm (31–35in)

WEIGHT 1.5–2kg (3¼–4½lb)

MIGRATION Migrant

HABITAT Inland saline and alkaline lakes, usually with extensive mudflats, and coastal lagoons

As its name suggests, the Lesser Flamingo is the smallest member of the flamingo family, the female being less than half the weight of the male Greater Flamingo (left). The Lesser Flamingo is pale to dark pink and has a characteristic deep-keeled, dark red bill, with the lower half appearing black at a distance. The bill is adapted to take only small algae, which the flamingo filters carefully from the water surface. Such a specialized feeding method is best carried out in calm water, which is why this species feeds at night to avoid strong daytime winds. Each flamingo consumes about 60g (2⅛oz) of algae a day. Some of the colonies of this species consist of over a million birds.

ADULT LESSER FLAMINGO

GREAT SITES

RIFT VALLEY LAKES

The Lesser Flamingo gathers in flocks on the alkaline lakes of the Great Rift Valley in East Africa. Outside the breeding season, huge feeding flocks of up to one million birds congregate at sites such as Lake Bogoria and Lake Nakuru in Kenya. The birds breed (often in alternate years and in response to rainfall) on Lake Natron (Tanzania) and Lake Magadi (Kenya).

ENORMOUS FLOCKS
Flocks of up to one million Lesser Flamingos, among the largest bird assemblies in the world, are among nature's most magnificent sights.

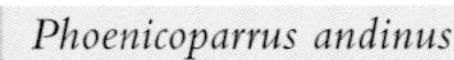

Phoenicoparrus andinus

Andean Flamingo

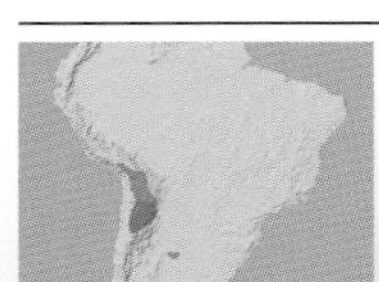

LENGTH 1m (3½ft)

WEIGHT 2–2.4kg (4½–5½lb)

MIGRATION Partial migrant

HABITAT High altitude salt-lakes mainly at 3,500–4,500m (11,500–14,800ft)

RED LIST CATEGORY Vulnerable

The Andean Flamingo is probably the rarest member of its family, with an estimated population of 34,000 birds breeding in only 10 localities. The species has undergone a rapid population decline due to exploitation and deterioration in habitat quality. The slow breeding of Andean Flamingos suggests that the legacy of past threats may persist in generations to come. The Andean Flamingo has a distinctive red-pink neck, breast, and wing coverts. A black triangular patch formed by the wings is clearly visible when the bird is at rest. Like the Lesser Flamingo (above), the Andean Flamingo has a deep-keeled bill, which helps it to feed on miniscule algae, sifted from tiny spaces between water and sediment. It lays a single chalky white egg on a mud mound. The young have straight bills at first and are fed liquid secretions from the adults' crop until their bills are fully developed.

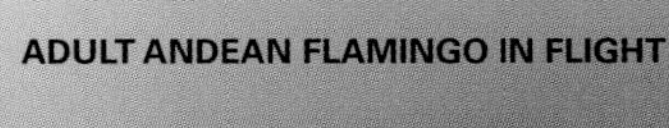

ADULT ANDEAN FLAMINGO IN FLIGHT

LAKE BOGORIA NATIONAL PARK

LOCATION In East Africa, 240km (150 miles) north of Nairobi, Kenya.

Part of a chain of lakes along the Great Rift Valley in East Africa, Lake Bogoria covers an area of 107 square km (41 square miles). The lake is dominated by many hot springs that pour superheated water into its highly alkaline waters. These caustic waters are devoid of fish and lack the flocks of migrant ducks, geese, and waders that stop to refuel on the region's freshwater lakes. In their place are up to a million Lesser Flamingos at times, plus smaller numbers of Greater Flamingos.

TOXIC FEEDING GROUND

The huge flocks of flamingos assemble to feed on the blue-green algae and swarms of brine shrimps that smother the surface of the lake. Due to the toxic environment, this vast food supply is unavailable to fish, amphibians, mammals, and most birds, so flamingos have exclusive access. Their populations can reach exceptionally high densities. For reasons that remain unclear, flamingo numbers at Lake Bogoria fluctuate dramatically from one season to the next. Without warning, virtually the lake's entire population of flamingos may shift to nearby lakes Nakuru or Naivasha, returning equally suddenly months later.

The only other birds to enter the lake are the Black-necked Grebe and Cape Teal, mostly where incoming springs lower the water's salinity. Large numbers of African Fish Eagles are attracted to the lake to hunt the flamingos – it is not unusual to see eight or more perched in a single tree at the water's edge. Other species that prey on the flamingos include Marabou Storks and Steppe and Tawny eagles.

Lake Bogoria National Reserve extends beyond the lake to incorporate a variety of other habitats that support a rich selection of tropical African birds, from bee-eaters and barbets to widowbirds, weavers, and hornbills. Resident birds of prey include the Secretarybird, while the reserve's wetlands attract water birds such as the Goliath Heron. In 2000, Lake Bogoria was designated a wetland of international importance under the Ramsar Convention on Wetlands.

FEASTING FLAMINGOS
Masses of Lesser Flamingos stand knee-deep in the hot, stinking waters of Lake Bogoria. The flamingos have tough skin on their legs to protect against caustic salts in the lake's waters.

WHAT TO SPOT

RED-AND-YELLOW BARBET
Trachyphonus erythrocephalus
(see p.321)

SECRETARYBIRD
Sagittarius serpentarius
(see p.186)

GOLIATH HERON
Ardea goliath
(see p.166)

AFRICAN FISH EAGLE
Haliaeetus vocifer
(see p.189)

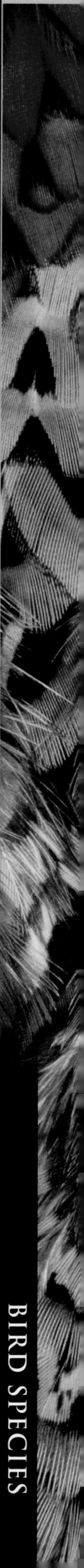

STORKS AND HERONS

ORDER	Ciconiiformes
FAMILY	3
SPECIES	115

LONG LEGS AND POWERFUL BILLS make storks and herons striking birds of freshwater habitats. This order also contains egrets, bitterns, ibises, and spoonbills. Molecular evidence suggests that New World vultures should be included, but customarily they are treated as birds of prey (see p.180). Most storks and herons are solitary hunters, stalking with stealth and patience, and attacking with lightning speed. At night, and during the breeding season, many congregate in trees.

WATERSIDE RETREAT
In an isolated tree, a small group of Painted Storks stand by their nests. Painted Storks often feed in water, sweeping their half-open bills from side to side to hunt for fish.

ANATOMY

Storks and their relatives show a great range in size. The smallest bitterns stand just 25cm (10in) high, while the largest storks measure 1.5m (5ft) from head to tail. One of these – the African Marabou – is second only to the Andean Condor in having the largest wingspan in any terrestrial bird. Few of these birds have much webbing on their feet. Instead, they have long flexible toes, which allow them to spread their weight on soft mud, as well as stand high up in trees. Apart from size, the feature that varies most is the shape of their bills. Storks and herons usually have straight bills, sometimes with a dagger-like tip. Ibises have decurved bills, while spoonbills are instantly recognizable, because their bills have rounded and flattened tips.

Most birds in this order fly well. The larger species have a leisurely flapping flight, sometimes interspersed with long bouts of soaring. Most herons and egrets retract their necks into an S-shape during flight, but storks fly with theirs fully extended. The long legs trailing behind are also a noticeable feature in flight.

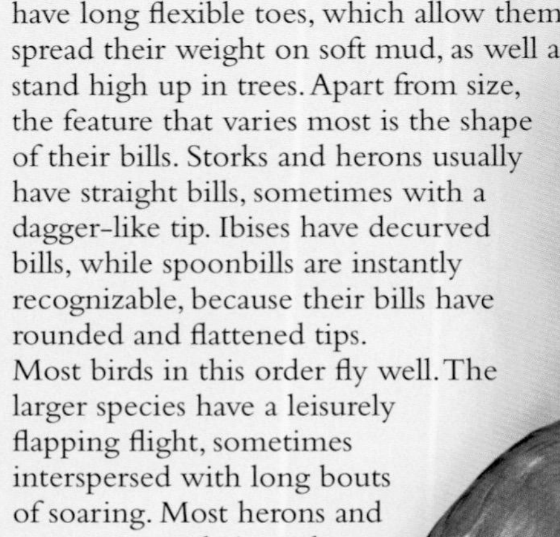

INSTANT STRIKE
With its long sinuous neck, the Tricoloured Heron can stab prey such as fish in a fraction of a second with its dagger-like bill.

BEHAVIOUR

All the birds in this order are carnivorous, and the majority feed on fish, frogs or other amphibians, and insects that they catch on or near water; some species will also eat small birds. Herons and bitterns are visual hunters, capable of waiting motionless for over an hour until prey comes within reach. Most of them hunt by day, but Night Herons are nocturnal, stalking prey with their unusually good night vision. Ibises and spoonbills feel for food in muddy water, using their highly sensitive bills to locate their prey, but storks often feed on land, striding warily through grass or marshy ground, and snapping up any small animals that they disturb. The largest storks have very different habits. They behave more like vultures, soaring high in the sky on immense wings as they search for dead remains.

BREEDING

Despite solitary feeding habits, many of the birds in this order breed in groups, and it is not unusual for several species to nest side by side. Most of the colonial species nest in trees or mangroves, creating an impressive spectacle with birds standing prominently near their nests. Storks and herons typically lay 4–6 eggs in a large platform of sticks, and the young remain in the nest for several weeks, fed by both parents. Contrasting with these species are bitterns, which nest on their own on marshy ground. They make nests from reeds and other waterplants, and are superbly camouflaged. When the breeding season is over, many species that nest in temperate regions migrate; herons often leave inland waterways and move to the coast.

FOCUSED HUNTER
Clinging to a branch with its slender toes, a Green Heron judges the right moment to strike. Its eyes can face forwards to help judge distances.

HUMAN IMPACT

THREATS AND CONSERVATION

A number of species in this order are currently listed as critically endangered. On the positive side, some species – such as the cattle egret – have benefited from the spread of pasture and paddy fields, which provides them with new feeding grounds.

ENDANGERED IBIS
Critically endangered stork species include the Northern Bald Ibis (shown here), which lives in eastern Europe, the Near East, and North Africa.

Mycteria americana

Wood Stork

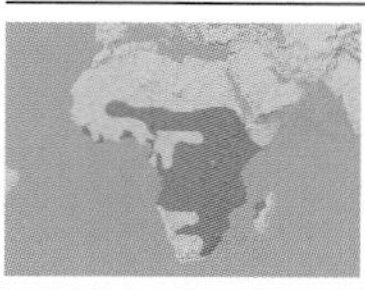

LENGTH 0.8–1.2m (2½–4ft)

WEIGHT 2–3kg (4½–6½lb)

MIGRATION Partial migrant

HABITAT Marshes, wet meadows, mangroves, lakes, and ponds

The only stork native to North America, the Wood Stork is also one of the largest wading birds to breed there. The juvenile's head is covered with white feathers and the bill is yellow. As it ages, the bill turns grey and the head becomes bare and grey. The adult is mostly white, with a contrasting black tail and flight feathers that are visible when the wings are spread. This stork catches small fish in water with its open bill submerged. When it catches a fish, its bill snaps shut in quick reaction.

JUVENILE WOOD STORK

Anastomus lamelligerus

African Openbill

LENGTH 80–94cm (31–37in)

WEIGHT 3–5kg (6½–11lb)

MIGRATION Partial migrant

HABITAT Mainly wetlands such as marshes, swamps, paddy fields, and margins of rivers and lakes

Named for its unusually shaped bill, the African Openbill is well equipped to feed on its diet of large aquatic snails. A special adaptation, its bill has an obvious gap between the two closed halves (mandibles), which curve away from each other. The snail shell is held in place by the upper mandible, while the lower mandible slices through the muscle that holds the snail in its shell. Predominantly black in colour, the African Openbill can often be seen wading in shallow water, searching for snails.

ADULT FEEDING

Mycteria ibis

Yellow-billed Stork

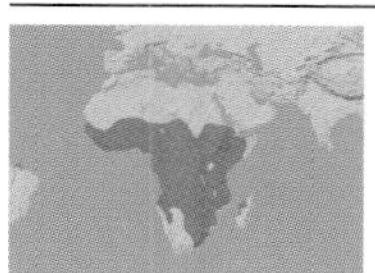

LENGTH 0.9–1.1m (3–3½ft)

WEIGHT 1.2–2.3kg (2¼–5½lb)

MIGRATION Non-migrant

HABITAT Margins of large rivers and lakes, swamps, paddy fields, lagoons, and coastal mudflats

This handsome stork, with its long, slightly decurved yellow bill and long red legs, is perfectly adapted to a life of wading in shallow water and mud in search of food, such as small fish, frogs, crustaceans, worms, and insects. It does not need to see its prey, but searches the water with its bill, which is very sensitive to movement, and then quickly snaps up its food. The sexes are quite similar, although the male is slightly larger. As the breeding season approaches, the red colour of the head and legs intensifies and the white of the plumage becomes suffused with a delicate pink.

ADULT IN BREEDING PLUMAGE

Ephippiorhynchus senegalensis

Saddle-billed Stork

LENGTH 1.4–1.5m (4½–5ft)

WEIGHT 6kg (13lb)

MIGRATION Non-migrant

HABITAT Mainly in large open wetland habitats, but also in open semi-arid areas

Aptly named, the Saddle-billed Stork has a huge black and red bill, with a yellow frontal "saddle". Its plumage is a contrast of white and an iridescent black. The female can be distinguished from the dark-eyed male by its bright yellow iris. The species inhabits the plains of Africa south of the Sahara desert, where it lives in pairs or small family groups. Juveniles closely follow their parents and learn to hunt by imitating them as they stab at fish and frogs.

MALE HUNTING WITH ITS YOUNG

Ciconia ciconia

White Stork

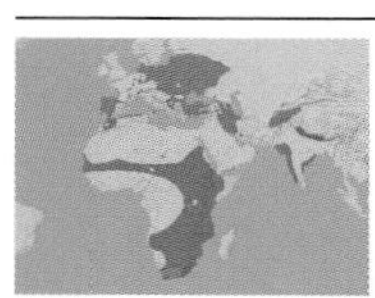

LENGTH 1m (3¼ft)

WEIGHT 2.3–4.4kg (5–9¾lb)

MIGRATION Migrant

HABITAT Variety of open areas, such as wetlands, grassland, pastures, banks of rivers and lakes

According to European folklore, the White Stork carries new-born babies to their parents, and throughout its range this bird is welcomed as a harbinger of good fortune. In areas where the storks breed, house owners often construct special rooftop platforms for them to nest on. Black and white in colour, this stork has a long red bill, black wing-tips, and red legs. Although not especially gregarious on its breeding grounds in Europe, White Storks gather in large flocks at favoured feeding sites on their wintering grounds in Africa and South Asia. Their diet varies from frogs, toads, and small rodents to grasshoppers. Swarms of locusts also attract large numbers of these storks, causing them to congregate in pursuit of a meal.

ADULT WHITE STORK

NESTING BEHAVIOUR

The White Stork builds a large, bulky nest of sticks on a high perch, such as a pole, tower, or rooftop. These storks tend to return to the same nest each year, the male usually arriving a few days before the female to repair the nest. If one of the pair does not return, the other finds a new mate.

Jabiru mycteria

Jabiru

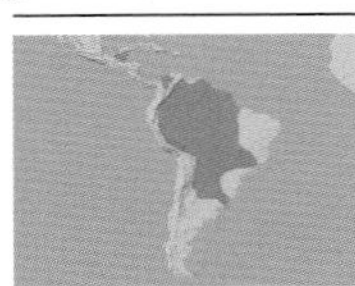

LENGTH 1.2–1.4m (4–4½ft)

WEIGHT 5–7kg (11–15lb)

MIGRATION Partial migrant

HABITAT Freshwater wetlands

A large stork with mainly white plumage, the Jabiru can be found from Mexico to Argentina. Its head and neck are featherless, with black skin above a thin band of red. The Jabiru also has an inflatable throat sac that it uses to indicate its excitement or irritation to other birds. The male is larger than the female and has a longer bill. The breeding season extends from December to May.

ADULT INFLATING THROAT SAC

Leptoptilos dubius

Greater Adjutant

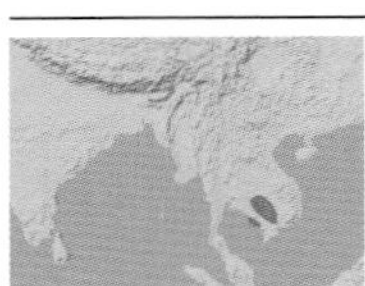

LENGTH 1.2–1.5m (4–5ft)

WEIGHT 5–8kg (11–18lb)

MIGRATION Migrant

HABITAT Mainly wetlands, but also dry areas such as grassland and open forest

RED LIST CATEGORY Endangered

This huge, dark stork has a very thick bill and large neck pouch, a distinctive white V-shaped neck ruff, and a combination of yellow and orange skin on its head. The Greater Adjutant is known for its scavenging habits – often it can be found feeding on carrion or at rubbish dumps. However, it will also feed on live prey such as large fish, frogs, reptiles, and injured birds.

The species is globally threatened, with a total population thought to number no more than a thousand individuals. Once common across much of Asia, it declined dramatically during the early 20th century, mainly due to habitat loss. Now, it is known to breed only in Assam, India and Cambodia.

ADULT GREATER ADJUTANT

Threskiornis molucca

Australian White Ibis

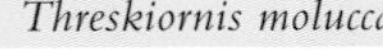

LENGTH 63–76cm (25–30in)

WEIGHT 1.5–2kg (3¼–4½lb)

MIGRATION Partial migrant

HABITAT Wetland areas, as well as dry open areas, particularly in towns and cities

AUSTRALIAN WHITE IBIS

As its common name suggests, the Australian White Ibis has white plumage, except for black tips to the wings, which are clearly visible in flight. Its head and long, decurved bill are also black. This species is very similar to the sacred ibis (*T. aethiopicus*) of Africa. Within Australia, however, the only species it can be confused with is the straw-necked ibis (*T. spinicollis*), which is easily distinguished by its dark upperparts.

A sociable species, this ibis is usually seen feeding in groups of around 40–200 birds. As well as scavenging on carrion and rubbish, it probes the ground with its bill in order to find insects or crustaceans. This common Australian species (which also occurs in New Guinea and the Solomon Islands) is frequently found near human habitation and in parks and gardens.

Leptoptilos crumeniferus

Marabou Stork

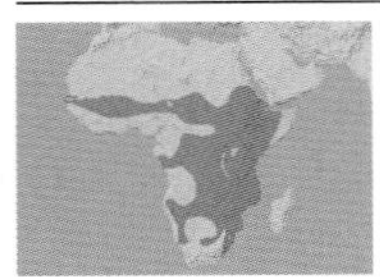

LENGTH 1.1–1.5m (3½–5ft)

WEIGHT 4–9kg (8¾–20lb)

MIGRATION Partial migrant

HABITAT Open dry savanna and grassland, as well as lake and river edges

Standing up to 1.5m (5ft) tall, the massive Marabou Stork is a familiar species in much of Africa. To some people, it is one of the world's ugliest birds, with its bald and scabby pink head and huge throat sac. However, once airborne, with a wingspan of almost 3m (10ft), it makes an impressive sight as it soars high above the plains.

The bare skin of its head and neck allows the Marabou Stork to feed on the carcasses of large mammals without getting its feathers soiled, in much the same way as vultures, alongside which the Marabou Stork often feeds.

ADULT MARABOU STORK

Nipponia nippon

Crested Ibis

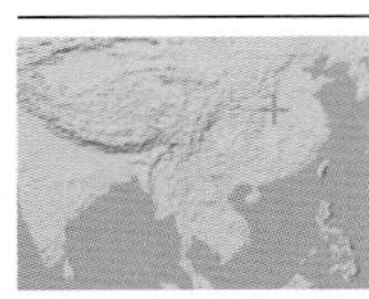

LENGTH 55–79cm (2½–31in)

WEIGHT 1.9kg (4½lb)

MIGRATION Non-migrant

HABITAT Marshes, streams, rivers, rice fields, and wetlands, close to large trees

RED LIST CATEGORY Endangered

A distinctive bird, the Crested Ibis has a bright red face and bushy crest. It is extremely rare, numbering only around 300 birds. Historically, the species occurred in the far east of Russia, as well as Japan and China. However, the only wild population is now confined to central mainland China, where in 1981 it numbered just seven birds. Through intensive conservation efforts, the number has now risen to around 150 birds and is slowly increasing.

Theristicus melanopis

Black-faced Ibis

LENGTH 70–75cm (28–30in)

WEIGHT 1.7kg (3¾lb)

MIGRATION Migrant

HABITAT Fields and grassland, as well as more marshy areas

With its rufous cap, black face, buff neck and breast, brown upperparts, and jet-black underparts, the Black-faced Ibis of South America is easy to identify. Very similar to it, however, is the more widespread Buff-necked Ibis (*T. caudatus*), which differs mainly in having extensive amounts of white on its wings. Unlike their close relative, most Black-faced Ibises are highly migratory, with birds breeding in Chile and southern Argentina, moving to the pampas of northern Argentina in winter. They are very sociable, often nesting in colonies with other birds such as cormorants and herons in a variety of habitats, from reedbeds to cliff ledges. The species is common in Chile and Argentina.

FORAGING BLACK-FACED IBIS

Eudocimus ruber

Scarlet Ibis

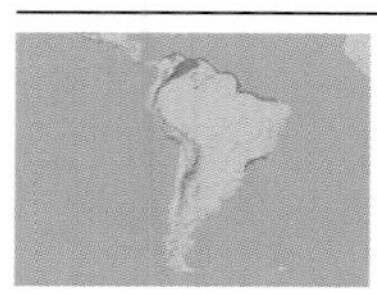

LENGTH 55–70cm (21½–28in)
WEIGHT 600–750g (21–27oz)
MIGRATION Partial migrant

HABITAT Estuaries, mudflats, and other wetlands; nests in mangroves or trees around inland wetlands

RED LIST CATEGORY Endangered

One of the world's most brightly coloured wetland birds, the Scarlet Ibis has scarlet plumage and legs, contrasting with its black bill. Some, however, consider it to be just a subspecies (or colour form) of the American White Ibis (*Eudocimus albus*): where the two forms overlap in Venezuela, mixed pairs have been recorded.

SCARLET IBIS

Platalea leucorodia

Eurasian Spoonbill

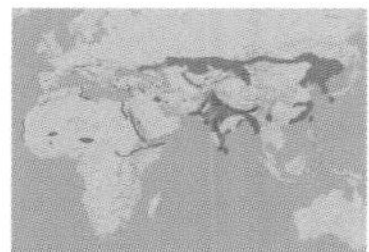

LENGTH 70–95cm (28–37in)
WEIGHT 1.1–1.9kg (2¼–4½lb)
MIGRATION Migrant

HABITAT Shallow wetlands

The Eurasian Spoonbill is a large all-white bird, except in its breeding plumage, when it acquires a variable yellow breast band and off-white crest. It has a distinctive long, black bill, with a spoon-shaped tip that is usually yellow in adults. Most populations of the species are highly migratory, although birds found in India and Sri Lanka are largely sedentary.

ADULT EURASIAN SPOONBILL

ADULT GLOSSY IBIS

Plegadis falcinellus

Glossy Ibis

LENGTH 50–65cm (20–26in)
WEIGHT 475–600g (17–21oz)
MIGRATION Migrant

HABITAT Favours freshwater wetlands, but also found in some coastal areas

The Glossy Ibis can appear dark and unobtrusive when seen in poor light or at a distance. However, when seen clearly, its plumage (particularly that of breeding adults) is a striking iridescent mixture of greens, purples, and browns. Like other ibises, it is a long-legged bird with an elongated, decurved bill that it uses to probe into the ground to search for food. The Glossy Ibis has a wide global distribution, being found in all inhabited continents, except South America (although it has bred in Venezuela). It is a highly migratory species, and as a result vagrant birds also often occur well outside their range, for example, New Zealand.

Platalea ajaja

Roseate Spoonbill

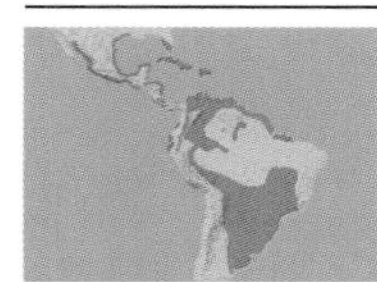

LENGTH 70–85cm (28–33in)
WEIGHT 1.4kg (3¼lb)
MIGRATION Partial migrant

HABITAT Prefers shallow coastal waters, although also found on inland freshwater wetlands

RED LIST CATEGORY Endangered

The beautiful Roseate Spoonbill is the world's only pink spoonbill. Its neck and upper back are white, graduating to a pale pink beneath. It has a striking bright pink bar across its wings and a large, black-spotted, pale grey bill. During the breeding season, the bare patch of skin on the head and face appears yellow. Juveniles are much paler – almost white, with just a few hints of pink on the wings – and have pink or yellow bills.

The species was common along the Gulf Coast of the USA till the middle of the 19th century. But by 1900, it was almost wiped out by plume hunters. It began to recolonize in the 20th century.

BILL SHAPE

All six species of spoonbills have long, straight, flattened bills that broaden out at the end into a distinctive "spoon" shape. They feed in a very characteristic way – swinging their heads from side to side, to increase the chance that the large surface area of the sensitive bill will come into contact with prey such as insects and small fish.

ADULT ROSEATE SPOONBILL

GREAT SITES

KEOLADEO NATIONAL PARK

LOCATION Rajasthan, northern India, about 190km (120 miles) south of New Delhi between the cities of Jaipur and Agra.

Keoladeo is named after an ancient Hindu temple in the park, and is also known as Bharatpur Sanctuary, after the nearest town. Formerly a duck-hunting reserve of the maharajas, this patchwork of seasonal marshes, tropical dry forest, and scrub lies in the Gangetic Plain, the vast lowland region covering much of north-central India. It is firmly established as one of the best birdwatching destinations in southern Asia. Nearly 380 bird species have been recorded within the park boundaries – around a quarter of the total number found in the entire Indian subcontinent. The park is an important breeding ground for thousands of storks, herons, and cormorants, which in winter are joined by large numbers of ducks and other migrant water birds from central Asia, China, and Siberia.

GREEN OASIS

Keoladeo's unspoiled natural appearance is misleading because the lush wetlands are of artificial origin. The landscape we see today was created in the 1850s to store the floodwaters of the summer monsoon. During the monsoon, water is channelled from the swollen Gambhir and Banganga rivers into a system of canals, sluices, and embankments to form extensive marshes and pools up to 2m (6½ft) deep. Following the banning of hunting in Keoladeo in the 1970s, around 29 square km (11 square miles) of the site became a national park in 1982, and three years later it was declared a World Heritage Site.

One of the reasons Keoladeo is a magnet for birds is the aridity of the surrounding countryside, which has a low rainfall and extremely hot, dry summers. For much of the year, the park becomes an oasis of green in an otherwise parched region. In its wetland areas, typical breeding birds include the Sarus Crane, Greater Adjutant, Painted Stork, Asian Openbill, Oriental Darter, Indian Pond Heron, and Pheasant-tailed Jacana, as well as various species of egret, spoonbill, ibis, pelican, and cormorant. Many birds of prey, including at least nine species of eagle, hunt in the park at different times of year and its dry areas are home to a rich array of land birds.

WHAT TO SPOT

INDIAN ROLLER
Coracias benghalensis
(see p.305)

PHEASANT-TAILED JACANA
Hydrophasianus chirurgus
(see p.227)

INDIAN POND HERON
Ardeola grayii

GADWALL
Anas strepera
(see p.130)

WETLAND NESTING SITE
Thickets of acacia trees scattered throughout the seasonal wetlands of Keoladeo provide ideal nest sites for colonies of water birds, such as these Painted Storks.

Tigriornis leucolopha

White-crested Tiger Heron

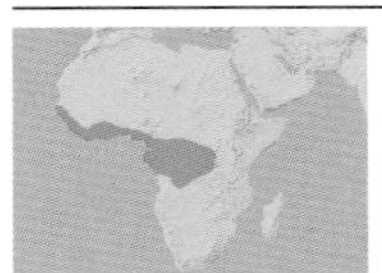

LENGTH 66–80cm (26–31in)

WEIGHT 1kg (2¼lb)

MIGRATION Non-migrant

HABITAT Marshy areas or streams within dense forest

Named for the stripes or bars all over its plumage, the White-crested Tiger Heron has a crest that is obscured by other feathers on its head. Generally, this heron is an uncommon species. Although it gives its presence away by its booming call, it is difficult to see due to its nocturnal habits and its partiality for dense rainforest streams. As a consequence, very little is known about the behaviour of this enigmatic species.

Tigrisoma lineatum

Rufescent Tiger Heron

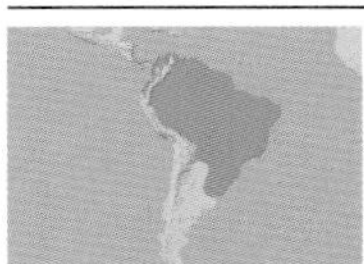

LENGTH 65–75cm (26–30in)

WEIGHT 800g (29oz)

MIGRATION Non-migrant

HABITAT Favours wooded, slow-flowing river banks; also found in marshy areas and mangroves

ADULT

The only tiger heron not to be noticeably striped, the Rufescent Tiger Heron is nevertheless an unmistakable species, with its rich chestnut head and breast, which is divided by a clear white stripe. The adult has a very long bill. The plumage of the juvenile is quite different and consists of black barring on a pale brown base. The Rufescent Tiger Heron wades near river banks and hides in undergrowth whenever it can and, like its close relatives, it is a secretive species that scientists know little about. Although it can be difficult to spot, the species is not thought to be uncommon, particularly in parts of Nicaragua, Colombia, and Venezuela.

Botaurus stellaris

Eurasian Bittern

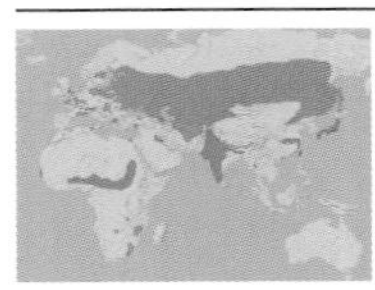

LENGTH 65–80cm (26–31in)

WEIGHT 1.2–1.5kg (2¾–3¼lb)

MIGRATION Partial migrant

HABITAT Breeds in extensive reedbeds; winters in a variety of well-vegetated wetlands

A rare and declining species, the Eurasian Bittern breeds only in extensive reedbeds. In winter, it is marginally easier to observe as it sometimes moves to more open areas.

During the spring and summer, the Eurasian Bittern is very difficult to see. Its presence is much more likely to be detected by the booming mating call emitted by the male, a loud and far-carrying, foghorn-like sound that can be heard from up to 5km (3 miles) away. This boom is often preceded by a couple of short, grunting noises, rather like a cough. Other unusual behaviour includes an impressive display when faced with a threat. The bird crouches with its neck arched backwards, wings spread, and its feathers held aloft so that it appears bigger. With the bird's dagger-like bill pointed menacingly in front of its body, this display must be an effective deterrent to intruders.

ADULT EURASIAN BITTERN

REEDBED CAMOUFLAGE

A secretive, difficult-to-see species, the Eurasian Bittern rarely ventures far from its favoured reedbed habitat during the breeding season. Its streaked, brown plumage and ability to freeze in an upright standing position, with its bill pointing upwards towards the sky, allow the bird to blend into its surroundings.

Ixobrychus minutus

Little Bittern

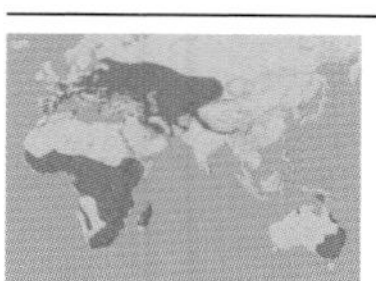

LENGTH 27–36cm (10½–14in)

WEIGHT 125g (4oz)

MIGRATION Migrant

HABITAT Variety of habitats, but prefers well-vegetated wetlands

As its name suggests, the Little Bittern is tiny – dwarfed by its larger relative, the Eurasian Bittern (opposite). However, unlike its relative, the male Little Bittern has plumage that is different from the female. It has a jet-black cap and back that contrast with its creamy brown underparts. The female is much more uniform and duller brown – although it has a black cap, it lacks the male's dark back. The Little Bittern feeds on large aquatic insects, fish, and amphibians, usually hunting in shallow water.

MALE LITTLE BITTERN

Cochlearius cochlearius

Boat-billed Heron

LENGTH 45–50cm (17½–19½in)

WEIGHT 600–700g (21–25oz)

MIGRATION Non-migrant

HABITAT Mangroves and other densely vegetated wetlands

The most striking feature of the Boat-billed Heron is its massive bill. This is used as a scoop to snatch up food such as shrimps, insects, and small fish – a feeding technique that is unique among the heron family. The Boat-billed Heron also has noticeably large eyes, which reflects the fact that the species is largely nocturnal. A number of different subspecies occur, which vary somewhat in their plumage tones. However, all have a distinctive black cap that extends down the back, contrasting with grey upperparts and white or brown underparts.

This species nests alone or in small colonies in mangrove trees, laying 2-4 eggs. Its calls include a deep croak and a high-pitched "pee-pee-pee".

ADULT BOAT-BILLED HERON

Nycticorax nycticorax

Black-crowned Night Heron

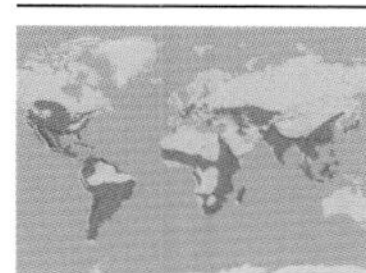

LENGTH 55–65cm (21½–26in)

WEIGHT 525–800g (19–29oz)

MIGRATION Migrant

HABITAT Wetlands

Although the male and female have similar plumage, including shades of grey and black, the female Black-crowned Night Heron is slightly smaller than the male. The juvenile is brown and streaked, with a pale yellow bill and greenish yellow legs and feet. This heron feeds on small fish, crustaceans, frogs, aquatic insects, and small mammals. A largely nocturnal species, perhaps to avoid competition for food from other, larger heron species, this heron has a wide global distribution.

ADULT BIRD

Butorides virescens

Green Heron

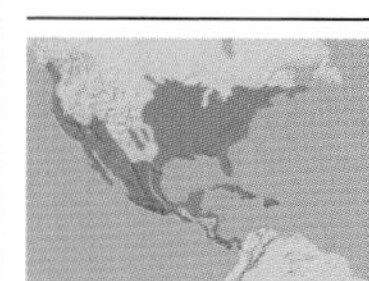

LENGTH 35–48cm (14–19in)

WEIGHT 200g (7oz)

MIGRATION Migrant

HABITAT Breeds in swampy thickets; winters mainly in coastal areas, particularly mangroves

A small wading bird, the Green Heron has a chestnut neck that contrasts with its green cap and black and white breast stripe. Its legs are bright yellow. The Green Heron is sometimes grouped together with about 30 similar forms found around the world (except Europe) as part of a species known as the Green-backed or Striated Heron (*B. striatus*). The Green Heron stands still at water edges, where it waits to ambush prey, which includes small fish, frogs, and aquatic insects. It often perches in trees. Its call is a loud and sudden "kyow". It is a common summer visitor to wetlands across much of North America, particularly eastern USA, as well as southern Canada. It winters further south, especially in Central and South America.

ADULT READY TO STRIKE

Ardeola ralloides

Squacco Heron

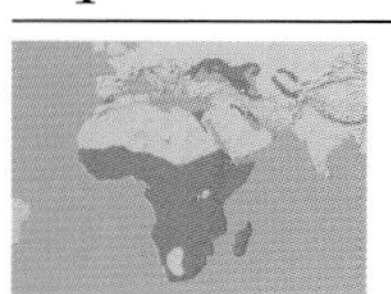

LENGTH 45cm (17½in)

WEIGHT 300g (11oz)

MIGRATION Partial migrant

HABITAT Mainly fresh water wetlands

An attractive bird, the Squacco Heron appears very much like an egret (see pp.166–167) in flight, due to its white wings. On the ground, however, its appearance is transformed: its upperparts are ginger in colour during the breeding season, with long-plumed nape feathers and thin black streaks on the back of its head. Adults in winter and juveniles are a duller brown with more extensive streaking.

This heron nests in small colonies on platforms of sticks in trees or shrubs. Migratory populations of the species breed in scattered locations across southern Europe and the Middle East, moving to tropical Africa for the winter. A number of non-migratory populations also occur in Africa. Small numbers of vagrant birds are usually seen annually in northern Europe.

ADULT IN BREEDING PLUMAGE

ADULT IN BREEDING PLUMAGE

Bubulcus ibis

Cattle Egret

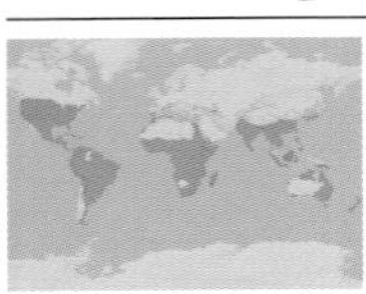

LENGTH 48–53cm (19–21in)

WEIGHT 300g (11oz)

MIGRATION Partial migrant

HABITAT Grassland and open cultivated country, often far from water

The Cattle Egret is the world's most abundant heron. In its original home in Africa, as well as more recently colonized regions, it has followed the clearance of land for farming, and exploits other open spaces, such as golf courses. Stumpy and short-legged with a large head and short, thick neck, it is found in drier places than other herons. Breeding Cattle Egrets develop buff plumes on the head and back.

Unlike most herons, the Cattle Egret feeds mostly on grasshoppers and other insects, although during the breeding season it feeds on frogs. Flocks in flight present a flickering, tight-packed effect, often looking much whiter than they appear on the ground.

FOLLOWING THE HERD

Throughout the world, the Cattle Egret is usually found very close to grazing animals. In Africa, these can be buffalo, antelope, zebra, or elephants. In many countries, domestic cattle fill the niche. The Cattle Egret walks close to the animal's shoulder, waiting for insects, frogs, and other prey to be flushed out.

TAKING A RIDE
The Cattle Egret sometimes rides on an animal's back, often probing its skin and ears for parasites and flies.

Ardea cinerea

Grey Heron

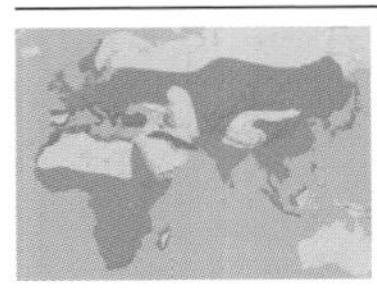

LENGTH 90–98cm (35–39in)

WEIGHT 1.4kg (3¼lb)

MIGRATION Partial migrant

HABITAT Shallow water along lakes, rivers, estuaries, and shorelines; also reed marshes and mangroves

ROOSTING GREY HERON

Eurasia's most widespread heron, the Grey Heron is the counterpart of the North American Great Blue Heron (below), the neotropical Cocoi Heron (*A. cocoi*), and the Australian white-necked herons. Less persecuted now than in the past, it is increasing both in numbers and in range.

This heron is usually seen hunting singly or spaced out along banks and shores. It stands for long periods and is most active at dawn and dusk. An opportunistic feeder, it takes fish, small mammals, and birds and catches insects on the wing. In winter, it can be found hunting earthworms, rats, and mice in fields. It nests colonially in trees, preferring high branches. Although its flight is heavy and slow, the Grey Heron can glide down nimbly to nests or feeding grounds.

GOLIATH HERON IN FLIGHT

Ardea goliath

Goliath Heron

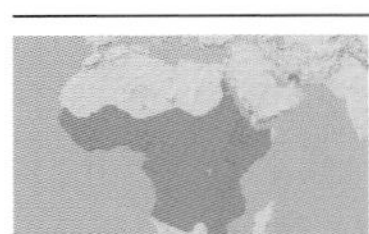

LENGTH 1.5m (5ft)

WEIGHT 4.4kg (10lb)

MIGRATION Non-migrant

HABITAT Rarely found far from water, both inland and on the coast

The world's largest heron, the Goliath Heron is nearly twice the size of the Purple Heron (*A. purpurea*) it superficially resembles. It may be found feeding in deeper water than other herons and can stand for hours waiting for the large fish that make up a major part of its diet. It is solitary and rarely found near settlements or other sources of human disturbance. The Goliath Heron flies slowly with legs held, not horizontally as in other herons, but at an angle below the body. Able to cover long distances, it flies with slow and heavy wingbeats.

Ardea herodias

Great Blue Heron

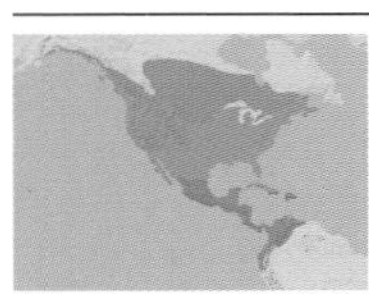

LENGTH 0.9–1.4cm (3–4½in)

WEIGHT 2.1–2.5kg (4½–5½lb)

MIGRATION Partial migrant

HABITAT Fresh and salt water, swamps, and dry land

Widespread in North America, the Great Blue Heron occurs in two colour forms: one dark grey-blue and the other all-white. Sometimes considered a subspecies of the Grey Heron (above), the Great Blue Heron is up to 40 per cent larger. The white form – sometimes called the Great White Heron – can be confused with the Great Egret (opposite). The white form of the Great Blue Heron can be distinguished by its heavier build, larger bill, and pale legs. In the breeding season, the adult Great Blue Heron has black plumes at the back of the crown – the courtship display includes fluffing up its feathers and striking odd poses. This heron is a generalist feeder, catching fish, frogs, small mammals, birds, and a wide variety of insects. It feeds by standing still in water for long periods or walking along waterways or through marshy vegetation and grassy fields. It can accumulate dangerous levels of toxic chemicals and is a good indicator of environmental quality.

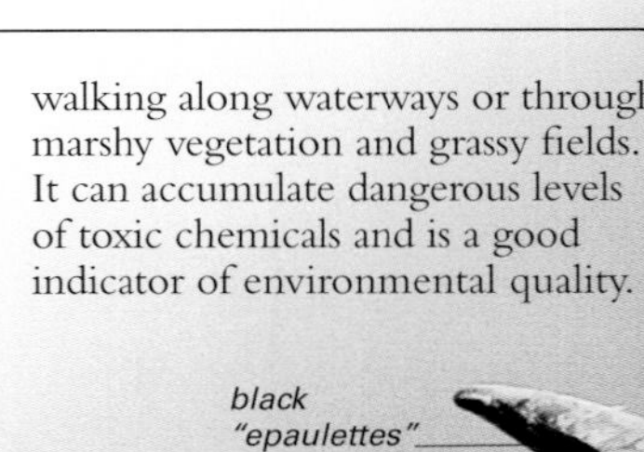

GREY-BLUE FORM

GREAT EGRET IN FLIGHT

Ardea alba

Great Egret

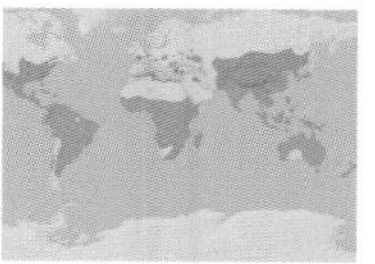

LENGTH 0.8–1m (2½–3¼ft)
WEIGHT 800–925g (29–33oz)
MIGRATION Partial migrant

HABITAT Marine and freshwater habitats and some manmade environments, such as fish ponds

The Great Egret, like several other species, specializes in searching out and killing small prey. Where the Great Blue Heron (opposite) and others wait patiently for hours to catch large fish, the Great Egret devotes most of its day to actively catching its prey – and when there are chicks to feed, much of the night too – seeking small fish as well as insects. Although gregarious and often found hunting in flocks, Great Egrets are aggressive, sometimes killing and eating neighbouring nestlings.

Breeding Great Egrets are easily distinguished from other white herons by the absence of head plumes. The Great Egret is less heavily built than the white form of the Great Blue Heron (opposite) and has a longer neck. Great Egrets have returned to their former numbers and range in the USA, after persecution for their plumes. In Europe, their numbers increased during the 1990s, with the range now extending to newly created habitats.

HUMAN IMPACT

VALUABLE PLUMAGE

In the late 19th and early 20th centuries, various species of white egret were slaughtered for their plumes. Widespread revulsion at this practice led to the founding of the RSPB in Britain and the Audubon Society in the USA.

EGRET PLUMES
Long white trains of lacy plumes extend along the back and beyond the tail of the Great Egret during the breeding season.

Egretta novaehollandiae

White-faced Heron

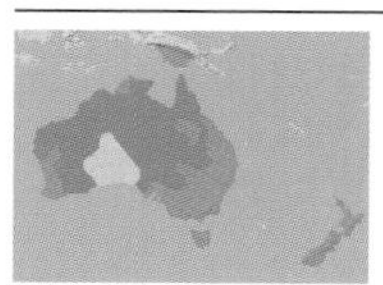

LENGTH 26–72cm (10–28in)
WEIGHT 525–600g (19–21oz)
MIGRATION Non-migrant

HABITAT Mainly inland on wetlands, salt lakes, and rice fields; less in mangroves and tidal mudflats

As its name suggests, this blue-grey heron has a white face. Australia's commonest heron, it is found in all parts of the continent, except for the driest interior. During the 20th century, these herons spread out from Australia to New Zealand, New Guinea, and other Pacific islands, taking advantage of the clearance of forests for agriculture, especially when irrigation was involved. The White-faced Heron has a varied diet, including insects at rubbish dumps, and in New Zealand, it preys on treefrogs. Its breeding season is linked to the arrival of the rains, and unusually for herons, it is a solitary nester. It also hunts alone and is highly territorial. However, it is less aggressive in winter and is sometimes seen feeding in flocks in alfalfa fields and paddocks.

Egretta garzetta

Little Egret

LENGTH 55–65cm (21½–26in)
WEIGHT 350–550g (13–20oz)
MIGRATION Migrant

HABITAT Watersides from rocky coasts to reedy lakes, especially open, muddy, and sandy shores

ADULT IN BREEDING PLUMAGE

This Little Egret is similar to the Snowy Egret (right) but appears larger because of its slightly longer neck and legs. It feeds in a more deliberate way than the Snowy Egret, which rushes about erratically when it forages. The Little Egret's prey includes small fish, frogs, snails, and other wetland animals. Breeding adults may be distinguished by two or three long, straight plumes growing from the back of their heads. Very sociable, this sparkling white egret of marshes, poolsides, and coasts is often found in small, loose feeding flocks and tends to form evening roosts in favoured spots.

Egretta thula

Snowy Egret

LENGTH 56–66cm (22–26in)
WEIGHT 375g (13oz)
MIGRATION Partial migrant

HABITAT All kinds of fresh and salt water; occasionally dry grassland

Following protection in the USA, the Snowy Egret has fully recovered from its former endangered status. In recent decades, it has expanded its breeding range northwards along the USA's east coast.

During the breeding season, the Snowy Egret has luxuriant "aigrette" plumes on its neck and back and shorter head-plumes forming a crest. This species feeds in shallow water and specializes in flushing out prey with its feet. It is among the most gregarious herons, feeding, roosting, and nesting in flocks, often with other herons. It is also highly vocal and very aggressive in defence of its feeding and nesting places.

ADULT SNOWY EGRET

GREAT EGRETS
During the breeding season, Great Egrets such as these develop a lime green lore (the patch of skin between the eyes and base of the bill).

PELICANS AND RELATIVES

ORDER	Pelicaniformes
FAMILY	8
SPECIES	64

DESPITE BEING RELATIVELY few in terms of species, pelicans and their relatives include some of the most striking and varied fish-eating birds. Pelicans fish from the surface, using an elastic pouch attached to a giant bill. This order also includes plunge-diving gannets and boobies, surface-diving cormorants and anhingas, and also tropicbirds and frigatebirds, which catch their food while on the wing. Found throughout the world on freshwater, coasts, and the open sea, they make up an ancient group, with a fossil history going back over 100 million years.

ANATOMY

From a distance, the birds in this order seem to have little in common, apart from the fact that they eat fish. However, they share a number of unusual features that suggest a common ancestry. One of these is the structure of their feet – uniquely among birds, all four toes are connected by webs. Nearly all species have a throat pouch, a feature that is most developed in pelicans and frigatebirds. They fly well, but move with difficulty on the ground. Compared to other fish-eaters, pelicans and their relatives are often large and conspicuous. The Dalmatian Pelican, for example, has a wingspan of nearly 3m (10ft), while the Australian Pelican has the largest bill of any bird, measuring up to 47cm (18½in) long. Frigatebirds have a wingspan of up to 2.3m (7½ft), despite weighing less than 1.6kg (3¼lb).

A LIFE ALOFT
Frigatebirds soar over the sea, but they avoid landing on it because their feathers become waterlogged, making it difficult to take off again.

SCOOPING FOR FISH
A Brown Pelican's pouch balloons outwards as it reaches underwater. As the pouch stretches and fills, the lower half of the bill bows outwards.

BEHAVIOUR

Pelicans and their relatives vary greatly in the way that they feed, and in the amount of time that they spend in the water. At one extreme, frigatebirds spend almost all the daylight hours in their air, soaring high over the sea. They snatch food from the surface, or from other birds, but hardly ever settle on the water. Cormorants and anhingas are exactly the opposite: they spend a lot of time on the surface, and can dive for several minutes as they search for food. Between these two extremes, gannets and boobies plunge through the surface into shoals of fish, hitting them in a simultaneous attack. Few of the birds in this order are true migrants, although some species, such as gannets, spend several years wandering at sea before they eventually return to land to breed.

PLUNGE-DIVING
Brown Boobies plunge into a shoal of fish off the coast of Peru. Air sacs under the skin cushion their impact.

BREEDING

Most birds in this order nest in colonies, often on rocky offshore islands. The largest colonies, formed by gannets, boobies, and cormorants, can contain hundreds of thousands of birds, with each breeding pair spaced just beyond pecking distance from their neighbours. Their courtship rituals are elaborate: gannets have conspicuous "sky-pointing" and greeting ceremonies, while male frigatebirds puff up their scarlet pouches like balloons. Pelicans usually nest on the ground, like most gannets and boobies do. Most birds in this order produce highly dependent young. They often feed their chicks regurgitated food, which allows them to spend several hours fishing before they have to return to the nest.

NESTING IN A CROWD
Gannets, such as these Northern Gannets, nest in huge colonies on rocky islets, often staining them white with their droppings.

FEEDING TIME
Newly hatched pelicans are blind and poorly developed. Here, a young pelican reaches deep into its parent's throat for a meal of partly digested fish.

Phaethon aethereus

Red-billed Tropicbird

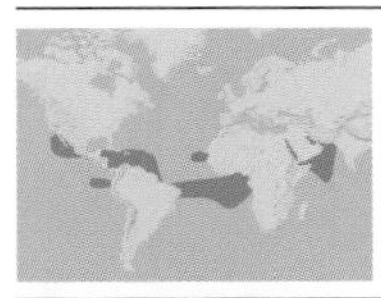

LENGTH 90–105cm (35–41in)

WEIGHT 650–700g (23–25oz)

MIGRATION Non-migrant

HABITAT Marine; breeds along rocky coastlines

The Red-billed Tropicbird is the largest member of a family of three distinctive species. The plumage of all three species is mainly white with black markings on the head and upperparts, but the Red-billed Tropicbird is distinguished by its red bill, black nape band, barred back, and white tail streamers. It has a long body, thick neck, and long, narrow wings. The tail is extraordinary, with the central pair of tail feathers elongated into elegant streamers that trail behind in flight. The bill is powerful, with a sharp, serrated edge.

The Red-billed Tropicbird has a powerful, direct flight with strong wingbeats. It often feeds far out to sea, plunge-diving to take prey on the water's surface. It also plunge-dives to catch fish and squid, and occasionally catches flying-fish in flight. The species occurs in all the subtropical and tropical oceans, although it has a restricted distribution in the Pacific Ocean. The Red-billed Tropicbird has been observed attempting to breed to the north of its normal range, and this change in breeding distribution may reflect increases in sea temperatures in these regions due to global warming.

RED-BILLED TROPICBIRD IN FLIGHT

Phaethon lepturus

White-tailed Tropicbird

LENGTH 70–90cm (28–35in)

WEIGHT 225–300g (8–11oz)

MIGRATION Non-migrant

HABITAT Tropical oceans; breeds on islands and atolls

Although the White-tailed Tropicbird has similar elegant white tail streamers – up to 45cm (17½in) long – to the Red-billed Tropicbird (above), it differs in its yellow bill and a much larger amount of black in the upper wing. It is monogamous and, like other tropicbirds, constructs its nest on the ground, well hidden under bushes, grass, and overhanging rocks in a wide variety of locations, including closed canopy forest. Nests are small unlined scrapes, but are vigorously defended by resident birds.

ADULT ON ITS NEST

Fregata andrewsi

Christmas Frigatebird

LENGTH 90–100cm (35–39in)

WEIGHT 1.5kg (3¼lb)

MIGRATION Non-migrant

HABITAT Tropical ocean; breeds in tall forest on shore terraces of Christmas Island

RED LIST CATEGORY Critically endangered

Both male and female Christmas Frigatebirds are mostly black with a white patch on the underparts, but the female also has a white collar and a white spur extending to the underwings. During the mating season, from December to June, the male displays its red throat pouch to attract females.

The Christmas Frigatebird has the most restricted range of the frigatebirds and breeds only on Christmas Island, in the Indian Ocean. Its distribution makes it vulnerable, and its numbers have declined as a result of forest clearance and phosphate mining.

Fregata minor

Great Frigatebird

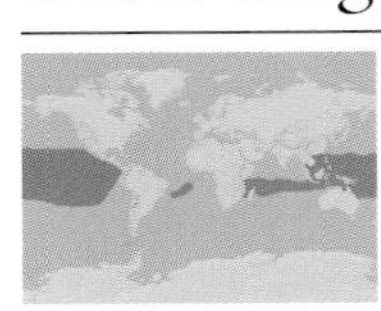

LENGTH 85–105cm (33–41in)

WEIGHT 1.2–1.6kg (2¼–3¼lb)

MIGRATION Non-migrant

HABITAT Tropical oceans; breeds on isolated well-vegetated islands and atolls

Mainly black in colour, the Great Frigatebird has a long blue-grey hooked bill. In the breeding season, the male's display is dramatic as it perches over a suitable nesting site to present an enormous inflated red gular (throat) sac at passing females, continuously shaking its wings as it does so.

With its remarkably light body, the Great Frigatebird is among the most aerial of all birds, rarely landing during the day, except when breeding. Famously, it obtains food by stealing it in flight from other seabirds, especially boobies. Target birds are harassed mercilessly until they regurgitate. The proportion of food collected in this way is probably small, but is more important when food is scarce.

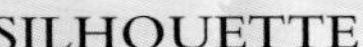

SILHOUETTE

The flight silhouette of the Great Frigatebird is very distinctive, with long, narrow, pointed wings and a deeply forked tail. Though it soars effortlessly for lengthy periods on thermals or flies purposefully with powerful wingbeats, it is ungainly on land and barely able to walk.

MALE DISPLAYING ITS RED THROAT SAC TO A FEMALE

BIRD SPECIES

Scopus umbretta

Hamerkop

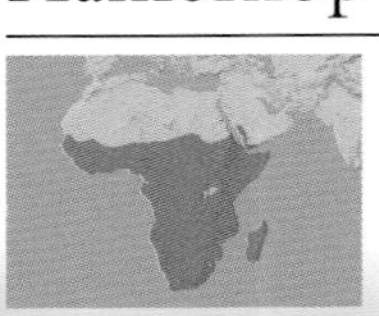

LENGTH 48–56cm (19–22in)

WEIGHT 475g (17oz)

MIGRATION Non-migrant

HABITAT Wide variety of swampy wetlands

Dull brown, with a pale chin and throat, the Hamerkop is named for its unusual shape – the word "Hamerkop" means "hammerhead" in German and aptly describes the bird's profile, with its strong bill and heavy crest at the back of its head. The Hamerkop feeds mainly on amphibians, using its strong bill to pick up frogs and fish from shallow water. Its nest is the largest roofed nest of any bird.

PAIR OF HAMERKOPS

NEST-BUILDING

Usually unobtrusive, the Hamerkop draws attention to itself by building huge nests of twigs and mud. These massive structures nestle in forked branches of large wetland trees and are built by both members of the pair. Equipped with a side entrance, these structures deter predators from gaining access to the egg-chamber.

Balaeniceps rex

Shoebill

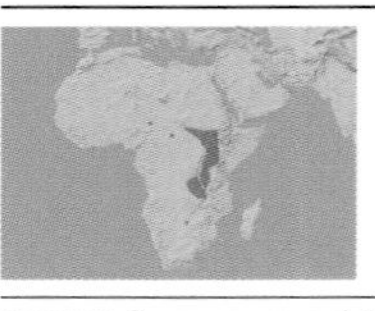

LENGTH 1.2m (4ft)

WEIGHT 5.5–6.5kg (12–14lb)

MIGRATION Non-migrant

HABITAT Swamps, especially with low, floating vegetation, in eastern and central Africa

RED LIST CATEGORY Vulnerable

A huge wetland bird standing over 1m (3¼ft) tall, the stork-like Shoebill is the sole member of its family. It has grey plumage. The enormous bill, shaped like a clog, gives rise to its name, and is used to catch fish, small reptiles, amphibians, and mammals. The Shoebill catches its prey by a powerful lunge at high speed into a pond or lake, with the bill and feet hitting the water at the same time. This species is threatened by habitat destruction and hunting.

ADULT SHOEBILL

ADULT GREAT WHITE PELICAN

Pelecanus onocrotalus

Great White Pelican

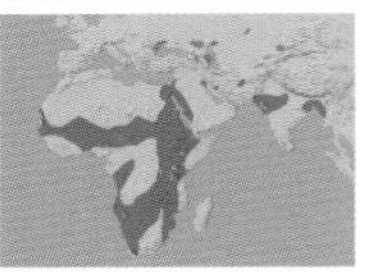

LENGTH 1.4–1.8m (4½–6ft)

WEIGHT 10–11kg (22–24lb)

MIGRATION Migrant

HABITAT Large, shallow wetlands, mostly freshwater, in warm lowlands

A typical member of its small but widespread family, the Great White Pelican has long, broad wings. At rest, these huge wings fit untidily against the body. This pelican has a bare pink facial patch around the eye, greyish white plumage, and pink legs. Adults develop a crest during the breeding season.

Juveniles are grey and have dark flight feathers. Pelicans are strong fliers, with deep wingbeats and the ability to glide occasionally. They can often be seen soaring in groups over suitable wetlands.

The feature the pelican is best known for is its huge, powerful bill and flexible gular (throat) pouch. The bill is used to catch fish rather as humans would use a dip net. The bird ducks its head under water or upends to scoop at shoals of fish. Water is then carefully spilled from the gular pouch, leaving only the fish, which are swallowed. Groups of pelicans can often be seen hunting co-operatively by herding shoaling fish together. The species is gregarious throughout the year and nests together in noisy colonies.

Pelecanus conspicillatus

Australian Pelican

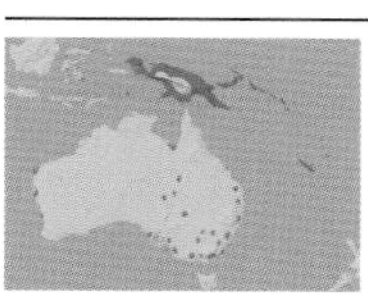

LENGTH 1.6–1.8m (5½–5¾ft)

WEIGHT 4–7kg (8¾–15lb)

MIGRATION Partial migrant

HABITAT Wide range of wetland habitats, including temporary lakes in arid areas

With its short grey crest, elongated hook-tipped bill, and a yellow or pink throat pouch, the Australian Pelican is distinctive. Its legs and feet are blue-grey in colour. A sociable bird, it feeds, roosts, and nests in large flocks. It is the only pelican to be found in Australia. All year, it is seen in the wetter parts of the country; migration occurs when huge inland lakes, such as Lake Eyre, fill up and become available for these birds.

ADULT AUSTRALIAN PELICAN

Pelecanus occidentalis

Brown Pelican

LENGTH 1.1m (3½ft)

WEIGHT 3.2–3.7kg (6½–7¾lb)

MIGRATION Partial migrant

HABITAT Coastal, marine habitats

Mainly silver-grey and brown, the Brown Pelican has a long bill with a pouch and a chestnut mane. It is unusual among the pelicans in that it feeds and breeds in coastal marine habitats. Indeed it is rare on inland wetlands and never found far out to sea. Its breeding behaviour is similar to that of other pelicans – the male will select a suitable nest site on the ground or in a tree or bush and display to attract a mate. Once paired, the male brings nesting material to the female, who constructs the nest.

ADULT BROWN PELICAN

PLUNGE-DIVING

While other pelicans swim and fish at the water's surface, the Brown Pelican is the only member of the family to feed by plunge-diving, a spectacular sight. When it spots a fish, it flies up as high as 10m (33ft) before folding back its wings and plunging into the sea to catch it. Brown Pelicans are gregarious, often hunting in this way in small flocks and herding shoaling fish together into a position where they can be caught with ease. In shallow water, however, they use their bills and throat pouches as dip nets, just as other pelicans do.

Pelecanus erythrorhynchos

American White Pelican

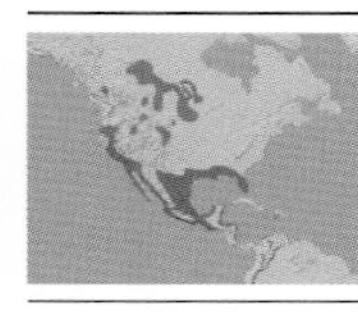

LENGTH 1.4–1.6m (4½–5½ft)

WEIGHT 5–6.5kg (11–14lb)

MIGRATION Migrant

HABITAT Breeds on freshwater lakes and shallow lagoons; winters on coasts and inland

The American White Pelican has the bill and gular (throat) pouch structure common to all pelicans. The upper mandible is flat with a strong ridge and is tipped with a sturdy hook. In breeding plumage, the American White Pelican's upper mandible is adorned with an additional keel-like knob. It can distend its large gular pouch at will using its tongue muscles, and can hold up to 10 litres (3 gallons) of water while feeding.

The American White Pelican breeds in wetlands throughout western North America. It winters in central California, along the Pacific coast to Guatemala, and on the shores of the Gulf of Mexico. Like many pelicans, it breeds in large colonies with other wetland birds. Such colonies are vulnerable to severe weather, which can cause high mortality in both adults and juveniles. Breeding in large colonies does, however, reduce the overall impact of predation by other creatures.

ADULT AMERICAN WHITE PELICANS

GREAT SITES

DANUBE DELTA

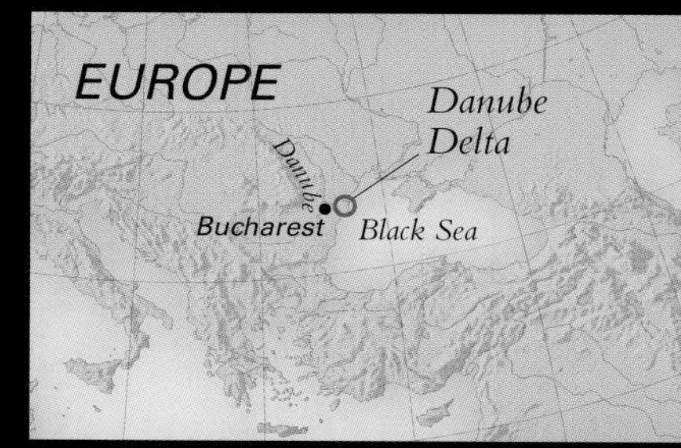

LOCATION At the mouth of the Danube River. on the western coast of the Black Sea, on the border between Romania and Ukraine.

Before draining into the Black Sea, the Danube River divides into three main branches and countless smaller channels to form the largest delta in Europe, covering 4,175 square km (1,610 square miles). This vast wetland is one of the last truly great European wildernesses. Heavily laden with silt, the murky brown river water disperses throughout the delta, giving rise to a complex mosaic of diverse habitats. More than 315 species of bird, including around 175 breeding species, have been recorded here, ensuring that the Lower Danube region ranks among the top birdwatching destinations in Europe. In 1991 approximately half of the delta's core area was inscribed as a UNESCO World Natural Heritage Site.

WATER BIRD DIVERSITY

The Danube Delta consists of a complex network of watercourses and shallow lakes and lagoons that are carpeted with water lilies in summer. There are also tree-fringed islands, and floating islets of decaying reeds called plaur, interspersed with extensive reedbeds, marshes, and seasonally flooded plains. The area is of massive importance for its breeding water birds. It supports significant numbers of Pygmy Cormorants and Dalmatian Pelicans, together with most of the European populations of Great White Egrets and White Pelicans. In addition, the delta's islands host large breeding colonies of Glossy Ibises, Eurasian Spoonbills, Eurasian Bitterns, and various herons. Whiskered Terns elegantly hawk for insects over the surface of virtually every pool, and the reedbeds are teeming with warblers. Patches of riverine woodland are home to nesting raptors and woodpeckers, while drier areas have shrikes, European Rollers, and Red-footed Falcons.

In April or early May, the northward passage through the delta of several million migratory birds can be spectacular and from November onwards, the delta provides shelter for wintering flocks of waterfowl, including at times 500,000 White-fronted Geese and 45,000 Red-breasted Geese – almost the entire world population of this rare species. But perhaps the most impressive resident is the White-tailed Sea-eagle, up to 40 of which overwinter in the delta.

PELICAN SANCTUARY
A group of White Pelicans gather on a nest-platform hidden amid the reedbeds. There are about 2,500 breeding pairs of this species in the Danube Delta.

WHAT TO SPOT

RED-BREASTED GOOSE
Branta ruficollis
(see p.126)

DALMATIAN PELICAN
Pelecanus crispus

RED-FOOTED FALCON
Falco vespertinus

EUROPEAN ROLLER
Coracias garrulus
(see p.304)

Morus bassanus

Northern Gannet

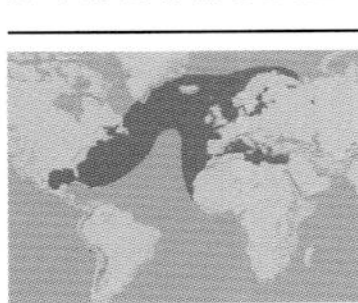

LENGTH 87–100cm (34–39in)

WEIGHT 2.4–3.6kg (5½–7¾lb)

MIGRATION Partial migrant

HABITAT Temperate marine waters; breeds on inaccessible islands and cliffs

A majestic seabird, the adult Northern Gannet is mainly white with black wing-tips and a buff-yellow tinge to the head. It has a streamlined shape that is used to good effect when it plunge-dives for fish from 10–40m (32–130ft) above the surface of the sea. During the dive, the Northern Gannet can plunge to 15m (50ft) below the surface. Air sacs around its throat and neck help to absorb the impact of such high-speed dives, and its nostrils can also be closed when diving. Dives are usually short-lived, lasting up to 20 seconds, while the bird catches its prey. It usually feeds on fish up to 30cm (12in) long, but also occasionally eats squid.

Northern Gannets breed on both sides of the Atlantic Ocean, and the populations have increased markedly since the early 20th century. Pairs may remain together for years and they also use the same nest for several years.

STREAMLINED SHAPE
With its torpedo-shaped body, long narrow wings, and a dagger-like bill, the Northern Gannet is well adapted to plunge-diving for fish.

BREEDING COLONIES

Northern Gannets nest in colonies that are usually situated on isolated rocks or small uninhabited islands. Colonies can also occur on steep inaccessible cliffs on larger islands and the mainland. The total population is estimated at 530,000 birds and a huge proportion of these nest in the largest colony on Boreray, an island in the St Kilda archipelago off northwest Scotland. This massive colony holds over 60,000 pairs.

NESTING FAMILY
A pair of gannets and their offspring are seen here at their nest – built on a cliff, it is made of marine flotsam, feathers, and droppings.

ADULT AUSTRALASIAN GANNET

Morus serrator

Australasian Gannet

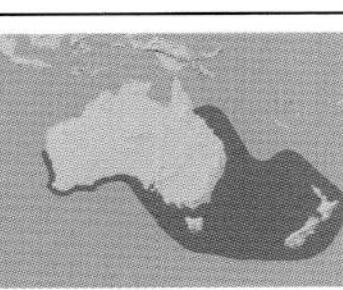

LENGTH 84–91cm (33–36in)

WEIGHT 2–2.8kg (4½–6½lb)

MIGRATION Migrant

HABITAT Marine, over continental shelf; breeds in isolated rocks, stacks and islands, and mainland cliffs

Similar to the Northern Gannet (left), the Australasian Gannet differs from it in having black secondary feathers when adult, and a black tail with white outer feathers. This species frequents the temperate waters around the east and south coasts of Australia and along the entire coastline of New Zealand. It is one of the least numerous of the gannets and boobies.

Sula dactylatra

Masked Booby

LENGTH 75–85cm (30–33in)

WEIGHT 2–2.5kg (4½–5½lb)

MIGRATION Migrant

HABITAT Marine; breeds on oceanic islands, atolls, and cays

The largest booby in the world, the Masked Booby has striking black and white plumage and a long yellow bill. Unlike the gannets that feed in shallow coastal zones, it is an oceanic wanderer, accustomed to the vastness of tropical and sub-tropical oceans. It breeds on remote oceanic islands and low-lying coral cays and atolls.

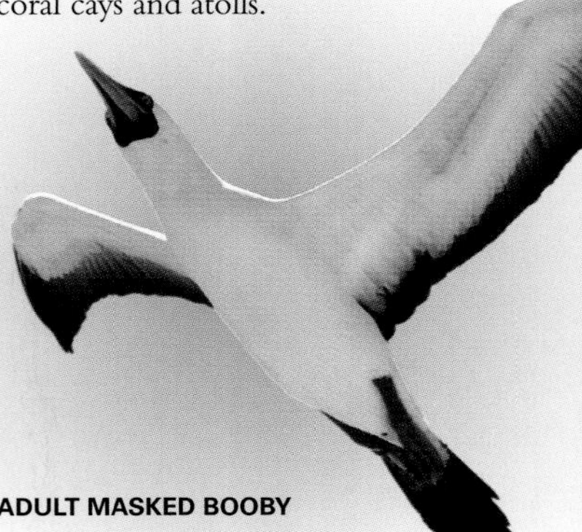

ADULT MASKED BOOBY

Sula nebouxii

Blue-footed Booby

LENGTH 76–84cm (30–33in)

WEIGHT 1.3–1.8kg (3¼–4½lb)

MIGRATION Non-migrant

HABITAT Marine; breeds on rocky coasts, cliffs, and islands

Aptly named for its bright blue feet, the Blue-footed Booby has pale brown plumage streaked in white and a white patch on its neck. It is monogamous, and strong bonds are maintained between male and female by repeated courtship displays at the nest site. The most impressive display is the "sky-pointing" ritual (pictured here). Both adults adopt a posture in which the bill is pointed skywards and the wing-tips and tail are raised. The adults walk in an exaggerated fashion and display each foot in turn, with their eyes focused downwards and the head moving slowly up and down. Sky-pointing is performed just before one of the pair flies out to sea. This species eats only fish caught by diving into the ocean, sometimes from great heights, and swimming underwater.

ADULTS PERFORMING SKY-POINTING COURTSHIP DISPLAY

PERUVIAN BOOBY BREEDING COLONY

Sula variegata

Peruvian Booby

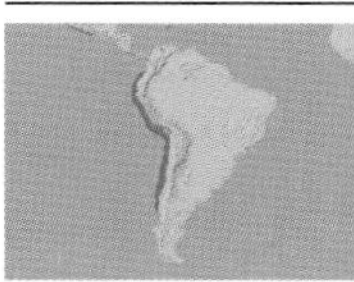

LENGTH 71–76cm (28–30in)

WEIGHT 1.5kg (3¼lb)

MIGRATION Partial migrant

HABITAT Marine (coastal), breeds on rocky islands and cliffs

The Peruvian Booby is white and brown in plumage, with a black patch around the bill. It is found down the west coast of South America and breeds along the coast between northern Peru and central Chile. This species once fed on just one type of fish, the anchoveta, which was very abundant in the productive, cool upwellings associated with the Humboldt Current. Overfishing up to the 1970s saw anchoveta stocks collapse completely and this was mirrored in the decline in populations of the Peruvian Booby. Since then, this bird seems to have successfully diversified its diet to include other fish species, but recent ocean-atmosphere climate fluctuations have resulted in further population declines. However, the Peruvian Booby is a robust species and its numbers appear to build up strongly after such reversals – it is currently not considered threatened. The species breeds throughout the year, with up to four eggs laid during nesting.

Sula sula

Red-footed Booby

LENGTH 70–80cm (28–31in)

WEIGHT 925–975g (33–35oz)

MIGRATION Non-migrant

HABITAT Tropical oceans, breeds on oceanic islands, atolls, and cays

The Red-footed Booby is unusual among the gannets and boobies in that there are two adult plumage types. In the brown form, the head, neck, upperwing, and underparts are pale brown. The flight feathers are darker brown and the tail is white. In the other form, the pale brown parts of the brown form are coloured white and only the flight feathers are dark. There is also a wide range of intermediate forms, which have varying amounts of brown and white in the plumage. However, it is easy to identify the Red-footed Booby by the coloration of its bare parts, which never varies; the pink-based blue bill and the striking red or orange feet. Unlike most species of booby, the Red-footed Booby nests in trees or shrubs and not on the ground. Its nest is made of twigs or other material and quickly becomes coated in guano (droppings).

ADULT (BROWN FORM)

Phalacrocorax pygmeus

Pygmy Cormorant

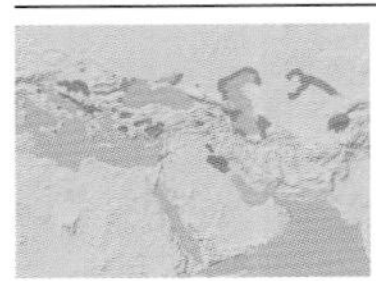

LENGTH 45–55cm ($17^1/_2$–$21^1/_2$in)

WEIGHT 750g (27oz)

MIGRATION Partial migrant

HABITAT Freshwater lakes and coastal deltas; more rarely on rivers and reservoirs

Black, with a bronzed neck, the Pygmy Cormorant is small-billed and short-necked. It normally fishes alone, usually by diving from low perches, and catches fish such as pike and carp. It nests in colonies, building a nest of twigs and grass in reeds or low trees. The species is at risk due to wetland drainage and the construction of river dams.

ADULT PYGMY CORMORANT

Leucocarbo aristotelis

European Shag

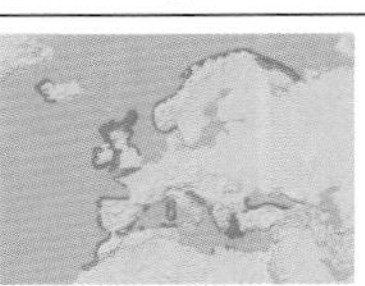

LENGTH 68–78cm (27–31in)

WEIGHT 2kg ($4^1/_4$lb)

MIGRATION Partial migrant

HABITAT Coastal cliffs and small marine islands, but sometimes on inland reservoirs, lakes, and rivers

PAIR OF ADULTS

This slender bird, with its green-glossed black plumage, has a tufted head and yellow gape on the sides of its thin, slightly hooked bill. It flies fast and low over water and is frequently seen perched on rocks. The species breeds in loose colonies and the nests are placed in caves or in the crevices between large boulders.

ADULT FLIGHTLESS CORMORANT

Phalacrocorax harrisi

Flightless Cormorant

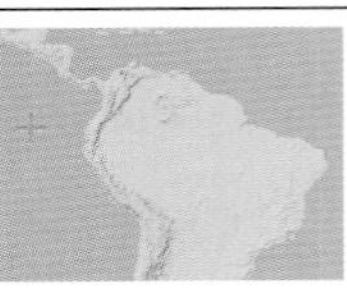

LENGTH 89–100cm (35–39in)

WEIGHT 3.5kg ($7^3/_4$lb)

MIGRATION Non-migrant

HABITAT Inshore waters; on land, always near the shoreline, on shingle and lava outcrops

With its tiny, ragged-looking wings, the Flightless Cormorant is unable to fly. Its habitat, the islands of Fernandina and Isabela in the Galapagos, was once free of predators, allowing the bird to lose its flying ability. It is dark in colour, with black upperparts and brown underparts, and has a hooked bill. The male is usually larger than the female.

These unusual cormorants nest in small groups of a few pairs, mainly in March to September, and on islands in the coldest waters, where food is plentiful. Its flightlessness increases the bird's vulnerability to oil spills and it is now threatened by the introduction of rats and cats in the Galapagos islands, where the species breeds. It can also be affected by environmental changes, as it is not known to disperse beyond its small range.

Phalacrocorax auritus

Double-crested Cormorant

LENGTH 74–89cm (29–35in)

WEIGHT 1.5–2.1kg ($3^1/_4$–$4^1/_2$lb)

MIGRATION Non-migrant

HABITAT Sheltered coasts; inland lakes and rivers

Largely black, with a green sheen, and brown upperparts with black scaling, the Double-crested Cormorant has bright orange skin around its bill. The ear tufts, to which its name refers, are a feature only of breeding birds. These tufts are largely white in birds of its western range but are typically black in eastern populations. In flight, this cormorant shows a prominent crook in its neck.

The species is highly sociable and usually occurs in flocks, although solitary birds are occasionally seen. The Double-crested Cormorant breeds in colonies, often placing its nest, made of twigs and grasses, low over water in mangrove swamps or other wooded places.

BREEDING ADULT

Leucocarbo bougainvillii

Guanay Cormorant

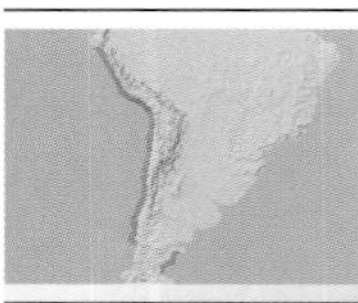

LENGTH 71–76cm (28–30in)

WEIGHT 2.5kg ($5^1/_2$lb)

MIGRATION Non-migrant

HABITAT Mainly marine; breeds on low, flat islands

Confined to the Humboldt Current region off western South America, Guanay Cormorants have been well known to local people for centuries, being one of the most famous of the "guano" birds, so-named for the economic value of their droppings, used as a fertilizer. In the early 20th century, a single breeding island of Guanay Cormorants could be worth several million dollars, due to the dense accumulation of guano.

The back of this cormorant is mainly black, with a green-blue iridescence, while its throat and chest are white. It also has a red patch around the eye and a grey bill. Guanay Cormorants form dense flocks, both in the water, where they feed en masse, and on land. Some colonies were once considered to number millions of birds, but the species is now declining.

ADULT GUANAY CORMORANTS

JUVENILE GREAT CORMORANT

Phalacrocorax carbo

Great Cormorant

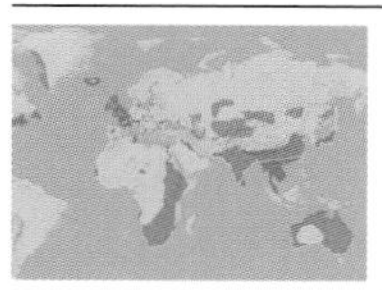

LENGTH 77–94cm (30–37in)

WEIGHT 1.9–3kg (4½–6½lb)

MIGRATION Partial migrant

HABITAT All types of coasts, but also on expanses of inland water, including reed marshes and reservoirs

The Great Cormorant has one of the most widespread territories in its family. Though it is generally black with a bright yellow throat patch, this is a species with a variable plumage. In the north of its range, the breeding adult is principally black, with a green gloss and white feathering on the head, but much browner and paler below in other seasons. Further south in the species' range, the adult has extensive white underparts.

Like most cormorants, this species breeds in colonies numbering up to 2,000 pairs. Nests are normally constructed of seaweed, twigs, or reeds, usually on elevated ground or on trees. It prefers to hunt in shallow water but can dive to depths of 30m (100ft).

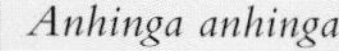

Anhinga anhinga

Anhinga

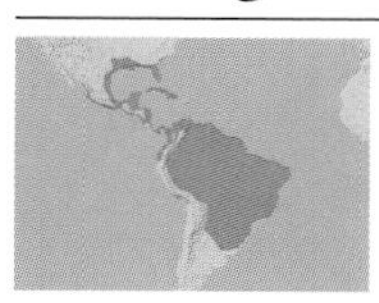

LENGTH 85–89cm (33–35in)

WEIGHT 1.2kg (2¼lb)

MIGRATION Non-migrant

HABITAT Usually calm bodies of fresh water, from large estuaries to small ponds

The Anhinga or Darter, as it is also known, has a slender, straight bill, elongated neck, and long tail. It is snake-like in appearance as it glides through the water, so low as to be almost invisible. When the adult is at rest and extends its wings to dry, the large white patches on its back and upper wing are noticeable. The juvenile is pale brown in colour, with paler underparts. Unlike cormorants, the Anhinga lacks a hook at the tip of its bill and is also different in flight, as it circles high on thermals like a bird of prey, flapping its large, broad wings.

The Anhinga constructs a nest of twigs and leaves. It is sociable when breeding, nesting in colonies with other tree-nesting birds, such as herons, ibises, and cormorants.

ADULT ANHINGA

IMPERIAL SHAG ON ITS NEST

Leucocarbo atriceps

Imperial Shag

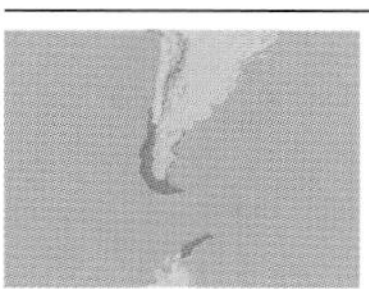

LENGTH 75cm (30in)

WEIGHT 2.5kg (5½lb)

MIGRATION Non-migrant

HABITAT Largely marine, but breeds on large flat-topped islands

A large black and white cormorant with a blue eye-ring, short crest, and yellow knobs above the bill, the Imperial Shag is one of many similar-looking species found mainly on islands and remote continental areas throughout the southern hemisphere.

The Imperial Shag breeds in large, dense colonies, which are often situated close to those of the Rockhopper Penguin (see p.139) and the Black-browed Albatross (see p.145), ensuring that such places produce a cacophony of sound. The nest is made of mud and algae, with a lining of grasses for the 2–4 eggs.

These cormorants travel great distances from their colonies to find food, mainly crustaceans and small fish that they catch by diving deep under water. Although their habitat is now used by fisheries, they do not appear to favour commercially exploited fish, thus avoiding conflict with humans.

FEEDING TECHNIQUE

The Anhinga feeds principally on fish, which it captures by using its long, spear-shaped, narrow bill. The bird swims stealthily through shallow water, stalking fish just below the surface, before stabbing one and raising it out of the water, still skewered by its bill. It then flips the fish in the air and swallows it head-first.

BIRDS OF PREY

ORDER	Falconiformes
FAMILY	3
SPECIES	304

WITH SOME SPECIES having enormous wingspans, birds of prey include the world's largest flying carnivores. Also known as raptors, most of them catch their food with their talons – something that requires superb eyesight and fast reactions, particularly when catching prey in mid-air. This large order contains eagles, hawks, kites, and falcons, together with carrion-eating vultures. As a group, they live throughout the world except in Antarctica.

ANATOMY

Birds of prey vary hugely in size. Some eagles have a wingspan of nearly 3m (10ft), compared to just 20cm (8in) for the smallest falconets from southeast Asia. Despite this huge difference in size, all birds of prey share a similar body plan, although with markedly different proportions, particularly in the shape of their wings. Birds of prey have powerful feet armed with sharp claws or talons, and their legs are often feathered as far as the ankle joint. All of them have strongly hooked bills, which they use for tearing up their food, rather than for catching their prey. They also have forward-facing eyes – a vital adaptation for judging distances accurately when they move in to make a kill. Owls have a similar anatomy, but unlike them, almost all birds of prey hunt by day.

WEDGE-TAILED EAGLE

RED KITE

PEREGRINE FALCON

WING SHAPES
With its widely spaced primary flight feathers, the Wedge-tailed Eagle is a typical soaring bird of prey. The Red Kite's kinked wings make it agile in the air, while the Peregrine Falcon's slender wings are shaped for speed.

WINGS AND FLIGHT

Even from the far distance, their distinctive wing shape and flight path help to identify different birds of prey. Eagles, buzzards, and vultures typically fly high in the sky, soaring effortlessly on their broad, outstretched wings. One species of African vulture – Rüppell's Vulture – is on record as the highest flier of this order of birds, after colliding with an aircraft at over 11,000m (36,000ft). However, such high-flying birds are an exception, because most birds of prey operate much closer to the ground. Kites and harriers criss-cross open country and woodland, flying at a leisurely pace relatively near the ground as they watch for potential prey below. Birds of the kestrel family are instantly recognizable, because they are among the few birds of prey that hover while they watch for food. Other birds of prey, such as peregrines and sparrowhawks, are pursuit hunters. These have a flight pattern more like that of a fighter plane: they burst through the air at high speed, diving or swooping on other birds, which are their main prey, and move on straight away if they fail to make a kill.

CLASSIFICATION

Birds of prey are classified in a single order. However, DNA and anatomical studies suggest that American vultures are not closely related to vultures from the Old World, and may be closer to storks. Their outward similarity to Old World vultures is probably the result of convergent evolution, creating similar body forms for similar ways of life.

A CASE OF CONVERGENCE
Like other American vultures, the King Vulture (right) has long legs and weak feet, without strongly curved toes. The Griffon Vulture (far right) is a typical Old World vulture, with grasping feet that are much more like those of eagles and buzzards.

HUNTING AND DIET

Despite their reputation as heavyweight hunters, some birds of prey have unusual and surprising diets. The Snail Kite, for example, lives entirely on freshwater snails, while the Palm-nut Vulture from Africa feeds on the fruit of oil and raffia palms. Small falcons often prey on dragonflies, while some large raptors – such as the Common Buzzard – will stoop to eating earthworms if the weather is too cold or wet for soaring. But given good conditions, most raptors are specialists, concentrating on particular kinds of prey. The fish-eating Osprey has spiny toes which help it to grip its catch, while snake eagles grip their prey just behind the head, preventing it from striking back. In tropical forests, Harpy Eagles snatch monkeys and sloths out of the treetops, carrying prey weighing up to 6kg (13lb) – about two-thirds of their own body weight. Aerial hunters, such as Peregrine Falcons and sparrowhawks, can kill birds substantially bigger than themselves. The latter grip their prey with their talons, but Peregrine Falcons slash it as they dive past, leaving the stricken bird to fall tumbling to the ground, where it is retrieved by the successful hunter.

BIRD EATS BIRD
The Eurasian Sparrowhawk flies low over hedges and woodland, preying on other birds. This adult female is feeding on a Grey Partridge. It plucks its victim's breast, eats the flight muscles, but leaves the rest.

SUCCESSFUL CATCH
The Osprey is one of the most widespread birds of prey. It fishes on lakes, reservoirs, and coasts, flying back to a favourite perch after making a catch.

NATURE'S RECYCLERS
Vultures are most common in dry, open habitats where columns of rising air make it easy to soar. These White-backed Vultures in Namibia have gathered around a zebra carcass.

HUMAN IMPACT

THREATS AND CONSERVATION

A quarter of all birds of prey are currently listed as vulnerable, threatened, or endangered. In southern Asia, some vultures have declined by over 95 per cent in less than a decade. Birds of prey are also threatened by habitat destruction – something that particularly affects large, tropical forest species.

CHECKING UP
A biologist fits a leg band to a Peregrine Falcon chick, so that its movements can be followed once it leaves the nest.

NESTING AND PARENTING

Birds of prey rarely build elaborate nests, and falcons often take over the disused nests of other birds. However, many species show great site tenacity, using the same nest year after year. These birds often add new nesting material each time they breed, creating enormous structures that can weigh over a tonne. Compared to other birds, birds of prey produce relatively few eggs, and they begin incubation as soon as the first is laid. In large eagles, the incubation period can be as long as seven weeks, but in all cases, it starts as soon as the first egg has been laid. Once the eggs have hatched, the chicks can take over two months to fledge. If food runs short during this period, the largest chick frequently eats its smaller siblings.

SWOOPING FOR THE KILL
With its wings, talons, and tail outstretched, a Golden Eagle swoops down onto its prey. Birds of prey instinctively attack mammals from behind, minimizing their chances of being seen until it is too late for their prey to escape.

GROWING FAMILY
High in a pine tree, an adult Northern Goshawk tends its three chicks. As with most birds of prey, the parents bring food back to the nest, and tear it up into pieces that are small enough for their chicks to swallow.

ADULT TURKEY VULTURE

Cathartes aura

Turkey Vulture

LENGTH 76cm (30in)

WEIGHT 1.4kg ($3^{1}/_{4}$lb)

MIGRATION Partial migrant

HABITAT Open or semi-open areas, often nesting on open ground where there are few other nests

A common bird of North and South America, the Turkey Vulture is so named because its bare-skinned head is similar to that of a Wild Turkey (see p.109). Its grey-brown plumage with two-tone wings contrast with its bright red to pink head and neck, and it has a hooked white bill. This vulture has a keen sense of smell, enabling it to locate prey even in thick jungle.

ROADSIDE SCAVENGERS

Well known for its habit of feeding on carcasses, the Turkey Vulture is a common roadside scavenger in its range, often seen feeding on roadkill. Its fondness for carrion probably accounts for its increase in populated areas.

Coragyps atratus

Black Vulture

LENGTH 60cm ($23^{1}/_{2}$in)

WEIGHT 2–2.7kg ($4^{1}/_{2}$–$5^{1}/_{2}$lb)

MIGRATION Non-migrant

HABITAT Open areas, including urban habitats, but avoids forests

The Black Vulture is predominantly a black bird, but the slightly iridescent feathers on its back make it appear green in bright light. The undersides of its wings are usually paler than the black plumage on the rest of its body, and it has long, grey-white legs. Its tail is short and squared, barely extending beyond the wing.

While its main food is carrion, it is also an opportunistic scavenger, eating even fruit and other birds' eggs. When alarmed, these vultures are able to regurgitate food to lighten their weight so that they can quickly escape. The Black Vulture is not agile in the air – its flight appears laboured, with long periods of gliding between a few wing flaps. It is often seen soaring on warm updraughts. The Black Vulture often forms large groups, usually together with Turkey Vultures (see above), although they are always dominant over the latter.

In the breeding season, the female lays two eggs in a suitable structure such as a tree stump, or in dark recesses like rocky crevices, hollow logs, tree cavities, and caves. However, the species is now often found nesting in sheltered parts of buildings. Its population is increasing, showing an expansion into urban areas. It is often seen in markets, fishing docks, and rubbish dumps and has adapted well to habitats disturbed by human activity.

ADULT BLACK VULTURE

Sarcoramphus papa

King Vulture

LENGTH 80cm (31in)

WEIGHT 3–3.8kg ($6^{1}/_{2}$–$8^{3}/_{4}$lb)

MIGRATION Non-migrant

HABITAT Forests and open areas to an altitude of 1.5km (1 mile)

This spectacular bird has contrasting black and white wings, which make it noticeable in flight, but its ornate black, yellow, and red markings on the bare head set the King Vulture apart from other vultures. It also has a fleshy growth above its beak that is often bright orange in mature individuals. Unlike many birds, both the males and females develop this growth, the main function of which is to show dominance when they gather with others to feed at a carcass.

Unusually for a scavenging bird, this species detects food by watching and then following other scavengers, not by using smell. It is not recorded as a true predator as it feeds only on carrion. Like most vultures, it has no voice box, its calls being limited to grunts and hisses.

WINGS ON DISPLAY
The King Vulture spreads its broad wings to display its impressive wingspan of 2m ($6^{1}/_{2}$ft).

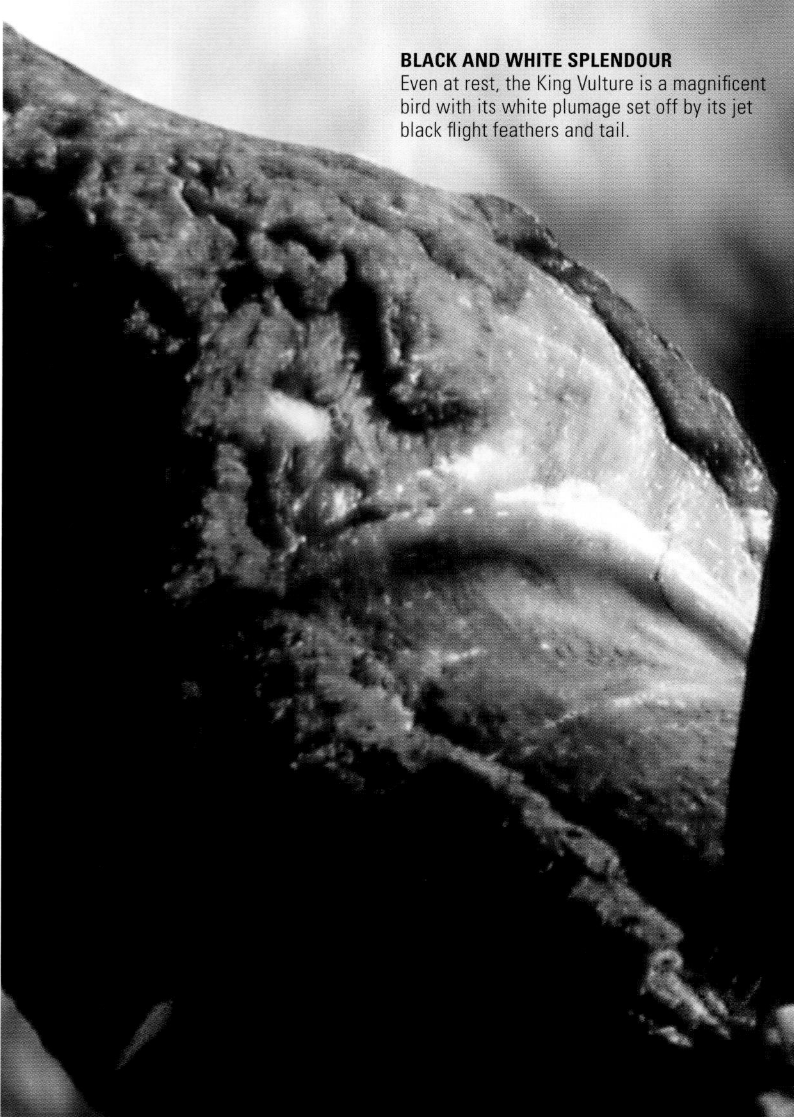

BLACK AND WHITE SPLENDOUR
Even at rest, the King Vulture is a magnificent bird with its white plumage set off by its jet black flight feathers and tail.

Gymnogyps californianus

California Condor

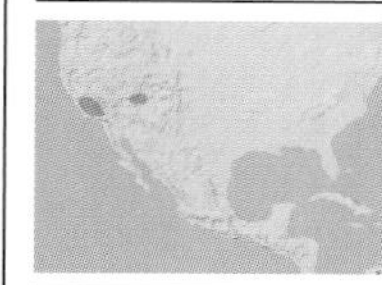

LENGTH 1.3m (4¼ft)

WEIGHT 9–11kg (20–24lb)

MIGRATION Non-migrant

HABITAT Open areas, but also wooded areas, scrubland, and rocky habitats.

RED LIST CATEGORY Critically endangered

Now found mainly in captivity or in controlled conditions in the wild, California Condors were on the brink of extinction, but despite some losses, are slowly increasing in number today (see panel, below). This species has black plumage with white-tipped wing feathers, a bare-skinned head tinged orange or pink, a black neck ruff, a hooked white bill, and pink legs and feet. It eats large carrion, but can survive several days without feeding.

CALIFORNIA CONDOR

HUMAN IMPACT

CAPTIVE BREEDING

To save the California Condor from extinction, all remaining birds in California were trapped for a captive breeding programme in 1987, which to some extent reduced this risk. When captive-bred birds are reintroduced in the wild, they are continually monitored by numbered wing-tags (see left) and radio transmitters.

Vultur gryphus

Andean Condor

LENGTH 1.2m (4ft)

WEIGHT 11–15kg (24–33lb)

MIGRATION Non-migrant

HABITAT Mountainous areas, but also found in lowlands to the west of the Andes

A huge bird, the Andean Condor has the largest wing area of any bird. The adult male has a prominent fleshy comb stretching from the beak to the top of the head. It also shows large areas of white to the trailing edge of the wing when seen from above.

Most populations are threatened due to the limited geographical range of the species and a slow breeding rate in remote sites. The Andean Condor has an important role in South American folklore yet persecution is widespread due to a perceived threat to livestock although many of the birds are in sparsely inhabited areas.

ADULT MALE

Caracara cheriway

Northern Crested Caracara

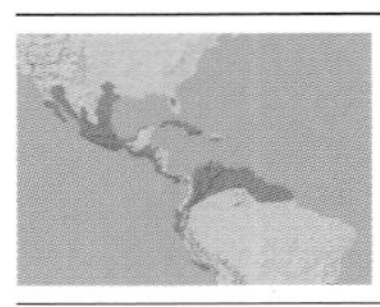

LENGTH 51–60cm (20–23½in)

WEIGHT 0.8–1.2kg (1¾–2¼lb)

MIGRATION Non-migrant

HABITAT Mainly open and semi-open country, such as grassland, bushland, farmland, and ranchland

The Northern Crested Caracara is not a fast-flying aerial hunter, but it uses its long legs to search for prey on ground. When excited, the bare skin on the face changes colour, from orange or shades of red to bright yellow. The sexes are similar, but the juvenile has a brown back, buff neck and throat, and pale breast streaked with brown. This species is omnivorous and will eat reptiles, amphibians, and carrion. It nests in a tree or on the ground, laying 2–4 eggs.

ADULT FEEDING ON A LIZARD

Milvago chimachima

Yellow-headed Caracara

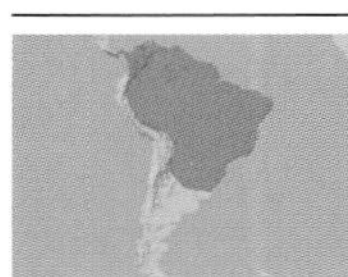

LENGTH 40–46cm (15½–18in)

WEIGHT 300–325g (11–12oz)

MIGRATION Non-migrant

HABITAT Ranchland, savanna, palm groves, and open country with scattered trees

ADULT BIRD

The Yellow-headed Caracara adult has a buff head and underparts, with contrasting dark brown upperparts, while the juvenile is mottled with brown on the underparts. It has a buoyant flight with even wingbeats and occasional sweeping glides. The call of the species is a screamed "schreee". It is omnivorous and is often seen feeding on roadkill. It will also take ticks from cattle, earning it the name of "tickbird".

Herpetotheres cachinnans

Laughing Falcon

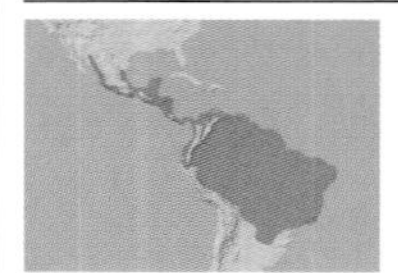

LENGTH 43–52cm (17–20½in)

WEIGHT 575–675g (21–24oz)

MIGRATION Non-migrant

HABITAT Forest edges and clearings, savanna, palm groves, and plantations

The common name of this unusual, large-headed Neotropical falcon comes from its cackling alarm call. It is a specialist snake-eater and often remains for hours on an exposed perch, on the lookout for food. It catches snakes by pouncing on them and then biting them just behind the head. It supplements its diet with lizards, small rodents, and also bats and centipedes. This falcon flies with quick, shallow wingbeats interspersed with glides and it seldom soars. It nests in rock- or tree-cavities, or uses the abandoned nests of other raptors.

ADULT LAUGHING FALCON

Polihierax semitorquatus

Pygmy Falcon

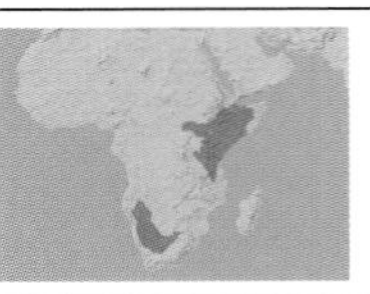

LENGTH 18–21 cm (7–8½in)

WEIGHT 60g (2⅛oz)

MIGRATION Partial migrant

HABITAT Dry acacia savanna, thornbush, and sub-desert scrub

This tiny falcon is closely associated with the Sociable Weaver (see p.452) and White-headed Buffalo Weaver (see p.454) colonies and breeds in their massed multi-chamber nests. It can often be seen scanning the ground from an exposed branch of a tree or a telephone pole and dropping in a quick swoop to catch large insects and small lizards. The male has a grey back, while the female's back is chestnut.

ADULT MALE

Falco tinnunculus

Common Kestrel

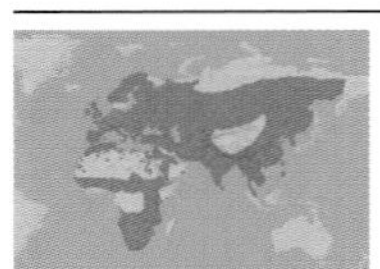

LENGTH 27–35cm (10½–14in)

WEIGHT 175–200g (6–7oz)

MIGRATION Partial migrant

HABITAT Wide range of areas, including farmland, forest edges, grassland, and suburban places

Often seen hovering over open country and along roadsides, the Common Kestrel is one of the most well-known birds of prey in Europe. The male has a blue-grey head and a red-brown back, spotted with black, while the female has a brown head and tail. The Common Kestrel's tail is slim, with a black band on each feather. This kestrel preys on small mammals, including voles, as well as small birds, large insects, earthworms, and frogs. Sensitive to ultraviolet rays, it can see the urine trails of rodents, which reflect ultraviolet light. It has excellent eyesight, and can see a beetle about 50m (165ft) from its perch. It nests on bare ledges on cliffs, quarries, tree-holes, unoccupied crows' nests, or even old, unused buildings.

HOVERING

While scanning the ground for its prey, the Common Kestrel can hover in one place for a long time, beating its wings very rapidly. As it hovers, its tail spreads out like a fan, displaying a black band across its feathers. The fan-shaped tail acts as a brake when it is about to land.

ADULT FEMALE

Falco rupicoloides

Greater Kestrel

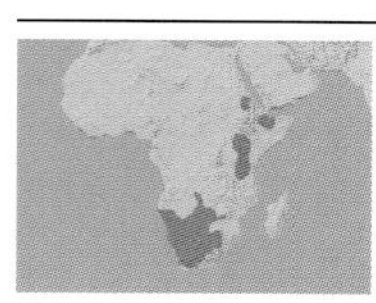

LENGTH 29–37cm (11½–14½in)

WEIGHT 250g (9oz)

MIGRATION Non-migrant

HABITAT Open grassland and savanna with scattered trees

The Greater or White-eyed Kestrel is widespread in Africa. As its name suggests, it has a pale eye, which helps to distinguish it from similar all-brown kestrels. The tail is grey, with thick black bars along its length. The juvenile has a browner tail and dark eye. There are three different subspecies, with well-defined ranges. The Greater Kestrel nests in trees, usually using the abandoned nest of another bird, and lays 3–5 eggs.

Falco columbarius

Merlin

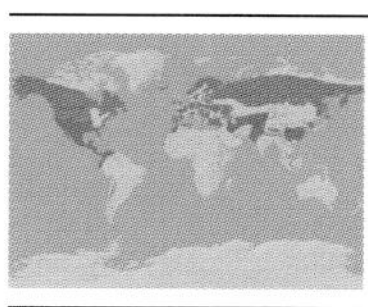

LENGTH 24–32cm (9½–12½in)

WEIGHT 175–225g (6–8oz)

MIGRATION Migrant

HABITAT Tundra, arctic-alpine, and temperate areas in summer; open places and coasts in winter

The Merlin relies on speed and agility to hunt its prey, which mainly consists of small birds such as larks and pipits, although it also eats a variety of large flying insects. It hunts by flying fast and low, often less than 1m (3¼ft) above the ground, in order to surprise its prey. The male Merlin is blue-grey above, and cream to rufous-buff below, with dark streaks; its pale grey tail has a black band. The female is brown above and has cream, brown-streaked underparts, its banded tail being brown and cream.

This species nests on the ground throughout most of its range, but also uses abandoned nests of other birds, especially crows' nests. It breeds from April to June and 3–6 eggs are laid. The male's call is a quick, sharp "kik-kik-ki-kik", while the female has a deeper, more nasal, "kee-kee-kee-kee", but both are quiet when nesting and in winter.

FEMALE MERLIN

Falco subbuteo

Eurasian Hobby

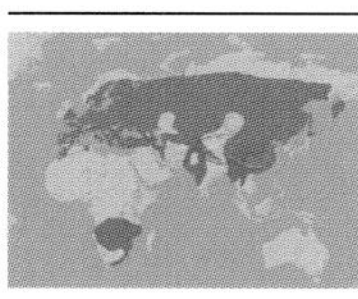

LENGTH 28–34cm (11–13½in)

WEIGHT 200–225g (7–8oz)

MIGRATION Migrant

HABITAT Edges of temperate forest and woodland in summer; grassland in winter

This sleek, sickle-winged falcon is a long-distance migrant, breeding from Europe to Russia and wintering mainly in southern Africa.

The adult has white cheeks that contrast with the black hood; it is slate-grey above and streaked below. At close range, the red vent and thigh feathers can be seen. The Eurasian Hobby is a fast and skilful hunter. It can be seen catching large dragonflies, which it eats in flight, and regularly preys on swallows and even swifts. The female uses abandoned nests of crows and other birds, laying 2–4 eggs. Its breeding season is carefully timed to feed its young – it has chicks in the nest when the recently fledged young of small birds are numerous, and the young leave the nest when there are plenty of dragonflies on the wing.

ADULT HUNTING INSECTS

Falco sparverius

American Kestrel

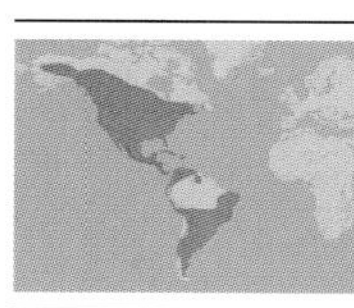

LENGTH 21–27cm (8–10½in)

WEIGHT 100–125g (3⅝–4½)

MIGRATION Migrant

HABITAT Wide variety of habitats, including urban areas, but not dense forests or tundra

This small and beautifully marked falcon is one of the most familiar raptors in its range. It has two vertical facial lines and its rufous back is barred in black. There are dark spots on its pale yellow breast.

The American Kestrel hunts from a perch or on the wing, and often hovers. It mainly eats large insects during the summer, while in winter, when insects are scarce, it turns to mice and small birds. It also takes young waterbirds, lizards, amphibians, and even scorpions. It is a noisy bird, uttering excited, high-pitched cries, including a series of 3–6 "klee" notes when alarmed. The American Kestrel often nests in a tree cavity and lays 3–7 eggs. Incubation takes 29 to 30 days and the young take their first flight about 30 days after hatching. Despite being hardy birds, American Kestrels in the wild are likely to have a life expectancy of no more than 2-5 years.

ADULT MALE

Falco biarmicus

Lanner Falcon

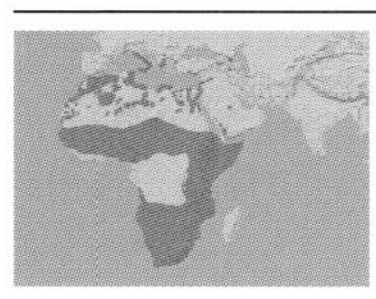

LENGTH 39–48cm (15½–19in)

WEIGHT 500–725g (18–26oz)

MIGRATION Partial migrant

HABITAT Open dry country, desert, semi-desert, rocky wadis, lightly wooded savanna, and grassland

A fast-flying bird, the Lanner Falcon preys on birds and bats. It has a black-bordered rufous cap and nape, which contrasts with steely-grey upperparts and white underparts. The juvenile is a bluish grey. This species usually hunts by horizontal pursuit. It is prized in falconry, as it displays a docile nature often lacking in more powerful falcons. It may be identified by its strident call, which has a repeated "kak-kak" sound.

Falco rusticolus

Gyrfalcon

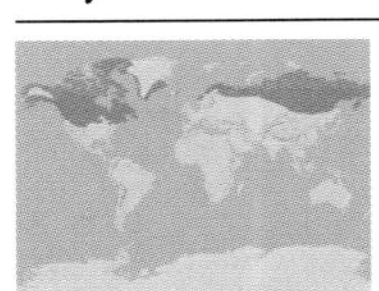

LENGTH
50–60cm (19½–23½in)

WEIGHT
1.2–1.7kg (2¼–3¾lb)

MIGRATION
Partial migrant

HABITAT From coastal cliffs to mountain crags, including tundra and woodland edges

The Gyrfalcon is the world's largest falcon and is found in three colour forms - white, grey, and dark. It feeds on birds and mammals, from small finches to large geese, and from voles to hares. It perches, watching for food, then flies low and fast to surprise its prey. Birds may be chased, but are usually caught on the ground or on water. This species is highly prized by falconers.

ADULT GYRFALCON

Falco mexicanus

Prairie Falcon

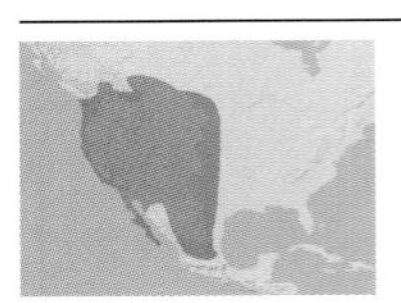

LENGTH
37–47cm (14½–18½in)

WEIGHT
600–900g (21–32oz)

MIGRATION
Partial migrant

HABITAT Grassland, prairies, desert, and wooded mountains, from high tundra down to sea level

The Prairie Falcon is a large, slim bird, with a grey-brown plumage. Outside the breeding season it can be highly nomadic, moving to where its food is plentiful. In some parts, its breeding is linked with the emergence of ground squirrels, an important prey item. As well as mammals and birds, it also eats lizards and large insects. It can be noisy and aggressive at times.

ADULT PRAIRIE FALCON

ADULT PEREGRINE FALCON

Falco peregrinus

Peregrine Falcon

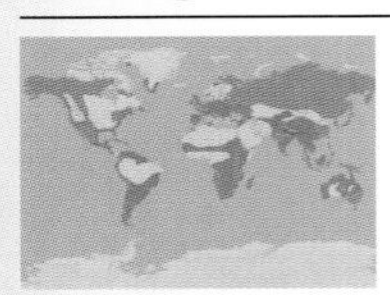

LENGTH
35–51cm (14–20in)

WEIGHT
0.5–1.2kg (1–2¼lb)

MIGRATION
Migrant

HABITAT Open country from mountains to coasts; large cities along rivers

The Peregrine Falcon is the fastest bird of prey, and can travel at speeds of up to 250kph (155mph), perhaps even faster. It will spot its prey from high in the sky, close its long wings, and dive down in a stoop. It preys mainly on birds, taking a wide variety, such as ducks, waders, pigeons, and parrots. The female is about double the size of the male and can catch larger prey. The upperparts of this bird are slate-grey and it is barred below. Its head has a helmeted pattern with a dark moustache.

The Peregrine Falcon has a wide distribution throughout the world. Arctic breeding birds will migrate south of the equator, while tropical populations are resident. There are 16 different subspecies, which vary in size and plumage.

Sagittarius serpentarius

Secretarybird

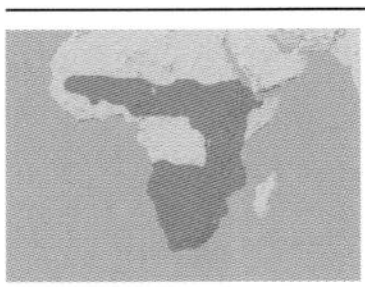

LENGTH
1.1–1.5m (3½–5ft)

WEIGHT
4kg (8¾lb)

MIGRATION
Non-migrant

HABITAT Open and bushy grassland, large cereal farms, and semi-desert with scrub

Unlike any other bird of prey, the Secretarybird has extraordinarily long legs, a long wedge-shaped tail, and a crest of black feathers on the back of its head. It gets its name from the crest, which resembles a row of quill pens, once used by secretaries. It spends most of its time on the ground and has the ability to run fast, taking off with a flapping run and sometimes soaring high on thermals, like other birds of prey.

Grasshoppers, beetles, small rodents, and snakes make up its main food items. Most of its prey is killed on the ground, sometimes with its bill, but also by stamping on it. It is often attracted to bush fires, where it will search for dead insects and other small animals. The Secretarybird does not migrate, but will move some distance to find food, responding to rainfall, fires, and cropping or grazing activities. It usually nests in the top of an acacia tree in a stick nest lined with grass, wool, and animal dung.

ADULT SECRETARYBIRD WITH PREY

SNAKE KILLER

The Secretarybird is famous for killing snakes, tackling even venomous species. It kills a snake by holding it under its feet and tearing it up, or flying up with the snake in its bill and dropping it on the ground.

STAMPING ON PREY
A fast runner, the Secretarybird chases its prey, which when caught, is stamped to death, the talons aiming at the head of the prey.

Pandion haliaetus

Osprey

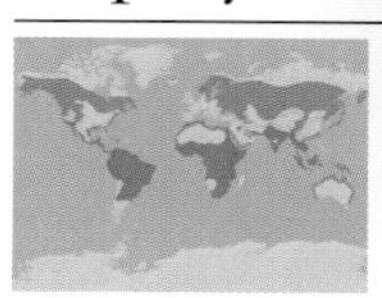

LENGTH 50–66cm (19½–26in)

WEIGHT 1.5kg (3¼lb)

MIGRATION Migrant

HABITAT Always found near water, salt or fresh; lakes, large rivers, estuaries, and coastal lagoons

Once known as the Fish-Hawk, the Osprey is well equipped to catch fish, which form its main diet. It hunts by flying or sometimes hovering over a lake, river, or estuary and then plunging into the water to grab a fish from close to the surface. Its claws are specially adapted to help it grasp its prey; the soles are spiny and the front outer talon is reversible and can be moved back to enable two talons to grip each side of the fish. The Osprey also has a strongly curved bill. Its other distinguishing features are its white head, a broad black mark through its cheek and the sides of its neck, its dark brown upperparts with a purple sheen, and its long tail with narrow bars.

It usually builds its nest at the top of a tree or on an island shore, and many nests are traditional, with pairs or their offspring returning to them year after year. The provision of nesting platforms has helped the Osprey to breed again in many areas from which it had vanished, due to past persecution and DDT poisoning.

This species is found in every continent except Antarctica. Most of the North American population migrate south to spend the winter in Central America and northern South America, while Eurasian birds fly to Africa, south of the Sahara.

OSPREY GRIPPING FISH WITH ITS TALONS

Pernis apivorus

European Honey Buzzard

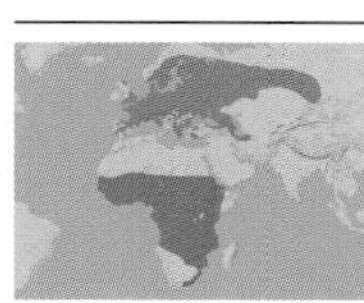

LENGTH 55cm (21½in)

WEIGHT 700g (25oz)

MIGRATION Migrant

HABITAT Lowland forest and woodland with glades and open areas

The European Honey Buzzard is not a true buzzard, in fact, it is more closely related to kites. Unusually for a bird of prey, it feeds on wasps, bees, and hornets as well as their nests, larvae, and pupae. Its forehead and face are covered with small scale-like feathers to protect it from stings. It has a shallow, curved bill and relatively underdeveloped talons.

In its courtship flight, called a "sky-dance", the male flies high, then swoops and dives down and up again in a undulating pattern, holding its wings high and quivering them.

MALE, FEMALE, AND YOUNG AT THEIR NEST

Elanoides forficatus

Swallow-tailed Kite

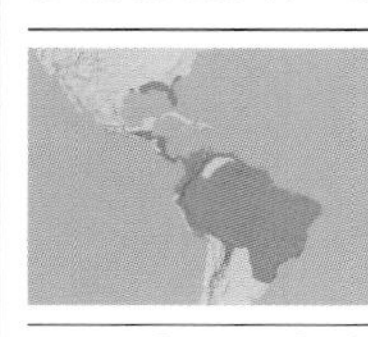

LENGTH 52–62cm (20½–24in)

WEIGHT 450g (16oz)

MIGRATION Migrant

HABITAT Over woodland, forest edges by rivers, wetland areas with trees and bushes

An agile flier, the Swallow-tailed Kite has long, pointed wings with black flight feathers and white wing linings. It catches most of its insect food on the wing, twisting its long, forked tail as it gracefully glides on high air currents. It often swoops down on water to drink. Its black bill, dark brown eyes, and black upperparts, contrasting with the white head and underparts, also make it easy to spot.

Birds that breed in southeastern USA and Central America migrate south to spend the winter in South America. Small groups may breed and feed together and flocks of several hundreds can be seen on migration. The nest of this species is usually built in a tree-top concealed by thick foliage. Lined with leaves and lichen, it is made of sticks, moss, and pine-needles and is built by both the male and female. The 2 or 3 eggs laid are incubated by both parents, but mostly by the female.

ADULT SWALLOW-TAILED KITE

Rostrhamus sociabilis

Snail Kite

LENGTH 40–45cm (15½–17½in)
WEIGHT 300–450g (11–16oz)
MIGRATION Partial migrant
HABITAT Freshwater lowland marshes

The Snail Kite has a specially adapted narrow, hooked bill enabling it to quickly and easily prise out the flesh from the shells of aquatic apple snails, which constitute most of its specialized diet. During droughts, when snails are scarce, the kite will switch to different prey such as crabs. The male and female differ in their plumage: the male is grey-black, while the female is dark brown, with white streaks on the face and breast. In flight, the white tail, with its broad dark tip is clearly visible. The bird flaps its large wings slowly as it flies above marshes, keeping its eyes pointed downwards in search of prey.

Populations from the south of the range are migratory – more northern populations move in response to drought conditions and in order to find food. The species is rare in the USA, where it is found only in Florida. Elsewhere, it occurs from Mexico and the Caribbean to the pampas of Argentina.

FEMALE SNAIL KITE

GREAT SITES

THE FLORIDA EVERGLADES

The entire North American population of Snail Kites is confined to Florida, where they number up to 500 birds in all. The shallow freshwater marshes of the Florida Everglades are the stronghold of the species, which is dependent on habitats that support aquatic apple snails, its staple food.

Ictinia mississippiensis

Mississippi Kite

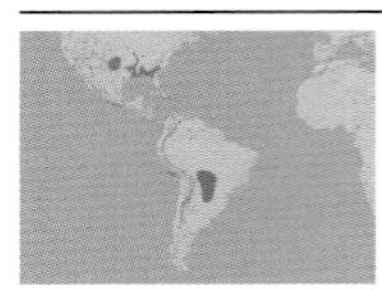

LENGTH 35–38cm (14–15in)
WEIGHT 250–300g (9–11oz)
MIGRATION Migrant
HABITAT Broad-leaved woodland; hunts in more open areas, such as farmland

Small and slender, the Mississippi Kite has a pale grey head (paler in the male) and breast, darker grey upperparts, long, pointed wings, and black wing-tips. The juvenile is brown and heavily streaked. The Mississippi Kite feeds mainly on small insects such as grasshoppers and cicadas, often eating them in mid-air, though larger prey, such as mice or small reptiles, are also taken. Its flight is smooth and graceful, with steady wingbeats and occasional glides.

The Mississippi Kite breeds in southern USA, nesting in loose colonies. Although it commonly occurs in the state of Mississippi, its name is actually derived from the fact that the first scientific specimen of the species was collected there. After breeding, the species undergoes a long-distance southerly migration to winter in Paraguay and northern Argentina. Flocks containing hundreds of these kites can be seen in winter, often together with other raptor species.

ADULT RED KITE

Milvus milvus

Red Kite

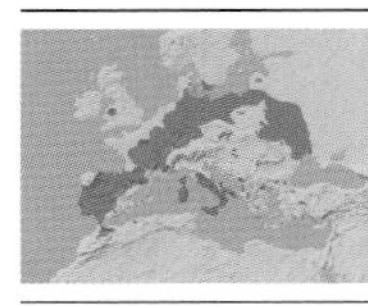

LENGTH 60–65cm (23½–26in)
WEIGHT 950–1200g (34–43oz)
MIGRATION Partial migrant
HABITAT Open woodland and farmland

This large and red-brown raptor, the Red Kite has a strikingly angular appearance in flight. When seen from below, the black tips and inner white feathers highlight the length of its wings. The species also has a long and distinctively forked tail, which is pale rust-red in colour. It flies in fast and twisting dives, with flexibility and elasticity in its movements.

The Red Kite is classified as near threatened due to a recent decline in its numbers, particularly in France, Spain, and Germany. In Britain, however, a successful reintroduction campaign has led to a growing population.

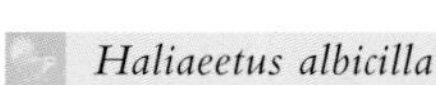

Haliaeetus albicilla

White-tailed Eagle

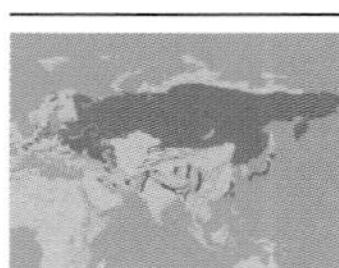

LENGTH 70–90cm (28–35in)
WEIGHT 4–5.5kg (8¾–12lb)
MIGRATION Partial migrant
HABITAT Diverse range of wetlands including coasts, lakes, large rivers, and marshes

The White-tailed Eagle is the largest eagle in northern Europe – it has a wingspan of 2.5m (8¼ft), and the female (which is heavier than the male) weighs up to 5.5kg (12lb). It is dark brown in colour, with a pale head, yellow bill, and a short white tail. The juvenile is a uniform darker brown, taking five to six years to attain adult plumage and a further two years before it acquires the white tail.

In flight, the White-tailed Eagle is often referred to as a "flying barn door", highlighting the fact that its long wings are exceptionally broad. The tips of the primary feathers are distinctly spread in flight, giving the bird a classic eagle profile. Its flight is heavy and direct, with deep wingbeats, and it soars on flat wings. The species prefers coastal habitats and can also be found inland near lakes and along rivers.

The White-tailed Eagle eats a variety of food. Fish, which are caught from the water's surface, probably form the bulk of its diet, but other prey, which include water birds and mammals (usually carrion), are also consumed.

In the north and east of its range, White-tailed Eagles are mainly migratory and winter gatherings can be up to 30 birds, but populations in Greenland, Iceland, and Norway are largely sedentary. This species builds its nest, made of sticks, seaweed, grasses, and bones of prey, on sea cliffs or in the flat crowns of large woodland trees.

SNATCHING PREY
Agile despite its size, the White-tailed Eagle dives for food, picking up fish and offal from the surface with its talons.

Milvus migrans

Black Kite

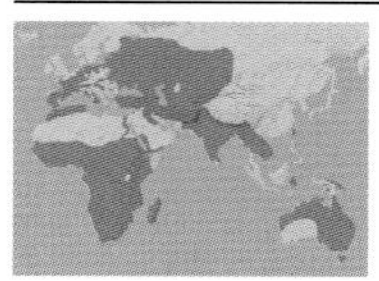

LENGTH 55–60cm (21½–23½in)

WEIGHT 550–950g (20–34oz)

MIGRATION Partial migrant

HABITAT Wide variety, from farmland to open woodland

Slightly smaller and less angular-looking than the Red Kite (opposite), the Black Kite also has a less deeply forked tail. Overall, its plumage is brown in tone, not black, as its name suggests. It feeds on dead or dying fish from water or from shores and is also a scavenger, snatching scraps and offal in quick swoops. The species has a wide global distribution, occurring across much of Europe, Asia, Africa, and Australia. The European population is highly migratory, but other populations are largely sedentary.

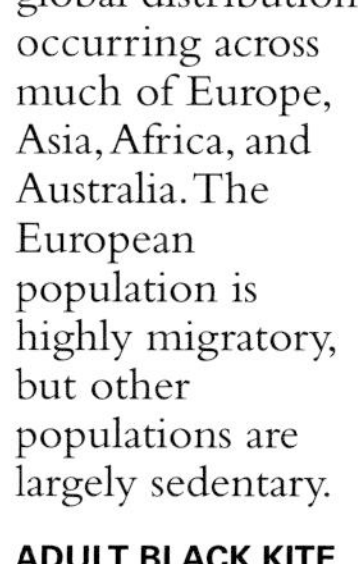

ADULT BLACK KITE

ADULT BRAHMINY KITE

Haliastur indus

Brahminy Kite

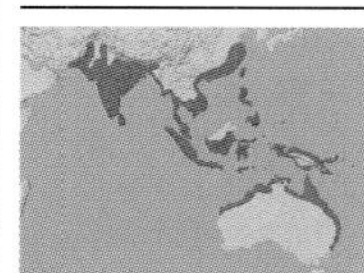

LENGTH 45–50cm (17½–19½in)

WEIGHT 325–650g (12–23oz)

MIGRATION Non-migrant

HABITAT Coastal wetlands and estuaries; also forest and farmland

A distinctive bird, the adult Brahminy Kite has rich chestnut upperparts that contrast with its snow-white neck, head, and breast. In flight, the white breast is particularly noticeable, set against its red-brown underwings and tail. The sexes are alike. The juvenile is brown in colour. The species feeds on fish, frogs, insects, and carrion. It nests in isolated trees near water.

Haliaeetus vocifer

African Fish Eagle

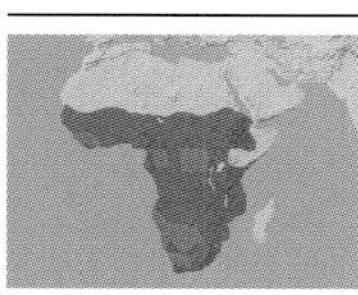

LENGTH 63–73cm (25–29in)

WEIGHT 2–3.5kg (4½–7¾lb)

MIGRATION Non-migrant

HABITAT Large rivers, lakes, dams, coastal estuaries

Widespread in Africa, south of the Sahara, the adult African Fish Eagle has a striking white head and breast, dark brown wings, and a chestnut belly and back. Its large bill is two-toned yellow and black in colour. The juvenile is mottled brown and much harder to distinguish from other eagles. A large bird, the African Fish Eagle has a wingspan of almost 2m (6½ft) and, similar to other raptors, the female is much bigger and heavier than the male. The species has a loud ringing call and is very vocal, both on its perch and in flight.

As its name suggests, the African Fish Eagle feeds mainly on fish. It scours the surface of the water from a perch, swooping down on to its prey with a backward swing of the feet, and seizing the fish in its large talons. It will also steal food from other species such as herons, and occasionally take other types of prey such as small mammals, young waterfowl, or carrion. It breeds during the dry season, building a large nest, made of sticks and pieces of wood on a tree. Incubation of the eggs takes about 42–45 days.

ADULT AFRICAN FISH EAGLE

TERRITORIAL DISPUTE
At sites where White-tailed Eagles gather for food, fights tend to break out – like this one between an adult (left) and juvenile (right).

Haliaeetus leucocephalus

Bald Eagle

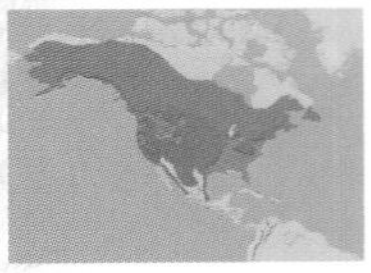

LENGTH 71–96cm (28–38in)

WEIGHT 3–6.5kg (6½–14lb)

MIGRATION Partial migrant

HABITAT Mostly near water, including rivers, lakes, and coastal sites to an altitude of 2,000m (6,500ft)

The conspicuous white head of the adult Bald Eagle, along with its white neck and tail, contrasts with the dark brown of its wings and back. Its massive beak and strong feet are yellow. The juvenile's plumage is in various shades of brown – it develops adult plumage at four years of age.

This fishing eagle snatches its prey from the water surface, using its sharp talons. It also takes small mammals or carrion on farmland and is known for scavenging on picnic litter and partly eaten fish left by bears.

Once an abundant species, the Bald Eagle was chosen as the national bird of the USA in 1782, but the population declined drastically in the 20th century due to the use of pesticides, over-hunting, and pollution of rivers. However, a successful recovery programme was initiated, and it is currently proposed for removal from the endangered species list.

BALD EAGLE AT ITS NEST

GATHERING TO FEED

In winter, large numbers of Bald Eagles gather at the spawning grounds of salmon, well before the fish have arrived. Hundreds of salmon die shortly after spawning, which makes it easy for these eagles to feast on dead or dying fish on the shore, without entering the water. They also steal food from other predatory birds and often fight among themselves for food.

Haliaeetus pelagicus

Steller's Sea Eagle

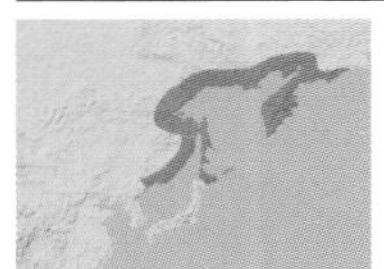

LENGTH 85–105cm (33–41in)

WEIGHT 6–9kg (13–20lb)

MIGRATION Partial migrant

HABITAT Confined entirely to coastal regions of eastern Asia

RED LIST CATEGORY Vulnerable

ADULT STELLER'S SEA EAGLE

A black and white bird with a powerful yellow beak, Steller's Sea Eagle is one of the world's largest birds of prey. The juvenile is more uniformly dark, but has a paler beak. The main threat facing this species is habitat loss, particularly on the Kamchatka Peninsula of eastern Russia, but a depletion in the numbers of salmon, its main food, is another serious factor. The population on the Kamchatka Peninsula is resident, whereas many of the other birds found on the Russian coast migrate to the Japanese islands during the winter.

Gypohierax angolensis

Palm-nut Vulture

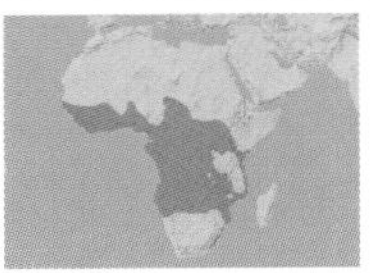

LENGTH 57–65cm (22½–26in)

WEIGHT 1.3–1.7kg (3¼–4½lb)

MIGRATION Non-migrant

HABITAT Forests and mangroves, always close to palm trees and water

Black and white in coloration, the Palm-nut Vulture develops an orange to red face patch at maturity, with the intensity of colour dictated by the amount of palm-nut oil the bird eats. Unusually for a vulture, it eats vegetable matter, such as the nut of the oil palm and raphia fruit husks, although it also takes fish and carrion.

ADULT PALM-NUT VULTURE

Gypaetus barbatus

Bearded Vulture

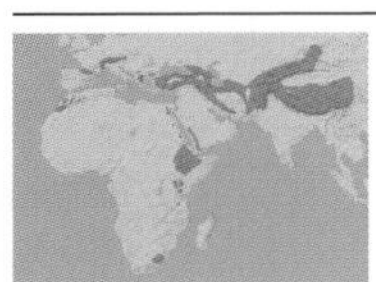

LENGTH 0.9–1.2m (3–4ft)

WEIGHT 5–7kg (11–15lb)

MIGRATION Non-migrant

HABITAT Mountainous areas and high steppes at altitudes of 1,000m–4,500m (3,300–14,500ft)

A large vulture, the adult Bearded Vulture has an orange front, from the base of the tail to the chin, while its upper back and wings are white. Its face is also white, with a black mask. The food it scavenges always contains bones and it will discard the flesh, preferring to extract the bone marrow. It does this by dropping bones or live tortoises on rocks to crush and break them.

ADULT BEARDED VULTURE

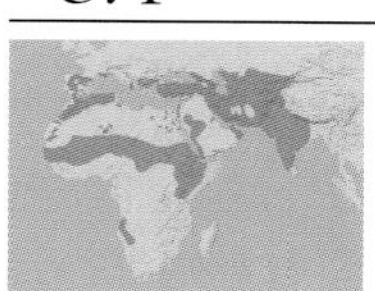

Neophron percnopterus

Egyptian Vulture

LENGTH 54–66cm (21½–26in)

WEIGHT 1.6–2.2kg (3¼–4½lb)

MIGRATION Migrant

HABITAT Plains, deserts, and rocky areas; also in towns and up to 2,500m (8,200ft) in mountains

Mostly white, with black flight feathers and a bare yellow face, which turns orange during nesting, the Egyptian Vulture is one of the smallest vultures found in Africa, Asia, and Europe. The juvenile, which matures at five years, has a speckled brown plumage which gradually gets lighter.

This vulture builds its nest of sticks, bits of debris, and skeletal remains on a rocky ledge or niche. It carries its nesting material in its beak, unlike most birds of prey, which use their talons for this purpose. Pairs mate for life and the female lays two eggs a few days apart.

The Egyptian Vulture is mostly a scavenger and feeds on carrion scraps left by other vultures because it is too small to compete for first place at a carcass. It is particularly well known for using stones as tools for breaking open the eggs of ostriches and other birds. It also actively hunts small mammals and reptiles, and drops tortoises on rocks to break their shells.

The species is not adapted to cold weather, despite sometimes being found at high altitudes, and the winter range of the migratory population is across central Africa and parts of India.

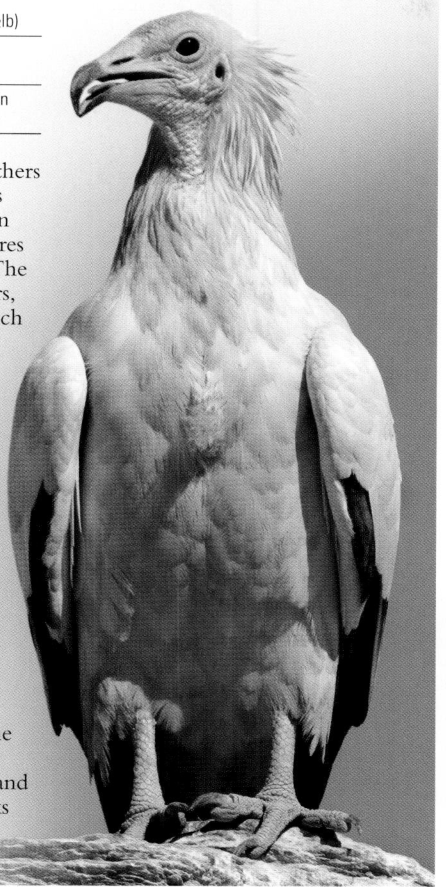

ADULT EGYPTIAN VULTURE

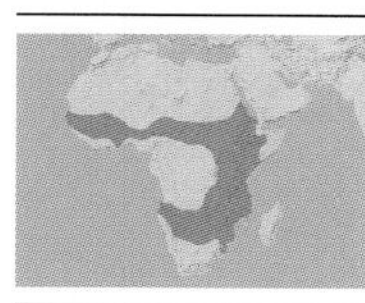

Gyps africanus

White-backed Vulture

LENGTH 78–90cm (31–35in)

WEIGHT 5.5kg (12lb)

MIGRATION Non-migrant

HABITAT Plains and savanna, but also at altitudes up to 3,000m (10,000ft)

A collar of white feathers on its upper back gives the White-backed Vulture its name, the white back and inner wing contrasting with the darker flight feathers. This vulture is the most widespread of the African vultures.

The White-backed Vulture is less dominant than other species when scavenging, being unable to open up a fresh carcass, and it has to jostle with other vultures to get its food. It nests in colonies and in trees, laying only a single egg. Its population has declined in some areas, the main threats being power lines and accidental poisoning.

ADULT WHITE-BACKED VULTURE

ADULT INDIAN VULTURE

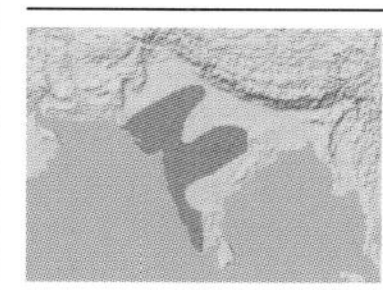

Gyps indicus

Indian Vulture

LENGTH 89–103cm (35–39in)

WEIGHT 5.5–6.5kg (12–14lb)

MIGRATION Non-migrant

HABITAT Semi-desert and dry areas up to 1,500m (4,900ft) but also around villages

RED LIST CATEGORY Critically endangered

Smaller and less heavily built than the Griffon Vulture (below left), this vulture has a long bill, broad wings, and a short tail. Its population has declined as a result of feeding on domestic animals treated with diclofenac, a drug now banned from veterinary use. An extensive captive breeding programme is now in place.

RUËPPELL'S VULTURE

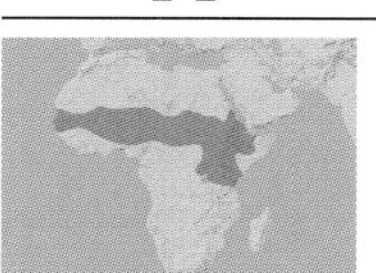

Gyps rueppellii

Ruëppell's Vulture

LENGTH 85–97cm (33–38in)

WEIGHT 7–9kg (15–20lb)

MIGRATION Non-migrant

HABITAT Mountains to 4,500m (14,800ft); open areas of savanna

The plumage of Ruëppell's Vulture is a dark mottled brown, with two rows of white spots across its wings. It flies at heights of over 6,000m (19,700ft), with a record of 11,300m (37,000ft) for a bird that collided with an aircraft. These vultures sometimes feed in groups of more than 100 birds. Aggressive at a carcass, they often gorge themselves until they can barely fly.

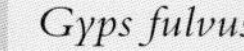

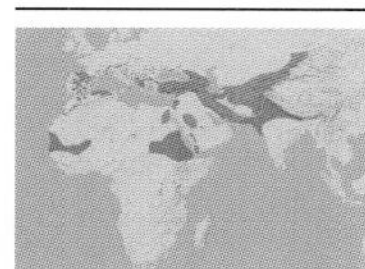

Gyps fulvus

Griffon Vulture

LENGTH 93–110cm (37–43in)

WEIGHT 6–10kg (13–22lb)

MIGRATION Partial migrant

HABITAT Mountains up to 3,000m (10,000ft) but also open plains and deserts

One of the larger vultures of Europe, Asia, and Africa, the Griffon Vulture has a pale brown head and neck, with a dull white ruff, contrasting with its sandy coloured body and wings. Like other vultures, it is a scavenger, feeding mainly on carrion. Its numbers are known to fluctuate in response to changes in the climate but the species is not a threatened one. The Griffon Vulture has been reintroduced into parts of Europe with reports of increasing numbers in Spain.

GROUP OF GRIFFON VULTURES

LAPPET-FACED VULTURES

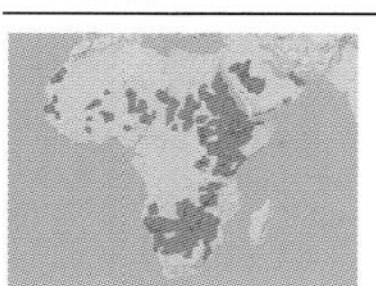

Aegypius tracheliotus

Lappet-faced Vulture

LENGTH 73–82cm (29–32in)

WEIGHT 14kg (31lb)

MIGRATION Non-migrant

HABITAT Open areas and semi-desert up to altitudes of 4,000m (13,100ft)

RED LIST CATEGORY Vulnerable

A powerful species that can open a fresh carcass and kill its own food, the Lappet-faced Vulture is usually dominant when feeding with other vultures. Its head and neck are bare of feathers. Pesticide poisoning and persecution has caused a decline in its population over most of its central and southern African range.

LAPPET-FACED VULTURE
The largest African vulture, the Lappet-faced Vulture uses its strong bill to open carcases. Not surprisingly, other vultures usually give way to it when feeding.

Circaetus pectoralis

Black-chested Snake Eagle

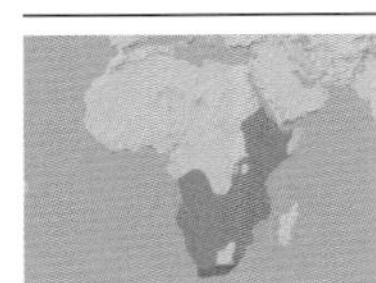

LENGTH 63–71cm (25–28in)

WEIGHT 1.2–2.3g (2¼–5½lb)

MIGRATION Partial migrant

HABITAT Wooded grassland, savanna, thornbush, and desert

Widespread in its range, this raptor has a distinctive black head and chest. The plumage of the adult is in a bold black and white pattern, while the juvenile is browner above and bright rufous below. As its name indicates, this bird feeds mostly on snakes, but will also prey on lizards, small mammals, and frogs.

ADULT BLACK-CHESTED SNAKE EAGLE

ADULT BIRD

Spilornis cheela

Crested Serpent Eagle

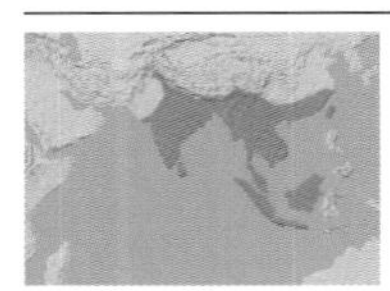

LENGTH 50–75cm (19½–30in)

WEIGHT 0.5–1.8kg (1–4½lb)

MIGRATION Partial migrant

HABITAT Broad-leaved evergreen, semi-deciduous, and deciduous forest

A conspicuous large raptor of south and southeast Asian forests, the Crested Serpent Eagle can often be heard giving it ringing cries while in flight. As its name suggests, it is a predator of reptiles, particularly snakes. The adult Crested Serpent Eagle has a black crest with white spots and reddish brown underparts with small white markings. The species builds a smaller nest than most raptors, made of sticks, and lined with green leaves.

Circus aeruginosus

Western Marsh Harrier

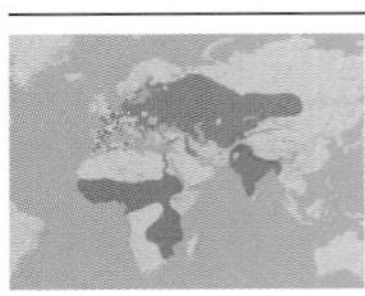

LENGTH 42–54cm (16½–21½in)

WEIGHT 600–825g (21–29oz)

MIGRATION Partial migrant

HABITAT Extensive reedbeds, marshland, swamps, reedy ditches through cultivated areas

Often simply called the Marsh Harrier, the Western Marsh Harrier, is a familiar sight over European marshlands. Like other harriers, it has long wings held in a shallow V-shape as it flies low. It is also similar to other harriers in that the male and female have different plumage. The male has a grey and brown wing pattern with black tips, a chestnut belly, and a grey tail. The female and the juvenile are mainly uniform brown, with creamy white head markings. The male is smaller than the female.

This harrier hunts small mammals, insects, and birds, catching them unawares as it drifts low over reedbeds and fields. It often perches on bush tops or trees for long spells, looking out for prey. The Western Marsh Harrier breeds in dense reedbeds. It is migratory, except in the mildest regions, and winters mainly in Africa.

MALE WESTERN MARSH HARRIER

Terathopius ecaudatus

Bateleur

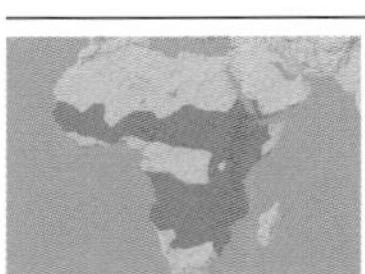

LENGTH 55–70cm (21½–28in)

WEIGHT 1.8–3kg (4½–6½lb)

MIGRATION Non-migrant

HABITAT Open savanna and grassland, desert thornbush, and open woodland

The only member of the genus *Terathopius*, the Bateleur is an unusual type of snake eagle, although it mainly eats mammals and birds. It also feeds on fish, reptiles, and insects – groups of these eagles may gather at termite mounds to feed. The female is similar to the male except that it has grey, rather than black, secondary flight feathers. Typically, the adult has rufous-chestnut upperparts, but a small number have creamy upperparts. The juvenile is plain brown with some white mottling and has pale green facial skin. It takes about seven or eight years to reach full maturity.

Named after its fast, gliding fight – the word "bateleur" means "acrobat" in French – in which it sways from side to side, this eagle displays a rocking and rolling flight during courtship, almost stopping in mid-air with the wings held open. It builds its large stick nest in an open-branched tree. A single egg is laid, which is incubated by the female alone, for about eight weeks. It takes another three to four months before the young are independent. The adults pair for life and will use the same nest for a number of years.

SILHOUETTE IN FLIGHT

Etched against the sky, the outline of the Bateleur is distinctive as the eagle glides in the air. The shape is formed by its disproportionately long, broad, bow-shaped wings with narrow, upturned tips, bulky head, and the extremely short tail, a combination of features that no other raptor shows. Its impressive wingspan extends to 1.75m (6ft).

PLUMAGE PATTERN
The gleaming white underwing feathers of this eagle contrast sharply with its black body and red face and feet.

MALE BATELEUR

FEMALE NORTHERN HARRIER

Circus cyaneus

Northern Harrier

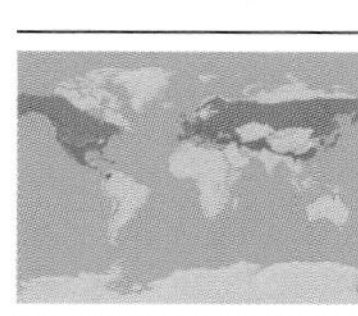

LENGTH 42–50cm (16½–19½in)

WEIGHT 300–525g (11–19oz)

MIGRATION Migrant

HABITAT Moorland, open taiga, steppes, marshes, and dunes in summer; various open areas in winter

A typical harrier, the Northern Harrier holds its long wings in a shallow V during its graceful flight. The male has a grey hood and upperparts and white underparts, showing conspicuous black wing-tips in flight. The female, as in other harriers, is different, with brown plumage that is heavily streaked and barred. This harrier hunts small mammals and birds, surprising them as it drifts low over open habitat.

GROUND NESTING

Unusually for a bird of prey, the Northern Harrier makes its nest on the ground, often among heather-like vegetation or grass. Made of sticks and grass and lined with fine material, the nest is built by both the male and the female. About 4–6 eggs are laid and are incubated for around four weeks. The dull brown plumage of the female (see right) helps keep it camouflaged on the nest.

Circus melanoleucos

Pied Harrier

LENGTH 43–50cm (17–19½in)

WEIGHT 300–400g (11–14oz)

MIGRATION Migrant

HABITAT Breeds in steppes and boggy scrub; winters in open areas, including marshland and farmland

ADULT MALE

With its boldly patterned black and white plumage, the male of this species is one of the most attractive harriers. Its eyes are yellow and the feet yellow to orange-yellow. The female is much less striking, being mostly brown and grey, with a streaky hood and barred wings, and the juvenile is a uniform dark brown. The species feeds mainly on small mammals, but also takes frogs, lizards, ground birds, and insects. The nest is built on the ground, and is made of grass, reeds, and weeds.

Polyboroides typus

African Harrier-Hawk

LENGTH 51–68cm (20–27in)

WEIGHT 575–700g (21–25oz)

MIGRATION Partial migrant

HABITAT Woodland, preferably with palm trees, and often near water; forest edges

This highly adapted relative of the harriers has a very flexible leg joint that allows it to forage on the branches and trunks of trees. It will hang onto tree branches by its feet, with its wings dangling down for balance, and probe for food with its slender bill. It can often be seen hanging from weaver nests, preying on the eggs and young. The adult is mainly grey, with black and white banding on the belly and tail. Its bare facial skin changes colour from yellow to deep crimson. The juvenile is brown in colour.

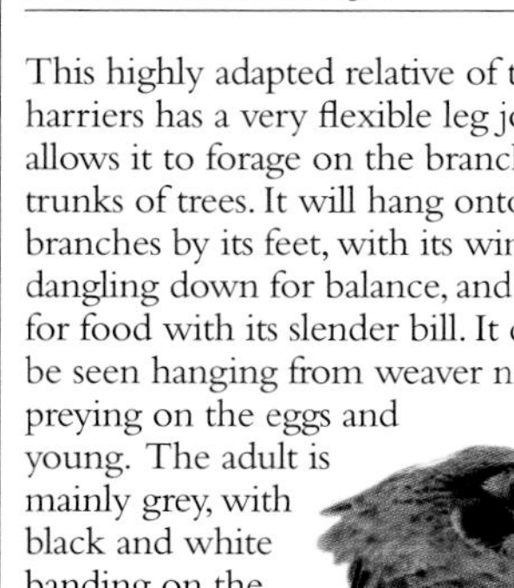

JUVENILE

ADULT SPOTTED HARRIER

Circus assimilis

Spotted Harrier

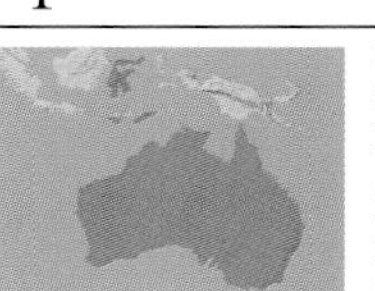

LENGTH 50–60cm (19½–23½in)

WEIGHT 475–675g (17–24oz)

MIGRATION Non-migrant

HABITAT Grassland, scrub, and woodland

This widespread Australian raptor is the world's largest harrier. Unlike most harriers, the adults have similar plumage. The upperparts are blue-grey with subtle darker markings, and there are striking white spots and bars on the chestnut underparts. The female, however, is larger. It glides slowly, with up-swept wings.

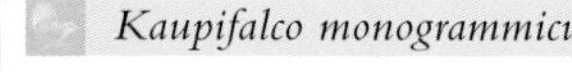

Kaupifalco monogrammicus

Lizard Buzzard

LENGTH 30–37cm (12–14½in)

WEIGHT 250–300g (9–11oz)

MIGRATION Non-migrant

HABITAT Broad-leaved woods with tall grass, savanna, and thornbush

Despite its name, the Lizard Buzzard is more closely related to the sparrowhawks and goshawks than the buzzards. It mainly preys on reptiles and large insects, but also feeds on small mammals and birds. It often sits quietly on a post or wire, or on a palm tree. The adult is largely grey, with a black and white banded tail and black and white barring on the belly. It is identifiable by the black stripe on its white throat. The juvenile is browner than the adult and has a fainter throat stripe.

ADULT LIZARD BUZZARD

ADULT DARK CHANTING GOSHAWK

Melierax metabates

Dark Chanting Goshawk

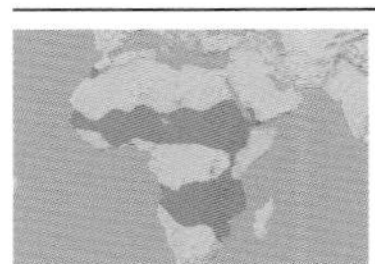

LENGTH 45cm (17½in)

WEIGHT 650–850g (23–30oz)

MIGRATION Non-migrant

HABITAT Broad-leaved woodland and wooded savanna, avoiding drier areas

A common bird in sub-Saharan Africa, the Dark Chanting Goshawk is a medium-sized, long-legged hawk. It hunts mostly small reptiles and rodents. However, it also takes birds and carrion. Prey is caught by gliding from a perch and is pursued on foot if missed during the swoop. Birds are caught in flight by a typical hawk technique of twisting through and between trees. It takes its name from the male's tuneful "chants" early in the breeding season.

Accipiter minullus

Little Sparrowhawk

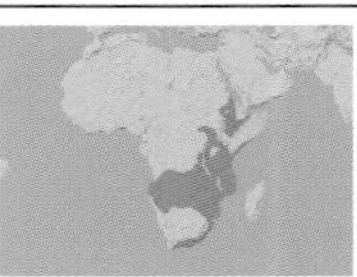

LENGTH 23–27cm (9–10½in)

WEIGHT 70–100g (2½–3⅝oz)

MIGRATION Non-migrant

HABITAT Mainly smaller wooded areas, typically along watercourses

Small and grey, with barred underparts, the Little Sparrowhawk hunts birds and bats in flight and is particularly agile among trees. A bold species, despite its relatively small size, it takes prey such as reptiles from the ground. The population is mostly found in southern Africa, but has a more northerly distribution to the east of the range. The Little Sparrowhawk is not a threatened species and readily colonizes exotic tree plantations.

ADULT BIRD

ADULT BESRA

Accipiter virgatus

Besra

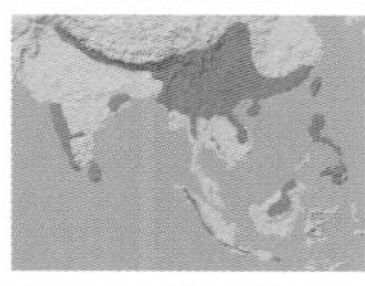

LENGTH 23–36cm (9–14in)

WEIGHT 85–150g (3–5oz)

MIGRATION Non-migrant

HABITAT Wide range of wooded habitats, from rainforest to pine and mangrove

Distinguished by its chestnut coloration and barred underwings, the Besra is a small species found throughout southern Asia from India to south China and Indonesia. The juvenile has browner upperparts than the adult. The species feeds mostly on birds, although insects and reptiles are also taken. It is a fast and agile bird-catcher.

Accipiter novaehollandiae

Grey Goshawk

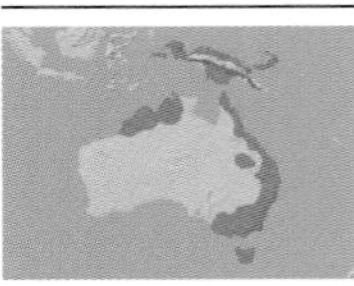

LENGTH 38–55cm (15–21½in)

WEIGHT 250–475g (9–17oz)

MIGRATION Non-migrant

HABITAT Rainforest, but some populations are found in drier forests or on woodland edges

Widespread in Australia, Tasmania, and New Guinea, the Grey Goshawk has a number of subspecies. Two forms are known – the grey form has a pale grey back, dark wing-tips, and white underparts with pale grey barring on the breast. The white form has an all-white plumage.

The Grey Goshawk takes its prey on the ground or by gliding from a perch. It feeds on birds up to the size of a heron or mammals as big as a rabbit. In the breeding season, it builds a nest of sticks, lined with leaves, and often uses the same nest the next season. It lays 2 or 3 eggs and fledging occurs within 30–42 days of hatching.

GREY GOSHAWK (WHITE FORM)

Accipiter nisus

Eurasian Sparrowhawk

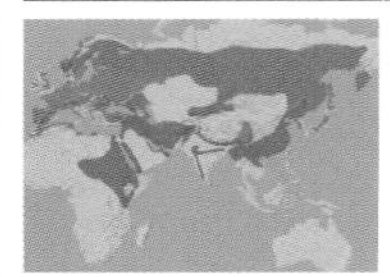

LENGTH 28–38cm (11–15in)

WEIGHT 100–350g (3⅝–13oz)

MIGRATION Partial migrant

HABITAT All types of woodland, including urban parks, and to the edge of the tree line on mountains

Feeding almost exclusively on other birds, the Eurasian Sparrowhawk often hunts around the edges of woodland or in clearings. The male is slate-grey above and barred reddish brown below, while the female has grey bars below. The male and female are significantly different in size and this is reflected in their choice of prey – the smaller male predominantly hunts smaller birds such as finches, buntings, and thrushes, while the female is capable of taking pigeons. European populations are largely resident, but Scandinavian birds and populations across Russia are migratory.

HUNTING STRATEGIES

The eight different hunting techniques of the Eurasian Sparrowhawk have been studied and described. It takes birds in flight, flying low and fast. It also catches its prey by dropping from a perch, co-operative hunting, or hunting from the ground. It kills smaller species by stabbing with its talons and kills larger prey mostly during consumption.

MALE EURASIAN SPARROWHAWK

ADULT COOPER'S HAWK

Accipiter cooperii

Cooper's Hawk

LENGTH 37–49cm ($14\frac{1}{2}$–$19\frac{1}{2}$in)
WEIGHT 225–600g (8–21oz)
MIGRATION Partial migrant

HABITAT Dense forest, but uses both coniferous and deciduous trees

A widespread species in North America, Cooper's Hawk is migratory in the northern part of the range, reaching Central America in winter. The adult has red-brown bars across the breast and belly. Like many hawks, the female Cooper's Hawk is larger than the male and may weigh twice as much.

Cooper's Hawk surprises and captures small and medium-sized birds from cover or while flying quickly through dense vegetation. It also feeds on lizards, frogs, snakes, and large insects, as well as small mammals such as squirrels and chipmunks.

The female sometimes breeds in its first year, although most birds do not reach maturity until the second year. The usual clutch size is 3–6 eggs and the young are fledged 27–30 days after hatching. The maximum observed lifespan is eight years, but it is thought that some birds live longer. This species is not globally threatened, although a significant decline in numbers was seen during the 1940s and 1950s due to the use of pesticides.

Butastur rufipennis

Grasshopper Buzzard

LENGTH 35cm (14in)
WEIGHT 300–375g (11–13oz)
MIGRATION Migrant

HABITAT Woodland edges, but also found in arid areas and over burnt grassland

Grey-brown above, with rufous underparts, the Grasshopper Buzzard has streaks on its plumage. It predominantly eats insects, but also takes some smaller vertebrates. Nearly all its prey are captured on the ground, although some insects are caught in flight as well. Hunting often takes place over freshly burned grass or in association with grazing animals or egrets. The species is common in sub-Saharan Africa and makes movements in response to rainfall levels.

ADULT BIRD

Accipiter gentilis

Northern Goshawk

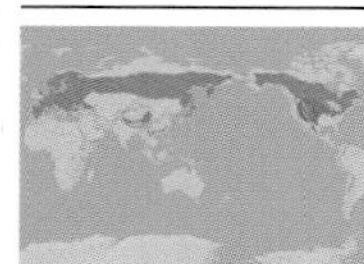

LENGTH 50–70cm ($19\frac{1}{2}$–28in)
WEIGHT 0.5–1.5kg (1–$3\frac{1}{4}$lb)
MIGRATION Non-migrant

HABITAT Mature woodland, mostly coniferous, but is also found in deciduous forest

The Northern Goshawk has a black crown with distinctive white eyebrows, a blue-grey back, and a long, rounded to wedge-shaped tail. It favours large prey such as grouse and crows, but will also take hares. Prey preferences vary according to the region, and reptiles are particularly important in parts of southern Europe. This species is found throughout the northern hemisphere, except in Greenland and Iceland. The range stretches through North America, Europe, and Russia. The species is not globally threatened.

ADULT BIRD

Geranospiza caerulescens

Crane Hawk

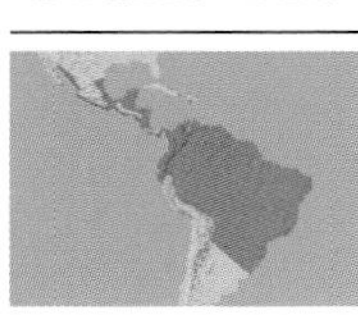

LENGTH 45–51cm ($17\frac{1}{2}$–20in)
WEIGHT 225–350g (8–13oz)
MIGRATION Non-migrant

HABITAT Rainforest and drier woodland or coastal mangroves, up to 730m (2,500ft).

The Crane Hawk is pale grey above and usually finely barred and darker grey below. It hunts a wide range of prey, such as lizards, snakes, and frogs, but large insects and bird nestlings are also taken. It catches its prey by reaching into tree-holes or between leaves for frogs. It has a vocal courtship display and a long breeding season in parts of its range.

ADULT CRANE HAWK

Leucopternis plumbeus

Plumbeous Hawk

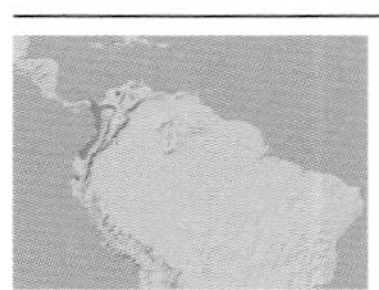

LENGTH 35cm (14in)

WEIGHT 500g (18oz)

MIGRATION Non-migrant

HABITAT Tropical rainforest

When perched, the Plumbeous Hawk appears dark grey with black wings. In flight, it has a conspicuous white band through its black tail, and when seen from below, its white underwings are clearly visible. Its legs and cere (the fleshy covering at the base of the upper mandible) are orange. The Plumbeous Hawk is a little-known species, with a small range in Panama, Colombia, Ecuador, and Peru.

Leucopternis albicollis

White Hawk

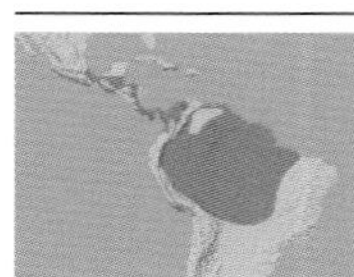

LENGTH 50cm (19½in)

WEIGHT 600–850g (21–30oz)

MIGRATION Non-migrant

HABITAT Mainly rainforest; also forest edges and pasture

The White Hawk has very broad wings and has a white head, body, and underwings. The upperwings are black, and the very short tail is black with a broad white band. It has a black bill and yellow legs. The sexes are similar, but the female is larger and heavier. The White Hawk hunts from a perch, often on the outskirts of a forest, and is easy to spot in Central and South America.

ADULT COMMON BLACK HAWK

Buteogallus anthracinus

Common Black Hawk

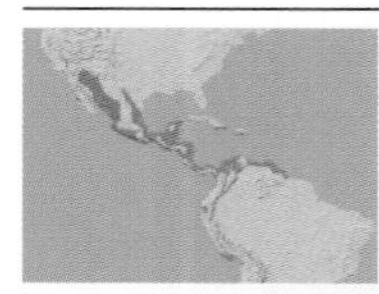

LENGTH 45–50cm (17½–19½in)

WEIGHT 0.8–1.2kg (1¾–2¼lb)

MIGRATION Partial migrant

HABITAT Dense wooded forests

The Common Black Hawk is found from southern USA through to northern parts of South America. Its plumage is a striking black or dark brown, with a yellow cere, legs, and lores (the area in front of the eye). Its tail has a distinctive horizontal white band that is conspicuous when it is in flight. The sexes are simlar, but the female is larger. The juvenile is browner above, with a dark-streaked pale front.

The Common Black Hawk feeds mainly on crabs, but also takes small vertebrates and eggs. Its nest is large, built with sticks in a mangrove tree. Its call is a distinctive "spink-speenk-speenk-spink-spink-spink".

Buteogallus meridionalis

Savanna Hawk

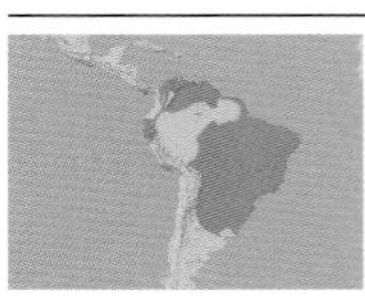

LENGTH 45–60cm (17½–23½in)

WEIGHT 825–1,050g (29–38oz)

MIGRATION Partial migrant

HABITAT Wide range of habitats from woodland to savanna

The Savanna Hawk is a distinctively coloured species. The plumage of the adult is primarily a pale cinnamon, with grey mottled areas on the back and fine dark barring on its underparts. It has a black and white banded tail and long yellow legs. The juvenile is much darker – with dark brown and rufous areas on the wings and a white eyebrow.

The Savanna Hawk is an opportunistic feeder, taking a wide range of small animals, reptiles, birds, and insects. It also scavenges prey from other bird species, such as storks, and is known to follow behind grass fires, picking up creatures trapped by the flames.

JUVENILE SAVANNA HAWK

Parabuteo unicinctus

Harris's Hawk

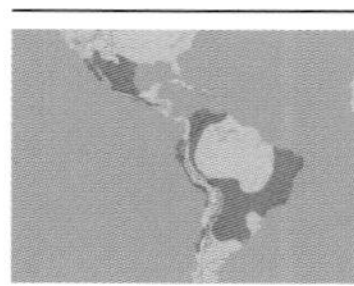

LENGTH 50–55cm (19½–21½in)

WEIGHT 725–1,000g (26–36oz)

MIGRATION Non-migrant

HABITAT Dry areas such as prairies and deserts

Harris's Hawk is a rich chocolate-brown colour overall, which contrasts with its bright rufous wings and leg plumage. In addition, the species has a two-tone black and white tail, as well as a bright yellow cere and legs. The female is bigger than the male. The juvenile is less distinctive and much more streaked. It stays with its parents for up to three years.

The striking plumage and the desirable social behaviour of Harris's Hawk are the reasons why the species is such a popular choice for falconry – although the main reason is probably its habit of hunting and feeding in groups. When the prey is flushed, these hawks work together to corner the animal, thereby compensating for their relatively low speed. In the wild, this behaviour is often shown by family parties of Harris's Hawk, which hunt co-operatively to increase their chances of catching larger prey, such as jack rabbits. It also takes a variety of other prey, including smaller birds and lizards. It nests in a tree or cactus, and usually lays 2–4 eggs.

JUVENILE HARRIS'S HAWK

ADULT BLACK-COLLARED HAWK

Busarellus nigricollis

Black-collared Hawk

LENGTH 45–50cm (17½–19½in)

WEIGHT 700–800g (25–29oz)

MIGRATION Non-migrant

HABITAT Around wetlands and rivers

Found throughout much of Central and South America, the Black-collared Hawk has an almost uniform rufous plumage, which contrasts with its pale head (whiter in the southern subspecies) and black throat patch. In flight, it looks unusual with its short tail and very broad black-tipped wings. The juvenile is browner and more streaked.

The Black-collared Hawk is often conspicuous as it perches in the open, waiting to swoop and catch a fish from the water's surface. Small spines on the undersides of its feet help the bird grasp its prey. Although it mainly eats fish, it will also take aquatic insects and snails, and, on rare occasions, lizards and rodents. The species breeds around swamps and marshes. Its nest is a large platform of sticks located up to 15m (50ft) high in a tree.

Harpyhaliaetus solitarius

Solitary Eagle

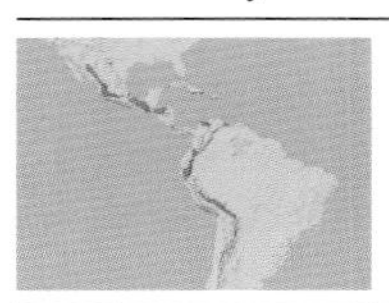

LENGTH 65–70cm (26–28in)

WEIGHT 3kg ($6^1/_2$lb)

MIGRATION Non-migrant

HABITAT Forested mountain slopes and upland forest

Also known as the Black Solitary Eagle, to help differentiate it from the similar (but paler) Crowned Solitary Eagle (*H. coronatus*), the Solitary Eagle is a Central and South American species that is rare throughout its restricted range.

In appearance, the adult Solitary Eagle is a uniform dark slate-grey, except for a white tail band and tip. It has a bright yellow eye, cere, and legs, which make a striking contrast to its dark plumage. The juvenile is dark brown above, with a streaked head and neck, pale streaked underparts, and a rufous back.

Buteo lineatus

Red-shouldered Hawk

LENGTH 45–60cm ($17^1/_2$–$23^1/_2$in)

WEIGHT 550–700g (20–25oz)

MIGRATION Partial migrant

HABITAT Lowland forest, close to water

The Red-shouldered Hawk is a forest-dwelling species, which is usually found near water. It is brightly coloured when seen at rest – orange below with a mottled brown back. Birds found in California are brighter, with more orange plumage tones. In flight, it has a number of narrow white bands across its dark tail. The juvenile is duller and more streaked. The species hunts mainly from perches, favouring small mammals as well as some amphibians and reptiles.

ADULT (ORANGE FORM)

GREAT SITES

HAWK MOUNTAIN

One of the best places to see the Red-shouldered Hawk is Hawk Mountain. Located in east-central Pennsylvania, the site is the venue for the spectacular migration of around 20,000 hawks, eagles, and falcons each autumn. The most commonly observed species is the Broad-winged Hawk (*B. platypterus*), but around 250 Red-shouldered Hawks are also usually seen.

Buteo galapagoensis

Galapagos Hawk

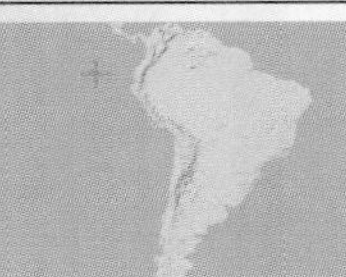

LENGTH 55cm ($21^1/_2$in)

WEIGHT 0.9–1.3kg (2–$3^1/_4$lb)

MIGRATION Non-migrant

HABITAT All island habitats, from barren lava fields to coastal areas

RED LIST CATEGORY Vulnerable

A plain, dark brown species, the Galapagos Hawk is the only raptor found in the Galapagos. It hunts and scavenges, and its prey includes seabirds, rats, centipedes, grasshoppers and even large iguanas. This hawk practises co-operative polyandry and as many as four males may mate with a single female, all of which aid the female in caring for the eggs and young. Up to three fledgelings may be raised at a time. The total world population of the Galapagos Hawk is thought to be no more than 500 birds.

ADULT GALAPAGOS HAWK

Buteo swainsoni

Swainson's Hawk

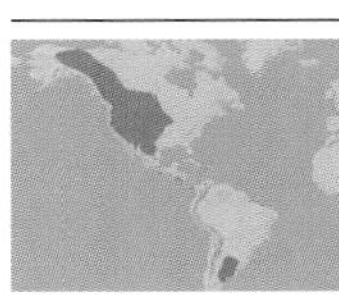

LENGTH 50–55cm ($19^1/_2$–$21^1/_2$in)

WEIGHT 850g (30oz)

MIGRATION Migrant

HABITAT Mainly open country

A slender hawk, with pointed wings and a relatively long tail, Swainson's Hawk occurs in three distinct colour forms – light, dark, and intermediate. Light-form birds, with their distinct chestnut chest patch and white face, are the most common. Swainson's Hawk is a very variable bird, which breeds in grasslands and open country in the western half of the USA, Canada, and Mexico, before migrating south to winter in South America (mainly north Argentina, southern Brazil, and Paraguay). On migration, the species can be seen in large flocks along its favoured routes.

ADULT (LIGHT-FORM)

Buteo albonotatus

Zone-tailed Hawk

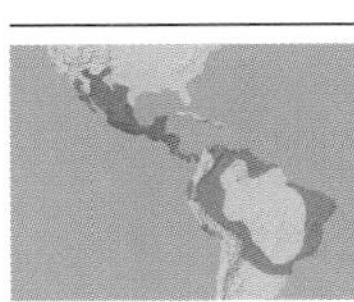

LENGTH 45–55cm ($17^1/_2$–$21^1/_2$in)

WEIGHT 600–900g (21–32oz)

MIGRATION Partial migrant

HABITAT Wooded canyons, riverside woodland, ranchland

The Zone-tailed Hawk is found from southern USA through to Central and South America. It is found primarily in wooded canyons and tree-lined areas along rivers in the USA, as well as other lowland woodland elsewhere in its range.

It is an all-dark, almost black, species, except for three pale bands on its tail. It has a yellow cere and feet. The sexes are similar in plumage. In flight, it is very similar to the more common Turkey Vulture (*Cathartes aura*), often soaring with its wings held in a V-shape. However, the Zone-tailed Hawk is smaller and darker than its vulture counterpart. The juvenile is similar to adults, also appearing all-dark, although it has some white spotting on its underparts.

RUFOUS FORM

Buteo jamaicensis

Red-tailed Hawk

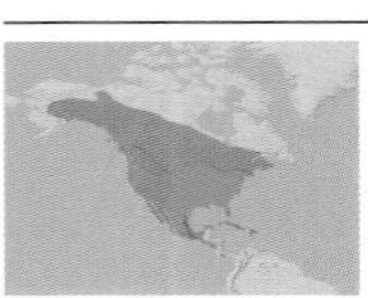

LENGTH 45–56cm (17½–22in)

WEIGHT 1–1.2kg (2¼lb)

MIGRATION Partial migrant

HABITAT Coniferous and tropical rainforest, prairies, and semi-deserts

Like other hawks and buzzards, the Red-tailed Hawk is very variable in plumage, with pale, dark, and rufous forms. A mostly white form is known as Krider's Hawk (*B. j. kriderii*) and the dark form found in Alaska is called Harlan's Hawk (*B. j. harlani*). Both these forms lack the distinctive red tail of the Red-tailed Hawk.

The most common large hawk in most of North America, the Red-tailed Hawk is an adaptable feeder, taking carrion, mammals (including hares), reptiles, amphibians, and the occasional fish. In deserts, snakes comprise up to half its diet. In open country, Red-tailed Hawks tend to hunt from perches, but in forests they ambush their prey from the air. They are equally adaptable nesters, using rocks with ledges, trees, cacti, and electricity pylons.

SNAKE-PROOF BOOTS

The tarsi (lower "legs") of species such as the Red-tailed Hawk that hunt snakes are protected by thick scales. Snake-eating raptors generally have short, strong toes to hold reptiles down while they are safely killed with the bill. Short toes also help the hawk to seize and hold onto rodents, which also form an important element of their diet.

STALKING ON GROUND
The feet of the Red-tailed Hawk are equally well adapted for walking on the ground, even in snow covered areas, where they stalk for prey.

FEEDING ON CARRION

Buteo buteo

Common Buzzard

LENGTH 50–57cm (19½–22½in)

WEIGHT 775–975g (28–35oz)

MIGRATION Partial migrant

HABITAT Woodland, open ground with trees, and woodland edges next to farmland

The Common Buzzard with its broad wings and a rather short, but ample tail is often seen perching on fence posts next to roads, waiting for prey to appear in the grass, but also well placed for roadkill. Its call is a ricocheting "pee-ow". Like the Red-tailed Hawk (left), it has many plumage variations, including light, rufous, and dark forms. These birds soar in pairs, and at the end of breeding, whole families take to the sky together.

ADULT LONG LEGGED BUZZARD

Buteo rufinus

Long-legged Buzzard

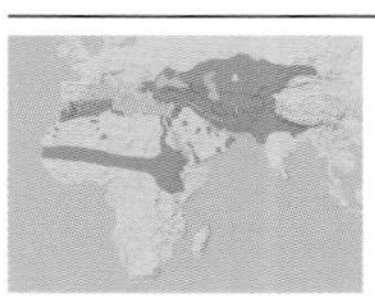

LENGTH 50–65cm (19½–26in)

WEIGHT 1–1.3kg (2¼–3¼lb)

MIGRATION Partial migrant

HABITAT Steppes, semi-desert, and other open uncultivated country; also scrub and open woodland

More likely to be seen on the ground than other buzzards, the Long-legged Buzzard stalks its prey on foot or waits at the entrance to burrows. Often described as sluggish, it spends a lot of time perching. But, like other buzzards, it also soars in circles on the lookout for prey. Sometimes seen over farmland in winter, it occasionally takes poultry. However, its diet consists mainly of rodents, reptiles, and insects.

Buteo regalis

Ferruginous Hawk

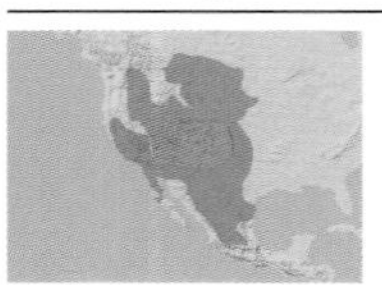

LENGTH 56–69cm (22–27in)

WEIGHT 1–1.7kg (2¼–3¾lb)

MIGRATION Migrant

HABITAT Dry open country, grassland, and farmland with nearby cliffs or rocky outcrops

Powerful and broad-chested, with a relatively big head, the Ferruginous Hawk is the largest hawk in North America. It has dark wing-tips, reddish brown upperparts, rufous legs that are fully feathered down to its yellow feet, and a pale tail.

Although this hawk will take meadowlarks and gamebirds, its breeding success and the overall size of its population is closely tied to the availability of ground squirrels, rabbits, prairie dogs, and gophers, which form the bulk of its diet. Fewer pairs will nest in the years when these mammals are scarce, and while three juveniles may be successfully reared when prey is plentiful, this number can fall to an average of less than one juvenile a nest. In areas where farmers control gopher and prairie-dog numbers, there can be a significant reduction in numbers or loss of the entire local Ferruginous Hawk population. These hawks have also suffered from the destruction of suitable nesting sites. The Ferruginous Hawk is a solitary nester and if disturbed, will abandon its nest before the eggs hatch. Fortunately, it takes readily to artificial nest platforms. Despite the local pressures that make it vulnerable, this hawk is not globally threatened, and its numbers have been growing since the late 1970s.

ADULT IN FLIGHT

rufous-streaked head

white underparts

Harpia harpyja

Harpy Eagle

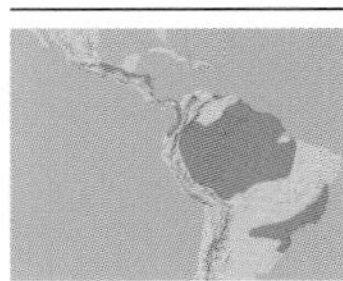

LENGTH 89–105cm (35–43in)

WEIGHT 4.8kg (11lb)

MIGRATION Non-migrant

HABITAT Tropical and sub-tropical rainforest with unbroken tree cover

One of the biggest and most powerful eagles, the Harpy Eagle has massive legs, feet, and talons capable of taking adult howler monkeys, small deer, and agoutis. Sloths make up to a third of its diet, captured as they come to the treetops in the early mornings. The Harpy Eagle mates for life but reproduces very slowly, breeding every two or three years.

JUVENILE HARPY EAGLE

PALE FORM

Morphnus guianensis

Crested Eagle

LENGTH 71–84cm (28–33in)
WEIGHT 1.8kg ($4^1/_2$lb)
MIGRATION Non-migrant

HABITAT Tropical and subtropical forest

This large bird of prey occurs in two colour forms: a pale form and a less common dark one. Like the Harpy Eagle (opposite), it has a twin-pointed crest. It can be distinguished in flight by its broad, rounded wings and long, pointed tail. The Crested Eagle hunts by scanning downwards from bare branches near the tops of trees, taking snakes, small monkeys and other mammals, birds, and tree frogs. The Crested Eagle is rare and near-threatened, poorly known, and probably decreasing. It usually nests high in tall trees but very few nests have been found and studied.

Pithecophaga jefferyi

Philippine Eagle

LENGTH 86–102cm (34–40in)
WEIGHT 4.4–6kg (10–13lb)
MIGRATION Non-migrant

HABITAT Primary tropical forest; now mainly confined to undisturbed forest in mountains

RED LIST CATEGORY Critically endangered

Long brown feathers adorn the head of the Philippine Eagle, giving it the appearance of a lion's mane. Its upperside is brown and the underside is white. Formerly called the Monkey-eating Eagle, its name was changed when it became the national bird of the Philippines. It feeds more often on flying lemurs and palm civets than monkeys. It also takes a range of other prey, which it finds as it moves from perch to perch.

ADULT PHILIPPINE EAGLE

Ictinaetus malayensis

Indian Black Eagle

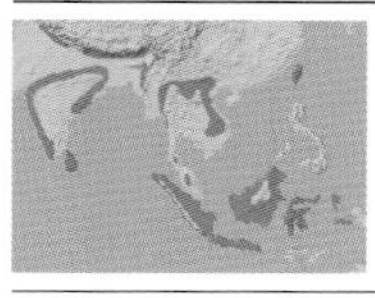

LENGTH 67–81cm (26–32in)
WEIGHT 1kg ($2^1/_4$lb)
MIGRATION Non-migrant

HABITAT Forested hills and mountains; clearings and regrown forest

The Indian Black Eagle with its long wings and tail is distinguished by its graceful, buoyant flight, during which it snatches prey from treetops. Its highly specialized feet with the outer toe helps it seize an entire nest and eat the nestlings and eggs in flight. It also attacks nests of ground-dwelling species and often takes bats and flying squirrels as prey. As part of its courtship display, it folds its wings in spectacular dives.

Aquila clanga

Greater Spotted Eagle

LENGTH 60–70cm ($23^1/_2$–28in)
WEIGHT 1.7–2.5kg ($3^3/_4$–$5^1/_2$lb)
MIGRATION Migrant

HABITAT Marshy forest and forest edges near swamps and wet meadows

RED LIST CATEGORY Vulnerable

This medium-sized to large eagle has a dark brown head and wings, and a white patch can often be seen on its upper wings. The species gets its name from the white spots on the juvenile. A raptor of wet places, the Greater Spotted Eagle lives on small aquatic creatures such as water voles, frogs, and fish, but will take other food, including carrion. It is a versatile hunter, soaring and diving down on its prey, or waiting on perches. It will also stalk on foot. Generally solitary, these eagles gather where large food sources suddenly become available, such as locust swarms or animals fleeing from grass fires.

JUVENILE GREATER SPOTTED EAGLE

Aquila heliaca

Asian Imperial Eagle

LENGTH 72–84cm (28–33in)
WEIGHT 2.5–4.5kg ($5^1/_2$–10lb)
MIGRATION Partial migrant

HABITAT Woodland with clearings and open country with scattered trees

RED LIST CATEGORY Vulnerable

A large eagle with yellowish white crown and neck feathers, the Asian Imperial Eagle has dark wings. The adult develops a white nape, while the juvenile is brown with dark flight feathers. The prey of the Asian Imperial Eagle consists largely of small to medium-sized mammals, such as ground squirrels and hamsters, and reptiles, including tortoises. It hunts from perches or by soaring, which helps it to find carrion, another regular part of its diet.

Over much of its range, the Asian Imperial Eagle has retreated to remote places. Originally a lowland species, it now inhabits higher altitudes because of human disturbance to its breeding sites and habitat loss due to the destruction of lowland forests. In winter, it seems to prefer wetlands.

The closely related Spanish Imperial Eagle is distinguishable from the Asian Imperial Eagle by its wings, which are more extensively white. Its diet consists of rabbits, on which it is dependent. Also listed as vulnerable, the Spanish Imperial Eagle (*A. adalberti*) has adapted to a more typically Mediterranean landscape, including scrub and dunes.

long wing feathers

JUVENILE ASIAN IMPERIAL EAGLE

Aquila chrysaetos

Golden Eagle

LENGTH
75–90cm (30–35in)

WEIGHT
2.8–6.5kg (6½–14lb)

MIGRATION
Partial migrant

HABITAT Open and deserted areas to an altitude of 5,500m (18,000ft) in parts of the range

An impressive wingspan of 2.3m (7½ft) makes the Golden Eagle one of the largest land eagles in the northern hemisphere. It gets its name from the tawny-golden feathers on its head and nape. Its plumage is dark brown, and it has feathered legs and yellow feet.

The Golden Eagle prefers medium-sized prey, such as hares, grouse, and reptiles, but has been known to injure or kill deer by swooping at them. Unusually for a bird of prey, it sometimes takes carnivores, such as wild cats and foxes. The species is mostly sedentary, but Golden Eagles in northern Russia, Canada, and Alaska are migratory, with some individuals being found up to the summer snow line in the Himalayas. Distribution in its range is mostly limited to mountainous areas or places that are not densely populated. Success in breeding is influenced by weather and the availability of food, and it is common for pairs to fail to breed in certain years. The chicks have a high mortality rate, but surviving adults have been known to live up to 38 years in the wild. The Golden Eagle is not globally threatened, but there have been historic declines in some parts of the range due to persecution.

ADULT HUNTING FOR PREY

AT THE NEST

The eyrie (nest) of the Golden Eagle is often built on an inaccessible cliff ledge. This nest is used for several years, with the eagle adding sticks to the structure each breeding season. Two eggs are laid, but the younger chick is often killed before fledging. The one that survives is dependent on the parents for several months or longer.

ADULT WEDGE-TAILED EAGLE

Aquila audax

Wedge-tailed Eagle

LENGTH
80–100cm (32–39in)

WEIGHT
2–5.5kg (4½–12lb)

MIGRATION
Non-migrant

HABITAT Wide range of habitats up to 2,000m (6,500ft); avoids densely populated areas

Australia's largest bird of prey, the Wedge-tailed Eagle has dark brown plumage and a long, graduated tail, which gives it a distinctive silhouette in flight. It hunts by soaring or swooping from a prominent perch. It takes a wide range of prey, but in the southern part of the range, it shows a preference for rabbits and hares. Young kangaroos and wallabies, domestic animals, large reptiles, and birds are also taken. It builds its nest on cliff ledges or in trees, lining it with leaves, but it has been known to breed on the ground in remote areas away from human habitation. Two eggs are usually laid, but only a single egg is produced by the bird in Tasmania.

Aquila verreauxii

Verreaux's Eagle

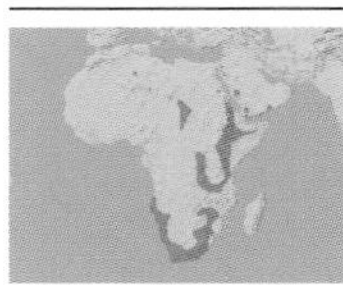

LENGTH
80–90cm (31–35in)

WEIGHT
3–6kg (6½–13lb)

MIGRATION
Non-migrant

HABITAT River gorges and rocky outcrops near colonies of hyrax (herbivorous mammals)

ADULT VERREAUX'S EAGLE

A spectacular black and white bird, the Verreaux's Eagle has a narrow wing base and broad primary feathers. It relies heavily on the rock hyrax for food and hunts on the wing, stooping on to its prey. Although not threatened, the patchy distribution of this species means that it is under pressure from human encroachment.

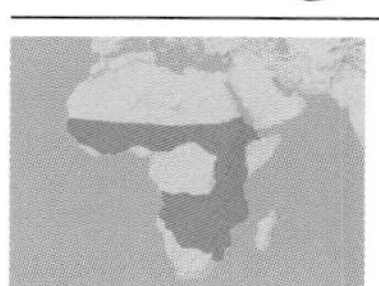

Hieraaetus wahlbergi

Wahlberg's Eagle

LENGTH 55–60cm (21½–23½in)

WEIGHT 450–1,400g (15–50oz)

MIGRATION Partial migrant

HABITAT Woodland and wooded savanna up to 1,800m (6,000ft)

Wahlberg's Eagle is a variable species and a number of colour forms have been described. The most common form is the dark form in which the birds are uniformly brown. The pale form (as shown here) is characterized by brown wings that contrast with its otherwise white or cream plumage. It is a slender species, resembling a kite when in flight. Its diet consists of mammals, reptiles, and birds, including large prey such as herons, goshawks, and owls. Breeding usually takes place between September and February (west African birds breed earlier) and is independent of rainfall. The clutch size is usually 1 or 2 eggs, and the period from incubation to fledging takes up to 120 days. Wahlberg's Eagle is found throughout much of sub-Saharan Africa, and while most of the population is sedentary or comprises short-distance migrants, some birds at the extremes of the range travel great distances to the north. Wahlberg's Eagle is one of Africa's most common eagle species but has suffered a moderate decline in numbers in parts of its range due to indirect human interference.

ADULT WAHLBERG'S EAGLE (PALE FORM)

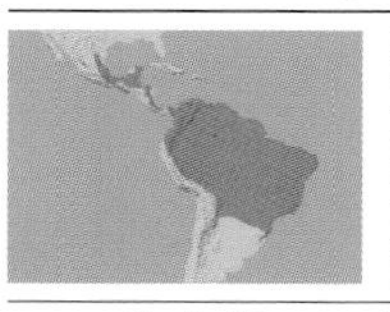

Spizastur melanoleucus

Black-and-white Hawk-Eagle

LENGTH 51–61cm (20–24in)

WEIGHT 850g (30oz)

MIGRATION Non-migrant

HABITAT Tropical forest and also in open areas of savanna

As its name indicates, this hawk-eagle is black and white in colour, with a white head and underparts and black upperparts. It also has a yellow patch around the bill. The Black-and-white Hawk-Eagle takes a wide range of prey, mostly small to medium-sized mammals and birds, usually on the edge of the tree line, where it can hunt by soaring and stooping from a height.

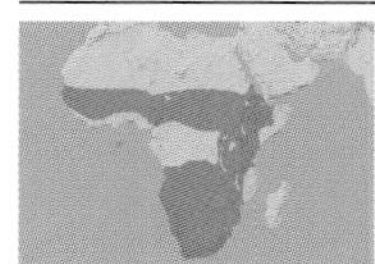

Polemaetus bellicosus

Martial Eagle

LENGTH 78–86cm (31–34in)

WEIGHT 3–6kg (6½–13lb)

MIGRATION Non-migrant

HABITAT Open areas including steppes, grassland, and woodland

One of the largest eagles in the world, the Martial Eagle has a crested appearance and prominent eyebrows. The adult's plumage is a contrasting dark grey and white, the white abdomen being marked with grey to black speckling. The juvenile is generally paler, showing grey instead of the black in the adult's plumage.

The Martial Eagle takes a wide range of vertebrate prey from 1–5kg (2¼–11lb) in weight, including gamebirds and waterfowl, or mammals to the size of small antelopes. It hunts almost exclusively in flight, with a shallow stoop to make the kill after extensive soaring. In the breeding season, a single egg is laid in a nest made of sticks, usually in small trees, but now increasingly on power pylons. The chick fledges more than 90 days after hatching and may remain dependent on the adults for up to one year after leaving the nest. The Martial Eagle is not migratory, but the juveniles disperse widely after they leave the nest.

ADULT MARTIAL EAGLE

Spizaetus philippensis

Philippine Hawk-Eagle

LENGTH 64–69cm (25–27in)

WEIGHT 1.1kg (2¼lb)

MIGRATION Non-migrant

HABITAT Lowland and hilly forests

RED LIST CATEGORY Vulnerable

The Philippine Hawk-Eagle has not been extensively studied and much information comes from studying related species in other areas. The adult has a prominent black crest at the back of the head, a streaked rufous-brown head and face, a white throat, dark brown upperparts, and rufous underparts. It also has finely barred feathered legs. However, it is difficult to distinguish from other species in the same range. Its prey consist of larger birds and some mammals, though its preferred mode of hunting has not been described.

JUVENILE PHILIPPINE HAWK-EAGLE

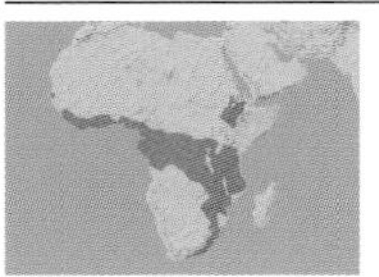

Stephanoaetus coronatus

Crowned Eagle

LENGTH 80–99cm (31–39in)

WEIGHT 2.7–3.6kg (5½–7¾lb)

MIGRATION Non-migrant

HABITAT Forests of all types, but hunts in more open areas

The rufous underwing feathers and boldly barred black and white outer wings and tail of the Crowned Eagle are clearly visible in flight. It has a large crest that is often raised. The Crowned Eagle mainly hunts mammals, including monkeys and small antelopes. Extremely powerful, it frequently takes prey larger than itself. Males often hunt cooperatively, using a range of strategies. Breeding may only take place in alternate years and the juvenile is dependent on the adults for up to a year.

GREAT SITES

KRUGER NATIONAL PARK

LOCATION In northeastern South Africa, bordered by Mozambique to the east and by Zimbabwe to the north.

One of Africa's oldest game reserves, Kruger was established as long ago as 1898, and in 1926 it became a national park that today covers almost 19,000 square km (7,350 square miles). The reserve lies within an enormous zone of grassland and scrub, which stretches across the highland plateau of northeastern South Africa and reaches into neighbouring Mozambique and Zimbabwe. This varied subtropical landscape, called bushveld, is a patchwork of open grassy areas and impenetrable thorny thickets, strewn with boulders, rocky outcrops, and stunted trees.

MIGRATION DESTINATION

Kruger National Park is best known for its herds of grazing animals and for the carnivores that hunt them, but it also supports an extraordinary diversity of bird life, so can rank among the most exciting birdwatching destinations in Africa. More than 520 species of bird have been recorded in the reserve, including around 250 species that occur year-round, together with a similar number of migratory species or nomadic wanderers. The majority of the area's seasonal visitors arrive in summer (October to March) along with the rains. They include many long-distance migrants from Europe and Central Asia, such as the Barn Swallow, European Roller, and Willow Warbler. Several European and Asian birds of prey also migrate to Kruger, such as the Eurasian Hobby and Red-footed Falcon.

A host of open-country African birds are found in Kruger all year, from the Secretarybird, which stamps on snakes and other prey with its extremely long legs, to a wide range of bee-eaters, shrikes, pipits, larks, and francolins. The wooded areas are home to species such as wood hoopoes, mousebirds, starlings, and the massive-beaked Southern Ground Hornbill. However, one of the main highlights of the reserve is its impressive variety of birds of prey.

During the winter dry season (April to September), birds concentrate at waterholes, rivers, and artificial dams. But in summer, birds are spread throughout the reserve and many species raise young.

MARTIAL COMBAT
A female Warthog defends its piglet from an attacking Martial Eagle. Kruger has one of the highest breeding densities of this powerful bird of prey anywhere in Africa.

WHAT TO SPOT

WHITE-FRONTED BEE-EATER
Merops bullockoides

PURPLE-CRESTED TURACO
Tauraco porphyreolophus
(see p.273)

NATAL SPURFOWL
Pternistis natalensis

SADDLE-BILLED STORK
Ephippiorhynchus senegalensis
(see p.159)

CRANES AND RELATIVES

ORDER	Gruiformes
FAMILY	11
SPECIES	199

STATUESQUE AND ELEGANT, the 15 species of cranes are by far the most charismatic species in this varied order of birds. Many cranes are threatened, and confined to scattered locations across the world. The gruiform order also contains 10 other families, including about 140 species of rails and crakes, as well as bustards, trumpeters, and several smaller groups. Externally, these birds look very different, with an enormous variation in size. Cranes themselves include a number of long-distance migrants, but some rails on remote islands have lost the ability to fly.

ANATOMY

In general, gruiform birds have short tails and rounded wings, and a relatively long neck. Some species of crane stand as tall as an adult man, while the smallest member of this order – the Inaccessible Island Rail – is no bigger than a newly hatched farmyard chick. Cranes and bustards have broad bodies, which in cranes accommodates the trachea coiled around inside the chest. This creates a resonating chamber that amplifies their calls. In many rails, the body is twice as deep as it is wide, creating an extraordinarily thin shape that slips easily between reeds. Gruiforms do not have webbed feet, but coots and finfoots have wide lobes on all of their toes. Not all species within this order can fly, but the ones that do keep their necks extended, and usually trail their legs behind them when in flight.

LOBED FEET
Coots have slender toes with broad lobes, which spread out as they kick against the water. They leave distinctive tracks in waterside mud.

FINAL APPROACH
With its wings spread and legs trailing, a Grey Crowned Crane comes in to land. Like most cranes, it often trumpets loudly as it flies.

BREEDING

Cranes and bustards are renowned for their elaborate courtship dances and displays. In crane species, entire flocks join in ritual dances, with birds leaping high into the air with their wings half-spread. These displays can take place at any time of the year, and young birds can be involved just as much as their parents. Bustards are more sedate, but the male's display can be bizarre. Parading in front of the female, the male Great Bustard suddenly seems to turns itself inside out, displaying white plumes that seem to transform it into a powder-puff on two legs. Among rails, courtship involves calls rather than dances: after dark, many of these birds produce strange wailing and grunting sounds from their hideaway among waterside plants. Almost all gruiform birds are ground-nesters, producing young that are well developed when they hatch. Birds of this order can be long-lived: the record lifespan for a crane is over 50 years.

DANCING ON ICE
Japan's Red-crowned Cranes often perform their ritual dances on the icy surface of frozen lakes.

BEHAVIOUR

Cranes and their relatives typically live in damp or wet habitats, but only a small number of them – including coots and moorhens – are fully aquatic birds. Cranes are highly social, and are usually seen in flocks, but rails and crakes are often solitary and secretive, hiding in dense vegetation by day, and emerging only at night. Cranes themselves eat a wide variety of food, including seeds, plant roots, and small animals, which they find by probing into soft ground with their strong beaks. Rails and crakes are also omnivorous, and some of the largest species, such as the Purple Swamphen, eat the eggs and young of other water birds. Two families of gruiforms – the bustards and seriemas – are birds of open and often dry grassland. Most of them run for safety if threatened, but bustards include some far-ranging migrants, and also some of the heaviest flying birds in the world.

HUMAN IMPACT

THREATS AND CONSERVATION

Over 20 species in this order have become extinct within the past few hundred years, and today a quarter or the remainder are either endangered or vulnerable. They include 10 species of crane, several bustards, and a large number of rails and crakes that have evolved on remote islands. Habitat change is the main threat to cranes, while introduced species are responsible for the decline of endemic rails and crakes.

NOT YET OUT OF DANGER
In the 1940s, the population of Whooping Cranes, (one is pictured here) dropped to 23 birds. The species is recovering, but is still in danger.

Otis tarda

Great Bustard

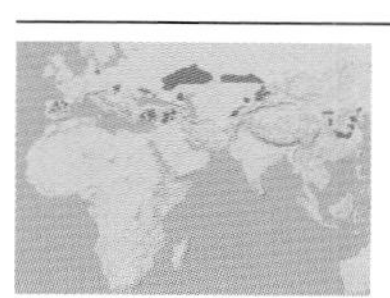

LENGTH 75–100cm (30–39in)

WEIGHT 3.3–18kg ($7^3/_4$–40lb)

MIGRATION Partial migrant

HABITAT Dry open grassland, crops, stubble.

RED LIST CATEGORY Vulnerable

Although largely terrestrial, the male of this impressive species is the heaviest of all flying birds. This distinction is sometimes claimed for both its relatives – the Kori Bustard (right) and the Trumpeter Swan (*Cygnus buccinator*), but the male Great Bustard probably has the greatest average weight. The adult male is brown above and white below, with a long grey neck and head. The breast and lower neck sides are chestnut. The female is smaller, with a buff neck and breast. With its powerful muscles, the Great Bustard is able to lift its bulk into the air. It has a stately slow walk, and tends to run when disturbed rather than fly. It is omnivorous, taking seeds, insects, and other small creatures, including frogs and beetles.

MALE GREAT BUSTARD

COURTSHIP DISPLAY

During courtship, the male Great Bustard withdraws its head and transforms itself into a huge shimmering ball of white, brown, and rusty-coloured fluff. It raises and spreads its tail, showing a large amount of white, mainly on the undertail. As part of this flamboyant display, the male inflates its throat-sac, up ends its tail, and turns its wings inside out to reveal the white feathers on its flanks.

Chlamydotis undulata

Houbara Bustard

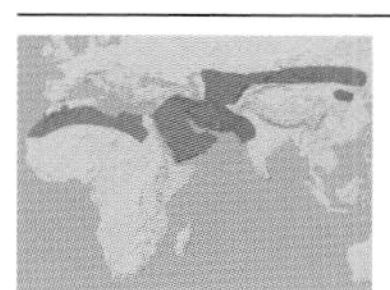

LENGTH 55–75cm ($21^1/_2$–30in)

WEIGHT 1.2–3.2kg ($2^1/_4$–$6^1/_2$lb)

MIGRATION Non-migrant

HABITAT Semi-desert, open grassland, cultivation

RED LIST CATEGORY Vulnerable

There are three subspecies of Houbara Bustard that are all very similar in appearance. The one pictured here is *C. u. macqueenii* of western Asia, which is sometimes regarded as a separate species on the basis of its DNA, vocalizations, and courtship behaviour. In its display, the male erects the long thread-like feathers on the top of its head and the sides of its neck.

ADULT HOUBARA BUSTARD

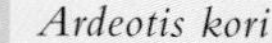

Ardeotis kori

Kori Bustard

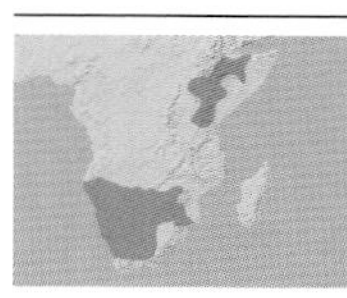

LENGTH 0.9–1.2m (3–4ft)

WEIGHT 6–19kg (13–42lb)

MIGRATION Non-migrant

HABITAT Dry open country with grass or scrub and adjacent crop fields

One of the largest of all flying birds, the Kori Bustard male performs a flamboyant display to attract a female. It tries to make itself look even bigger by inflating its neck to four times its usual size. If successful, pairing lasts only a brief few seconds, after which the female is left to lay the eggs, incubate, and care for the young alone, while the male returns to the display ground.

NECK RUFF INFLATED IN DISPLAY

ADULT AUSTRALIAN BUSTARD

Ardeotis australis

Australian Bustard

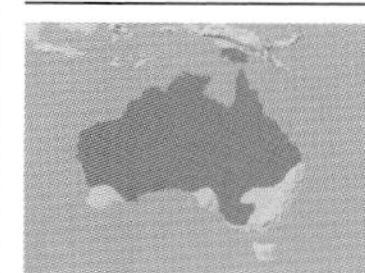

LENGTH 0.9–1.2m (3–4ft)

WEIGHT 2.8–8kg ($6^1/_2$–18lb)

MIGRATION Non-migrant

HABITAT Grassland, savanna, open woodland, and among shrubs

The Australian Bustard has a long, white neck, a black cap on its head, and orange-brown wings, with mottled black and white markings. Its diet includes seeds, fruit, insects, molluscs, lizards, young birds, and small rodents. Once common throughout much of Australia, its population still exceeds 100,000, but is thinly distributed.

Afrotis afraoides

Northern Black Korhaan

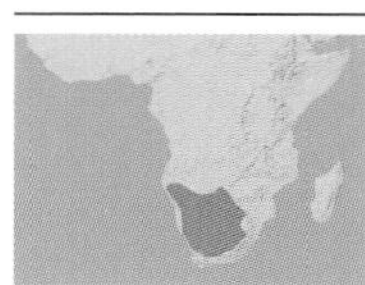

LENGTH 50cm ($19^1/_2$in)

WEIGHT 700g (25oz)

MIGRATION Non-migrant

HABITAT Dry coastal scrub, open grassland, sparse thornveld, and cropland

The Northern Black Korhaan has a black neck and underparts and a strikingly patterned back. It is adept at hiding in its scrubby habitat. When it spreads its wings, a white patch in the outer wing can be seen, which distinguishes it from the similar Southern Black Korhaan (*A. afra*).

ADULT BIRD

Tetrax tetrax

Little Bustard

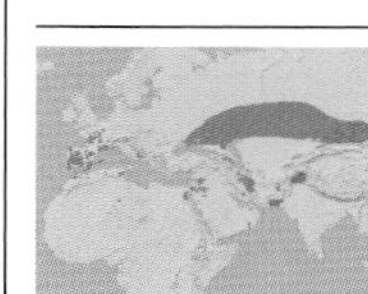

LENGTH 43cm (17in)

WEIGHT 675–975g (24–35oz)

MIGRATION Partial migrant

HABITAT Steppes, open grassland, and crops

MALE LITTLE BUSTARD

In winter, the male Little Bustard loses its distinctive black and white neck and breast patterns and assumes a buff plumage with dark markings, similar to the protectively patterned female. The dull coloration makes it much more difficult to see in its preferred habitat, where the vegetation conceals it from predators. The species is sociable, feeding in large flocks.

MALE SUBDESERT MESITE

Monias benschi

Subdesert Mesite

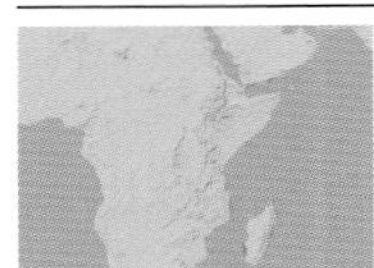

LENGTH 32cm (12½in)

WEIGHT 125–150g (4–5oz)

MIGRATION Non-migrant

HABITAT Lowland spiny forest and subdesert thickets

RED LIST CATEGORY Vulnerable

Of the three species of mesite, all of which occur only in Madagascar, the Subdesert Mesite is the only one in which the plumage of the male and female differ. Compared to the male, the female has extensive rufous colouring on the throat and breast. A terrestrial bird, the Subdesert Mesite may be either polyandrous or polygynous, or both. The mesites are threatened, mainly due to forest loss.

Rhynochetos jubatus

Kagu

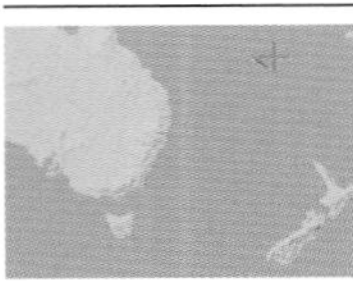

LENGTH 55cm (21½in)

WEIGHT 900g (32oz)

MIGRATION Non-migrant

HABITAT Found only in forested areas, although occasionally ventures into tall shrubland

RED LIST CATEGORY Endangered

Widespread across New Caledonia prior to the arrival of Europeans in the late 18th century, the Kagu is now restricted to humid forests in the south of the island, where fewer than 1,000 birds survive. Grey in colour, the Kagu has black, red, and white bars on its wings and a long crest. It feeds by probing the soil with its large bill.

ADULT KAGU

GREAT SITES

RIVIÈRE BLEU

Current conservation efforts to protect the Kagu revolve around the creation of reserves. By far the most important of these is Rivière Bleu, which is also the most frequently visited by birdwatchers. The aim is to control predators, such as dogs, cats, and pigs, and prevent habitat loss due to fires and mining.

Cariama cristata

Red-legged Seriema

LENGTH 75–90cm (30–35in)

WEIGHT 1.5kg (3¼lb)

MIGRATION Non-migrant

HABITAT Open country, including sparsely wooded areas, fields, savanna, and ranchland

The Red-legged Seriema has a crest of stiff, raised feathers. As its name indicates, this bird has red legs. It is mainly grey-brown, with white underparts, and banded wings and tail. An omnivore, this species kills small birds, rodents, and snakes by beating them on the ground with its bill. An extremely vocal bird, its songs are often heard in the grasslands of southern South America. It is capable of running at a high speed in pursuit of prey and in response to danger. The Red-legged Seriema nests in trees.

ADULT BIRD

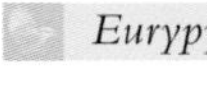

Eurypyga helias

Sunbittern

LENGTH 43–48cm (17–19in)

WEIGHT 175–225g (6–8oz)

MIGRATION Non-migrant

HABITAT Humid forest in areas near water; either streams, ponds, rivers, or oxbow lakes

Like the Kagu (above), the Sunbittern has soft, lax flight feathers, which account for the species being almost silent in flight. At first glance, a Sunbittern may be taken for a heron, with its long straight pointed bill, slender neck, and long legs. When it spreads its wings and fans its tail, it reveals bright orange-chestnut on its wing feathers.

It is wary, but not shy, of humans, tending to freeze and melt into the background or slink off quietly if disturbed. It flies with quick flicks of the wings if surprised at close quarters. The breeding behaviour has been closely studied in some areas.

Nests are built on tree branches, using mud, grass, and leaves. The female lays two eggs, occasionally one, which are incubated by both sexes for about a month. The adult feeds its chicks a wide range of invertebrate and vertebrate prey, including crabs, cockroaches, lizards, spiders, frogs, beetles, and fish. Remarkably, the young moult directly into adult plumage while still in the nest, which is extremely unusual in any bird species. They leave the nest three to four weeks after hatching.

ADULT SUNBITTERN

Crex crex

Corncrake

LENGTH 27–30cm (10½–12in)
WEIGHT 125–200g (4–7oz)
MIGRATION Migrant

HABITAT Breeds in dry to moist meadows and among cereal crops; winters in dry grassland

The rasping, double-note calls of this bird were once a familiar sound throughout the night in its breeding range. The Corncrake has declined dramatically in recent decades, but is now making a slow comeback due to conservation programmes. The male has a tawny back with bold black streaks, while the female has white and brown bars on the flanks. One of the latest migrants to reach northern Europe in spring, the species returns to Africa relatively early. During its brief sojourn in Europe, it raises two broods, with the black downy young leaving the nest after just a few days of care by the female.

ADULT CORNCRAKE

Gallirallus okinawae

Okinawa Rail

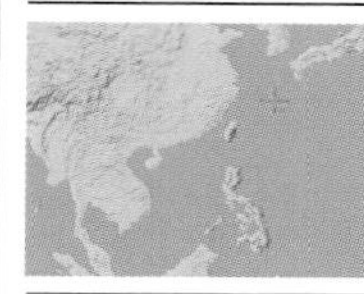

LENGTH 30cm (12in)
WEIGHT 425g (15oz)
MIGRATION Non-migrant

HABITAT Evergreen forest with dense undergrowth and water nearby; also scrub and cultivated areas

RED LIST CATEGORY Endangered

The striking red bill and legs of the Okinawa Rail contrast deeply with its dark plumage, especially the black face and heavily dark-barred underside. It has dark olive-brown upperparts. However, like all rails, it is shy and difficult to spot. Like many island-inhabiting rails, the Okinawa Rail is almost flightless and is now in danger of attacks by introduced predators, such as cats, dogs, and mongooses. It has also learned the habit of roosting in trees to combat predation by snakes. Nonetheless, the Okinawa Rail remains common within its tiny range in Japan, where it is largely confined to uninhabited forests.

This species is mainly insectivorous, although it supplements this diet with lizards and small invertebrates. During the breeding season, from May to July, it builds a nest on the forest floor and lays 2 or 3 eggs, but most aspects of the Okinawa Rail's breeding cycle remain unknown to ornithologists.

ADULT OKINAWA RAIL

Gallirallus philippensis

Buff-banded Rail

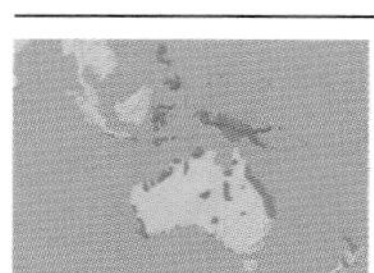

LENGTH 25–33cm (10–13in)
WEIGHT 125–300g (4–11oz)
MIGRATION Partial migrant

HABITAT All types of wetland but also grassland, wooded areas, crops, heaths, and even golf courses

Over its wide range, the Buff-banded Rail is quite a variably marked species; some forms, for example, that found on the Indonesian island of Flores, even lack the buff breast-band, from which the species takes its name. The white eyebrow and chestnut eye-stripe of this rail make up its striking head pattern. Some populations, especially those on small islands, are threatened by habitat loss, hunting, and predators such as cats and rats. However, the bird's wide range means that the species is not threatened.

ADULT BUFF-BANDED RAIL

ADULT WATER RAIL

Rallus aquaticus

Water Rail

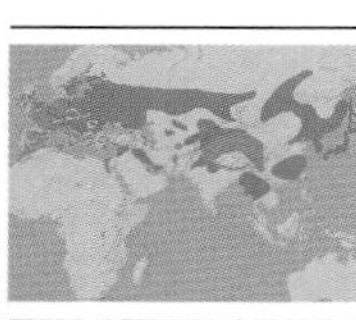

LENGTH 25–28cm (10–11in)
WEIGHT 75–200g ($2^5/_8$–7oz)
MIGRATION Partial migrant

HABITAT Dense wetlands of all types, from fresh to salt water; occasionally in other habitats in winter

Largely grey below, the Water Rail has black and white barred flanks and brown upperparts, which are streaked in black, and bright red legs. Its long, decurved bill is also red, with a black tip. A widespread species, it is able to tolerate a range of conditions and is omnivorous in its eating habits, feeding on plants, seeds, and fruit, as well as a variety of aquatic insects and other invertebrates, amphibians, fish, and birds.

Rallus limicola

Virginia Rail

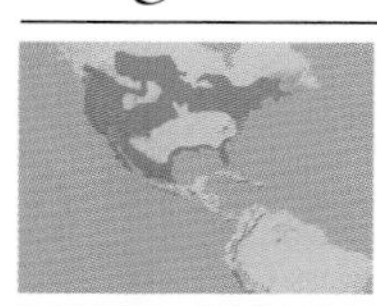

LENGTH 20–25cm (8–10in)
WEIGHT 60–125g ($2^1/_8$–4oz)
MIGRATION Partial migrant

HABITAT Freshwater, brackish, and salt marshes; prefers shallow water and flooded grassland

The Virginia Rail has grey cheeks, a cinnamon-rufous throat and breast, and bright buff-coloured underparts. It has a long, slim red bill, a short tail, and long toes. These birds probe with their bill in mud or shallow water searching for food. They mainly eat insects and aquatic animals. While populations in the USA are largely migratory, the birds are more likely to be resident farther south. Like many species of rail, it is threatened locally by the destruction of its wetland habitats, although its large range is some insurance against the negative effects of these changes.It has a number of calls, including a harsh "kuk kuk kuk", usually heard at night.

ADULT VIRGINIA RAIL

ADULT BAILLON'S CRAKE

Porzana pusilla

Baillon's Crake

LENGTH 17–19cm (6½–7½in)

WEIGHT 35g (1¼oz)

MIGRATION Partial migrant

HABITAT Densely vegetated freshwater and saltwater wetlands

Baillon's Crake is a small, typically elusive, crake. The adult is a rich mix of colours: a bright red eye, chocolate-brown upperparts streaked with black and white flecks, and grey underparts. The juvenile is duller and browner below. Found in Europe, Asia, Africa, and Australasia, the species has a wide global distribution. However, it is not easy to observe.

Porzana carolina

Sora

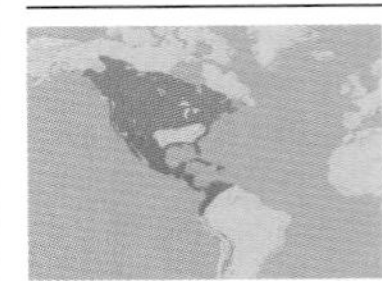

LENGTH 19–25cm (7½–10in)

WEIGHT 75g (2⅝oz)

MIGRATION Migrant

HABITAT Freshwater wetlands, but also brackish and saltwater marshes

A compact rail found only in the Americas, the Sora can be distinguished from other rails and crakes by its black face and throat and contrasting bright yellow bill. The juvenile is browner below and does not have any black on the face. The Sora eats mainly plant life such as seeds, wild rice, and algae, but also feeds on insects, spiders, snails, and small crustaceans. It breeds in Canada and northern USA, before migrating to spend its winters in the southern USA, the Caribbean, and Central and northern South America.

ADULT SORA

Porphyrio porphyrio

Purple Swamphen

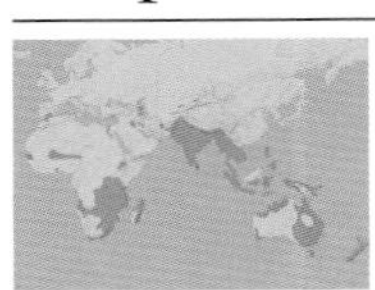

LENGTH 38–50cm (15–19½in)

WEIGHT 550–1100g (20–39oz)

MIGRATION Non-migrant

HABITAT Sheltered fresh or brackish wetlands

ADULT (AUSTRALIAN FORM)

With a wide global distribution, the Purple Swamphen has a variety of distinctive subspecies. As a result, the species has different common names. These include the Purple Gallinule in Europe and the Maori "Pukeko" in New Zealand. However, there is considerable variation among the different geographical forms, with some subspecies appearing more brown or green above. Purple Swamphens are predominantly vegetarian, preferring the shoots, stems, and leaves of aquatic plants, although they also eat small numbers of insects, molluscs, fish, and sometimes even small birds, rodents, and lizards. Pairs nest in swamps, clumps of rushes in paddocks, or long, unkempt grass. Several females lay eggs in one nest and share the incubation duties. Each bird can lay 3-6 speckled eggs and a communal nest may contain up to 12 eggs.

Porphyrio hochstetteri

Takahe

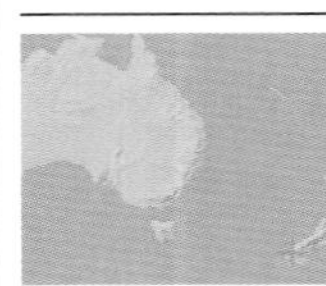

LENGTH 63cm (25in)

WEIGHT 2–3kg (4½–6½lb)

MIGRATION Non-migrant

HABITAT Alpine tussock grassland; also translocated to predator-free offshore islands

RED LIST CATEGORY Endangered

New Zealand's Takahe is remarkable in many ways: it is the world's largest living rail, standing half a metre high, like an inflated blue and green football, with a huge prehistoric-looking red bill. It is flightless with tiny stumpy wings. The species was thought to be extinct until it was rediscovered in 1948, when a small population of 250–300 birds was found in the mountainous Fiordland of New Zealand's South Island. The numbers, however, declined rapidly soon after their rediscovery, possibly partly due to predation by stoats and possums.

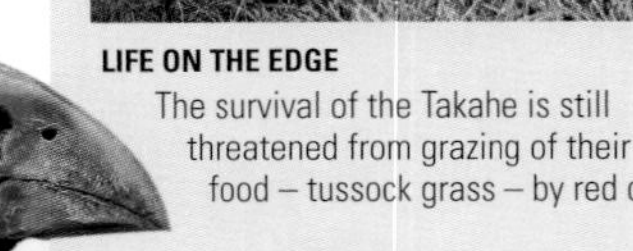
ADULT TAKAHE

HUMAN IMPACT

CAPTIVE BREEDING

A number of Takahes were taken from the wild in the 1980s and a captive-breeding programme was started. Today, new populations have been established on predator-free offshore islands and a special conservation area has also been set up in New Zealand's Murchison Mountains.

LIFE ON THE EDGE The survival of the Takahe is still threatened from grazing of their main food – tussock grass – by red deer.

ADULT PURPLE GALLINULE

Porphyrio martinica

Purple Gallinule

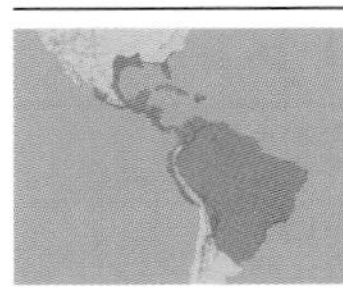

LENGTH 27–36cm (10½–14in)

WEIGHT 200–275g (7–10oz)

MIGRATION Partial migrant

HABITAT Lush marshes, swamps, and grassy wetlands

The Purple Gallinule is an American species, not to be confused with the larger Purple Swamphen (left), confusingly given the same name sometimes. The adult Purple Gallinule is just over half the size of the Purple Swamphen, with a yellow-tipped red bill, a pale blue facial shield, and bright yellow legs and feet. Its wings are green, contrasting with its blue head and underparts. An omnivore, the Purple Gallinule feeds on a variety of plant and animal matter, including seeds, leaves, and the fruit of both aquatic and terrestrial plants, as well as insects, frogs, snails, spiders, earthworms, and fish.

Gallinula chloropus

Common Moorhen

LENGTH 30–38cm (12–15in)

WEIGHT 175–325g (6–12oz)

MIGRATION Partial migrant

HABITAT All freshwater wetlands

This medium-sized gallinule has a wide global distribution and is found on all inhabited continents, except Australia, where it is replaced by the similar Dusky Moorhen (*G. tenebrosa*). As a result, a number of different subspecies occur, all very similar in plumage, but varying in size. The adult Common Moorhen appears black from a distance, with a broken white line along the flanks and a white undertail. Its head and underparts are black, with dark brown plumage above. It has a small red frontal shield extending just onto the forehead and a yellow-tipped red bill. Its legs and feet are a dull greenish yellow. Juvenile and immature birds are paler and browner, lacking the bright red bill and facial shield; the chicks are fluffy and black, with tiny red and yellow bills.

The Common Moorhen is a noisy bird, with a wide variety of clucks and harsh chattering calls, the most familiar being a crowing, two-syllable "kurr-ikk", usually uttered during the breeding season to advertise the bird's presence. It is a sociable bird with intricate courtship rituals, as well as frequent displays of aggression that help to establish hierarchy. Unusually, the females compete for males, rather than the other way round. The heaviest female tends to win and prefers small males with large fat reserves, as they can incubate eggs for longer. The Common Moorhen is also aggressive towards other species that infringe on its territory. The species is normally resident, but movements take place in many parts of its range, particularly in response to harsh weather.

PAIR OF FIGHTING MOORHENS

ADULT EURASIAN COOT

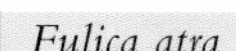

Fulica atra

Eurasian Coot

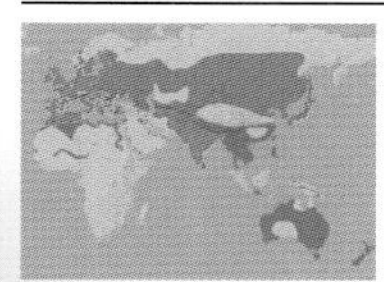

LENGTH 36–39cm (14–15½in)

WEIGHT 500–900g (18–32oz)

MIGRATION Partial migrant

HABITAT Wetlands, but prefers large, open freshwater areas

Yet another species that appears all black from a distance, the Eurasian Coot is actually black only on the head and breast, with the rest of its plumage being a dark slate-grey. The species has a bone-white bill and large white facial shield that extends up to the forehead. The Eurasian Coot has lobed feet, which are large and partially webbed, reflecting the amount of time the coot spends swimming in the water. It builds a nest of reeds and grasses near the water's edge or on underwater vegetation protruding from the water, laying up to 10 eggs. The Eurasian Coot is an omnivore, and will take a variety of small live prey, as well as the eggs of other waterbirds. It is a noisy species, with a wide repertoire of crackling, explosive or trumpeting calls, often given at night. It is found throughout most of Europe, Asia, Australia, and New Zealand, as well as parts of North Africa and the Middle East.

AGGRESSION

During the breeding season, the Eurasian Coot is notoriously aggressive. Even the slightest violation of a boundary by another coot or waterbird will provoke a tremendous show of strength and aggression. It displays its white frontal shield and splashes water, the fights involving violent striking and clawing with the feet and stabbing with the bill. These fights can result in injury and even death.

ADULT AFRICAN FINFOOT

Podica senegalensis

African Finfoot

LENGTH 35–59cm (14–23in)

WEIGHT 350–875g (13–31oz)

MIGRATION Non-migrant

HABITAT Still or slow-moving water in overgrown mangroves, forest, and savanna

Elusive, but not uncommon, the African Finfoot is thinly distributed over its wide range. The plumage of this aquatic bird varies according to the subspecies, generally being dark brown above and paler below. It has a sharp bill, a long neck with white streaks, and legs and feet that are bright orange or red. A claw on its wing helps it to climb scrub or trees, making it agile on land.

MALE SUNGREBE

Heliornis fulica

Sungrebe

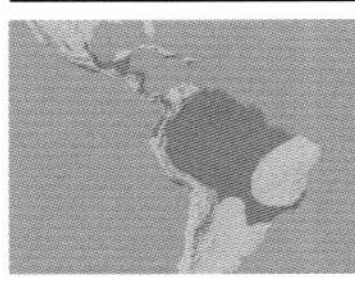

LENGTH 26–33cm (10–13in)

WEIGHT 125–150g (4–5oz)

MIGRATION Non-migrant

HABITAT Forest rivers and streams, lakes and ponds, with overhanging vegetation

In an adaptation that is unique, the male Sungrebe carries its young in skin pockets under its wings in flight. Its bill is black above and buff below and it has yellow eyelids, while the female has red eyelids and a red bill. Both the male and female are mainly brown in colour, with yellow and black stripes on the legs and feet. The smallest of the finfoots, the Sungrebe feeds, like its larger relatives, on aquatic insects and their larvae, crustaceans, frogs, and small fish. Although a non-migrant, it is occasionally seen in places outside its normal range, such as Trinidad.

Heliopais personatus

Masked Finfoot

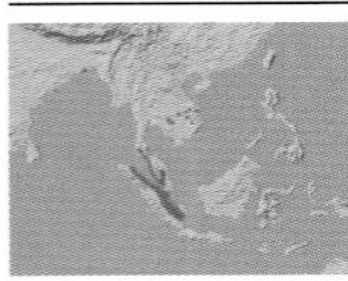

LENGTH 43–55cm (17–21½in)

WEIGHT Not recorded

MIGRATION Partial migrant

HABITAT Coastal and inland wetlands, including mangroves, flooded forest, swamps, and lakes

RED LIST CATEGORY Vulnerable

The Masked Finfoot's feet are a distinctive pea-green. It has a black mask and eyebrows that contrast with its white eye-ring and throat stripe. Its back and wings are brown. The male grows a small fleshy knob over its bill during breeding. The diet of the species consists of aquatic invertebrates, frogs, and small fish. A very shy bird, little is known about its breeding habits, although it probably breeds in areas where it was thought to be only a winter visitor. The species has disappeared from many parts of its range, including Myanmar (Burma), where large numbers once bred. It is intolerant of human disturbance and has also suffered from changes to its wetland habitat.

Psophia leucoptera

Pale-winged Trumpeter

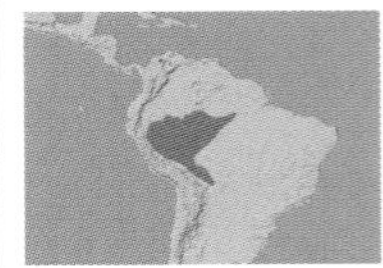

LENGTH 45–52cm (17½–20½in)

WEIGHT 1075g (38oz)

MIGRATION Non-migrant

HABITAT Dense lowland tropical rainforest

Pale in colour, with a green patch on its back and green-tipped wings, the Pale-winged Trumpeter has long, strong legs and feet that are well adapted to a life spent mostly on the ground; it prefers walking and running to flying. It is a sociable species, travelling in small groups of 3–12 birds. Although it eats carrion, insects, and small vertebrates, the Pale-winged Trumpeter is largely a fruit-eater, often feeding on dropped fruit below trees where monkeys are active. As a result, it may be indirectly affected by a decline in the number of monkeys. Although not yet considered threatened, it is declining because of deforestation and the spread of human settlement.

GREAT SITES

TAMBOPATA RESERVE

Tambopata Reserve is home to over 575 bird species. Here you can see the Pale-winged Trumpeter and visit the world's largest mineral clay lick, where more than a dozen species of macaw and parrot can be seen every day. BirdLife International has designated the park as an Important Bird Area, harbouring the globally threatened Black Tinamou and Southern Helmeted Curassow.

Aramus guarauna

Limpkin

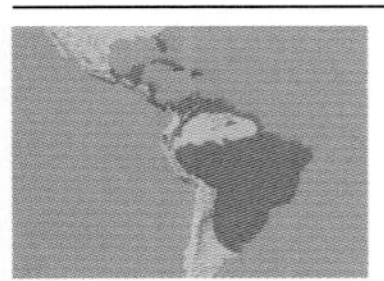

LENGTH 56–71cm (22–28in)

WEIGHT 1–1.5kg (2¼–3¼lb)

MIGRATION Partial migrant

HABITAT Shallow water with plentiful supplies of molluscs, especially apple snails

Brown in colour, with a spangled grey head and neck, the Limpkin gets its common name from its limping walk. The amount of white speckling on its oily plumage varies: the North American subspecies is heavily spotted, while birds from South America have little or no white markings. It has a slender, sharp, yellow bill that is twisted at the tip, enabling it to extract apple snails from their shells with ease.

The Limpkin has a range of calls, including rattles and shrieks. The male's windpipe has loops to extend its length, which amplifies its call. While trying to attract a mate, it calls throughout the day and night. This species is unaggressive, except when the male defends its breeding territory. It charges at intruders, fighting with its feet and uttering mournful calls. The nest is a platform of reeds and grass and 4–8 eggs are usually laid. Breeding pairs often stay together year after year. Once almost hunted to extinction in parts of its range, the Limpkin now faces a threat from invading alien plants, which oust the native aquatic plants that sustain apple snails, its main food item.

LIMPKIN (NORTH AMERICAN SUBSPECIES)

Turnix tanki

Yellow-legged Buttonquail

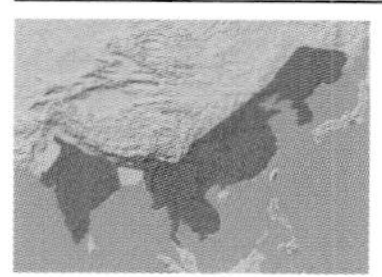

LENGTH 17cm (6½in)

WEIGHT 35–125g (1¼–4oz)

MIGRATION Partial migrant

HABITAT Grassland, scrub, and cropland

Mainly grey in colour, the Yellow-legged Buttonquail has a yellow bill, barred back, spotted underparts, and yellow legs. The female Yellow-legged Buttonquail has a red collar and, like other buttonquails, is much larger than the male and more brightly coloured. The female leaves hatching and bringing up chicks to the male – when several males are about, it may practise "serial polyandry", moving on to a new mate as soon as its eggs are laid. This species superficially resembles a true quail, but lacks a hind toe – a feature it shares with other birds that spend their time walking or running. Buttonquails are found singly, in pairs, or small family groups, which roost together. Relying on its camouflage, they will freeze rather than fly when threatened.

ADULT YELLOW-LEGGED BUTTONQUAIL

Ortyxelos meiffrenii

Quail-plover

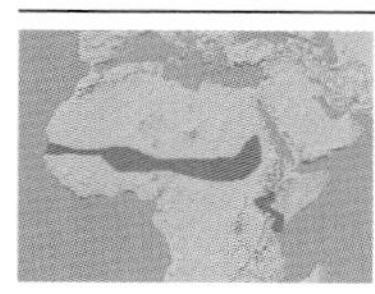

LENGTH 10–13cm (4–5in)

WEIGHT 16–20g (9/16–11/16oz)

MIGRATION Partial migrant

HABITAT Dry, semi-arid, and coastal grassland, savanna, and scrub

A small bird, the Quail-plover has pale yellow cheeks and mottled brown markings on the back and chest. In flight, it shows a black and white pattern on the wings. It skulks on the ground in tall grass and if flushed, flies up with a jerky movement. Its nest is a shallow scrape in the ground lined with grass, in which two eggs are laid.

Grus japonensis

Red-crowned Crane

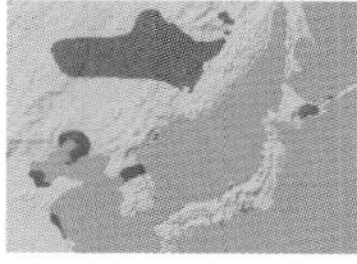

LENGTH 1.5m (5ft)

WEIGHT 7–12kg (15–26lb)

MIGRATION Migrant

HABITAT Reed and sedge marshes, bogs, and wet meadows; rivers and coastal marshes in winter

RED LIST CATEGORY Endangered

The heaviest of all crane species, the Red-crowned Crane is the second rarest after the Siberian Crane. Named for its red crown, it has snow-white plumage and a grey neck and tail. It prefers deeper water than other cranes and nests among standing reeds in water. A generalist feeder, like other cranes, it tends to have more animal than plant food in its diet – insects, fish, frogs, and small mammals, as well as aquatic invertebrates. In winter, the Red-crowned Crane forages for waste grain on cropland, and in Japan, the birds will also come to feeding stations, where rice is put out for them. This is perhaps one reason why the Japanese population of Red-crowned Cranes has increased from just 33 in 1954 to around 800 today. Elsewhere, the species faces many threats. China's huge dam projects threaten water levels that might flood or dry out its wetland habitats. In Russia and China, reed and grass fires in spring destroy nesting grounds. Another threat is pollution from oil fields.

DANCING ON ICE

The courtship dance of the Red-crowned Crane starts with the trumpeting calls of the birds as they stand side-by-side. The dance is a series of bows, head bobbing, leaps, and various other gestures. Both sexes leap into the air and display, raising their wings and tail feathers. Sometimes, these cranes pick up grasses, sticks, or feathers and toss them in the air.

JUVENILE (LEFT) AND ADULT (RIGHT) RED-CROWNED CRANE

Balearica regulorum

Grey Crowned Crane

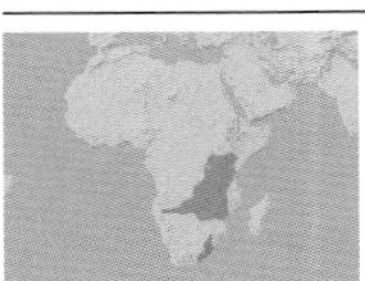

LENGTH 1m (3¼ft)

WEIGHT 3.5kg (7¾lb)

MIGRATION Non-migrant

HABITAT Mixed wetland and grassland habitats and cultivated land with irrigation

The Grey Crowned Crane and the closely related Black Crowned Crane (*B. pavonina*) differ from all other cranes in two striking respects. They lack the long, coiled windpipe that other cranes have and, therefore, cannot produce their far-carrying "bugling" calls, and, unlike other cranes who stand on the ground or in water, these species are able to perch in trees due to their long hind toes.

With its short bill, crown of golden bristles, red wattles, and predominantly grey plumage, the Grey Crowned Crane is a familiar sight in cultivated fields. It is considered sacred in Kenya, and is the national bird of Uganda.

This crane has adapted well to landscapes modified by humans. Outside the rainy season, when it breeds, it generally moves about in search of standing water, but where dams and irrigation systems provide permanent sources, it moves less. However, the intensification of agriculture, greater use of pesticides, fewer fallow periods, and heavy grazing have caused a decline in its population. Conservationists are working with communities to restore its numbers.

ADULT WITH CHICK

ADULT SIBERIAN CRANES

Grus leucogeranus

Siberian Crane

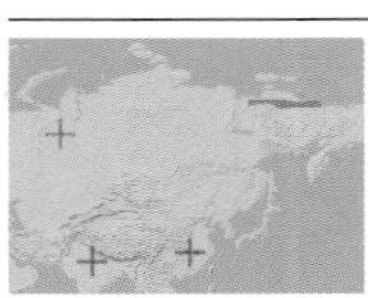

LENGTH 1.4m (4½ft)

WEIGHT 6.5kg (14lb)

MIGRATION Migrant

HABITAT Wide shallow wetlands with good visibility

RED LIST CATEGORY Critically endangered

The Siberian Crane has a red face and pure white plumage, with black wing-tips. It is also the most specialized of the cranes in its habitat requirements for breeding, feeding, and roosting: it eats cranberries, insects, and fish in its breeding grounds, but is vegetarian during migration and while wintering.

Numbers of Siberian Cranes are dwindling rapidly, and it is now one of the rarest cranes – the large population in its wintering site in China is threatened by hydrological changes caused by the Three Gorges Dam, built on the Yangtze river. Oil exploration is a further threat to its breeding grounds.

HUMAN IMPACT

MIGRATION TRAINING

Experimental conservation techniques are now being applied to save the Siberian Crane, including the use of microlight aircraft to show young captive-bred cranes the traditional migratory route from Russia to Central Asia. The aircraft lead the young birds on their journey.

READY TO FLY
Young Siberian Cranes reared in captivity undergo training to follow microlight aircraft on migratory routes.

Grus antigone

Sarus Crane

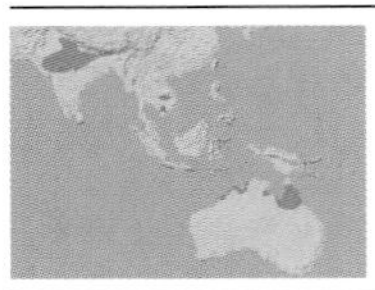

LENGTH 1.5m (5ft)

WEIGHT 6.5kg (14lb)

MIGRATION Partial migrant

HABITAT Marshes, floodplains, high altitude wetlands, paddy fields, and other cultivated land

RED LIST CATEGORY Vulnerable

The tallest of the cranes, the Sarus Crane is found in three separate populations in the Indian subcontinent, southeast Asia, and Australia, but has disappeared from Thailand, Malaysia, and the Philippines. The species has mainly grey plumage with a bare red head and upper neck, a powerful grey bill, and pink legs. It prefers a combination of flooded and dry ground for nesting and feeding, and moves seasonally with the monsoon and droughts. The bond between a pair is particularly strong – a crane stays with its dead or injured mate for a long time.

PAIR OF SARUS CRANES

Grus rubicunda

Brolga

LENGTH 1.6m (5¼ft)

WEIGHT 7kg (15lb)

MIGRATION Non-migrant

HABITAT Brackish and freshwater wetlands and irrigated land

The Brolga is a mainly grey bird with a broad red band from its bill to the back of the head, a grey-green crown, and red throat pouch. The juvenile lacks the red band. In the dry season, the staple food of the Brolga consists of the tubers of the bulkuru sedge, but it also eats plants, snails, molluscs, insects, frogs, lizards, and small mammals. Although non-migratory, it makes extensive seasonal movements because of Australia's extreme climate.

ADULT BROLGA

Grus canadensis

Sandhill Crane

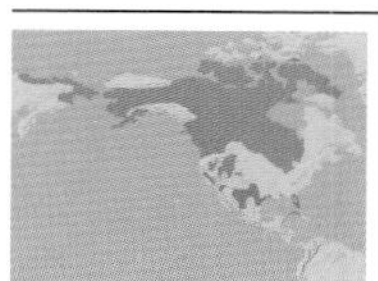

LENGTH 88–95cm (35–37in)

WEIGHT 3.3–6kg ($7^{3}/_{4}$–13lb)

MIGRATION Partial migrant

HABITAT Marshes, lake margins, and river deltas, from the Arctic to the tropics

One of the longest-surviving bird species (bones identical to those of the modern Sandhill Crane have been found in fossil deposits up to nine million years old), the Sandhill Crane is the most abundant of the world's cranes. The six subspecies vary greatly in size, the smallest being the Lesser Sandhill Crane (*G. c. canadensis*), while the largest, the Greater Sandhill Crane (*G. c. rowani*), can be almost twice as heavy.

The Sandhill Crane is a grey bird with a red forehead and a relatively short bill. In parts of its range, iron-rich mud gets plastered on its feathers and turns them a rusty red.

The Sandhill Crane can live more than 20 years in the wild, and twice as long in captivity. Omnivorous like other cranes, it eats insects, frogs and other aquatic animals, seeds, and berries. Outside the breeding season, it forages in large flocks.

"DANCING" SANDHILL CRANES

broad white patch behind eye

long grey neck

ADULT COMMON CRANE

Grus grus

Common Crane

LENGTH 1.1–1.3m ($3^{1}/_{2}$–$4^{1}/_{4}$ft)

WEIGHT 5.5kg (12lb)

MIGRATION Migrant

HABITAT Breeds in large wetlands; winters in open country, including cultivated land

A large and stately bird that moves with slow, dignified footsteps, the Common Crane is easily distinguished from the Grey Heron (see p.166), with which it shares much of its range. The Common Crane has a black head and neck, with a white stripe running down the nape and a red spot on the crown. Its plumage is slate-grey in colour.

Outside the breeding season when pairs defend their territories, this crane is very gregarious and can gather in thousands where food is abundant. It feeds on crops, eating large quantities of grain, acorns, and even olives. During breeding, it is more carnivorous, eating insects, frogs, rodents, snakes, and small birds. In the breeding season, the courtship display involves dancing with the wings uplifted. The nest is built by both male and female, who remain a pair throughout the year.

ADULT FEEDING

Grus americana

Whooping Crane

LENGTH 1.3m ($4^{1}/_{4}$ft)

WEIGHT 6kg (13lb)

MIGRATION Migrant

HABITAT Breeds in prairie wetlands, marshes, and mudflats; winters in brackish coastal wetlands

RED LIST CATEGORY Endangered

The tallest bird in North America, the Whooping Crane has red bare skin on its crown, a black moustache, a heavy yellow bill, and long black legs. In flight, the adult shows black outer flight feathers that contrast with its otherwise snow-white plumage. It is an opportunist feeder, taking in a variety of plant and animal food. The courtship ceremony involves elaborate dances by pairs of breeding adults.

By the middle of the 20th century, the population of Whooping Cranes in the USA had declined to a tiny number, but by the early 21st century, there were more than 200 birds in the wild.

GREY CROWNED CRANES
A fan of stiff golden feathers makes up the crown of this beautifully coloured crane. The bright red throat pouch is inflated when the bird calls.

WADERS, GULLS, AND AUKS

ORDER	Charadriiformes
FAMILY	16
SPECIES	344

THIS LARGE AND VARIED ORDER includes some of the commonest birds of coasts and fresh water, as well as some species that feed far inland. Waders (or shorebirds) – which make up nearly two-thirds of the total number of species in the order – typically have long legs and beaks, and feed by probing in sand or mud. Gulls and their relatives generally search for food on the wing, while auks chase fish under water, using their wings to swim. Many birds in this order nest in groups, and many are long-distance migrants.

WADER
With its thin legs and lightweight body, the White-tailed Plover is a typical wader. This species breeds on damp ground in the Middle East and around the Caspian Sea.

GULL
Compared to most waders, gulls have shorter legs, and longer, narrower wings. This Slender-billed Gull, from North Africa, Europe, and Asia, often breeds far inland.

AUK
The Razorbill is a typical member of the auk family, with its black and white plumage. Unlike waders and gulls, auks are restricted to the North Atlantic, North Pacific, and Arctic Ocean.

ANATOMY

Birds within this order vary a great deal in shape, and also in size. The Great Black-backed Gull has the largest wingspan, measuring up to 1.7m (5½ft), while the smallest auks are only 16cm (6in) long. Waders usually have lightly built bodies, carried on long legs with slender toes, but their most distinctive feature is often their beak, which can be straight or curved – upwards, downwards, or – uniquely in the case of the Wrybill – even sideways. Gulls and auks have similarly compact bodies, but their wings are of quite different types. A gull's wings are long and slender, designed for gliding and soaring, while an auk's are short and stubby – a shape that allows them to propel the bird under water as well as in the air. With a few notable exceptions, such as the Ruff and Eurasian Dotterel, males and females of species in this order have plumage of very similar coloration.

FLIGHT AND MIGRATION

Waders, gulls, and auks include some fast and agile fliers. Among them are some record-breaking migrants, such as the Arctic Tern, which makes a return trip between both polar regions every year. In general, waders spend a large amount of their lives on their feet, but they fly strongly and well. Many species breed in the northern tundra, dispersing along coasts farther south during the rest of the year. Gulls are renowned for their skill at soaring, and they can be surprisingly agile when fighting over a catch. Skuas – their close relatives – take this even further, chasing other birds through the air, and often tugging at their tails until they disgorge their food. For controlled flight, few birds can rival skimmers, which zig-zag across calm water, slicing through the surface with their bills. Auks also fly well, despite having much smaller wings in relation to their bodies. Their flight is usually fast and direct, but their wings also double up as flippers, powering them under water when they dive after fish.

SPEED AND AGILITY
By far the most elegant species in the skua family, the Long-tailed Skua is both a predator and a parasite. In summer, it feeds mainly on lemmings in its breeding grounds in the Arctic tundra. After breeding, it migrates as far south as the Southern Ocean, and gets much of its food by stealing from other seabirds.

HABITATS

Most waders live either on coasts, by shallow bodies of fresh water, or in marshy ground. However, some winter out at sea, and at the other extreme, a number of species – including stone curlews and dikkops, coursers, and seedsnipes – have completely terrestrial lifestyles, and rarely if ever wade in water. Gulls are much more aquatic, but they are not always tied to the sea. Many roam far inland, and an increasing number make a good living on farmland and by scavenging in urban areas. By contrast, auks are truly marine birds. They get all their food from the sea, and once they have finished breeding, they move offshore, often staying far beyond sight of land.

FAVOURED SHALLOWS
Like many waders, Pied Avocets feed in shallow water. Slender toes help to spread their weight on soft muddy sediment.

FEEDING

When similar birds share the same habitat, evolution often makes them diverge so that they exploit different types of food. This is exactly the case with coastal waders: with their different beaks and feeding methods, up to a dozen species can live close together without engaging in direct competition. Avocets feed in the water itself, while many other waders extract small animals from soft mud. Turnstones search for food along the tideline, while sanderlings repeatedly scuttle down the shore, picking up food revealed behind each retreating wave. The charadriiform order includes two main groups of fish eaters: terns, which dive onto fish from the air, and auks, which pursue them under water. Gulls typically live as much by scavenging as by catching their own food. Many of them will eat anything they can swallow, including dead fish along the tideline or waste at landfill sites. However, large gulls are aggressive predators. They attack other seabirds and their young, and will also eat mammals as big as rabbits. Skuas have similar feeding habits, and also indulge in aerial piracy.

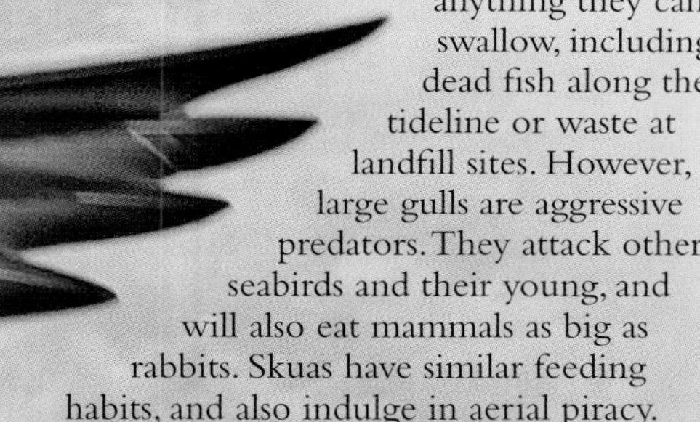

LONG-BILLED LIFESTYLE
With a beak up to 22cm (8½in) long, the North American Long-billed Curlew can probe far into tidal mud to find molluscs and worms.

SHORELINE SCAVENGER
This Lava Gull from the Galapagos Islands has a wide-ranging diet that includes dead remains on the shore, small lizards, and the young of other birds.

UNDERWATER HUNTERS
Groups of guillemots often dive in pursuit of fish. Their feeding method is remarkably similar to that of penguins, although guillemots can fly.

HUMAN IMPACT

COMPETITION ON THE SEAS

Gulls often benefit from human activities, but as a group, waders and their allies are easily harmed by habitat change. Inland species, such as lapwings, have difficulty raising their young in intensive farmland, while auks face stiff competition for small fish at sea. Sand-eel fishing, in particular, has had a damaging effect on Atlantic Puffins, Razorbills, and guillemots, all of which feed sand-eels to their chicks.

SHIP FOLLOWERS
Gulls often follow fishing boats inshore, but auks are not natural scavengers, and will feed only on fish that they have caught themselves.

NESTING AND PARENTING

Few birds in this order make elaborate nests, most laying their eggs directly on rocky ledges or on the ground. Waders usually nest on their own, but gulls and auks often gather in nesting colonies, returning to the same sites year after year. The biggest of these, formed by Least Auklets in the Aleutian Islands, off Alaska, can contain over a million birds. Waders typically lay four eggs, so well camouflaged that they can be difficult to see against the ground. Terns also use camouflage for protection, laying their eggs directly on shingle or sand. Many of these ground-nesters guard their nests vigorously, either attacking intruders, or luring them away with distraction displays. In the auk family, the number of eggs is usually just one, or more rarely two. Young Atlantic Puffins typically leave the nest when around six weeks old, but Guillemots and Razorbills leave at the age of just two weeks. At this age, their wings are still tiny, so they leap off their cliff ledges as darkness falls, to avoid being caught by gulls.

GUILLEMOT COLONY
Guillemots nest on narrow cliff ledges, laying a single egg directly on the bare rock. Even if there is spare space, the adults are often tightly packed – a way of preventing predatory gulls finding enough space to land.

Burhinus oedicnemus

Eurasian Stone-curlew

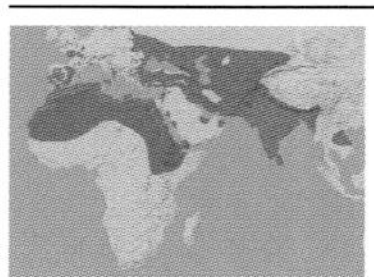

LENGTH 40–44cm (15½–17½in)

WEIGHT 450–500g (16–18oz)

MIGRATION Migrant

HABITAT Areas of low or sparse vegetation, including heaths, pastures, bare sand, and dry mudflats

A typical member of its family of "thick-knees", named after their distinctive swollen knee joints, the Eurasian Stone-curlew has a dull plumage, large head, and big, bulging eyes. It is largely nocturnal, foraging actively from dusk till dawn. It has a far-carrying call.

NESTING EURASIAN STONE-CURLEW

ADULT BEACH STONE-CURLEW

Esacus magnirostris

Beach Stone-curlew

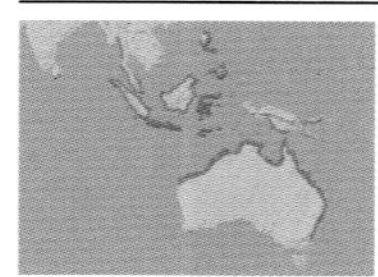

LENGTH 53–57cm (21–22½in)

WEIGHT 1kg (2¼lb)

MIGRATION Non-migrant

HABITAT Sandy beaches, especially those with a mangrove or reef exposed to tides

A large bird, the Beach Stone-curlew has a prominent white eyebrow, grey-brown upperparts, with black and brown streaks, and creamy white underparts. Like other "thick-knees", it feeds at night, searching for crabs and small marine invertebrates in sand or on reefs. It can be seen on tropical beaches from Malaysia to northern Australia, but a decline in its numbers has been noted in parts of its range.

Chionis albus

Snowy Sheathbill

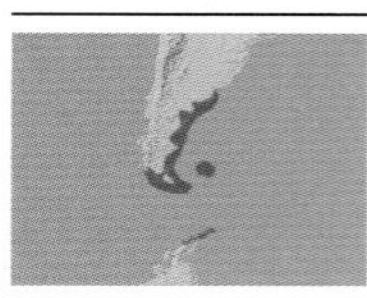

LENGTH 40cm (15½in)

WEIGHT 625–725g (22–26oz)

MIGRATION Partial migrant

HABITAT Coastal areas

The Snowy Sheathbill is a snow-white bird found in the dense breeding colonies of birds and seals in the Antarctic. Agile and quick on the ground on its unwebbed feet – the only Antarctic species that does not have webbed feet – it is a scavenger, stalking about in penguin rookeries and cormorant and seal colonies in search of food. It eats anything it can find, such as scraps, faeces, carrion, chicks, seal afterbirth, and the occasional stolen egg. It even harasses penguins into regurgitating the food they bring for their young. Typically for a bird with such eating habits, its facial skin is largely featherless. In the breeding season, both the male and female incubate the 2–4 eggs.

ADULT SNOWY SHEATHBILL

Pluvianellus socialis

Magellanic Plover

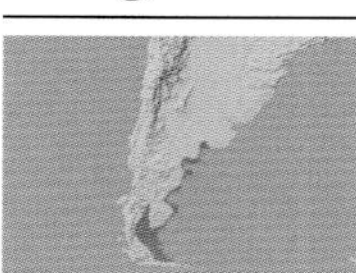

LENGTH 19–22cm (7½–8½in)

WEIGHT 80–90g (2⅞–3¼oz)

MIGRATION Partial migrant

HABITAT Freshwater or brackish water; winters in coastal areas

Mainly dove-grey in colour, the Magellanic Plover has a black bill, white throat and underparts, and pink legs. A rare bird, perhaps numbering only 1,000 birds in all, it inhabits a small range at the very southern tip of South America. It is unusual in several ways, such as its habit of scratching or digging for food with its powerful legs, in the manner of a domestic chicken. It also feeds its young by regurgitating food, which is unknown in other shorebirds.

ADULT MAGELLANIC PLOVER

ADULTS FEEDING

Haematopus ostralegus

Eurasian Oystercatcher

LENGTH 40–45cm (15½–17½in)

WEIGHT 450–650g (16–23oz)

MIGRATION Migrant

HABITAT Inter-tidal zones and a variety of freshwater wetlands and adjacent habitats

Black and white in colour, the Eurasian Oystercatcher is a typical member of a widespread family. The 11 species of oystercatcher are either pied or black and all have the trademark strong, blunt, laterally flattened orange bill, which they use to feed on molluscs. In flight, the white patches on the wings and tail of the Eurasian Oystercatcher are clearly visible. The juvenile is browner than the adults, with a white neck collar and a duller bill. The call of the species is a distinctive loud piping.

It is the most widely distributed member of the family, breeding from Iceland and western Europe to eastern Asia, and it is highly migratory, moving south in winter to the shorelines of West Africa, the Gulf States, and India. While it is mainly a coastal wader, the species can also be found breeding inland – in wetland habitats along rivers or on large bodies of water.

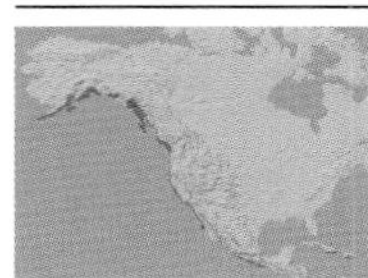

Haematopus bachmani

Black Oystercatcher

LENGTH 43–45cm (17–17½in)

WEIGHT 550g (20oz)

MIGRATION Non-migrant

HABITAT Exposed rocky coasts, reefs, and islands

ADULT BLACK OYSTERCATCHER

Predominantly black, with a slightly brown cast to its upperparts, the Black Oystercatcher has a blood-red bill, a glowing yellow eye, an orange-red eye-ring, and pink legs and feet. When it is feeding quietly, its coloration can make it difficult to pick out against dark rocks. It is found only along the Pacific coast of North America, where it frequents tide-line rocky outcrops, reefs, and beaches.

ADULT CRAB-PLOVER

Dromas ardeola

Crab-plover

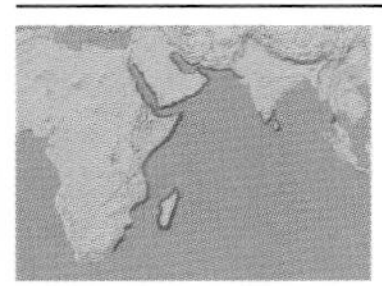

LENGTH 38–41cm (15–16in)

WEIGHT 325g (12oz)

MIGRATION Partial migrant

HABITAT Sandy shores and inter-tidal mud

Easy to distinguish from other shorebirds, the Crab-plover has a heavy, dagger-like black bill (specially adapted to eating crabs), black and white plumage, and long grey legs.
The only member of its family, it has a number of characteristics that are different from other wading birds, such as its habit of nesting in underground chambers and laying only a single, pure white, unmarked egg. It is a noisy bird, calling frequently while at its breeding sites and on its wintering grounds.

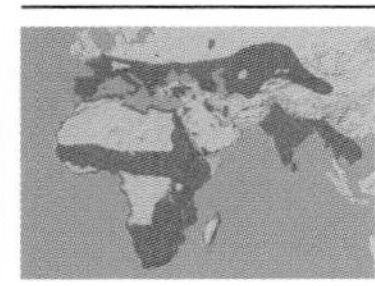

Himantopus himantopus

Black-winged Stilt

LENGTH 35–40cm (14–15½in)

WEIGHT 150–200g (5–7oz)

MIGRATION Migrant

HABITAT Variety of wetland habitats in mostly subtropical and tropical regions

Distinctive for its extremely long, wax-pink legs, which enable it to wade knee-deep in water in search of prey, the Black-winged Stilt is black and white in colour, with red eyes and a straight, black bill. It is found throughout the subtropical and tropical regions of the world. It hunts by sight or touch, using its bill to detect prey, mainly aquatic insects, in water. This social species breeds in loose colonies in marshy ground or mudflats near water and incubates 3 or 4 eggs.

BLACK-WINGED STILT AT ITS NEST

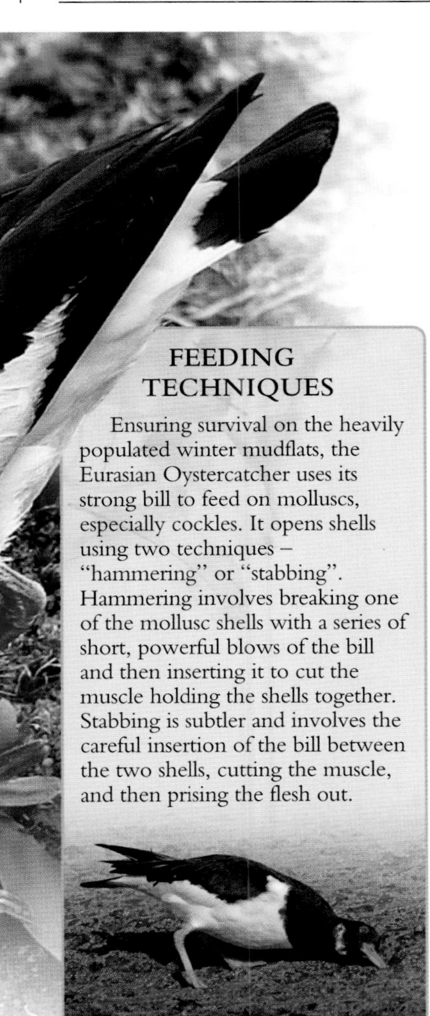

FEEDING TECHNIQUES

Ensuring survival on the heavily populated winter mudflats, the Eurasian Oystercatcher uses its strong bill to feed on molluscs, especially cockles. It opens shells using two techniques – "hammering" or "stabbing". Hammering involves breaking one of the mollusc shells with a series of short, powerful blows of the bill and then inserting it to cut the muscle holding the shells together. Stabbing is subtler and involves the careful insertion of the bill between the two shells, cutting the muscle, and then prising the flesh out.

ADULT IBISBILL

Ibidorhyncha struthersii

Ibisbill

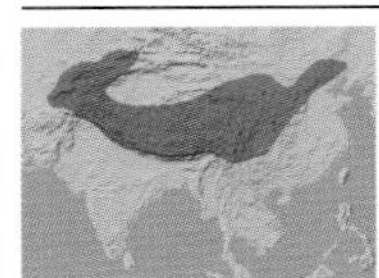

LENGTH 38–41cm (15–16in)

WEIGHT 300g (11oz)

MIGRATION Partial migrant

HABITAT High-altitude rivers with flat, stony alluvial floodplains; some winter in rocky lowland rivers

With its grey plumage that provides a surprising degree of camouflage, the Ibisbill can be very difficult to spot when it is feeding quietly in mid-stream or resting among rocks. It has a long, thin, decurved bill, a black face, and a black breast-band. The sole member of its family, the Ibisbill breeds in the high mountain river valleys of central Asia and the Himalayas, at heights of up to 4,400m (14,500ft) above sea level.

LONG LEGS

The Black-winged Stilt has the longest legs in relation to its body size of any bird in the world. The long legs allow it to feed in deeper water than most other waders. The potential length of the legs is obvious as soon as the chicks hatch. Before their bills and legs reach the extraordinarily long adult size, the young are dependent on their parents, who provide a large proportion of their food.

Cladorhynchus leucocephalus

Banded Stilt

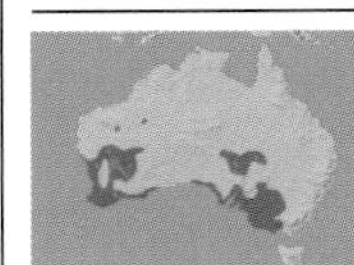

LENGTH 36–45cm (14–17½in)

WEIGHT 200–225g (7–8oz)

MIGRATION Partial migrant

HABITAT Saline wetlands and commercial saltpans; occasionally on estuaries

Named for the red-chestnut band that is prominent across its breast in the breeding season (usually fading or disappearing after breeding), the Banded Stilt has a slender black bill and a white head, back, and underparts. In flight, a white trailing edge is visible on its black wings. Its long legs are pink or orange.

Native to Australia, the species follows an unusual breeding strategy. It waits until the huge temporary salt lakes in the arid interior are filled up during the rains. Flocks then quickly move in and huge colonies develop along the shorelines, feeding almost exclusively on brine shrimps, which are abundant in the lakes.

ADULT BANDED STILT

GREAT SITES

MORECAMBE BAY

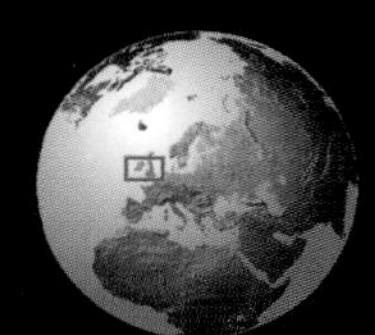

LOCATION A wide bay on the Irish Sea coast of northwest England, UK.

Set against the magnificent backdrop of windswept salt marshes and the rolling hills of the southern Lake District, Morecambe Bay is one of the largest and most important estuarine areas for birds in Europe. The intertidal mudflats and sandflats of this vast shallow bay teem with abundant invertebrate life such as lugworms, cockles, mussels, and shrimps, attracting enormous numbers of waders, ducks, and geese to feed. During peak migration periods, thousands of shorebirds pause here to rest and feed when moving up and down the UK's west coast in spring and autumn, and the bay is also a vital overwintering or breeding location for a wide variety of species.

INTERTIDAL BIRD LIFE

Morecambe Bay is fed by five main rivers – the Leven, Kent, Keer, Lune, and Wyre – and their estuaries merge into a single, funnel-shaped tidal system. At extreme low tides in spring the sea may drain up to 12km (7 miles) away from the high-water mark and the exposed mud and sand stretch to the horizon – the biggest continuous intertidal area in Britain, covering around 305 square km (118 square miles). On the bay's north and east sides, the tidal flats are bordered by low-lying salt marshes.

Morecambe Bay hosts globally significant numbers of 11 species of bird, including ducks such as Northern Pintail and Common Shelduck and waders such as Red Knot, Dunlin, Eurasian Curlew, Eurasian Oystercatcher, and Common Redshank. Some of these waders use the bay as a stop-over during their migrations; others remain throughout the winter. The bay regularly supports 65,000–70,000 Red Knots in winter – over 15 per cent of the species' entire wintering population in Europe and North Africa.

At high tide, when the mudflats are flooded by the incoming sea, the salt marshes and raised shingle beaches that fringe the bay offer a temporary refuge to masses of waders. Occasionally a Peregrine Falcon or Merlin triggers alarm among the wader flocks.

The fast-moving waters and treacherous quicksands of Morecambe Bay have caused many fatalities; crossing the bay is safe only at low tide and with a professional guide.

RISING WATERS
When the bay's mudflats and shallow winding creeks are submerged by the incoming tide, waders, such as these Eurasian Oystercatchers, gather in tightly packed flocks.

WHAT TO SPOT

MERLIN
Falco columbarius
(see p.185)

DUNLIN
Calidris alpina
(see p.230)

COMMON RINGED PLOVER
Charadrius hiaticula
(see p.225)

EURASIAN WIGEON
Anas penelope

Recurvirostra avosetta

Pied Avocet

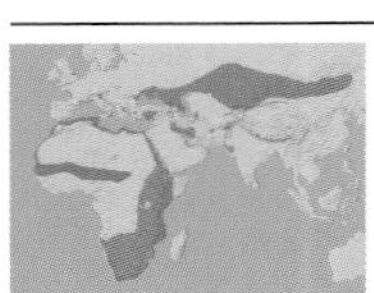

LENGTH 42–45cm (16½–17½in)

WEIGHT 250–300g (9–11oz)

MIGRATION Migrant

HABITAT Brackish and saline wetlands

With its black and white plumage, slender, upcurved bill, and bluish grey legs, the Pied Avocet is a distinctive bird. Its long bill is specially adapted to sift through shallow water or mud to feed on a range of invertebrates. It breeds in large colonies on wetlands, where it is noisy and aggressive, seldom tolerating the presence of intruders and often driving much larger birds away.

ADULT PIED AVOCET

Recurvirostra novaehollandiae

Red-necked Avocet

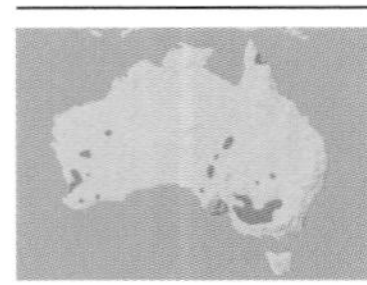

LENGTH 43–46cm (17–18in)

WEIGHT 325g (12oz)

MIGRATION Partial migrant

HABITAT Shallow brackish or saline lakes and lagoons; occasionally on estuaries

Also called the Australian Avocet, the Red-necked Avocet breeds in Australia, where it is widespread. The dark chestnut-red head and neck, white-ringed eyes, pied upperparts, white underparts, and bright blue legs make this avocet a colourful and easily recognizable bird.

A sociable species, it feeds in large flocks – foraging for crustaceans, aquatic insects, molluscs, and worms – and nests in loose colonies. Its nest is a shallow scrape lined with vegetation found near water. Like other avocets, it frequents shallow freshwater or saltwater lagoons and lakes, which are found in the arid interior of Australia, especially in wet years. Red-necked Avocets make full use of these temporary interior salt lakes, often moving in and out of inland areas.

ADULT RED-NECKED AVOCET

FEEDING TECHNIQUE

A long, upcurved bill is common to all the avocets and is used to good effect when they forage for food. An avocet mainly feeds by sweeping its bill and head from side to side in shallow water and loose mud, holding it slightly open and locating its prey by touch. It lunges forwards to catch its food, usually small crustaceans, aquatic insects, worms, and molluscs.

ADULT MASKED LAPWING

Vanellus miles

Masked Lapwing

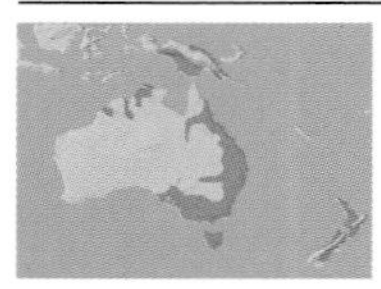

LENGTH 33–37cm (13–14½in)

WEIGHT 400g (14oz)

MIGRATION Partial migrant

HABITAT Open habitats with low vegetation

Notable for the huge yellow wattles in front of its eyes and the curious long, yellow spurs protruding from the bend in both wings, the Masked Lapwing is a large black-headed bird. Native to Australia, it has benefited from scrub clearance for agriculture and has colonized both Papua New Guinea and New Zealand in recent times.

ADULT NORTHERN LAPWING

Vanellus vanellus

Northern Lapwing

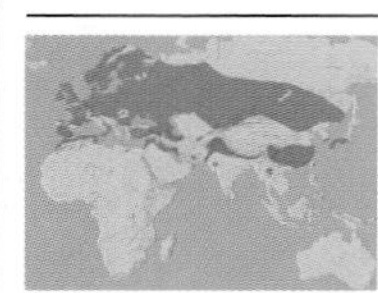

LENGTH 28–31cm (11–12in)

WEIGHT 200–225g (7–8oz)

MIGRATION Migrant

HABITAT Open areas of wet or damp grassland, arable farmland, and steppes

Its raised, pointed crest, along with its black and white breast and iridescent green and purple back, make the Northern Lapwing easy to identify. It feeds by walking about and probing the soil surface, while practising "foot-trembling", in which one foot is vibrated up and down on the ground to attract prey to the surface. In the breeding season, it is highly vocal, especially the territorial male, which is known for its enthusiastic and noisy aerial display.

Vanellus armatus

Blacksmith Plover

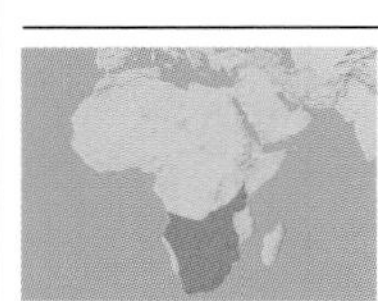

LENGTH 28–31cm (11–12in)

WEIGHT 150g (5oz)

MIGRATION Non-migrant

HABITAT Wetlands and open grassy areas

Resident in the wetlands of southern Africa, the strongly contrasting black, white, and grey plumage makes the Blacksmith Plover an easy bird to identify. It derives its common name from the metallic, ringing nature of the alarm call, which sounds like a hammer repeatedly hitting an anvil. Like most plovers, it is noisy and aggressive during the nesting season and vigorously defends its territories and its young from intruders. Mostly found patrolling the edges of fresh and saline bodies of water, it may sometimes feed in open grassy areas.

ADULT BLACKSMITH PLOVER

Vanellus chilensis

Southern Lapwing

LENGTH 31–38cm (12–15in)

WEIGHT 325g (12oz)

MIGRATION Partial migrant

HABITAT Tropical and temperate lowland grassland and wetlands

The only South American shorebird with a crest, the Southern Lapwing has a grey head, black throat and breast, and an iridescent bronze wing patch. It has red spurs at the bend of its wing, which it displays in a show of aggression. When nesting, the Southern Lapwing greets intruders with strident alarm calls and may even attempt to lure away potential predators from nests by feigning injury. It is resident in tropical regions, but those breeding in cooler latitudes migrate north in the winter.

ADULT SOUTHERN LAPWING

Pluvialis dominica

American Golden Plover

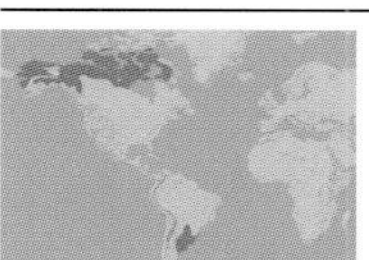

LENGTH 24–25cm (9½–10in)

WEIGHT 150g (5oz)

MIGRATION Migrant

HABITAT Arctic and subarctic tundra; winters in grassland, mudflats, rivers, and lakeshores

ADULT AMERICAN GOLDEN PLOVER

Named for the golden hue of its brown upperparts, the American Golden Plover has a broad white stripe above its eyes. It is similar to the European Golden Plover (above right). The species is a long-distance migrant, breeding at high latitudes in the tundra of North America and wintering as far south as the grasslands of Patagonia.

Vanellus spinosus

Spur-winged Lapwing

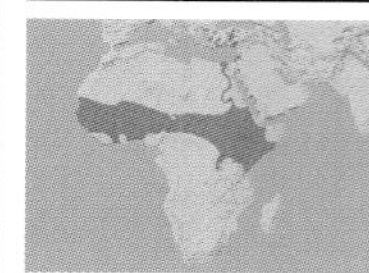

LENGTH 25–28cm (10–11in)

WEIGHT 175–200g (6–7oz)

MIGRATION Partial migrant

HABITAT Wide variety of fresh and saline wetlands, mostly inland

As its name suggests, the Spur-winged Lapwing, or Plover, has a sharp spur on the bend of its wing. It shares this feature with a number of other lapwings, including the Masked (p.224) and Southern (left) Lapwings. Both its striking black, white, and brown plumage and its sharp spurs are used for display during breeding. Typically hunch-backed in posture, this lapwing can be seen throughout its fragmented range in Africa. Curiously, in recent times, the species has expanded its range into Turkey and Greece and these populations, unlike those resident in Africa, are migratory.

ADULT SPUR-WINGED LAPWING

Pluvialis squatarola

Grey Plover

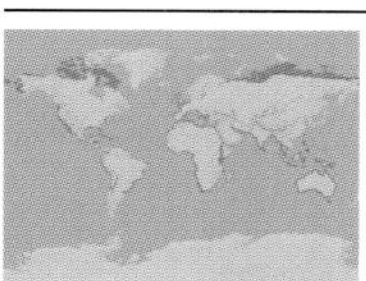

LENGTH 27–30cm (10½–12in)

WEIGHT 200–350g (7–13oz)

MIGRATION Migrant

HABITAT Breeds in high Arctic tundra; winters on inter-tidal marine areas

Easily distinguished from the other "golden" plovers by its much stouter black bill, black "armpits" (seen only when in flight), grey plumage, and white rump, the Grey Plover is the largest of the *Pluvialis* genus of plovers.

ADULT IN NON-BREEDING PLUMAGE

This plover is a truly cosmopolitan species, being highly migratory. It breeds throughout the high Arctic tundra zone, where it chooses dry grassy or lichen-covered tundra, prefering broken terrain and rocky slopes to nest in. After the breeding season, it migrates to areas such as southern Australia and South Africa and is a common sight on beaches and tidal mudflats around the world in winter. Some birds defend their winter territories vigorously and return to them year after year. The male Grey Plover defends its territory by performing a beautiful song display while in flight.

Pluvialis apricaria

European Golden Plover

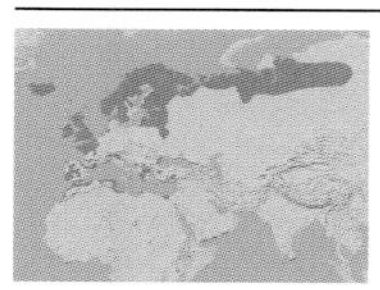

LENGTH 26–29cm (10–11½in)

WEIGHT 225g (8oz)

MIGRATION Migrant

HABITAT Breeds in moorland and tundra; winters in wet lowland grassland and agricultural fields

A bulky, gold-spangled plover, the European Golden Plover has a variable breeding plumage. Some southerly breeding birds show less black in their plumage. European Golden Plovers breed in a variety of upland, Arctic, and tundra habitats and migrate southwest to winter in large flocks in permanent grasslands and agricultural areas of western Europe.

BREEDING PLUMAGE OF SOUTHERN FORM

Charadrius hiaticula

Common Ringed Plover

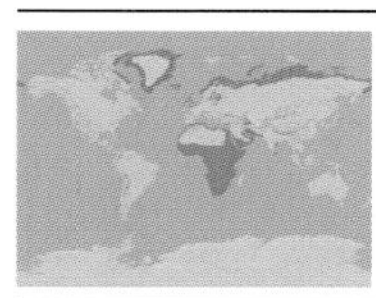

LENGTH 18–20cm (7–8in)

WEIGHT 55–75g (2–2⅝oz)

MIGRATION Migrant

HABITAT Coastal in Arctic, subarctic, and temperate zones; also breeds in tundra areas and along rivers

The Common Ringed Plover has pronounced head markings, a white collar, and a broad black band on its breast. The male has a larger band than the female. This bird is a classic "leap-frog" migrant – the most northerly breeding populations winter the farthest south, and the birds that breed further south undertake progressively shorter migrations.

ADULT COMMON RINGED PLOVER

ADULT KILLDEER

Charadrius vociferus

Killdeer

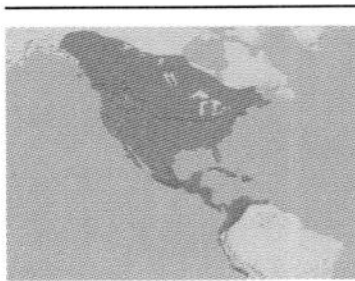

LENGTH 23–26cm (9–10in)

WEIGHT 90–100g ($3^1/_4$–$3^5/_8$oz)

MIGRATION Partial migrant

HABITAT Inland pools, grassland, fields, car parks, and other open areas

Easily distinguished from all other American plovers by its two black breast-bands, the Killdeer gets its common name from its call – a two-syllabled "kill-dee". It has adapted well to living in close proximity to humans and can often be seen on farmland, and in airports, car parks, and other such man-modified open areas. It even nests on flat, gravelled rooftops. It is found singly or in pairs, but small flocks may gather outside the breeding season.

DISTRACTION PLOY

Like many other birds, when its eggs or young are threatened by a predator, the Killdeer performs a distracting display to draw the intruder away from the nest. It acts like a crippled bird with one or both wings dragging and often limps, rapidly calling out constantly while remaining just out of reach.

Charadrius alexandrinus

Kentish Plover

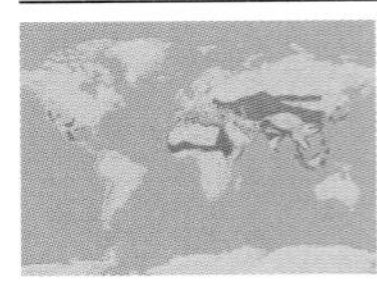

LENGTH 15–18cm (6–7in)

WEIGHT 40g ($1^7/_{16}$oz)

MIGRATION Partial migrant

HABITAT Mainly coastal areas: beaches and saline or brackish wetlands.

One of the smaller members of its genus, the Kentish Plover has an incomplete breast-band, which appears as a dark elongated patch at the side of the breast. In the breeding season, this patch becomes a well-defined black bar on the male. This partial band and the bird's forecrown and eye-stripe become black during the breeding season. The female has a dusky eye patch with a brown chest patch. The legs of this plover are relatively long and dark and the bill is fine and black.

The Kentish Plover prefers sandy beaches along the sea coast, although it will also nest inland on the shores of saline or brackish wetlands. Most inland breeding birds move to the coast in winter. It nests in shallow hollows in sand, lined with pebbles or shell fragments.

Charadrius australis

Inland Plover

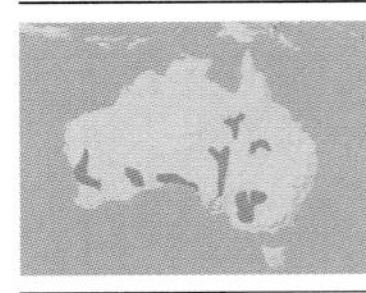

LENGTH 19–23cm ($7^1/_2$–9in)

WEIGHT 85g (3oz)

MIGRATION Partial migrant

HABITAT Deserts and semi-deserts

This long-legged plover is unusual in that it is a nomadic bird of the arid Australian outback, where it lives on the sparsely vegetated plains. Compared with most other birds, its eyes are relatively large, which helps it to see well in the dark. The Inland Plover is mainly active when darkness falls, searching for and feeding on nocturnal insects and spiders. It is most often seen on dirt roads at night. A tame bird that tends to rely on its dull plumage for protection, it will allow the observer to approach closely before running away.

INLAND PLOVER

Anarhynchus frontalis

Wrybill

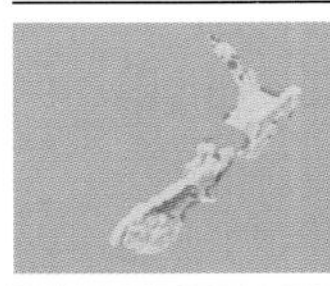

LENGTH 20cm (8in)

WEIGHT 60g ($2^1/_8$oz)

MIGRATION Migrant

HABITAT Breeds on stony riverbeds; winters on seashores

The Wrybill is unique among birds in that it has a bill that is bent to one side. In all individuals of this species, the tip of the bill is twisted to the right at an angle of about 12 degrees. This is considered to be an adaptation that helps the Wrybill find food in its breeding ground, where it walks in clockwise circles, turning over stones to hunt for the insects and worms that live under them.

ADULT WRYBILL

MALE GREATER PAINTED SNIPE

Rostratula benghalensis

Greater Painted Snipe

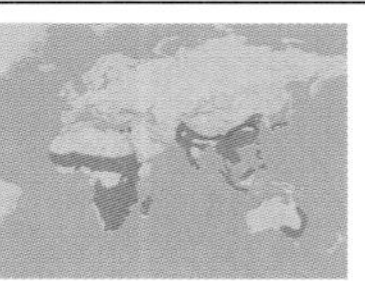

LENGTH 23–26cm (9–10in)

WEIGHT 125g (4oz)

MIGRATION Non-migrant

HABITAT Overgrown shallow wetlands, marshes, and paddy fields

A small, plump, and colourful wading bird, the Greater Painted Snipe inhabits muddy marshy areas. Its long bill is used to probe deep into soft mud in search of the molluscs, crustaceans, and worms that form the greater part of its prey. It also feeds by swishing its bill from side to side in shallow water to pick up small animals and vegetable matter. It is most active at dawn and dusk, when it forages singly, in pairs, or in small, loose groups.

Although similar in appearance to snipes, in some ways this species is more closely related to the jacanas. Both, the Greater Painted Snipe and the jacanas are unusual in that the female is larger and more brightly coloured than the male. This is a consequence of the fact that the rusty-chested female is more dominant of the pair and fights with other females for territory and mates, the biggest and most brightly coloured female emerging as the winner. The female mates with more than one male and then lays several clutches of eggs.

Actophilornis africanus

African Jacana

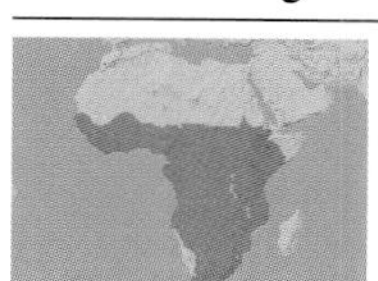

LENGTH 30cm (12in)

WEIGHT 150–250g (5–9oz)

MIGRATION Non-migrant

HABITAT Both large and small wetlands with floating vegetation

A denizen of shallow sub-Saharan wetlands with emergent vegetation, this lanky-legged bird is equipped with exceptionally long toes and claws. These spread the bird's weight across a larger surface area, enabling it to walk on floating aquatic vegetation, such as the pads of water-lilies (which is why it is also known as the Lily Trotter). When seen from a distance, the bird can appear to be "miraculously" walking along the surface of the water.

The upperparts of the adult African Jacana are a rich chestnut colour, often with a green sheen. Its neck and face are white with a black stripe through the eye, which joins up with the black of the crown, nape, and hindneck. A band of gold adorns the breast, while the bill and frontal shield glow in a vivid pale blue. The olive-green of the long legs completes the splendid colour scheme of this bird's plumage. Never a strong flier, it moults all of its flight feathers at once and cannot fly at all until new feathers grow. The African Jacana breeds in sub-Saharan Africa and lays four brown eggs that have black markings.

ADULT AFRICAN JACANA

CARRYING CHICKS

The adult male African Jacana protects its chicks and keeps them warm and dry by pressing them closely between its wings and body. Its bone structure is adapted for this purpose, and it can also walk about while carrying up to two chicks under each wing. The male bird can even manage to move eggs, one at a time, to a new nest if this becomes necessary.

UNDER FATHER'S WING
A close look at this photograph will reveal the leg of a chick protruding from beneath the shielding wing of its parent.

ADULT IN BREEDING PLUMAGE

Hydrophasianus chirurgus

Pheasant-tailed Jacana

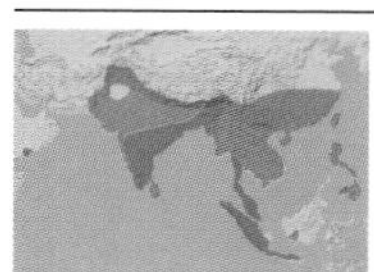

LENGTH 31–58cm (12–23in)

WEIGHT 125–200g (4–7oz)

MIGRATION Partial migrant

HABITAT Shallow wetlands with plenty of vegetation, particularly water-lilies

With its long, gracefully curved tail, the Pheasant-tailed Jacana is unmistakable.

The sexes look alike, although the female is somewhat larger than the male, as befits the dominant partner. Unlike other jacanas, it has a different non-breeding plumage – its tail becomes much shorter, and its colours become subdued. The Pheasant-tailed Jacana spends most of its time walking on the floating vegetation of its aquatic habitat, only occasionally coming on to dry land or swimming in the water. At such times it remains remarkably inconspicuous, but when it takes flight, the dazzling white of the outstretched wings makes the bird stand out sharply from its surroundings. When it is at rest, this whiteness may be visible as a panel down the flank, although it is often partly hidden by the brown feathers of the wing coverts, which protect the wings as the bird walks through grass and reeds. Another feature that usually remains hidden beneath the wings is the sharp spur at the bend of the wing, which it uses during fights with rivals in the breeding season.

Attagis malouinus

White-bellied Seedsnipe

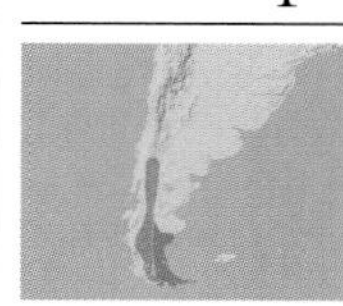

LENGTH 26–29cm (10–11½in)

WEIGHT 350g (13oz)

MIGRATION Non-migrant

HABITAT High mountain steppes, moorland, and peat-bogs

A bird of open windswept moorland and montane scree slopes at the southernmost tip of South America, the White-bellied Seedsnipe survives by foraging on the sparse small berries and plants growing in its inhospitable mountain habitat. Its belly is a bright white, but the muted mottled brown, black, and buff plumage of the upperparts allows the bird to blend in beautifully with its surroundings, especially when it crouches down and becomes immobile when a potential predator appears. Although its total population is not large, the species is not regarded as endangered since it inhabits inaccessible regions that are relatively free from human interference.

WHITE-BELLIED SEEDSNIPE

Scolopax minor

American Woodcock

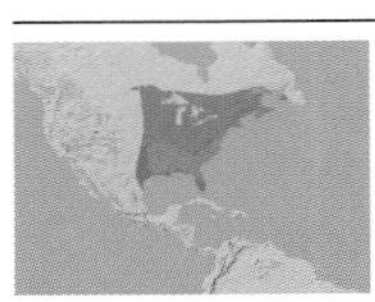

LENGTH 26–30cm (10–12in)

WEIGHT 175–225g (6–8oz)

MIGRATION Migrant

HABITAT Mixed or deciduous woodland, damp fields, and marshes

Well camouflaged by its dull plumage, marked by black and brown barring, the small American Woodcock has a long, thin, pinkish brown bill. The species breeds throughout the eastern half of North America in spring, when each male carries out a complex courtship display. On bare ground in a clearing, it calls repeatedly and, at short intervals, rises up to 100m (330ft) in the air on noisy wings as it circles, hovers, twitters, and chirps before spiralling to the ground.

ADULT AMERICAN WOODCOCK

Lymnocryptes minimus

Jack Snipe

LENGTH 17–19cm (6½–7½in)

WEIGHT 45–55g (1⅝–2oz)

MIGRATION Migrant

HABITAT Breeds in open boreal marshes, such as floating bogs; winters on inland freshwater marshes

Differing significantly from the other snipes, such as the Common Snipe (below), the diminutive Jack Snipe is placed in its own genus, *Lymnocryptes*. It is much smaller and has a shorter bill and wings than its near relatives. Unusually for snipes, it has a purple and green sheen on its upperparts.

The breeding grounds of the Jack Snipe stretch from Norway to the east, up to Siberia. The male advertises and defends its large territory with an aerial song-flight display, its rhythmic song, also uttered from the ground, sounding like a distant galloping horse. In winter, the Jack Snipe is difficult to observe as it seldom flies during the day, is very well camouflaged by the pale markings on its upperparts, and keeps to dense vegetation in wet, muddy areas. Often, the only way to see it is to try and flush it out.

ADULT JACK SNIPE

Gallinago gallinago

Common Snipe

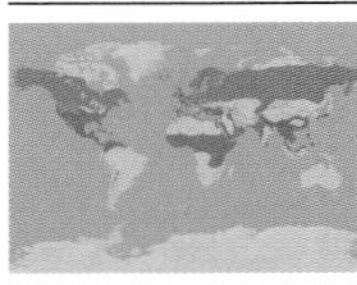

LENGTH 25–27cm (10–10½in)

WEIGHT 95–125g (3⅜–4oz)

MIGRATION Migrant

HABITAT Tussocky, fresh, and brackish marshes; also damp farmland and other wetlands in winter

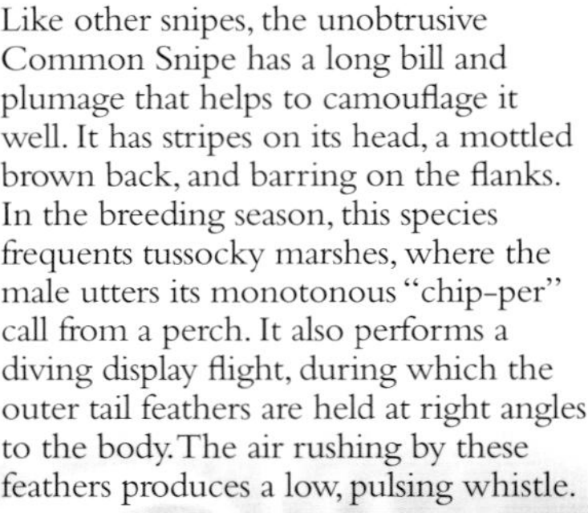

Like other snipes, the unobtrusive Common Snipe has a long bill and plumage that helps to camouflage it well. It has stripes on its head, a mottled brown back, and barring on the flanks. In the breeding season, this species frequents tussocky marshes, where the male utters its monotonous "chip-per" call from a perch. It also performs a diving display flight, during which the outer tail feathers are held at right angles to the body. The air rushing by these feathers produces a low, pulsing whistle.

COMMON SNIPE INCUBATING ITS EGGS

Limnodromus griseus

Short-billed Dowitcher

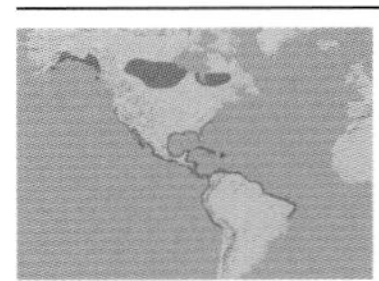

LENGTH 25–29cm (10–11½in)

WEIGHT 100–125g (3⅗–4oz)

MIGRATION Migrant

HABITAT Open marshes and bogs; winters in coastal inter-tidal areas

Until the 1950s, the two North American dowitcher species – the Long-billed Dowitcher (*L. scolopaceus*) and the Short-billed Dowitcher – were considered to be a single species and are confusingly similar in their breeding plumage. Both have long, straight bills, but the Short-billed Dowitcher differs from its long-billed cousin in its mellow "tu-tu-tu" call (the Long-billed Dowitcher utters a single "keek"), its paler plumage, and its paler tail with wider white bars. The Short-billed Dowitcher feeds with a rapid, snipe-like probing action. It usually stands in water to feed or swims, often submerging its head entirely.

Breeding takes place in subarctic Canada, from northern Quebec through the centre to the northwest, and southern Alaska. There are three distinct subspecies in these areas.

Limosa haemastica

Hudsonian Godwit

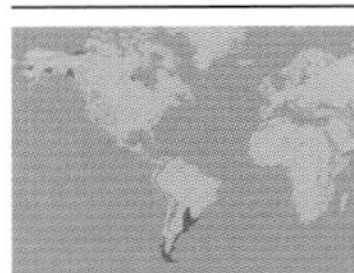

LENGTH 37–39cm (14½–15½in)

WEIGHT 225–450g (8–16oz)

MIGRATION Migrant

HABITAT Arctic and subarctic coastal and riverine marshes; winters on coastal mudflats

ADULT IN BREEDING PLUMAGE

The Hudsonian Godwit has a showy, chestnut-red breeding plumage, a long, pointed bill, and long legs. When not in its breeding plumage, it is superficially similar to other godwits, but can easily be identified in flight when its black and grey underwing is visible. The Hudsonian Godwit breeds at scattered locations across northern North America and gathers in large flocks to migrate in August.

ADULT IN BREEDING PLUMAGE

Limosa lapponica

Bar-tailed Godwit

LENGTH 37–39cm (14½–15½in)

WEIGHT 225–450g (8–16oz)

MIGRATION Migrant

HABITAT Low-lying coastal tundra; winters in muddy and sandy inter-tidal areas

Easily recognizable for its beautiful brick-red breeding plumage, the Bar-tailed Godwit can be distinguished from other godwits by its tapering, upcurved bill, uniform wing pattern, barred tail, and short legs. Outside the breeding season, it has a pale, mottled brown plumage. The female is larger than the male, with streaked, pale chestnut underparts and a longer bill, but both sexes are grey in winter.

The species nests in the Arctic from Scandinavia to Alaska. Wintering birds favour estuarine habitats and feed along the water's edge, probing the mud with a side-to-side action.

Numenius arquata

Eurasian Curlew

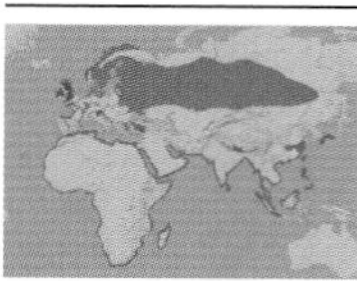

LENGTH 50–60cm (19½–23½in)

WEIGHT 750–875g (27–31oz)

MIGRATION Migrant

HABITAT Damp and wet open areas of short vegetation; winters in marine coastal habitats

With its very long, thick, and decurved bill, the Eurasian Curlew is well equipped to search for and feed on its prey in mud or sand (see panel, above right). The brown-streaked plumage of this curlew is dull, but its white back and rump are clearly visible when it is in flight. It gets its common name from its call, a repeated loud, rich, ringing "courli", which is heard throughout the year. A variation of this call, extending into a bubbling trill, is part of its breeding display song-flight, sometimes also heard on its wintering grounds on the coast.

The winter range of the species stretches from western Europe and West Africa across Asia to Japan and the Philippines, where Eurasian curlews can be found along coasts on tidal mudflats and sandy beaches in the north of its range and on rocky shores and mangroves in the tropics.

ADULT PROBING FOR PREY

FEEDING ON THE SHORELINE

The Eurasian Curlew uses three feeding techniques: pecking the soil surface; jabbing deeper with its bill; and prolonged probing with its entire bill immersed in mud, sand, or shallow water. The extremely long bill allows it to extract insects, worms, shellfish, and crustaceans (especially shrimps and crabs) buried so deep that other shorebirds cannot reach them.

ADULT IN WINTER PLUMAGE

Numenius phaeopus

Whimbrel

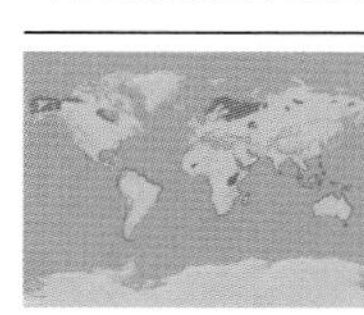

LENGTH 40–42cm (15½–16½in)

WEIGHT 325–375g (12–13oz)

MIGRATION Migrant

HABITAT Poorly vegetated and exposed boreal and low Arctic habitats; winters in coastal areas

It is the splendid decurved bill of the Whimbrel that clearly identifies it as one of the curlews. It is smaller than the Eurasian Curlew (above), is more slender, and has a noticeably shorter bill and legs. The Whimbrel can be recognized by its distinctive head stripes and a grey back mottled in white and buff. Its call is a characteristic far-carrying, rippling series of seven "pu" notes, an easily identified sound that is often heard when the birds first start migrating in spring and autumn.

Despite having a long bill, the Whimbrel rarely probes deeply into mud and sand. Instead, it gleans seeds from plants and picks up insects, worms, molluscs, and crustaceans from the soil surface. In winter, it mainly feeds on crabs along the seashore.

Numenius americanus

Long-billed Curlew

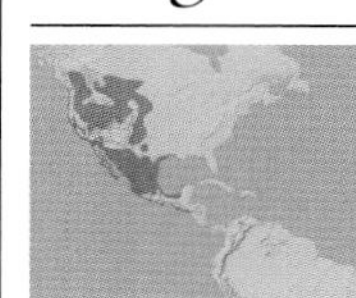

LENGTH 50–65cm (19½–26in)

WEIGHT 525–650g (19–23oz)

MIGRATION Migrant

HABITAT North American prairies, winters in estuaries; occasionally inland farmland

Aptly named, the Long-billed Curlew has a delicate cinnamon tint to its brown head, neck, breast, and mottled upperparts. The population levels of this species are declining due to widespread loss of its natural prairie breeding habitat. Globally, curlews are a fragile group, with three of the eight species considered to be under threat of extinction.

ADULT LONG-BILLED CURLEW

ADULT GREATER YELLOWLEGS

Tringa melanoleuca

Greater Yellowlegs

LENGTH 29–33cm (11½–13in)

WEIGHT 150g (5oz)

MIGRATION Migrant

HABITAT Breeds in open areas with ponds and scattered trees; winters in varied wetland habitats

A tall, graceful bird with long, brightly coloured legs, the Greater Yellowlegs is ideally suited to a life of wading in shallow water, where it searches for small creatures such as fish, frogs, and insects. It may hunt its prey by sight, picking it from the surface of the water, or by feel, sweeping its submerged bill from side to side. It is distinguished from the Lesser Yellowlegs (*T. flavipes*) by its bill, which is thicker, slightly paler-based, and faintly upturned.

Tringa totanus

Common Redshank

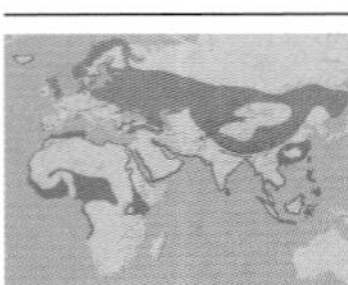

LENGTH 27–29cm (10½–11½in)

WEIGHT 125g (4oz)

MIGRATION Migrant

HABITAT Wide variety of wetland habitats

This is a common and widespread wading bird of Europe, Africa, and Asia, named for its distinctive bright orange-red legs. In flight, it shows a distinguishing broad white trailing edge to the wing. Being a noisy bird by nature, it is often the first in a gathering of birds to give the alarm at the appearance of an intruder, its ringing "tyew-yew-yew" call and variants being familiar sounds in many wetlands. When displaying, the bird performs a rising and falling flight on quivering, downcurved wings while calling out a slow "tyoo tyoo tyoo", which turns into a yodelling "tu-ludl" on landing.

ADULT COMMON REDSHANK

Heteroscelus incanus

Wandering Tattler

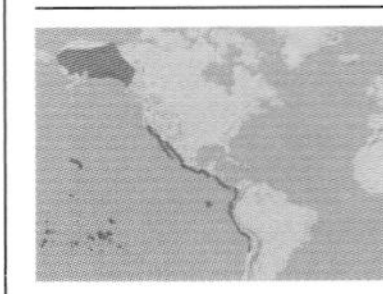

LENGTH 26–29cm (10–11½in)

WEIGHT 100g (3⅝oz)

MIGRATION Migrant

HABITAT Breeds along mountain streams; winters on rocky seashores, reefs, and adjacent habitats

ADULT WANDERING TATTLER

The Wandering Tattler nests in summer along mountain streams in Alaska and northwestern Canada. When winter approaches it "wanders" southwards, spreading out from the American west coast to islands throughout vast reaches of the Pacific Ocean, as far as the Australian Barrier Reef. During this season, it frequents rocky coasts and coral reefs, where it feeds on crustaceans, molluscs, small fish, and insects. It is one of the most characteristic waders of remote Pacific islands. The unmarked, completely dark, upperparts distinguish this species from most other shorebills. In breeding plumage it has a heavily barred face and underparts. The female is larger than the male.

Calidris alpina

Dunlin

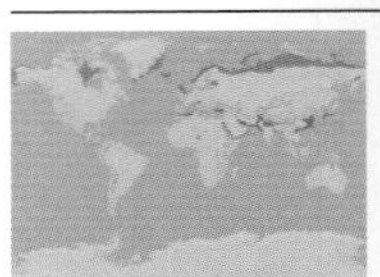

LENGTH 16–22cm (6½–8½in)

WEIGHT 45–60g (1⅝–2⅛oz)

MIGRATION Migrant

HABITAT Breeds on tundra, moors and marshes; winters mainly on muddy coastal habitats

One of the most familiar shorebirds, the Dunlin's breeding plumage is characterized by a conspicuous black patch on its white belly. At this time of year, in common with many other waders, its upperpart feathers are dark brown, scalloped with broad rufous and white fringes. Its long, decurved bill is black, as are its short legs. The juvenile has black and cream stripes on its back and black streaks on its buff underparts.

In summer, the Dunlin is a truly circumpolar species, breeding in the northernmost parts of Alaska, Scandinavia, and Russia. With the approach of autumn, it migrates south to winter chiefly on coastal wetlands in temperate parts of the northern hemisphere.

Outside the breeding season, it often gathers in enormous flocks on favoured feeding grounds. In flight, such flocks are often compact and seem to wheel and circle as one entity, with the birds executing sudden changes of direction in perfect unison. The Dunlin's cry is a thin, reedy, vibrant "shree" or rasping "treerrr". It usually lays about four eggs.

DUNLIN IN BREEDING PLUMAGE

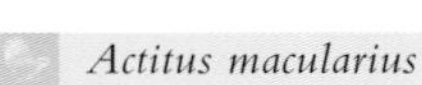

Actitus macularius

Spotted Sandpiper

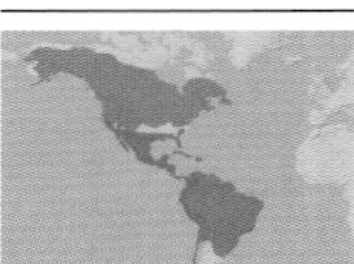

LENGTH 18–20cm (7–8in)

WEIGHT 40g (1 7/16oz)

MIGRATION Migrant

HABITAT Riverbanks, shorelines of lakes, and ponds, and adjoining habitats

In summer, this species has a black-spotted breast and belly, turning a pale grey in autumn and winter. It is a very common, widespread bird and can be found along the shores of rivers, lakes, pools, and ponds – almost anywhere from the middle of a suburban sprawl to the farthest wilderness of the Alaskan tundra.

ADULT IN SUMMER PLUMAGE

Philomachus pugnax

Ruff

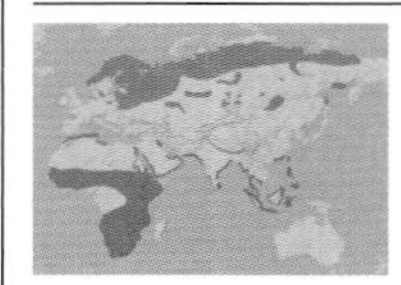

LENGTH 20–32cm (8–12½in)

WEIGHT 100–175g (3⅝–6oz)

MIGRATION Migrant

HABITAT Breeds on freshwater swamps, damp meadows; winters mainly on inland muddy areas

The male Ruff undergoes one of the most spectacular avian transformations each year; from a winter bird in subdued greys to a colourful summer garb. Each Ruff has differently coloured head plumes and broad, feathery neck collars, which it puffs up on the lek, a traditional display ground, where it tries to outdo the other Ruffs in attracting the reeves (females). The Ruff lays four eggs in a grass-lined scrape, well hidden in deep vegetation at marsh edges.

NON-BREEDING PLUMAGE
During winter, the male Ruff is very subdued in appearance.

BREEDING MALE RUFF
In breeding plumage, the male Ruff, with its collar of long showy feathers, is the most spectacular of all waders.

Calidris canutus

Red Knot

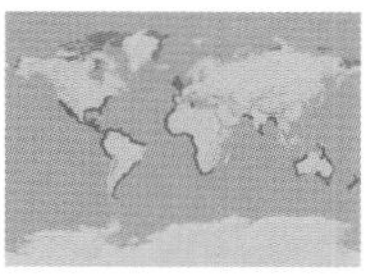

LENGTH 23–25cm (9–10in)

WEIGHT 150g (5oz)

MIGRATION Migrant

HABITAT Breeds on high Arctic tundra and stony areas; winters along coasts

A relative of the Dunlin (above), this stout, medium-sized shorebird is very much a maritime coastal species in winter. One of the largest of all sandpipers of the genus *Calidris*, the Red Knot has grey plumage in winter, with a pale stripe over the eye, a pale grey back, and white underparts. During the breeding season, its face and underparts turn brick-red, while the upperparts are dark and spotted with pale chestnut. The juvenile's plumage is patterned in pale grey and white, with orange-tinged underparts.

Sociable at all times, these shorebirds form enormous flocks, especially during migration (see panel, right). They typically swarm over mudflats or estuaries, slowly and steadily picking their way across feeding grounds, with their heads down. They take insects and plant material, obtained from surface peckings, in summer and molluscs and worms in winter.

BREEDING ADULT

LONG MIGRATION

The Red Knot undertakes one of the longest migrations of any bird; all the way from northernmost Alaska to the southern tip of Tierra del Fuego, a round trip each year of over 30,000km (18,600 miles). At staging posts these birds gather in huge flocks, numbering up to 50,000 birds.

Eurynorhynchus pygmeus

Spoon-billed Sandpiper

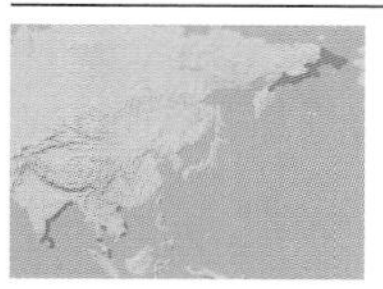

LENGTH 14–16cm (5½–6½in)

WEIGHT 30–35g (1 1/16–1¼oz)

MIGRATION Migrant

HABITAT Breeds on coastal tundra; winters on coastal mudflats and saltpans

RED LIST CATEGORY Endangered

The distinctive spoon-shaped bill of this rare and endangered species distinguishes it from other waders. Mainly pale brownish grey in colour, with white underparts, its plumage turns rufous in the breeding season. It breeds in remote areas near the coast of northeastern Russia, where there are estimated to be fewer than 1,000 breeding pairs spread over an extensive area.

ADULT SPOON-BILLED SANDPIPER

Phalaropus lobatus

Red-necked Phalarope

LENGTH 18–19cm (7–7½in)

WEIGHT 35–40g (1¼–1 7/16lb)

MIGRATION Migrant

HABITAT Breeds on freshwater bogs and marshes; winters mainly at sea

MALE ON NEST

Also known as the Northern Phalarope, this bird breeds throughout much of the Arctic region wherever there are marshy areas. The female is similar in appearance to the male, with a white chin, red neck, and dark grey back, but is more brightly coloured. She mates with different males, leaving each one to incubate the eggs and care for the young.

SPOTTED SANDPIPER
This Spotted Sandpiper chick is nestling among dead leaves in the Yukon valley. The species is found near fresh water throughout North and South America.

Pluvianus aegyptius

Egyptian Plover

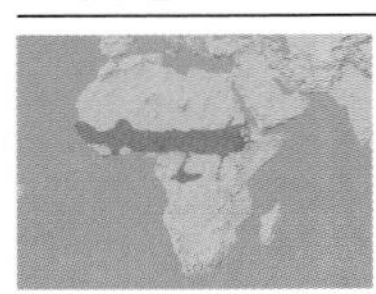

LENGTH
19–21cm (7½–8½in)

WEIGHT
75–90g (2⅝–3¼oz)

MIGRATION
Partial migrant

HABITAT Wide lowland tropical rivers, with sand or gravel bars

Unlike any other wader, the Egyptian Plover has a striped head, prominent black breast-band, grey back, and yellow underparts. In flight, its black crown and band contrast vividly with its grey wings, and the black wing-bar is clearly visible. When nesting, the adult buries its eggs under sand.

The name of this species is a misnomer because it is not a plover, but is usually placed with the coursers (although some scientists regard it as the only member of its genus). It has been extinct in Egypt from the early 20th century, although it is common in a wide band across central Africa. It is also known as the "crocodile-bird", as it is supposed to pick pieces of food from between the teeth of crocodiles (though this behaviour has never been documented).

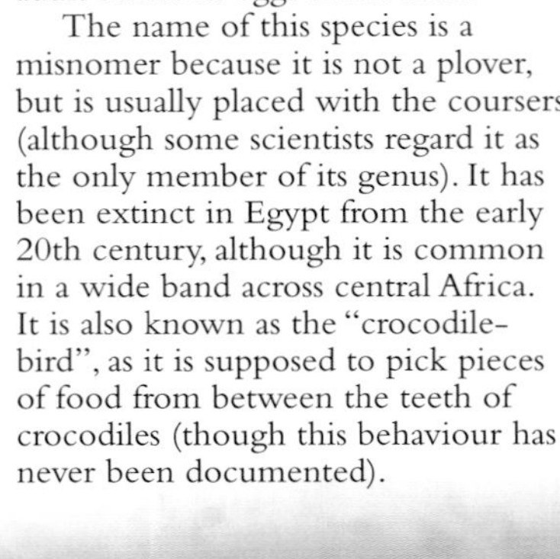

ADULT EGYPTIAN PLOVER

Glareola pratincola

Collared Pratincole

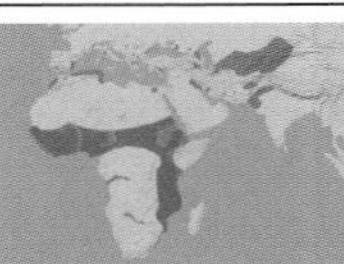

LENGTH
22–25cm (8½–10in)

WEIGHT
85g (3oz)

MIGRATION
Migrant

HABITAT Open areas such as ploughed fields, steppes, plains, grassland; usually near water

With its brown head, back, and wings, the Collared Pratincole is very similar to the Black-winged Pratincole (*G. nordmanni*), which has a black, rather than chestnut underwing, and the Oriental Pratincole (*G. maldivarum*), which has a much shorter tail. The Collared Pratincole also has a noticeable white trailing edge to the wing, which is absent in the other species. They also have a distinct black-lined "bib" when in breeding plumage. In flight, all three are long-winged and rather hawk-like and all gather in large flocks during migration to feed on swarms of flying ants and other insects.

ADULT IN BREEDING PLUMAGE

ADULT CREAM-COLOURED COURSER

Cursorius cursor

Cream-coloured Courser

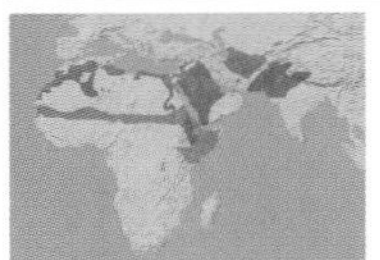

LENGTH
19–22cm (7½–8½in)

WEIGHT
100–150g (3⅝–5oz)

MIGRATION
Migrant

HABITAT Arid, flat open areas of semi-desert and desert

A striking inhabitant of desert areas, the Cream-coloured Courser has sandy plumage and pale legs, which allow it to blend perfectly with its habitat. However, it stands out against green vegetation. It has a noticeable black and white stripe at the back of its eye, which leads to its grey nape. Its flight is identifiable by its relaxed wingbeats, pointed wings, and dark underwing. Loose congregations of up to 30 birds gather to feed, hunting their insect prey by running and stopping at intervals. The nest of this species is a scrape in the ground where the female lays two eggs. When disturbed, the adults run swiftly, stopping now and then to rise on tiptoe, stretching their necks to check for intruders.

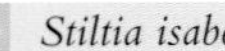

Stiltia isabella

Australian Pratincole

LENGTH
22cm (8½in)

WEIGHT
65g (2⅜oz)

MIGRATION
Partial migrant

HABITAT Breeds on arid plains; winters on grassy and flooded plains, mudflats, and beaches

The elegantly postured Australian Pratincole has a very slim, attenuated body shape and long legs. It is sandy-brown with very long, pointed black wings, and a white belly and vent with a chestnut and black patch at the side. The legs are grey to red. When breeding, the bill is bright red at the base. Non-breeding birds are duller, with a mostly black bill, black spotting on the throat, and smaller flank markings. When feeding, this bird dashes after insects, such as spiders and centipedes, often bobbing its head as it goes. It has special glands, which enable it to drink fresh or saline water. The female lays its eggs on bare ground, sometimes lining the nest with pebbles, dry vegetation, or rabbit dung.

ADULT AUSTRALIAN PRATINCOLE

Larus modestus

Grey Gull

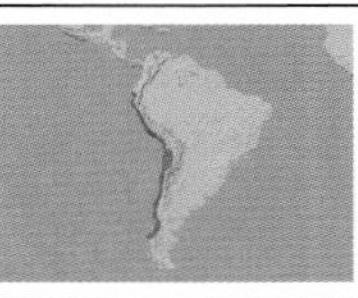

LENGTH
45cm (17½in)

WEIGHT
350–400g (13–14oz)

MIGRATION
Non-migrant

HABITAT Nests up to 50km (32 miles) from the coast in barren desert; feeds along sandy beaches

Identifiable by its dark grey body that contrasts with its white head and black bill, wing-tips, and legs, the Grey Gull is abundant in Chile and is also found further north in Peru and Ecuador. It breeds in large, dense colonies of about 60,000 pairs in upland deserts near the coast. One of the pair tends the nest during the day, providing shade to the clutch of 1 or 2 eggs by standing over them.

Larus canus

Mew Gull

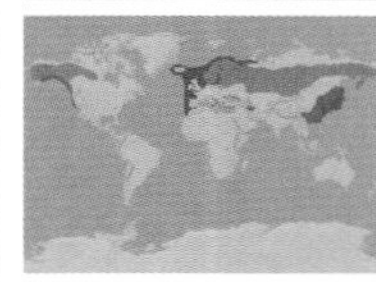

LENGTH
40–46cm (15½–18in)

WEIGHT
350–500g (13–17oz)

MIGRATION
Partial migrant

HABITAT Coasts, estuaries, farmland, lakes, and reservoirs

Its nasal call has given the Mew Gull its name. In Europe, the species is also known as the Common Gull, but it is by no means the most commonly occurring member of its family. The adult in breeding plumage has a clean, white appearance with a yellow bill, dark eyes, grey black-tipped wings with small white spots, and yellow legs. The juvenile Mew Gull has dark brown plumage.

ADULT MEW GULLS IN FLIGHT

HERRING GULLS FIGHTING OVER FOOD

Larus argentatus

Herring Gull

LENGTH 55–67cm (21½–26in)

WEIGHT 1–1.5kg (2¼–3¼lb)

MIGRATION Partial migrant

HABITAT Mainly coastal; also inland on large lakes or reservoirs, farmland, and rubbish tips

A large, noisy bird, the Herring Gull is known for its honking or bugling call, a familiar sound around coastal towns in Europe and eastern North America, where it is now one of the most common coastal birds. The species takes four years to acquire its adult plumage, which consists of a white head and underparts, a pale grey back and wings, and black wing-tips with white spots ("mirrors"). The Herring Gull has pale yellow eyes, a broad yellow bill with a red spot on its tip, and pink legs. It will eat anything from rubbish and carrion to earthworms, although fish, molluscs, and algae form the bulk of its diet along the sea coast. Like other gulls, it carries hard-shelled molluscs into the air, then drops them on land to break open shells. Inland, it eats insects, rodents, and the eggs and young of other birds.

During the breeding season, these gulls usually nest in colonies on cliffs. The adults build untidy nests made up of vegetation and scraps of refuse and both the male and female incubate the eggs for 23–27 days.

FEMALE AND CHICK

Larus dominicanus

Kelp Gull

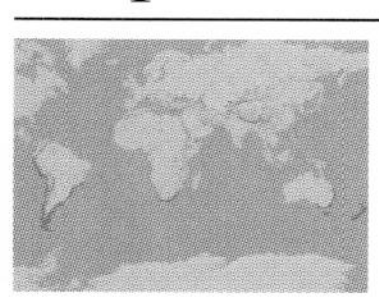

LENGTH 55–65cm (21½–26in)

WEIGHT 0.8–1.1kg (2–2½lb)

MIGRATION Partial migrant

HABITAT Mainly coastal

This large gull is found exclusively in the southern hemisphere, around the coasts of South America, Africa, Antarctica, and Australia. It has a heavy yellow bill, a white head and underparts, a dark, slate-grey back, and yellow legs. The Kelp Gull is a skilled scavenger and has increased markedly throughout its range as a result of more farming and fisheries.

Larus marinus

Great Black-backed Gull

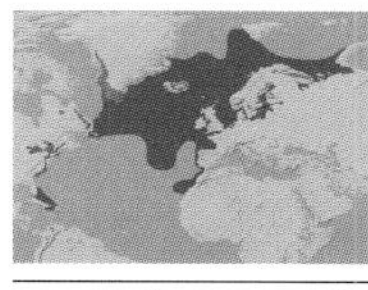

LENGTH 68–79cm (27–31in)

WEIGHT 1.4–2.2kg (3¼–4½lb)

MIGRATION Partial migrant

HABITAT Coasts, estuaries, large inland waters, and agricultural fields

The world's largest gull, the Great Black-backed Gull has a bulky appearance. It has a massive white head, a huge red-spotted yellow bill, a slaty black back and wings, and pink legs. Like many other large gull species, it takes four years to acquire adult plumage and becomes gradually less streaked as it ages. With its large wingspan of 1.5m (5ft), the flight of the Great Black-backed Gull is heavy and powerful, with slow, deep wingbeats. This gull has a very varied diet, which includes fish, shellfish, and carrion (see panel, right).

The species breeds on the east coast of North America from Labrador to New York. Farther east, it also breeds in Greenland and Iceland, and from Britain to Norway and neighbouring parts of Russia. Although very aggressive towards other birds, it often nests together with other gulls in loose colonies or may occasionally build solitary nests. The nest is a large pile of feathers, debris, sticks, seaweed, and grasses, often sheltered in cliff ridges, and is built by both the male and female.

PREDATORY BEHAVIOUR

Although the Great Black-backed Gull can often be seen scavenging around rubbish tips, it is highly predatory and will frequently pursue and take live prey as large as adult seabirds (including puffins, shearwaters, and cormorants) and rabbits. It also steals food from other birds and often makes a meal of their eggs and young.

ADULT GREAT BLACK-BACKED GULLS

ADULT IN SUMMER PLUMAGE

Larus ridibundus

Common Black-headed Gull

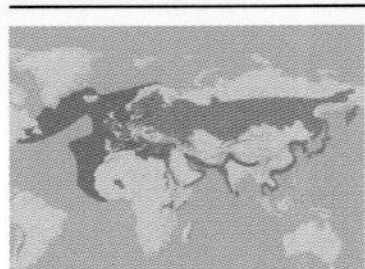

LENGTH 37–43cm (14½–17in)

WEIGHT 275g (10oz)

MIGRATION Partial migrant

HABITAT Coasts, inland wetlands, marshes, agricultural land, and open areas in towns

Named somewhat misleadingly, the Common Black-headed Gull is never truly black-headed – it has a dark brown hood in summer (appearing black from a distance). As well as the brown hood, the summer plumage of the adult includes a white crescent around the eye, a dark red bill and legs, a very pale grey back, and grey wings. In winter, the Common Black-headed Gull has a pale head, a distinct dark spot behind the eye, and black on the trailing edge of its wings.

A small, highly adaptable species of gull, it is common around urban areas in much of its range. It breeds in May and June, building its nest on the ground, hidden in vegetation. A number of very similar species (sometimes considered races of the Common Black-headed Gull) occur elsewhere in the world, including the Brown-hooded Gull (*L. maculipennis*) in South America and the Brown-headed Gull (*L. brunnicephalus*) in Asia.

Larus atricilla

Laughing Gull

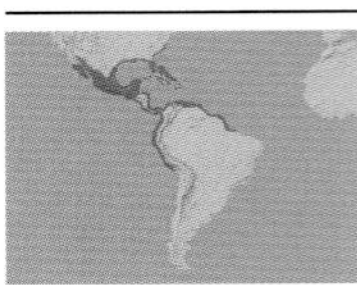

LENGTH 39–46cm (15½–18in)

WEIGHT 275–325g (10–12oz)

MIGRATION Partial migrant

HABITAT Coasts; also visits nearby habitats such as rubbish tips and parks

In summer, the adult Laughing Gull has a black hood, a powerful dark brown bill, a dark grey back, and dark red legs. Non-breeding adults have a white head, smudged with dark markings, and a dark red bill. The species is named after its call, a long drawn-out strident laugh. It forms large colonies with thousands of nests, breeding in the USA, the Caribbean, and Central America and wintering as far south as Peru.

ADULT IN BREEDING PLUMAGE

ADULT IVORY GULL

Pagophila eburnea

Ivory Gull

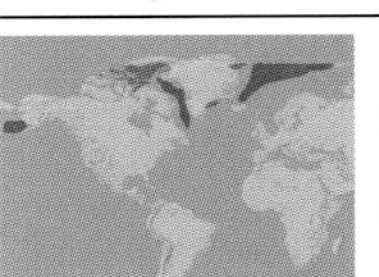

LENGTH 44–48cm (17½–19in)

WEIGHT 550g (20oz)

MIGRATION Partial migrant

HABITAT Breeds mainly on sea cliffs; winters on the edge of drifting and pack ice

With its overall pure white plumage, black eyes, and yellow-tipped dark bill, the adult Ivory Gull is easily identified. The juvenile has dark markings around the face, as well as some dark spotting on the back and wings and acquires the all-white plumage only in its second year. This Arctic species is declining in numbers, probably due to shrinking areas of pack ice and is now globally classified as near-threatened.

Rhodostethia rosea

Ross's Gull

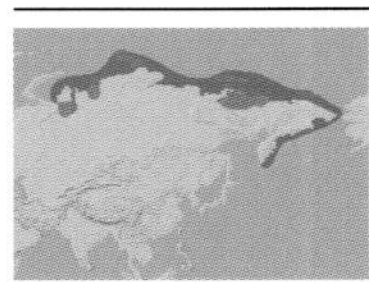

LENGTH 29–32cm (11½–12½in)

WEIGHT 175–200g (6–7oz)

MIGRATION Partial migrant

HABITAT Breeds on river deltas in tundra and taiga; winters in open seas around pack ice

Small and delicate, Ross's Gull has a distinctive summer plumage. The adult has a black collar that sweeps over the forehead and around the neck (as if marking out a hood). It usually has a pink wash to the breast and bright red legs. In flight, its long, pointed wings with white trailing edges and its wedge-shaped tail are clearly visible. In winter, the adult lacks the black collar, with just a small black smudge behind the eye. The juvenile has a black ear spot, a black tail tip, and more black than the adult on the wings and tail.

ADULT IN SUMMER PLUMAGE

Creagrus furcatus

Swallow-tailed Gull

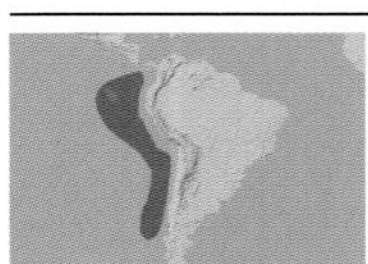

LENGTH 51–57cm (20–22½in)

WEIGHT 610–780g (21–28oz)

MIGRATION Migrant

HABITAT Breeds on cliffs and steep slopes in Galapagos Islands; winters on coast or open sea

The Swallow-tailed Gull has a black hood, red eye-ring, and pale-tipped black bill (with a white spot at its base) during the breeding season. It has two white lines along its shoulders that show out against the dark grey plumage on its back. In flight, a distinct two-colour pattern can be seen on its wings – black at the tips, with a broad triangular white patch in the centre, contrasting with its grey back.

This gull nests on the Galapagos Islands, usually on cliffs or steep slopes. After breeding, the adult leaves its colony to winter along the coast of mainland South America, or to spend time at sea. It returns to the islands about five months later, usually to its previous nest site. The most nocturnal member of its family, it has large eyes adapted to see clearly in the dark. Its favoured food is squid, which is plentiful near the water surface at night.

ADULT IN BREEDING PLUMAGE

ADULT BLACK-LEGGED KITTIWAKE

Rissa tridactyla

Black-legged Kittiwake

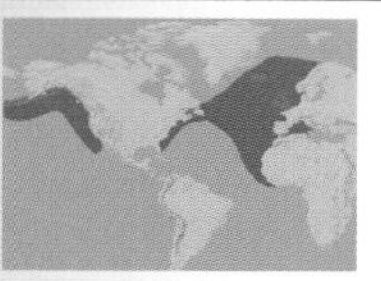

LENGTH 38–40cm (15–15½in)

WEIGHT 400–425g (14–15oz)

MIGRATION Migrant

HABITAT Breeds mainly on steep cliffs (and, increasingly, on buildings); winters at sea

With an estimated global population of 6–7 million pairs, which is continuing to increase, the Black-legged Kittiwake is the world's most abundant species of gull. It is a clean-looking gull with a plain face, unmarked yellow bill, and a grey mantle and wings. In winter, the adult has a dark smudge across the nape. The juvenile shows a distinct black "M" pattern across its upperwing in flight and has a black-tipped tail. The name "Kittiwake" is onomatopoeic, referring to the ever-present screeching call heard at its nesting colonies.

SEABIRD CITIES

As the world's most numerous gull species, it is no surprise that the Black-legged Kittiwake nests in huge colonies, usually on cliffs, many of which exceed 10,000 pairs, some numbering up to 100,000. They build nests of seaweed, which sticks to the rock surface when it dries. The Black-legged Kittiwake is also expanding its range by nesting on buildings and structures such as piers.

Sterna nilotica

Gull-billed Tern

LENGTH 33–43cm (13–17in)

WEIGHT 170–240g (6–9oz)

MIGRATION Migrant

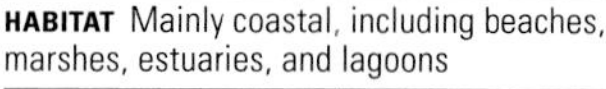

HABITAT Mainly coastal, including beaches, marshes, estuaries, and lagoons

ADULT GULL-BILLED TERN

A rather squat tern, with a short black bill, the Gull-billed Tern has a black crown and nape, pale grey upperparts, white underparts, and long black legs and feet. Its wings are broad and rounded and its short tail is forked. In summer, the adult has a black cap that extends below the eyes, while in winter, the head is white with faint dark streaks.

The Gull-billed Tern has a varied diet and is more insectivorous than other tern species. Small fish form part of its diet, together with small reptiles, frogs, and even small voles. Its most favoured food includes dragonflies and grasshoppers. The species has a wide, but patchy, near-global distribution.

ADULT CASPIAN TERN

Sterna caspia

Caspian Tern

LENGTH 48–56cm (19–22in)

WEIGHT 650g (23oz)

MIGRATION Migrant

HABITAT Coastal areas as well as larger inland wetlands

The Caspian Tern is the world's largest species of tern – its wingspan of almost 1.5m (5ft) is similar to that of the Herring Gull (see p.235). The species has a thick, bright red bill, with a small black tip, and a black cap that covers its head from bill to nape. In flight, it shows bold black markings on the tips of its underwing. It is not as sociable as other tern species, although it sometimes breeds in large colonies. Usually, however, it is seen singly or in pairs.

The Caspian Tern is found in all continents, except South America (where only a few birds winter) and Antarctica. It is likely to be confused with the Royal Tern (*S. maxima*) from Africa and the Americas; however, the Royal Tern is smaller and has a more orange bill, without a black tip.

Sterna paradisaea

Arctic Tern

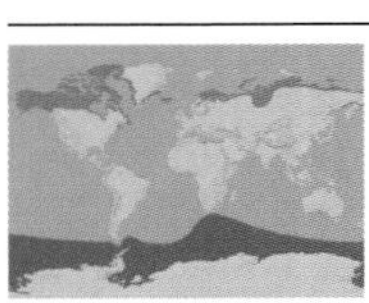

LENGTH 33–36cm (13–14in)

WEIGHT 85–125g (3–4oz)

MIGRATION Migrant

HABITAT Nests on shingle beaches, tundra, lakes, and coastal lagoons; usually winters at sea

Mainly grey and white in colour, the Arctic Tern has a black cap and nape. Non-breeding birds have a white forehead and a red bill and feet. Its deeply forked tail is white, with grey outer margins. It feeds on small fish and marine crustaceans. The Arctic Tern is the world's most long-distance migratory bird. The species breeds around the Arctic Circle from Siberia to Greenland, and Iceland to Norway. It leaves its breeding grounds each year to embark on a 40,000km (25,000 mile) round trip that involves a journey to the Antarctic. As a result, the species experiences two summers each year and more daylight than any other creature on the planet. During its lifetime, the average Arctic Tern will travel a distance equivalent to that from the Earth to the Moon and back.

ADULT ARCTIC TERN WITH CHICKS

Sterna dougallii

Roseate Tern

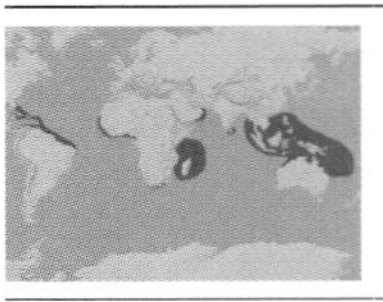

LENGTH 33–43cm (13–17in)

WEIGHT 90–125g (3¼–4oz)

MIGRATION Migrant

HABITAT Breeds on rocky, sandy, or coral islands, sometimes densely vegetated; winters at sea

ADULT ROSEATE TERN

It is the pink flush to its underparts, which can only be seen early in the breeding season, that gives the Roseate Tern its name. Apart from this feature, the species is a typical *Sterna* tern, with pale grey plumage and long tail streamers. Individuals usually have an all-dark bill, with varying amounts of red at the base, depending on the subspecies and the time of year. The Roseate Tern feeds by plunge-diving for fish.

ANTARCTIC TERN IN SUMMER PLUMAGE

Sterna vittata

Antarctic Tern

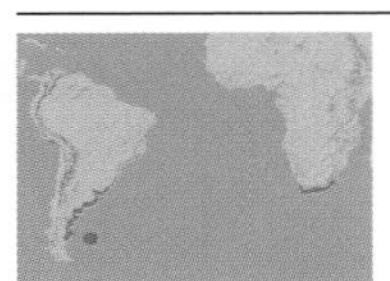

LENGTH 35–40cm (14–15½in)

WEIGHT 150–175g (5–6oz)

MIGRATION Migrant

HABITAT Breeds on rocky islets, otherwise favours edges of ice, rocky coasts, and beaches

Before migrating to the tip of South America and Africa, the Antarctic Tern breeds on islands in the Southern Ocean. In its breeding plumage, this bird is very similar to the Arctic Tern (left), although it is larger and bulkier. A non-breeding Antarctic Tern is distinguished from its close relative by its grizzled crown, white forehead, and a red bill and legs. The plumage of the juvenile is white, with a black bill and legs.

Sterna fuscata

Sooty Tern

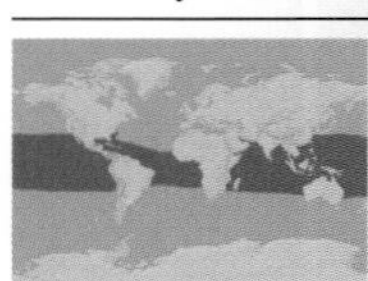

LENGTH 36–45cm (14–17½in)

WEIGHT 150–250g (5–9oz)

MIGRATION Migrant

HABITAT Tropical and subtropical waters; breeds on islands

With its striking black and white coloration, the Sooty Tern is one of the world's most abundant seabirds. Several colonies contain more than a million pairs. Once the chicks have fledged, these terns leave the colony, spending the next two or three months at sea, before returning for the next breeding season. During this time at sea, it is believed that the species sleeps on the wing.

COURTING PAIR

NESTING PAIR OF BLACK TERNS

Chlidonias niger

Black Tern

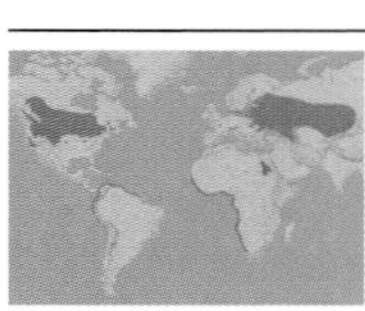

LENGTH 23–28cm (9–11in)

WEIGHT 60–75g (2⅛–2⅝oz)

MIGRATION Migrant

HABITAT Breeds on inland marshes, lakes, and pools; found in coastal areas and on marshes during winter

The Black Tern is one of three species referred to collectively as the "Marsh Terns", the other two being the White-winged Black Tern (*C. leucopterus*) and the Whiskered Tern (*C. hybrida*). All three have a wide global range and favour marshy inland locations. They are smaller than *Sterna* terns (above) and have short forked tails that lack streamers. In its breeding plumage, the Black Tern is distinctively dark, with a jet-black head and breast, dark grey wings, and a small patch of white on the undertail. In winter, it has a black crown and ear-patch and a white collar.

It mainly eats insects and fish, but unlike the *Sterna* terns, this bird does not dive for fish, but forages on the wing, picking up items at or near the water's surface or catching insects on the wing.

Anous stolidus

Brown Noddy

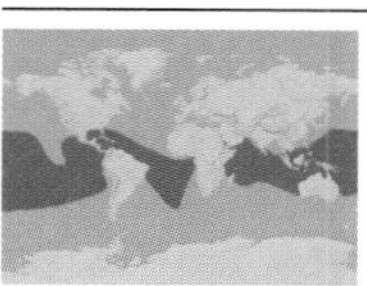

LENGTH 38–45cm (15–17½in)

WEIGHT 150–275g (5–10oz)

MIGRATION Migrant

HABITAT Breeds on tropical and subtropical islands and coral reefs; disperses to sea after breeding

ADULT BROWN NODDY

One of three similar-looking representatives of the genus *Anous*, the Brown Noddy's name is derived from its habit of nodding to its mate during courtship. These dark-coloured terns are usually found far out to sea, often in large flocks. They hover over the water's surface before swooping and snatching small fish and squid.

Gygis alba

Angel Tern

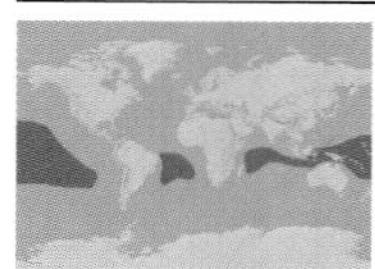

LENGTH 25–30cm (10–12in)

WEIGHT 95–125g (3⅜–4oz)

MIGRATION Partial migrant

HABITAT Usually nests in trees or bushes on islands; sometimes also cliffs and rocky slopes

Also known as the Fairy Tern, the Angel Tern is a graceful, almost ethereal species, with a stunning snow-white plumage, which is only punctuated by its large black eyes and delicate, slightly upturned black bill. In flight, its wings look almost translucent. Away from its tropical island nesting sites, where it is a solitary nester, the Angel Tern lives out at sea. It feeds mainly on small fish.

ADULT ANGEL TERN

PAIR OF ADULT INCA TERNS

Larosterna inca

Inca Tern

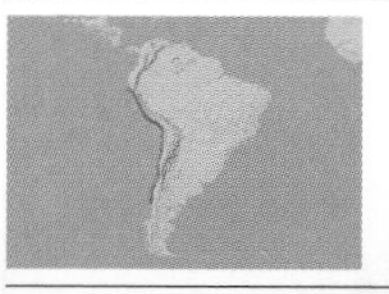

LENGTH 39–42cm (15½–16½in)

WEIGHT 175–200g (6–7oz)

MIGRATION Non-migrant

HABITAT Pacific coast of South America; usually rocky shores and sandy beaches

With its dark grey plumage and bright red bill and legs, the Inca Tern is very noticeable. It has a distinctive white stripe that curls down from the bill to the side of the neck, adjacent to a small area of bare yellow facial skin. In flight, the species displays a paler area on the underwing and a prominent white trailing edge to the wing. The juvenile is dark all over, lacking the adult's facial characteristics. The size of a small gull, the species often flies near fishing boats, where it forages for scraps and offal. However, its natural diet consists of small fish and plankton and it feeds by plunge-diving for fish. The call of an Inca Tern is a cat-like mew. It breeds on rocky cliffs and nests in a hollow or burrow and lays one or two eggs, which it incubates for about four weeks.

Rynchops niger

Black Skimmer

LENGTH 41–46cm (16–18in)

WEIGHT 300–375g (11–13oz)

MIGRATION Migrant

HABITAT Coastal wetlands in North America; also found inland, for example, by rivers in South America

The Black Skimmer is the American representative of the skimmer family, the other two being the African Skimmer and the Indian Skimmer. All three have a front-heavy appearance, with a massive bill and heavy head. They also have strikingly pied plumage with black upperparts and bright white underparts. The Black Skimmer has a two-coloured bill, with a red base and a black tip. It is long-winged, but short-tailed – a feature that adds to its oddly proportioned appearance. The female is smaller and the juvenile has a brown mottled back.

The Black Skimmer is found only in the Americas (including limited parts of the Caribbean), ranging from coastal areas of the USA to Argentina and Chile. All skimmers are sociable birds that breed in loose colonies and roost together. Unlike other gulls and terns, flocks of skimmers synchronize their movements in flight, twisting and circling together in a spiral of black and white wingbeats. Its call is a barking "yip". Although the Black Skimmer is active throughout the day, it is more so at dawn and dusk, and even during night.

BLACK SKIMMERS DIVING FOR PREY

UNUSUAL BILL SHAPE

All three species of skimmer have distinctive bills, with the lower mandible longer than the upper one. This is an adaptation for their special feeding method. Skimmers fly low over the water with their bills held open, the lower mandible ploughing through the water until it strikes a fish. Then the upper part of the bill snaps shut, trapping the fish.

Stercorarius longicaudus

Long-tailed Skua

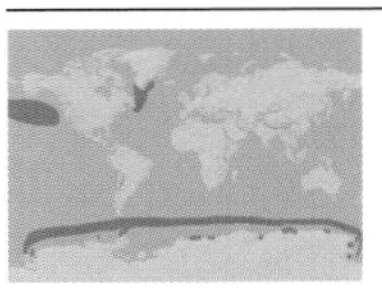

LENGTH 48–53cm (19–21in)

WEIGHT 225–350g (8–13oz)

MIGRATION Migrant

HABITAT Mostly marine; breeds on tundra or coastal grassland

The most noticeable feature of the Long-tailed Skua is its pair of long central tail streamers, although these are visible only in adults. They have pale greyish brown upperparts and long slender wings. The juvenile has a short tail and is difficult to distinguish from other species.

Unlike other skuas, the Long-tailed Skua hunts for food itself, rather than stealing from other birds. It feeds mainly on lemmings, but fish, insects, eggs, and young birds are taken when lemmings are scarce. Breeding is linked to the availability of its main food, being unsuccessful in years when lemming numbers are low. However, the population of this species is generally stable. Juveniles become sexually mature when they reach four years of age, but little is known of their movements outside the breeding season. The nest sites of this skua are found in areas that are further inland than those of other skuas.

ADULT LONG-TAILED SKUA

Stercorarius maccormicki

South Polar Skua

LENGTH 50–55cm (19½–21½in)

WEIGHT 0.9–1.6kg (2–3¼lb)

MIGRATION Migrant

HABITAT Mostly marine; breeds on snow-free areas; sometimes associated with penguin rookeries

SOUTH POLAR SKUA

A powerful bird, the South Polar Skua is dark brown to grey in colour and has broad, rounded wings. It preys on penguin chicks and eggs, although it mainly eats fish. The population is thought to be stable, but the breeding sites are limited and are vulnerable to human disturbance and pollution. This skua lays two eggs, but the older chick will often kill the younger one and breeding success is often low.

PAIR OF PARASITIC SKUAS

Stercorarius parasiticus

Parasitic Skua

LENGTH 41–46cm (16–18in)

WEIGHT 325–600g (12–21oz)

MIGRATION Migrant

HABITAT Mostly marine in winter; coastal in summer, close to sea bird colonies

Brown above, with white underparts, the Parasitic Skua has a dark crown and two pointed and extended central tail feathers. It is solitary off breeding grounds, but is well known for its spirited defence of its nest and has been known to chase away or even strike an intruder. Most of the nests are in coastal areas, but it also nests inland, where the bird is a predator, taking lemmings and insects.

FOOD THEFT

Aptly named, the Parasitic Skua gets most of its food by stealing from other birds, in a behavioural pattern known as kleptoparasitism. It waits for another bird to return from a fishing trip and harasses its victim until it regurgitates the food it has eaten. Another strategy it uses is to watch fishing birds closely and then snatch any fish that they bring to the surface to feed on.

ADULT GREAT SKUA

Stercorarius skua

Great Skua

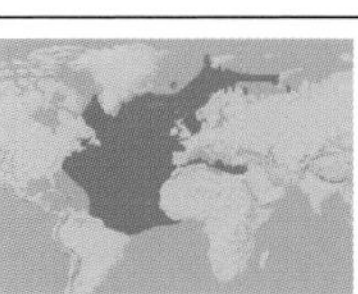

LENGTH 53–58cm (21–23in)

WEIGHT 1.1–1.7kg (2¼–3¼lb)

MIGRATION Migrant

HABITAT Mostly marine in winter; on islands close to sea bird colonies in summer

The Great Skua has streaked greyish brown plumage and broad wings. A large and aggressive bird, it will vigorously defend its nest site, often injuring human intruders. Most of its food is gathered by stealing from other birds and it has also been known to kill small gulls and auks. Scavenging around fishing vessels is also common, although Great Skuas avoid areas of human activity when inshore.

Fratercula arctica

Atlantic Puffin

LENGTH
26–36cm (10–14in)

WEIGHT
450g (16oz)

MIGRATION
Migrant

HABITAT Sea cliffs in summer, but in oceans and open seas outside the breeding season

Also known as the "parrot of the sea" for the extravagant red, yellow, and blue colours of its bill in summer, the Atlantic Puffin has a pale grey to white face and cheeks, black upperparts, white underparts, and red-orange legs and feet.

The Atlantic Puffin is ungainly on land and lacks agility in the air, but it is at home in the sea, "flying" through the water with ease. It can dive down to 20m (66ft) and can remain under water for up to 30 seconds.

In the nesting season, a single egg is laid and is incubated by both adults in turn, taking about 42 days to hatch. The development of the young to fledglings depends on food supplies and takes between 38 and 59 days with some fledglings leaving the nest before all the feathers have grown. The species feeds on crustaceans and small fish, breeding birds being heavily reliant on sand eels, which are captured within 100km (60 miles) of the nest.

HUMAN IMPACT

FACING THREATS

A combination of fishing pressures and changing sea temperatures through climatic shift have caused severe reduction in breeding success in some years. The Atlantic Puffin has a limited feeding range in summer and increases in water temperature have sometimes pushed the normal food beyond the reach of colonies. Some Atlantic Puffin colonies have witnessed close to 100 per cent failure rates in the more extreme years with the frequency increasing in recent decades.

brightly coloured bill in summer

black collar

ATLANTIC PUFFIN CARRYING SAND EELS

Alle alle

Little Auk

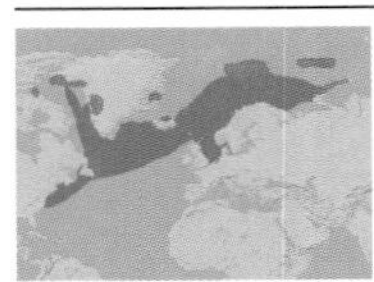

LENGTH 22cm (8½in)
WEIGHT 175g (6oz)
MIGRATION Migrant

HABITAT Open seas; breeds on scree-slopes of coastal cliffs

One of the smallest members of its family, but also one of the hardiest, the Little Auk or Dovekie breeds in huge colonies on islands in the high Arctic. The species moves south in winter, but storms regularly carry these birds south of their normal range. The black and white Little Auk has a short bill and stubby wings. Its flight is very fast and direct, low over the sea. Its diet consists of crustaceans, especially copepods, but also other small invertebrates and fish.

ADULT LITTLE AUK

GUILLEMOT NESTING COLONY

Uria aalge

Guillemot

LENGTH 42cm (16½in)
WEIGHT 1kg (2¼oz)
MIGRATION Partial migrant

HABITAT Open seas; breeds on sea-cliffs

With its long, pointed bill, the Guillemot, or Murre, is the most familiar cliff-nesting auk in Europe. It is dark brown to black on the head and upperparts and has white underparts. Some birds have distinct white "spectacles". In winter, the neck and throat are white. It finds its food by swimming underwater, where it mainly catches small schooling fish under 20cm (8in) in length and crustaceans, marine worms, and squid, as it dives to depths of about 50m (160ft). The Guillemot is gregarious and breeds in tightly packed colonies, laying its eggs on bare rock ledges (see panel, right).

POINTED EGGS

The eggs of the Guillemots have evolved a long shape, with one end broad and rounded and the other narrow and sharply pointed. This makes the eggs roll in a circle when disturbed, preventing them from falling off the steep cliff ledges.

MULTI-COLOURED EGGSHELLS
A variety of colours – such as blues, greens, and whites – and patterns, from spots to speckles, adorn the Guillemot's eggs.

Alca torda

Razorbill

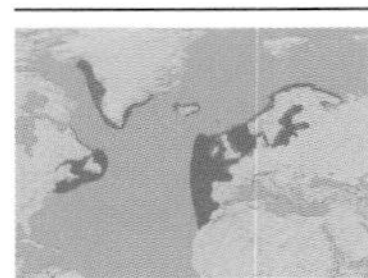

LENGTH 43cm (17in)
WEIGHT 725g (26oz)
MIGRATION Partial migrant

HABITAT Open seas; breeds on sea cliffs

The only member of the genus *Alca*, the Razorbill resembles the Common Guillemot (above), but is smaller and darker. There are pale bands on its short, thick, flattened bill, and a white line from the bill-base to the eye. In winter, the neck and throat are white rather than black. It swims underwater, catching fish and also crustaceans and marine worms.

ADULT RAZORBILL

Cephus grylle

Black Guillemot

LENGTH 33cm (13in)
WEIGHT 375g (30oz)
MIGRATION Partial migrant

HABITAT Coastal waters, sea cliffs, and coastal boulder- and scree-slopes

With its sleek black breeding plumage, white shoulders, and distinctive bright red feet, the Black Guillemot (also known as Tystie) is one of the most attractive auks. In winter, it looks quite different, with much of the body being white. It dives for its food like other auks, and mainly eats fish and crustaceans, as well as some molluscs, insects, and plant material. Compared to other auks, it is a relatively solitary nester and prefers to lay its eggs in rock-crevices, often not very high above the surface of the sea.

ADULT IN BREEDING PLUMAGE

BREEDING ADULT

Cerorhinca monocerata

Rhinoceros Auklet

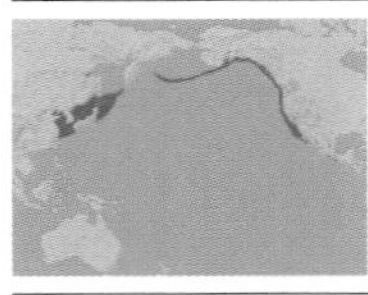

LENGTH 37cm (14½in)
WEIGHT 450–500g (16–18oz)
MIGRATION Partial migrant

HABITAT Open seas; breeds on maritime and inland grassy slopes, sometimes on forest floors

The Rhinoceros Auklet gets its name from the unusual horn-like protrusion on top of its bill. When breeding, the adult sports two white head-stripes and an orange-tinted eye and bill. In winter it looks duller and the horn shrinks. It feeds on fish, krill, and squid and nests in an excavated burrow or natural cavity, where it lays just a single egg.

SANDGROUSE

ORDER Pteroclidiformes
FAMILY 1
SPECIES 16

BIRDS OF DRY, open habitats with plump bodies and pointed wings, sandgrouse are found in southern Europe, Africa, and Asia. Gregarious and fast-flying, they nest and feed on the ground. Sandgrouse feed entirely on seeds, and in times of scarcity, they may be found far outside their normal range.

SANDGROUSE IN FLIGHT
Startled by a sudden noise, a group of Burchell's Sandgrouse burst into the air, flying rapidly on fast-beating wings.

ANATOMY

Sandgrouse look like a cross between pigeons and gamebirds, with small heads and deep bodies. Their short legs are fully feathered. Females lay their eggs on the ground, and their young are well developed when they hatch. Adult males have absorbent breast feathers, which they use to collect water, delivering it to their chicks.

CRYPTIC PLUMAGE
Despite its conspicuous breast-band, the Namaqua Sandgrouse blends in well in its habitat of semi-desert and dry savanna.

Pterocles coronatus

Crowned Sandgrouse

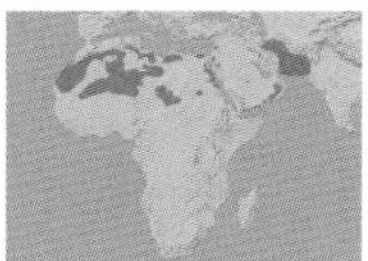

LENGTH 27–30cm (10½–12in)
WEIGHT 250–300g (9–11oz)
MIGRATION Non-migrant
HABITAT Stony and sandy desert and semi-desert

Truly a desert bird, the Crowned Sandgrouse is found in some of the hottest and driest regions of north Africa and the Middle East, tolerating temperatures of over 50°C (122°F).

The male Crowned Sandgrouse is cream-spotted, and has a bright rufous head with a black and white face and blue-grey stripe above the eye. The female lacks the black on the face, and is much more intricately patterned in black, brown, and buff.

The Crowned Sandgrouse is a very short-legged bird, and forages on the ground for seeds and plant-shoots. When breeding, it lays 2 or 3 eggs on the ground. The eggs are incubated by both parents, but the male takes over at night as it is not as well camouflaged.

FLOCK GATHERED AT WATER HOLE

Pterocles lichtensteinii

Lichtenstein's Sandgrouse

LENGTH 24–26cm (9½–10in)
WEIGHT 175–250g (6–9oz)
MIGRATION Non-migrant
HABITAT Scrubby semi-desert and desert, semi-wooded dry ravines and hillsides

MALE LICHTENSTEIN'S SANDGROUSE

The distinctive plumage of Lichtenstein's Sandgrouse gives it camouflage protection in the exposed open habitat that it prefers. Both sexes are very heavily marked with black and brown, but the male has black and white bands on the forecrown and a buff breast with a double black band. During the heat of the day, it sits motionless on the ground and is difficult to see. In the early mornings and evening, these birds gather in flocks to visit the nearest water hole. The belly feathers are adapted to retain water, and in the breeding season, the chicks are able to drink from the wet feathers of the adults.

Pterocles alchata

Pin-tailed Sandgrouse

LENGTH 31–39cm (12–15½in)
WEIGHT 200–400g (7–14oz)
MIGRATION Partial migrant
HABITAT Semi-desert, treeless steppes, dry mudflats, and arable farmland

This sandgrouse gets its common name from the male's long, narrow tail streamers. The female has a shorter tail than the male, is more heavily patterned above, lacks the dark throat, and shows two dark neck bands (the male has one). The flight of the species is fast and direct, and its wings are very long and pointed. It uses a simple depression in the ground for a nest, and lays three well-patterned eggs. Both sexes incubate them for about three weeks.

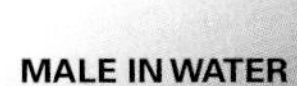

MALE IN WATER

GREAT SITES

SPANISH STEPPES

A patchwork of dry scrub, rough grassland, and low-scale cultivation, the steppe grasslands of central and southern Spain are among the richest and least disturbed grassland habitats in Europe. The mosaic of vegetation, largely undisturbed, provides a hospitable environment for many bird species and is home to a great number of Pin-tailed Sandgrouse.

SAINT PAUL ISLAND

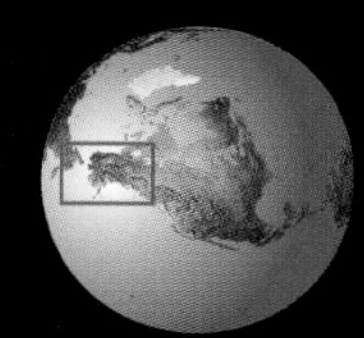

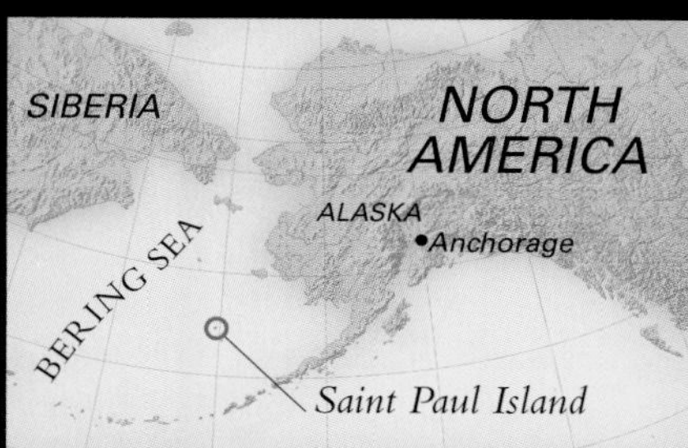

LOCATION The Bering Sea, about 450km (280 miles) off the coast of southwest Alaska and 800km (500 miles) east of Siberia.

Saint Paul Island is the largest of the Pribilofs, an isolated group of four islands, lying to the north of the Aleutians, a great arc of volcanic islands strung out across the Bering Sea. This rocky outpost in the heart of the Bering Sea hosts some of the most important seabird colonies in the northern hemisphere. Each year during the brief subarctic summer Saint Paul's rugged coastline comes to life as huge numbers of ocean-going birds return to land to breed. For three short months its sea cliffs reverberate with the cacophony created by tens of thousands of puffins, guillemots, auklets, murrelets, cormorants, and kittiwakes.

CLIFF-TOP BREEDING GROUNDS

Saint Paul Island has sandy beaches, coastal mudflats, craggy peaks of basalt rock, wet bogs, and treeless rolling hills covered with sparse tundra vegetation. Its 105 square km (40 square miles) remain a pristine, barely populated environment, but it is the surrounding ocean that makes the island so special for birds. The cold waters around the Pribilofs are extremely rich in nutrients and support one of the world's most productive fisheries, attracting several million seabirds from a dozen main species, as well as whales, fur seals, Walrus, and sea lions.

Throughout the winter, pack ice covers the Bering Sea as far south as Saint Paul Island. The trigger for seabirds to begin breeding is when rising temperatures force the ice front to retreat north. By the height of summer there are up to 19 hours of daylight, giving parent birds more time to forage for their offspring. The cliff-nesting species form a complex community, in which each species uses a particular nesting zone. Narrow cliff ledges are crowded with Black- and Red-legged Kittiwakes, Northern Fulmars, Red-faced Cormorants, Guillemots, and Thick-billed Murres; Crested and Least Auklets nest among rubble at the base of the cliffs; Horned Puffins occupy deep crevices on the cliff-face; and Tufted Puffins dig burrows on the cliff-top. More than 240 species of bird have been seen on Saint Paul Island, including migratory ducks, waders, and passerines.

CROWDED CLIFF LEDGE
Thick-billed Murres, also known as Brunnich's Guillemots, are the most abundant seabird on the cliffs of Saint Paul Island, crowding the cliff ledges during the breeding season.

WHAT TO SPOT

RED-LEGGED KITTIWAKE
Rissa brevirostris

TUFTED PUFFIN
Fratercula cirrhata

RUDDY TURNSTONE
Arenaria interpres

PECTORAL SANDPIPER
Calidris melanotos

PIGEONS AND DOVES

ORDER	Columbiformes
FAMILIES	1
SPECIES	298

THROUGHOUT THE WORLD pigeons and doves are familiar, thanks to the spread of feral pigeons. They make up a large, distinctive order of plant-feeding birds and, technically, there is no difference between them, the smaller species that tend to be known as doves. Their small heads bob backwards and forwards as they walk; they feed in trees, or on the ground; and escape danger with a noisy take-off, on fast-flapping wings. They build flimsy nests from sticks, in trees, on ledges, or on buildings.

BEHAVIOUR

Pigeons and doves are gregarious birds, and often feed in flocks. Left undisturbed, they may eat methodically, taking all food within reach before moving on. In dry regions, most species feed primarily on seeds; in the humid tropics, the majority eat fruit. They almost always swallow their food whole – even with fruit the size of a golfball. Unlike most birds, they drink by sucking up water, rather than tipping back their heads. Pigeons typically lay up to three eggs, and their young grow rapidly, some flying when just two weeks old. On the nest, parents feed the young on a secretion produced from the lining of the crop.

LIQUID MEAL
Reaching into its parent's throat, a young Woodpigeon feeds on pigeon "milk", a secretion stimulated by the hormone prolactin, which triggers milk-production in mammals.

ANATOMY

Pigeons and doves show wide variations in colour, from greys and browns, to rich and vivid mixtures of hues – oriental fruit-doves are particularly colourful. Despite these differences, pigeons and doves all have the same recognizable shape, with plump body, small head, and a fleshy base to the bill. Their flight muscles are exceptionally powerful, making them some of the fastest flying land birds. Most pigeons have small bills, often with a fleshy cere. A few are ornamented with feathery crests.

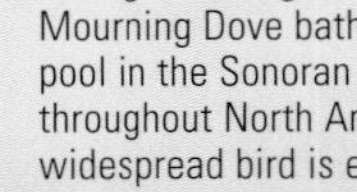

REFRESHING DIP
Taking advantage of spring rain, a Mourning Dove bathes in a temporary pool in the Sonoran Desert. Found throughout North America, this widespread bird is equally at home in deserts and suburban backyards.

HUMAN IMPACT

THREATS AND CONSERVATION

The world's most famous extinct bird – the Dodo – was a giant flightless pigeon, and the Passenger Pigeon became extinct in 1914. Now, 26 species of pigeon and dove are endangered; 11 are on the critical list. Most of these birds come from the tropics, particularly the western Pacific. The biggest threats are hunting, introduced predators, and deforestation.

MINDANAO BLEEDING-HEART
Found only in the Philippines, this fruit-eating dove has undergone a catastrophic decline as a result of trapping, and of forest clearance. Many other pigeons, especially island residents, face similar problems.

Columba guinea

Speckled Pigeon

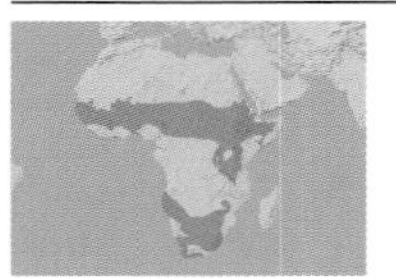

LENGTH 32–35cm (12½–14in)
WEIGHT 225–400g (8–14oz)
MIGRATION Non-migrant

HABITAT Open country, from savanna to gardens, including highland regions

ADULT AT WATER HOLE

Taking its name from its white-spotted wings, the Speckled Pigeon has a bifurcated neck collar and bare red or purple skin around the eye. It gathers in large flocks to feed on harvested grain and may also take snails. It mainly nests in the dry season, sometimes building a robust stick nest, but occasionally just using a bare scrape. The Speckled Pigeon is generally common and appears to be increasing in many areas. It is expanding into towns and agricultural areas, from its traditional habitat of wild, rocky areas.

Columba janthina

Japanese Wood Pigeon

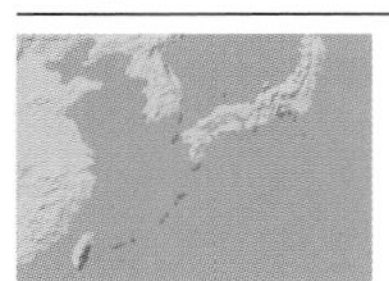

LENGTH 37–44cm (14½–17½in)
WEIGHT 400g (14oz)
MIGRATION Non-migrant

HABITAT Heavily dependent on mature forest

The Japanese Wood Pigeon is sooty black, with green and purple iridescences on the head and neck, and has a long tail. It lives mainly on seeds, buds, and fruits, taken from trees or the ground. Unlike many pigeons, it is not a sociable bird. It lays a single egg in a nest constructed in a tree-hole or rock crevice. The species is declining due to ongoing deforestation, which has already led to its extinction on some islands.

TYPICALLY SOLITARY ADULT

Columba livia

Common Pigeon

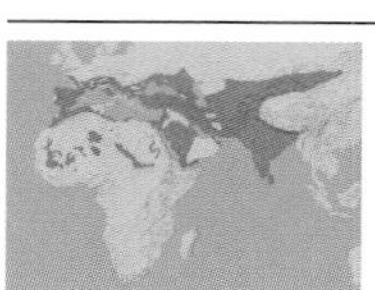

LENGTH 31–34cm (12–13½in)

WEIGHT 175–350g (6–13oz)

MIGRATION Non-migrant

HABITAT Wild, rocky regions (wild populations); cities (domestic birds)

The Common Pigeon is familiar in urban areas throughout the world. The domestic form is one of the world's most successful birds. In contrast, pure-bred wild populations, which are restricted to Eurasia and Africa, are now increasingly rare due to interbreeding with feral birds. The wild form of the species is generally grey, with iridescent areas on the neck and upper breast, but urban Common Pigeons are variable. Urban birds may nest all year-round.

URBAN COMMON PIGEONS

HUMAN IMPACT

URBAN PIGEON

The original homing pigeons, the Common Pigeon has adapted to life in towns and cities across the world. However, there are concerns that the species' sheer abundance and habit of roosting communally may create public health problems in some areas or drive out other bird species.

ADULT MALE

Columba palumbus

Common Wood Pigeon

LENGTH 41–45cm (16–17½in)

WEIGHT 275–700g (10–25oz)

MIGRATION Partial migrant

HABITAT Woodland, especially in arable farmland; parks and gardens, including urban areas

The Common Wood Pigeon can be identified by its white neck patch, pink breast, grey back, and white bands in the wings. Its wing-clapping displays and hollow calls are familiar sights and sounds of the countryside in its range. In recent decades, the species has expanded its range northwards and into towns and cities.

Nesoenas mayeri

Pink Pigeon

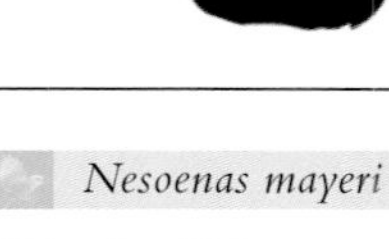

LENGTH 40cm (15½in)

WEIGHT 300–325g (11–12oz)

MIGRATION Non-migrant

HABITAT Native forest on the island of Mauritius

RED LIST CATEGORY Endangered

Once brought to the brink of extinction by deforestation, the population of the Pink Pigeon has recovered in recent years due to dedicated conservation efforts. This large pigeon has a white face and forehead, a strong bill with a hooked tip, and brown wings. It has a soft pink body, but the female and juvenile are a duller pink than the male.

ADULT MALE

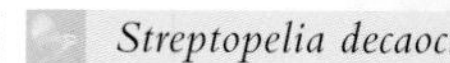

Streptopelia decaocto

Eurasian Collared Dove

LENGTH 30–32cm (12–12½in)

WEIGHT 125–200g (4–7oz)

MIGRATION Non-migrant

HABITAT Originally arid country, but now common in towns, villages, and even large cities

One of the most remarkable avian success stories, Eurasian Collared Dove's have spread dramatically across Europe from its original Asian range within the last 100 years, and is now in the process of colonizing North America. The most conspicuous marking on this principally grey and buff bird is the dark partial neck ring. Its food is mainly seed-based, supplemented with beetles, flies, and molluscs. It constructs fragile stick nests and sometimes begins its nesting season in midwinter.

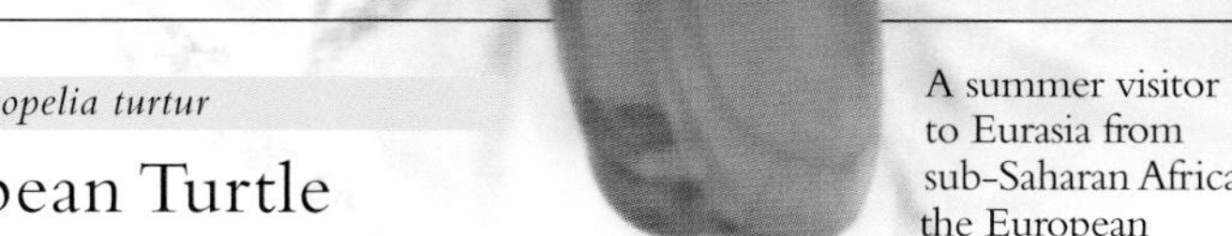

ADULT WITH FEATHERS FLUFFED-UP

Streptopelia turtur

European Turtle Dove

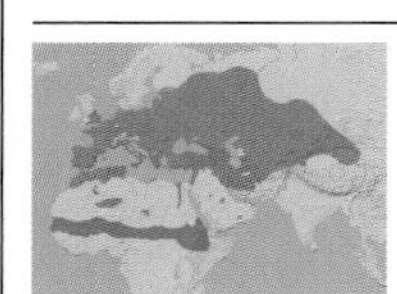

LENGTH 27–29cm (10½–11½in)

WEIGHT 100–175g ($3^5/_8$–6oz)

MIGRATION Migrant

HABITAT Principally found in woodland, but also open country with some trees; avoids dense forest

A summer visitor to Eurasia from sub-Saharan Africa, the European Turtle Dove's range is declining in several European countries due to changing agricultural practices and hunting. Its head, neck, and rump are blue-grey, with a black and white striped patch on the sides of its neck, and its wings are beautifully patterned in cinnamon and black. It breeds in bushes or trees and feeds on seeds, fruit, insects, worms, and snails.

ADULT EUROPEAN TURTLE DOVE

Oena capensis

Namaqua Dove

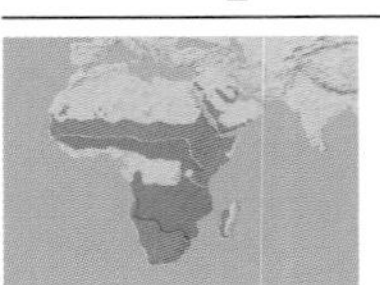

LENGTH 28cm (11in)

WEIGHT 40g ($1^{7}/_{16}$oz)

MIGRATION Partial migrant

HABITAT Open savanna and thorn-scrub, particularly in sandy areas; cultivated areas

The small Namaqua Dove has a very long, tapered black tail, and its plumage is mostly grey, apart from a white belly and black wing spots. The male also has a black face, throat, and breast. Its song is a quiet, mournful "kuh-whooo", which is frequently repeated. The Namaqua Dove usually forages on open ground and roadsides, seeking out small seeds. These doves are usually solitary or found in pairs, but form flocks at waterholes.

ADULT MALE NAMAQUA DOVE

Phaps chalcoptera

Common Bronzewing

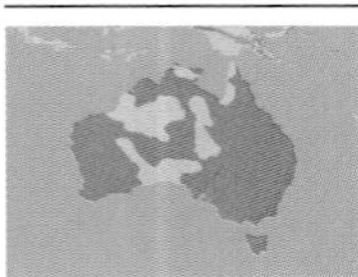

LENGTH 28–36cm (11–14in)

WEIGHT 325–350g (12–13oz)

MIGRATION Non-migrant

HABITAT Almost every habitat type, except for very barren areas, very dense rainforest, and urban areas

The beautiful iridescent wing markings give this bird its name. Depending on the light, these markings are green, turquoise, bronze, red, or purple. Both sexes have black and white eye-lines. The male has a buff-white forehead and pink breast, while in the female these parts are grey. A large pigeon, the Common Bronzewing is found in most parts of Australia.

Pairs or small flocks of Common Bronzewings forage on the ground for seeds and other vegetable matter, They are rarely found far from water and frequently visit water holes. The Common Bronzewing is a ground-feeder, and is also capable of very fast flight. This shy bird tends to feed quietly until disturbed, then remains still, blending into the ground and leaf litter until the potential predator comes too close, at which point it flies up with a noisy flapping of wings, before continuing in a low, direct flight.

Both parents share the incubation of the creamy white eggs and feed the young. The call of the Common Bronzewing is a mournful "whooo", repeated at intervals.

MALE COMMON BRONZEWING

Geophaps plumifera

Spinifex Pigeon

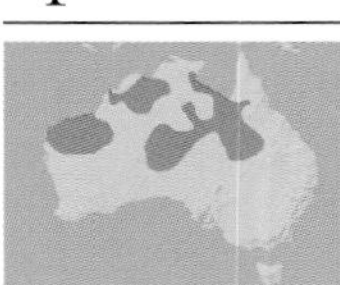

LENGTH 20–24cm (8–$9^{1}/_{2}$in)

WEIGHT 100g ($3^{5}/_{8}$oz)

MIGRATION Non-migrant

HABITAT Dry grassland dominated by tussock-forming spinifex grasses; open woodland with rocky ridges

A very long wispy crest and its tiny size distinguish the Spinifex Pigeon. This pigeon is mainly rust in colour, blending with the red soil of the arid areas that it inhabits. It has bright red facial skin, a bold white chin-strap, and pale blue-grey and black markings on the head. Its upperparts are marked by black and pale blue-grey bands. The male and female are similar.

There are three different subspecies, each showing different amounts of rufous coloration on the underparts. The Spinifex Pigeon lives mainly on the ground and, when flushed, rises with a quail-like whirr of the wings. It is almost exclusively a seed-eater and is dependent on seasonal water holes for its survival. Its call is a high-pitched "coo" or a deep "coo-r-r-r".

The nest is a simple scrape, sheltered by a spinifex clump, bush, or rock.

ADULT SPINIFEX PIGEON

ADULT DIAMOND DOVE

Geopelia cuneata

Diamond Dove

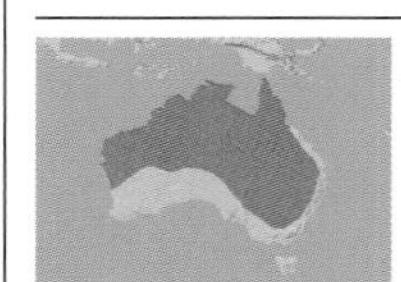

LENGTH 19–24cm ($7^{1}/_{2}$–$9^{1}/_{2}$in)

WEIGHT 30g ($^{7}/_{8}$oz)

MIGRATION Non-migrant

HABITAT Lightly wooded, semi-arid or arid grassland near water

This tiny, long-tailed dove is widespread across Australia. Its grey head and neck offset a red eye-ring and its wings are sprinkled with white spots. Flocks of 20–30 Diamond Doves can often be seen feeding on the ground on grass seeds, as well as other vegetable matter and even ants. Their calls are slow and mournful, and the flight style is strong and direct. The flimsy nest is built from interwoven grasses and twigs, and holds two white eggs. Chicks are usually fully feathered and are able to fly within two weeks after hatching.

Leucosarcia melanoleuca

Wonga Pigeon

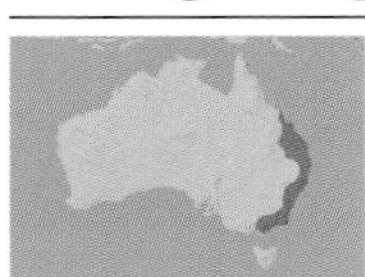

LENGTH 38–45cm (15–$17^{1}/_{2}$in)

WEIGHT 400–450g (14–16oz)

MIGRATION Non-migrant

HABITAT Dense forest and shrub in gullies or open woodland with a dense understorey

The large, plump Wonga Pigeon has a short neck, long tail, and boldly patterned grey and white plumage. There is a broken grey breast-band below an incomplete white V-shape on the neck and breast. It has black spots on the belly. The eyes are dark red-brown in colour, with pink eye-rings encircling them. A terrestrial bird, it is very elusive and more often heard than seen, producing a loud, high-pitched "coo", as well as explosive wing-claps. When males display, they bow and coo.

ADULT WITH TYPICAL CHEST MARKINGS

Zenaida macroura

Mourning Dove

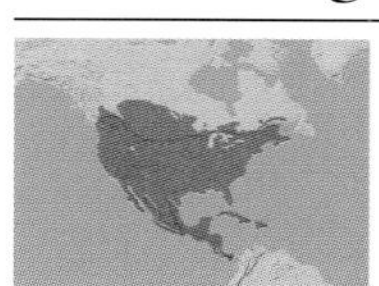

LENGTH 23–34cm (9–13½in)

WEIGHT 125g (4oz)

MIGRATION Partial migrant

HABITAT Wide range of open and semi-open habitats, including urban areas

Common and widespread in North America, the Mourning Dove has grey-brown plumage, a black spot on the cheek, distinctive black spotting on the wings, and black and white markings on its long tail. It calls with a clear, mournful "woo-oo-oo-oo", from which it gets its common name. Northern birds are migratory – those from Canada travel the furthest, probably wintering in Mexico or further south.

ADULT MOURNING DOVE

FRAGILE NEST

The Mourning Dove builds a very thin, twig nest typical of this family in the branches of a tree, shrub, or cactus. Sometimes, however, it makes its nest on the ground. The female usually lays two white eggs, which are incubated for about two weeks. After hatching, the chicks stay in the nest for 12–14 days. "Pigeon's milk", a fluid secreted from the crop lining of both parents is fed to the young.

Scardafella inca

Inca Dove

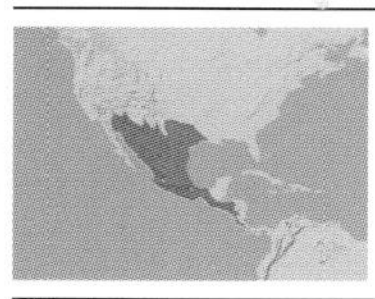

LENGTH 19–22cm (7½–8½in)

WEIGHT 50g (1¾oz)

MIGRATION Non-migrant

HABITAT Open dry areas, brushy woodland, and cultivated areas

Small and slim, the Inca Dove has a grey-brown body covered in black scaly markings. The male is flushed with pink on the forehead and breast, but this colour is less obvious on the female's plumage. The tail is quite long and square-ended, with white feather edges that show in flight. When it takes off, the wings make a distinctive quiet, rattling noise. This is a terrestrial species that primarily eats seeds, grain, and some fruit and grit. This species may obtain much of the liquid it needs to survive from fruit. It is seldom seen in flocks. The song is a forceful cooing "cowl-coo" or "poo-pup", usually from a tree, wire, or other open high perch such as a television aerial. The flimsy twig nest is built 1-8m (3¼–26ft) high in a tree, often a thorny one, and two white eggs are normally laid.

Despite being named after the Inca empire, this species does not occur in any of the areas that constituted it. The Inca Dove is found in Central America and southern USA, but is expanding its range to the north and south.

FEMALE INCA DOVE

Leptotila verreauxi

White-tipped Dove

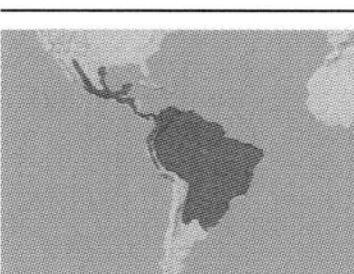

LENGTH 24–30cm (9½–12in)

WEIGHT 150g (5oz)

MIGRATION Non-migrant

HABITAT Arid or semi-arid forest edges, open woodland, and scrub, including cultivated areas

This widespread Neotropical dove has a specially shaped primary feather on its forewing, which enables it to quickly change speed and direction when faced with an obstacle. It is rather nondescript, apart from its pale underside and white-tipped tail, the adult White-tipped Dove has a grey crown and a grey hindneck that glistens with a purple iridescence, while the wing linings are chestnut in colour. It has purple-red legs and feet. The eye-ring ranges from red to blue in the southernmost populations. Its song resembles a small deep-sounding foghorn, "oo-whooooo" or "hu' woo wooooo".

This species feeds mainly on the ground and eats fallen tree seeds and fruit, grasses, prickly pear cacti, some cultivated grains, and large insects such as grasshoppers and crickets. It is either solitary or found in pairs, never in flocks. Both parents incubate the eggs for 14 days and feed and rear the juveniles.

ADULT WHITE-TIPPED DOVE

ADULT KEY WEST QUAIL-DOVE

Geotrygon chrysia

Key West Quail-dove

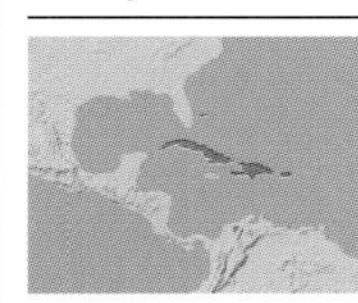

LENGTH 27–31cm (10½–12in)

WEIGHT 175g (6oz)

MIGRATION Non-migrant

HABITAT Semi-arid woodland and scrub forest; wet lower montane forest

This small, short-tailed ground-dwelling dove was first discovered in Key West, hence its name. Although it no longer breeds in Florida, it still turns up there as a vagrant. It has a green iridescence on its crown and hindneck and purple iridescence on the mantle. The white facial stripe is a distinctive feature. This bird forages on the ground, eating seeds and fruit. It nests in a low shrub or on the ground, and lays two buff-coloured eggs.

Starnoenas cyanocephala

Blue-headed Quail-dove

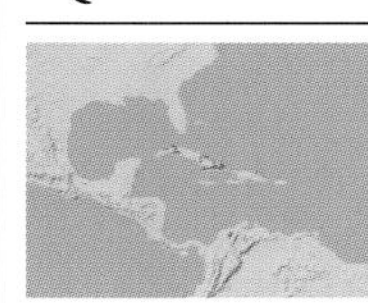

LENGTH 29–35cm (11½–14in)

WEIGHT 225g (8oz)

MIGRATION Non-migrant

HABITAT Understorey and floor of lowland forest, including wet swamps

RED LIST CATEGORY Endangered

This stunning ground dove is an endangered species due to habitat loss and over-hunting. It sports a bright blue cap, bold black and white stripes on the face, black and blue stripes on the neck, and a black bib with a white fringe. The bill is red with a blue tip. These doves feed on seeds, berries, and snails and live on the ground in pairs.

ADULT BIRD

Caloenas nicobaricus

Nicobar Pigeon

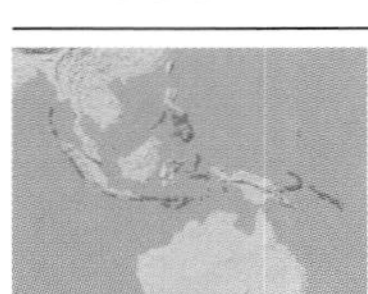

LENGTH 32–35cm ($12\frac{1}{2}$–14in)

WEIGHT 500–600g (18–21oz)

MIGRATION Non-migrant

HABITAT Various forested small tropical islands

Distinguished by its dark green-and copper-glossed plumage, long neck feathers (hackles), and short white tail, this pigeon has a curious knob on top of its bill. With its strong legs, it is well adapted to its ground-dwelling existence, seeking out seeds, fruit, and insects. It lays a single faintly blue-tinged, white egg. Some DNA studies suggest that the Nicobar Pigeon is the closest living relative of the extinct Dodo.

ADULT NICOBAR PIGEON

ADULT VICTORIA CROWNED PIGEON

Goura victoria

Victoria Crowned Pigeon

LENGTH 66–74cm (26–29in)

WEIGHT 2.5kg ($5\frac{1}{2}$lb)

MIGRATION Non-migrant

HABITAT Swamp and sago palm forests and also drier forests

RED LIST CATEGORY Vulnerable

With its stunning crest, blue plumage, and pale tail spots, this enormous red-eyed pigeon is distinctive. It lives mainly on the ground, but noisily flies up to perch on a branch when disturbed. It is found in pairs or small groups, and feeds on insects and fallen fruit, figs, and seeds. The nest is relatively neat and solid for a pigeon, being constructed of leaves as well as twigs and stems. The single egg takes four weeks to hatch.

LACE-LIKE CREST

The spectacular crest of lacy feathers on the head of the Victoria Crowned Pigeon consists of laterally compressed white-tipped blue feathers in small individual fan-shaped clusters. When the crest is raised, it fans out, giving the appearance of an exquisite lacey crown, so large and beautiful that it has led to widespread hunting of the species.

Gallicolumba luzonica

Luzon Bleeding-heart

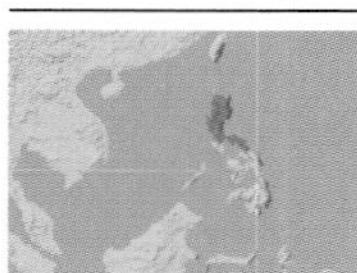

LENGTH 30cm (12in)

WEIGHT 200g (7oz)

MIGRATION Non-migrant

HABITAT Primary and secondary broad-leaved evergreen forest

This secretive, ground-dwelling dove gets its name from the vivid blood-red patch at the centre of its white breast, which gives the impression of a bleeding wound. Its plumage is grey above and buff below. It walks on the forest floor in search of seeds, small fruit, and grubs, rarely leaving the ground, except when nesting. It usually lays two eggs.

ADULT LUZON BLEEDING-HEART

Treron calva

African Green Pigeon

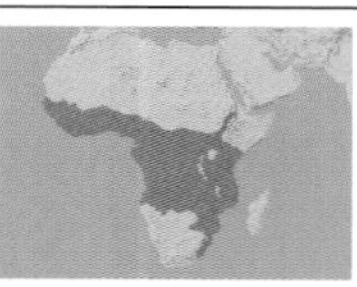

LENGTH 25–30cm (10–12in)

WEIGHT 175–225g (6–8oz)

MIGRATION Non-migrant

HABITAT Various types of forest and woodland, forest edges, and mangroves

ADULT AFRICAN GREEN PIGEON

With its bright red bill base and feet, combined with green upperparts, this African Green Pigeon is easily spotted. There are at least 17 subspecies, which differ in the amount of grey in the plumage and the colour of the feet. African Green Pigeons live in small flocks in dense foliage. Quiet, shy, and almost entirely arboreal, they rarely come to the ground. A fruit-loving species, they often gather in large numbers to feed on fruiting fig trees.

Ptilinopus magnificus

Wompoo Fruit Dove

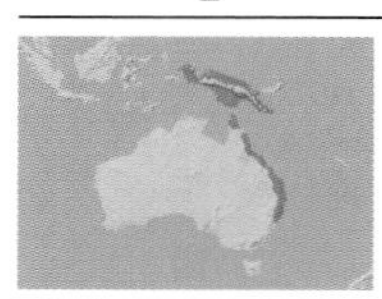

LENGTH 29–45cm ($11\frac{1}{2}$–18in)

WEIGHT 175–200g (6–7oz)

MIGRATION Non-migrant

HABITAT Lowland tropical rainforest; also eucalyptus forest and farmland in winter

The impressive Wompoo Fruit Dove is the largest of its family. In addition to its size, its yellow wing markings and a long tail also help to make it prominent. The head of this fruit dove is grey, the bill red and yellow, and the underparts purple with a yellow vent. The sexes look similar, but juveniles have a duller plumage compared to the adults. Despite all these bright colours, however, the bird can be very hard to see in the dense canopy foliage. The only signal revealing its presence is its call, a very human-sounding deep "wollack-wa-hoo".

Like other fruit doves, it feeds on fruit-bearing trees, such as figs. The Wompoo Fruit Dove can eat large fruit whole, and is also able to collect fruit by acrobatically springing forward from trees and vines. The nest of twigs, a sturdy construction placed on leafy branches, is built by both the male and female. A single white egg is laid, and the parents share the incubation and care of the chick. If the chick dies, the doves usually have time to try to breed again. Eight different subspecies are recognized, the largest birds being in the south of its range and lowland New Guinea.

ADULT WOMPOO FRUIT DOVE

Ptilinopus regina

Rose-crowned Fruit Dove

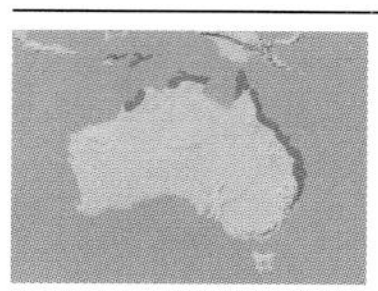

LENGTH 22–24cm (9–9½in)

WEIGHT 100g (3⅝oz)

MIGRATION Non-migrant

HABITAT Variety of forest types; mangroves

ADULT ROSE-CROWNED FRUIT DOVE

The Rose-crowned Fruit Dove is one of a number of vividly coloured fruit doves that are found in Indonesia and Australasia. Its most distinctive features are its streaky grey breast and orange belly. The red crown, with a yellow band behind it, is only shown by three of the five subspecies. The male and female are similar, but young birds are greener with no red on the crown.

The Rose-crowned Fruit Dove eats a wide variety of fruit. It calls with a loud, explosive "hookcoo" or "woo-hoo", which becomes a rapid "coocoocoocoocoo".

ADULT MALE

Ptilinopus superbus

Superb Fruit Dove

LENGTH 21–24cm (8½–9½in)

WEIGHT 125g (4oz)

MIGRATION Non-migrant

HABITAT Tropical broad-leaved evergreen forest, mangroves, and plantations

Despite the bright colours of its plumage, this dove can be surprisingly well camouflaged in the dense foliage of the rainforest canopy. The brilliantly coloured male has a purple cap, green ear-feathers, orange-red collar, and blue and green bands on the underparts. The female is mostly green with a small blue-black patch at the back of the crown. Large numbers of these doves sometimes gather in the canopy of fruiting trees to feed. The nest is a small platform of twigs. The call of this species is a steady "coo-coo-coo-coo".

Alectroenas madagascariensis

Madagascar Blue Pigeon

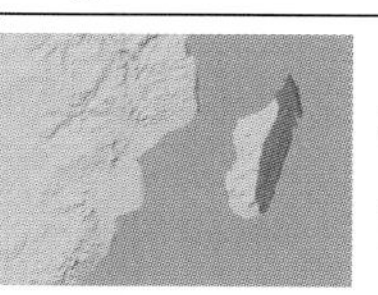

LENGTH 25–28cm (10–11in)

WEIGHT 175g (6oz)

MIGRATION Non-migrant

HABITAT Undisturbed primary and degraded tropical broad-leaved evergreen forest

This species is found only in the diminishing tropical forests of eastern Madagascar. The Madagascar Blue Pigeon has beautiful silvery blue-grey plumage. It has a patch of red skin around the eye and a blood-red tail and undertail feathers. Little is known about the habits of the Madagascar Blue Pigeon, but it lives in pairs or small flocks of up to 12 or more. It searches for fruiting trees, where it prefers to feed in the treetops. This bird breeds from July to March.

ADULT IN A FRUIT TREE

Ducula aenea

Green Imperial Pigeon

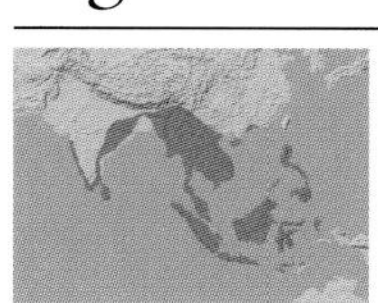

LENGTH 40–47cm (16–18½in)

WEIGHT 545g (20oz)

MIGRATION Non-migrant

HABITAT Various types of forest, forest edges, and mangroves

ADULT BIRD

A large bird, the Green Imperial Pigeon has a pale grey head, neck, and underparts, while the upperparts, wings, and tail are mostly green. Its flight is rapid and direct and it utters a deep, booming call. This pigeon lives in the canopy of tropical forests, where it forages for fruit.

Lopholaimus antarcticus

Topknot Pigeon

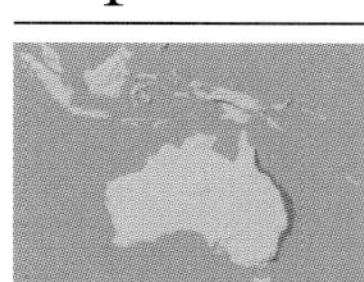

LENGTH 40–45cm (15½–17½in)

WEIGHT 450–525g (16–19oz)

MIGRATION Non-migrant

HABITAT Rainforest, sometimes in more open areas during nomadic movements

This large Australian Pigeon has an unusual crest of elongated feathers on its forecrown. This crest bulges out and then sweeps back over the crown, blending into a second crest of rufous and black feathers that hangs over the nape. Otherwise, it is mainly grey, but has a narrow silver-grey band on its slaty-black tail.

A nomadic species, the Topknot Pigeon is generally found in flocks that can number up to hundreds, making seasonal movements in search of food. It tends to feed on fruit in the canopy, but often rests on exposed branches. This species can get water by drinking raindrops trapped in foliage. Breeding occurs from July to January, when a nest of long, loose twigs is built high up in a rainforest tree. One large, slightly glossy egg is laid.

ADULT TOPKNOT PIGEON

Hemiphaga novaeseelandiae

New Zealand Pigeon

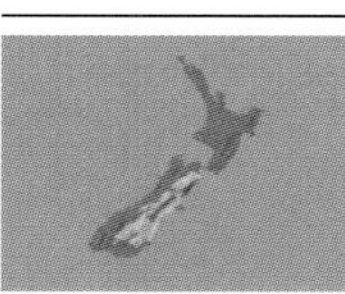

LENGTH 46–50cm (18–19½in)

WEIGHT 650–800g (23–29oz)

MIGRATION Non-migrant

HABITAT Lowland native forest and plantations; also rural and city gardens and parks

The New Zealand Pigeon is the second largest member of the Columbidae family. Its plumage is mostly shiny greenish purple, with a contrasting white belly and vent. The bill is red to orange, and the eyes and feet are red.

The call of this pigeon is a soft "coo". It mainly feeds on fruit from trees. It plays an important ecological role in the regeneration of native forests, as it is the only species of bird capable of eating the largest fruit and dispersing the seeds intact. It also browses on leaves and buds, particularly when breeding. The species breeds predominantly in summer and nests in trees, laying a single egg in a twig nest. The egg is incubated for 28 days, and the young take five weeks to leave the nest.

PARROTS

ORDER	Psittaciformes
FAMILY	1
SPECIES	352

NOISY, GREGARIOUS, and often brilliantly coloured, parrots are some of the most eyecatching tropical birds of all. They are native to every continent except Europe, in a variety of different habitats, but the greatest numbers live in forests, particularly in southeast Asia and Australasia. Prized for their beauty, intelligence, and ability to mimic human speech, they continue to be threatened by collectors and deforestation.

CONSPICUOUS CRESTS
Unlike typical parrots, this Major Mitchell's Cockatoo has a crest that it can raise or lower. Cockatoos are often placed in a separate family, as they share a number of distinctive features.

ANATOMY

Parrots vary in length from about 8cm (3in), in the case of pygmy parrots, to over 1m (3¼ft) in the case of large macaws. Unlike some birds, they share a number of visible physical features that make them easy to recognize. Among these characteristics are plump bodies, short necks, and strongly decurved bills with a fleshy cere (region of bare skin) at the base. Their feet have four fleshy toes, with two pointing forwards and two pointing behind. Some parrots have long, sharply pointed wings, while in others they are broad and rounded. In parakeets, lorikeets, and macaws, the tail is long and graduated, but in some other species it is short and square.

CLASSIC FEATURES
The White-cheeked Rosella, from Australia, is a typical medium-sized parrot. Like all parrots, it has a decurved bill, with the maxilla closing over the mandible. Its legs are fairly short, but its toes are well developed, with strong claws.

GETTING A GRIP
Holding a nut in one of its feet, this Blue-throated Macaw demonstrates the extraordinary dexterity shown by many parrots.

PLUMAGE

Parrot plumage is often boldly coloured – a feature particularly noticeable in macaws, lorikeets, and rosellas, species that have long been prized as cage-birds. Many of these colours are created by the microscopic structure of the feathers, rather than by chemical pigments. However, not all parrots are this flamboyant. A number of species of Australian cockatoo are almost entirely white and others are a dull brownish black. Whatever their colour, all parrots have large quantities of powder down, which gives their feathers a dusty feel. In the majority of parrots, males and females are similar or identical. Where the sexes do differ, the males are usually brighter than the females.

HABITATS

The majority of parrots are birds of forests and open woodland, with the largest number found in rainforest and cloudforest in the tropics, but in the southern hemisphere they are widespread in temperate regions as well. Some parrots have successfully adapted to open grassland, such as the savanna-like cerrado of Brazil or the Australian "outback", where a scattering of trees allows them to nest. Australia's parrots include a number of species that feed on the ground, while New Zealand is the home of the endangered Kakapo – the world's heaviest parrot, and the only species that has lost the ability to fly. Parakeets have successfully established themselves as urban birds in some parts of the world, including in Europe and North America.

MOUNTAIN PARROT
The Kea, from New Zealand, is one of the few parrots that tolerates temperatures close to freezing. It lives in the mountains of the country's South Island, sometimes above the snowline.

SETTING UP HOME
Having found a suitable nest-hole, a male Budgerigar feeds the female – a common part of parrot courtship behaviour. Budgerigars live in open grassland and scrubland, where tree-holes can be hard to find. They often nest in fallen branches, or in old fenceposts.

NESTING AND PARENTING

As a group, parrots share remarkably similar nesting habits. Most species lay their eggs – which can number up to 10 – in tree-holes, using little or no nesting material. One of the few exceptions to this is the Monk Parakeet, from Argentina and southern Brazil. In this species, several dozen birds work together to build a giant nest from twigs, with each pair occupying a separate "apartment". Initially, young parrots are naked when they hatch, but they soon grow a covering of down. Their heads and beaks are well developed, and their parents feed them by regurgitation. For many parrots, the supply of suitable nest-holes has a pronounced effect on breeding success. Many parrots take over old woodpecker holes, but in Australasia, where there are no woodpeckers, parrots sometimes use old termite nests instead.

FEEDING AND SOCIAL LIFE

Most parrots feed on plants. Large macaws and cockatoos can crack open nuts the size of golf balls, while at the other end of the scale, small parrots such as Budgerigars eat grass-seeds, using their tongues to roll each seed around in their beaks, so that they can discard the husk. Lorikeets specialize in feeding on pollen and nectar, which they collect with tongues that have brush-like tips. Pygmy parrots are unusual in eating insects, which they prise from crevices in bark, but New Zealand's parrots excel in unusual eating habits. The flightless Kakapo feeds on the juices from grasses, while the Kea is a natural opportunist, feeding on carrion and leftover food. The Antipodes Parakeet scavenges dead remains in penguin colonies, and even kills storm petrels in their burrows.

Parrots are highly social birds, and are rarely seen on their own. Many species live in pairs, or in noisy flocks, setting off shortly after dawn in search of food. Large parrots, such as macaws, typically fly in groups of 2–20 birds, but some species – such as Galahs – gather in much larger numbers, and can be serious agricultural pests.

GALAHS FEEDING
Small, highly sociable cockatoos, Galahs are a common sight in open country throughout Australia, including the edges of towns. Unlike most parrots, they have benefited from the spread of farming.

PAIRED FOR LIFE
Parrots are long-lived birds, and they typically pair up for life. In the wild, Scarlet Macaws can live to be 50, but their life expectancy in captivity is even longer, sometimes reaching 80 years.

HUMAN IMPACT

ENDANGERED SPECIES

Parrots include a large number of threatened birds. Altogether, over 90 species are listed as being vulnerable or endangered, and of these, 17 are in imminent danger of becoming extinct in the wild. The two chief threats facing parrots are habitat destruction – particularly in tropical forests and on remote islands – and trapping for the cage-bird trade.

DWINDLING NUMBERS
Found only in a small part of eastern Brazil, Lear's Macaw is critically endangered, with fewer than 500 birds left in the wild.

ADULT KEA

Nestor notabilis

Kea

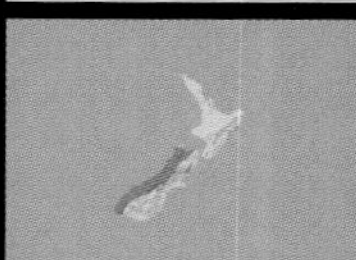

LENGTH 48cm (19in)

WEIGHT 800–950g (29–34oz)

MIGRATION Non-migrant

HABITAT Upland scrub and grassland in summer; wooded valleys in winter

RED LIST CATEGORY Vulnerable

Found only on New Zealand's South Island, the Kea is a large, stocky mountain bird. It is olive-green in colour, with dark-edged feathers and bright red underwings. It has a sharp, elongated, hooked bill, with a long upper mandible, and well-developed feet for foraging on the ground.

The Kea is an inquisitive species that can often be found near ski lodges or car parks, waiting to pick up food scraps. In these situations, the parrot can soon be a nuisance as it can easily strip rubber wiper blades and window trims from cars. Only about 5,000 individuals now remain. The species was protected in 1970 after more than 150,000 birds were legally shot when some birds were found to be feeding on sick sheep.

Strigops habroptila

Kakapo

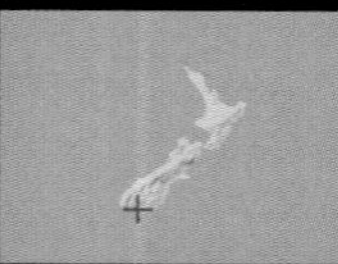

LENGTH 64cm (25in)

WEIGHT 1.5–3kg (3¼–6½lb)

MIGRATION Non-migrant

HABITAT Currently confined to forests on predator-free offshore islands

RED LIST CATEGORY Critically endangered

New Zealand's Kakapo is one of the most remarkable species of bird. As well as being nocturnal and flightless, it is very long-lived and is the world's heaviest parrot. The Kakapo has a rounded face that has led to its alternative name – the Owl-Parrot. It has barred green plumage and short wings. It breeds only once in every three to five years, when its favoured feeding plants are fruiting. The males gather at mating grounds (leks), where they excavate a series of bowl-shaped holes in the ground and make loud, booming calls to attract females.

Before human colonization, the Kakapo was found throughout New Zealand. However, by 1976 only 18 male birds remained. Conservationists then decided to take all the remaining birds into captivity under a breeding programme (see panel, below).

HUMAN IMPACT

KAKAPO RECOVERY PLAN

All remaining Kakapos have been transferred to a predator-free offshore island, where they are supervised by teams of dedicated conservationists. This has proved to be very successful and at the end of 2005, the birds numbered around 85 individuals – their highest level in more than 25 years.

ADULT KAKAPO

Loriculus vernalis

Vernal Hanging Parrot

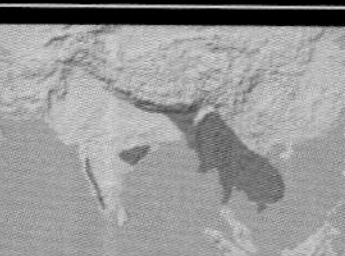

LENGTH 13cm (5in)

WEIGHT 35g (1¼oz)

MIGRATION Partial migrant

HABITAT Forest, woodland, orchards, bamboo thickets, and tall scrub

This small, squat species is found in much of coastal India and parts of China and Indochina. Its plumage is largely bright green, with slightly paler underparts. It has an orange-red bill, a pale blue patch on its throat, a red rump and tail patch, and orange-red legs. The eye stands out in the bird's plain face due to its noticeable pale iris. The female is paler and has little or no blue on its throat. The juvenile has a duller rump, and lacks the throat patch. This parrot nests in holes in trees and lays 2–4 white eggs.

MALE VERNAL HANGING PARROT

Probosciger aterrimus

Palm Cockatoo

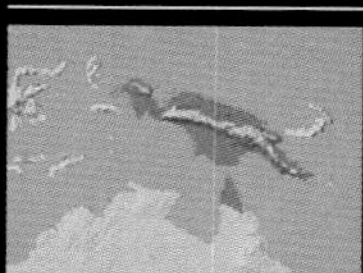

LENGTH 55–60cm (21½–23½in)

WEIGHT 850g (30oz)

MIGRATION Non-migrant

HABITAT Tropical foresr

The Palm Cockatoo is found in Papua New Guinea and Australia's Cape York peninsula. It is a large, all-black species, except for its bright red cheek patches: these are actually areas of bare skin that become darker in colour when the bird is alarmed or excited, giving the appearance of blushing. The male and female are similar in appearance, and have an impressive head crest of long, back-curved feathers. However, the most noticeable feature is the massive hooked bill, which, aided by very strong jaw muscles, is capable of exerting tremendous pressure to crush or crack tough nuts and seeds.

ADULT PALM COCKATOO

Calyptorhynchus banksii

Red-tailed Black Cockatoo

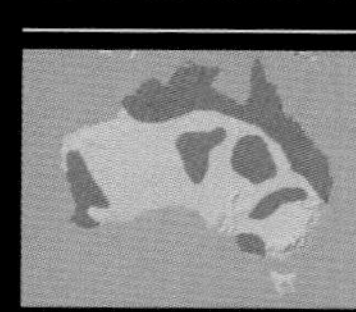

LENGTH 50–65cm (19½–26in)

WEIGHT 650–775g (23–28oz)

MIGRATION Non-migrant

HABITAT Forests, woodland, farmland, and semi-arid inland areas

A large, long-winged species, the Red-tailed Black Cockatoo appears almost like a hawk in flight. The male is all black, except for two bright red undertail patches. The female is browner, with yellow spotting on the head and shoulder and yellow barring on the breast. Its orange undertail feathers are barred, while the male has bold scarlet panels on the undertail. Both sexes have a rounded crest and a stubby bill. They nest in the large hollows of gum trees. The species is found only in Australia, where it has a wide but fragmented range.

MALE RED-TAILED BLACK COCKATOO

JUVENILE MALE

Callocephalon fimbriatum

Gang-gang Cockatoo

LENGTH 32–37cm (12½–14½in)

WEIGHT 275g (10oz)

MIGRATION Partial migrant

HABITAT Tall dense woodland, as well as parks and gardens in some areas

Noticeably different in appearance to the female, the male Gang-gang Cockatoo has a bright scarlet head, with a distinctively upturned, fluffy crest. The rest of the male's plumage is predominantly grey, appearing scaly (except on the all-dark tail) as the feathers are pale-edged. The female is less striking in appearance, with a grey head and crest. In contrast to the male, the female is brighter below, with buff-grey and red barring on the breast, and barring on the underside of the tail. The juvenile is similar to the female, although young males display a variable amount of pinkish red on the crest and crown. The call of the Gang-gang Cockatoo is a drawn-out, creaking rasp that sounds like a gate swinging on a rusty hinge.

This cockatoo is restricted to the southeastern corner of Australia. Although not an uncommon species, it can be difficult to see as it is usually silent, even when it is feeding. The Gang-gang Cockatoo is perhaps easiest to see in the botanical gardens of Canberra (see p. 361).

PAIR OF ADULT LITTLE CORELLAS

Cacatua sanguinea

Little Corella

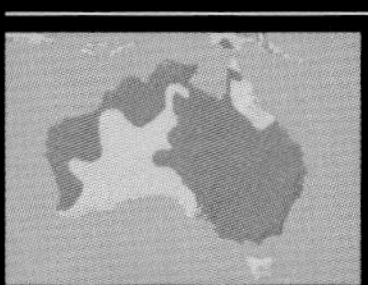

LENGTH 36–39cm (14–15½in)

WEIGHT 450–575g (16–21oz)

MIGRATION Non-migrant

HABITAT Grassland, farmland, and open woodland

When seen at rest, the Little Corella appears almost completely white. A number of subspecies occur, but all share a number of key features: a short bill, a small, pointed crest, an area of bare blue skin that circles the eye, and no pink or red on the throat. In flight, the Little Corella looks different from different angles: when seen from above, its wings are all-white; but when seen from below, a lemon-yellow underwing and tail are visible.

A very sociable species, these birds gather in large flocks in Australia's agricultural heartland and congregations of over 30,000 birds have been reported. As a result, the species is often regarded by farmers as a pest. The Little Corella is an abundant species throughout much of the interior of Australia, as well as being common in feral flocks in many urban areas of the east coast. The species is also found in southern Papua New Guinea.

Cacatua galerita

Sulphur-crested Cockatoo

LENGTH 45–55cm (17½–21½in)

WEIGHT 800–975g (29–35oz)

MIGRATION Non-migrant

HABITAT Forest, woodland, and farmland

The Sulphur-crested Cockatoo is a common sight in much of eastern and northern Australia; it also occurs throughout Papua New Guinea. It is a large white species with a striking lemon-yellow crest, a pale yellow tint behind the eye, and a strong dark bill. The crest is usually held flat, but can be raised as a tall, forward-curving adornment. The species flies with a stiff-winged series of flaps that are followed by long, swooping glides. When seen from below, a yellow wash to the underside of its wings and tail is visible. The calls of the species are a collection of raucous, noisy screeches that vary from ear-piercing squawks to guttural grunts.

In parts of southern Australia, the species forms huge flocks of hundreds of birds that roost along tree-lined watercourses, emerging en masse when disturbed, in an impressive cloud of white feathers and a cacophony of screeching sounds. However, in tropical Australia and New Guinea, the species is seldom seen in flocks of more than 20 birds. The Sulphur-crested Cockatoo's normal diet consists of berries, seeds, nuts, and roots.

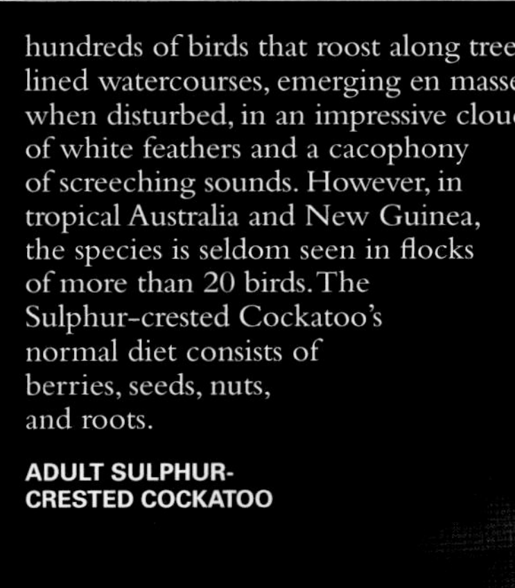

ADULT SULPHUR-CRESTED COCKATOO

Eolophus roseicapilla

Galah

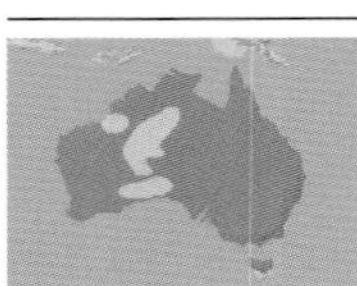

LENGTH 35cm (14in)

WEIGHT 350g (13oz)

MIGRATION Non-migrant

HABITAT Woodland, farmland, scrub, parks, and gardens

Found throughout most of Australia, the Galah has plumage in a splendid combination of grey and pink, its pinkish white cap and deep rose-pink underparts contrasting with its pale grey upperparts. The male and female are similar in appearance, differing only in eye colour – brown in the male and red in the female. In flight, the Galah is long-winged, appearing hawk-like from certain angles. The top part of the tail and rump appear a paler grey when seen from above. This bird flies in different ways – sometimes with deep wingbeats that carry it in a direct path; at other times, it flies erratically and randomly across the sky. The Galah has a distinctive metallic, high-pitched screeching call, and gives out harsher, scolding screeches when alarmed.

Galah is an aboriginal name for the species but has now entered common Australian usage to imply a "fool" or "idiot". The term is probably derived from the species's playful behaviour – it is not uncommon, for instance, for a Galah to hang upside-down from a branch or wire by one leg or for flocks of Galahs to be seen fighting and screeching at one another.

GALAH FLOCK

GREGARIOUS GALAHS

A very sociable species, Galahs are found in large flocks of up to a thousand birds. The flocks can be a nuisance when they descend to feed on agricultural crops. On a hot day, the birds gather for shelter among trees, which they often strip of bark and leaves. Large flocks form communal roosts, engaging in noisy acrobatics before settling down for the evening.

Trichoglossus haematodus

Rainbow Lorikeet

LENGTH 25–30cm (10–12in)

WEIGHT 85–125g (3–4oz)

MIGRATION Partial migrant

HABITAT Woodland, rainforest, open country with trees, mangroves, parks, and gardens

One of the most spectacularly plumaged of all parrots, the Rainbow Lorikeet is a brightly coloured bird in a stunning mixture of a flecked blue head, bright red eye and bill, bright yellow or orange collar, green upperparts, orange breast, and blue belly. The male and female are indistinguishable in appearance. Found across a wide range, this species includes a large number of different subspecies – at least 20 – some of which are much plainer and greener than the eastern Australian bird pictured here.

As the Rainbow Lorikeet darts through the trees, it shows a distinctive flight silhouette with its long tail and thin wings, which are angled back. Noisy in flight with loud screeches and chattering calls, it is quieter and more subdued when feeding or at rest. The Rainbow Lorikeet feeds mainly on flowers, searching out trees in blossom to feast on pollen and nectar. Massive flocks of birds also gather (and are a popular tourist attraction) in parts of Australia where sweet food is offered to them.

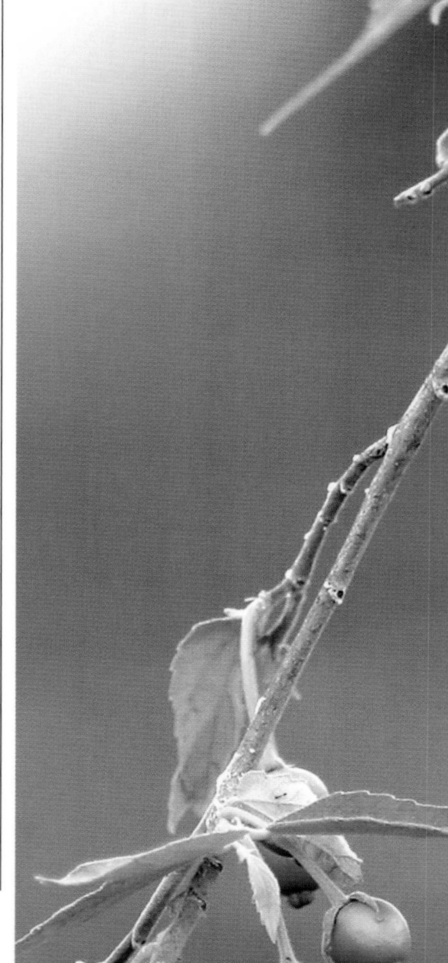

ADULT RAINBOW LORIKEET (EASTERN AUSTRALIAN SUBSPECIES)

Nymphicus hollandicus

Cockatiel

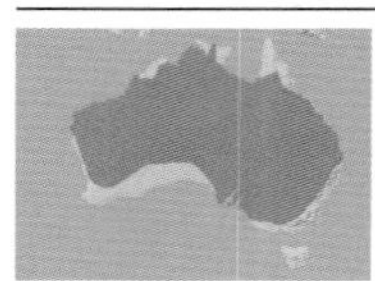

LENGTH 33cm (13in)

WEIGHT 80–100g ($2^{7}/_{8}$–$3^{5}/_{8}$oz)

MIGRATION Non-migrant

HABITAT Dry open country close to water, including open woodland, grassland, and farmland

A small, graceful cockatoo, the Cockatiel has a pointed bright yellow crest, a yellow face and throat, a large orange ear spot behind the eye, and a long tail. The rest of the plumage is pale grey, except for a large white wing-bar. The male and female are similar in appearance, although the male has more striking marks on the head. The Cockatiel has a swift direct flight. It usually forages for fruit and seeds in pairs or small groups.

MALE COCKATIEL

ADULT RED LORY

Eos rubra

Red Lory

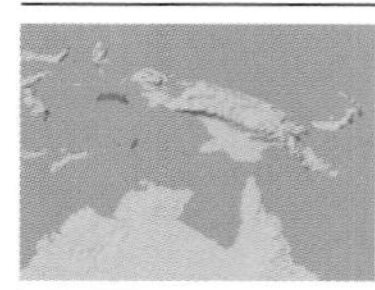

LENGTH 31cm (12in)

WEIGHT 150g (5oz)

MIGRATION Non-migrant

HABITAT Lowland forest, mangroves, and plantations

Found only in the Molucca islands of Indonesia, the Red Lory is a small, bright scarlet parrot with an orange bill, a blue patch on the wings, dark flight feathers, and dull grey legs. The species is usually found in flocks of up to 30 birds, gathering at flowering trees to feed on nectar with their brush-tipped tongues. Small parties frequently move between islands in parts of its range.

MALE VARIED LORIKEET

Psitteuteles versicolor

Varied Lorikeet

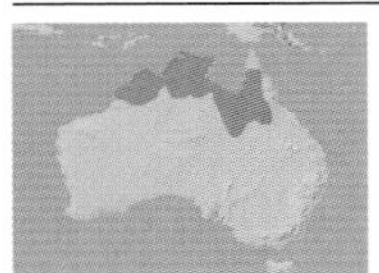

LENGTH 19cm (7½in)
WEIGHT 50–60g (1¾–2⅛oz)
MIGRATION Partial migrant

HABITAT Tropical woodland, particularly along watercourses

Found only in tropical northern Australia, the Varied Lorikeet is tiny and predominantly bright green, with generous yellow flecks on its plumage. The male has a bright scarlet cap, a white eye-ring, a yellow spot behind the eye, a mauve-pink patch on the upper breast, and paler plumage below. The female has less red on the crown, and the juvenile is duller overall.

The Varied Lorikeet feeds on flowers and fruit. Consequently, it is nomadic, moving about to find suitable trees in flower. A gregarious species, it is usually seen in family parties or small groups, although large flocks often gather to feast on nectar. The Varied Lorikeet is noisy when feeding, with its chattering, sharp screeches, and softer scolding calls. It can be quite aggressive, driving off other nectar-feeding species, such as honeyeaters.

Glossopsitta concinna

Musk Lorikeet

LENGTH 22cm (8½in)
WEIGHT 50–65g (1¾–2⅜oz)
MIGRATION Non-migrant

HABITAT Coastal woodland

FEMALE MUSK LORIKEET

The Musk Lorikeet is found only in a small coastal belt of southeastern Australia (including parts of Tasmania). It is a small, bright green parrot, with a crimson red forehead and "mask" behind the eye, and a yellow flash down the side of the breast. The male has a bright blue crown, which is turquoise and less well-defined in the female. The Musk Lorikeet is often found feeding in mixed flocks with other small species of lorikeet.

Charmosyna papou

Papuan Lorikeet

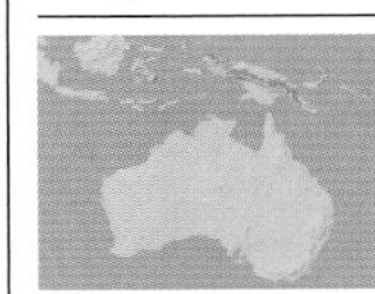

LENGTH 36–42cm (14–16½in)
WEIGHT 75–100g (2⅝–3⅝oz)
MIGRATION Non-migrant

HABITAT Upland forest

The Papuan Lorikeet has a bright red forehead, neck, breast, and back; green wings; dark blue flanks and crown; and a long tail with extravagant yellow streamers. The male and female are alike, except for the bright yellow back of the female. The juvenile is duller. A darker form of the species also occurs (apparently at higher altitudes) in which the red areas of plumage are replaced with black.

ADULT PAPUAN LORIKEET

Northiella haematogaster

Bluebonnet

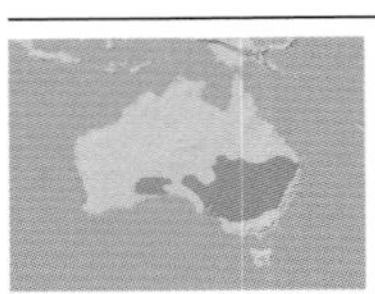

LENGTH 26–30cm (10–12in)

WEIGHT 95g (3$\frac{3}{8}$oz)

MIGRATION Non-migrant

HABITAT Woodland and open areas, including farmland; scrub and riverine forest

A spectacular bird while in flight, the Bluebonnet has a blue face and a bright orange and yellow belly, which is splendidly displayed when the bird is in the air. Its primary wing feathers are blue. The juvenile is also brightly coloured, but lacks some of the contrasting tones seen in the adult. This species feeds in pairs or small groups. It breeds in July–December; the female incubates the 4–7 eggs and is fed by the male for 20 days. Four subspecies of the Bluebonnet have been identified.

ADULT BLUEBONNET

MALE RED-FRONTED PARAKEET

Cyanoramphus novaezelandiae

Red-fronted Parakeet

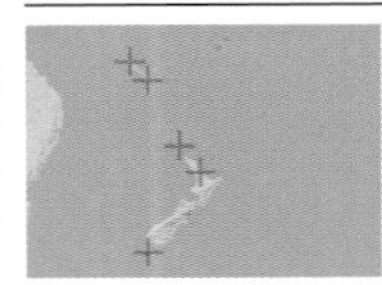

LENGTH 23–28cm (9–11in)

WEIGHT 70–125g (2$\frac{1}{2}$–4oz)

MIGRATION Non-migrant

HABITAT Native forest or scrub on islands

RED LIST CATEGORY Vulnerable

The Red-fronted Parakeet is mainly green in colour. However, it has a red eye-stripe, crown, and forehead. It feeds on fruit and seeds, and usually nests in a cavity, such as a rock crevice. Large clutches of up to 10 eggs have been reported, but the average is five eggs, laid in October–December. The female incubates the eggs but the male helps to feed the young.

Platycercus elegans

Crimson Rosella

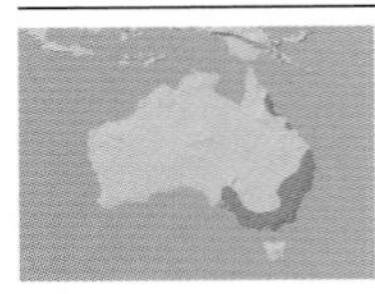

LENGTH 32–37cm (12$\frac{1}{2}$–14$\frac{1}{2}$in)

WEIGHT 125–150g (4–5oz)

MIGRATION Non-migrant

HABITAT Forested hills, up to 1,900m (6, 200ft)

Deep crimson and dark blue in colour, the Crimson Rosella is striking in appearance. Both sexes look similar, but the rich red colour is replaced by green in the juvenile. Three subspecies have been described in the species' natural range, which is largely restricted to the eastern and southeastern coast of Australia, although an isolated population exists in northeast Australia. The Crimson Rosella is often found in pairs or in small groups. Although the adults prefer to stay in the same area for years, the younger ones are nomadic, usually wandering in flocks of up to 30. Outside the breeding season, the species tends to disperse rather than be truly migratory. The diet of the Crimson Rosella is varied; it feeds on flowers and seeds of grasses, trees, and shrubs and even strips tree bark looking for insect larvae.

The male Crimson Rosella's courtship display consists of wing fanning, tail-wagging, and head-bobbing. The breeding season takes place between August and February, when 3–8 eggs are laid in a tree-hole. The male feeds the female during incubation and for a short period after the eggs hatch. The male also actively feeds the young for the period up to fledging.

FEEDING IN FLOCKS
Groups of Crimson Rosellas gather to feed on tree blossoms and the seeds of eucalyptus trees.

Psephotus varius

Mulga Parrot

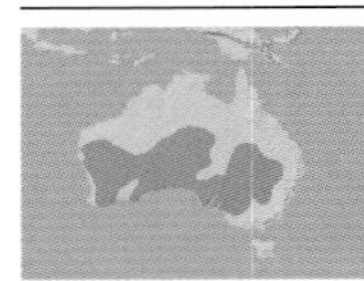

LENGTH 26–31cm (10–12in)

WEIGHT 60g (2$\frac{1}{8}$oz)

MIGRATION Non-migrant

HABITAT Dry woodland, open areas, and cultivated land

The Mulga Parrot is also known as the Varied Parrot, reflecting its spectacular contrasts of colour. Its plumage is mainly green, but it has a yellow forehead and upper face, with a red nape and rump. The breeding season lasts from July to December, although it also breeds during the rains. The young remain with the parents to form family groups after fledging.

PAIR OF MULGA PARROTS

Psephotus haematonotus

Red-rumped Parrot

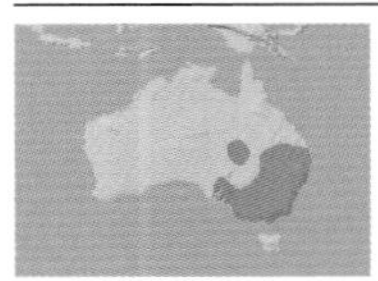

LENGTH 25–28cm (10–11in)

WEIGHT 60g (2$\frac{1}{8}$oz)

MIGRATION Non-migrant

HABITAT Wet areas up to 1,000m (3,300ft) and suburban habitats

MALE RED-RUMPED PARROT

The Red-rumped Parrot is not really an apt name for this bird, because its most spectacular feature is the bright mix of green, blue, and yellow in its plumage. The red rump is clearly visible only when the bird is in flight, and is not present in the female and the juvenile. The bird breeds in small colonies, although it is territorial around the nest and defends individual branches. Breeding usually takes place between July and January.

Neophema petrophila

Rock Parrot

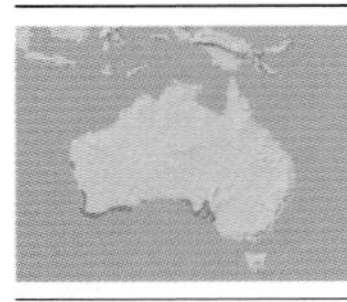

LENGTH 21–24cm (8$\frac{1}{2}$–9$\frac{1}{2}$in)

WEIGHT 55g (2oz)

MIGRATION Non-migrant

HABITAT Coastal scrub and grassland

The plumage of the Rock Parrot is mainly subtle shades of olive and yellow, accented by a blue face, wings, and tail. The female is generally duller in coloration. Seldom found away from the sea at any time of the year, the Rock Parrot has no natural waterproofing in its feathers and can get waterlogged on damp days. The Rock Parrot's nest is usually found between boulders or in the burrows of seabirds.

MALE ROCK PARROT

BRILLIANT COLOURS
With its crimson head, back, and belly and bright blue wings with bold black markings, the Crimson Rosella is a stunning bird.

Purpureicephalus spurius

Red-capped Parrot

LENGTH 35–38cm (14–15in)

WEIGHT 125g (4oz)

MIGRATION Non-migrant

HABITAT Eucalyptus forest

Named for the bright red cap of the male (the female has a purple cap), the Red-capped Parrot usually has a yellow face, although it is bright green in some birds. There is a startling contrast between its dark blue front and bright green back. Both the sexes have a red vent. Although the sexes are similar in appearance, the head of the female is generally duller in colour. This parrot feeds mainly on fruit, but also takes insects and blossoms. It breeds between August and December, when the male performs a display consisting of raising the head feathers to show off its red crown. It constantly feeds the female as part of the courtship. It also feeds the young two weeks after they hatch.

ADULT RED-CAPPED PARROT

Melopsittacus undulatus

Budgerigar

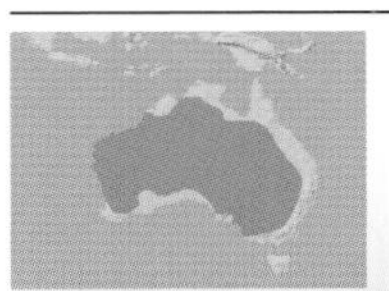

LENGTH 18–20cm (7–8in)

WEIGHT 30g (1¹⁄₁₆oz)

MIGRATION Non-migrant

HABITAT Wide range of habitats, including arid areas, but usually close to water

Despite being confined to Australia as a naturally breeding bird, the Budgerigar is probably the most familiar parrot in the world – it is also one of the smallest. The plumage of the wild Budgerigar is a combination of a black-barred head and back and a yellow face contrasting with a bright green front and a blue tail. The Budgerigar is a swift-flying bird. It mostly feeds on grass seeds from the ground. Budgerigars are thought to be able to survive for long periods without water, although many die during prolonged drought. There is no distinct breeding season; it depends much on the availability of food. The bird breeds in small colonies, nesting in tree hollows or cavities, and 4–8 eggs are laid. The male supplies food for the female during this time.

ADULT BUDGERIGAR (WILD SPECIES)

COLOUR FORMS

Domesticated Budgerigars are commonly bred in various shades and hues that are rarely found in the wild species. These colour variants are derived by breeding the birds selectively rather than by controlling their diets. The variety ranges from blue, green, yellow, and white to pied and multicoloured plumage.

Psittinus cyanurus

Blue-rumped Parrot

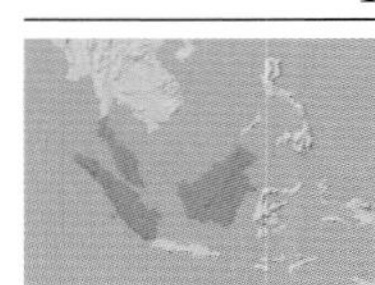

LENGTH 18cm (7in)

WEIGHT 100g (3⅝oz)

MIGRATION Partial migrant

HABITAT Lowland rainforest, forest edges, plantations, and occasionally mangroves

A stout bird with a short tail, the Blue-rumped Parrot is among the most widely distributed species in its genus. The male has a bright red bill, with a blue head, dark upper back, and a blue rump, with the rest of the plumage in bright green. The female has a brown bill and head, with a green upper back, and a smaller, less noticeable blue rump. The male in the subspecies found on the islands off Sumatra, has less blue on its head, with paler green plumage on its back, and an all-green rump. This bird is considered to be near-threatened, due to the alarming rate at which its primary rainforest habitat is being logged. Cage-bird traders are also known to hunt and capture large numbers of the species.

ADULT MALE

Aprosmictus erythropterus

Red-winged Parrot

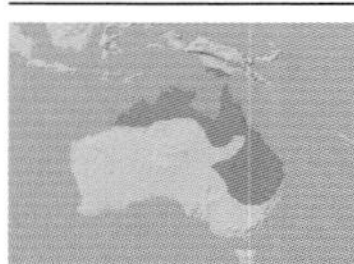

LENGTH 30cm (12in)

WEIGHT 150g (5oz)

MIGRATION Partial migrant

HABITAT Open woodland, forest, and scrub

Mainly an Australian species, though also found in southern Papua New Guinea, the Red-winged Parrot is a large bird. The male's bill and eyes are red, which contrast with the bright green head and underparts. This bird's back is almost black and it has a broad scarlet wing patch. The male Red-winged Parrot has a blue upper rump that is usually hidden from view when the bird is perching, but is visible in flight. Although both the sexes are broadly similar, the female is not so well marked.

The Red-winged Parrot has a distinct and erratic flight action, pausing after each wingbeat and weaving around in a buoyant, jerky manner. The bird is usually seen in pairs or small groups, feeding on seeds and fruit among trees.

MALE FEEDING

Prioniturus discurus

Blue-crowned Racquet-tail

LENGTH 27cm (10½in)

WEIGHT 175g (6oz)

MIGRATION Non-migrant

HABITAT Rainforest

The Blue-crowned Racquet-tail is a small parrot with a variable amount of bright blue on its head and green plumage. However, the Blue-crowned Racquet-tail's most noticeable feature is its remarkable tail. Its two central tail feathers are long, with bare shafts that have dark racquet-shaped tips. The male has longer tail feathers than the female. These parrots form small flocks, feeding together on banana and other fruiting trees.

ADULT BLUE-CROWNED RACQUET-TAIL

MALE ADULT

Alisterus scapularis

Australian King Parrot

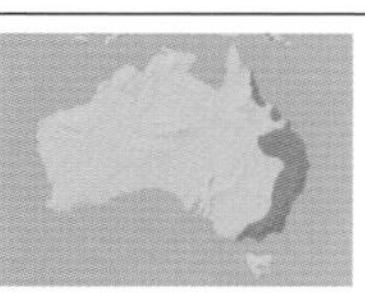

LENGTH 42–44cm (16½–17½in)

WEIGHT 200–275g (7–10oz)

MIGRATION Non-migrant

HABITAT Rainforest, woodland, and scrub

With its sharp, hooked bill and bright plumage, the male Australian King Parrot must rank as one of the most attractive parrots in Australia. Its scarlet head, with bright green upperparts, green underparts, purple rump, along with a dark tail, and two pale green tramlines down its back, create a stunning contrast. The female is duller, with a green head, and the scarlet plumage restricted to the belly.

Tanygnathus lucionensis

Blue-naped Parrot

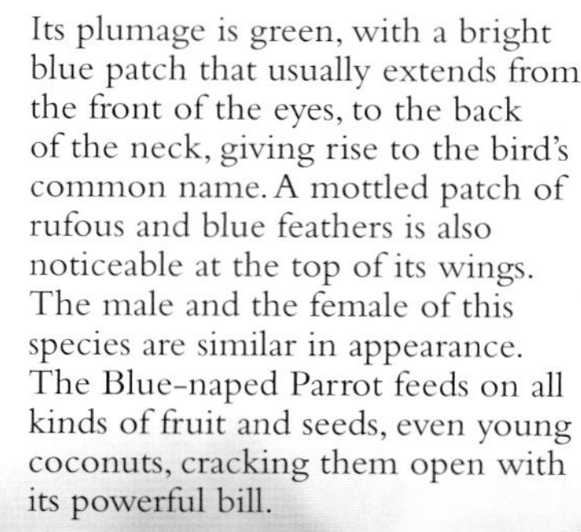

LENGTH 30cm (12in)

WEIGHT 150–225g (5–8oz)

MIGRATION Non-migrant

HABITAT Lowland forest, plantations, scattered trees in agricultural areas, and mangroves

The Blue-naped Parrot has a heavy, bright red bill, a white eye-ring that stands out, a thick neck, and a short tail.

Its plumage is green, with a bright blue patch that usually extends from the front of the eyes, to the back of the neck, giving rise to the bird's common name. A mottled patch of rufous and blue feathers is also noticeable at the top of its wings. The male and the female of this species are similar in appearance. The Blue-naped Parrot feeds on all kinds of fruit and seeds, even young coconuts, cracking them open with its powerful bill.

ADULT BLUE-NAPED PARROT

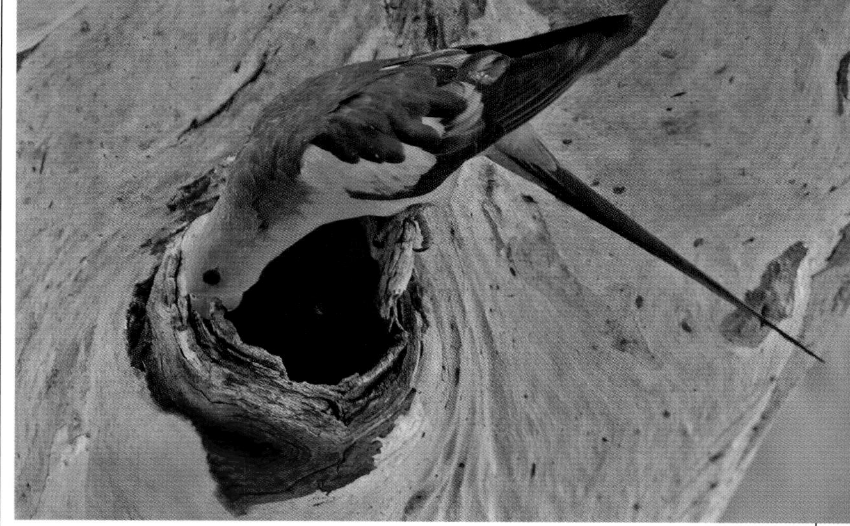

MALE REGENT PARROT AT NEST HOLE

Polytelis anthopeplus

Regent Parrot

LENGTH 40cm (15½in)

WEIGHT 100g (3⅝oz)

MIGRATION Partial migrant

HABITAT Eucalyptus woodland, mallee scrub, and coastal forest

A large, long-winged, long-tailed bird, the Regent Parrot looks particularly impressive in flight because of the contrast between its bright yellow plumage, the dark wings, and the tail. The male is a spectacular-looking bird, with its yellow head and shoulders, dark olive-green upperparts, bright yellow underparts, and a salmon pink bar across the black-tipped wings. While both sexes look similar, the female Regent Parrot is slightly less gaudy in appearance than the male.

The Regent Parrot is a social species that nests in small colonies, usually in large hollows in gum trees. The female lays 3–8 eggs and rarely leaves the nest while it is incubating the eggs, waiting for the male to feed it. Outside the breeding season, these parrots form large flocks, particularly when the species comes in to roost. The Regent Parrot is found only in Australia, where it has a fragmented distribution. The bird occurs in the mallee scrub of South Australia, New South Wales, and Victoria, with a separate population on the other side of the continent in the coastal forest of southwest Australia.

Polytelis swainsonii

Superb Parrot

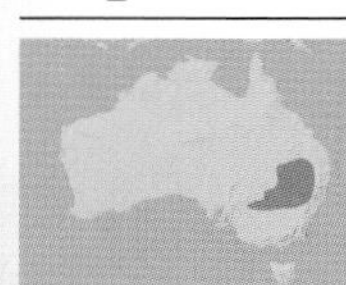

LENGTH 40cm (15½in)

WEIGHT 125–150g (4–5oz)

MIGRATION Partial migrant

HABITAT Box woodland; breeds in River Red Gum forest

RED LIST CATEGORY Vulnerable

Confined to southeast Australia, the Superb Parrot is a rapidly declining species, currently numbering only around 6,500 birds. It is a bright green parrot with a long tail. The male has a yellow forehead, with a face that is bordered below by a broad scarlet crescent that extends across its throat. The female has a plain green face with a blue tint, and is dull overall. However, it has red feathering on its thighs, a feature lacking in the otherwise brighter male. The Superb Parrot has a swift, direct flight. When seen from below, the female shows a rose-pink tint on the underside of its tail, while the male shows black.

FLOCK OF SUPERB PARROTS

GREAT SITES

GULPA STATE FOREST

One of the best places for a glimpse of the Superb Parrot is the Gulpa State Forest in southwest New South Wales. The species is present in this region most of the year, although it can be quite scarce during summer.

Psittacula cyanocephala

Plum-headed Parakeet

LENGTH 33–37cm (13–14½in)

WEIGHT 55–85g (2–3oz)

MIGRATION Non-migrant

HABITAT Moist deciduous woodland

The Plum-headed Parakeet is a brightly coloured species that is found throughout the Indian subcontinent and Sri Lanka. The male has a striking head coloration: crimson above the bill and graduating through purple, before becoming blue at the top of the neck. This "hood" is further separated from the body by a well-defined but thin black border. In addition to its well-marked head, the male Plum-headed Parakeet also has two small maroon patches at the top of the wing that are not present in the female. It has a long blue tail, and a hint of blue on the rump. The female Plum-headed Parakeet is less striking, with a purple-grey head that has no black edging; instead it has an indistinct yellow neck-ring. The juvenile has a green head, with a small amount of orange on the crown.

This species is sometimes considered to be a pest as large flocks of several hundred birds can gather and cause damage to agricultural crops. Usually, however, its main food consists of wild fruit, seeds, buds, and nectar.

MALE PLUM-HEADED PARAKEET

Psittacula krameri

Rose-ringed Parakeet

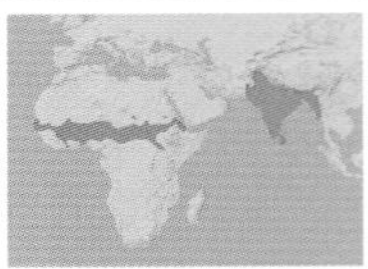

LENGTH 37–43cm (14½–17in)

WEIGHT 100–150g (3⅝–5oz)

MIGRATION Non-migrant

HABITAT Mainly deciduous woodland and forest; also farmland

Also known as the Ring-necked Parakeet, the Rose-ringed Parakeet is a common species that naturally occurs in large parts of Africa and Asia. Many feral populations have also become established in other locations around the world, such as Europe and North America. It is a slim-bodied, mainly green parrot, with a long tail. The male has a bright red bill, red eye, a pink collar around its neck, and a black chin. The female Rose-ringed Parakeet is plainer and lacks the distinctive head pattern of the male.

MALE ROSE-RINGED PARAKEET

Agapornis roseicollis

Rosy-faced Lovebird

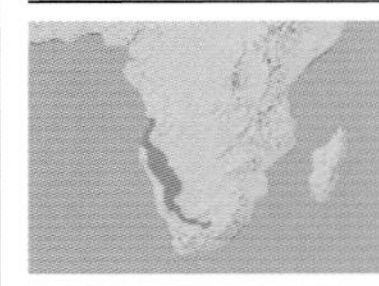

LENGTH 15–18cm (6–7in)

WEIGHT 45–65g (1–2⅜oz)

MIGRATION Non-migrant

HABITAT Arid woodland, tree-lined rivers, and scrubby hillsides

FLOCK OF ADULT ROSY-FACED LOVEBIRDS

The Rosy-faced Lovebird is a small parrot, with a noticeable white eye-ring, a pale-coloured bill, a pink face and throat, and a bright blue rump. It is mainly green in colour. Both sexes are similar in appearance, but the juvenile is browner.

The Rosy-faced Lovebird is found in arid, rocky terrain in southern Africa and is specifically located in a narrow band stretching from Angola and Namibia to South Africa. Although it is found in dry habitats, the species requires access to water and often visits watering holes for baths. It is also sociable and feeds in small groups. Commonly kept as cage-birds, large numbers have been taken from the wild, contributing significantly to the decline of the species.

Agapornis canus

Grey-headed Lovebird

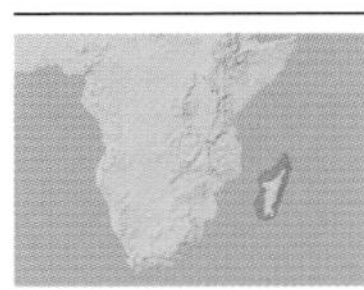

LENGTH 15cm (6in)

WEIGHT 25–30g (⅞–1 1/16oz)

MIGRATION Non-migrant

HABITAT Forest edges, scrub, and semi-wooded areas near the coast

This tiny, short-tailed parrot is the only species of lovebird to occur in Madagascar and is the smallest of the lovebirds. The male Grey-headed Lovebird has dark green upperparts, a pale lime-green belly, and a contrasting pale grey head and breast. The female and juvenile are much less distinctive: entirely dark green above and pale green below, without any grey on the head and breast. The adult has a greyish white bill, but in the juvenile, the bill is more yellow in tone and has a black base.

This lovebird feeds mainly on seeds and can often be found foraging on the ground. It also consumes some fruit and the species has been known to cause damage to rice crops.

PAIR OF GREY-HEADED LOVEBIRDS

ADULT GREATER VASA PARROT

Coracopsis vasa

Greater Vasa Parrot

LENGTH 50cm (19½in)
WEIGHT 525g (19oz)
MIGRATION Non-migrant
HABITAT Forest, coconut plantations, savanna, scrub, and open areas adjacent to woodland

This distinctive and unusual-looking parrot is found only in Madagascar and the neighbouring Comoros Islands. It is a large, dark brown bird that is almost black on the breast and back, with slightly paler feathering on its wings and long tail. Both sexes are alike, while the juvenile is generally browner. During the breeding season, some individuals lose most of their facial feathers, their bald heads revealing bare yellow-orange skin below.

Poicephalus rueppellii

Rüppell's Parrot

LENGTH 22–25cm (8½–10in)
WEIGHT 100–150g (3⅝–5oz)
MIGRATION Non-migrant
HABITAT Dry woodland

A distinctive parrot with an unusual colouring combination, Rüppell's Parrot is a bird of southwest Africa, found only in Angola and Namibia. The female is pale grey on the head and breast; dark grey on the wings and back, with a bright yellow vertical wing-bar; and bright blue on the belly and undertail. The male lacks the blue plumage below – instead, its underparts are a uniform grey.

Eclectus roratus

Eclectus Parrot

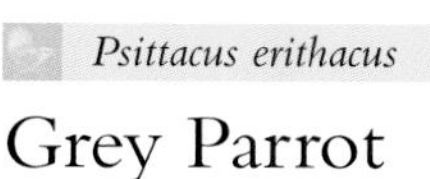

LENGTH 35–42cm (14–16½in)
WEIGHT 350–600g (13–21oz)
MIGRATION Non-migrant
HABITAT Woodland canopy

The Eclectus Parrot is found throughout much of New Guinea and neighbouring islands of Indonesia. The species also occurs in the very tip of Australia's Cape York Peninsula. Although it is still a common bird in many areas, excessive trapping for the cage-bird trade has led to considerable decline in parts of its range. There are several subspecies and the female's colour patterns show a variety of noticeable plumage differences according to the subspecies. These parrots feed on fruit, seeds, nuts, berries, leaf buds, blossoms and nectar, all of which are procured mainly in the treetops.

FEMALE ECLECTUS PARROT

CONTRASTING COLOURS

The Eclectus Parrot provides one of the most extreme examples of plumage differences between the sexes. For many years, the male and female were regarded as different species. Unusually, the female has the brightest plumage: bright scarlet with a blue band across the chest and back, while the male is predominantly green.

Psittacus erithacus

Grey Parrot

LENGTH 28–39cm (11–15½in)
WEIGHT 400–500g (14–18oz)
MIGRATION Non-migrant
HABITAT Damp lowland forest

The Grey Parrot (also known as the African Grey Parrot) is a common bird in captivity. Although much of this popularity can be attributed to its distinctive appearance, it is probably largely due to the species' propensity for mimicry. Parrots are now generally regarded as one of the most intelligent bird families – and the Grey Parrot's powers of speech certainly seem to offer supporting evidence. Individual captive Grey Parrots with a vocabulary of more than 500 words have been recorded, with some individuals reputedly able to invent their own words and phrases in order to communicate – using language in the same way that a human would.

The Grey Parrot is a medium- to large-sized species of parrot with barred grey plumage. It has white facial feathering, black wing-tips and a scarlet tail. Birds of the subspecies *P. e. timneh*, from parts of Sierra Leone and Ivory Coast, are smaller and darker, with a grey-red tail. The Grey Parrot feeds primarily on nuts and fruit, supplemented by leafy matter. Each clutch consists of 3–5 eggs, which are laid in a tree-cavity high above the ground. The female incubates the eggs for 30 days and is fed by the male during this time. Both parents feed the young.

ADULT GREY PARROT

CAPTIVE SPIX'S MACAW

Cyanopsitta spixii

Spix's Macaw

LENGTH 55–57cm ($21^1/_2$–$22^1/_2$in)

WEIGHT 300–400g (11–14oz)

MIGRATION Non-migrant

HABITAT Gallery woodland within the caatinga (dry shrubland and thorn forest) zone

RED LIST CATEGORY Critically endangered

Named after a 19th-century German naturalist-explorer who spent three years in Brazil, Spix's Macaw is the smallest of the blue macaws. It has a black bill, silvery grey head, with dark grey skin surrounding the eyes, a darker back and wings, and a long, pointed tail. It feeds on seeds, nuts, and fruit and is a creature of habit, perching all day on a favoured treetop. Spix's Macaw was perhaps partially nomadic, although it has always been restricted to a small and remote corner of northeast Brazil, where the last known wild bird disappeared a few years ago; approximately 50 are now in captivity.

Ara macao

Scarlet Macaw

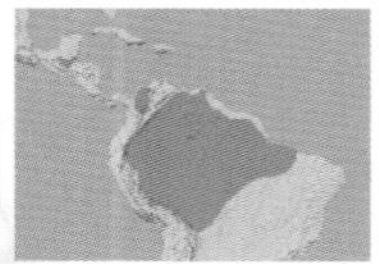

LENGTH 84–89cm (33–35in)

WEIGHT 0.9–1.5kg (2–$3^1/_4$lb)

MIGRATION Non-migrant

HABITAT Humid evergreen forest and gallery woodland; occasionally pine forest and mangroves

It is difficult to distinguish the Scarlet and Red-and-green Macaws (right), from each other, especially as the two species often occur together in the same forests. Mostly bright red in colour, the Scarlet Macaw has an unmarked bare white face and bright yellow feathers on its blue wings. Its wide-ranging diet has been well studied and the bird is known to consume the seeds of a great many tree species, as well as the fruit, flowers, leaves, and even the sap and bark. In some areas, it even eats pine-seeds. It is totally reliant on tree cavities for nesting. The numbers of this magnificent bird have declined in many areas, especially in Central America, where in many countries the species is now on the verge of extinction.

ADULT SCARLET MACAW

Ara ararauna

Blue-and-yellow Macaw

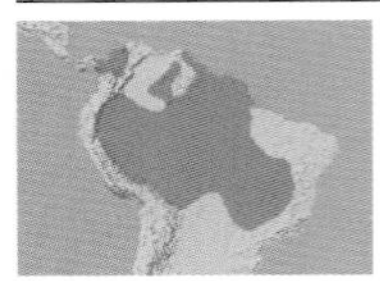

LENGTH 86cm (34in)

WEIGHT 1–1.5kg ($2^1/_4$–$3^1/_4$lb)

MIGRATION Non-migrant

HABITAT Seasonally flooded and gallery forest, palm groves in savanna; rarely in deciduous forest

Unlike many macaws, which have declined in numbers, the Blue-and-yellow Macaw is still common over much of its large range, despite depletion due to trappers and habitat loss. Named for its plumage colours, it has a green forehead, a black chin, blue feathers on its upperparts, and yellow underparts. The species is dependent on palms for its nest sites, although it feeds on a variety of fruit, flowers, and nectar of other trees; it moves seasonally in search of food. The breeding cycle lasts four to five months and 1–3 eggs are laid.

BLUE-AND-YELLOW MACAW

PAIR OF RED-AND-GREEN MACAWS

Ara chloroptera

Red-and-green Macaw

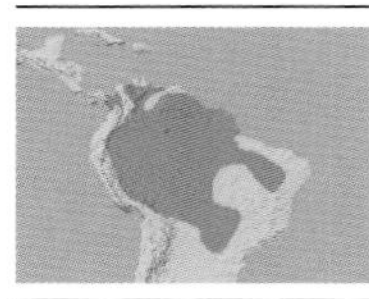

LENGTH 90–95cm (35–37in)

WEIGHT 1–1.7g ($2^1/_4$–$3^1/_4$lb)

MIGRATION Non-migrant

HABITAT Humid tropical and gallery forests in lowland and foothills

Often mistaken for the Scarlet Macaw (left), the breast of the Red-and-green Macaw is bright red, but the lower feathers of the wings are green. It has red lines around its eyes, formed by rows of tiny feathers on its face. It usually feeds in the canopy on fruit, seeds, and nuts. It is more adaptable than the Scarlet Macaw as far as its choice of nest sites is concerned and will also utilize holes in cliffs, both natural and those it partially excavates.

CLAY LICKS

This macaw is one of several parrots known to visit clay cliffs in forests, usually along watercourses, in order to scrape off and swallow particles of clay. The reason for this unusual behaviour is not definitely known, but it has been suggested that the clay helps make some unripe fruit more palatable or, even more remarkably, counters the stimulant effects of some elements of its diet.

Primolius maracana

Blue-winged Macaw

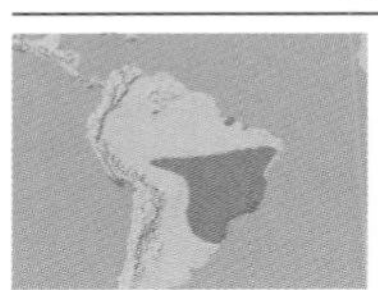

LENGTH 36–43cm (14–17in)
WEIGHT 250–275g (9–10oz)
MIGRATION Non-migrant

HABITAT Edges of lowland forest; also in palm groves and gallery woodland

Mainly green in colour, the Blue-winged Macaw has a heavy black bill, a bare whitish yellow face, a red forecrown and patch on its belly, and blue on its forewing and on the tip of its tail. It mainly feeds on seeds but also takes fruit and nuts. Two eggs are laid and are incubated for about a month. This macaw has been known to reach the age of 50–60 years.

PAIR OF BLUE-WINGED MACAWS

Diopsittaca nobilis

Red-shouldered Macaw

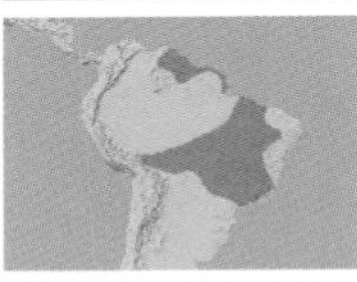

LENGTH 30cm (12in)
WEIGHT 125–175g (4–6oz)
MIGRATION Non-migrant

HABITAT Savanna and marshy areas, with gallery woodland and groves of palms

ADULT RED-SHOULDERED MACAW

The Red-shouldered Macaw is one of several smaller macaws with mostly green plumage and a bare area of white skin around the eye. This species has a pale blue crown and an orange-red shoulder patch. Its nest is sited either in a palm tree or an arboreal termite nest. Four eggs are laid and are incubated for about a month.

Aratinga aurea

Peach-fronted Parakeet

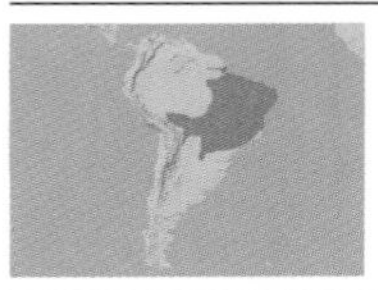

LENGTH 23–28cm (9–11in)
WEIGHT 75–95g (2⅝–3⅜oz)
MIGRATION Non-migrant

HABITAT Open savanna, with palms, gallery forest, dry woods, and tall scrub

The genus *Aratinga* is one of the two largest genera of South American parakeets and the Peach-fronted Parakeet is one of its most widespread and common representatives. Mainly green in colour, the forehead to mid-crown is peachy orange and separated from the pale yellow-orange ring around the eye by a strip of dull green feathers. The underparts are mainly greenish yellow, becoming more buff on the throat and upper breast. The Peach-fronted Parakeet is a very sociable bird, frequently occurring in flocks, except when breeding. The nesting season occupies much of the second half of the year. The bird excavates a hole in a disused termite's nest, either on the ground or, less commonly, in a tree and 2–4 eggs are laid, with incubation lasting just over three weeks. The young take almost seven weeks to reach fledging. Nestlings are often taken as pets, as the nests are easily accessed. The Peach-fronted Parakeet is often seen foraging on the ground, as well as in trees and low bushes, taking seeds, flowers, and leaves, but also, to a much lesser extent, termites, moths, beetles, and various insect larvae. It also visits crops such as rice, soya, and maize, which are about to be harvested, bringing the bird into conflict with local farmers, especially in Argentina, where the species is still listed as a pest.

Whereas many species, including a number of parrots, are declining as a result of deforestation, this adaptable species is actually increasing in Brazil as a result of such clearance.

FEEDING TOGETHER
Like many parrots, Peach-fronted Parakeets feed communally, with one bird serving as a lookout for danger.

A STRONG GRIP
The Peach-fronted Parakeet has very dextrous feet, which it uses to hold its food.

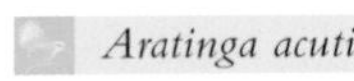

Aratinga acuticaudata

Blue-crowned Parakeet

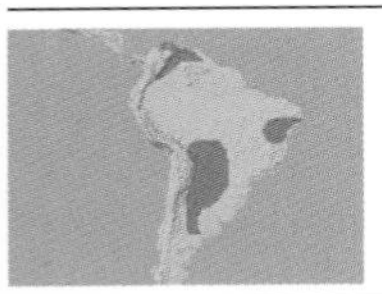

LENGTH 33–38cm (13–15in)
WEIGHT 175g (6oz)
MIGRATION Non-migrant

HABITAT Dry woodland and cactus scrub, and open savanna with palm groves

Principally green, the Blue-crowned Parakeet has a dull blue head, a white ring around the eye, and some red on its tail. It feeds on cacti fruit, berries, and seeds, but also on mangoes and some crops, moving widely in search of food. This parakeet has suffered at the hands of the cage-bird trade, especially in the south of its range, with large numbers being exported from Argentina.

GROUP OF BLUE-CROWNED PARAKEETS

GREAT SITES

MANÚ NATIONAL PARK

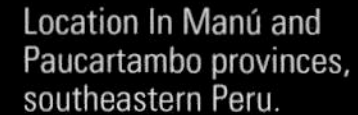

Location In Manú and Paucartambo provinces, southeastern Peru.

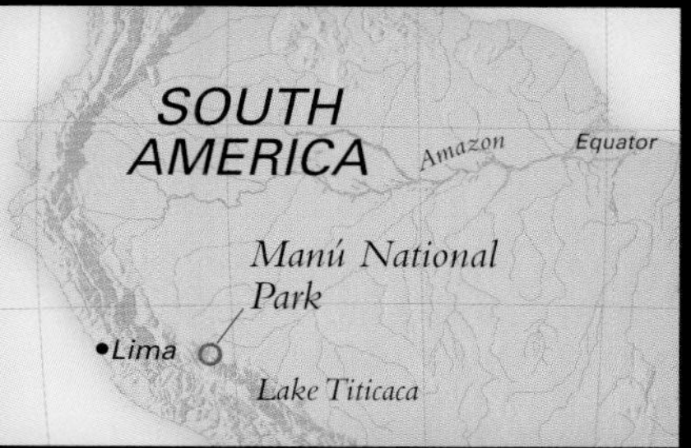

Manú is the world's largest tropical rainforest reserve and supports a greater diversity of birds than any other national park. More than 850 species of bird have been recorded here, including many that are globally threatened. This total is equivalent to around 10 per cent of all bird species in the world. On the eastern slopes of the Andes in Peru, Manú National Park and the adjacent Biosphere Reserve and Cultural Zone form a vast protected area of 18,800 square km (7,250 square miles). It comprises virtually the entire watershed of the Río Manú and most tributaries of the Río Madre de Dios, two of the major rivers in the western Amazon basin.

RANGE OF HABITATS

Manú's extraordinary species richness is due to its altitudinal variation and range of habitats, from tundra-like puna grassland and stunted elfin forest at high altitudes, humid temperate forest and cloudforest at mid-altitudes, humid upper tropical forest in the foothills, and primary rainforest and swamp forest in the lowlands.

Some of Manú's birds, such as the Black-faced Cotinga and Rufous-fronted Antthrush, are found nowhere else, while this is among the best areas in the Amazon basin to see many other species, from tanagers to toucans, woodcreepers, hummingbirds, quetzals, cotingas, and parrots. In addition to its resident birdlife, Manú hosts huge numbers of warblers and other migrant birds from North America throughout the northern winter, and in late July and August during the dry season its exposed river banks provide a valuable feeding and resting place for migrating North American shorebirds.

A highlight of the lowland rainforest at Manú is the flocks of macaws that visit favoured cliffs and river banks, reaching a peak in August and September. Another of Manú's most spectacular birds is the Andean Cock-of-the-Rock, which inhabits the frequently mist-shrouded cloudforest.

Classified as a World Heritage Site in 1987, Manú is famous among birdwatchers for offering one of the most intense and varied experiences anywhere in the Amazon.

FLOCKING AT CLAY LICKS
In early morning raucous flocks of Scarlet and Red-and-green Macaws assemble at clay licks, often exposed cliffs or river banks, in the lowlands of Manú National Park.

WHAT TO SPOT

HOATZIN
Opisthocomus hoazin
(see p.272)

ORINOCO GOOSE
Neochen jubata
(see p.128)

ANDEAN COCK-OF-THE-ROCK
Rupicola peruvianus
(see p.339)

HARPY EAGLE
Harpia harpyja
(see p.200)

Anodorhynchus hyacinthinus

Hyacinth Macaw

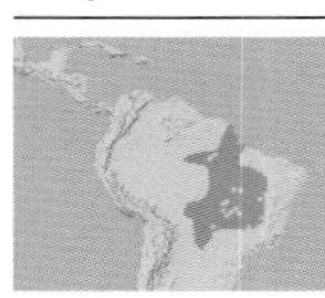

LENGTH 100cm (39in)

WEIGHT 1.5kg (3¼lb)

MIGRATION Non-migrant

HABITAT Tropical lowland forest, gallery forest, and palm groves

RED LIST CATEGORY Endangered

The largest parrot in South America, the Hyacinth Macaw displays its enormous size to great effect when it is in flight. It has a massive "bone-crushing" bill, deep cobalt-blue plumage, violet wings, and grey on the underparts of the tail and wings. A yellow patch around the eye and at the base of the bill provides a spectacular contrast. The sexes show no difference in plumage, but the juvenile has paler yellow skin on the face and a shorter tail.

This species mostly feeds on palm fruit, although occasionally it also eats other fruit, as well as snails. Most foraging is done on the ground, where it walks jauntily on its short legs with the tail held low. It nests either in tree-holes or on cliffs. Only 2 or 3 eggs are laid, and incubation lasts just under a month. The young remain in the nest for three months before fledging.

The status of this species is a source of conservation concern, as populations have declined steadily due to illegal trade in cage birds.

ADULT HYACINTH MACAW

SMALL FLOCKS

A very gregarious bird, the Hyacinth Macaw can frequently be seen travelling in small flocks of one to eight pairs, which call loudly to one another. In the wild, Hyacinth Macaws often flock to areas of exposed clay known as macaw licks. When disturbed, these bright birds screech loudly and circle overhead with their long tails streaming. In the breeding season, however, pairs will break away from the group. The species is monogamous, and pairs remain bonded for life.

Cyanoliseus patagonus

Burrowing Parakeet

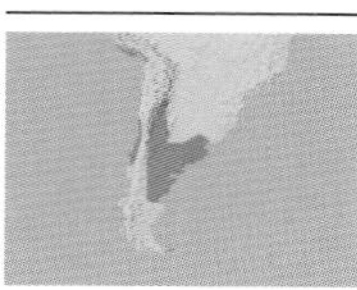

LENGTH 39–52cm (15½–20½in)

WEIGHT 250–300g (9–11oz)

MIGRATION Non-migrant

HABITAT Dry wooded savanna, thorn scrub, and other arid lowland, especially along watercourses

Most parakeets tend to be relatively small, but the Burrowing Parakeet is an exception. It has an olive-brown head and breast and has yellow over the rest of the underparts, with a red "stain" on the central belly. Its back and wings are yellow and its flight feathers are blue. It feeds on seeds, foraging on the ground, and is persecuted in some areas because it is seen as a crop pest.

CLIFF-NESTING

Burrowing Parakeets are so named for their habit of nesting in sandstone, limestone, or earth cliffs, sometimes well above the ground, and frequently in close proximity to water, including the sea. The burrows are often interconnected, forming a sort of mini-labyrinth.

LARGE FLOCK OF BURROWING PARAKEETS

ADULT REDDISH-BELLIED PARAKEET

Pyrrhura frontalis

Reddish-bellied Parakeet

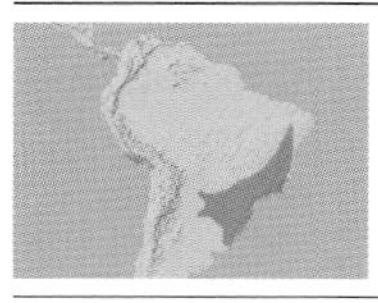

LENGTH 24–28cm (9½–11in)

WEIGHT 70–95g (2½–3⅜oz)

MIGRATION Non-migrant

HABITAT Montane evergreen forest; also parkland and gallery woodland

As its name indicates, the Reddish-bellied Parakeet has a red belly. It has a white eye-ring, a yellowish green neck and breast, blue flight feathers, and a reddish brown undertail. It mostly feeds on the nuts of the monkey-puzzle tree in some parts of its range, although a variety of other fruit are also taken. The female lays five eggs in a tree-hole, and the incubation process takes almost one month. It is one of the most common parrots in southern Brazil.

Myiopsitta monachus

Monk Parakeet

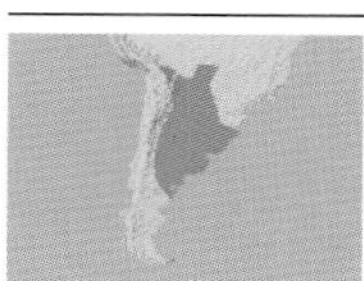

LENGTH 29cm (11½in)

WEIGHT 90–150g (3¼–5oz)

MIGRATION Non-migrant

HABITAT Gallery forest, savanna woodland, scrub, parkland, and orchards; often near or in urban areas

The Monk Parakeet is mostly green, with a pale grey face and crown, yellowish pink bill, and brown breast feathers that are fringed with grey. It has a varied diet, with thistles often an important component during the breeding season. In some areas, it is considered a serious pest of agricultural crops.

ADULT MONK PARAKEET

COMMUNAL NESTS

The Monk Parakeet's nesting system is atypical of parrots. The species makes communal nests of spiny sticks, which are cut from bushes and are often placed on top of trees, especially the eucalyptus. The nests contain multiple chambers that are occupied all year round, being used by different pairs in rotation, and sometimes also by non-breeding individuals. Rarely is a nest used by a lone pair.

Brotogeris chiriri

Yellow-chevroned Parakeet

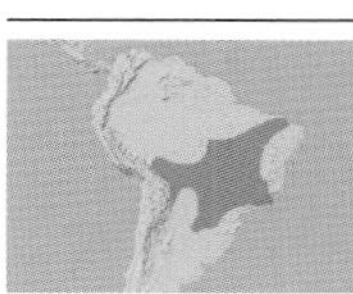

LENGTH 20–25cm (8–10in)

WEIGHT 60g (2⅛oz)

MIGRATION Non-migrant

HABITAT Patches of forest, including riparian woodland and in open country; frequently enters towns

The two most noticeable features of the Yellow-chevroned Parakeet are its bright pink bill and the yellow stripe in each wing, which is more conspicuous in flight. It is green in colour overall, and a paler green on the underparts. The sexes are similar in plumage. The high-pitched screeching calls of an overhead flock are often the first indication of the Yellow-chevroned Parakeet's presence. It mostly feeds on seeds and fruit.

ADULT YELLOW-CHEVRONED PARAKEET

Forpus xanthopterygius

Blue-winged Parrotlet

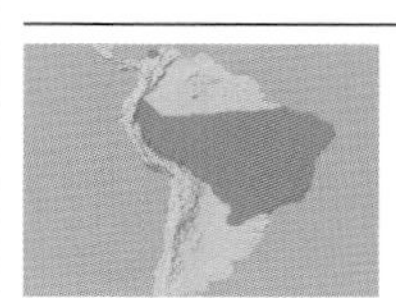

LENGTH 13cm (5in)

WEIGHT 30g (1⅙oz)

MIGRATION Non-migrant

HABITAT Lightly wooded areas, including savanna, pastures, parkland, and town suburbs

ADULT BLUE-WINGED PARROTLET

This small parrot is green all over, and slightly yellower below. The blue wing patches that gives the bird its name are actually hard to see, except in flight, and are only present in males. There is also some blue on the rump. The Blue-winged Parrotlet feeds primarily on seeds and fruit, including grass seeds taken on the ground, and also shows a preference for catkins. It lays 4–7 eggs in a hole in a tree, or sometimes in an old termite nest. Only the female incubates the eggs.

Touit purpuratus

Sapphire-rumped Parrotlet

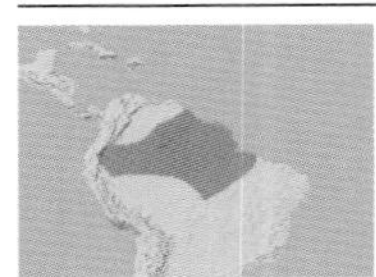

LENGTH 18cm (7in)

WEIGHT 55–65g (2–2³⁄₈oz)

MIGRATION Non-migrant

HABITAT Montane evergreen forest, seasonally flooded and savanna forests, and forest edges

This squat, short-tailed, and small-billed parrot is most frequently seen in high flight between feeding and roosting areas in early morning and late afternoon. The Sapphire-rumped Parrotlet is mainly green, relieved by an olive-brown head, violet-blue edges to the wings and rump, and a brown line at the edge of the back, with red patches on the tail. The sexes differ only in the pattern of red and green on the tail.

Pionopsitta vulturina

Vulturine Parrot

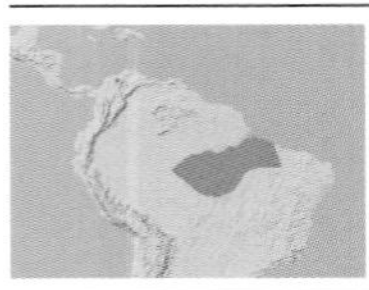

LENGTH 23cm (9in)

WEIGHT 150–175g (5–6oz)

MIGRATION Non-migrant

HABITAT Amazonian forest, both seasonally flooded and permanently dry areas

Found only in east Amazonian Brazil, the Vulturine Parrot has a distinctive head, which is mostly bare, but is covered by black bristles that become yellow-orange near the bill base. It is unclear what purpose the bare head serves, but it is speculated that the juice from the fruit the bird feeds on would otherwise mat the bird's feathers. The Vulturine Parrot's plumage is largely green, with a yellow feathered collar and small patches of red, orange, and blue in the wings and tail.

ADULT BLUE-HEADED PARROT

Pionus menstruus

Blue-headed Parrot

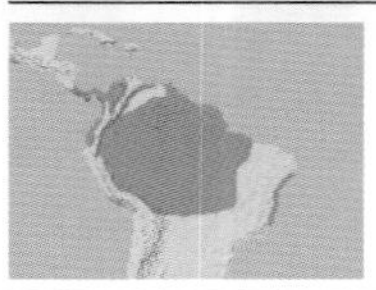

LENGTH 24–28cm (9½–11in)

WEIGHT 200–300g (7–11oz)

MIGRATION Non-migrant

HABITAT All types of woodland, including seasonally flooded and savanna forest and tall second growth

One of the most common parrots across its broad South American range, the Blue-headed Parrot is easily identified by its size and relatively squat appearance, especially when it is perching. It has a strikingly blue head and some red on the undertail feathers. The juvenile has a mainly green head. Ornithologists recognize three subspecies, which differ only in the intensity of the blue on the head and breast.

The Blue-headed Parrot's whistled calls serve to defy the common misconception that all parrots utter loud, raucous vocalizations. It mainly feeds on seeds and fruit of a variety of plant species, but in some areas it also searches out sugar-rich flowers and even corn. In the breeding season, the nest is placed in the stump or hole of a dead or living palm, usually well above the ground. Typically, four eggs are laid and these are incubated by the female alone for almost a month. Once the eggs have hatched, both adults bring food to the nestlings, which take almost two months to fledge.

ADULT TURQUOISE-FRONTED AMAZON

Amazona aestiva

Turquoise-fronted Amazon

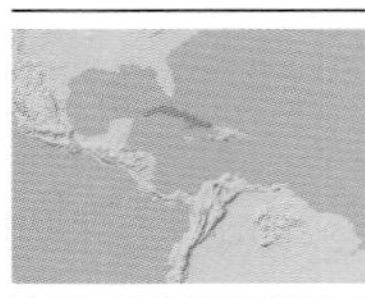

LENGTH 37cm (14½in)

WEIGHT 350–450g (13–16oz)

MIGRATION Non-migrant

HABITAT Savanna and gallery forest, palm groves and other wooded areas; requires tall trees

This typically noisy parrot is an excellent mimic of human and other sounds in captivity; large numbers have been taken from the wild for export, particularly in Argentina, in recent decades. The turquoise-blue forecrown, from which the species derives its name, is difficult to see at a distance. The male and the female are similar in plumage. Two subspecies are recognized, which differ primarily in the colour of the shoulder patch: it is orange-red in one and yellow in the other. The species gathers in flocks at regular night-time roosts, but mated pairs always stay close together.

Amazona leucocephala

Cuban Amazon

LENGTH 32cm (12½in)

WEIGHT 225–325g (8–12oz)

MIGRATION Non-migrant

HABITAT Woodland and forest, especially on limestone, also mangroves, plantations, and gardens

With the beautiful pink coloration on its face, throat, and upper breast and its green back, this parrot is a common and popular cage-bird, especially in Cuba. The only one of its family to be found in the Bahamas and Caymans, the Cuban Amazon is one of only two parrot species in Cuba. It mainly feeds on fruit and seeds, including cultivated species, such as mango and papaya. It usually requires tall trees for nesting, but in the Bahamas it nests in holes on the ground.

ADULT CUBAN AMAZON

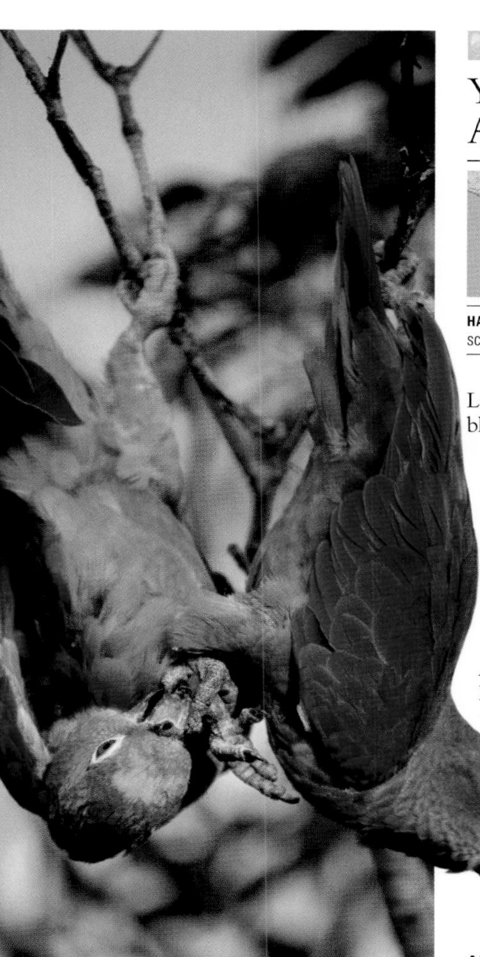

Amazona ochrocephala

Yellow-crowned Amazon

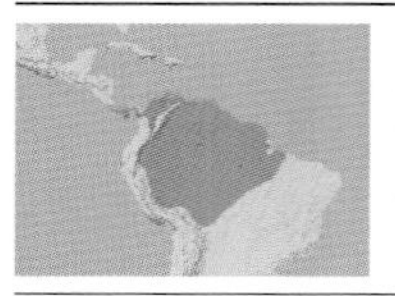

LENGTH 35–38cm (14–15in)

WEIGHT 350–550g (13–20oz)

MIGRATION Non-migrant

HABITAT Forest, savanna and gallery woodland, thorn scrub, and cultivated land with patchy woodlots

Largely green in colour, with violet-blue wing feathers, the Yellow-crowned Amazon is a remarkably variably coloured parrot: some birds may have almost completely yellow heads, others have yellow solely on the crown, and still others have yellow confined to the back of the neck. The result of this variation is that ornithologists are unable to agree whether the Yellow-crowned Amazon is just one species or three. It feeds primarily on fruit, seeds, and flowers of cultivated plants, such as mangoes, bananas, and avocados. This parrot's "talking" abilities have led to its over-exploitation for the pet trade in some areas, while habitat destruction and degradation are further threats.

ADULT YELLOW-CROWNED AMAZONS

ADULT RED-FAN PARROT

Deroptyus accipitrinus

Red-fan Parrot

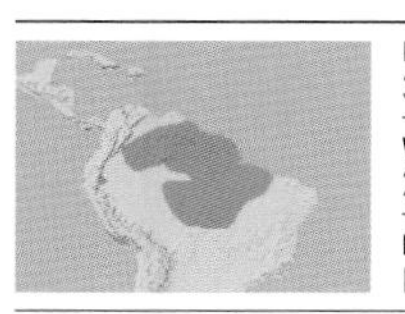

LENGTH 36cm (14in)

WEIGHT 200–300g (7–11oz)

MIGRATION Non-migrant

HABITAT Primary dryland tropical forest, sometimes in clearings and at edges

The unusual plumage of the Red-fan Parrot has led to its placement in its own genus. Two subspecies are distinguished, one of which has a white forecrown. The distinctive head pattern of the species immediately draws attention, and has led to it being heavily trapped in some regions. The underparts present a rich mosaic of maroon feathers with pale blue tips and edges. The back and wings are green.

FAN-LIKE CREST

At rest, the Red-fan Parrot's remarkable head pattern is inconspicuous, but when the parrot is alarmed or excited, it raises its elongated neck and nape feathers to create a ruff-like effect. The blue-tipped red feathers fan out across its head, adding to its raptor-like shape, which has given rise to the bird's alternative name – the Hawk-headed Parrot.

Cyclopsitta diophthalma

Double-eyed Fig Parrot

LENGTH 13–16cm (5–6½in)

WEIGHT 25–55g (⅞–2oz)

MIGRATION Non-migrant

HABITAT Forested areas, including mangroves and open woodland, sometimes in parks and gardens

Most of this small parrot's plumage is in varying shades of green, but the vast array of different head patterns displayed by the Double-eyed Fig Parrot has led to ornithologists naming eight different subspecies. These range from those with primarily red on the face and crown to others that have either mainly blue or yellow on the head. Some of these subspecies are restricted to small islands, though ironically, the Double-eyed Fig Parrot is one of the mainland Australian subspecies that gives most cause for conservation concern, due to the dwindling area of habitat available to it.

As indicated by its name, the Double-eyed Fig Parrot feeds mainly on figs, although it consumes the seeds rather than the flesh. The nesting cycle of the species is poorly known, but it generally seems to lay just two eggs.

ADULT DOUBLE-EYED FIG PARROT

CUCKOOS AND TURACOS

ORDER	Cuculiformes
FAMILIES	3
SPECIES	161

FOUND MAINLY IN woodlands and forests, cuckoos and turacos form two distinctive but related families of birds. Cuckoos are found worldwide, and include well known migrants, while turacos are confined to sub-Saharan Africa. The Hoatzin, from South America, is thought to be related to cuckoos and turacos.

ANATOMY

Cuckoos and turacos are heavy-bodied birds with small heads and beaks, broad wings, and long tails. Cuckoos themselves are often drab, but many turacos have brilliant plumage, coloured by red and green pigments that are unique to the turaco family. All have strong legs, and feet with two toes pointing forwards and two pointing back, enabling them to climb as well as perch. Hoatzins have a different foot anatomy, and their young are unique in having two small claws on the leading edge of each wing. They use these claws to clamber about in trees after they have left the nest.

BEHAVIOUR

Most cuckoos and turacos live and feed away from the ground. Exceptions are the ground cuckoos, which include the Greater Roadrunner. Arboreal cuckoos feed mainly on insects, but ground cuckoos tackle larger prey, including lizards and snakes. Turacos are fruit-eaters, but they occasionally take insects and grubs. Turacos build large nests high in trees, but about half the species in the cuckoo family are brood parasites, using other birds to raise their young. In North America, Cowbirds parasitize over 100 species of small songbird.

BROOD PARASITISM
Bracing itself with its feet, a young cuckoo ejects the last of its foster parents' eggs. Having disposed of the competition, it eats all the food that the adult birds bring to the nest and will quickly be bigger than they are.

SPECIALIZED TASTES
Cuckoos specialize in eating caterpillars – particularly those that are protected by allergenic hairs. Like its relatives, this Squirrel Cuckoo can swallow, without coming to any harm, food that would be poisonous to other birds.

Opistohocomus hoazin

Hoatzin

LENGTH 61–66cm (24–26in)
WEIGHT 700g (25oz)
MIGRATION Non-migrant

HABITAT Well-vegetated riverbanks and edges of swamps and lakes

An interesting bird to look at, the Hoatzin's appearance is reminiscent of a prehistoric creature. This bird is the size of a pheasant with a spiky crest, a long neck, and a long tail. It nests in small colonies, laying 2 or 3 eggs. It is, however, an unusual bird in many respects. One such oddity is that it digests its vegetarian diet of leaves using bacterial fermentation, in a similar way to cows.

ESCAPE CLAWS

The Hoatzin chicks are uniquely equipped with two claws on each of their wings. When threatened, the chicks escape by falling into the water below the nest. When the danger passes, they use the claws on their wings to clamber back to the nest.

ADULT HOATZIN

Tauraco persa

Guinea Turaco

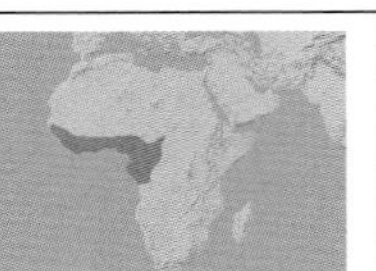

LENGTH 40–43cm (15½–17in)
WEIGHT 300g (11oz)
MIGRATION Non-migrant

HABITAT Lowland, lower montane, and gallery forest

Also called Green Turaco, the Guinea Turaco typically has green plumage. It has a small but thick red bill, a green crest, and prominent eye-rings. This bird has crimson patches on its primary feathers and a long tail. Although the Guinea Turaco is a common and a noisy bird, it can be difficult to spot as it frequents the canopy and can easily become inconspicuous. The bird usually feeds on fruit and blossoms. It lays two eggs in a tree platform nest.

ADULT GUINEA TURACO

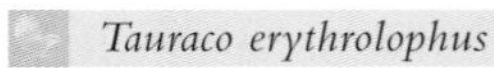

Tauraco erythrolophus

Red-crested Turaco

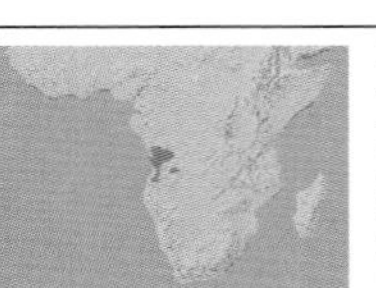

LENGTH 40cm (15½in)
WEIGHT 225g (8oz)
MIGRATION Non-migrant

HABITAT Tall tropical forest and forest edge; savanna

The Red-crested Turaco has a yellow bill, a white face, and bright crimson flight feathers. But its most noticeable feature is its splendid white-tipped red crest, from which the bird takes its name. This bird is an omnivore and its diet is mostly made up of fruit, leaves, and invertebrates. The chicks hatch at the beginning of the wet season when the food is readily available. This allows them to feed on a high proportion of protein-rich insects, important for their development.

ADULT FISCHER'S TAURACO

Tauraco fischeri

Fischer's Turaco

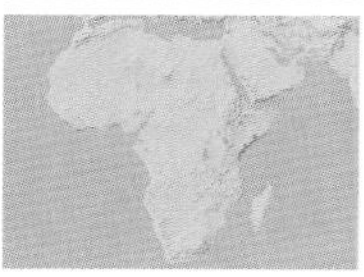

LENGTH 40cm (15½in)

WEIGHT 250g (9oz)

MIGRATION Non-migrant

HABITAT Coastal lowland forest

This bird is easily distinguished from other similar species by its beautiful head markings. Fischer's Turaco has a diagnostic short white-tipped red crest extending back to the nape, which gives it a stunning appearance. This species is considered to be near threatened. As the suitable forest areas within the bird's range become increasingly fragmented, a further decline in its population is inevitable. Its re-classification as a threatened species is also likely in the near future.

Gallirex porphyreolopha

Purple-crested Turaco

LENGTH 40–46cm (15½–18in)

WEIGHT 225–250g (8–9oz)

MIGRATION Non-migrant

HABITAT Coastal and gallery forest, and broad-leaved woodland

The Purple-crested Turaco is aptly named for its dark violet crest. Its irridescent plumage is mainly green and violet in colour. It has bright red flight feathers. In the past, these red primary feathers were much prized as adornments by the Zulu tribe. The Purple-crested Turaco feeds mainly on fruit and berries, but also accepts food from feeding stations in suburban gardens. The bird is generally found in pairs or in small family parties, though larger congregations also occur.

ADULT PURPLE-CRESTED TURACO

Corythaixoides concolor

Grey Go-away-bird

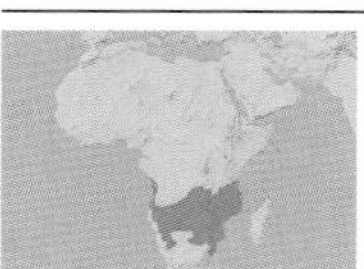

LENGTH 48cm (19in)

WEIGHT 250g (9oz)

MIGRATION Non-migrant

HABITAT Acacia savannna and dry, open woodland

As its name suggests, the Grey Go-away-bird has a uniform grey plumage. However, the bird does have a few notable features such as the long tail and an impressively long, pointed shaggy crest that the bird raises and lowers according to its mood. The Grey Go-away-bird tends to occupy drier, more open habitats in its range in southern Africa than its more colourful, forest-dwelling relatives. But even while the Grey Go-away-bird is a dry country specialist, it is dependent on suitable water sources and shuns truly dry areas. The common name of this species is derived from its call, a harsh nasal "kay-waaaay" or "go away".

ADULT GREY GO-AWAY-BIRD

ADULT GREAT BLUE TURACO

Corythaeola cristata

Great Blue Turaco

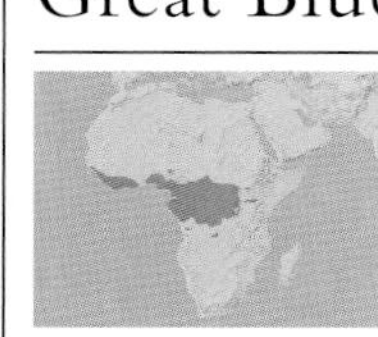

LENGTH 75cm (30in)

WEIGHT 975g (35oz)

MIGRATION Non-migrant

HABITAT Tall forest and secondary growth

Extremely popular with bird-watchers, the Great Blue Turaco is the largest member of the extraordinary turaco family. The bird has green, blue, and yellow plumage, a bright yellow red-tipped bill, a blue and black crest, and a broad long, black-tipped tail. Although the sexes look similar, the female is larger than the male. The juvenile is noticeably duller, with a smaller crest.

The Great Blue Turaco is usually found feeding high in the tree canopy in pairs or in small family groups. This bird moves with surprising speed and agility for its size, and is also adept at leaping about in the canopy. Fruit forms the bulk of its diet but when it becomes temporarily scarce, the bird feeds on flowers, leaves, and even algae. This species is considered a delicacy and is hunted for the bush meat trade. Other threats to it include trapping for the cage-bird trade and forest degradation. The bird's large range, however, acts a buffer for its population, and at present, it is not considered to be at risk.

Clamator jacobinus

Jacobin Cuckoo

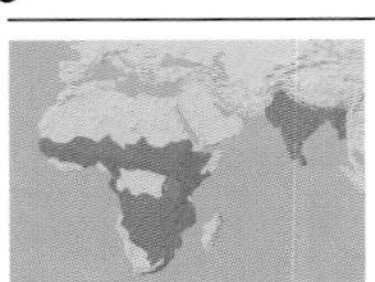

LENGTH 34cm (13½in)

WEIGHT 65–70g (2⅜–2½oz)

MIGRATION Migrant

HABITAT Open woodland and scrub; also dry plains up to 2,000m (6,500ft)

The Jacobin Cuckoo is a black and white bird, sporting a prominent crest and a long tail. It feeds on a range of insects such as caterpillars, in trees or on the ground. It is a brood parasite and its hosts consist of several species of babbler in India, while bulbuls, shrikes, and chatterers are usually targeted in Africa. The eggs of the host are sometimes ejected by the juvenile. A noisy species, its call is a persistent and loud "pipew pipew pipew".

Clamator glandarius

Great Spotted Cuckoo

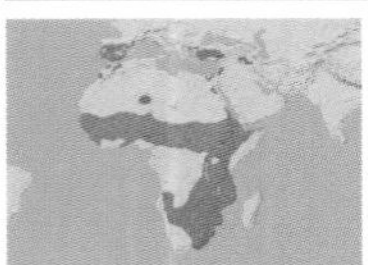

LENGTH 35–39cm (14–15½in)

WEIGHT 125g (4oz)

MIGRATION Migrant

HABITAT Mainly semi-dry areas of woodland and scrub, but also rocky hillsides

The Great Spotted Cuckoo is found in southern Europe, the Middle East, and southern Africa as a summer migrant. It has a silvery grey crest, dark neck, white markings on the back, and white-spotted wings. Its throat is pale yellow and its underparts are white. It commonly feeds on the ground, taking a range of insects and small reptiles. This cuckoo is a brood parasite, laying its eggs in the nests of crows, magpies, and starlings. Its egg has a shorter incubation period than the host's, which means that the young cuckoos grow faster and get a larger share of food from their foster parents. The adult Great Spotted Cuckoo will sometimes lay a second egg in the host nest, but the younger bird usually starves.

ADULT GREAT SPOTTED CUCKOO

Hierococcyx varius

Common Hawk-Cuckoo

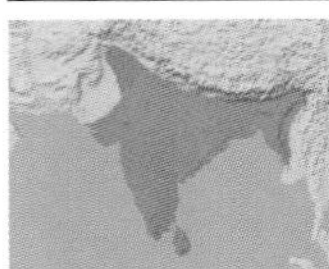

LENGTH 33cm (13in)

WEIGHT 100g (3⅝oz)

MIGRATION Non-migrant

HABITAT Wooded areas of deciduous and semi-evergreen forest; also gardens and tree plantations

Found throughout much of India, Bangladesh, and Sri Lanka, the Common Hawk-Cuckoo has a hawk-like appearance, with a grey head, brown back, rufous breast, and a long, barred tail. It feeds on insects and small lizards. It lays its eggs in the nests of babblers and laughing thrushes, and the cuckoo nestling ejects the young of the host species from the nest.

ADULT COMMON CUCKOO

Cuculus canorus

Common Cuckoo

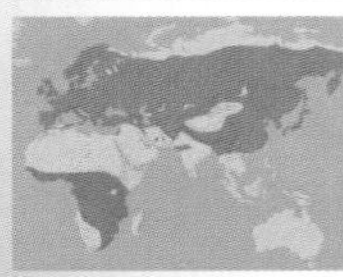

LENGTH 33cm (13in)

WEIGHT 125g (4oz)

MIGRATION Migrant

HABITAT Wide variety of habitats from woodland to reedbeds and open country to 2,000m (6,500ft)

The male Common Cuckoo is dark grey above, with a blackish brown tail, spotted and tipped with white and unevenly barred in black. The female is similar, although it is rufous on its upper breast. There are four subspecies, identified by the areas where they breed and winter: the geographical breeding sites of this cuckoo stretch from western Europe to east Asia and its wintering grounds are in southern Africa, India, and southeast Asia.

The call of the species, consisting of two notes, is a familiar sound of spring. The adult has the unusual ability to feed on hairy caterpillars, which are plentiful in woodland in summer. The global population is not threatened, although the numbers of western European Common Cuckoos declined in the 20th century.

BROOD PARASITE

Like all cuckoos, the Common Cuckoo is a brood parasite. It lays its eggs in the nests of other bird species. The hosts are typically insectivorous birds, such as flycatchers, pipits, warblers, wagtails, and buntings. They feed the cuckoo nestlings, who usually throw the host's eggs and chicks out of the nest.

Cuculus poliocephalus

Lesser Cuckoo

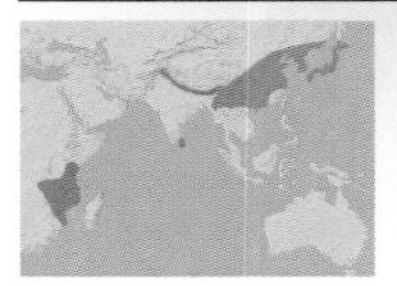

LENGTH 25cm (10in)

WEIGHT 50g (1¾oz)

MIGRATION Migrant

HABITAT Broad-leaved or coniferous forest between 1,500m (4,900ft) and 3,500m (11,500ft)

Although smaller, the male Lesser Cuckoo is generally similar to the Common Cuckoo (above) in appearance. However, the female is sometimes rufous in colour and the juvenile has a black face. The call is a loud chattering sound. The breeding sites are typically at an altitude of more than 1,000m (3,300ft) to 3,500m (11,500ft) in the Himalayas, and they range stretch from Japan to Nepal. Like other members of its family, the Lesser Cuckoo is a brood parasite and lays its eggs in the nests of warblers, wren-babblers, and other small species. Its eggs are generally unmarked, but can vary in colour. The adult feeds on caterpillars, beetles, and other insects.

This species migrates mainly towards the southwest, and some birds reach East Africa, where it is the only cuckoo found in pine forests. Its global population is not threatened, although local populations are influenced by trends within the host species.

ADULT LESSER CUCKOO

Cacomantis variolosus

Brush Cuckoo

LENGTH 21–28cm (8½–11in)

WEIGHT 35g (1¼oz)

MIGRATION Non-migrant

HABITAT Rainforest, secondary forest, and mangroves, up to 2,000m (6,500ft)

The Brush Cuckoo is found through much of southeast Asia and in northern and western Australia, but does not reach Tasmania. Its head and upperparts are brownish grey. It has rufuous underparts, with a grey throat and upper breast. The male and female have similar plumage.

The Brush Cuckoo is a brood parasite, laying its eggs in the nests of over 60 different bird species. The selection of hosts depends on the species that nest in the same range as this cuckoo and vary from sunbirds to shrikes. The Brush Cuckoo's eggs are white, with varying patterns of brown spots, which match the eggs of the host species. The host's eggs or young are ejected by the young cuckoo, which hatches after an incubation period of just 13 days. The young are fed by the host bird for up to a month after fledging. The adult Brush Cuckoo mainly feeds on caterpillars, but also takes a variety of large insects and spiders from the foliage of trees and bushes.

ADULT BRUSH CUCKOO

Chrysococcyx cupreus

African Emerald Cuckoo

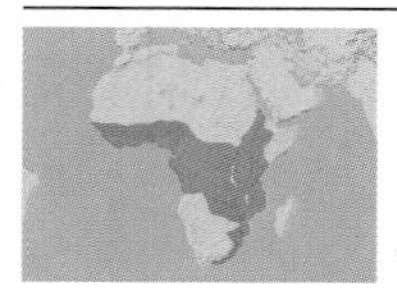

LENGTH 20cm (8in)

WEIGHT 35–45g (1¼–1⅝oz)

MIGRATION Partial migrant

HABITAT Evergreen forest, open woodland, and cultivation

As its common name suggests, the male African Emerald Cuckoo is mostly a glossy green on the head and upperparts. The female is duller, with a brown head and barred undersides, although the wings and tail retain some green coloration.

The African Emerald Cuckoo is a brood parasite and mainly targets insectivorous species such as bulbuls, warblers, robin-chats, and weavers. The female cuckoo removes a single egg from the host's nest with the young cuckoo ejecting the rest of the eggs or young of the host after hatching at 13–14 days. The young birds fledge at 18–20 days and remain with the host for up to two weeks. A solitary bird, this cuckoo mainly feeds on caterpillars gleaned from the forest canopy. It is found in Africa, south of the Sahara, but has declined over parts of the range.

ADULT HORSFIELD'S BRONZE CUCKOO

Chrysococcyx basalis

Horsfield's Bronze Cuckoo

LENGTH 17cm (6½in)

WEIGHT 20g (11/16oz)

MIGRATION Partial migrant

HABITAT Open woodland and scrub, mainly in arid or semi-arid areas

Both the male and female of this species are greenish brown with paler, barred underparts, and a bold, dark eye-stripe. This cuckoo lays its eggs in the nests of around 28 bird species, choosing hosts that construct domed, rather than open, nests. The adult cuckoo forages on the ground and in foliage, taking mainly caterpillars and a variety of insects.

Scythrops novaehollandiae

Channel-billed Cuckoo

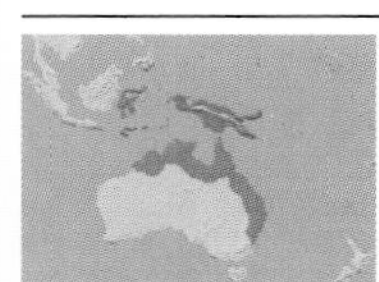

LENGTH 60cm (23½in)

WEIGHT 600–625g (21–22oz)

MIGRATION Migrant

HABITAT Edges of forest or along rivers and other open areas, particularly damp or semi-dry areas

ADULT CHANNEL-BILLED CUCKOO

Named after its large curved bill, an unusual feature in the cuckoo family, the Channel-billed Cuckoo is grey in colour, with a long, barred tail. The adult feeds mainly on fruit, such as figs. It is a brood parasite, choosing hosts that are similar in size, such as crows and magpies. It is not known whether the young cuckoos eject the host's eggs and young, although the adult cuckoos are known to damage the eggs of the host when targeting the nest.

Eudynamys scolopaceus

Asian Koel

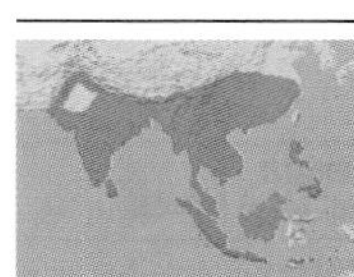

LENGTH 39–46cm (15½–18in)

WEIGHT 225g (8oz)

MIGRATION Partial migrant

HABITAT Damp forest and scrub, sometimes around human habitation

Mainly a brood parasite of larger species such as crows, the Asian Koel also targets mynas, figbirds, and drongos. The male commonly distracts the host species to allow the female to lay eggs, but the host's eggs and young are not ejected. The male Asian Koel has ruby-red eyes and glossy black plumage. The female and the juvenile are dark grey-brown, with white spots on the throat and white bars on the underparts. The adults mostly feed on fruit, although some invertebrates are taken. The call of the Asian Koel is a loud "ko-el ko-el ko-el" crescendo.

MALE ASIAN KOEL

Piaya cayana

Squirrel Cuckoo

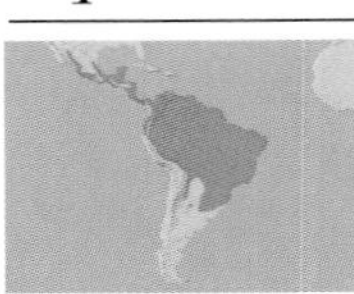

LENGTH 46cm (18in)

WEIGHT 100g (3$\frac{5}{8}$oz)

MIGRATION Non-migrant

HABITAT Range of forests and plantations, but generally avoids denser lowland forest

The Squirrel Cuckoo has a pale throat and chest, brown upperparts, and grey underparts. The tail is long, with its underside marked by alternating black and white chevrons. It mainly feeds on caterpillars, although a range of insects are also taken, including army ants. The species builds a platform nest made of leaves and branches. Its range stretches through much of South America, including coastal Central America.

ADULT SQUIRREL CUCKOO

Centropus superciliosus

White-browed Coucal

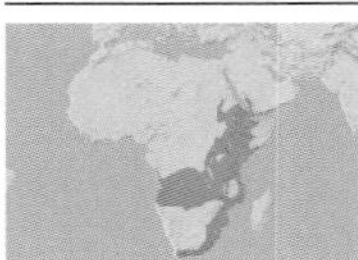

LENGTH 36–42cm (14–16$\frac{1}{2}$in)

WEIGHT 150–175g (5–6oz)

MIGRATION Non-migrant

HABITAT Dense bush beside rivers and in other wetland areas

ADULT WHITE-BROWED COUCAL

Named for the white stripe above its eye, the White-browed Coucal is a rich brown colour on its back, with a streaked dark head. The female is larger than the male, although there is little difference in plumage. Its diet ranges from insects to small reptiles, mice, frogs, and small birds. The White-browed Coucal sometimes patrols the edges of burnt grass after a fire to catch trapped prey. When disturbed, the young are able to emit a foul-smelling liquid.

ADULT BIRD

Centropus phasianus

Pheasant Coucal

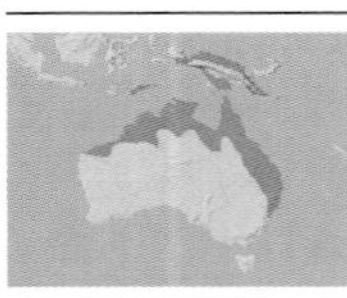

LENGTH 53–80cm (21–31in)

WEIGHT 200–500g (7–18oz)

MIGRATION Non-migrant

HABITAT Damp grassland and forest in lowland areas, particularly around rivers and marshes

Named for its striking pheasant-like appearance, the Pheasant Coucal is black, with contrasting streaked reddish brown upperparts and wings. The female is larger than the male. This species collects most of its food on the ground. Its diet includes insects, reptiles, nestling birds, and young mammals. The nest is made up of grass stems and is constructed on the ground.

Coua gigas

Giant Coua

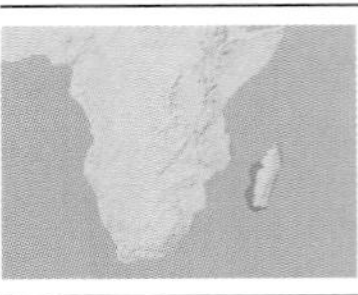

LENGTH 58–62cm (23–24in)

WEIGHT 425g (15oz)

MIGRATION Non-migrant

HABITAT Deciduous forest and scrub in areas of calcium-rich soil

The largest species of a family entirely confined to Madagascar, the Giant Coua is more like a pheasant than a cuckoo. Mainly brown on the upperparts with a rufous belly, it has an ornate unfeathered face, its dark eye framed by a blue area with a pink patch at the rear of the eye. Its call is a deep repetitive sound delivered from the ground or a low tree.

The main food of this species consists of insects and seeds gathered by foraging through the leaf layer on the forest floor. The birds usually forage in pairs, but also alone or in family groups. Despite the ground-living existence of the adults, the nest, constructed from leaves and twigs, is placed 3–10m (10–33ft) above the ground. The Giant Coua is less common in the southern part of its range due to hunting. Birds within the protected parts of its range are surrounded by areas where deforestation is advancing rapidly.

ADULT GIANT COUA

Crotophaga sulcirostris

Groove-billed Ani

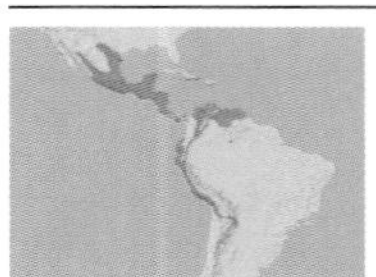

LENGTH 32cm (12$\frac{1}{2}$in)

WEIGHT 70–80g (2$\frac{1}{2}$–2$\frac{7}{8}$oz)

MIGRATION Non-migrant

HABITAT Scrub from sea-level to 2,500m (8,500ft), particularly in disturbed areas of growth

Found in Central America and northern South America, the Groove-billed Ani is a glossy, black bird with a heavy, curved bill. The male is slightly larger than the female. The bird takes a wide range of insects and small reptiles when foraging on the ground. Insects are also taken from cow dung and, less commonly, ticks are taken from the backs of cattle. The breeding season varies, depending on the part of the range, but coincides with the rainy season in drier areas.

A sociable species, the Groove-billed Ani is a communal breeding bird, with up to five pairs breeding together. Up to 18 eggs have been recorded in some nests, although each female lays only 3 or 4. A male may have several mates, and also takes part in incubation. Fledging occurs 10 days after hatching, but the young are tended for three weeks after leaving the nest.

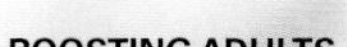

ROOSTING ADULTS

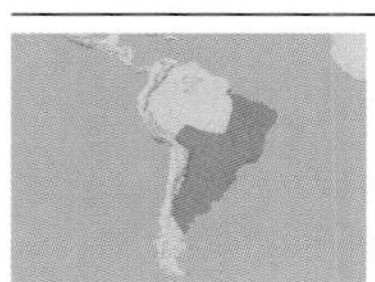

Guira guira

Guira Cuckoo

LENGTH 36cm (14in)

WEIGHT 150g (5oz)

MIGRATION Non-migrant

HABITAT Scrub from sea-level to more than 1,200m (4,000ft); also more open areas

A row of prominent feathers around the head give the Guira Cuckoo a striking appearance. Both the male and female have an orange-yellow bill and a bright orange head crest, although the female is slightly larger. Two forms exist, which differ only in the colour of the bill, being either yellow or orange. The Guira Cuckoo feeds mainly on insects, but also on mice, small reptiles, and the young of other birds. A highly sociable species, this bird feeds and roosts in large groups of up to 20 birds, often huddling together for warmth. The Guira Cuckoo is not a brood parasite, but has been known to lay its eggs in the nests of other species, sharing incubation with the host. It also breeds in groups, with up to 10 eggs being found in some communal nests.

ADULT GUIRA CUCKOO

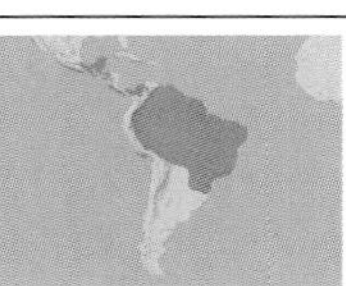

Dromococcyx phasianellus

Pheasant Cuckoo

LENGTH 36cm (14in)

WEIGHT 80g ($2^{7}/_{8}$oz)

MIGRATION Non-migrant

HABITAT Tropical forest up to 1,500m (4,900ft)

Dark brown above, with pale brown underparts, the Pheasant Cuckoo has a prominent white stripe running from the eye to the back of the head and a long graduated tail. The male and female are similar and do not differ in size. The diet of the Pheasant Cuckoo mainly consists of large insects, such as grasshoppers, and lizards. It is a brood parasite, often laying its eggs in the nests of tyrant-flycatchers.

The Pheasant Cuckoo is not common and is localized in distribution. Its range stretches from south Mexico to Argentina and Paraguay, with the Central American subspecies being described as distinct by some scientists. The Pheasant Cuckoo is a resident bird and there are no known migratory movements, but it is a solitary, secretive species that is difficult to study.

ADULT GREATER ROADRUNNER

Geococcyx californianus

Greater Roadrunner

LENGTH 56cm (22in)

WEIGHT 300–325g (11–12oz)

MIGRATION Non-migrant

HABITAT Arid areas, including scrub and more open areas, to an altitude of 2,500m (8,202ft)

The Greater Roadrunner prefers to run rather than fly and is able to run for short distances at a speed of 30kph (18mph). It has a prominent dark crest, a heavy, hooked bill, and its plumage is mainly streaked in brown and white. Its long tail reveals white tips when it is spread. The male is larger, but its plumage is similar to that of the female. The species "sunbathes" by positioning its feathers so that the black skin on its back can absorb sunlight.

During courtship, the male Greater Roadrunner performs an unusual display, parading before the female as it bows and alternately lifts and drops its wings. The nest is constructed on a site raised 1–3m ($3^{1}/_{4}$–10ft) above the ground. The female lays 2–6 eggs. Larger clutches are produced after the rains.

PREY BATTERING

An opportunistic carnivore, the Greater Roadrunner collects a wide variety of food from the ground, including carrion from roadkill, large invertebrates (even venomous tarantulas and scorpions), reptiles, small birds, and mammals. It batters its prey with its strong, pointed bill or smashes it against a rock, and eats it whole. It tackles scorpions by seizing the tail.

OWLS

ORDER	Strigiformes
FAMILY	2
SPECIES	194

FOUND IN EVERY CONTINENT except Antarctica, owls are predatory birds with forward-facing eyes and sharp, grasping claws. Externally, they resemble birds of prey, but their closest living relatives are thought to be nightjars and allied species. Most owls hunt at night; their secretive habits – together with distinctive calls – mean that they are heard more often than they are seen. By day, they usually roost in trees, using camouflaged plumage to remain hidden. Owls feed almost entirely on live animals. Most catch rodents and small mammals but, as a group, their diet includes nocturnal insects, songbirds, and fish. They can find food even in winter and few migrate.

DAYLIGHT HUNTER
Swooping on its prey, a Northern Hawk Owl stands out against the late snows of spring. Some owls search for prey on the wing, but many launch themselves from a perch.

ANATOMY

Owls' most striking features are upright posture and large, forward-facing eyes. Set in a flattened face, the eyes widen inside the skull, so that the saucer-shaped retinas almost touch. The retinas are packed with photoreceptors, allowing owls to spot prey in very low levels of light. Their ears are also sensitive, and may be positioned asymmetrically, which helps to pinpoint the source of a sound. Some species, such as Barn Owls, can catch their prey in total darkness. Owls fly almost silently, thanks to soft, muffling fringes on their flight feathers. However, during the breeding season, they may produce far-carrying cries – hooting, piercing screeches, or trills. In some species, pairs take part in long duets.

ASYMMETRICAL EARS
Several groups of owls, including barn owls, have ear openings that differ both in position and in size. This unusual asymmetry helps an owl to pinpoint sounds in the vertical plane – in other words, sounds from straight ahead of them when they are on the wing.

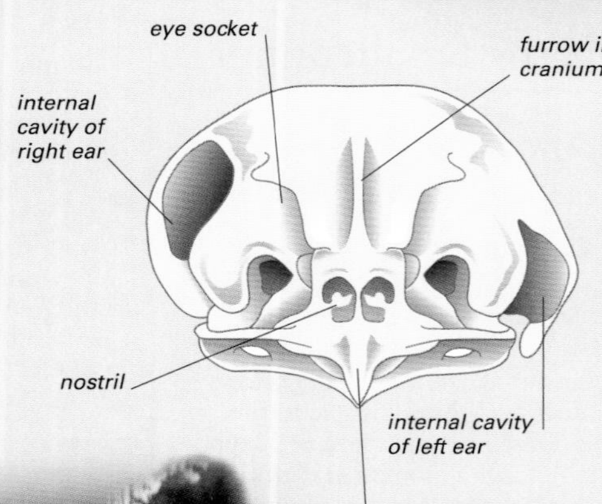

EAR TUFTS
Owls may have feathery tufts that look like ears: in this Long-eared Owl they are particularly well developed. However, as in all birds, the true ear openings are hidden beneath their plumage, where they lead to cavities inside the skull, which amplify sounds.

FEEDING

Most owls wait for darkness before hunting. However, some species – such as Short-eared Owls – emerge before dusk, and can be seen on the wing long after dawn. Another exception are owls that live in the far north. Here, nights are short during the summer breeding season, forcing the owls to hunt by day. All owls share the same technique for making a kill. An owl grips the prey with its talons and usually takes it back to a perch. If the animal is small, the owl swallows it whole; if not, it uses its hooked bill to tear it apart. Once it has finished feeding, it digests all the soft tissue, but regurgitates bones, feathers, and fur as pellets.

OWL PELLETS
Pellets are formed in an owl's gizzard, where hard remains become trapped. The gizzard compresses them into a smooth shape, for regurgitation.

BREEDING

In the far north, Snowy Owls nest in open tundra, choosing a slight rise where they have a good view. However, this kind of behaviour is unusual among owls. Some take over abandoned hawks' or crows' nests, but most are cavity nesters, bringing up their young in tree-holes, under rocky overhangs or, more rarely, in burrows. Owls use little or no nesting material, and lay up to a dozen white, rounded eggs. The eggs hatch in sequence, producing chicks of varying age and size. Once hatching begins, both parents deliver food to the young. If food is short, the oldest chick gets the most – which ensures that at least some of the young survive. Owl chicks can take up to eight weeks to leave their nest.

STAGGERED HATCHING
Three Great Grey Owl chicks look out from their nest. Flanked by its larger siblings, the one in the middle is the least likely to survive to adulthood if the parents have difficulty finding food.

Tyto novaehollandiae

Australian Masked Owl

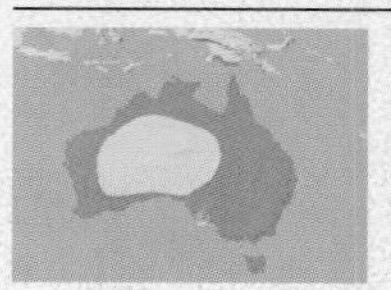

LENGTH 33–57cm (13–$22\frac{1}{2}$in)
WEIGHT 425–1250g (15–45oz)
MIGRATION Non-migrant
HABITAT Forests and open woodland, as well as farmland with large trees

The Australian Masked Owl is similar to the Barn Owl (below), but is larger, with a rounder, black-bordered face, a more powerful bill and talons, and completely feathered legs. It is blackish brown with grey and white spots on the upperparts. The underparts are white with brown spots. The female is a darker colour than the male. The Tasmanian subspecies (*T. n. castanops*) is a much darker brown than the pale birds found on the mainland and is also larger; the female being the largest of the *Tyto* genus.

Tyto alba

Barn Owl

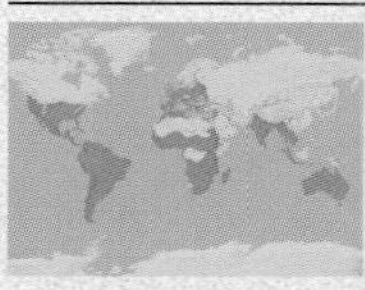

LENGTH 30–45cm (12–$17\frac{1}{2}$in)
WEIGHT 275–600g (10–21oz)
MIGRATION Non-migrant
HABITAT Widespread, but favours lowland areas with some cover

The Barn Owl is one of the world's most widely occurring owl species. There are many subspecies, which differ considerably in size and the overall darkness of their plumage. The typical Barn Owl, however, is a pale creamy white bird with a distinctive heart-shaped face. It has a fluttering, almost moth-like flight. The species feeds over open areas, quartering the ground as it looks for prey – usually small rodents – before plunging in a flurry of wingbeats. The Barn Owl is sometimes also referred to as the Screech Owl, reflecting its notable, high-pitched call.

ADULT BARN OWL

powerful thin, hooked bill

spotting and speckling on back

SILENT HUNTER

The Barn Owl is equipped with both excellent vision and hearing, making it a fearsome predator. Its ability to locate prey by using sound is aided by its asymmetrically placed ears, which allows it to localize sounds generated by its prey. It either flies slowly over an area, listening for movements of its prey, or perches in wait, before swooping to attack it.

Megascops asio

Eastern Screech Owl

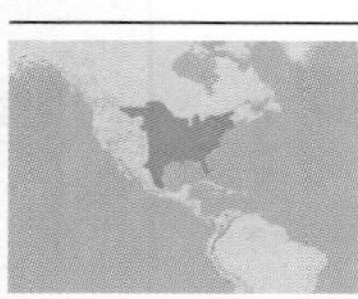

LENGTH 16–25cm ($6\frac{1}{2}$–10in)
WEIGHT 175–200g (6–7oz)
MIGRATION Non-migrant
HABITAT Woodland, parks, and gardens

Small and stocky with prominent ear tufts, the Eastern Screech Owl occurs in two main colour forms: a greyish brown and a more striking rufous form. The species is found in the eastern half of USA and southern Canada. The closely related Western Screech Owl occurs in the west of the continent. However, the eastern species can be told apart from the western species by its paler bill, black-edged facial disc, and less patterned underparts.

ADULT (GREY FORM)

ADULT EURASIAN SCOPS OWL

Otus scops

Eurasian Scops Owl

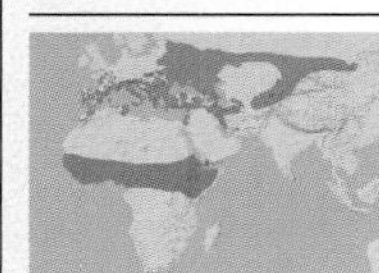

LENGTH 16–20cm ($6\frac{1}{2}$–8in)
WEIGHT 60–125g ($2\frac{1}{8}$–4oz)
MIGRATION Migrant
HABITAT Open woodland, orchards, parkland, and gardens

This small, tufted owl with grey-brown plumage breeds from southern Europe to the Middle East and also North Africa. The territorial call of the male is very distinct – a short, low "teu" that is repeated every two to three seconds, rather like a car alarm. Duets with the female, which has a higher-pitched call, are frequent.

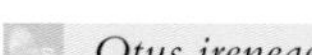

Otus ireneae

Sokoke Scops Owl

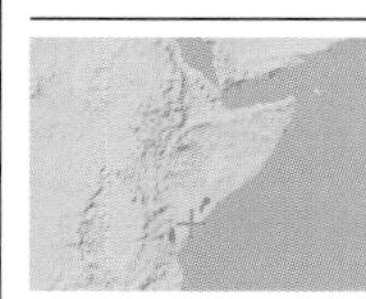

LENGTH 15–18cm (6–7in)
WEIGHT 50g ($1\frac{3}{4}$oz)
MIGRATION Non-migrant
HABITAT Forest
RED LIST CATEGORY Endangered

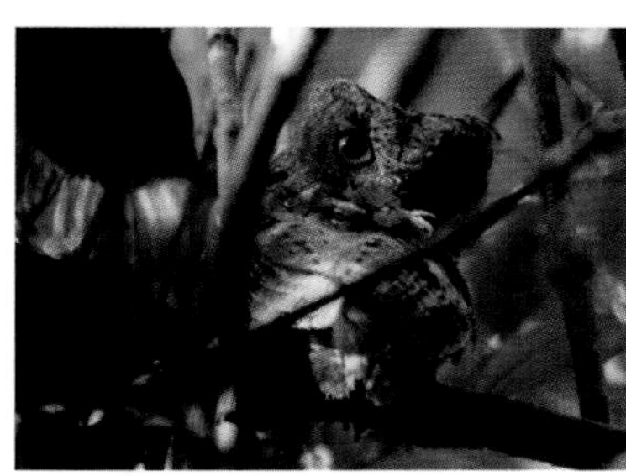

ADULT SOKOKE SCOPS OWL

The tiny Sokoke Scops Owl occurs in greyish brown and rufous colour forms. It has very slight ear tufts. The species was believed to occur only in the Arabuko-Sokoke Forest of coastal Kenya, but has recently also been found in the East Usambara Mountains of Tanzania. The species is classified as endangered as its forest habitat in Tanzania is being rapidly cleared. In Kenya, its habitat is protected.

Ptilopsis granti

Southern White-faced Owl

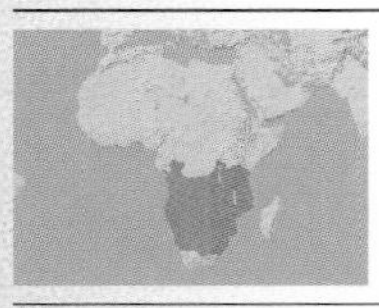

LENGTH 22–25cm ($8\frac{1}{2}$–10in)
WEIGHT 175–275g (6–10oz)
MIGRATION Non-migrant
HABITAT Dry woodland, savanna, and semi-desert

The Southern White-faced Owl is a distinctive species with long black-centred ear tufts, bright orange eyes, a black-bordered white face, and a white line that stretches along the wing. It also has a tuft of white facial feathers that looks like a moustache. The species is largely resident and is found in southern Africa. A very similar species, the Northern White-faced Owl (*P. leucotis*) is found in Central Africa. The northern species is slightly paler in coloration, with less contrasting face markings.

ADULT SOUTHERN WHITE-FACED OWL

Bubo virginianus

Great Horned Owl

LENGTH 51–60cm (20–23½in)

WEIGHT 0.9–1.5kg (2–3¼lb)

MIGRATION Partial migrant

HABITAT Most forest types, grassland, shrubland, and rocky areas with steep gorges

This large, mainly nocturnal, owl has large erect ear tufts, and its grey-brown plumage is mottled above and barred below, helping it roost undetected during daytime. It has rust-brown facial discs and a white chin and throat.

Occuring throughout the Americas, from the northern tree line south to Patagonia, the Great Horned Owl occupies the widest habitat range of any owl. This is because it takes a wide variety of prey and will use virtually any nesting site – including rockfaces and old buildings – that offers sufficient cover.

ADULT GREAT HORNED OWL

EAR TUFTS

Several owls, including the Great Horned Owl, have prominent ear tufts or "horns", as they are also called. The function of these tufts remains hotly disputed. Some argue that they aid daytime camouflage, breaking up the shape of the owl and blending it with its perch. Others believe that the tufts are used for behavioural signalling and species recognition. What appears clear, however, is that they have no role in hearing.

Bubo lacteus

Verreaux's Eagle-owl

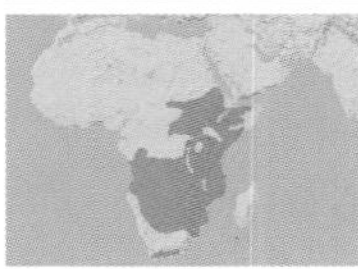

LENGTH 60–65cm (23½–26in)

WEIGHT 1.7–2.6kg (3¾–5½lb)

MIGRATION Non-migrant

HABITAT Open savanna and semi-desert areas, including adjacent riparian areas and woodland

Africa's largest owl, Verreaux's Eagle-owl, is also known as the Giant or Milky Eagle-owl and occurs over much of the continent south of the Sahara. Apart from its distinct ear tufts, it can be distinguished by its deep pink eyelids, white throat, and pale grey-brown plumage.

An opportunistic hunter, it takes any available prey. In the southwest of its range, herons are its favoured prey, while elsewhere, a variety of mammals, reptiles, and birds are taken at night. It will also wade into water in search of fish and insects.

PERCHING ADULT

Bubo bubo

Eurasian Eagle-owl

LENGTH 60–75cm (23½–30in)

WEIGHT 2.3–3kg (5½–6½lb)

MIGRATION Partial migrant

HABITAT Rocky country with cliffs, wooded patches, and quarries, all far from human habitation

A powerful and voracious predator, the Eurasian Eagle-owl is the largest owl in the world. Also known as the Great, Common, or Northern Eagle-owl, it has large ear tufts (upright in the male, but drooping in the female). It usually hunts at night and feeds on small or medium-sized mammals (especially hares) and even preys on large birds such as herons and buzzards.

ADULT MALE

Bubo scandiaca

Snowy Owl

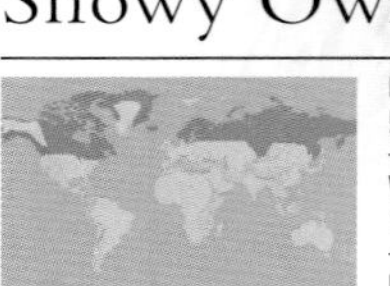

LENGTH 55–70cm (21½–28in)

WEIGHT 1.8–2.3kg (4½–5½lb)

MIGRATION Migrant

HABITAT Open tundra with terrestrial perches and sparse low vegetation, usually in lowland

A spectacular white owl of the northern polar tundra, the Snowy Owl is named for its white plumage. The male is entirely white, with narrow grey or brown barring on the upperparts. The female is larger and is also white, but with extensive barring on the upperparts and spotting on the crown. Both sexes have bright golden or orange irises and heavily feathered legs and toes. The nestling is grey with a white face. The first year bird is white with heavy, dark barring. Males and females become whiter as they get older.

The Snowy Owl feeds on mammals up to the size of hares, particularly lemmings and voles, and birds up to the size of geese. The Snowy Owl hunts at dusk and dawn, making a long powerful swoop from a low perch to snatch its prey off the ground. It occasionally takes fish, amphibians, crabs, and insects. Its call is a series of chattering, barking notes.

The Snowy Owl is usually monogamous and often pairs for life. The male's courtship flight is undulating and consists of flaps followed by a glide. The size of the clutch depends on prey availability: the more prey there is, the more eggs the female will lay. Breeding success is dependent on food supply and the timing of the spring thaw.

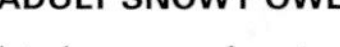

ADULT SNOWY OWL

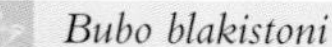

Bubo blakistoni

Blakiston's Fish Owl

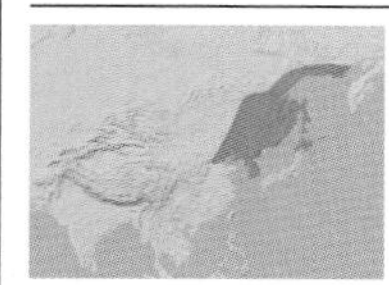

LENGTH 60–70cm (23½–28in)

WEIGHT 1.7–2.3kg (3¼–5½lb)

MIGRATION Non-migrant

HABITAT Dense mixed or broad-leaf forest and forested valleys along clear rivers

RED LIST CATEGORY Endangered

ADULT BLAKISTON'S FISH OWL

Blakiston's Fish Owl or the Eagle-owl is one of the largest and rarest of all owls, with just 500 pairs remaining. The destruction of its habitat has contributed to its decline, as has the depletion of the stocks of fish that form much of its diet. Its habit of concentrating around fish holes in the winter ice also makes it susceptible to persecution. Pairs mate for life and occupy distinct territories within their forest habitat. The female usually lays two eggs, which she incubates while the male stands guard and feeds her.

ADULT PEL'S FISHING OWL

Scotopelia peli

Pel's Fishing Owl

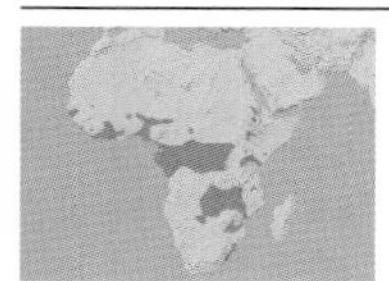

LENGTH 55–63cm (21½–25in)

WEIGHT 1.7–2.2kg (3¼–4½lb)

MIGRATION Non-migrant

HABITAT Forest edges along lowland rivers, swamps, lakes, and estuaries

The largest of the fishing owls, Pel's, or African Fishing Owl, has a round head and lacks ear tufts. Generally pale chestnut in colour, there is substantial individual variation in plumage colour and in barring. This species hunts by night from a perch about 1m (3¼ft) above water, gliding to snatch its food from the surface, its curved talons helping to grasp its slippery prey. Its main quarry is fish, but it also takes crabs and frogs.

Strix nebulosa

Great Grey Owl

LENGTH 59–69cm (23–27in)

WEIGHT 0.8–1.7kg (1¾–3¾lb)

MIGRATION Partial migrant

HABITAT Boreal or coniferous forest with open areas such as montane meadows

ADULT AND CHICK

The Great Grey Owl, also known as the Dark Wood-owl or Lapland Owl, is a stunning inhabitant of the northern taiga forests. The adult has a large, round head with concentric grey circles on its facial disc and small pale "staring" eyes.

This owl can detect movement upto 60cm (2ft) under the snow. When it hears a movement, it glides up to 100m (330ft) before pouncing, breaking through the snow-covered ground to extract a vole or other small mammal. It also takes birds up to the size of a grouse. The Great Grey Owl is usually monogamous, and its young are fed by both sexes. It breeds in boggy northern forests.

CAMOUFLAGED PLUMAGE

The thick white plumage, and heavily feathered feet of the Snowy Owl make it well adapted for life north of the Arctic Circle. This owl nests on the ground, usually on a mound or boulder with good visibility and access to hunting. Its white plumage helps to camouflage it, concealing it from its prey and also allowing it to roost undisturbed in the day.

Strix aluco

Tawny Owl

LENGTH 37–39cm ($14^1/_2$–$15^1/_2$in)

WEIGHT 425–525g (15–19oz)

MIGRATION Non-migrant

HABITAT Deciduous, mixed, and coniferous woods; towns with parks and large gardens

Widespread across Europe, Asia, and North Africa, the Tawny Owl is one of the world's most familiar owls. It exhibits a range of colour forms, from a rich rufous through all shades of brown to pale grey, although these are rarely observed as this is a nocturnal species. The Tawny Owl has a large, round head, large black eyes, white bristles around the bill, an obvious facial disc, white marks on the shoulders, and a short tail.

The male uses a long drawn-out hooting call during courtship or to communicate with its mate. More often heard is, however, the "ke-wick!" call used by both the male and the female to keep in contact with other Tawny Owls. These owls mate for life and stay together throughout the year. They nest in holes in trees, old buildings, and cliffs and defend their nests aggressively, even attacking humans who come too close. The 2–5 eggs in the clutch are laid between April and June, and the female tends to the young until they are grown. A night hunter, the Tawny Owl drops down from its perch to take voles, mice, rats, and frogs from the ground or catches small birds as they roost or incubate eggs at night. Its flight is silent, strong, and direct.

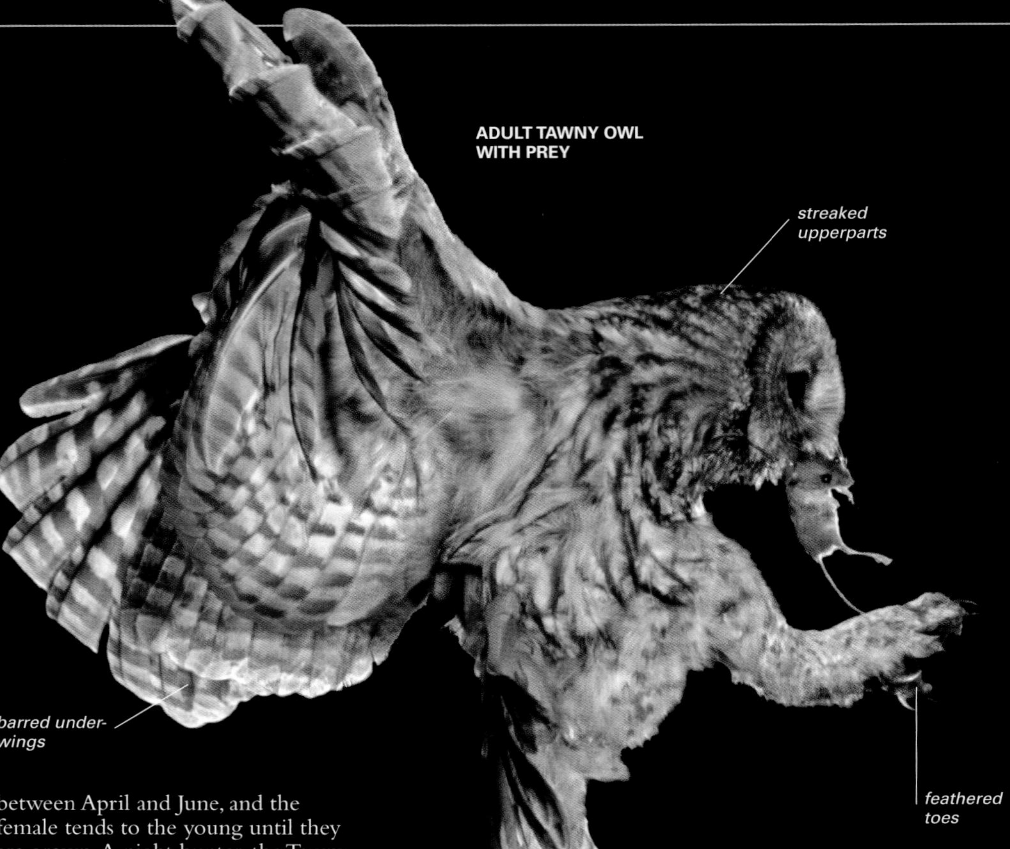

ADULT TAWNY OWL WITH PREY

Strix uralensis

Ural Owl

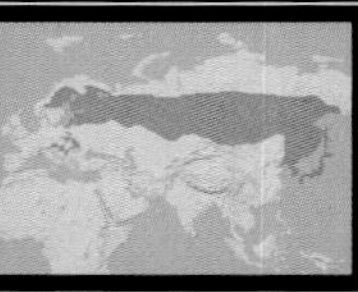

LENGTH 58–62cm (23–24in)

WEIGHT 700–875g (25–31oz)

MIGRATION Non-migrant

HABITAT Pine, beech, and mixed woods with clearings, and forest edges

ADULT URAL OWL

The Ural Owl resembles a large Tawny Owl (above), with the same kind of facial disc, but with a relatively longer tail. The breeding cycle of the Ural Owl is linked to fluctuations in vole populations, but it will also eat other mammals and birds such as young hares, wood pigeons, and grouse. It is nocturnal and nests in hollow trees.

Lophostrix cristata

Crested Owl

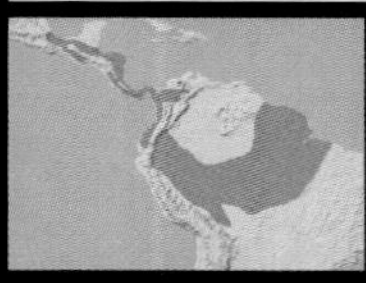

LENGTH 38–43cm (15–17in)

WEIGHT 475–625g (17–22oz)

MIGRATION Non-migrant

HABITAT Lowland primary or secondary rainforest with undergrowth, mostly near water

The Crested Owl has distinctive white ear-tufts extending into white eyebrows. Otherwise, its plumage is chocolate or reddish brown. A grey subspecies is found in Mexico and Central America.

Mainly nocturnal, the Crested Owl responds when disturbed at its daytime roost by stretching its body and raising its ear-tufts. Dependent on rainforest, it is disappearing from deforested parts of its range.

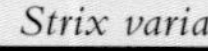

Strix varia

Barred Owl

LENGTH 50–60cm ($19^1/_2$–$23^1/_2$in)

WEIGHT 625–800g (22–29oz)

MIGRATION Non-migrant

HABITAT Dense mature woodland, but also spreads into areas cleared by logging

Related to the Ural Owl (left), but with a less pronounced facial disc and shorter tail, this owl's name comes from the distinctive horizontal bars on its upper breast. The Barred Owl hunts mainly from perches, swooping down on small mammals and birds, but also feeds on insects and other invertebrates.

A nocturnal species, the Barred Owl roosts high in trees, nestled against the trunk or on large branches. It nests and roosts in holes and also in the abandoned nests of large raptors. It is aggressive in defence of its nest.

ADULT BARRED OWL

ADULT SPECTACLED OWL

Pulsatrix perspicillata

Spectacled Owl

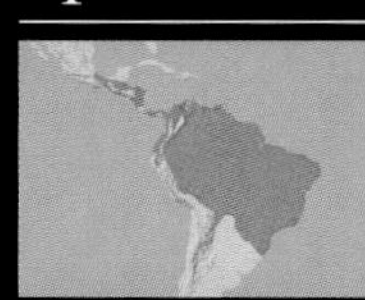

LENGTH 41–48cm (16–19in)

WEIGHT 775–900g (28–32oz)

MIGRATION Non-migrant

HABITAT Old-growth tropical and sub-tropical forest and plantations

The contrast with the dark plumage of the head and upperparts makes this owl's white "spectacles" particularly striking. Its throat is also white. The Spectacled Owl is active at night. It hunts mainly from perches, flying between branches, where it waits for prey. It preys on roosting birds up to the size of pigeons, and ground- and tree-living mammals, as big as opossums, and will also pounce on insects. The Spectacled Owl is disappearing from parts of its range where old-growth forest has been cleared.

Surnia ulula

Northern Hawk-Owl

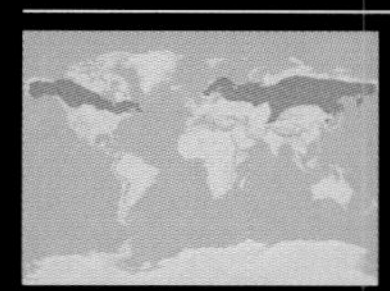

LENGTH 36–41cm (14–16in)

WEIGHT 300–350g (11–13oz)

MIGRATION Non-migrant

HABITAT Boreal coniferous forest and open country with trees

A slim, long-bodied, long-tailed owl, the Northern Hawk-Owl often flies by day. The hawk-like appearance is reinforced by its yellow eyes and falcon-like wing shape.

Like other owls of the boreal forest, the Northern Hawk-Owl's breeding success is dependent on the number of voles and lemmings available for it to feed on, and it shifts its territories from year to year accordingly. Although these owls do not migrate, they can be found a long way south of their usual range in years when the small rodent population decreases.

This species generally nests in hollow trees, often choosing abandoned woodpecker nests, but it takes readily to nest boxes. About 5–13 eggs are laid, and the female remains on the nest to incubate the eggs, while the male hunts for food.

FULL-TIME HUNTER

Often mistaken for a diurnal bird of prey, the Northern Hawk-Owl hunts both during day and night. It flies swiftly, close to the ground, alternately flapping its wings in rapid beats and gliding. It waits on a perch and uses its rapid flight to overtake its prey. During courtship, the males will often try to impress females by hunting for food and bringing it to them.

DIVING FOR ITS PREY
The Northern Hawk-Owl has exceptional hearing and can plunge into the snow to capture rodents below the surface.

ADULT NORTHERN HAWK-OWL

Glaucidium californicum

Northern Pygmy Owl

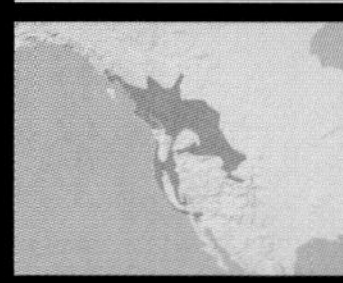

LENGTH 17cm (6½in)

WEIGHT 60–75g (2⅛–2⅝oz)

MIGRATION Non-migrant

HABITAT Taiga and other coniferous forest; mixed forest with pines, aspens, and beeches

One of the smallest owls in its range, this sparrow-sized owl is mostly active at dawn and dusk, although it is also seen in daylight. In fact, its night vision is believed to be poor. Often seen in the open, on posts or bare branches, this owl hunts mammals and insects by dropping down from a perch and ambushes birds by bursting out of concealment. The Northern Pygmy Owl will tackle prey much larger than itself, such as ground squirrels and quails. Although not migratory, in mountainous regions it will move to lowlands in winter.

Glaucidium brasilianum

Ferruginous Pygmy Owl

LENGTH 17–20cm (6½–8in)

WEIGHT 65–75g (2⅜–2⅝oz)

MIGRATION Non-migrant

HABITAT Tropical and subtropical forest; grassland with trees, parks, and gardens

The name "ferruginous", which means rusty, covers only one colour form of this widely distributed species, which varies from a rich reddish brown to a dull grey. It is small and stocky with disproportionately large talons. Its round head is covered with stripes. Often seen in daylight, it is most active at dawn and dusk.

Hunting from a perch, it swoops down on insects, frogs, mammals, and birds, sometimes taking prey bigger than itself with its relatively powerful claws.

ADULT

Glaucidium capense

African Barred Owlet

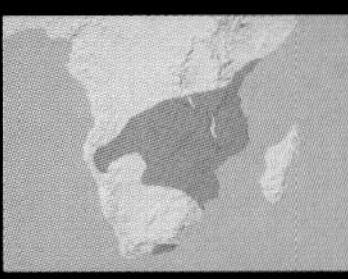

LENGTH 22cm (8½in)

WEIGHT 125g (4oz)

MIGRATION Non-migrant

HABITAT Woodland edges and riverside forests; one subspecies lives in primary forest

Despite its name, the barring on the upper breast of this owl is less striking than the spots that cover the rest of its underparts. The African Barred Owlet is active at dawn and dusk and is also seen in daylight. Its feet are relatively small, which restricts its range of prey to insects and the smallest frogs, lizards, birds, and mammals. Secretive about the whereabouts of its nest, it feeds its young only after dark. There are four subspecies of this owl, which vary in size, colour, and in their calls.

ADULT AFRICAN BARRED OWLET

Xenoglaux loweryi

Long-whiskered Owlet

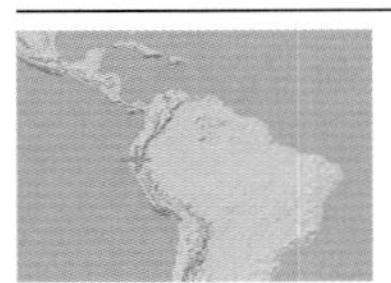

LENGTH 14cm (5½in)

WEIGHT 45–50g (1⅝–1¾oz)

MIGRATION Non-migrant

HABITAT Cloudforest at 1,900m–2,200m (6,200–7,200ft)

One of the smaller owl species, the Long-whiskered Owlet is confined to a tiny range in Peru. The common name refers to the wispy feathers on its face, originating around the eyes and the bill. The golden-brown eyes are emphasized by prominent eyebrow stripes, and it has a collar of white spots. The plumage of the Long-whiskered Owlet is dark brown, with dark mottling on the upperparts and white markings on the belly.

Very little information is available but its diet is presumed to mostly include insects. It is not considered to be globally threatened despite its limited range, although habitat loss could be a serious threat in the future. No reliable figures exist for the population of the species; it may not be uncommon within its range.

ADULT ELF OWL

Micrathene whitneyi

Elf Owl

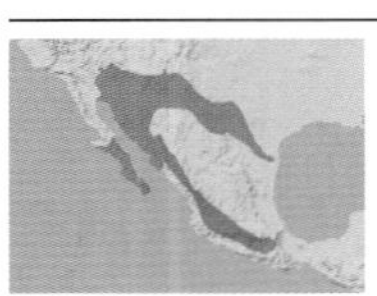

LENGTH 14cm (5½in)

WEIGHT 40g (1 7/16oz)

MIGRATION Partial migrant

HABITAT Desert containing cacti or dry woodland up to 2,000m (6,600ft)

Similar to the Long-whiskered Owlet (left) but more distinctly marked, the Elf Owl has a pronounced facial disc and several white markings on the back and wings with blurry streaks below. Its food is entirely made up of invertebrates. Four subspecies are known, ranging from a migratory population in southwest USA to a resident population in Mexico.

ADULT BURROWING OWL

Athene cunicularia

Burrowing Owl

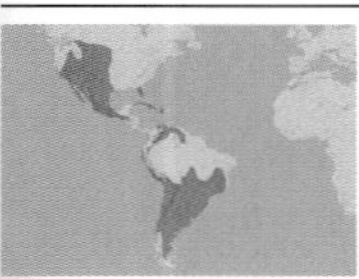

LENGTH 19–25cm (7½–10in)

WEIGHT 120–250g (4–9oz)

MIGRATION Partial migrant

HABITAT Dry open habitats, including manmade ones, such as airports

Unlike other owls, this species makes its home underground (see panel, below). It also spends much of its time hunting on the ground, its diet varying according to the time of year and the availability of prey, such as insects, small mammals, and reptiles. It has white eyebrows, a prominent white stripe on the chin, and bars and spots on its breast and belly. This owl is migratory in North America, wintering in Central America; the South American population is sedentary.

NEST BURROWS

Although capable of excavating its own burrow, the Burrowing Owl nests in a wide range of burrows dug and abandoned by small mammals, such as the Ground Squirrel, or in larger ones made by the American Badger. It clears and tidies unused burrows by kicking dirt backwards. It has occasionally been known to share burrows with mammals or other owls, although each hole is isolated from other nests.

Athene noctua

Little Owl

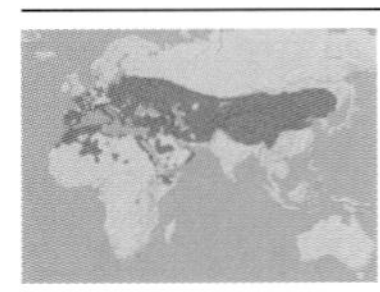

LENGTH 21–23cm (8½–9in)

WEIGHT 55–60g (2–2⅛oz)

MIGRATION Non-migrant

HABITAT Wide range of open habitats from semi-desert to farmland

Small, flat-headed, and short-tailed, the Little Owl can appear quite round when perched in the day. It has large, pale yellow eyes circled with black and a brown back with buff spots. Its food includes invertebrates, small reptiles, and mammals. A vocal species, these birds can be heard calling to each other in daylight, although they tend to be most active in the evening.

ADULT LITTLE OWL

ADULT NORTHERN SAW-WHET OWL

Aegolius acadicus

Northern Saw-whet Owl

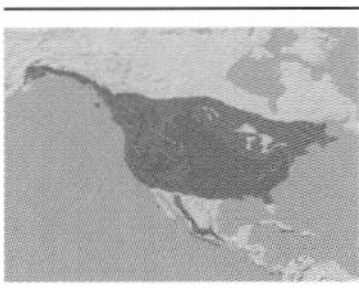

LENGTH 18–20cm (7–8in)

WEIGHT 100g (3⅝oz)

MIGRATION Migrant

HABITAT Woodland, prefers coniferous forest

The Northern Saw-whet Owl has a white patch between the eyes, brown facial discs, and chestnut-brown upperparts, with white and buff spots, and brown streaks and blotches on its underparts. It feeds on small rodents, large insects, and bats. Found across much of North America, it winters in the mid-west of the USA.

Ninox boobook

Southern Boobook

LENGTH 25–36cm (10–14in)

WEIGHT 250–300g (9–11oz)

MIGRATION Non-migrant

HABITAT Wide range of habitats from forest to farmland, up to 2,300m (7,500ft)

Named for its high-pitched, two-syllable "boobook" call, the Southern Boobook has a pale brown, heart-shaped face, which contrasts with the heavily streaked dark brown upperparts. It is white below, with rufous-brown streaks and spots. It roosts in trees during the day and feeds at dusk, hunting insects and birds in mid-air, although small mammals and reptiles make up most of its diet. It is found throughout Australia and islands to the north, including parts of New Guinea and Timor. Up to 10 subspecies have been listed but some are disputed.

ADULT SOUTHERN BOOBOOK

Pseudoscops grammicus

Jamaican Owl

LENGTH 27–34cm (10½–13½in)

WEIGHT Not recorded

MIGRATION Non-migrant

HABITAT Open woodland, forest edges, or parkland

Confined entirely to Jamaica, this bird is dark brown on the back to red-brown on the breast and belly. The ear tufts and the facial discs, which have a pale lower rim, are well developed. It is nocturnal and feeds on invertebrates, frogs, lizards, and mice. Eggs are laid between December and June in a nest built in a tree-cavity, which is usually well concealed by vegetation. Its limited range makes it vulnerable to habitat loss.

ADULT JAMAICAN OWL

Uroglaux dimorpha

Papuan Hawk-owl

LENGTH 30–33cm (12–13in)

WEIGHT Not recrded

MIGRATION Non-migrant

HABITAT Lowland rainforest and forest edges to 1,500m (4,900ft)

Limited to Papua New Guinea and Irian Jaya, this bird is rarely seen, sparsely distributed, and under threat from deforestation. When relaxed, its sleek build and long tail give it a hawk-like appearance, which is further emphasized by the streaked brown plumage. Its diet includes insects, mammals, and medium-sized birds almost as large as the owl. Little is known about its breeding cycle, although downy chicks have been observed during August.

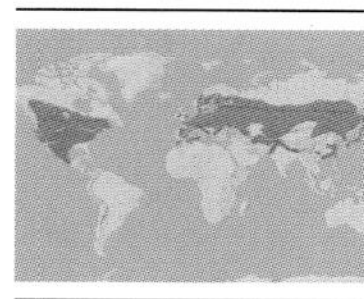

Asio otus

Long-eared Owl

LENGTH 35–40cm (14–16in)

WEIGHT 225–450g (8–16oz)

MIGRATION Partial migrant

HABITAT Dense vegetation close to open areas or a wider range of habitats in winter

The Long-eared Owl is found throughout much of the northern hemisphere to the subarctic tree limits in summer. There are a number of subspecies with different plumage tones, but all have the distinct facial discs and ear tufts. This owl mainly preys on small mammals and is nocturnal or crepuscular during the breeding season. It often forms loose social groups. The male tends to supply more food to the young than the female, and the process continues even after they have fledged. It is a long-lived species.

ADULT LONG-EARED OWL

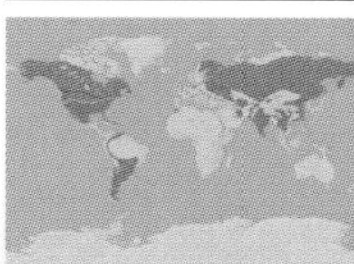

Asio flammeus

Short-eared Owl

LENGTH 38cm (15in)

WEIGHT 200–500g (7–18oz)

MIGRATION Migrant

HABITAT Open country such as tundra, marsh, and grassland

The summer range of the Short-eared Owl extends well into treeless Arctic regions. Wintering birds are found in southern USA and in subtropical parts of Africa and Asia. The plumage varies with the subspecies, but the rounder facial discs and smaller ear tufts differentiate the species from the Long-eared Owl (above). It feeds on small mammals but has been known to eat small birds. The bird almost exclusively roosts on the ground or in low bushes. Pairs tend to form in late winter, with the male embarking on an aerobatic display accompanied by wing-clapping. The female almost always builds the nest – unusual in this family of owls – and incubates the eggs, the usual clutch size being 5 or 6 eggs. Fledglings take 50 days to become independent.

JUVENILE IN DEFENSIVE POSTURE
The young Short-eared Owl raises its wings when threatened so that it appears larger than normal.

ON THE LOOKOUT
The Short-eared Owl hunts in daylight. It flies with deep wingbeats and glides on stretched wings a few feet above the ground, pouncing on prey when it is located.

NORTHERN SAW-WHET OWL
This Northern Saw-whet Owl has made its nest in a birch tree. Found in many North American woodlands, the species often uses holes made by woodpeckers.

NIGHTJARS AND FROGMOUTHS

ORDER	Caprimulgiformes
FAMILIES	5
SPECIES	115

ACTIVE AT DUSK OR after dark, nightjars, frogmouths, and their relatives feed mainly on insects caught in mid-air or on the ground. They roost by day in trees or on the ground, relying on their superb camouflage to avoid detection. Frogmouths build rudimentary nests in tree-forks, but nightjars lay their eggs directly on the ground, without making a nest of any kind.

ANATOMY

Nightjars and their relatives have rounded bodies, with large heads and short necks. They have large eyes, and their bills are short but very wide, giving them an enormous gape. Their wings are narrow and sharply pointed, creating a hawk-like silhouette in flight. Apart from Australian Owlet-Nightjars, all have short legs and tiny feet. Mottled and streaked in brown and grey, their plumage includes some of the finest examples of bird camouflage, enabling them to roost on the ground or on dead branches with little risk of being seen. Many have distinctive and repetitive calls, to be heard after dark during the breeding season.

FEEDING

Nightjars trawl the air for insects, using their funnel-like bills to catch prey. Their mouths are fringed with bristles, which help them to trap their food. They fly silently and buoyantly, pursuing individual insects – particularly moths – a few metres above the ground. Other members of this order, including potoos and frogmouths, dart out from a perch, catching insects in mid-air, or small animals on the ground. The South American Oilbird is the only vegetarian in the group. It feeds on oil palm fruit and nests deep in caves, using echolocation to navigate in darkness.

GIANT GAPE
With an enormous gape for its size, the Common Potoo can swallow the largest tropical moths.

ROOSTING NIGHTJAR
Superbly camouflaged, a Slender-tailed Nightjar waits for dusk, to start to feed.

Podargus strigoides

Tawny Frogmouth

LENGTH 34–53cm ($13^1/_2$–21in)
WEIGHT 275–350g (10–13oz)
MIGRATION Non-migrant

HABITAT Forest, mallee scrub, open land with trees, including farmland and parks

The only frogmouth species in Australia and Tasmania, the Tawny Frogmouth varies in colour and size across its range. The grey plumage is mottled in red or brown, blending in with the colour of branches. A boldly marked subspecies is found in east and southeast Australia. It is up to twice the size of the delicately marked subspecies in the north of the country.

The Tawny Frogmouth hunts from perches, where it waits patiently for prey. Its huge mouth allows it to tackle relatively large creatures, including scorpions, spiders, frogs, lizards, snakes, and mice, which it captures by diving silently upon them. Prey that is not killed outright is beaten to death against the perch. Active after dusk and before dawn, it roosts on bare branches and tree trunks during the day.

ADULT AND YOUNG AT NEST

CAMOUFLAGE

The Tawny Frogmouth spends the day roosting on a bare branch, in a semi-upright position at an angle to the branch. When disturbed, it stiffens itself and sleeks down its body feathers, so that with its dull coloration and the tufts of feathers on its face, it looks exactly like the stump of a branch. Although it may appear to be asleep, the bird is very alert, and follows the movements of an intruder through slitted eyes, moving its head very slightly.

CONVINCING DISGUISE
The streaked plumage of the Tawny Frogmouth mimics the rough, fissured texture of the bark of a tree, while the bill and facial tufts look exactly like the broken end of a branch.

TYPICAL ROOSTING POSITION

Steatornis caripensis

Oilbird

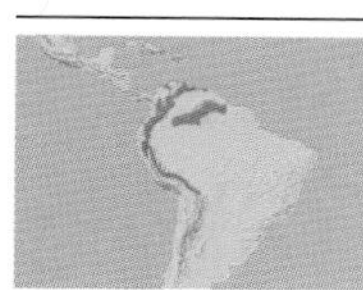

LENGTH 40–50cm (15½–19½in)

WEIGHT 350–475g (13–17oz)

MIGRATION Non-migrant

HABITAT Nests in caves and deep rocky clefts; feeds in undisturbed forest

Reddish brown in colour, the Oilbird has white markings on the head, throat, and wings. Unlike other nightjars and their allies, the Oilbird is a fruit-eater. Also, unlike them, it nests colonially in caves, where it finds its way about by echolocation. Oilbirds can travel long distances in search of fruit. Although they do not migrate, some oilbirds disperse away from their caves after breeding. The colonies contain thousands of pairs of birds, which emerge together at dusk, providing a spectacle to tourists. In the past, young birds were harvested to be boiled into oil, which was used for cooking or to fill lamps. Oilbirds are now protected across most of their range, but continue to be at risk from the destruction of the primary forest in which they feed on fruit.

Aegotheles cristatus

Australian Owlet-Nightjar

LENGTH 21–25cm (8½–10in)

WEIGHT 45g (1⅝oz)

MIGRATION Non-migrant

HABITAT Open woodland, mallee and other scrub, waterside trees

Active at dusk and dawn, the Australian Owlet-Nightjar has distinctive dark markings on its face and head. The barred plumage is grey in the male and brown in the female. It eats beetles, caterpillars, spiders, and millipedes, which it catches by swooping from a branch and snatching them from the ground or from trees. It also feeds on ants on the ground. In cold weather, it may become torpid, to conserve energy.

ADULT AUSTRALIAN OWLET-NIGHTJAR

Nyctibius griseus

Common Potoo

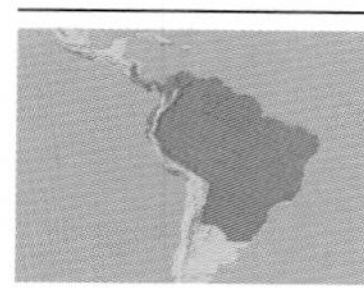

LENGTH 33–38cm (13–15in)

WEIGHT 150–175g (5–6oz)

MIGRATION Non-migrant

HABITAT Forest, mangroves, scrub, savanna, and other open habitats with trees

The melancholy call of the Common or Grey Potoo has misled many hearers into believing they were listening to a mammal – or even a human voice. Its grey-brown plumage with a fine black and buff pattern provides effective camouflage against tree bark. With its big head and outward-bulging eyes, it can be mistaken for an owl. It feeds on insects, which it catches in the air. The Common Potoo nests in a knot-hole or depression in a branch.

COMMON POTOO AT NEST

Chordeiles minor

Common Nighthawk

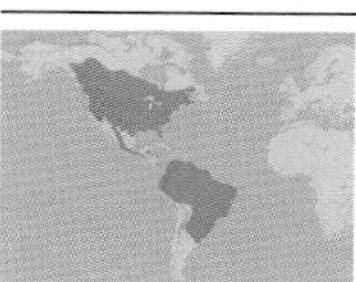

LENGTH 22–25cm (8½–10in)

WEIGHT 45–100g (1⅝–3⅝oz)

MIGRATION Migrant

HABITAT Open, dry country, grassland, farmland, and other human-modified landscapes

Tolerating a wide range of climates and habitats, from the sub-tropics to central Canada, the Common Nighthawk is found from sea-level up to 2600m (8,500ft). It has large eyes and mottled, brown, black, and white plumage. It has adapted well to human changes to the environment, using flat roofs for nesting and roosting. The Common Nighthawk hunts where insects gather, such as over water, around street lamps, or where ants are swarming. The display of the male includes a booming sound produced by the wind rushing through its wings as it dives.

ADULT COMMON NIGHTHAWK

Nyctidromus albicolis

Pauraque

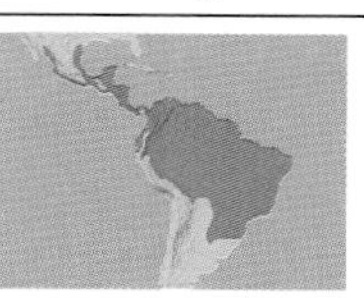

LENGTH 22–28cm (8½–11in)

WEIGHT 45–90g (1⅝–3¼oz)

MIGRATION Partial migrant

HABITAT Forest, forest edges and clearings, scrub, plantations, and mangroves

Not just the most common, the Pauraque is also one of the most frequently encountered nightjars across much of its vast range. It has a grey-brown to rufous-brown plumage, rounded wings, and a long tail. The buff eye-ring and facial stripe contrast with the reddish sides of the face. Unusually among nightjars, which move awkwardly on the ground, the Pauraque has relatively long legs and can run fast – although it prefers to fly. It roosts and nests on the ground, under bushes.

PAURAQUE ROOSTING ON THE GROUND

Phalaenoptilus nuttali

Common Poorwill

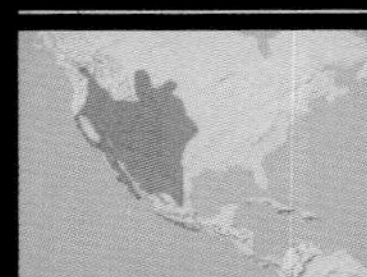

LENGTH 18–20cm (7–8in)

WEIGHT 30–60g (1 1/16–2 1/8oz)

MIGRATION Migrant

HABITAT Arid and semi-arid country, woodland, and forest clearings

The Common Poorwill is the smallest American nightjar, and the only bird in the world known to "hibernate" for extended periods. It breeds in western North America from Canada to Mexico. When the weather becomes cold and food short, it becomes torpid for periods of weeks or months, spending the entire winter in parts of its range tucked into clefts in rocks. Torpid birds have even been found incubating eggs when it is unusually cold during breeding. This dramatically reduces the birds' consumption of body fat.

The plumage of the Common Poorwill is mostly grey, patterned with black on the upperparts. The sexes look similar, but the male has bolder white tips to the tail than the female. Like other nightjars, this species hunts at dawn and dusk, starting around half an hour after sunset. It is also active on moonlit nights. It catches insects, such as beetles and moths, by flying up from the ground or from a low perch on a branch or rock. Its flight is noiseless and moth-like. On the ground it hops, or waddles awkwardly.

The song from which the bird's name comes is often rendered as "poor-jill" rather than "poor-will". From nearby, an extra syllable can be heard: "poor-will-ow" or "poor-jill-ip". The male sings from the ground or low branches, beginning before breeding starts, to attract a mate and establish its territory. Some individuals will sing throughout the year. The Common Poorwill roosts on the ground. Although it is usually solitary, sometimes pairs and families are found together. Both parents incubate the eggs. It has a threat display, which involves fluffing up its feathers, opening its wide mouth, and hissing like a snake or growling.

ADULT COMMON POORWILL

DISTRACTION DISPLAY

The Common Poorwill relies on its dull coloration to hide from predators. But if an intruder comes too close to a nest, the female will sometimes perform a distraction display. This involves beating one wing against the ground and flopping awkwardly on its belly – to suggest that it is injured and will be easy to catch. All the while, it tries to lead the intruder away from its eggs.

Caprimulgus carolinensis

Chuck-will's-widow

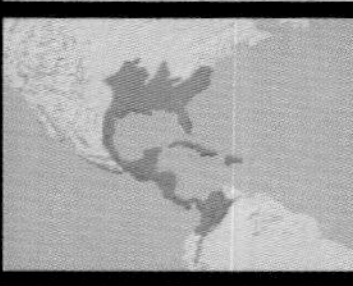

LENGTH 27–34cm (10 1/2–13 1/2in)

WEIGHT 95–125g (3 3/8–4oz)

MIGRATION Migrant

HABITAT Deciduous and mixed woodland, forest edges, pastures, and open country

A large, stout nightjar, the Chuck-will's-widow has a brownish red throat and buff-brown mottling all over its plumage. Most active after dusk and before dawn, it feeds on flying insects and small birds, including sparrows and warblers, sometimes hunting for cicadas on tree-tops. The three-note song, which gives the bird its name, is repeated up to 30 times a minute. The male has regular song posts on branches or fences.

ADULT CHUCK-WILL'S-WIDOW

Caprimulgus vociferus

Whip-poor-will

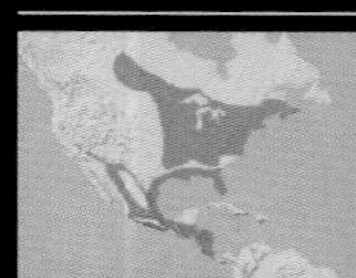

LENGTH 22–27cm (8 1/2–10 1/2in)

WEIGHT 40–70g (1 7/16–2 1/2oz)

MIGRATION Partial migrant

HABITAT Forest and open woodland, in lowland and mountains, dry and humid climates

A resting Whip-poor-will can be told apart from the similarly sized Common Nighthawk (see p.289) by the length of the wing. The Nighthawk's folded wings extend beyond the end of its tail, while the Whip-poor-will's tail extends beyond its wing-tips. It has a mottled plumage of grey, black, and brown upperparts and grey and black underparts. When displaying, the male flashes its white outer tail feathers.

The Whip-poor-will hunts by sallying from the ground or from perches, but also flies about, "hawking" after insects in clearings and open woodlands. It may swallow grit to aid digestion. The whistled "Whip-poor-will" or "whip-pr-weeea" rises in pitch at the end and is often mixed with sharp "quit!" notes, the phrase being repeated many times.

Caprimulgus sericocaudatus

Silky-tailed Nightjar

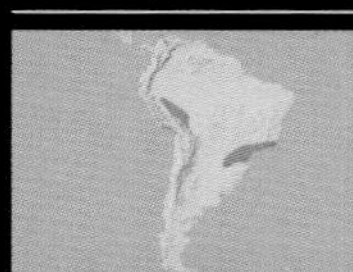

LENGTH 24–30cm (9 1/2–12in)

WEIGHT 55–85g (2–3oz)

MIGRATION Non-migrant

HABITAT Forest clearings and forest edges

The Silky-tailed Nightjar is closely related to the Tawny-collared (*C. salvini*) and Yucatan (*C. badius*) Nightjars. These birds differ from one another, and from other nightjars, by small variations in plumage and size. Such visual clues are of little help in distinguishing these birds in poor light, when they are active, so the song is much more important for field identification. The male has a repeated three-note song; "doh, wheeo, eeeo", repeated without variations or pauses for minutes on end.

The Silky-tailed Nightjar hunts on the ground, or from perches. Although there are few details of its foraging methods and food habits, its prey includes beetles, crickets, grasshoppers, and flying ants.

ADULT SILKY-TAILED NIGHTJAR

ADULT EUROPEAN NIGHTJAR

Caprimulgus europaeus

European Nightjar

LENGTH 26–28cm (10–11in)

WEIGHT 65–100g (2³/₈–3⁵/₈oz)

MIGRATION Migrant

HABITAT Heathland, open woodland, young or recently logged forestry plantations

Habitat loss and the decline in insect numbers due to pesticide use have led to a decrease in the population of the European Nightjar. It is recognized by its brown plumage, mottled with black and grey, and large, pointed wings. It pursues its insect prey in sustained flight, swooping up at them from below. Occasionally, it hovers and swoops down. When insects are scarce, the European Nightjar may conserve energy by hunting from a perch, or from the ground to catch flightless insects and spiders. The call is a cricket-like churring, audible at long distances but difficult to locate. The courtship display of the male involves a slow, fluttering flight, with clapping of the wings. The male plays an active part in raising the young.

CAMOUFLAGE

Seen close-up, the European Nightjar's upper plumage is an intricate blend of browns, greys, buff, and cinnamon, overlaid with bold black streaks. This blends perfectly into the leaf litter on which it nests and roosts during daylight, mimicking the pattern of light and shade thrown by trees and bushes. Relying on this camouflage, the European Nightjar responds to disturbance by flattening itself to the ground to conceal its shape and reduce its shadow, and closing its large eyes to slits.

Caprimulgus eximius

Golden Nightjar

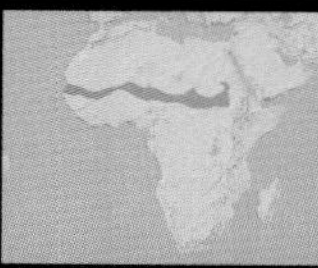

LENGTH 23–25cm (9–10in)

WEIGHT 65g (2³/₈oz)

MIGRATION Non-migrant

HABITAT Lowland semi-desert, rocky or sandy country with sparse grass and scattered scrub

The golden colouring of the upperparts, from which the Golden Nightjar gets its name, is unique among nightjars. The sexes are similar in plumage. It is far better suited to the dry, sandy country in which it is mostly found than the typical nightjar plumage, which is adapted for concealment in leaf litter. This nightjar avoids areas of thick scrub or trees.

The Golden Nightjar forages at dusk, often close to or over water. Its prey includes moths, grasshoppers, mantises, and beetles. Its eggs are laid on the bare ground, often near a clump of grass or some other vegetation providing cover. Although generally non-migratory, birds in parts of the range may wander after the breeding season. Its numbers vary across its large range.

MALE IN DISPLAY FLIGHT

Macrodipteryx longipennis

Standard-winged Nightjar

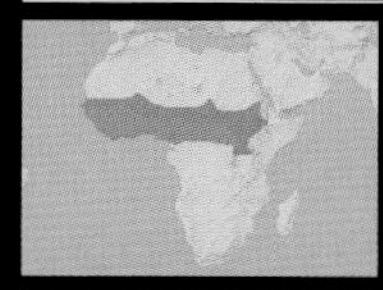

LENGTH 22cm (8¹/₂in)

WEIGHT 50g (1³/₄oz)

MIGRATION Migrant

HABITAT Savanna with trees and thorn scrub, open ground, sometimes farmland

While several nightjar species have elongated tails, the "standards" of the breeding male Standard-winged formed from the second innermost primary feather of each wing, which is bare except near the tip. These can be up to 54cm (21¹/₂in) long. When males and females gather at display grounds, the male performs its aerial courtship display, involving one or more birds flying slowly in circles or figures of eight around the females, with their wing standards raised. Outside the breeding season, the male moults its standards, which grow longer each year.

The Standard-winged Nightjar feeds on small moths, beetles, and other winged insects. It follows insect swarms, and hunts insects disturbed by

Macropsalis forcipata

Long-trained Nightjar

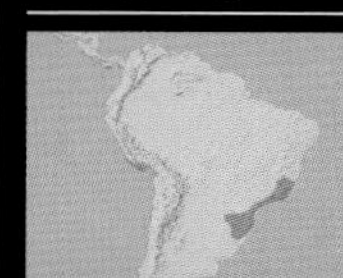

LENGTH 28–31cm (11–12in)

WEIGHT Not recorded

MIGRATION Non-migrant

HABITAT Rainforest, forest edges, and forests re-generating after logging, from lowland to mountains

The distinctively elongated outer "retrices" or tail feathers, 48–68cm (19–27in), of the male Long-trained Nightjar can be more than twice the length of its body. They are used in a courtship display, during which the males puff out their throats and raise their tail feathers at the right angle, when the white inner edges form a conspicuous V. The diet of the Long-trained Nightjar has not been studied in detail, but it has been observed flying close to trees to snatch insects from the leaves, hawking for flying insects in clearings, and making sallies from bare patches of ground. It has also been recorded lurking near street lamps to catch insects attracted to the light.

The calls include a high-pitched, repetitive "tsip, tsip, tsip, tsip", given by both sexes. No actual nest is made, but eggs are laid on leaf litter in the shade of bushes. When disturbed, the female may perform a distraction display, feigning injury to lead intruders away from the eggs or young. Endemic to the rainforests of southeastern Brazil and northeastern Argentina, the Long-trained Nightjar is rare in some parts of its range and locally common elsewhere.

SWIFTS AND HUMMINGBIRDS

ORDER	Apodiformes
FAMILY	3
SPECIES	429

SOME ORNITHOLOGISTS CLASSIFY swifts, treeswifts, and hummingbirds in two separate orders. However, these fast-flying birds share some important features, particularly in the wing structure. Swifts and treeswifts feed on flying insects, and include the most aerial of all land birds. Hummingbirds feed mainly on nectar from flowers, but catch insects to feed to their young.

ANATOMY

Swifts and hummingbirds both have tiny legs and feet – apodiformes means "without legs". Their wings are long compared to their bodies, but also narrow. Internally, the wing bones have unusual proportions, with the shoulder joint and elbow joint very close together. A swift has a short bill with a wide gape, making an effective trap for flying insects. Hummingbird bills are more variable, but all work like tubes, allowing the birds to suck up the nectar with their tongues.

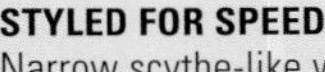

STYLED FOR SPEED
Narrow scythe-like wings and a forked tail make the Common Swift one of the fastest of all aerial insect-eaters.

extended "hand" bones
humerus
wrist
shoulder
shoulder girdle
forearm bones
"elbow" close to body

HUMMINGBIRD WING
In hummingbirds and swifts, the "elbow" joint is close to the body, giving the wing muscles greater leverage and allowing the wing to tilt. Hummingbirds use this when they hover.

BEHAVIOUR

Typical swifts spend most of their lives in the air, while tree swifts catch insects by darting out from a perch. Hummingbirds are better than swifts at perching, but normally hover when feeding. Hummingbirds are restricted to the Americas; swifts are found worldwide, although in temperate regions they are summer visitors, departing as soon as they have bred. Treeswifts fasten their nests to branches, but typical swifts build in many different places, including chimneys, attics, sandy banks, and caves. Most use material collected on the wing, glued together with saliva; Cave Swiftlets use saliva alone. Hummingbirds make exquisite cup-shaped nests, and lay two tiny eggs.

FEEDING TIME
A female Ruby-throated Hummingbird feeds a nestling in a nest made from lichen, moss, and spiders' silk.

HIGH-ENERGY FOOD
A Broad-tailed Hummingbird sips nectar from orchids. With fast-digesting sugars, nectar is hummingbird aviation fuel.

Hydrochous gigas

Waterfall Swift

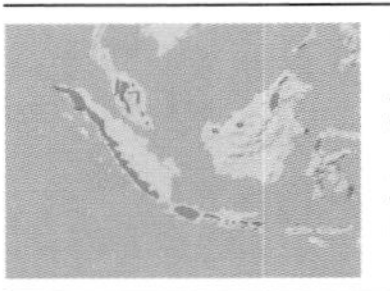

LENGTH	16cm (6½in)
WEIGHT	35–40g (1¼–1 7/16oz)
MIGRATION	Non-migrant

HABITAT Mountainous rainforest to 1,500m (5,000ft)

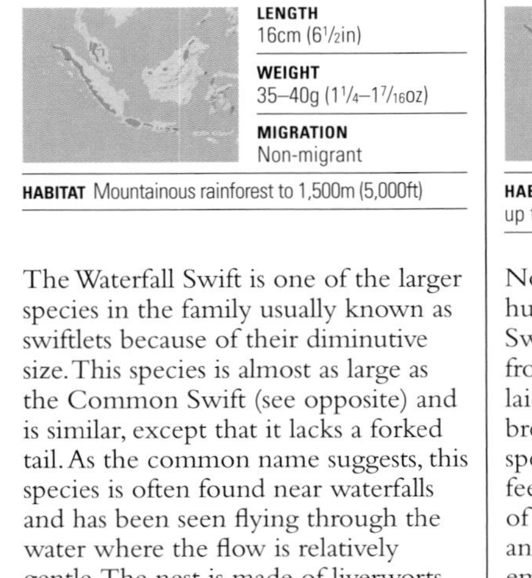

The Waterfall Swift is one of the larger species in the family usually known as swiftlets because of their diminutive size. This species is almost as large as the Common Swift (see opposite) and is similar, except that it lacks a forked tail. As the common name suggests, this species is often found near waterfalls and has been seen flying through the water where the flow is relatively gentle. The nest is made of liverworts and moss cemented with saliva and is usually located behind a waterfall. Typically, a single egg is laid, but little is known regarding development periods. The Waterfall Swift has excellent poor-light vision, and most of its foraging activity is done at dawn or dusk.

Collocalia linchi

Cave Swiftlet

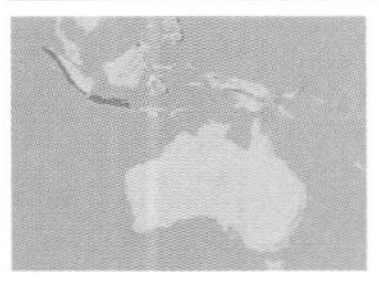

LENGTH	10cm (4in)
WEIGHT	Not recorded
MIGRATION	Non-migrant

HABITAT Forest and open country from sea-level up to 500m (1,640ft)

Noted for its square tail and the green hue to its black plumage, the Cave Swiftlet nests in caves, building a nest from plants and saliva. Two eggs are laid, but little is known about the breeding season. It is a gregarious species and tends to form large feeding flocks. A wide variety of flying insects is taken in and around the crowns of emergent and fruiting trees, such as figs. It is not globally threatened, but is thought to be extinct in the Malay peninsula, previously part of its range.

ADULT CAVE SWIFTLET

Aerodramus fuciphaga

Edible-nest Swiftlet

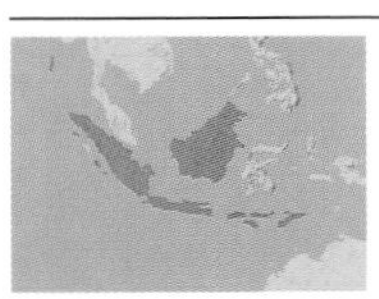

LENGTH	12cm (4½in)
WEIGHT	15–18g (9/16–5/8oz)
MIGRATION	Non-migrant

HABITAT Cleared and forested areas on the coast or inland up to 2,800m (9,000ft)

This swiftlet is so named because its nests are harvested in many parts of the range (they are used in Chinese cuisine). Its white, opaque nest is made by the male from its gelatinous saliva, which it winds into a cup-shaped structure and attaches to a cave wall. A slender bird, the adult Edible-nest Swiftlet is relatively plain, with a combination of a brown back and paler underparts typical of swifts, but lacks the forked tail characteristic of this group. It forages mainly in dim light. The species is not migratory, but long flights in search of food between islands or to the mainland have been reported. Its numbers have declined to an alarming extent due to over-exploitation.

ADULT WHITE-RUMPED SPINETAILED SWIFT

Zoonavena sylvatica

White-rumped Spinetailed Swift

LENGTH 11cm (4½in)
WEIGHT 13g (7/16oz)
MIGRATION Non-migrant

HABITAT Up to 1,700m (5,000ft) in Himalayas and a variety of forest habitats and plantations

The White-rumped Spinetailed Swift is named for the white rump band that extends from its white undersides. It forages in small groups above the tree canopy or close to forested areas, with up to 50 birds in a flock. It constructs solitary nests in hollow tree trunks, with 3 or 4 eggs being produced, mainly between March and April.

Chaetura pelagica

Chimney Swift

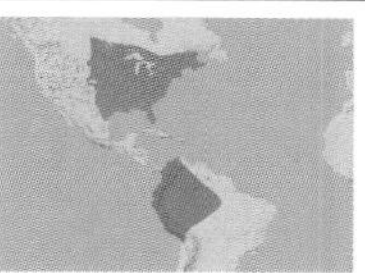

LENGTH 12–14cm (4½–5½in)
WEIGHT 21g (11/16oz)
MIGRATION Migrant

HABITAT Forest edges near rivers, but mostly urban areas

ADULT CHIMNEY SWIFT

It is its habit of nesting in urban structures that has given the Chimney Swift its common name; nesting in natural tree-holes is now rare for this bird. It is uniformly grey-brown above, with a pale grey throat and dark brown underparts. The breeding season is from early May to July, but only a single clutch of 4 or 5 eggs is produced.

Hirundapus caudacutus

White-throated Needletail

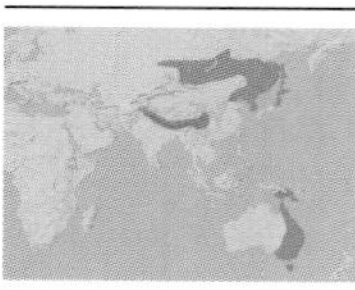

LENGTH 19–20cm (7½–8in)
WEIGHT 100–150g (3⅝–5oz)
MIGRATION Migrant

HABITAT Wooded lowland, hills, and valleys; up to 4,000m (13,123ft) in the Himalayas

The tail of the White-throated Needletail looks square-shaped when the bird is at rest. The throat and undertail are white and its back is pale. The White-throated Needletail is gregarious when feeding, but rarely associates with other species. Two subspecies have been identified on the basis of plumage details and geographical range. The northern subspecies is migratory, travelling from Siberia and Japan to New Guinea and Australia. The nest is a scrape in debris of tree hollows and 2–7 eggs are produced.

ADULT WHITE-THROATED NEEDLETAIL

NEEDLE TAIL

The common name of the White-throated Needletail derives from the needle-like feather spines that lack the usual feather vanes in its tail. The spines can project up to 6mm (¼in) beyond the normal tail feathers. They help to give the bird stability when it clings to vertical surfaces, without compromising the flexibility of the tail in flight.

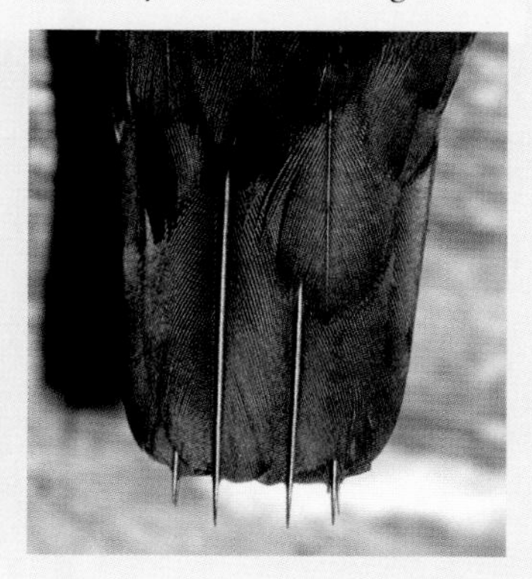

ALPINE SWIFT IN FLIGHT

Tachymarptis melba

Alpine Swift

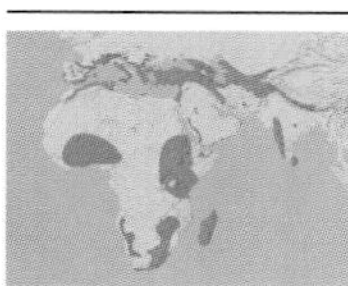

LENGTH 20–22cm (8–8½in)
WEIGHT 100g (3⅝oz)
MIGRATION Migrant

HABITAT Wide range of habitats; typically to 1,500m (5,000ft), but up to 3,700m (12,000ft) when feeding

This is a large species with dark brown upperparts, white chin, throat, and belly, and dark undertail. The Alpine Swift typically forages at an altitude higher than that frequented by other species, but it has also been known to feed closer to the ground when the weather is unfavourable. Its food consists of the larger insect species. The breeding season varies, depending on the range, but the species usually has a single brood of three eggs laid in a shallow nest lined with feathers. The nest is usually built on a horizontal surface, but often also in cracks or cavities on vertical rock surfaces. Range expansions have been noted in Europe, and the species is stable and common over much of the range.

Tachornis furcata

Pygmy Swift

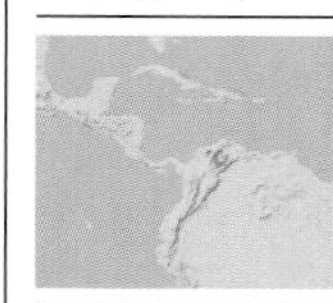

LENGTH 10cm (4in)
WEIGHT Not recorded
MIGRATION Non-migrant

HABITAT Tropical lowland evergreen or secondary forest

As the common name suggests, the Pygmy Swift is a small species and appears slender in flight. Its upperparts are uniformly dark and its pale throat and belly are separated by a darker band on the upper breast. This species feeds on insects in flight. Little is known about its breeding season and habits. The Pygmy Swift is not globally threatened, despite its limited range on the border between northern Colombia and Venezuela.

Apus apus

Common Swift

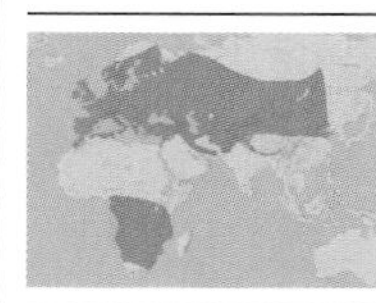

LENGTH 16–17cm (6½in)
WEIGHT 35–50g (1¼–1¾oz)
MIGRATION Migrant

HABITAT Wide range of habitats from sea-level to high altitude; areas with trees and buildings

The Common Swift has a short head, with almost no bill, a white chin, an all-dark body (which becomes browner in late summer), and a deeply forked tail, with fine white feather edges. The bird feeds on insects in the air and foraging has been recorded up to 4,000m, (13,000ft) with migrating birds higher still at 5,700m (19,000ft). Its breeding range occurs throughout Europe, extending to China and it winters exclusively in southern Africa. The nest is a feather-lined cavity and it produces only a single brood of 2 or 3 eggs a year, leaving soon after the young fledge. This means that the birds are on the breeding range for as little as 12–14 weeks. Although not threatened, the numbers of this swift have declined in Europe.

ADULT COMMON SWIFT

Eutoxeres aquila

White-tipped Sicklebill

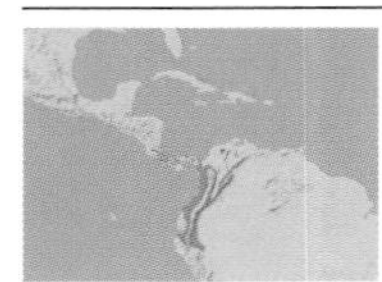

LENGTH 12–14cm (4½–5½in)

WEIGHT 8–13g (5/16–7/16oz)

MIGRATION Non-migrant

HABITAT Forest understorey, forest edges, and near rivers

Named after its extraordinary bill, which is strongly decurved over about two-thirds of its length, this bird mainly feeds on heliconia flowers, using its bill to probe into their curved blooms. It has a predominantly green plumage, dark-streaked underparts, and a white-tipped tail with green outer tail-feathers. Unlike many hummingbirds, which feed while hovering, the sicklebill perches to sip nectar from flowers.

Phaethornis eurynome

Scale-throated Hermit

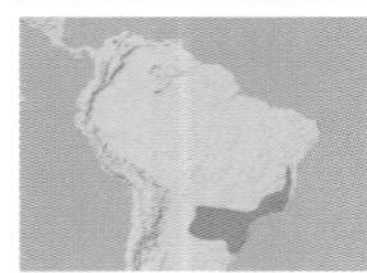

LENGTH 14cm (5½in)

WEIGHT 4–6g (5/32–7/32oz)

MIGRATION Non-migrant

HABITAT Understorey of primary forest and old secondary growth

A medium-sized hermit, the Scale-throated Hermit is named for the appearance of its dark throat feathers. It has a curved bill and long white tail-streamers. The female has a slightly more curved bill and shorter wings. This species is likely to be seen in flight or hovering at a forest flower. Its nest is a cone-shaped cup of plant material and cobwebs attached to the tip of a leaf.

SCALE-THROATED HERMIT

Phaethornis superciliosus

Eastern Long-tailed Hermit

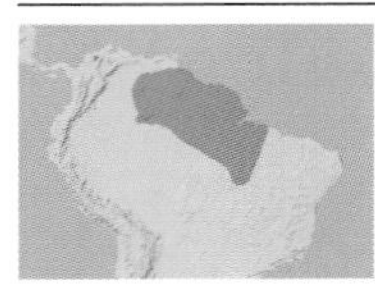

LENGTH 14cm (5½in)

WEIGHT 4–6g (5/32–7/32oz)

MIGRATION Non-migrant

HABITAT Understorey of all types of lowland rainforest, including areas near rivers

Mainly brown above, the Eastern Long-tailed Hermit has dark wings, buff underparts and rump, and a white-tipped tail with long white central tail-feathers. Like most of the medium-sized hermits, its bill is long and slightly decurved. It feeds by trap-lining (foraging in circuits), regularly visiting large tubular-shaped flowers, such as heliconias and passionflowers, scattered over a particular area.

Phaethornis pretrei

Planalto Hermit

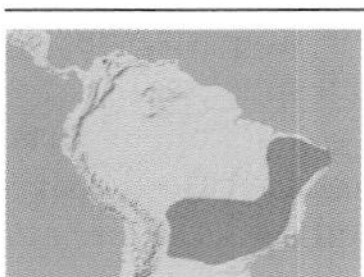

LENGTH 14cm (5½in)

WEIGHT 4–6g (5/32–7/32oz)

MIGRATION Non-migrant

HABITAT Dry forest and other well-vegetated areas in montane regions, including gardens

This species takes its unusual common name from the plateau region of interior Brazil, which forms its core range. Within most of its distribution, the Planalto Hermit is the only hermit with a long bill and tail and is further distinguished by its warm buff coloured underparts. Its nest is cone-shaped, typical of most hermits, but is constructed on vertical structures, such as wires and waste-water pipes, under bridges, or on roots and twigs protected by a rock overhang. Two eggs are laid and incubated for about two weeks by the female alone, and the chicks fledge after a further 20 days.

ADULT PLANALTO HERMIT

Campylopterus hemileucurus

Violet Sabrewing

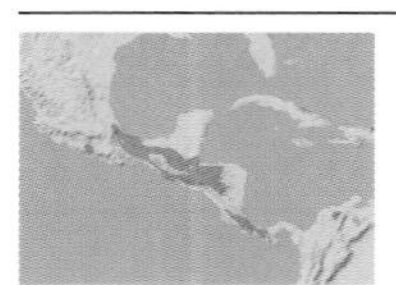

LENGTH 13–15cm (5–6in)

WEIGHT 10–12g (3/8–7/16oz)

MIGRATION Non-migrant

HABITAT Humid forest, secondary growth, and small banana plantations in foothills and on slopes

MALE VIOLET SABREWING

Both sexes of this large hummingbird are distinctive, but only the male Violet Sabrewing has largely violet plumage. In contrast, the female has grey and green underparts and blue discs on the throat. It has a more decurved bill than the male. Both sexes have a white spot behind the eye and white in the tail. The Violet Sabrewing feeds on nectar from banana flowers and also gleans arthropods from foliage and spiderwebs. Its nest, built mainly in the wet season, is a cup made of green moss and plant fibres, bound with cobwebs. In this season, males form leks of up to 12 birds to display and sing to potential mates.

ADULT HOVERING TO FEED

Eupetomena macroura

Swallow-tailed Hummingbird

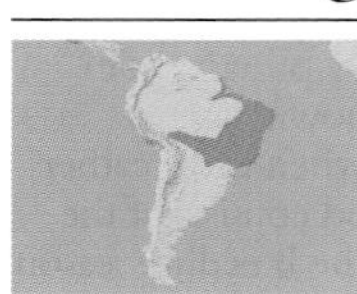

LENGTH 15–17cm (6–6½in)

WEIGHT 6–9g (7/32–11/32oz)

MIGRATION Non-migrant

HABITAT All types of open and non-forested areas, including towns and cities

This large hummingbird, with the long, forked tail that gives it its name, is a common sight even in large cities, where it feeds on trees that line busy streets. It has a black bill and is deep blue and green in colour, with dark wings. The sexes are quite alike, although the female is slightly smaller and has duller plumage. This bird is dominant at nectar-rich flowers, defending its feeding territory aggressively and attacking other hummingbirds that try to feed at the same flowers. It can also catch insects in flight. The male utters long but low chirps as it perches on a branch. During courtship, the male sings just before sunrise in a lek.

Most Swallow-tailed Hummingbirds build their nests between October and March, although breeding has been recorded in southern Brazil even in June (midwinter). The nest is constructed on a horizontal branch; two eggs are laid and are incubated by the female for up to 16 days.

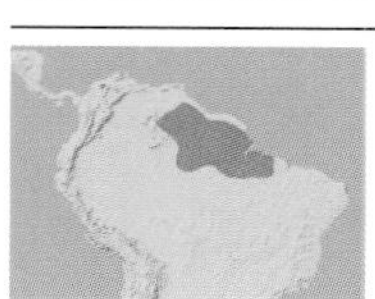

Topaza pella

Crimson Topaz

LENGTH 21–23cm (8½–9in)

WEIGHT 10–14g (3/8–½oz)

MIGRATION Non-migrant

HABITAT Canopy of lowland rainforest, frequently around granite outcrops and along rivers

One of the most striking hummingbirds, the male Crimson Topaz has a glittering crimson-to-purple breast and upperparts. Its head is black and its throat green, while the tail has scissor-like central tail-feathers. All-black individuals are not uncommon in some areas. In comparison, the female is almost nondescript, being mainly green with golden-green throat discs and red outer tail-feathers.

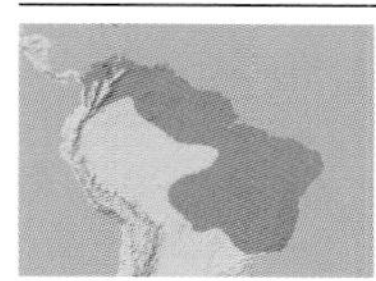

Chrysolampis mosquitus

Ruby Topaz

LENGTH 9cm (3½in)

WEIGHT 5g (3/16oz)

MIGRATION Partial migrant

HABITAT Savanna-like vegetation with scattered trees; gardens and cultivated land

Brilliantly coloured, the Ruby Topaz has a scarlet-red crown, yellow throat and breast, orange-red tail, and otherwise brown-black plumage. However, the male looks virtually all black if seen against the light or at a distance. The female shares the largely red tail, but has green upperparts and grey-white underparts. When displaying, the male circles around the female with its crown feathers raised and its tail fanned out. The Ruby Topaz is a true migrant. North to south migrations are known in Brazil and the species is seemingly absent from parts of Colombia and Trinidad and Tobago in certain seasons.

ADULT RUBY TOPAZ

FEMALE PLOVERCREST

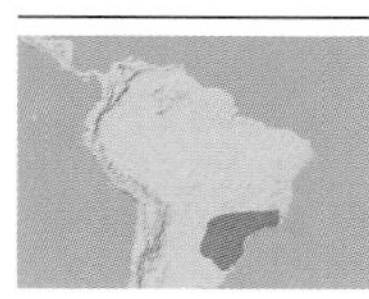

Stephanoxis lalandi

Plovercrest

LENGTH 9cm (3½in)

WEIGHT 2–4g (1/16–5/32oz)

MIGRATION Non-migrant

HABITAT Forest understorey and scrub; occasionally along watercourses

Unlike the male, which has an elongated crest, the female Plovercrest has only a short crest. The female also has a white spot behind the eye and lacks the purple breast and underparts of the male. The diet of this species consists principally of nectar, which it obtains from both native and introduced plants in its habitat. However, it is also capable of catching both airborne insects and those that can be gleaned from leaves.

The males form leks during the breeding season, where their chipping calls may be heard almost all day. The clutch of two eggs is tended by the female and nesting lasts for about six weeks from the laying of eggs to the fledging of the young.

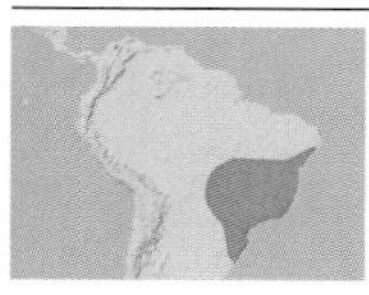

Lophornis magnificus

Frilled Coquette

LENGTH 8cm (3¼in)

WEIGHT 3g (1/8oz)

MIGRATION Non-migrant

HABITAT Plantations and forest edges, secondary growth, and gardens

A tiny hummingbird, the male Frilled Coquette has a rufuous crest and a fan-like ruff or frill of white feathers tipped with iridescent green that contrast dramatically with the rich chestnut crown feathers. It has a black-tipped red bill. The female lacks the crest and frill and has a darker red bill than the male. The Frilled Coquette readily adapts to manmade habitats, often eating at sugar-water feeders, but mainly feeds on small arthropods and the nectar of a wide range of flowers.

MALE FRILLED COQUETTE

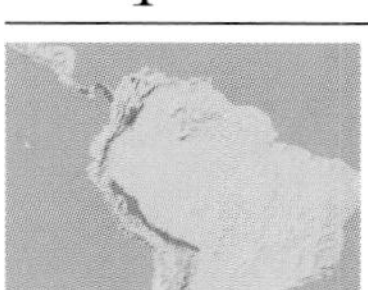

Lophornis delattrei

Rufous-crested Coquette

LENGTH 7cm (2¾in)

WEIGHT 3g (1/8oz)

MIGRATION Non-migrant

HABITAT Semi-open habitats, including humid forest edges and clearings

With its dark-tipped rufous crest, the male Rufous-crested Coquette is very distinctive. The female has a bright rufous face and a dark-spotted throat. Both sexes have a white rump-band.

Whereas most coquettes are lowland birds, the Rufous-crested Coquette is found in the Andes at altitudes up to 2,000m (6,500ft). Like most other coquettes, the species is known to hawk insects in flight as well as to visit a variety of trees and plants to obtain nectar. It is not frequently seen, and not much is known about its breeding behaviour.

MALE RUFOUS-CRESTED COQUETTE

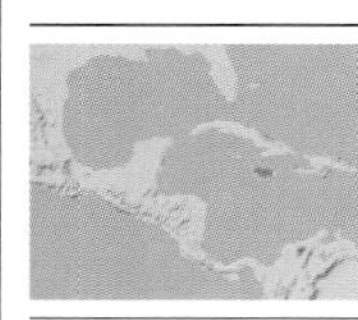

Trochilus polytmus

Red-billed Streamertail

LENGTH 11–30cm (4½–12in)

WEIGHT 5g (3/16oz)

MIGRATION Non-migrant

HABITAT Principally forested areas in highlands, but found in most well-vegetated areas

Found only in Jamaica, the Red-billed Streamertail is named for the black tail of the male. It has extremely elongated streamers that trail well behind the bird's body and account for almost half its total length. The male is spectacular, with its glittering grass-green plumage, black head, and dark wings. The female, by contrast, has no tail streamers and has a duller plumage, being chiefly green above and white-grey below, with a red tone to the bill. The species feeds on insects that are airborne, caught in spiderwebs, or gleaned from leaves, and also visits flowers and bird-feeders for nectar. While courting, the male waves its tail streamers from side to side.

Thalurania glaucopis

Violet-capped Woodnymph

LENGTH
8–11cm (3¼–4½in)

WEIGHT
5g (3/16oz)

MIGRATION
Non-migrant

HABITAT Forest and scrub of all types; and suburbs of towns

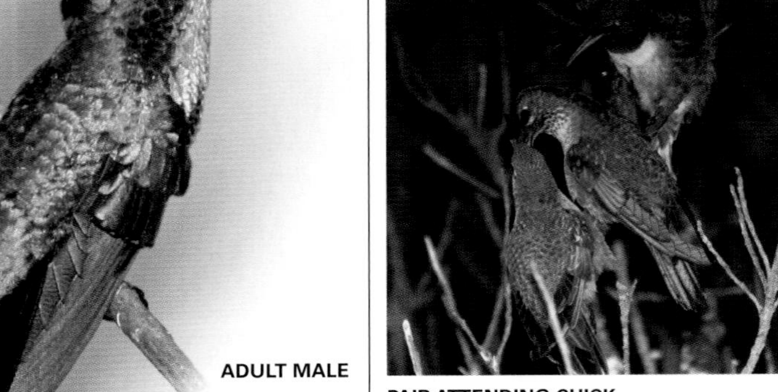

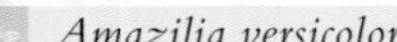

ADULT MALE

The male of this species has a violet-blue crown that gives rise to its common name. It also has brilliant green underparts. The female lacks the crown and has grey-white underparts. Both sexes have a long, forked tail. This hummingbird takes nectar from plants and trees and also feeds on insects.

PAIR ATTENDING CHICK

Oreotrochilus chimborazo

Ecuadorian Hillstar

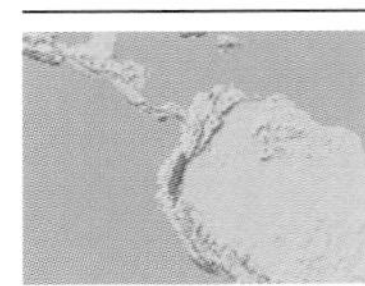

LENGTH
13cm (5in)

WEIGHT
8g (5/16oz)

MIGRATION
Non-migrant

HABITAT Highland grassland between the tree line and the snow line

Despite its name, the Ecuadorian Hillstar is not exclusive to Ecuador. Three subspecies have been described from different mountain ranges, the subspecies differing in the colour of the throat - two with varying amounts of green and the other being entirely iridescent purple. The Ecuadorian Hillstar is found at altitudes of up to 5,200m (17,000ft). In order to combat the extremely low night-time temperatures, it roosts in caves and crevices and becomes quite torpid during darkness. It is very aggressive, being territorial over its chosen patch of flowers. It feeds on nectar by clinging to the plants with its comparatively large feet and also catches insects in flight.

FEMALE VERSICOLORED EMERALD

Amazilia versicolor

Versicolored Emerald

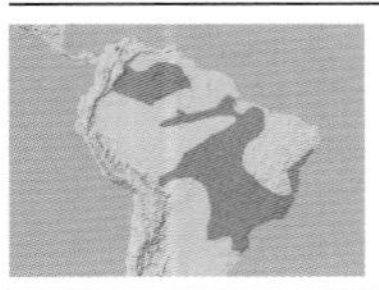

LENGTH
8–10cm (3¼–4in)

WEIGHT
4g (5/32oz)

MIGRATION
Partial migrant

HABITAT Open and semi-open habitats; also found at rainforest edge

Four subspecies of the Versicolored Emerald are recognized, and while most of these are principally green with or without a white throat, a subspecies in Venezuela and Guyana is quite different. It has a turquoise head and bright white throat. It visits a wide variety of plant species, but prefers those with short tubular flowers. It hawks insects in flight and also gleans them from leaves.

Ensifera ensifera

Sword-billed Hummingbird

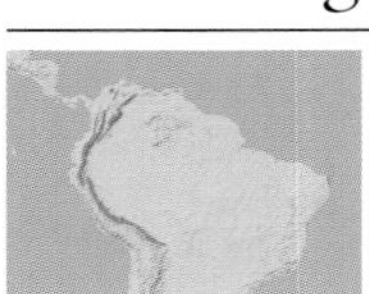

LENGTH
17–23cm (6½–9in)

WEIGHT
12–15g (7/16–9/16oz)

MIGRATION
Non-migrant

HABITAT Montane forest and its edges; patches of shrubs

Almost half the length of this hummingbird is constituted by its remarkable bill, the longest of any within its family. The Sword-billed Hummingbird is dark green in colour, with a deeply forked black tail. The tail of the male is more forked than that of the female. The sexes differ slightly, with the female showing some white in the throat and underparts and more white behind the eye than the male. The species appears to be closely related to the incas and strafrontlets. It is a locally common species capable of adapting to manmade habitats such as gardens. Despite this, its nesting ecology is practically unknown.

FEMALE SWORD-BILLED HUMMINGBIRD

NECTAR FEEDER

The long bill of the Sword-billed Hummingbird is an adaptation that allows it to extract nectar from flowers with long, pendant corollas that other hummingbirds are unable to access. The male shown here is sipping nectar from a *Datura* flower, but the species visits flowers of at least seven other genera.

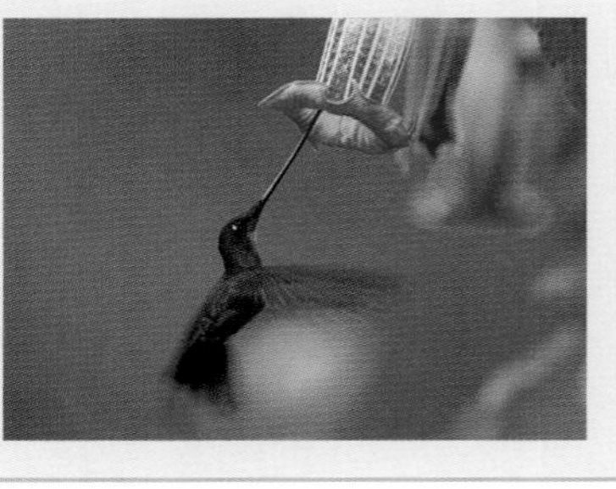

Coeligena torquata

Collared Inca

LENGTH
15cm (6in)

WEIGHT
7g (¼oz)

MIGRATION
Non-migrant

HABITAT Montane cloud forest and their borders in the Andes

The *Coeligena* genus consists of a dozen species of incas and starfrontlets, all of which occur solely in the Andes. Of these, the Collared Inca is one of the most widespread and is easily identified by its bright white throat patch and white tail markings. Six subspecies have been described, which differ principally in their slightly different head and throat patterns. The Collared Inca feeds on nectar and also catches arthropods at lower levels in forests and forest edges. The breeding season is variable, but it is generally in spring and summer.

FEMALE COLLARED INCA

Patagona gigas

Giant Hummingbird

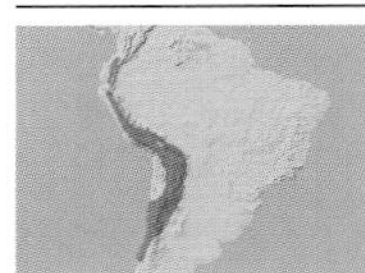

LENGTH
20–22cm (8–8½in)

WEIGHT
18–20g (5/8–11/16oz)

MIGRATION
Partial migrant

HABITAT Arid open and semi-open areas with a few trees at higher altitudes

As its name suggests, this hummingbird, the sole representative of its genus, is relatively large. The sexes are generally similar in plumage, both with brown upperparts, but the male Giant Hummingbird has warm orange underparts and a much larger white rump patch. Despite its size, this hummingbird constructs a small nest and the clutch usually consists of two eggs.

FEMALE ON NEST

Leucochloris albicollis

White-throated Hummingbird

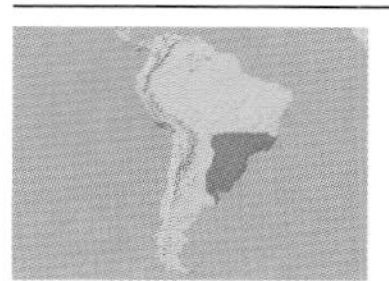

LENGTH 10–12cm (4–4½in)
WEIGHT 5g (3/16oz)
MIGRATION Non-migrant

HABITAT Forest edges, but also scrub, parks, and gardens

Unlike a great many hummingbirds, in which the male is characterized by its more elaborate and brighter plumage, both sexes of the White-throated Hummingbird have almost identical plumage, a distinctive white throat, and a white belly. Only the juvenile has underparts that are a dull grey.

The species forages for nectar at a variety of both native and introduced plants and trees, visiting parks and gardens to feed. It also catches insects by hawking. Like most birds in southern Brazil, it nests in spring to late summer, building a small cup-shaped nest of plant down and moss, decorated with lichens and bound with cobwebs. It is sited on a horizontal branch. Two eggs are laid, and they are incubated for two weeks by the female alone. The young fledge in just over three weeks. The White-throated Hummingbird is common, adapting well to human-modified habitats and is easily identified, even in flight, by its distinctive calls.

ADULT BIRD

Adelomyia melanogenys

Speckled Hummingbird

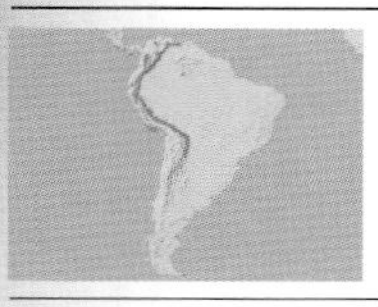

LENGTH 9cm (3½in)
WEIGHT 5g (3/16oz)
MIGRATION Non-migrant

HABITAT Forest and its edges, especially around watercourses and thickets

Among the most common of its family in the Andes, the Speckled Hummingbird is also one of the more widespread hummingbirds. The sexes are basically alike, with a dark ear patch and speckling on the breast. Up to seven subspecies are recognized, most of which differ in the amount of speckling and colour of the underparts. This bird frequently perches to sip nectar at flowers and also hawks insects in flight or gleans them from foliage.

ADULT SPECKLED HUMMINGBIRD

Heliodoxa leadbeateri

Violet-fronted Brilliant

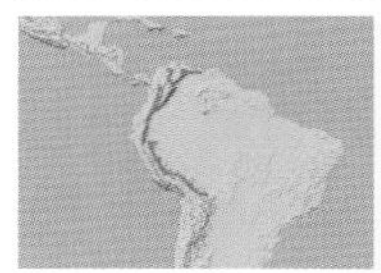

LENGTH 11–13cm (4½–5in)
WEIGHT 6–9g (7/32–11/32oz)
MIGRATION Non-migrant

HABITAT Forest, including cloud forest and edges, as well as second growth and shade coffee plantations

The so-called brilliants are a group of about nine species of hummingbird, all of which are characterized by their predominantly dark green plumage. Like the other species in this group, all of which belong to the genus *Heliodoxa*, the Violet-fronted Brilliant shows little difference between the sexes. However, the male has a violet forecrown and green underparts, while the female lacks the violet forecrown and has white underparts, thickly spotted with golden-green discs. While hummingbirds (unlike most non-passerines) have many subspecies, the Violet-fronted Brilliant is considered monotypic, which means that no subspecies are recognized.

This species mainly feeds on flowers at low levels and, unlike some hummingbirds, is usually found singly, rather than congregating at flowering trees. It also frequently catches insects in flight. The female lays two eggs and incubates them alone. The Violet-fronted Brilliant is a common bird in the Andes and adjacent mountain ranges, where it is found from low in the foothills up to about 2,400m (7,900ft).

MALE VIOLET-FRONTED BRILLIANT

ADULT GREENISH PUFFLEG

Haplophaedia aureliae

Greenish Puffleg

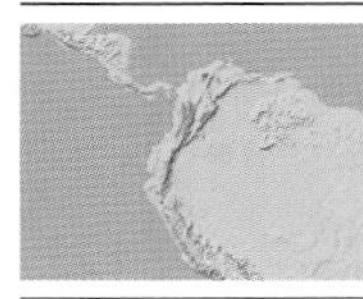

LENGTH 10cm (4in)
WEIGHT 5–7g (3/16–1/4oz)
MIGRATION Non-migrant

HABITAT Understorey of humid forest and forest borders

Like all of the pufflegs, a group of 14 species of hummingbird, this bird has puffy white feathering on its legs. The Greenish Puffleg is one of the more widespread species in the group. Three different subspecies have been described, some of which have a copper tinge to the head and neck. Like most hummingbirds, this species lays two eggs in a cup-shaped nest of moss and fine plant material bound together with cobwebs.

Lesbia victoriae

Black-tailed Trainbearer

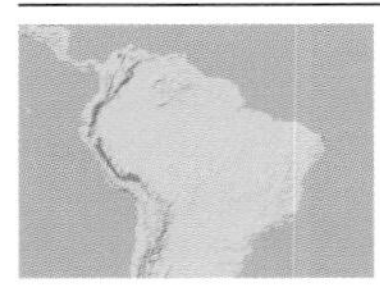

LENGTH 15–26cm (6–10in)

WEIGHT 5g (3/16oz)

MIGRATION Non-migrant

HABITAT Mountain forest edges at 2,500–4,000m (8,200–13,000ft)

As its name indicates, the Black-tailed Trainbearer has a spectacular, deeply forked tail, which makes up as much as three-quarters of the total length of the bird's body in the male. The female has a shorter tail, but this still represents around half of its total length. The male has a bright green plumage, with pale undersides, dark wings, and a black tail. The undersides of the female are white and distinctly marked with green discs.

A nectar-feeder, the Black-tailed Trainbearer mainly feeds at flowers, although it is also known to feed on eucalyptus trees. It also takes insects on the wing by hawking. While foraging, the male utters high-pitched notes and when courting it spreads its tail as it chases a female, calling as it does so. The Black-tailed Trainbearer's nest is a cup-shaped structure, made from plant fibres and a covering of moss and lichens. The usual location of its nest is beneath a twig, fern, or a rock. The female lays a single egg, and the incubation takes 18–19 days, with a further 30 days for fledging, a prolonged period for a bird of its size. The breeding season varies widely among the different populations (about three subspecies have been identified in its range), with the longest season stretching from October to March. The species is not globally threatened, although much of the habitat has been modified by human activity.

MALE FEEDING AT A FLOWER

MALE LONG-TAILED SYLPH

Aglaiocercus kingi

Long-tailed Sylph

LENGTH 10–19cm (4–7½in)

WEIGHT 5g (3/16oz)

MIGRATION Non-migrant

HABITAT Variable forest and gardens from 1,000–3,000m (3,300–10,000ft)

The Long-tailed Sylph is a very colourful bird. The male has a variety of blue and green shades in its plumage. Its green tail makes up to 12cm (4½in) of its total length. The female has a white throat with prominent green patches, and a yellow breast and belly. However, it lacks the long tail of the male. Both the sexes have dark wings.

The bird feeds on nectar by piercing the base of the flower, rather than the conventional way of taking nectar from the front of the bloom. In addition, it feeds by perching on the flowers as well as hovering to feed. The bird takes insects in flight by hawking from a perch.

Its breeding has been recorded between February and October, but it is thought that this bird breeds throughout the year. Its nest is a domed structure, with a side entrance built from moss and plant fibres.

Mellisuga helenae

Bee Hummingbird

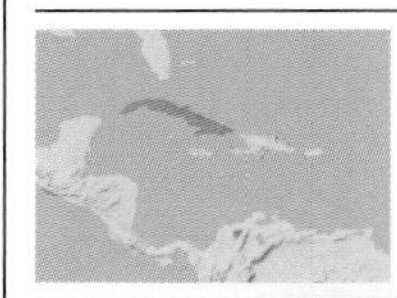

LENGTH 5cm (2in)

WEIGHT 2g (1/16oz)

MIGRATION Non-migrant

HABITAT Mature woodland, gardens, and wet areas, but also in more open areas

FEMALE BEE HUMMINGBIRD

The smallest bird in the world, the male Bee Hummingbird has a striking fiery red head and throat, with a green body. The female is slightly larger and lacks the red head markings. Its uppersides are a bluish green and the undersides are greyish white. The bird takes nectar from a wide range of plants, although it also feeds on insects, and the chicks eat insects that come within the range of the nest. Its breeding season is March to June and it lays two eggs at an interval of one day. The incubation is for about 22 days and the chicks have a full set of feathers by 14 days, leaving the nest after about 5 days of flight practice. The species is confined to Cuba and the nearby Isla de la Juventud, and is not migratory.

PLAINER FEMALE
The female does not have a red throat. It is larger and has a longer bill than the male.

BRIGHTLY COLOURED MALE
Identifiable by the iridescent red patch on its throat, the male Ruby-throated Hummingbird is more vividly coloured than the female.

Archilochus colubris

Ruby-throated Hummingbird

LENGTH 9cm (3½in)

WEIGHT 3g (⅛oz)

MIGRATION Migrant

HABITAT Deciduous and mixed forest in breeding season; tropical forest in winter

Named after the red throat of the male, this hummingbird has a green crown and upperparts and greyish white underparts. The female lacks the red throat and black face of the male, and with its paler underparts, appears much plainer than the male. The Ruby-throated Hummingbird feeds primarily on nectar and over 30 species of flowers have been identified as important food sources. It also takes some insects and spiders.

The summer breeding range of this species stretches up to much of eastern USA and into southern Canada, with the wintering birds mostly found in Central America. The male arrives on the breeding grounds between April and May, ahead of the female. It makes a courtship flight, but the female builds the nest. It lays two eggs in a cup-shaped nest, made of plant material, moss, and spider webs built on a horizontal branch. The incubation takes 16 days from the laying of the second egg, and the fledging follows after 15–20 days.

Calypte anna

Anna's Hummingbird

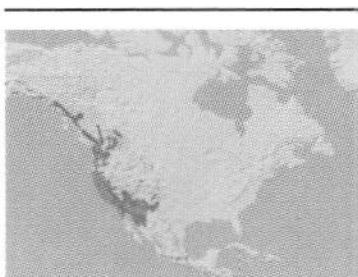

LENGTH 10cm (4in)

WEIGHT 3–6g (⅛–7/32oz)

MIGRATION Partial migrant

HABITAT Oak woodland and shrub or more open woodland

A stunning bird, the male Anna's Hummingbird has an iridescent deep red head and face, a pale throat and belly, and an iridescent green back. In contrast, the female lacks the red head of the male and has pale green plumage, with pale grey underparts.

Anna's Hummingbird feeds on nectar, visiting a wide range of flowers, especially in gardens, with fuchsias being a preference. It hovers to gather nectar from flowers and the male occupies a feeding territory where there are rich sources of nectar. While feeding on nectar, they also help in pollination. This species also catches insects by hawking.

The male's courtship display consists of hovering before the female, flying up in a high arc, and then diving rapidly towards her, with a loud "chirp".

MALE ANNA'S HUMMINGBIRD

FEEDING NESTLINGS

Nesting on its own, without any help from the male, the female Anna's Hummingbird builds a cup-shaped nest made of soft materials such as plant down, feathers, hair, and spider webs. Two eggs are laid and incubated by the female for 14–19 days. To feed the nestlings, the female selects flowers that have nectar with a high sugar content. It then regurgitates nectar, as well as small insects and spiders, into their bills, after stimulating them to open their mouths. The young birds make begging calls only after they leave the nest.

FEEDING A YOUNG NESTLING
When it hatches, the Anna's Hummingbird nestling is blind and does not make begging calls. The female stimulates it to feed by touching its bill.

FEEDING AN OLDER NESTLING
At a later stage, the nestling clings to the nest, perching on its side, and feeds after its mother stimulates it to gape by hovering above the nest.

MOUSEBIRDS

ORDER	Coliiformes
FAMILIES	2
SPECIES	6

FOUND ONLY IN SUB-SAHARAN AFRICA, mousebirds are grey or brown, and move in a rodent-like, scuttling way when feeding. They have conspicuous crests, well developed legs, and feet with an outer toe that can swivel to point backwards or forwards. Instead of perching, they often hang vertically or upside down from a branch. Mousebirds feed mainly on buds, fruit, and seeds. However, rarely they eat insects, and even the young of other birds. They typically live in flocks of up to 30, which break up at the beginning of the breeding season, and reform when the nestlings are fully fledged. The young clamber out of the nest when a few days old, returning to it at night.

WHITE-HEADED MOUSEBIRDS
Found in Kenya and Somalia, these birds have long, tapering tails that are typical of all mousebirds.

Colius striatus

Speckled Mousebird

LENGTH 30–36cm (12–14in)
WEIGHT 35–80g (1¼–2⅞oz)
MIGRATION Non-migrant

HABITAT Open woodland and forest edges; secondary growth, abandoned cultivation, and scrub

The Speckled Mousebird is remarkable for its disproportionately long tail. It has a mainly brown plumage. The chin and throat are usually darker than the rest of the plumage, and there is a paler area on the cheeks, which are white or grey, depending on the subspecies. It feeds on insects and fruit, as well as buds, flowers, and blossoms. It breeds almost year-round and some females may be capable of producing a clutch as many as eight times in a single year.

ADULT SPECKLED MOUSEBIRD

Urocolius macrourus

Blue-naped Mousebird

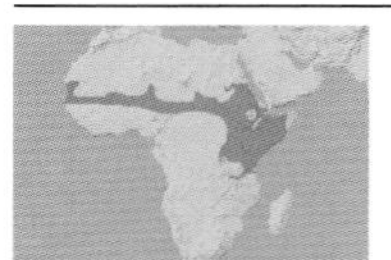

LENGTH 33–36cm (13–14in)
WEIGHT 35–60g (1¼–2⅛oz)
MIGRATION Non-migrant

HABITAT Open woodland in semi-arid regions, thornbush and wooded savanna, and even gardens

The Blue-naped Mousebird has largely blue-grey upperparts, including its long graduated tail, and much darker-coloured wings. It has a striking tufty crest, and a largely red bill. As befits its name, it has a blue nape patch (lacking in juveniles and adults of some subspecies), and pale buffy underparts. It breeds throughout the year. The nest is a shallow cup of twigs, lined with grass, placed in a tree or bush. It usually lays 2 or 3 eggs, which are incubated for 11 days, and the young leave the nest in about 10 days.

TROGONS

ORDER	Trogoniformes
FAMILY	1
SPECIES	39

WITH THEIR LUSTROUS plumage, trogons include some of the world's most richly coloured tropical forest birds. The largest number live in the Americas, but they are also found in southern Asia, with three species in sub-Saharan Africa. All have short bills, rounded wings and tails, and an unique foot anatomy – the inner toe points backwards, a feature not found in any other group of birds. They feed on insects and fruit, typically spending long periods on one perch, interrupted by brief flights to collect food. Trogons nest in cavities, excavating tree holes, or taking over abandoned insect nests.

MALE MASKED TROGON
Despite their brilliant colours, trogons can be surprisingly difficult to spot among foliage and flowers, because they often stay still for long periods of time.

SECOND-HAND NEST
After pecking an opening, this Violaceous Trogon has taken over a disused termite nest.

Apaloderma narina

Narina Trogon

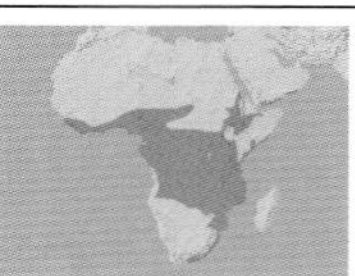

LENGTH 30–32cm (12–12½in)
WEIGHT 50–95g (1¾–3¼oz)
MIGRATION Non-migrant

HABITAT Forested areas, including gallery forest and savanna woodland, often along watercourses

Like many members of its family, the Narina Trogon is mainly green above, the colour extending to the breast in the male, which has bright red underparts. The female, however, has red confined to the belly and a brown face and throat, becoming pink on the breast. Both sexes have a bright yellow bill. This bird perches quietly for long periods, looking for prey and feeds on insects, including larvae, but also spiders, small lizards, and frogs.

MALE RED-HEADED TROGON

Harpactes erythrocephalus

Red-headed Trogon

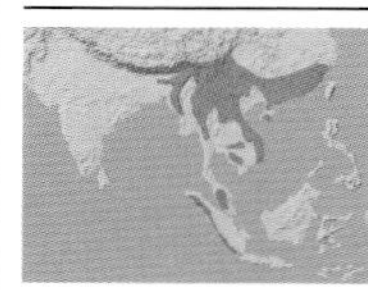

LENGTH 31–35cm (12–14in)
WEIGHT 75–100g (2⅝–3⅝oz)
MIGRATION Non-migrant

HABITAT Well-shaded areas in the mid-storey and lower canopy of dense forest to mid-altitudes

Mainly red in colour, the male Red-headed Trogon has grey-black wings, but males of some subspecies have a brown back. The female has a brown head and breast and mainly brown upperparts. The Red-headed Trogon is one of the most common trogons in Asia. It feeds mainly on insects, but also takes small berries. It catches insects and moths while it is in flight and preys upon invertebrates on the ground by swooping from a perch. Its call is a series of "chaup chaup" sounds. The species nests in spring and summer, usually in an unlined hollow in a rotten tree trunk, where it lays 2–4 eggs. Surprisingly, little else is known of the Red-headed Trogon's breeding biology.

Trogon rufus

Black-throated Trogon

LENGTH
23–25cm (9–10in)

WEIGHT
50–55g (1³/₄–2oz)

MIGRATION
Non-migrant

HABITAT Understorey and mid-levels of rainforest, occasionally in secondary growth or plantations

One of the most widespread representatives of the family in its range, the male Black-throated Trogon has a green head, upper breast, and back, a dark face and throat, and golden yellow underparts. The female has a brown head and breast and mainly brown upperparts, but is yellow below. Unlike most Neotropical trogons, this bird is not only a fruit-eater – it also takes insects, beetles, and caterpillars.

ADULT MALE

Trogon elegans

Elegant Trogon

LENGTH
28–30cm (11–12in)

WEIGHT
65–70g (2³/₈–2¹/₂oz)

MIGRATION
Non-migrant

HABITAT Canopy of woodland, including pine-oak forest, from lowland to highland

The only one of its family to breed regularly in the USA, the Elegant Trogon is also widespread and common in Central America. The male has a green chest and back, with grey wings, which have a latticed pattern. It has bright red underparts and a dark-tipped tail, while the female has brown upperparts. Both sexes have a narrow, white breast-band. The nest of this bird is usually sited in a cavity in a rotten tree, but occasionally in an earth bank, and 2 or 3 eggs are laid. The young are fed on insects, but at other times of the year, the diet consists only of fruit.

MALE ELEGANT TROGON

Pharomachrus mocinno

Resplendent Quetzal

LENGTH
36–65cm (14–26in)

WEIGHT
175–200g (6–7oz)

MIGRATION
Non-migrant

HABITAT Montane and cloud forests, usually in the canopy or subcanopy

With its extravagant colours, the Resplendent Quetzal outshines even the brightly coloured trogons. The male has a yellow bill, a predominantly emerald-green plumage, and red breast. It has truly extraordinary streamers, which constitute almost half the overall length of its body. These feathers are not actually part of the tail, but are some of its undertail feathers. In comparison to the flamboyant male, the female has a dark bill, a shorter tail, and no filamentous wing-feathers. It lacks a bushy crest and has brown underparts.

The Resplendent Quetzal is largely fruit-eating, although insects, small frogs, lizards, and snails offer some variation to the diet. The young are fed almost exclusively on insects for the first 10 days of their lives. Although mainly sedentary, the Resplendent Quetzal performs altitudinal movements in response to the seasonal fruiting of trees. Studies have revealed that it may undertake complex local migrations in Costa Rica, covering different altitudinal zones.

MALE RESPLENDENT QUETZAL

NESTING

The Resplendent Quetzal nests in decaying trees or in deep hollows, but usually uses more open holes. Just 1 or 2 eggs are laid and the nesting period lasts almost two months. The mortality rate of the young is 80 per cent – one study found that many chicks die without leaving the nest and that 80 per cent of the survivors fail to reach adulthood.

A CONTORTION ACT
In the nest-hole, the male Resplendent Quetzal accommodates its tail by holding it upright against the back wall of the cavity.

GREAT SITES

MONTEVERDE CLOUDFOREST PRESERVE

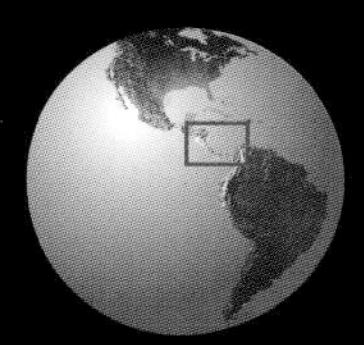

LOCATION In northern Costa Rica, northwest of the capital, San José

Costa Rica has a fabulously varied birdlife. Although it is a small country, 830 species of bird have been recorded there and over a quarter of its surface is managed for conservation. The Monteverde Cloudforest Preserve is a large protected area of mountain forest in north-central Costa Rica, covering around 10,500 hectares (26,000 acres). Much of the land that now makes up the reserve was originally bought by a group of Quakers, who emigrated from the USA in 1951.

MEETING OF WEST AND EAST

Monteverde straddles the upper slopes of the Cordillera de Tilarán, the spine of mountains down the centre of Costa Rica. The area is a meeting place where birds from both west and east can be seen, together with a wide range of species found only in uplands. The gain in altitude through the reserve brings changes in both temperature and humidity, producing six main forest zones – each with its own wildlife – in horizontal bands up the slopes.

The cloudforest that dominates the mid-altitudes is by far the most spectacular habitat. Here, the air is cool and drenched with mist and rain almost all year, and the majestic trees are festooned with masses of orchids, ferns, mosses, and trailing vines. This is the home of the elusive Resplendent Quetzal. Its favourite food is the fruit of the wild avocado tree, which thrives in the cloudforest. Another fruit-eating resident is the Three-wattled Bellbird, whose bizarre ringing call can carry over 3km (2 miles) across the area's forested ravines.

Monteverde is on a major north-south flyway of migratory birds from North America, especially birds of prey, such as the Broad-winged Hawk, and songbirds, such as vireos and New World warblers. Some migrants pause only briefly on their journey south, but many birds remain for several months, often forming colourful flocks with resident local species such as tanagers and euphonias.

RESPLENDENT RESIDENT
One of Monteverde's most famous residents, the Resplendent Quetzal (a male is pictured here) often nests near to a wild avocado tree, which ensures a reliable source of food for its young.

WHAT TO SPOT

EMERALD TOUCANET
Aulacorhynchus prasinus
(see p.282)

ORANGE-FRONTED PARAKEET
Aratinga canicularis

BROWN VIOLETEAR
Colibri delphinae

COMMON POTOO
Nyctibius griseus
(see p.254)

KINGFISHERS AND RELATIVES

ORDER	Coraciiformes
FAMILY	11
SPECIES	208

BRIGHTLY COLOURED BIRDS WITH LARGE and distinctive bills, kingfishers and their relatives are found throughout the world. They show a huge range of size, from tiny Caribbean todies, which can weigh as little as 5g (1/5oz), through bee-eaters, kingfishers, rollers, and hoopoes, to the largest hornbills from southeast Asia, which have a wingspan of up to 1.5m (5ft). Apart from large hornbills, coraciiform birds are essentially carnivorous, feeding on a wide variety of animals from fish to insects, including wasps and bees. All are cavity-nesters, and some breed in extended family groups.

ANATOMY

Coraciiform birds typically have large heads compared to their bodies, and their bills reinforce this "front-heavy" look. This is most marked in hornbills, which have exceptionally large bills, often topped by a horny shield, or casque. Most birds in this order have broad, rounded wings, but those of bee-eaters are sharply pointed – an adaptation that gives them speed and manoeuvrability for catching insects in mid-air. Internally, kingfishers and their relatives have some unusual anatomical features, including a characteristic pattern of feather tracts – feather-producing regions of the body that are separated by "islands" of bare skin. Another shared feature is their foot structure, with three forward-pointing toes connected for part of their length. Although their feet are small, most of these birds perch well; some spend all their lives in trees.

AERIAL STRIKE
With its wings swept back, a Eurasian Kingfisher dives to catch a fish. Kingfishers spot their prey either by tracking over the water's surface, or by watching from a perch.

BEHAVIOUR

Despite marked differences in size and habitat, many coraciiform birds share the same "spot-and-swoop" hunting technique, often taking off and returning to a favourite perch. Having made a catch, they typically beat it against a branch. Kingfishers use this behaviour to subdue fish, and animals such as lizards, before swallowing them head-first. Bee-eaters catch food in mid-air, then return to a perch to deactivate insect stings. Bee-eaters live and feed in noisy flocks like many of the loud and gregarious birds in this order – kookaburras, in particular, are famous for their laughing calls. Several species will fearlessly try to drive away intruders.

GROUND HUNTING
Heaviest of Africa's hornbills, the Southern Ground Hornbill is a terrestrial hunter, pecking up small animals as it strides through grasslands and open woodlands.

BREEDING

Kingfishers and their relatives rarely use any nesting material, but they often devote considerable energy to excavating burrows. Bee-eaters and river kingfishers dig long tunnels in banks of earth, while many others in this family nest in cavities in trees. Once the female is installed in the nest, some male hornbills "imprison" their partner by sealing the entrance with mud; a small opening left in the wall allows the male to deliver food. Coraciiformes lay up to 10 eggs each time they breed, and their young are blind and naked on hatching.

CARMINE BEE-EATER COLONY
Nesting colonies of bee-eaters can contain hundreds of birds, often divided into smaller groups, known as clans.

Coracias garrulus

European Roller

LENGTH 31cm (12in)
WEIGHT 150g (5oz)
MIGRATION Migrant

HABITAT Breeds on sunny lowlands with patches of woodland; winters on dry, wooded African savanna

Predominantly electric blue, with a chestnut back and wing patches, the European Roller is a large-headed, long-necked roller. It spends long periods on a perch looking for prey. It is an intercontinental migrant; almost the entire population winters south of the Sahara. In spring, the species makes spectacular mass movement northwards along the East African coast.

ADULT EUROPEAN ROLLER

Coracias spatulatus

Racquet-tailed Roller

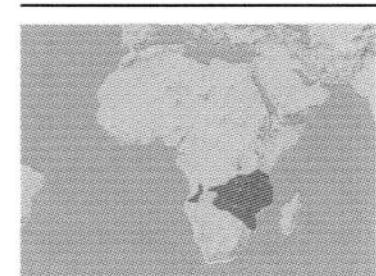

LENGTH 36cm (14in)
WEIGHT 100g (3 5/8oz)
MIGRATION Non-migrant

HABITAT Undisturbed, mature woodland and well-wooded savanna

The Racquet-tailed or "Weigall's" Roller is the smallest and lightest roller. It has long tail streamers, which have an elongated outer tail feather with a spoon-like tip. In flight, its dark blue wings contrast with a bright azure wing-stripe. It swoops to the ground to take locusts, beetles, and small lizards. It is primarily a species of the dense woodland.

ADULT INDIAN ROLLER

Coracias benghalensis

Indian Roller

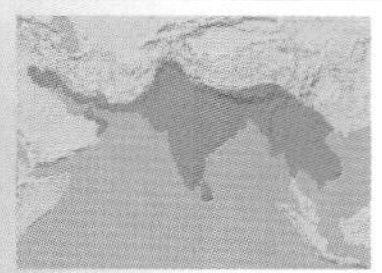

LENGTH 32cm (12½in)

WEIGHT 150–175g (5–6oz)

MIGRATION Partial migrant

HABITAT Open farmland, wooded groves, roadsides, villages, parks, and other open areas

A stocky bird with a brown back, the Indian Roller is particularly spectacular in flight; its azure stripe across the wings being visible from a distance. Its crown, inner wing, belly, and outer tail are turquoise and the flight feathers are mostly dark blue. The throat is streaked white. It feeds on insects, rodents, and reptiles.

ADULT ORIENTAL DOLLARBIRD

Eurystomus orientalis

Oriental Dollarbird

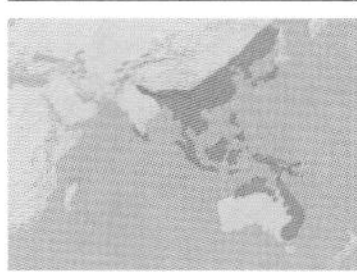

LENGTH 30cm (12in)

WEIGHT 125–150g (4–5oz)

MIGRATION Partial migrant

HABITAT Various types of woodland, savanna, parks, wasteland, and farmland with scattered trees

A swift flier and aerially dextrous, the Oriental Dollarbird, also known as the Red-billed or Eastern Broad-billed Roller, hawks after insects or carries out spectacular territorial and display flights. It gets its name from the large, coin-like white mark on each underwing, which is conspicuous in flight. It is blue-green in colour, with a black cap.

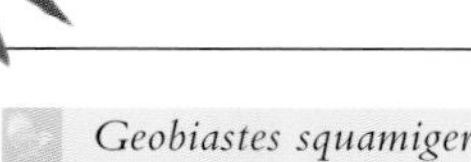

Geobiastes squamiger

Scaly Ground Roller

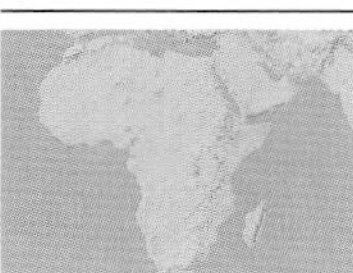

LENGTH 28cm (11in)

WEIGHT 150g (5oz)

MIGRATION Non-migrant

HABITAT Dark, humid rainforest up to mid-altitudes, sometimes in secondary growth

RED LIST CATEGORY Vulnerable

The Scaly Ground Roller is the second largest rainforest member of its family. It is endemic to Madagascar. A thickset, terrestrial bird, most of its plumage is covered by dark scaling and its wings are short and rounded. Rummaging through dense leaf litter, it feeds on invertebrates such as earthworms.

ADULT SCALY GROUND ROLLER

ADULT MALE

Leptosomus discolor

Cuckoo-roller

LENGTH 45cm (17½in)

WEIGHT 250g (9oz)

MIGRATION Non-migrant

HABITAT Variety of forested and woodland habitats, sometimes open country

The male Cuckoo-roller has a flamboyant velvety purple and grey plumage, with a shiny dark green back, wings, and tail. The female and juvenile are mostly brown, marked with darker streaks. The plaintive call of the Cuckoo-roller is frequently heard as it circles and glides over the forests of Madagascar.

MALE GALATEA PARADISE KINGFISHER

Tanysiptera galatea

Galatea Paradise Kingfisher

LENGTH 38cm (15in)

WEIGHT 50g (1¾oz)

MIGRATION Non-migrant

HABITAT Primary lowland rainforest, narrow strips of forest in savanna, all in lowlands

Also known as Common or Rossel Island Racquet-tail, the Galatea Paradise Kingfisher is a spectacular bird. It is dark blue above, with a shiny blue crown and a red bill. The male has white central tail feathers that extend up to 20cm (8in) longer than the rest of the tail. The call of this species – four evenly pitched, long, mournful whistles that accelerate into a trill – is very different from other kingfishers. It is mainly a "wait and see" predator. It feeds by concealing itself in the forest before pouncing on terrestrial invertebrates.

Dacelo novaeguinae

Laughing Kookaburra

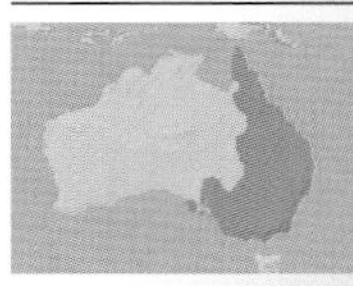

LENGTH 40cm (15½in)

WEIGHT 325–350g (12–13oz)

MIGRATION Non-migrant

HABITAT Eucalyptus forest and woodlands, often along watercourses; also parks and farmland

Few bird calls are as well known as that of the Laughing Kookaburra. The choruses of this very large kingfisher are normally uttered at dawn and dusk by two or more birds, usually in response to a neighbouring group. The "laugh" comprises a complex sequence of repetitive chuckles, shrieks, and cackles with "ooo" sounds, each lasting around two seconds and rising in intensity to a loud laugh. The result is a cacophony of sound.

The Laughing Kookaburra has a large, heavy, hook-tipped bill and has a distinctive plumage: both the male and female have a dark crown and eye-mask contrasting with the white head and underparts, brown wings mottled in blue, and a rufous uppertail. The male has a blue patch on the rump and a barred tail, while the female has a brown rump patch.

These birds are monogamous and pair for life, defending their territory all year. They are often helped to raise chicks by male offspring from earlier broods, who also defend the nest.

ADULT LAUGHING KOOKABURRA

EXTENDED FAMILIES

Most kookaburra species tend to live in extended family units. A Laughing Kookaburra offspring stays around its territory, helping its parents incubate, hunt, brood, feed, and raise the next generation of offspring.

Pelargopsis capensis

Stork-billed Kingfisher

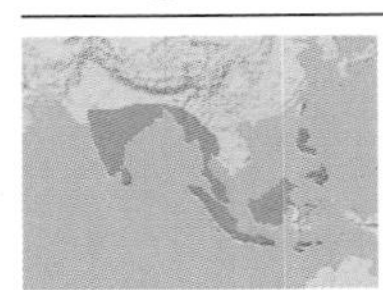

LENGTH 35cm (14in)

WEIGHT 150–200g (5–7oz)

MIGRATION Non-migrant

HABITAT Lowland watercourses, both within deep forest and in open country such as paddy fields

With the distinction of having the largest bill of any kingfisher, the Stork-billed Kingfisher is a heavy-looking bird. Its large head and bill lend it a top-heavy appearance. Despite its size, however, it can be inconspicuous as it sits quietly in the forest understorey, watching for prey. Its main prey is fish and crustaceans. However, it will also use its bill to advantage in dispatching lizards, rodents, and young birds. It immobilizes its prey by hitting it against a branch before swallowing. It defends its territory aggressively, chasing away birds as big as storks and eagles.

ADULT STORK-BILLED KINGFISHER

Todirhamphus chloris

Collared Kingfisher

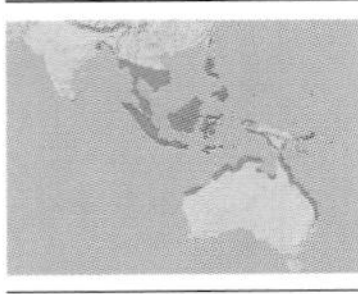

LENGTH 24cm (9½in)

WEIGHT 55–80g (2–2⅞oz)

MIGRATION Partial migrant

HABITAT Mangroves and other coastal vegetation, sometimes penetrating inland to open areas

A common bird in its large range of southeast Asia to Australia, the Collared Kingfisher is also known as the White-collared, Sordid, or Black-masked Kingfisher. The plumage varies across the 49 races of the species, with differences in the blueness or greenness of the upperparts, the extent of the pale spot above the bill, and the whiteness of the underparts.

ADULT COLLARED KINGFISHER

Halcyon leucocephala

Grey-headed Kingfisher

LENGTH 22cm (8½in)

WEIGHT 40g (1 7/16oz)

MIGRATION Partial migrant

HABITAT Woodland and thickets, especially along watercourses, bushy grassland, and parkland

A relatively small kingfisher, the Grey-headed or Chestnut-bellied Kingfisher has a distinctive plumage. Its head and breast are grey, its back is black, and its belly is chestnut. The wings, rump, and tail are bright blue. The male is slightly brighter than the female. The Grey-headed Kingfisher is primarily insectivorous, preying on grasshoppers, crickets, and locusts in particular. Most prey is taken from the ground, but some insects are caught in flight. Small prey are swallowed whole, while larger insects may be smashed against a perch. Pairs display by singing from a treetop and flicking open their vivid blue wings. They also circle high above the ground, calling constantly, before diving back to a tree.

The timing and extent of the species' migratory movements vary across its African range. Only birds in Cape Verde, the East African coast, and perhaps in equatorial Africa are resident, while those at mid-latitudes and some southern areas undertake a complex three-stage migration.

ADULT DISPLAYING ITS WINGS

ADULT RUDDY KINGFISHER

Halcyon coromanda

Ruddy Kingfisher

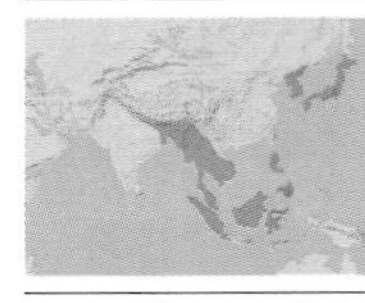

LENGTH 25cm (10in)

WEIGHT 80g (2⅞oz)

MIGRATION Partial migrant

HABITAT Evergreen forest and temperate woodland around streams; also in mangroves in the south

This shy, medium-sized kingfisher has a distinctive plumage. It has a large bright red bill, a pale rufescent head and underparts, violet-tinged wings and mantle, and a contrasting azure rump. Its legs are red. The male and female are similar in plumage, although the male may be brighter.

Its prey depends on its habitat. In forests away from water, it will catch beetles, grasshoppers, cicadas, and small lizards. In aquatic habitats, it feeds on mayflies, fish, frogs, and crustaceans. The Ruddy Kingfisher is resident in the tropical south of its range, but migratory in the temperate north.

Todirhamphus sanctus

Sacred Kingfisher

LENGTH 22cm (8½in)

WEIGHT 45–65g (1⅝–2⅜oz)

MIGRATION Partial migrant

HABITAT Eucalyptus and open woodland, scrub, forest edges, farmland, and coastal habitats

The Sacred, Wood, Tree, or Green Kingfisher has a prominent black eye mask and a green back, wings, and tail, with pale underparts. Its diet includes insects, worms, small fish, lizards, birds, and mice, which it spots by perching on a vantage point and scouring the area below for movement.

ADULT BIRD

Syma torotoro

Yellow-billed Kingfisher

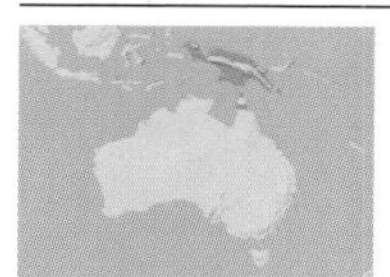

LENGTH 20cm (8in)

WEIGHT 40g (1 7/16oz)

MIGRATION Non-migrant

HABITAT Primary and secondary rainforest, monsoon, and mangrove forest, and mature plantations

The Yellow-billed, Lowland, or Saw-billed Kingfisher is found in the forests of New Guinea. This small kingfisher often raises its crown feathers, creating an alarmed appearance. It has a strong orange-yellow bill, white throat, rufous head and underparts, greenish blue upperparts, and a dark blue tail. The juvenile has a dark grey bill.

The species feeds primarily on insects, but will also take worms, small lizards, snakes, and reptile eggs. It perches in the canopy, higher than many kingfishers, swaying from side to side as it searches for prey. When it spots a movement, it swoops and grabs its prey. Its call is a whistling trill.

ADULT YELLOW-BILLED KINGFISHER

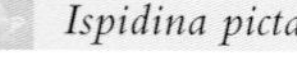

Ispidina picta

African Pygmy Kingfisher

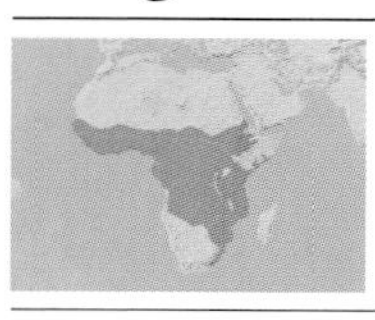

LENGTH 12cm (4 1/2in)

WEIGHT 11–14g (3/8–1/2oz)

MIGRATION Migrant

HABITAT Dense forest, woodland, and grassland

One of the smallest of all kingfishers, the African Pygmy or Miniature Kingfisher is predominantly blue and rufous in its plumage and has an orange bill. The juvenile has a black bill. This kingfisher inhabits dense forest, where it sits quietly on a perch 1m (3 1/4ft) above the ground, flicking its tail or bobbing its head as it searches for prey. It mostly takes insects, but will also eat small lizards and frogs. Unusually among kingfishers, it will follow and prey on ant swarms.

ADULT AFRICAN PYGMY KINGFISHER

Alcedo atthis

Common Kingfisher

LENGTH 16cm (6 1/2in)

WEIGHT 25–35g (7/8–1 1/4oz)

MIGRATION Partial migrant

HABITAT Still or slow-flowing water, including streams, small rivers, canals, small lakes, and ponds

In most of its range, the Common, River, or Eurasian Kingfisher is the only small blue kingfisher present. It is thus one of the most familiar of the world's kingfishers. It has a bright orange cheek patch, a white throat, and a white patch on the neck sides. Its crown and wings are greenish blue, the back and tail bright cobalt blue, and the underparts bright orange. The male has a black bill. Despite these bright colours, this bird can be difficult to spot as it sits motionless on a shady waterside branch.

From its perch 1–2m (3 1/4–6 1/2ft) above the water, the Common Kingfisher will spot a fish and dive steeply into the water, catching its prey to a depth of 1m (3 1/4ft). Where no suitable waterside vantage point is available, it will hover before diving. Its prey is mainly fish up to about 12cm (4 1/2in) long, but the Common Kingfisher will also take shrimps, aquatic insects, amphibians, and butterflies. Adults carry fish, with the head facing outwards, in their bills, so that the meal can easily be passed to, and swallowed by, hungry chicks. Chicks are fed every 45 minutes at first, which reduces to every 15 minutes until they are 18 days old. The nest is in a tunnel chamber in a sandy bank, with chicks sitting on a bed of fish-bones.

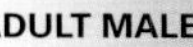

DIVE-FEEDING

On spotting a fish underwater, the Common Kingfisher dives vertically, streamlining its body by drawing its wings back just before it fully submerges. Underwater, its eyes are covered with protective membranes. After catching its prey, it rises vertically back to its perch.

ADULT MALE

ADULT LITTLE KINGFISHER

Alcedo pusilla

Little Kingfisher

LENGTH
11–13cm (4¼–5in)

WEIGHT
10–15g (⅜–⁹⁄₁₆oz)

MIGRATION
Non-migrant

HABITAT Wooded channels and coastal mangroves; occasionally gardens

Despite its bright blue and white plumage, the Little Kingfisher is an inconspicuous inhabitant of pools and streams in forests, usually in coastal areas. It is well named, being one of the smallest and shortest-tailed member of its family. The male and female have broadly similar plumage, but the juvenile has a green wash tinging its back, a buff spot above the bill, and a rufous blaze on its neck. This species has a white spot next to its eyes and one on each side of the neck. It has black legs, feet, and bill. Several races have been described, generally differing only in their shades of blue coloration and the presence (or lack) of a complete blue band on the breast.

Breeding is throughout the wet season, particularly January. The Little Kingfisher excavates its own nest holes, either in streamside banks, rotten wood, or in termite nests, and lays around 3–5 eggs. Food is brought to the nest by both adults, as frequently as every five minutes, to meet the needs of the demanding chicks, which give buzzing calls. Some of the races have very small ranges, sometimes being restricted to just one island. Although the Little Kingfisher is usually common, it is threatened in some places due the destruction of its habitat by the clearance of mangroves.

FOREST AND WATER

A bird of lowland rainforest streams, the Little Kingfisher inhabits shaded areas with overhanging vegetation. It is also found near lakes and estuaries and shows a preference for coastal mangroves. As befits its size, the Little Kingfisher feeds on tiny fish, insect larvae, small crustaceans, and shrimps. It sits on a low perch, such as a branch overlooking a pool, lake, or stream, and often bobs its head and wings while watching for prey. Once it spots its prey, it plunges into the water, catches its food, and returns to its perch.

Chloroceryle americana

Green Kingfisher

LENGTH
20cm (8in)

WEIGHT
30–40g (1¹⁄₁₆–1⁷⁄₁₆oz)

MIGRATION
Non-migrant

HABITAT Wooded streams and rivers, but also lakes, marshes, mangroves, and coasts

MALE GREEN KINGFISHER

The male Green Kingfisher has white underparts, a broad chestnut breast band, and green spots on the flanks. The female has buff-white underparts with two green chest bands, which link to the green spots along the sides of the belly. Some subspecies show more white on the wings. Often spotted on a bare branch or other open perch, the Green Kingfisher is noticeable as it bobs its head or flicks its tail. It flies low and straight just above the water surface and then dives to catch its prey, mostly small fish. It also eats aquatic insects.

These kingfishers are solitary, rarely seen in pairs or groups. However, their perches, where they spend long periods of time looking out for prey, are often close together. The species utters a distinctive "choot" or "chew" call. It also has a alarm call, which is a soft, ticking rattle. It nests near water in tunnels, which it excavates itself, and 3 or 4 eggs are laid. It feeds its young on small fish and insects.

Megaceryle torquata

Ringed Kingfisher

LENGTH
40cm (15½in)

WEIGHT
250–325g (9–12oz)

MIGRATION
Non-migrant

HABITAT Rivers, streams and lakes, usually in open areas

The largest kingfisher in the Americas, this species is distinguished from the superficially similar Belted Kingfisher (opposite) by the all-red underparts in the male and the grey and white bands on the female's breast. The male has a pale grey head with a white spot in front of the eye and a narrow line beneath; grey back and wings; and grey and white upper tail feathers. Both the male and the female have a white collar. The juvenile is similar to the female. The Ringed Kingfisher is noisy and easy to see, often perching on powerlines and other manmade structures. It is an extremely patient hunter, often waiting for hours on its perch for a fish. It dives down to capture its food, returning to its perch before swallowing its prey head-first. Its large bill enables it to devour crabs and lizards, as well as fish, and it sometimes hunts far from water.

MALE RINGED KINGFISHER

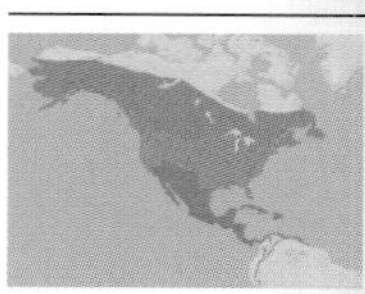

Megaceryle alcyon

Belted Kingfisher

LENGTH 28–33cm (11–13in)

WEIGHT 125–150g (4–5oz)

MIGRATION Partial migrant

HABITAT Stretches of clear water, from streams to garden ponds and tidal creeks; lowlands to highlands

The most widespread of North America's kingfishers, the Belted Kingfisher is a noisy and conspicuous bird, which is remarkably resistant to habitat change. It is even tolerant of some pesticides and other pollutants, and in recent years the population has expanded due to the creation of sand and gravel pits. While the female has reddish underparts, the male is largely white below, with a grey-blue band across the breast.

This bird eats a wide variety of fish, but also consumes frogs, salamanders, insects, crustaceans, and even young birds and small mammals. To catch fish, it dives into the water from a perch or by hovering above it, and will sometimes follow egrets, catching small prey disturbed by them. This species nests in holes in banks, sometimes in mudslides.

FEMALE BELTED KINGFISHER

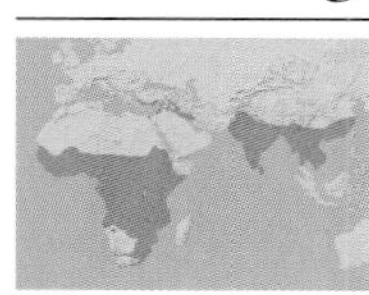

Ceryle rudis

Pied Kingfisher

LENGTH 25cm (10in)

WEIGHT 70–100g ($2^1/_2$–$3^5/_8$oz)

MIGRATION Non-migrant

HABITAT From lakes, rivers, and estuaries to mangroves, ditches, marshes, and reservoirs

With striking black-and-white plumage, the Pied Kingfisher is probably one of the most numerous of its family, its raucous calls drawing attention in wetlands throughout its range. The female has only one black band on the breast, whereas the male has two. Fish are its main prey, but this adaptable bird also takes frogs, tadpoles, crabs, and molluscs. The nests of this species are sometimes grouped in small colonies and "helpers" may tend the young, especially if food is scarce.

ADULT PIED KINGFISHER

HOVERING FOR PREY

The Pied Kingfisher has mastered the art of hovering in one spot above the water for long periods of time, even when it is windy, while it looks out for prey. It does not need to return to its perch and can exploit additional food resources, including fish species only found far from shore, which are unavailable to other kingfishers.

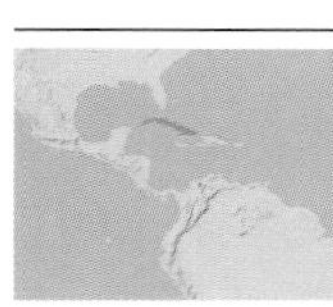

Todus multicolor

Cuban Tody

LENGTH 10cm (4in)

WEIGHT 5–7g ($^3/_{16}$–$^1/_4$oz)

MIGRATION Non-migrant

HABITAT All types of woodland, wet and dry, deciduous and evergreen, and orchards

CUBAN TODY

The Cuban Tody has the most striking pattern in its genus, characterized by its bright blue lower cheeks and pink flanks. Its food mostly consists of insects, often taken by flycatching in mid-air, and supplemented by small lizards and sometimes fruit. The Cuban Tody usually excavates its own burrows for nesting, but occasionally uses natural cavities or old crab burrows.

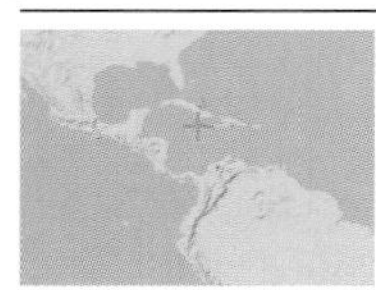

Todus todus

Jamaican Tody

LENGTH 11cm ($4^1/_2$in)

WEIGHT 7g ($^1/_4$oz)

MIGRATION Non-migrant

HABITAT All forest types, except plantations and the highest areas of the island

Found only in Jamaica, the Jamaican Tody is a small and colourful bird, predominantly green above, with a red throat and yellow underparts, with some pink on the sides. It has a large head and a long, flat bill. It perches on small branches, with its bill upturned and, like its Cuban relative (above), takes insects, larvae, and fruit. The Jamaican Tody nests in burrows, which it excavates in muddy banks or rotten wood.

ADULT JAMAICAN TODY

Momotus momota

Blue-crowned Motmot

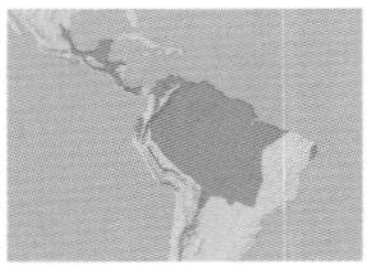

LENGTH 39cm (15½in)

WEIGHT 125g (4oz)

MIGRATION Non-migrant

HABITAT Humid rainforest and forest edges; some dry plantations

Often seen perching quietly and motionless in the shady forest, usually in the lower or middle parts of trees, the Blue-crowned Motmot will sometimes announce its presence with a soft "hoop-hoop" call and may slowly swing its tail from side-to-side. In common with most other motmots, its two long central tail feathers have a bare shaft section that is featherless, leaving a paddle-shaped vane at the tip of each feather. Its plumage is green and it has a blue cap and a black eye-stripe.

Its nest is inside a long burrow up to 4m (13ft) long, excavated in the side of a bank, or hollow, with the entrance well hidden. It excavates its nest during the rainy season (August–September) when the soil is soft. By the time nesting takes place in March, the tunnel entrance does not look new and is less likely to be noticed by predators.

ADULT BLUE-CROWNED MOTMOT

FEEDING HABITS

Looking out for prey from a perch, the Blue-crowned Motmot glides down to the ground to take earthworms, spiders, insects, and even small lizards and snakes. It also takes insects from among leaves. Some motmots will even come to bird-feeders for fruit.

Baryphthengus ruficapillus

Rufous-capped Motmot

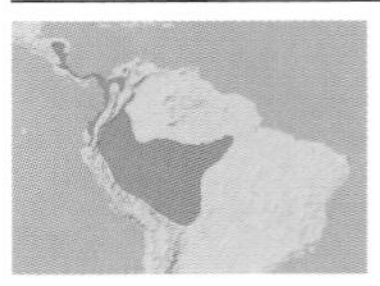

LENGTH 44cm (17½in)

WEIGHT 150g (5oz)

MIGRATION Non-migrant

HABITAT Humid and wet tropical rainforest, as well as semi-open areas with regenerating forest

One of the largest of the motmots, the Rufous-capped Motmot is easily distinguished from other types by its bright rufous crown, black face mask, and lack of "paddles" at the end of its tail. Its soft, hooting "hoorooroo" call is quite distinctive. It feeds on the ground and its bill has a coarse serrated edge in the centre of the upper mandible, which enables it to grasp beetles and fruit easily.

ADULT RUFOUS-CAPPED MOTMOT

As a fruit-eater, it helps plants to disperse their seeds. In common with all motmots, it has each middle toe fused to the adjacent outer one.

Eumomota superciliosa

Turquoise-browed Motmot

LENGTH 34cm (13½in)

WEIGHT 65g (2⅜oz)

MIGRATION Non-migrant

HABITAT Forest edges and scrubland

Mostly green in colour, with a rufous back and underparts, this motmot has tail feathers that look like pendulums as the adult swings its tail from side to side. The juvenile has complete central tail feathers, but loses part of the feathering where the vane is more brittle. Confined to Central America, the Turquoise-browed Motmot is the national bird of both Nicaragua and El Salvador. It is more easily seen than most motmots because of its habit of perching on branches and fences.

ADULT TURQUOISE-BROWED MOTMOT

Nyctyornis amictus

Red-bearded Bee-eater

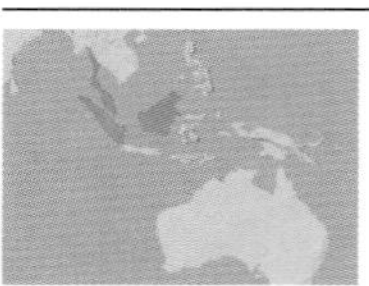

LENGTH 29cm (11½in)

WEIGHT 80g (2⅞oz)

MIGRATION Non-migrant

HABITAT Lowland evergreen forest near streams, swamps, or lagoons

Named for its red throat feathers, which resemble a beard when they are are puffed out, the Red-bearded Bee-eater is mainly green in colour. Its bill is the largest and most curved of all the bee-eaters. Unlike most bee-eaters, it is not a colonial breeder. Its nest burrows are about 1.2m (4ft) long and while many may be excavated, only one is actually used. It hunts for food alone or with its mate, chasing after insects from a concealed perch. It often sits motionless, but gives its descending "ka-ka-ka-ka" call.

Merops hirundineus

Swallow-tailed Bee-eater

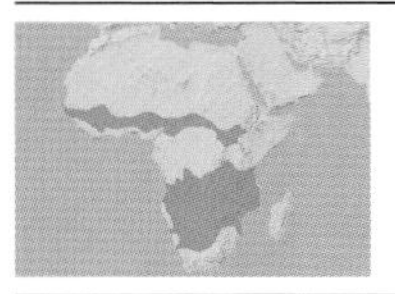

LENGTH 21cm (8½in)

WEIGHT 20g (11/16oz)

MIGRATION Partial migrant

HABITAT Mature woodland with grassy clearings, mainly in lowland areas

Recognizable by its deeply forked tail, the colourful Swallow-tailed Bee-eater is mainly green in colour with a black eye-stripe, a yellow throat, and blue throat-band. It moves from place to place in search of insect prey, largely honeybees, but also beetles, butterflies, and dragonflies. It hawks for insects from a high treetop or telegraph wire. A sociable species, this bird breeds in pairs or small groups and forms small family flocks of 8–10 birds.

ADULT SWALLOW-TAILED BEE-EATER

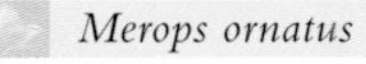

Merops ornatus

Rainbow Bee-eater

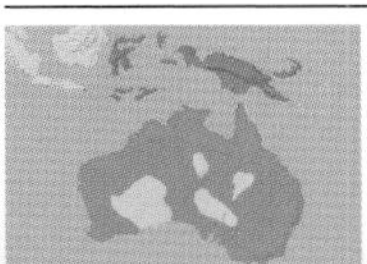

LENGTH 20cm (8in)

WEIGHT 30g (1 1/16oz)

MIGRATION Partial migrant

HABITAT Pastures and lightly wooded open countryside, even city parks

Also known as the Rainbowbird for its vibrant green, blue, violet, and yellow plumage, the Rainbow Bee-eater is the only one found in Australia. In common with other bee-eaters it enjoys basking in the sun with its wings spread, feathers raised, bill open, and head to one side. It digs its nesting burrow with its bill, pushing loose material out by the feet. A pair stays together for life and some pairs have one or more helpers at the nest.

Merops apiaster

European Bee-eater

LENGTH 24cm (9½in)

WEIGHT 45–80g (1⅝–2⅞oz)

MIGRATION Migrant

HABITAT River valleys, pastures, and cultivated land with bushes, as well as open wooded areas

This common and widespread species is one of the largest and most colourful of the bee-eaters. Its plumage is green and it has a black eye-stripe, a yellow throat, and a bluish green tail. Like many bee-eaters, its two central tail feathers are elongated.

It is a very sociable species, breeding in colonies, migrating in noisy flocks, and also wintering together. Some pairs have helpers who assist them in raising their young. When a mate returns to its partner, they greet each other by fanning and vibrating their tails, while giving excited calls. The bird usually hunts from a perch, but may hawk, gliding at a considerable height. Honeybees form a major part of its diet and a bee-eater will "de-sting" them before eating by rubbing the tip of the bee's abdomen against its perch.

ADULT EUROPEAN BEE-EATER

Merops nubicoides

Southern Carmine Bee-eater

LENGTH 26cm (10in)

WEIGHT 60g (2⅛oz)

MIGRATION Migrant

HABITAT Bushy and wooded grassland, flood plains, marshes, and lake shores

ADULT SOUTHERN CARMINE BEE-EATERS

Vivid red (carmine) in colour, with a greenish blue crown and a black stripe around the eyes, the Southern Carmine Bee-eater has a black bill and tail streamers that can reach 12cm (4½in) in length. While its diet includes honeybees, this species also feeds on grasshoppers and locusts. It perches on the backs of animals and waits for them to flush out larger insects. Cattle, antelopes, elephants, ostriches, bustards, and secretary birds are some of its favourite perches. This species also feeds high in the air, sometimes up to 100m (325ft), staying aloft for as long as 10 minutes. It also picks up grit and shells from the ground. A very sociable species, this bird breeds in large colonies numbering hundreds, even thousands, of nests.

Upupa epops

Eurasian Hoopoe

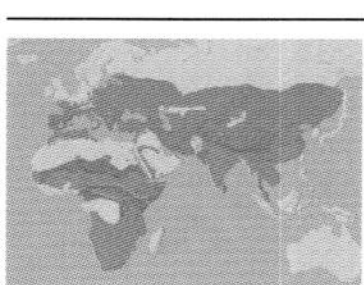

LENGTH 26–32cm (10–12½in)

WEIGHT 50–90g (1¾–3¼oz)

MIGRATION Migrant

HABITAT Open country and parkland; even treeless steppes, provided there are walls in which to nest

When it takes flight, the Eurasian Hoopoe reveals its the splendid black and white bars on its wings. Its bill is slim and slightly curved and it has a handsome black-tipped crest that is briefly raised into a fan-shape when it lands, but is otherwise kept closed. Its plumage is pink-beige in colour, its rump is white, and its black tail has a broad white band. The juvenile is duller and has off-white wing-bars.

The Eurasian Hoopoe spends most of its time on the ground, foraging in short grass and open lawns. It uses its long bill to probe for invertebrates and small vertebrates, such as insects, worms, small reptiles, rodents, and sometimes even carrion. It nests in a hole in a tree or wall (see panel), and sometimes lines the nest with plants, feathers, and wool. The Eurasian Hoopoe's call is a low, soft, far-carrying "oop, oop, oop", which is often repeated. It calls from a rooftop or tree, with its crest raised, but is usually very quiet.

A familiar bird in its range because of its association with human habitation, the Eurasian Hoopoe is found in pairs or in groups. The species is widespread in Europe, Asia, and Africa. Some populations are resident, but birds in the northern range migrate south to the tropics during winter.

ADULT EURASIAN HOOPOE

NESTING

The Eurasian Hoopoe can produce up to three broods in a year. Nests are usually placed in tree-holes, but cavities in walls, buildings, or in rocks are also used. Up to seven eggs are laid and both parents bring food to the nest, although only the female incubates the eggs. Incubation takes about 15 days and the nesting period lasts for about four weeks.

ADULT GREEN WOOD HOOPOE

Phoeniculus purpureus

Green Wood Hoopoe

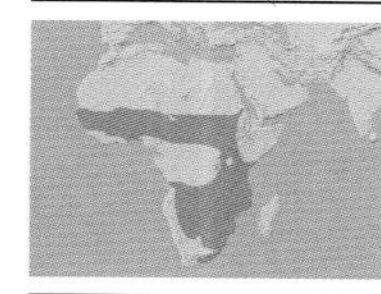

LENGTH 33–37cm (13–14½in)

WEIGHT 55–100g (2–3⅝oz)

MIGRATION Non-migrant

HABITAT Savanna, palm groves, open woodland, and gardens with large trees

The largest and most widespread of the eight species of Africa's wood hoopoes, the Green Wood Hoopoe has black plumage with a violet-green iridescence and white spots on the tail. It has a long red bill, which it uses to prise out insects and larvae from crevices in the bark of trees.

Tockus leucomelas

Southern Yellow-billed Hornbill

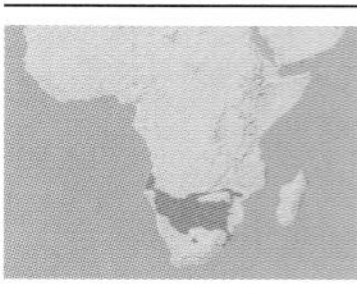

LENGTH 40cm (15½in)

WEIGHT 150–250g (5–9oz)

MIGRATION Non-migrant

HABITAT Open savanna woodland and semi-desert with trees

This relatively small, long-tailed hornbill is one of several African species with a yellow bill, though females differ from males in having a smaller bill with much-reduced casque on top. It has a black crown with black markings on the neck and breast. Its back and wings have white spots and stripes. It has a distinctive area of red skin around its eyes and on both sides of the lower mandible. Juvenile birds have mottled bills.

The Southern Yellow-billed Hornbill forages mainly on the ground, sometimes even digging into it. Its large bill is used to catch scorpions and some rodents, but it principally eats arthropods, fruits, seeds, and its diet even extends to predating birds eggs. It nests in natural cavities in trees. The female lays 3 or 4 eggs and incubates them for about 25 days. The Southern yellow-billed Hornbill is rather common and widespread in the savannas of southern Africa.

ADULT MALE

ADULT FEMALE

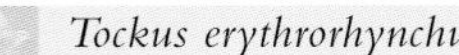

Tockus erythrorhynchus

Red-billed Hornbill

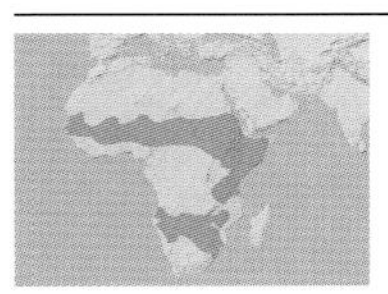

LENGTH 40–48cm ($15\frac{1}{2}$–19in)

WEIGHT 100–225g ($3\frac{5}{8}$–8oz)

MIGRATION Non-migrant

HABITAT Dry woodland and savanna, usually with little ground vegetation

One of the most common and widespread of Africa's savanna-dwelling hornbills, the Red-billed Hornbill has a striking plumage of grey, white, and black. The male has a black patch on the lower part of the bill. In some areas, in the dry season, the species may congregate in groups of up to several hundred birds. Such flocks may make local movements in search of food, which is mainly taken on the ground.

Tockus fasciatus

African Pied Hornbill

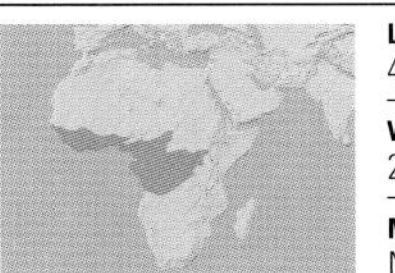

LENGTH 48–55cm (19–$21\frac{1}{2}$in)

WEIGHT 200–325g (7–12oz)

MIGRATION Non-migrant

HABITAT Forest, including secondary growth and even plantations and wooded farmland

The African Pied Hornbill is a glossy black bird with a white belly and white outer tail feathers. It has blue skin around the eye. Its bill is mostly yellow with a red or black tip, depending on the subspecies. The female is smaller and has a black bill tip. Insects and fruit form the bulk of this species' diet, but frogs, mice, lizards, and even bats are taken.

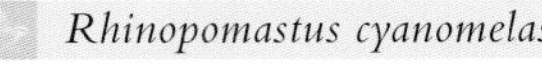

Rhinopomastus cyanomelas

Common Scimitarbill

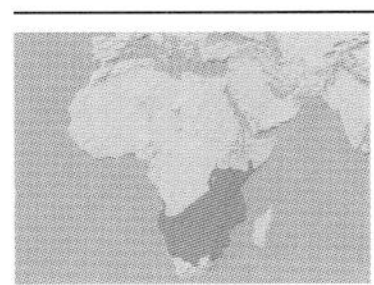

LENGTH 26–30cm (10–12in)

WEIGHT 25–40g ($\frac{7}{8}$–$1\frac{7}{16}$oz)

MIGRATION Non-migrant

HABITAT Wooded areas, including savanna; rarely found in dense forest

Mainly black in colour, with a blue and violet iridescence, the Common Scimitarbill is a long-tailed bird. It has a narrow, decurved bill, which is longer in the male. The female and juveniles have brown coloration on the head. One subspecies has white in the wings. The Common Scimitarbill is acrobatic, frequently hanging upside-down to find food, and it feeds on insects and other invertebrates. It nests in tree-cavities where 2–4 eggs are laid and the chicks hatch after an incubation period of about 16 days. Most of the food is brought by the male, while the female remains in the nest, tending the young.

ADULT COMMON SCIMITARBILL

Ocyceros birostris

Indian Grey Hornbill

LENGTH 50–61cm ($19\frac{1}{2}$–24in)

WEIGHT 375g (13oz)

MIGRATION Non-migrant

HABITAT Deciduous woods, parkland, and thorn forest, cultivated areas, and gardens

As its name suggests, this relatively small-billed hornbill has grey plumage set off by a dark decurved bill with a pale yellow tip, black eye-stripes, and a long tail. The female is typically smaller with a less obvious casque on the bill. The Indian Grey Hornbill mainly lives on small fruit, but it also takes insects in flight, lizards on the ground, and even preys on the nestlings of other birds. In the breeding season, a pair of Grey Hornbills may be assisted by an additional male to help bring food to the nest. The most widespread hornbill in the Indian subcontinent, it is quite common as it is able to adapt to human-modified areas.

ADULT BIRD

ADULT GREAT HORNBILL

Buceros bicornis

Great Hornbill

LENGTH 95–105cm (37–41in)

WEIGHT 1.2kg (2¼lb)

MIGRATION Non-migrant

HABITAT Tropical evergreen forest up to 2,000m (6,500ft)

The Great Hornbill is the largest member of the hornbill family and is named for its huge yellow bill, which has a double-pointed yellow casque. A black band encircles the base of the lower bill as well as the face, the lower underparts and tail are white, and the black wings have a white band across them. Both male and female look similar, although the female is smaller, and has a dull white iris; the male can be identified by its red iris. This bird's main food is fruit, although it also feeds on small mammals, birds, reptiles, and insects. The normal clutch size is two eggs, but as many as four have also been recorded. The incubation takes 38–40 days, with a total nesting cycle of up to 140 days.

Buceros rhinoceros

Rhinoceros Hornbill

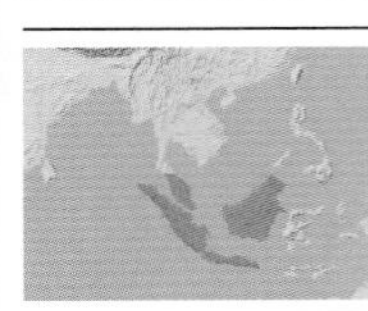

LENGTH 80–90cm (31–35in)

WEIGHT 2–3.5kg (4½–7¾lb)

MIGRATION Non-migrant

HABITAT Primary and taller secondary evergreen forest up to 1,400m (4,600ft)

The male Rhinoceros Hornbill is characterized by the large casque on its long bill, which is red at the base. It has a black head, breast, and back and a white abdomen. The female shares the same plumage, but the front of its casque is rounded and less decorative. This bird feeds on fruit, small animals, and birds' eggs. This species is fast declining in numbers.

MALE RHINOCEROS HORNBILL

CURVED CASQUE

The Rhinoceros Hornbill has one of the most ornate casques in the hornbill family. The male has a bright orange bony structure, resembling the horn of a rhinoceros, with an upcurved point at the front. It displays the casque to the female during courtship, although it is also used as a jousting weapon by competing males.

Aceros waldeni

Walden's Hornbill

LENGTH 60–65cm (23½–26in)

WEIGHT 1.2kg (2¼lb)

MIGRATION Non-migrant

HABITAT Evergreen forest with closed canopy

RED LIST CATEGORY Critically endangered

Like other hornbills, Walden's Hornbill has a distinctive casque on its bill. This bird is mainly black in colour, with a rufous head, neck, and upper breast. It is known to eat fruit such as figs. It often nests in an old woodpecker hole. Walden's Hornbill has a restricted range of just a few islands in the Philippines and was hardly recorded for 80 years following its discovery in the 1870s. It is under considerable pressure by hunters today.

Bycanistes bucinator

Trumpeter Hornbill

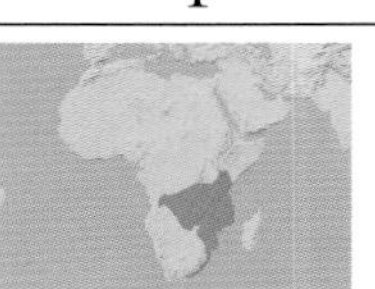

LENGTH 50–55cm (19½–21½in)

WEIGHT 450–675g (16–24oz)

MIGRATION Non-migrant

HABITAT Coastal and riverine forest into deciduous woodland up to 2,200m (7,200ft)

Found in southern Africa, the Trumpeter Hornbill is considered to be an intelligent bird. The red skin around its eyes and the black casque are the bird's noticeable features. Its plumage is mainly black, with white underparts and a white rump. The Trumpeter Hornbill is known to feed on as many as 14 different types of fruit, as well as insects and small animals taken from foliage or sometimes while in flight. It is highly gregarious and can be found in flocks of two to five individuals, sometimes even up to 50. The nest is protected by both the sexes, and the complete nest cycle takes 88–117 days. The female incubates the 4 or 5 eggs in the clutch. Although thinly spread over a wide range, the species can be locally common in some areas.

ADULT TRUMPETER HORNBILL

Bucorvus leadbeateri

Southern Ground Hornbill

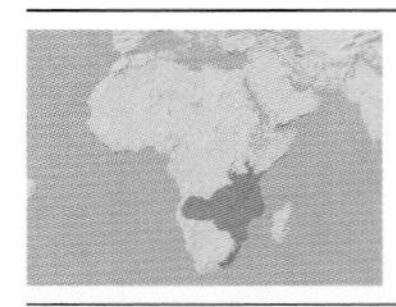

LENGTH 90–100cm (35–39in)

WEIGHT 2.2–6kg (4½–13lb)

MIGRATION Non-migrant

HABITAT Woodland and savanna up to an altitude of 3,000m (10,000ft)

Despite having a casque that is lighter in weight than other hornbills, the Southern Ground Hornbill is one of the largest and heaviest. Both sexes have red skin patches beneath the bill, but the female differs in its smaller skin patch with an area of blue. It usually nests in a cavity; two eggs are laid, but the younger chick usually starves within a week.

FEEDING ADULTS

WOODPECKERS AND TOUCANS

ORDER	Piciformes
FAMILIES	5
SPECIES	396

WOODPECKERS AND TOUCANS are highly distinctive forest and woodland birds. Woodpeckers are unrivalled at chiselling into tree trunks, while toucans are instantly recognizable by their gigantic, colourful bills. Together with jacamars, puffbirds, honeyguides, and barbets, they form a large order centred in the tropics. Only woodpeckers are widespread in temperate regions, while the order is absent from Madagascar, Australia, and New Zealand. Piciformes feed mainly on insects or on fruit, but honeyguides specialize in beeswax.

FLAP AND FOLD
Like all its relatives, the Black Woodpecker flies by flapping its wings in brief bursts, and then folding them by its sides.

ANATOMY

All piciformes have well-developed bills, and strong feet with two toes pointing forwards and two backwards. Woodpeckers and barbets use their toes to cling vertically to tree trunks and branches, while woodpeckers also have stiffened tail feathers, to help brace them as they feed. Barbets have short bills, but woodpecker bills are straight and sharp, with powerful neck muscles delivering the force needed to hammer into wood. Woodpecker skulls are extra thick to cushion the brain – vital for birds that peck thousands of times a day. Unusually among birds, many woodpeckers have long, prehensile tongues, with barbed or sticky tips. Using these, they can probe into ants' nests, or tunnels made by wood-boring insects. Puffbirds and jacamars use their sharp-tipped bills to catch flying insects, but a toucan's bill acts like gigantic forceps for collecting fruit. Aracaris and toucanets have similar bills, but smaller and less conspicuous.

BEHAVIOUR

Toucans and aracaris often feed and roost in small groups, while Acorn Woodpeckers live in extended families, each with their own shared territory. However, in general, piciform birds live alone or in pairs. Most feed in trees, and move clumsily on the ground, although there are exceptions. Ground Woodpeckers have evolved a terrestrial lifestyle, feeding mainly on termites and ants, using trees only as a refuge. When airborne, piciformes tend to fly in short bursts, flapping their wings for several seconds, then folding them by their sides – which produces a characteristic up-and-down flight. Apart from northern woodpeckers, few species migrate. Honeyguides are remarkable: having located a bees' nest, they attract ratels or humans to it, by fluttering and calling. Once the nest has been broken open, the honeyguide feeds on the wax.

BREEDING

Jacamars and puffbirds nest in burrows, but apart from these, most piciform birds nest in cavities in trees. Woodpeckers can hack their way into hard, living wood, but barbets usually choose wood that is dead, and soft, making excavating easier work. Toucans cannot use their bills in this way: instead, they nest in natural tree holes, or holes that woodpeckers have used and abandoned. All piciformes lay white, rounded eggs, and typically both parents share the task of incubation. However, honeyguides are brood parasites, laying their eggs in the nests of other birds. When a honeyguide hatches, it has a sharp hook at the end of its bill, which it uses to kill any other young birds in the nest. As a result, it gets all the food that its foster parents deliver.

JACAMAR BILLS
Jacamars have long, finely pointed bills, often held with an upward slant. They use them to catch large flying insects, including dragonflies and butterflies.

TOUCAN BILLS
Relative to their bodies, toucans have some of the bulkiest bills of all birds. An internal structure similar to honeycomb means that they are lighter than they look, so a toucan can lean forward without tipping over.

BARBET BILLS
Barbets have large, heavy, bristly bills. They eat insects and plants, and may peck into wood in search of a meal. They also use their bills to dig nest holes.

BRACE POSITION
Clinging to a tree, this Pileated Woodpecker demonstrates the sturdy "tripod" stance formed by its two feet and its strong, stiff tail.

SECOND-HAND HOME
An Emerald Toucanet looks out of its nest hole. Toucans and aracaris use existing holes, creating fierce competition when they are scarce.

Aulacorhynchus prasinus

Emerald Toucanet

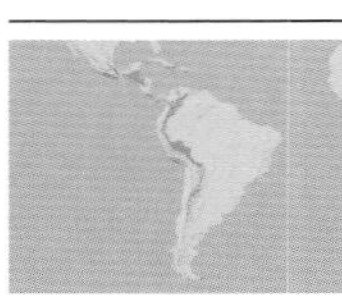

LENGTH 30–37cm (12–14½in)

WEIGHT 100–250g (3⅝–9oz)

MIGRATION Non-migrant

HABITAT Wet montane forest to altitudes over 3,000m (10,000ft)

As its common name suggests, the plumage colour of the Emerald Toucanet is predominantly green. Its lower face is bright blue and the upper mandible of the bill is yellow, with a purple base. The diet mainly consists of fruit, but some insects, small reptiles, and eggs of other bird species are also taken, with small flocks foraging in a trailed flight through trees. The nest is made in an unlined tree-cavity and both parents incubate the eggs.

Aulacorhynchus sulcatus

Groove-billed Toucanet

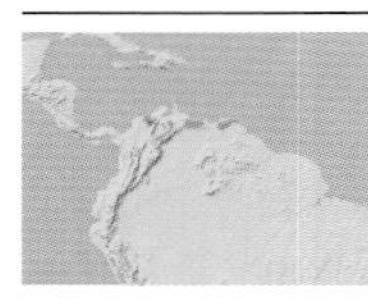

LENGTH 33–37cm (13–14½in)

WEIGHT 150–200g (5–7oz)

MIGRATION Non-migrant

HABITAT Tropical montane forest, typically 900–2,000m (3,000–6,500ft)

The three geographical subspecies of the Groove-billed Toucanet have different bill characteristics. The sexes are similar, but the female has a shorter bill and tends to be slightly smaller. Mainly a brilliant green in colour, this bird has a blue patch around the eyes and a white throat. Its diet is varied, although it takes more birds' eggs than the Emerald Toucanet (above). It is even known to form raiding parties for this type of feeding. The breeding behaviour is not well known.

MALE GROOVE-BILLED TOUCANET

Pteroglossus castanotis

Chestnut-eared Aracari

LENGTH 43–47cm (17–18½in)

WEIGHT 225–300g (8–11oz)

MIGRATION Non-migrant

HABITAT Wet forest around rivers and lakes, occasionally over 1,000m (3,300ft)

The Chestnut-eared Aracari is named for the rich brown facial coloration behind its eye. The bill is ornate, with bands of yellow on black in front of a blue face. The female has a shorter bill.

The diet of the Chestnut-eared Aracari is varied, consisting mainly of fruit, but also includes nestlings and eggs – this species is known to raid nests of other birds. It can be spectacularly acrobatic when feeding on fruit, even hanging upside-down. The range of the species includes much of central South America, particularly in the Amazonian region. This bird is not migratory, though there is some movement within the range during the winter.

ADULT CHESTNUT-EARED ARACARI

ADULT COLLARED ARACARI

Pteroglossus torquatus

Collared Aracari

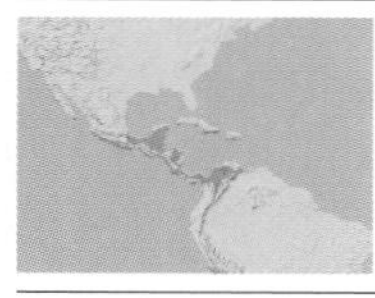

LENGTH 43–48cm (17–19in)

WEIGHT 150–300g (5–11oz)

MIGRATION Non-migrant

HABITAT Wet primary forest up to 1,000m (3,300ft), occasionally, 1,500m (4,900ft)

Similar to the Chestnut-eared Aracari (above), the Collared Aracari differs in that it has a paler upper mandible and a bright red rump. The head is dark and the facial pattern around the eye is orange, with variations in geographical subspecies. The female is darker and has a shorter bill, with its size range relating to differences in the subspecies. The diet is varied and includes fruit, birds' eggs, small reptiles, and insects. It systematically rips open any nest that is encountered, irrespective of whether the nest is occupied or not.

Pteroglossus frantzii

Fiery-billed Aracari

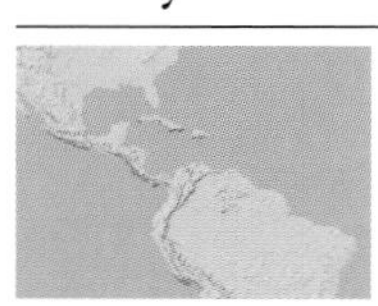

LENGTH 45cm (17½in)

WEIGHT 225–275g (8–10oz)

MIGRATION Non-migrant

HABITAT Wet lowland forest and secondary forest, mostly below 1,200m (4,000ft)

The red upper mandible differentiates the Fiery-billed Aracari from the similar Collared Aracari (left). There is some range overlap, although the Fiery-billed Aracari is confined to Costa Rica and Panama. The limited range means the birds require constant monitoring as a contraction in their range has been recorded. Its diet is varied, and it raids the nests of other species.

ADULT FIERY-BILLED ARACARI

Selenidera maculirostris

Spot-billed Toucanet

LENGTH 33–37cm (13–14½in)

WEIGHT 150–200g (5–7oz)

MIGRATION Non-migrant

HABITAT Subtropical moist forest and palm groves

MALE SPOT-BILLED TOUCANET

The Spot-billed Toucanet is named for the black markings on its yellow-tipped bill. The sexes are markedly different – the male has a black head divided by a yellow stripe at the back of the head, stretching from the pale green face. The female is smaller, with an orange head and front.

Andigena laminirostris

Plate-billed Mountain-toucan

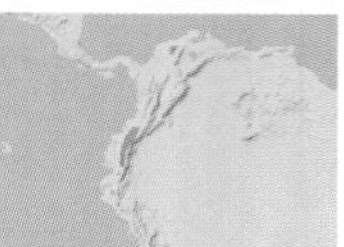

LENGTH 46–51cm (18–20in)

WEIGHT 275–350g (10–13oz)

MIGRATION Non-migrant

HABITAT Moist montane forest, mainly at 1,300–2,500m (4,300–8,200ft)

A colourful species, the Plate-billed Mountain-toucan has a blue neck, the front extending to a pale blue and yellow face and a black hood. The bill is predominantly black, but the basal area is chestnut, with a yellow patch on the upper mandible. It has brown wings, a yellow rump, and a green tail tipped in orange. The female has similar plumage, but is generally smaller and has a shorter bill.

Nearly all the dietary requirements of the adults are met by fruit, although a greater proportion of animal prey from insects, small reptiles, and birds' eggs is provided for the young. The range of the species is limited to small areas of Colombia and Ecuador, with the breeding season varying in the two countries. Pairs sometimes rear two broods in a season, but may not breed annually. Both sexes feed the young.

ADULT PLATE-BILLED MOUNTAIN-TOUCAN

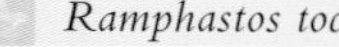

Ramphastos toco

Toco Toucan

LENGTH 55–61cm (21½–24in)

WEIGHT 500–850g (18–30oz)

MIGRATION Non-migrant

HABITAT Riverine and forest edges, orchards, and rarely, in urban areas up to 1,750m (5,750ft)

One of the largest species of toucan, the Toco Toucan has an enormous yellow bill tipped with a black patch, which looks heavy but is actually hollow. The face is pale orange and the lower face and throat are white. The rest of the plumage is black, with a white uppertail and orange vent. The female is similar to the male. The food of the species is varied, from fruit and insects to birds' eggs taken in the canopy or on the ground in small foraging groups.

ADULT TOCO TOUCAN

ADULT GREEN-BILLED TOUCAN

Ramphastos dicolorus

Green-billed Toucan

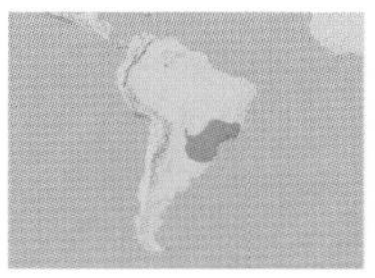

LENGTH 42–48cm (16½–19in)

WEIGHT 250–400g (9–14oz)

MIGRATION Non-migrant

HABITAT Tropical and subtropical montane forests mainly between 1,000–1,500m (3,300–4,900ft)

Named after its pale green bill, the Green-billed Toucan has a bright red front, a yellow to orange upper breast and throat, and red vent. The face is orange and its back, wings, and tail are black. The female is similar, but has a shorter bill. The differences in size between the sexes is a reflection of the size variation in the species across the geographical range. The main food is fruit, but insects and small birds are also taken – captive birds have been recorded feeding on birds that invade their cages. Foraging is largely in pairs or small groups, although larger groups, numbering over 20 birds, have been recorded. The breeding season varies across the range, from October to February in the south and January to June in the north. Pairs have been known to raise up to three broods in a season and the species is highly territorial. The young are fed on insects at first, but this gives way to fruit, although little is known about the behaviour following fledging. Individuals have been known to live over 16 years in captivity, but it is not known how long birds live in the wild.

Ramphastos sulfuratus

Keel-billed Toucan

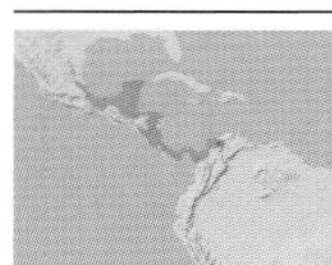

LENGTH 46–51cm (18–20in)

WEIGHT 275–550g (10–20oz)

MIGRATION Non-migrant

HABITAT Wet lowland forest, usually below 800m (2,600ft), but up to 1,600m (5,200ft) in some areas

A dramatically coloured species even within a spectacular family, the Keel-billed Toucan's main feature is a bright green bill tipped in red, but with a bright orange patch on the upper mandible. The face is green, with a bright yellow throat and breast. The underparts, back, and tail are black and the rump is white. The diet is varied, but mostly consists of fruit, including introduced varieties. The female is smaller and chooses a nest site that the male cannot easily enter.

ADULT KEEL-BILLED TOUCAN

TOCO TOUCAN
The Toco Toucan uses its spectacular orange bill to reach for food, mainly fruit, on the ends of branches that are too thin to support its weight.

Capito niger

Black-spotted Barbet

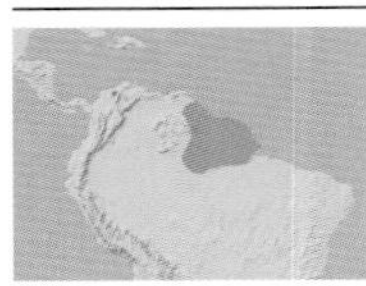

LENGTH
16–19cm (6½–7½in)

WEIGHT
40–70g (1 7/16–2½oz)

MIGRATION
Non-migrant

HABITAT Forest and tall secondary growth, including gardens and plantations

The Black-spotted Barbet has a red forehead and throat. The female is more heavily spotted than the male, which lacks noticeable streaking or spotting on the breast and has much darker cheeks and wings, with a pale bar on the wings. Like all South American barbets, the Black-spotted Barbet inhabits treetops where it moves sluggishly, flicking its tail and head periodically. It nests in a hole, excavated high in a tree, and feeds on a variety of fruit, especially figs, as well as nectar and various insects.

FEMALE BLACK-SPOTTED BARBET

Psilopogon pyrolophus

Fire-tufted Barbet

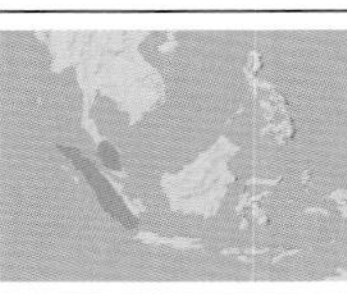

LENGTH
29cm (11½in)

WEIGHT
100–150g (3 5/8–5oz)

MIGRATION
Non-migrant

HABITAT Upland forest, principally on the edges, in dense vines and creepers

Well named for its striking head, bill pattern, and red tuft of feathers at the base of its pale yellow, black-barred bill, the Fire-tufted Barbet is uncommon and localized within its small range in southeast Asia. The bird feeds on figs and other fruit as well as on insects, sometimes hanging down precariously to reach for food. Very little is known about its breeding habits.

ADULT FIRE-TUFTED BARBET

red throat

MALE RED-THROATED BARBET

Megalaima mystacophanos

Red-throated Barbet

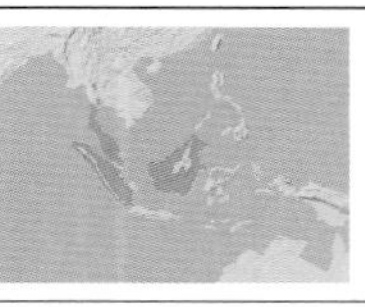

LENGTH
23cm (9in)

WEIGHT
60–95g (2 1/8–3 3/8oz)

MIGRATION
Non-migrant

HABITAT Forest and tall secondary growth, large gardens, and rubber and cacao plantations

Predominantly green in colour, the Red-throated Barbet has a long, heavy bill and a red crown. The male has a red throat, while the female usually has a blue face, with the red restricted to the crown. This species probably breeds year-round, but little is known about its breeding habits in the wild. Like many lowland forest birds of its native range, it is at risk from deforestation.

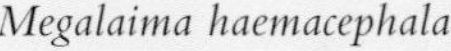
Megalaima haemacephala

Coppersmith Barbet

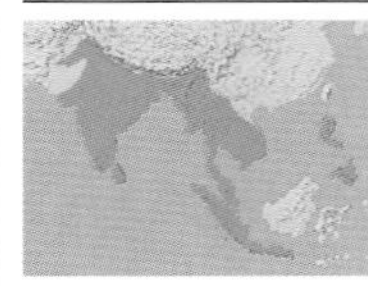

LENGTH
15–17cm (6–6½in)

WEIGHT
30–55g (1 1/16–2oz)

MIGRATION
Non-migrant

HABITAT Forest, usually on edges, and drier country; also scrub, plantations, gardens, and mangroves

The most widespread of the Asian barbets, the Coppersmith Barbet is small and much less dependent on forest habitats than its relatives. Considerable variations in plumage have led scientists to recognize as many as nine different subspecies. Some of these show a red head marked with black lines, while others show a yellow head marked with black and a contrasting red forehead. All have green upperparts and are pale with dark streaks below.

ADULT (NORTHERN PHILIPPINES SUBSPECIES)

The Coppersmith Barbet sings persistently, even on moonlit nights. The song is a series of low "tok" or "tonk" notes, although the tempo may vary. During courtship, it puffs out its throat feathers, bobs and turns its head, and flicks its tail. The nesting season is long, and many pairs probably have two broods. Three eggs are normally laid and both sexes incubate them, with the young hatching in about two weeks. Thereafter, both adults take an active part in nesting duties, feeding the young and removing their faecal sacs.

The Coppersmith Barbet mainly feeds on a diverse range of fruit, from figs to mangoes. However, it also takes insects, which it catches in flight, and their larvae. Large groups of these birds may congregate at abundant food sources, such as areas rich in fruit-bearing trees.

Pogoniulus chrysoconus

Yellow-fronted Tinkerbird

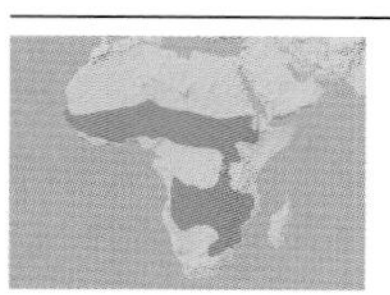

LENGTH 12cm (4½in)

WEIGHT 8–20g (5/16–11/16oz)

MIGRATION Non-migrant

HABITAT Dry woodland and scrub, riverine and montane forest, and wooded savanna

The Yellow-fronted Tinkerbird is distinguished from its close relatives by the yellow forehead patch found in both sexes. The plumage is heavily streaked and spotted black and white. It aggressively defends its feeding areas, driving off other small barbets, although occasionally joining mixed-species flocks. The species feeds mainly on fruit and insects. It nests above head level in a stump or dead branch; the young fledge usually in just over four weeks.

ADULT YELLOW-FRONTED TINKERBIRD

yellow underparts

black-bordered red throat

ADULT (RED-HEADED FORM)

Lybius torquatus

Black-collared Barbet

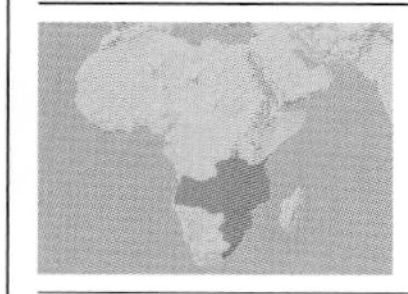

LENGTH 18cm (7in)

WEIGHT 35–50g (1¼–1¾oz)

MIGRATION Non-migrant

HABITAT Most wooded habitats, but avoids dense forest, including farmland and gardens

The Black-collared Barbet has several subspecies and two different forms – the typical red-headed form (shown above) and the yellow-headed variety with a whiter belly. In complete contrast, one subspecies has a dark, pale-spotted head, often with a white back. The Black-collared Barbet gleans and probes for insects on the bark and leaves of trees, and occasionally flycatches from a perch. It is a prolific breeder, with some pairs producing up to four broods in a single nesting season. Its habitat, however, is shrinking.

Lybius dubius

Bearded Barbet

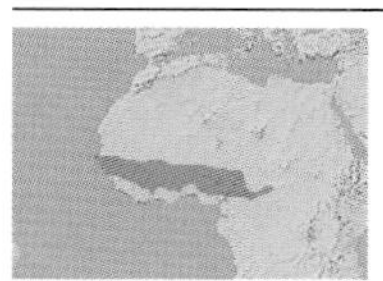

LENGTH 26cm (10in)

WEIGHT 80–100g (2⅞–3⅝oz)

MIGRATION Non-migrant

HABITAT Wooded areas, from sea level to high ground, and garden

Like most African barbets, the Bearded Barbet has pronounced teeth-like grooves in its large yellow bill. Its plumage is principally red and black in colour and the male and the female are similar in overall appearance. The Bearded Barbet lives in groups and is generally common. However, its breeding behaviour and diet are surprisingly little known.

ADULT BEARDED BARBET

Trachyphonus erythrocephalus

Red-and-yellow Barbet

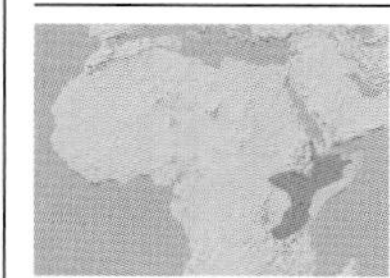

LENGTH 20–23cm (8–9in)

WEIGHT 40–75g (1 7/16–2⅝oz)

MIGRATION Non-migrant

HABITAT Open woodland and wooded savanna, even desert-like terrain, but with trees

One of the most distinctive barbets, the Red-and-yellow Barbet has a striking head pattern and bold white spots on its upperparts and tail. It is also known for its ability to live in close proximity to humans, taking advantage of the feeding opportunities presented by household waste. Its natural diet, however, includes fruit, seeds, insects, lizards, and even small birds and their eggs. The bird mainly forages on the ground, moving in groups that methodically search and probe natural and manmade crevices for food. The Red-and-yellow Barbet is dominant over other species of barbet within its range.

NESTS IN TERMITE MOUNDS

The Red-and-yellow Barbet builds its nest in an earth bank or termite mound, with the nest chamber reached by a short tunnel slightly less than 1m (3½ft) long. In each group, the primary male mates with one female and also incubates the eggs. The rest of the group act as "helpers", bringing food and, perhaps, excavating the chamber.

ADULT RED-AND-YELLOW BARBET

Indicator indicator

Greater Honeyguide

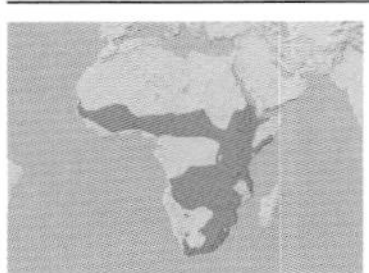

LENGTH 20cm (8in)

WEIGHT 50g (1¾oz)

MIGRATION Non-migrant

HABITAT Open woodland, wooded edges, bushland, plantations, gardens, and riparian woodland

As indicated by its name, the Greater Honeyguide can lead humans to bee nests with its piping call. Once it has broken open the nest and eaten its fill, the honeyguide moves in to feed on beeswax, honeybee grubs, and eggs. However, such behaviour is erratic and in some places, does not occur at all – some adult birds never "guide" this way.

The male is dark grey-brown, with white underparts and streaked wings, a black throat, and a yellow shoulder patch, while the female is duller and lacks the black throat.

MALE GREATER HONEYGUIDE

Picumnus minutissimus

Guianan Piculet

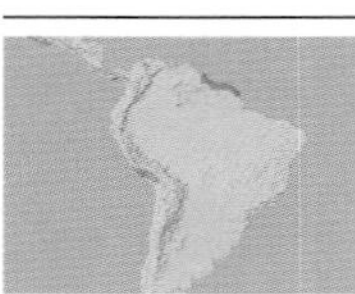

LENGTH 10cm (4in)

WEIGHT 13.5g (7/16oz)

MIGRATION Non-migrant

HABITAT Wide variety of habitats, including secondary forest, plantations, mangroves, riparian vegetation

This is the world's smallest woodpecker. It inhabits coastal lowlands from Guyana east to French Guiana. Its has lightly barred olive-brown upperparts, scaly underparts, and a finely barred throat. The male has a red crown patch. It forages like a tit, hanging from small branches, searching for ants and small beetles.

Jynx torquilla

Eurasian Wryneck

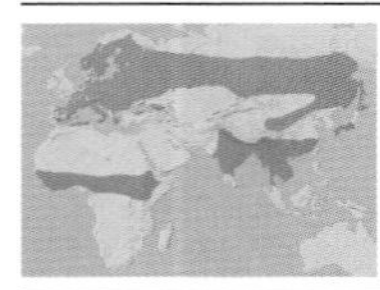

LENGTH 16cm (6½in)

WEIGHT 35g (1¼oz)

MIGRATION Migrant

HABITAT Open forest, clearings, woodland, wooded pasture; migrants in open, treeless habitats

A small, long-tailed woodpecker with a dull plumage marked by bars, mottling, and dark stripes, the Eurasian Wryneck can be identified by the prominent dark stripe around its eye. It gets its common name from its ability to turn its head by almost 180 degrees. When disturbed at the nest, pairs of Eurasian Wrynecks use this snake-like head movement as a threat display along with hissing sounds.

Unlike most woodpeckers, the Eurasian Wryneck does not climb using its tail as a support, but perches perpendicular to horizontal branches.

With its short, narrow, pointed bill, the Eurasian Wryneck chisels soil or decaying wood rather than digs for prey. Its food is mainly ants, especially larvae and pupae, and it will forage on the ground, often opening up anthills with its bill. Other prey ranges from aphids and beetles to occasional molluscs and tadpoles.

Although not globally threatened, the species has declined rapidly in central and western Europe. This may be due to climate changes such as wetter summers.

ADULT EURASIAN WRYNECK

Picumnus temminckii

Ochre-collared Piculet

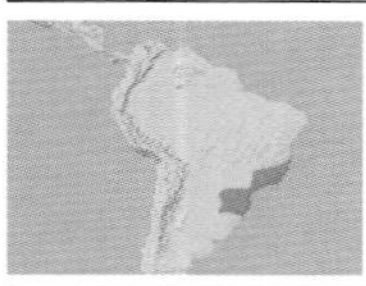

LENGTH 10cm (4in)

WEIGHT 12g (7/16oz)

MIGRATION Non-migrant

HABITAT Humid forest, especially forest edges, scrub, and bamboo

A tiny woodpecker of the Atlantic forests of southeast South America, the Ochre-collared Piculet is relatively poorly known. Aptly named for its ochre neck collar, which differentiates it from the similar White-barred Piculet (*P. cirratus*), it has a black crown that is spotted white at the back. In the male, the forecrown is red. Both sexes have olive-brown upperparts, white underparts barred in black, and a black tail with white outer feathers. Foraging in the lower levels on thin branches and stalks, the species feeds on ants and insect larvae. The sound of light tapping, as it seeks to excavate a small hole in a branch, is often the first clue to this diminutive woodpecker's presence.

MALE OCHRE-COLLARED PICULET

Sasia abnormis

Rufous Piculet

LENGTH 9cm (3½in)

WEIGHT 9g (11/32oz)

MIGRATION Non-migrant

HABITAT Secondary forest with decaying trees, swamp forest, bamboo stands, and low vegetation

A woodpecker with colourful plumage, the Rufous Piculet has an olive-green rear crown and a rufous-orange head. The upperparts are olive-green and the underparts are rufous-orange. The male is distinguishable by its yellow forehead.

The reason why the Latin name of this species suggests that the Rufous Piculet is abnormal is because it has only three toes (most other woodpeckers have four). The purpose of this adaptation is unclear, but what is certain is that it does not hinder its rapid movement on trees.

As with other piculets, this species can be detected by its incessant tapping as it excavates small holes in trees. It inserts its long tongue in the holes to extract ants, larvae, spiders, and small beetles.

ADULT RED-HEADED WOODPECKER

Melanerpes erythrocephalus

Red-headed Woodpecker

LENGTH 24cm (9½in)

WEIGHT 80g (2⅞oz)

MIGRATION Partial migrant

HABITAT Lowland forest with dead trees, open areas and understorey; wooded savanna and swamps

As its name suggests, the Red-headed Woodpecker has an entirely red head and throat. The back, forewings, and tail are black, contrasting with the white rear wings, underparts, and rump. This species is one of the most omnivorous woodpeckers, taking a very wide range of prey. It flycatches for insects, snatches worms and lizards from the ground, and also feeds on nuts, fruit, and seeds. Unlike many other woodpeckers, it does not bore holes in trees for food.

Melanerpes formicivorus

Acorn Woodpecker

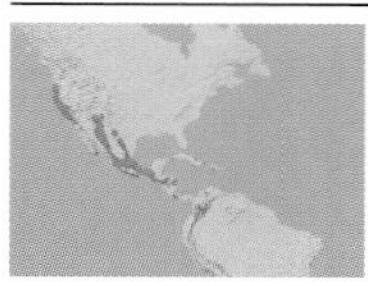

LENGTH 23cm (9in)

WEIGHT 80g (2⅞oz)

MIGRATION Partial migrant

HABITAT Oak and pine woodland, Douglas fir and redwood stands; in open areas on migration

Some woodpeckers are so dependent on a particular food source that they store a sufficient amount to see them through the winter. The Acorn Woodpecker provides an excellent example of this practice (see panel, below).

This noisy and gregarious woodpecker has a striking appearance. The white iris contrasts with a broad black eye-stripe, pale yellow forehead and throat, and a red crown. The rest of the plumage is dark blue, black, and white. As its common name suggests, acorns are the primary food source for this woodpecker. However, this species will also eat pine-seeds, insects, and, occasionally, eggs and lizards. It also drinks sap and nectar.

ADULT ACORN WOODPECKER

STORING FOOD

Acorns form half the winter diet of northern populations of the Acorn Woodpecker. This species sets up "granaries" of acorns to help it through the winter months. Over the years, birds drill up to 50,000 holes in an old tree. They insert acorns into these and retrieve them when hungry. A granary is excavated, used, and defended by a group of birds, often family members.

Melanerpes flavifrons

Yellow-fronted Woodpecker

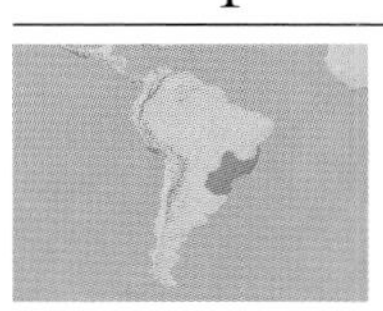

LENGTH 17cm (6½in)

WEIGHT 55–65g (2–2⅜oz)

MIGRATION Non-migrant

HABITAT Humid forest, secondary forest, forest edge and orchards

This small, brightly coloured woodpecker is a noisy denizen of the Atlantic forests of eastern South America. The Yellow-fronted Woodpecker has a yellow forehead, eye-ring, and throat, contrasting with a blue-black eye mask and upperparts. The breast is olive, the flanks barred black, and the belly is red. The male's crown is red and the female's is blue-black: a classic difference for sexually dimorphic woodpeckers. Like other members of its genus, the Yellow-fronted Woodpecker sometimes stores its food (fruit, berries, seeds, and insects).

MALE YELLOW-FRONTED WOODPECKER

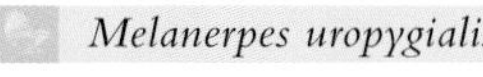

Melanerpes uropygialis

Gila Woodpecker

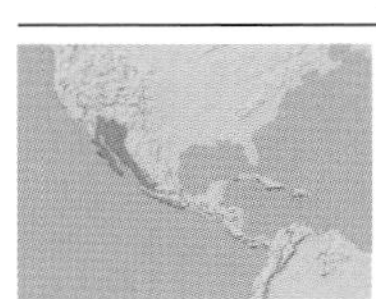

LENGTH 23cm (9in)

WEIGHT 60–70g (2⅛–2½oz)

MIGRATION Non-migrant

HABITAT Arid habitats with scattered trees or cacti, including desert, subtropical forest, and urban areas

The Gila Woodpecker is distinctive in appearance and behaviour. It has a tan head, throat, breast, and belly. The back, wings, rump, and vent are barred black and white, and the male has a neat red cap. Unlike other woodpeckers, the Gila Woodpecker thrives in deserts, with almost no trees. This species usually nests in mesquite or saguaro cacti. It is omnivorous and eats food items ranging from ants to eggs and nestlings, from cactus fruit to household scraps. Accordingly, it forages at all levels – from ground to "canopy" and uses various techniques. Individuals call noisily to one another, with their abrasive, high-pitched calls, advertising their territory.

ADULT ON CACTUS

MALE YELLOW-BELLIED SAPSUCKER

Sphyrapicus varius

Yellow-bellied Sapsucker

LENGTH 19–21cm (7½–8½in)

WEIGHT 50g (1¾oz)

MIGRATION Migrant

HABITAT Breeds in deciduous and mixed coniferous forests; winters in forests and more open areas

As its name suggests, the Yellow-bellied Sapsucker has pale yellow underparts. The patterns on its head, in red, black, and white, are also distinctive. The species can be conspicuous during the early spring, when males drum territorially, occasionally on manmade objects, such as metal street signs and lamp-posts.

This is one of four similar species that nest only in North America, but is the most migratory of them, breeding in a belt stretching west from Newfoundland to Alaska and south to below the Great Lakes and spending its winters in southern USA, Central America, and the Caribbean. This species feeds on tree sap, extracting it by making two types of holes in trees: deep, round ones that extend into the tree; or shallower, rectangular holes that need to be tended so that the sap flows.

Campethera cailliautii

Green-backed Woodpecker

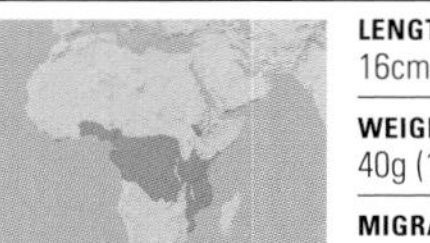

LENGTH 16cm (6½in)

WEIGHT 40g (1 7/16oz)

MIGRATION Non-migrant

HABITAT Wide range of habitats, from savanna to forest

This woodpecker belongs to the same genus as the Nubian Woodpecker (above right). Although the ranges of the two species overlap, there is little scope for confusion as the Green-backed Woodpecker is much smaller and lacks the noticeable cheek stripe of its larger relative, giving it a more plain-faced appearance. The Green-backed Woodpecker also tends to feed high in the canopy, mainly on ants and termites. The species is largely resident, although some short-distance movements have been recorded.

FEMALE NUBIAN WOODPECKER

Campethera nubica

Nubian Woodpecker

LENGTH 23cm (9in)

WEIGHT 60g (2⅛oz)

MIGRATION Non-migrant

HABITAT Dry bushland, grassland, woodland, and savanna

One of nine similar African woodpeckers, which have red caps, olive-green upperparts, and white-speckled underparts, the Nubian Woodpecker is one of the larger members of its genus. It feeds mostly on ants and termites on tree trunks. The most familiar call of the Nubian Woodpecker is a loud, metallic "weee-weee-weee-kweek", used by pairs to communicate with each other.

Sphyrapicus ruber

Red-breasted Sapsucker

LENGTH 20–22cm (8–8½in)

WEIGHT 60g (2⅛oz)

MIGRATION Partial migrant

HABITAT Mixed coniferous and deciduous forests, particularly aspen and ponderosa pine

The least migratory of the four sapsucker species, the Red-breasted Sapsucker is found in a thin coastal belt from Alaska to northern California and western Nevada. The male and female of this medium-sized sapsucker are similar, both with a striking scarlet "helmet" that extends downwards to the neck and chest and a line of white spots that stretches from the mantle to the rump. The upperparts are black, barred with white. The southern form can be easily identified by its white moustache stripe.

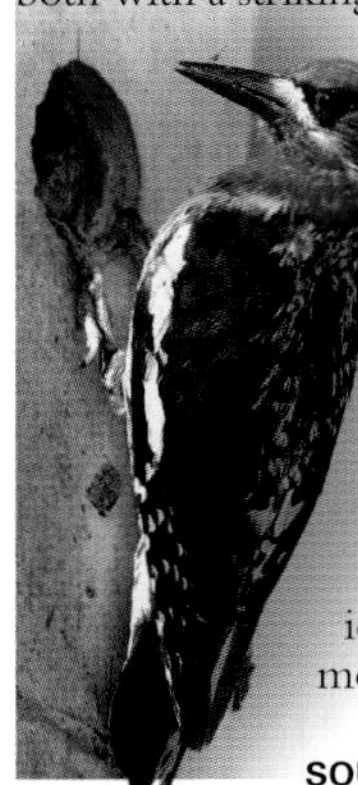

SOUTHERN FORM

Geocolaptes olivaceus

Ground Woodpecker

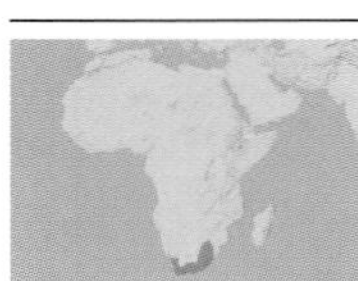

LENGTH 22–30cm (8½–12in)

WEIGHT 125g (4oz)

MIGRATION Non-migrant

HABITAT Open rocky upland areas, usually at about 1,200–2,000m (4,000–6,500ft)

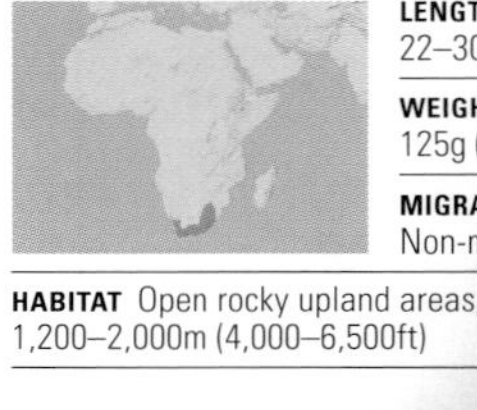

ADULT GROUND WOODPECKER

Restricted to upland areas of South Africa, the Ground Woodpecker feeds largely on ants. It is usually seen in pairs or small groups of up to six birds. It mainly feeds on the ground, usually moving by hopping, appearing to know the exact location of ant nests within its large territory. When it flies, its red rump is clearly visible.

GREAT SITE

WAKKERSTROOM

Once a sleepy rural backwater, the Wakkerstroom area has become one of South Africa's top bird-watching destinations. One of the best places to observe the Ground Woodpecker, it has many other rare species, such as Rudd's and Botha's Larks, the Yellow-breasted Pipit, and a range of bustards and cranes.

Dendropicos fuscescens

Cardinal Woodpecker

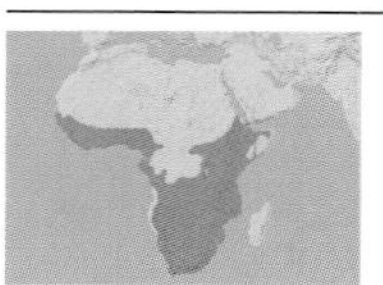

LENGTH 14–16cm (5½–6½in)

WEIGHT 25g (⅞oz)

MIGRATION Non-migrant

HABITAT Woodland and bushland

Found in much of the continent of Africa, south of the Sahara, this bird is Africa's most widespread species of woodpecker. This species has a brown-green back with white barring and pale underparts that are densely streaked with white and brown flecks. The male has a red cap and the female a dark one. The Cardinal Woodpecker often hangs upside-down when foraging for insects and moths in tree crevices. It sometimes calls to contact its mate or family group. Both sexes often drum softly.

MALE CARDINAL WOODPECKER

WHITE-BARRED BACK

Dendrocopos kizuki

Japanese Pygmy Woodpecker

LENGTH 13–15cm (5–6in)

WEIGHT 19g ($^{11}/_{16}$oz)

MIGRATION Non-migrant

HABITAT Deciduous and coniferous woodland and forest

Also known as the Japanese Spotted Woodpecker, this species occurs throughout Japan and is the most common woodpecker found in Japan. It is also found in smaller numbers in China and Siberia. A small black and white woodpecker, its most distinctive feature is its dusky face, enlivened by a striking small, white highlight just behind the eye.

Dendrocopos major

Great Spotted Woodpecker

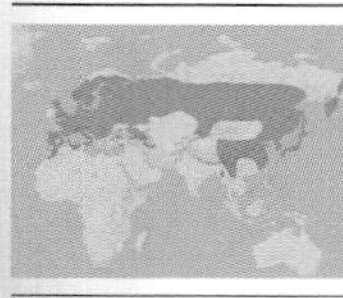

LENGTH 20–24cm (8–9½in)

WEIGHT 70–80g (2½–2⅞oz)

MIGRATION Partial migrant

HABITAT All types of woodland and forest, parks, and gardens

The Great Spotted Woodpecker is found across Europe (though not in Ireland) and parts of Asia to Siberia and Japan. Throughout much of its range, it is the most abundant woodpecker. Its most distinctive features are the broad white bar down the back and striking scarlet vent and undertail. The male has a small red patch on the back of the head (the nape) that is absent in the female. Juveniles display an entirely red crown.

The species can easily be detected by a regular metallic "chik" call during its short, undulating bursts of flight. This woodpecker also drums vociferously, particularly in early spring. Indeed it is the fastest drummer among the European woodpeckers, with up to 15 strikes per second. Drumming usually takes place on dead branches and trunks. Although it is largely a resident species, shortages of food often cause northern populations to migrate periodically.

MALE GREAT SPOTTED WOODPECKER

Picoides villosus

Hairy Woodpecker

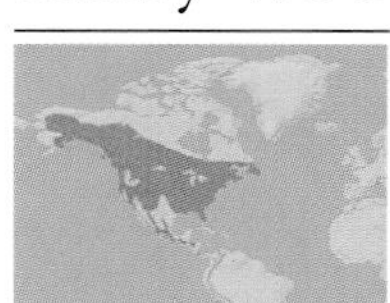

LENGTH 16–26cm (6½–10in)

WEIGHT 50–80g (1¾–2⅞oz)

MIGRATION Non-migrant

HABITAT Wide range of forest types, occasionally parks and gardens

This woodpecker is named for its white nasal tufts, although these are difficult to see in the field. However, they are not unique to the species – for instance, the similar Downy Woodpecker (*P. pubescens*) also has these tufts. The Hairy and Downy Woodpeckers are typical pied woodpeckers, but can be told apart from other similar species by their white backs. Distinguishing the two is more difficult – the Hairy Woodpecker is much larger, with a stronger bill and completely white outer tail feathers. Like other black and white woodpeckers, the male displays a small red patch on the back of the head, which is absent in the female and juveniles. Its call is a high-pitched "keek", sometimes rolled into a series of notes. Both sexes drum on trees.

ADULT MALE

Picoides tridactylus

Eurasian Three-toed Woodpecker

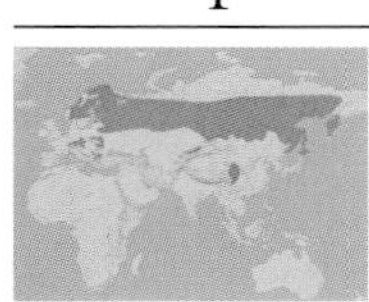

LENGTH 20–24cm (8–9½in)

WEIGHT 60–70g (2⅛–2½oz)

MIGRATION Partial migrant

HABITAT Mature northern coniferous forest

An unmistakable black and white woodpecker, this bird has only three toes – hence its name. The male has a distinct yellow crown and both sexes are boldly striped. As well as feeding on insects and larvae, the Three-toed Woodpecker also punctures the bark of trees to get at underlying sap, often leaving a pattern of holes on coniferous tree trunks. Males and females frequently drum during the late winter and early spring.

Shy and elusive, this generally northern species is found in coniferous boreal forests in Scandinavia and across northern Russia and Siberia to Japan. It is also found in mountainous areas in central and eastern Europe.

The Three-toed Woodpecker also occurs in North America but the American birds are generally smaller, with males displaying less yellow on the head. American birds also apparently feed less on sap (preferring beetle larvae) – probably due to the competition from sapsuckers.

Many populations of the species are sedentary, though some (particularly northern ones) do perform long-distance migrations when conditions dictate.

ADULT MALE

Piculus aurulentus

Yellow-browed Woodpecker

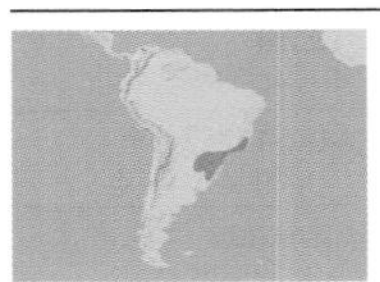

LENGTH 22cm (8½in)

WEIGHT 75g (2⅝oz)

MIGRATION Non-migrant

HABITAT Humid montane forest

The Yellow-browed Woodpecker is one of seven closely related South and Central American species belonging to the genus *Piculus*. All are small in size and yellowish green above, barred beneath, and with red head markings that vary in size and number. The Yellow-browed Woodpecker can be distinguished from the others by the two yellow head stripes that give the species a masked appearance. It also has a rufous patch on the wing. The male has a bright red forehead and cap that extends to the back of the head. In the female, this red patch is restricted to the back of the head, the front being the same yellowish green as the upperparts.

The species feeds either singly or in pairs, mainly on ants and their larvae. The Yellow-browed Woodpecker is an uncommon, secretive bird that is difficult to observe in its forest habitat.

ADULT MALE

Piculus rubiginosus

Golden-olive Woodpecker

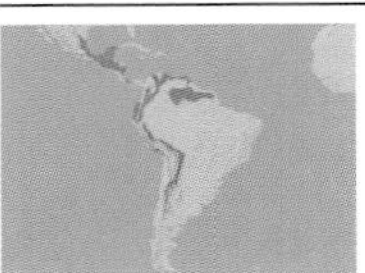

LENGTH 18–23cm (7–9in)

WEIGHT 55g (2oz)

MIGRATION Non-migrant

HABITAT Wide range of habitats from humid rainforest to dry deciduous forest

Predominantly olive-green above and barred yellow and black beneath, the Golden-olive Woodpecker has a dark forehead, red nape, and striking white face patch. An adaptable species, it is often found in trees that border coffee plantations and agricultural fields. The Golden-olive Woodpecker has a patchy distribution that ranges from Mexico to Argentina.

ADULT FEMALE

Colaptes auratus

Northern Flicker

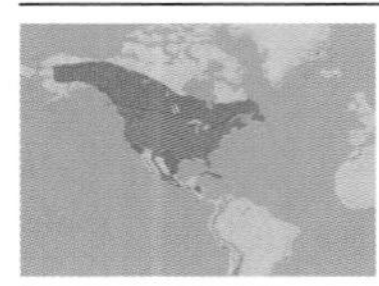

LENGTH 30–35cm (12–14in)

WEIGHT 125–150g (4–5oz)

MIGRATION Partial migrant

HABITAT Mainly forest edges and other open areas

This large woodpecker has a long, pointed bill, a brown back, wings with dark bars, spotted grey underparts, and a white rump patch. There are two forms of this species, varying mainly in size and head patterns – the Northern Red-shafted Flicker (*C.a.cafer*) and the Northern Yellow-shafted Flicker (*C.a.auratus*), so named for the colour of the feather shafts in the wings. Birds from the southern part of its range are mainly resident, but those from further north migrate south for the winter.

Colaptes campestris

Campo Flicker

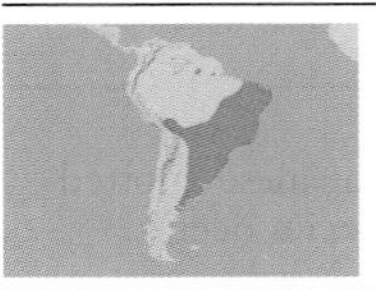

LENGTH 28–31cm (11–12in)

WEIGHT 150g (5oz)

MIGRATION Non-migrant

HABITAT Grassland and farmland

Both male and female Campo Flickers are striking, with distinctive barred plumage that contrasts with their black heads and yellow faces. The Campo Flicker feeds mainly on ants and termites. It is often seen surveying its grassland habitat from a suitable lookout on a tree or fence post. It forages predominantly on the ground, walking while searching for food and hopping longer distances in a rather comical manner. A sociable species, it is often seen in small groups of up to eight birds. As a bird of open areas, this is one of the few species that has benefited from forest clearance in South America.

ADULT MALE

Celeus elegans

Chestnut Woodpecker

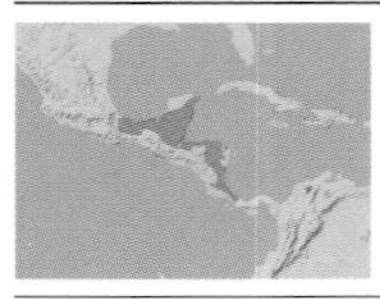

LENGTH 26–32cm (10–12½in)

WEIGHT 150g (5oz)

MIGRATION Non-migrant

HABITAT Wide variety of forests

As its name suggests, the Chestnut Woodpecker has a beautiful chestnut-coloured plumage with a noticeable brownish yellow crown and crest that contrasts with the rest of the plumage and the bright red cheek patch of the male. It has a striking blue eye-ring, formed by a patch of bare skin as well as a pale ivory-coloured bill.

Although the species lives mainly on ants and termites, it also regularly feeds on fruit. When fruit crops are abundant, these woodpeckers will often ignore their usual invertebrate food, switching to a completely vegetarian diet. Despite its large size, the species is very dextrous, easily clinging to thin branches as it strips fruit right down to the stone.

ADULT MALE

Dryocopus lineatus

Lineated Woodpecker

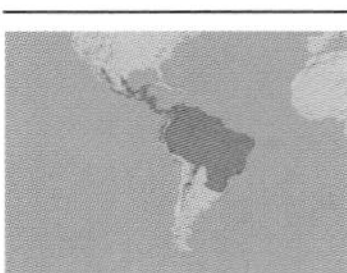

LENGTH 30–36cm (12–14in)

WEIGHT 175–200g (6–7oz)

MIGRATION Non-migrant

HABITAT Generally humid open areas such as forest edges

The Lineated Woodpecker is a medium-to-large member of its family, found throughout much of Central and South America. The male is black above except for a bright red crest, crown, and forehead, and a grey patch behind the eye. It also has two separate white stripes: one on the shoulder, and another that curves round from the base of the bill to the neck. Its underparts are off-white in colour, with horizontal black barring. The female is smaller, with a black stripe below the bill and a black forehead.

MALE LINEATED WOODPECKER

Dryocopus martius

Black Woodpecker

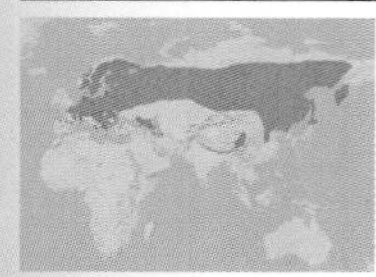

LENGTH 45–55cm (17½–22½in)

WEIGHT 325 (12oz)

MIGRATION Partial migrant

HABITAT Mature forest

As its name suggests, the Black Woodpecker is mainly black in colour, with the exception of variable bright red markings on the head: the male has a complete red cap, but the female has just a few markings on the back of the head. The largest woodpecker in Europe, this species has a slender neck and a dark-tipped pale bill that is shaped like a dagger. The Black Woodpecker can be detected by its loud calls or its drumming, which is usually loud and lasts for a long time.

The Black Woodpecker feeds mainly on ants, although other insects are also consumed. It is said to be expert at locating ant colonies within its territory – apparently it can even detect nests beneath deep snow. The bird feeds mainly low down on the trunks of trees, or often on dead branches lying on the ground.

CHISELLING OUT PREY
Probing deep into tree trunks with its strong bill, the Black Woodpecker (the female is shown here) digs out insects.

ADULT ON THE WING
The Black Woodpecker's flight is straight, not dipping like other woodpeckers, and it can be confused with a small crow while flying.

It peels off large fragments of bark with its powerful bill, searching underneath for its favoured food, and uses its tail as a prop when it perches upright. This woodpecker plays an important role in forest ecology as it creates holes in trees that are used for nesting by many other species. Its own nest is in a large oval hole.

The Black Woodpecker is found across most of Europe (except Britain and Ireland) across Russia and Siberia to northern parts of Japan. Most Black Woodpeckers are resident, although northern populations are partially migratory (particularly juveniles). Birds also move during autumn and winter, with distances of up to 1,000km (620 miles) being recorded.

Picus flavinucha

Greater Yellownape

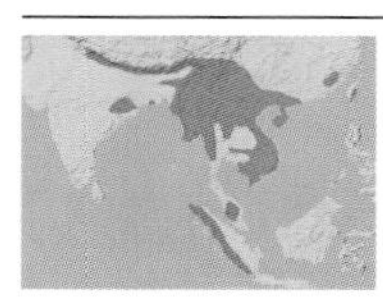

LENGTH 34cm (13½in)

WEIGHT 150–200g (5–7oz)

MIGRATION Non-migrant

HABITAT Various forest types

An attractive species of woodpecker that occurs in southeast Asia, the Greater Yellownape has an olive-green forehead and crown and a yellow nape that contrasts with its green upperparts and grey underparts. At rest, its green plumage blends into foliage. The tail of the Greater Yellownape is black and the wings are barred in red. The males of some subspecies of this woodpecker have a yellow "moustache" that extends onto the throat, while in the females, this feature is rufous in colour.

ADULT FEMALE

Picus awokera

Japanese Woodpecker

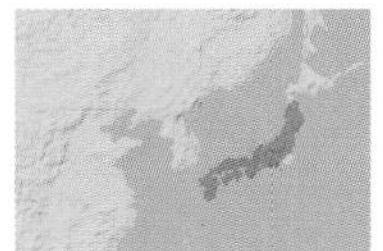

LENGTH 30cm (12in)

WEIGHT 150g (5oz)

MIGRATION Non-migrant

HABITAT Variety of reasonably open forests

The Japanese Woodpecker is only found in Japan and occurs on all the main islands, except Hokkaido, where it is replaced by the similar Grey-headed Woodpecker (*P. canus*). The Japanese Woodpecker differs primarily by the dense black barring that covers its belly. The red cap on male birds also extends right down to the back of the neck whereas on the Grey-headed Woodpecker, this is confined to between the bill and the forehead.

Confusingly, the female Japanese Woodpecker actually has a grey forehead, with a small amount of red on the back of its head and neck. However, both male and female Japanese Woodpeckers have a red "moustache" – a feature that is black in the Grey-headed Woodpeckers. The Japanese Woodpecker also feeds much less frequently on the ground than its close relative and is usually seen clinging to the side of a tree trunk.

Picus viridis

European Green Woodpecker

LENGTH 31–33cm (12–13in)

WEIGHT 175g (6oz)

MIGRATION Non-migrant

HABITAT Semi-open areas such as woodland edges, heaths, and parks

Pale in colour, the European Green Woodpecker has a barrel-shaped body. The male can be distinguished from the female by its red "moustache", which is black in the female, while juveniles are barred and streaked. In many parts of Britain, it is known as the "yaffle", an imitation of its distinctive high-pitched, ringing laugh.

Like other members of its family, it has a tongue that is specially adapted to help it feed. More than double the length of its bill, the tip is covered with a sticky fluid to help trap ants, its favourite prey. It generally feeds on the ground, hopping short distances before undertaking its distinct undulating flight. Levaillant's Woodpecker (*P. vaillantii*), which occurs in North Africa, is considered by some authorities to be a subspecies of the European Green Woodpecker. It is greyer beneath, with a black and white facial pattern.

FEMALE FEEDING ITS YOUNG

FEMALE LESSER GOLDENBACK

Dinopium benghalense

Lesser Goldenback

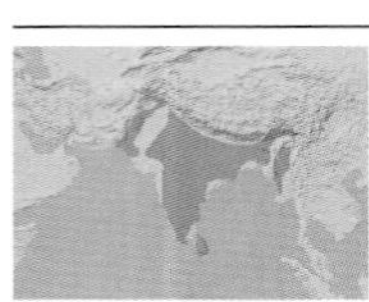

LENGTH 26–29cm (10–11½in)

WEIGHT 85–125g (3–4oz)

MIGRATION Non-migrant

HABITAT All types of woodland, including more open areas with trees; avoids arid zones and dense forest

Unlike several races of this woodpecker that have golden-yellow upperparts, the Lesser Goldenback has a deep crimson-red back. Males in all races have a red crown, while females have a black forecrown. The species chiefly feeds on ants, which it takes from the bark and leaves of trees, but also eats spiders, caterpillars, fruit, and nectar. Both adults take turns to excavate the nest hole, which is often located low down in a tree. Two or three eggs are laid and are incubated by both parents. Although virtually restricted to the Indian subcontinent, the Lesser Goldenback is one of the commonest woodpeckers within its range.

Reinwardtipicus validus

Orange-backed Woodpecker

LENGTH 30cm (12in)

WEIGHT 150–175g (5–6oz)

MIGRATION Non-migrant

HABITAT Primarily lowland rainforest; also found in coastal vegetation and mature plantations

The somewhat uncommon Orange-backed Woodpecker is one of the most attractive Asian members of its family. The crest and underparts in the male are mostly red and it has a white back, with orange-red tipped feathers. It also has very dark wings, with red markings, and a dark tail. The female is similar, but is much browner on the head and underparts. Both sexes have a large and mostly yellow bill.

Mulleripicus pulverulentus

Great Slaty Woodpecker

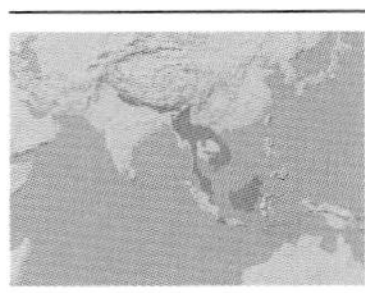

LENGTH 50cm (19½in)

WEIGHT 350–550g (13–20oz)

MIGRATION Non-migrant

HABITAT Tall, semi-open woodland in lowlands and foothills; also swamp-forests and mangroves

Named for its plumage, which is almost entirely slate-grey, the Great Slaty Woodpecker is the largest of the woodpeckers. It has a large, sharp bill, pale buff chin and throat, a very long neck, and a long tail. The male is distinguished by its red cheek-spot. Despite its size, this woodpecker feeds mainly on insects, supplemented with small fruit, and it forages in parties of four to six.

ADULT MALE

Chrysocolaptes lucidus

Greater Goldenback

LENGTH 28–34cm (11–13½in)

WEIGHT 100–225g (3⅝–8oz)

MIGRATION Non-migrant

HABITAT Most types of woodland, including forest and mangroves near rivers

A large golden, red, black, and white woodpecker, the Greater Goldenback has a black band from its eyes to its throat, a black-scalloped golden back, and white underparts. It also has a red patch on the rump and lower back, although this is often hard to see, being partially concealed by the wings. The male has a raised red crest (shown here), while the female has a much darker crown.

There are several similar species of the woodpecker in Asia. However, these birds are not always close relatives. Despite its name, the Greater Goldenback is perhaps only marginally larger than some other species of Goldenback, and in any case there is considerable size (and plumage) variation within the species across its range. Some subspecies have a yellow crown.

The Greater Goldenback generally lives in pairs or family parties, but it frequently associates with other woodpeckers. It forages largely on big trees, but often descends to the ground, taking large caterpillars, wood-boring larvae, and other insects as prey, but also nectar from flowers. It lays two eggs in a nest that is excavated by both adults, the work of preparing the nest hole sometimes taking up to four weeks, and the eggs are incubated for a month.

ADULT RUFOUS-TAILED JACAMAR

Galbula ruficauda

Rufous-tailed Jacamar

LENGTH 19–25cm (7½–10in)

WEIGHT 18–30g (⅝–1$^{1}/_{16}$oz)

MIGRATION Non-migrant

HABITAT Wooded areas, even a few trees along a creek, but rarely in deep forest

One of the widest-ranging of its family, the Rufous-tailed Jacamar has a long bill, a rufous belly, but otherwise glittering metallic green and red plumage and a red undertail. It tends to sit quietly in a shady spot for most of the day, usually in pairs or family groups, betraying its presence only by an occasional darting flight in pursuit of an insect.

Galbula cyanescens

Bluish-fronted Jacamar

LENGTH 20–23cm (8–9in)

WEIGHT 20–25g ($^{11}/_{16}$–$^{7}/_{8}$oz)

MIGRATION Non-migrant

HABITAT Beside streams or other bodies of water; edges of primary forest or in secondary growth

Among the prominent features of the Bluish-fronted Jacamar is its metallic blue forecrown and bib. The upperparts are green, while the underparts, including the undertail, are rufous. The female is similar, but has ochre underparts. In plumage, this species is similar to several other jacamars, including the Rufous-tailed Jacamar (opposite), but the species have ranges that do not overlap.

Like other jacamars, this species generally feeds on insects caught in flight, although it often perches much higher up than the Rufous-tailed Jacamar, which can often be found close to the ground. Its nesting habits are unknown – in fact, the Bluish-fronted Jacamar is a poorly known bird because it is confined to an inaccessible area in western Amazonia.

MALE BLUISH-FRONTED JACAMAR

Jacamerops aureus

Great Jacamar

LENGTH 25–30cm (10–12in)

WEIGHT 55–75g (2–$2^{5}/_{8}$oz)

MIGRATION Non-migrant

HABITAT Primary forest, more occasionally in tall secondary growth, but rarely at borders and edges

The largest and most impressive of the jacamars, the Great Jacamar has a more massive, slightly shorter, and marginally more curved bill than the other jacamars. Its throat is white, its upperparts are predominantly an iridescent green, and its underparts are red. Usually solitary or found in pairs, it is sluggish in its behaviour, perching in one place for long periods of time. It is capable of taking prey up to the size of small lizards.

Notharchus macrorhynchos

White-necked Puffbird

LENGTH 25cm (10in)

WEIGHT 80–100g ($2^{7}/_{8}$–$3^{5}/_{8}$oz)

MIGRATION Non-migrant

HABITAT Many types of woodland and edge habitats, high treetops

Almost entirely black and white with a relatively massive bill, the White-necked Puffbird has a white neck that is separated from its white underparts by a deep black breast-band. The White-necked Puffbird takes a variety of prey from insects to small vertebrates. It nests in tree cavity or a termite nest, or, more occasionally, a hole in the ground.

Nystalus chacuru

White-eared Puffbird

LENGTH 22cm ($8^{1}/_{2}$in)

WEIGHT 50–65g ($1^{3}/_{4}$–$2^{3}/_{8}$oz)

MIGRATION Non-migrant

HABITAT Open country and forest edges, including agricultural areas, but prefers native vegetation

Found in the interior of South America, this charismatic bird has a red bill with a dark tip and hook as well as the distinctive white "ears". In Brazil, its habit of waiting quietly on an open perch for a lizard or other similar prey has lead to it being named "João-bobo" (literally "sitting duck"). Surprisingly, for such a common bird, its nesting habits are poorly known, but the nest is made in a hole in a bank or ground, and up to four eggs are laid.

ADULT WHITE-EARED PUFFBIRD

Nonnula rubecula

Rusty-breasted Nunlet

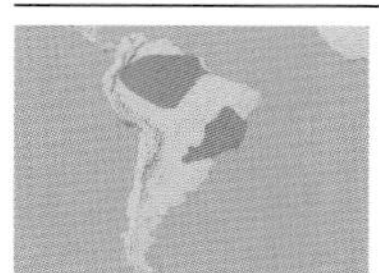

LENGTH 14–16cm ($5^{1}/_{2}$–$6^{1}/_{2}$in)

WEIGHT 17–20g ($^{5}/_{8}$–$^{11}/_{16}$oz)

MIGRATION Non-migrant

HABITAT Midstorey of humid rainforest; occasionally in more open woodland and secondary growth

ADULT RUSTY-BREASTED NUNLET

Of the six species of nunlet (small puffbirds with generally brown and grey plumage), the Rusty-breasted Nunlet is the most widespread and is one of only two species to occur (in its case partially) outside of Amazonia. The Rusty-breasted Nunlet is a generally unobtrusive bird due to its small size, dull plumage, and its habit of hunting quietly. It feeds on beetles, small crabs, and other arthropods, and sometimes follows flocks of other birds. Its nest is a burrow constructed in a tree cavity or a hole in a bank.

Monasa nigrifrons

Black-fronted Nunbird

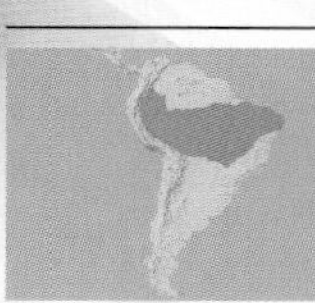

LENGTH 26–29cm (10–$11^{1}/_{2}$in)

WEIGHT 70–100g ($2^{1}/_{2}$–$3^{5}/_{8}$)

MIGRATION Non-migrant

HABITAT Forest usually along rivers and woodland that is seasonally flooded

Four species of nunbird (generally black puffbirds with red or yellow bills) are known from Amazonia and its fringes. The Black-fronted Nunbird is one of the two most widespread and common species, and is the only one to have entirely black feathering. Amongst the noisiest of the forest's avian inhabitants, the Black-fronted Nunbird spends most of its time sitting on a prominent perch, looking for arthropods, small lizards, and insects.

ADULT BLACK-FRONTED NUNBIRD

Chelidoptera tenebrosa

Swallow-winged Puffbird

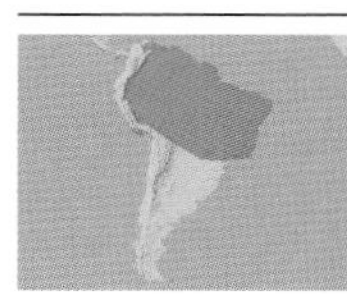

LENGTH 15cm (6in)

WEIGHT 30–40g ($1^{1}/_{16}$–$1^{7}/_{16}$oz)

MIGRATION Non-migrant

HABITAT All types of open wooded areas, with a preference for those on sandy soil

ADULT SWALLOW-WINGED PUFFBIRD

Several subspecies of the Swallow-winged Puffbird have been described and these principally differ in the pattern of the underparts: some have a narrow white band separating the dark throat and red belly; the colour of the plumage also varies in intensity, some subspecies being much paler than others. The Swallow-winged Puffbird is often the most abundant and easy to see of the puffbirds in its wide South American range, due to the fact that this bird habitually perches in the open atop a dead tree or even a telephone wire. It bears a superficial resemblance to a swallow with a short tail.

The Swallow-winged Puffbird catches flying insects, by making short aerial sorties, usually either on a level with, or higher than, its perch. It nests in short tunnels, dug in a bank or in flat ground, and lays at most two eggs, incubated in two weeks. However, like many other puffbirds, little more is known about this bird's nesting behaviour.

PASSERINES

ORDER	Passeriformes
FAMILY	92
SPECIES	over 5,200

OVER HALF THE WORLD'S BIRDS belong to this enormous order, commonly known as the perching birds. All share one of nature's most successful innovations – slender and highly specialized four-toed feet. Compared to other birds, perching birds tend to be small, but are often highly active. Species of this varied order are found in almost every terrestrial habitat, from forests to tundra, but none live at sea.

ANATOMY

The passerine order takes its name from the Latin word for the House Sparrow (*Passer domesticus*) – a typical example of a perching bird. Like sparrows, most passerines tend to be small; some of the lightest weigh less than 5g (1/5oz). However, this order also includes some large and heavily built birds, such as oropendolas and crows. Whatever their size, all passerines have four-toed feet with three toes pointing forwards, and one backwards, all four meeting at the same level. Their toes are never webbed. When a perching bird settles on a branch or twig, its toes automatically lock into position, stopping it falling off even when it is asleep. Passerines usually have between nine and ten flight feathers in their wings, and 12 feathers in their tails. However, one of their most significant features is their voicebox, or syrinx. In the majority of passerines, known as oscines or songbirds, the syrinx is highly developed, with complex membranes and muscles. This allows songbirds to create a huge variety of sounds. The remaining passerines, often known as suboscines, have a less elaborate syrinx, but even so, many of them also have intricate songs and calls.

BALANCING ACT
Grasping tightly with its toes, this American Yellow Warbler perches on a twig. Passerine toes are very flexible, allowing these birds to hold onto the slenderest of perches, such as grass stems or telephone wires.

PLUMAGE AND COLORATION

Passerines include many species that are small and drab, but also some of the most vividly coloured birds in the world. This is particularly true in the tropics, but even in the temperate world, birds such as cardinals and goldfinches never fail to catch the eye. In many passerines, males and females look identical, but in a number, males and females look so different that they could be mistaken for different species. These differences reach an extreme in birds-of-paradise: the females are relatively dowdy, while the males look almost overloaded by their flamboyant plumage. Plumage differences usually reflect the different roles played by male and female birds. The male's plumage has evolved to attract a mate, while the female's dull coloration camouflages her while she is on the nest. In many species, plumage differences are a year-round feature, but in some the male adopts an "eclipse" plumage much more like the female's after his post-breeding moult.

FEMALE SUPERB FAIRYWREN

MALE SPLENDID FAIRYWREN

DRESSED TO IMPRESS
During the breeding season, male and female fairywrens show a striking difference in plumage. After breeding, the iridescent blue males (such as the Splendid Fairywren, left) develops an "eclipse" plumage, becoming almost identical to the female.

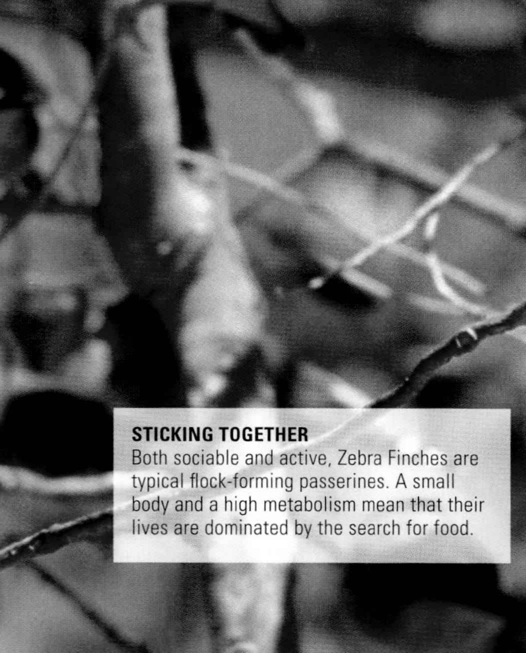

STICKING TOGETHER
Both sociable and active, Zebra Finches are typical flock-forming passerines. A small body and a high metabolism mean that their lives are dominated by the search for food.

WINGS AND FLIGHT

The small size of most passerines affects the way they fly. Most have short, broad wings, which allow them to take off in a fraction of a second – something that is often vital for their survival. This wing shape also gives them good manoeuvrability as they swerve through vegetation, and rapid braking when they come in to land on a perch. Although many passerines migrate, they are more often seen flying in short bursts, and very few of them have the gliding or soaring flight seen in large birds. The main exceptions to this rule are aerial insect-eaters, such as swallows and martins, and large birds such as ravens, which often stay in the air for several hours at a time. Up until the relatively recent past, there was in existence a flightless passerine – the Stephens Island Wren of New Zealand. However, this unique bird was wiped out in 1895 by feral cats.

RAPID TAKEOFF
Seen from below, this Northern Wheatear clearly shows the short, broad wing shape and powerful pectoral muscles, shared by many passerines, which enables them to take off very quickly.

BILLS AND FEEDING

Most passerines eat compact, energy-rich food – the kind that can be collected quickly and swallowed whole, before predators have a chance to move in. Seeds and insects both meet these requirements, and passerine birds eat them in huge quantities. Seed-eating passerines generally have blunt bills, often with a conical shape. Many of these birds roll seeds between their bill's margins, cracking off the husk before they swallow the kernel. In warm parts of the world, several families of passerines – including sunbirds and honeyeaters – feed on nectar, another high-energy plant-based food. Sunbirds have specialized bills that give them a striking resemblance to hummingbirds, which are unrelated but share a similar way of life.

Insect-eating passerines can be found over most of the globe, although in temperate regions, many of them migrate. Most of them have short, slender bills – the ideal tool for prising insects out of crevices. The order also includes birds that eat earthworms and other invertebrates, as well as some that hunt larger prey. Shrikes use their hooked bills to catch small mammals and reptiles, while crows and ravens scavenge anything they can swallow – often including the eggs and young of other passerine birds.

EURASIAN NUTHATCH

RED CROSSBILL

MARICO SUNBIRD

BILL SHAPES
As with other orders, bill shape in passerines is tailored to diet. Nuthatches have small, straight bills, which they use for pecking open seeds and prising insects from bark. The crossbill's bill is a highly specialized implement, used for extracting seeds from the cones of pines, spruces, and other coniferous trees. The long, decurved bill of a sunbird is ideally suited to extracting nectar from flowers.

NESTING COLONIES

The nests of passerines are usually well hidden, and also well spaced from their neighbours. However, some species, such as martins, oropendolas, and weavers, nest in colonies. Most of them make independent nests, but Social Weavers take colonial life even further, and work together to build a giant shared nest with many compartments.

OROPENDOLA COLONY
Montezuma Oropendolas build some of the largest nests of all passerines. Woven from grass and leaves, they can be 1m (3¼ft) long.

NESTING AND PARENTING

Passerines typically nest in trees or bushes, and they often make complex nests to protect their nestlings from the weather and from predators. The "standard" passerine nest is cup-shaped, with a warm lining made from feathers, moss, or mud, but many passerines build covered or suspended nests, which give their young even greater protection. Cliff swallows make flask-shaped nests out of mud, while weavers show extraordinary dexterity in tying and manipulating grass. Tailorbirds, from southeast Asia, turn large leaves into nest-shaped funnels by sewing their edges together, using their bills as needles.

Passerine nestlings hatch while they are still poorly developed. Naked and blind, they unable to use their legs or wings, and also unable to control their body temperature. However, they grow up at an extraordinary speed, fuelled by a constant supply of food. In some small insect-eaters, such as tits and chickadees, the parents make up to 2,000 food deliveries a day. With this prodigious food supply, some young passerines are ready to fly just 10 days after they hatch.

SUSPENDED NEST
The Eurasian Reed Warbler builds a cup-shaped nest, expertly slung between three or four reed stems.

ATTENTIVE PARENT
Like all passerines, this Eurasian Reed Warbler will feed its young until they have fledged. Young reed warblers clamber out of their nest before they can fly, making it harder for predators to spot them.

SONG AND SINGING

All passerines have their own calls, but sophisticated songs are a characteristic of oscines (songbirds), which make up by far the largest number of species in the passerine order. Not all songbirds are melodious: crows and jays, for example, are well known for their harsh and grating croaks. However, some species – such as the Eurasian Skylark – are legendary not only for the beauty of their singing, but also for their sheer vocal power. Songbirds also include some astoundingly gifted mimics, such as mynas, lyrebirds, and the Marsh Warbler. Songs are often produced by males only, and are used for attracting mates and deterring rivals. The great advantage of this form of communication is that the singer can remain hidden. The Common Nightingale is a good example of this. One of the most renowned European songbirds, it has an extremely loud, fluid song, but is almost impossible to spot inside the thickets where it sings.

Most songbirds hatch with the innate ability to produce a basic song. As a young bird grows up, it refines its performance by listening to adult birds, and often acquires a regional "accent" in the process. As a result, songs are highly species-specific, and even where two species are physically very similar, their songs are often a valuable aid in telling them apart.

SMALL SIZE, LOUD VOICE
Small songbirds are able to produce extraordinarily loud songs for their size. In most species, only the male sings, but this female Pied Flycatcher is responding to the male's call.

COURTSHIP FEEDING
Having successfully attracted a partner, a male Blue Tit gives the female a gift of food. This behaviour, known as courtship feeding, not only cements the pair bond, but also serves a practical role in helping the female to build up enough reserves to produce a clutch of up to a dozen eggs. Blue Tits raise just one family each breeding season, but some small passerines can raise as many as three successive broods.

COURTSHIP

For many passerines, song is the trigger that brings male and female together. Males typically sing from within a territory, which contains all the resources needed to raise a family. Drawn by the male's song, the female inspects the territory, as well as its occupant. If she is satisfied with both, courtship soon gets underway. The division of duties between partners varies enormously in the passerine world. With Blue Tits, the female builds the nest and incubates the eggs, and the male throws all his energy into collecting food for the young. With weavers, the male usually builds the nest entirely on his own – this, rather than a territory, is the main attraction for the female. But with some species, including birds-of-paradise, lyrebirds, and many cotingas, males use their flamboyant plumage to attract partners, but play no part in nest-building or in rearing the young.

ROOSTING QUELEAS
Packed tightly together in a clump of bamboo, Red-billed Queleas, a flock-forming African species, settle down to pass the night. With their slender toes locked in position, they can sleep quite comfortably on perches that are almost upright.

SOCIAL GROUPS

Once most young passerines have left their nest, the bond between them and their parents is soon broken, and the young take up life on their own. With cooperative breeders – such as the White-winged Chough – family life is different; the young stay with the family group, and help to incubate and feed the next generation of young. But for the majority of passerines, social life centres around flocks – groups of birds that often feed and roost together. Some passerines form permanent flocks, but in most, flocking occurs outside the breeding season, when parents are no longer tied to their nests. The largest feeding flocks are formed by seed-eating birds. In North America, Red-winged Blackbirds gather in huge flocks. Common Starlings are also well known for their flocking behaviour, particularly in winter when they gather in enormous numbers to roost. Flocking helps small passerines to avoid being singled out by predators, and it also improves their chances of finding scattered food.

READY FOR DEPARTURE
Every year, many passerines migrate enormous distances to breed. Here, dozens of Barn Swallows prepare to set off on their journey to warmer latitudes.

HUMAN IMPACT

THREATS AND CONSERVATION

About 10 per cent of the world's passerines are currently listed by the IUCN as endangered or vulnerable. The decline in the numbers of songbirds is largely the result of loss of habitat, often caused by deforestation, the spread of towns and cities, or the intensification of farming.

DISAPPEARING SKYLARK
Once common, the Eurasian Skylark has declined rapidly in recent years. Because it nests on the ground, it is at risk from farm machinery. Intensive farming also makes it harder for these birds to find enough food.

CLASSIFYING PASSERINES

Anatomical and genetic evidence clearly show that passerine birds form a single natural group, having evolved from the same original ancestor at some point in the distant past. Most ornithologists agree that passerines fall into two clear-cut groups. One group contains the "primitive" passerines, also known as suboscines, while the other contains the oscines or songbirds. Of these two groups, the songbirds are by far the largest, comprising about 4,000 species. However, at the family level, the classification of songbirds is in a state of flux, as DNA studies continue to throw new light on the way different species are related. The list of families and their classification on this page reflects much of this new research, and is used throughout the section on passerine bird species that follows.

SUBOSCINE
The Eastern Kingbird is a typical suboscine. It belongs to the Tyrant Flycatcher family, a group found from Canada to Patagonia.

OSCINE
Like most oscines, the Rufous-tailed Rock Thrush has a flowing musical song. It is found across Europe and northern parts of Asia.

SUBOSCINES

Also called "primitive" passerines, suboscines make up the suborder Tyranni. Their songs are innate, or "hard-wired" at hatching. The majority live in Central or South America. The New Zealand Wrens show many features not found in other suboscines, and sometimes are put in a suborder of their own.

Group	Family	Species
NEW ZEALAND WRENS	Acanthisittidae	3
BROADBILLS	Eurylaimidae	14
ASITIES	Philepittidae	4
PITTAS	Pittidae	30
MANAKINS	Pipridae	48
COTINGAS	Cotingidae	96
TYRANT FLYCATCHERS	Tyrannidae	430
ANTBIRDS	Thamnophilidae	205
GNATEATERS	Conopophagagidae	8
TAPACULOS	Rhinocryptidae	55
ANTPITTAS AND ANTTHRUSHES	Formicariidae	60
OVENBIRDS	Furnariidae	236
WOODCREEPERS	Dendrocolaptidae	52

OSCINES

This worldwide group, known as songbirds, forms the suborder Passeri. These birds have a highly developed syrinx, and can produce elaborate, varied songs. The basic song is developed by learning.

Group	Family	Species
LYREBIRDS	Menuridae	2
BOWERBIRDS	Ptilonorhynchidae	18
SCRUBBIRDS	Atrichornithidae	2
AUSTRALASIAN TREECREEPERS	Climacteridae	7
AUSTRALSIAN WRENS	Maluridae	28
HONEYEATERS	Meliphagidae	174
BRISTLEBIRDS	Dasyornithidae	3
PARDALOTES	Pardalotidae	4
THORNBILLS AND GERYGONES	Acanthizidae	60
AUSTRALASIAN BABBLERS	Pomatostomidae	5
LOGRUNNERS	Orthonychidae	3
SATINBIRDS	Cnemophilidae	3
BERRYPECKERS	Melanocharitidae	12
WATTLED CROWS	Callaeatidae	2
WHIPBIRDS AND RELATIVES	Eupetidae	10
QUAIL-THRUSHES	Cinclosomatidae	5
WATTLE-EYES AND BATISES	Platysteiridae	28
HELMETSHRIKES AND PUFFBACKS	Malaconotidae	52
BOATBILLS	Machaerirhynchidae	2
VANGAS	Vangidae	22
BUTCHERBIRDS	Cracticidae	13
WOODSWALLOWS	Artamidae	10
IORAS	Aegithinidae	4
BRISTLEHEAD	Pityriasidae	1
CUCKOOSHRIKES	Campephagidae	81
SITELLAS	Neosittidae	3
SHRIKETITS	Falcunculidae	4
WHISTLERS	Pachycephalidae	41
SHRIKES	Laniidae	30
VIREOS AND RELATIVES	Vireonidae	52
ORIOLES	Oriolidae	29
SHRIKETHRUSHES AND RELATIVES	Colluricinclidae	14
DRONGOS	Dicruridae	22
FANTAILS	Rhipiduridae	43
MONARCHS	Monarchidae	87
CROWS AND JAYS	Corvidae	117
MUDNESTERS	Corcoracidae	2
BIRDS-OF-PARADISE	Paradisaeidae	40
AUSTRALASIAN ROBINS	Petroicidae	45
BALD CROWS	Picathartidae	2
WAXWINGS AND RELATIVES	Bombycillidae	8
PALMCHAT	Dulidae	1
TRUE TITS	Paridae	54
PENDULINE TITS	Remizidae	10
LONG-TAILED TITS	Aegithalidae	11
SWALLOWS AND MARTINS	Hirundinidae	84
LARKS	Alaudidae	92
CISTICOLAS	Cisticolidae	110
BULBULS	Pycnonotidae	118
OLD WORLD WARBLERS	Sylviidae	280
BABBLERS AND RELATIVES	Timaliidae	273
WHITE-EYES	Zosteropidae	95
FAIRY-BLUEBIRDS	Irenidae	2
GOLDCRESTS	Regulidae	6
WRENS	Troglodytidae	76
GNATCATCHERS	Polioptilidae	14
NUTHATCHES	Sittidae	25
TREECREEPERS	Certhiidae	8
MOCKINGBIRDS AND THRASHERS	Mimidae	34
PHILIPPINE CREEPERS	Rhabdornithidae	2
STARLINGS	Sturnidae	114
THRUSHES	Turdidae	175
CHATS AND FLYCATCHERS	Muscicapidae	275
DIPPERS	Cinclidae	5
LEAFBIRDS	Chloropseidae	8
FLOWERPECKERS	Dicaeidae	44
SUNBIRDS	Nectariniidae	127
SUGARBIRDS	Promeropidae	2
OLD WORLD SPARROWS & SNOWFINCHES	Passeridae	40
WEAVERS	Ploceidae	108
WAXBILLS AND RELATIVES	Estrildidae	130
WHYDAHS	Viduidae	20
WAGTAILS AND PIPITS	Motacillidae	64
ACCENTORS	Prunellidae	13
FINCHES AND RELATIVES	Fringillidae	168
NEW WORLD WARBLERS	Parulidae	118
NEW WORLD BLACKBIRDS	Icteridae	98
BANANAQUIT	Coerebidae	1
BUNTINGS AND AMERICAN SPARROWS	Emberizidae	308
TANAGERS	Thraupidae	202
CARDINALS AND GROSBEAKS	Cardinalidae	42

NEW ZEALAND WRENS

ORDER	Passeriformes
FAMILY	Acanthisittidae
SPECIES	3

FOUND ONLY IN New Zealand, these stocky, almost tailless birds are not closely related to any other passerines. They include the New Zealand Rockwren, which lives on South Island on high mountain slopes, and the Rifleman, which is abundant throughout New Zealand. The Bushwren, used to replace the New Zealand Rockwren in forests at lower altitudes and is probably now extinct.

BEHAVIOUR

The New Zealand wrens are all very weak fliers, spending much of their time on the ground or creeping around boulders and tree trunks to search for spiders and other invertebrate prey. Combined with their dull, greenish brown upperparts, this can make them difficult to spot. Their ground-living lifestyle may have evolved because New Zealand has no native mammal predators of small birds – in the absence of this threat, the New Zealand wrens lost much of their ability to fly. A fourth species in this family, Stephen's Island Wren, was probably flightless, but it became extinct within a year of its discovery in 1894, when introduced feral cats killed its entire population.

Acanthisitta chloris

Rifleman

LENGTH 7–9cm (3–3½in)

WEIGHT 6–8g (7/32–5/16oz)

MIGRATION Non-migrant

HABITAT Forest, especially of beech, but also in scrub and pine plantations

MALE RIFLEMAN

Found only in New Zealand, the Rifleman is a beautiful and intriguing bird. The male has an unmarked green back, while the female is brown above with black streaking. This noticeable difference between the male and the female is thought to stem from the slightly different foraging niches the sexes occupy during the nesting season – the male tends to search for food in leaves and moss, while the female is found probing the bark of trunks. Birds of this species constantly flick their wings, but fly only short distances.

Despite its small size, the Rifleman builds a comparatively large domed nest in a cavity in the branch or dead stump of a tree. Both sexes share in the workload of constructing the nest, which has a short entrance tunnel. The female lays 2–5 eggs. Although this is essentially a monogamous species, some pairs appear to attract "helpers" that help to feed the young, usually with insects. Nests are sometimes preyed upon by weasels. The average lifespan of the species is about two years for males, and almost four months less in females.

BROADBILLS

ORDER	Passeriformes
FAMILY	Eurylaimidae
SPECIES	14

BROADBILLS ARE NAMED for the very wide, flattened, hooked bill in many species. Most are plump birds with squat bodies and short, rounded tails. They occur in forests, mangrove swamps, scrub, and thickets from West Africa eastwards as far as the Philippines, with ten species in Asia and the rest in Africa. The majority live in lowland areas, but a few, including Whitehead's Broadbill of Borneo and the rare Grauer's Broadbill of Central Africa, which was unknown to Western science until 1909, are restricted to humid mountain forests.

HIDDEN BILL
A thick clump of long feathers conceal most of the Green Broadbill's upper mandible, giving it a curiously top-heavy appearance. Its plumage is superbly camouflaged among rainforest foliage.

ANATOMY

This family's unusual bill-shape is shared with trogons (see p.300) and frogmouths (see p.288). It is a design suited to hunting large insects, which broadbills catch during a mid-air sally from a perch or by scooping them off branches and leaves. The Black-and-red Broadbill also feeds on crabs and fish. In Asia, the three green broadbill species in the genus *Calyptomena* have a very different diet – they eat mainly fruit, especially figs.

Smithornis capensis

African Broadbill

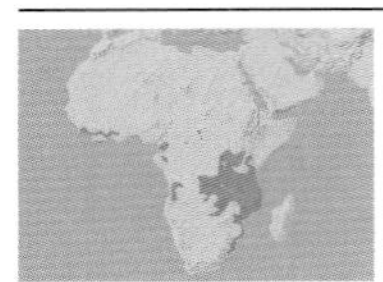

LENGTH 12–14cm (4½–5½in)

WEIGHT 17–30g (5/8–1 1/16oz)

MIGRATION Non-migrant

HABITAT Most forest types as well as in plantations; even cultivation and open country around villages

The African Broadbill is the most widespread of the four broadbill species found in Africa. It has largely dark brown plumage, with a dark head and pale underparts with dark streaks. It feeds mainly on insects that are caught in flight. It is an unobtrusive bird, except for the loud display performed by both sexes – a very fast trilling noise produced by vibrating the wing-feathers that stops abruptly. In courtship, this species hangs upside-down from its perch and uses its wings to produce a klaxon-like noise. It constructs a nest shaped like a bag.

AFRICAN BROADBILL AT NEST

GREAT SITES

MKUZI RESERVE

Lying close to the border with Mozambique, the Mkuzi Game Reserve in KwaZulu-Natal is a stronghold of the African Broadbill. Along with several other species that are restricted in range, the African Broadbill is found mainly in sand-forest in the area, such as the Tongaland sand-forest close to the Reserve's main camp. Sand-forest is a habitat unique to this part of South Africa and southern Mozambique.

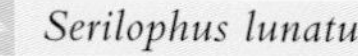

Calyptomena viridis

Green Broadbill

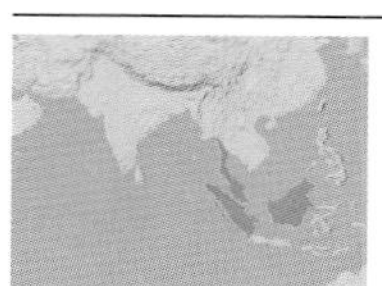

LENGTH 14–19cm (5½–7½in)

WEIGHT 45–75g (1⅝–2⅝oz)

MIGRATION Non-migrant

HABITAT Understorey and lower levels of rainforest; plantations, mainly in lowlands

Both sexes of Green Broadbill have predominantly leaf-green plumage, a strange bump-shaped head, and near-tailless appearance. The male has delicate deep black markings on the head and wings. The female's plumage is relieved by its yellower underparts. It feeds almost entirely on fruit, mainly figs, supplemented with some insects, including winged termites, which are caught in flight. Although essentially sedentary, the Green Broadbill is nomadic in response to fruit availability. The female takes on most of the nesting responsibilities, including constructing the neat gourd-shaped nest and incubating the 1–3 eggs that it lays.

Psarisomus dalhousiae

Long-tailed Broadbill

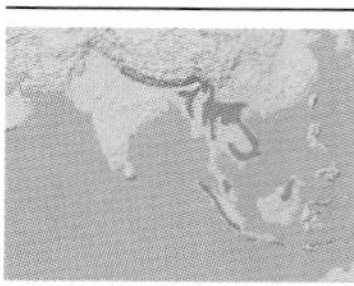

LENGTH 23–26cm (9–10in)

WEIGHT 50–65g (1¾–2⅜oz)

MIGRATION Non-migrant

HABITAT Forested areas, including pine- and bamboo-dominated woodland

With its long tail and well-marked head pattern, the Long-tailed Broadbill is one of the most striking birds found in Asian forests. It has black plumage on the top and rear of the head with a white collar around the neck. It has green underparts and a dark green back. The Long-tailed Broadbill feeds mainly on invertebrates, especially insects, but occasionally, it will also eat frogs, berries, and fruit. In the non-breeding season, it is typically found in parties of up to 15 birds, and is sociable even in the breeding season. Both the male and female build a bulky, conspicuous nest of roots, creepers, and dead leaves. A typical clutch consists of 4–8 eggs.

ADULT LONG-TAILED BROADBILL

Serilophus lunatus

Silver-breasted Broadbill

LENGTH 16cm (6½in)

WEIGHT 25–35g (⅞–1¼oz)

MIGRATION Non-migrant

HABITAT Sometimes in gardens, but prefers forests of all types, including those selectively logged

The male and female Silver-breasted Broadbill are essentially alike. The hood is all black, relieved by a yellow eye-ring, narrow white collar, and pale bill. The underparts are pinkish buff, and the upperparts are black, offset with rich yellow markings on the wings and back. There is also a blue patch in the wings. The diet of the Silver-breasted Broadbill consists mainly of insects and fruit, with most prey being gleaned from the foliage while it perches. The species' range has contracted and its numbers have declined due to ongoing deforestation throughout much of its range.

ASITIES

ORDER	Passeriformes
FAMILY	Philepittidae
SPECIES	4

THIS SMALL FAMILY is restricted to evergreen forests on Madagascar, particularly in the wetter eastern part of the island. They are short, compact-bodied birds, and in the nesting season the males develop unique fleshy wattles around the eye, unlike those in any other birds. Two species – the Common Sunbird-Asity and Yellow-bellied Sunbird-Asity – have long, decurved bills for feeding on nectar and insects. The other two species – the Velvet Asity and Schlegel's Asity – eat fruit and have shorter bills.

FLOWER FEEDER The spectacular bill of the Common Sunbird-Asity enables it to exploit a food out of reach to most Madagascan birds.

Philepitta castanea

Velvet Asity

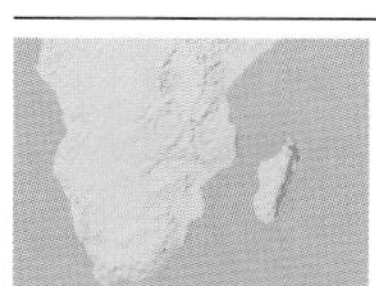

LENGTH 14–7cm (½–⅝oz)

WEIGHT 25–45g (⅞–1⅝oz)

MIGRATION Non-migrant

HABITAT Rainforest and its edges, often in areas with a relatively open understorey

MALE VELVET ASITY

The Velvet Asity has a short bill and tail. The breeding male has all-black plumage, with a wattle of deep green skin above the eye. In the non-breeding season, the male has yellow tips to the black feathers. The female is mainly brown above and buff with dark brown streaks below and undertakes the bulk of the breeding duties. Fruit forms the main part of this species' diet. Males gather in dispersed leks to display and call and the successful male mates with several females.

Neodrepanis coruscans

Common Sunbird-Asity

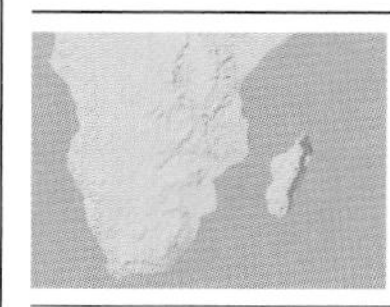

LENGTH 9–11cm (11/32–⅜oz)

WEIGHT 5–7g (3/16–¼oz)

MIGRATION Non-migrant

HABITAT Canopy and subcanopy of lower montane rainforest

MALE COMMON SUNBIRD-ASITY

Like real sunbirds, the male and female Common Sunbird-Asity differ greatly in appearance. The female has a drab brown and yellow plumage in contrast to the male, who has bright plumage and a sky-blue wattle. Both sexes have a long, strikingly decurved bill. It feeds mainly on nectar, although it also catches flies in flight and joins mixed-species flocks to feed on insects, gleaned from the foliage. The female constructs a nest of moss, leaves, and small twigs, suspended from a branch.

PITTAS

ORDER	Passeriformes
FAMILY	Pittidae
SPECIES	30

THE PITTAS HAVE SPECTACULARLY beautiful plumages, often with iridescent areas that shimmer like jewels when seen from certain angles. Birds of this family are round-bodied with a strong bill, very short tail, and long legs that give them a distinctive upright stance – an adaptation to living among leaf litter on the forest floor. Their eyes are large and, unusually for passerines, they possess an excellent sense of smell, to help them find invertebrate prey in the dimly lit forest interior. Most pittas are found in southeast Asia, but notable exceptions include the African Pitta and three species from northern Australia. In spite of their brilliant coloration, pittas are rarely seen, due to their shy habits and tendency to "freeze" or quietly slip away into the undergrowth when alarmed.

MIGRATORY SPECIES
Despite being reluctant fliers, several pittas are migratory. They include the Indian Pitta (right), one of the strongest migrants in the family. It breeds in the Himalayas and northeastern India and travels to southern India for the winter. Some make the sea crossing to Sri Lanka.

Pitta erythrogaster

Red-bellied Pitta

LENGTH 16–18cm (6 1/2–7in)
WEIGHT 45–70g (1 5/8–2 1/2oz)
MIGRATION Non-migrant

HABITAT Primary forest; also scrub and degraded areas of woodland

With its colourful plumage pattern consisting of a red belly and metallic blue breast-band and wings, the Red-bellied Pitta is a distinctive bird. Although there are 23 subspecies that have red bellies and blue breast-bands, their head and back patterns vary. It hops on the forest floor, looking for snails, beetles, and other insects to feed on. It is silent, except in the breeding season, when it utters whistling calls.

ADULT RED-BELLIED PITTA

ADULT BLUE-WINGED PITTA

Pitta moluccensis

Blue-winged Pitta

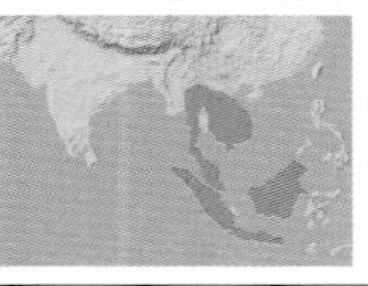

LENGTH 18–20cm (7–8in)
WEIGHT 50–150g (1 3/4–5oz)
MIGRATION Migrant

HABITAT Dry primary forest, mangroves, and scrub; gardens and plantations on migration

Aptly named, the Blue-winged Pitta has striking electric blue wings. It has a black crown, with a black stripe running through the eyes, separated by a brown band. Its throat is white, its back is green, and its buff underparts become crimson around the belly. It has a very short tail. Both the sexes look alike. The diet of this bird is varied and includes insects and their larvae. It also feeds on crustaceans and snails, cracking their shells open with a stone, which it uses as an anvil. It makes a nest on the ground and lays 4–6 eggs.

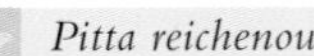

Pitta reichenowi

Green-breasted Pitta

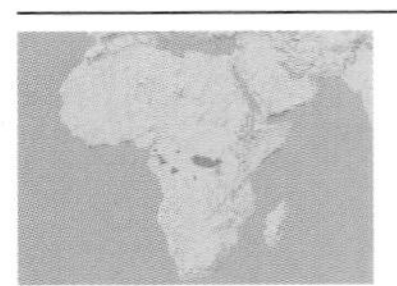

LENGTH 17–19cm (6 1/2–7 1/2in)
WEIGHT 70g (2 1/2oz)
MIGRATION Non-migrant

HABITAT Forest with dense undergrowth and thickets; also tall, secondary woodland

ADULT GREEN-BREASTED PITTA

Very shy and rarely seen, the Green-breasted Pitta is a poorly known bird. Its plumage is largely green, but it has buff stripes above the eyes, joining at the back of the head, a white throat, with a small black patch, and chestnut underparts. This pitta feeds on caterpillars, beetles, snails, and worms. Its voice is a bell-like whistle, given at regular short intervals. Little is known about its breeding habits.

ADULT NOISY PITTA

Pitta versicolor

Noisy Pitta

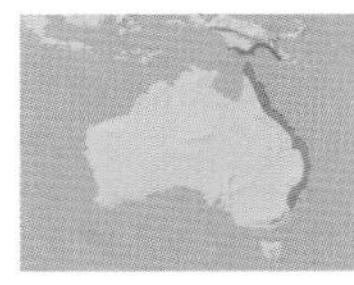

LENGTH 19–21cm (7 1/2–8 1/2in)
WEIGHT 70–125g (2 1/2–4oz)
MIGRATION Partial migrant

HABITAT Wet gulleys in lowland rainforest with thick undergrowth; also wet eucalyptus forest

The Noisy Pitta has a black face and a brown crown with a central black streak. Its back is green and its underparts are buff. The Noisy Pitta is no more vocal than many other pittas, but its low-whistled calls and cat-like purrs are distinctive. It forages on the forest floor and eats insects, woodlice, worms, and snails, as well as berries and fruit. Placed on the ground, its nest is a large, domed structure. It is constructed between October and April. The female Noisy Pitta lays 3 or 4 eggs and both the male and female incubate the eggs, which takes just over 14 days. It is one of the three pitta species that breeds only in Australia.

Pitta brachyura

Indian Pitta

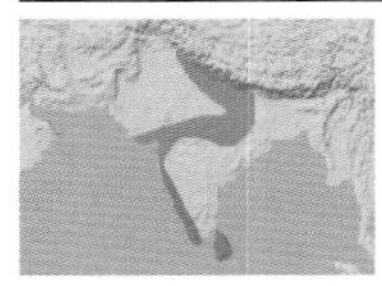

LENGTH 18cm (7in)
WEIGHT 45–65g (1 5/8–2 3/8oz)
MIGRATION Migrant

HABITAT Dense undergrowth in lowland, and deciduous and evergreen forest in foothills

The Indian Pitta is the only bird of the pitta family to be found in the Indian subcontinent. It has a black face, with green upperparts and yellow-buff underparts. The bird arrives at its breeding grounds in May, and starts building its large, oval nest with leaves, roots, grass, and twigs. It lays up to six eggs, which are incubated by both adults. The young are fed on insects, their larvae, and worms.

ADULT INDIAN PITTA

MANAKINS

ORDER Passeriformes
FAMILY Pipridae
SPECIES 48

THIS FAMILY OF SMALL forest birds is confined to the American tropics, from southern Mexico southwards to northern Argentina. The majority of species live in lowland rainforest, and nearly all are year-round residents. Manakins have a large head and a short bill and tail. Males are colourful, with an erectable throat patch or a crest in some species, whereas females are dull green and all look much alike.

TAIL DEVELOPMENT
The Blue Manakin is one of a few manakins in which mature males develop long central tail feathers, absent in younger males.

BEHAVIOUR

Manakins live in the lower levels of the forest and are highly active, flitting among branches to pluck fruit, their main food. They also eat a few insects. Males perform an elaborate courtship display that may include wing-flicking, acrobatic jumps, and butterfly-like flights, depending on the species. These often vigorous displays may in some species be carried out in groups of males, on the ground or lined up on a branch, where each tries to outperform its rivals.

FEMALE PIN-TAILED MANAKIN

Ilicura militaris

Pin-tailed Manakin

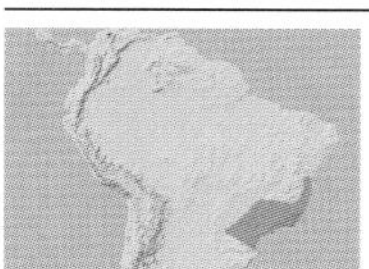

LENGTH 11–13cm ($4^1/_2$–5in)
WEIGHT 13–15g ($^7/_{16}$–$^9/_{16}$oz)
MIGRATION Non-migrant
HABITAT Humid Atlantic forest, in lowland and foothills

Found only in the Brazilian Atlantic forest, the Pin-tailed Manakin is a quiet bird. The male is distinctive, with its red forecrown, black head, and startling yellow eyes. Its underparts are white, with a red rump, black wings, and sharp, pointed central tail-feathers. The males have a lek system, in which each bird displays within the hearing distance of its neighbour.

Chiroxiphia caudata

Blue Manakin

LENGTH 15cm (6in)
WEIGHT 25g ($^7/_8$oz)
MIGRATION Non-migrant
HABITAT Humid forest and second growth in the Atlantic forest, usually in lowland and on slopes

An attractive bird, the male Blue Manakin has a brilliant red crown and black and blue plumage. The male's elongated central tail-feathers are also a distinctive feature. The female is drabber, being entirely clad in olive-green. However, its colouring is an effective camouflage, especially when it is nesting, because it solely tends to the young. One of the most common forest birds of southern Brazil, the Blue Manakin has a whining, almost cat-like call at leks. The male performs an intricate courtship dance before a female.

MALE BLUE MANAKIN

Antilophia galeata

Helmeted Manakin

LENGTH 15cm (6in)
WEIGHT 20–25g ($^{11}/_{16}$–$^7/_8$oz)
MIGRATION Non-migrant
HABITAT Woodland along streams or rivers in savanna areas

MALE HELMETED MANAKIN

The male Helmeted Manakin is a large, long-tailed manakin, with an all-black plumage, except for a spectacular red crest, which runs across its upper back and ends in bristle-like feathers on the forehead. The female shares its tufty forecrown feathers and long tail, but is entirely olive-green. Fruit and insects constitute the Helmeted Manakin's diet. Its nest, like those of its relatives, is a shallow, fragile-looking cup of twigs and leaves suspended up to 10m (33ft) above the ground. It lays two eggs, but little else is known about this bird's breeding habits. It has a rollicking, throaty call that is a common sound in its favoured savanna woodland.

MALE BAND-TAILED MANAKIN

Pipra fasciicauda

Band-tailed Manakin

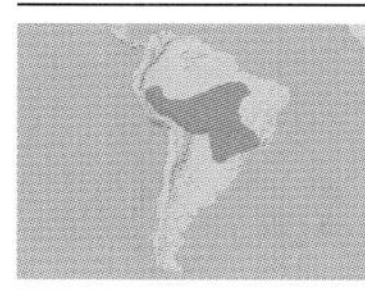

LENGTH 11cm ($4^1/_2$in)
WEIGHT 10–20g ($^3/_8$–$^{11}/_{16}$oz)
MIGRATION Non-migrant
HABITAT Seasonally flooded lowland forest and gallery forest in savanna

A small, unobtrusive bird, the male Band-tailed Manakin has striking red, yellow, and black plumage, with a neat white tail-band, which also gives the species its name. The female, however, is a dull green bird with patches of yellow on its throat and breast. Three different subspecies have been named, based on the amount of red on the underparts in males. Like most manakins, the Band-tailed Manakin feeds mainly on small fruit and seeds, as well as on insects, which it usually takes in flight. This species is one of the lekking manakins, and the males gather at the group display grounds for the right to mate with a female. However, only an older, dominant male is successful in the courtship process.

COTINGAS

ORDER	Passeriformes
FAMILY	Cotingidae
SPECIES	96

THE COTINGAS VARY HUGELY in size, appearance, and the way they breed, making them one of the most diverse bird families of the New World tropics. The largest cotingas – umbrellabirds – are as big as small crows, while the smallest species are the size of tits or chickadees. Male cotingas are often brilliantly coloured, and include several of the most spectacular South American birds, such as the two bright orange cock-of-the rock species. Many are adorned with decorative plumes or crests, and a few have extraordinary fleshy wattles on the forehead or hanging below the bill. In contrast, female cotingas generally have drab plumage.

FAR-CARRYING CALL
The male Three-wattled Bellbird is remarkable for its strange facial wattles and for its extremely loud call, which reverberates through the treetops.

BEHAVIOUR

Cotingas live in lowland rainforest and highland cloudforest, particularly in the treetops, but an exception to this rule are the plantcutters, which are found in fields and on dry, shrub-covered slopes in the Andes. Most cotingas feed on fruit, and to help them swallow this food some species, such as the fruiteaters and fruitcrows, have a very wide gape. However, plantcutters eat plant buds, leaves, and seeds, and the becards and tityras are insect-eaters. Many male cotingas have loud courtship or territorial vocalizations. For example, bellbirds utter repetitive calls that can be heard over a kilometre away, while the Capuchinbird has a mooing call and also produces a bizarre droning noise. Males of several species are polygamous and assemble at a lek to attract females. Their displays may be mainly visual, as in cocks-of-the-rock, or can take the form of competitive singing bouts, as in the drab-coloured pihas.

INSECT EATER
Some cotingas, such as this Black-and-white Becard, glean large insects from foliage, or dart from a perch to snatch them in mid-air, like a flycatcher.

Schiffornis turdina

Thrush-like Schiffornis

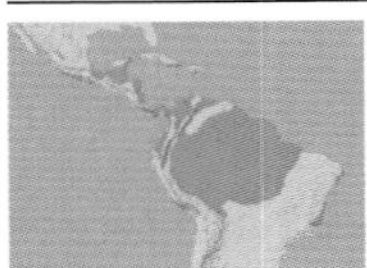

LENGTH 16cm ($6\frac{1}{2}$in)
WEIGHT 25–35g ($\frac{7}{8}$–$1\frac{1}{4}$oz)
MIGRATION Non-migrant

HABITAT Interior of humid forest; more occasionally, tall secondary growth

The Thrush-like Schiffornis is mainly brown, although some of the 13 subspecies currently recognized have grey heads. It can be overlooked in the forest because of its dull plumage, unless the male gives away its presence by its song, an unmistakable whistled phrase. It is a solitary feeder, foraging on fruit and insects. Its nest is a bulky cup of dead leaves and rootlets, usually set in a hollow, in which the bird lays two eggs and incubates them for three weeks. The nestlings are notable for their long, copious black down.

ADULT THRUSH-LIKE SCHIFFORNIS

Phytotoma rara

Rufous-tailed Plantcutter

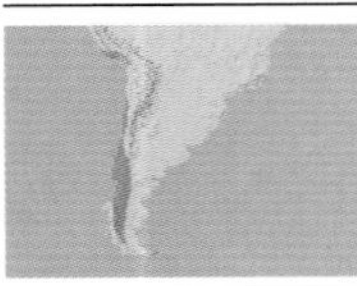

LENGTH 18–20cm (7–8in)
WEIGHT 40–45g ($1\frac{7}{16}$–$1\frac{5}{8}$oz)
MIGRATION Partial migrant

HABITAT Thorn scrub, woodland edges, and clearings, as well as farmland and orchards

Of the three species of plantcutters, the Rufous-tailed Plantcutter has, perhaps, the most striking appearance. The male has a rufous crown, "beady" red eyes, and black cheeks with bold white markings. Its bill is short and thick with serrated edges, which it uses to strip off buds, leaves, and fruit. Its underparts are rufous with black wings. In contrast, the female is less distinctive, being mainly brown above and on the head, and buffy below streaked brown, though it shares the bright red eyes of the male.

The bird feeds mainly on grass, buds, shoots, and leaves, taken both on the ground and in the bushes. The adults and the young also occasionally feed on insects. The Rufous-tailed Plantcutter's nest is a shallow cup-shaped structure made of twigs, placed in a dense thorn shrub, where the bird lays up to four eggs. This bird gathers in groups during the non-breeding season, when the populations in the extreme south of its range move north.

MALE RUFOUS-TAILED PLANTCUTTER

Pipreola arcuata

Barred Fruiteater

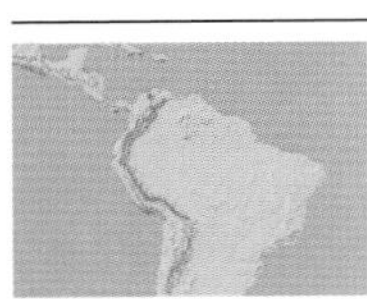

LENGTH 23cm (9in)
WEIGHT 100–125g ($3\frac{5}{8}$–4oz)
MIGRATION Non-migrant

HABITAT Montane forest and its borders

MALE BARRED FRUITEATER

The male Barred Fruiteater has a striking appearance, with its red bill and pale eyes. It has a black head, and green and yellow barred underparts. The female shares most of these features, but lacks the black hood. The Barred Fruiteater, as its name sugggests, seems to eat only fruit, taken while it is perching. Its song is an extremely high, thin, almost hissing "se-e-e-e-e-a-a-a". Its nesting behaviour is almost completely unknown.

Oxyruncus cristatus

Sharpbill

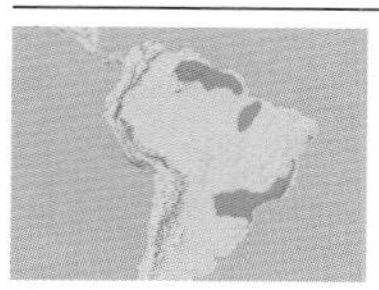

LENGTH 17cm ($6\frac{1}{2}$in)

WEIGHT 40g ($1\frac{7}{16}$oz)

MIGRATION Non-migrant

HABITAT Tropical forest mainly in lowland, but also in lower hills

The Sharpbill has a broad-based sharp bill, with a narrow crest of red feathers on its head. It has mainly green upperparts and yellow or white underparts, spotted and streaked with black. The crest of red feathers is less dense in the female and completely absent in young birds. The bird forages on moss and epiphytes, as well as on rolled dead leaves in search of invertebrates and seeds. It also feeds on fruit.

The Sharpbill is much more frequently heard than seen. Its most characteristic song is a descending whistle with the quality of a falling bomb. In the breeding season, several males assemble to take part in lekking. They sing in close proximity, but are not in sight of each other. Over the years, there has been considerable debate over which family the Sharpbill belongs to. DNA tests, however, have indicated that it is a member of the cotinga family.

ADULT SHARPBILL

Cotinga amabilis

Lovely Cotinga

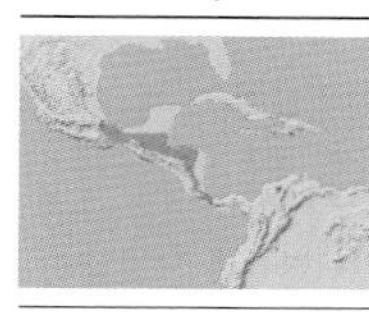

LENGTH 18cm (7in)

WEIGHT 65–75g ($2\frac{3}{8}$–$2\frac{5}{8}$oz)

MIGRATION Non-migrant

HABITAT Mainly the canopy of humid, tropical evergreen forest

Aptly named, the male Lovely Cotinga has largely deep turquoise-blue plumage, with a large purple throat patch and an even larger patch on its breast and the belly. Its wings are mainly black. The female, like several of its relatives, has a mainly brown head and upperparts, white-grey underparts with brown streaks and spots, and neat white feather tips on its back. As the bird spends most of its time in the canopy of tall forest, its natural history is not well known. The Lovely Cotinga feeds on fruit taken from the tree while the bird is in flight, as well as on some insects and even small lizards. The Lovely Cotinga has a strong flight. Its outer wing feathers produce a rattling sound, which also features in the bird's courtship display flights. Only one nest belonging to the Lovely Cotinga has ever been found, and that, too, was impossible to observe closely as it was sited more than 30m (98ft) above the ground.

MALE LOVELY COTINGA

Rupicola peruvianus

Andean Cock-of-the-rock

LENGTH 30–32cm (12–$12\frac{1}{2}$in)

WEIGHT 200–275g (7–10oz)

MIGRATION Non-migrant

HABITAT Montane forest, especially in ravines

Few birds are more symbolic of South America, or simply as beautiful, as the Andean Cock-of-the-rock. The male Andean Cock-of-the-rock has a vivid red or orange plumage with black and white wings and a black tail. Due to the casque-like crest that topples forward over the bird's forehead, it appears almost bill-less. Like many other cotingas, the female Andean Cock-of-the-rock is far less colourful than the male, although its plumage is nevertheless distinctive. The female is usually deep chestnut-brown, with pale eyes and a slightly less exaggerated crest. This bird feeds on large insects, fruit, and small vertebrates.

ADULT MALE

MUD NESTS

The Andean Cock-of-the-rock builds its nest with mud, in the form of a truncated cone that is usually attached to a rock face. The nest's cup is lined with vegetable fibre. Several nests may be sited in close proximity to one another.

SINGLE PARENT

The female builds the nest, incubates the egg, and feeds the young on her own; the male does not help with raising the young.

MALE THREE-WATTLED BELLBIRD

Procnias tricarunculatus

Three-wattled Bellbird

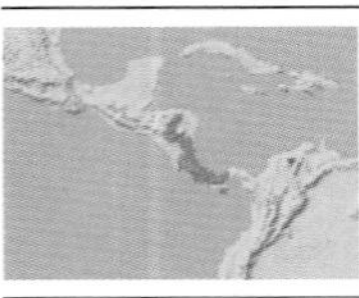

LENGTH 25–30cm (10–12in)

WEIGHT 150–200g (5–7oz)

MIGRATION Migrant

HABITAT Montane forest, moving lower in the non-breeding season

RED LIST CATEGORY Vulnerable

Most of the male Three-wattled Bellbird's plumage is warm chestnut, contrasting markedly with its brilliant white head and neck. Three black wattles hang limply from the base of the bill. The female, in contrast, is mainly olive-green, blending easily with foliage. This species feeds mainly on fruit and berries. While many cotingas move seasonally, primarily following fruit availability, the Three-wattled Bellbird is a pronounced migrant, mainly altitudinally, moving to much lower ground in the non-breeding season but those in northern Costa Rica also move into lowland Nicaragua. Ironically, it is this adaptability which has been the cause of its decline, as destruction of lowland forest in its range is continuing apace.

Procnias nudicollis

Bare-throated Bellbird

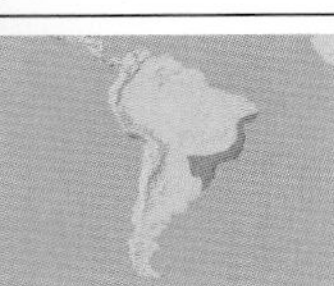

LENGTH 27–29cm ($10^{1}/_{2}$–$11^{1}/_{2}$in)

WEIGHT 150–225g (5–8oz)

MIGRATION Partial migrant

HABITAT Primary forest in both lowland and foothills

Unlike the other three species of bellbird, the Bare-throated Bellbird lacks wattles. With the exception of the naked green throat skin, the male is almost entirely white, which makes it easy to identify, especially when it is perched above the forest canopy, giving its metallic "bock" calls that sound like an anvil being hit. The female and the juvenile male are mainly olive-green. The species is a rather popular cagebird.

ADULT MALE SINGING

Cephalopterus penduliger

Long-wattled Umbrellabird

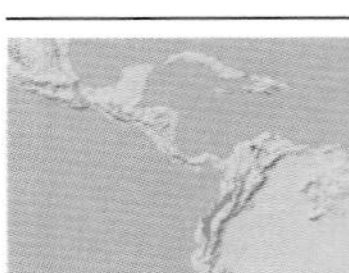

LENGTH 36–41cm (14–16in)

WEIGHT 350g (13oz)

MIGRATION Non-migrant

HABITAT Forest, but also found in secondary growth and even adjacent farmland

RED LIST CATEGORY Vulnerable

The Long-wattled Umbrellabird is among the largest passerines found in South America and the most threatened of the three species of umbrellabird, all of which are characterized by a feathered wattle hanging from the throat. In the Long-wattled Umbrellabird, this densely feathered wattle may reach up to 35cm (14in) long in males, but is much reduced or almost absent in females. In flight, the wattle is retracted into the body. Both sexes are mainly black with a blue gloss; at a glance they might be mistaken for a crow, except for the striking brushy parasol-like crest, which is larger and more upright in the male.

This species feeds mainly on the fruit of palm and laurel trees, but also takes insects, lizards, and even small snakes. In the breeding season, the territorial male utters deep, far-carrying booming calls in display, together with up to 10 other males, which gather in the same area well above the forest floor. When calling, the male leans forward to show off his crest and wattle.

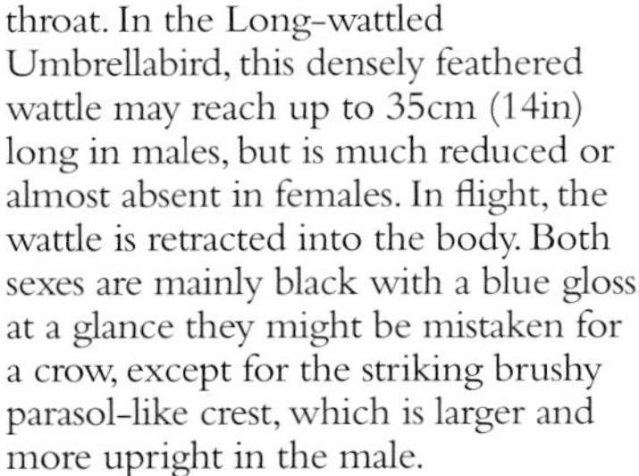

MALE LONG-WATTLED UMBRELLABIRD

Phibalura flavirostris

Swallow-tailed Cotinga

LENGTH 22cm ($8^{1}/_{2}$in)

WEIGHT 45–50g ($1^{5}/_{8}$–$1^{3}/_{4}$oz)

MIGRATION Partial migrant

HABITAT Woodland, forest, and open areas, including gardens with trees, from sea level to highland

MALE SWALLOW-TAILED COTINGA

In a family rich in unmistakably plumaged birds, the Swallow-tailed Cotinga still stands out with its black, yellow, and green plumage and its deeply forked tail. The male has a brighter plumage than the female. This species feeds on insects and fruit and its nest is a tiny cup on a branch.

Carpodectes nitidus

Snowy Cotinga

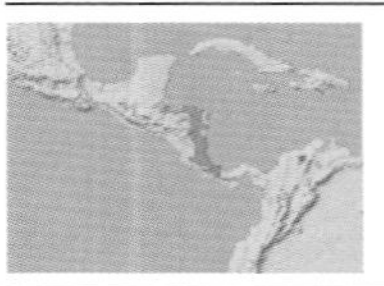

LENGTH 19–21cm ($7^{1}/_{2}$–$8^{1}/_{2}$in)

WEIGHT 90–125g ($3^{1}/_{4}$–4oz)

MIGRATION Non-migrant

HABITAT Tall secondary growth and, more especially, the canopy in humid forest

The Snowy Cotinga is one of three mainly white cotingas, which are restricted as a group to southern Central America and extreme northwest South America. The male Snowy Cotinga has a bluish grey cast to the crown and mantle, whereas the female is mainly grey, with a black tail and wings, which have many white fringes to the feathers. The juvenile male has some dark patches on the wings. Its diet is mainly fruit and the species is known to wander widely in search of rich feeding sources.

JUVENILE MALE SNOWY COTINGA

TYRANT FLYCATCHERS

ORDER	Passeriformes
FAMILY	Tyrannidae
SPECIES	430

THESE SMALL AND MEDIUM-SIZED birds make up the largest bird family in the New World. They occur from the taiga of Alaska and Canada south to Patagonia, in virtually every habitat. Most species live in the tropics, and those that breed in temperate regions, including the 30 species that nest in North America, usually migrate there in winter. Tyrant flycatchers are typically brown, olive-green, pale yellow, or grey in colour, and some are so similar that they can be identified only by their calls or song.

HOLE-NESTER
Species in the genus *Myiarchus*, such as this Great Crested Flycatcher, are unusual among the tyrant flycatchers due to their hole-nesting habits. This bird has brought an insect back to its nest-hole.

BEHAVIOUR

This diverse family gets the "tyrant" part of its name from the noisy, aggressively territorial behaviour of a few species, especially kingbirds. Above all, however, it is skill at catching insects and other invertebrates that unites the tyrant flycatchers. They hunt by hawking: they sit patiently on a perch, quickly dart away to snatch a passing insect, then return to the same perch. Every species has its own variation of this technique – some pluck prey off leaves, some drop to the ground or the surface of water, and others chase insects in mid-air. As a result, many different species can share the same habitat, with each exploiting a different food source. The majority of tyrant flycatchers form monogamous breeding pairs, and generally both sexes raise the young. The nest is usually cup-shaped, but can be spherical or a "bag" suspended below a branch.

VARIED BILLS
Bill shape reflects a bird's diet. The Great Kiskadee (above) has a broad, triangular bill, suited to large prey. Bristle-like feathers around the bill guard its face from struggling prey.

ADULT YELLOW-BELLIED ELAENIA

Elaenia flavogaster

Yellow-bellied Elaenia

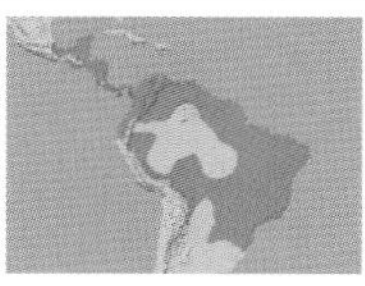

LENGTH 17cm (6½in)

WEIGHT 20–30g (11/16–1 1/16oz)

MIGRATION Non-migrant

HABITAT Wooded habitats, including second growth, scrub, savanna, and brush; absent from dense forest

One of the most common in its group, the Yellow-bellied Elaenia is easily identified by its conspicuous crest, and distinctive voice. It has olive-brown upperparts and pale yellow lower underparts. This bird feeds on insects and berries. The nest is cup-shaped and usually placed on a low branch; two eggs are laid and sometimes two broods are attempted.

Suiriri islerorum

Chapada Suiriri

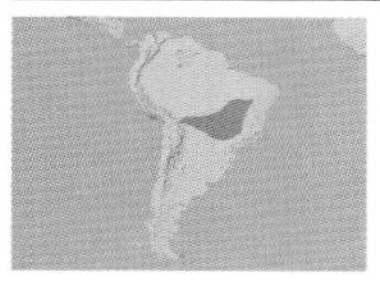

LENGTH 16cm (6½in)

WEIGHT 20–25g (11/16–7/8oz)

MIGRATION Non-migrant

HABITAT Well-wooded savanna areas

The description of the Chapada Suiriri by scientists, in 2001, was the answer to a long-standing mystery, as anomalous specimens of its close relative, the Suiriri Flycatcher (*S. suiriri*), had baffled ornithologists for almost 75 years. It was possible to identify the Chapada Suiriri by its call (a distinctive male-female duet), only because of modern techniques used to record birds' voices. A classic example of what scientists refer to as a "cryptic" species, which are often very similar in plumage but different in voice and behaviour, the Chapada Suiriri has a small bill and is principally grey above and paler below, with a pale band across the tip of the otherwise dark tail. It is named after a region of Brazil where it is particularly abundant. Details about its lifestyle are yet to be assembled, but it is known to feed mainly on fruit and small arthropods. Aspects of its breeding habits are, however, almost entirely unknown as yet.

ADULT CHAPADA SUIRIRI

Pseudotriccus ruficeps

Rufous-headed Pygmy Tyrant

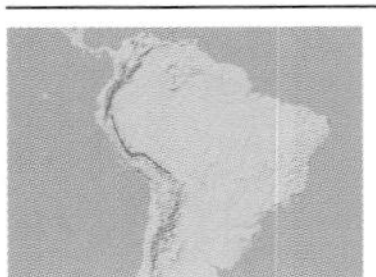

LENGTH 11cm (4½in)
WEIGHT 11g (⅜oz)
MIGRATION Non-migrant
HABITAT Humid mountain or dense cloud forest, usually at 1,850–3,500m (6,000–11,500ft)

Aptly named for its bright orange-rufous head and throat, the Rufous-headed Pygmy Tyrant is easily identified. The upperparts are dark olive, and the breast and flanks are greyish olive. It has dark chestnut wings and tail with rufous edging and feathering. It has short, rounded wings that are typical of a bird that needs to fly only short distances – from perch to perch.

This species forages on insects close to the ground in the forest understorey, snatching prey from leaves in sudden vertical sallies and making strange snapping noises with its bill as it does so. Common in some parts of its Andean range, but uncommon in others, the Rufous-headed Pygmy Tyrant is found in several protected areas, such as the Machu Picchu Historical Sanctuary in Peru.

Phylloscartes paulista

Sao Paulo Tyrannulet

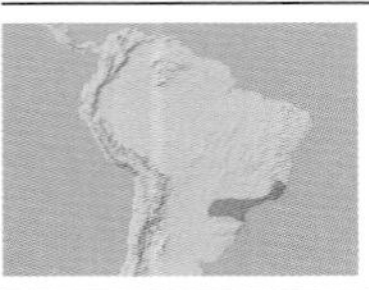

LENGTH 11cm (4½in)
WEIGHT 10g (⅜oz)
MIGRATION Non-migrant
HABITAT Humid tropical forest and forest borders, usually below 400m (1,300ft)

The most distinctive feature of the Sao Paulo Tyrannulet's plumage is the broad black crescent on the ear feathers, which contrasts with the pale yellow eyebrow and sides of the nape. The pale wing-bars are usually indistinct, not contrasting greatly with the olive wings. The San Paulo Tyrannulet darts forward from its perch for insects in the forest. It is usually is found singly or in pairs, often with flocks of other species.

This enigmatic species is found in the lowland Atlantic forest, one of the world's most threatened ecosystems. Although the remaining forests continue to be destroyed for agriculture, industrialization, and mining, the Sao Paulo Tyrannulet is common in several protected areas, particularly in Brazil.

ADULT SAO PAULO TYRANNULET

GREY-HOODED FLYCATCHER

Mionectes rufiventris

Grey-hooded Flycatcher

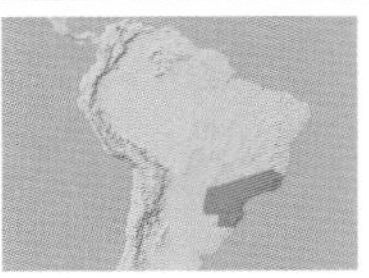

LENGTH 14cm (5½in)
WEIGHT 13g (7/16oz)
MIGRATION Non-migrant
HABITAT Humid forest and secondary growth in understorey, below 1,000m (3,300ft)

Easily recognized by its grey head, the Grey-hooded Flycatcher has a grey chest and olive upperparts. During courtship, males sing in dispersed groups of two or three to attract females. The song, unusual among tyrant flycatchers, starts slowly, accelerates rapidly, and then stops abruptly. When a female enters the "lek" (display area), the male displays by jumping and wing-flicking.

Myiornis auricularis

Eared Pygmy Tyrant

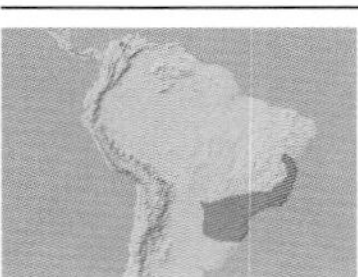

LENGTH 7cm (2¾in)
WEIGHT 5g (3/16oz)
MIGRATION Non-migrant
HABITAT Humid forest and dense shrubby growth along forest edges, up to 1,250m (4,100ft)

One of the smallest of all tyrant flycatchers, the Eared Pygmy Tyrant weighs even less than some hummingbirds. It has a rounded grey head, and the most distinguishable feature of its plumage is the large, crescent-shaped black ear patch, which gives the species its common name. It is found in the forests of Brazil, Paraguay, and Argentina.

ADULT EARED PYGMY TYRANT

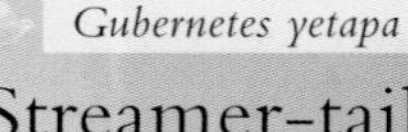

Gubernetes yetapa

Streamer-tailed Tyrant

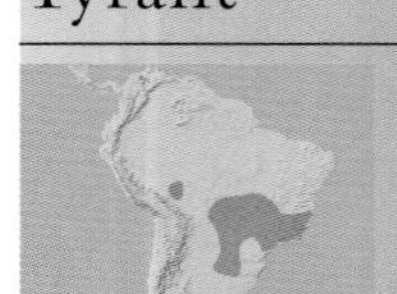

LENGTH 35–42cm (14–16½in)
WEIGHT 70g (2½oz)
MIGRATION Non-migrant
HABITAT Damp grassland and marshes, with nearby shrubland, in lowland areas

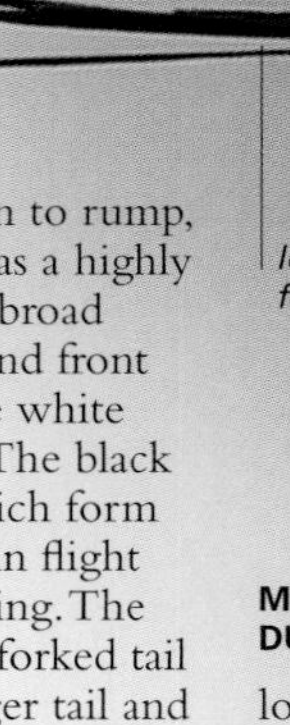

wings raised in display

long, deeply forked tail

MALE AND FEMALE IN DUETTING DISPLAY

Mostly pale grey from crown to rump, the Streamer-tailed Tyrant has a highly distinctive plumage. It has a broad chestnut-brown eye-stripe and front collar that contrasts with the white throat and grey underparts. The black wings have rufous bases, which form an obvious panel on the main flight feathers when the bird is flying. The long, graduated, and deeply forked tail is black. The male has a longer tail and brighter plumage than the female.

Pairs of Streamer-tailed Tyrants often perform a spectacular duetting ritual that probably signals territory ownership but may also have a role in courtship or pair-bonding. The pairs sit 10–50cm (4–19½in) apart on a prominent perch, facing each other or in opposite directions. Each bird lowers its head, rhythmically lifts and lowers its long tail, and raises both wings overhead, while whistling "tewear-tee-tear" or warbling "tea-whittle, tea-whittle" in an excited manner.

This bird flies after large insects from the tops of bushes and trees, usually hunting over marshy ground and taking insects in flight.

ADULT COMMON TODY-FLYCATCHER

Todirostrum cinereum

Common Tody-Flycatcher

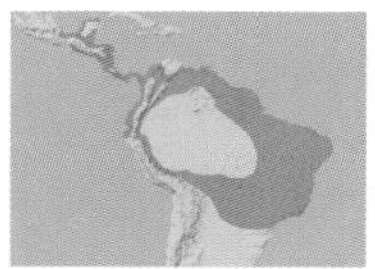

LENGTH 10cm (4in)

WEIGHT 6g (7/32oz)

MIGRATION Non-migrant

HABITAT Open and semi-open areas with trees, particularly gardens, and woodland

A familiar bird in Central and South America, the tiny Common Tody-Flycatcher has a dark grey face, a long bill, bright yellow irises, and yellow underparts.

The bird has a peculiar foraging action: the bird moves sideways along a perch, with its wings drooped and the tail cocked over the head, which it then wags from side to side. It can look quite comical as it flutters and shuffles around the vegetation of its habitat.

Platyrinchus mystaceus

White-throated Spadebill

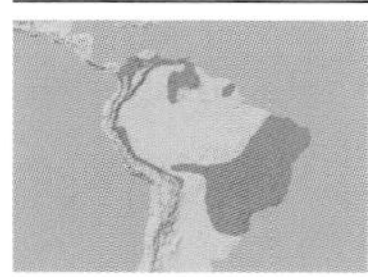

LENGTH 10cm (4in)

WEIGHT 10g (3/8oz)

MIGRATION Non-migrant

HABITAT Understorey of humid and dry forest, sometimes in thickets along forest edges

Despite being widespread, the tiny White-throated Spadebill is easily overlooked in its dark forest habitat. As its common name suggests, this bird has a shovel-shaped bill. As is typical of its genus, the White-throated Spadebill also has large eyes, bristles around its bill, and a short tail. Its contrasting face pattern comprises dark stripes around the bill and ear, black ear feathers, and a pale eye-ring. It has a semi-concealed yellow crown patch (smaller in the female), which is sometimes raised in the shape of a fan when a male is singing animatedly. The song is a high, thin rattling trill, rising slightly and then descending. It forages low in the undergrowth, rapidly darting upwards to glean insects from the undersides of leaves, snapping its bill upon capture. These birds usually occur in pairs and rarely join mixed-species flocks.

ADULT WHITE-THROATED SPADEBILL

Onychorhynchus coronatus

Royal Flycatcher

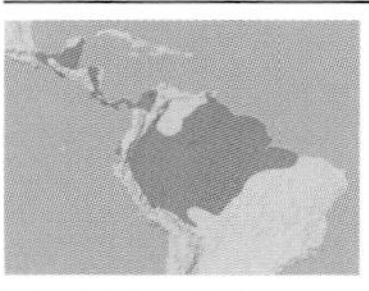

LENGTH 15–18cm (6–7in)

WEIGHT 14g (1/2oz)

MIGRATION Non-migrant

HABITAT Evergreen and deciduous forest and woodland, especially near shady watercourses

The identifiable feature of the Royal Flycatcher, also known as the Amazonian Royal Flycatcher, is its concealed crest. When revealed – during display or when it behaves aggressively – the crown of this hammer-headed bird resembles the fan of a peacock. Each crest feather is elongated, coloured red in the male and orange in the female, with violet-black tips. The effect is enhanced when the bird sways its head and slowly opens and closes its bill to reveal a bright orange mouth.

Hirundinea ferruginea

Cliff Flycatcher

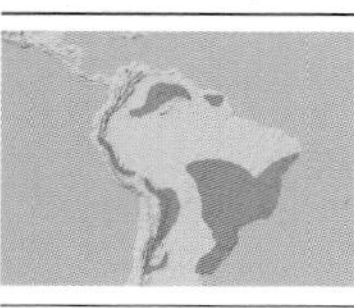

LENGTH 16–19cm (6 1/2–7 1/2in)

WEIGHT 30g (1 1/16oz)

MIGRATION Partial migrant

HABITAT Cliffs, rocky outcrops, slopes affected by landslides, and steep banks, bordered by forest

It is in flight that the Cliff Flycatcher reveals the most distinctive feature of its plumage: the broad rufous band on the wings. It is otherwise largely brown, although some subspecies have chestnut on the belly, rump, and uppertail. Unlike its relatives in its choice of habitat, the Cliff Flycatcher habitually breeds on rockfaces after it finds a suitable ledge and constructs a ring of stones to provide stability to its nest. The Cliff Flycatcher has adapted easily to manmade equivalents of its natural haunts, and its population and distribution are probably increasing as a result. It even nests on high-rise flats in the city of Sao Paulo, Brazil.

The species is also unusual for its foraging behaviour, which it conducts from an exposed perch, such as a rocky outcrop or telephone wire, hunting for insects in spectacular aerial flycatching sallies, as it swoops and glides on its triangular wings.

ADULT CLIFF FLYCATCHER

Sayornis phoebe

Eastern Phoebe

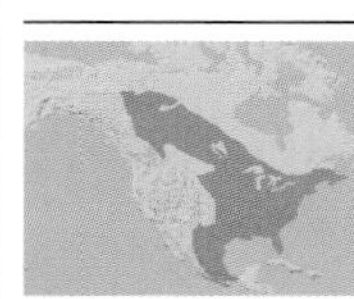

LENGTH 12–16cm (4 1/2–6 1/2in)

WEIGHT 20g (11/16oz)

MIGRATION Partial migrant

HABITAT Forest and forest edges and open deciduous woodland near water; also open areas in winter

Greyish olive on its upperparts, the Eastern Phoebe has a dark crown and chest and white or grey underparts. It has a long, dark tail, which it constantly moves up and down. The male finds and displays potential nest sites to the female, who chooses the site, usually a manmade structure such as a bridge or building, and constructs the nest. This affinity for houses means that the Eastern Phoebe is a familiar bird across much of North America. It has also meant that the species has been able to expand its range and population, despite the clearance of riverside vegetation.

A solitary species, the Eastern Phoebe forages mainly for small flying insects from exposed perches in open areas. Outside the breeding season, it will eat fruit in cold weather. It is a partial migrant – northern populations migrate south to southern USA and Mexico, while southern birds are resident.

ADULT EASTERN PHOEBE

EASTERN PHOEBE
Named after its song (a hoarse "fee-bee"), the Eastern Phoebe often hunts for insects near water. It typically flicks its tail up and down while perching.

Contopus sordidulus

Western Wood Pewee

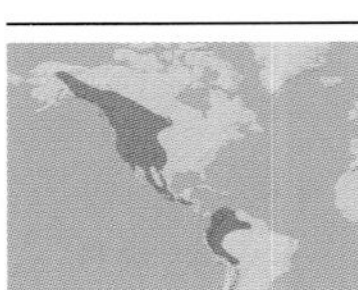

LENGTH 14–16cm (5½–6½in)

WEIGHT 13g (7/16oz)

MIGRATION Migrant

HABITAT Breeds in semi-open mature woodland; winters in tropical forest and forest edges

The Western Wood Pewee's plumage is mainly dark grey-brown, with two indistinct wing-bars and slightly paler eye-ring, belly, and undertail feathers. This bird makes flycatching sallies from exposed perches, taking insects in the air or gleaning prey from foliage. It is a long-distance migrant. It breeds in western USA and migrates through Central America to wintering grounds, mainly in northwest South America.

The Western Wood Pewee is almost identical to its closely related species, the Eastern Wood Pewee (*C. virens*), which is found mainly in southeastern North America. The two species are reliably distinguishable only by song – the Western Wood Pewee has a soft, nasal whistle – although the Western Wood Pewee is darker and has narrower and duller wing-bars.

ADULT WESTERN WOOD PEWEE

Empidonax flaviventris

Yellow-bellied Flycatcher

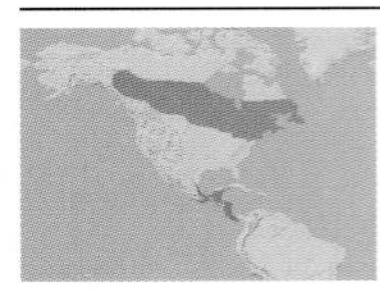

LENGTH 12–15cm (4½–6in)

WEIGHT 12g (7/16oz)

MIGRATION Migrant

HABITAT Breeds in upland coniferous and mixed forest and swamps; winters in dense vegetation

Dull olive above and yellow beneath, the Yellow-bellied Flycatcher has white wing-bars that contrast with its dark wings. It also has a distinct pale eye-ring. It is distinguished from the Acadian Flycatcher (right), a species of the same genus, by its smaller bill, shorter tail, and yellower underparts and differs from the Pacific-slope Flycatcher (below) by its call and brighter upperparts.

A long-distance migrant, the Yellow-bellied Flycatcher breeds in western Canada and northeastern USA, and winters in Central America. Males have longer wings than females and arrive on breeding grounds about four days earlier; it is probable that males and females winter in different areas.

Empidonax virescens

Acadian Flycatcher

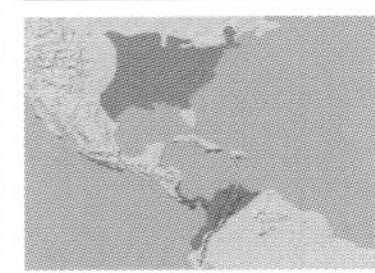

LENGTH 15cm (6in)

WEIGHT 13g (7/16oz)

MIGRATION Migrant

HABITAT Breeds in mature forest, often near water; winters in lowland forest or shady plantations

The Acadian Flycatcher has the longest wings of the *Empidonax* tyrant flycatchers and, accordingly, it migrates the furthest south in winter. It also has the longest and broadest bill of the genus. The Acadian Flycatcher differs in plumage from other members of its genus by its brighter green upperparts and whiter underparts.

ADULT ACADIAN FLYCATCHER

ADULT PACIFIC-SLOPE FLYCATCHER

Empidonax difficilis

Pacific-slope Flycatcher

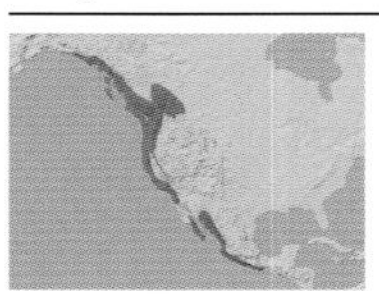

LENGTH 14–17cm (5½–6½in)

WEIGHT 11g (3/8oz)

MIGRATION Migrant

HABITAT Breeds mainly in dense forest with pine trees, often near water; winters in tropical forests

The characteristics of the Pacific-slope Flycatcher – its white eye-ring, yellow throat, and olive green upperparts – epitomize the subtlety of differences between the tyrant flycatchers of the *Empidonax* genus. Formerly considered the same species as the Cordilleran Flycatcher (*E. occidentalis*) of interior western North America, because of the almost identical plumage, the Pacific-slope Flycatcher is now recognized as a separate species, identifiable by its call.

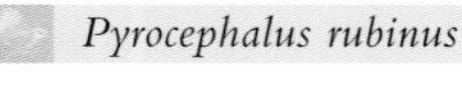

Pyrocephalus rubinus

Vermilion Flycatcher

LENGTH 14cm (5½in)

WEIGHT 14g (½oz)

MIGRATION Partial migrant

HABITAT Variety of open areas, often near water, with scrub, bushes, or trees

With its bright red crown and underparts, contrasting with a dark brown eye mask, ear feathers, and upperparts, the male Vermilion Flycatcher is the most vividly coloured member of a family with largely dull plumage. The female has very different plumage from the male, being pale grey above and white below. This pattern is offset by a dark eye mask, streaked chest, and pink belly and vent.

Widespread from southern North America to northern Patagonia, the Vermilion Flycatcher is a familiar inhabitant of open areas. The male is visible at long range and often attracts attention with its impressive courtship display: its bushy crest raised and chest puffed out, it flutters upwards to about 20m (66ft), singing all the time, before descending.

As might be expected for a species with such a large range, there is considerable variation among its 12 subspecies, two of which are endemic to the Galapagos Islands and are sometimes treated as separate species. Both are considerably smaller than mainland birds, and the females differ considerably in plumage.

MALE VERMILION FLYCATCHER

ADULT WHITE-FRONTED GROUND TYRANT

Muscisaxicola albifrons

White-fronted Ground Tyrant

LENGTH 21cm (8 1/2in)

WEIGHT 35g (1 1/4oz)

MIGRATION Non-migrant

HABITAT Montane grassland, barren rocky or grassy slopes, and bogs at 4,000–5,600m (13,000–18,400ft)

The largest member of its genus, the White-fronted Ground Tyrant has long wings that – at rest – extend a long way down its tail. In a largely homogeneous genus comprising species that look almost identical, the White-fronted Ground Tyrant is relatively distinctive. It has a conspicuous white forehead merging into white eyebrows. The upperparts are grey and the wings silvery, while the underparts are grey, becoming white on the belly and vent. The central tail feathers are dark, and the outer ones are white.

This ground tyrant occurs at perhaps the highest altitude of any member of its family. It is terrestrial, running after prey or chasing it in short flights. Perhaps because of its restricted and inaccessible distribution, this species is not well known.

Xolmis velatus

White-rumped Monjita

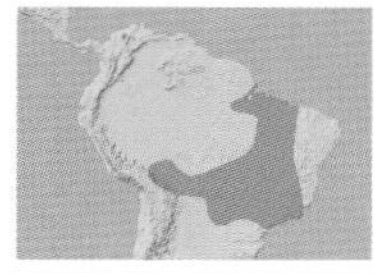

LENGTH 20cm (8in)

WEIGHT 30g (1 1/16oz)

MIGRATION Non-migrant

HABITAT Savanna and semi-open areas with bushes or trees, often near water or buildings or both

Named for its broad white rump, the White-rumped Monjita has a white tail base that contrasts with the black uppertail and the brownish grey back. In flight, a prominent white wing stripe is visible across the base of the flight feathers. The underparts are white, as is most of the head.

The White-rumped Monjita is typical of the monjitas in that it inhabits open grassland areas with scattered bushes or trees. A tame species, it allows observers a close approach as it perches conspicuously on a bush, branch, wire, or fence-post. From these vantage points, the White-rumped Monjita drops to the ground or hovers in search of its insect prey.

While the species is mainly silent, it has a surprisingly intense dawn song, sometimes heard at night, consisting of a whistled "jew" delivered at 1-5 second intervals. Little is known about the breeding habits of the White-rumped Monjita, although in the Brazilian "cerrado" (savanna), the species may use holes in termite mounds that have been excavated by other species, such as Campo Flickers (see p.326) or Orange-fronted Parakeets (*Aratinga canicularis*).

ADULT WHITE-RUMPED MONJITA

ADULT MASKED WATER TYRANT

Fluvicola nengeta

Masked Water Tyrant

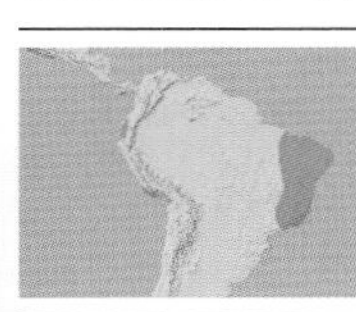

LENGTH 15cm (6in)

WEIGHT 20g (11/16oz)

MIGRATION Non-migrant

HABITAT Semi-open lowland near bodies of fresh water

The Masked Water Tyrant is conspicuous for its bold plumage, which is white in colour, except for the contrasting black eye-stripe, wings, and tail, which has a broad white tip.

The Masked Water Tyrant has an impressive courtship display. Pairs of these birds face each other with their tails spread out and also raised, bobbing up and down continuously. Sometimes the male fans its tail and spreads its wings horizontally to reveal the black underside.

Unusually for most tyrant flycatchers, the Masked Water Tyrant is rarely seen away from water and is even happy standing in it. These birds feed singly or in pairs, on open scrubby ground, marshes, usually along the edges of watercourses, and even on floating vegetation. They hunt aquatic insects typically by darting forward and striking at their prey. A usually tame species, Masked Water Tyrants are found in Brazil, Ecuador, and Peru.

Megarynchus pitangua

Boat-billed Flycatcher

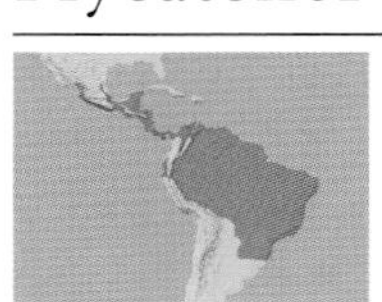

LENGTH 21–24cm (8 1/2–9 1/2in)

WEIGHT 70g (2 1/2oz)

MIGRATION Partial migrant

HABITAT Various wooded and forest habitats, and semi-open areas with tall trees

Almost identical to the common and widespread Great Kiskadee (see p.348), although the two are not closely related, the Boat-billed Flycatcher has a black crown with a concealed orange patch, white eyebrow, black eye-stripe, white throat, brownish olive upperparts, and yellow underparts. However, it differs from the Great Kiskadee in being larger with greener upperparts and browner wings and tail; most noticeably, it also has a curved bill that is stouter and broader than that of the Great Kiskadee. The Boat-billed Flycatcher has the biggest bill of all the tyrant flycatchers and uses it to catch large insects and even small reptiles and amphibians, which are bashed against a perch before being consumed.

The Boat-billed Flycatcher nods its head as it calls: the most distinctive sound is a nasal, repeated "nay-nay" – when a pair calls together, the duet is poorly synchronized. It also has a distinctive dawn song.

Colonia colonus

Long-tailed Tyrant

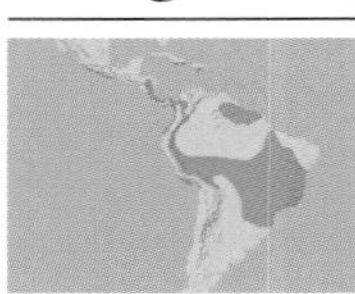

LENGTH 18–28cm (7–11in)

WEIGHT 18g (5/8oz)

MIGRATION Partial migrant

HABITAT Edges and clearings in humid tropical forest, secondary woodland

Aptly named for its most peculiar feature – the elongated, blade-shaped central tail feathers – the Long-tailed Tyrant is distinctive. These feathers are flicked up and down when the bird calls and appear to be ornamental in function. The male is predominantly black with a white forehead, crown, and rump, while the female is greyer, with shorter tail streamers.

Found in Brazil, the Long-tailed Tyrant spends much of its time in the forest canopy, mostly on an exposed branch or on dead tree stumps with holes or cavities that it can use for nesting. From a high perch, it undertakes flycatching sallies of up to 10m (33ft) in length, specializing in catching stingless sweatbees.

ADULT MALE

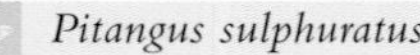

Pitangus sulphuratus

Great Kiskadee

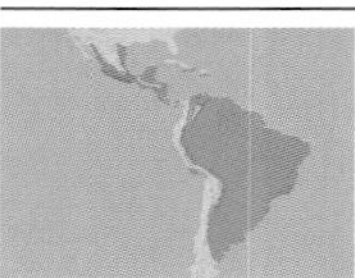

LENGTH 20–23cm (8–9in)

WEIGHT 65g (2 3/8oz)

MIGRATION Partial migrant

HABITAT Wide variety of habitats from urban areas to open grassland and forest edges

The call of the Great Kiskadee is one of the most familiar sounds of South America: the loud, shrill "kiss-ka-dee" gives the species its common name. The Great Kiskadee is a large, boldly patterned, and colourful tyrant flycatcher. Its black crown (with a semi-concealed yellow crown patch) and broad black eye mask contrast with the striking white eyebrow and throat. The upperparts are olive-brown, with rufous edges to the tail and wings, and the underparts are a vivid yellow. It has a broad black bill.

The Great Kiskadee's diet is the most varied of all tyrant flycatchers, cementing its place as the family's top ecological generalist. While it mainly flycatches for insects and eats fruit, this species will also catch small vertebrates such as nestling birds, lizards, snakes, frogs, and mice. Uniquely among its family, the Great Kiskadee also dives for fish like a kingfisher, usually beating its prey on a perch before eating it.

The broad range of habitats used by the Great Kiskadee means that it has benefited from human activities. It has spread into urban areas and uses manmade fibres to build its nest.

ADULT GREAT KISKADEE

ADULT CATTLE TYRANT

Machetornis rixosa

Cattle Tyrant

LENGTH 19cm (7 1/2in)

WEIGHT 30g (1 1/16oz)

MIGRATION Partial migrant

HABITAT Semi-open and open areas, including agricultural land and city parks

With mainly dull olive-brown upperparts and a darker eye-stripe, the Cattle Tyrant has pale yellow underparts. Like several other tyrant flycatchers, it has a concealed red or orange crest. As its name suggests, the Cattle Tyrant is best known for its affinity with cattle, feeding on insects they disturb and even using them as look-out perches. However, the Cattle Tyrant predates the arrival of livestock in the South American continent, so its association with animals must have started with native mammals, such as the Capybara. The Cattle Tyrant is a bird of open areas, often seen running after insects in urban green spaces.

In plumage, it resembles the *Tyrannus* kingbirds, such as the Tropical Kingbird (below). However, unlike the arboreal kingbirds, it is a terrestrial species. Its physical characteristics – short, rounded wings and long legs – also differ. Moreover, research shows that there is no particular genetic affinity between the two species.

Tyrannus melancholicus

Tropical Kingbird

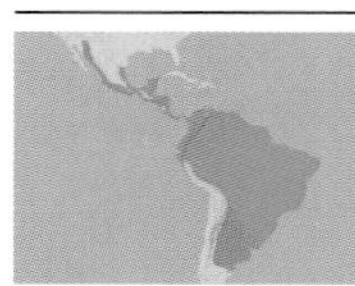

LENGTH 18–24cm (7–9 1/2in)

WEIGHT 35g (1 1/4oz)

MIGRATION Partial migrant

HABITAT Almost any form of open or semi-open area with trees, often near water

The Tropical Kingbird is the largest and most common kingbird, with an estimated population of 200 million occurring over a very large range. This kingbird has a grey crown and nape, with a darker eye mask that contrasts with its white throat. In common with many tyrant flycatchers, it also has a concealed reddish orange crown patch. The mantle and wings are grey-green, the underparts bright yellow, and the notched tail is brown.

The species' tendency to act aggressively with larger birds – even up to the size of a vulture – has given rise to both its genus name (like a tyrant) and its common name (the king of birds). Almost exclusively insectivorous, it catches its prey in the air, with its sallies starting almost always from a high perch, usually above 25–30m (80–100ft). It often perches near flowers and muddy areas to target the butterflies that congregate at such sites.

ADULT TROPICAL KINGBIRD

Tyrannus forficatus

Scissor-tailed Flycatcher

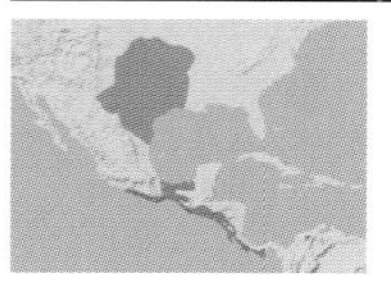

LENGTH 19–38cm ($7^1/_2$–15in)

WEIGHT 40g ($1^7/_{16}$oz)

MIGRATION Migrant

HABITAT Open and semi-open grassland and savanna with scattered bushes and trees

A spectacular species, the Scissor-tailed Flycatcher is a common sight in open areas of North and Central America. The highly elongated outer tail feathers, from which the species derives its name, occur in just four tyrant flycatchers. The purpose of this adaptation, as with swallows, appears to be to aid manoeuvrability in the air. The deeply forked tail helps the bird twist for flying insects during its hawking sallies from an exposed perch. But such an impressive appendage also serves in the male's zigzag courtship display: sexual selection may favour longer tails. The male's plumage is as distinguishable as its tail length: the very pale grey head and back are offset by dark upperwings and salmon-pink underwings and vent.

The Scissor-tailed Flycatcher occurs singly or in pairs during the breeding season, but large flocks form during migration and in winter.

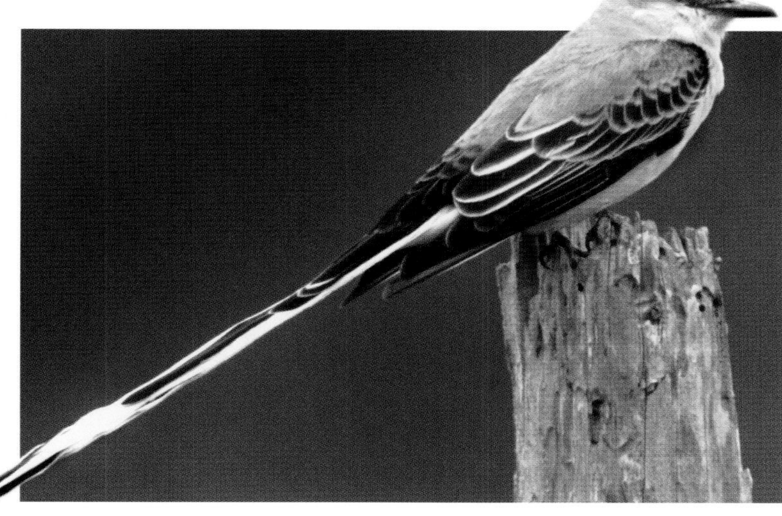

MALE SCISSOR-TAILED FLYCATCHER

Tyrannus tyrannus

Eastern Kingbird

LENGTH 19–23cm ($7^1/_2$–9in)

WEIGHT 40g ($1^7/_{16}$oz)

MIGRATION Migrant

HABITAT Forested and open terrain, ranging from humid forest edges to gardens

A familiar bird across the Americas, with perhaps 13 million breeding throughout North America and wintering in South America, the Eastern Kingbird differs in plumage from most kingbirds. While other kingbirds are mostly grey and yellow, the Eastern Kingbird is essentially black and white. It has black ear feathers and a black crown, dark grey mantle and wings, and a white-tipped black tail. The underparts are mainly white, although the breast is grey. The wings are relatively short and narrow, creating a distinctive shape in flight. The attenuated primary feathers probably cause the wing whirrs that can often be heard.

While solitary or forming pairs on breeding grounds, the Eastern Kingbird is gregarious on wintering grounds. Huge flocks of thousands of birds may gather at fruiting trees, particularly in the west Amazonian area where the largest numbers winter. On breeding grounds, the Eastern Kingbird hawks for insects from any available perch. On migration and wintering grounds, however, it eats fruit and seeds.

BREEDING PAIR

black and white plumage

Myiarchus crinitus

Great Crested Flycatcher

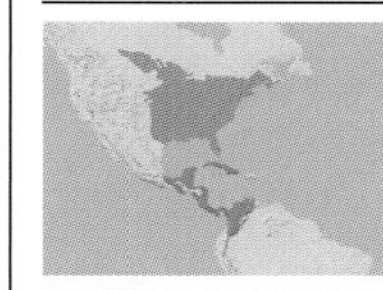

LENGTH 21cm ($8^1/_2$in)

WEIGHT 30g ($1^1/_{16}$oz)

MIGRATION Migrant

HABITAT Open deciduous woodland and edges of clearings; also in humid tropical forest in winter

One of the largest and most richly patterned of the relatively homogeneous group of *Myiarchus* flycatchers, the Great Crested Flycatcher has the same basic plumage pattern as other species in this group. It is olive-green above, with its grey head and chest sharply demarcated from a yellow belly and undertail feathers. It has rufous wings, pale wing-bars, and a rufous tail, which together with its contrasting underparts help distinguish it from the closely related Brown-crested Flycatcher (*M. tyrannulus*). As is typical of *Myiarchus* flycatchers, the rear of its crown is peaked, creating a crested appearance.

ADULT GREAT CRESTED FLYCATCHER

ANTBIRDS

ORDER	Passeriformes
FAMILY	Thamnophilidae
SPECIES	205

ANTBIRDS ARE SO NAMED because some species follow swarms of army ants to eat the insects and other small animals flushed out by the ants. They are found in Central America and in the northern half of South America, with the greatest diversity of species in the Amazon Basin. Some authorities place them in the same family as antpittas and antthrushes (see p.354). They are also closely related to gnateaters (see p.352). Most antbirds live in dense forest, but some species occur in forest clearings, thickets, gardens, and savanna.

ANATOMY

There are several distinct groups of antbird, which differ in both size and structure. The antwrens and antvireos are small birds with a slender, warbler-like bill that they use to pick insects off leaves in lower and middle levels of the forest. Antshrikes are larger, longer-tailed birds with a strong, hooked bill, like that of true shrikes (see p.382). They live in open habitats as well as forest, and often drop to the ground to catch prey. Most antbirds are grey, black, or brown, but some antshrikes have bold patterns of bars and stripes.

IDENTIFICATION CHALLENGE
The Unicolored Antwren is one of several dozen similar species that can be very hard to separate in the field.

PLUMAGE DIFFERENCES
In many species of antbird the male and female look strikingly different. This is a female Giant Antshrike; the male of this species is black-and-white barred above and grey below.

BEHAVIOUR

Antbirds live in monogamous breeding pairs and usually mate for life, sharing nest-building and the feeding of the two or three young. They defend a nesting territory, but often join mixed-species flocks to travel through the forest in search of food. These flocks are largest in the early morning and late afternoon and may contain hundreds of individuals, including representatives of numerous other species of antbird, as well as other forest birds. Some antbirds are known as "professional ant-followers", because they feed almost entirely by following columns of army ants across the forest floor.

CUP-SHAPED NEST
A female Slaty Antwren brings food for her chicks. All antbirds make an open nest in the fork of a branch, often low down or among the undergrowth.

Myrmotherula gularis

Star-throated Antwren

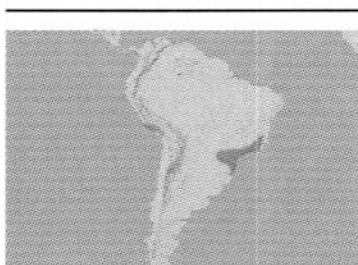

LENGTH 8.5–9.5cm (3¼–3¾in)
WEIGHT 10–12g (3/8–7/16oz)
MIGRATION Non-migrant
HABITAT Understorey of evergreen forest

Distinguishable by its black and white speckled throat, the Star-throated Antwren has a dark eye and grey face, brown upperparts with a distinct white-lined black patch on the wing, and grey underparts. Like other antwrens it has a short-tailed, round-bodied appearance. Confined to the Atlantic forest of Brazil, the species is uncommon, although not considered to be globally threatened.

ADULT STAR-THROATED ANTWREN

Biatas nigropectus

White-bearded Antshrike

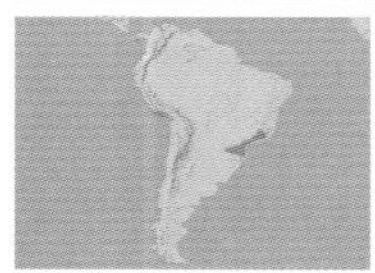

LENGTH 18cm (7in)
WEIGHT 25–35g (7/8–1¼oz)
MIGRATION Non-migrant
HABITAT Understorey of bamboo-rich, evergreen forest, in the understorey and edges of thickets
RED LIST CATEGORY Vulnerable

A rare bird, the White-bearded Antshrike is found only in the Atlantic forest of southeast Brazil and northeast Argentina. Its entire global population is estimated at fewer than 10,000 individuals and this number is thought to be decreasing due to the rapid destruction of the species' habitat, which has been converted to agricultural use, mining, and urban expansion.

The male has a striking black cap and triangular black breast patch, separated by a broad white band under the bill. The rest of its plumage is largely brown. The female lacks any black, and has a chestnut cap and a plain white throat that contrasts with its buff underparts. The diet of this species consists mainly of spiders, as well as ants and other insects.

MALE WHITE-BEARDED ANTSHRIKE

MALE GREAT ANTSHRIKE

Taraba major

Great Antshrike

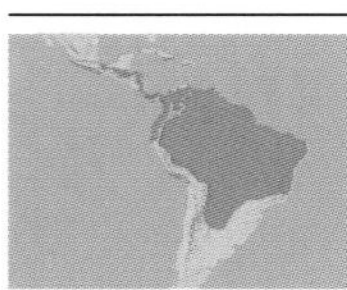

LENGTH 20cm (8in)
WEIGHT 50–70g (1¾–2½oz)
MIGRATION Non-migrant
HABITAT Understorey of dense thickets

One of the most widely distributed members of its family, the Great Antshrike is found from Mexico to Argentina. The male is a striking bird, jet-black above and white below, with a bright red eye and three prominent white wing-bars. The female is different, being chestnut above and pale buff below. This antshrike is an opportunistic feeder, eating a varied diet that includes snails, slugs, and even small rodents and fish.

ADULT FEMALE
With black and white barring on the sides of the head and the neck only, the female is plainer than the male.

ADULT MALE
In contrast to the female, the male has a black crown and striking horizontal black and white bars all over its body.

Thamnophilus doliatus

Barred Antshrike

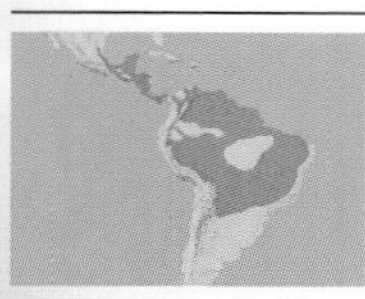

LENGTH 16cm (6 1/2in)

WEIGHT 25–30g (7/8–1 1/16oz)

MIGRATION Non-migrant

HABITAT Understorey and mid-levels of mainly deciduous forest

Like most antbirds, the male and female Barred Antshrikes have very different plumage. The male Barred Antshrike has the barred black and white plumage implied by its name. The female, however, has a much plainer plumage with chestnut brown upperparts and slightly paler orange-buff underparts. Both sexes sing, the female often echoing the male.

The Barred Antshrike is usually found in pairs, hopping about in vegetation or searching for food in foliage. It can often be seen on a perch, scanning for beetles or other insects before deftly swooping to pick one up. It also eats fruit and seeds. This bird nests in shrubs. The female lays two eggs, which are incubated by both parents. The Barred Antshrike is a common bird throughout most of its large range, which stretches from Mexico to northern Argentina.

MALE SQUAMATE ANTBIRD

Myrmeciza squamosa

Squamate Antbird

LENGTH 15cm (6in)

WEIGHT 16–20g (9/16–11/16oz)

MIGRATION Non-migrant

HABITAT Forest floor in a variety of woodland types

An attractive species, the male Squamate Antbird is rufous-brown above with a black face and throat. Its breast is also black and flecked with crescent-shaped white markings. The female has a black patch around the eye and a white throat and breast with scalloped markings. The species is confined to the Atlantic forest of southeast Brazil.

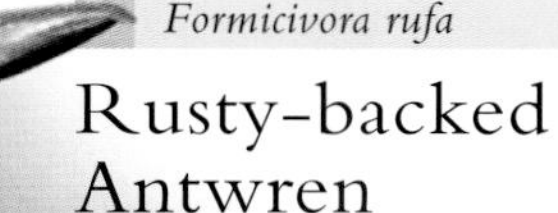

Formicivora rufa

Rusty-backed Antwren

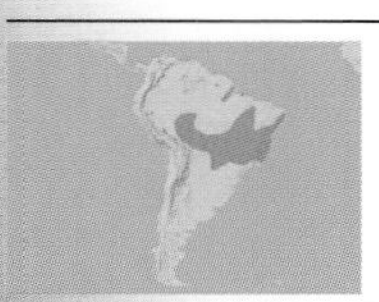

LENGTH 13cm (5in)

WEIGHT 12–14g (7/16–1/2oz)

MIGRATION Non-migrant

HABITAT Undergrowth in a variety of scrubland habitats

The male Rusty-backed Antwren has a black face, a rufous crown and upperparts, and underparts that are bordered by a distinct white line. Its wing has a broad, noticeable dark bar covered with white spots. The female lacks the black face and breast; instead, it has pale, heavily streaked underparts. The male juvenile resembles the female, but has spotted, rather than streaked, underparts.

The Rusty-backed Antwren is an active bird, hopping and fluttering in short bursts, often pausing to look for insects. Pairs or small family groups are usually seen together, feeding low down in small trees, scrub, or grass, their tails characteristically cocked – pairs sing loudly to communicate with each other. After swallowing its prey, this bird has been observed to wipe its bill on a branch. Although generally common, the Rusty-backed Antwren has a rather fragmented range in Peru, Brazil, Bolivia, and Paraguay.

MALE RUSTY-BACKED ANTWREN

Drymophila ferruginea

Ferruginous Antbird

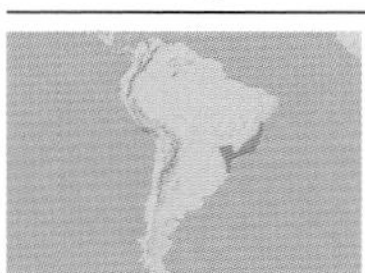

LENGTH 13cm (5in)

WEIGHT 10g (3/8oz)

MIGRATION Non-migrant

HABITAT Bamboo thickets in evergreen forest

The Ferruginous Antbird is common throughout most of its range in southeast Brazil. It has a striped black and white head, rufous-orange underparts, black wings with a distinct white bar, and a black tail. The female is slightly paler and more streaked than the male, though this is not always easy to see. The Ferruginous Antbird is very similar to Bertoni's Antbird (*D. rubricollis*), also found in southeast Brazil and parts of Paraguay and Argentina. However, the Ferruginous Antbird has black markings on its back and a darker tail. It is usually found in pairs or small family groups, as well as in mixed-species flocks. It is a very active forager, moving around in short hops, before pausing to scan for prey. It usually feeds a few metres off the ground, on various kinds of insects. Like many of its close relatives, the Ferruginous Antbird is found exclusively in bamboo thickets.

ADULT FERRUGINOUS ANTBIRD

Pithys albifrons

White-plumed Antbird

LENGTH 11–13cm (4 1/2–5in)

WEIGHT 18–25g (5/8–7/8oz)

MIGRATION Non-migrant

HABITAT Understorey of humid evergreen forest

With magnificent white facial plumes on its black face, the White-plumed Antbird is one of the most unusual members of its family. It has grey upperparts and orange-brown underparts. It feeds on insects and is dependent on army ants to obtain its food, waiting for huge swarms to flush out small creatures in their path. The bird then darts out to snatch up its food, quickly retreating to cover. This species nests in trees, laying 2 or 3 eggs, which are incubated by both parents.

Gymnopithys leucaspis

Bicoloured Antbird

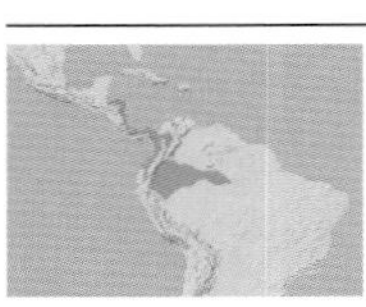

LENGTH 14–15cm (5 1/2–6in)

WEIGHT 30–35g (1 1/16–1 1/4oz)

MIGRATION Non-migrant

HABITAT Understorey of humid forest and old secondary growth

Both the male and female Bicolored Antbird have white throats and underparts, but there is geographical variation in the darkness of the flanks and sides and the colour of the area around the eyes. This bird follows army-ants, feeding on insects, spiders, and even small frogs and lizards disturbed by the ants.

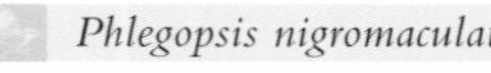

ADULT BICOLOURED ANTBIRD

Phlegopsis nigromaculata

Black-spotted Bare-eye

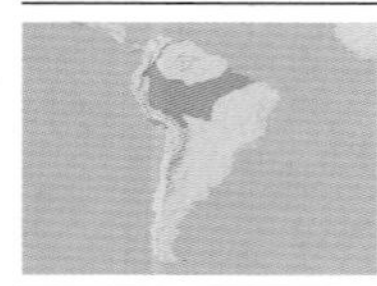

LENGTH 17–18cm (6 1/2–7in)

WEIGHT 40–50g (1 7/16–1 3/4oz)

MIGRATION Non-migrant

HABITAT Understorey of humid lowland forest; occasionally in seasonally flooded areas

The loud, harsh calls of the Black-spotted Bare-eye signal the presence of an ant swarm, which it follows, feeding on the insects that it disturbs. Up to 20 birds may attend a single swarm, where it is one of the most dominant antbird species, because of its large size, but there is a "pecking order" within the species, too. Both male and female have a patch of red skin around the eyes and the same combination of deep black on the head and breast, and brown on the back and wings.

ADULT BLACK-SPOTTED BARE-EYE

Hylophylax naevioides

Spotted Antbird

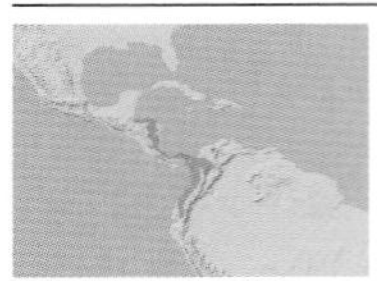

LENGTH 11–12cm (4 1/2in)

WEIGHT 15–18g (9/16–5/8oz)

MIGRATION Non-migrant

HABITAT Understorey of humid forest and tall secondary growth in lowland and foothills

The male Spotted Antbird has a dark grey head, chestnut back and wing-bars, and white underparts that are spotted black. The female is similar, but has a paler spotting and a brown head. The species follows ant swarms in pairs or family groups, darting through the low foliage above and around the ants, looking for insects and arthropods fleeing from the path of the swarm. Being a small antbird, it is subordinate to the larger ant-following species.

Phaenostictus mcleannani

Ocellated Antbird

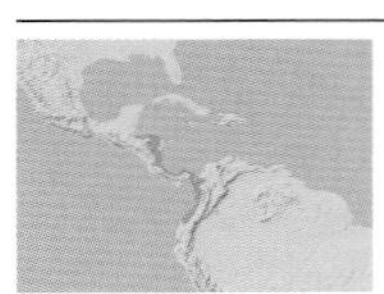

LENGTH 19–20cm (7 1/2–8in)

WEIGHT 50–55g (1 3/4–2oz)

MIGRATION Non-migrant

HABITAT Understorey of humid forest, tall second growth in lowlands; occasionally in shaded plantations

Both sexes of the Ocellated Antbird are alike, with a large patch of naked blue skin around the eyes, heavily spotted brown back, wings, and rufous underparts. The Ocellated Antbird is an ant swarm follower and dominates many smaller antbirds, although it is subordinate to some other species that periodically attend the ants to find easy prey. This species shows complex social behaviour – up to eight, often young, birds congregate around a pair which tolerates their presence for unknown reasons. Both sexes incubate the eggs, and the young attend swarms just 2 or 3 weeks after hatching.

ADULT OCELLATED ANTBIRD

GNATEATERS

ORDER	Passeriformes
FAMILY	Conopophagidae
SPECIES	8

DUE TO THEIR extremely short tails and their shy, ground-living lifestyle in the dense forests of tropical South America, the gnateaters are rather like small antpittas (see p.354), with which they used to be grouped. These birds are insect-eaters and feed in the leaf litter. The male has a simple, sweet-sounding song, and forms a stable breeding pair with the female. The birds remain in the same area of forest all year.

SHORT TAIL
A stumpy tail helps gnateaters, such as this male Black-cheeked Gnateater, to creep and flutter through tangled rainforest undergrowth.

Conopophaga lineata

Rufous Gnateater

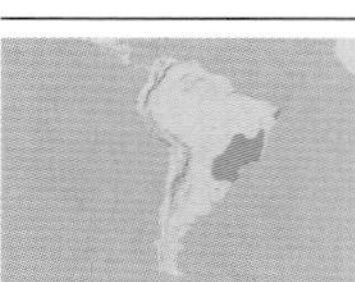

LENGTH 11–14cm (4 1/2–5 1/2in)

WEIGHT 16–25g (9/16–7/8oz)

MIGRATION Non-migrant

HABITAT Forest and well-developed secondary growth; often found in or close to bamboo

This robin-like bird is rufous-chestnut on the front and underparts, with an earth-brown back and wings, and a short, stubby tail. The male has well-developed grey eyebrows. The female lays two eggs and incubates them at night and for part of the day, with the male sitting on the nest for the rest of the day. The young hatch after 14 days and fledge in two weeks, although juveniles may remain with their parents for another one and a half months.

MALE RUFOUS GNATEATER

TAPACULOS

ORDER Passeriformes
FAMILY Rhinocryptidae
SPECIES 55

UNIQUE TO SOUTH AMERICA, tapaculos are found mostly in the continent's cooler, temperate regions, especially on forested slopes in the Andes and in woodland and scrub in the south. Some tapaculos resemble wrens, but others are fatter-bodied. They live on or near the ground, scraping around with their feet, like gamebirds, to find seeds and invertebrates. These weak fliers often hold their tail vertical. One of the most distinctive features of tapaculos, not visible from a distance, is a movable flap of loose skin covering each nostril.

HUMID HABITAT
The Ocellated Tapaculo lives in impenetrable bamboo thickets and damp, mossy forests on the slopes of the western Andes.

Rhinocrypta lanceolata

Crested Gallito

LENGTH 21cm (8½in)
WEIGHT 51–64g (1¾–2⅜oz)
MIGRATION Non-migrant

HABITAT Open thorn brush and undergrowth in Chaco woodland

The Crested Gallito has a finely spotted, white-streaked head, a spiked crest, grey breast, and slightly rufous belly and flanks. The upperparts and long tail are brown. It lives mainly on the ground hopping or running through the undergrowth, but sings from a low perch. The nest is a spherical structure of grass, weeds, and bark, in which two eggs are laid. Being large in size, it is one of the few tapaculos to be a target for brood parasitism by the Shiny Cowbird.

Scytalopus unicolor

Unicolored Tapaculo

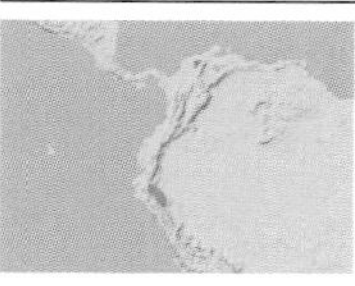

LENGTH 11cm (4½in)
WEIGHT 17–19g (⅝–11/16oz)
MIGRATION Non-migrant

HABITAT Dense shrubbery within montane forest

The life history of this bird is almost completely unknown, despite having been described more than 110 years ago. Most of the small tapaculos in the genus *Scytalopus* are known for their lack of plumage features, but the Unicolored Tapaculo is perhaps the most nondescript. It is darker grey above and paler grey below; the juvenile is browner above, with barring on the tail. Although confined to a tiny area in the Andes, it is fairly common and not threatened.

MALE SLATY BRISTLEFRONT

GREAT SITES

ITATIAIA NATIONAL PARK

Situated between Rio de Janeiro and São Paulo, but in most part untouched by humankind, this national park is one of the oldest in Brazil and a haven for the rich birdlife of the Atlantic forest region. The Slaty Bristlefront is just one of several tapaculos found here.

Merulaxis ater

Slaty Bristlefront

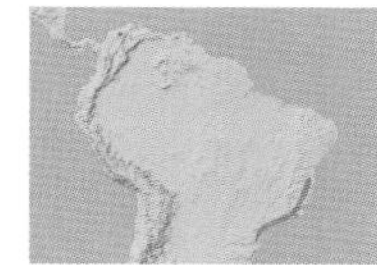

LENGTH 19cm (7½in)
WEIGHT 35–40g (1¼–1 7/16oz)
MIGRATION Non-migrant

HABITAT Understorey of humid forest and tall secondary growth in lowland and mountains

The Slaty Bristlefront is an unusual tapaculo, the male and female being different in plumage. The male is virtually all grey with brown on the rear, and the female is mainly brown with warmer-coloured underparts. Unlike other tapaculos, it has a tuft of bristles above the base of the bill and a long and broad tail. Pairs keep close together, in continuous vocal contact. The bird's song is considered one of the most lovely of the Brazilian Atlantic Forest.

Liosceles thoracicus

Rusty-belted Tapaculo

LENGTH 20cm (8in)
WEIGHT 40–45g (1 7/16–1⅝oz)
MIGRATION Non-migrant

HABITAT Ground-level in rainforest, mainly in dry areas, and often around treefalls

The male and female Rusty-belted Tapaculo are alike, with a white eyebrow and throat, mottled cheeks, brown upperparts, rufous breast-band, and scaled underparts. Three different subspecies have been described, but variation between them is not well marked. The Rusty-belted Tapaculo is usually found alone or in pairs, walking or hopping across the forest floor, searching for bugs in the litter or along fallen logs. Very little is known about its breeding behaviour, and only one nest has ever been found. The nest is spherical, with an opening at the top, and made up of small twigs, grass, lichen, and moss. Within its range, the Rusty-belted Tapaculo is uncommon to locally fairly common.

ADULT RUSTY-BELTED TAPACULO

ANTPITTAS AND ANTTHRUSHES

ORDER	Passeriformes
FAMILY	Formicariidae
SPECIES	60

SELDOM SEEN, these secretive birds live on the forest floor and among thick undergrowth in South and Central America, particularly in the rainforests of the Amazon region and in the cloudforests of the Andes mountains. They are related to antbirds (see p.350), and some ornithologists group them in a single family. Unlike antbirds, however, most antpittas and antthrushes do not seek out swarms of army ants. Their loud, far-carrying calls, which are often melancholy whistles, can be the only way to locate well-hidden birds.

ANATOMY

The birds in this family live almost exclusively on the ground, and are well adapted to this lifestyle. They have an upright posture, with strong legs and feet, and their short, rounded wings are ideal for a rapid burst of flight into cover when disturbed. Antpittas are virtually tailless, in this respect resembling the pittas (see p.336) of the Old World, but the antthrushes have a fairly long tail, which they hold cocked in an upright position. Antpittas hop across the forest floor, pausing regularly to inspect the leaf litter for invertebrate prey, whereas antthrushes walk, flicking their tail as they go. In all species, the sexes are alike, with a subdued plumage in brown, rufous, grey, or black tones.

AN ELUSIVE FAMILY
Antpittas and antthrushes, such as this Yellow-breasted Antpitta, are among the hardest South American birds to see.

Formicarius analis

Black-faced Antthrush

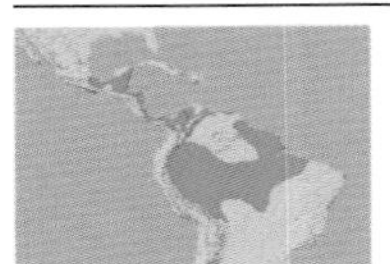

LENGTH 17cm (6½in)
WEIGHT 45–70g (1⅝–2½oz)
MIGRATION Non-migrant
HABITAT Humid mature forest and secondary growth, and lowlands

Largely grey below and brown above, the Black-faced Antthrush has a small black patch on its face, with occasional rufous colouring on its cheeks, blue skin around the eye, and a rufous patch under the tail. The male and female are alike in plumage. These birds have short, cocked tails, their heads and tails bobbing up and down as they feed on ants and insects on the ground and walk on leaf litter. The call is a whistle, with a descending "wu-wu-wu-wu". There are geographical variations in the plumage and song of this species.

Pittasoma rufopileatum

Rufous-crowned Antpitta

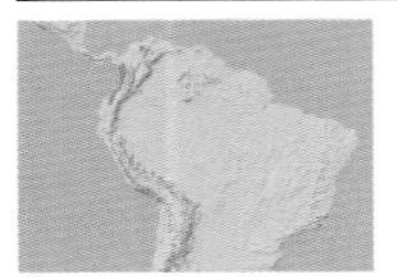

LENGTH 16–18cm (6½–7in)
WEIGHT 95g (3⅜oz)
MIGRATION Non-migrant
HABITAT Lowland and foothills, in wet forest and secondary growth

Unlike other pittas, which have brown or grey plumage, most subspecies of the Rufous-crowned Antpitta have an entirely rufous head, with a long black eyebrow, except for birds in Ecuador, which have only a rufous crown. The upperparts are dark brown, streaked with black, and the underparts are either white or buff, barred with black, or are pale and unmarked. The female usually has white spots on the black eyebrow. The species mainly feeds by following columns of army ants, taking the insects flushed out by them.

Grallaria alleni

Moustached Antpitta

LENGTH 17cm (6½in)
WEIGHT 65–80g (2⅜–2⅞oz)
MIGRATION Non-migrant
HABITAT Ravines and steep slopes of wet, moss-laden primary growth in mountains
RED LIST CATEGORY Endangered

Named for its bold white moustache, the Moustached Antpitta has a bluish grey crown and nape, white feathering on the lower throat, and warm buff-coloured underparts. Its call is a series of deep whistles, sounding like "hu-u hu-u", as it increases in volume before trailing off. Until 1990, this antpitta was known only from two specimens, but it was rediscovered in Ecuador and subsequently the species has been found in national parks and other protected areas in Ecuador and Colombia.

ADULT MOUSTACHED ANTPITTA

OVENBIRDS

ORDER	Passeriformes
FAMILY	Furnariidae
SPECIES	236

THE OVENBIRDS are a large, diverse group of rather drably coloured insect-eaters, most of which have plain brown upperparts and pale underparts. They live throughout South and Central America, in virtually all habitats. The family is named for the domed mud nests, which resemble traditional bread ovens, made by true ovenbirds.

BEHAVIOUR

Many ovenbirds, including the horneros, miners, and cachalotes, are found in dry, open country such as savanna or scrub. A few species are reluctant fliers that prefer to run across the ground. The cinclodes live beside fresh water or along the seashore. Most other members of the family live in forest, in the canopy or in the undergrowth.

DARK PLUMAGE
The Blackish Cinclodes is an unusually dark member of the ovenbird family, found in Tierra del Fuego and on the Falkland Islands. It lives on rocky coasts and in areas of tussock grass.

Geositta cunicularia

Common Miner

LENGTH 14–17cm (5½–6½in)
WEIGHT 20–35g (11/16–1¼oz)
MIGRATION Non-migrant
HABITAT Grassland and scrub from coasts to the high Andes, usually in areas with sandy soil and rocks

Like many ground-dwelling birds, Common Miners can be quite variable in their coloration. However, all subspecies have a slender, slightly decurved bill, a white eyebrow, some rufous colouring in the wings, and dark markings on the breast. The call of this bird is a rapid trill. It feeds on insects and seeds gleaned from the ground. The species nests in holes excavated in earth banks, and may raise two broods of 2–3 young in each. It is generally common to abundant over most of its range.

Pseudoseisura unirufa

Grey-crested Cachalote

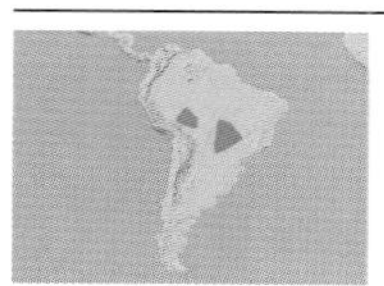

LENGTH 20cm (8in)
WEIGHT 40–55g (1 7/16–2 oz)
MIGRATION Non-migrant
HABITAT Gallery forest and seasonally flooded savanna, often near water and habitation

Despite its small range at the junction of the borders of Brazil, Bolivia, and Paraguay, the Grey-crested Cachalote is not rare. It does not shun contact with humans and often constructs its oblong stick nests in trees around human dwellings. Its presence is often made known by its song, which is audible at some distance. The plumage is unremarkable – it is entirely deep rufous-brown, relieved only by the prominent grey crest and bright yellow eyes. The Grey-crested Cachalote feeds mainly on arthropods dug from the ground, as well as fruit and seeds.

Most aspects of the species' behaviour are not very well known, largely because the Grey-crested Cachlote has only recently been recognized as a species. It was formerly considered to belong to the same species as *P. cristata*, found in northeast Brazil, which, however, lacks the grey crest and has a different song. The two species may also differ in their breeding systems – unlike the Grey-crested Cachlote, *P. cristata* is a cooperative breeder.

ADULT GREY-CRESTED CACHALOTE

Furnarius rufus

Rufous Hornero

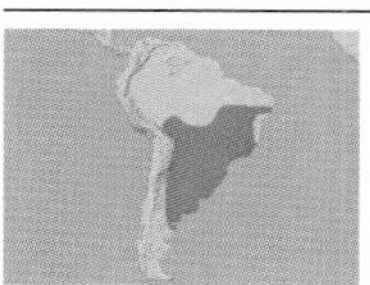

LENGTH 16–23cm (6½–9in)
WEIGHT 30–65g (1 1/16–2 3/8 oz)
MIGRATION Non-migrant
HABITAT Open habitats, from city parks to agricultural areas and scrub, mainly in lowlands

With its jaunty gait and vociferous calls sung by pairs in duets, the Rufous Hornero is common in populated areas, seeming at home in the busiest parks and gardens in cities. It is rufous-brown above, with a faint white eyebrow, dull white chin, a red-rufous tail, and pale underparts. Like other horneros, it has a long, strong, and slightly curved bill, which it uses to dig out invertebrates, seeds, insect larvae, and arthropods on the ground, often foraging in pairs. It flies up into trees when disturbed. Its nest may be sited on high branches.

ADULT RUFOUS HORNERO

MUD NESTS

Dome-shaped like a charcoal oven called a "horno" in South America, the mud and clay nest of the Rufous Hornero may have one or two openings. Often sited on top of a fence or post, it may remain there for several years, though it is used only once.

SPIKY TAIL AND RUFOUS EYEBROW

Aphrastura spinicauda

Thorn-tailed Rayadito

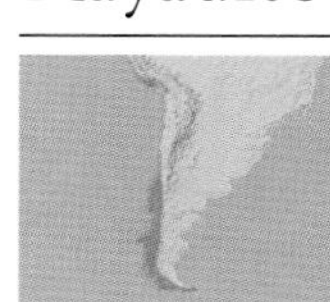

LENGTH 14cm (5½in)
WEIGHT 10–13g (3/8–7/16 oz)
MIGRATION Non-migrant
HABITAT Southern beech forest in lowland and foothills, but also less-vegetated areas

This diminutive bird can be recognized by its broad rufous-buff eyebrow, jagged wing pattern, and spiky rufous tail. The Thorn-tailed Rayadito frequently forms flocks in the non-breeding season. In constant movement as it gleans the foliage and bark of trees, it often acts as a nucleus for other species of birds to join into foraging groups. It nests in tree-holes or behind bark.

Cinclodes antarcticus

Blackish Cinclodes

LENGTH 19–23cm (7½–9in)
WEIGHT 45g (1 5/8 oz)
MIGRATION Non-migrant
HABITAT Coastal beaches, usually with rocks, and especially near seabird or seal colonies

True to its name, the Blackish Cinclodes is readily identified by its dark plumage. One of the southernmost breeding passerines in the world, it makes its living along shorelines, where it feeds on marine invertebrates and their larvae, pecking through holes in kelp debris with its long, decurved bill. In some areas, it also feeds on fish scraps and on the cracked eggs of penguins and cormorants.

ADULT BLACKISH CINCLODES

Asthenes pudibunda

Canyon Canastero

LENGTH 15–17cm (6–6½in)
WEIGHT 13–17g (7/16–5/8 oz)
MIGRATION Non-migrant
HABITAT Arid montane scrub and *Polylepis* woodland in the high Andes; favours ravines

Mainly brown above, with a pale eyebrow behind the eye and greyish buff underparts, the Canyon Canastero has rufous wings and a long rufous-brown tail. The sexes do not differ in plumage. It is a poorly known bird – for example, almost nothing is known of its breeding habits. It forages for arthropods either alone or in pairs, searching the ground or low vegetation methodically. Although not considered globally threatened, it has a highly restricted range in the Peruvian Andes, just reaching north Chile.

ADULT CANYON CANASTERO

Synallaxis spixi

Spix's Spinetail

LENGTH 16cm (6½in)
WEIGHT 13g (7/16oz)
MIGRATION Non-migrant

HABITAT Secondary growth, scrub, cerrado, and woodland edges, often near water

A typical member of its genus of spinetails, Spix's Spinetail (also known as the Chicli Spinetail) has a dark throat patch and a contrasting rufous crown and wings. The tail structure is also typical of the genus, being long and steeply graduated, with sharply pointed individual feathers, the central pair thinning towards the tip. The nest is cylindrical in shape, with a long lateral entrance tube. It is made from thorny sticks, has a dense roof to provide protection from rain, and is lined with leaves, moss, and hair.

ADULT SPIX'S SPINETAIL

Anumbius annumbi

Firewood-gatherer

LENGTH 19cm (7½in)
WEIGHT 40g (17/16oz)
MIGRATION Non-migrant

HABITAT Agricultural land, second-growth scrub, seasonally inundated grassland, and pastures

Frequently seen carrying sticks to its nest, the Firewood-gatherer is aptly named. It interweaves thorny twigs to build a conspicuous nest that can be 2m (6½ft) tall. The nest is placed low in a tree or a telegraph pole and the entrance hole is decorated with artificial objects such as glass and threads. This species breeds twice per year. The young from the first nest are usually ejected from the territory, but sometimes stay to help their parents raise the second brood.

The Firewood-gatherer is an unusual ovenbird, with its striped mantle and long, graduated tail. It has a conspicuous white eyebrow and white throat patch with a dark-spotted border.

Philydor lichtensteini

Ochre-breasted Foliage-gleaner

LENGTH 16cm (6½in)
WEIGHT 20g (11/16oz)
MIGRATION Non-migrant

HABITAT Tropical evergreen forest and secondary forest in lowlands

Foraging in the mid-storey and canopy, the Ochre-breasted, or Lichtenstein's, Foliage-gleaner often forms part of mixed flocks. It is rufous-brown above and ochre below, with a broad buff eyebrow that contrasts with the grey-brown crown and forehead. It uses its bill – the shortest of its genus – to glean arthropods from leaves.

ADULT BIRD

Automolus leucophthalmus

White-eyed Foliage-gleaner

LENGTH 20cm (8in)
WEIGHT 35g (1¼oz)
MIGRATION Non-migrant

HABITAT Tropical evergreen forest and tall secondary growth in lowlands and mid-altitudes

A large, chunky ovenbird, the White-eyed Foliage-gleaner is distinguished from its near relatives by its striking white throat and white iris, which gives rise to its common name. Its upperparts are warm brown, its tail rufous, and its underparts are warm buff. It specializes in foraging in dead leaves and debris on the ground, searching for nocturnal arthropods that take daytime shelter there. The nest is a shallow cup sited at the end of a 60-cm (23½-in) long tunnel.

ADULT WHITE-EYED FOLIAGE-GLEANER

Xenops minutus

Plain Xenops

LENGTH 11cm (4½in)
WEIGHT 11g (3/8oz)
MIGRATION Non-migrant

HABITAT Tropical lowland, flooded evergreen forest, and tropical deciduous forest

The short, wedge-shaped bill of the Plain Xenops is formed by a sharp, upturned lower mandible. The bill is also compressed laterally and the shape helps the bird with its foraging technique; hammering twigs to get at its invertebrate prey. As its common name suggests, this bird lacks any prominent streaking, although it has a white cheek stripe.

ADULT PLAIN XENOPS

WOODCREEPERS

ORDER Passeriformes
FAMILY Dendrocolaptidae
SPECIES 52

AS THEIR NAME SUGGESTS, these forest birds from Central and South America climb up tree trunks and creep along branches to find food, much as treecreepers (see p.427) do in North America and Eurasia. In common with treecreepers and also with woodpeckers, their tails have long, stiff feathers that act as a prop against the trunk when climbing, and their claws are long and strong for gripping bark. Most woodcreepers are brown or olive in colour. Species differ mainly in the amount of pale spots and streaks on the head, back, and underparts, and in the length and shape of their bill, which varies from straight or slightly decurved to very long and scythe-shaped.

UPWARDLY MOBILE
Woodcreepers, such as this White-throated Woodcreeper, methodically search trees for food, using their long bills to prise insects from under the bark.

Dendrocincla fuliginosa

Plain-brown Woodcreeper

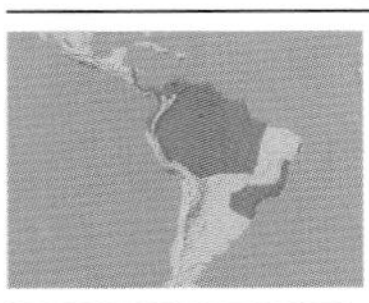

LENGTH 19–23cm (7½–9in)
WEIGHT 40g (17/16oz)
MIGRATION Non-migrant

HABITAT Forest in lowland and foothills

As indicated by its name, this medium-sized woodcreeper has a nondescript plumage pattern, without any streaking. Like the slightly larger Planalto Woodcreeper (opposite), it follows ant swarms, waiting for ants passing through its territory to force fleeing insects into the open for it to eat.

Lepidocolaptes falcinellus

Scalloped Woodcreeper

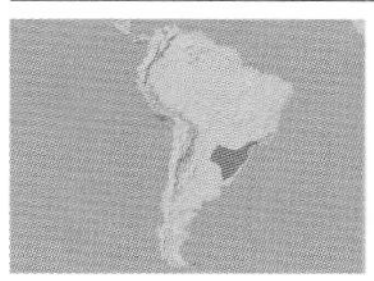

LENGTH 17–20cm (6½–8in)
WEIGHT 30g (1¹⁄₁₆oz)
MIGRATION Non-migrant

HABITAT Atlantic rainforest, montane evergreen and semi-deciduous forests, and *Araucaria* forest

A medium-sized woodcreeper, the Scalloped Woodcreeper has a long, decurved bill. Its white throat contrasts with its buff crown and ear feathers, and its upperparts are rufous-brown. The underparts of this species are olive, with bold and broad buff stripes, each stripe edged with brown, producing a "scaly" pattern.

The classification of woodcreepers is in a constant state of flux and the Scalloped Woodcreeper is no exception. Until recently, it was considered the same species as the Scaled Woodcreeper (*L. squamatus*), but has been differentiated by its measurements, upperpart coloration, and crown pattern – the plumage of the Scalloped Woodcreeper has a smaller number of streaks and spots than the Scaled Woodcreeper.

ADULT SCALLOPED WOODCREEPER

Dendrocolaptes platyrostris

Planalto Woodcreeper

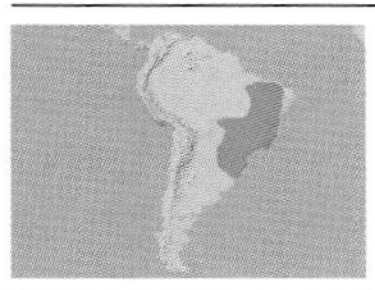

LENGTH 26cm (10in)
WEIGHT 60g (2⅛oz)
MIGRATION Non-migrant

HABITAT Lowland and montane forest, semi-deciduous woodland, and palm swamps

A slender woodcreeper with a long tail and straight bill, the Planalto Woodcreeper has a white-streaked dark brown head and a white eyebrow that contrasts with its black forehead. Its upperparts and underparts are brown. This species follows ant swarms, waiting to swoop on any invertebrate that the ants flush from cover, the female appearing more dominant than the male while capturing prey.

ADULT PLANALTO WOODCREEPER

Sittasomus griseicapillus

Olivaceous Woodcreeper

LENGTH 13–20cm (5–8in)
WEIGHT 10–18g (⅜–⅝oz)
MIGRATION Non-migrant

HABITAT Various wooded habitats from lowland evergreen rainforest to cerrado and mangroves

The Olivaceous Woodcreeper is a small and slim bird, with stiff tips to its tail feathers, an adaptation that helps it to climb trees. It has a short, thin bill, and its plumage varies from grey-olive to ochre, but its wings, lower back, and tail are rufous in colour. It forages on tree trunks, usually alone, and feeds on insects and spiders. The only species in its genus, it is taxonomically complex and some scientists believe that it should be split into three or four separate species according to the differences in size, weight, vocalizations, and plumage.

ADULT OLIVACEOUS WOODCREEPER

Campylorhamphus trochilirostris

Red-billed Scythebill

LENGTH 22–28cm (8½–11in)
WEIGHT 40g (1⁷⁄₁₆oz)
MIGRATION Non-migrant

HABITAT Wooded habitats, including gallery forest, forest islands, cerrado, chaco forest, and scrub

Possibly the most impressive member of a spectacular genus, the Red-billed Scythebill is renowned for its very long, slim, deeply decurved red bill. This adaptation aids foraging and feeding strategies such as gleaning prey from leaves or probing for food on tree trunks. The Red-billed Scythebill mainly feeds on arthropods, especially spiders, but also takes vertebrates, such as small frogs. It often smashes larger prey against tree trunks before eating. Like other woodcreepers, it has stiffened shafts on its tail feathers that help it to climb trees and strong feet and sharp claws that enable it to maintain its grip on tree trunks.

The plumage of the Red-billed Scythebill is similar to that of other woodcreepers, being olive- to rufous-brown, with rufous wings. The head and underparts are streaked in buff or white, the boldness of the streaks varying across the 12 subspecies. This woodcreeper is solitary or is found in pairs, sometimes feeding in mixed flocks. It builds its nest in a tree hole and lays 2 or 3 eggs, both parents incubating the eggs and feeding their young. It has a wide range, occurring in Panama, Venezuela, Colombia, Ecuador, Peru, Bolivia, Brazil, Paraguay, and northern Argentina.

ADULT RED-BILLED SCYTHEBILL

LYREBIRDS

ORDER	Passeriformes
FAMILY	Menuridae
SPECIES	2

THESE CHICKEN-SIZED birds are famous for the extraordinary song and courtship display of males, but are unobtrusive at other times. They live in eastern Australia in subtropical and temperate rainforest, wooded gorges, and dense scrub, and forage for invertebrates on the ground, using their strong feet to dig for prey. Of the two species, the Superb Lyrebird is fairly common, while the more rufous Albert's Lyrebird has a small range in mountain forest and is listed as vulnerable.

SINGLE PARENT
The female Superb Lyrebird defends her own territory and takes care of her single young for up to a year, with no help from the male.

BEHAVIOUR

Male lyrebirds take up to eight years to acquire their full adult plumage, including a spectacularly long tail with a central pair of lyre-shaped feathers. Mature males are polygamous and defend large territories that overlap with those of several females. They start displaying in winter, and rotate between a number of different 1–2m (3–5ft) wide display mounds, or arenas, raked up on the forest floor. During his display, the male throws his tail up and over his back, quivering it while pouring out a stream of song. Outside the breeding season, lyrebirds form small feeding parties of both sexes, together with young birds.

Menurus novaehollandiae

Superb Lyrebird

LENGTH 0.7–1m (2¼–3¼ft)

WEIGHT 0.9–1.1kg (2–2¼lb)

MIGRATION Non-migrant

HABITAT Cool temperate and subtropical rainforest

At first glance, the Superb Lyrebird, with its large size and long tail, could be mistaken for a pheasant but it is actually one of the world's largest songbirds. It has dark brown upperparts with a coppery tinge on the wings. The adult male has a distinctive train of lacy tail plumes with two long outer feathers. The Superb Lyrebird utters loud alarm whistles and other vocalizations common to the species, interspersed with phenomenal mimicry of other birds, mammals, and even machinery. The male sings throughout the year but the singing increases in frequency during the breeding season.

MALE SUPERB LYREBIRD

COURTSHIP DISPLAY

The male Superb Lyrebird tries to attract and mate with as many females as possible. It first prepares a dancing arena, which it uses to stage its display. It sings loudly and thrusts its tail horizontally over the head and back while side-stepping and jumping.

BOWERBIRDS

ORDER	Passeriformes
FAMILY	Ptilonorhynchidae
SPECIES	18

BOWERBIRDS OCCUR throughout New Guinea, and in Australia (excluding the south). Most species live in forests. They are stout-billed and eat mainly fruit, and smaller quantities of nectar, flowers, seeds, and invertebrates. The three species of catbird form monogamous breeding pairs, but in all other bowerbirds, males are polygamous. To attract mates, males of these species build complex bowers in a variety of styles. They decorate their bower with objects such as berries, flowers, shells, or discarded litter. Having inspected the bower and mated, the female builds her nest elsewhere.

BIRD ARCHITECT
A male Great Bowerbird, his pink crest raised, attracts a female to inspect his avenue-shaped bower, decorated with snail shells.

Ailuroedus crassirostris

Green Catbird

LENGTH 26–30cm (10–12in)

WEIGHT 175g (6oz)

MIGRATION Non-migrant

HABITAT Rainforest, usually in upland areas

A robust, emerald green bird with a red eye, the Green Catbird has a pale bill, a dark head with small buff spots, black cheeks, and well-spotted olive-green underparts. It is not a typical bowerbird as it does not construct a display ground like the other members of the family and is in fact monogamous. The male indulges in true territorial singing while perched close to the ground. Typical calls include a cat-like wailing vocalization, from which the species gets its common name. The breeding season is from September to January. The male Green Catbird is not involved in nest construction, incubation, and brooding, but does provide food for the female and young.

ADULT GREEN CATBIRD

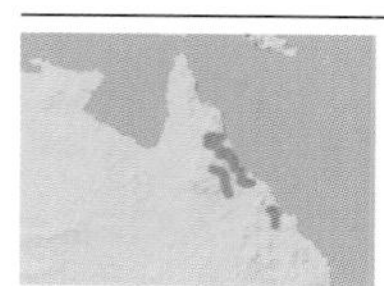

Prionodura newtoniana

Golden Bowerbird

LENGTH 23cm (9in)
WEIGHT 75–85g ($2^5/_8$–3oz)
MIGRATION Non-migrant
HABITAT Tropical upland rainforest

The glossy plumage of the male Golden Bowerbird glitters when it catches the sunlight. The male has golden-olive upperparts broken by a bright yellow rear crown and nape and golden yellow underparts. The female is drab, being olive-brown above and grey below. The impressive bower built by the male is the largest constructed by any Australian bowerbird. When displaying, the male hovers vertically in the vicinity of the bower and adopts a variety of elaborate postures on the central perch.

MALE GOLDEN BOWERBIRD

THE MAYPOLE BOWER

The bower of the Golden Bowerbird is a U-shaped construction consisting of two columns of sticks up to 3m (10ft) high. These are built up around vertical saplings that are about 1m (3ft) apart and join at the base. The horizontal display-perch between the two columns, is adorned with lichens and orchids.

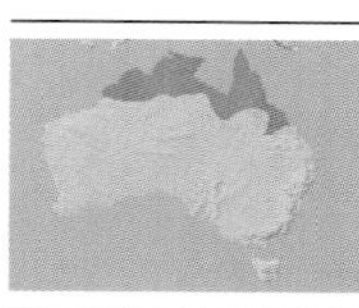

Chlamydera nuchalis

Great Bowerbird

LENGTH 34–38cm ($13^1/_2$–15in)
WEIGHT 175–225g (6–8oz)
MIGRATION Non-migrant
HABITAT Dry eucalyptus woodland, scrub, and thickets, close to water

A large bird, the Great Bowerbird has a strong bill, unmarked fawn underparts, and fawn and brown upperparts that have white tips, giving it a heavily spotted appearance. It has a lilac crest on the nape, which is spread like a fan during territorial and threat displays, but is usually only visible as just a small patch. The female is smaller, less spotted, and lacks the lilac crest.

The male Great Bowerbird builds a large "avenue" bower under the cover of a shrub or low branch. The bower consists of a platform of twigs on which two arched walls sit, forming an avenue up to 1.2m (4ft) long and 15cm (6in) wide. At each end of the platform, extensive display grounds contain huge numbers of bones, shells, and other items such as broken glass.

ADULT GREAT BOWERBIRD

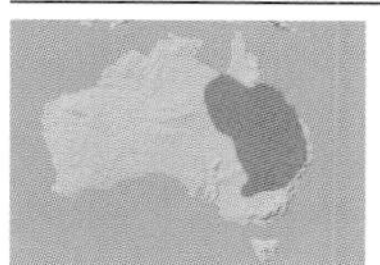

Chlamydera maculata

Spotted Bowerbird

LENGTH 25–30cm (10–12in)
WEIGHT 150g (5oz)
MIGRATION Non-migrant
HABITAT Inland scrub and dry, open woodland

The Spotted Bowerbird is a robust dry-country bowerbird. The male is largely brown with bold rufous spots on the upperparts and a pink crest on the nape that is usually seen only in display. The female is similar but usually has a smaller crest. Males build an "avenue" bower decorated with shiny red and white objects. Bowers near human habitation often include a treasure trove of nails, spoons, and coins.

ADULT BIRD

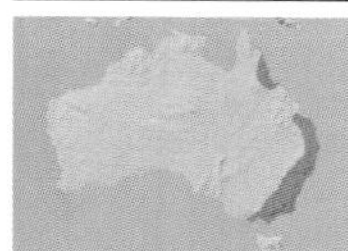

Ptilonorhynchus violaceus

Satin Bowerbird

LENGTH 28–32cm (11–$12^1/_2$in)
WEIGHT 200–225g (7–8oz)
MIGRATION Non-migrant
HABITAT Rainforest and wet eucalyptus and other woodland

Entirely glossy blue-black, the male Satin Bowerbird has striking blue eyes, a stout yellow bill with a black base, and greenish yellow legs. The female and young male are blue-grey to olive-green above, with brown wings and tails, and pale, scaly underparts. The bower is the typical "avenue" construction of bowerbirds. The walls are decorated with macerated plants and other material and the display area is covered with a variety of blue, blue-green, or yellow objects, from flowers to scraps of paper and pieces of glass. During the display, the female stands motionless at the rear of the avenue while the male holds a display object in its bill as it poses and dances.

PRACTICE MAKES PERFECT
A young male practises the skills required to build the complex bower. It attains adult plumage when it is seven years old.

MALE AT WORK
The male spends hours decorating the interior of the bower with a paste of green leaves, wood pulp, or charcoal.

SCRUBBIRDS

ORDER	Passeriformes
FAMILY	Atrichornithidae
SPECIES	2

DUE TO THEIR subdued brown coloration, their small, inconspicuous wings held against the body, and their habit of scuttling across the ground, scrubbirds can seem more like rodents than birds. They are capable of only weak, fluttering flight, and this has made them vulnerable to wildfires. The two species have a curious distribution, at opposite ends of Australia: one lives in mountain forests on the east coast; and the other in coastal scrub in the far southwest. Both are rare and localized.

Atrichornis rufescens

Rufous Scrubbird

LENGTH 17–19cm ($6^1/_2$–$7^1/_2$in)

WEIGHT 25g ($^7/_8$oz)

MIGRATION Non-migrant

HABITAT Wet gulleys, ridges, and escarpments in subtropical and temperate forest

A highly terrestrial bird, the Rufous Scrubbird has dark rufous brown, barred plumage, which serves as an effective camouflage on the forest floor. Both sexes have a pale off-white throat, but only the male, which is also slightly larger, has a black triangle of feathers on the breast and belly. The wings of the Rufous Scrubbird are short, the legs and feet sturdy, and the tail is comparatively long.

The Rufous Scrubbird searches for invertebrates by scurrying in a mouse-like manner through leaf litter on the ground and lifts the debris with its stout bill, using its head like a shovel. Its nest is a dome of dead grasses placed near the ground in sedges or tree ferns and built solely by the female, who also incubates the two eggs that are laid.

AUSTRALASIAN TREECREEPERS

ORDER	Passeriformes
FAMILY	Climacteridae
SPECIES	7

THIS SMALL FAMILY is represented in all of Australia's wooded habitats; one species, the Papuan Treecreeper, is confined to New Guinea. There are no woodpeckers in Australasia, and so these birds have evolved to fill a similar role. They climb trees to find ants and other insects, helped by their strong feet and toes. Some species breed co-operatively – the offspring remain to help their parents raise the next brood.

CAVITY NESTER
Like all treecreepers, the White-throated Treecreeper, shown here feeding an insect to its young, nests inside small tree-holes.

Climacteris picumnus

Brown Treecreeper

LENGTH 16–18cm ($6^1/_2$–7in)

WEIGHT 25–35g ($^7/_8$–$1^1/_4$oz)

MIGRATION Non-migrant

HABITAT Dry forest and woodland, especially areas with much fallen timber

Despite its name, the Brown Treecreeper is equally at home foraging on the ground as it is on trees, feeding in pairs or small groups. Two main plumage types occur: brown-backed forms in the south of the range and black-backed forms in the north, which differ only in the overall darkness of the head, upperparts, and tail. The sexes differ only slightly; the male has a patch of dark streaks on the lower throat, which are rufous in the female. This treecreeper nests in a grass-lined hollow and lays 2 or 3 eggs, which the female incubates.

MALE BROWN TREECREEPER

AUSTRALASIAN WRENS

ORDER	Passeriformes
FAMILY	Maluridae
SPECIES	28

ALTHOUGH UNRELATED to true wrens (see p.424), these small, long-tailed birds have the same habit of holding their tail in an upright position. One group of species, known as fairywrens, have colourful males, often with areas of brilliant iridescent blue, black, red, or purple in their plumage, and dull brown females. They are insect-eaters, and live in a wide variety of habitats. Another group, the grasswrens, are seed-eaters of arid country, including desert. Their plumage is mainly brown and streaked, and the sexes look alike. Most members of this family build domed grass nests, and several form extended family groups.

MUTUAL PREENING
This male Red-backed Fairywren is preening a female to cement their pair bond. Fairywrens usually live in small groups, but only one of the adult females will breed.

Clytomyias insignis

Orange-crowned Fairywren

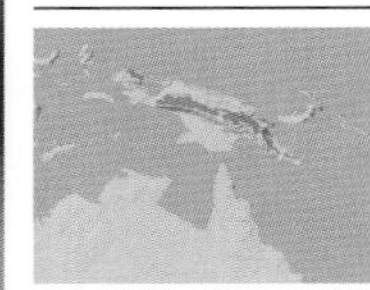

LENGTH 14cm ($5^1/_2$in)

WEIGHT 10–14g ($^3/_8$–$^1/_2$oz)

MIGRATION Non-migrant

HABITAT Montane rainforest, usually in thickets of vine and bamboo, and in small clearings

Endemic to New Guinea, this bird is lesser known among the fairywrens. It has an orange crown, olive-brown upperparts, and buff-orange underparts; its wings, and graduated tail are olive-brown. It rarely flies and walks in small groups through dense foliage with its tail half cocked. The Orange-crowned Fairywren does not join mixed-species foraging flocks, preferring to remain in groups of its own species, gleaning the underside of leaves for invertebrates. Its breeding biology is not known. Although not endangered, deforestation poses a potential threat to its survival.

Malurus lamberti

Variegated Fairywren

LENGTH 15cm (6in)

WEIGHT 8–9g ($^5/_{16}$–$^{11}/_{32}$oz)

MIGRATION Non-migrant

HABITAT Shrubby thickets

The most widespread of the fairy wrens, the Variegated Fairywren is divided into five subspecies, consisting of two groups: those with grey-brown females and variable males, some with lavender on the flanks; and the rock-inhabiting forms, in which the female has white or chestnut eyepatches and is more blue-grey on the upperparts. All female Variegated Fairywrens have pale underparts, but the intensity of the blue on the head varies in males, being brightest in the northern birds and darkest in the southeastern ones. This species moves in small groups consisting of a dominant male and its mate, less brightly coloured subordinate males, and often plainer juveniles. It constructs a nest of grass and bark on dead branches or in bushes and lays 3 or 4 eggs.

ADULT MALE

ADULT MALE AND FEMALE

Malurus cyaneus

Superb Fairywren

LENGTH 14cm (5½in)

WEIGHT 9–11g ($^{11}/_{32}$–$^3/_8$oz)

MIGRATION Non-migrant

HABITAT Patchy undergrowth in forest and woodland, but open spaces for feeding

This species is the only fairywren found in Tasmania. The male has a black bill, blue and black throat and upperparts, and a grey-white belly. The female has a dull orange-red eyepatch and a brown bill and upperparts. Like its relatives, these fairywrens live in small groups. It was recently discovered that these groups did not consist of males with a harem of females, but just one female mated to the dominant male, the rest being young males, who remain in drab plumage (like the dominant male in the non-breeding season); young females are driven from the territory to disperse widely.

GREAT SITES

BOTANIC GARDENS, CANBERRA

With its many native plants and range of habitats, the Australian National Botanic Gardens, Canberra, is home to a rich variety of birds, providing them with food and protection. A common sight among the shrubs and low-growing bushes are the Superb Fairywrens; hundreds inhabit the grassy woodland area of the Gardens, where they feed on small insects.

Malurus splendens

Splendid Fairywren

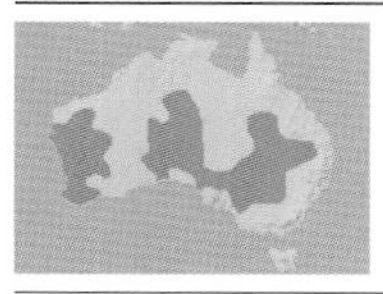

LENGTH 14cm (5½in)

WEIGHT 9–11g ($^{11}/_{32}$–$^3/_8$oz)

MIGRATION Non-migrant

HABITAT Undergrowth of eucalyptus forest, as well as in mallee scrub

ADULT MALE WITH BLUE BACK

As with other fairywrens, several subspecies of the Splendid Fairywren are recognized. The differences are most easily spotted when the male is in breeding plumage – divided into those with turquoise or blue throats and blue or black backs. Males in eclipse plumage in the non-breeding season have pale underparts like the females, only retaining some blue in the wings and tail. Females have rufous coloration around the eyes and only have blue on the tail. Like other fairywrens, the Splendid Fairywrens also live in groups and build untidy, but well-concealed, domed nests of grass, laying 2–4 eggs.

Amytornis striatus

Striated Grasswren

LENGTH 15–18cm (6–7in)

WEIGHT 20g ($^{11}/_{16}$oz)

MIGRATION Non-migrant

HABITAT Spinifex scrub in mallee and on undulating sandhills or rocky slopes, always in arid areas

Well named for its plumage, with prominent white, black, or rufous streaks, the Striated Grasswren varies in appearance. As with other Australian grasswrens, several subspecies occur, differing in the coloration of the upperparts (brown or rufous), while some species have warmer brown bellies or shorter tails. All subspecies show a black moustache stripe. These wrens are furtive and difficult to see, but in the breeding season, the male sings its trilling warbles from an exposed perch. The species feeds mainly on insects, beetles, and seeds taken on the ground.

ADULT STRIATED GRASSWREN

HONEYEATERS

ORDER	Passeriformes
FAMILY	Meliphagidae
SPECIES	174

THIS FAMILY IS UNIQUE to the southwest Pacific, being principally confined to Australia, where its members have radiated to occupy most niches and habitats, from mangroves and tropical forests to subalpine woodland and semi-arid areas provided there are trees. Such diversification has enabled the family to become among the most numerous avian inhabitants. In certain areas of Australia, sometimes up to ten species occur in a single hectare. The social behaviour of honeyeaters is also varied, ranging from living in monogamous pairs to complex groups.

SWEET TOOTH
Many honeyeaters, such as this Bridled Honeyeater, eat a large proportion of fruit with their diet.

ANATOMY

Most honeyeaters are slender, streamlined birds, with long, pointed wings. All species possess a rather long, protrusible tongue, a feature that is unusual among perching birds. The tip of the tongue has a brush-like tip, which is used to extract nectar from flowers. Bill shape varies with the species' chosen diet. Most honeyeaters are clad in dull green, grey, or brown feathers, but some have more striking black, white, or yellow markings, and almost all known species are further adorned by patches of bare, coloured skin on the gape, eye-ring, or face patch. There are relatively few species in which plumage differs between the sexes, although in many species, males are larger.

SHORT BILL
The Noisy Miner has a short and stubby bill well-suited to its diet that consists largely of fruit and insects.

LONG BILL
The Eastern Spinebill is a good example of a fine-billed species. This shape of bill is ideal for extracting nectar from flowers, on which this bird feeds.

BEHAVIOUR

Honeyeaters do not eat honey, but they principally rely on nectar-bearing plants for their energy requirements, as well as other sugary substances found on certain invertebrates and on eucalyptus trees. A few species consume significant quantities of fruit. In order to follow flowering and fruiting seasons, many honeyeaters, in common with a large number of Australian birds, are to some extent nomadic or migratory. Unusually among passerines, honeyeaters have undulating flight patterns. Most honeyeaters are rather vocal and it is surprisingly often the smallest species that utter the most musical songs, while some of the larger species, such as the wattled honeyeaters, have much less attractive vocalizations, including hawk-like and other raucous notes, which these group-living species use to maintain contact between the flock members.

BREEDING

Shredded bark, grasses, twigs, spiderwebs, and plant down are typical materials used to construct the cup-shaped nest, which is sited in a tree fork and usually lined with some softer materials. Their nests are often untidy or flimsy-looking. However, a few species construct a bulky, domed nest with an entrance at the top, and at least one species, the Blue-faced Honeyeater, frequently uses the old nest of another bird in which to lay its eggs, although it is capable of building its own. Among the group-living species, as many as ten birds may attend a single nest. On an average, honeyeaters lay two eggs, but the number in any given clutch varies between one and five; eggs are typically white, pinkish or buff, often with reddish brown spots. The eggs are incubated for up to 17 days, and the young remain in the nest from anything between one and a half to four weeks.

FEEDING THE YOUNG
The Bell Miner is a co-operative breeder in that non-breeding adults may help look after the young. Here, an adult, who may not be a parent, feeds the young with an insect.

YELLOW EDGES
Many honeyeaters show yellow edges to the wing and tail feathers, but in six species, including the New Holland Honeyeater pictured here, this feature is unusually prominent.

Notiomystis cincta

Stitchbird

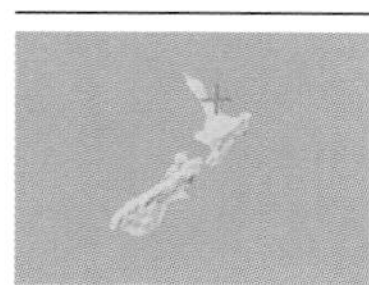

LENGTH 18cm (7in)

WEIGHT 30–40g ($1\frac{1}{16}$–$1\frac{7}{16}$oz)

MIGRATION Non-migrant

HABITAT Restricted to predator-free islands

RED LIST CATEGORY Vulnerable

MALE STITCHBIRD

Once widespread across New Zealand's North Island, the Stitchbird has a single surviving natural population numbering 500 to 2,000 individuals on Little Barrier Island. Captive breeding programmes have established populations on three other predator-free islands. The plumage of the male Stitchbird is a mix of black above and pale below, with a yellow band across the chest, while the female is mainly brown.

Lichenostomus chrysops

Yellow-faced Honeyeater

LENGTH 16–18cm ($6\frac{1}{2}$–7in)

WEIGHT 17g ($\frac{5}{8}$oz)

MIGRATION Partial migrant

HABITAT Mainly forest, woodland, and scrub

ADULT YELLOW-FACED HONEYEATER

A small, delicate bird, the Yellow-faced Honeyeater has a predominantly brown plumage. However, it has a distinct facial pattern: a yellow patch sandwiched between two black lines, with a small yellow mark just below the eye. Its ringing calls often combine to form a brisk song. A number of species are rather similar, particularly the Eungella and Bridled Honeyeaters (*L. hindwoodi* and *L. frenatus*), which are larger and have restricted ranges. However, the likeliest confusion in identification is with the brighter-plumaged Singing Honeyeater (*L. virescens*), which has a black stripe through, rather than below, its eye.

Manorina melanocephala

Noisy Miner

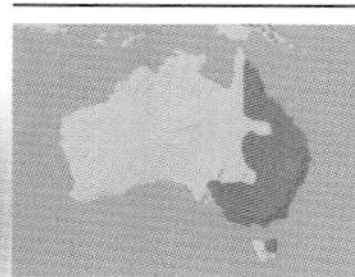

LENGTH 24–27cm ($9\frac{1}{2}$–$10\frac{1}{2}$in)

WEIGHT 55–65g (2–$2\frac{3}{8}$oz)

MIGRATION Non-migrant

HABITAT Open forest, heaths, camp grounds, parks, and gardens

This is a common honeyeater from eastern Australia, found in open forests and, increasingly, suburban areas. It is told from the similar looking Yellow-throated Miner (below) by its white forehead, black crown, and grey rump. The bill and the areas around and behind its eyes are yellow. The species nests in groups or colonies of 4–12. It aggressively defends its area, harassing and chasing away larger invaders such as magpies, currawongs, or crows. It eats mostly nectar, fruit, and insects.

Meliphaga analoga

Mimic Honeyeater

LENGTH 16–19cm ($6\frac{1}{2}$–$7\frac{1}{2}$in)

WEIGHT 20–25g ($\frac{11}{16}$–$\frac{7}{8}$oz)

MIGRATION Non-migrant

HABITAT Rainforest, secondary forest, coffee plantations, and gardens

Found throughout New Guinea, the Mimic Honeyeater is also known as the Mimetic Honeyeater. A yellow streak runs from its slender bill to just below its eye. It has olive upperparts with greenish yellow markings on the wing and tail, grey underparts, and a pale yellow ear-spot. The male and female are similar in plumage, although the male is larger. The species is most frequently seen in singles, pairs, or small parties.

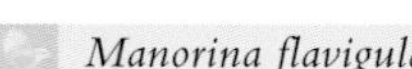

Manorina flavigula

Yellow-throated Miner

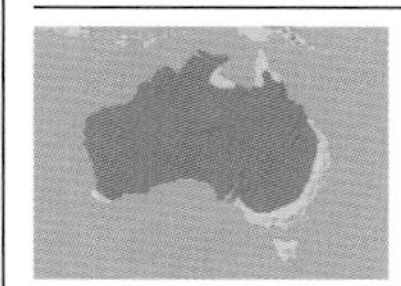

LENGTH 25–28cm (10–11in)

WEIGHT 50–65g ($1\frac{3}{4}$–$2\frac{3}{8}$oz)

MIGRATION Non-migrant

HABITAT Drier woodland, dry mallee scrub, heath, and grassland

ADULT YELLOW-THROATED MINER

A common bird throughout most of arid Australia, the Yellow-throated Miner is absent only from Tasmania and wetter areas of the east coast. It has a black smudge behind the eye, and its bill, eye skin, side of the throat, legs, and feet are yellow. In flight, it displays a pale rump, which distinguishes it from the similar Noisy Miner (above).

The Yellow-throated Miner is a sociable species that lives in tight-knit groups, forming colonies of 12 to 50 birds. These groups mostly forage together in small bands, flying noisily from one tree to another. Unlike most honeyeaters, their diet consists mainly of insects. They breed communally and breeding pairs are often assisted by other members of the same group.

ADULT LEWIN'S HONEYEATER

Meliphaga lewinii

Lewin's Honeyeater

LENGTH 19–21.5cm ($7\frac{1}{2}$–$8\frac{1}{2}$in)

WEIGHT 30–40g (1–$1\frac{3}{8}$oz)

MIGRATION Partial migrant

HABITAT Rainforest, dense woodland, coastal scrub, orchards, and gardens

This medium-sized, dark-plumaged honeyeater is named after John Lewin, an English settler who painted the birds of Australia in the early 1800s. It is mostly olive-grey, with a stout black bill, a cream streak running from its bill to below its eye, and a pale yellow ear patch. The species is one of the most common, frequently heard birds of Australia's eastern rainforests, and its long, rattling song is often likened to a machine-gun. It eats mainly fruit and nectar and regularly raids orchards.

ADULT BLUE-FACED HONEYEATER

Entomyzon cyanotis

Blue-faced Honeyeater

LENGTH
30–32cm (12–12½in)

WEIGHT
95–125g (3⅜–4oz)

MIGRATION
Partial migrant

HABITAT Woodland, gardens, parks, plantations, orchards, and farmland

This large honeyeater is commonly found in the north and east of Australia, although it is generally absent from drier outback areas. The species is uncommon in the south of its range and absent from Tasmania; outside Australia, it also occurs in southern New Guinea. The adult Blue-faced Honeyeater has an unmistakable facial pattern – a two-toned area of bare blue skin surrounding prominent white eyes. The rest of its head is mostly black, except for a white band around the nape and a white moustache stripe. It has a large black bib, which stands out from the rest of the pure white breast. The back, wings, and tail are olive-green in colour. The juvenile, unlike the adult, has yellow facial skin. Blue-faced Honeyeaters in the Northern Territory range also have a large white patch on the underwing that is prominent in flight.

These aggressive, gregarious birds are frequently found in small flocks. They are commonly seen in gardens or campsites, searching for any available food. Their diet usually consists of insects, but nectar, pollen, and fruit such as bananas and grapes also prove a great attraction. The species is noisy and flocks can often be located by their loud, raucous whistles.

HUMAN IMPACT

PLANTATION PEST

In tropical areas where the banana tree grows, the Blue-faced Honeyeater is also known as the "banana bird" – a name that reflects the species' penchant for the fruit. It is a pest on banana plantations, where small groups forage not only on the ripe fruit, but also on the flowers of the tree, extracting their nectar.

Melithreptus lunatus

White-naped Honeyeater

LENGTH
13–15cm (5–6in)

WEIGHT
13–15g (7/16–9/16oz)

MIGRATION
Partial migrant

HABITAT Eucalyptus forest and woodland

The White-naped Honeyeater is a small, neat species usually found feeding in pairs or flocks in the canopy, where it searches for nectar and insects, as well as sugar-rich honeydew secretions. The species is olive-green above and white below, with a black cap and short white band across the back of the neck. Different subspecies can be distinguished by the colour of bare skin around the eye; this is red in the abundant subspecies that is found on the eastern coast (*M.l. lunatus*) and white in the western subspecies (*M.l. chlorosis*).

ADULT (EASTERN SUBSPECIES)

Anthornis melanura

New Zealand Bellbird

LENGTH 20cm (8in)
WEIGHT 25–35g (7/8–1 1/4oz)
MIGRATION Non-migrant

HABITAT Forest, orchards, parks, gardens, and scrub

Mostly green in colour, the New Zealand Bellbird has a short decurved bill. The male is slightly brighter in its plumage with red eyes and a darker head, wings, and tail, and in particular, a dark throat. The female has brown eyes and shows a faint white moustache stripe. The species is found only in New Zealand (on both the main islands), but unlike many of the country's native birds is not threatened. Its ringing notes are particularly impressive when a group of birds calls in unison – a melodious chorus that can be heard at dusk or dawn.

FEMALE NEW ZEALAND BELLBIRD

ADULT TUI

Prosthemadera novaeseelandiae

Tui

LENGTH 30cm (12in)
WEIGHT 90–150g (3 1/4–5oz)
MIGRATION Non-migrant

HABITAT Forest and scrub, as well as parks and gardens (particularly outside breeding season)

The Tui is endemic to New Zealand, where it occurs on both the main islands, as well as the Chatham, Kermadec, and Auckland Islands. The species was once known as the Parson Bird; at a distance it appears all black except for a small white bib on its throat, which resembles a parson's collar. The Tui's plumage is more elaborate than plain black, however, with a green and purple sheen to its feathers. Its song melds a variety of extraordinary croaks, coughs, and clicks with rich, melodious notes.

Although much of New Zealand's native forest has disappeared, the Tui has adapted well to changes caused by human impact and has taken advantage of the abundance of flowering plants around human habitations as a new source of food.

Philemon corniculatus

Noisy Friarbird

LENGTH 31–35cm (12–14in)
WEIGHT 100g (3 5/8oz)
MIGRATION Partial migrant

HABITAT Forest, scrub, parks, and gardens

With its featherless black head, the Noisy Friarbird has a most unusual appearance, almost like that of a tiny vulture, earning it the alternate name of "leatherhead". It is a large honeyeater with a grey-brown plumage and a powerful bill, which is adorned with a prominent triangular casque (bump) on the upper mandible. The adult also has a red eye and silvery white plumes on the neck and breast. The juvenile is duller and lacks the casque. As its name suggests, the species is noisy, uttering a variety of harsh-sounding calls. It is aggressive and social, often seen in small parties or flocks.

The Noisy Friarbird is found along Australia's east coast (as well as New Guinea), with birds in the southern part of its range being breeding migrants. Farther north, the Noisy Friarbird is nomadic, moving to places with flowering trees in order to feed on their nectar. It also eats fruit, insects, and, occasionally, the eggs or chicks of other birds. The female builds the nest and incubates the eggs, but both parents feed the young, up to three weeks after fledging.

Three similar species occur in Australia: the Little Friarbird (*P. citreogularis*); the Silver-crowned Friarbird (*P. argenticeps*) found in tropical Queensland and the Northern Territories; and the Helmeted Friarbird (*P. buceroides*).

ADULT NOISY FRIARBIRD

Acanthagenys rufogularis

Spiny-cheeked Honeyeater

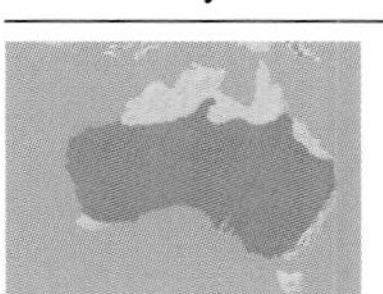

LENGTH 22–26cm (8 1/2–10in)
WEIGHT 50g (1 3/4oz)
MIGRATION Non-migrant

HABITAT Arid woodland and scrub

ADULT SPINY-CHEEKED HONEYEATER

Named for the spiny bristles on its cheek, this common bird of Australia's arid interior has a black-tipped pink bill, an apricot breast, streaked sides to neck and flanks, and a noticeable white rump in flight. It is a noisy species, with a variety of mellow whistles. Like many of Australia's desert-dwelling birds, this species is nomadic, moving around in search of food and water.

Anthochaera carunculata

Red Wattlebird

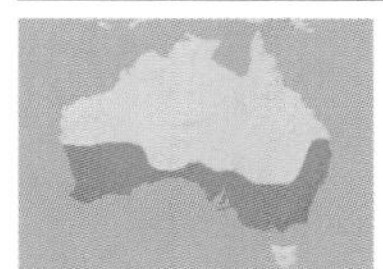

LENGTH 33–36cm (13–14in)
WEIGHT 100–125g (3 5/8–4oz)
MIGRATION Partial migrant

HABITAT Woodland, forest, scrub, heath, orchards, parks, and gardens

One of the largest of Australia's honeyeaters, the Red Wattlebird is found in a band across the southern coast of the continent, except for Tasmania, where it is replaced by the Yellow Wattlebird (*A. paradoxa*). It is generally a brown species with prominent white streaks, a yellow belly, and a fleshy red wattle hanging just below its eye. It feeds mainly on flowering trees and takes insects and other small creatures as well. It is an increasingly common visitor to parks and gardens in urban areas.

ADULT RED WATTLEBIRD

Acanthorhynchus tenuirostris

Eastern Spinebill

LENGTH 14–16cm (5 1/2–6 1/2in)
WEIGHT 9–12g (5/16–7/16oz)
MIGRATION Partial migrant

HABITAT Forest, woodland, heath, parks, and gardens

The Eastern Spinebill is a brightly coloured honeyeater, which is often only seen briefly as it darts after insects or hovers around flowers. Its most noticeable feature is its delicate, decurved bill. This, combined with its fleeting flight is reminiscent of a hummingbird. The Eastern Spinebill is a beautifully plumaged bird, with its red eyes and contrasting striped breast, dark upperparts, and rufous underparts. Although the male and female are similar, the male has a brighter plumage and more distinct markings. The species is found in the coastal belt (including Tasmania) from just north of Adelaide in South Australia to northern Queensland. In the southwest tip of Western Australia, it is replaced by the closely related Western Spinebill (*A. superciliosus*), in which the male is even more brightly coloured.

MALE EASTERN SPINEBILL

Phylidonyris novaehollandiae

New Holland Honeyeater

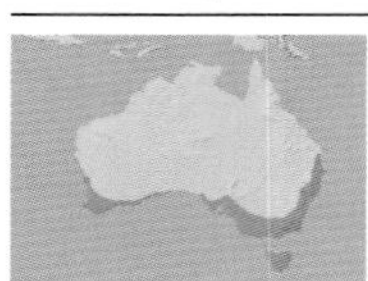

LENGTH 18cm (7in)

WEIGHT 20g (11/16oz)

MIGRATION Non-migrant

HABITAT Woodland, scrub, parks, gardens, and heaths

The New Holland Honeyeater has white eyes set in a black face, with white eyebrows extending from behind the eyes to the back of the head, white ear-tufts, whiskers, and a long black bill. Its upperparts are mostly black, except for a large golden yellow wing patch and a yellow-edged, white-tipped tail. In flight, its wings and tail appear yellow. The juvenile is duller, with brown upperparts and less conspicuous eyes. One of the most common and often-encountered honeyeaters in southeast Australia and the southwestern tip of Western Australia, this honeyeater is unafraid of people, and consequently, common in towns and cities within its range. It is a noisy species, giving out a variety of piercing and whistling calls.

ADULT MALE

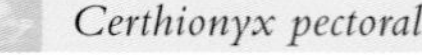

Certhionyx pectoralis

Banded Honeyeater

LENGTH 12–14cm (4½–5½in)

WEIGHT 10g (3/8oz)

MIGRATION Non-migrant

HABITAT Grassy woodland, coastal scrub, mangroves, and watercourse vegetation

The Banded Honeyeater has a striking pied appearance. It has black upperparts, white underparts, and a black band across the breast. Its bill appears heavy compared to many other small honeyeaters. Male and female are similar. The juvenile is a dull imitation of the adult: brown above with a faint brown band across the breast and a buff-yellow face. In flight, both the male and female of the species display a noticeable white rump.

The Banded Honeyeater is found only in Australia and is common throughout the tropical north of the continent – wherever there are flowering paperbark or eucalyptus trees. It is a nomadic species that constantly undertakes journeys in search of food, the only exception being when it is nesting. Large gatherings of birds can occur when suitable trees are heavily in flower.

Myzomela sanguinolenta

Scarlet Myzomela

LENGTH 10cm (4in)

WEIGHT 9g (11/32oz)

MIGRATION Partial migrant

HABITAT Rainforest, woodland, heathland, scrub, parks, and gardens

This species is also known as the Scarlet Honeyeater. The male has a blood-red head and breast contrasting with its white belly and black wings and tail. In flight, it shows off the white-edged feathers of its black wings and a scarlet rump. The thin black band between its bill and eye gives it a masked appearance. The female is a plain tawny-brown colour, with just a faint pink tint to the chin. The juvenile is similar, although young males gradually acquire their bright plumage, developing areas of red first on the head and back, and finally on the breast. The Scarlet Myzomela is seen alone or in flocks, hovering to feed at flowers with fast beating wings.

MALE SCARLET MYZOMELA

Epthianura tricolor

Crimson Chat

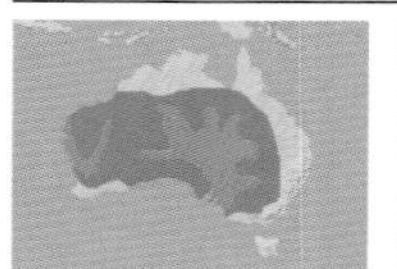

LENGTH 10–12cm (4–4½in)

WEIGHT 11g (3/8oz)

MIGRATION Partial migrant

HABITAT Scrubland, grassland, dry open woodland, edges of salt lakes, and roadsides

This species is most commonly seen foraging on the ground for insects and seeds, or perched low on bushes. The Crimson Chat has a brush-tipped tongue, which allows it to feed on nectar when outback flowers are in bloom. The male can be identified by its bright crimson crown, breast, and rump; its contrasting pale eyes and white throat; and its dark mask, wings, and back. The female is different in its plumage, being brown above with small areas of pink on the forehead, breast, and rump. The juvenile does not have pink tones on its plumage and is plain in appearance.

The Crimson Chat is one of the few small species of Australian birds that walk and run rather than hop across the ground. A nomadic inhabitant of Australia's arid interior, it sometimes appears in very large numbers in areas where it has recently rained.

MALE CRIMSON CHAT

Ashbyia lovensis

Gibberbird

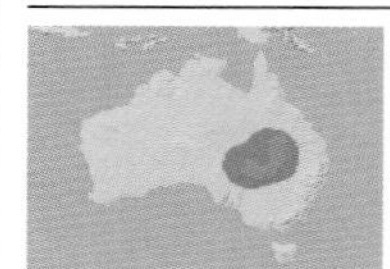

LENGTH 13cm (5in)

WEIGHT 17g (5/8oz)

MIGRATION Non-migrant

HABITAT Sparsely vegetated rocky desert plains

The Gibberbird is so named not because it chatters incessantly but after "gibber", an Australian term for the type of flat, rocky desert it favours. Also called the Desert Chat, the Gibberbird is pale and plain in appearance and blends effortlessly into its dusty, desert surroundings. Mottled grey-brown above, it has pale yellow eyes, a brighter yellow face and underparts, and a white-tipped dark tail. The female is only slightly duller than the male, making it difficult to distinguish the sexes. The Gibberbird is a nomadic species that dwells almost entirely on the ground, although it will occasionally fly to catch an airborne insect. It is often seen in pairs or small groups, running short distances before pausing to stand upright, flicking its tail.

ADULT IN A TYPICAL UPRIGHT STANCE

BRISTLEBIRDS

ORDER Passeriformes
FAMILY Dasyornithidae
SPECIES 3

BRISTLEBIRDS ARE shy residents of heathland, thickets, and scrub in the coastal strip of southern and eastern Australia, usually close to the sea or a short distance inland. They are named for a group of stiff, bristle-like feathers at the base of the bill. They have a subdued, brownish grey plumage and a long, rounded tail. The three different species are restricted to small ranges located far apart from each other, which suggests that at one time they were more widespread. Two species – the Western and Rufous Bristlebirds – are endangered, due to extensive urban development on the coast. The relationship of bristlebirds to pardalotes (see below) and to thornbills and gerygones (see p.368) is much debated, and sometimes all these closely related birds are placed together in the same family,

BEHAVIOUR

Bristlebirds feed mainly on invertebrates and spend most of their time walking or hopping through grass tussocks and other low vegetation, moving quickly and often breaking into a short run. They seldom fly for more than about 20m (60ft), soon dropping back down into cover. Due to this secretive lifestyle, the birds' penetrating, melodious song and harsh contact calls are often the sole indication of their presence. The breeding behaviour of bristlebirds is poorly known. They build a domed or globular nest from grasses and sticks, among grass or low down in a shrub, and the female lays two eggs.

Dasyornis broadbenti

Rufous Bristlebird

LENGTH 24–27cm ($9^1/_2$–$10^1/_2$in)
WEIGHT 70g ($2^1/_2$oz)
MIGRATION Non-migrant

HABITAT Coastal scrub and heath

Commonest of the three members of its family, the swift-running Rufous Bristlebird is usually shy, although some individuals are rather tame and can be seen at sites frequented by people. It has a rich rufous cap and wings, pale grey scalloped underparts, and a broad paddle-shaped tail. The *D. b. litoralis* race of the species was formerly found in southwestern Western Australia, but now appears to be extinct.

ADULT RUFOUS BRISTLEBIRD

Dasyornis brachypterus

Eastern Bristlebird

LENGTH 20–22cm (8–$8^1/_2$in)
WEIGHT 40g ($1^7/_{16}$oz)
MIGRATION Non-migrant

HABITAT Dense coastal scrub, woodland, and heaths

RED LIST CATEGORY Endangered

A medium-sized bird, the Eastern Bristlebird is mainly grey-brown in colour, with faint eyebrows and dark cinnamon-brown upperparts. Its underparts are pale, with a greyer wash. Its long tail is usually held horizontally, but is sometimes raised when the bird is excited. With its small, rounded wings, it is capable of flying only for very short distances.

The Eastern Bristlebird is a shy, ground-dwelling species that moves quickly and quietly along the floor of its dense heath habitat. It is more likely to be heard than seen – its voice consists of repeated ringing calls or a loud and melodious series of high-pitched whistles, which often end with a whip-like crack. The Eastern Bristlebird is found in just a few small, fragmented populations on Australia's east coast, and its total population is estimated to be around only 1,500 individuals.

PARDALOTES

ORDER Passeriformes
FAMILY Pardalotidae
SPECIES 4

THESE COLOURFUL BIRDS are found in many kinds of woodland and scrub throughout Australia, including golf courses, parks, and gardens. They have a small, compact body and a strikingly short, stubby bill – both features similar to flowerpeckers (see p.449). Three of the species are common and widespread, but the rare Forty-spotted Pardalote is confined to southeastern Tasmania. Some authorities group pardalotes with the thornbills and gerygones (see p.368).

BEHAVIOUR

Pardalotes are highly active birds that move through woodland in pairs or small parties, often high up in the tree canopy. Their diet includes small insects plucked off foliage and a sugary solution collected from the surface of eucalypt leaves. They breed in pairs or co-operatively – with extra birds assisting the main pair. Both sexes help to build the nest and raise the young.

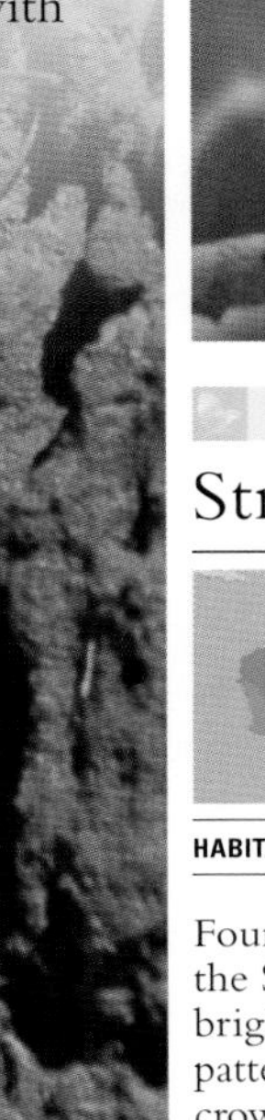

NESTING TUNNEL
Like other pardalotes, the Striated Pardalote digs a nesting chamber in an earth bank, often beside a creek or in a road cutting. Holes in walls and tree trunks are also used.

ADULT STRIATED PARDALOTE

Pardalotus striatus

Striated Pardalote

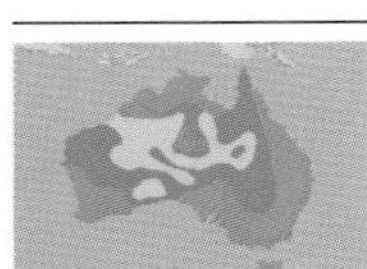

LENGTH 9–12cm ($3^1/_2$–$4^1/_2$in)
WEIGHT 12g ($^7/_{16}$oz)
MIGRATION Partial migrant

HABITAT Woodland, forest, scrub, parks, and gardens

Found throughout most of Australia, the Striated Pardalote is a small, brightly coloured bird with attractive patterns on its plumage. It has a black crown (in some subspecies streaked white) and thick white eyebrows that have a patch of gold in front of each eye. The species has pale brown upperparts, with a yellow wash on its pale breast and throat, and a mustard-yellow rump. Its black wings show a broad white stripe and small red spots (yellow in Tasmanian birds). The short, stubby bill is characteristic of this species. The juvenile lacks the distinctive black and white facial pattern of the adult. The Striated Pardalote forages mainly for insects in the tops of trees, often in pairs or small groups. Its favoured prey is the lerp, a type of sap-sucking insect.

THORNBILLS AND GERYGONES

ORDER	Passeriformes
FAMILY	Acanthizidae
SPECIES	60

MANY OF THE COMMONEST small Australian birds belong to this large and diverse family. Its members can be roughly divided into two main groups. One group is formed by the thornbills, gerygones, whitefaces, and Weebill, all of which are under 13cm (5in) in length. They have fine, pointed bills and most feed by searching for insects among foliage; some hover frequently while feeding. The second group consists of the scrubwrens, Pilotbird, and a few other species. These birds are somewhat larger and longer-tailed, and many feed on the ground among leaf litter. Cooperative breeding is common among all species in this family.

CONCEALED NEST
A Southern Whiteface brings food for its chicks, hidden in its nest inside a hollow tree stump. This species is known as the "squeaker" due to the twittering calls given constantly by birds on the move.

Pycnoptilus floccosus

Pilotbird

LENGTH 16–18cm (6½–7in)
WEIGHT 30g (1 1/16oz)
MIGRATION Non-migrant
HABITAT Wet forest and drier coastal woodland

Predominantly brown in colour, with a rufous-brown forehead and breast, the Pilotbird has deeper brown underparts, which are lightly scalloped. Its eyes are red and it has a long tail. A large scrubwren, which feeds mostly on the ground, the Pilotbird forages for invertebrates in leaf litter. It gets its unusual name from its habit (in certain areas) of following the Superb Lyrebird (see p.358) as it forages in the forest, similar to a pilotfish alongside a shark, and picking out insects and earthworms that the larger bird disturbs. It has a characteristic sweet, far-carrying song, sounding like "guinea-a-week". The Pilotbird is generally a secretive species that favours damp gullies and eucalyptus forest in the southeast of Australia (Victoria and New South Wales).

Oreoscopus gutturalis

Fernwren

LENGTH 13–15cm (5–6in)
WEIGHT 20g (11/16oz)
MIGRATION Non-migrant
HABITAT Rainforest above 600m (2,000ft)

The Fernwren is mainly rich dark brown in colour and has a thin white line above the eye, a noticeable white throat, and a black breast patch. As a result, the bird has a "masked" appearance. The female is less clearly marked than the male, while the juvenile is a very uniform brown, lacking any distinct markings on the breast and throat, with just a thin, pale line above the eye.

Difficult to spot, the Fernwren skulks and hops through the ferns and dense undergrowth of the rainforest, feeding in damp leaf litter as it flicks its tail and bows its head. The species is usually located by its high-pitched, penetrating whistles and buzzing sounds. It is found only in the Atherton Tablelands of northeast Queensland.

JUVENILE FERNWREN

ADULT WHITE-BROWED SCRUBWREN

Sericornis frontalis

White-browed Scrubwren

LENGTH 11–13cm (4½–5in)
WEIGHT 12–16g (7/16–9/16oz)
MIGRATION Non-migrant
HABITAT Undergrowth of woodland and scrub, as well as mangroves, heath, and gardens

In appearance, the male White-browed Scrubwren has a distinct pale eye and a dark facial mask between two white stripes. It is dark brown on its back and wings and a paler buff below (though birds of the Western Australian subspecies are streaked from throat to breast). It also has a small but distinct white mark on the edge of the wing. The female and juvenile are duller than the male.

Although it feeds low down in its dense scrubby habitat, the White-browed Scrubwren is often heard, being noisy and uttering a variety of buzzing calls. It feeds on insects and seeds, usually in pairs. Breeding takes place in July to January each year. The cup-shaped nest is lined with feathers and has a side entrance tunnel. It is usually located on or near the ground in thick vegetation, but may be in a tree fork a few metres high. One of the most common and widespread members of its family, the White-browed Scrubwren is found in a wide coastal belt in Australia.

Smicrornis brevirostris

Weebill

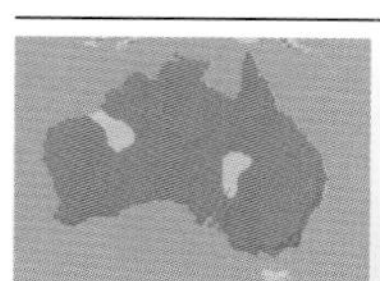

LENGTH 8cm (3¼in)

WEIGHT 5g (3/16oz)

MIGRATION Non-migrant

HABITAT Dry woodland and scrub

Australia's smallest bird, the Weebill gets its name from its short, stubby bill. This tiny bird is olive-green above and pale buff to lemon below. It has a noticeably pale eye and a dark band and white tip to the end of its tail. Birds from the southeast of the country are paler and less yellow in their overall plumage tone.

The Weebill is often found feeding in mixed flocks alongside other species, and its presence is usually announced by a distinctive loud whistle. It is an active bird, preferring to forage in the outer edges of the tops of trees, where it feeds predominantly on insects. Although the species is generally sedentary, it does undertake nomadic local movements from time to time.

HOODED NEST

During its long breeding season, from July to February, the Weebill makes a neat, tightly woven dome-shaped nest from grasses, plant down, and leaves. It has a narrow entrance, rather like a spout, situated at the top of the structure. Inside, it is cushioned with feathers and other soft material, and 2 or 3 pale, brown-flecked eggs are laid.

ADULT WEEBILL

Acanthiza pusilla

Brown Thornbill

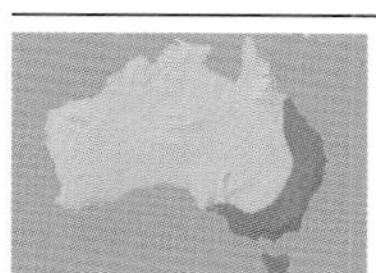

LENGTH 10cm (4in)

WEIGHT 7–9g (¼–11/32oz)

MIGRATION Non-migrant

HABITAT Rainforest, eucalyptus woodland, scrub, mangroves, parks, and gardens

ADULT BROWN THORNBILL

Pale brown above and finely streaked on its forehead and breast, the Brown Thornbill has a noticeable dark red eye, an off-white unstreaked belly, a dull cinnamon rump, and a pale tip to its grey-brown tail.

A common species in most wooded habitats along the Australian east coast, the Brown Thornbill frequents undergrowth – rarely in the canopy. It forages on its own, or in pairs, feeding mainly on insects, but also taking seeds, nectar, and fruit. It can be confused with the very similar Inland Thornbill (*A. ewingii*) found in the west of Australia, which is slightly greyer and holds its tail angled more upwards.

ADULT, WITH DISTINCTIVE YELLOW RUMP

Acanthiza chrysorrhoa

Yellow-rumped Thornbill

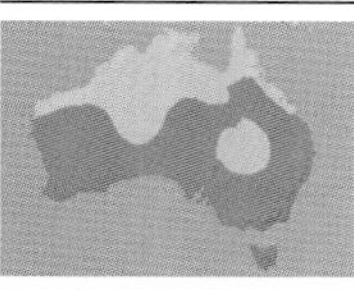

LENGTH 11–13cm (4½–5in)

WEIGHT 9–11g (11/32–3/8oz)

MIGRATION Non-migrant

HABITAT Grassy woodland edges, scrub, farmland, golf courses, parks, and gardens

Although a small bird, the Yellow-rumped Thornbill is the largest species of thornbill. It has a distinctive facial pattern, with a white-streaked dark crown and white eyebrow. It is olive-grey above with pale greyish white underparts. However, its most obvious feature, and the one after which it is named, is its yellow rump. This is visible when the bird is in flight – it flies short distances with a low, bouncing movement when flushed. The bright rump is also highlighted due to the contrast with the bird's white-tipped black tail.

A sociable species, this thornbill is usually found hopping on the ground in pairs or small flocks, preferring short grass; in recent years, it has become a familiar sight on golf courses. It has a tinkling song and a two-syllable "check-check" flight call. Its nest, made of grass and bark, is dome-shaped, with a hidden entrance and a decoy cup-shaped structure on top to protect it from predators.

ADULT WHITE-THROATED GERYGONE

Gerygone olivacea

White-throated Gerygone

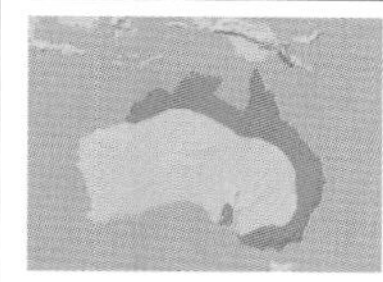

LENGTH 10–12cm (4–4½in)

WEIGHT 7g (¼oz)

MIGRATION Partial migrant

HABITAT Woodland, scrub, and trees along rivers

A slender bird, the White-throated Gerygone has a white throat, greyish brown upperparts, and yellow underparts. It is perhaps best known for its lilting, cascading song, the word "gerygone" meaning "born of sound". The White-throated Gerygone is found along the north coast of Australia, from the Kimberley region in Western Australia, right along the east coast to Adelaide in South Australia.

Aphelocephala leucopsis

Southern Whiteface

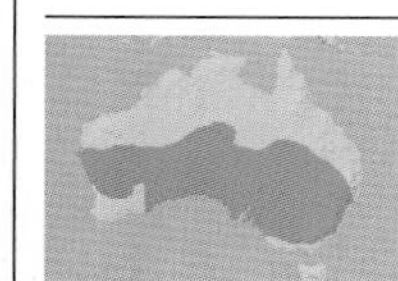

LENGTH 10–12cm (4–4½in)

WEIGHT 11–13g (3/8–7/16oz)

MIGRATION Non-migrant

HABITAT Dry, open forest and scrub

Of the three Australian whitefaces, the Southern Whiteface is the plainest and the most common. It does not really have a white face, but a white forehead that is lined above with a black band. It also has a stubby bill, off-white breast, olive-buff flanks, and a black tail. The Southern Whiteface occurs patchily across the southern half of Australia; the Banded Whiteface (*A. nigricincta*) is found in the interior; and the rare Chestnut-breasted Whiteface (*A. pectoralis*) is confined to a small area of inland South Australia.

ADULT SOUTHERN WHITEFACE

AUSTRALASIAN BABBLERS

ORDER	Passeriformes
FAMILY	Pomatostomidae
SPECIES	5

FOUND ONLY IN Australia and New Guinea, this family of birds is unrelated to the Asian babblers in the family Timaliidae (see p.418). Like them, however, they are highly social and extremely vocal. They are named for their strident calls and their loud, chattering, warbling, or miaowing songs. Pairs of these birds may sing duets, and often several members of a group join in. Australasian babblers live in forest and scrub in groups of up to 15 birds, and always feed and roost together. They breed cooperatively, building several domed stick-nests. One is used to raise young, and the others for roosting.

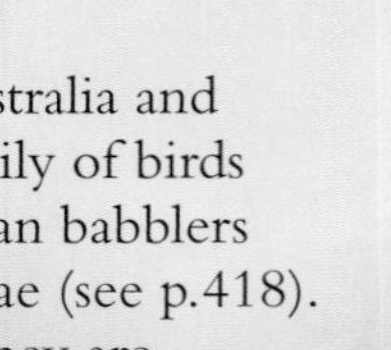

SHARED NESTS
A Grey-crowned Babbler adds sticks to one of the communal nests belonging to its group.

Pomatostomus temporalis

Grey-crowned Babbler

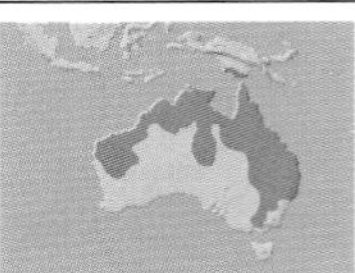

LENGTH 29cm (11½in)
WEIGHT 75g (2⅝oz)
MIGRATION Non-migrant
HABITAT Open woodland, farmland, and scrub

The Grey-crowned Babbler is a very sociable species, usually encountered in large family parties consisting of a primary breeding pair along with several non-breeding birds. These groups are noisy and energetic as they forage high in trees or on the ground. There are two races of Grey-crowned Babbler, which differ quite considerably in their appearance. The race in eastern Australia has grey upperparts and a greyish brown lower breast. It has a distinct white stripe above the eye, a dark grey mask across the face, a white throat and breast, and a long, rounded tail with a white band around the entire tip. The pale yellow eyes stand out from the middle of the dark mask. This race also has a long, heavy, decurved bill. The race that predominates in Western Australia and the Northern Territories is much warmer-looking than its eastern counterpart: it differs in its rufous breast and brown upperparts. Both races are vocal with a large selection of rather nasal calls, one of which is often described as sounding like "yahoo", giving rise to an alternative name sometimes used for the species.

WESTERN ADULT

LOGRUNNERS

ORDER	Passeriformes
FAMILY	Orthonychidae
SPECIES	3

THESE GROUND-LIVING birds have beautifully camouflaged plumage that helps them to blend in with the leaf litter of their rainforest home. They are weak fliers, so their cryptic plumage and secretive behaviour are their chief protection against predators. Logrunners feed on invertebrates, using their strong legs and bills to rake around vigorously for hidden prey, such as spiders and worms. While digging, they often lean on their stiff, spiny-tipped tail feathers as a prop. Two species of logrunner are found in eastern Australia, and the third occurs in New Guinea.

MOTTLED JUVENILE
This downy Northern Logrunner, or Chowchilla, chick is moulting into its juvenile plumage. Logrunners usually nest on the ground and produce broods of one or two young.

ADULT MALE

Orthonyx temminckii

Australian Logrunner

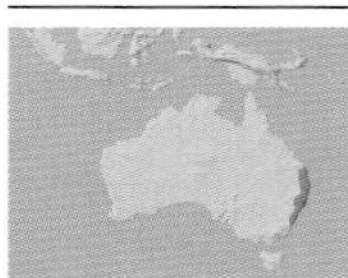

LENGTH 18–20cm (7–8in)
WEIGHT 55–60g (2–2⅛oz)
MIGRATION Non-migrant
HABITAT Leafy subtropical rainforest floors

The Australian Logrunner is a small, stocky bird. It is attractively plumaged with intricately patterned markings that can often be difficult to discern among the shadows of the rainforest floor. The male has a mottled black and rufous back, as well as a rufous rump and flanks. It has a grey face, with a thick black line that extends downwards along the side of the throat and breast. The throat itself is white. The black wings have grey wingbars and it has a broad, dark tail, with short spines at the tip. The female is similar to the male except that it has an orange throat. Immature birds are similar in structure, but browner and densely scalloped on the face and underparts.

The Australian Logrunner lives mainly on the forest floor, where it scratches noisily among the leaf litter with its large, strong feet, leaving a tell-tale trail of small, leafless circles – flinging debris aside with first one foot, then the other. It can be a noisy species, particularly at dawn, when its rapid piping song can often be heard.

SATINBIRDS

ORDER	Passeriformes
FAMILY	Cnemophilidae
SPECIES	3

THE SATINBIRDS are a group of three species formerly thought to be part of the birds-of-paradise family (see p.396), but they were given their own family when differences in their DNA came to light. Unlike birds-of-paradise, they build domed nests, have weak legs and feet, and eat nothing but fruit at all ages, even when young chicks. Two species, the Silken and Antenna Satinbirds, have brilliantly coloured males, while the male Velvet Satinbird is glossy black. Females are dull and inconspicuous. All three satinbird species live in the mountain forests of New Guinea.

SINGLE PARENT
Here, a female Antenna Satinbird builds her globular nest on her own. She will also care for her single chick alone, as is the norm in satinbirds.

Cnemophilus macgregorii

Antenna Satinbird

LENGTH 25cm (10in)
WEIGHT 100g ($3\frac{5}{8}$oz)
MIGRATION Non-migrant
HABITAT Mountain rainforest and forest edge

The Antenna Satinbird is also known as the Crested Cnemophilus or the Sickle-crested Bird-of-Paradise. Males of this species are striking birds. They have orange-yellow or golden plumage on the top of the head and upperparts, which contrasts with their jet-black underparts. They also have a short orange crest. Females are olive coloured all over. Although it is thought to be fairly common in its limited range, little is known about the species, since it inhabits relatively inaccessible upland areas and is surprisingly inconspicuous in its rainforest home.

ADULT MALE

BERRYPECKERS

ORDER	Passeriformes
FAMILY	Melanocharitidae
SPECIES	12

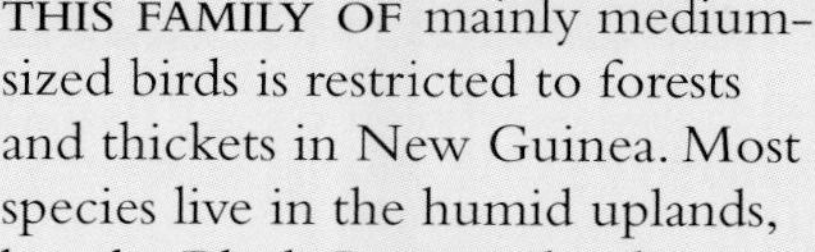

THIS FAMILY OF mainly medium-sized birds is restricted to forests and thickets in New Guinea. Most species live in the humid uplands, but the Black Berrypecker has a lowland range. Apart from two unusually colourful species, these birds have rather dull plumages, typically in shades of brown, grey, olive, pale yellow, or black and white.

BEHAVIOUR

Eight of the species in this family have short, fairly heavy bills, and look like drab members of the honeyeater family (see p.362). They occur at all levels of the forest, from ferns and shrubs near the ground up to the treetops, and are usually seen alone or in pairs. Most of their diet consists of fruit, which is supplemented with a few insects. The remaining four species, called longbills, are quite different. Their very long, decurved bills are similar to those of sunbirds (see p.450), and are suited to their insect-based diet.

BRIGHTLY PATTERNED
The Tit Berrypecker is one of only two colourful species in its diverse but poorly known family.

Toxorhamphus poliopterus

Slaty-headed Longbill

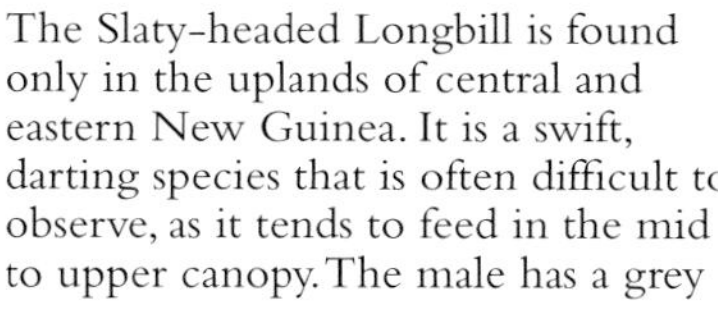

LENGTH 12.5cm ($4\frac{3}{4}$in)
WEIGHT 10–12g ($\frac{3}{8}$–$\frac{7}{16}$oz)
MIGRATION Non-migrant
HABITAT Upland rainforest

The Slaty-headed Longbill is found only in the uplands of central and eastern New Guinea. It is a swift, darting species that is often difficult to observe, as it tends to feed in the mid to upper canopy. The male has a grey head and wings, a grey throat, a bright yellow breast, and duller yellow belly. Females are very similar to males but slightly smaller and paler. The most noticeable feature of the Slaty-headed Longbill is its very long, decurved bill, which it uses for catching insects and drinking nectar.

ADULT SLATY-HEADED LONGBILL

ADULT MALE

Melanocharis versteri

Fan-tailed Berrypecker

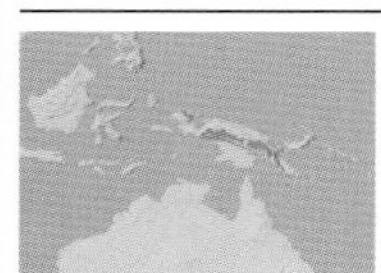

LENGTH 14–15cm ($5\frac{1}{2}$–6in)
WEIGHT 12–18g ($\frac{7}{16}$–$\frac{5}{8}$oz)
MIGRATION Non-migrant
HABITAT Upland rainforest and dense secondary forest growth

The male Fan-tailed Berrypecker has glossy blue-black upperparts that contrast with its off-white underparts. It has a long, rounded tail. Females are similar in shape but are a dull olive green above. The white markings on the outer tail feathers are conspicuous, especially in flight. As well as feeding on berries as its name suggests, the Fan-tailed Berrypecker also takes insects, sometimes by hovering. The species builds an impressive large, cup-shaped nest mainly out of ferns. It is decorated on the outside with lichen.

WATTLED CROWS

ORDER Passeriformes

FAMILY Callaeatidae

SPECIES 2

THESE RARE NEW ZEALAND birds, also known as wattlebirds, are named for the prominent fleshy wattles that hang from the face, either side of the bill. These are orange in the Saddleback and blue in the Kokako; the Kokako's South Island subspecies had orange wattles, but this population probably died out in the late 1960s. A third species of wattled crow, the Huia, was last seen in 1907 and is now considered extinct. It was remarkable for being the world's only bird in which each sex had a differently shaped bill – thin and decurved in females, or straight and pointed in males.

BEHAVIOUR

Wattled crows live in thick forest and feed at all levels of this habitat, particularly on and near to the ground. Their varied diet includes berries, nectar, leaf buds, and insects, with a greater proportion of fruit in summer. They make short gliding flights, but tend to prefer to bound along on their strong legs. Both the Saddleback and the Kokako form monogamous breeding pairs. The male and female share the task of feeding their nestlings, and stay with their young for up to a year after they fledge.

DEVELOPMENT OF YOUNG
The disc-shaped wattles are already clearly visible in these Kokako nestlings. The young stay in the nest for 30–45 days.

ADULT KOKAKO

Callaeas cinerea

Kokako

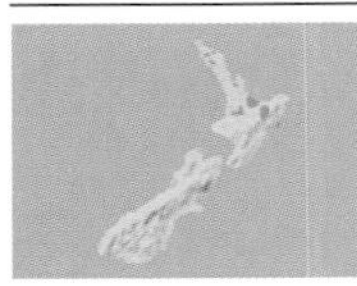

LENGTH 38cm (15in)

WEIGHT 225g (8oz)

MIGRATION Non-migrant

HABITAT Native lowland hardwood and podocarp (subtropical) forest

RED LIST CATEGORY Endangered

A large blue-grey bird with a short, stubby black bill and a black face, the Kokako has remarkable blue facial wattles. Structurally, it is an unusual species with long legs, short rounded wings, and a long tail. The bird, therefore, tends to climb the top of trees, only taking very short flights. Its call is a series of melodious piping notes, similar to the sounds of an organ, sometimes sung in a duet.

The numbers of this species have increased slightly in recent years, due to intensive conservation action, though the Kokako is still classified as endangered.

Philesturnus carunculatus

Saddleback

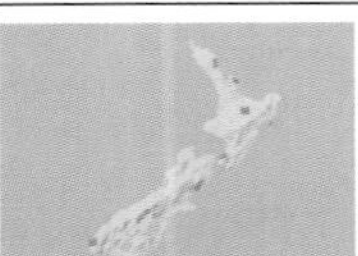

LENGTH 25cm (10in)

WEIGHT 70–80g ($2^1/_2$–$2^7/_8$oz)

MIGRATION Non-migrant

HABITAT Forest and scrub floor on offshore islands

The Saddleback is an attractive, glossy black bird with a very strong bill. Its back, rump, and the undertail are a bright chestnut colour. The adult Saddleback has orange red wattles that hang from just below the base of its bill. The juvenile is brown rather than black, and does not have the wattles. The Saddleback is usually found feeding on the ground, or bounding (rather than flying) between low branches. The bird takes fruit, insects, and nectar. It builds its nest in epiphytes, on the tops of tree ferns, and holes in the tree trunks. The nest is made from twigs and leaves and is lined with fibrous material such as fern scales or bark fibre. The bird lays between 1–4 eggs. The species became extinct on the New Zealand mainland in the early 1900s, but many healthy populations exist on offshore islands.

ADULT SADDLEBACK

WHIPBIRDS AND RELATIVES

ORDER	Passeriformes
FAMILY	Eupetidae
SPECIES	10

THIS SMALL BUT DIVERSE family of insectivorous, ground-dwelling birds includes whipbirds, wedgebills, jewel-babblers, and the Malaysian Rail-babbler. They are confined to Australia and New Guinea, except for the latter species, which is secretive and seldom-seen, and which ranges from Thailand south to Sumatra and Borneo. Most species live in dense forest, but wedgebills inhabit open, arid country.

BEHAVIOUR

The members of this family display a wide variety of behaviour, but are usually feeble or reluctant fliers that prefer to hop briskly or run when foraging. Wedgebills fly more readily than their relatives, gliding between bushes with their tail spread. They form loose flocks, whereas other species are typically more solitary and territorial. Most species have loud, distinctive calls.

HIGHLY VOCAL
The Chirruping Wedgebill from Australia is named for its frequent chattering. Small parties often set up a noisy chorus while perched on bushes.

Psophodes olivaceus

Eastern Whipbird

LENGTH	25–30cm (10–12in)
WEIGHT	60–70g (2$^{1}/_{8}$–2$^{1}/_{2}$oz)
MIGRATION	Non-migrant

HABITAT Rainforest, wet eucalyptus forest, and scrub

The Eastern Whipbird is an elusive bird with a loud, ringing whip-crack call, which gives the species its common name. The bird has a black crest and head, with a thick white strip below its eyes. Its throat and the breast are also black, with a variable amount of white streaking on its belly, and its back and tail are olive-green. These birds hop through the thick undergrowth of the forest floor, foraging among the leaf litter.

ADULT EASTERN WHIPBIRD

Ptilorrhoa castanonota

Chestnut-backed Jewel-babbler

LENGTH	23cm (9in)
WEIGHT	70g (2$^{1}/_{2}$oz)
MIGRATION	Non-migrant

HABITAT Hill forest

A shy but attractive bird, the Chestnut-backed Jewel-babbler is a long-legged bird with a rich blue-grey plumage, chestnut crown and back, black wing feathering, and a long tail. It forages on the floor, tossing aside fallen leaves to uncover insects. More likely to be heard than seen, the bird's calls include a series of loud, ringing down-slurring notes, whip-cracks, and rapid machine gun-like whistles.

ADULT CHESTNUT-BACKED JEWEL-BABBLER

QUAIL-THRUSHES

ORDER	Passeriformes
FAMILY	Cinclosomatidae
SPECIES	5

THE QUAIL-THRUSHES are retiring, medium-sized birds that spend all their life on the ground. There are four Australian species, found in heathland, scrub, stony terrain, and dry, open woodland, and a single New Guinean species, which occurs only in rainforest. The birds' camouflaged upperparts match the ground colour of their habitat. In all species, males have black throat patches, while females are grey-throated.

BEHAVIOUR

Quail-thrushes are insect-eaters, and forage in pairs or small groups, probing the earth, stones, or fallen leaves with their bill. In inland Australia, they also eat the seeds of spinifex plants. Like quails, they crouch low and freeze when disturbed, then burst into the air in a flurry of wingbeats and fly fast and low to cover. Quail-thrushes are normally silent, and so tend to pass unnoticed, but males have a far-carrying song. The nest is a simple cup in the ground, and in open areas is often placed in the shade of a shrub or rock.

Cinclosoma punctatum

Spotted Quail-thrush

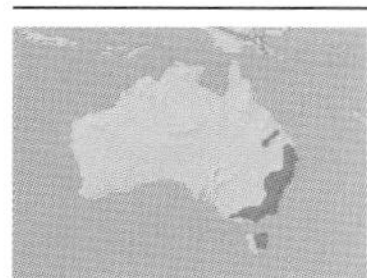

LENGTH	25–28cm (10–11in)
WEIGHT	100–125g (3$^{5}/_{8}$–4oz)
MIGRATION	Non-migrant

HABITAT Dry forest and woodland with plentiful leaf and twig litter

The Spotted Quail-thrush is a distinctively patterned species. The male has a black face and throat, with a large white patch below and a white stripe above the eyes. Its neck and breast are blue-grey and it has a sandy-coloured back, flecked with black streaking. The female lacks the male's facial pattern.

ADULT SPOTTED QUAIL-THRUSH

WATTLE-EYES AND BATISES

ORDER	Passeriformes
FAMILY	Platysteiridae
SPECIES	28

THESE SMALL birds from sub-Saharan Africa are also called puffback flycatchers, and used to be placed in the chats and flycatchers family, Muscicapidae (see p.440). The wattle-eyes are named for the fleshy growths around their eyes, which can be bright red, pink, blue, or violet, depending on the species. Most of them are black above and white below, but some species have yellow underparts, and females may be brown. Batises are also pied, with a black breast-band, and some have rufous or grey areas.

NEAT NEST
DNA studies have confirmed the Black-throated Wattle-eye (right) as a member of this family. Like other species within this family, it makes a tiny nest cup, tightly woven with spider's silk.

BEHAVIOUR

Wattle-eyes and batises are insect-eaters of all kinds of open wooded country, including savanna, bush, gardens, and forest clearings, although some live in dense forest. They are restless, active birds, which normally catch insects in mid-air, during an aerobatic sally from an exposed perch, but sometimes they snatch their prey off leaves or drop to the ground. Usually, they are seen in pairs or small groups. The male and female form a monogamous breeding pair, with both sexes helping to build the cup-shaped nest, incubate the 2 or 3 eggs, and feed the young.

Batis capensis

Cape Batis

LENGTH 12cm (4½in)

WEIGHT 11–12g (3/8–7/16oz)

MIGRATION Partial migrant

HABITAT Mainly evergreen forest

ADULT MALE CAPE BATIS

This small, active bird is found in a fragmented range from southeast Tanzania to southwest South Africa. The Cape Batis is an intricately patterned species, and has a grey head, black face-mask, red eyes, and greyish brown upperparts. The female is slightly different, with rufous tinges on its throat and a rufous, rather than black, breast-band. The juvenile is similar to the female, but duller. There are many similar species of the *Batis* genus, but most do not overlap with the Cape Batis and have subtle plumage differences as well as easily distinguishable calls.

Platysteira cyanea

Brown-throated Wattle-eye

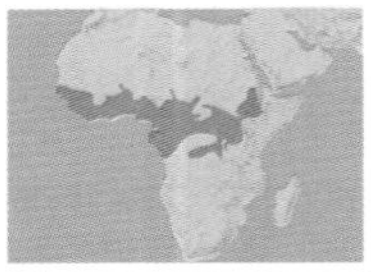

LENGTH 12–14cm (4½–5½in)

WEIGHT 15g (9/16oz)

MIGRATION Non-migrant

HABITAT Forest clearings and open woodland areas

A small black-and-white bird, the Brown-throated Wattle-eye has a distinctive fleshy red wattle above the eye. The male has a black head and a contrasting white throat and upperparts, which are separated by a thick black breast-band. It also has a long white bar that extends along the length of the wing. The female has a dark chestnut-brown throat and breast and grey upperparts. The juvenile is duller and greyer, with off-white underparts and no red wattle.

The Brown-throated Wattle-eye is a widespread species south of the Sahara, and is found in a band extending from Senegal in the west to Kenya in the east.

FEMALE BROWN-THROATED WATTLE-EYE

HELMETSHRIKES AND PUFFBACKS

ORDER	Passeriformes
FAMILY	Malaconotidae
SPECIES	52

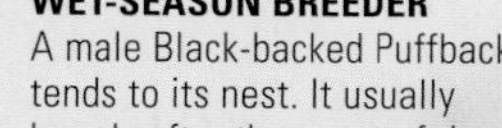

THIS FAMILY contains some of Africa's most colourful birds. Many are bright yellow, orange, red, or green, generally in both sexes. Helmetshrikes are black and white, with a large crest and fleshy wattles around the eyes. Despite their bold plumage, these birds can be hard to see, because they often stay hidden in scrub or forest – their calls are the best way to locate them. As well as helmetshrikes and puffbacks, the family includes boubous, gonoleks, bushshrikes, and tchagras. All of them eat invertebrates, but larger species also catch small vertebrates. Helmetshrikes breed co-operatively.

WET-SEASON BREEDER
A male Black-backed Puffback tends to its nest. It usually breeds after the onset of the rainy season when food is plentiful, like many other members of this family.

Prionops plumatus

White-crested Helmetshrike

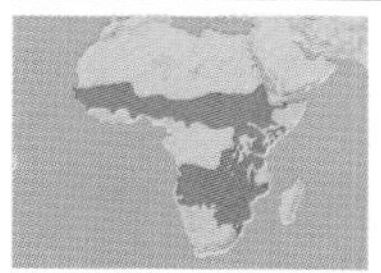

LENGTH	19–25cm (7$\frac{1}{2}$–10in)
WEIGHT	30–35g (1$\frac{1}{16}$–1$\frac{1}{4}$oz)
MIGRATION	Non-migrant

HABITAT Mainly open woodland

The White-crested Helmetshrike is a medium-large member of the *Prionops* genus, which is widespread in open woodland throughout much of sub-Saharan Africa. The adult has a white crest, head, and neck, black neck collar, a yellow eye-ring and a black crescent behind the eye, white underparts, and black wings and tail with white outer-tail feathers. The juvenile has dark eyes and brown upperparts. There are at least nine subspecies, differing in plumage as well as size: for instance, birds found in Ethiopia and Sudan lack the white wing-bar common in other subspecies, whereas some southerly birds have a grey head without a crest. The White-crested Helmetshrike has a complex and variable set of different calls.

ADULT BIRD

Telophorus zeylonus

Bokmakierie

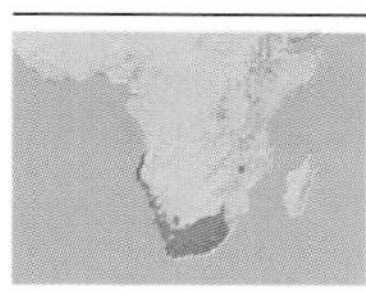

LENGTH	23cm (9in)
WEIGHT	60–65g (2$\frac{1}{8}$–2$\frac{3}{8}$oz)
MIGRATION	Non-migrant

HABITAT Mainly open habitat such as scrub, thickets, grassland, parks, and gardens

ADULT BOKMAKIERIE

A large species of bushshrike, the Bokmakierie is found in southern Africa. The adult has a grey head and neck and yellow eyebrows, throat, and underparts, with a black eyebrow extending down into a breast-band. The upperparts and wings are olive-green. In flight, its yellow tail-tips can be clearly seen. It is most frequently seen on the ground, on its own or in pairs. It is a shy bird, but will perch on exposed sites such as rocks and shrubs when giving its ringing calls.

Chlorophoneus dohertyi

Doherty's Bushshrike

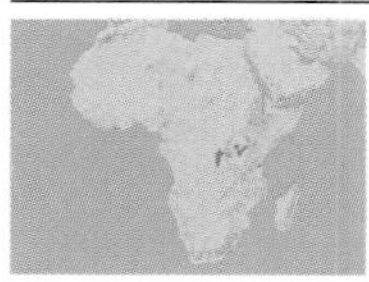

LENGTH	19cm (7$\frac{1}{2}$in)
WEIGHT	30–40g (1$\frac{1}{16}$–1$\frac{7}{16}$oz)
MIGRATION	Non-migrant

HABITAT Thick scrub and undergrowth, generally in upland areas

A shy species that inhabits thick scrub and undergrowth and limited to a tiny range, Doherty's Bushshrike is not often seen. The adult is striking, with its crimson face and forehead sandwiched by a black face-mask and breast-band. These features contrast with its green upperparts and yellow underparts. Very rarely, some adults have a yellow throat and forehead. The juvenile is a plain olive-green above, and a paler yellow below.

ADULT DOHERTY'S BUSHSHRIKE

Tchagra senegalus

Black-crowned Tchagra

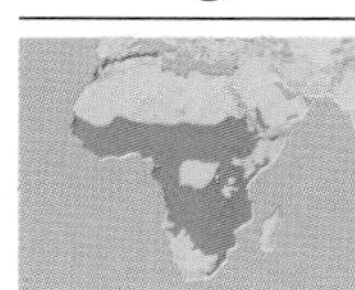

LENGTH	20–23cm (8–9in)
WEIGHT	50g (1$\frac{3}{4}$oz)
MIGRATION	Non-migrant

HABITAT Scrubby semi-desert, thickets, open forest, woodland, and gardens

The Black-crowned Tchagra is a medium-large species of thin-billed bushshrike. The adult has an intricate head pattern: a white stripe above and a black stripe through the eye, topped with a black crown. The underparts are cream-coloured or off-white, the upperparts are brown or grey, and the wings show a variable amount of chestnut-brown. The tail is black with a white outer border that is clearly visible in flight. The sexes are similar, but the juvenile is less distinctive than the adult, with a brown crown and duller underparts. The Black-crowned Tchagra is a solitary, shy species that is usually found low down in the undergrowth or on the ground. It creeps, runs, and hops around in search of insects, sometimes also turning over leaves to look for food. It has a variety of calls, ranging from trills to harsher notes. However, its most common song is a loud, mellow whistle.

The Black-crowned Tchagra builds its nest in a tree or bush. It lays 2 or 3 eggs, which are incubated for 12–15 days mainly by the female, it takes another 15 days for the chicks to fledge. The species is widespread south of the Sahara, it also occurs in north Africa, and a small population is also found in the Middle East.

ADULT BLACK-CROWNED TCHAGRA

BOATBILLS

ORDER	Passeriformes
FAMILY	Machaerirhynchidae
SPECIES	2

BOATBILLS ARE SMALL, boldly marked forest birds that behave like flycatchers. Males are mostly yellow and black, while females have green and grey upperparts. There are only two species: the Yellow-breasted Boatbill of northeastern Australia and New Guinea; and the Black-breasted Boatbill, found in the mountains of New Guinea. These birds are named for their wide, flattened bill, which is almost shovel-like in profile.

SMALL BROODS
A female Yellow-breasted Boatbill visits her nest. Boatbills make hammock-shaped nests from twigs and produce small broods of two young.

Machaerirhynchus flaviventer

Yellow-breasted Boatbill

LENGTH 11–13cm ($4^1/_2$–5in)

WEIGHT 10g ($^3/_8$oz)

MIGRATION Non-migrant

HABITAT Forested areas, including dense second growth and edges, mainly in the lowlands

The Yellow-breasted Boatbill bears a resemblance to the Tody-flycatcher (see p.306) of South America, both in coloration and in its wide flat bill. The male has a white throat and bright yellow underparts. The female is much paler, both above and below, and several subspecies lack the thick black stripe through the eye. This bird frequently joins mixed-species flocks to search for insect prey, largely in the mid-storey of forests. The nest is a frail-looking basket of rootlets bound with cobwebs, and 2 or 3 eggs are laid.

MALE YELLOW-BREASTED BOATBILL

VANGAS

ORDER	Passeriformes
FAMILY	Vangidae
SPECIES	22

UNIQUE TO MADAGASCAR, vangas have evolved over many generations to occupy a wide range of different habitats and ecological niches on the island. One species, the Blue Vanga, is also found in the nearby Comoros Islands. Although all vangas live in or near trees, some live in more open areas such as savanna, while others are confined to dense humid forest.

ANATOMY

Vangas range in size from shrikes to small crows, and their coloration also varies markedly – some are drab but three species are mainly blue. However, the feature that differs most is their bill shape. Several species have stout, hooked bills, and are generalist insect-eaters. The Sickle-billed Vanga has an extremely long, decurved bill to winkle food from cracks, and the Helmet Vanga's massive bill enables it to kill large prey.

POWERFUL BILL
The Helmet Vanga's huge, deep bill is blue in adults and brown in juveniles. It can tackle larger prey than other vangas – including land crabs, tree frogs, and chameleons.

Vanga curvirostris

Hook-billed Vanga

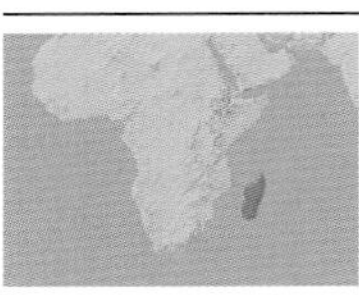

LENGTH 25–29cm (10–$11^1/_2$in)

WEIGHT 65–75g ($2^3/_8$–$2^5/_8$oz)

MIGRATION Non-migrant

HABITAT Often found in dense forest and scrub, but also recorded in plantations

With its long heavy bill and pied plumage, the Hook-billed Vanga is unmistakable. The male and female are alike in appearance. A predatory bird of Madagascan forests, this species feeds on large insects, including cicadas, as well as chameleons, and even mouse lemurs. It either beats its prey against a branch before consuming it, or impales it on a thorn before tearing at its flesh with its bill. In the breeding season, it builds bulky cup-shaped nests lined with spiderwebs and placed prominently in a tree. Both sexes incubate the eggs and care for the 3 or 4 young.

ADULT HOOK-BILLED VANGA

Cyanolanius madagascarinus

Blue Vanga

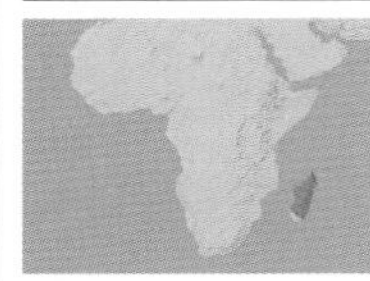

LENGTH 16cm ($6^1/_2$in)

WEIGHT 25g ($^7/_8$oz)

MIGRATION Non-migrant

HABITAT Primary evergreen forest, often around clearings

Aptly named, the male Blue Vanga is a brilliant blue above, with a bright blue bill and eye-ring and a black line through the eye. The underparts are white. The female differs in having a brown bill, some brown tones in the upperparts, and off-white to buff-coloured underparts. This vanga regularly joins mixed-species flocks, gleaning insects from the foliage.

Euryceros prevostii

Helmet Vanga

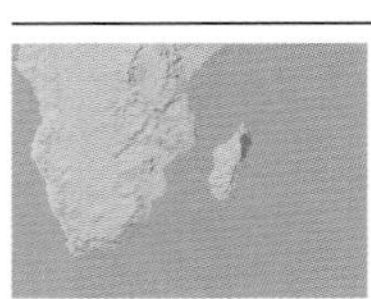

LENGTH 28–31cm (11–12in)

WEIGHT 85–100g (3–$3^5/_8$oz)

MIGRATION Non-migrant

HABITAT Found in the mid-storey of humid evergreen forest in lowland and foothills

A distinctive member of its family, the adult Helmet Vanga has a massive blue bill, with a black tip, and pale yellow eyes. It has a black head, wings, and underparts and a deep chestnut-brown back and tail. The black parts of the adult are buff in the juvenile. This species moves in mixed flocks with other large vanga species, but also perches quietly for long periods.

Schetba rufa

Rufous Vanga

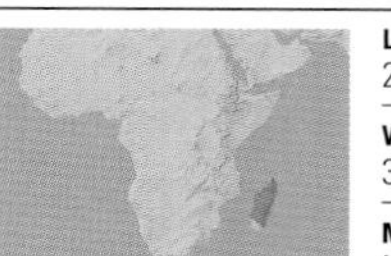

LENGTH 20cm (8in)

WEIGHT 35–40g ($1^1/_4$–$^7/_{16}$oz)

MIGRATION Non-migrant

HABITAT Primary evergreen forest, usually in areas with tall trees and an open understorey

This medium-sized vanga is renowned for its rich vocalizations. Its back and tail are rusty red and the underparts are white. The male differs from the female in an entirely black head and upper breast. The species feeds on small vertebrates and insects. The nest is constructed by both adults, in the low fork of a tree, and both parents tend the young.

ADULT FEMALE AT THE NEST

Hypositta corallirostris

Nuthatch Vanga

LENGTH 14cm ($5^1/_2$in)

WEIGHT 14g ($^1/_2$oz)

MIGRATION Non-migrant

HABITAT Humid lowland forest

Also known as the Coral-billed Nuthatch, the Nuthatch Vanga is endemic to Madagascar. The plumage is almost entirely blue, but the female is more buff in colour, especially below. The male has black around the eye and the base of the bill. This species hugs and climbs the bark of medium to large trees, but unlike typical nuthatches, it does not descend headfirst. Also, unlike nuthatches, the nest is a cup-shaped structure attached to the main trunk, and not in a hole.

JUVENILE NUTHATCH VANGA

BUTCHERBIRDS

ORDER	Passeriformes
FAMILY	Cracticidae
SPECIES	13

THESE AUSTRALASIAN birds look much like crows due to their heavy, triangular bill, well-built body, and strong legs and feet. Most of them are black, grey, or white. Several species, particularly the Australian Magpie, have adapted to life in cities. Apart from this abundant species, the family also contains seven butcherbirds, three currawongs, and two shieldbills, which are endemic to New Guinea and, unlike the rest of the family, resemble small, all-dark woodswallows (see p.378).

BEHAVIOUR

These bold, aggressive birds often become tame, and are highly vocal. They live in most habitats, but are especially numerous in eucalypt woodland, farmland, and suburban areas. They have a varied diet, including fruit, small animals, and carrion. Butcherbirds are named for their habit of wedging prey between fence wires or into a tree fork. Currawongs get their name from the wailing call of the Pied Currawong.

DISMEMBERING PREY
By hanging their food on a tree, butcherbirds can tear apart larger prey than would otherwise be possible. A Grey Butcherbird is pictured (left).

Cracticus nigrogularis

Pied Butcherbird

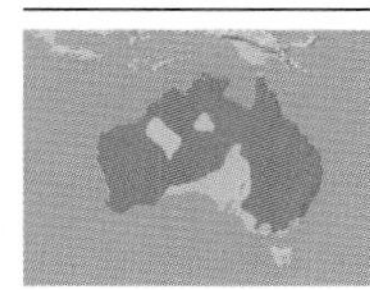

LENGTH 32–35cm ($12^1/_2$–14in)

WEIGHT 125g (4oz)

MIGRATION Non-migrant

HABITAT Woodland, farms, plains with trees and even towns and roadsides

Whereas the adult Pied Butcherbird is immediately recognizable by its striking black and white plumage, the juvenile is mainly grey-brown. The melodious fluting and piping songs of the Pied Butcherbird disguise a fierce predatory disposition. It is well-named for it impales its prey – insects, mice, lizards, or small birds – on a broken branch before tearing it into shreds, using its hooked bill. The nest is an untidy cup lined with grass and placed in the upright fork of a tall tree. The female incubates the eggs alone and is fed by the male during this time. About 3–5 young birds usually remain with their parents for up to 15 months and help the adults to raise the next brood.

ADULT PIED BUTCHERBIRD

Gymnorhina tibicen

Australian Magpie

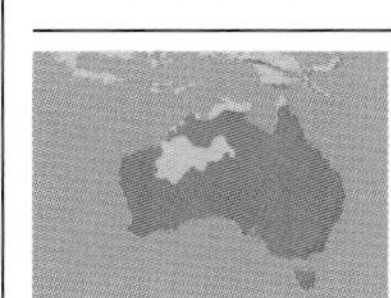

LENGTH 34–44cm ($13^1/_2$–$17^1/_2$in)

WEIGHT 275g (10oz)

MIGRATION Non-migrant

HABITAT Common in woodland, urban areas, and clearings

The Australian Magpie is found in a striking array of about five forms, all of which are basically black and white. They are distinguished in adult plumage by the varying amount of white in the wings and on the back, and the length of the bill, which is pale, with a dark tip. It is often found around human settlements, where it can become tame, but during the nesting season it may attack humans.

BLACK-BACKED FORM

Strepera graculina

Pied Currawong

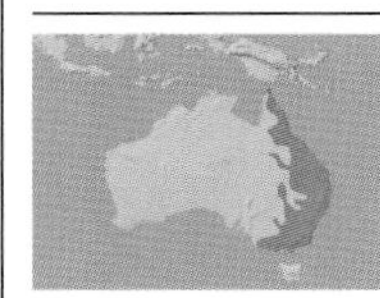

LENGTH 41–51cm (16–20in)

WEIGHT 300g (11oz)

MIGRATION Partial migrant

HABITAT Forested and wooded areas, but also around rural and urban areas with trees

At rest, despite its name, the Pied Currawong appears almost all black, except for the white at the tip and the base of the tail. In flight, however, when the long wings are also apparent, white flashes in its long wings and a white rump can be seen. The bill is long and conical, and like other currawongs, the eyes are pale. The Pied Currawong is often seen in flocks, which may number up to 100 birds in winter, but each pair breeds alone and is well separated from its neighbour. The nest is a large flat cup of sticks, lined with softer material, into which the female lays three eggs.

WOODSWALLOWS

ORDER	Passeriformes
FAMILY	Artamidae
SPECIES	10

THESE GRACEFUL FLIERS from southeast Asia, New Guinea, and Australia are not related to swallows and martins (see p.405), but, like them, spend long periods on the wing catching flying insects. They have broad, pointed wings and are among the few songbirds able to soar. Woodswallows also feed on nectar, which they gather at flowering trees using the brush-like tip to their tongue.

CLOSE CONTACT
Like all of their family, White-breasted Woodswallows preen and roost in close-packed rows, perhaps for safety.

Artamus personatus

Masked Woodswallow

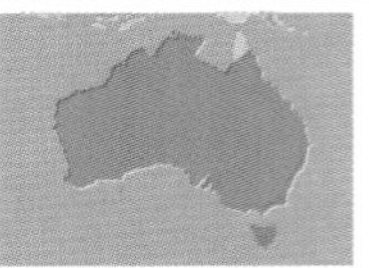

LENGTH 20cm (8in)

WEIGHT 34g ($1^1/_4$oz)

MIGRATION Partial migrant

HABITAT Open forest and woodland, scrub, heath, farmland, and vineyards

The male Masked Woodswallow has a dark face, which contrasts with its slate-grey upperparts and paler underparts. It has a thick, black-tipped bill and a white tip to its tail. The female is a paler version of the male, but has a dark grey face and brown-tinged underparts. The diet of this species consists mainly of flying insects, but it also takes prey from the ground. The Masked Woodswallow is highly nomadic, and moves in response to changes in rainfall and temperature.

MALE MASKED WOODSWALLOW

IORAS

ORDER	Passeriformes
FAMILY	Aegithinidae
SPECIES	4

IORAS ARE SMALL insect-eating birds found from India, through southeast Asia, south as far as Java. They make up one of only four bird families unique to the Indomalayan realm (see p.70), and formerly were lumped together with one of the others – the leafbirds (see p.448). Ioras of both sexes are greenish yellow or green with white wingbars. The males have black upperparts. This plumage provides effective camouflage amid sun-dappled foliage.

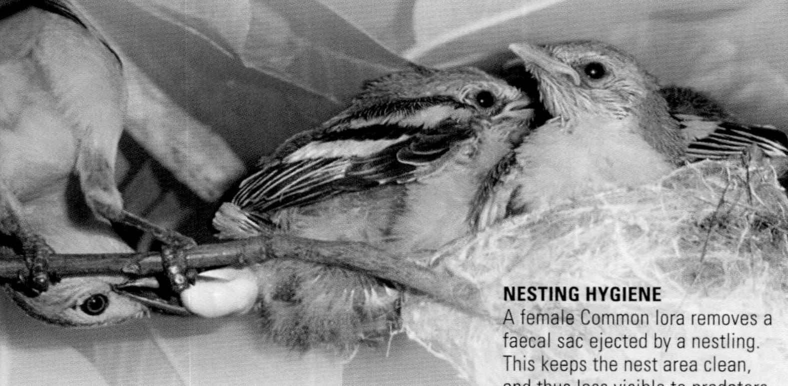

NESTING HYGIENE
A female Common Iora removes a faecal sac ejected by a nestling. This keeps the nest area clean, and thus less visible to predators.

BEHAVIOUR

These birds live mostly in forest and lightly wooded habitats, and in cleared or cultivated areas such as agricultural land, orchards, parks, and gardens. One species, Marshall's Iora from northwestern India, occurs in arid scrubland. Ioras move quickly and acrobatically through the trees, searching the leaves for spiders, caterpillars, and small insects. During the breeding season, they are territorial and usually seen in pairs, although within their local area a pair will often join mixed feeding flocks of other small birds, such as minivets and tits. The climax of the male's courtship display is a slow, spiralling glide from a high perch to a lower one, with the lower back feathers fluffed up.

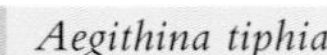

Aegithina tiphia

Common Iora

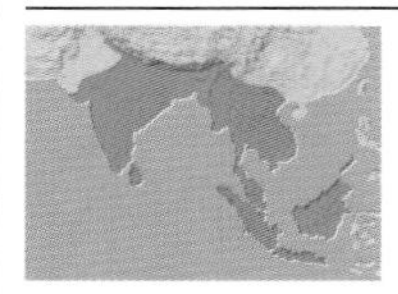

LENGTH 13–14cm (5–$5^1/_2$in)

WEIGHT 12–17g ($^1/_2$–$^3/_4$oz)

MIGRATION Non-migrant

HABITAT Mangrove forests, woodland, scrub, bamboo thickets, and orchards

This widespread and variable species is found throughout south and southeast Asia. There are a number of subspecies of the Common Iora differing quite considerably in their appearance. Generally, the adult Common Iora has a strong decurved bill, olive-green upperparts, dark wings with a double white wing-bar, and bright yellow underparts. The male tends to be brighter and blacker-backed than the female, although this difference is more noticeable in certain subspecies. The males of some subspecies have a dark cap and upperparts during breeding, but moult to a female-like plumage after breeding has taken place.

The Common Iora builds a cup-shaped nest, which is held in place by cobwebs attached to nearby branches, and 2–4 eggs are usually laid. Both the male and female provide food for the nestlings, tending to them and sheltering them from the elements.

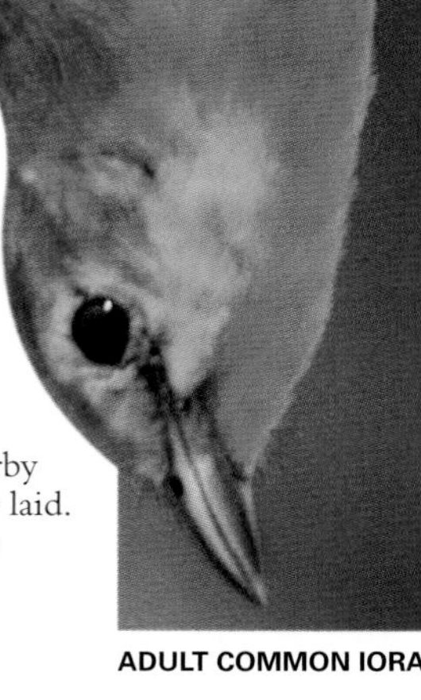

ADULT COMMON IORA

BRISTLEHEAD

ORDER	Passeriformes
FAMILY	Pityriasidae
SPECIES	1

THE BORNEAN BRISTLEHEAD is one of only three passerines to be given its own family. Its relationship to other birds is much debated, and based on biochemical studies of its DNA some authorities suggest it is allied to the woodswallows (opposite) or butcherbirds (see p.377). The bristlehead's rarity and elusive, canopy-living habits add to the difficulty of its classification, but most ornithologists agree it is sufficiently unusual to be treated as a family in its own right.

Pityriasis gymnocephala

Bornean Bristlehead

LENGTH 25cm (10in)

WEIGHT 120–140g (4–5oz)

MIGRATION Partial migrant

HABITAT Lowland primary rainforest; also other higher-level wooded areas

This unusual bird is the sole member of its family and is found only on the island of Borneo. In appearance, the Bornean Bristlehead is a bare-headed, crow-like bird, with a massive hooked bill and short tail. The species gets its name from the short yellow bristles on its orange-yellow crown. It has a predominantly glossy black plumage that contrasts with its red face, throat, neck, and thighs. The Bornean Bristlehead is a noisy bird, and uses a variety of contact calls within its group. Very little is known about its breeding patterns.

The species is classified as globally near-threatened due to the almost complete destruction of its native lowland peat-swamp forest. However, it appears able to survive in less threatened upland forest areas.

CUCKOOSHRIKES

ORDER	Passeriformes
FAMILY	Campephagidae
SPECIES	81

THIS LARGE GROUP of birds are not in fact allied with cuckoos (see p.272) or shrikes (see p.382). The family's name comes from the stout, hooked, shrike-like bill of species in the genus *Coracina*, and the rather cuckoo-like plumage and shape of many of these birds, most noticeable in flight. The family can be split into two groups. In the largest group are the cuckooshrikes, cicadabirds, and trillers (including all of the genus *Coracina*); these occur in Africa, southern and southeast Asia, Australasia, and islands in the western Pacific. The second group contains the 13 species of minivet, found only in Asia.

BLACK-FACED CUCKOOSHRIKE
Cuckooshrikes in the genus *Coracina* are mainly soft grey or black, with slim bodies, long, pointed wings, and fairly long tails.

BEHAVIOUR

Minivets are small, active insect-eaters that often gather in parties of up to 20 birds, constantly calling to each other as the flock moves through forest or open woodland. Males of most species are scarlet and black, or orange and black, while females are duller yellow, orange, and grey. The cuckooshrikes and cicadabirds also live in forest or wooded habitats, often in groups, but they are slower-moving and many of them eat fruit as well as insects. A few species feed on the ground. All members of the family form monogamous pairs, and lay two to five eggs.

WATCHFUL PARENTS
A pair of Small Minivets (the male is on the right) watch over their three young nestlings. This species is less colourful than most other minivets.

ADULT BLACK-FACED CUCKOOSHRIKE

Coracina novaehollandiae

Black-faced Cuckooshrike

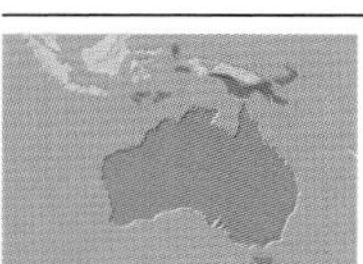

LENGTH 32–35cm (12½–14in)

WEIGHT 100–150g (4–5oz)

MIGRATION Migrant

HABITAT Open forest, grassland, scrub, farmland, parks, and gardens

The adult Black-faced Cuckooshrike has a distinct black facial mask and throat, slate-grey upperparts, and paler grey underparts. The juvenile is more barred, with a duller dark mask and pale throat. The species feeds on insects, fruit, and seeds. The nest is a shallow saucer of sticks and bark, bound together with cobwebs. Both parents care for the young birds.

Coracina lineata

Barred Cuckooshrike

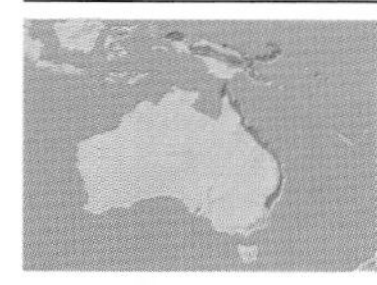

LENGTH 22–29cm (8½–11½in)

WEIGHT 65–100g (2½–3¾oz)

MIGRATION Partial migrant

HABITAT Rainforest and other wooded areas

A dark, neatly marked species, the adult Barred Cuckooshrike has a narrow black line separating its yellow eyes and dark bill. It is slate-grey on the upperparts and breast, with a finely barred black and white belly. The juvenile has dark eyes and pale off-white underparts. Some Barred Cuckooshrikes found in Australia undertake nomadic movements in search of fruiting trees. Little is known about the movements of other populations, although they are thought to be largely sedentary.

ADULT BARRED CUCKOO-SHRIKE

Coracina tenuirostris

Common Cicadabird

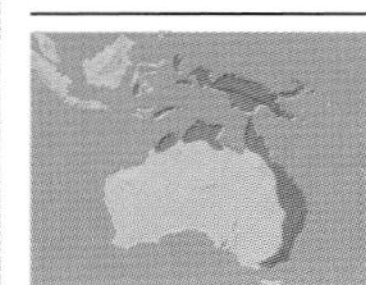

LENGTH 24–27cm (9½–10½in)

WEIGHT 55–75g (2–2¾oz)

MIGRATION Partial migrant

HABITAT Rainforest canopy, eucalyptus forest, and other wooded and semi-wooded areas

An elusive species, the Common Cicadabird is most likely to be heard, its staccato buzzing noise similar to the sounds made by a cicada. The male is a uniform dark grey, while the female has a thin white line above and below the eye, brown upperparts, and pale barred underparts. The juvenile is similar to the female, but is paler brown above. The species is a migrant breeding bird in southeastern Australia, and a year-round resident in north Australia, New Guinea, and Indonesia.

Lalage sueurii

White-shouldered Triller

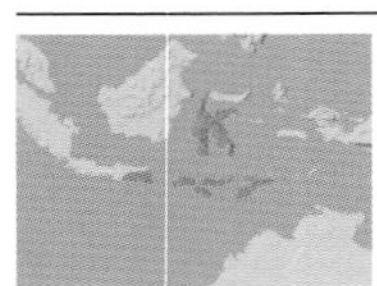

LENGTH 18cm (7in)

WEIGHT 25g ($^{7}/_{8}$oz)

MIGRATION Non-migrant

HABITAT Lightly wooded areas and mangroves

A small bird, the male White-shouldered Triller has a striking pied plumage, with a wide white shoulder patch and a grey-white rump. Most males show a white eyebrow, but in some, like the bird pictured below, it is absent. The female is drabber, with brown plumage and faint barring on the flanks. The species feeds on insect larvae, which it gleans from foliage. Not considered threatened, it is only found in central Indonesia.

ADULT MALE

Campephaga phoenicea

Red-shouldered Cuckooshrike

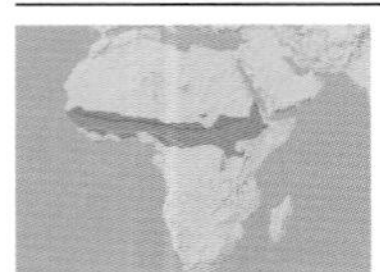

LENGTH 20cm (8in)

WEIGHT 25g ($^{7}/_{8}$oz)

MIGRATION Non-migrant

HABITAT Wooded savanna and narrow strips of forest

The Red-shouldered Cuckooshrike is a typical representative of this African genus of cuckooshrike. It has glossy black plumage and striking yellow cheeks. As the name of the species indicates, the male Red-shouldered Cuckooshrike differs from other members of the *Campephaga* genus by its conspicuous red shoulder patch. The female is grey-brown above, with densely barred pale underparts and yellow-edged wing and tail feathers and, unlike the male, cannot be easily distinguished from near relatives.

Pericrocotus ethologus

Long-tailed Minivet

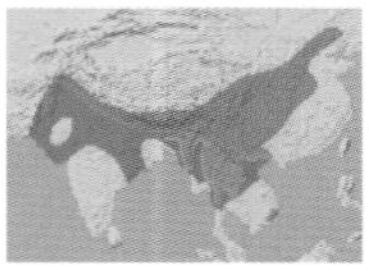

LENGTH 20cm (8in)

WEIGHT 18–20g ($^{5}/_{8}$–$^{11}/_{16}$oz)

MIGRATION Partial migrant

HABITAT Open broad-leaved and coniferous forest, often lower in winter in secondary wooded habitats

One of a group of red and black minivets found in southern Asia, the Long-tailed Minivet is a small, arboreal bird. Only the adult male of the species is red and black, with a red U-shaped patch on its black wings, and red underparts. The female is largely grey and yellow, its pale grey throat and yellow eyebrow distinguishing it from other minivet species. The juvenile is similar to the female, except for a red tinge that is present on the rump of the juvenile male.

JUVENILE MALE

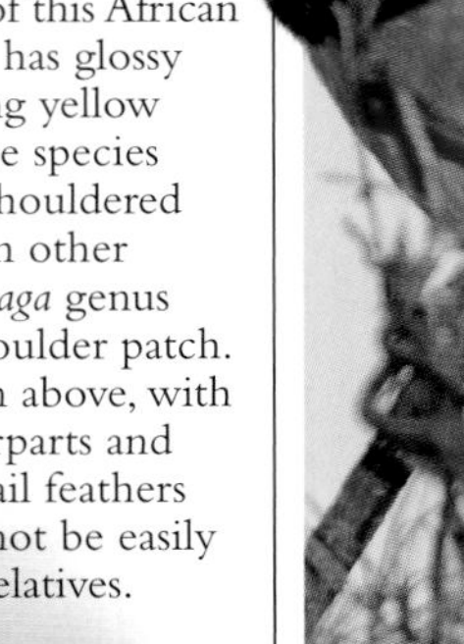

MALE SCARLET MINIVET

Pericrocotus flammeus

Scarlet Minivet

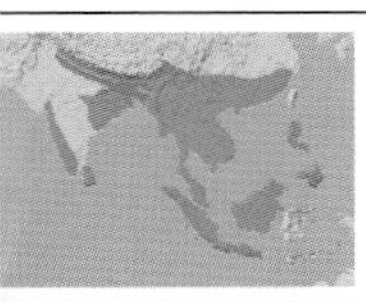

LENGTH 20–22cm (8–8$^{1}/_{2}$in)

WEIGHT 25g ($^{7}/_{8}$oz)

MIGRATION Non-migrant

HABITAT Open tropical, subtropical, and temperate broad-leaved forest; occasionally in conifers

The male Scarlet Minivet is a striking red and black bird that can be told apart from its similar relatives by its larger size, stocky build, and orange-red underparts. Viewed close up, its red wing patch reveals an outlying blob of red on the wing-tips, which is an identifying feature of the bird. The female is grey and yellow above, with yellow underparts. Highly social, this species forms large flocks during the non-breeding season, often joining mixed-species flocks as it feeds in the canopy.

SITELLAS

ORDER Passeriformes

FAMILY Neosittidae

SPECIES 3

OF THE THREE SPECIES of sitellas, two are found in New Guinea and the third in Australia (in most of the continent). Sitellas bear a superficial resemblance to nuthatches (p.472) in structure, and sometimes in plumage, but a much greater similarity in their feeding behaviour. This family is highly social, feeding, breeding, and roosting together. Nests are well-camouflaged cups attached to a tree fork, moulded to resemble a knot on the bark.

CLINGING HEAD-DOWNWARDS
A Varied Sitella works its way down a tree, in a typical "rocking-horse" motion, in search of insects.

Daphoenositta chrysoptera

Varied Sittella

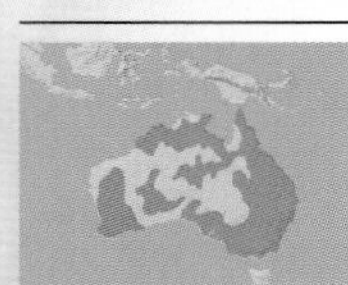

LENGTH 11–13cm (4$^{1}/_{2}$–5in)

WEIGHT 12g ($^{7}/_{16}$oz)

MIGRATION Non-migrant

HABITAT Eucalyptus woodland, forest, and scrub; avoids dense rainforest

Well named for the wide variety of plumage types throughout its range in Australia, the subspecies of the Varied Sittella differ in the colours of the head and wing patches and in the amount of streaking on the underparts. Most adults of the species, however, have long, slender bills and are gray above and white below. There are five distinct subspecies. The subspecies *D. c. leucocephala* (shown here) is named for its white head; in addition, it has a white neck, an orange wing patch, and streaked underparts. The Varied Sittella forms noisy groups that carefully search for invertebrates on the surfaces of trunks and branches.

VARIED SITTELLA (*D. C. LEUCOCEPHALA*)

SHRIKETITS

ORDER Passeriformes
FAMILY Falcunculidae
SPECIES 4

SHRIKETITS COMPRISE a group of four species: three in Australia and the fourth in the highlands of New Guinea. These have only recently been recognized as constituting their own family separate from the whistlers and shrikethrushes; they were formerly regarded as a single species that included several subspecies. Among their other close relatives are the Australasian sitellas. Shriketits are principally forest-based species, although they do not shun more open habitats, such as parks and golf courses, as long as they contain trees. These short-tailed Australian birds are fairly round-bodied and have a formidable stout and strongly hooked bill. The clear, animated songs of the shriketits often contain much mimicry of other bird species, according to the locality. The nest, constructed during the summer months by the Australian species, is a deep cup, located well above head height in a tall tree and supported by a vertical stem. The birds usually lay two or three well-spotted eggs.

Falcunculus frontatus

Crested Shriketit

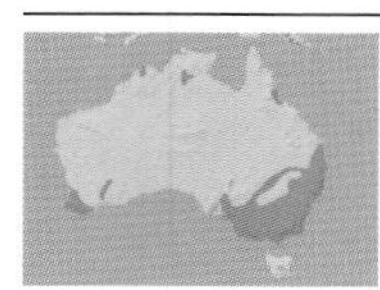

LENGTH 18–19cm (7–$7\frac{1}{2}$in)
WEIGHT 25–30g ($\frac{7}{8}$–$1\frac{1}{16}$oz)
MIGRATION Non-migrant

HABITAT Eucalyptus forest and woodland, gardens, and coastal scrub

Distinguished by its black crest, the Crested, or Eastern, Shriketit has two broad white stripes on its head and a large bill, with a patch of white at its base. The sexes are very similar, except for the throat, which is black in the male and green in the female. The Crested Shriketit uses its strong, notched bill to open seedpods, caterpillar cocoons, and galls and to pick insects from branches. It also tears off loose bark as it searches for its insect prey, making quite a noise as it does so. It nests in groups, making a nest of bark and spiders' webs, usually placed near the top of a tree.

MALE CRESTED SHRIKETIT

WHISTLERS

ORDER Passeriformes
FAMILY Pachycephalidae
SPECIES 41

WHISTLERS OCCUR FROM India through southeast Asia and Indonesia, but most species are found in Australia and New Guinea. Most species within this family are sedentary, but some are long-distance migrants. The family name hints at the vocal capacity of this group, which boasts some of Australia's finest songsters.

ANATOMY

All whistlers are characterized by their strong feet. They usually have relatively large and robust, hooked or stubby bills, which are used for catching prey, mainly insects, but they also eat small vertebrates, other birds' eggs and nestlings, and fruit. Whistlers typically also have large, rounded heads, giving rise to their alternative name, thickheads. Most are brown, olive, green, or grey in coloration, but some species are more striking, with yellow, rufous, and black plumage.

TREE-FORK NEST
Birds of this family, such as this Rufous Whistler, generally build nests from grasses, lichen, and twigs in a fork in a bush or tree.

Pachycephala pectoralis

Golden Whistler

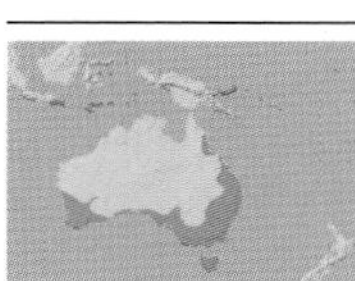

LENGTH 17cm ($6\frac{1}{2}$in)
WEIGHT 20–50g ($\frac{11}{16}$–$1\frac{3}{4}$oz)
MIGRATION Non-migrant

HABITAT Rainforest, open forest, and woodland; low scrub and coastal vegetation

Green and yellow in colour, the male Golden Whistler has a splendid black head, white throat, and golden nape. The female is largely dull brown, although some races have yellow-tinged underparts. The Golden Whistler is highly vocal during the breeding season, producing a range of mellifluous notes, many being strong and ending in sharp cracks. It often sings in response to sudden loud noises, giving rise to its other name of Thunderbird. The Golden Whistler shows much variation in size across its vast geographical range, as indicated by its large weight range.

MALE GOLDEN WHISTLER

NESTING

The nest of the Golden Whistler is a shallow cup built from twigs, grass, and bark, lined with finer grass and bound together with spiders' webs. Both parents share the incubation and care of the young, and feed them on insects, spiders, and other small arthropods. Berries are also given. Most food is picked from the leaves and bark of the lower or middle levels of a tree.

Pachycephala rufiventris

Rufous Whistler

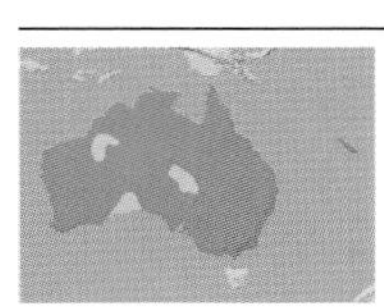

LENGTH 17cm ($6\frac{1}{2}$in)
WEIGHT 20–25g ($\frac{11}{16}$–$\frac{7}{8}$oz)
MIGRATION Non-migrant

HABITAT Wide range of open forest and woodland environments

The male Rufous Whistler has a white throat, a black breast-band, grey upperparts, and rufous underparts. The female is dull grey to brown, with heavily streaked underparts. Like other whistlers, this species is very vocal during the breeding season. Its robust song consists of sharp "chik" notes, bursts of whiplash-like and explosive "ee-chong" notes, and loud sections of more melodic song. It breeds in monogamous pairs and both the male and the female incubate the eggs.

SHRIKES

ORDER	Passeriformes
FAMILY	Laniidae
SPECIES	30

ALTHOUGH BIRDS OF this family are widespread across northern Eurasia and Africa, only two species of shrike occur in the Americas, both in North America. They are principally birds of open country, using prominent lookouts such as tall bushes or posts to search for their prey, which ranges from small birds and mammals, to beetles, lizards, and frogs. However, a handful of species are forest-dependent, including one of the rarest members of the family, the São Tomé Fiscal, which is listed as critically endangered.

BEHAVIOUR

The majority of species of this family of large-headed and sharp-clawed birds, are in the genus *Lanius*, which in Latin means butcher. This name is reflected in the alternative English name for shrikes and butcherbirds, and is a reference to their apparently brutal habit of securing their prey on a twig or barb on a fence so that they can more easily tear off small pieces, using their typically hooked beak. The prey is stored for future meals.

SHRIKE LARDER
Shrikes impale their prey on thorn bushes or barbed wire for later consumption; the food store is known as a "larder".

Corvinella corvina

Yellow-billed Shrike

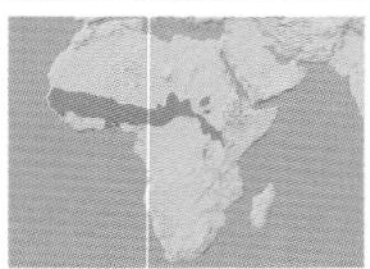

LENGTH 30cm (12in)
WEIGHT 65g (2 3/8oz)
MIGRATION Partial migrant

HABITAT Grassland and scrub with scattered trees, as well as open woodland

Named for its bright yellow bill, the Yellow-billed Shrike is a large shrike, with a brown mask and an overall streaky-brown coloration. It has small wings with a rufous wing patch that is very noticeable in flight. The long, tapering tail is 18cm (7in) long. The sexes are similar in plumage and differ only in the central flank feathers – rufous in the male but cinnamon or maroon in the female. These are exposed when the birds preen or display. The juvenile has buff fringes on the wings.

The Yellow-billed Shrike is a sociable bird that is usually found in small groups of 6–15, often sitting conspicuously on exposed perches, From these perches, it keeps a lookout for insects, the main part of its diet. It also feeds on spiders, slugs, and lizards. A rather noisy bird, the species has a complex repertoire of buzzing and chattering calls. The cup-shaped nest is placed in a bush or tree and 4 or 5 eggs are laid. At a given time, only one female in a group breeds, and the other members provide food and protection to the female in the nest and the nestlings.

Lanius collurio

Red-backed Shrike

LENGTH 18cm (7in)
WEIGHT 30g (1 1/16oz)
MIGRATION Migrant

HABITAT Breeds in open areas of scrubland, heath, and farmland; winters mainly in arid savanna

Although of a similar size, the sexes of this species differ considerably in appearance. The male has a grey head, a thick black face mask, a red-brown back, pale unstreaked underparts, a grey rump, and black tail. The female and juvenile are brown above with scalloped markings on their underparts. This shrike feeds on insects and small animals such as frogs, birds, and bats, which it hunts by swooping from a perch.

MALE RED-BACKED SHRIKE

BREEDING BEHAVIOUR

In spring, the male Red-backed Shrike arrives at the breeding site a few days before the female, advertising its presence with a song. Once a suitable mate has been attracted, a complex courtship commences, with the male performing a zigzag fluttering display. Both sexes co-operate to build the nest and feed the young. Sometimes, non-breeding birds also help to feed the chicks.

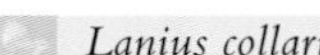

Lanius collaris

Common Fiscal

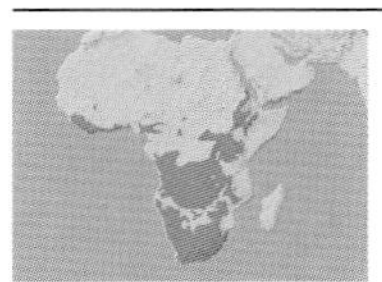

LENGTH 21–23cm (8 1/2–9in)
WEIGHT 30–40g (1 1/16–1 7/16oz)
MIGRATION Non-migrant

HABITAT Wide variety of open spaces and low ground cover, including urban areas

Found throughout southern Africa, the Common Fiscal is a medium-sized black and white bird. The adult is all white below and black above, displaying a varying amount of white on the head and wings. The juvenile has barred rufous-brown upperparts and pale, brown-barred underparts. This is a familiar species, often found in close association with human habitations, and a number of different forms occur. It is a solitary bird, usually found sitting on exposed perches.

ADULT COMMON FISCAL

ADULT LOGGERHEAD SHRIKE

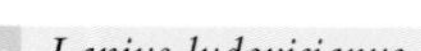

Lanius ludovicianus

Loggerhead Shrike

LENGTH 22cm (8 1/2in)
WEIGHT 50g (1 3/4oz)
MIGRATION Migrant

HABITAT Wide variety of habitats; prefers open areas with scattered bushes and trees

The Loggerhead Shrike is a medium-sized songbird that shows some geographical variations. However, most subspecies have a grey head, with a distinct black mask, white underparts, and a grey back and rump. It has black wings marked with small white patches and a black tail. The juvenile is brown with fine barring above and below. This species feeds largely on insects. Northern populations in the USA are migratory, while those from further south are largely sedentary.

VIREOS AND RELATIVES

ORDER	Passeriformes
FAMILY	Vireonidae
SPECIES	52

VIREOS, A FAMILY exclusive to the Americas, are generally dull-plumaged birds, mainly rather small in size, but with fairly heavy beaks. They inhabit scrub and forests. Only one or two species have colourful plumage. Their songs are repetitive and rarely musical. Three species are of conservation concern, the San Andrés and Chocó vireos, both from Colombia, and the Black-capped Vireo, which breeds in the southern USA.

WARBLING VIREO NEST
All vireos construct bag-like nests, of bark, leaves, moss, and grass, bound with spider silk.

BEHAVIOUR

Vireos and their relatives are insectivores. They feed principally by gleaning arthropods and insects from foliage and bark, as well as taking some fruit when available. One species, the Grey Vireo of North America, takes some of its food on the ground. This species is also notable for the fact that both sexes sing, a feature that is unique within this family of passerines. Many species are long-distance migrants, moving to Central and even South America for the winter after breeding in North America, but several others are endemic to single islands. Some vireo species habitually join mixed-species foraging flocks, especially in winter.

ADULT BIRD

Cyclarhis gujanensis

Rufous-browed Peppershrike

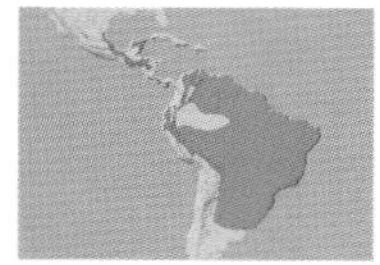

LENGTH 15–17cm (6–6$\frac{1}{2}$in)
WEIGHT 30g (1$\frac{1}{16}$oz)
MIGRATION Non-migrant
HABITAT Forest, woodland, and scrub

Despite its name, the Rufous-browed Peppershrike is actually a member of the vireo family. It has a grey head with a broad rufous-brown stripe above the eyes, pale lemon breast, off-white belly, and olive-green upperparts. However, its most distinctive feature is its thick, pale bill, which is strongly hooked to help it feed on insects and fruit. It has a varied series of loud calls and song and is more commonly heard than seen, as it usually feeds high in the canopy.

Vireo olivaceus

Red-eyed Vireo

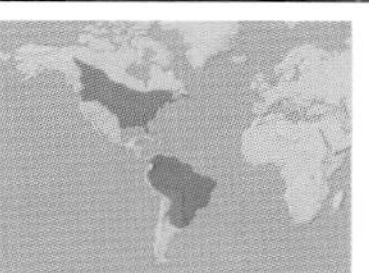

LENGTH 15cm (6in)
WEIGHT 17g ($\frac{5}{8}$oz)
MIGRATION Migrant
HABITAT Woodland

The Red-eyed Vireo has a strong bill and a distinctive head pattern – a dark-bordered grey crown with a white stripe above and a dark line through its noticeably red eyes. Its upperparts are green, strongly contrasting with its white breast. Its wings are long.

The Red-eyed Vireo is a very vocal bird and is strongly territorial in its summer breeding grounds. In summer, it gleans insects from treetop foliage. In contrast, on its wintering grounds, it does not sing and feeds mainly on fruit, especially before migration. During the breeding season, the male displays by swaying with fluffed up feathers and a fanned out tail and the female calls out to respond to the display. The nest is a cup in a fork of a branch. The species breeds from southern Canada down through eastern USA to Florida. It winters in South America.

ADULT RED-EYED VIREO

Vireo flavifrons

Yellow-throated Vireo

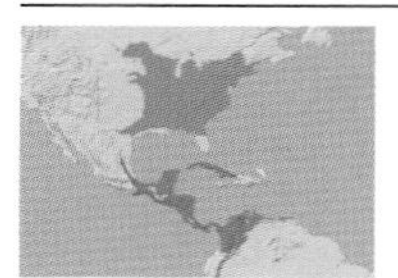

LENGTH 14cm (5$\frac{1}{2}$in)
WEIGHT 18g ($\frac{5}{8}$oz)
MIGRATION Migrant
HABITAT Forest and woodland

The Yellow-throated Vireo has distinctive facial patterning: a short black line between its eye and stout bill, and yellow "spectacles" surrounding its dark eye. It has a bright yellow throat and breast, which contrast with its white belly and undertail. Its upperparts graduate in colour from olive-green to greyish green. The wings are darker, with two distinct broad, white wing-bars. It forages alone or in pairs for insects and sometimes fruit.

Vireo gilvus

Warbling Vireo

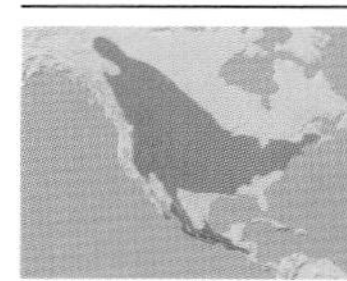

LENGTH 14cm (5$\frac{1}{2}$in)
WEIGHT 12g ($\frac{7}{16}$oz)
MIGRATION Migrant
HABITAT Breeds mainly in deciduous woodland; occurs in more varied habitat while on passage

A small, plain songbird, the Warbling Vireo has a characteristic pale stripe above its eyes. It is olive-brown above and paler below, with brighter, more yellow flanks. Birds in the western part of its range are slightly smaller than those found in the east. The Warbling Vireo forages for insects in trees but feeds on fruit as well, especially before migration. Its song is a long, rapid warble. It makes a deep cup-shaped nest, suspended from a tree branch or shrub, and the male helps the female with the incubation of the eggs.

ADULT WARBLING VIREO

ORIOLES

ORDER	Passeriformes
FAMILY	Oriolidae
SPECIES	29

THE NAME ORIOLE is derived from the Latin word for golden, which admirably suits the generally yellow or red and black plumage of the males, although females have duller plumage. Orioles comprise two genera, one of which, figbirds, is confined to Australasia. Species of the other genus range across much of Europe, Asia, and sub-Saharan Africa. Despite the often colourful plumage of the males, they are not easy to glimpse in their forested habitats, but their flute-like songs are a good guide to their presence.

NESTING DUTIES
Female orioles, such as this African Golden Oriole, take responsibility for most of the nesting duties.

ANATOMY

Most European and African species of oriole show varying coloration and patterning in black and yellow (males) or green and yellow (females). Species from Indonesia and New Guinea exhibit a much wider array of colours, from all black with a chestnut vent to dull yellowish-green. Male figbirds have bare red skin around the eyes. While Eurasian and African orioles have very slightly decurved and mid-length bills, Australian figbirds possess short stout beaks with a hooked tip. The latter eat fruit and insects, with most species showing a predilection for large hairy caterpillars.

Sphecotheres vieilloti

Australasian Figbird

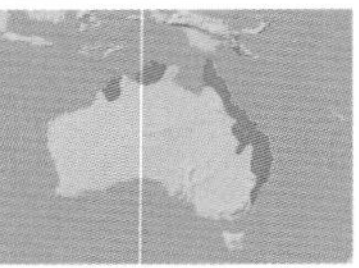

LENGTH 27–30cm (10½–12in)

WEIGHT 100–125g (3⅝–4oz)

MIGRATION Non-migrant

HABITAT Rainforest edges, woodland, mangroves, orchards, parks, and gardens

The male Australasian Figbird has a black head, with a large area of bare red skin around the eye, a grey chin and breast, green upperparts, paler underparts, and red legs. The male of the subspecies found in northern Australia is more yellow below. The female is dull in comparison – green above, with a streaked breast and grey legs. The Australasian Figbird is a very social species, living in small groups during the breeding season and larger flocks during the winter. The flocks feed on fruiting trees and show a preference for figs, hence the bird's name. It is parrot-like in its behaviour, climbing to treetops and hanging from branches as it feeds on fruit and insects. It is a noisy bird with loud squeaky calls.

MALE AUSTRALASIAN FIGBIRD

Oriolus flavocinctus

Yellow Oriole

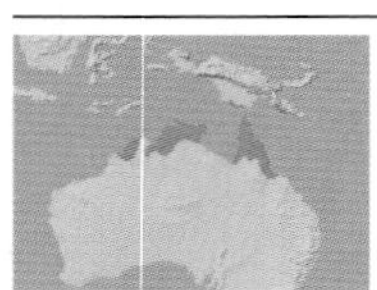

LENGTH 26–30cm (10–12in)

WEIGHT 90g (3¼oz)

MIGRATION Non-migrant

HABITAT Tropical rainforest, woodland, mangroves, riverside vegetation, parks, and gardens

The Yellow Oriole, also known as the Green Oriole, is common in tropical Queensland and northern Australia. The adult bird is a uniform yellowish green, with numerous black flecks and dark wings. It has a pink bill and conspicuous red eyes. The juvenile is duller, with dark eyes and a brown bill. Despite its bright coloration, the Yellow Oriole is inconspicuous and elusive as its plumage blends into the foliage of the forest canopy. The species has a loud, bubbling call that is usually the first sign of its presence.

Breeding takes place during the wet season from October to March, and the nest is a deep cup constructed from strips of bark and vines and slung between leafy branches. The Yellow Oriole typically lays two eggs. Another species of oriole, the Olive-backed Oriole, is also found throughout much of eastern and northern Australia. Although similar in appearance to the Yellow Oriole, it is duller above and paler underneath.

Oriolus oriolus

Eurasian Golden Oriole

LENGTH 24cm (9½in)

WEIGHT 80g (2⅞oz)

MIGRATION Migrant

HABITAT Deciduous lowland woodland, parks, and gardens

The male Eurasian Golden Oriole is a striking bird with a golden yellow head, back, and underparts. Its flight feathers are black with yellow edgings and patches. It has a pink bill and a distinct black area in front of the eye. The female is olive-green above and black-flecked below, with a brighter yellow rump and undertail. Despite the gaudy appearance of the male, the Eurasian Golden Oriole can be difficult to see in the dappled yellow and green leaves of the canopy. However, it is easily identified by its song, an almost ethereal flute whistle that carries over a considerable distance. A solitary bird, it frequents the upper areas of trees.

STREAKY FEMALE
The female is much less stirking than the male with its olive-green upperparts and pale underparts with dark streaks.

GOLDEN MALE
The male Eurasian Golden Oriole reveals brilliant yellow plumage that contrasts strongly with its jet-black wings.

INTRICATE ENGINEERING

The Golden Oriole makes an impressive nest, usually in the fork of a thin branch high in the tree. The nest is slung from the fork like a hammock. Its base of plant fibres, grass, leaves, and moss is held together by long woven strands of bark or grass, or sometimes glued together by saliva. The species usually lays a clutch of 3 or 4 eggs.

SHRIKETHRUSHES AND RELATIVES

ORDER Passeriformes
FAMILY Colluricinclidae
SPECIES 14

THIS IS A RELATIVELY small group of species that is often included within an expanded family of whistlers (see p.381). The grouping reaches its highest diversity in New Guinea, where 9 of the 14 species and a great many subspecies occur; two other species, about which little is known, are restricted to single Indonesian islands.

BEHAVIOUR

Most species within this family are forest dwellers. Many shrikethrushes are somewhat unusual among passerines in constructing their carefully woven stick nests in the same locality year after year. Typically, the female alone is responsible for the nest's construction, and one species, the Crested Bellbird, goes to the unusual length of adorning the rim of the nest with paralysed hairy caterpillars, possibly as a defensive measure.

RENOWNED SONGSTER
The Crested Bellbird is known for its distinctive and unusual song that ends with a cow-bell-like note.

JUVENILE GREY SHRIKETHRUSH

Colluricincla harmonica

Grey Shrikethrush

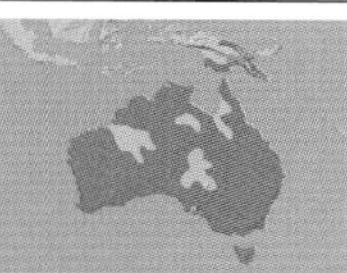

LENGTH 22–25cm ($8\frac{1}{2}$–10in)
WEIGHT 65–75g ($2\frac{3}{8}$–$2\frac{5}{8}$oz)
MIGRATION Non-migrant
HABITAT Widespread from coastal scrub to tropical forest and arid inland woodland

The Grey Shrikethrush is known for its song, which is a series of loud ringing whistles and mellow musical notes. Grey overall with more olive on its upperparts, the male is distinguished from the female by its black bill and small white area in front of the eye. The juvenile has a pale brown eyebrow and streaking on the throat and breast.

Oreoica gutturalis

Crested Bellbird

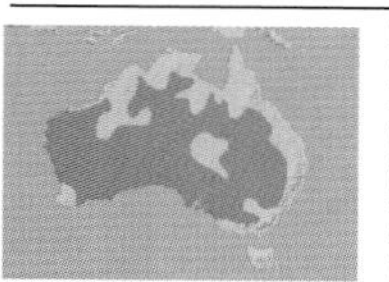

LENGTH 20–22cm (8–$8\frac{1}{2}$in)
WEIGHT 60–65g ($2\frac{1}{8}$–$2\frac{3}{8}$oz)
MIGRATION Non-migrant
HABITAT Arid interior woodland and scrub

The male Crested Bellbird has a black cap and breast that contrasts with its white face and throat and bright yellow eyes. The female is duller, lacking the black patch on the breast. The Crested Bellbird is a common bird of dry inland Australia, though it is more often heard than seen as it forages inconspicuously on the ground. Its song is a series of piping, rhythmic notes. It is usually solitary, but can be found in pairs during the breeding season. Small family parties may form for short periods.

MALE CRESTED BELLBIRD

DRONGOS

ORDER Passeriformes
FAMILY Dicruridae
SPECIES 22

THIS FAMILY OCCURS in sub-Saharan Africa, southern and southeast Asia, New Guinea and coastal eastern Australia. Most drongos have uniformly black plumage with a green or purple gloss. Species are distinguished by tail shape (forked, square, or with elongated feathers) and whether there is a crest or not. Sexes are alike in all species.

BEHAVIOUR

Drongos prefer wooded habitats, but some species have adapted to more open country. They often perch apparently lethargically on the same branch for long periods, before sallying forth to feed on fruit or take an insect in flight. Drongos fiercely defend their nests from all-comers, even large raptors, but several species are frequent victims of cuckoo brood parasitization.

FLIMSY NEST
Drongos, such as this Spangled Drongo, build flimsy stick nests, usually sited in the fork of a tree. Both parents incubate the eggs and care for the young.

Dicrurus forficatus

Crested Drongo

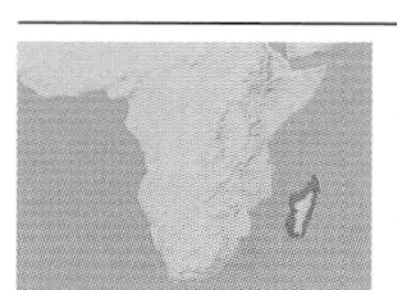

LENGTH 26cm (10in)
WEIGHT 45–50g ($1\frac{5}{8}$–$1\frac{3}{4}$oz)
MIGRATION Non-migrant
HABITAT Sparsely wooded terrain

The adult Crested Drongo is glossy black, with a blue sheen to its plumage and brown tips to the wings, and has red eyes and a forked tail. Its most noticeable feature, which also gives it its name, is the erect tuft of feathers that sprouts from its forehead. The juvenile is browner and lacks this head tuft. The species is usually solitary, though it is sometimes seen in pairs and mixed-species flocks. The Crested Drongo is a dextrous bird that performs aerial acrobatics in order to catch its insect prey. An aggressive species, it attacks intruders that venture too close to its nest – including eagles, dogs, and even humans. The Crested Drongo is the only member of its family found in Madagascar (as well as the island of Anjouan in the Comoros).

ADULT CRESTED DRONGO

FANTAILS

ORDER	Passeriformes
FAMILY	Rhipiduridae
SPECIES	43

FANTAILS ARE FOUND from southern Asia to New Zealand and across the Pacific to Fiji and Samoa, with half of all species occurring in New Guinea. This is a uniform group of relatively small, slim-bodied, birds with short bills. They are notable for their long tails that, as their name suggests, are frequently fanned and waved from side to side, exposing white tail spots. Most species are a mixture of black, brown, and grey, often relieved by white throat patches or eyebrows, although some species are rufous to an extent.

BEHAVIOUR

Fantails are almost exclusively insectivorous, catching their prey in acrobatic sallies from the understorey or canopy of their forested habitats. One species frequently resorts to gleaning insects from the backs of sheep. Breeding occurs almost year-round, and nests are constructed of bark and moss, and lined with a variety of soft materials.

TYPICAL BROOD
This Rufous Fantail parent is feeding an insect to its nestlings. Most fantails have a brood of two chicks.

Rhipidura albicollis

White-throated Fantail

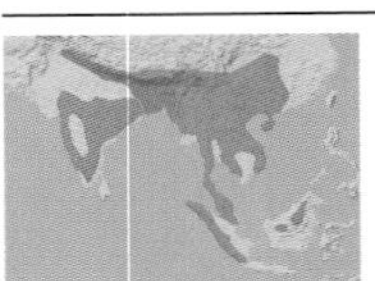

LENGTH 17–20cm (6½–8in)
WEIGHT 13g (7/16oz)
MIGRATION Non-migrant

HABITAT Variety of wooded areas from broad-leaved evergreen forest to parks and gardens

The White-throated Fantail is predominantly black, except for its narrow white eyebrows, white chin and throat, and white-tipped tail feathers. The juvenile shows a much smaller pale area on the throat and has a browner tail. The species forages on small flying insects, tending to feed in the undergrowth or lower levels of the canopy. It frequently catches flies in flight and joins mixed-species feeding flocks. Although generally a resident species that can be found at the same sites all the year round, birds that breed in higher mountainous areas move to lower altitudes during winter. The White-throated Fantail is a relatively large member of its family and a common species throughout its extensive range.

JUVENILE WHITE-THROATED FANTAIL

Rhipidura albiscapa

Grey Fantail

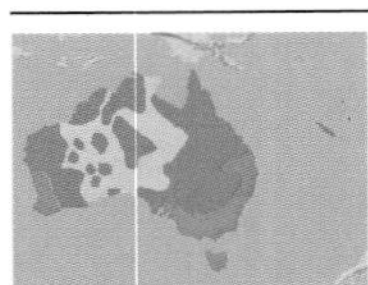

LENGTH 14–17cm (5½–6½in)
WEIGHT 8g (5/16oz)
MIGRATION Partial migrant

HABITAT Forest, woodland, scrub, parks, and gardens

An inquisitive and tame species, the Grey Fantail is one of Australia's more common small songbirds, occurring throughout most of the continent, except the drier deserts. It has a long tail that is constantly flicked and fanned. The overall plumage tone of the Grey Fantail varies from pale to slate-grey. It has short white eyebrows, faint white marks behind the eyes, white edges to the wing feathers, and a dark breast-band.

ADULT GREY FANTAIL

Rhipidura leucophrys

Willie Wagtail

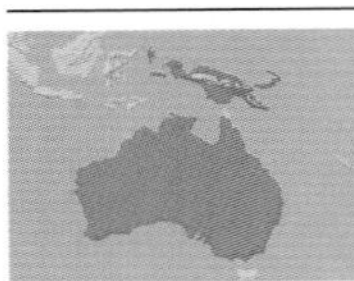

LENGTH 19–21cm (7½–8½in)
WEIGHT 17–25g (5/8–7/8oz)
MIGRATION Non-migrant

HABITAT Almost anywhere, except dense forest

Both the male and the female of this species have black upperparts that contrast with their thin white eyebrows and white underparts. However, when seen at close range, the Willie Wagtail also shows some faint pale spotting on the wings and a hint of a moustache stripe. It is a tame, fearless bird that is quite at home in urban areas, where it can be observed darting about in parks and gardens. The Willie Wagtail is one of Australia's most familiar birds, found throughout most of the continent, except for Tasmania. The name "Wagtail" is confusing, because although it flicks and wags its tail from side to side, it is actually a member of the fantail family, and not one of the wagtails of Europe and Asia.

ADULT WILLIE WAGTAIL FEEDING CHICKS

GROUND-FEEDING

The Willie Wagtail captures most of its preferred insect and larvae food at or around ground level. As a result, up to three quarters of its time is spent foraging on the floor. It often runs around quickly and erratically, before suddenly stopping and flicking its wings in a characteristic fashion to disturb its prey. At other times, it makes short flights from a low perch in order to catch flying insects on the wing.

MONARCHS

ORDER	Passeriformes
FAMILY	Monarchidae
SPECIES	87

INHABITANTS OF FOREST and woodland, with many species confined to single islands or small archipelagos, monarchs are a highly threatened group. Of the almost 90 species, some 19 are classed as being at some risk of extinction. In most cases, the threat is a result of human activity, either through habitat loss and land development, or the introduction of non-native species.

ANATOMY

This group, which includes the paradise flycatchers, is characterized by their flat broad bills, small feet, and steep foreheads, with some species having crests or long tails or both. The long tails that distinguish some species appear to have a sexual role, as particularly long-tailed males appear to be most successful at mating with neighbouring females. Plumage is typically striking, with different species displaying various combinations of blue, black, rufous, white, and yellow. Several of the paradise flycatchers have different colour forms within a species. Most species within the monarch family show no plumage differences between males and females, and juveniles may take some time to acquire full adult plumage.

CRESTED APPEARANCE
Most paradise flycatchers, such as this African Paradise Flycatcher are rufous above with shaggy crests, bare skin around the eyes, and long tails.

BEHAVIOUR

Most birds within this family feed at different heights within the forest, and in some species, the two sexes occupy different foraging niches. Most monarchs are principally insectivores, but a few species also take fruit. Nesting duties are usually shared between the sexes. The territories of sedentary species may be defended year-round with vocalizations and visual displays. Most monarchs are monogamous, but a few are polygamous or have communal breeding systems.

PIED MONARCH NEST
Monarchs typically construct cup-shaped nests, with walls festooned with lichens, moss, cocoons, or spiderwebs.

Hypothymis azurea

Black-naped Monarch

LENGTH 15–17cm (6–6½in)
WEIGHT 9–13g (11/32–7/16oz)
MIGRATION Non-migrant
HABITAT Forested areas, especially bamboo

Bright blue above, except for a small black spot at the back of the head and the black base of the bill, the male Black-naped Monarch has a white belly and undertail. The female is duller, with only a faint blue tint to the upperparts, and brown wings. It also lacks the black nape spot of the male. A bird of lowland forest, it feeds only on insects, expertly spotting and catching them in the air. The breeding season is between April and July, with the female laying 3 or 4 eggs.

MALE BLACK-NAPED MONARCH

Eutrichomyias rowleyi

Cerulean Paradise Flycatcher

LENGTH 18cm (7in)
WEIGHT 15g (9/16oz)
MIGRATION Non-migrant
HABITAT Broad-leaved, tropical hill rainforest
RED LIST CATEGORY Critically endangered

Both male and female Cerulean Paradise Flycatchers are brightly coloured – cerulean blue above and paler blue below, with a white eye-ring and a bluish black bill. The species mainly feeds on insects and small invertebrates. It is found only on the island of Sangihe, Indonesia, and until recently, was feared extinct, as it had not been sighted with certainty since 1878. However, an expedition discovered a population of at least 19 birds in 1998. It is endangered because much of its rainforest habitat on the island has been cleared for agriculture.

Terpsiphone viridis

African Paradise Flycatcher

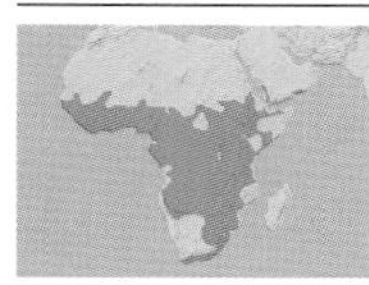

LENGTH 18cm (7in)
WEIGHT 12–14g (7/16–½oz)
MIGRATION Partial migrant
HABITAT Mainly open woodland

ADULT FEMALE

The male and female African Paradise Flycatchers are similar in plumage, except for the elongated central tail feathers of the male, which project 10–18cm (4–7in) beyond other feathers. It is a variable species, with a number of different subspecies – most have a noticeable pale blue ring around the eye, a black head and breast, and rufous upperparts. The species is found in most of sub-Saharan Africa.

Terpsiphone paradisi

Asian Paradise Flycatcher

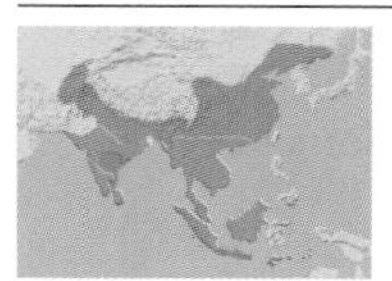

LENGTH 20cm (8in)
WEIGHT 20–25g (11/16–7/8oz)
MIGRATION Migrant
HABITAT Forest, mangroves, gardens, and parks

The male Asian Paradise Flycatcher has an exceptionally long tail, with two central feathers extending up to 30cm (12in) beyond the other feathers. A black head and throat contrasts sharply with a blue eye-ring, rufous upperparts, and white underparts. A white form has white feathers instead of the rufous plumage. The female lacks the tail streamers and has a duller, less glossy plumage.

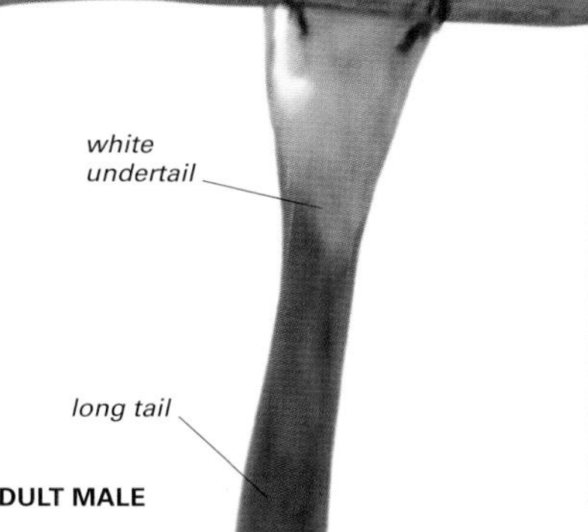

ADULT MALE

BIRD SPECIES

Chasiempis sandwichensis

Elepaio

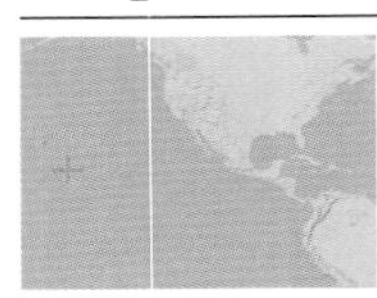

LENGTH 14cm (5½in)

WEIGHT 12–18g (7/16–5/8oz)

MIGRATION Non-migrant

HABITAT Woodland, preferably at high altitude

RED LIST CATEGORY Endangered

The Elepaio adult is a blend of black, white, and rufous, with a distinctive wing-bar. The juvenile is plainer and more rufous. It feeds on insects, gleaning them from foliage or catching them on the wing. It constructs a cup-shaped nest in the branches of a wide variety of trees.

Although the Elepaio is one of Hawaii's most abundant native songbirds, it is still classed as endangered due to severe recent declines. The species occurs only on three Hawaiian islands: Big Island, Oahu, and Kauai. The main threat to the Elepaio is habitat destruction.

JUVENILE ELEPAIO

Monarcha melanopsis

Black-faced Monarch

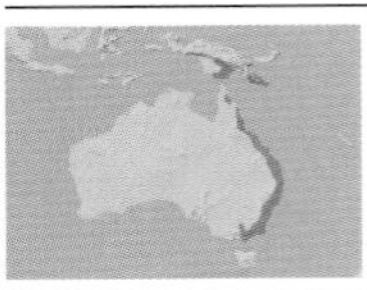

LENGTH 16–19cm (6½–7½in)

WEIGHT 20–30g (11/16–1 1/16oz)

MIGRATION Partial migrant

HABITAT Lowland rainforest

The Black-faced Monarch breeds on the east coast of Australia, with many birds moving north to winter in New Guinea. The adult bird is blue-grey above and rufous-orange below. It has a black face, eye-rings, and throat, separated from its large black eyes by a paler area. The juvenile is duller, with a completely grey face that lacks the black areas of plumage. Unlike many similar flycatcher species, the Black-faced Monarch is slow and unobtrusive as it forages for insects in the mid-level of the rainforest canopy. It is usually seen singly or occasionally in pairs.

ADULT BLACK-FACED MONARCH

Monarcha trivirgatus

Spectacled Monarch

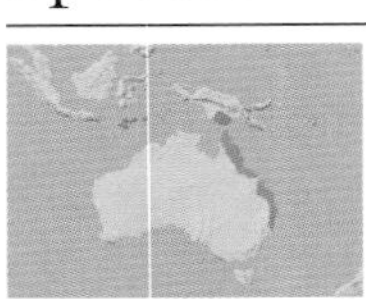

LENGTH 14–16cm (5½–6½in)

WEIGHT 10–15g (3/8–9/16oz)

MIGRATION Partial migrant

HABITAT Rainforest

A medium-sized flycatcher, the Spectacled Monarch has a grey back, orange breast, white belly, and white undertail. When seen from above its grey tail has prominent white outer tips. However, the species' most distinctive feature is the black face-mask of the adult bird, which also extends to the throat. The juvenile lacks this dark area of facial plumage and instead has a grey face and throat.

The Spectacled Monarch is highly active as it darts and hovers around the middle of the canopy, searching for insects. It often spreads and waves its tail as it is feeding, showing off the noticeable white tip. It breeds from October through February and builds a nest made of bark, spider webs, and roots. Its most distinctive call is a series of strong, upward whistles.

The Spectacled Monarch is found in Australia, as well as parts of New Guinea, Timor, and Indonesia. In Australia, it is partially migratory across most of its range, though it is resident in northern Queensland.

ADULT SPECTACLED MONARCH

Arses kaupi

Pied Monarch

LENGTH 16cm (6½in)

WEIGHT 13–15g (7/16–9/16oz)

MIGRATION Non-migrant

HABITAT Rainforest and vine scrub

FEMALE PIED MONARCH

The Pied Monarch is found only in Australia's northern Queensland. It has distinctive black and white plumage, with a black head, face, breast-band, wings, and tail, which contrast with its fluffy white neck collar, crescent-shaped white back marking, underparts, and rump. The female has an incomplete neck collar and broader black breast-band. Both sexes have a blue area of bare skin that forms a ring around the eye. Although usually seen alone or in pairs the species is also sometimes seen displaying in excited groups of 3–5 birds that fluff out their white neck frills and back patches.

FEMALE MAGPIELARK

Grallina cyanoleuca

Magpielark

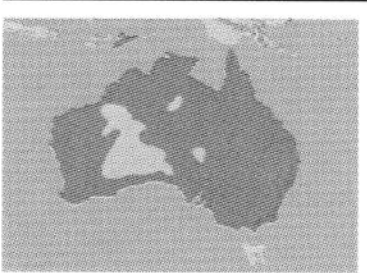

LENGTH 26–30cm (10–12in)

WEIGHT 80g ($2^{7}/_{8}$oz)

MIGRATION Non-migrant

HABITAT Wide variety, except for very dry areas

One of the most conspicuous of Australia's birds, the Magpielark is also resident on the island of Timor. Both sexes are black and white in their plumage, though they have some subtle differences that distinguish them – the male has a thin white eyebrow and an entirely black forehead and throat, whereas the female has a more open-faced appearance due to its white forehead and throat. The juvenile resembles the female, but lacks the distinct white eye-ring of the adult. The Magpielark feeds on worms, larvae, and insects, usually foraging on the ground. It is fearless and tame, commonly found around human habitation, where its loud metallic calls are one of the most familiar bird sounds.

BOWL-SHAPED NEST

The Magpielark builds a distinctive large, bowl-shaped nest. It is made from grass and other plant material, bound together with wet mud, and placed on a flat branch. Both the male and female build the nest and also share the incubation of the 3–4 eggs and care of the young.

Myiagra alecto

Shining Flycatcher

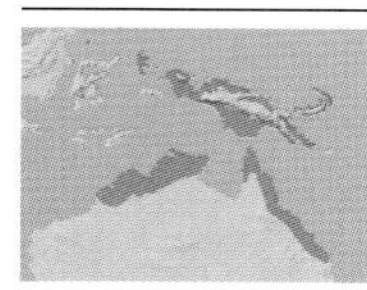

LENGTH 17–19cm ($6^{1}/_{2}$–$7^{1}/_{2}$in)

WEIGHT 20g (11/16oz)

MIGRATION Non-migrant

HABITAT Rainforest, mangroves, creeks, and swamps, usually around water

The Shining Flycatcher is found in eastern and northern Australia, New Guinea, and Indonesia. The male is a uniform, iridescent glossy blue-black in colour, except for the bright orange-red inside its mouth that can sometimes be seen when the bird is calling. The female has a blue-black head that contrasts with its bright rufous-chestnut back and tail, and white underparts. It also has dark rufous-chestnut wing-tips. The juvenile is similar to the female, but shows variable amounts of rust-coloured plumage on its underparts.

Usually found in close proximity to water, the Shining Flycatcher is an active species that tends to feed low down in the understorey, often foraging among bare areas of mud on tidal areas or around the roots of mangroves. As it feeds, it calls frequently, flicking its tail and wings in order to disturb its prey, which largely consists of insects. The song of the Shining Flycatcher comprises of a diverse series of clear musical whistles and buzzing croaks. However, its most common call is a fast series of clear whistles that gradually increases in volume.

PAIR AT NEST

Myiagra inquieta

Restless Flycatcher

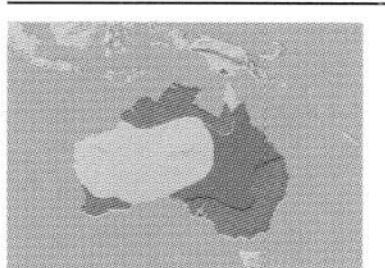

LENGTH 20cm (8in)

WEIGHT 20g ($^{11}/_{16}$oz)

MIGRATION Partial migrant

HABITAT Open forest and woodland, farmland, and scrub; usually near water

As its name suggests, the Restless Flycatcher is an active species that is constantly on the move, rapidly fluttering its wings and waving and spreading its tail. In appearance, the male and female Restless Flycatcher are similar – sleek-looking, medium-sized, long-tailed birds with a peaked crown. In terms of plumage they have a glossy blue-black head, back, and tail; grey-brown wings; and largely white underparts, except for a variable buff tint on the flanks. The juvenile is similar to the adults, but slightly duller, with some pale edging to the wing feathers. It feeds close to the ground, hovering over grass and foliage, constantly calling before snatching its insect prey from the ground or a plant. The species also uses perches from which it sallies forth, swooping in different directions. It is usually seen alone or in pairs, but also joins mixed foraging flocks with other species.

The Restless Flycatcher makes a diverse collection of distinctive sounds, the most common being a clear, high-pitched, musical "tu-whee". Other calls include a harsh buzzing. It also utters a series of metallic sounds, given while the bird is hovering, which usually end with a deep rattling.

ADULT RESTLESS FLYCATCHER

Lamprolia victoriae

Silktail

LENGTH 12cm ($4^{1}/_{2}$in)

WEIGHT 15–20g ($^{9}/_{16}$–$^{11}/_{16}$oz)

MIGRATION Non-migrant

HABITAT Wet rainforest

The Silktail is is currently classified as a short-tailed monarch flycatcher. It is a striking species that has iridescent entirely black plumage, except for its white rump and short, rounded tail. The feathers of its head and breast are spangled with metallic blue-green feathers. The Silktail is restricted to just two Fijian islands, Taveuni and Vanua Levu, and is considered to be near-threatened.

CROWS AND JAYS

ORDER	Passeriformes
FAMILY	Corvidae
SPECIES	117

THIS FAMILY CONSISTS OF a mixture of some of the most familiar species, such as the Eurasian Magpie of Europe and Blue Jay of North America, as well as some of the rarest and most poorly known birds on Earth. Many are highly adaptive and successful, but others are dependent on a single, often threatened habitat and have small ranges. Their scavenging habits have perhaps led to their role as birds of ill omen in folklore and legend. Crows are comparatively long-lived passerines, with some species living for up to ten years.

FEEDING TOGETHER
The nimble Azure-winged Magpie usually occurs in family groups and is omnivorous, feeding on insects and berries.

ANATOMY

Crows and jays are among the largest of passerines, though most of the American representatives of the family are rather smaller, some of them being no bigger than large thrushes. While most crow species live in wooded habitats and are principally arboreal, one group, the ground jays of central Asia, are exclusively ground-dwelling and are noted for being swift runners (preferring not to take to the air in the face of danger) and for having rather long, slim, and slightly decurved bills. Although many Eurasian and North American species are notable for their almost entirely black or black and grey plumage, and best distinguished by overall body size, bill shape and size, and calls, other species, principally of Asia and South America have much more colourful plumage, exhibiting blue, bright green, and many other colours. Some species are characterized by their long tails, and are usually referred to as magpies or treepies. Crows are strong fliers, though few are migratory, and some are able to remain aloft for long periods, engaging in wild and tumbling flights.

TYPICAL SILHOUETTE
This Hooded Crow is typical of many crows, with its broad-based wings, well-fingered wingtips, bulky body, and large head and bill.

BEHAVIOUR

Crows are famed for their adaptability and this characteristic is perhaps best observed in their diets and feeding behaviour. In line with their reputation for intelligence, crows are often among the first birds to learn to take advantage of a new food resource. Their diet includes both plant- and animal-based foods, including nuts, large insects, and even such diverse items as mussels. Food is usually manipulated using the feet, but some crows are capable of fashioning "tools", including hooks, to prise open certain types of nut. Other species wash their food first, possibly as a means of softening harder items. Several crows time their nesting seasons to take advantage of peak food supplies for their young. Rooks often lay their eggs in early spring, when earthworms are abundant.

PLAYING OR FIGHTING?
Crows can be aggressive when feeding, but they are also one of the few birds known to engage in "playful" behaviour.

COLOURFUL CROW
One of the most colourful of crows is the Common Green Magpie, an Asian species that defies the widespread misconception of crows being largely black, grey, and white birds.

SOCIAL INTERACTION
Many crow species roost in large flocks and nest colonially. Even those that nest alone form communal roosts and feed in flocks during the non-breeding season.

Platylophus galericulatus

Crested Jay

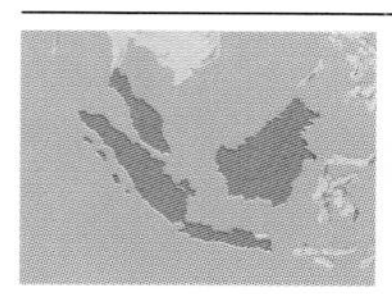

LENGTH 31–33cm (12–13in)

WEIGHT 80g (2 7/8oz)

MIGRATION Non-migrant

HABITAT Lowland forest

The Crested Jay has the longest crest of all jays. Another distinctive feature is the crescent-shaped white patch on its neck that contrasts prominently with its dark plumage. Some scientists consider the Crested Jay to be one of the most primitive of the crow family. Like the other members of this group, it is an inquisitive and noisy bird, with a loud call. It is usually found in pairs or small family groups.

ADULT CRESTED JAY

Cyanocitta stelleri

Steller's Jay

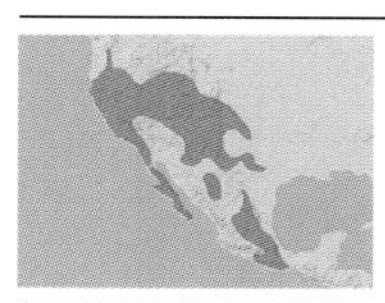

LENGTH 28–32cm (11–12 1/2in)

WEIGHT 125g (4oz)

MIGRATION Non-migrant

HABITAT Pine woods; mixed conifer and oak woods

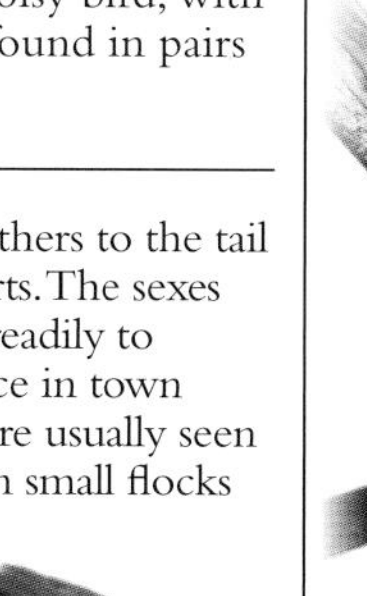

SOUTHERN COLOUR FORM

Steller's Jay is common in western North America. Its range extends from Alaska to Central America, with the northernmost birds being darkest and greyest, becoming more blue the farther south they are found. Generally a shy bird, Steller's Jay can become tame when regularly fed – at bird tables, campsites, and roadside picnic places. However, it depends for most of its food on acorns and the seeds found in pine cones. Like other jays, it is an omnivore and a scavenger, and will also rob nests and eat insects and frogs. It uses mud to anchor its bulky nest of twigs together.

Aphelocoma californica

Western Scrub Jay

LENGTH 27–31cm (10 1/2–12in)

WEIGHT 75–80g (2 5/8–2 7/8oz)

MIGRATION Non-migrant

HABITAT Open country with trees and bushes, from desert to canyon sides

There are many different subspecies of Scrub Jay, varying in size and in the shades of blue and pattern of their plumage. The lack of a crest distinguishes it from other American jays. It has a white eyebrow over the dark eye patch and a smoky brown back. The Western Scrub Jay is territorial and usually found in pairs or small family groups. Like most other jays, it depends on acorns and pine-nuts, but it also robs the nests of other birds, taking eggs and nestlings. Its diet also consists of insects, frogs, lizards, and mice. When feeding on the ground, it stays close to cover. During courtship, the male hops around the female in an upright posture, with its head erect and its tail spread and dragging on the ground. The clutch size ranges from 2 to 6 eggs. The female incubates them for about 15 to 17 days and is fed by the male during this time.

ADULT WESTERN SCRUB JAY

Cyanocitta cristata

Blue Jay

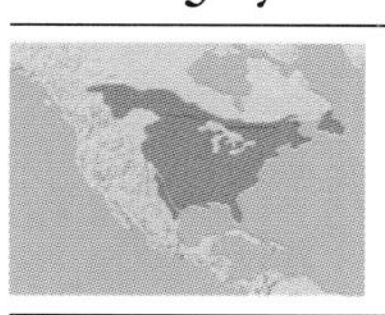

LENGTH 25–28cm (10–11in)

WEIGHT 88g (3 1/4oz)

MIGRATION Partial migrant

HABITAT Woods, parks, and gardens

The Blue Jay is the most common and widespread of North American jays. When in flight, the white spots on its blue wings and tail are visible. Black barring extends from its flight feathers to the tail and it has white underparts. The sexes are alike. Blue Jays adapt readily to people, taking up residence in town parks and gardens. They are usually seen alone or in pairs, but form small flocks after breeding, and larger groups on migration.

ADULT BLUE JAY

Gymnorhinus cyanocephalus

Pinyon Jay

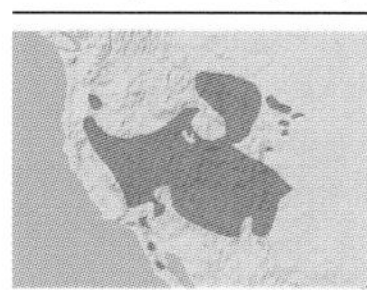

LENGTH 25–28cm (10–11in)

WEIGHT 100g (3 5/8oz)

MIGRATION Non-migrant

HABITAT Pinyon pine woods

RED LIST CATEGORY Vulnerable

An unusual jay because of its plain dull-blue plumage, the Pinyon Jay is a highly social bird. Flocks of these jays may consist of up to 200 birds, which forage and roost together and nest in colonies. Their breeding time is closely tied to the availability of pine-seeds, but they supplement their diet with fruit, berries, and insects.

ADULT PINYON JAY

Garrulus glandarius

Eurasian Jay

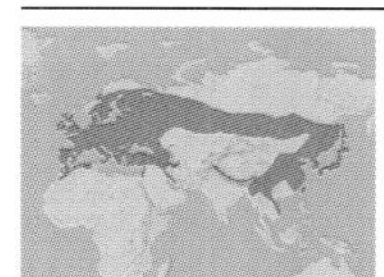

LENGTH 35cm (14in)

WEIGHT 175g (6oz)

MIGRATION Non-migrant

HABITAT Forests, parks, and gardens

A common bird across much of Europe and Asia, from the near-Arctic and Himalayan foothills to the tropical forests of Myanmar and Thailand, the Eurasian Jay in one area may be quite different in colours and patterns to another. There are more than 30 subspecies in a wide range of colours and with either black or streaked crowns. However, all the subspecies have a blue patch on their forewing. A shy bird, the Eurasian Jay is almost always seen flying away, when the white wing patches on its otherwise black hindwings and the white rump, contrasting with the black tail, make it easy to identify. Like other jays, it is an omnivorous opportunist and dependent for its winter survival on the success of the acorn crop. In years and in areas where acorns fail, it can spread out from its normal home range in search of better supplies. When acorns are plentiful, it stores them by burying them. It has a good memory, usually remembering where the buried acorns are. However, it often does not return to its food store, thereby playing an important role in the regeneration of oak forests.

ADULT EURASIAN JAY

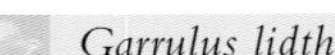

Garrulus lidthi

Lidth's Jay

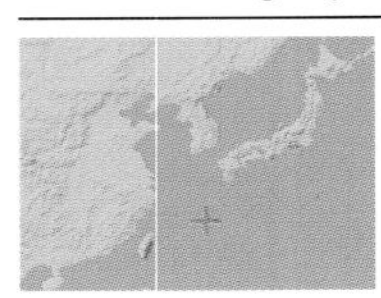

LENGTH 38cm (15in)

WEIGHT 175–200g (6–7oz)

MIGRATION Non-migrant

HABITAT Woodland, including pine woods and cultivated areas

RED LIST CATEGORY Vulnerable

This striking black, blue, and chestnut bird is only found on a few Japanese islands, where it is called the Ruri-kakesu (meaning the "lapis lazuli Jay"). It mainly eats acorns and some insects and is usually found in pairs or small groups, although larger flocks have been seen. Unlike other jays, Lidth's Jay habitually builds its nest in a large tree-hole, using twigs and sticks, and then lines it with softer material. Although once hunted for its plumage, Lidth's Jay is now fully protected.

ADULT AZURE-WINGED MAGPIE

Cyanopica cyanus

Azure-winged Magpie

LENGTH 35cm (14in)

WEIGHT 75g (2⅝oz)

MIGRATION Non-migrant

HABITAT Woodland, especially pines, and also open country with olive and cork oak groves

Confined to Spain, Portugal, and eastern Asia, the Azure-winged Magpie is smaller and more delicate than other magpies. It has a glossy black head and a white throat. Its back and underparts are pale grey-brown in colour, while its wings and the feathers of its long tail are azure blue, giving rise to its common name. It often flicks its wings and tail when excited. It has a variety of calls: high whistles and deeper notes.

The Azure-winged Magpie feeds largely on insects, but also takes seeds, fruit, and scraps, usually from the ground, and stores food for later use. It is a very sociable species, feeding in family parties after the breeding season, often forming flocks of 30 or more birds. It breeds in colonies and other members of the flock may assist a pair during the breeding season. The nest is built in the fork of a branch near the top of a tree and more than one pair may nest in the same tree.

Urocissa erythrorhyncha

Red-billed Blue Magpie

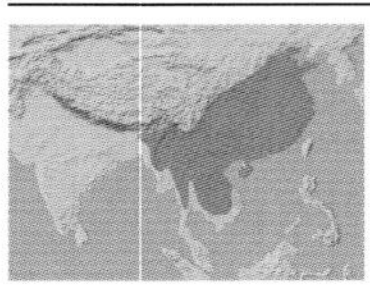

LENGTH 68cm (27in)

WEIGHT 150g (5oz)

MIGRATION Non-migrant

HABITAT Jungle, forest, and scrub, as well as cultivated areas with trees and gardens

The black head, white nape, orange-red bill, and the two long blue, white-tipped central tail feathers are characteristic of the Red-billed Blue Magpie. When flying, it glides with its tail spread. On the ground, it hops with its tail held high. A noisy bird, it lives in small flocks, feeding on insects, fruit, and carrion. It whistles, screeches, and chatters, and will also mimic other birds.

Cissa chinensis

Common Green Magpie

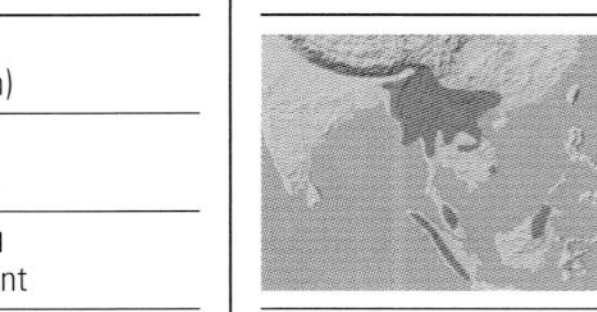

LENGTH 38cm (15in)

WEIGHT 125g (4oz)

MIGRATION Non-migrant

HABITAT Evergreen forest and bamboo jungle as well as open scrub and gardens

A striking green bird, the Common Green Magpie has chestnut-red wings and a bright red eye-ring, and legs. Usually shy, it whistles, shrieks, and chatters noisily, making it more easily heard than seen. It forms small groups and sometimes joins other species to feed in trees or on the ground. It eats invertebrates, small mammals, young birds and eggs, and carrion.

ADULT EURASIAN MAGPIE

Pica pica

Eurasian Magpie

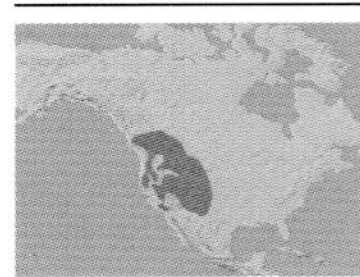

LENGTH 45cm (17½in)

WEIGHT 225g (8oz)

MIGRATION Non-migrant

HABITAT Woodland, open ground with bushes and hedges, and urban gardens

The Eurasian Magpie has a black head, upper breast, back, rump, and tail and a white belly. The dark wings have a blue, purple, and green sheen, and a broad white wing stripe is evident when the bird is at rest. It feeds on a wide range of animal and vegetable food, including insects, seeds, young birds and eggs, and scraps. It is notorious for liking shiny objects. Magpies give loud chattering and rattling calls, but also have a quiet song. The Eurasian Magpie is a territorial bird and will form flocks after the breeding season and roost in groups. Three species of magpies are in the *Pica* genus: Black-billed, Yellow-billed, and Eurasian.

Nucifraga columbiana

Clark's Nutcracker

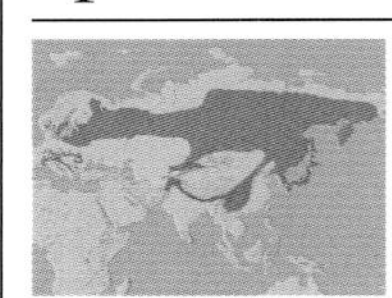

LENGTH 30cm (12in)

WEIGHT 125g (4oz)

MIGRATION Partial migrant

HABITAT Coniferous forest

A stocky bird, Clark's Nutcracker is mainly grey in colour, with black-and-white wings and tail, the outer tail feathers being white. It eats conifer seeds rather than nuts, and its long pointed beak enables it to probe into pine cones, which it holds with one foot while prising the seeds out. It will also eat insects, eggs, and young birds, and will even come to bird-feeders for peanuts and suet. Clark's Nutcracker has a pouch under its beak that enables it to carry 60 or more seeds at a time. In winter, it habitually stores food, usually in the ground, retrieving it when supplies are short. If seed crops fail and its stores run out, it will irrupt, moving a considerable distance away from its usual range to lower ground, even into desert areas.

In the breeding season, a pair is territorial, keeping other birds away, but in winter, the species can be found feeding in large groups, especially when irrupting. Unlike a magpie or jay, Clark's Nutcracker walks rather than hops and its flight is undulating.

Nucifraga caryocatactes

Spotted Nutcracker

LENGTH 33cm (13in)

WEIGHT 175g (6oz)

MIGRATION Partial migrant

HABITAT Coniferous woodland, sometimes mixed with deciduous trees

The Spotted Nutcracker has a dark brown cap. Its face, back, and underparts are heavily spotted, with white markings and its vent is white, as are the tips of the tail feathers. The male and female are similar in plumage. The Spotted Nutcracker feeds largely on pine seeds, but also eats hazelnuts. Before opening a pine cone or nut, it holds it in its foot or keeps it wedged in the fork of a branch. Birds can travel many miles in search of food; any food shortage triggering irruptions. The Spotted Nutcracker is territorial when breeding, but will form feeding flocks in autumn. Unlike other members of the crow family, a pair shares parental duties, with both birds incubating the eggs and feeding the young.

ADULT SPOTTED NUTCRACKER

PAIR OF RED-BILLED CHOUGHS

Pyrrhocorax pyrrhocorax

Red-billed Chough

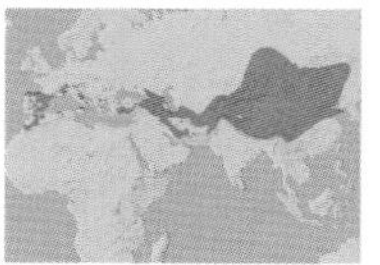

LENGTH 39cm (15½in)

WEIGHT 300g (11oz)

MIGRATION Non-migrant

HABITAT Rocky areas, from mountains to quarries and coastal cliffs with nearby grass

The range of the Red-billed Chough extends from the Himalayas to western Europe. It is a distinctive glossy black bird, with red bill and legs. It feeds mostly on the ground, eating insects and other invertebrates as well as some seeds. Its nest is usually built in a rock crevice or cave. A skilled flier, it soars high, swoops steeply, and performs aerial twists and tumbles.

Corvus splendens

House Crow

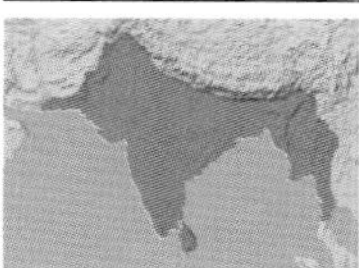

LENGTH 42cm (16½in)

WEIGHT 275–325g (10–12oz)

MIGRATION Non-migrant

HABITAT Wooded hills to coastal mangroves; also thrives in urban areas

ADULT HOUSE CROW

Widely distributed in southern Asia, this slim, long-bodied crow has been introduced to the Middle East and Europe, where it thrives. It has a glossy jet black face, crown, and throat, while its neck, back, and underparts are grey. It gathers in flocks throughout the year and roosts communally.

The House Crow is omnivorous, eating insects, seeds, and carrion, but also taking advantage of the waste in towns and cities, scavenging on rubbish tips and around markets, farms, and fisheries. It will even enter buildings to steal food. It nests close to human habitation, often in trees, but will readily use buildings, pylons, cranes, and street lamps as nesting sites. Natural nests are built from sticks and twigs, while in urban areas, they may be entirely made up of wire and other metal. Like many crows, the House Crow is intelligent and, unlike most birds, is able to recognize a hunter with a gun, flying off immediately.

Corvus brachyrhynchos

American Crow

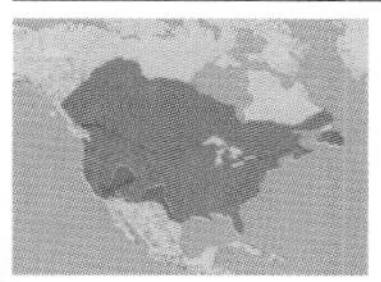

LENGTH 45cm (17½in)

WEIGHT 500g (18oz)

MIGRATION Partial migrant

HABITAT Open woodland, farmland and parks, and urban areas

The American Crow has jet black plumage, dark eyes, and a large black bill. It is omnivorous and a scavenger, feeding on seeds, insects, reptiles, mammals, and the eggs and young of other birds. While it does eat crops, it also removes harmful insect pests. On the coast, it drops shellfish onto rocks to crack them open.

This intelligent bird is very sociable, roosting communally and forming large family groups. These groups consist of offspring from previous years, who help their parents rear later broods.

ADULT AMERICAN CROW

Ptilostomus afer

Piapiac

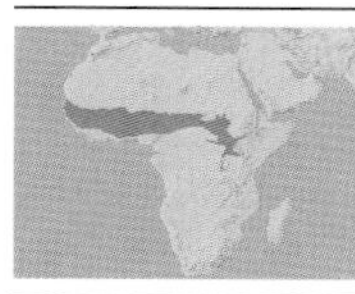

LENGTH 46cm (18in)

WEIGHT 125g (4oz)

MIGRATION Non-migrant

HABITAT Open country, cultivated fields, pasture, and lawns in towns and villages

A slender, long-tailed glossy black crow, with a black bill, the Piapiac is sometimes called the Black Magpie. Unlike other crows, it has only 10 tail feathers. It feeds on insects, often from around the feet of cattle, and it will even take parasites from a cow's back. It breeds cooperatively, with several adults and juveniles attending one nest. It is agile and runs along tree branches and also hops and runs on the ground.

ADULT PIAPIAC

ADULT WESTERN JACKDAW

Corvus monedula

Western Jackdaw

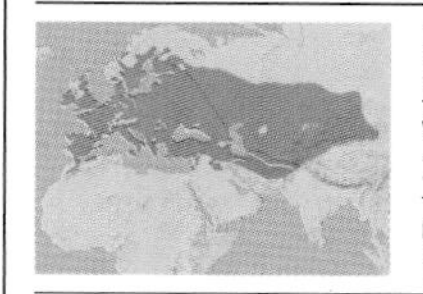

LENGTH 33cm (13in)

WEIGHT 250g (9oz)

MIGRATION Partial migrant

HABITAT Open woodland, cultivated fields, pasture, parks in villages and towns, and sea coasts

An agile flier, the Western Jackdaw is a small crow with a quick wingbeat. Its plumage is greyish black except for the cheeks, nape, and neck, which are pale grey. It feeds on insects, seeds, and grain. A hole-nesting bird, it usually chooses a tree hole or rock crevice, but has also taken to building large nests of sticks in chimneys and lofts.

Corvus frugilegus

Rook

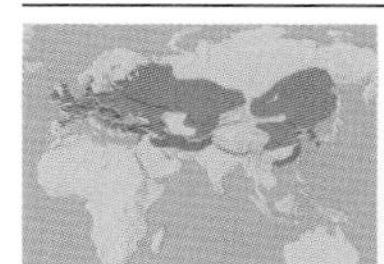

LENGTH 45cm (17½in)

WEIGHT 400–475g (14–17oz)

MIGRATION Partial migrant

HABITAT Open country and pasture with woods or clumps of trees

ADULT ROOK

Also called the Bare-faced Crow, due to the grey-white skin around the base of its bill in front of the eyes, the Rook has black plumage with a purple-blue sheen and its bill is grey-black. Its call is a loud, raucous cawing and its flight direct and steady. It has long been regarded as an agricultural pest because it eats worms and grain, but it also consumes insect larvae that would otherwise be damaging to crops.

SOCIAL BONDS

Like many members of the crow family, the Rook is a highly social bird. Its communal nesting place is called a "rookery", where there can be several hundred nests. Courtship involves singing, bowing, and display flights. The pair will preen and feed each other to maintain the bond between them. Both parents build the nest and feed the young, but only the female incubates the eggs.

ADULT CARRION CROW AT A CARCASS

Corvus corone

Carrion Crow

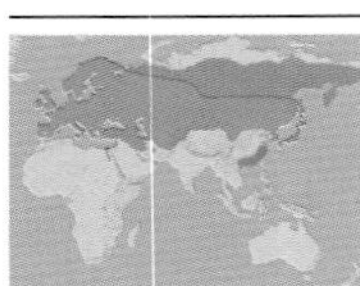

LENGTH 48–52cm (19–20½in)

WEIGHT 400–600g (14–21oz)

MIGRATION Non-migrant

HABITAT Open farmland, coasts, and uplands; parks and gardens

A common bird throughout its very wide range, the Carrion Crow includes three distinct subspecies. One is all black, another is grey and black, and the third is similar to the Hooded Crow, but has a heavier bill, longer throat feathers, and much paler grey parts. As its common name suggests, the Carrion Crow feeds on carcasses but, like others of the family, has a wide-ranging diet including vegetable matter and will even steal food (kleptoparasitize) from smaller birds. It may drop shellfish onto rocks in order to get to their fleshy part and there is even a record of a crow seizing a bat in flight.

The call of the Carrion Crow is a loud, harsh "caw krra krra krra" and its bold, upright stance is characteristic of the species.

Corvus albicollis

White-necked Raven

LENGTH 50–54cm (19½–21½in)

WEIGHT 900g (32oz)

MIGRATION Non-migrant

HABITAT Cliffs and gorges in mountainous areas, including open forest

The largest crow in its African range, the White-necked Raven is identifiable by its white neck patches and deep-based, arched bill. In flight, the broad-based wings and short tail are clearly outlined. As in most crows, there is no difference between the male and the female. The species is highly gregarious, forming small flocks in the non-breeding season, which may swell to as many as 800 in number. The White-necked Raven joins other crows, kites, and vultures at animal carcasses and also congregates at locust swarms. Like the Carrion Crow (left), the species' varied diet includes small birds, lizards and other reptiles, fruit and berries, and seeds. In some areas, the bird may scavenge in towns and villages.

PAIR OF ADULTS

Corvus corax

Northern Raven

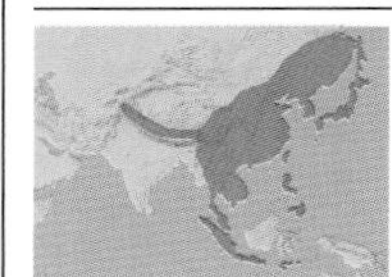

LENGTH 58–69cm (23–27in)

WEIGHT 0.9–1.6kg (2–3¼lb)

MIGRATION Non-migrant

HABITAT Rugged mountains, coastal cliffs, steppes, and semi-desert

Achieving the distinction of reaching one of the highest altitudes on record for a passerine bird, the Northern Raven has been sighted at well over 6,000m (19, 600ft) on Mount Everest. It is a large, black bird with a robust bill and a ruff of feathers on its throat called "hackles". The tail is wedge-shaped. Both the sexes look similar. A bird of the mountains, it shies away from areas modified or settled by humans.

A powerful bird in the air, the Northern Raven is well known for its playful manouevres and effortless acrobatic displays, especially during early spring. It has been seen rolling down a snowbound hillside, apparently for "enjoyment". It is a solitary nester, although the species is sociable and large flocks gather occasionally, especially at nocturnal roosts. It begins its nest-building and display activities by late February or even earlier in most areas. Both parents care for the young, which may remain with them for up to six months after fledging.

SCAVENGING

Like many crows, despite its ability to forage for food, the Northern Raven is first and foremost a scavenger, taking all kinds of carrion, from dead sheep, cattle, and rabbits, to fish. At a kill on the ground, it waddles and occasionally hops into position, jostling for space near the carcass.

ADULT NORTHERN RAVEN

ADULT LARGE-BILLED CROW

Corvus macrorhynchos

Large-billed Crow

LENGTH 48–59cm (19–23in)

WEIGHT 450–650g (16–23oz)

MIGRATION Non-migrant

HABITAT Woodland and forest, in some areas more coastal and in others, principally around habitation

Like many of its relatives, the Large-billed Crow has a dull black plumage, although in some areas it may be glossy. It is chiefly recognizable by its long bill, steep forehead, and its long, wedge-shaped tail. A gregarious bird, it is usually found in pairs or small groups, but larger flocks are also common at feeding places or roosting sites. A pair of Large-billed Crows may remain together for life. The nest is built in a solitary site, usually in the fork of a large tree, and consists of a platform of twigs. The female incubates the eggs, but both sexes feed the young. The Himalayan populations perform fantastic aerobatic displays.

Corvus albus

Pied Crow

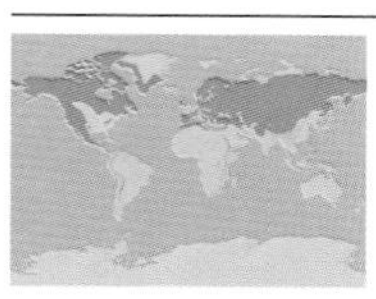

LENGTH 46–50cm (18–19½in)

WEIGHT 500–600g (18–21oz)

MIGRATION Non-migrant

HABITAT Open country with forest or cultivation, towns and villages, semi-desert areas with oases

The Pied Crow is distinguished by its black plumage, which contrasts with its bold white collar and breast. It is similar to the White-necked Raven (opposite), which may occasionally show some white on the breast, but has a much larger bill.

The Pied Crow is a gregarious species, with as many as 1,000 birds gathering at rubbish dumps and slaughterhouses, without any fear of humans. In addition to its habitual scavenging activities, this crow eats a high proportion of vegetable matter and is capable of taking insects on the wing or even of killing fruit bats roosting in the tree canopy. Its nests are well separated from other birds, but may be parasitized by the Great Spotted Cuckoo (see p.274), a species that frequently targets crows.

PAIR OF ADULT PIED CROWS

MUDNESTERS

ORDER Passeriformes

FAMILY Corcoracidae

SPECIES 2

BOTH SPECIES IN THIS Australian family are highly social birds that live in tight-knit family groups and breed co-operatively. Each group consists of a dominant adult male paired with one or more adult females, plus three to eight young from previous years. All members of the group work together to build a large, bowl-shaped mud nest, and the younger birds help the breeding adults to incubate the eggs and feed the next generation of nestlings. Outside the breeding season, several groups may join together to form larger flocks.

CLOSE CONTACT
White-winged Choughs stay in touch with other group members using a variety of soft whistles and clicking sounds.

ADULT WHITE-WINGED CHOUGH

Corcorax melanorhamphos

White-winged Chough

LENGTH 45cm (17½in)

WEIGHT 350g (13oz)

MIGRATION Non-migrant

HABITAT Eucalyptus woodland, forest, and mallee scrub

In flight, the white wing feathers that give the White-winged Chough its name, are clearly visible. It is black in colour and has a long tail. It moves in small groups, usually of 4–8 birds, foraging in leaf litter with a sideways sweep of the bill, or probing the soil for invertebrates. Its breeding is communal, with the group consisting of a dominant male, several females, and offspring of previous years, all helping to build the large mud-bowl nest.

Struthidea cinerea

Apostlebird

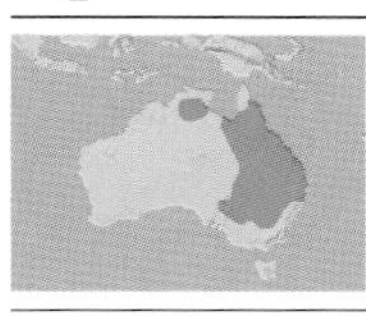

LENGTH 29–32cm (11½–12½in)

WEIGHT 125g (4oz)

MIGRATION Non-migrant

HABITAT Woodland and shrubland, especially in Cypress and Casuarina stands; never far from water

The Apostlebird has a black stout bill, grey plumage, brown wings, and a black tail. Both the sexes look alike. The Apostlebird mainly eats insects or mice, often taken from roadsides, but in winter, it switches to small seeds.

Like the White-winged Chough (left), it lives communally in groups of up to 20, but may form feeding flocks of hundreds. Its nest is a large bowl of grass, heavily plastered with mud and attached to a horizontal branch; 2–5 eggs are laid. All members of the group incubate and feed the young, which remain dependent on the adults for food for several months.

It inhabits the eastern and southeastern inland regions of Australia and in recent years, the Apostlebird has been spreading its range westwards.

PAIR OF APOSTLEBIRDS

BIRDS-OF-PARADISE

ORDER Passeriformes
FAMILY Paradisaeidae
SPECIES 40

FEW BIRDS ARE MORE charismatic than the birds-of-paradise. As a family, they are almost entirely restricted to New Guinea, with less than a handful of species occurring in the rainforests of northeastern Australia and a few in Indonesia. Four species are currently categorized by the IUCN as Near Threatened.

IMPRESSIVE DISPLAY
This male Raggiana Bird-of-Paradise, a polygynous species, commences his elaborate display to the much duller female that has just arrived at its lek.

PLUMAGE

Species within the birds-of-paradise family are either polygynous or monogamous. In the latter group, males and females have similar plumage, with all seven species being either entirely blue-black or largely black. However, in the other, much larger group, males have far brighter, gaudier, and more magnificent plumage than females because they compete to mate with more than one female. They also sport an amazing array of dazzling colourful plumes, head or tail wires, and other adornments. Each of the 14 genera represented in the polygynous grouping has a basic male plumage that is peculiar to the species and that is manipulated in these courtship displays.

BEHAVIOUR

Birds-of-paradise are diverse in body size and bill shape, the latter ranging from stout and crow-like to long and sickle-shaped. Some species also exhibit significant bill differences between the sexes, which prevent males and females of the same species competing for food. Most species in this family are fruit-eaters, but many also take some arthropods, leaves, and buds. Birds-of-paradise typically build open cup- or bowl-shaped nests of stems, vines, and leaves, and lay up to three eggs, which in polygynous species are incubated by the female unaided.

LONG-BILLED FEMALE
The female Victoria Riflebird usually has a longer bill than the male.

Astrapia mayeri

Ribbon-tailed Astrapia

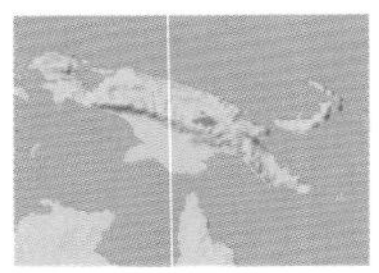

LENGTH 32cm (12½in)
WEIGHT 125–150g (4–5oz)
MIGRATION Non-migrant
HABITAT Mountain forests and forest fragments, including disturbed forest

The male Ribbon-tailed Astrapia has the longest tail feathers in relation to its size of any bird – up to 1m (3½ft) long; three times the length of the bird itself. Appearing black from a distance, its plumage is in fact brilliantly iridescent, with yellow, green, blue, and purple on the head, and olive-green on the back. The brown female also has iridescent head plumage.

The Ribbon-tailed Astrapia has a varied diet, including fruit, insects, spiders, reptiles, and small mammals. Its courtship display includes flicking its tail during an undulating flight, while another display involves jumping repeatedly between branches.

The Ribbon-tailed Astrapia was not discovered until 1938, making it the most recently described of all the birds-of-paradise. It is locally threatened by hunting for its tail plumes and by large-scale logging. However, in other areas it is protected by the fact that some of its range is remote and inaccessible.

Cicinnurus respublica

Wilson's Bird-of-Paradise

LENGTH 16cm (6½in)
WEIGHT 55–60g (2–2⅛oz)
MIGRATION Non-migrant
HABITAT Mostly hill forest, sometimes also found in lowland forest

This very small bird-of-paradise is also called the Bare-headed Little King Bird-of-Paradise, and is closely related to the King Bird-of-Paradise (opposite). The male Wilson's Bird-of-Paradise has a bare blue crown with a pattern of criss-crossing lines on it. The cobalt blue of its head is said to be so vivid that it is visible at night. It has a red back and wings and yellow mantle. Its short tail is black and it has two spiral tail wires. The female also has a blue cap and black head, but the wings and back are grey-brown and the underparts are barred. However, the inconspicuous behaviour of this species means that it is more easily located by its calls.

The male chooses a display ground, usually a small clearing in dense forest, which it keeps clear of leaves and litter. The emerald green breast-shield is thrust forward, and the spiral tail feathers flicked during the display.

MALE WILSON'S BIRD-OF-PARADISE

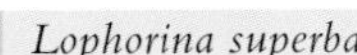

Lophorina superba

Superb Bird-of-Paradise

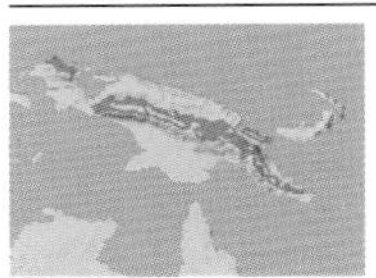

LENGTH 26cm (10in)
WEIGHT 65–85g (2⅜–3oz)
MIGRATION Non-migrant
HABITAT Mountain forests, including disturbed forest

The Superb Bird-of-Paradise is the sole member of its genus. When the displaying male stands fully erect, it shows gleaming black cape feathers covering its back and an iridescent greenish blue breast-shield. When at rest, the male is mostly black with a green breast-shield and crown. The female is quite different, and is largely brown with barred underparts. The male Superb Bird-of Paradise is polygamous, mating with as many females as it can attract to its solitary territory. Other parts of the display include pushing out its breast-shield and flicking its cape over its head, without expanding it.

The Superb Bird-of-Paradise is extensively hunted for its plumage, but remains one of the most common birds-of-paradise. It is found in virtually all the upland forests of New Guinea.

ADULT VICTORIA RIFLEBIRD

Ptiloris victoria

Victoria Riflebird

LENGTH 25cm (10in)

WEIGHT 85–100g (3–3⅝oz)

MIGRATION Non-migrant

HABITAT Lowland and hill rainforest, swamp forest

This species is named after Britain's Queen Victoria. The male is a velvet jet-black with a green head and the female is red-brown. The male Victoria Riflebird fans and raises both wings to form a complete circle, and opens its bill to display its yellow gape, while simultaneously raising and lowering itself on its legs. To attract the female, the male gives a loud call. The species eats insects, other invertebrates, fruit, and flowers.

ADULT MALE

Paradisaea minor

Lesser Bird-of-Paradise

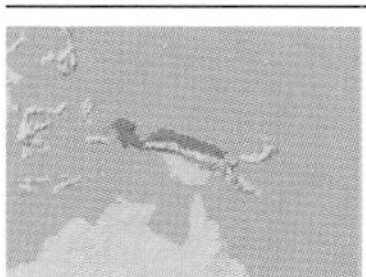

LENGTH 32cm (12½in)

WEIGHT 150–300g (5–11oz)

MIGRATION Non-migrant

HABITAT Island forest

The Lesser Bird-of-Paradise is widespread in the north and west of New Guinea. The elongated, yellow flank plumes and cape of the male are distinctive and are used in courtship displays. It also has two long wire-like tail feathers. The brown female is almost crow-like. Several males display together at a lekking ground, mating with as many females as they can.

Ptiloris paradiseus

Paradise Riflebird

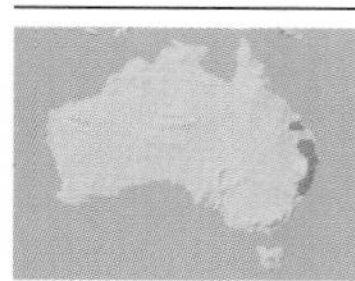

LENGTH 30cm (12in)

WEIGHT 100–150g (3⅝–5oz)

MIGRATION Non-migrant

HABITAT Subtropical and temperate rainforest

FEMALE PARADISE RIFLEBIRD

The most southerly of all the birds-of-paradise, the Paradise Riflebird is a member of the same genus as the very similar Victoria Riflebird (left). The male is black with an iridescent greenish blue crown, throat, and central tail feathers. The female is brown with black barred underparts. The courtship display of the male includes fanning and extending its wings in front of itself. The male may spend much of the day on a chosen display perch on prominent branches high above the ground. It forages rather like a treecreeper (see p.427), climbing trunks and branches in search of insects, spiders, and centipedes.

Seleucidis melanoleuca

Twelve-wired Bird-of-Paradise

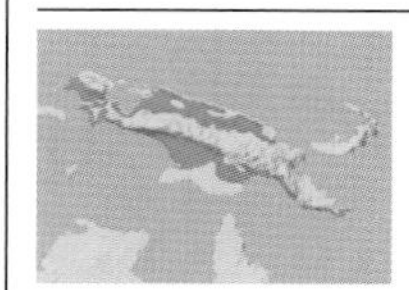

LENGTH 33cm (13in)

WEIGHT 150–200g (5–7oz)

MIGRATION Non-migrant

HABITAT Lowland forest

Six flank plumes on each side of the male Twelve-wired Bird-of-Paradise are elongated into the wires that give the bird its name, and which radiate around the bird. The display involves pushing out its breast-shield and raising its flank-plumes in a way that changes it from a mostly black bird to a mostly yellow one. The female is largely brown. The trachea includes a unique, elastic section, which enables it to make its "advertising" calls heard at a long distance. The bird is generally shy, more often heard than seen.

ADULT MALE

JUVENILE MALE

Cicinnurus regius

King Bird-of-Paradise

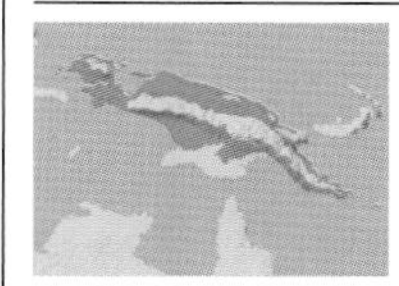

LENGTH 19cm (7½in)

WEIGHT Not recorded

MIGRATION Non-migrant

HABITAT Lowland forest, including disturbed areas

The smallest bird-of-paradise, this species is a mostly crimson bird, with white underparts, a green breast-shield, and bright blue feet. Two tail feathers are elongated into wires tipped with metallic green discs. The courtship display includes spreading its wings and hanging upside down from the perch, swinging its tail feathers. Despite its vivid colour the male is inconspicuous, but it can be tracked by its calls.

Paradisaea raggiana

Raggiana Bird-of-Paradise

LENGTH 34cm (13½in)

WEIGHT 150–275g (5–10oz)

MIGRATION Non-migrant

HABITAT Primary and secondary forest in lowland, hills, and lower flanks of mountains; also in gardens

The male Raggiana Bird-of-Paradise has lush orange flank plumes, a yellow cowl, and an emerald green throat. It is similar in appearance and colour to the Great (*P. apoda*) and Lesser (left) Birds-of-Paradise, but lacks their yellow flank plumes. Males gather and display at a communal lek, where the females visit them to mate. The males play no part in nesting or raising the young. The Raggiana Bird-of-Paradise is the national bird of Papua New Guinea.

MALE RAGGIANA BIRD-OF PARADISE

FLOWER DISPLAY

In its courtship display, the male Raggiana Bird-of-Paradise turns its head downwards and fans out its wings. When it does so, the wings form a flower-like shape and the bird appears to be surrounded by "petals".

AUSTRALASIAN ROBINS

ORDER	Passeriformes
FAMILY	Petroicidae
SPECIES	45

THIS FAMILY OF AUSTRALIAN, New Zealand, and New Guinean birds occupy a range of habitats from dry savanna to montane forests. Some have exceptionally dull plumage, but others very bright. Most are insectivores that use a perch-and-pounce method of acquiring prey. Species within this family have high-pitched, short and staccato songs, or give drawn-out whistles or trills. Most Australian robins build small, shallow cup-shaped nests sited low in the vegetation, although some nest high in trees or on the ground. A clutch of 2 or 3 eggs is usual.

FEEDING YOUNG
Here, a Rose Robin is bringing food to the young in the nest, a cup-shaped construction typical of those made by birds of this family.

Eopsaltria australis

Eastern Yellow Robin

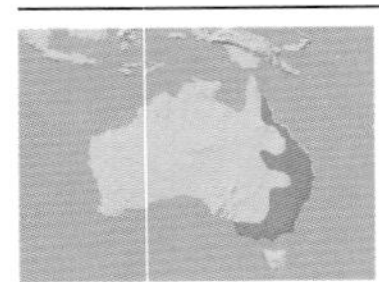

LENGTH 15cm (6in)

WEIGHT 18–20g ($^5/_8$–$^{11}/_{16}$oz)

MIGRATION Non-migrant

HABITAT Wide range of coastal and sub-coastal habitats, particularly damp places or near water

ADULT EASTERN YELLOW ROBIN

One of the larger Australasian robins, the brightly coloured Eastern Yellow Robin is also one of the most easily observed birds. It has a grey back and head and striking yellow underparts. Like all Australasian robins, it is found in dark, shady places and employs a perch-and-pounce hunting technique, feeding on a wide range of small invertebrates, but mostly insects. Breeding mostly takes place in the spring and is often communal. The nest is a well-finished cup, placed in a branch fork, and is neatly plastered with lichen, moss, and bits of bark.

Petroica phoenicea

Flame Robin

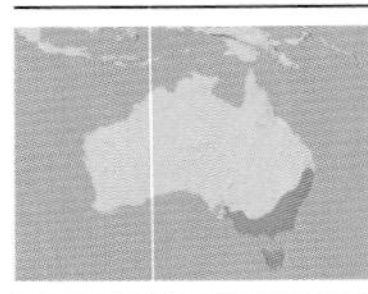

LENGTH 14cm (5$^1/_2$in)

WEIGHT 13g ($^7/_{16}$oz)

MIGRATION Partial migrant

HABITAT Breeds in open forest and woodland, and montane areas, dispersing to open grassy plains

Easily distinguished by its bright orange-red throat plumage, the male Flame Robin has a noticeable white forehead spot, slate-grey upperparts, and white markings on its wings and tail. The female is plain grey-brown, with paler underparts, and smaller white wing markings than the male. The Flame Robin mainly eats insects. It will remain motionless for long periods on a perch, scanning the ground for prey, before pouncing to catch it. During the breeding season, it is found in pairs, but will band together in large groups to feed in more open areas during the winter. The usual call is a short "peep".

The species is a partial migrant, mostly breeding in and around the Great Dividing Range and in the Tasmanian highlands. When autumn arrives, most birds disperse to lower and warmer areas, some travelling as far as eastern South Australia, southern Queensland or, in the case of some Tasmanian birds, Victoria. Birds breeding in warmer climates tend to be year-round residents.

MALE FLAME ROBIN

Microeca fascinans

Jacky Winter

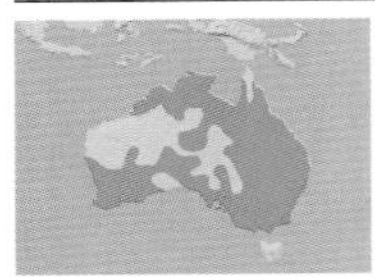

LENGTH 13cm (5in)

WEIGHT 16g ($^9/_{16}$oz)

MIGRATION Non-migrant

HABITAT Dry open forest and woodland, with bare ground, mallee scrub, farmland, and parks

A small flycatcher, the Jacky Winter has a faint pale eye-ring, grey-brown upperparts, and a white throat and belly, with white in the wings and tail. It sits upright on an exposed perch, wagging its tail from side to side, uttering its "peter-peter" call. Its feeding strategy is to dart out from a perch to catch flying insects, but it also pounces on worms and beetles on the ground. Its cup-shaped nest is often placed on an exposed dead tree branch.

ADULT JACKY WINTER

Petroica australis

New Zealand Robin

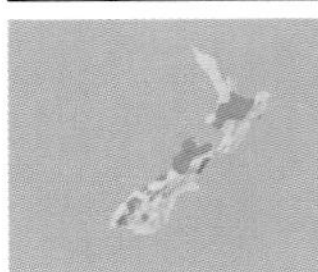

LENGTH 18cm (7in)

WEIGHT 35–40g (1$^1/_4$–1$^7/_{16}$oz)

MIGRATION Non-migrant

HABITAT Forest fringes; green belts of urban areas

The male New Zealand Robin is dark slate-grey, with a cream-white belly, while the female is a dark grey-brown. This robin eats small insects and worms found in leaf litter. The nest is built against the bole of a tree and if the young are threatened, the parents perform an extravagant distraction display, hopping about the intruder with outspread wings, uttering piping notes.

MALE NEW ZEALAND ROBIN

BALD CROWS

ORDER	Passeriformes
FAMILY	Picathartidae
SPECIES	2

THERE ARE TWO SPECIES of bald crows, or rockfowl, both confined to West Africa and considered vulnerable according to the IUCN. Male and female bald crows are similar and the two species mainly differ in the colour of the bald head. They feed on invertebrates, as well as frogs and lizards, found in the leaf litter as they hop through their forest habitats. Their wings are rarely used for flight, but are important for maintaining balance on vines, further aided by their long tail, which is at least twice as long as the body. Birds of this family are colonial nesters, usually on remote cliffs, rock faces, or cave roofs far from human settlements. The one or two eggs are laid in the cup-shaped mud nest during the wet season.

YOUNG ROCKFOWL
A young Grey-necked Picathartes peeps out of its mud nest. The rufous colour of its bald head, characteristic of this species, is visible.

Picathartes gymnocephalus

White-necked Picathartes

LENGTH 40cm (16in)
WEIGHT 200g (7oz)
MIGRATION Non-migrant

HABITAT Primary and secondary forest, forest clearings, and gallery forest in rocky, hilly terrain

RED LIST CATEGORY Vulnerable

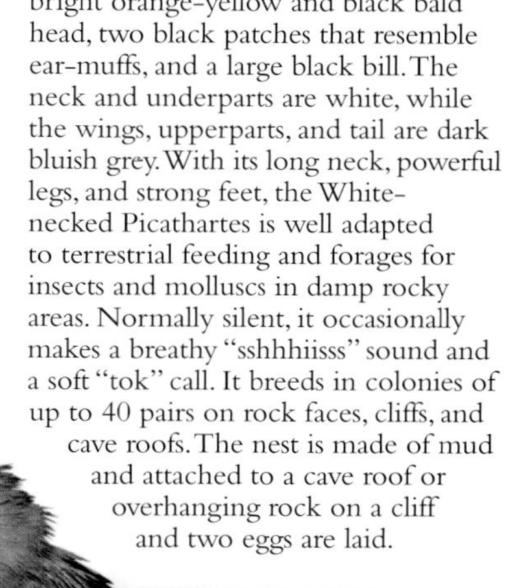

This long-legged crow-like bird has a bright orange-yellow and black bald head, two black patches that resemble ear-muffs, and a large black bill. The neck and underparts are white, while the wings, upperparts, and tail are dark bluish grey. With its long neck, powerful legs, and strong feet, the White-necked Picathartes is well adapted to terrestrial feeding and forages for insects and molluscs in damp rocky areas. Normally silent, it occasionally makes a breathy "sshhhiisss" sound and a soft "tok" call. It breeds in colonies of up to 40 pairs on rock faces, cliffs, and cave roofs. The nest is made of mud and attached to a cave roof or overhanging rock on a cliff and two eggs are laid.

ADULT WHITE-NECKED PICATHARTES

WAXWINGS AND RELATIVES

ORDER	Passeriformes
FAMILY	Bombycillidae
SPECIES	8

THESE ARE SLEEK, medium-sized songbirds found across the Northern Hemisphere. The three true waxwing species (Bohemian, Cedar, and Japanese) are similar in appearance with mainly buff plumage, a fluffy crest, and black chin and face masks. They live mainly on fruit and berries, often gathering in large flocks to feed. The silky-flycatchers and the Hypocolius are also included in this group.

WINTER FEAST
Waxwings, such as this Bohemian Waxwing, are renowned for their winter travels in search of berries, often to areas where they do not normally occur.

Hypocolius ampelinus

Hypocolius

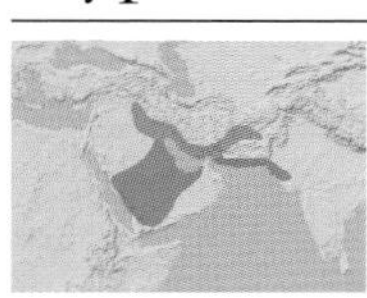

LENGTH 23cm (9in)
WEIGHT 50g ($1^3/_4$oz)
MIGRATION Non-migrant

HABITAT Breeds in lowland woodland areas, especially with fruiting trees

An unusual bird, the Hypocolius is sometimes placed in a separate family. It has a long, black-tipped tail. The male has a black mask on its face, pale blue-grey upperparts, and white tips to the wings. The female is brown in colour and much plainer, lacking the black mask. The juvenile is a pale, sandy colour. The Hypocolius eats mainly fruit and berries, with fallen date palms forming an important part of its diet.

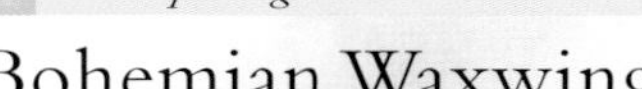

Bombycilla garrulus

Bohemian Waxwing

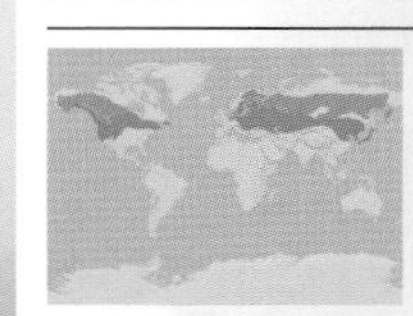

LENGTH 18–21cm (7–$8^1/_2$in)
WEIGHT 50–55g ($1^3/_4$–2oz)
MIGRATION Migrant

HABITAT Breeds in mature coniferous forest in damp mossy terrain; winters in more open lowland areas

A sleek bird, the Bohemian Waxwing has bright red bead-like tips to the secondary wing feathers, which resemble drops of sealing wax, giving rise to its common name. Its wings have yellow and white markings. Pinkish brown in colour, with a wispy, upright crest, it has a narrow black mask underlined with white. It has bright yellow tips on its tail feathers, with chestnut undertail feathers. This bird mainly feeds on berries, supplemented by insects. It usually nests high up in a conifer tree.

ADULT BOHEMIAN WAXWING

BOHEMIAN WAXWINGS
Waxwings are generally sociable birds. Berries form a large part of their diet, and a feeding flock of waxwings can rapidly strip a bush or tree of its fruit.

PALMCHAT

ORDER	Passeriformes
FAMILY	Dulidae
SPECIES	1

THE PALMCHAT IS THE ONLY member of its family and is found solely on the Caribbean island of Hispaniola. It is a noisy resident, particularly when close to the nest where its large repertoire of calls cannot fail to be heard. There is considerable debate as to which other bird families the Palmchat is most closely related to, with current opinion suggesting that the waxwings and silky-flycatchers (see p.399) may be its nearest relatives.

BEHAVIOUR

The Palmchat is a highly social species throughout the year. It builds massive communal nests – sometimes reaching up to two metres (6$\frac{1}{2}$ft) in diameter. These vast structures are also used outside the breeding season as places to roost. The nest is constantly repaired and extended by the resident birds. Up to 50 pairs of Palmchats may occupy the structure, but 4–10 pairs is the more usual occupancy. Pairs of birds usually inhabit individual chambers accessible by their own separate entrance tunnel. Occasionally, other species of bird are permitted to build their own nests on top of the Palmchat's communal nest.

Dulus dominicus

Palmchat

LENGTH 18–20cm (7–8in)

WEIGHT 40–50g (1$\frac{7}{16}$–1$\frac{3}{4}$oz)

MIGRATION Non-migrant

HABITAT Mainly open areas of royal palm trees; also other open areas, including parks and gardens

A medium-sized songbird, the Palmchat has a mixture of olive-brown and green upperparts. It is pale below, but heavily streaked with brown. It has a noticeable red eye and a strong, ivory-coloured bill. The males and female are similar in appearance and the juvenile has a darker throat.

This bird builds a huge, domed nest high in the crown of the royal palm tree (hence the name Palmchat). These nests are usually occupied by up to ten pairs, each living in a separate chamber. The palmchat is the only member of its family and is found solely on the West Indian island of Hispaniola.

ADULT PALMCHAT

TRUE TITS

ORDER	Passeriformes
FAMILY	Paridae
SPECIES	54

THIS LARGE GROUP of small, stocky songbirds occurs in Europe, Asia, and Africa. In North America they are referred to as "titmice" or "chickadees". Many members of the family are predominantly brown with black and white head markings, but a number of species are spectacularly coloured. Some have noticeable crests.

BEHAVIOUR

Tits are small and agile. They tend to feed quite high up in the trees on a mixed diet of insects and seeds, although increasingly in urban areas, many species now obtain much of their sustenance from bird food put out by humans. Peanuts, suet mixes, and coconuts are among the favourite high-energy foodstuffs that are used to attract these favourite visitors into the garden. Tits are tame, sociable birds. Consequently, it is often easy to observe large groups, often comprising a variety of species.

FEEDING UPSIDE DOWN
Blue Tits are adept at hanging upside down from feeders and branches, to get food out of the reach of less agile birds.

ADULT BLACK-CAPPED CHICKADEE

Poecile atricapillus

Black-capped Chickadee

LENGTH 13cm (5in)

WEIGHT 11g ($\frac{3}{8}$oz)

MIGRATION Non-migrant

HABITAT Woodland and forest, particularly deciduous and mixed; parks and gardens

As its name suggests, the Black-capped Chickadee has a black cap. It has a large black bib that contrasts with its white cheeks and a short, black bill. It is grey-brown on its back, with a pale wing bar, and has a pale breast and buff flanks. The species has a complex series of calls, which include a low, husky, and drawn out "chick-a-dee-dee-dee" and a clear, fluted "fee-bee".

This species often joins foraging flocks that consist of other species and feeds on insects, insect eggs, and seeds from conifers and bayberry trees. It is a common and familiar garden bird throughout most of Canada and the northern USA – in southeast USA, it is replaced by the similar, but duller Carolina Chickadee (*P. carolinensis*) and sometimes hybridizes with it.

Poecile cincta

Grey-headed Chickadee

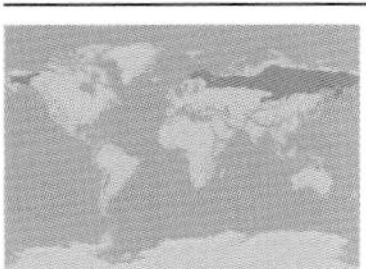

LENGTH 14cm (5$\frac{1}{2}$in)

WEIGHT 12g ($\frac{11}{16}$oz)

MIGRATION Non-migrant

HABITAT Coniferous forest

Also known as the Siberian Tit, this species is the only tit to occur in both Europe and America. A separate population is also found in Alaska. The Grey-headed Chickadee has a short bill, grey-brown cap and back, white cheeks, dark (almost black) bib, white-edged wings, and cinnamon flanks. In Europe, there are no species that can be confused with it; in Alaska, the similar Boreal Chickadee (*P. hudsonica*) also has a brown cap, but a much smaller white cheek patch. The diet of this species consists of a range of seeds and invertebrates. The Grey-headed Chickadee stores food for the winter in crevices or cracks in trees or among lichens. It nests in cavities of trees.

PERCHING GREY-HEADED CHICKADEE

ADULT VARIED TIT

Poecile varia

Varied Tit

LENGTH 10–13cm (4–5in)
WEIGHT 17g (5/8oz)
MIGRATION Non-migrant

HABITAT Forest

This species has a number of different subspecies that vary in appearance. Birds of the most widespread subspecies are orange below, with a grey back. Its white cheeks and forehead contrasts with its black bib, crown, and nape. The darkest race occurs on Japan's Outer Izu Islands, where it has a dark rufous forehead, cheeks, and underparts. Birds found in Taiwan are dark rufous below, but have a white forehead and cheeks.

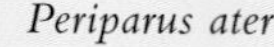

Periparus ater

Coal Tit

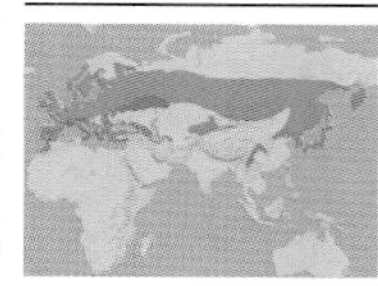

LENGTH 11cm (4½in)
WEIGHT 9g (11/32oz)
MIGRATION Non-migrant

HABITAT Coniferous forest; also found in other types of woodland, parks, and gardens

The Coal Tit is found throughout Europe and eastwards across a wide belt of Asia to Japan. It has white (or off-white) cheeks, a black cap, with a white stripe along the back of the head, a black bib, buff underparts, and a greenish olive back with two contrasting white-spotted wingbars. Birds found in the Himalayas have a noticeable black crest. The juvenile has a yellow tinge to the pale areas of its plumage.

ADULT COAL TIT

Lophophanes cristatus

European Crested Tit

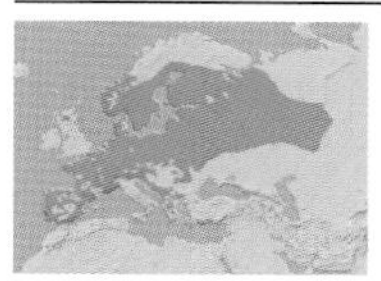

LENGTH 12cm (4½in)
WEIGHT 10–12g (3/8–7/16oz)
MIGRATION Non-migrant

HABITAT Mainly coniferous forest (though other types of woodland in some parts of its range)

With its distinctive crest and pied head pattern, the European Crested Tit stands out among the European members of its family. Its black crest is neatly streaked with white, giving it a scaly appearance. It has a black eye stripe that extends into an inverse "C" shape and its thick black bib is joined together by a thin circular black line that extends around the back of the neck. The European Crested Tit is pale below with a brown back, although some populations (such as those in Brittany, France) are more buff below. The sexes are very similar, but the female has a slightly shorter crest. The juvenile appears slightly duller than the adult. The species is found in most of Europe, but is absent from Italy, Ireland, and most of Britain.

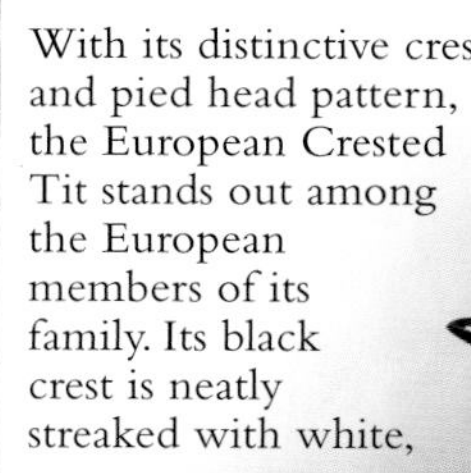

ADULT EUROPEAN CRESTED TIT

Cyanistes caeruleus

Blue Tit

LENGTH 12cm (4½in)
WEIGHT 10g (5/8oz)
MIGRATION Partial migrant

HABITAT Wide range of habitats, including woodland, scrub, parks, and gardens

A bright and attractive bird, the Blue Tit is one of the most familiar small birds across much of Europe, although it is also found in North Africa, the Middle East, and parts of Central Asia. Although a number of quite varied subspecies occur, this is a distinct species. Blue Tits found in Europe are bright yellow below, with a distinct facial pattern: white cheeks, a blue cap, a blue band around the back of the neck, and a thin stripe through the eye. The back is greyish green, with blue tail and wings. The juvenile lacks any blue or white, appearing dirty yellow below and greenish grey above. The birds found in North Africa and the Canary Islands are generally darker above with almost black head markings.

The Blue Tit often visits garden birdfeeders and nestboxes. Outside the breeding season, the species can usually be found foraging in large (often mixed) flocks. The Blue Tit has a large repertoire of calls including scolding alarms and high-pitched whistles, as well a number of piping and trilling songs.

ADULT BLUE TIT

ADULT TUFTED TITMOUSE

Baeolophus bicolor

Tufted Titmouse

LENGTH 16cm (6½in)
WEIGHT 20g (11/16oz)
MIGRATION Non-migrant

HABITAT Deciduous and mixed woodland, parks, and gardens

The Tufted Titmouse is the largest member of its family in the Americas. It is an attractive species with a distinct grey crest and an "open-faced" appearance. It is quite a plain bird: grey above and white below, with rufous-buff flanks. The adult has a small black area above the bill that is not present in the plainer, shorter-crested juvenile. One of the subspecies found in Texas and northeast Mexico has a distinct black crest and is often treated as a separate species: the Black-crested Titmouse.

The Tufted Titmouse has a number of high-pitched nasal calls and a clear, low-pitched song. It is often found foraging in groups with other birds.

Melanochlora sultanea

Sultan Tit

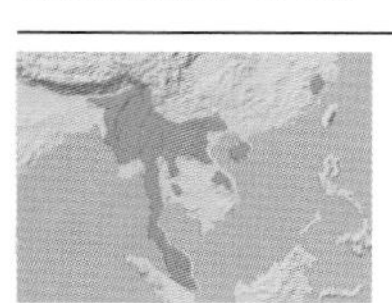

LENGTH 20cm (8in)
WEIGHT 40g (17/16oz)
MIGRATION Non-migrant

HABITAT Forest, scrub, and bamboo

Not only is the striking Sultan Tit of Asia the largest member of its family, it is also quite unlike any of its relatives in its plumage. The male has a glossy blue-black bib and upperparts that contrast with its bright yellow underparts and impressive crest. The female has duller plumage. The juvenile is even more dull in coloration and has a shorter crest. The adult of the isolated subspecies found in southern Laos and central Vietnam has a dark crest that is the same colour as its upperparts. Like other members of the tit family, the Sultan Tit is an active, social species but can be inconspicuous due to its preference for canopy-feeding.

MALE SULTAN TIT

PENDULINE TITS

ORDER	Passeriformes
FAMILY	Remizidae
SPECIES	10

MOST SPECIES OF THE penduline tit family are found in Europe, Africa, and Asia although there is one from North America. The name "penduline" comes from their pendulous bag-shaped nests, which hang from trees or reeds, usually over water. All have short, rather delicate pointed bills enabling them to take insects, spiders, and small seeds.

BEHAVIOUR

Penduline tits are constantly active, foraging over reeds, twigs, and leaves, and keeping in contact with one another with thin, sibilant calls. They are usually found in pairs or small groups. Eurasian Penduline Tits may be monogamous, or a single male may mate with more than one female, and a female with more than one male. In other species, the large numbers of eggs in one nest, suggest that more than one female may contribute.

BAG-LIKE NEST
The tear-drop-shaped nest hangs from a single attachmemt to a willow twig. It has its entrance near the top.

Remiz pendulinus

Eurasian Penduline Tit

LENGTH 11cm (4½in)
WEIGHT 8–13g (5/16–7/16oz)
MIGRATION Migrant

HABITAT Variety of tall wetland vegetation, including reedbeds and rushes; scrub

MALE EURASIAN PENDULINE TIT

A typical member of its small family, the Eurasian Penduline Tit is a diminutive, compact bird with a broad, black "bandit's mask" (the female has a narrower mask than the male) and a short, conical bill. It has a pale grey head, red-brown back, buff underparts, and a dark tail. In flight, it shows a deep red-brown band across its wings.

During the summer, this tit feeds largely on invertebrates, which it takes while it forages in tall emergent vegetation and the outermost twigs and branches of trees and bushes. Plant material, especially reed seeds, feature in its diet during winter. Its nest, made of plant down and cobwebs, is flask-shaped, with a short entrance tube. The species breeds throughout mainland Europe, extending into southwest Siberia and northwest Kazakhstan. During the 20th century, a dramatic westerly and northerly expansion in its range occurred, enabling its colonization of southern Scandinavia and the Netherlands.

Auriparus flaviceps

Verdin

LENGTH 10cm (4in)
WEIGHT 6–9g (7/32–11/32oz)
MIGRATION Non-migrant

HABITAT Well-vegetated desert, including dry washes and watercourses

Found in the deserts of southwest USA and adjacent Mexico, the Verdin is mainly grey, with a bright yellow head and throat and chestnut shoulder patches. Like the other penduline tits, it has a sharply pointed bill. It is a shy and inconspicuous bird, but its presence at a site is revealed by its spherical nest. This large, elaborate structure is made of thorny twigs that act as the first line of defence against would-be predators. It is built by the male, well above the ground.

BUSHTITS

ORDER	Passeriformes
FAMILY	Aegithalidae
SPECIES	11

THIS GROUP OF VERY SMALL songbirds is found mostly in Europe and Asia (particularly the Himalayas), with just one species, the American Bushtit, occurring in North America. They are sociable birds, always on the move in noisy, bounding flocks. They build intricate hanging woven nests out of grass and twigs, which are usually lined with feathers and moss. These birds have long tails in relation to the size of their bodies.

FAMILY PARTIES
These young Long-tailed Bushtits will continue to act sociably when they are older, foraging and feeding together in noisy, restless flocks.

Aegithalos caudatus

Long-tailed Bushtit

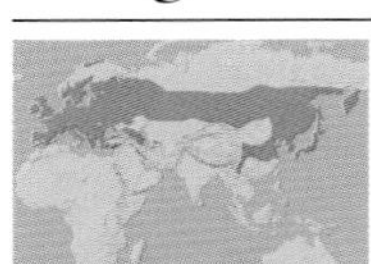

LENGTH 13–16cm (5–6½in)
WEIGHT 6–11g (7/32–3/8oz)
MIGRATION Non-migrant

HABITAT Edges of mixed and deciduous woodland, scrub, heathland, and hedgerows

ADULT BIRD (NORTHERN SUBSPECIES)

The most widespread member of its small family, the Long-tailed Bushtit has a white crown, with black and brown upperparts and dull white underparts. A gregarious species, it is often found in noisy family parties of up to 30 birds, which form the core of mixed-species feeding flocks in the winter months. The "white-headed" northern birds (shown here) sometimes wander away from their breeding areas in the winter, perhaps in response to cold weather.

Psaltriparus minimus

American Bushtit

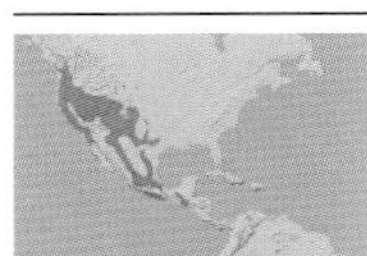

LENGTH 10cm (4in)
WEIGHT 5g (3/16oz)
MIGRATION Non-migrant

HABITAT Open deciduous and mixed woodland

One of North America's smallest birds, the tiny American Bushtit is grey-brown overall and has a short stubby bill and a long graduated tail. Like its close relative the Long-tailed Bushtit (left), it shows a great deal of geographical variation throughout its range. Another similarity with the Long-tailed Bushtit is its gregarious behaviour and corresponding complex social system. Flocks of up to 40 birds, consisting only of family members, are on record. These flocks vociferously defend their territories against rival groups and individuals attempting to join a group from outside are invariably driven away.

ADULT AMERICAN BUSHTIT

SWALLOWS AND MARTINS

ORDER	Passeriformes
FAMILY	Hirundinidae
SPECIES	84

COLLECTIVELY KNOWN as hirundines, swallows and martins are generally quite small, long-winged birds that spend most of their time on the wing feeding on insects. They vary in appearance, though most tend to have dark upperparts, which often contrast with paler plumage below. Many species also have a forked tail and very long tail streamers. Some swallows and martins are very sociable, nesting in large colonies such as excavated holes in cliffs or riverbanks.

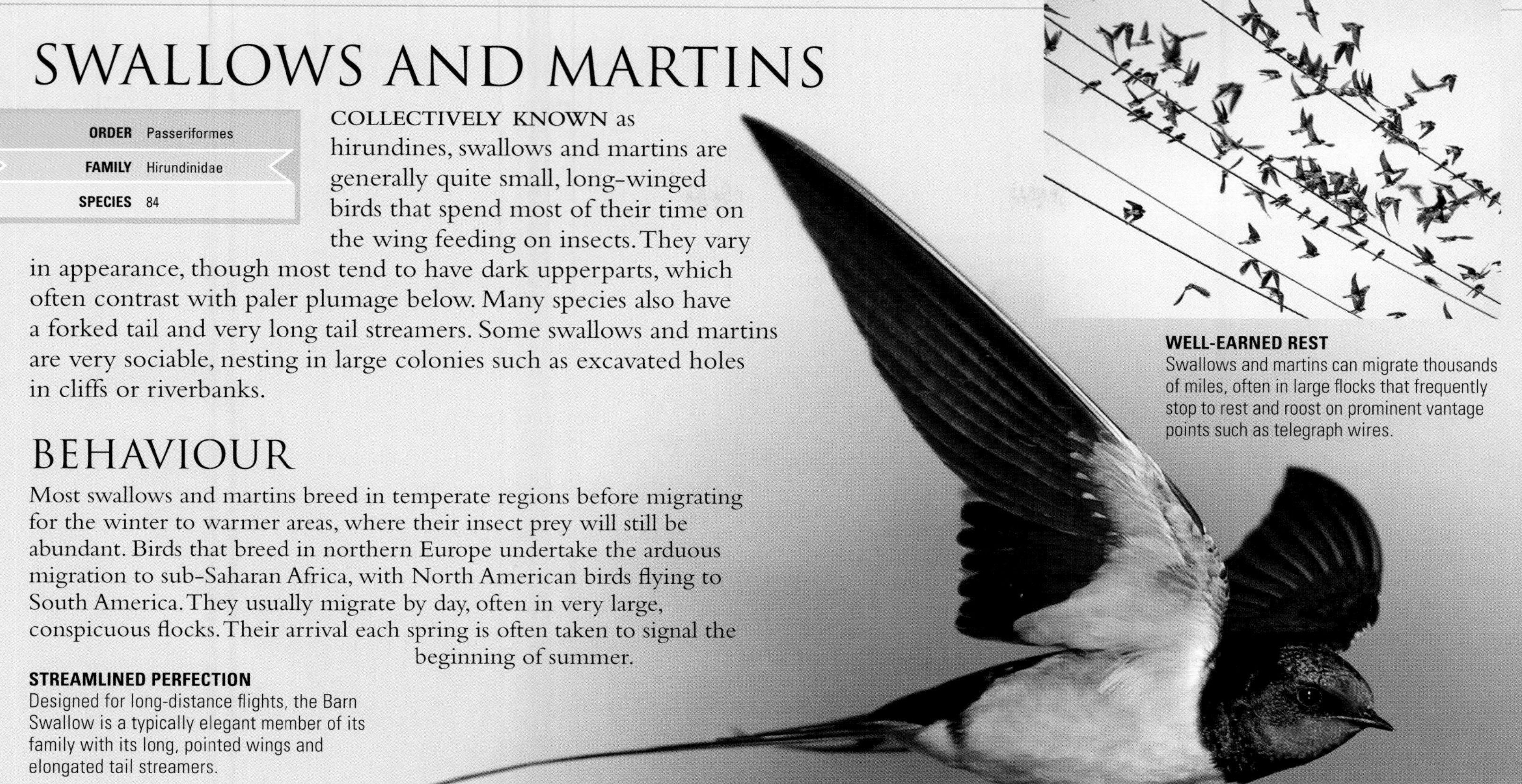

WELL-EARNED REST
Swallows and martins can migrate thousands of miles, often in large flocks that frequently stop to rest and roost on prominent vantage points such as telegraph wires.

BEHAVIOUR

Most swallows and martins breed in temperate regions before migrating for the winter to warmer areas, where their insect prey will still be abundant. Birds that breed in northern Europe undertake the arduous migration to sub-Saharan Africa, with North American birds flying to South America. They usually migrate by day, often in very large, conspicuous flocks. Their arrival each spring is often taken to signal the beginning of summer.

STREAMLINED PERFECTION
Designed for long-distance flights, the Barn Swallow is a typically elegant member of its family with its long, pointed wings and elongated tail streamers.

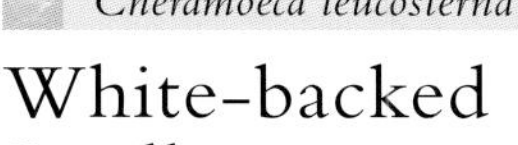

Cheramoeca leucosterna

White-backed Swallow

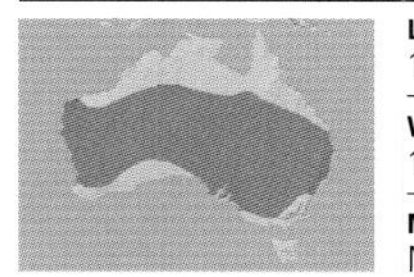

LENGTH 15cm (6in)
WEIGHT 12–16g (7/16–9/16oz)
MIGRATION Non-migrant
HABITAT Open country, usually near water

Like many swallows, the White-backed Swallow has a streamlined body, a short neck, a short broad bill, long pointed wings, short legs, and a forked tail. Found only on the island continent of Australia, it stands out within its range because of its distinctive pied coloration.

The White-backed Swallow inhabits dry, open country throughout sub-tropical Australia. Its distribution is strongly linked to areas with suitable nesting sites, usually on sandy cliffs and riverbanks, and favourable breeding sites may encourage small colonies to develop. This swallow excavates nest burrows down to 60cm (23½in), the burrow ending in an enlarged chamber with a rudimentary nest of dried grass and leaves. Unlike some bank-nesting swallows, it seems to prefer natural breeding sites and has been slow to take advantage of artificial breeding sites.

ADULT WHITE-BACKED SWALLOW

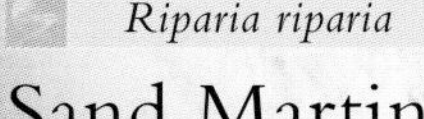

Riparia riparia

Sand Martin

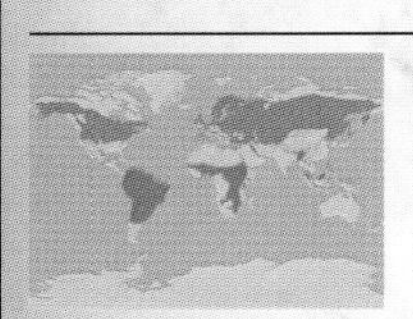

LENGTH 12cm (4½in)
WEIGHT 11–20g (3/8–11/16oz)
MIGRATION Migrant
HABITAT Lowland habitats near water

A common species throughout its range, the Sand Martin, or Collared Sand Martin, is one of the most widespread of the world's swallow species. It has a black bill, brown upperparts, white underparts, with a narrow brown band on the breast, and a slightly forked tail. Its choice of breeding sites is strongly linked to the availability of suitable nesting banks. In some areas, these are provided by erosion through natural river processes, but it has switched to artificial sites where floodplain management has taken places, mostly provided by the sand and gravel extraction industry. It breeds throughout temperate Eurasia and North America.

ADULT AT NEST HOLE

Petrochelidon pyrrhonota

American Cliff Swallow

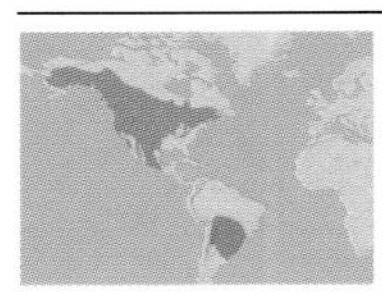

LENGTH 13cm (5in)

WEIGHT 18–25g (5/8–7/8oz)

MIGRATION Migrant

HABITAT Open areas of farms and towns; also in mountainous areas

Similar to the more widespread Barn Swallow (opposite), the American Cliff Swallow has a short black bill, white forehead, and dark brown throat. A band of paler plumage at the nape separates the blue of the head and back, and it has white underparts with grey-brown flanks, blue-black wings, and a pale pink rump. However, the most notable characteristic of this swallow is the short, squared-off tail, which is completely overlapped by the wing feathers when the bird is at rest.

This species eats flying insects, catching them in flight, or occasionally, forages on the ground for berries. The American Cliff Swallow breeds in North America and has expanded its range from its natural rocky habitat in mountainous regions to farms and towns. Further expansion of its range has been facilitated by large-scale human constructions such as dams and bridges, which it uses as nesting sites, adapting remarkably well to the change in its environment. The majority of the breeding population is now found in association with human activity over much of its range. It spends the winter in South America, south of the Amazonian rainforest up to the eastern slopes of the Andes. Migrating birds have been recorded out at sea, on the Caribbean islands, and even as far south as Tierra del Fuego.

ADULT AMERICAN CLIFF SWALLOW

MUD NESTS

Typically, the Cliff Swallow plasters its conical mud nests on vertical rockfaces, although most of these birds now nest on buildings. Each nest is a complex construction of mud pellets with a tubular entrance on one side. On natural rock surfaces, the nests are spaced at a discreet distance from one another and can sometimes number up to several thousand in a single colony.

Tahchycineta bicolor

Tree Swallow

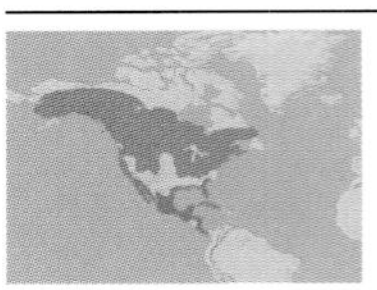

LENGTH 13cm (5in)

WEIGHT 16–25g (9/16–7/8oz)

MIGRATION Migrant

HABITAT Open or wooded areas, often near water

A short-tailed species, the Tree Swallow has black wings that overlap the tail when at rest. It has a white throat and chest, with the back varying from iridescent deep blue to greener colours around the wing margins.

Most of this swallow's nest sites are found close to water but occasionally in drier areas of the prairies. It shows a preference for natural nest sites such as tree cavities, although many birds now prefer to use artificial nest boxes, particularly on open farmland. Extremely territorial in behaviour, the male Tree Swallow has been known to eject juveniles from other nests nearby if the resident male is absent. Nevertheless, this species is gregarious in migration and is often seen in large flocks outside the breeding season. The Tree Swallow mainly eats flying insects, but may also feed on spiders and crustaceans. In winter, this species will also eat berries.

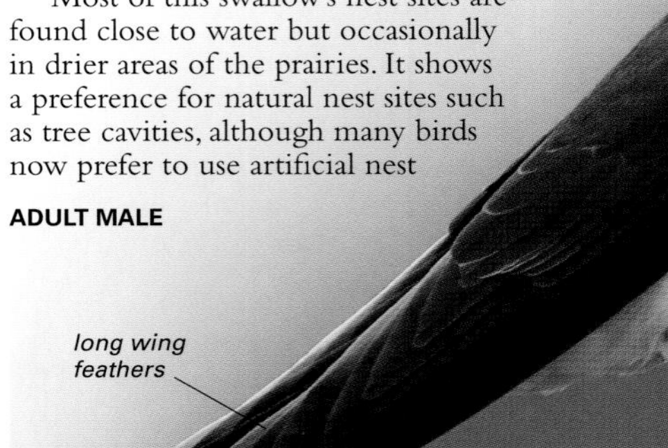

ADULT MALE

Progne subis

Purple Martin

LENGTH 19cm (7½in)

WEIGHT 50–65g (1¾–2⅜oz)

MIGRATION Migrant

HABITAT Open or semi-open areas, mostly near water

One of the largest swallows found in North America, the Purple Martin is uniformly dark and lacks the pale chest seen in many other swallow species. Its iridescent plumage glistens in various shades of blue, green, or purple. The Purple Martin has benefited from the provision of artificial nest boxes. It migrates to South America in the winter.

ADULT PURPLE MARTIN

Notiochelidon cyanoleuca

Blue-and-white Swallow

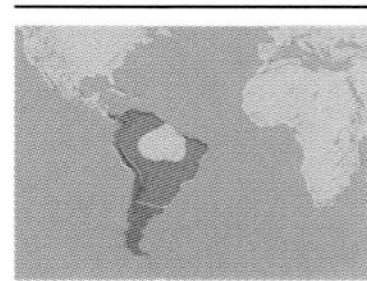

LENGTH 12cm (4½in)

WEIGHT 9–13g (11/32–7/16oz)

MIGRATION Migrant

HABITAT Open areas near water; often associated with human habitation

Similar to the Tree Swallow (above), the Blue-and-white Swallow has a more distinct fork to the tail in flight. However, it is easy to distinguish the two species because there is little, if any, overlap in their ranges. This swallow is found in the Andes and central South American pampas regions. The northern subspecies are resident but the migratory subspecies tend to move through mountainous areas rather than along coasts. Nesting takes place in small groups or in isolation, although large flocks form outside the breeding season.

Hirundo neoxena

Welcome Swallow

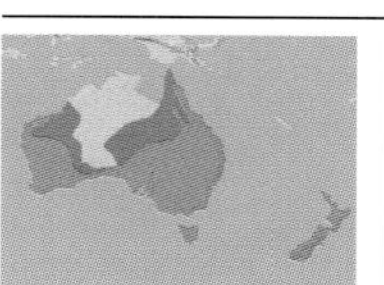

LENGTH 15cm (6in)

WEIGHT 12–17g (7/16–5/8oz)

MIGRATION Partial migrant

HABITAT Mostly found close to water, including coastal caves

The Welcome Swallow of Australia is very similar to the Barn Swallow (right). However, its red facial markings extend onto the upper breast and there is no dark band separating this area of colour from the pale front. The Welcome Swallow extended its range into New Zealand during the 1950s due to its preference for artificial nest sites. There are also signs that the population of this species is increasing in the islands to the north of Australia. Nesting usually takes place in isolation or in small colonies, but the birds form communal flocks outside the breeding season.

ADULT MALE

MALE WIRE-TAILED SWALLOW

Hirundo smithii

Wire-tailed Swallow

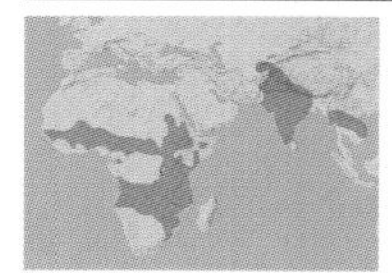

LENGTH 14cm (5 1/2in)

WEIGHT 11–17g (3/8–5/8oz)

MIGRATION Partial migrant

HABITAT Open areas such as grassland, usually near water

An elegant species, the Wire-tailed Swallow is notable for the long, wire-like tail feathers of the male, which gives the species its common name. It also has a striking chestnut cap, which contrasts with the unbroken bright blue of the back and wings.

The Wire-tailed Swallow is resident in much of equatorial Africa but is an irregular migrant on the Indian subcontinent and southeast Asia. Some breeding sites are found at altitudes of more than 2,000m (6,500ft) in Asia and up to 3,000m (10,000ft) in Africa. Pairs are usually solitary nesters. Most nests are now found on buildings.

Hirundo rustica

Barn Swallow

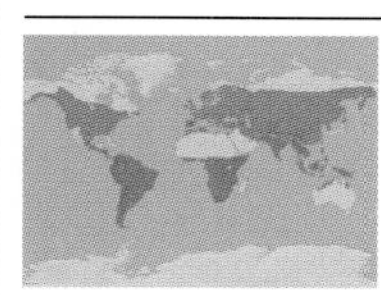

LENGTH 18cm (7in)

WEIGHT 14–25g (1/2–7/8oz)

MIGRATION Migrant

HABITAT Open farmland and savanna, especially near water; also urban areas

SWALLOW SONG
The Barn Swallow utters a repetitive clipped "chi-dit, chi-dit" or "wit-wit".

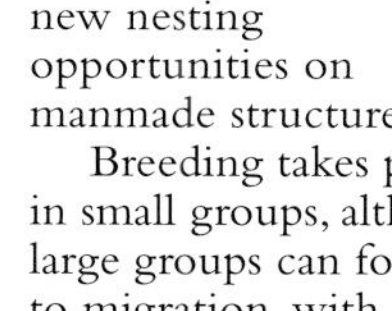

A distinctive species, the Barn Swallow has blue upperparts, with a band of blue extending beneath the throat. Its facial markings are chestnut-coloured. Long tail feathers are more pronounced in the male but can also been seen on the female. Some races have red or pink chests – instead of the white chest of most swallows – but all Barn Swallows have a dark throat-band.

The Barn Swallow population has declined in some parts of its range due to a reduction of land devoted to agriculture. However, this factor has been offset by the Barn Swallow's adaptation to new nesting opportunities on manmade structures.

Breeding takes place in small groups, although large groups can form prior to migration, with non-breeding birds forming large communal roosts in places such as reedbeds. The Barn Swallow generally feeds at low levels, close to the grass or just above water. It is known to pick insects off vegetation or from the ground during periods of colder weather. Some subspecies are known to migrate from as far off as Hawaii, northern Alaska, and the islands of the Atlantic Ocean – the longest migration undertaken by any passerine.

FEATHERS IN FLIGHT
In flight, the Barn Swallow spreads its forked tail, revealing the white spots that form a white band across its tail feathers.

Delichon urbicum

Common House Martin

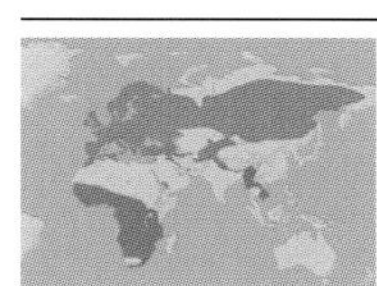

LENGTH 13cm (5in)

WEIGHT 13–25g (7/16–7/8oz)

MIGRATION Migrant

HABITAT Urban areas and open areas such as farmland

A small species, the Common House Martin has a uniformly blue back and dark wings, interrupted by a white rump. The birds are highly vocal around their nests and when feeding in large groups. Breeding birds are found through much of Europe, Asia, and North Africa. This species is vulnerable to extreme weather events, such as drought in sub-Saharan Africa. Other threats include the over-use of fungicides and pesticides on farmland, although the population as a whole is not endangered.

COMMON HOUSE MARTIN

Cecropis cucullata

Greater Striped Swallow

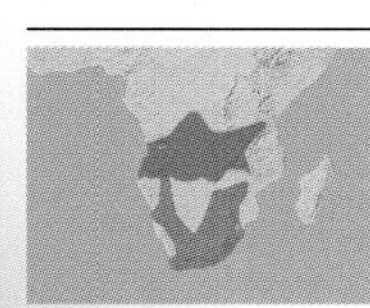

LENGTH 18–20cm (7–8in)

WEIGHT 15–20g (9/16–11/16oz)

MIGRATION Migrant

HABITAT Open areas of mountainous regions; also suburban areas

The Greater Striped Swallow is a long-tailed species with a chestnut crown extending down to the nape of the neck. It has a pale red rump, but the most noticeable feature is its finely streaked chest. Nesting is usually in isolation and buildings or other manmade structures are sometimes used. The breeding season often stretches from August to March, usually with up to three broods, and about two months spent on nest construction.

MALE GREATER STRIPED SWALLOW

LARKS

ORDER	Passeriformes
FAMILY	Alaudidae
SPECIES	92

THESE BIRDS OF open country are well-represented in Europe, Africa, and Asia. In these regions they are often a familiar sight on farms and pastures, though many species are most at home in arid areas, including some of the world's most inhospitable deserts. Generally quite small, there is considerable variation in size within the family, with some species reaching a weight of up to 75g (2½oz). Larks have generally rather drab plumage – a mixture of pale browns and buffs, although a few species have areas of black. Their bills vary from long and thin to short and thick.

SINGING ON THE WING
The Eurasian Skylark delivers its famous song as it ascends, hovers, and then gradually descends.

GROUND NEST
All species of lark nest on the ground in well-concealed nests, although the number of eggs in a typical clutch varies between species.

NESTING CAMOUFLAGE
The patterned plumage of the Horned Lark blends in with the background when the bird is on the nest.

BEHAVIOUR

Larks are usually seen on the ground. Their generally streaky, brown plumage means that the birds are often difficult to pick out as they scurry along the ground, foraging for seeds and invertebrates, the main elements of their diet. Birds of this family are ground-nesters, often in natural grassland or areas of cultivation. The nest can vary from a shallow depression to the more elaborate domed structure built by the Clapper Lark. The preference of some species, such as the Eurasian Skylark, for farmland makes them vulnerable to the effects of intensive agriculture, which in some areas has decimated lark populations. However, numbers of some species have actually benefited from agricultural development in the form of deforestation by increasing the area of their preferred habitat. Many larks are migrants or partial migrants, although some of the species that inhabit warm regions are sedentary.

Mirafra apiata

Clapper Lark

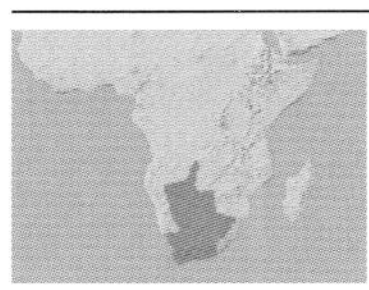

LENGTH 12–15cm (4½–6in)

WEIGHT 25–45g (⅞–1⅝oz)

MIGRATION Non-migrant

HABITAT Well-vegetated areas, sometimes on rocks, and also in fallow fields

This lark is named for its wing-clapping flight-display, in which it flies up with a loud rattling of its wings and then dives whistling loudly. It may repeat this display every 15–30 seconds. A solitary bird, the Clapper Lark forages for insects and seeds on the ground. It also nests on the ground, building a domed structure of grass and rootlets, with a side entrance. It breeds from October to February, after the rainy season. However, several aspects of this bird's nesting behaviour are poorly known, in spite of it being a common bird.

ADULT CLAPPER LARK

Chersomanes albofasciata

Spike-heeled Lark

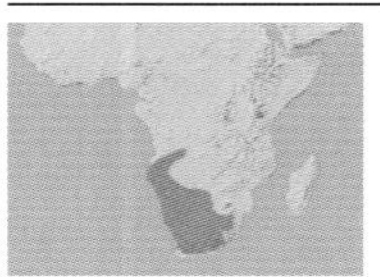

LENGTH 13cm (5in)

WEIGHT 20–35g (11/16–1¼oz)

MIGRATION Non-migrant

HABITAT Open areas, from highland grassland to lowland deserts and semi-deserts

A long-billed bird with an upright stance, the Spike-heeled Lark has orange-buff to white upperparts. Its back and wings may vary from very dark to a very pale sandy colour. Its tail has prominent white tips. The male and female are similar in their plumage.

The female Spike-heeled Lark builds its nest on the ground, usually in a small shady bush. In some areas, breeding is co-operative, with birds attending each nest in threesomes, although this does not appear to influence the number of nests. The female usually lays 2–5 eggs, and the entire nesting period lasts for less than one month. Despite the general unobtrusiveness of this species, it falls prey to small mammals, such as mongooses, shrikes, and small falcons. These larks mob potential predators from the air, hovering and calling repeatedly.

MALE SPIKE-HEELED LARK

ADULT GREATER HOOPOE-LARK

Alaemon alaudipes

Greater Hoopoe-lark

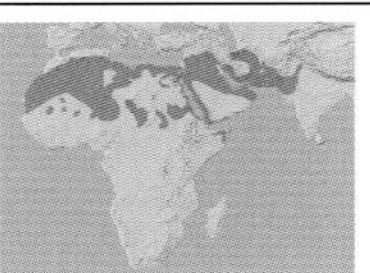

LENGTH 19–23cm (7½–9in)

WEIGHT 30–50g (1 1/16–1¾oz)

MIGRATION Non-migrant

HABITAT Deserts and semi-deserts, often in almost wholly barren areas, typically on gravel plains

Taking its name from its long and slightly decurved bill, which resembles the Eurasian Hoopoe's (see p.312) bill, the long-legged Greater Hoopoe-lark is a common bird that feeds on insects, seeds, and small lizards. In spring, from dawn, when the desert is still cold, the male often engages in a dramatic "rolling" display, during which the white in its wings is revealed.

Melanocorypha calandra

Calandra Lark

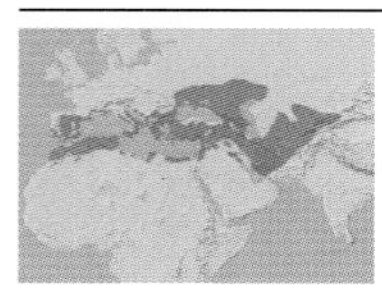

LENGTH 18–20cm (7–8in)

WEIGHT 45–75g (1 5/8–2 5/8oz)

MIGRATION Partial migrant

HABITAT Open plains and steppes, semi-deserts and cultivated areas

ADULT CALANDRA LARK

The Calandra Lark is characterized by its heavy bill, white eyebrows, black markings on the sides of its neck, long broad wings, and short tail. These larks form large flocks, especially after the breeding season, but also nest in proximity to one another. The male sings on the wing, displaying from great heights (almost invisible to the human eye). The female incubates the eggs, but the male also feeds the chicks.

Alauda arvensis

Eurasian Skylark

LENGTH 16–19cm (6 1/2–7 1/2in)

WEIGHT 25–50g (7/8–1 3/4oz)

MIGRATION Partial migrant

HABITAT Mainly farmlands, but also occupies heaths, moors, meadows, and steppes, even forest clearings

One of the traditional harbingers of spring in Europe, the Eurasian Skylark commences its song-flights before daybreak, and may continue all day, especially in the early breeding season. It has a rich melodious song. In contrast, its plumage looks rather similar to that of many other small larks. Like the Woodlark (right), this species switches from a mainly insectivorous diet in summer to a vegetarian one in winter. It takes food mainly on the ground, usually in pairs or alone. These larks may also form larger groups, numbering up to 1,000 in flocks mixed with other lark species, in autumn and winter.

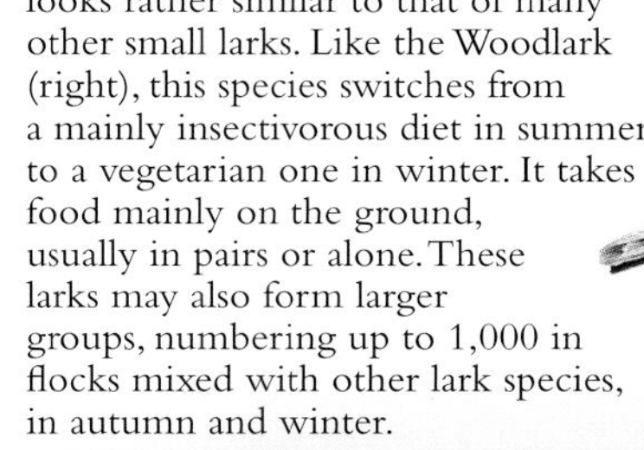

ADULT EURASIAN SKYLARK

HUMAN IMPACT

AGRICULTURE

Once a very common bird, the Eurasian Skylark is now seen less often. Its population has declined massively, especially since the 1960s. This can largely be attributed to modern methods of intensive agriculture, which have reduced nesting opportunities and affected the food supplies of this species. This threat, combined with that of over-hunting in some areas, is putting the species at increased risk.

Lullula arborea

Woodlark

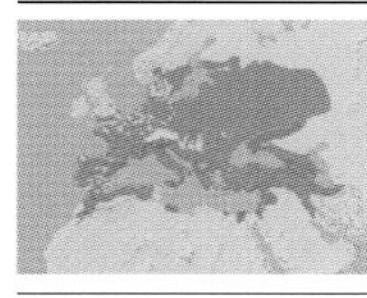

LENGTH 14–15cm (5 1/2–6in)

WEIGHT 25–35g (7/8–1 1/4oz)

MIGRATION Partial migrant

HABITAT Variety of open areas, but prefers heaths, young plantations, and open woodland and scrub

The Woodlark's plumage is generally brown, with paler underparts and a streaked breast. The male and female look very similar. The white eyebrows, which meet on the back of its neck and its rufous cheeks are among the subtle differences that distinguish this species from the more familiar, slightly larger, Eurasian Skylark (below left). The Woodlark forages on the ground, eating mainly small invertebrates during the nesting season, but vegetable matter becomes a far more important part of the diet in winter. During the breeding season, the male performs butterfly-like song-flights, while the female incubates the eggs. Although this species is not generally threatened by humans, its conservation is a concern in Europe.

ADULT AND CHICKS AT NEST

Eremophila alpestris

Horned Lark

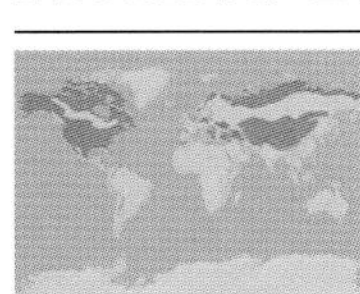

LENGTH 14–17cm (5 1/2–6 1/2in)

WEIGHT 30–40g (1 1/16–1 7/16oz)

MIGRATION Migrant

HABITAT Barren land with very short vegetation, such as tundra and beaches

ADULT HORNED LARK

One of the most common birds in the lark family, the Horned Lark, like many of its relatives, displays much plumage variation across its wide range. The differences mainly involve the depth of the upperpart coloration, and the amount of yellow and black on the face. Like other larks, such variation is strongly related to the type of soils on which the different populations are found. The Horned Lark is the only lark species to have successfully colonized arctic and tundra habitats. In the breeding season it is regularly found at heights well over 5,000m (16,400ft) in the Himalayas.

Galerida cristata

Crested Lark

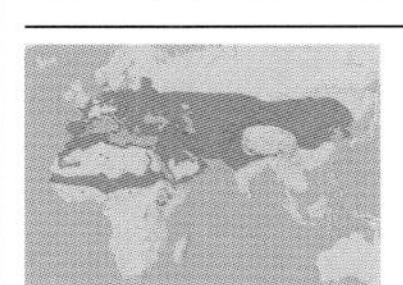

LENGTH 17–19cm (6 1/2–7 1/2in)

WEIGHT 35–50g (1 1/4–1 3/4oz)

MIGRATION Non-migrant

HABITAT Farmland, dry plains with sparse cover, including bushes, warm semi-deserts, and steppes

Seen near roadsides in many areas, the Crested Lark is familar in its range. Its plumage coloration can vary, chiefly due to the different soil types and humidity levels the bird encounters in its wide range. Compared to the Eurasian Skylark (above left) and the Woodlark (above), this bird is distinguished by its long, spiky crest. Its diet comprises seeds, invertebrates, and vegetable matter. The female incubates the eggs, but both sexes feed the young and may even be assisted by a "helper" at the nest.

ADULT CRESTED LARK

CISTICOLAS

ORDER	Passeriformes
FAMILY	Cisticolidae
SPECIES	110

THIS WIDESPREAD FAMILY of passerines is found in southern Europe, Asia, Africa, and Australia. They are tiny birds with thin, pointed bills, relatively long tails, and a rather delicate appearance overall. Their plumage varies considerably. Grass and scrubland cisticolas are usually streaky and brown, and can be very difficult to identify – differences in calls are often the best way to distinguish these well-camouflaged birds. However, some of the forest-dwellers are more brightly coloured.

BEHAVIOUR

Cisticolas and their relatives feed mainly on small insects. Beetles and their larvae are thought to be one of the main items of prey, though weevils, grasshoppers, caterpillars, moths, flies, and spiders are all regularly consumed. Some cisticolas also visit flowers, possibly to feed on nectar, although it is also likely they are just there to catch the insects that have gathered at the spot.

HEALTHY APPETITE
This Rattling Cisticola has caught itself a good meal – an insect that is relatively large in comparison to its own small size.

Cisticola exilis

Golden-headed Cisticola

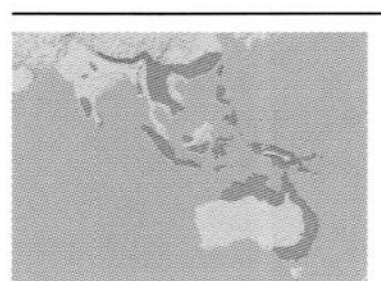

LENGTH 10cm (4in)
WEIGHT 10g ($^{3}/_{8}$oz)
MIGRATION Non-migrant
HABITAT Wetland areas with dense vegetation

The Golden-headed Cisticola is named for the orange head that develops in the male during the breeding season. The female and non-breeding male are streaked brown, with a pale yellow nape and rump. The diet of this bird mainly consists of insects collected on the ground in dense grass, although it also eats some seeds.

MALE IN BREEDING PLUMAGE

It makes its nest by weaving grasses and other vegetation together, which has earned the bird the other common name of Tailorbird. The nest entrance is on the side but close to the top of the structure, which is usually lined with down. Both parents build the nest, but only the female incubates the eggs.

Cisticola juncidis

Zitting Cisticola

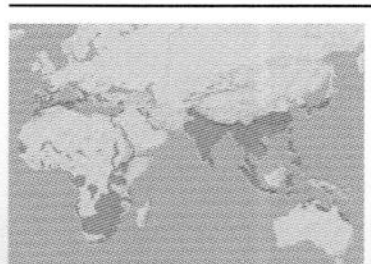

LENGTH 10cm (4in)
WEIGHT 10g ($^{3}/_{8}$oz)
MIGRATION Partial migrant
HABITAT Tropical and subtropical grassland in dry and damp areas

Also known as the Fan-tailed Cisticola, the Zitting Cisticola is named after the monotonous song that it utters when in flight. Both sexes are alike with heavily streaked upperparts and paler underparts. The nest is a woven cup-shaped structure and often has a canopy of leaves to camouflage it. The species has a wide distribution from southern Europe, Africa, across Asia, and northern Australia. It is difficult to distinguish the subspecies because there is little difference in plumage across the range.

ADULT ZITTING CISTICOLA

Prinia gracilis

Graceful Prinia

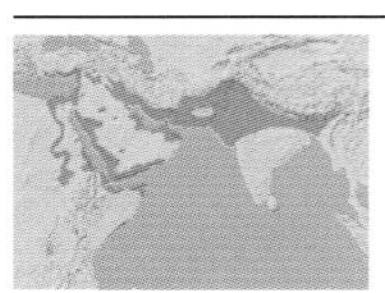

LENGTH 11cm ($4^{1}/_{2}$in)
WEIGHT 7g ($^{1}/_{4}$oz)
MIGRATION Non-migrant
HABITAT Dense grassland and shrubs

The male and female Graceful Prinia are alike in plumage, the upperparts being grey, streaked with brown, while the underparts are plain. The bird has a short, black bill and the tail is long, with distinct alternating bands on the underside. It feeds on insects, often on the ground, and moves in pairs or in small groups. The woven nest is usually placed in a bush and 3–5 eggs are laid. The young are fed on insects. The global population of this species is widespread, with many subspecies, including one found in southern Turkey that is darker in plumage than the others.

ADULT GRACEFUL PRINIA

Apalis thoracica

Bar-throated Apalis

LENGTH 13cm (5in)
WEIGHT 12g ($^{7}/_{16}$oz)
MIGRATION Non-migrant
HABITAT Mostly wooded areas, also found in gardens

Named for its black throat-band, the Bar-throated Apalis has a dark grey area surrounding its yellow eye and dark grey upperparts. The female of the species is less brightly coloured, often with a narrower throat-band. The Bar-throated Apalis mainly feeds on invertebrates taken on the ground, on the wing, or in foliage, although fruit and seeds are also eaten. It is monogamous and the oval-shaped nest is constructed in the branches of trees, with 2–4 eggs being laid. There are very few details available about the timing of the breeding period due to the scattered distribution of this species.

The Bar-throated Apalis is found in southern Africa, extending to parts of eastern Africa. Several subspecies have been identified while others have been given the status of separate species. Although this bird is not considered to be endangered, the patchy distribution makes some regional populations vulnerable. However, many subspecies are protected in national parks.

ADULT BAR-THROATED APALIS

Camaroptera brachyura

Green-backed Camaroptera

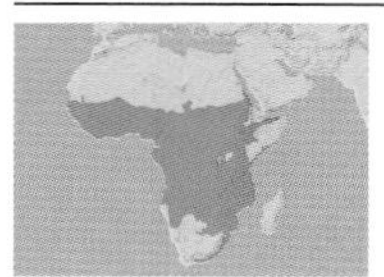

LENGTH 12cm (4½in)

WEIGHT 9–12g (11/32–7/16oz)

MIGRATION Non-migrant

HABITAT Deciduous and evergreen forest with dense undergrowth

Also known as the Bleating Warbler, the Green-backed Camaroptera is predominantly grey in colour. Its most conspicuous features are its red eyes and its green back and wings. The male and female are similar in plumage. This bird mainly feeds on insects as it forages in vegetation. It is a shy bird and more often heard than seen. It builds its nest by weaving grass and leaves together, using spider silk. The nest is usually placed in dense cover and 2–4 eggs are laid. The species is widespread throughout its range in sub-Saharan Africa.

ADULT GREEN-BACKED CAMAROPTERA

Orthotomus sutorius

Common Tailorbird

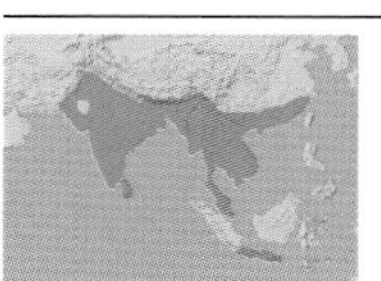

LENGTH 13cm (5in)

WEIGHT 8g (5/16oz)

MIGRATION Non-migrant

HABITAT Open woodland, scrub, and gardens

An attractive species, the Common Tailorbird has bright green plumage and an elegant long tail that is held erect. Both sexes have a chestnut crown, but the female lacks the long central tail feathers that are a feature of the male in the breeding season. The bird mainly feeds on insects but fruit and seeds are also taken. The common name of this bird comes from its nesting habit, which involves stitching leaves together to form a platform for the nest of woven grass.

ADULT COMMON TAILORBIRD

BULBULS

ORDER	Passeriformes
FAMILY	Pycnonotidae
SPECIES	118

BULBULS ARE FOUND throughout most of Africa, Asia, and the Middle East, and a number of introduced species have also colonized urban areas in other parts of the world. They are medium-sized passerines with relatively long tails, short legs, rounded wings, and quite long, moderately powerful bills. Most species have rather dull plumage – mixtures of dark browns and olives – though there are exceptions. Many show a slight crest on top of the head. In some species, such as the Red-whiskered Bulbul, this crest is exaggerated, and is the bird's most noticeable feature.

BEHAVIOUR

Many species of bulbul are common and conspicuous birds, and are consequently well known across Africa and Asia. Their calls are loud and repeatedly given, forming a near-continuous background noise in many parts of their range. Bulbuls are adaptable birds that are common in both rural and urban environments. Their behaviour is boisterous and they are relatively bold in relation to humans; some species show little fear as they scavenge around houses and people in search of stray scraps. In rural areas, some species of bulbul are considered agricultural pests as a result of their tendency to feed on fruit and other crops in large numbers.

FAMILIAR VISITOR
The Common Bulbul is a familiar sight in most of Africa, as it has adapted to human settlements.

Pycnonotus zeylanicus

Straw-headed Bulbul

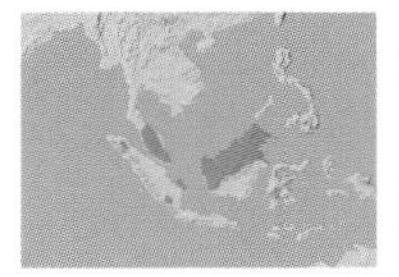

LENGTH 29cm (11½in)

WEIGHT 60g (2⅛oz)

MIGRATION Non-migrant

HABITAT Variety of wooded areas, close to water

RED LIST CATEGORY Vulnerable

One of the larger species in the family of bulbuls, the Straw-headed Bulbul is named for its yellow head. The sexes are similar in plumage, which is mainly brown, with streaked underparts. There is a black stripe behind the bill. It feeds on fruit and insects and breeding takes place throughout the year. Two eggs are laid and three adults co-operatively feed the young. The species is classified as vulnerable due to habitat loss.

ADULT STRAW-HEADED BULBUL

Pycnonotus jocosus

Red-whiskered Bulbul

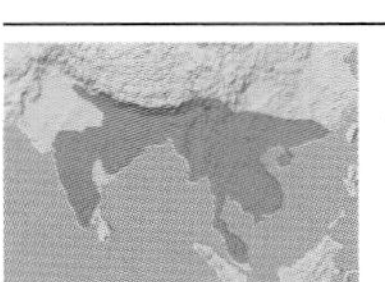

LENGTH 20cm (8in)

WEIGHT 30g (1 1/16oz)

MIGRATION Non-migrant

HABITAT Lightly wooded areas, scrub, and farmland

The Red-whiskered Bulbul gets its common name from the red facial patch behind the eye. Its plumage also includes a crest on the black head, a dark collar, and a lower white facial patch and throat. The male and female are similar and have dark brown upperparts with paler underparts. The main food is fruit, nectar, and insects and flocks of up to 50 birds can sometimes be seen feeding together. It produces 2 or 3 broods in the breeding season, and the nest is usually situated in a tree fork, often low down. Both adults incubate the eggs and feed the young. The Red-whiskered Bulbul is popular as a cage-bird but is not yet globally threatened.

ADULT RED-WHISKERED BULBUL

HUMAN IMPACT

TRADING IN CAGE-BIRDS

Popular as a cage-bird because of its attractive appearance and full-throated, cheerful song, the Red-whiskered Bulbul can often be seen in captivity in bird markets. As the species is captured in large numbers, this has led to a serious decline of the population and measures are being proposed for greater protection.

BIRDS FOR SALE
A common sight in Asia is a bird market with hundreds of caged birds; many species are threatened by trapping for the cage-bird trade.

ADULT SOMBRE BULBUL

Andropadus importunus

Sombre Bulbul

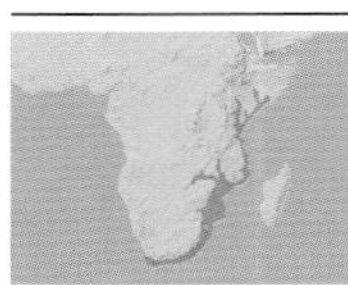

LENGTH 15–18cm (6–7in)

WEIGHT 20–40g ($^{11}/_{16}$–$1^{7}/_{16}$oz)

MIGRATION Non-migrant

HABITAT Dense coastal scrub, inland along riverine bush, and forest up to 2,000m (6,500ft)

The Sombre Bulbul is plain, apart from the pale eye that stands out against its dark plumage. The sexes are alike in plumage and size, but there is a lot of variation in size in the four subspecies. It feeds mainly on fruit, including berries collected in the canopy or undergrowth, but also hawks for insects. Highly sedentary, ringed individuals have been recaptured in the same locality for up to 10 years.

Pycnonotus barbatus

Common Bulbul

LENGTH 15–20cm (6–8in)

WEIGHT 30–40g ($1^{1}/_{16}$–$1^{7}/_{16}$oz)

MIGRATION Non-migrant

HABITAT All woodland types containing fruiting trees up to 2,300m (7,500ft)

Both sexes of the Common Bulbul are alike, though the female is generally smaller. Its 10 subspecies have varying intensities of black head markings. Some subspecies show yellow markings at the base and below the tail. Its main food is fruit, but it also feeds on nectar and invertebrates, such as termites and ants. Although not globally threatened, it has declined over some areas of its range due to heavy deforestation.

ADULT COMMON BULBULS

Bernieria madagascariensis

Long-billed Bernieria

LENGTH 17–20cm ($6^{1}/_{2}$–8in)

WEIGHT 20–40g ($^{11}/_{16}$–$1^{7}/_{16}$oz)

MIGRATION Non-migrant

HABITAT Primary evergreen and dry deciduous forest to 1,300m (4,200ft)

Entirely confined to Madagascar, the Long-billed Bernieria has a long bill that is an adaptation for feeding primarily on invertebrates. Its plumage is very warbler-like – olive-green above and paler green on below. The species is not threatened but is less common in southwestern parts of its range.

Bleda eximius

Green-tailed Bristlebill

LENGTH 21–23cm ($8^{1}/_{2}$–9in)

WEIGHT 45–50g ($1^{5}/_{8}$–$1^{3}/_{4}$oz)

MIGRATION Non-migrant

HABITAT Lowland forest

RED LIST CATEGORY Vulnerable

The Green-tailed Bristlebill is named for the bristles at the base of its stocky bill. It is a striking bird, with bright yellow underparts. Its diet mostly comprises arthropods but small frogs are also taken close to the ground, rarely higher than 3m (10ft). The species is considered vulnerable due to its limited range and habitat preference.

Hemixos castanonotus

Chestnut Bulbul

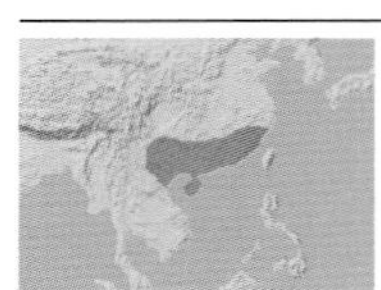

LENGTH 22cm ($8^{1}/_{2}$in)

WEIGHT Not known

MIGRATION Non-migrant

HABITAT Broad-leaved evergreen forest.

A striking bird, the Chestnut Bulbul has a rich chestnut-coloured body and black cap, wings, and tail. Its diet is made up of berries and insects that are flushed from vegetation and chased in flight. Three eggs are laid in a nest built entirely by the female. Little is known about the incubation period or development of the young.

ADULT CHESTNUT BULBUL

Hypsipetes leucocephalus

Black Bulbul

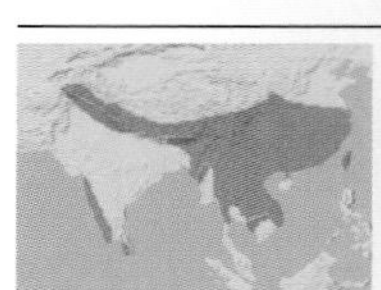

LENGTH 23–27cm (9–$10^{1}/_{2}$in)

WEIGHT Not recorded

MIGRATION Migrant

HABITAT Broad-leaved evergreen and mixed deciduous forest

This bulbul is sometimes called the Himalayan Black Bulbul to reflect its uncertain relationship with other Indian species. Ten subspecies have been recognized, each with varying amounts of white plumage on the head. Its diet comprises a wide range of berries, nectar, and invertebrates and is collected in large flocks, particularly outside the breeding season. In this season, the various subspecies often mix while feeding in the upper branches of tall trees. Some subspecies are sedentary but migration patterns in others are erratic, resembling nomadic movements that vary with changing food supplies.

ADULT BLACK BULBUL

OLD WORLD WARBLERS

ORDER	Passeriformes
FAMILY	Sylviidae
SPECIES	280

THESE SMALL, slender birds have thin bills and a variety of plumages. Most species are rather plain in appearance, with dull browns being the predominate colour. There are exceptions, however, and a number of species have quite striking plumages. As their family name suggests, many species have attractive, warbling songs.

BEHAVIOUR

Although warblers build a variety of different nests, most build open, cup-shaped structures from grasses, reeds, and small twigs. Other materials such as moss and leaves, and even artificial materials such as plastic or string are also woven into the nest by a number of species. Some nests are rather loose and precarious, whereas others resemble tightly knit bags. Many are suspended between plant or reed stems, but can also hang suspended from branches. Some species nest in natural crevices or holes in walls.

HUMAN IMPACT

MIGRATION MONITORING

Around 80 species of Old World warblers undertake large-scale migrations (for example, that of the Common Chiffchaff from northern Europe to sub-Saharan Africa). Ornithologists study these patterns of movement by trapping the birds and attaching small metal identification rings around their legs and then releasing them to continue their journey.

COMMON CHIFFCHAFF "RINGED"
If this Common Chiffchaff is recaptured, scientists will be able to gather information about its travels based on its number.

SHALLOW NEST
A Garden Warbler attends its brood. The nest is a typically skimpy construction made from grasses and moss.

Megalurus gramineus

Little Grassbird

LENGTH 13cm (5in)
WEIGHT 14g (1/2oz)
MIGRATION Non-migrant
HABITAT Swamps and marshes

ADULT LITTLE GRASSBIRD

Another name for the Little Grassbird is the Striated Grassbird because of its streaked brown back. It feeds mostly on insects and other small invertebrates. It is solitary, always remaining in dense cover, and as a consequence, is difficult to see. Two subspecies are known, the western subspecies tending to be darker and more strongly streaked. The population in Tasmania is uniformly dark on the upper- and underparts. Nests have been found throughout the year. Birds of this species also take over the abandoned nests of other warblers.

MALE BROWN SONGLARK

Cincloramphus cruralis

Brown Songlark

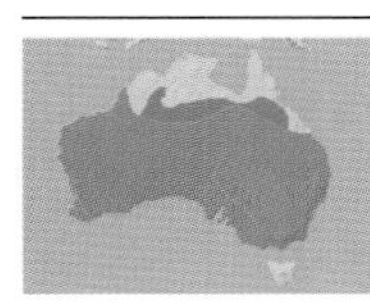

LENGTH 19–25cm (7 1/2–10in)
WEIGHT 30–75g (1 1/16–2 5/8oz)
MIGRATION Non-migrant
HABITAT Open plains, grassland, and savanna with few trees

The Brown Songlark is a plain bird with a long tail. The male is less strongly marked on the head and is significantly larger. The size difference is so great that when early specimens arrived in Europe, they were thought to belong to two separate species. It feeds mainly on insects and seeds collected from the ground. The breeding season lasts from September to February. The male performs a display flight and song. The nest is a simple hollow in the ground, lined with grass.

Eremiornis carteri

Spinifexbird

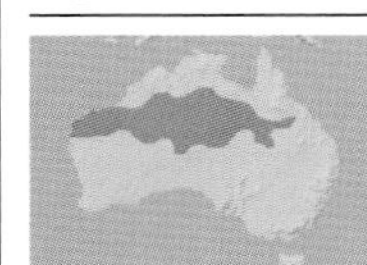

LENGTH 15cm (6in)
WEIGHT 12g (7/16oz)
MIGRATION Non-migrant
HABITAT Grassland, particularly along water courses

The Spinifexbird has a rich brown cap, golden brown streaked wings, and a long tail. Both sexes are alike. Its diet comprises a variety of insects and seeds collected in porcupine grass. This species flies weakly, with its tail drooping. It tends to be solitary, and therefore, is not migratory. The breeding season of the Spinefexbird stretches from August to November and the nest is a shallow cup built in grass stems close to the ground. It usually contains two eggs. Not globally threatened, the species may be common in suitable habitats.

ADULT SPINIFEXBIRD

ADULT CETTI'S WARBLER

Cettia cetti

Cetti's Warbler

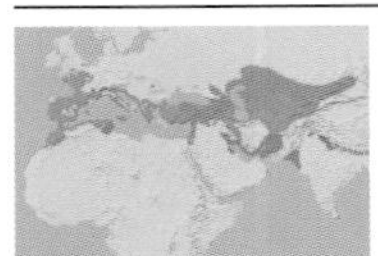

LENGTH 14cm (5½in)

WEIGHT 8–16g (5/16–9/16oz)

MIGRATION Partial migrant

HABITAT Reedbeds and denser trees by water, usually at low level

Nondescript in appearance, with its brown plumage and grey underparts, Cetti's Warbler is difficult to see. It has a darker eye stripe and broad tail, which is either cocked or flicked up and down. The male is slightly larger although there is considerable overlap in the size ranges of both sexes. The Cetti's Warbler song is explosive and metallic in character with rapidly delivered alternating notes. It forages in dense cover, feeding on insects, spiders, snails, and some seeds. Its nest is a deep cup of grass and leaves in vegetation and 3–5 eggs are laid.

Sphenoeacus afer

Cape Grassbird

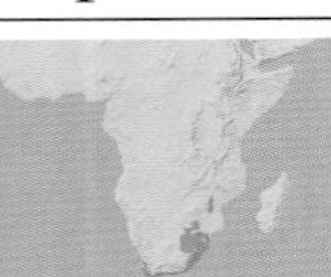

LENGTH 17–19cm (6½–7½in)

WEIGHT 30g (1 1/16oz)

MIGRATION Non-migrant

HABITAT Dry grassland in mountainous and coastal areas; fynbos (shrubland)

With its bright chestnut head, which contrasts with its striped chin, and its white underparts and wings streaked in combinations of grey and brown, the Cape Grassbird is an attractive species. Like most warblers, its main food is insects but seeds are also taken at certain times of the year. A shy bird, it is difficult to see. Nevertheless, it is extremely vocal, although its song is relatively simple for a member of the warbler family.

Found only in Cape Town, the Cape Grassbird is endemic to South Africa and inhabits a type of shrubland called "fynbos". It is one of many African warblers that has been the subject of molecular studies to determine the true family affinities of the various species. Other African species that are also called grassbirds are no longer considered to be closely related to the Cape Grassbird. Because of its limited geographical range and the non-migratory nature of its behaviour, the Cape Grassbird could be used as an indicator of the health of its environment.

ADULT CAPE GRASSBIRD

Locustella naevia

Common Grasshopper Warbler

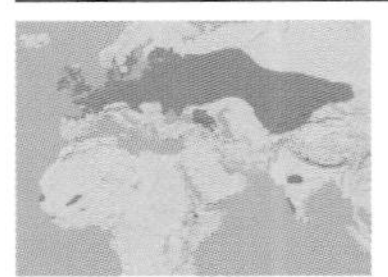

LENGTH 13cm (5in)

WEIGHT 11–15g (3/8–9/16oz)

MIGRATION Migrant

HABITAT Scrub, marshy areas, and artificial plantations

The Common Grasshopper Warbler is a green-brown bird flecked with darker colours on its upperparts and paler on the underparts. More likely to be heard than seen, this species is named after its reeling call that has been likened to that of a grasshopper or a fishing reel. The call is so high-pitched that it may be beyond the hearing range of some people. This nocturnal migrant may make very long individual flights when on the move.

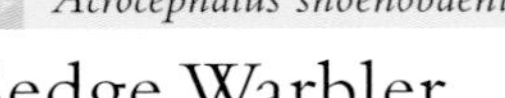

COMMON GRASSHOPPER WARBLER

Acrocephalus shoenobaenus

Sedge Warbler

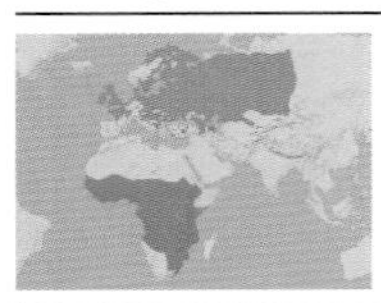

LENGTH 13cm (5in)

WEIGHT 10–13g (3/8–7/16oz)

MIGRATION Migrant

HABITAT Reedbeds, cereal fields, and artificial plantations

A pale eyebrow stripe divides the dark crown and face of the Sedge Warbler. Its upperparts are a flat brown with the underparts shading from pale tan to white. Its loud song consists of a great deal of mimicry, and is usually delivered from a prominent plant, such as a reed. The Sedge Warbler is found throughout much of Eurasia from Scandinavia to west Asia and the Middle East. Wintering birds are found in sub-Saharan Africa. The birds cross the desert in a single flight in both directions. The Sahel region of Africa is an important feeding ground for birds preparing to cross the Sahara in spring.

ADULT SEDGE WARBLER

Acrocephalus agricola

Paddyfield Warbler

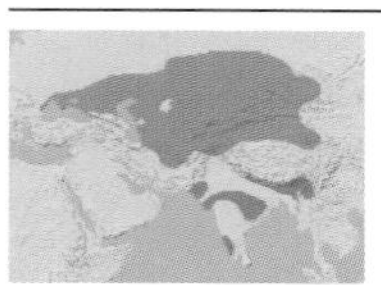

LENGTH 13cm (5in)
WEIGHT 10g (3/8oz)
MIGRATION Migrant

HABITAT Steppe grassland, shrubs near water, and damp agricultural land

A plain brown bird, the Paddyfield Warbler has a bold eyebrow stripe. Its bill is short with a dark tip. Its crest is raised and its tail is cocked almost always, which can be an aid to identification. It mainly feeds on insects. Although it sometimes feeds in the open, it tends to skulk in long grass and reeds, climbing stems of vegetation but often dropping back into cover. The Paddyfield Warbler lays 4 or 5 eggs in a nest in grass. Its song is smooth and soft and also includes mimicry, lacking the harsher rattling notes of many other similar species.

ADULT PADDYFIELD WARBLER

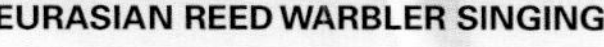

EURASIAN REED WARBLER SINGING

Acrocephalus scirpaceus

Eurasian Reed Warbler

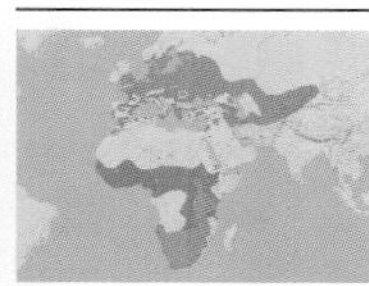

LENGTH 13cm (5in)
WEIGHT 10–15g (3/8–9/16oz)
MIGRATION Migrant

HABITAT Wetland areas, mainly reedbeds

The Eurasian Reed Warbler is a plain bird, with an unstreaked brown back and buff underparts. The male and female are identical, as with most warblers, but the juvenile has richer buff underparts. The dull colours of this warbler make it difficult to distinguish it visually from similar species. However, its loud song – a slow, chattering "jit-jit-jit" with whistles and a great deal of mimicry – is distinctive. The Eurasian Reed Warbler often delivers its call when moving through vegetation, rather than from a perch.

This bird is insectivorous, but will take other small food items, including seeds and berries. It lays 3–5 eggs and nests outside reedbeds tend to have a higher breeding success rate. It is a common host for cuckoos.

GRASS NEST

A deep cup woven from grasses and anchored around reed stems, the nest of the Eurasian Reed Warbler is constructed over shallow water to protect it from predators. However, this is not enough protection from cuckoos, who watch out for warblers carrying nest material to a site and often check the stage of construction. The depth of the cup is an adaptation to prevent eggs and the young from being accidentally dislodged.

Acrocephalus australis

Australian Reed Warbler

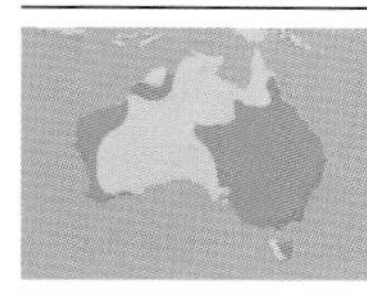

LENGTH 16cm (6 1/2in)
WEIGHT 18g (5/8oz)
MIGRATION Non-migrant

HABITAT Mainly wet grassland and often in reedbeds

The Australian Reed Warbler is similar to other species in the warbler family, although its white throat is distinctive. The species is confined to Australia and is particularly notable for having been studied extensively. The Australian Reed Warbler is a suitable parasitic host for several cuckoo species. Adult birds are able to detect alien eggs by their weight and appearance. This bird is also known to build two types of nest: one is used as a demonstration or courtship structure and the other is a significantly different breeding nest.

Hippolais pallida

Eastern Olivaceous Warbler

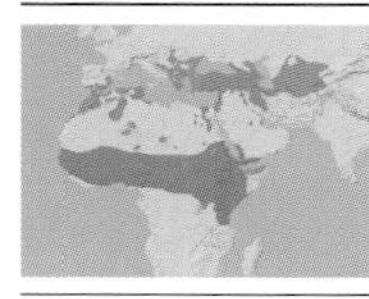

LENGTH 13cm (5in)
WEIGHT 8–13g (5/16–7/16oz)
MIGRATION Migrant

HABITAT Dry areas of scrub, but also in woodland and orchards close to water

Uniformly coloured apart from paler areas on the throat and rump, the Eastern Olivaceous Warbler has plain wings and white sides to its tail. It feeds in a purposeful manner, reaching and lunging towards food, such as insects and fruit. Its song, delivered from an exposed perch or in flight, is prolonged and includes repeated phrases and mimicry. The song flight also serves as a display, with the singing bird ascending vertically and changing direction to make a diagonal descent to a new perch.

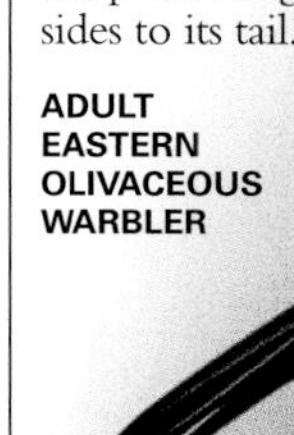

ADULT EASTERN OLIVACEOUS WARBLER

Hippollais icterina

Icterine Warbler

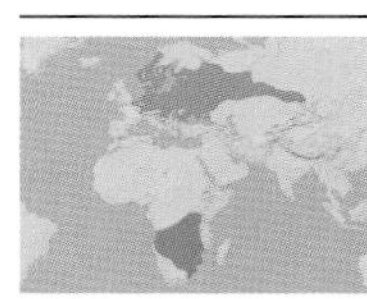

LENGTH 13cm (5in)
WEIGHT 13g (7/16oz)
MIGRATION Migrant

HABITAT Forest edges, orchards, and gardens

Broad-billed, slender, and square-tailed, the Icterine Warbler has plumage that varies between a colourful green to a more drab brown. The upperparts are darker and contrast with the pale underparts, which have yellow tones from the chin to the tail. Its song is melodious and prolonged, containing a great deal of repetition and mimicry and is usually delivered from a concealed place, rarely from an exposed perch. It feeds mainly on insects, catching them in flight in a similar way to flycatchers, or gleaning them from foliage. The species is found through much of continental Europe, including southern Scandinavia.

ICTERINE WARBLER SINGING

Phylloscopus collybita

Common Chiffchaff

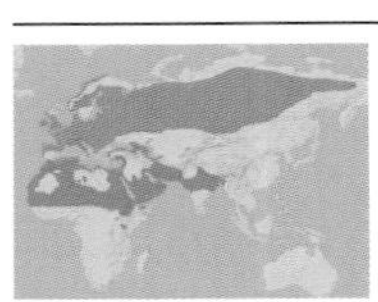

LENGTH 11cm ($4^1/_2$in)

WEIGHT 6–9g ($^7/_{32}$–$^{11}/_{32}$oz)

MIGRATION Partial migrant

HABITAT Wooded areas, but more open places outside the breeding season

One of the earliest migrants, the Common Chiffchaff is named after its loud, even-paced song, a repetitive "chip-chap-chip-chap-chap-chup", when it first appears from its wintering grounds. Its plumage is dull green or pale brown and varies between geographical subspecies. Several subspecies have been identified, although most are difficult to distinguish in the field other than by variations in calls. The species is insectivorous, taking insects and spiders from foliage. The male plays very little part in the breeding cycle, with nest-building, incubation, and care of the young undertaken by the female.

ADULT COMMON CHIFFCHAFF

Phylloscopus borealis

Arctic Warbler

LENGTH 12cm ($4^1/_2$in)

WEIGHT 11g ($^3/_8$oz)

MIGRATION Migrant

HABITAT Arctic and subarctic woodland and scrub

The Arctic Warbler is slightly duller coloured species than the similar Wood Warbler (above). It has pale yellow eyebrows extending beyond the eyes. Greyish green above and off-white below, it has a pale yellow bar across its wings.

ADULT ARCTIC WARBLER

The Arctic Warbler mainly feeds on insects collected in the tree canopy, although it also forages on the ground. The species is strongly territorial and small groups almost always consist of families. In the breeding season, a nest of dried grass is built by the female in dense cover, favouring mature birch forest, although some birds breed close to lakes. The female also incubates the eggs, usually up to seven in number, but both adults feed the brood. The young become independent at just two weeks as an adaptation to the short Arctic season. Arctic Warblers breed across northern Europe, northern Asia, and Alaska. The species has one of the longest migration routes of the warblers. The wintering grounds are in southeast Asia and the whole population winters in the same region.

Phylloscopus sibilatrix

Wood Warbler

LENGTH 13cm (5in)

WEIGHT 7–12g ($^1/_4$–$^7/_{16}$oz)

MIGRATION Migrant

HABITAT Deciduous woodland; broad-leaved woodland in the breeding season

One of the larger leaf warblers, the Wood Warbler is unusual in having two different songs: a low plaintive "sioo sioo sioo" and a vibrant trill "ti-ti-ti-ti-ti-ik-ik-irrrrrrr". It has a distinct wide, creamy white eye-stripe and its plumage is greyish green.

ADULT WOOD WARBLER

The species mainly breeds in European countries and migrates to central and eastern Africa. In the breeding season, lasting from May to June, it builds a simple domed grass nest, with no feather lining, on the ground. A single brood is produced with a clutch of up to seven eggs.

Phylloscopus ijimae

Ijima's Leaf Warbler

LENGTH 10cm (4in)

WEIGHT 9g ($^{11}/_{32}$oz)

MIGRATION Migrant

HABITAT Evergreen forest, but also breeds in broad-leaved woodland

RED LIST CATEGORY Vulnerable

ADULT IJIMA'S LEAF WARBLER

Entirely confined to certain areas in the Japanese islands, this warbler has a long orange bill, a greenish grey crown, green upperparts, green wings and tail, and white underparts. The greatest threat to the species has occurred on its breeding grounds, where it is vulnerable to habitat clearance, introduced predators, and pesticides.

Eremomela icteropygialis

Yellow-bellied Eremomela

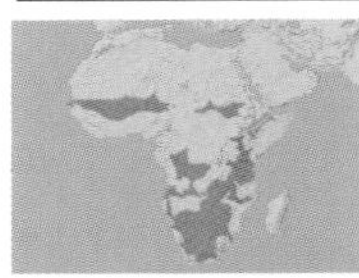

LENGTH 10cm (4in)

WEIGHT 7g ($^1/_4$oz)

MIGRATION Non-migrant

HABITAT Woodland, forest edges, scrub, and gardens

Mainly grey across the head, back, and wings, the Yellow-bellied Eremomela has a dark eye-line and yellow underparts. It is an insectivorous species, collecting food in the tree canopy. Its nest is a deep cup, shaped from plant down and spider silk and it times its nesting to coincide with the rainy season. Both adults feed the young.

ADULT YELLOW-BELLIED EREMOMELA

Sylvietta brachyura

Northern Crombec

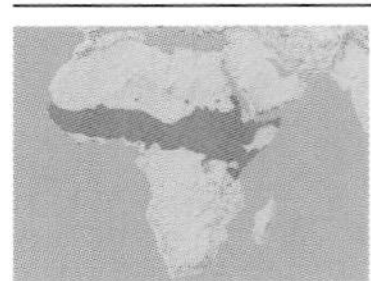

LENGTH 8cm ($3^1/_4$in)

WEIGHT 8g ($^5/_{16}$oz)

MIGRATION Non-migrant

HABITAT Wooded areas, but also in scrub and gardens

A grey bird with a bold white eyebrow stripe and pale rufous underparts, the Northern Crombec has a very short tail, which gives it a rather stubby appearance. Its main diet consists of insects, which it gleans from the foliage of thorn trees, moving from tree to tree. These birds are mostly solitary or move around in pairs, but mixed-species flocks are also recorded. They are fairly common over most of their range, but are not found above 2,000m (6,500ft).

ADULT NORTHERN CROMBEC

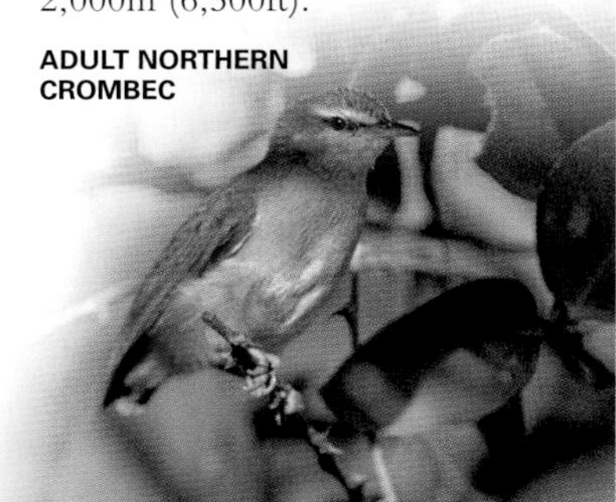

Sylvia atricapilla

Eurasian Blackcap

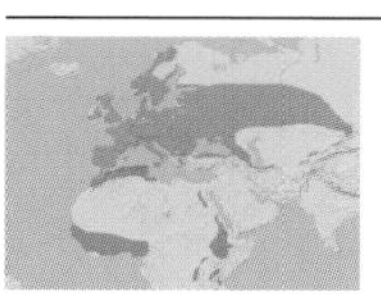

LENGTH 13–15cm (5–6in)

WEIGHT 17g (5/8oz)

MIGRATION Migrant

HABITAT Woodland, parks, and gardens.

"Blackcap", the common name of this species, refers to the characteristic black cap of the male, its black crown contrasting with its plain grey and brown plumage. Confusingly, the female has a brown cap and is sometimes mistaken for a separate species. The species mainly eats insects, but fruit and seeds are eaten during the winter. It is a short-distance migrant, breeding in much of Europe and wintering in southern Europe and North Africa.

MALE EURASIAN BLACKCAP

MALE COMMON WHITETHROAT

Sylvia communis

Common Whitethroat

LENGTH 13–15cm (5–6in)

WEIGHT 15g (9/16oz)

MIGRATION Migrant

HABITAT Low hedges, scrub, and woodland edges

The male Common Whitethroat has a distinctive combination of colours in its plumage. It has a slate-grey head in contrast to the white throat (and which gives the species its common name), dark brown back and wings, and a pink hue on its pale undersides. The female differs in that it has a dull brown head. The song of this species is scratchy and grating, but it also gives a monotonous call. It picks insects from foliage and also eats berries and some seeds. Its nest, a small cup made from grass and stems, is constructed in low-growing vegetation. The species breeds in much of Europe and western Asia, wintering in Africa, Arabia, and India.

Sylvia nisoria

Barred Warbler

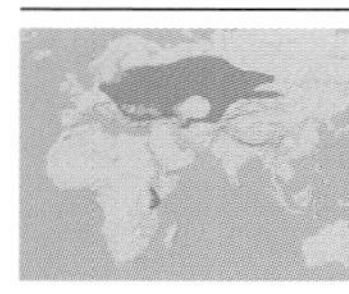

LENGTH 15cm (6in)

WEIGHT 25g (7/8oz)

MIGRATION Migrant

HABITAT Open areas containing scrub and bushes

A series of dark bars cross the pale grey chest of the Barred Warbler, which has a dark grey back and wings. Its yellow eye is accentuated by a darker area around the face. The female has less distinct bars, while the grey-brown juvenile does not have any.

The main food of this species consists of insects, with fruit and seeds being less important. The Barred Warbler tends to stay well concealed in thickets, where it collects much of its food. Its song, a long, bright, musical warble, is delivered from a prominent perch or in a display flight, offering the best chance to see the male. The species nests in dense cover, such as bramble bushes. Normally, 3–7 eggs are laid and just a single brood is produced, although a second brood is known to be produced when a clutch is lost in the early stages of nesting. The female incubates the eggs for up to 14 days, but after hatching, both parents feed the young for the remaining 10 or 11 days of their development.

MALE BARRED WARBLER FEEDING ON INSECT

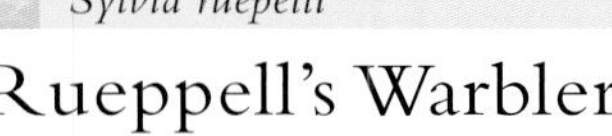

Sylvia ruepelli

Rueppell's Warbler

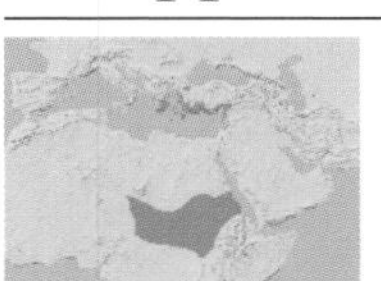

LENGTH 13cm (5in)

WEIGHT 11g (3/8oz)

MIGRATION Migrant

HABITAT Dry shrub and open areas

Rueppell's Warbler is one of a number of similar warbler species characterized by a black head and slate-grey body. However, Rueppell's Warbler is distinct in having a white stripe dividing its dark grey face from the black throat. The female is less striking but, like the male, has distinctly red eyes. The species breeds in Europe, where it is a summer visitor to Greece and Turkey from its wintering quarters in northeast Africa. Insects form the main diet. It is a bird of Mediterranean maquis, or dry scrub. The total population may be as high as half a million pairs; the species is not globally threatened despite hunting pressures on other species in the region.

ADULT RUEPPELL'S WARBLER

Sylvia undata

Dartford Warbler

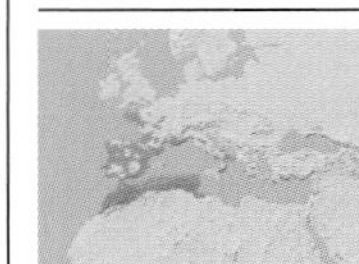

LENGTH 13cm (5in)

WEIGHT 11g (3/8oz)

MIGRATION Partial migrant

HABITAT Heathland and other areas of low-growing vegetation

Named after a part of the British Isles where the bird was first described, the Dartford Warbler, ironically, almost died out in that area in the 1960s. The male is dark grey on the upperparts and a deep chestnut to red colour from the throat to belly. The female and juvenile have less contrasting colours. Although it is difficult to see, the male appears briefly on top of vegetation when singing. It often builds a courtship nest, but the main structure is built by the female. The species is not globally threatened, but is vulnerable to habitat loss.

MALE DARTFORD WARBLER

BABBLERS AND RELATIVES

ORDER	Passeriformes
FAMILY	Timaliidae
SPECIES	273

THIS IS ONE OF THE largest and most varied passerine families. Its relationship to other families is still being debated: the family has in the past been grouped with chats and flycatchers (see p.440), and some species have been considered as Old World Warblers (see p.413) or thrushes (see p.436).

ANATOMY

Babblers are quite varied in size with species ranging from small wren-sized birds up to others as big as small crows. Nearly all have large, strong legs and many have stout bills. Their wings tend to be short, rounded, and held close to the body. The body plumage of most species is loose and fluffy. Most babblers are muted shades of brown and grey and there is usually little difference between the sexes in size or plumage. Unlike most passerines, juveniles do not have a markedly different plumage than adults.

LAUGHINGTHRUSH
The Streaked Laughingthrush uses a wide variety of calls to communicate with other individuals.

BEHAVIOUR

Among the most social and gregarious of birds, babblers usually occur in small groups of 3–30 individuals. The family's name comes from the many vocalizations birds use to maintain contact which each other. These groups tend to stay together for extended periods of time and defend their territory against other groups of babblers. Group members roost together at night in small trees and shrubs and they often preen each other. The individuals in roosting groups are so close that the birds are usually in physical contact with each other. Many babblers breed co-operatively, with the non-breeding birds assisting the parents in incubating the eggs and feeding the young.

WING SHAPE
The Jungle Babbler has the short, rounded wings typical of most babblers. A few migratory babblers have longer wings.

Illadopsis rufipennis

Pale-breasted Illadopsis

LENGTH 15cm (6in)
WEIGHT 18–30g (5/8–1 1/16oz)
MIGRATION Non-migrant

HABITAT Undergrowth in forest, coastal thickets, cocoa plantations at 500–2,500m (1,700–8,300ft)

The Pale-breasted Illadopsis belongs to a small genus of African babblers that inhabit low undergrowth. This species is often only detected by its call, a series of ascending whistled notes. There are few birds that conceal themselves more effectively or are more drab in plumage than this African babbler and its close relatives.

Mostly active at dawn and dusk, the Pale-breasted Illadopsis moves in pairs or small parties, foraging on or close to the ground, turning over dead leaves and debris in search of small insects, crickets, woodlice, spiders, and molluscs. It also joins flocks of other birds, following driver ant columns, which flush out potential prey. In the breeding season, it builds a compact, deep, cup-shaped nest on the ground, well hidden among leaves or in a small shrub or the crown of a tree-fern. The bird lays two eggs, and the female incubates the eggs for 14 days.

Pomatorhinus erythrogenys

Rusty-cheeked Scimitar-Babbler

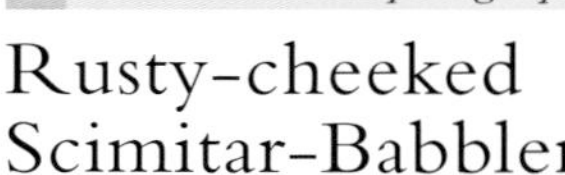

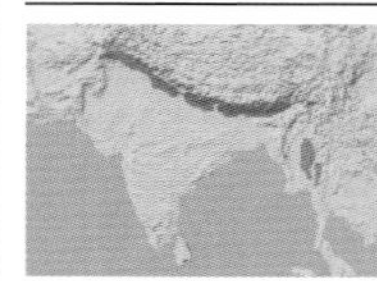

LENGTH 22–26cm (9–10in)
WEIGHT 60–70g (2 1/8–2 1/2oz)
MIGRATION Non-migrant

HABITAT Scrub in open forest, bush-clad hillsides, bushes bordering fields, and abandoned cultivation

Distinguished by its rufous-chestnut face, sides, and vent, the Rusty-cheeked Scimitar-Babbler has a pale bill and eyes, olive-brown upperparts, and an unspotted breast. The bird's curved bill helps it to probe into cracks and crevices in bamboo and tree branches.

It lives in pairs or small groups, and feeds on insects, larvae, and chrysalises, as well as seeds and berries. A pair sings a duet, with the male uttering a melodious "whi-u", followed by the female's "u", the combined "whi-u-u" sounding like only one bird is calling. The large, dome-shaped nest is placed on the ground or among low vegetation and 2–4 eggs are laid.

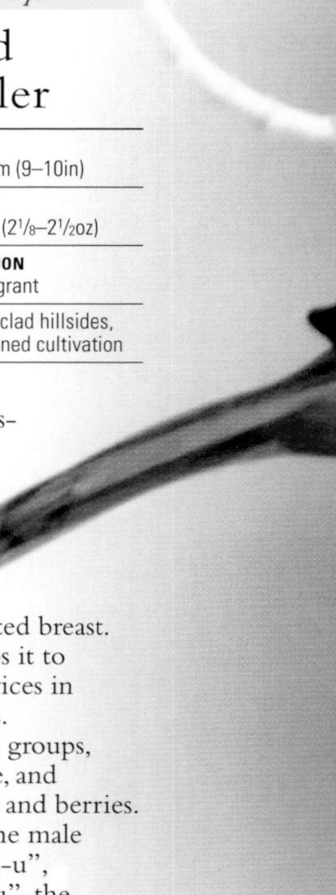

ADULT RUSTY-CHEEKED SCIMITAR-BABBLER

Stachyris ruficeps

Rufous-capped Babbler

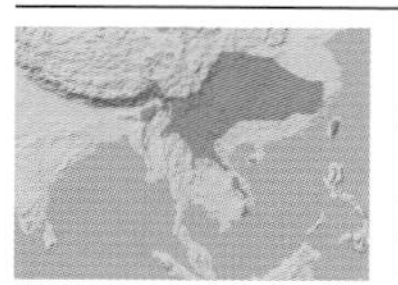

LENGTH 12cm (4¾in)

WEIGHT 7–12g (¼–7/16oz)

MIGRATION Non-migrant

HABITAT Understorey of broad-leaved forest and secondary growth at 460–2,900m (1,500–9,600ft)

This busy little babbler is identifiable by its bright rufous cap, the greenish yellow tones of its plumage, and pale legs. It has a pleasant hollow, piping song. The Rufous-capped Babbler is found in small flocks, and feeds on insects close to the ground. It also joins large flocks consisting of several species. This bird lays 3–5 eggs in a ball-shaped nest.

ADULT RUFOUS-CAPPED BABBLER

Leiothrix argentauris

Silver-eared Leiothrix

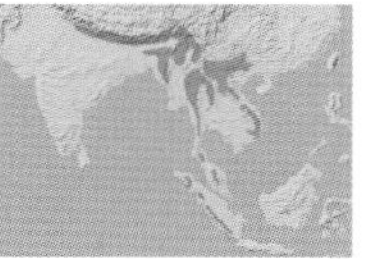

LENGTH 18cm (7in)

WEIGHT 20–30g (11/16–1 1/16oz)

MIGRATION Non-migrant

HABITAT Broad-leaved evergreen forest, pine forest, and tea plantations at 175–2,000m (600–6,600ft)

ADULT SILVER-EARED LEIOTHRIX

One of the most strikingly marked babblers, the Silver-eared Leiothrix has a yellow bill, a black head with contrasting silvery ear feathers, red and yellow wing patches, yellow legs, and a dark grey tail. Different subspecies show varying amounts of red on the neck and throat and yellow on the forehead. It has an extended, descending song and is arboreal, travelling through bushy and mid-storey vegetation in small flocks.

ADULT WRENTIT

Chamaea fasciata

Wrentit

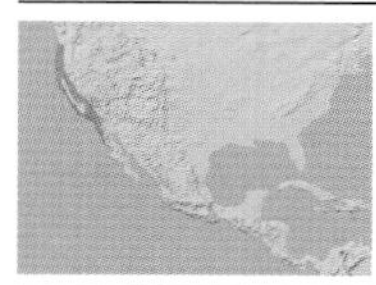

LENGTH 14–16cm (5½–6½in)

WEIGHT 14g (½oz)

MIGRATION Non-migrant

HABITAT Dense brushy areas, thickets along streams or on moist slopes, dense shrubs mixed with trees

A small, noisy songbird with a short, black bill, the Wrentit is the only North American babbler. It has small white spots above and below its pale eyes, dark grey upperparts, and lightly streaked, greyish brown underparts. Its tail is long and dark. The male sings a series of loud notes that speed into a trill, while the song of the female has no trill. The Wrentit feeds on insects, although berries form half its diet in autumn and winter. It mates for life and defends its territory throughout the year. Its nest is a deep cup among the twigs of a shrub and nesting activities are shared by the male and the female.

Turdoides caudata

Common Babbler

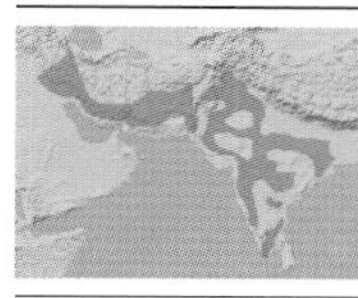

LENGTH 20–26cm (8–10in)

WEIGHT 30–40g (1 1/16–1 7/16oz)

MIGRATION Non-migrant

HABITAT Semi-desert, sandy floodplains with tamarisk clumps at 1,200m (4,000ft)

Slim, with a white throat, streaked brown upperparts and breast, and a dark graduated tail, the Common Babbler is a gregarious and noisy bird. It lives in flocks of 6–20 all year round and hops on the ground with a bouncing gait, scuttling about under vegetation. It flies low, gliding between rapid flaps of the wings. It feeds on insects, grain, berries, and also nectar. Its nest is a small, deep cup with thick walls, where it lays 3–5 eggs.

Garrulax pectoralis

Greater-necklaced Laughingthrush

LENGTH 27–35cm (10½–14in)

WEIGHT 100–175g (3⅝–6oz)

MIGRATION Non-migrant

HABITAT Mixed deciduous, broadleaved, and coniferous forest; bamboo; 75–1,850m (250–6,100ft)

A vocal bird, the Greater-necklaced Laughingthrush is medium-sized, with short, rounded wings and strong legs. It has brown upperparts, a broad black breast-band, deep orange underparts, and a floppy tail. It is usually found in flocks and forages through leaf-litter and low vegetation for insects. Its nest, placed on a bush or low tree, is cup-shaped and bulky.

ADULT GREATER-NECKLACED LAUGHINGTHRUSH

Minla cyanouroptera

Blue-winged Minla

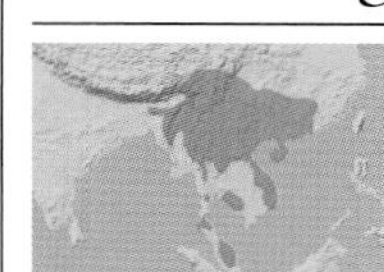

LENGTH 14–16cm (5½–6½in)

WEIGHT 14–30g (½–1 1/16oz)

MIGRATION Non-migrant

HABITAT Bushy growth and broad-leaved evergreen, pine, and mixed forest at 250–3,000m (800–10,000ft)

One of the widespread arboreal forest babblers, the Blue-winged Minla is also known as the Blue-winged Siva. It has prominent black eyes, a black-edged and streaked blue crown, pale brown upperparts, with striking blue wings, and a square-ended, blue tail. Small flocks of this babbler move through thick mid-storey foliage in search of insects, berries, and seeds. It builds a small cup-shaped nest between March and August, and lays 2–5 eggs, which it incubates for 14 days.

ADULT BLUE-WINGED MINLA

Minla strigula

Bar-throated Minla

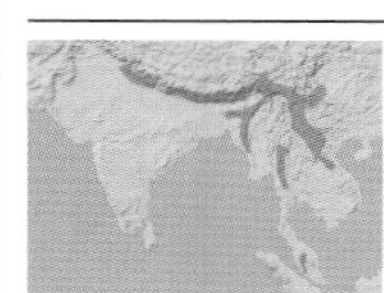

LENGTH 16–18.5cm (6½–7½in)

WEIGHT 14–24g (½–⅞oz)

MIGRATION Non-migrant

HABITAT Broad-leaved evergreen, coniferous, and open forest at 1,300–3,750m (4,300–12,400ft)

ADULT BAR-THROATED MINLA

The Bar-throated Minla has a high-domed chestnut crown, olive brown upperparts, black, white, and chestnut patterned wings, and a chestnut-centred black tail with yellow edgings. It is an arboreal species that travels in mixed-species feeding flocks, foraging on moss- and lichen-covered branches in search of beetles, caterpillars, and other insects, as well as berries, seeds, and nectar from rhododendron flowers.

Alcippe castaneceps

Rufous-winged Fulvetta

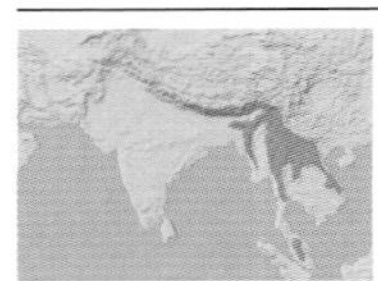

LENGTH 8–10cm (3¼–4in)

WEIGHT 13g (7/16oz)

MIGRATION Non-migrant

HABITAT Broad-leaved evergreen forest, secondary growth, and bamboo

A distinctive olive-coloured fulvetta, the Rufous-winged Fulvetta has a streaked chestnut crown, long white eyebrow, black eye-stripe, and largely rufous wings. Typically for a fulvetta, it is most often encountered in large active flocks of up to 30 birds, which forage in forests, often joining mixed-species feeding flocks. It feeds by clinging to moss- and lichen-covered trunks while searching for food items, cheeping repeatedly all the while. It also has a three-note song.

ADULT WHITE-EARED SIBIA

Heterophasia auricularis

White-eared Sibia

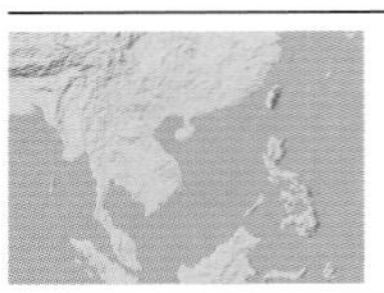

LENGTH 23cm (9in)

WEIGHT 35g (1¼oz)

MIGRATION Non-migrant

HABITAT Mid-elevation natural broad-leaved forest at 1,200–3,000m (4,000–10,000ft)

Found only on the island of Taiwan, the White-eared Sibia is distinguishable by the white blaze across its face that extends into long plumes projecting from the ear feathers. Its throat, breast, and upper back are grey. Its underparts are pinkish cinnamon, with an orange-rufous rump. It is largely arboreal and small flocks sometimes gather to feed in fruiting and flowering trees. The White-eared Sibia is common and easy to observe in the middle to upper levels of mid-elevation broad-leaved forests. During the winter, it may occur at lower altitudes.

ADULT STRIATED YUHINA

Yuhina castaniceps

Striated Yuhina

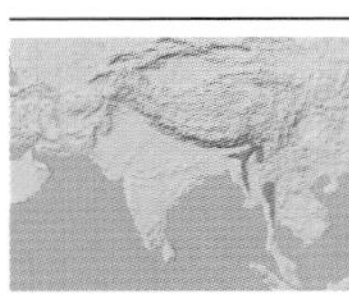

LENGTH 12cm (4½in)

WEIGHT 12g (7/16oz)

MIGRATION Non-migrant

HABITAT Broad-leaved evergreen forest, forest edges, secondary growth, and scrub

A small babbler, the Striated Yuhina has prominent chestnut cheeks and barely discernible narrow, white streaks on its brown upperparts. It has a short crested crown, which is either chestnut or grey, depending on the subspecies. The Striated Yuhina has a smaller crest than other yuhinas, and is the only one to show white on its tail. As indicated by its alternative name, White-browed Yuhina, it has a short white eyebrow. There is some geographical variation in the plumage of this species throughout its range, but this is largely restricted to the colour of the crown. This yuhina is found in hill and mountainous forests from India into southern China and southeast Asia.

Like many other yuhinas, the Striated Yuhina is often encountered in large, noisy, active groups within mixed-species flocks. It gleans insects from the middle storey of forests or feeds on fruit and nectar.

Panurus biarmicus

Bearded Reedling

LENGTH 13cm (5in)

WEIGHT 12–18g (7/16–5/8oz)

MIGRATION Partial migrant

HABITAT Wetlands, especially reedbeds and other emergent vegetation

A small, short-winged, long-tailed babbler, the Bearded Reedling has a stubby bill and orange-brown plumage, the spectacular black moustache of the adult male giving rise to the common name of the species. It inhabits dense reedbeds and often calls out in a metallic "ping" or in a loud, ringing chorus. During the autumn, the species gathers in small flocks, which depart from the breeding grounds noisily during the day.

MALE BEARDED REEDLING

Paradoxornis webbianus

Vinous-throated Parrotbill

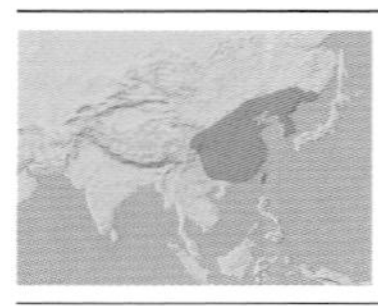

LENGTH 11–13cm (4½–5in)

WEIGHT 11g (3/8oz)

MIGRATION Non-migrant

HABITAT Scrub, grassland, and bamboo thickets

A typical small parrotbill, the Vinous-throated Parrotbill has a stubby bill and long tail. The plumage is muted, with brown tones predominating, but the bird has a striking pinkish brown face and a brilliant pale pink, faintly streaked throat and upper breast. Like other parrotbills, it is often found in very active, small flocks that feed low in undergrowth on insects, fruit, and seeds. It constructs a deep bowl-shaped nest and 3–5 eggs are laid. Its call is a very soft chirping. The Vinous-throated Parrotbill is found in East Asia, occurring in China, North and South Korea, eastern Russia, and northern Vietnam.

ADULT VINOUS-THROATED PARROTBILL

Chaetops frenatus

Cape Rockjumper

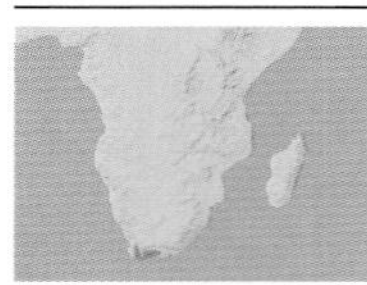

LENGTH 23–25cm (9–10in)

WEIGHT 50–60g (1¾–2⅛oz)

MIGRATION Non-migrant

HABITAT Rocky slopes and scree in upland areas

One of the most enigmatic of the African birds, the Cape Rockjumper's classification has been the cause of great debate. It is currently included within the babbler family, but was, until recently, considered to be a thrush. The male has a dark grey head and a broad white moustache. Its back and wings are dark grey and the underparts and rump are rufous red. It has a long, black tail. The female and juvenile have a duller head pattern, a paler grey head, upperparts, and wings, an orange rump, and buff underparts. The Cape Rockjumper is found only in South Africa, where it is restricted to rocky mountain slopes. It occurs in small family groups, in which the young are reared by a dominant pair.

MALE CAPE ROCKJUMPER

WHITE-EYES

ORDER	Passeriformes
FAMILY	Zosteropidae
SPECIES	95

WIDESPREAD IN THE OLD WORLD, white-eyes are found from sub-Saharan Africa and its offshore islands, across southern Asia, and to many islands in the Pacific. Most species are non-migratory, but the birds' tendency to congregate in groups and wander probably explains the family's occurrence on so many oceanic islands. In the Pacific, many islands have endemic species and subspecies of white-eyes. In the 1850s, the Silvereye made the jump from Tasmania to New Zealand, where it is now common.

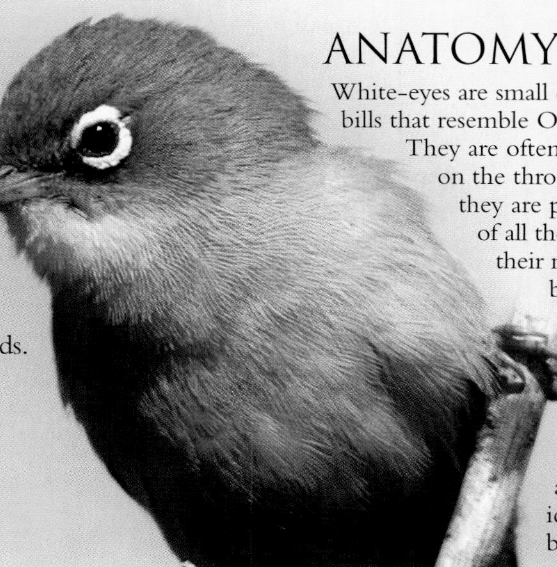

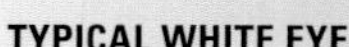

TYPICAL WHITE EYE
The distinctive white eye that gives this family of passerines its common name is actually formed by a ring of white feathers around the eye.

ANATOMY

White-eyes are small olive-green birds with pointed bills that resemble Old World warblers (see p. 413). They are often yellow underneath, particularly on the throat. In structure and appearance, they are probably the most homogeneous of all the passerine families. Contrary to their name, most species have dark eyes, but nearly all species have rings of white feathers around the eye. This white ring, usually broken at the lores, is very prominent in some species, and absent in a few island species. The similarity in appearance often makes identification difficult except by range and voice.

Zosterops pallidus

Cape White-eye

LENGTH 12cm ($4\frac{1}{2}$in)
WEIGHT 11g ($\frac{3}{8}$oz)
MIGRATION Non-migrant

HABITAT Woodland, forest, plantations, scrub, and gardens

In common with nearly all the members of the white-eye family, the most striking feature of the Cape White-eye is its very obvious white eye-ring. It is also similar to many of the world's white eyes in its plumage, with its yellow throat, the black patch around its eye, green upperparts, grey breast and belly, and yellow rump. Within its range in southern Africa it is, however, easily distinguished from its relatives. The male and the female are alike and the juvenile resembles the adults. The Cape White-eye is a common resident in well-wooded habitats throughout its range in Botswana, Lesotho, Mozambique, Namibia, South Africa, and Swaziland.

ADULT CAPE WHITE-EYE

Zosterops montanus

Mountain White-eye

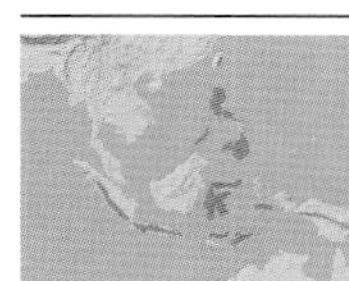

LENGTH 12cm ($4\frac{1}{2}$in)
WEIGHT 11g ($\frac{3}{8}$oz)
MIGRATION Non-migrant

HABITAT Montane forest, forest edges, secondary growth, and wooded cultivation

With a plumage similar to many of the white-eyes, the Mountain White-eye is best identified by its distribution and its call. This species has a curious distribution, being found in an arc from the Philippines through the islands of Indonesia to Sumatra, without occurring on the neighbouring island of Borneo. It is found in well-wooded mountainous habitats and tends to feed in the upper levels of trees. Like many white eyes, the Mountain White-eye is gregarious and travels in large, noisy flocks that often form the core of even larger mixed-species feeding flocks. These huge flocks, or "bird-waves", are occasionally encountered in forests throughout the tropics.

MOUNTAIN WHITE-EYE

Zosterops palpebrosus

Oriental White-eye

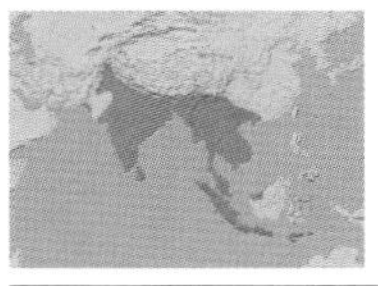

LENGTH 9cm ($3\frac{1}{2}$in)
WEIGHT 9g ($\frac{11}{32}$oz)
MIGRATION Non-migrant

HABITAT Well-wooded habitats, including gardens and mangroves

Notable among a homogenous family for its small size, the Oriental White-eye is a tiny golden-olive bird. It has a broad white eye-ring, bright yellow throat and vent, and silvery grey breast and belly. Plumage variations occur throughout its range. The Oriental White-eye has a huge range, occurring from Afghanistan, through India and China, Thailand, Malaysia, and into eastern Indonesia. This obvious geographical variation is likely to attract the attention of taxonomists and many of the subspecies may be elevated to full species status.

Zosterops japonicus

Japanese White-eye

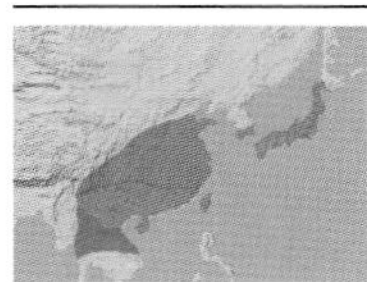

LENGTH 10–12cm (4–$4\frac{1}{2}$in)
WEIGHT 11g ($\frac{3}{8}$oz)
MIGRATION Partial migrant

HABITAT Well-wooded areas, including gardens, parks, and cultivated land

The Japanese White-eye has a yellow throat and chin, and its cap, back, and tail are olive-green. Like other members of the family, the Japanese White-eye is highly gregarious and in the non-breeding season flies in fast-moving, noisy flocks. Individuals forage acrobatically on a range of food items, including small invertebrates, fruit, and berries. It also feeds on seasonally blossoming trees, and many individuals have brush-tipped tongues to facilitate extraction of pollen and nectar. The Japanese White-eye has a large range that includes Japan, central, eastern, and southern China, South Korea, and the northern parts of southeast Asia. Many northern breeding birds migrate south in winter and occur outside the breeding range, mostly in southeast Asia.

PAIR OF JAPANESE WHITE-EYES

SEASONAL FEEDING

The diet of the Japanese White-eye changes during the year, according to seasonal abundance. In summer, it consists of insects gleaned from shrubs and low trees; in the autumn, berries and small fruit are favoured; and in winter and early spring, blossoms, particularly of camellia and cherry trees, are eaten.

FEEDING ON NECTAR
Shown above is a Japanese White-eye feeding on the nectar of a flower of an African Tulip tree.

ADULT SILVEREYE FEEDING

Zosterops lateralis

Silvereye

LENGTH 9.5–12cm (3¾–4½in)

WEIGHT 13g (7/16oz)

MIGRATION Non-migrant

HABITAT Wide variety of wooded habitats, including natural woodland, orchards, and parks

Named for the white ring surrounding its dark eye, the Silvereye has a dark green back and pale undersides. It mainly feeds on fruit, but insects and nectar also form part of its diet. The species is mostly solitary or forages in small flocks, but larger flocks have been known outside the breeding season, which stretches from August to February. It constructs a neat nest of grass and hair and lays 2 or 3 eggs. The Silvereye usually has a single brood every year, but it can make adjustments when conditions are favourable, producing up to three broods in some years. Although not migratory, there is some movement of the birds from the southern part of its range in autumn, with the birds returning in late winter.

Woodfordia superciliosa

Bare-eyed White-eye

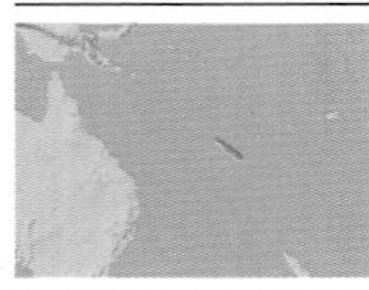

LENGTH 15cm (6in)

WEIGHT Not recorded

MIGRATION Non-migrant

HABITAT Primary forest, forest edges, and secondary growth

A colourful species, the Bare-eyed White-eye has olive-green upperparts and a paler breast and belly. The face is black, emphasized by a white border. The species is endemic to Rennell Island in the Solomon Isles, but is common and widespread within its limited range. It mainly feeds on insects, but also eats some small fruit in the tree canopy or in the open.

Lophozosterops dohertyi

Crested Ibon

LENGTH 12cm (4½in)

WEIGHT Not recorded

MIGRATION Non-migrant

HABITAT Primary forest up to 1,400m (4,500ft)

This species derives its name from its inconspicuous grey crest. The Crested Ibon has a white eye-stripe and the undersides to its face are bright yellow. The birds are mostly seen in pairs but occasionally form feeding flocks with other birds. It generally feeds in the understorey or in dense shrubs and is so quiet when feeding that it is often overlooked.

Chlorocharis emiliae

Mountain Blackeye

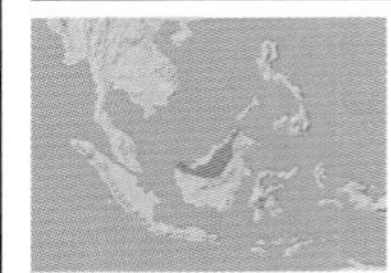

LENGTH 12cm (4½in)

WEIGHT Not recorded

MIGRATION Non-migrant

HABITAT Mountain scrub between 1,600–3,600m (5,200–12,000ft)

As the common name suggests, the Mountain Blackeye lacks a white eye-ring, even though it is part of the white-eye family. It has a pale yellow bill and its plumage is a uniform olive-green colour. It feeds on insects and small fruit collected from the forest understory or the ground and will also feed in the vicinity of humans.

GREAT SITES

MOUNT KINABALU NATIONAL PARK

Set up in 1964, this National Park on the island of Borneo is important as it preserves montane habitats. The Mountain Blackeye has been studied here and found to be an important pollinator of rhododendrons, although it sometimes raids nectar from the base of the flowers.

ADULT FEEDING ON NECTAR

FAIRY-BLUEBIRDS

ORDER	Passeriformes
FAMILY	Irenidae
SPECIES	2

FAIRY-BLUEBIRDS ARE stunningly beautiful forest birds from tropical Asia, but they can be surprisingly inconspicuous due to their treetop lifestyle and their habit of perching quietly. They eat mainly fruit, especially wild figs, and gather to feast in the crown of fruiting trees in parties of up to ten birds, often with other fruit-eating species. They also gather nectar from tree blossom, and eat a few insects. Fairy-bluebirds used to be grouped with another family unique to southern and southeast Asia – the leafbirds (see p.448).

BREEDING PAIR
Only the female fairy-bluebird (left in this picture) builds the nest, but both sexes feed the 2 or 3 young.

Irena puella

Asian Fairy-bluebird

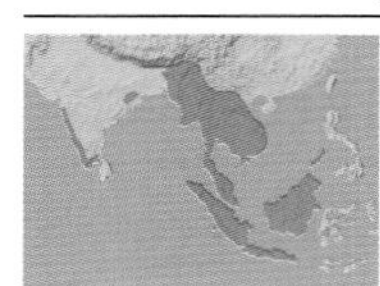

LENGTH 24–27cm (9½–10½in)

WEIGHT 65g (2⅜oz)

MIGRATION Non-migrant

HABITAT Broad-leaved evergreen forest

The male Asian Fairy-bluebird shows a combination of dark and bright blue plumage that has an iridescent quality. The eye is red against the dark face. The female is a dull blue-green or purple. The main diet is fruit and nectar, but a few insects are also taken. This species is particularly fond of figs, with large flocks gathering on fruiting fig trees. It feeds mainly in the canopy, with some foraging at lower levels. The birds split into pairs during the breeding season and a flimsy platform is built in a tree fork. Two or three eggs are laid, and the young are exclusively fed on insects. The species is not migratory, but there are movements to areas where fruit becomes available.

MALE ASIAN FAIRY-BLUEBIRD

GOLDCRESTS

ORDER	Passeriformes
FAMILY	Regulidae
SPECIES	6

THIS FAMILY contains two species of kinglet and four species of "crest" – including the Goldcrest itself. These tiny birds live in the forests of North America, Europe, and Asia, especially the coniferous forests of the taiga zone in the far north and in highland regions further south. They are olive-green above and greyish-buff below, often with prominent black or white stripes on the face. Males have a bright red or yellow blaze through their crown, which is not always visible but is flared like a crest during their courtship display. This feature gives the family its name, and a duller version is also present in the females of some species.

BEHAVIOUR

These active insect-eaters are always on the move – they flit energetically among the foliage, hover frequently, and often hang upside-down to inspect the underside of pine cones or leaves. In cold weather, they huddle together at night in a sheltered spot to conserve valuable body heat. Northern populations migrate south to avoid harsh winter conditions, and, despite being such small birds, they are capable of long flights across the sea. The female lays 7–12 eggs, and usually produces two clutches each breeding season.

GLEANING FOOD
Goldcrests use their miniature, needle-like bill to examine the surface of pine needles, pine cones, seed heads, and bark for small insects.

Regulus regulus

Goldcrest

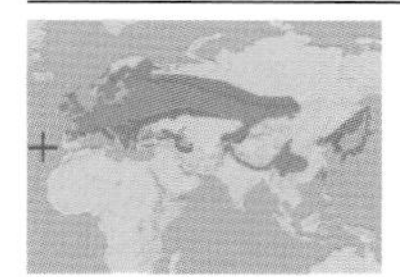

LENGTH 9cm (3½in)

WEIGHT 5–7g (3/16–1/4oz)

MIGRATION Partial migrant

HABITAT Coniferous woodland, parks, and gardens

One of the smallest birds in Europe and Asia, the Goldcrest is remarkable for its incredible migratory movements over part of its range. Scandinavian and Siberian birds head to central Europe and the British Isles, making huge crossings of 200km (125 miles) or more in autumn and return to the breeding grounds in spring. The Goldcrest has olive-green plumage, with a bright cap that can be raised into a crest. The crest of the female is yellow, flanked by black stripes, while the male has an orange crest that is apparent when the bird displays. It has a conspicuous black eye.

The wintering Goldcrest often joins mixed feeding flocks, although it tends to stay on the edge of the flock. The main diet is small arthropods and slow moving invertebrates picked up from the bark of trees. The Goldcrest is constantly in motion when foraging and gives out a high-pitched call to stay in contact with other birds in the flock. Seven or eight eggs are laid in a delicate nest woven from spider webs, moss, and other soft material. As the nest is extremely fragile, it is often built in heavily armoured plants such as brambles and also dense conifers.

The Goldcrest suffers tremendous losses in cold winters, but the ability to exploit artificial conifer plantations has led to a large expansion of range. In addition to the birds ranging across Europe and Asia, there are three subspecies on five islands in the Azores.

MALE GOLDCREST

FEMALE GOLDEN-CROWNED KINGLET

Regulus satrapa

Golden-crowned Kinglet

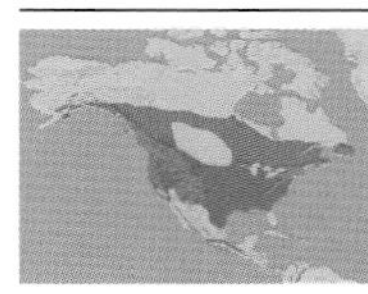

LENGTH 8–11cm (3¼–4½in)

WEIGHT 4–8g (5/32–5/16oz)

MIGRATION Partial migrant

HABITAT Coniferous woodland; less commonly, parks and gardens

An active bird, the Golden-crowned Kinglet forages continuously and intensively throughout the day, searching for spiders and insects and their eggs and larvae. The male has a large orange patch in the centre of the crown, its upperparts are grey, and the underparts a mix of olive-green and white. The female is somewhat smaller than the male and similar in colour, except that its crown patch is canary yellow.

The Golden-crowned Kinglet actively defends its feeding and breeding places, driving away other kinglets and much larger warblers and sparrows. It makes full use of the short breeding season – immediately after the first brood of typically 8 or 9 young birds leave the nest, the female begins to lay a second clutch, leaving the care of the still-dependent fledglings to the male.

WRENS

ORDER	Passeriformes
FAMILY	Troglodytidae
SPECIES	76

A FAMILY OF SMALL insect-eating birds, wrens are generally brown and streaked in appearance, often with areas of black and white plumage. They have loud rattling songs, often consisting of extensive repertoires of sounds, which are surprisingly loud for such a small bird. Wrens are found almost exclusively in the Americas, with the exception of one species, the Winter Wren, which is widespread in Europe and Asia. Wrens inhabit a wide variety of habitats from deserts to thick woodland.

CACTUS WREN
The Cactus Wren makes its nest in a hole in a cactus, where it builds a large pouch-shaped structure protected by the spikes of the plant.

ANATOMY

Usually the tail is quite short and stout, making up around a quarter of overall body length. It is often held cocked and aloft. However, in some species such as the Cactus Wren the tail can make up half its length, whereas other species, such as the ground-dwelling Nightingale Wren, appear almost entirely tailless. Another noticeable feature of wrens is the long, thin bill. This is usually fine and slightly decurved, although this can vary depending on the preferred food and lifestyle of the different species.

CLASSIC POSE
This Winter Wren has adopted the classic wren singing pose: tail cocked upwards, wings held down, and head thrown back to produce its extraordinarily loud song.

BEHAVIOUR

Despite their small size, wrens are masterful and noisy songsters. Some calls consist of short, jarring "chucks", which contrast with their longer rich, fluid songs. Most species of wren learn these remarkable songs by imitating adult birds around them. A single male can have a repertoire of more than 100 different songs. Many wren species spend much of their time close to the ground, where they forage among leaves for invertebrates. Some tropical members of the family follow swarms of army ants, feasting on any insects that are flushed out. A few wren species can also be found searching for insects high in the trees. The majority of wrens build oval-shaped nests with an entrance hole at the side, although a number of species make their nests in a cavity.

Campylorhynchus brunneicapillus

Cactus Wren

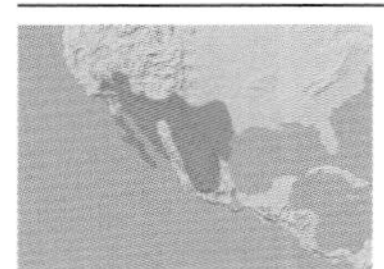

LENGTH 18cm (7in)
WEIGHT 35–45g (1¼–1⅝oz)
MIGRATION Non-migrant
HABITAT Semi-desert with cacti

A large member of the wren family, the Cactus Wren has a long, pointed bill and a prominent white stripe above the eye. It has streaked upperparts and a well-spotted dull white breast. The male and female look alike. The Cactus Wren does not raise its tail vertically in the typical wren fashion, but holds it horizontally. As its name suggests, the species is usually found around cacti. It prefers to remain near the ground, flying low and hunting for invertebrates. Although most of its diet consists of small insects, it also plays a significant part in dispersing the seeds of these desert-dwelling plants.

Unlike many other wrens, the Cactus Wren is monogamous. It usually nests in cavities in cacti, building a large pouch-shaped structure that is lined with fur or feathers and has an entrance on one side. Even though the nest is conspicuous, the sharp spikes of the plant are a deterrent to predators such as raccoons. The call of this wren is a monotonous, repetitive "chut".

ADULT CACTUS WREN

Salpinctes obsoletus

Rock Wren

LENGTH 14–16cm (5½–6½in)
WEIGHT 15–18g (9/16–5/8oz)
MIGRATION Partial migrant
HABITAT Rocky terrain, including boulder-strewn slopes or manmade areas such as quarries

A number of subspecies occur in the Rock Wren species, which show a variable amount of streaking. Generally, however, it is a plain, predominantly brown bird. It can be distinguished from other wrens by its cinnamon rump and buff tips on the outer tail feathers. The Rock Wren, like many other members of its family, has a melodious voice – the song of the male is a fluid combination of a hundred different sounds, usually attracting a potential mate. One note is repeated three or four times, followed by a short pause before the song begins again with a new note. It should not be confused with the similarly named species from New Zealand, which actually belongs to a different family.

MALE ROCK WREN

Cistothorus platensis

Sedge Wren

LENGTH 9–12cm (3 1/2–4 1/2in)
WEIGHT 8–10g (5/16–3/8oz)
MIGRATION Partial migrant

HABITAT Damp sedge meadows in North America; wider variety of habitats in South America

The tiny Sedge Wren is a buff-tinged bird that is plain below, with streaked upperparts. It has an "open-faced" appearance and a short spiky tail that is often held cocked. The most interesting aspect of the Sedge Wren's behaviour is found in birds of the North American subspecies: the most northerly populations breed before migrating farther south to nest again.

ADULT SEDGE WREN

MALE BEWICK'S WREN

Thryomanes bewickii

Bewick's Wren

LENGTH 12–14cm (4 1/2–5 1/2in)
WEIGHT 8–12g (5/16–7/16oz)
MIGRATION Non-migrant

HABITAT Variety of habitats from suburban areas to woods

A small species, Bewick's Wren has a prominent white stripe above the eye and is greyish brown above, with a more rufous rump. It is off-white below, with a barred tail, which it wags from side to side. This bird feeds largely on insects, but also eats a small amount of vegetable matter, particularly in winter. It makes a stick nest in a cavity and lays 5–7 eggs. The male Bewick's Wren has a repertoire of between 10 to 20 loud, melodious songs that consist of a mixture of buzzes and repeated notes. The species is common in many parts of North and Central America.

Thryothorus ludovicianus

Carolina Wren

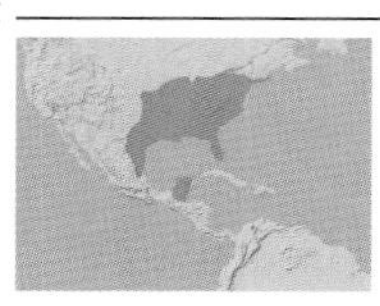

LENGTH 12–14cm (4 1/2–5 1/2in)
WEIGHT 15–20g (9/16–11/16oz)
MIGRATION Non-migrant

HABITAT Damp woodland; also found in a variety of other scrubby areas

Superficially similar to Bewick's Wren (left), the Carolina Wren is larger, with warmer-toned plumage, including buff underparts. It has a conspicuous white stripe above the eyes. The species is not confined to the Carolinas, but is found from southeast Canada, down the east coast of the USA to northeast Mexico. It is largely sedentary, with pairs occupying the same territory throughout the year.

ADULT CAROLINA WREN

Troglodytes aedon

House Wren

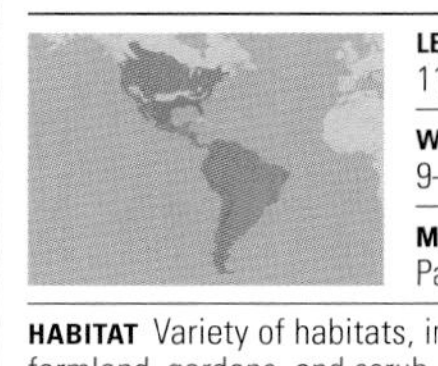

LENGTH 11–13cm (4 1/2–5in)
WEIGHT 9–14g (11/32–1/2oz)
MIGRATION Partial migrant

HABITAT Variety of habitats, including forest, farmland, gardens, and scrub

The different populations of the House Wren are sometimes treated as separate species - the Northern and Southern House Wrens. Both are, however, very similar: rufous-brown above with a grey face and pale black barring on the wings and tail. The House Wren can be distinguished from Bewick's Wren (left) by the absence of a white stripe above the eye.

ADULT HOUSE WREN

Troglodytes troglodytes

Winter Wren

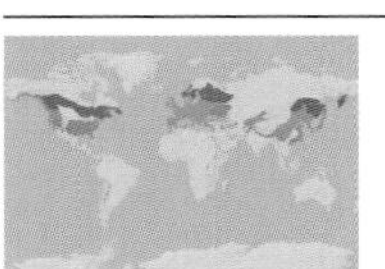

LENGTH 10cm (4in)
WEIGHT 6–12g (7/32–7/16oz)
MIGRATION Partial migrant

HABITAT Variety of habitats from woodland to gardens

Also known as the Northern Wren, reflecting its distribution across the northern hemisphere, the Winter Wren is a common garden bird in some areas. Its plumage is rufous brown above, grey below, and barred with dark brown and grey. The legs are pale brown. Despite its small size, it is often seen due to its aggressive posturing – bobbing its head with its tail cocked, delivering its loud, staccato song or churring alarm call. In winter, the species roosts communally to preserve body heat.

ADULT WINTER WREN

SOAKING UP THE SUN

Although the Winter Wren is usually seen feeding low down in the undergrowth, it sunbathes whenever it can find a sunlit spot to bask in. The Winter Wren shown here has found a suitably warm place on a tree trunk. It spreads its wings and raises the feathers on its head to ensure that most of its plumage is directly exposed to sunlight.

Catherpes mexicanus

Canyon Wren

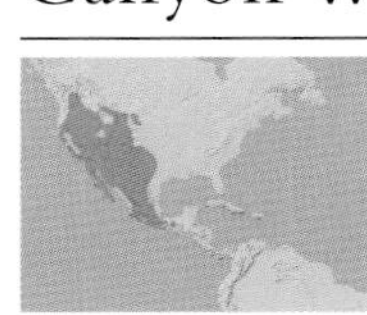

LENGTH 13–15cm (5–6in)
WEIGHT 9–18g (11/32–5/8oz)
MIGRATION Non-migrant

HABITAT Rocky areas such as canyons; occasionally sea cliffs

The medium-sized Canyon Wren feeds exclusively on insects and this is reflected in its specially adapted bill: long, fine, and slightly decurved, to allow it to probe into the crevices of its rock-strewn habitat. The species is one of the more attractive members of its family, with its bright white throat and upper breast, barred orange plumage, and broad tail.

ADULT CANYON WREN

ADULT BLACK-CAPPED DONACOBIUS

Donacobius atricapilla

Black-capped Donacobius

LENGTH 22cm (8 1/2in)
WEIGHT 30–40g (1 1/16–1 7/16oz)
MIGRATION Non-migrant

HABITAT Brushy areas along rivers

This large songbird is unlikely to be confused with any other wrens, with its bright yellow eyes, dark upperparts, pale buff-yellow underparts, chestnut rump, and white outer-tail feathers. The Black-capped Donacobius is a noisy bird, with pairs often singing duets in a series of whistles or performing loud, ritualized courtship displays, fanning their tails. They forage in pairs, often near water.

GNATCATCHERS

ORDER	Passeriformes
FAMILY	Polioptilidae
SPECIES	14

GNATCATCHERS ARE FOUND only in the Americas. They are small, predominantly grey plumaged birds with slender pointed bills and long tails. Most species tend to have some areas of black plumage on their otherwise grey heads. Three species (the gnatwrens from South America) are browner in appearance with very long bills and short, cocked tails.

BEHAVIOUR

Despite their name, gnatcatchers rarely catch gnats or other flying insects. They are insectivorous, however, usually foraging for small arthropods among the foliage. All gnatcatchers tend to hold their tail in a cocked position, frequently fanning and flicking it from side to side, exposing the white outer tail feathers. This behaviour is thought to startle hidden prey, allowing it to be more easily caught.

INSECT PREY
This male Blue-grey Gnatcatcher, the commonest member of its family in North America, has found a tasty insect snack.

Polioptila caerulea

Blue-grey Gnatcatcher

LENGTH 10cm (4in)
WEIGHT 6g ($^{7}/_{32}$oz)
MIGRATION Partial migrant

HABITAT Deciduous and pine forest, orchards, swamps, and mesquite scrub

A tiny bird with a hooked bill, the Blue-grey Gnatcatcher has bluish grey plumage, with a black and white tail. It forages restlessly through leaves, feeding on small insects, caterpillars, and spiders, sometimes hovering to catch its prey. Its nest, built by both the male and female, is held together with spiders' webs and caterpillar silk, and is camouflaged with lichen. It is the most northerly species of gnatcatcher in its range.

ADULT BLUE-GREY GNATCATCHER

NUTHATCHES

ORDER	Passeriformes
FAMILY	Sittidae
SPECIES	25

NUTHATCHES HAVE THE UNIQUE ability to climb down trees and rocks head first, which distinguishes them from woodpeckers and treecreepers. They have big heads, short tails, and large powerful bills and feet. Many species have a similar coloration of blue-grey backs, buff undersides with rufous flanks, and dark eye-stripes. Most are woodland birds, though some, like the rock nuthatches, are adapted to open rocky places. The Wallcreeper is entirely adapted to rocks, cliffs, and buildings.

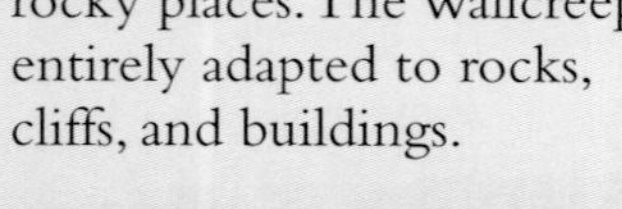

EURASIAN NUTHATCH AT NEST
Nuthatches nest in holes in trees, often abandoned woodpecker holes, lined with leaves and loose bark.

Sitta europaea

Eurasian Nuthatch

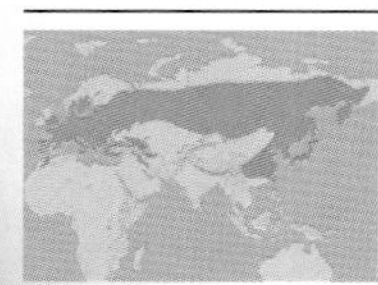

LENGTH 14cm ($5^{1}/_{2}$in)
WEIGHT 25g ($^{7}/_{8}$oz)
MIGRATION Non-migrant

HABITAT Mature deciduous and mixed forest, parks, and large gardens; conifers in north of range

There are many subspecies of nuthatch across the species' vast range – some have white underparts, while others are orange-buff underneath – with many intermediate forms. The Eurasian Nuthatch has a distinctive black stripe running from the base of the bill to the sides of the head.

An excitable bird, it gives itself away with its loud, fluting calls and conspicuous jerky movements. It walks head first down tree trunks as it probes crevices and lifts bark in search of invertebrates. Its strong bill enables it to feed easily on nuts. It stores food by hoarding seeds and other food in holes and cracks in walls and trees.

The Eurasian Nuthatch nests in holes, often taking over old woodpecker nests. The female may reduce the size of the entrance to the hole with mud. The species is often seen in pairs, which remain together in vigorously defended territories throughout the year.

EURASIAN NUTHATCH AT NEST-HOLE

Sitta canadensis

Red-breasted Nuthatch

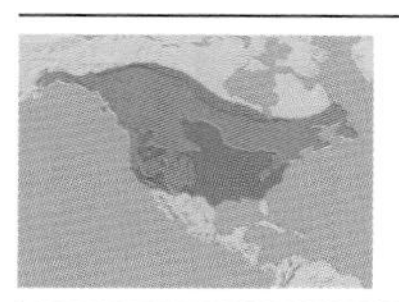

LENGTH 12cm (4½in)

WEIGHT 10g (⅜oz)

MIGRATION Migrant

HABITAT Breeds in coniferous forest; in winter, also in deciduous and mixed woods, parks, and gardens

The Red-breasted Nuthatch is the most migratory nuthatch and in isolated cases, has even been known to cross the Atlantic. It has a black cap and the back, wings, and short tail are blue-grey. The underparts are rust-coloured. In summer, it forages mostly in the tree canopy in search of insects, and sometimes catches flies in flight. It is an important predator of caterpillars of the spruce budworm, a pest which can defoliate huge tracts of forest. In winter, the Red-breasted Nuthatch moves further down the trees, and to the ground in search of pine-seeds and beech nuts. It hoards food in cracks in trees, and it excavates its own nest-holes in decaying wood.

ADULT RED-BREASTED NUTHATCH

Tichodroma muraria

Wallcreeper

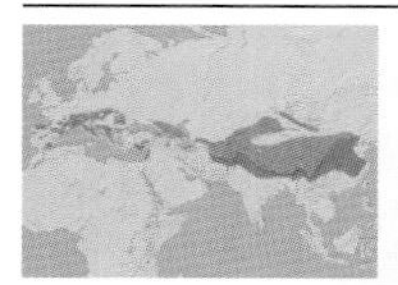

LENGTH 16cm (6½in)

WEIGHT 18g (⅝oz)

MIGRATION Migrant

HABITAT Cliffs and rocky slopes in mountainous regions; quarries, river beds, and towns in winter

Constantly flicking its wings to show red patches on an otherwise grey plumage, the Wallcreeper forages over rocks in a series of short, jerky rushes, disappearing into holes and clefts. In the air, while fluttering its long rounded wings, it can seem erratic, but it is able to manoeuvre precisely around rocky outcrops and cliff faces.

The Wallcreeper has been described as combining the characteristics of treecreepers and nuthatches. The long, slightly decurved bill resembles that of a treecreeper, but the jerky movements recall a nuthatch. Some authorities place the Wallcreeper in its own single-species family. It nests in clefts in rocks and on cliff faces, out of the reach of predators, such as stoats and martins. For the rest of the year, it is solitary, but is sometimes seen in family groups; flocks of up to 50 birds have been seen in late autumn.

ADULT WALLCREEPER

TREECREEPERS

ORDER	Passeriformes
FAMILY	Certhiidae
SPECIES	8

THE TREECREEPERS ARE small woodland birds with long, thin bills, and streaked brown plumage. Adapted for foraging over rough tree bark, they have long toes and short legs, and stiff tail feathers, which they use for support. The family includes the true treecreepers and the Spotted Creeper. The Brown Creeper is the only American species.

BEHAVIOUR

Foraging treecreepers make their way up tree trunks and large branches in a spiral. They probe crevices and flakes of bark in search of invertebrates. After finishing with one tree, they fly to the base of another and begin again. They often build nests behind loose bark. In spring and summer, they are usually found in pairs and family groups.

FAMILY GROUP
A Eurasian Treecreeper family huddles together on a tree trunk. Families may stay together for several weeks after the young have fledged.

Certhia familiaris

Eurasian Treecreeper

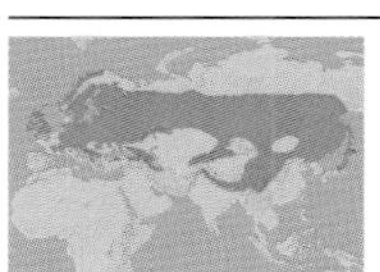

LENGTH 13cm (5in)

WEIGHT 9g ($^{11}/_{32}$oz)

MIGRATION Partial migrant

HABITAT Deciduous, coniferous, and mixed woodland that contains trees with loose, rough bark

The Eurasian Treecreeper has a narrow, slightly decurved bill, mottled brown upperparts, and white underparts. It works its way up and around the trunks and large branches of trees in a spiral. Well before reaching the top, it flies to another tree, and begins again. It searches loose and fissured bark for insects and spiders; in winter, it looks for seeds. It nests behind flaps of bark.

ADULT EURASIAN TREECREEPER

Certhia americana

Brown Creeper

LENGTH 13cm (5in)

WEIGHT 8g ($^{5}/_{16}$oz)

MIGRATION Partial migrant

HABITAT Coniferous, deciduous, and mixed old-growth forest; parks and gardens with mature trees

BROWN CREEPER AGAINST BARK

Also known as the American Treecreeper, the Brown Creeper is the only treecreeper found in the USA. Like other treecreepers, the Brown Creeper is perfectly camouflaged as it moves spirally up the trunks of trees, searching the bark for small insects and spiders with its tweezer-like bill. It will also come to feeding stations, where it feeds on fat and sometimes on seeds. It nests and roosts behind loose bark, particularly in the scales of bark on mature pines and other conifers.

MOCKINGBIRDS AND THRASHERS

ORDER	Passeriformes
FAMILY	Mimidae
SPECIES	34

THIS IS A FAMILY OF medium-sized, rather thin-looking birds with long, powerful bills. Their plumage tends to be streaky, particularly on the underparts, though they vary quite considerably in their coloration from the bright blue of the Blue Mockingbird to the rich chestnut of the Brown Thrasher. Mockingbirds and thrashers are found only in the Americas and Caribbean (as well as the Galapagos Islands). Many species are urban birds, finding homes in parks and gardens. They are famous for their exceptional songs that are constantly varied over time and often mimic other birds in the area.

BEHAVIOUR

Most mockingbirds and thrashers are well adapted for life on the ground, with their long tails providing excellent balance as they run along the floor foraging for insects, seeds, and fruit. In fact, most things will be consumed, even small vertebrates such as lizards or frogs, or the eggs of other birds. The least terrestrial members of the family are the two species of catbird, which are dark in plumage and have relatively short tails.

A MEAL OF EGGS
Espanola Mockingbirds on the Galapagos Islands break open the eggs of seabirds with their sharp bills.

ADULT GREY CATBIRD

Dumetella carolinensis

Grey Catbird

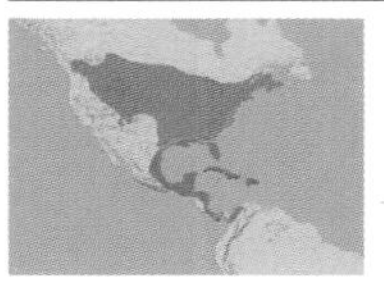

LENGTH	23cm (9in)
WEIGHT	35g (1¼oz)
MIGRATION	Migrant

HABITAT Dense shrub, woodland edges, secondary growth, and well-vegetated urban areas

One of the smallest members of the mimidae family, the Grey Catbird is predominantly dark grey in colour. It has a black crown, short wings, chestnut undertail feathers, and a long, black tail. Both the sexes look alike, but the juvenile's plumage is a mottled brown-grey. Best known for its hoarse, cat-like mewing call, its song is a long series of rambling, stuttering warbles that are sometimes harsh and squeaky, but also musical and mellow. It can mimic birds, frogs, and mechanical sounds.

The Grey Catbird is an omnivore, feeding mainly on fruit and berries in late summer, when migrating, and on tropical wintering grounds. It feeds on insects at other times. Although the Grey Catbird is less terrestrial than other species of its family, it forages for insects on the ground, using its short bill to toss aside leaf litter. It constructs a bulky cup-shaped nest and usually lays 2 or 3 eggs.

This species undertakes the longest migration of the mimidae, making a "leapfrog" journey, with birds breeding in the extreme northeast of its range flying the farthest south to winter in the extreme southwest. The bird usually returns to the same wintering and breeding sites in successive years.

Mimus polyglottos

Northern Mockingbird

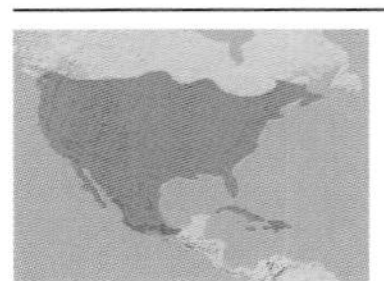

LENGTH	26cm (10in)
WEIGHT	50g (1¾oz)
MIGRATION	Partial migrant

HABITAT Low, scrubby, and open vegetation, including suburban gardens, and thorn scrub

As its scientific name suggests, the Northern Mockingbird is one of the nature's true polyglots (*polyglottos* means "many-tongued"), with enormously varied songs and is an adept mimic of other birds' songs and calls (see panel, right). It is known for singing on moonlit nights.

The Northern Mockingbird has pale grey upperparts, dull white underparts, and a long tail. Its dark wings have two white wingbars and large white patches which, together with the white tail sides, are clearly visible when it is in flight. It feeds on insects and fruit, often jerking its wings over its back as it forages, to flush out insects. The male performs a courtship display in which it flashes its wings by repeatedly extending them.

EXPERT MIMIC

Renowned as a mimic, the Northern Mockingbird can imitate dog barks, frog calls, bird calls, sounds of machinery, bells, and whistles. It learns sounds quickly, integrating them into its own song. So varied is its repertoire, that no two songs are the same. Mimicry is crucial for sexual selection – the larger the male's repertoire, the greater is its attractiveness to females.

ADULT NORTHERN MOCKINGBIRD

Oreoscoptes montanus

Sage Thrasher

LENGTH 22cm (8½in)
WEIGHT 45g (1⅝oz)
MIGRATION Migrant

HABITAT Dry brushland and deserts; breeds in plains with sagebrush or saltbush

The smallest bird in its family, the Sage Thrasher has a short bill, a faintly streaked nape, grey-brown upperparts, and dull white underparts with bold brownish grey streaks. The tail is dark with white tips. It forages for insects on the ground, often digging for food under bushes and in leaf litter. Its song is a series of warbled phrases, including mimicry of various sounds, lasting up to 20 minutes. It usually sings from a perch and sometimes in flight.

ADULT SAGE THRASHER

Mimodes graysoni

Socorro Mockingbird

LENGTH 25cm (10in)
WEIGHT 65g (2⅜oz)
MIGRATION Non-migrant

HABITAT Moist dwarf forest and ravines with shrubs and trees above 600m (2,000ft)

RED LIST CATEGORY Critically endangered

The Socorro Mockingbird has grey-brown upperparts, slightly darker wings with two wing-bars, white underparts, and a dark brown tail. Endemic to Socorro in the Revillagigedo Islands near Mexico, this bird is the rarest member of its family. Surveys held as recently as 1994 found just 350 Socorro Mockingbirds in the area – a catastrophic decline given that it was once the most abundant landbird on the island. This decline is thought to be primarily due to sheep-grazing.

ADULT BROWN THRASHER

Toxostoma rufum

Brown Thrasher

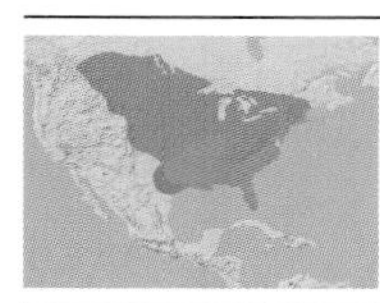

LENGTH 24–31cm (9½–12in)
WEIGHT 70g (2½oz)
MIGRATION Partial migrant

HABITAT Woodland edges, well-vegetated urban areas, dense shrubbery, and riparian woodland

This common yet inconspicuous bird, the official bird of the American state of Georgia often remains hidden inside dense vegetation. A large member of its family, it has a long, slightly decurved bill, long legs, and a long tail. Its face is grey, its upperparts are bright rufous brown, and its underparts are pale white, with bold black and rufous stripes. It wings are marked by two black and white wingbars. The yellow iris lends the Brown Thrasher a penetrating gaze.

The Brown Thrasher forages on the ground, feeding on insects, fruit, and seeds. Its song is a series of loud, musical phrases, and a rather inaccurate mimicry of the calls of other birds.

Melanotis caerulescens

Blue Mockingbird

LENGTH 25cm (10in)
WEIGHT 65g (2⅜oz)
MIGRATION Non-migrant

HABITAT Lowland riverine brushland, tall thorn scrub, low tropical deciduous woodland, and forest edges

Aptly named for its deep blue plumage, the Blue Mockingbird has a black eye mask that contrasts with its vivid red eyes. Its crown, throat, and breast are streaked with pale blue.

ADULT BLUE MOCKINGBIRD

Both the sexes look similar, but the juvenile is dull grey in colour.

This bird usually sings from deep cover, uttering a series of phrases in varied notes that are slowly and deliberately repeated. It forages low down in undergrowth or on the ground, and is mainly insectivorous during the breeding season. Although a resident of Mexico, occurring north of the isthmus of Tehuantepec, vagrants have been found several hundred kilometres outside its normal range.

Toxostoma curvirostre

Curve-billed Thrasher

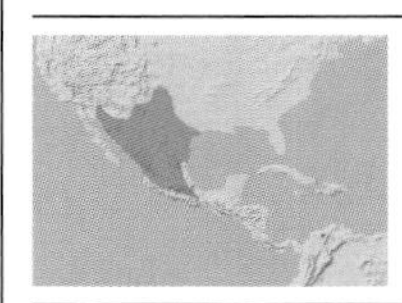

LENGTH 27cm (10½in)
WEIGHT 80g (2⅞oz)
MIGRATION Non-migrant

HABITAT Deserts with cacti, emergent trees, dry scrubland, thorn scrub, and open woodland

Named for its long, curved bill, the Curve-billed Thrasher has sandy brown plumage that blends in well with its desert habitat. The bird's pale iris gives it a beady-eyed look. It feeds on nectar from agave plants and on the fruit of cacti, both foods being necessary to provide it with water and vital nutrients in its barren environment. It feeds mainly on the ground. A noisy bird, the Curve-billed Thrasher's song is a series of loud, melodious phrases, occasionally including mimicry of songs of other birds.

ADULT CURVE-BILLED THRASHER

Cinclocerthia ruficauda

Brown Trembler

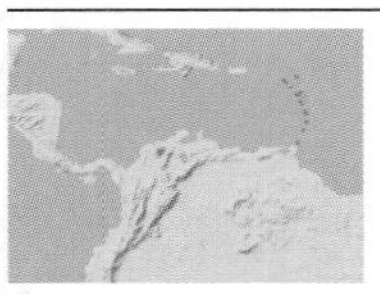

LENGTH 25cm (10in)
WEIGHT 55g (2oz)
MIGRATION Non-migrant

HABITAT Humid rainforest and montane forest; occasionally plantations

The Brown Trembler is the only true denizen of humid rainforest in its family. The bird has a very long, slightly decurved bill. Its plumage is rufous brown on the upperparts, grey buff on the throat, and grey-brown on the breast. It has a short tail, which is often held cocked. In its characteristic display, the Brown Trembler keeps its wings drooped and quivers them. Both sexes display, the purpose of which may be to maintain the pair's bond.

PHILIPPINE CREEPERS

ORDER	Passeriformes
FAMILY	Rhabdornithidae
SPECIES	2

THE CLASSIFICATION OF these two species of forest birds from the Philippines is unclear. Somewhat similar in appearance to nuthatches (see p.426) and treecreepers (see p.427), they were formerly grouped with those birds. Some ornithologists suggest they may be related to the babblers (see p.418), but these small, streaked brown birds are now usually placed in their own family. The uncertainty in relationships extends to the English names of the birds, with some authors calling them creepers, while others prefer the name rhabdornis because the birds are not true creepers – the birds only occasionally creep along tree trunks. They primarily forage for insects among the leaves, flowers, and small branches of the forest canopy.

Rhabdornis inornatus

Stripe-breasted Creeper

LENGTH 17cm (6½in)

WEIGHT 40–80g (1 7/16–2 7/8oz)

MIGRATION Non-migrant

HABITAT Lowland and montane forest, often over 800m (2,600ft)

As its name indicates, the Stripe-breasted Creeper has boldly streaked underparts. It has a prominent dark brown mask cutting across its white face and grey throat. Its upperparts are a uniform, rich brown colour, extending from the top of the head to the back. The sexes are alike in plumage but the male is significantly larger than the female. The Stripe-breasted Creeper usually forages in the middle and high levels of the forest and occasionally gathers in large numbers to feed on flying ants. Otherwise, the diet consists of fruit and other insects. These birds often forage at lower altitudes in response to fruit availability. The species is gregarious and, particularly outside the breeding season, forms large roosting flocks in the tree canopy. Not much is known about the breeding ecology of the Stripe-breasted Creeper, although breeding birds have been observed in March and April. The nest is constructed in a tree-cavity.

The Stripe-breasted Creeper is found only in six island regions in the southern Philippines. The species is not globally threatened but its range is limited and it is not common on any of the islands.

STARLINGS

ORDER	Passeriformes
FAMILY	Sturnidae
SPECIES	114

INHABITANTS OF MANY different habitats, from grassland and semi-desert to tropical forest, starlings were originally found in Europe, Africa, and Asia, with one genus in Australasia. However, they have been introduced to North America and many Atlantic and Pacific islands. Starlings are sturdily built, small to medium-sized birds, with short wings and short tails, strong legs and long straight bills. Some are brilliantly colourful, but even the dark or black species have glossy and sometimes iridescent plumage gleaming with many different colours. Some have vividly-coloured patches of bare skin on their faces.

STARLING FEEDING
Common Starlings take worms and insects, or fruit and seeds according to season.

BEHAVIOUR

Some starlings are specialist fruit-eaters, but the more widespread and common species tend to be opportunistic, generalist feeders, eating mostly insects during spring and summer, and switching to fruit and seeds in autumn and winter. Most members of this family are gregarious, nesting in colonies, and feeding, travelling, and roosting in flocks. They nest in holes in trees, rock crevices, and in buildings. Many are excellent mimics, and incorporate the calls of other birds in their songs.

SHOWY STARLINGS
The Superb Starling is one of the most colourful species of the starling family. The plumage includes glossy, iridescent greens and blues.

Aplonis panayensis

Asian Glossy Starling

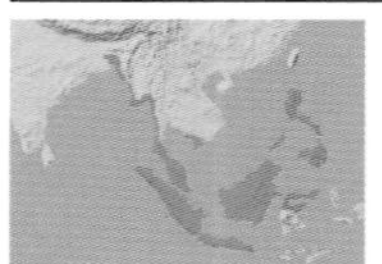

LENGTH 19–22cm (7½–8½in)

WEIGHT 55g (2oz)

MIGRATION Non-migrant

HABITAT Coastal scrub, secondary growth, and cultivation, mostly in lowland areas

A slim-bodied bird, the Asian Glossy Starling is named for its spectacular glossy blue plumage, but its red eyes are equally striking. The sexes are alike in plumage, but the juvenile is heavily streaked on the underparts. The diet of this starling is mainly made up of fruit and it seems to have a preference for figs. Most of the fruit is collected in the tree canopy, but flocks occasionally descend to the ground to pick up fallen fruit. It may also feed on insects.

The Asian Glossy Starling is a highly gregarious species, feeding and roosting in flocks that are compact and move quickly. It can mimic the calls of other birds. In the breeding season from February to August, it nests in colonies, usually in sheltered places high above the ground. The nest is built in a tree-hole or the crown of a palm but artificial sites such as buildings and pylons are also used. The female lays 3 or 4 eggs.

ADULT ASIAN GLOSSY STARLING

ADULT GOLDEN MYNA

Mino anais

Golden Myna

LENGTH 24cm ($9\frac{1}{2}$in)

WEIGHT 150g (5oz)

MIGRATION Non-migrant

HABITAT Open, lowland forest

The Golden Myna is a spectacular bird with a striking combination of a black face, body, and wings, contrasting with its yellow cap, neck, and undertail area. The breeding season is from February to October and a pair stays together for life. The nest is built in a tree-hole and the main food is fruit, collected from the tree canopy. The Golden Myna is bred in captivity, but does not seem to be threatened and is not considered to be globally at risk.

ADULT COMMON MYNA

Acridotheres tristis

Common Myna

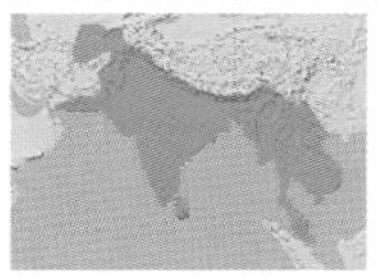

LENGTH 25cm (10in)

WEIGHT 125g (4oz)

MIGRATION Non-migrant

HABITAT Dry and grassy areas up to 1,500m (5,000ft)

A dark bird overall, the Common Myna has a yellow mask and a pale yellow bill. The species is naturally found in India and southeast Asia but has been widely introduced in other regions across the world. The diet consists of insects and fruit collected in the tree canopy. The nest is an untidy platform built in a tree crown and 4–6 eggs are laid.

Gracula religiosa

Common Hill Myna

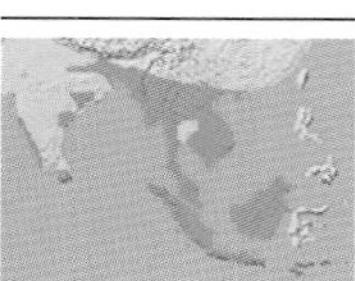

LENGTH 27–31cm ($10\frac{1}{2}$–12in)

WEIGHT 200g (7oz)

MIGRATION Non-migrant

HABITAT Broad-leaved evergreen and deciduous forest, usually below 600m (2,000ft)

The Common Hill Myna has black plumage contrasted by yellow facial stripes and a white or yellow undertail area. Its natural food consists of fruit, nectar, and insects collected in the tree canopy. The breeding season is from September to June and 3 or 4 eggs are laid in a tree-hole that is often used year after year. The species is well known for its ability to mimic various sounds, including human speech. A familiar cage-bird, the Common Hill Myna has a long association with humans, although for many years it was mainly a hunted bird.

ADULT COMMON HILL MYNA

Leucopsar rothschildi

Bali Myna

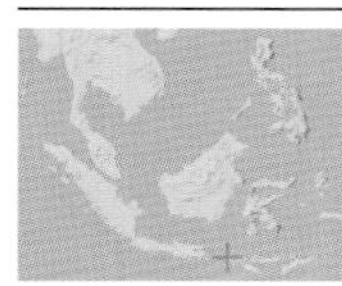

LENGTH 25cm (10in)

WEIGHT 85–90g (3–$3\frac{1}{4}$oz)

MIGRATION Non-migrant

HABITAT Dry lowland forest

RED LIST CATEGORY Critically endangered

The long head plumes and white plumage make the Bali Myna an attractive bird. It has a bright blue face stripe and the bill is pale yellow. Fruit, seeds, and insects make up the bulk of its diet and the nest is normally built in an abandoned woodpecker hole. The breeding season is from January to March and although 2 or 3 eggs are produced, it is common for only a single chick to survive to fledging. The species was never very widely distributed and habitat destruction has further reduced its range. However, it is now protected under Indonesian law to arrest the losses to the illegal bird trade. It has also been widely bred in various zoos around the world.

ADULT BALI MYNA

Lamprotornis superbus

Superb Starling

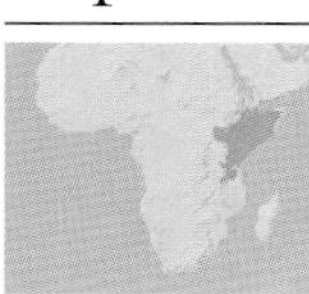

LENGTH 19cm ($7\frac{1}{2}$in)

WEIGHT 65g ($2\frac{3}{8}$oz)

MIGRATION Non-migrant

HABITAT Semi-arid open woodland and grassland; also towns

Aptly named, the Superb Starling has an iridescent blue back, green wings, and bright orange underparts. It has a black face that is emphasized by its white eyes. It usually feeds on insects and berries collected in vegetation or on the ground. This bird is able to run or hop when moving on the ground. The breeding season varies across the range and begins with the male Superb Starling making a hopping display, with the neck outstretched, and trailing the wings on the ground. The nest is a bulky structure, usually built in a thorny tree. If the tree does not have enough thorns or the nest is built in a cliff hole, the bird builds a barricade around the nest. Four eggs are produced, and both the male and female share incubation and feeding.

ADULT SUPERB STARLING

Sturnus philippensis

Chestnut-cheeked Starling

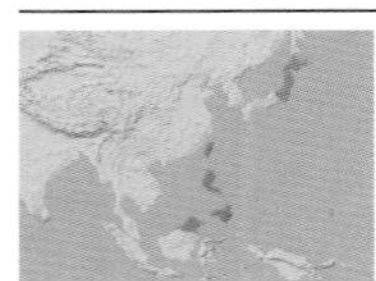

LENGTH 18cm (7in)
WEIGHT 75g ($2^{5}/_{8}$oz)
MIGRATION Migrant

HABITAT Open deciduous and mixed woodland; winters in gardens and wooded cultivation

Bright and colourful, the male Chestnut-cheeked or Violet-backed Starling has a white or buff head, chestnut cheeks that extend to the side of the throat and breast, a violet back, and a white wing patch. The female is different, with a head mottled with brown or white and a greyish brown back and rump. This bird moves in small flocks and eats fruit and insects. Larger flocks congregate in its wintering grounds.

ADULT ROSY STARLING

Sturnus roseus

Rosy Starling

LENGTH 22cm (9in)
WEIGHT 65–90g ($2^{3}/_{8}$–$3^{1}/_{4}$oz)
MIGRATION Migrant

HABITAT Steppes, semi-desert, and dry grassland

The beautiful Rosy Starling has pink plumage and a glossy black head, wings, and tail. However, it turns dusky in winter. Its bill and legs are also pink. The juvenile can be distinguished by its short yellow bill and paler plumage. Highly gregarious, this starling breeds in large, noisy, and often erratically occupied colonies that resemble those of cliff-nesting seabirds. Nest sites include cliff faces, gorges, and manmade structures with cavities. It feeds on seeds, fruit, and nectar. In the breeding period, its diet consists of locusts and grasshoppers, and adults fly up to 10km (6 miles) to feed on swarms of these insects.

Sturnus vulgaris

Common Starling

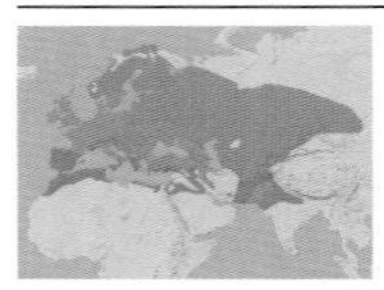

LENGTH 21–22cm ($8^{1}/_{2}$–9in)
WEIGHT 60–90g ($2^{1}/_{8}$–$3^{1}/_{4}$oz)
MIGRATION Migrant

HABITAT Open habitats and areas of fruit-bearing shrubs and trees

The Common Starling with its shiny black, white-spotted plumage is a familiar bird to many as it has adapted readily to manmade structures and habitats. This starling feeds on a variety of animal and plant material. Its diet changes seasonally according to the abundance of different food – invertebrates and their larvae are important in spring and form the high-protein core of the nestlings' diet. The Common Starling mostly forages on the ground in open areas with short turf by probing for food on, or just below, the surface or among grass roots. Plant material, especially seeds, becomes important during the autumn and winter, when this starling's gut actually elongates to accommodate the change in diet. Introductions have extended its natural range to North America.

ADULT FEEDING ITS YOUNG

Creatophora cinerea

Wattled Starling

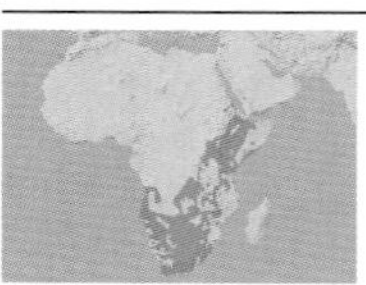

LENGTH 19–21cm ($7^{1}/_{2}$–$8^{1}/_{2}$in)
WEIGHT 70–75g ($2^{1}/_{2}$–$2^{5}/_{8}$oz)
MIGRATION Partial migrant

HABITAT Grassland, savanna, and open, broad-leaved woodland

The Wattled Starling has a pale grey bill and legs and a white rump. The male has a patch of bare yellow skin behind and below the eye and bare black patches on the throat. In the breeding season, the male may lose all its head and neck feathers and develop pendulous black wattles from the bare skin on the throat; sometimes smaller wattles form above the bill too, with a range of individual variations occurring in the shape and size of these wattles. The female largely resembles a non-breeding male.

The Wattled Starlings are omnivorous and appear to feed opportunistically on a range of food items. In some areas, they prey on locusts and other swarming grasshopper species. They also eat a range of other invertebrates and take berries and seeds where available. They can be viewed as pests when they feed on grapes in vineyards. The Wattled Starlings are found throughout eastern, central, and southern Africa and appear to be expanding their range in the west, presumably in response to forest clearance, which extends their habitat.

MALE WATTLED STARLING

BIRD SPECIES

Lamprotornis nitens

Cape Starling

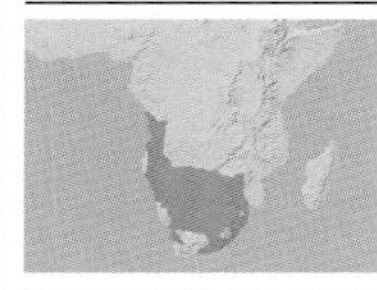

LENGTH 25cm (10in)

WEIGHT 85g (3oz)

MIGRATION Non-migrant

HABITAT Savanna and riverine bush, forest edges, plantations, parks, and gardens

The Cape Starling, also known as the Red-shouldered Starling, has glossy blue-green plumage with few obvious markings. Its bill, legs, and feet are black. The identifying features, however, are two rows of dark spots on the wing feathers and the small bronze-purple epaulette. Young birds have some amount of gloss on their feathers. This bird nests in natural or manmade cavities, such as tree-holes and pipes, and under roofs. The Cape Starling's nest, lined with materials such as snakeskins and feathers, is made of animal dung and dry grass. The young birds from earlier broods often help to feed the young.

ADULT CAPE STARLING

Buphagus africanus

Yellow-billed Oxpecker

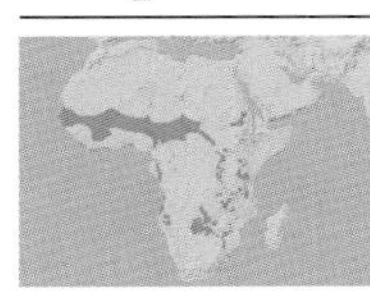

LENGTH 19–22cm ($7^1/_2$–9in)

WEIGHT 55–70g (2–$2^1/_2$oz)

MIGRATION Non-migrant

HABITAT Thorn scrub and broad-leaved woodland, often near water; often in association with game

As indicated by its name, this starling has a striking yellow bill, ending in a stout, bright red tip. It has red eyes, grey-brown upperparts, and a contrasting pale buff lower back and rump that are distinctive. It feeds mainly on parasites, especially ticks, and on the wounded tissue of host animals (see panel, below), a strong association that extends to the oxpeckers' choice of roost sites, many spending the night perched on a large mammal.

ADULT YELLOW-BILLED OXPECKER

PICKING OUT PARASITES

Feeding almost exclusively on external parasites found on large mammals, the Yellow-billed Oxpecker is often found perched on a cow or a wild herbivorous animal, such as a giraffe (pictured right). In this mutually beneficial association, host animals generally tolerate these birds as they remove troublesome ticks, lice, and fleas from their hair.

Onychognathus tristramii

Tristram's Starling

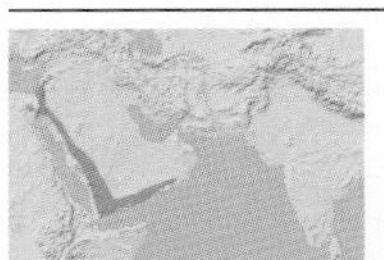

LENGTH 25cm (10in)

WEIGHT 125g (4oz)

MIGRATION Non-migrant

HABITAT Arid rocky areas with cliffs and ravines, increasingly in urban areas in parts of range

A sturdy glossy black bird, Tristram's Starling has striking chestnut patches on the wing. Its repeated loud musical whistles often give this bird's presence away. It is the only "red-winged" starling that is found outside Africa and is common throughout its small range, which covers the western Arabian peninsula from Yemen to Israel. Population increases have been noted in Israel in response to the cultivation of arid desert areas. A growing dependence on humans and an associated tameness has also been noted. Tristram's Starling has a varied diet, feeding mainly on fruit and invertebrates. It occasionally cracks snail shells on an "anvil", such as a rock, and also takes external parasites from livestock and wild mammals. In cultivated areas, it feeds on dates, prickly pear fruit, and grapes, and often frequents rubbish dumps.

ADULT TRISTRAM'S STARLING

BIRD SPECIES

COMMON STARLINGS
In open country, typically just before sunset, Common Starlings can form huge flocks of up to a million birds. They fly in tight formation with no apparent leader.

THRUSHES

ORDER	Passeriformes
FAMILY	Turdidae
SPECIES	175

THRUSHES ARE A VERY variable family with a widespread global distribution. Generally they are small to medium-sized with quite long tails and a wide variety of plumages. Most thrushes are predominantly brown; many are streaked and spotted, often showing quite detailed patterning. Other members of the family display a fantastic array of bright colours ranging from electric blue to vivid orange. Thrushes are famous for their songs, including a number of species regarded as among the most beautiful songsters in the bird world.

NESTING

The majority of thrushes are territorial and monogamous, with each sex having a clearly defined role. First, the male bird finds and establishes a territory (which varies in size between species). Once a suitable area has been found, the male sings to attract a mate. The female bird then builds a nest and sits on the eggs while the male defends the territory. Nests vary in location (some are on the ground, others in trees) and structure, though most are cup-shaped and made out of dead leaves and twigs (some smaller species nest in holes in trees or in nest boxes).

AMERICAN ROBIN FEEDING YOUNG
Earthworms are a staple food of adult thrushes, which feed smaller worms to their offspring, often gathering up a beak-full before returning to the nest.

IN FLIGHT
Like a number of its relatives, the Eastern Bluebird has a rich warbling song. This is often delivered by the male while in flight, a characteristic shared by many members of the family that inhabit open countryside.

TYPICAL CLUTCH
Typical of its family, the Redwing usually lays 4–6 pale greenish blue eggs with fine brown speckling. The nest is usually on the ground or low down in a bush.

FEEDING

Thrushes employ a variety of tactics to find food, but most species within this stout-legged family can usually be found running, walking, and hopping along the ground in search of invertebrates and other favourite foods, from berries and seeds to small reptiles. Worms are particularly sought-after by many species such as the Common Blackbird of Europe and the American Robin of the Americas. Others, such as the European Song Thrush, have a fondness for snails, breaking open their shells on rocks or "anvils". Some species, such as the Redwing and Fieldfare, gather in loose flocks to feed, especially during autumn when berries are plentiful in hedges.

ANATOMY

Most thrushes have no spectacular features that mark them out for a particular lifestyle. Although the majority spend most of their time feeding on the ground, they are also quite at home among the trees. Equally, although invertebrates form the staple diet, most thrushes also eat large quantities of fruits and berries. Variations in anatomy between different species reflect differences in habitat and behaviour. For example, migratory species have longer, more pointed wings than more sedentary species; and the Long-billed Thrush has a longer bill than its relatives, an adaptation to its diet of earthworms.

THE EARLY BIRD
The speckle-breasted Fieldfare is a familiar sight in many towns and cities in Russia and Scandinavia, where it can often be observed pulling worms from the lawn of a garden or park.

MALE EASTERN BLUEBIRD

Sialia sialis

Eastern Bluebird

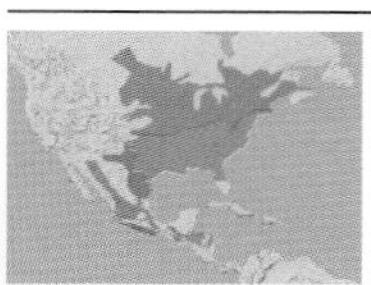

LENGTH 17–21cm (6½–8½in)

WEIGHT 25–30g (⅞–1¹⁄₁₆oz)

MIGRATION Partial migrant

HABITAT Open woodland, including orchards, plains, pastures, pine forests, and swampy ground

Like many thrushes, the male and female Eastern Bluebirds have different plumage, the male being more brightly coloured than the drab female. It has a brilliant blue head and upperparts, and chestnut-orange underparts that turn white on the abdomen, while the female has a grey head, much paler blue wings, and dull orange underparts.

This species mainly feeds on beetles, spiders, and caterpillars in spring and summer, but switches to a fruit-based diet in autumn and winter. An adaptable bird, it also takes small snakes, shrews, and lizards. Many of these birds move south in winter, migrating in small flocks, but also in larger groups of up to 100 birds.

Sialia currucoides

Mountain Bluebird

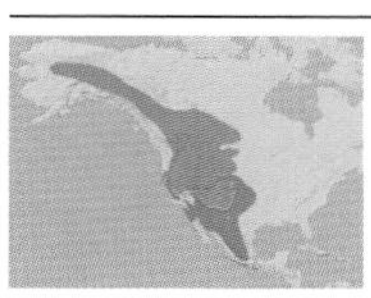

LENGTH 17–20cm (6½–8in)

WEIGHT 25–35g (⅞–1¼oz)

MIGRATION Partial migrant

HABITAT Breeds at the tree line in open areas; winters in farmland and lowland areas

The male Mountain Bluebird is truly the bluest of its genus, being pale blue below and a deeper skyblue on the upperparts. The female is largely grey-brown with a white eye-ring and an ultramarine tail. This bird feeds on insects and takes berries in autumn and through the winter. It often chooses an elevated lookout as a song-perch and sings for long periods.

MALE MOUNTAIN BLUEBIRD

GREAT SITES

YELLOWSTONE NATIONAL PARK

Situated in northwest Montana, in the heart of the Rocky Mountains, are the rugged highlands of the Yellowstone National Park. The extensive forest and grassland offer a haven for the Mountain Bluebird and many other birds of the hills and mountains of western USA. This famous park is the centre of the Greater Yellowstone Ecosystem, the largest intact ecosystem in the northern temperate zone.

ADULT BLUE WHISTLING THRUSH

Myophonus caeruleus

Blue Whistling Thrush

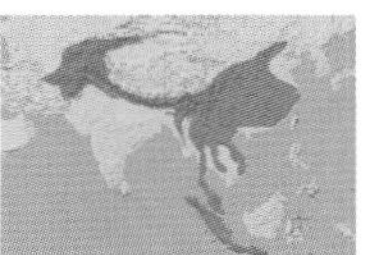

LENGTH 29–35cm (11½–14in)

WEIGHT 125–225g (4–8oz)

MIGRATION Partial migrant

HABITAT Forested highland, usually in undergrowth and near water, occasionally in lowland in winter

Far more easily heard than seen, the Blue Whistling Thrush is a large thrush with very deep blue-black plumage that is spotted grey and white, red eyes, and a black or yellow bill, the colours of the bill varying in the subspecies. As its name indicates, its song is a fluid whistle. Most Blue Whistling Thrushes have two broods a year, except those that inhabit the highest altitudes. The nest is a bulky cup of moss and roots woven with grass and leaves, – it is occasionally reused in consecutive years and up to five eggs are laid.

Zoothera citrina

Orange-headed Thrush

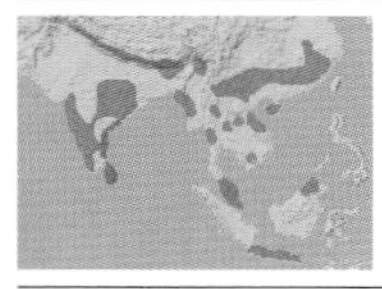

LENGTH 20–23cm (8–9in)

WEIGHT 45–65g (1⅝–2⅜oz)

MIGRATION Partial migrant

HABITAT Forest, especially dense understorey, often in bamboo thickets and near running water

The Orange-headed Thrush shows a great deal of plumage variation across its range. Some subspecies have black vertical lines through the eye and cheeks or white on the face. The orange tone to the head and underparts also vary. The Orange-headed Thrush shown here has a brick-red head and underparts. The female differs from the male in its matt brown, rather than grey-blue, back.

ADULT ORANGE-HEADED THRUSH

Catharus guttatus

Hermit Thrush

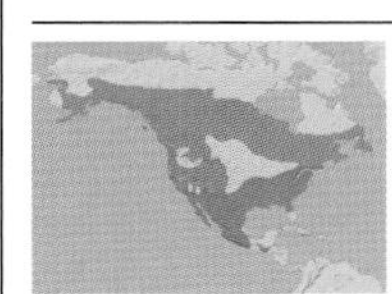

LENGTH 16–18cm (6½–7in)

WEIGHT 18–35g (⅝–1¼oz)

MIGRATION Migrant

HABITAT Boreal forest and parkland; the understorey of open woodland in winter

Like several other North American thrushes, the Hermit Thrush has predominantly olive-brown upperparts, dark-spotted underparts, and a rufous tail. The male and female are similar in their plumage. This thrush mainly feeds on berries. Although the male may sing from a tall conifer treetop, the Hermit Thrush is principally a ground-dweller, favouring the understorey and well-vegetated areas. Even the bulky nest of grass and leaves is placed on the ground. Usually 4–6, eggs are laid, but like many North American songbirds, its nesting success is limited due to brood parasitization by Brown-headed Cowbirds (*Molothrus ater*), and other losses to squirrels, chipmunks, and weasels.

ADULT HERMIT THRUSH

ADULT WOOD THRUSH

Hylocichla mustelina

Wood Thrush

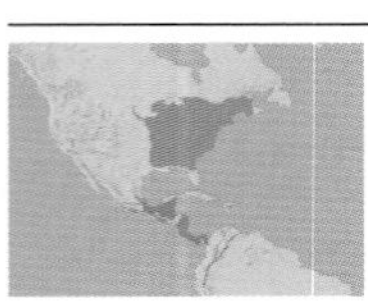

LENGTH 13–20cm (5–8in)

WEIGHT 50g ($1^3/_4$oz)

MIGRATION Migrant

HABITAT Breeds in broad-leaved woodland; winters in humid forests

Larger, and with more boldly spotted underparts than other North American thrushes, the short-tailed Wood Thrush has a white eye-ring, black streaking on its white face, and reddish brown upperparts. Its song, one of the most melodious thrush songs, sounds like a flute, with the middle note lower than the first and the last note a high trill. It feeds on the ground, eating insects, spiders, and fruit. The Wood Thrush is a common summer migrant to much of southeast Canada and the eastern USA and spends its winters in Central America from Mexico to Panama.

MALE RING OUZEL

Turdus torquatus

Ring Ouzel

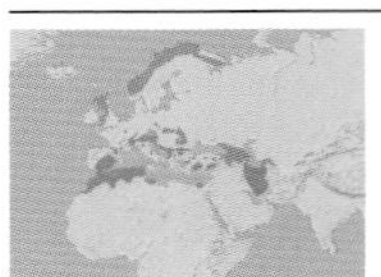

LENGTH 24cm ($9^1/_2$in)

WEIGHT 100g ($3^5/_8$oz)

MIGRATION Migrant

HABITAT Rocky upland and moorland

An upland relative of the Common Blackbird (below), the Ring Ouzel has pale edges to its flight feathers and underparts. The male can be identified by its broad white breast-band, a feature that is less noticeable in the female and entirely lacking in the juvenile. The species breeds largely in northern and eastern Europe.

Turdus cardis

Japanese Thrush

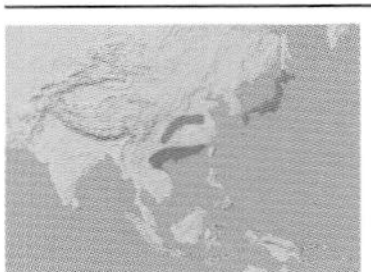

LENGTH 21–23cm ($8^1/_2$–9in)

WEIGHT 60g ($2^1/_8$oz)

MIGRATION Migrant

HABITAT Dense upland forest

The male Japanese Thrush is rather like a cross between a blackbird and a song thrush. Its upperparts are jet-black, contrasting vividly with its spotted white belly. It has a yellow bill. Young males are similar, but usually have slightly paler or slate-grey wings, back, and tail. The female is plain in comparison to the male, and is a typical streaked, brown thrush. The Japanese Thrush has a rich, clear song that consists of a series of musical, flute-like trills and whistles. This species is widely distributed and breeds in Japan and central China before spending the winter in southern China and Vietnam.

Turdus merula

Common Blackbird

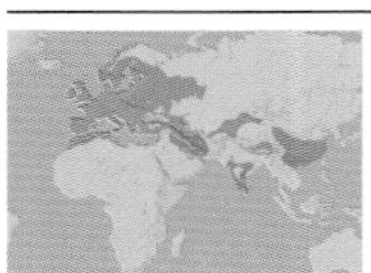

LENGTH 24–29cm ($9^1/_2$–$11^1/_2$in)

WEIGHT 125g (4oz)

MIGRATION Partial migrant

HABITAT Deciduous woodland, scrub, parks, and gardens

A familiar bird throughout most of Europe, as well as parts of Asia and north Africa, the Common Blackbird is also quite common in southeast Australia and New Zealand, where it was introduced in the 19th century by colonists. The male has an unmistakable all-black plumage, with an orange beak, eye-ring, and legs. The female is a uniform dark brown, with dark streaks on the throat and mottled underparts. The Common Blackbird's song is a very musical, full-throated warbling and as it roosts it makes loud, sharp "chak-chak" calls. It noisily explores leaf litter for worms and insects and also feeds on fruit and berries. Its nest is a grass and mud cup, lined with grass.

MALE IN SONG

Turdus viscivorus

Mistle Thrush

LENGTH 28cm (11in)

WEIGHT 100–125g ($3^5/_8$–4oz)

MIGRATION Partial migrant

HABITAT Woodland, farmland, orchards, parks, and gardens

Larger and a paler brown colour than the similar Song Thrush (left), the Mistle Thrush has a pattern of spots on its breast that is also subtly different from that of the Song Thrush, with larger, less regular black marks, a distinct wing pattern, and an obvious grey rump. Its undulating flight is distinct and much heavier than that of the Song Thrush.

One of the first indications of the species' presence is its harsh, rattling call. Its melancholy song is a flute-like series of whistles, resembling the song of the Common Blackbird (left), but with a more limited repertoire of phrases. It is not particularly sociable and is usually seen singly or in pairs.

ADULT MISTLE THRUSH

Turdus philomelos

Song Thrush

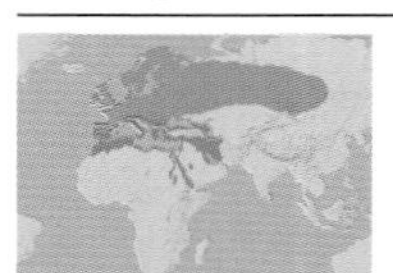

LENGTH 20–24cm (8–$9^1/_2$in)

WEIGHT 65g ($2^3/_8$oz)

MIGRATION Partial migrant

HABITAT Woods, hedgerows, thickets, parks, and gardens

Named after its famous voice, the Song Thrush sings a loud, clear series of musical, ringing notes mingled with harsher phrases. Occasionally, it will also mimic other birds and sounds. In appearance, both sexes are the same; warm brown above with large black spots on the underparts. The species is smaller and darker than the similar Mistle Thrush (right). In flight, its orange underwing is noticeable. The Song Thrush is partially migratory, with northern and eastern populations, in particular, moving south and west to escape harsh conditions.

ADULT SONG THRUSH

EATING SNAILS

The Song Thrush is omnivorous and feeds out in the open on a wide range of insects, worms, snails, and also on berries. Since it cannot crush the snail shells with its bill or swallow them whole, it has learned how to smash them open (see below) to get at the flesh within. It usually feeds on the banded snail of the *Cepaea* genus.

SNAIL-SMASHING TECHNIQUE
The Song Thrush picks up a shell with its bill and repeatedly smashes it on an "anvil" such as a stone, wall, or path to break it open.

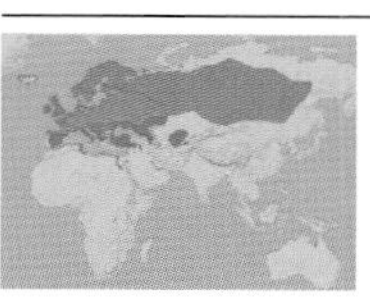

Turdus pilaris

Fieldfare

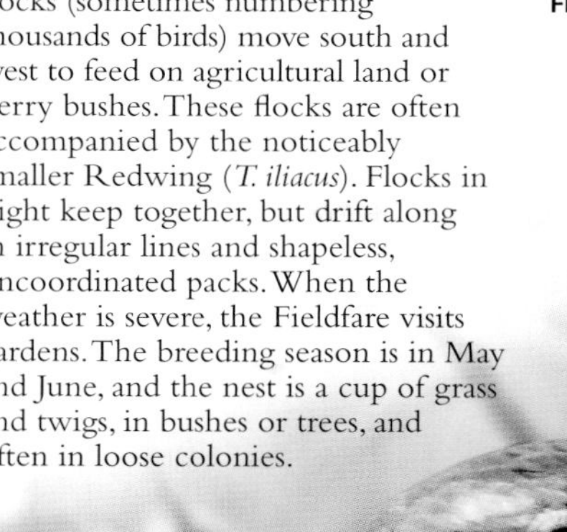

LENGTH
25–27cm (10–10½in)

WEIGHT
100g (3⅝oz)

MIGRATION
Migrant

HABITAT Breeds in woodland, parks, and gardens; winters in more open areas

A large and striking thrush, the Fieldfare has a grey head, a black mask, and wing markings that contrast with its mainly brown upperparts and speckled belly. In flight, it displays a large white patch on the underwing, a useful feature for identification. The sexes are virtually alike. The Fieldfare is a noisy bird, often emitting a scolding "chuck" or cackling "chack-chack". In the summer, its song is reminiscent of the Common Blackbird (opposite), but is far less melodious. The male sometimes performs a song flight as a part of the courtship ritual.

The Fieldfare is a common breeding bird in much of northern Europe, often found in city centre parks in Scandinavian towns and cities and in wooded areas. In winter, large flocks (sometimes numbering thousands of birds) move south and west to feed on agricultural land or berry bushes. These flocks are often accompanied by the noticeably smaller Redwing (*T. iliacus*). Flocks in flight keep together, but drift along in irregular lines and shapeless, uncoordinated packs. When the weather is severe, the Fieldfare visits gardens. The breeding season is in May and June, and the nest is a cup of grass and twigs, in bushes or trees, and often in loose colonies.

FEEDING ADULT

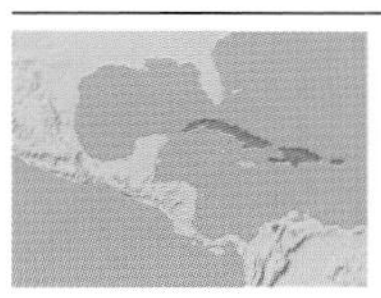

Turdus plumbeus

Red-legged Thrush

LENGTH
26cm (10in)

WEIGHT
75g (2⅝oz)

MIGRATION
Non-migrant

HABITAT Rainforest edges, coastal woodland, scrub, mangroves, pinewoods, plantations, and parks

ADULT RED-LEGGED THRUSH

A Caribbean species, found in most of the West Indies from Dominica to Cuba and the Bahamas (though not Jamaica), the Red-legged Thrush is large and distinctly marked with black and white streaks on the throat. There is some variation between the different island forms, although all are generally slate-grey in colour with a noticeable red bill, eye-ring, and legs. The male's bill changes from red to black in the breeding season.

Generally found alone or in pairs, the species is often shy when encountered in forests, but has become tamer and more accustomed to people in parks and gardens. It is a fruit-eater, but spends most of its time feeding noisily among leaf litter looking for insects, including caterpillars, beetles, ants, crickets, wasps, although it occasionally forages for snails, lizards, and bird eggs. It is most active at dawn or dusk. The Red-legged Thrush builds a nest of leaves and grass, usually in a tree.

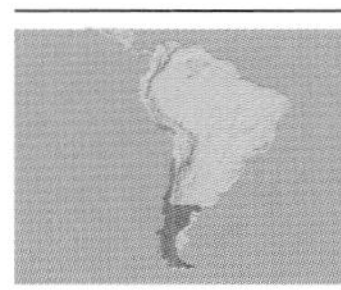

Turdus falcklandii

Austral Thrush

LENGTH
23–27cm (9–10½in)

WEIGHT
95g (3⅜oz)

MIGRATION
Non-migrant

HABITAT Tussock-grass near rocky beaches (Falklands race); woodland (South American race)

Two main races occur of the medium-sized Austral Thrush – *T. f. falklandii* is found in the Falkland Islands, the only resident thrush there, and *T. f. magellanicus* in Chile and Argentina. The birds on the South American mainland have paler, more orange underparts and a more heavily streaked throat than the Falkland Island birds. Both races have black heads, yellow bills, and olive-brown backs, wings, and tails. The females of both races are generally similar to the males, but sometimes have browner heads. Juveniles of both races are brown and spotted. Both races are also rather different in behaviour – mainland birds are usually found in woodland and forests, and even in gardens, whereas those on the Falklands favour areas of tussock-grass and beaches, often feeding around rotting seaweed. The diet of the Austral Thrush consists mostly of worms, larvae, insects, and snails, although it will also sometimes feed on berries and fruit. It has learned to visit bird tables in parts of its range. The call of this species is a melodious, whistled song.

ADULT AUSTRAL THRUSH

Turdus migratorius

American Robin

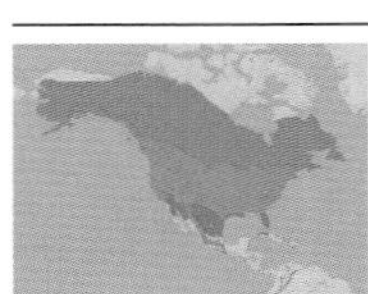

LENGTH 25–28cm (10–11in)
WEIGHT 75g ($2\frac{5}{8}$oz)
MIGRATION Partial migrant

HABITAT Forest, wooded swamps, farmland, parks, urban and suburban gardens

MALE IN BREEDING PLUMAGE

The most common and widespread large thrush of North America, the American Robin shares only a red breast with its European namesake. In build and movements, it most closely resembles the Common Blackbird (see p.438). The sexes are similar, although the male acquires a black head during breeding, and the female is generally paler, with an orange breast rather than the male's deep brick red. Not all American Robins migrate, despite the scientific name. Even those that breed in Canada and Alaska may stay on through the winter, when berries and other fruit are in plentiful supply. They use garden nest boxes and shelves. During breeding, the male may roost communally while the female remains at the nest.

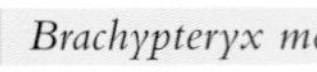

Brachypteryx montana

White-browed Shortwing

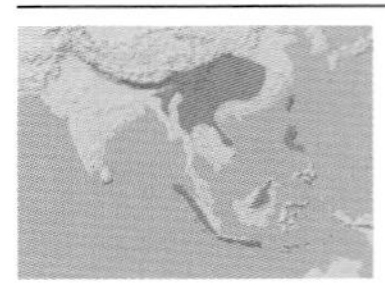

LENGTH 13cm (5in)
WEIGHT 17g ($\frac{5}{8}$oz)
MIGRATION Non-migrant

HABITAT On mountains in dense undergrowth, bamboo thickets, oak, fir, and rhododendron forest

Unlike most of the thrush family, shortwings run rather than hop. The 14 subspecies vary greatly in plumage. The male has grey-blue plumage with distinctive white eyebrows. Most females are rufous-brown with pale underparts, but the female of the north Borneo subspecies has a blue back and reddish chestnut face and underparts. The species hunts for small insects and their larvae, and snails and worms.

MALE WHITE-BROWED SHORTWING

ADULT RED-THROATED ALETHE

Alethe poliophrys

Red-throated Alethe

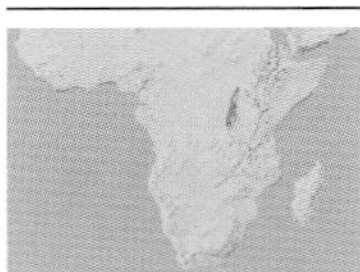

LENGTH 15cm (6in)
WEIGHT 35g ($1\frac{1}{4}$oz)
MIGRATION Non-migrant

HABITAT Mountain forest and wooded ravines

One of the restricted-range species confined to the Albertine Rift Mountains Endemic Bird Area, the Red-throated Alethe is locally common. Both sexes have a red throat. The Red-throated Alethe hunts by rushing at insects, worms, and snails, mainly on the ground. Sometimes it tosses fallen leaves aside in search of prey. It also follows and feeds on columns of soldier ants.

Cochoa viridis

Green Cochoa

LENGTH 25–28cm (10–11in)
WEIGHT 90–125g ($3\frac{1}{4}$–4oz)
MIGRATION Non-migrant

HABITAT Dense broad-leaf evergreen forest, often near trees

The Green Cochoa is vivid green with a blue head. It perches motionless for long periods in the middle storey of its dense forest home. Fruit makes up a good proportion of the Green Cochoa's diet, and its wide gape enables it to eat large berries whole. It has also been seen foraging for insects. When sighted, it is often in pairs or small family groups. Its distinctive call is very thin and high-pitched. The nest is a shallow cup of green moss, leaves, and fibres in a tree.

CHATS AND FLYCATCHERS

ORDER	Passeriformes
FAMILY	Muscicapidae
SPECIES	275

THIS LARGE GROUP of small songbirds is found in Europe, Africa, and Asia. The family includes the chats, previously classified with the thrushes (see p.436). This varied group of small songbirds includes such well-recognized and tame species as the European Robin and the very plain Common Nightingale, which is renowned for its beautiful song.

ANATOMY

Chats and flycatchers are characterized by their short bills. Most flycatchers have quite dull plumage, although there are a number of vibrantly coloured exceptions. Males and females of the Muscicapidae family are often differently plumaged, and some species have different summer and winter plumages. Many species are agile in flight as they dart through the air after their flying insect prey. The method of hunting favoured by many species is to wait on a prominent lookout perch before undertaking circular flights, which usually culminate back on the same perch, often accompanied by the sound of the bird's bill snapping shut on its insect prey.

BEHAVIOUR

Birds of this family nest in a variety of locations. Some nest in holes in trees and walls, while others build a cup-shaped nest in a tree or hedge. Some members of this family build a nest of twigs and leaves on the ground, hidden by the surrounding leaf litter. The family includes many migrants and partial migrants.

EUROPEAN ROBIN
A typical European Robin's nest is hidden in a hedge, camouflaged by the surrounding vegetation.

SWALLOWING A FLY
A Spotted Flycatcher rests on its perch to consume the insect that it has just caught during one of its short sallies.

Erithacus rubecula

European Robin

LENGTH 14cm (5½in)

WEIGHT 15–20g (9/16–11/16oz)

MIGRATION Partial migrant

HABITAT Deciduous, mixed, and coniferous woodland, parks, and gardens

The plump breast – orange rather than red – round head, and confiding manner have made the European Robin a favourite bird of many bird-lovers. The sexes are very similar in appearance. Juvenile robins are brown and speckled, and without the red breast. Despite its friendly image, the European Robin is solitary, territorial, and very aggressive. The orange-coloured breast is used in a threat display and boundary disputes can end in injury. In autumn, the female sings in defence of its territory.

The European Robin eats invertebrates such as beetles and ants, which it picks from the ground, or hunts from perches. It does not turn over leaves or the soil by itself, which is why it perches expectantly near human gardeners or large woodland mammals. Gardens are favoured because they provide the European Robin's preferred mixture of habitats – shade and cover, moist ground, and open areas. It uses holes in buildings and trees for nesting.

ADULT EUROPEAN ROBIN

COURTSHIP FEEDING

Playing an important part in strengthening pair bonds and reducing aggression between birds, courtship feeding is a ritual practised by European Robins. Such feeding begins during nest-building and continues through egg-laying. The provision of food for the female during incubation of the eggs provides her with nourishment when demands on her are heavy. It ends only after the brooding process is over. The female begs from the male, adopting the posture of a chick begging its parents for food.

Erithacus akahige

Japanese Robin

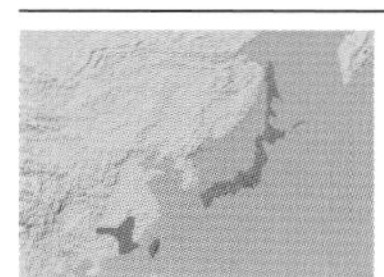

LENGTH 15cm (6in)

WEIGHT 17g (5/8oz)

MIGRATION Migrant

HABITAT Undergrowth, broad-leaf evergreen, mixed and deciduous mountain forest, parks, and gardens

Once a popular cage-bird, the Japanese Robin is still locally common in Japan, mostly in mountains. The male has an orange-red face and upper breast with a black breast-band. The female is similar to the male, but its face and breast are a duller orange-red. It forages on ground in search of its prey, mainly beetles. It is known as the Komadori in Japan.

MALE JAPANESE ROBIN

Luscinia megarhynchos

Common Nightingale

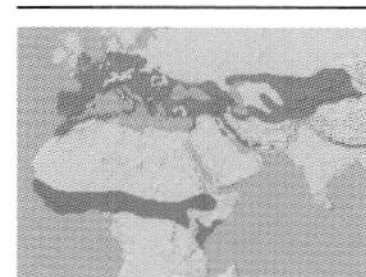

LENGTH 17cm (6½in)

WEIGHT 17–25g (5/8–7/8oz)

MIGRATION Migrant

HABITAT Thickets, scrub, and coppiced woodland offering cover and open ground, often near water

Larger than the European Robin (above), the Common Nightingale is more thrush-like in shape, with a smaller head and longer tail. It has brownish buff upperparts and a rusty red tail. It is more often heard than seen, skulking and singing from damp undergrowth, riverside thickets, tangled bushes, and densely packed stems of coppiced woodland, where it breeds.

It feeds on the ground, moving in a series of long and short hops, with a thrush-like, upright stance. It will also hunt by dropping from perches on its prey, generally insects such as ants and beetles and other invertebrates, although in autumn it also eats fruit. Normally solitary, the Common Nightingale is territorial. The male remains faithful to the same sites year after year. These birds also sing to establish their winter territories.

SWEET SONG

The song of the Common Nightingale is richly varied and powerful, a mixture of melody, chuckling, and occasional harsh notes, with sequences of slowly repeated notes that build in volume. Studies suggest that the male sings during the day to communicate with rival males, and at night to attract females.

PAIR OF COMMON NIGHTINGALES

Luscinia svecica

Bluethroat

LENGTH 15cm (6in)

WEIGHT 18g (5/8oz)

MIGRATION Migrant

HABITAT Damp upland forest; bushes, reeds, and grass near water

A distinctive bird, the male Bluethroat has a blue bib bordered below by bands of black, white, and orange across the breast. The upperparts are plain brown except for the black tail, which has a conspicuous rufous edge at the base. The female has a dark breast-band. Ten subspecies of the Bluethroat are recognized. In some of the subspecies, known as Red-spotted Bluethroats, the breeding male has a red spot in the middle of the blue throat (as shown below), while in other subspecies, the breeding male has a white spot – these are therefore called White-spotted Bluethroats.

MALE BLUETHROAT

MALE WHITE-THROATED ROBIN

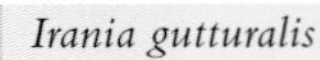

Irania gutturalis

White-throated Robin

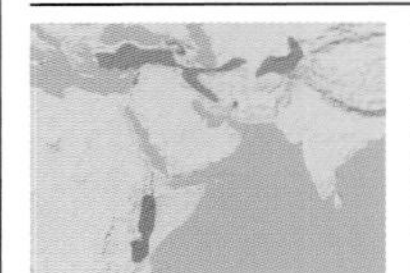

LENGTH 18cm (7in)

WEIGHT 20g (11/16oz)

MIGRATION Migrant

HABITAT Stony hillsides and scrub

The male White-throated Robin has bluish grey upperparts, bright rusty-red underparts, and a black tail that is often cocked. The sides of the face are black, contrasting strongly with a bold white stripe down the centre of the throat. A delicate white eyebrow completes the head pattern. The female of the species is similar, but has more subdued colours and diffuse patterns, the upperparts and face being brownish grey and only the sides of the belly and breast tinged orange.

The White-throated Robin feeds on insects gathered mainly on the ground, but also from bushes and trees. It breeds on open stony hillsides and valleys with scattered bushes up to an altitude of about 2,000m (6,500ft) in the Middle East and western Central Asia. The nest is a cup woven from grass, twigs, and leaves, lined with hair, down and feathers, paper, rags, and other scraps. It is usually built in a bush, shrub, or low tree, with the female laying 4 or 5 eggs. The female does most of the incubating, though the male may take over when the female leaves the nest. At the end of the summer, the species migrates to eastern Africa, where it winters in thick scrub and undergrowth.

ADULT RUFOUS-TAILED SCRUB ROBIN

Cercotrichas galactotes

Rufous-tailed Scrub Robin

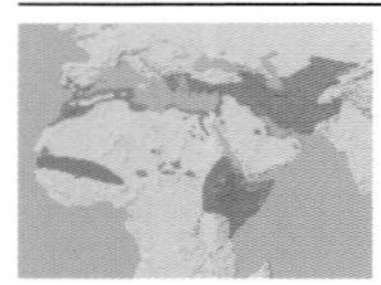

LENGTH 17cm (6½in)

WEIGHT 20g (11/16oz)

MIGRATION Partial migrant

HABITAT Variety of habitats, including dry scrub, stony ground, parks, gardens, and vineyards

The most striking feature of this small bird of dry scrubby areas is its long, slightly fan-shaped rufous tail, with white tips and dark bars on the feathers. It frequently cocks its tail in a vertical position or tilts it so far back that it almost touches the rear of its head, revealing the white feathers of the undertail. The Rufous-tailed Scrub Robin runs and hops beneath bushes, searching for insects and may also perch out in the open, looking for prey.

Copsychus saularis

Oriental Magpie-Robin

LENGTH 20cm (8in)

WEIGHT 25g (7/8oz)

MIGRATION Non-migrant

HABITAT Parks, gardens, scrub, and forest

Also known as the Dayal, or Dial Bird, the Oriental Magpie-Robin is a common bird throughout much of tropical Asia. The male (shown below) has a black head, throat, and upperparts, with a white shoulder patch. The female is similarly patterned to the male, but its upperparts and underparts are grey. It is much shyer than the bold male and seen much less often. The male has a melodious song, its musical notes often heard as it sings on a perch in the breeding season.

A pugnacious bird, the Oriental Magpie-Robin moves about singly or in loose pairs and defends its territory against intruders of the same species. Its feeds mainly on insects.

MALE ORIENTAL MAGPIE-ROBIN

MALE INDIAN ROBIN

Saxicoloides fulicatus

Indian Robin

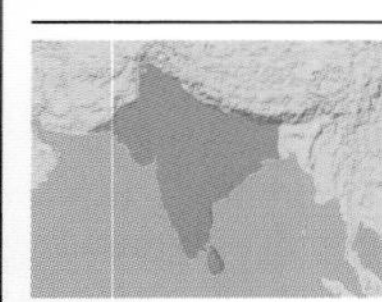

LENGTH 16cm (6½in)

WEIGHT 17g (5/8oz)

MIGRATION Non-migrant

HABITAT Dry scrubland

A common bird in the Indian subcontinent, the Indian Robin is frequently seen around villages and in fallow or waste ground in towns. The male is a shiny black and brown bird with a white patch on its wing and a chestnut rump, while the female is brownish grey. This robin tends to run along the ground in short spurts or fly short distances from one low bush to another. Sometimes, it perches on a rock or tree, where it cocks its long tail to reveal its chestnut rump. It mainly feeds on insects such as cockroaches and beetles.

ADULT MALE (EUROPEAN SUBSPECIES)

Phoenicurus ochruros

Black Redstart

LENGTH 14cm (5½in)

WEIGHT 17g (⅝oz)

MIGRATION Partial migrant

HABITAT Breeds in open montane habitats and towns and industrial areas; winters in coastal areas

The Black Redstart belongs to the genus *Phoenicurus*, all species of which have the characteristic rufous tail (the word "start" is an old English word for tail). They differ slightly from each other in their plumage patterns. There are a number of of subspecies of Black Redstart. However, in most European birds, the adult male Black Redstart is bluish grey on the crown, nape, and back. The sides of the face, forecrown, throat, and breast are black, fading to bluish grey on the belly, and the wings have a white patch. The female is a uniform dusky brownish grey, but also has the rufous redstart tail. Like most of its relatives, the Black Redstart usually perches upright and frequently vibrates or "shivers" its tail.

HUMAN IMPACT

BREEDING IN URBAN AREAS IN EUROPE

Although cliffs and rocky mountainous areas comprise the natural breeding habitat of the Black Redstart, this bird has now taken to breeding in urban areas. In much of Europe, manmade constructions serve as nesting sites and the nests of Black Redstarts are now commonly seen on the rooftops of houses and in industrial complexes, the nest usually being placed in a niche or hole in the building.

Phoenicurus phoenicurus

Common Redstart

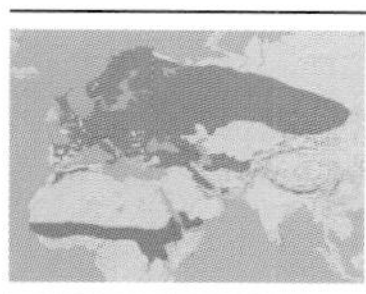

LENGTH 14cm (5½in)

WEIGHT 15g (9/16oz)

MIGRATION Migrant

HABITAT Breeds in woodland, forest, parks, and gardens; winters in open savanna and scrub

Superficially similar to the Black Redstart (left), the male Common Redstart is distinguishable by its white forecrown and orange breast. The female is browner overall, and unlike the male, lacks the bluish grey tones of the Black Redstart. The bill of the Common Redstart is short and slim, a general-purpose tool for preying on insects. The bird has several methods of foraging – it may glean insects from tree foliage or out of bark crevices. At times, it hunts for beetles and other small mammals on the ground or perches on a low lookout to pounce on prey below. Most often, however, it plucks winged insects in the air. It then returns and beats the insect against the perch to remove the wings before consuming it. The song of the Common Redstart is a brief musical warble ending in a trill.

MALE COMMON REDSTART

ADULT WHITE-CAPPED REDSTART

Chaimarrornis leucocephalus

White-capped Redstart

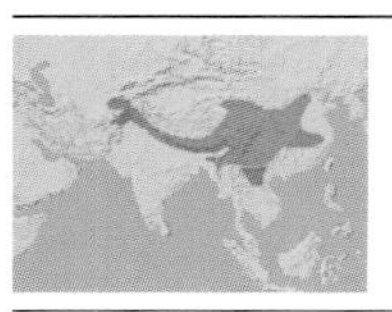

LENGTH 19cm (7½in)

WEIGHT 20g (11/16oz)

MIGRATION Partial migrant

HABITAT Mountains, near streams and rivers

Also known as the River Chat, this colourful bird is well-known to all those familiar with the mountains of Central Asia, the Himalayas, and northeast China. It has a white crown, black back, wings, and breast with rufous underparts and a black-tipped rufous tail. It sallies forth from its perch to twist and turn, chasing after an insect borne along by the swirling air currents above streams and rivers.

Myiomela leucura

White-tailed Robin

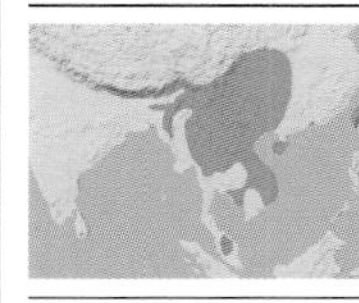

LENGTH 17cm (6½in)

WEIGHT 20g (11/16oz)

MIGRATION Non-migrant

HABITAT Damp gullies, ravines, and undergrowth in montane, broad-leaved evergreen forest

The White-tailed Robin is a shy and secretive denizen of undergrowth in damp ravines and gullies, often near water. The male is blue-black in colour, the blue of the forehead and shoulder patches being clearly visible in bright sunlight. Its eyes and bill are also black. The white in the tail, which gives the bird its name, only becomes apparent when the bird spreads its long, broad, black tail, perhaps to display the fan to a female or to startle an insect into movement. The female has the same tail pattern as the male, but is brown, with a thin white band across the throat and a brown breast-band.

Found singly or in pairs, the White-tailed Robin forages on the ground, feeding on insects and berries, and flies up into trees if disturbed. Its calls are a low, quiet "tuk" and a thin whistle, while its song is an undulating and rapid series of notes.

ADULT WHITE-TAILED ROBIN

ADULT MALE

Enicurus leschenaulti

White-crowned Forktail

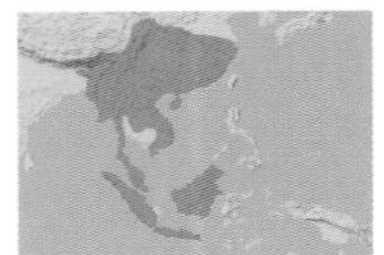

LENGTH 25–28cm (10–11in)

WEIGHT 35g (1¼oz)

MIGRATION Non-migrant

HABITAT Near fast-flowing rivers and streams

This elegant bird has a black mantle and breast and its tail is banded black and white. It has pink legs and a black bill. The White-crowned Forktail feeds along rivers and streams, searching for insects and larvae. It nests in crevices or hollows in trees and rocks. Its nest is built of moss and leaves and both the male and the female incubate the eggs.

MALE EURASIAN STONECHAT

Saxicola torquatus

Eurasian Stonechat

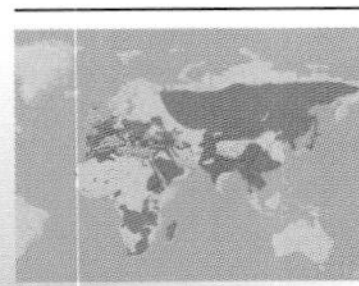

LENGTH 13cm (5in)

WEIGHT 11–15g (3/8–9/16oz)

MIGRATION Partial migrant

HABITAT Open, often barren habitats, such as heathland and mountain

Also known as the Common Stonechat, the Eurasian Stonechat is found from Ireland to Japan and Siberia to South Africa. Within this huge range, there are many distinctive subspecies, some of which are often treated as separate species. The male and female are quite distinct in appearance: the male has a dark hood, generally a rufous front, a dark brown back, and varying amounts of white on the wings and collar, while the female has fewer white markings and a browner head. Pairs are often seen together, prominently perched on bushes and other lookouts.

Some European populations (such as those in Britain) are largely sedentary, but many birds move south for the winter, particularly to North Africa. Many Asian populations also tend to move long distances, while southern African ones tend to be non-migratory.

Saxicola caprata

Pied Bush Chat

LENGTH 14cm (5½in)

WEIGHT 15g (9/16oz)

MIGRATION Partial migrant

HABITAT Open terrain such as scrub, grassland, and steppes

Mainly black, apart from the white wing-bar, rump, and undertail, the male Pied Bush Chat is a striking bird. The female is much plainer and browner. The species feeds in a typical chat fashion, flying down to the ground to take insects spotted from a vantage point. In the west of its range, it is largely migratory, with eastern birds tending to be mainly resident.

MALE PIED BUSH CHAT

Oenanthe leucura

Black Wheatear

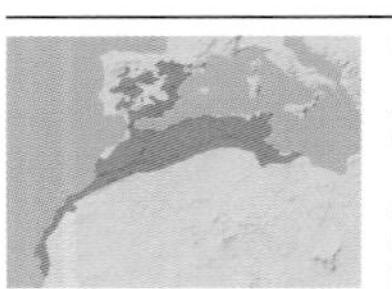

LENGTH 18cm (7in)

WEIGHT 40g (17/16oz)

MIGRATION Partial migrant

HABITAT Steep rocky hillsides, cliffs, ravines, and ruins

ADULT BLACK WHEATEAR

An upland bird, the Black Wheatear has taken its love of rocks to extremes. The male often fetches and arranges large numbers of pebbles near the entrance to its nest as a demonstration to the female of its suitability as a mate. At one nest, more than 9,000 stones were counted, including one weighing more than half the bird's own weight. Unlike other wheatears, the male and female are similar in appearance, but the male is glossier, while the female is duller and browner.

Oenanthe oenanthe

Northern Wheatear

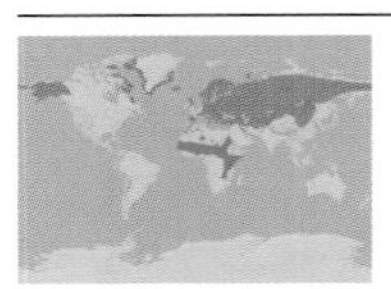

LENGTH 15cm (6in)

WEIGHT 20–30g (11/16–11/16oz)

MIGRATION Migrant

HABITAT Breeds in open ground, including heathland and rocky hillsides; winters in a range of habitats

ADULT NORTHERN WHEATEAR

Recognizable by its white rump and the black inverted T-pattern on its tail, the Northern Wheatear is a remarkable species, being one of the most northerly occurring songbirds and one of the world's great migrants. It breeds in inhospitable places such as Greenland, Alaska, and northern Siberia, before moving south to spend the winter in sub-Saharan Africa.

Monticola saxatilis

Rufous-tailed Rock Thrush

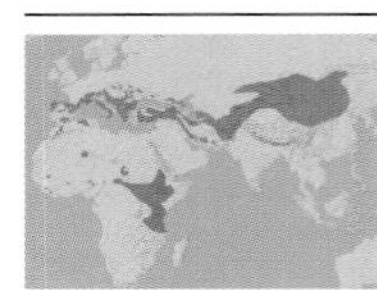

LENGTH 16–19cm (6½–7½in)

WEIGHT 50g (1¾oz)

MIGRATION Migrant

HABITAT Breeds on rocky slopes and hillsides; occurs more widely in winter, usually in wooded savanna

The male Rufous-tailed Rock Thrush has a combination of blue-grey upperparts (with a white patch on the back) and orange underparts, while the female is brown and has a scaled appearance. The species breeds in southern Europe and eastern China, with most birds migrating to sub-Saharan Africa for the winter.

MALE RUFOUS-TAILED ROCK THRUSH

Muscicapa striata

Spotted Flycatcher

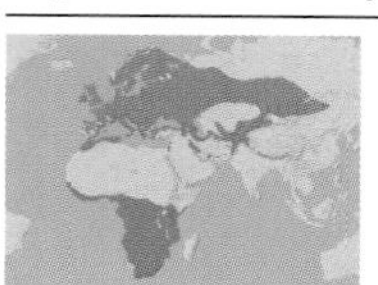

LENGTH 70–90cm (28–35in)

WEIGHT 16g ($^{9}/_{16}$oz)

MIGRATION Migrant

HABITAT Deciduous woodland, parks, and gardens

ADULT SPOTTED FLYCATCHER

An elegant, but rather plain bird, the Spotted Flycatcher has a subtly streaked head, a brown back, with a noticeable pale wing-bar, and creamy white underparts. It might be more appropriately named "Streaked Flycatcher", since the markings on its breast are vertical streaks rather than spots. Its tail is long and points downwards. The species is the most common and widespread flycatcher throughout Europe.

Ficedula hypoleuca

European Pied Flycatcher

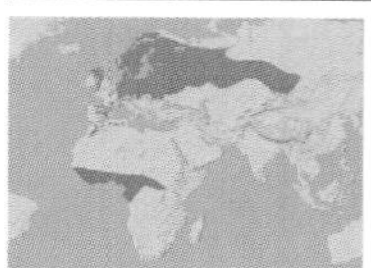

LENGTH 13cm (5in)

WEIGHT 12–15g ($^{7}/_{16}$–$^{9}/_{16}$oz)

MIGRATION Migrant

HABITAT Mainly deciduous woodland, parks, and gardens

The plumage of the male European Pied Flycatcher is a striking combination of black and white; it is black above and white below, with small white spots above the bill and a large white wing-bar. The female is plainer and browner, but also has a distinct white wing-bar that distinguishes it from the Spotted Flycatcher (left). The female makes a loose nest of moss, roots, and strips of bark, lined with feathers. It lays about 1–11 pale blue eggs with red speckles. Like other flycatchers, the species performs a circular sally for insects from its perch, its bill clicking as it snaps shut on its prey. A long-distance migrant, it winters south of the Sahara in West Africa.

MALE EUROPEAN PIED FLYCATCHER

NESTING

A hole-nesting species, the European Pied Flycatcher likes tree-holes made by woodpeckers or crevices that are created when rotten branches fall away from the trunk. It often takes over abandoned Willow-Tit nest sites, particularly in Scandinavia, probably because they are just the right size. Nest boxes, however, are increasingly favoured, even over natural sites.

FEMALE BRINGING FOOD
This female European Pied Flycatcher is feeding its young, which are safely ensconced in a nest inside an old woodpecker hole.

Ficedula parva

Red-breasted Flycatcher

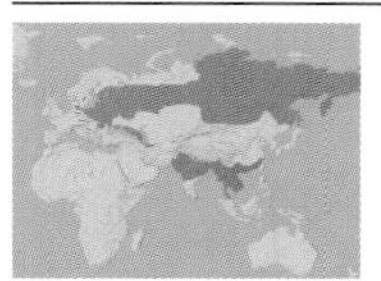

LENGTH 11cm (4$^{1}/_{2}$in)

WEIGHT 10g ($^{3}/_{8}$oz)

MIGRATION Migrant

HABITAT Mainly deciduous woodland; breeds in tall deciduous or mixed forest

MALE RED-BREASTED FLYCATCHER

The Red-breasted Flycatcher is the smallest flycatcher found in Europe. It frequently pumps and spreads its tail to reveal a distinct pattern of bold white patches that contrast with the dark centre and tip. Only the mature adult male has a striking red throat; the female and juvenile have pale underparts. A very mobile species, it flits around tree canopies.

Cyanoptila cyanomelana

Blue-and-white Flycatcher

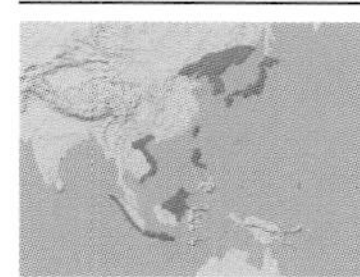

LENGTH 17cm (6$^{1}/_{2}$in)

WEIGHT 25g ($^{7}/_{8}$oz)

MIGRATION Migrant

HABITAT Deciduous and mixed forests, near streams

Glossy blue upperparts and a black face and breast, which contrast spectacularly with its bright white underparts, make up the distinctive plumage of the male Blue-and-white Flycatcher. The female is mainly brown, with a white throat and belly and a distinct pale eye-ring.

The call of the Blue-and-white Flycatcher is a melodious warble.

ADULT MALE

Niltava sundara

Rufous-bellied Niltava

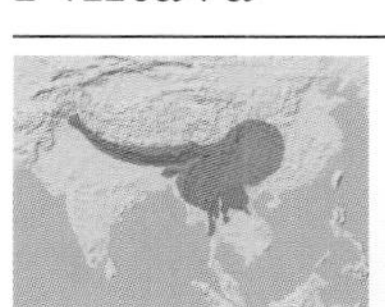

LENGTH 18cm (7in)

WEIGHT 20g ($^{11}/_{16}$oz)

MIGRATION Partial migrant

HABITAT Deciduous or mixed forest

The Rufous-bellied Niltava is also known as the Beautiful Niltava, in recognition of the stunning bright orange underparts and dark blue upperparts of the male, which are topped by a brilliant pale blue cap. It has a black throat with a tinge of blue. The female is drab and brown with a small blue patch on the side of the neck that is often difficult to see, while the juvenile has brown upperparts with buff spots and buff-brown underparts.

MALE RUFOUS-BELLIED NILTAVA

The Rufous-bellied Niltava hunts for insects, such as ants and beetles, in low scrub and forest undergrowth. Largely resident from the Himalayas to southwest China, the species also breeds in the Himalayas and can be found at altitudes of 1,800–2,300m (6,000–7,000ft). Its nest is usually built close to the ground. Its call is a sharp "psi psi".

NORTHERN WHEATEARS
Northern Wheatears arrive in northern Europe (these birds were photographed in Finland) in summer, having spent the winter in Africa.

DIPPERS

ORDER	Passeriformes
FAMILY	Cinclidae
SPECIES	5

THE FIVE SPECIES OF dipper have a wide, but patchy, global distribution, being found in much of Europe and Asia, some western areas of North and South America, and small areas of North Africa and the Middle East. They are medium-sized, stocky birds, with short, cocked tails and mainly dark plumage. All dippers are highly adapted for life in and near fast-flowing water.

BEHAVIOUR

Birds of this family spend their entire lives around clear, fast-flowing rivers and streams. They dive under the water and swim around in search of invertebrate prey such as larvae and insect nymphs that can be found among the rocks and stones. Dippers have many special adaptations to this lifestyle. Their squat shape and short, powerful wings are ideally suited to swimming, and they have a dense covering of well-oiled and waterproof feathers.

DIPPER DIVING
A White-throated Dipper swims along a riverbed looking for insects and larvae among the rocks and stones.

Cinclus mexicanus

American Dipper

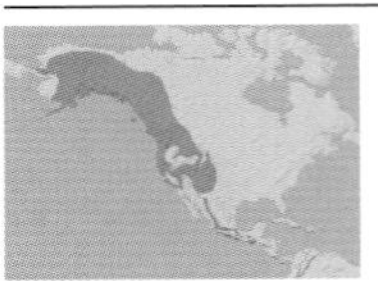

LENGTH	19cm (7½in)
WEIGHT	55–60g (2–2⅛oz)
MIGRATION	Non-migrant

HABITAT Rocky streams in mountainous areas

Closely resembling its European counterpart, the White-throated Dipper (right) in behaviour, the American Dipper differs in its plumage, which is a uniform grey. It has a straight black bill and pink legs. It feeds on aquatic insects and their larvae, and may also take tiny fish. Between feeding bouts, it can be seen perching on rocks, bobbing its whole body up and down. Its nest, built by the female, is a large ball with a side entrance, often situated behind a waterfall or under a bridge.

ADULT AMERICAN DIPPER

ADULT FEEDING ON AN INSECT

Cinclus cinclus

White-throated Dipper

LENGTH	19–21cm (7½–8½in)
WEIGHT	55–65g (2–2⅜oz)
MIGRATION	Partial migrant

HABITAT Rivers and streams in or near woodland or forest, from sea-level to high mountain areas

Like other dippers, this plump, short-tailed bird is equipped with an extra eyelid called a nictitating membrane, which allows it to see under water, and scales that close its nostrils when it is submerged. The adult White-throated Dipper is dark brown and slate-grey, with a white throat and breast. The juvenile is a more uniform grey, apart from pale feather tips.

LEAFBIRDS

ORDER	Passeriformes
FAMILY	Chloropseidae
SPECIES	8

LEAFBIRDS ARE FOUND only in south and southeast Asia. They get their name from their predominantly green "leaf-coloured" plumage. They are quite delicate birds with a rather upright stance. In the majority of leafbird species the male has a dark face and throat. Females and juveniles are usually a uniform green in coloration.

BRUSH-SHAPED TONGUE
The tongue of this Golden-fronted Leafbird is a useful adaptation for feeding on nectar-rich flowers.

BEHAVIOUR

The bright green plumage that is shared by the various leafbirds affords them excellent camouflage as they move through the leafy canopy of the forest. Leafbirds feed on a variety of foods including insects, nectar, and fruit. Smaller fruits are swallowed whole, but larger ones are speared on the lower mandible of the bill and then rotated to loosen the contents and fluid into the throat.

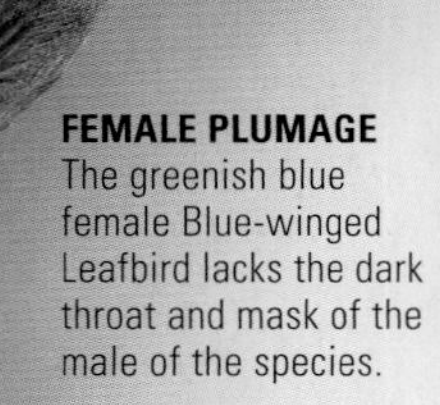

FEMALE PLUMAGE
The greenish blue female Blue-winged Leafbird lacks the dark throat and mask of the male of the species.

Chloropsis aurifrons

Golden-fronted Leafbird

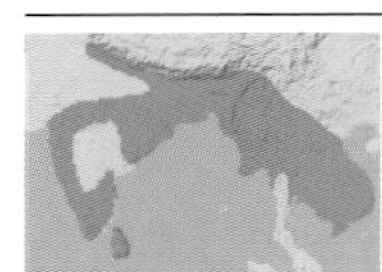

LENGTH	18cm (7in)
WEIGHT	30–35g (1$^{1}/_{16}$–1¼oz)
MIGRATION	Non-migrant

HABITAT Canopy of deciduous, broad-leaved, evergreen and mixed forests, and secondary growth

Predominantly green in colour, both sexes of the Golden-fronted Leafbird are alike, with a purple-blue throat encircled by black, and a pronounced orange forehead. This leafbird can be found searching for insects and fruit in pairs or small groups and often joins mixed-species feeding flocks. It builds a simple cup-shaped nest in a tree, and lays 2 or 3 cream to buff eggs with pale red markings. The male and the female take turns in incubating the eggs until they are hatched, which is usually after two weeks of incubation.

ADULT GOLDEN-FRONTED LEAFBIRD

FLOWERPECKERS

ORDER	Passeriformes
FAMILY	Dicaeidae
SPECIES	44

FLOWERPECKERS OCCUR mainly in Asia, from India to the Philippines. One species, the Mistletoebird, occurs in Australia. The rarest member of the family is the Cebu Flowerpecker, a critically endangered black, white and red species that is found only on the island of Cebu in the Philippines, and numbers only around 100 individuals. Birds of this family are generally brightly coloured, although some (such as the aptly named Plain Flowerpecker) are rather dull in appearance. Males and females usually have similar plumage.

ANATOMY

Although these small, and short-tailed birds feed on berries and insects, nectar from flowers forms an important part of the diet in many species, hence the family name. This dietary preference is aided by the short, fine bill, which can easily probe inside flowers, and the split, tubular-shaped tongue. The design of the tongue of this family of birds is invaluable when feeding on nectar by helping to channel the sticky fluid into the bird's throat. The sharp bill is also an effective tool for piercing fruit, allowing the bird to extract the sweet juices.

CONTRASTING COLOURS
The male Crimson-breasted Flowerpecker has yellow underparts and a contrasting scarlet breast patch.

Dicaeum percussus

Crimson-breasted Flowerpecker

LENGTH 10cm (4in)

WEIGHT 9g ($^{11}/_{32}$oz)

MIGRATION Non-migrant

HABITAT Canopy of broad-leaved evergreen forest, forest edges, forest gaps, up to 1,200m (4,000ft)

With its dark blue and yellow plumage, and bright red crown and breast patches, the Crimson-breasted Flowerpecker is one of the most striking southeast Asian flowerpeckers. The female is greenish olive above, with a fainter red crown patch, and duller below, without the red breast patch. This flowerpecker is mostly seen feeding on small fruit in the canopy, giving high-pitched chipping calls. The nest is oval and is suspended from the twigs of a tree branch.

ADULT MALE

Dicaeum hirundinaceum

Mistletoebird

LENGTH 10cm (4in)

WEIGHT 9g ($^{11}/_{32}$oz)

MIGRATION Non-migrant

HABITAT Various types of forest and woodland and other vegetation supporting mistletoe

The Mistletoebird is the only species of flowerpecker in Australia. The male is blue-black with a red throat, upper breast, and vent, and shows a vertical black stripe on the centre of its pale grey abdomen. Very different from the male, the female Mistletoebird is mostly grey, with a contrasting orange vent and a white instead of red throat. It is a restless bird that moves quickly about the tree-tops, uttering its sharp "dzee" call-note.

The nest is a pear-shaped purse with a slit-like entrance on one side, and is suspended from leafy twigs. It is constructed solely by the female; 3 or 4 white eggs are laid and the female incubates them alone for about two weeks. However, both parents feed the young for a further two weeks.

MALE MISTLETOEBIRD

FEEDING HABITS

As the common name suggests, the Mistletoebird eats a variety of mistletoe-like berries. The seeds pass through its tiny body quickly and fall off in sticky droppings that are wiped onto the branches of trees. The seeds then germinate and form new mistletoe plants.

FEMALE EATING BERRY
Adapted to a diet of mistletoe berries, the species lacks a muscular gizzard (food-grinding organ), allowing whole seeds to come out in droppings.

SUNBIRDS

ORDER	Passeriformes
FAMILY	Nectariniidae
SPECIES	127

FOUND IN FORESTS and gardens in Africa, southern and southeast Asia, and northernmost Australia, sunbirds are the Old World equivalent of hummingbirds in the New World, but evolved entirely separately from them. Like hummingbirds, these are small, fast-moving birds with long, decurved bills and long tongues suited to feeding on flower nectar, spiders, and insects. The spiderhunters have much longer bills for picking prey from spiders' webs. Most male sunbirds are brightly coloured, often with iridescent areas of plumage on the head, throat, and back, whereas the females are typically dull green, brown, or grey.

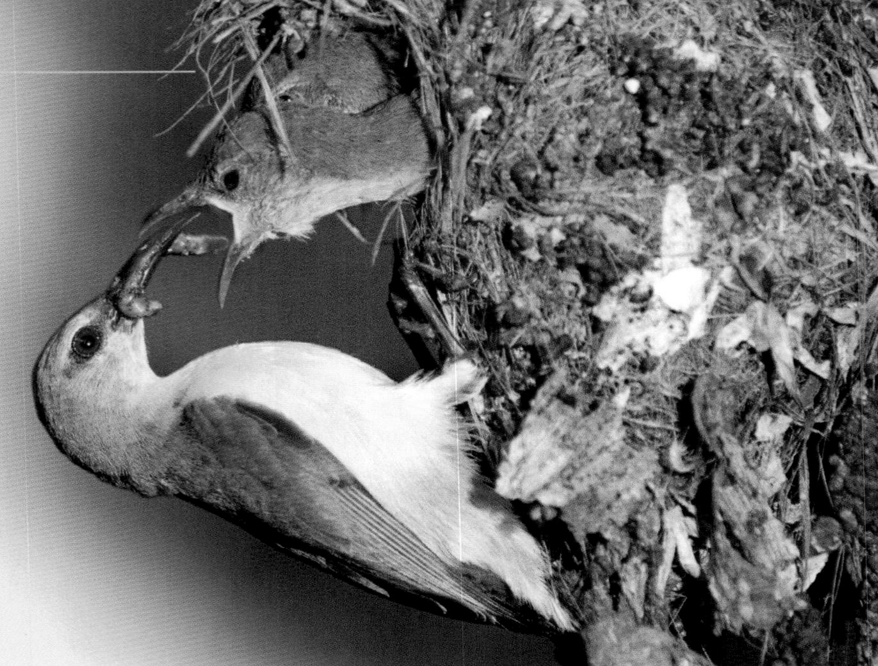

PROTEIN-RICH DIET
A Purple-rumped Sunbird gives a caterpillar to its chicks. Sunbirds feed their nestlings entirely on invertebrates.

MALE PYGMY SUNBIRD

Hedydipna platura

Pygmy Sunbird

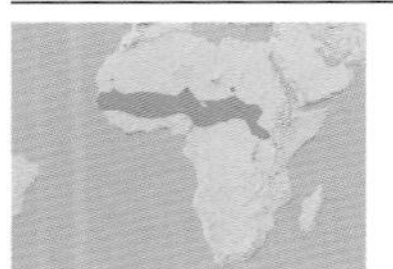

LENGTH 9–17cm ($3^1/_2$–$6^1/_2$)
WEIGHT 7g ($^1/_4$oz)
MIGRATION Non-migrant

HABITAT Arid savanna, riverine scrub, and gardens

Although a very small bird, the Pygmy Sunbird is noticeable because of its extremely long tail streamers, which are up to 7cm (3in) long. The male's plumage is two-toned, with a green throat and upperparts and golden-yellow underparts, while the female has drabber plumage, with grey-brown upperparts and yellow underparts. It also has a faint yellow eyebrow.

Leptocoma zeylonica

Purple-rumped Sunbird

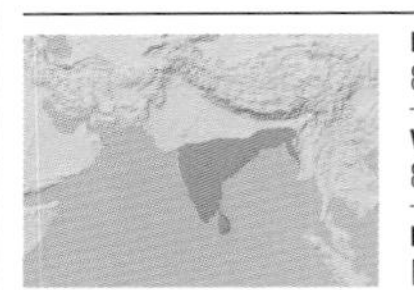

LENGTH 8cm ($3^1/_4$in)
WEIGHT 8g ($^5/_{16}$oz)
MIGRATION Non-migrant

HABITAT Open deciduous woodland, secondary woodland and well-wooded cultivation, and gardens

The distinguishing features of this medium-sized sunbird include the pale yellow underparts and white flanks and undertail feathers, which are shown by both sexes. The male Purple-rumped Sunbird has bright iridescent feathering in its plumage. It is dark maroon above, with a thin maroon breast-band. The crown is glossy blue-green as is the bend in the wing and it has violet patches on the throat and rump. The female is dull brown above, and has a white throat, which contrasts strongly with the yellow underparts. These birds feed on insects and fruit and are considered pests in grape-growing regions. They are usually encountered in pairs and breed during the wet season or monsoon.

MALE PURPLE-RUMPED SUNBIRD

Chalcomitra balfouri

Socotra Sunbird

LENGTH 15cm (6in)
WEIGHT 15 ($^9/_{16}$oz)
MIGRATION Non-migrant

HABITAT Arid wooded hillsides

Named after the small island of Socotra off the Horn of Africa, to which it is endemic, the Socotra Sunbird is a large, drab-coloured sunbird. This sunbird has red eyes and a black chin. Its breast is barred in black and it has grey-brown, streaked upperparts and white underparts. Both sexes are similar, except for the yellow tufts on the male's chest, which remain hidden under the wings unless the bird is displaying. Although much of its primary habitat on Socotra has been drastically modified by clearance and over-grazing, this species appears to be faring well and is not currently considered to be threatened.

ADULT SOCOTRA SUNBIRD

Nectarinia kilimensis

Bronzy Sunbird

LENGTH 12–22cm (4½–8½in)

WEIGHT 14–17g (½–⅝oz)

MIGRATION Non-migrant

HABITAT Upland grassland, heaths, forest edges, clearings, and gardens

FEMALE BRONZY SUNBIRD

A familiar upland bird throughout its range, the Bronzy Sunbird is frequently seen feeding in gardens. The male is largely black, with a gold, bronze, and green sheen on the head, throat, and mantle. The female is brown-green above, with a dark mask and pale eyebrow and throat. The underparts are yellow, with brown streaks. Feeding largely on nectar, the Bronzy Sunbird favours tubular flowers, such as the red-hot poker, but also frequents sugar-water feeders.

MALE MALACHITE SUNBIRD

Nectarinia famosa

Malachite Sunbird

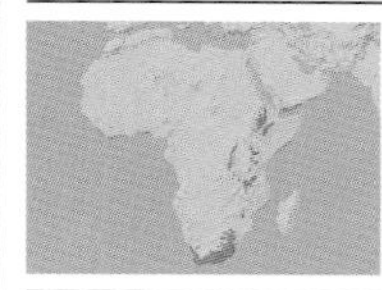

LENGTH 15–24cm (6–9in)

WEIGHT 14–18g (½–⅝oz)

MIGRATION Non-migrant

HABITAT Upland grassland, scrub, and forest edges; lower in cool, wet months

The Malachite Sunbird is a large, long-tailed mountain species. The breeding male is bright emerald green, with darker flight feathers and elongated central tail feathers. It has bright yellow breast tufts but these are usually hidden, except during display. Like the Bronzy Sunbird (left), this species favours plants with tubular flowers.

Cinnyris jugularis

Olive-backed Sunbird

LENGTH 12cm (4½in)

WEIGHT 8–10g (5/16–3/8oz)

MIGRATION Non-migrant

HABITAT Lowland open deciduous woodland, mangroves, coastal scrub, and cultivated land

Named for the olive upperparts, other features of the male Olive-backed Sunbird include yellow underparts. The male also has metallic blue coloration on its forehead, throat, and upper breast. The female lacks the blue coloration, which is replaced by yellow. This sunbird mainly feeds on nectar, extracting it from flowers with its long, slender, decurved bill and deeply cleft tongue.

MALE OLIVE-BACKED SUNBIRD

ADULT MALE (A.G. ISOLATA)

Aethopyga gouldiae

Mrs Gould's Sunbird

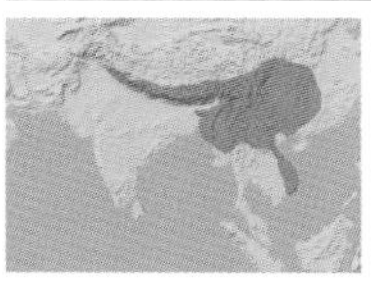

LENGTH 11–17cm (4½–6½in)

WEIGHT 5–7g (3/16–1/4oz)

MIGRATION Non-migrant

HABITAT Mid-montane broad-leaved evergreen forest, forest edges, and secondary growth

This shy species shows marked variations across its large range. The male (shown here) is of the subspecies *A. g. isolata*, found in northeast India, Bangladesh, and Myanmar (Burma). It differs from the other three subspecies in its very narrow red breast-band and violet-blue, instead of glossy blue, tail streamers. Otherwise, the males are similar, with small patches of violet on the crown, throat, and cheeks, rich red upperparts, and bright, iridescent rumps and tails. Largely insectivorous, this species also feeds on parasitic plants.

Aethopyga siparaja

Crimson Sunbird

LENGTH 10–12cm (4–4½in)

WEIGHT 6–8g (7/32–5/16oz)

MIGRATION Non-migrant

HABITAT Open wooded areas, secondary growth, groves, mangroves, and gardens

The male Crimson Sunbird often, like the bird shown here, has a metallic blue cap and moustache stripe, an unstreaked red throat and breast, dark red upperparts, a large yellow rump patch, and a uniform olive belly and vent. However, marked variations exist across this sunbird's huge range. The female has a uniform olive plumage. Both the male and female have slender and decurved bills.

The Crimson Sunbird's diet is a mixture of invertebrates and nectar – it seems to prefer feeding at red flowers. Like many insectivorous birds, it has been recorded piercing flowers to get directly at the nectar, instead of entering from the front, thereby assisting pollination. It forages in pairs or small family groups, frequenting lower levels of vegetation. The nest is a finely woven hooded grass pocket hanging from exposed roots on a bank and two eggs are laid.

ADULT MALE

Cinnyris asiatica

Purple Sunbird

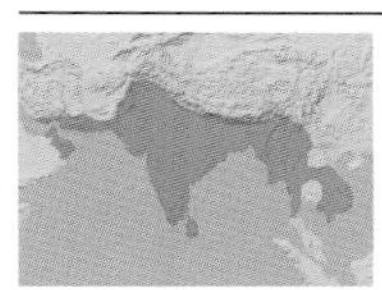

LENGTH 7–9cm (2¾–3½in)

WEIGHT 9g (11/32oz)

MIGRATION Non-migrant

HABITAT Dry deciduous forest and woodland, scrub, and gardens

The male Purple Sunbird in breeding plumage (as shown here) is very dark, with a metallic purple head, mantle, and breast. It mostly feeds singly, or in pairs, on nectar and fruit, and is often found in the vicinity of flowering trees and clumps of mistletoe. It perches to feed, but also hovers at flowers. These birds also congregate in large numbers at flying insect swarms to feed on them.

BREEDING MALE

SUGARBIRDS

ORDER	Passeriformes
FAMILY	Promeropidae
SPECIES	2

SUGARBIRDS ARE FOUND only in South Africa. They have been classified with such diverse families as honeyeaters (see p.362), starlings (see p.430) and thrushes (see p.436), but recent DNA evidence suggests they are most closely related to the sunbirds (see p.450). The habits of sugarbirds are closely tied to the various species of the African shrubs of the genus *Protea* since their main food is the nectar found in the flowers.

ANATOMY

There is little difference in coloration between male and female sugarbirds but the sexes are easily distinguished by the much longer tails of the males. The length of tail alone of a male Cape Sugarbird can be greater than the entire length of a female of the same species. When feeding, the sugarbird often faces into the wind so that the breeze does not blow around its long tail. The male displays his tail prominently in courtship flights, jerking it rapidly up and down until the long feathers whip above and below the bird's body.

CAPE SUGARBIRD
Sugarbirds time their nesting to coincide with the peak flowering season of their favourite flowers.

Promerops cafer

Cape Sugarbird

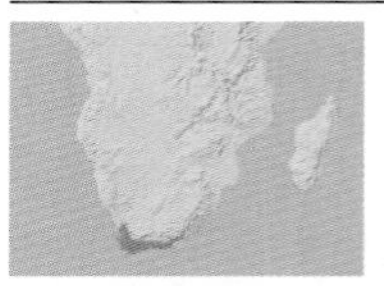

LENGTH 28–43cm (11–17in)

WEIGHT 35g (1¼oz)

MIGRATION Non-migrant

HABITAT Fynbos shrubland, gardens, and plantations

Its extraordinarily long tail distinguishes the male Cape Sugarbird from other birds, except the closely related, and shorter-tailed, Gurney's Sugarbird (*P. gurneyi*). The male Cape Sugarbird has a brown head and back and a brown stripe on the white throat. It has a yellow vent and the long tail is dark brown. The female has a white breast and shorter tail. Researchers have found that the longest-tailed males are most attractive to females and that females that mate with the longest-tailed males lay the most eggs. The Cape Sugarbird feeds on flowers but also eats spiders, beetles, and flying insects.

FEMALE CAPE SUGARBIRD

IMPORTANT POLLINATOR

With its long curved bill and even longer brush-tipped tongue, the Cape Sugarbird is perfectly adapted to extracting nectar from the tube-shaped florets that make up the flowers of *Protea* ("sugarbush") shrubs. As they move from plant to plant, they transfer pollen from the flowers.

OLD WORLD SPARROWS AND SNOWFINCHES

ORDER	Passeriformes
FAMILY	Passeridae
SPECIES	40

THESE ARE BIRDS OF OPEN country, including savanna, semi-desert, grassland, and farmland. The family was originally confined to Eurasia and Africa, but House and Tree Sparrows have been introduced to every continent except Antarctica. With their short, strong conical beaks, they are adapted to a diet of seeds; several species have extended their ranges following human cultivation of cereal crops. Sparrows feed and roost in large flocks, and nest in colonies.

SNOWFINCHES FEEDING
These White-winged Snowfinches feed on insects and seeds, including pine nuts. This alpine species is often found around mountain villages and ski resorts.

Philetairus socius

Sociable Weaver

LENGTH 14cm (5½in)

WEIGHT 25g (⅞oz)

MIGRATION Non-migrant

HABITAT Open savanna and grassland, with large trees for nesting

The Sociable Weaver has a brown body, black face mask, a patterned back and wings, and black speckled sides. It forages in groups for seeds and insects. Up to 500 birds may be involved in building the huge haystack-like nests, some of which have been in use for over 100 years. These nests maintain a constant temperature, even when night-time temperatures outside drop to freezing. This thermal efficiency cuts food needs and, in arid regions, water consumption. Living up to its name, the Sociable Weaver often plays host to other small birds.

ADULT SOCIABLE WEAVER

Passer moabiticus

Dead Sea Sparrow

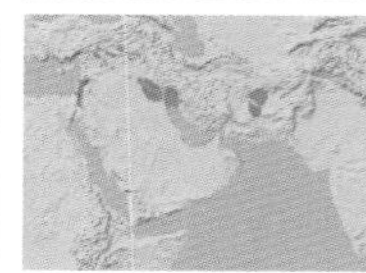

LENGTH 12cm (4½in)

WEIGHT 15g (9/16oz)

MIGRATION Partial migrant

HABITAT Scrub, especially with tamarisk, usually near water; also cultivated land

The smallest and most colourful of the *Passer* genus, the Dead Sea Sparrow has extended its range in recent decades. The male has a grey crown, cheeks, neck, and back and a small black bib. Its upperparts are reddish brown, with dark streaks, and the underparts are grey-white. The female is like a House Sparrow (opposite), but has a smaller bill and paler plumage. Like other sparrows, this sparrow is mainly a seed-eater, and also takes insects, particularly when breeding.

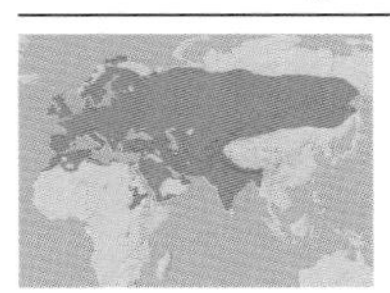

Passer domesticus

House Sparrow

LENGTH 15cm (6in)

WEIGHT 30g ($1^1/_{16}$oz)

MIGRATION Non-migrant

HABITAT Wide variety of habitats; tolerates extremes of climate and altitude

MALE HOUSE SPARROW

The House Sparrow has followed human settlement around much of the world and has been introduced in the Americas and Australia. Grain and food scraps supplement or even replace its natural diet of grass and weed seeds, and it readily adapts to nesting in holes in buildings and nest boxes instead of cavities in trees and rocks. Sturdy and aggressive, it can evict other hole-nesting species. It has one of the shortest incubation periods of any bird, and can produce 3–4 broods, each of up to seven young, in a season. The male House Sparrow is rufous-brown at the back of the head, with a grey crown. A black bib extends over the chest and the underparts are grey. The female is browner overall with a pale stripe behind each eye.

While it has become a major agricultural pest in the USA, eating and spoiling grain and animal feed, the House Sparrow has declined sharply in much of western Europe. Although intensive farming has reduced its winter feeding opportunities, the reason for its sudden decline in Europe is not yet known.

ADULT EURASIAN TREE SPARROW

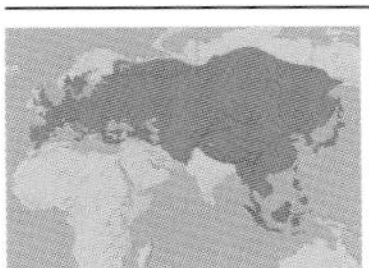

Passer montanus

Eurasian Tree Sparrow

LENGTH 14cm ($5^1/_2$in)

WEIGHT 25g ($^7/_8$oz)

MIGRATION Partial migrant

HABITAT Farmland and woodland in open country with scattered trees

Outside the breeding season, the Eurasian Tree Sparrow mixes with the House Sparrow (above) in foraging flocks on farmland. It is easily told apart as it is more slender and "neater" in appearance, with a chestnut cap, characteristic black cheek patches on a white face, dark streaks on the back, and a plain brown tail. The male and the female are similar.

The Eurasian Tree Sparrow nests colonially in holes in trees, cliff faces, and old buildings, and sometimes among twigs forming the nests of larger birds like crows and herons. The rounded nest is made of straw and grass. Introduced by settlers to the USA, it has also extended its range to northern Europe, the Mediterranean islands, and new areas in the Middle East. However, its numbers are declining in western Europe.

Petronia petronia

Rock Sparrow

LENGTH 14cm ($5^1/_2$in)

WEIGHT 30g ($1^1/_{16}$oz)

MIGRATION Partial migrant

HABITAT Rocky hills and mountains and the fringes of deserts; on farmland in winter

The Rock Sparrow is similar in size to a House Sparrow (above), but with a longer, more stout bill and larger head. Its face and crown have lined markings. It is also a more powerful flier, with wings that are strikingly longer than the House Sparrow's. It subsists on grass and weed seeds, supplemented by berries in the autumn and insects in spring, and while breeding. The young are fed on insects. Many sparrow species are promiscuous, with both sexes mating outside the pair. But the Rock Sparrow is polygynous, and the male mates with a second and even third female after the first has begun nesting. The female builds the nest by herself. These sparrows breed in scattered colonies, sometimes sharing suitable sites with House Sparrows and other hole-nesting species. The Rock Sparrow is often seen on the ground, where it runs as well as hops. Its call is nasal and repetitive.

ADULT PROVISIONING A NEST

Montifringilla nivalis

White-winged Snowfinch

LENGTH 17cm ($6^1/_2$in)

WEIGHT 30g ($1^1/_{16}$oz)

MIGRATION Non-migrant

HABITAT Mountains, in rocky and grassy areas between the tree line and the snow line

ADULT WHITE-WINGED SNOWFINCH

The highly variegated plumage of the White-winged Snowfinch is mainly grey-brown in colour. Its white wings are black-tipped and its tail is white with a narrow black centre. It is similar to the Snow Bunting (see p.475) but lives so high in the alpine regions of Europe and Asia that the two species are unlikely to be seen together.

The White-winged Snowfinch has been described as an alpine counterpart of the House Sparrow (above), because of its successful exploitation of human changes to its habitat. It is often found near mountain villages and ski resorts and readily takes food put out for it. It nests on rock faces, often alongside swifts, but also takes readily to the roof cavities of occupied buildings. After breeding, the birds form flocks that can number 100 or more.

WEAVERS

ORDER	Passeriformes
FAMILY	Ploceidae
SPECIES	108

WEAVERS OCCUR IN both open country and forests across sub-Saharan Africa, with a handful of species in Madagascar and southern Asia. They are related to the Old World sparrows (see p.452), waxbills (see p.458), and whydahs (see p.462), all of which were formerly placed in the same family.

ANATOMY

Most weavers are sparrow-like in size and shape. Their bills vary from small and thick in the seed-eating, open country species to more slender and pointed in the insectivorous, forest dwelling birds. Some show extreme sexual dimorphism with the breeding males brightly coloured while the females are a muted brown.

SEXUAL DIMORPHISM
The male Southern Red Bishop is a stunning crimson and black, while the female is a muted brown. Outside the breeding season, males resemble females.

BEHAVIOUR

True to their name, weavers build their nests by weaving together strips of plant material into elaborate, covered nests. After bridging the space between two supports, the bird will stand on this structure and weave the bowl of the nest. The entrance is a tunnel woven to the side or underneath. Some species of buffalo weaver build large communal nests with multiple nesting chambers in trees, while others nest singly. Weavers are often found in mixed species flocks with starlings and other weavers.

NEST BUILDING
Southern Masked Weavers build oval nests by weaving together strips of grass that they attach to vertical reeds, shrubs, or papyrus stalks. The floor of the nest is cushioned with plant down.

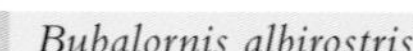

Bubalornis albirostris

White-billed Buffalo Weaver

LENGTH 23cm (9in)
WEIGHT 70g ($2^1/_2$oz)
MIGRATION Non-migrant

HABITAT Mainly dry savanna, but also on farmland or near villages

Its thick white bill gives the White-billed Buffalo Weaver its name. The undertail and rump feathers are black, with white flecks on the back and wings. The species is highly colonial and a nest structure can contain up to 10 separate chambers woven within it. Its main food is seeds, mostly cereals such as millets, but juveniles feed only on insects.

ADULT WHITE-BILLED BUFFALO WEAVER

ADULT SPECKLE-FRONTED WEAVER

Sporopipes frontalis

Speckle-fronted Weaver

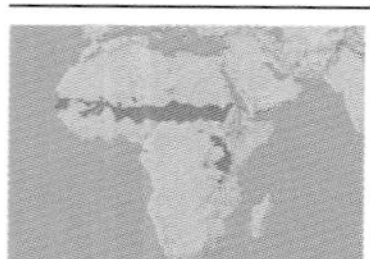

LENGTH 12cm ($4^3/_4$in)
WEIGHT 15–20g ($^9/_{16}$–$^{11}/_{16}$oz)
MIGRATION Non-migrant

HABITAT Dry bush and open thorn-scrub; also found around villages

The Speckle-fronted Weaver has a distinct orange-brown hood with a black forehead. The underparts are flat grey with brown variegated wings. The sexes are alike, although juveniles tend to be paler. This bird mainly feeds on seeds from the ground and insects. This is mostly a solitary nesting species although small colonies are also seen. The nest is an untidy ball-shaped structure with a long side entrance.

Dinemellia dinemelli

White-headed Buffalo Weaver

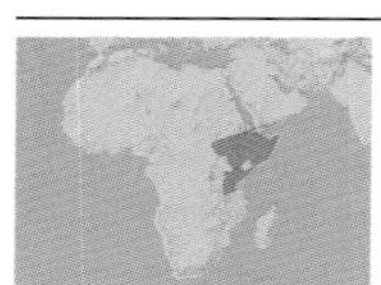

LENGTH 18cm (7in)
WEIGHT 60–80g ($2^1/_8$–$2^7/_8$oz)
MIGRATION Non-migrant

HABITAT Mainly dry bush and open acacia savanna

Although mostly white, the White-headed Buffalo Weaver has a contrasting black facial mask, wings, and tail. The undertail and rump feathers are orange or red in the male but often paler in the juvenile. The nesting behaviour of this species is complex, and co-operative breeding has been recorded in captive birds. The dome-shaped nest is built from grass and has a short entrance tube leading to an inner chamber. Both sexes build the nest – several different structures are built by a pair of birds or unoccupied nests of other weavers are used, with the species often nesting in groups within the same tree. The diet consists of insects, but seeds and berries are also eaten. Sometimes the birds form foraging flocks with other species.

ADULT WHITE-HEADED BUFFALO WEAVER

Ploceus capensis

Cape Weaver

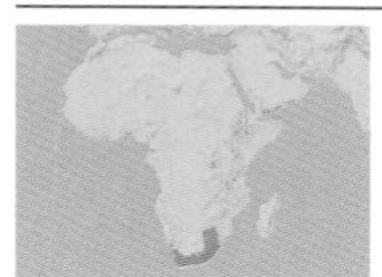

LENGTH 18cm (7in)

WEIGHT 35–55g ($1^1/_4$–2oz)

MIGRATION Non-migrant

HABITAT Open country with trees, mostly near water

The male Cape Weaver has dark-streaked wings, yellow underparts, an orange tinge to the face and white eyes. The female and the juvenile, however, have an olive-yellow head and breast, shading to pale yellow on the lower belly, and brown eyes. The bill of the Cape Weaver is long and conical, helping it to feed on a variety of seeds, grains, and insects.

The Cape Weaver is a colonial nesting bird, and up to seven females have been recorded breeding with a single male. The male is strongly territorial around the nest, despite the tendency of the species to build nests close to other birds. The nest is a kidney-shaped structure built from woven grass and reeds, with an entrance on the underside. The chamber is lined with finer grass and down, usually taken from neighbouring nests. The population of this species has increased in its range as a result of human activity, but the range has not expanded.

MALE CAPE WEAVER

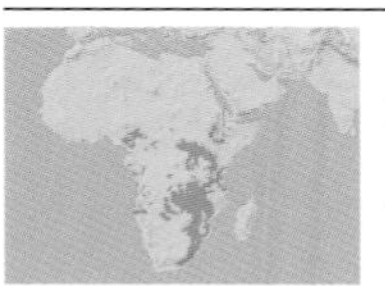

ADULT SPECTACLED WEAVER

Ploceus ocularis

Spectacled Weaver

LENGTH 16cm ($6^1/_2$in)

WEIGHT 25g ($^7/_8$oz)

MIGRATION Non-migrant

HABITAT Open woodland and forest margins, but also in more open areas and gardens

A mainly yellow bird, the Spectacled Weaver has a contrasting black bib and black eye-rings that give the species its common name. Its nest is built of woven grass and consists of a side chamber adjoining a long downward-facing entrance tube. Its food is mostly insects, but it has been known to take chicken feed on the ground and termites in flight.

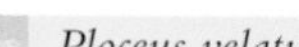

Ploceus velatus

Southern Masked Weaver

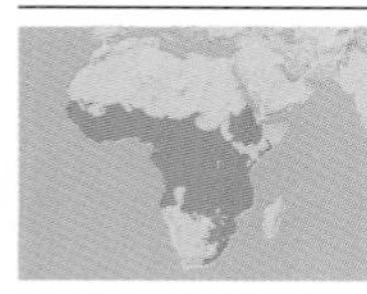

LENGTH 15–16cm (6–$6^1/_2$in)

WEIGHT 30–35g ($1^1/_{16}$–$1^1/_4$oz)

MIGRATION Non-migrant

HABITAT Dry savanna woodland and scrub with mature trees

The Southern Masked Weaver is a striking bird, with a sharply contrasting yellow and black face mask. The wings and back are also streaked black or dark green. The female has no face mask and has paler, olive-green plumage. The species is gregarious, often building clusters of nests at the ends of branches. The nest is a woven gourd-shaped structure, with the entrance on the underside, which makes it difficult for nest predators to reach.

ADULT MALE

Euplectes jacksoni

Jackson's Widowbird

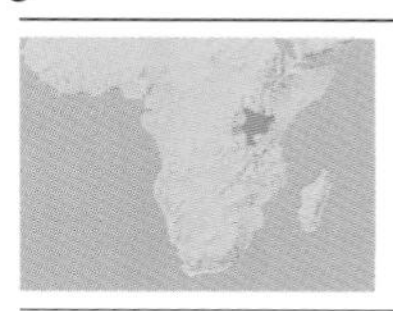

LENGTH 14–30cm ($5^1/_2$–12in)

WEIGHT 30–45g ($1^1/_{16}$–$1^5/_8$oz)

MIGRATION Non-migrant

HABITAT Open grassland, typically at an altitude of 1,500–3,000m (5,000–10,000ft)

During its courtship flight, the male Jackson's Widowbird raises and displays its decorative tail feathers. It also performs a display on the ground in which it jumps up in the air and then falls back again, rattling its wings and swaying. The male is territorial and will mate with several females. The spherical nest is built of woven grass, with a side entrance, close to the ground.

Quelea quelea

Red-billed Quelea

LENGTH 12cm ($4^3/_4$in)

WEIGHT 15–30g ($^9/_{16}$–$1^1/_{16}$oz)

MIGRATION Partial migrant

HABITAT Semi-arid zones but also wet and dry habitats on rare occasions

Named for its prominent and thick red bill, the Red-billed Quelea has a plumage that is mainly brown. The undersides are plain and the wings are variegated with a darker brown.

Its diet consists of insects and seeds, but it is also considered an agriculture pest. The behaviour of the Red-billed Quelea is influenced by food levels that are in turn, influenced by the weather. This results in unpredictable and large-scale movements of these birds.

The species has been studied in detail due to its adverse effects on human agriculture. In the breeding season the Red-billed Quelea builds a grass-woven nest, which is a ball-shaped structure with an entrance on the upper side, under a porch.

RED-BILLED QUELEA

LARGE FEEDING FLOCKS

The Red-billed Quelea is usually found in large numbers. Feeding flocks can devastate large areas of cultivated crops, which has led to its unofficial name of Locust Bird or Feathered Locust. Large numbers are culled annually without much impact on the overall population. Problems occur when they move in response to weather patterns.

SOUTHERN MASKED WEAVERS
The Southern Masked Weaver builds nests in colonies of up to 100 pairs. The nests are sometimes positioned over water to discourage some predators.

WAXBILLS AND RELATIVES

ORDER	Passeriformes
FAMILY	Estrildidae
SPECIES	130

THEIR BRIGHT COLOURS and the ease with which they breed in captivity have made many species of this family popular cage-birds. Native to warmer regions, there are three main groups: the waxbills of Africa and Asia, the grass finches of Australia, and the munias and mannikins of southern Asia and the southwest Pacific. The latter are not to be confused with the unrelated New World manakins (see p.337).

NEST CONSTRUCTION
A Blue Waxbill works on its elaborate nest made of twigs and other plant material. The nest has a domed roof and an entrance on the side.

ANATOMY

All members of the family are small birds, nearly all with thick, finchlike bills used for cracking open seeds. Most of the birds known as waxbills have bright red bills, while many other members of the family display striking crimson patterns, especially on the head. Nestlings have distinctive patterns of coloured lines and dots in their mouths specific to each species.

CLOSE PAIR BOND
Many waxbills, such as these colourful Orange-cheeked Waxbills, make a lifelong pair bond.

BEHAVIOUR

Waxbills and their relatives form very stable pairs, many species probably mating for life. Males engage in a courtship display in front of the females, in which they bob up and down, sometimes jumping up off the branch before returning to the same spot. Often the male will hold a piece of nest-building material in his bill during the display and will sing while performing. Displays also occur outside the mating season and seem to strengthen the pair bond. These displays have added to the popularity of the birds as pets. Nests are dome-shaped masses of twigs. Often a smaller, incomplete version of the nest is built over the real nest. Sometimes a dead nestling or insect is placed at the entrance of the false nest, perhaps to distract predators from the real nest.

Pytilia melba

Green-winged Pytilia

LENGTH 12–13cm (4¾–5in)
WEIGHT 15g (9/16oz)
MIGRATION Non-migrant

HABITAT Open and dry areas, including grassland, savanna, and semi-desert

The male Green-winged Pytilia has a red bill and face, bright green wings, grey barred underparts, and a red upper tail. The female lacks the red face of the male, while the juvenile is a duller version of the female. The diet of the Green-winged Pytilia mainly consists of small seeds, but some insects are also taken from the ground. It feeds in pairs or small family groups that seldom fly more than a few metres between bouts of feeding. It is not migratory, but there is nomadic movement outside the breeding season. The species is found in central and southern Africa, except in the extreme desert areas and lowland forests.

FEMALE GREEN-WINGED PYTILIA

FEMALE AND MALE ADULTS

Amadina fasciata

Cut-throat Finch

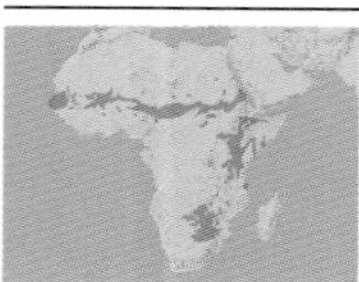

LENGTH 12cm (4½in)
WEIGHT 18g (5/8oz)
MIGRATION Non-migrant

HABITAT Dry bush and acacia savanna; also in villages

The male Cut-throat Finch has a bright red throat set against a barred head and back, a sand-coloured chest, and dark underparts. The female is similar, but has a mottled grey throat. Both sexes have a large, pale bill. The juvenile is similar to the adults, but the red throat of the juvenile male is patchy and the plumage of the juvenile female is more delicately barred. The song of the species is a low buzz or hum, often delivered continuously. These birds forage in groups and make frequent visits to water when feeding on seeds and termites. Large mixed-species feeding flocks are sometimes formed with other finches, weavers, and queleas. The pair bond between the male and the female is strong and the two sexes are seldom far apart.

The Cut-throat Finch is found in a belt to the south of Sahara and in eastern and southeastern Africa. It is not migratory, but results from ringing these birds show that long-distance movement takes place outside the breeding season

Hypargos margaritatus

Pink-throated Twinspot

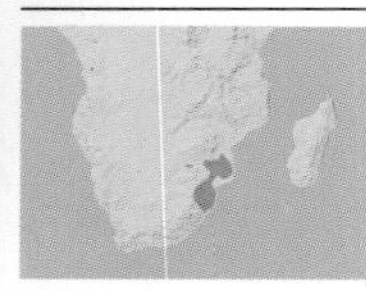

LENGTH 13cm (5in)
WEIGHT 15g (9/16oz)
MIGRATION Non-migrant

HABITAT Thorny scrub, dry savanna, and tangled forest edges

ADULT PINK-THROATED TWINSPOT

It is the male Pink-throated Twinspot that gives the species its common name, as the female has a grey throat. The male has a dark belly, with white spots, while the female has a pale belly with heavily outlined spots. Both the male and female have brown upperparts and a pink tail. This species feeds mainly on seeds, although young birds are fed on insects. The breeding season begins in January. Its nest, an oval structure made mostly of leaves, is lined with feathers, and the usual clutch size is three eggs.

Spermophaga haematina

Western Bluebill

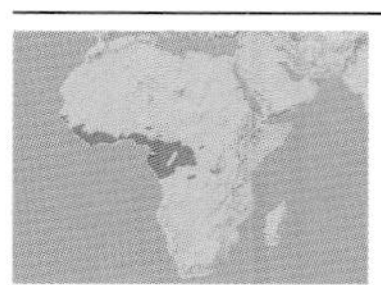

LENGTH 15cm (6in)

WEIGHT 23g (7/8oz)

MIGRATION Non-migrant

HABITAT Forest edges or secondary forest

Aptly named for its blue bill, which has a red tip, the Western Bluebill has brightly coloured plumage. The male Western Bluebill has a spectacular scarlet breast set against its black head, upperparts, wings, and tail. The female is similar, but has barred underparts instead of the continuous black markings of the male. The female also has a mottled red and black face. Juveniles of either sex are similar to the adults. The song of the Western Bluebill is a series of sharp notes, extending into a trill before fading away, and is delivered from cover.

The species is usually seen in small parties or in pairs that make constant contact calls. It usually feeds low down in the understorey and in dense cover, its diet consisting of seeds, fruit, and insects. It is distributed in the western parts of southern and central Africa in damp areas, but avoids swamps and open areas.

MALE WESTERN BLUEBILL

Lagonosticta senegala

Red-billed Firefinch

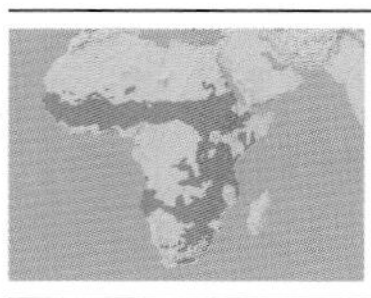

LENGTH 10cm (4in)

WEIGHT 8g (5/16oz)

MIGRATION Non-migrant

HABITAT Acacia grassland, but often in association with human habitation

A striking red bird, the male Red-billed Firefinch has dark wings. The female is olive-green with a small red face and red uppertail. This species feeds on smaller seeds and sometimes on insects. The Red-billed Firefinch travels in pairs or small parties, together with other species. It is often found close to human settlements and in suburban gardens and its range stretches throughout sub-Saharan central and southern Africa.

MALE RED-BILLED FIREFINCH

NESTING

A characteristic bulky structure, the nest of the Red-billed Firefinch is usually built in a bush or a wall. Made of dried woven grass, it has a thatched domed roof that serves as protection from rain and a side entrance to keep off predators. However, the nest is often parasitized by the Village Indigobird (*Vidua chalybeata*). It deposits its egg, adding to the clutch of the host birds' 3–6 eggs.

Uraeginthus ianthiongaster

Purple Grenadier

LENGTH 14cm (5½in)

WEIGHT 14g (½oz)

MIGRATION Non-migrant

HABITAT Dense, thorny bush and dry scrub

ADULT MALE PURPLE GRENADIER

The male Purple Grenadier has a blue face, with a red eye-ring that extends onto the bill, and a chestnut head and throat. Its upperparts and wings are brown and its chest and underparts are bright blue. The female is uniformly brown with a barred belly. These birds feed on the ground in pairs or small parties, and occasionally as solitary birds. Their main food is seeds, particularly of grasses, although insects are also eaten. The Purple Grenadier is shy of humans, but can be tame when familiar with people. The species is widespread in east Africa.

Estrilda troglodytes

Black-rumped Waxbill

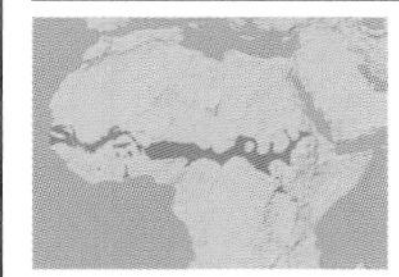

LENGTH 10cm (4in)

WEIGHT 8g (5/16oz)

MIGRATION Non-migrant

HABITAT Savanna and dry, open areas

The Black-rumped Waxbill is named for the black uppertail and rump area contrasting with its pale brown wings. The underparts are white, extending to the lower face and the belly, while the chest of the male is lightly streaked with pale pink. The bill is sometimes pink and paler than the prominent red eye-stripe. The Black-rumped Waxbill feeds mainly on small seeds such as millet, but will also take smaller insects and ant pupae. The pair bond is strong, although the birds tend to be more loosely associated outside the breeding season. The nest is an elongated structure made of grass and contains a compartment used by the non-incubating partner.

PAIR OF BLACK-RUMPED WAXBILLS

Amandava subflava

Orange-breasted Waxbill

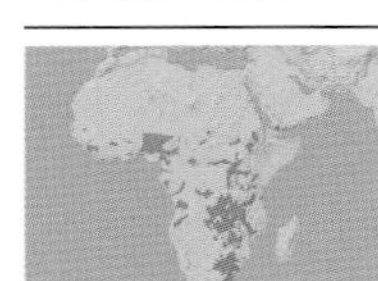

LENGTH 9–10cm (3½–4in)

WEIGHT 7g (¼oz)

MIGRATION Partial migrant

HABITAT Tall grassland, swamps and marshes, including rice fields

The male Orange-breasted Waxbill has a red eyebrow, brown upperparts with barred flanks, pink underparts, and a red upper tail. The female lacks the facial markings and pink underparts; both sexes have the bright red bill. It is distributed throughout sub-Saharan Africa and is not found in drier areas. Its main food is grass seeds; insects are rarely taken. It feeds in small groups, but larger flocks can form outside the breeding season. The species is largely nomadic, but some birds make regular migratory movements in response to rainfall.

FEMALE AND MALE ORANGE-BREASTED WAXBILLS

Emblema pictum

Painted Finch

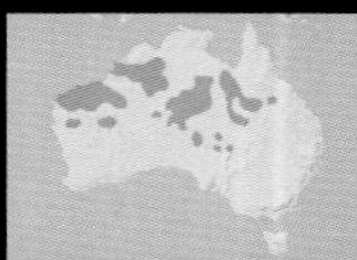

LENGTH 11cm ($4^{1}/_{2}$in)

WEIGHT 10g ($^{3}/_{8}$oz)

MIGRATION Non-migrant

HABITAT Dry rocky country, including stone deserts, gorges, acacia scrub, and spinifex

Both sexes of the Painted Finch have red faces, although the female has a smaller face. A glowing red rump contrasts with the white-spotted black breast and flanks. They are hard to see until disturbed, which is when the red rump is distinctive. Usually seen in pairs or small flocks outside the breeding season, the Painted Finch is locally common. It is very selective about its habitat, being absent from apparently suitable areas within its range. This species spends much of its time on the ground, feeding on the seeds of spinifex grass and other small seeds.

MALE PAINTED FINCH

Neochmia temporalis

Red-browed Finch

LENGTH 11cm ($4^{1}/_{2}$in)

WEIGHT 11g ($^{3}/_{8}$oz)

MIGRATION Non-migrant

HABITAT Woodland with clearings, gardens, eucalyptus forest near water, and mangroves

Different features of this bird have led to it having different names– it is also known as the Red-browed Firetail and the Red-browed Waxbill. Despite its brilliant red brow, bill, and tail, the otherwise olive-green and grey colouring of the Red-browed Finch helps it to go unnoticed among vegetation, until it flies. A bold and confident bird, it has moved easily into the gardens of towns and cities in Eastern Australia.

The Red-browed Finch is seen in pairs, family groups, and small flocks, which stay loyal to the same areas throughout the year. In winter, these flocks gather together, often mixed with other finches, around good feeding sites where grass and other small seeds are abundant. Feeding mostly on the ground or clinging to the stalks of grasses and weeds, it also approaches bird tables and feeders. It is seldom seen far from cover, and when disturbed, makes for the nearest bush with a bouncing flight.

Popular aviary birds in their homeland, escaped Red-browed Finches have become common in other parts of Australia, and have been introduced to Tahiti and the Marquesas.

Taeniopygia guttata

Zebra Finch

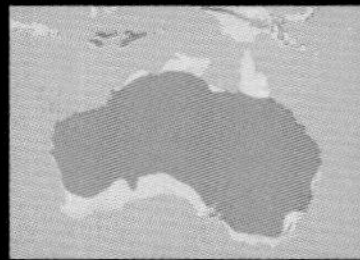

LENGTH 10cm (4in)

WEIGHT 12g ($^{7}/_{16}$oz)

MIGRATION Non-migrant

HABITAT Scrub, open woodland, cultivated land, orchards, and gardens

The most common of Australia's "grass finches", the Zebra Finch is used by researchers to study bird physiology, reproduction, and behaviour. Unlike most other birds, it drinks by sucking rather than scooping water up with its bill. It can, however, go without water for several days. Although its bill is adapted for seed-eating, it also feeds on insects, catching termites on the wing. A noisy and sociable bird that breeds after the rains, the Zebra Finch nests in shrubs and branches, holes in trees and rocks, rabbit burrows, termite mounds, and even the ground. Its shrill, buzzing call has been the subject of much research into birdsong.

MALE ZEBRA FINCH

Erythrura trichroa

Blue-faced Parrot-Finch

LENGTH 12cm ($4^{1}/_{2}$in)

WEIGHT 14g ($^{1}/_{2}$oz)

MIGRATION Non-migrant

HABITAT Rainforest, mangroves, and eucalyptus forest, also grassland and cultivated land

There are ten species of parrot-finch that share the same green body colour. Several have blue faces, and in some, the blue extends to the breast or the entire underside. Others have red faces or a combination of blue and red. The red tail of the Blue-faced Parrot-Finch is shared by many species. Despite these vivid colours, the Blue-faced Parrot-Finch is an inconspicuous bird, and mist-nesting sometimes reveals larger numbers than expected. It feeds on grass seeds, including bamboo, flocking together when seeds are abundant.

Erythrura gouldiae

Gouldian Finch

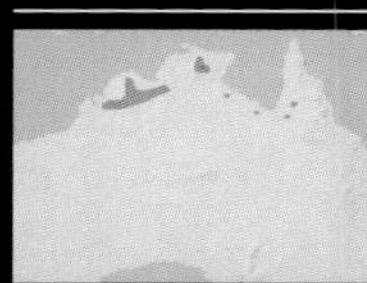

LENGTH 13cm (5in)

WEIGHT 14g (½oz)

MIGRATION Partial migrant

HABITAT Grassy plains with trees, woods and scrub, and spinifex

RED LIST CATEGORY Endangered

HUMAN IMPACT

IN RAPID DECLINE

From millions of birds in the 1950s, the Gouldian Finch has declined steadily. Loss of feeding habitat due to inappropriate development, cattle-grazing, and unfavourable fire regimes have deprived it of its primary food and reduced its numbers drastically. Infection with a parasitic mite is also a major threat to the bird.

The Gouldian Finch can have a red, black, or more rarely, orange-yellow face, but is distinctive in all variants. Black-faced birds make up most of the population. Throughout the year, the Gouldian Finch depends upon grass seeds as its primary food. It builds nests in tree-holes in open, grassy woodland. Outside the breeding period, it is found in a wide variety of woodland habitats. In the dry season, it gathers to drink at water holes.

This once abundant finch has, however, been reduced to fewer than 2,500 birds in the wild, possibly because of its popularity as a cage-bird. Conservationists are trying to re-establish wild breeding populations from this captive stock. This is more complicated than it sounds. A high proportion have been bred as colour mutants, and there has been inevitable genetic drifts, with birds becoming less able to look after themselves and more prone to disease. Aviculturalists are trying to provide a genetically variable stock for the release programme. Other initiatives include fencing cattle out of the finch's habitat and researching the role of fire in the ecosystem (fire regimes) that will provide a year-round supply of suitable habitat and seeds.

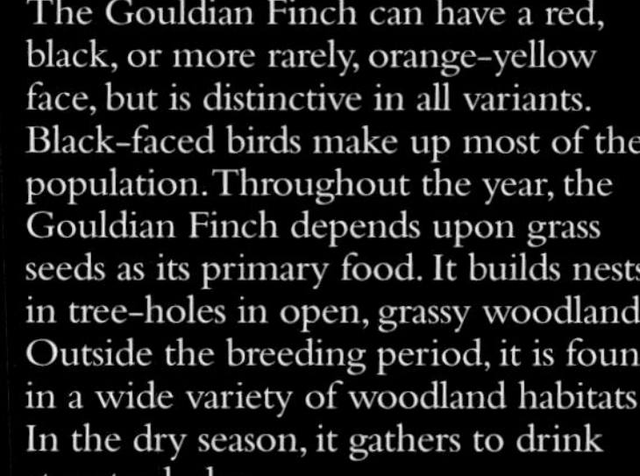

MALE GOULDIAN FINCH

Lonchura atricapilla

Chestnut Munia

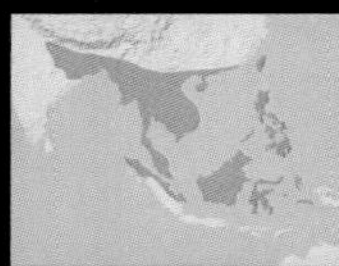

LENGTH 12cm (4½in)

WEIGHT 13g (7/16oz)

MIGRATION Non-migrant

HABITAT Swamps and marshes, mangroves, reedbeds, and rice fields; the edges of forest

The Chestnut Munia has many different forms, varying in size and colour, and tolerating a wide range of habitats and altitudes, from sea-level to over 2,000m (6,560ft). Outside the breeding season, it can assemble in huge flocks, and for this reason, in some places it has become a serious pest of rice crops. In addition to its already huge range across tropical south and southeast Asia, the Chestnut Munia has been introduced or has established itself from cage-bird escapes in Australia, Japan, Hawaii, Jamaica, Guam, Puerto Rico, and Florida.

Lonchura orizyvora

Java Sparrow

LENGTH 17cm (6½in)

WEIGHT 25g (7/8oz)

MIGRATION Non-migrant

HABITAT Lowland grassland and open woods; farmland

RED LIST CATEGORY Vulnerable

The black head, huge pink bill, white cheeks, pearl-grey back, and pink belly makes the Java Sparrow a popular cage-bird, which has proved disastrous for the species. It is also killed as an agricultural pest. Its habit of forming large flocks at roost sites near cultivated land around towns and villages makes it easy to trap in large numbers. The species has all but disappeared from large parts of its former range in Java and Bali. Conservation work includes protecting surviving populations, controlling pet trade, and meeting demands for the bird from the cage-bird trade.

MALE JAVA SPARROW

WHYDAHS

ORDER	Passeriformes
FAMILY	Viduidae
SPECIES	20

RESIDENTS OF THE OPEN woodlands of sub-Saharan Africa, whydahs and indigobirds, which are also placed in this family, are close relatives of waxbills (see p.458). Males and females are usually strikingly different in plumage. Male indigobirds are uniformly black and are difficult to tell apart; male whydahs can be boldly patterned and all have long, often elaborate tails. The females have generally plain brown plumage.

BEHAVIOUR

All members of the family are brood parasites, laying their eggs in the nests of other birds, usually a species of waxbill. Most species of whydah and indigobird specialist parasites, targeting only one species of waxbill. The structure and coloration of the nestling's mouthparts are often distinctively patterned and tend to closely match the mouthparts of the young of the host species. The young also mimic the begging behaviour of the host species' young. Adult birds feed almost exclusively on grass seeds they find by kicking the dirt and sand with both feet.

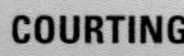

COURTING
A male Pin-tailed Whydah courts a female by fluttering up and down to display his greatly elongated, central tail feathers.

Vidua macroura

Pin-tailed Whydah

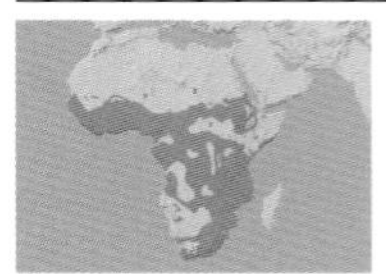

LENGTH 11–32cm (4½–12½in)

WEIGHT 12–18g (7/16–5/8oz)

MIGRATION Non-migrant

HABITAT Open areas of scrub; also cultivated areas

This species gets its name from the two very long tail feathers displayed by the male Pin-tailed Whydah during the breeding season, when it courts with a bouncing flight to show off its tail. Its breeding plumage also includes a black cap and breast-band, a white collar, and a broad white wing-bar. However, the female and non-breeding male lack the long tail feathers and are streaked brown on the upperparts, with pale underparts. The bill is bright red throughout the year in both sexes, but the juvenile has a grey bill.

One of the most adaptable brood parasites, the Pin-tailed Whydah mainly targets waxbills. The host egg is eaten and replaced by a single egg, which the female lays one by one in different nests; 2–4 eggs are laid in a single brood and up to 25 eggs can be produced in a season. The young Pin-tailed Whydahs are raised in the host brood and mimic the host's young, fooling them into believing they are one of their own. The main food of this species is grass seeds and the eggs of host species, but it also takes some invertebrates.

MALE PIN-TAILED WHYDAHS

WAGTAILS AND PIPITS

ORDER	Passeriformes
FAMILY	Motacillidae
SPECIES	64

THIS FAMILY HAS MEMBERS on every continent and several species breed on the Arctic tundra. Pipits occur from rocky seashores to the highest mountains. Usually found near water, most are birds of open country, but there are a number of forest species. Pipits are usually streaked, brown birds, while the wagtails are more colourful, especially the males.

BEHAVIOUR

All species within this family walk or run rather than hop. Wagtails bob their long tails continuously. Although most feed on insects on the ground, they will also catch flies in the air. Species with longer tails, being more manoeuvrable, are thought to spend more time hunting in flight. Most species are fiercely territorial when breeding, but roost communally, and form flocks for migration and feeding at other times.

GREY WAGTAIL AT NEST
Wagtails and pipits build their nests at ground level. Both male and female wagtails feed the young.

MALE DISPLAYING AND CALLING

Motacilla cinerea

Grey Wagtail

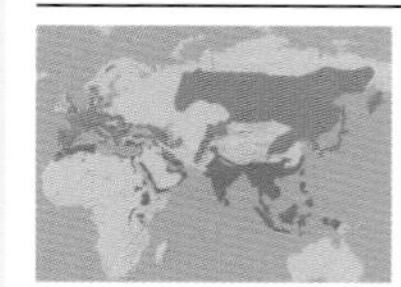

LENGTH 17–20cm (6½–8in)

WEIGHT 14–20g (½–11/16oz)

MIGRATION Partial migrant

HABITAT Fast-flowing upland water courses; also slow and still water habitats in winter

The slimmest of the wagtails, the Grey Wagtail also has the longest tail. It has a white stripe across the eye and its slate-grey upperparts contrast with its bright yellow underparts. The males of some subspecies show a strong black throat area that is absent in the female and juvenile.

The Grey Wagtail mainly feeds on insects and insect larvae collected around water, although terrestrial invertebrates are also taken. It nests in crevices in cliffs and rocks, laying 3–6 eggs. Its range stretches from the resident populations of western Europe to the strongly migratory races of Siberia and central and eastern Asia. There are also indications of vertical migration in the resident populations.

MALE GOLDEN PIPIT

Tmetothylacus tenellus

Golden Pipit

LENGTH 14–16cm (5 1/2–6 1/2in)
WEIGHT 18–20g (5/8–11/16oz)
MIGRATION Partial migrant

HABITAT Acacia scrub; open scrub and grassland

The male Golden Pipit is mainly yellow, with brown streaked upperparts and wings and a prominent black breast-band. The female is plain with uniform brown underparts. Its diet consists mainly of insects taken from vegetation and open ground. Much of the population is non-migratory but the species may irrupt periodically to appear in areas outside the normal range. Birds in the northern part of the species' range are known to make seasonal movements during the dry season.

Macronyx capensis

Cape Longclaw

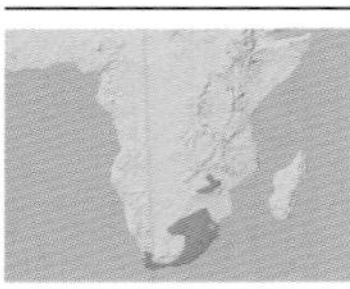

LENGTH 20cm (8in)
WEIGHT 45–55g (1 5/8–2oz)
MIGRATION Non-migrant

HABITAT Mainly dry grassland up to 2,300m (7,500ft), but also some wet areas

The most striking feature of the Cape Longclaw is the bright red throat patch surrounded by a black band in the male and a smaller, paler area in the female. The plumage of this bird is brown, with streaked upperparts. It feeds on a wide variety of invertebrates taken from the ground in grasslands or flushed out by fires or by farming activity.

ADULT MALE

Anthus pratensis

Meadow Pipit

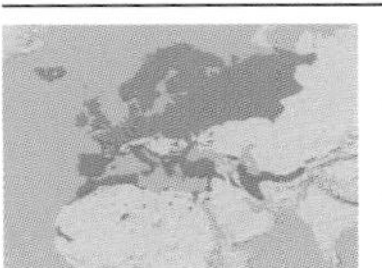

LENGTH 15cm (6in)
WEIGHT 18–20g (5/8–11/16oz)
MIGRATION Migrant

HABITAT Wide range of open habitats with dense low-level cover

This species is common in parts of its range. It has dark, almost black streaks on the dark grey-brown upperparts and creamy white underparts. The Meadow Pipit feeds mainly on invertebrates but plant seeds are also taken. The male has a display flight incorporating a courtship song that begins from a prominent perch. It rises sharply into the air and makes a shallower descent, usually in a straight rather than spiral flight. The Meadow Pipit nests on the ground (see panel) and 4 or 5 eggs are laid. Populations in western Europe are sedentary, although the birds form nomadic flocks outside the breeding season. Northern populations ranging from Iceland, northern Scandinavia, and Russia are migratory, wintering in southern Europe, North Africa, and the Middle East.

pink legs

streaked underparts

FEEDING ADULT

GROUND-NESTING MEADOW PIPIT

The Meadow Pipit builds a nest in a hollow in the ground, building a partial canopy of grass over it, which can be a substantial structure. Some birds use a natural hollow beneath a stone instead. The female incubates the eggs, while the male helps the female to feed the young after the eggs hatch.

Anthus novaeseelandiae

New Zealand Pipit

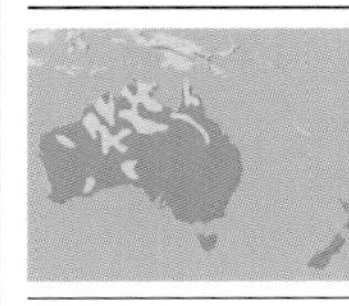

LENGTH 18cm (7in)
WEIGHT 25g (7/8oz)
MIGRATION Non-migrant

HABITAT Open and short grassland, including roadsides, dunes, and artificial areas such as airfields

The New Zealand Pipit is not confined to New Zealand as its name would suggest. It has a strong, pale eyebrow stripe, brown streaked upperparts, and underparts that are plain, apart from some streaking around the throat. However, there are variations between subspecies. Its diet mostly consists of invertebrates, including small crabs. The breeding season is from August to December. Each pair produces two or three broods, each consisting of 2–5 eggs, in a season.

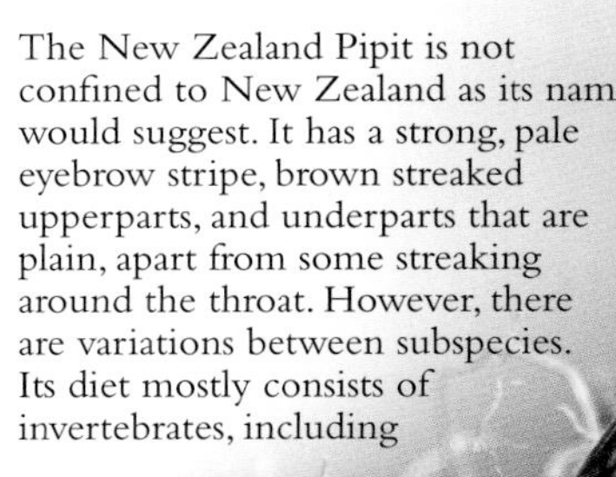

ADULT NEW ZEALAND PIPIT

Anthus spinoletta

Water Pipit

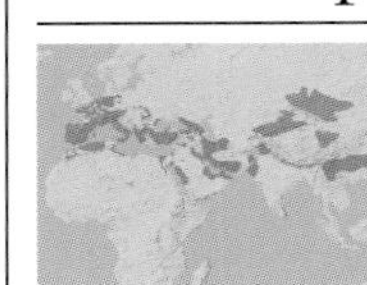

LENGTH 15–17cm (6–6 1/2in)
WEIGHT 19–25g (11/16–7/8oz)
MIGRATION Migrant

HABITAT Alpine pastures and meadows above 600–3,200m (2,000–10,500ft)

The Water Pipit has dark grey upperparts and is fairly uniform in colour, except for the wings that are heavily marked and some streaking on the underparts. Recognized as a separate species only in the second half of the 20th century, it has three subspecies in a range stretching from western and southern Europe to central Asia. It feeds on insects and small invertebrates on the ground. The nest is a grass-lined cup and 4 or 5 eggs are laid.

ADULT WATER PIPIT

Anthus cervinus

Red-throated Pipit

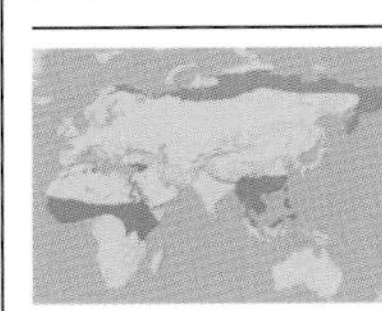

LENGTH 15cm (6in)
WEIGHT 16–30g (9/16–11/16oz)
MIGRATION Migrant

HABITAT Willows, sedges, and marshy tundra

The Red-throated Pipit has dark brown, streaked upperparts and a heavily streaked belly and lower breast. The red-brown throat, which gives the bird its name, stretches from the chin to the upper breast; it is less extensive in the female. The male has two display flights: it flies up to 20m (65ft) and makes a parachuting descent and has a horizontal flight of about 50m (165ft) when it delivers its courtship song. The nest of this species is a grassy cup and a single brood of 2–7 eggs is produced during the short Arctic summer.

ADULT RED-THROATED PIPIT

ACCENTORS

ORDER	Passeriformes
FAMILY	Prunellidae
SPECIES	13

ACCENTORS ARE A FAMILY of small, streaky brown birds that are often seen hopping along the ground. A number of species have noticeable facial masks. Accentors occur predominantly in Europe and Asia, with most species preferring mountainous areas above the tree line. Only one species, the Dunnock, is common in lowland temperate areas, being a common garden bird in much of Europe.

BEHAVIOUR

Although many accentors are quite plain to look at, recent research has shed new light on their complex mating behaviour. In the humble Dunnock, for example, easily overlooked as it skulks along a hedgerow or hops across a flowerbed, promiscuous males will mate with several females, unaware that the female birds are acting in a similar fashion, mating with a number of males.

NOT SO PLAIN
The breeding behaviour of the unobtrusive Dunnock has cast new light on its previous image as a boring brown bird. Here, a typical brood of five chicks is fed by an adult bird.

Prunella rubida

Japanese Accentor

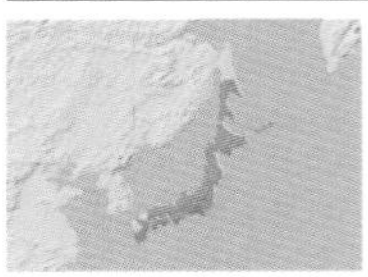

LENGTH 15cm (6in)

WEIGHT 17g (5/8oz)

MIGRATION Partial migrant

HABITAT Thickets, scrub, and forest undergrowth

This Japanese species is a typical accentor: a superficially nondescript brown and chestnut bird, with a thin, pointed bill, and a pleasant song. The female sings particularly melodiously and like the male, often sings from an exposed perch to attract mates. The female may mate with several different males, and sometimes two males may assist a female in raising a single brood. The Japanese Accentor forages on the ground, never far from cover, or in the branches of bushes. It is an "altitudinal migrant", coming down from the mountains in winter, when it can be found in lowland thickets and on coastal flats.

ADULT JAPANESE ACCENTOR

GREAT SITES

MOUNT FUJI

At the base of Japan's highest mountain is a bird reserve that is home to more than 175 bird species, over 100 of which breed there. The first bird reserve in the area was established in 1924. Important birds include the endemic Japanese Accentor, Alpine Accentor, Nutcracker, Red-flanked Bluetail, Japanese Green Pigeon, Brown Thrush, and several species of cuckoos and flycatchers.

FINCHES AND RELATIVES

ORDER	Passeriformes
FAMILY	Fringillidae
SPECIES	168

FINCHES ARE SMALL, STOCKY birds with stout cone-shaped bills. They come in a huge variety of plumages. Many species have rather plain and brown plumage, while others display a range of gaudy colours from bright golden yellows to rich scarlets. Numerous finches are familiar visitors to garden feeders, where they supplement their natural diet.

ANATOMY

Among the most conspicuous features shared by members of the finch family are their bills. Generally finches have thick, conical bills that are adapted for cracking open seeds. However, there is considerable variation among the family. For instance, the European Goldfinch has a fairly typical conical bill that is used to open small seeds. In contrast, the Hawfinch has a massive bill (complemented by large muscles at the side of the skull) that is specially adapted for splitting large, hard seeds such as cherry stones. Variations include the unique cross-tipped beak of the crossbills.

HAWFINCH
Strong bill and cheek muscles capable of splitting hard tree seeds.

GOLDFINCH
Cone-shaped bill, ideal for dealing with most small seeds.

CROSSBILL
Crossed bill adapted for prising open spruce and pine cones.

FIGHTING FINCHES
Although European Greenfinches are sociable, fights do occasionally break out, particularly between male birds during the breeding season.

BEHAVIOUR

Many species of finch are extremely sociable, often forming large flocks, particularly outside the breeding season. For example, huge flocks of Bramblings, numbering around one million birds, have been known to take up temporary residence near forests containing an abundant supply of beech nuts. Smaller gatherings, often comprising a variety of finch species, are more commonplace. In the breeding season, however, many species become less sociable.

ADULT (EUROPEAN SUBSPECIES)

Fringilla coelebs

Common Chaffinch

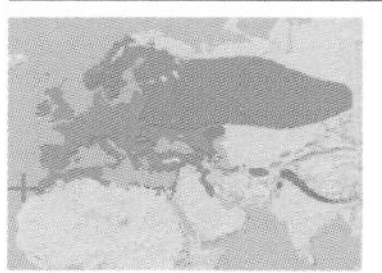

LENGTH 15cm (6in)
WEIGHT 25g ($^7/_8$oz)
MIGRATION Partial migrant

HABITAT Deciduous and coniferous woodland, farmland, parks, and gardens

An abundant species, the Common Chaffinch is often seen across its extensive range. Its plumage varies considerably between subspecies in western Europe, Africa, and the Canary Islands, but the black and white pattern of its wings and tail and its characteristic jerky, nodding walk are unmistakable. It feeds on insects, seeds, and shoots.

Fringilla montifringilla

Brambling

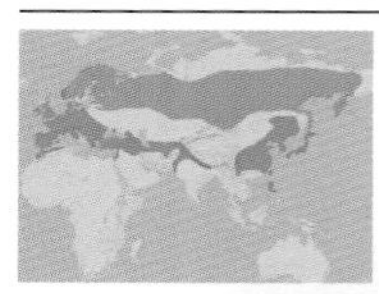

LENGTH 15cm (6in)
WEIGHT 25g ($^7/_8$oz)
MIGRATION Migrant

HABITAT Breeds in northern birch and birch-conifer forests; winters in woodland and farmland

In winter plumage, the Brambling is superficially similar to the Common Chaffinch (left), with a black and white wing pattern, although it can be distinguished by its white rump and all-black tail. The breeding male Brambling has a distinctive jet-black head and mantle.

In summer, the Brambling eats insects and their larvae. It also feeds on weed seeds and berries, and in alpine regions, seeds from spruce cones. When snow is thick on the ground, it digs tunnels, using its wings and bills to reach food. It also takes beech nuts from their cups on the trees, sometimes hovering to do so.

MALE IN BREEDING PLUMAGE

Carduelis pinus

Pine Siskin

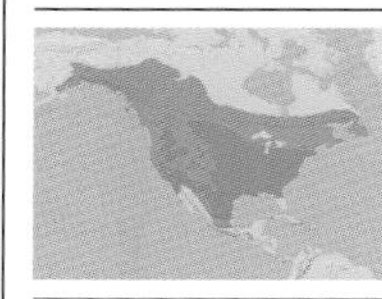

LENGTH 13cm (5in)
WEIGHT 13g ($^7/_{16}$oz)
MIGRATION Partial migrant

HABITAT Conifer forests, mixed woodland, and alder thickets

Locally abundant in one year, Pine Siskins may be absent from the same area in the next. Their irregular movements are related to the supply of hemlock, spruce, and birch buds and seeds. The Pine Siskin has a narrow, pointed bill, dark streaks all over its plumage, and yellow in its wings and tail. A sociable species, it nests colonially.

ADULT PINE SISKIN

Carduelis chloris

European Greenfinch

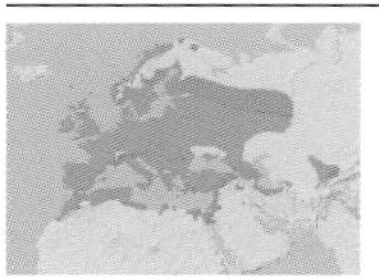

LENGTH 16cm (6$^1/_2$in)
WEIGHT 25g ($^7/_8$oz)
MIGRATION Partial migrant

HABITAT Woodland, farmland, parks, and gardens

Larger and sturdier than other green-coloured finches in its range, the European Greenfinch is also more uniformly green, the colour varying from the rich green of the breeding male to the olive-brown of the female and juvenile. It has striking yellow patches on the wings and tail. The European Greenfinch has a powerful bill and can easily feed on large, hard seeds. It is a familiar visitor to gardens, taking sunflower seeds, seed mixes, and peanuts from bird-tables. It also feeds on rosehips, picking out the seeds and leaving the fruit. In early spring, the male flies slowly at treetop height, rolling from side to side while it sings. It also sings from a perch. The nest of the European Greenfinch is bulky and made of grass and twigs.

Originally a woodland-edge species, these birds have exploited human changes to the landscape, taking advantage of irrigation on farmland.

ADULT MALE

MALE IN BREEDING PLUMAGE

Carduelis tristis

American Goldfinch

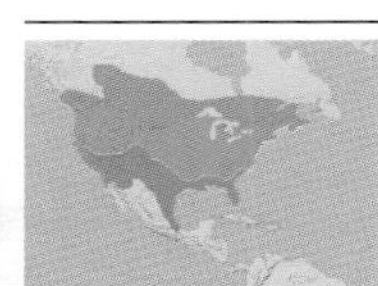

LENGTH 11cm (4$^1/_2$in)
WEIGHT 13g ($^7/_{16}$oz)
MIGRATION Partial migrant

HABITAT Woodland, farmland, gardens, and open ground with plentiful weeds

In the USA, the American Goldfinch is also known as the Wild Canary because of the brilliant canary yellow plumage of the breeding male. In winter, the adult male looks more like the female, which is grey and brownish yellow in colour. In mid- to late summer, while other songbirds are coming to the end of breeding, the American Goldfinch begins to nest – it does not begin to breed until the seeds of thistles, teasels, dandelions, and burdock are widely available. In winter, it feeds on seeds of trees, such as alder and birch, and is often found feeding in flocks.

Carduelis carduelis

European Goldfinch

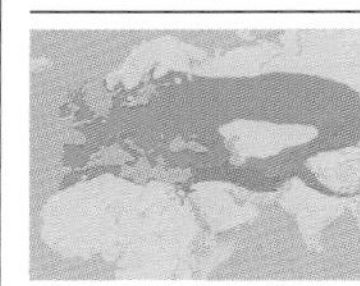

LENGTH 14cm (5$^1/_2$in)
WEIGHT 16g ($^9/_{16}$oz)
MIGRATION Partial migrant

HABITAT Mixed and coniferous woodland, farmland, gardens, and wasteland with weeds

A brilliantly coloured bird, the adult European Goldfinch has a red face and yellow, black, and white plumage. In flight, the broad yellow band on its wings is clearly visible. The juvenile has a grey head and duller wings than the adult. The slender bill of this species is ideal for extracting small seeds that are inaccessible to other birds. Its call is a liquid, lilting, slightly metallic twittering.

ADULT EUROPEAN GOLDFINCH

MALE MEALY REDPOLL

Carduelis flammea

Common Redpoll

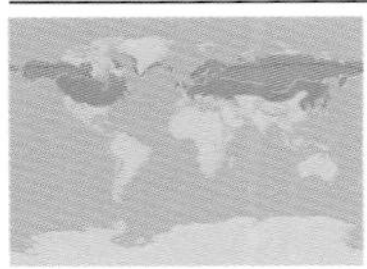

LENGTH 12–15cm (4½–6in)

WEIGHT 12g (7/16oz)

MIGRATION Partial migrant

HABITAT Mainly heath and woodland (both coniferous and deciduous)

The Redpoll's name literally means "red head", referring to its bright red cap, characteristic of the male and female but absent in the plainer, brown-streaked juvenile. Birds that breed from Scandinavia and Siberia across to North America are slightly larger and paler than those found in western Europe and are often referred to as Mealy Redpolls. The largest Common Redpolls are Greenland Redpolls, which breed in Greenland and Iceland. Common Redpolls are quite abundant in New Zealand, where they were introduced in the 19th century by European colonists.

This species is often found in large flocks – in winter, as it moves between treetops for seeds, and during migration. It is often seen with other bird species. It is a non-territorial bird, and breeding pairs nest close to one another. The call is "sweet-ee-et", while its flight song is a rattling "chit-chit-chit".

Carduelis cannabina

Common Linnet

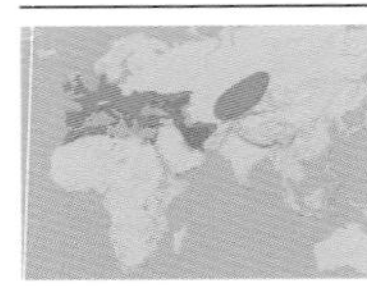

LENGTH 14cm (5½in)

WEIGHT 20g (11/16oz)

MIGRATION Partial migrant

HABITAT Mainly lowland, usually in farmland, scrub, and heath, up to 2,500m (8,200ft)

This attractive small finch is a common bird across most of Europe (and as far east as Afghanistan). The male varies in plumage, with a pale red forehead and pink-red chest in the breeding season in summer. In winter, its chest turns paler and its head becomes brown. Both the male and female have pale brown cheek spots, but the female has streaked brown plumage throughout the year. In the summer, the Common Linnet's song is musical, which is why it was once a popular cage bird. When the breeding season is over, it can often be found feeding on waste ground in flocks of up to several thousand birds.

ADULT MALE IN SUMMER PLUMAGE

Carpodacus cassinii

Cassin's Finch

LENGTH 16cm (6½in)

WEIGHT 25g (7/8oz)

MIGRATION Partial migrant

HABITAT Mountainous coniferous forest

Unusually for male birds in their first breeding year, young male Cassin's Finches do not attain their stunning bright red plumage, appearing similar to the much drabber, brown-streaked female. Both the male and the female have brown wings and short, forked tails. These finches mainly feed on seeds, berries, and insects. They breed in the mountainous west of Canada and the USA, and then many move to northern Mexico for the winter. The species is named after John Cassin, a famous 19th-century American ornithologist, who described nearly 200 species.

ADULT MALE CASSIN'S FINCH

Rhodospiza obsoleta

Desert Finch

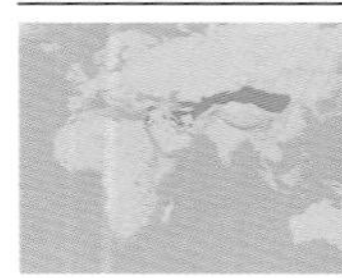

LENGTH 15cm (6in)

WEIGHT 25g (7/8oz)

MIGRATION Non-migrant

HABITAT Deserts and semi-arid areas

A large finch, found mainly in Asia, the Desert Finch has pale brown plumage that blends in with its desert habitat. The adult has a strong, dark bill (paler in juveniles) and a distinctive pink, white, and black wing coloration. The species feeds in large flocks, sometimes with other finches, on seeds and insects.

ADULT MALE DESERT FINCH

Carpodacus roseus

Pallas's Rosefinch

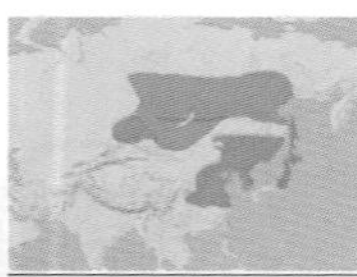

LENGTH 17cm (6½in)

WEIGHT 30g (1 1/16oz)

MIGRATION Migrant

HABITAT Coniferous forests, alpine meadows, mountains, scrub, and taiga

The male Pallas's Rosefinch is an attractive small bird. Its rump and underparts are scarlet-pink, with silvery edging to the feathers of its throat and forehead. Its back and neck are covered with dark streaking; its wings are predominantly brown, with a pink double wing-bar and pale edging to the feathers. It has a pale bill. The female is much less distinct than the male: it is a streaky brown bird that is difficult to distinguish from other rosefinches. However, it shows a pale pink rump, a pale orange forehead, and generally warmer brown plumage tones than its relatives. Another useful identification feature of Pallas's Rosefinch is its rather plain face that lacks any eye-stripes.

ADULT MALE PALLAS'S ROSEFINCH

BIRD SPECIES

Pinicola enucleator

Pine Grosbeak

MALE PINE GROSBEAK

LENGTH 20cm (8in)

WEIGHT 55g (2oz)

MIGRATION Partial migrant

HABITAT Boreal forest

The Pine Grosbeak is a large, thrush-sized finch. The male is predominantly bright scarlet in colour, while the female and juvenile are duller and browner. Despite its striking appearance, the species is often overlooked as it forages silently on the ground, feeding mainly on berries and seeds. Although most populations are resident, large irruptions occur periodically during autumn and winter as the birds move south to search for food.

Haematospiza sipahi

Scarlet Finch

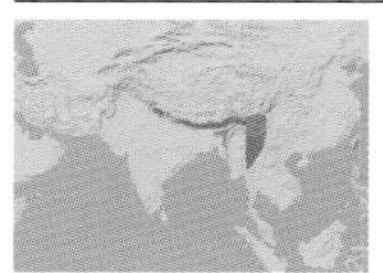

LENGTH 18cm (7in)

WEIGHT 40g (1[7]/[16]oz))

MIGRATION Partial migrant

HABITAT Fir and oak forests – particularly edges and clearings

As its name suggests, the male Scarlet Finch is predominantly bright red in its coloration, except for a small amount of dark plumage in front of the eye (the lores); and black feathering on its wings and tail. It has a large, powerful yellow bill that it uses to prise open seeds. The females is olive-green, with paler tips to the feathers and a striking bright yellow rump. The bill is duller than that of the male. Young male birds are rather like the female, but with a more orange tint to their plumage and an orange-yellow rump.

This uncommon bird is only found in the Himalayas, where it usually inhabits upland forests. The Scarlet Finch is generally a solitary species, although it can occasionally be found in small flocks numbering up to 30 birds. In winter, the species retreats to lower levels and has been recorded away from its usual range as a scarce visitor.

Loxia curvirostra

Red Crossbill

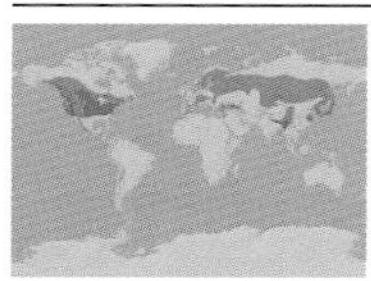

LENGTH 17cm (6½in)

WEIGHT 35–40g (1¼–1[7]/[16]oz)

MIGRATION Partial migrant

HABITAT Coniferous forest

Named after its distinctive strong, crossed beak, which is specially adapted to prise seeds out of spruce and pine cones (see panel, below), the Red Crossbill has other adaptations to help it to feed: its legs and toes are adapted for grasping and holding cones, while its agility allows it to move easily on dense coniferous branches. As its breeding season is linked to the ripening of cones, it is one of the earliest species of songbird to breed, often as early as February. In the breeding season, these birds are found in pairs. Although usually seen feeding high among coniferous trees in flocks, they are often seen drinking from puddles on the ground. They also eat insects and caterpillars.

ADULT MALE RED CROSSBILL

CROSSED BILL

The tips of the upper and lower mandibles of the Red Crossbill's bill overlap each other to form an efficient tool to help it feed. Using its sharp, hooked bill, this bird extracts dry seeds from ripe pine or spruce cones on which it thrives. It places the tips of its slightly open bill under a cone scale and bites down. The crossed tips of the bill push the scale up, while its tongue scoops the seed into its mouth.

MALE DISPLAYING ITS UNDERWING

Pyrrhula pyrrhula

Eurasian Bullfinch

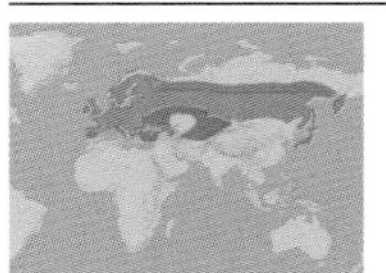

LENGTH 15–17cm (6–6½in)

WEIGHT 20–25g ([11]/[16]–⅞oz)

MIGRATION Partial migrant

HABITAT Woodland, scrub, orchards, hedgerows, and gardens

This shy species is often seen in pairs, offering the observer the chance to compare the bright male with its duller female companion. The male Eurasian Bullfinch has bright pink underparts and cheeks, and a slate-grey back that contrasts with its black wings. The female is browner. Both sexes, however, are distinguished by their large powerful bill and conspicuous black cap and face.

MALE HAWFINCH

Coccothraustes coccothraustes

Hawfinch

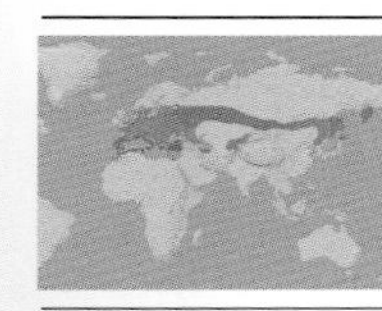

LENGTH 18cm (7in)

WEIGHT 55–60g (2–2⅛oz)

MIGRATION Partial migrant

HABITAT Deciduous and mixed woodland, parks, and gardens

The Hawfinch is found across Europe and parts of Asia to Japan. Its most noticeable feature is its massive, powerful bill. This adaptation enables it to crack open hard seeds (such as cherry stones) and get at the kernel. Despite its strength, the bill is also a precision tool capable of rotating fruit to strip them of their pulp. The plumage of the Hawfinch is a subtle mix of browns, greys, and whites. The male is slightly brighter than the female, with a purple gloss to its black flight feathers. In the plumage of both the male and female, the primaries (wing-tips) have a scaled appearance.

Compared to other finches, it is notoriously wary and difficult to observe; despite its large size and distinctive markings, it can often sit in the tops of trees, unseen.

ADULT JAPANESE GROSBEAK

Eophona personata

Japanese Grosbeak

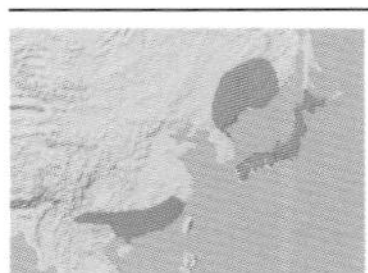

LENGTH 23cm (9in)

WEIGHT 80g (2 7/8oz)

MIGRATION Migrant

HABITAT Various types of forest and woodland, also scrub

A large, striking finch, the Japanese Grosbeak has a largely lilac grey plumage that contrasts with its black head, wings (with small white patches), white vent, and tail. This bird has an enormous deep-based yellow bill, which it uses to crack open fruit, nuts, and seeds – the main elements of its diet. Although common in its range incorporating Japan and parts of China, the Japanese Grosbeak is not always easy to spot.

Hesperiphona vespertina

Evening Grosbeak

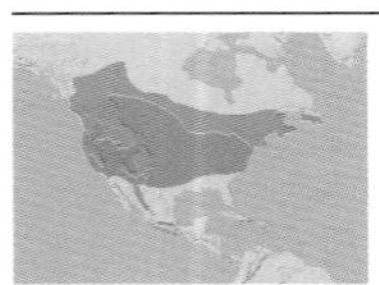

LENGTH 19cm (7 1/2in)

WEIGHT 55–60g (2–2 1/8oz)

MIGRATION Non-migrant

HABITAT Dense coniferous and mixed forest, suburban gardens in winter

The male Evening Grosbeak is a striking bird with a deep, conical bill and yellow eyebrows. It has an olive yellow plumage, which is darkest on its head and the breast, with contrasting black and white wings, and a black tail. The female Evening Grosbeak is more subdued in its appearance. Its plumage is silver-grey, with yellow patches on the nape, sides, and the rump. Its underparts are pale grey in colour, with white patches on the wing feathers, and it has a black tail. The Evening Grosbeak forages in trees, bushes, and sometimes on the ground. It feeds on nuts and seeds that it cracks open with its stout bill, and also takes fruit and insects. It is an irregular visitor to feeding stations and gardens, especially in winter. An irruptive migrant, its population cycle closely follows that of a key prey item, the larvae of the spruce budworm, which is a pulpwood forest.

MALE EVENING GROSBEAK

Pseudonestor xanthophrys

Maui Parrotbill

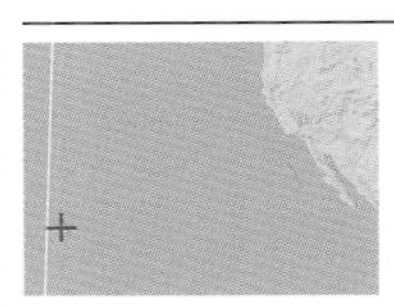

LENGTH 14cm (5 1/2in)

WEIGHT 20–25g (11/16–7/8oz)

MIGRATION Non-migrant

HABITAT Montane mesic and wet forest at 1,200–2,000m (4,000–6,500ft) altitude

RED LIST CATEGORY Critically endangered

A rare honeycreeper, the Maui Parrotbill is best known for its large, parrot-like bill. The upper mandible is decurved, with the lower mandible tapering to a chisel-like tip, helping the bird to pry open twigs and probe bark for food. The male has bright yellow-green plumage.

Vestiaria coccinea

Iiwi

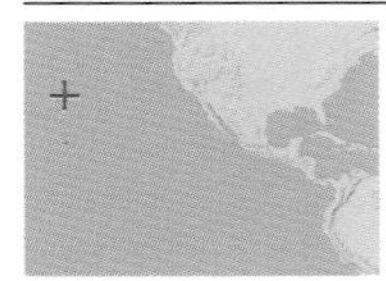

LENGTH 15cm (6in)

WEIGHT 15–20g (9/16–11/16oz)

MIGRATION Non-migrant

HABITAT High altitude wet forest with 'ohi'a and koa trees; also dry mamane forest

One of the most common of Hawaii's endemic landbirds, the Iiwi has bright red plumage and its wings and tail are black. It once extracted nectar from Hawaiian lobelioids, using its long, decurved bill. However, with the plant becoming extinct, it now feeds on 'ohi'a nectar, for which its bill is less well adapted.

NEW WORLD WARBLERS

ORDER	Passeriformes
FAMILY	Parulidae
SPECIES	118

THESE BRIGHTLY COLOURED insectivorous birds are restricted to the New World and are unrelated to the generally much plainer Old World warblers (see p.413). Despite their name, many species have songs that are more insect-like than warbling. Most species frequent the tops of trees, while some use the middle levels. Others stay close to or on the trunks, and a few have become primarily terrestrial.

SPRING MIGRATION
The Black-and-white Warbler is one of the most common – and most often seen – warblers during spring migration in New York City's Central Park.

BEHAVIOUR

About half of the New World warblers are migratory, breeding in North America and wintering in Central and South America. During the peak of spring migration in the eastern USA, 20–30 species can be found in a single morning in some urban parks. The autumn migration is more dispersed, and some species, such as the Blackpoll Warbler, make nonstop, 36-hour flights over the Atlantic Ocean from North to South America.

ENDANGERED WARBLER
The only place to hear a singing male Kirtland's Warbler is in young jack pines, 1.5–7.5m (5–25ft) tall, in the lower peninsula of Michigan, USA.

Vermivora peregrina

Tennessee Warbler

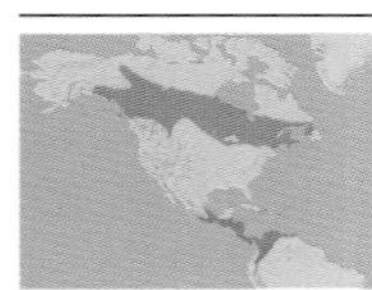

LENGTH 12cm (4 1/2in)

WEIGHT 9g (11/32oz)

MIGRATION Migrant

HABITAT Open or young woodland with mossy or weedy understorey; migrants in brushy habitat

A dainty warbler of the North American boreal forest, the Tennessee Warbler was named after the American state where it was first discovered. However, the bird does not breed within the state. The male Tennessee Warbler has a slender bill, grey crown, white eyebrows with dark patches around its eyes, and a bold white stripe above the eye. It has olive upperparts and wings, while the underparts and the undertail feathers are white in colour. In autumn, the male, female, and the juvenile have pale yellow underparts.

The bird primarily feeds on the Spruce Budworm, a pulpwood forest pest. It is solitary when nesting and its cup-shaped nest is usually placed at the bottom of a small tree or shrub.

MALE NORTHERN PARULA

Parula americana

Northern Parula

LENGTH 11cm (4½in)

WEIGHT 8g (5/16oz)

MIGRATION Migrant

HABITAT Coniferous, deciduous, and mixed hardwood forest, particularly near water, with lichens

A small and compact denizen of the lichen-strewn canopy, the Northern Parula has a striking plumage. The male of the species has a blue head, with a broken white eye-ring, and black patches around the eyes. Its throat and breast are yellow, with a dark red "necklace". It has blue-grey upperparts with a bronze-green mantle and the blue wings show two short white wing-bars. In comparison, the female and the juvenile are much duller. The Northern Parula has a long, sharp bill. The lower mandible is a conspicuous orange colour.

This bird is insectivorous, feeding mainly on spiders and caterpillars by gleaning them from foliage, twigs, and branches. It also sallies or hovers for insects. The Northern Parula's nest is a cup-shaped structure sited at the tip of a tree limb. There are two breeding populations: the northern is associated with beard moss or lace lichen, the southern with Spanish moss.

Dendroica petechia

American Yellow Warbler

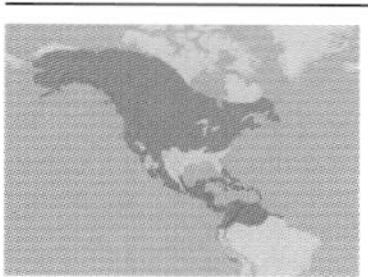

LENGTH 13cm (5in)

WEIGHT 10–12g (3/8–7/16oz)

MIGRATION Partial migrant

HABITAT Various brushy and semi-open habitats, especially if shady and near water; also mangroves

As the name suggests, the American Yellow Warbler has yellow plumage. The migratory subspecies is bright yellow with slightly duller upperparts and broad red streaks below. The males in a few of the over 40 subspecies, have varying amounts of rufous coloration on their heads, throat, and breast. The females and the juveniles of all the subspecies are duller than the males. The bird's courtship is intense, with the male having been recorded singing over 3,000 times every day. The American Yellow Warbler feeds on insects and spiders.

MALE (MIGRATORY SUBSPECIES)

Dendroica fusca

Blackburnian Warbler

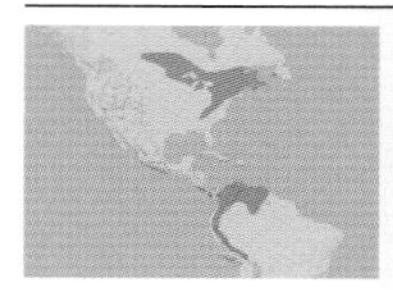

LENGTH 13cm (5in)

WEIGHT 10g (3/8oz)

MIGRATION Non-migrant

HABITAT Coniferous or mixed woodland; winters in forest canopy and borders and secondary woodland

Named after an English botanist, the Blackburnian Warbler is an attractive species. The male has a glowing plumage of black, white, and orange. It has a black face mask, with a flaming orange throat, black upperparts with a yellow belly, a white wing panel, and a white vent. The female is a duller version of the male, with a pale orange-ochre eyebrow, pale orange sides of the head, and dark grey-olive upperparts. The juvenile is duller than the female.

The Blackburnian Warbler's song is a thin, high-pitched ascending trill in two or three parts, ending with a "seep seep seep titi zeeee". It gleans insects, particularly lepidopteran larvae, in the canopy, taking prey from branches, twigs, and foliage. It sometimes catches insects in flight. While solitary in its wintering grounds, the species may join mixed foraging flocks after breeding. It is territorial on its breeding grounds, building a solitary nest of small sticks, lichen, and plant down, lined with bark pieces and small roots. It is placed on a horizontal branch and 4 or 5 eggs are laid. The female builds the nest and incubates the eggs, but both parents feed the young. One brood a year is produced.

ADULT BIRD

GREAT SITES

CENTRAL PARK, NEW YORK

It may seem unlikely, but Central Park, in the middle of New York's Manhattan, is a bird haven. During spring migration, it becomes an oasis for warblers, including the Blackburnian Warbler, tanagers, and grosbeaks. Birds stop for a day or two in this green oasis amid a concrete desert, before continuing their journey. The spectacle of colours and forms is a magnet for bird-lovers.

Mniotilta varia

Black-and-white Warbler

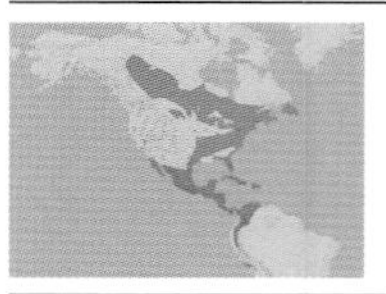

LENGTH 13cm (5in)

WEIGHT 11g (3/8oz)

MIGRATION Migrant

HABITAT Mature deciduous or mixed forest; winters in forest borders and secondary woodland

True to its name, the Black-and-white Warbler has pied black and white plumage. It has a striped head and a slightly decurved bill. The bill's shape helps this warbler to probe into deep crevices. The Black-and-white Warbler has an unusually long hind toe and claw on each foot. This adaptation enables it to clamber safely along the bark surface, while its short, stout legs serve a similar purpose

As distinctive in behaviour as in its plumage, the bird forages for insects while climbing along the trunks and larger branches of trees. Therefore, it is also often referred to as the Black-and-white Creeper. It lays 4 or 5 eggs in a cup nest on the ground.

MALE BLACK-AND-WHITE WARBLER

Setophaga ruticilla

American Redstart

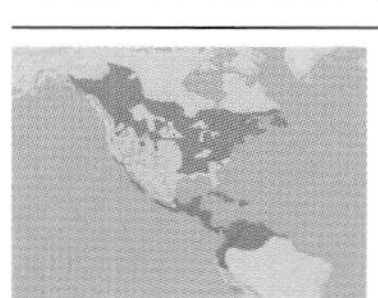

LENGTH 13cm (5in)

WEIGHT 8g (5/16oz)

MIGRATION Migrant

HABITAT Moist, second-growth hardwood forest, especially near streams; tropical lowland woodland

The American Redstart, a boldly patterned warbler, gets its name from the male's bright markings on its tail – "start" being an old word for tail. The male American Redstart is black, with orange patches on the breast sides, the wings, and the tail. The female and the juvenile have grey plumage with yellow patches. A young male resembles a female until its second autumn; some yearlings nevertheless hold territories and sing to attract mates.

The American Redstart is an active forager, always on the move, flicking its wings and tail while feeding. The resulting flash of bright colour flushes the insect prey from the foliage. The bird mostly gleans its prey, but also catches them in the air.

ADULT MALE

Protonotaria citrea

Prothonotary Warbler

LENGTH 13cm (5in)

WEIGHT 14g (1/2oz)

MIGRATION Migrant

HABITAT Mangroves, woodland, and scrub, especially near water

Once called the Golden Swamp Warbler because it is found in flooded forests, the Prothonotary Warbler is named for its plumage, in reference to the golden robes of the protonotaries (papal officials). The golden yellow of its head, neck, and underparts is offset by its olive-green back and blue-grey wings and tail. The species nests in tree-holes or cavities and lays 4–6 eggs.

MALE PROTHONOTARY WARBLER

ADULT OVENBIRD

Seiurus aurocapilla

Ovenbird

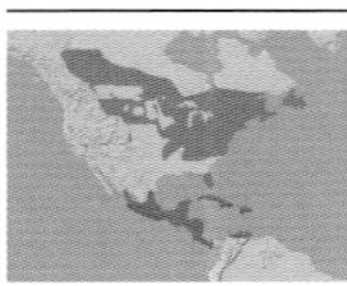

LENGTH 14cm (5 1/2in)

WEIGHT 19g (11/16oz)

MIGRATION Migrant

HABITAT Mature deciduous or mixed forests with sparse shaded undergrowth

Named after its small oven-shaped nest, the Ovenbird has olive upperparts and white underparts, with thick black stripes. It usually sings from an elevated perch, its loud, repetitive "tea-cher, tea-cher, tea-cher" often ringing through the forest. It is a ground-feeding bird, with a distinctive gait – high-stepping and head-bobbing, with its tail raised – as it forages for insects, earthworms, caterpillars, seeds, and fruit.

Seiurus noveboracensis

Northern Waterthrush

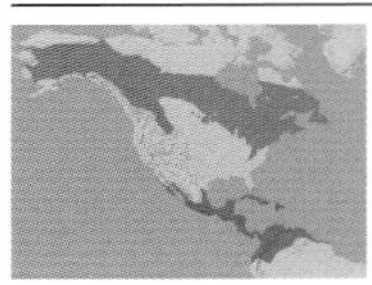

LENGTH 14cm (5 1/2in)

WEIGHT 16g (9/16oz)

MIGRATION Migrant

HABITAT Dense shrubbery, small trees, woodland and mangroves near slow-moving or standing water

Uniformly dark brown above, this species has white or creamy yellow underparts, with bold black stripes. Its head is marked with a prominent pale yellow eyebrow. It feeds on the ground at the edges of water or in damp places, walking sedately, with the rear of its body and its tail slowly moving up and down. The Northern Waterthrush eats aquatic and terrestrial insects, caterpillars, and worms. It also takes crustaceans, molluscs, and small fish.

ADULT NORTHERN WATERTHRUSH

Zeledonia coronata

Wrenthrush

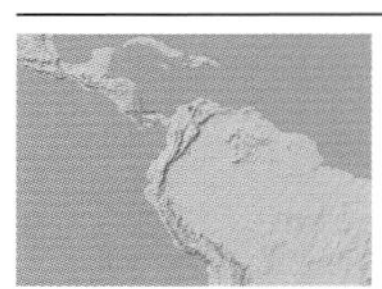

LENGTH 12cm (4 1/2in)

WEIGHT 20g (11/16oz)

MIGRATION Non-migrant

HABITAT Dense undergrowth of montane humid forest and forest borders

A plump little bird with a short tail, the Wrenthrush, or Zeledonia, is the only member of its genus. A secretive bird, it skulks in forest undergrowth, hopping along the ground or from perch to perch, flicking its wings, and very rarely flying. It has a distinctive golden-tawny crown, slate-grey face and necksides, dark olive-brown upperparts, and slate-grey underparts. Its nest is a domed structure made mainly of moss.

Geothlypis trichas

Common Yellowthroat

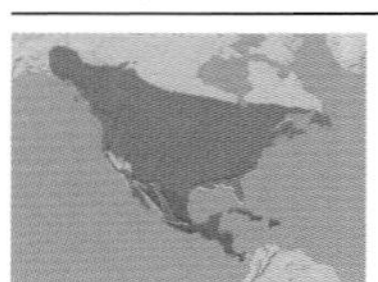

LENGTH 12cm (4 1/2)

WEIGHT 10g (3/8oz)

MIGRATION Partial migrant

HABITAT Dense vegetation in wet marshes, wet fields, and bushy areas

A shy warbler found in damp thickets, the Common Yellowthroat has a bright yellow chin, throat, and breast, and olive-brown upperparts. The male has a bold black face mask, edged with white, which varies in size. This is an important feature during courtship because a male with a large mask is likely to attract the most females.

The Common Yellowthroat is more often heard than seen. Its cheerful song – "wichity-wichity-wichity" – can be heard throughout its vast range. It usually feeds close to the ground. In the breeding season, the male performs a display flight, particularly in the late afternoon. It flies up to 7m (21ft) in the air, uttering a jumble of high-pitched notes, then parachutes down, calling out its song. When nesting, the parent Common Yellowthroat foils predators by dropping down into thick grass away from the nest, in the opposite direction.

MALE COMMON YELLOWTHROAT

Icteria virens

Yellow-breasted Chat

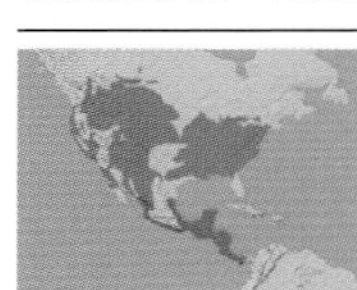

LENGTH 18cm (7in)

WEIGHT 25g (7/8oz)

MIGRATION Migrant

HABITAT Dense bushes and hedgerows in open, sunny areas near deciduous woodland

The largest warbler of North America, the Yellow-breasted Chat is the only member of its genus and is unusual among warblers in being relatively large, and having a stout bill, stocky body, and long tail. Olive-grey above, the bird has a bright yellow throat and breast, and a white belly and rump. Prominent white "spectacles" on its face contrast with a black patch around its bill. The female is similar to the male, but has a grey patch around the bill.

The song of the Yellow-breasted Chat is varied, consisting of a series of up to 10 simple notes, with long pauses, odd liquid whistles, and harsh, rasping notes. Unlike most warblers, it mimics other birds' calls and often sings at night in addition to daytime. It forages in dense vegetation for insects, insect larvae, and berries. The male performs a display flight in the breeding season, pumping its tail up and down as it sings.

MALE YELLOW-BREASTED CHAT

NEW WORLD BLACKBIRDS

ORDER	Passeriformes
FAMILY	Icteridae
SPECIES	98

NEW WORLD BLACKBIRDS are unrelated to the Common Blackbird, a species of thrush (see p.436) native to Europe, just as the New World orioles are unrelated to the Old World orioles (see p.384). To avoid confusion, members of this family are referred to as icterids (an anglicized version of the scientific family name).

ANATOMY

Pointed, conical bills powered by strong muscles allow icterids to eat a wide variety of food. In the caciques and oropendolas, the base of the upper mandible is enlarged into a frontal shield. Some members of this family have all-black but iridescent plumage. Others are patterned in yellows and reds, while the meadowlarks that frequent open country, tend to be streaked brown on the back. In many species, the males and the females have different plumage.

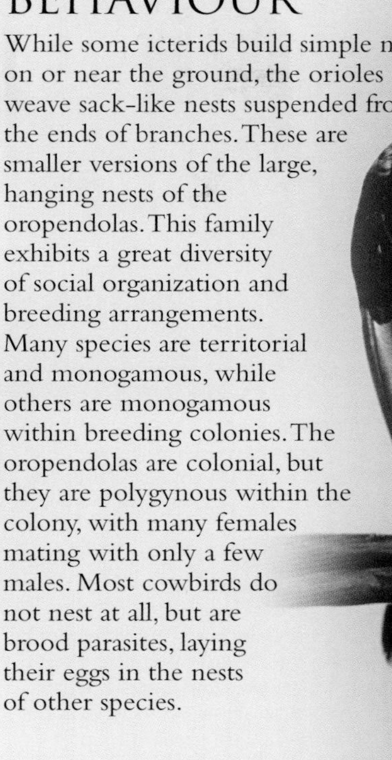

PERCHING MEADOWLARK
Meadowlarks (a Western Meadowlark is pictured) often seek elevated perches from which to sing.

BEHAVIOUR

While some icterids build simple nests on or near the ground, the orioles weave sack-like nests suspended from the ends of branches. These are smaller versions of the large, hanging nests of the oropendolas. This family exhibits a great diversity of social organization and breeding arrangements. Many species are territorial and monogamous, while others are monogamous within breeding colonies. The oropendolas are colonial, but they are polygynous within the colony, with many females mating with only a few males. Most cowbirds do not nest at all, but are brood parasites, laying their eggs in the nests of other species.

GRACKLE COURTSHIP
A calling, displaying Common Grackle puffs up its chest and opens its wings to show off the iridescence on the chest.

MALE YELLOW-RUMPED CACIQUE

Cacicus cela

Yellow-rumped Cacique

LENGTH	23–29cm (9–11½in)
WEIGHT	70–100g (2½–3⅝oz)
MIGRATION	Non-migrant

HABITAT Forest edges, woodland, and semi-open areas with scattered trees

A slender long-tailed bird, the Yellow-rumped Cacique has black plumage that contrasts with its yellow lower belly, wing patches, rump, and tail base. Its eyes are blue and its bill is white. It breeds colonially, with up to 100 bag-shaped nests in a tree, usually near a wasp's nest for protection. A sociable species, these birds feed in flocks.

Psarocolius decumanus

Crested Oropendola

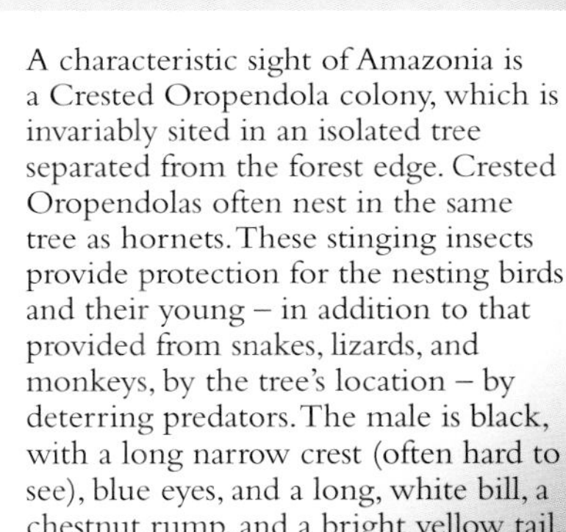

LENGTH	34–49cm (13½–19½in)
WEIGHT	150–275g (5–10oz)
MIGRATION	Non-migrant

HABITAT Edges and clearings of lowland rainforest, deciduous woodland; farmland with scattered trees

HANGING NESTS

The Crested Oropendola, as all oropendolas, is a colonial breeder. The female builds a hanging woven nest, more than 1.2m (4ft) long, high in a tree, usually near a hornet's nest. Each colony has a dominant male, which mates with many females, after an elaborate bowing display. In a colony there may be 15–30 females and only 3 or 4 males.

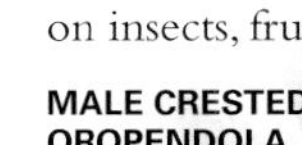

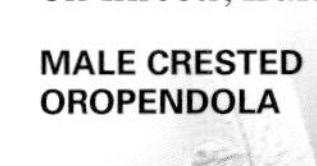

A characteristic sight of Amazonia is a Crested Oropendola colony, which is invariably sited in an isolated tree separated from the forest edge. Crested Oropendolas often nest in the same tree as hornets. These stinging insects provide protection for the nesting birds and their young – in addition to that provided from snakes, lizards, and monkeys, by the tree's location – by deterring predators. The male is black, with a long narrow crest (often hard to see), blue eyes, and a long, white bill, a chestnut rump, and a bright yellow tail. The female is smaller and duller, and lacks the crest. This species feeds on insects, fruit, and berries.

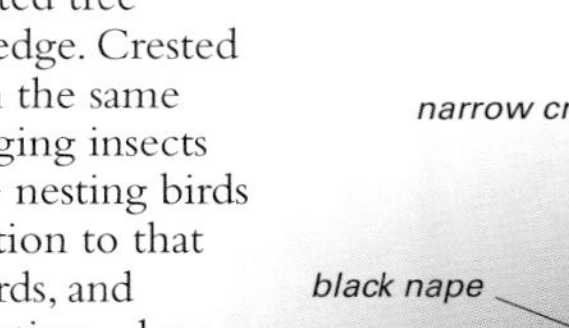

MALE CRESTED OROPENDOLA

Icterus galbula

Baltimore Oriole

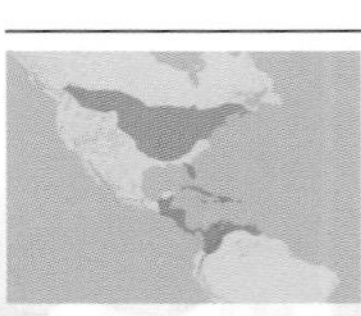

LENGTH 20–22cm (8–8½in)

WEIGHT 30–35g (1¹⁄₁₆–1¼oz)

MIGRATION Migrant

HABITAT Breeds in open woodland and winters in rainforest; roosts in tall grass or cane; gardens

The Baltimore Oriole is the commonest oriole breeding in eastern North America, but has had a chequered history as a species. It was frequently grouped with Bullock's Oriole (*I. bullockii*), a similar species found in western USA, but DNA studies suggest that the two orioles are not close relatives. The only bright orange and black oriole north of Florida, the male has an orange-yellow shoulder patch and black wings, with white edging. The female is mainly olive in colour, with pale orange underparts, and the juvenile is similar. Like most orioles, the Baltimore Oriole forages by gleaning insects and caterpillars from the leaves of trees, but it also searches for food in grass and plants. It switches to a diet of mainly nectar in winter, supplemented with berries.

In the breeding season, the displaying male spreads its wings and tail and bows to the female. These orioles nest in trees and four eggs are laid in mid- to late May. Although the female is largely responsible for parental duties, it abandons the young just before they become independent, in order to commence its post-breeding moult. The species is a long-distance migrant, and southbound migration from breeding grounds begins as early as the end of July.

ADULT MALE
The adult male has bright orange-red underparts, a deep black head and back, and white on the wings, especially when breeding.

ADULT FEMALE
With its paler underparts and back and plain head, the female is less colourful than the male.

Euphagus cyanocephalus

Brewer's Blackbird

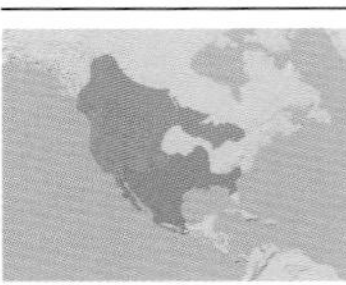

LENGTH 21–23cm (8½–9in)

WEIGHT 60–65g (2⅛–2⅜oz)

MIGRATION Partial migrant

HABITAT Open farmland, alpine meadows and beaches; very common in urban areas

In contrast to the grey-brown female, the male Brewer's Blackbird is all black with a green and purple-blue gloss. The male has yellow eyes; these are usually brown in the female. A gregarious bird, it forms large foraging and roosting flocks in winter and during migration, often joining mixed-species flocks. It is a colonial nester, a strategy that appears to reduce nest predation, although the Brown-headed Cowbird (below) parasitizes this species. The nest is made of dry grass, held together with mud, and usually placed in a bush or occasionally, on the ground.

ADULT MALE

Quiscalus quiscula

Common Grackle

LENGTH 12–13cm (4½–5in)

WEIGHT 90–125g (3¼–4oz)

MIGRATION Partial migrant

HABITAT Open areas, such as fields, marshes, and parks; common in suburban areas

The Common Grackle appears completely black from a distance, but there is a purplish blue or even bronzy hue to its metallic plumage. The female is slightly smaller and duller than the male. Both sexes have pale yellow eyes and a long keel-shaped tail. In a characteristic display, the male spreads out its wings and tail and fluffs up its body feathers, which then resemble a ruffed collar. It also displays in flight.

ADULT COMMON GRACKLE

Molothrus ater

Brown-headed Cowbird

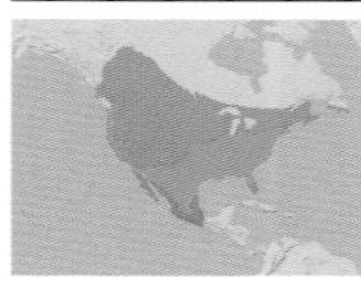

LENGTH 19–20cm (7½–8in)

WEIGHT 30–50g (1¹⁄₁₆–1¾oz)

MIGRATION Partial migrant

HABITAT Open woodland and grassland; gardens

The Brown-headed Cowbird is one of the most numerous birds in North America, with an estimated population of 20–40 million. Whereas the male is metallic green-black with a contrasting brown head, the female is mainly grey-black and paler below. This species is gregarious, foraging and roosting in flocks. It walks on the ground to forage, feeding on insects, grain, and fruit.

The Brown-headed Cowbird is an aggressive brood parasite and the expansion of its colonies in the eastern states in the 20th century has led to a decline in many songbird species. In some areas, control programmes have been initiated to protect rare host species (a total of more than 220 species have been recorded as hosts). Cowbird eggs are generally laid in the morning. The female usually appears to be extremely fertile.

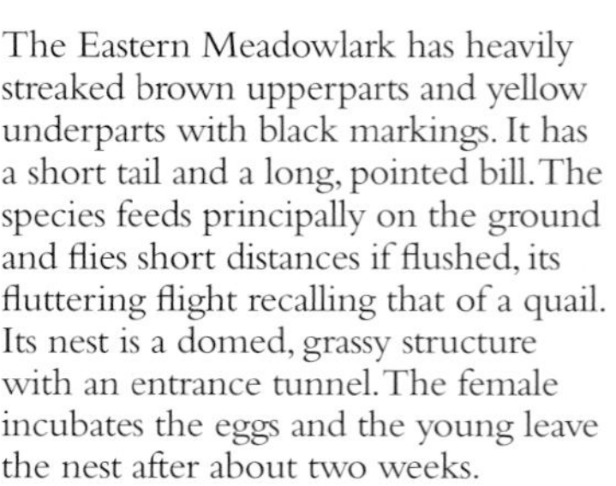

ADULT MALE

Sturnella magna

Eastern Meadowlark

LENGTH 22–25cm (8½–10in)

WEIGHT 75–100g (2⅝–3⅝oz)

MIGRATION Partial migrant

HABITAT Native grassland, pastures, meadows, and old fields

The Eastern Meadowlark has heavily streaked brown upperparts and yellow underparts with black markings. It has a short tail and a long, pointed bill. The species feeds principally on the ground and flies short distances if flushed, its fluttering flight recalling that of a quail. Its nest is a domed, grassy structure with an entrance tunnel. The female incubates the eggs and the young leave the nest after about two weeks.

ADULT EASTERN MEADOWLARK

Dolichonyx oryzivorus

Bobolink

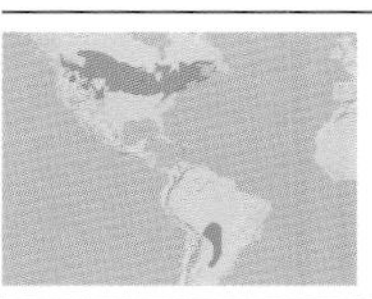

LENGTH 18–21cm (7–8½in)

WEIGHT 30–35g (1¹⁄₁₆–1¼oz)

MIGRATION Migrant

HABITAT Breeds in grassy prairies and fallow fields; winters in rice fields, grassland, and marshes

The Bobolink undertakes a very long migration, travelling to south of the equator each autumn, moving up to 10,000km (6,200 miles) from its breeding to its wintering grounds. The breeding male is a mixture of black and white, with a buff nape patch; the female is principally yellow, with a striped head pattern and streaked upperparts. The Bobolink's name reflects its song, which the male utters in flight over breeding territories. The species shows strong site fidelity, nesting on the same grounds year after year.

ADULT MALE BOBOLINK

Agelaius phoeniceus

Red-winged Blackbird

LENGTH 20–22cm (8–8½in)

WEIGHT 40–65g (1⁷⁄₁₆–2⅜oz)

MIGRATION Partial migrant

HABITAT Breeds in dense freshwater vegetation; also occurs in fields and woodland edges

In contrast to the extremely boldly patterned male, the female Red-winged Blackbird is dark brown to charcoal black above, with heavily streaked underparts, and sometimes wedge-shaped flashes of red on the wings. The species lives in colonies and is one of the earliest harbingers of spring in North America. The male generally arrives first and immediately begins to establish a territory. The nest is made in reed and sedge beds just above the water surface and is usually woven around the stalks of cat-tails. The period from the start of incubation – carried out by the female – until the young fledge, is less than a month.

The song of both sexes is a series of ringing and scratchy, buzzy trills; when the whole colony is active, there is a cacophony of sound. Most populations north of Mexico are migratory, while the tropical birds are largely sedentary.

MALE RED-WINGED BLACKBIRD

LARGE ROOSTING FLOCKS

Gregarious at roosts all year round, the Red-winged Blackbird gathers in large flocks – in its wintering grounds, some roosts may number in the millions. It also forages in flocks, sometimes up to a distance of 80km (50 miles) from the roost site. In the breeding season, roosts are smaller and attended only by young, non-breeding males.

BANANAQUIT

ORDER	Passeriformes
FAMILY	Coerebidae
SPECIES	1

THE BANANAQUIT IS one of the most common and familiar birds of the Caribbean, although it is absent from Cuba. It is also widespread in Latin America. Its relationship to other birds has long been debated. It has in the past been considered one of the New World warblers (see p.468) or a tanager (see p.481). However, many ornithologists now put it in a family of its own.

BEHAVIOUR

Bananaquits use their tubular tongues to suck nectar after piercing the base of a flower with their decurved, sharply pointed bill. They pierce fruit in a similar manner to feed on the juice. Males and females both build globular nests that are often used as sleeping quarters with separate nests used for breeding. Members of a pair sleep separately in different nests, but they do not sleep in the same nest night after night. Sometimes groups of birds that are not mates share a sleeping nest as a kind of dormitory.

FLOWERY FEAST
Nectar-filled, tubular flowers are a favourite food source for Bananaquits, which use their sharp bills to pierce the flower base.

Coereba flaveola

Bananaquit

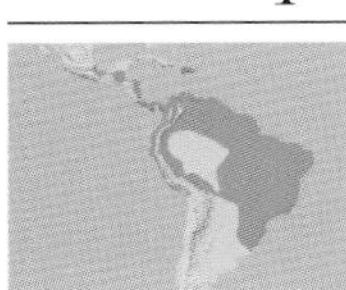

LENGTH 10–12cm (4–4½in)

WEIGHT 8–11g (⁵⁄₁₆–⅜oz)

MIGRATION Non-migrant

HABITAT Any form of wooded or well-vegetated habitat, including gardens, but generally not tall forest

Commonly known as "sugarbird" or "nectar robber", due to its propensity to visit sugar-water feeders intended for hummingbirds, the Bananaquit is a familiar tropical bird. It usually has a white eyebrow, dark upperparts, and yellow and white underparts. However, there is extraordinary variation in its plumage, which has led scientists to recognize as many as 40 different subspecies. Some of these deviate quite dramatically from the "usual" plumage features. For example, the subspecies found on the island of St. Vincent is entirely black. This has led to the view that as many as nine different species of the Bananaquit should be recognized.

While the Bananaquit is difficult to miss, its voice is easily overlooked, the song being a "wispy" insect-like trill. The bird is usually seen alone or in pairs, which maintain only loose contact with each other. The nest is an untidy structure of dry grass suspended from a tall bush, and is also frequently used as a roosting site.

ADULT BANANAQUIT

BUNTINGS AND AMERICAN SPARROWS

ORDER	Passeriformes
FAMILY	Emberizidae
SPECIES	308

THIS FAMILY INCLUDES BOTH the New World sparrows and the Old World buntings. Once treated as a sub-family of the Finches (see p.464), they are now recognized as a family in their own right. American sparrows are believed to have evolved in the Americas, subsequently spreading to most of the world, except for Madagascar, southeast Asia, and Australasia. Many species have relatively drab and subdued body plumage, streaked with browns, blacks, and whites for camouflage. However, the males especially tend to have striking head patterns.

COURTSHIP AND MATING
Corn Buntings are known to be promiscuous, with both males and females mating with more than one partner. Males play no part in raising young.

ADAPTIVE RADIATION
Among Galapagos ground finches, bills have evolved to take advantage of all available food sources, including large and small seeds and insects.

ANATOMY

Generally larger and more sturdily built than finches, these birds vary in size from the tiny grassquits, weighing less than 10gm ($\frac{1}{3}$oz), to buntings and towhees (sparrows) weighing three to six times as much. They have strong, short conical bills for seed eating. These bills may be adapted for small seeds, as in smaller species, such as the grassquits, whose light weight enables them to cling to the seedheads of grasses. But they also include some very powerful bills capable of tackling large, hard seeds. The most extreme examples are found among ground finches from the Galapagos islands (known as Darwin's ground finches), where an original ground finch ancestor has evolved to occupy many different seed-eating and insect-eating niches. The Woodpecker Finch actually extends the reach of its bill by using a sharp twig or cactus spine to probe for invertebrates.

BEHAVIOUR

Like most other seed-eating birds, buntings and New World sparrows switch to a diet of mostly insects when feeding young. Most species feed on or near the ground, and hop on their relatively large feet, although some walk and run. Usually seen singly or in pairs in the breeding season, during winter and on migration they form small groups and, less frequently, large flocks, sometimes joining with other species. Most buntings and American sparrows have simple, jangling songs given from a perch and, more rarely, in a song-flight. Most species within this family are highly territorial, using their songs to mark and defend their territories as well as to attract mates.

ACTIVE PARENT
The Lapland Longspur (above) is a ground-nesting species which breeds in the Arctic tundra, where the continual daylight of high summer means parents can be active at all hours.

YELLOWHAMMERS FEEDING
In winter, many buntings such as these Yellowhammers form flocks for feeding and roosting. Changes in farming practice have led to a reduced availability of winter food, which in turn has been responsible for a decline in populations of many species.

Emberiza citrinella

Yellowhammer

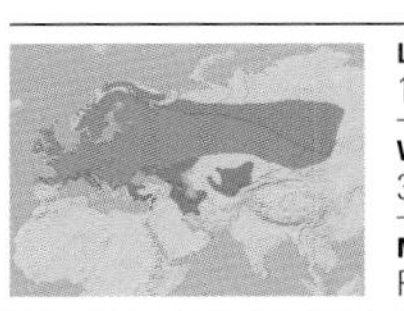

LENGTH 17cm (6 1/2in)

WEIGHT 30g (1 1/16oz)

MIGRATION Partial migrant

HABITAT Farmland, bushy areas, heaths, and woodland edges; also on coasts

The Yellowhammer is characterized by its long tail. The male, with its mainly yellow head and breast, cannot be easily confused with other species. The female is distinctive too, with a partly yellow head, the rest of the plumage being streaky brown.

Like many buntings, Yellowhammers are social birds, especially in winter, when they forage on the ground in large flocks for grain and seeds, flying up to the nearest cover at the slightest disturbance. In summer, they move in pairs and nest low down either in a bush or on the ground. The Yellowhammer is best known for its song, which was formerly a commonplace sound in rural areas.

MALE YELLOWHAMMER

ADULT MALE

Emberiza schoeniclus

Common Reed Bunting

LENGTH 14–16cm (5 1/2–6 1/2in)

WEIGHT 17–20g (5/8–11/16oz)

MIGRATION Partial migrant

HABITAT Reeds or wet areas; also breeds among young conifers and crops

The male Common Reed Bunting has a striking black and white head, rusty-brown upperparts, and pale underparts, while the female is plainer, with cream and brown streaks on its back. In spring, the male sings from a tall reed or bush, staking out its territory. The male can be polygamous, but both sexes incubate the eggs and feed the young. However, the female builds the nest.

Calcarius lapponicus

Lapland Longspur

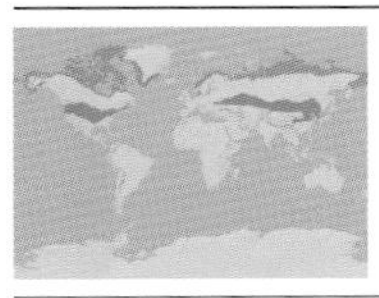

LENGTH 14–16cm (5 1/2–6 1/2in)

WEIGHT 30g (1 1/16oz)

MIGRATION Migrant

HABITAT Breeds in upland and tundra; winters on coasts and cultivated steppes

In winter, the Lapland Longspur has red-brown cheeks and pale brown plumage. However, in summer, the male (pictured here) has a black and white facial pattern and a bright rufous nape. Compared to the summer male, the breeding female has a plainer face pattern, with virtually no black. This species is wary and flies long distances when it is disturbed.

MALE IN SUMMER PLUMAGE

Plectrophenax nivalis

Snow Bunting

LENGTH 15–18cm (6–7in)

WEIGHT 35–55g (1 1/4–2oz)

MIGRATION Migrant

HABITAT Breeds in dry rocky areas of the Arctic; winters in fields and on shores to the south

Named by the famous Swedish naturalist, Carl Linné (better known as Linneaus), the dainty Snow Bunting often appears completely white when it is in flight. The male Snow Bunting has a white head and shoulders, black upperparts, long black and white wings, and a white rump. The female has a white head, with brown streaks, and greyish black upperparts tinged with brown. Both sexes have white underparts.

The Snow Bunting is the most northerly-breeding songbird in the world. This bird is among the last to reach its breeding grounds and does not start nesting until late May. It is usually monogamous, remaining in pairs during the breeding season. The nest is on the ground and sheltered from the elements in a crevice; up to nine eggs are laid. Incubation and nest-building duties, as with many other bunting species, are carried out solely by the female.

In winter, these birds prefer to form flocks limited to their own species, but in areas where they are less common, they may band with longspurs or other seed-eating birds. In harsh weather, they may take shelter in a hole.

MALE IN SUMMER PLUMAGE

SEASONAL PLUMAGE

In summer, the male Snow Bunting is strikingly black and white, while in winter, it has a yellow bill and assumes a less conspicuous garb of warm buff-brown and white (pictured right). The female is similar to the male in this season, but shows much less white in the wing, while in summer, when it is nesting, it is largely grey below and dark brownish grey on the upperparts.

Calamospiza melanocorys

Lark Bunting

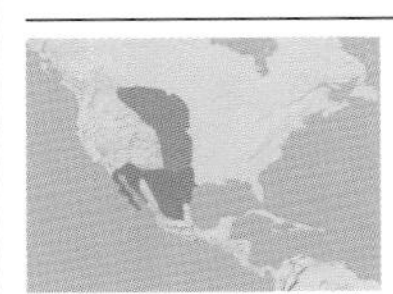

LENGTH 14–18cm (5 1/2–7in)

WEIGHT 30–50g (1 1/16–1 3/4oz)

MIGRATION Migrant

HABITAT Breeds in short-grass prairies; winters in open grassland and farmland

MALE LARK BUNTING

The male Lark Bunting is mainly black, with large, white wing patches. The female Lark Bunting has brown-streaked plumage with a pale wing-panel. In the early breeding season, the male performs display flights, ascending high up in the air, singing all the while, and then parachuting down. These sparrows breed colonially; the male sometimes has more than one mate and the female is responsible for nest-building and incubating the eggs.

ADULT FOX SPARROW (EASTERN SUBSPECIES)

Passerella iliaca

Fox Sparrow

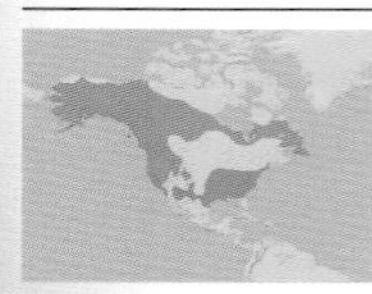

LENGTH 15–19cm (6–7½in)

WEIGHT 25–50g (⅞–1¾oz)

MIGRATION Migrant

HABITAT Breeds in deciduous thickets or firs; winters in brush and chaparral

In recent years, some scientists have been in favour of treating Fox Sparrows as four different species, principally based on the wide variation in plumage coloration. The most widespread variant is the eastern subspecies pictured here (the so-called Red Fox Sparrow), with its grey crown and red-streaked chest and back. The other subspecies are the Sooty Fox Sparrow, which is dark brown, the grey Slate-coloured Fox Sparrow, and the Thick-billed Fox Sparrow, although the two latter forms are very similar.

The Fox Sparrow mainly feeds in bushes and brush, but occasionally ventures to the ground where, in winter, it may be heard scratching for food in the dry leaves. It forms small, loose flocks at this season, but is less sociable than many North American sparrows. The Fox Sparrow generally nests on the ground, but occasionally in trees, and constructs a bulky cup of twigs, rootlets, and grasses. The female alone incubates the 3–5 eggs.

Melospiza melodia

Song Sparrow

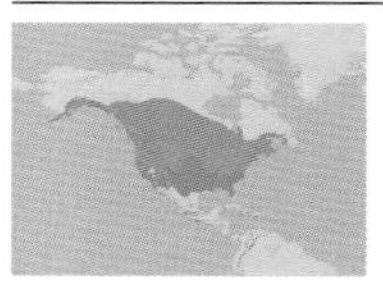

LENGTH 12–17cm (4½–6½in)

WEIGHT 12–55g (7/16–55oz)

MIGRATION Partial migrant

HABITAT Open brushy areas, woodland edges, coastal marshes, and beaches

The plumage of the Song Sparrow is mainly reddish brown and grey, with a well-marked grey and brown striped head pattern. Some populations are greyer and paler above and below. The species is variable in size and plumage. Its song varies too, but is usually a whistle ending in a trill. It is a sociable bird, forming flocks often in combination with other species in winter. It may have up to three broods in a season, with the young fledging in as little as a week.

ADULT SONG SPARROW

Zonotrichia albicollis

White-throated Sparrow

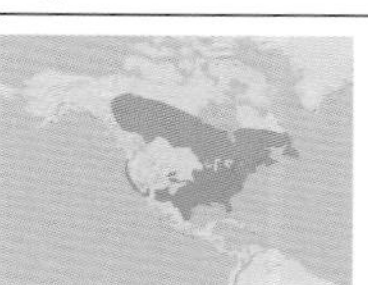

LENGTH 15–17cm (6–6½in)

WEIGHT 19–35g (11/16–1¼oz)

MIGRATION Migrant

HABITAT Brushland and semi-open woodland, including plantations and bogs; often in clearings

The White-throated Sparrow is identifiable principally by its complex head pattern of white crown-stripes and white eyebrows, with a yellow patch in front of the eyes, and a white throat patch. However, different forms exist, and some birds have tan-coloured crown-stripes and eyebrows. In breeding grounds, the male sings constantly, even at night.

ADULT MALE

Junco hyemalis

Dark-eyed Junco

LENGTH 13–17cm (5–6½in)

WEIGHT 14–25g (½–⅞oz)

MIGRATION Partial migrant

HABITAT Semi-open woodland and edges, brushy country, urban areas, and gardens

Writing in the 1700s, the American naturalist John James Audubon remarked that there was not a person in the country who did not know this little sparrow and it remains one of the most common and ubiquitous birds of North America. The Dark-eyed Junco was formerly known as the Snow-bird or Winter Finch. This was probably because over much of the more populous eastern states, where it is primarily a winter visitor, its numbers increase during severe winter. This species has a variable appearance (see panel), although all forms have dark eyes. The sexes are alike, but the juvenile has a streaked plumage.

The species feeds on seeds, berries, and invertebrates. The male Dark-eyed Junco sings almost year-round, but most frequently between February and June, coinciding with the main breeding period. As winter turns to spring, the flocks of this species begin to disband and pairs leave to breed. The nest is usually well concealed, built on a tree and occasionally on the ground or even in a building. It is built by the female, who also takes sole responsibility for incubating eggs that can number up to six. These hatch after less than two weeks and the young take up to two weeks to fledge. They are fed by both parents.

ADULT DARK-EYED JUNCO

VARIABLE SPECIES

Striking plumage differences exist between the five forms of the Dark-eyed Junco. The commonest form is the Slate-coloured Junco, but the four other recognized forms are the Pink-sided, White-winged, Grey-headed, and Oregon (shown here) Juncos. However, since they interbreed, they are still considered as a single species.

ADULT CHIPPING SPARROW

Spizella passerina

Chipping Sparrow

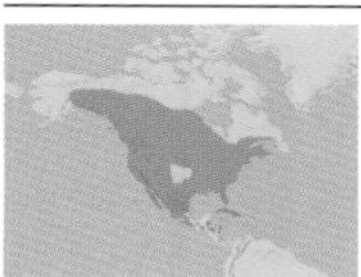

LENGTH 12–14cm (4½–5½in)

WEIGHT 11–15g (3/8–9/16oz)

MIGRATION Partial migrant

HABITAT Widespread in open woodland, edges, grassy fields, and parkland

One of the most common North American sparrows, the Chipping Sparrow is a small, slim bird. It has a rusty crown and striking white eyebrows in summer, but in winter, its face pattern is less well marked and the crown is a duller brown. It is named after its repetitive rattle, a series of "chip chip" sounds that is among the most frequently heard bird songs. The species breeds from March in southern USA. The female builds the nest on a branch, well above the ground.

Amphispiza belli

Sage Sparrow

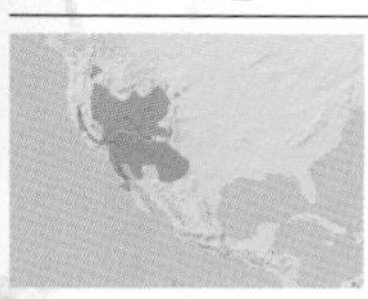

LENGTH 14–16cm (5½–6½in)

WEIGHT 14–19g (½–11/16oz)

MIGRATION Partial migrant

HABITAT Sagebrush desert and chapparal, with some populations moving to higher altitudes in summer

Both the male and female Sage Sparrow have the same plumage, with predominantly dark head, a white moustachial stripe and spot in front of the bill, and dark brown-grey upperparts. This sparrow spends most of its time foraging unobtrusively on the ground in small flocks. Two subspecies are now recognized: the Bell's Sparrow of coastal areas and the larger, paler form in the interior.

ADULT SAGE SPARROW

Aimophila aestivalis

Bachman's Sparrow

LENGTH 12–16cm (4½–6½in)

WEIGHT 18–25g (5/8–7/8oz)

MIGRATION Non-migrant

HABITAT Dry open woodland and scrub, especially closely associated with pines

Formerly known as the Pine-woods Sparrow, this typical North American sparrow has a grey head and back heavily streaked with chestnut and dark brown and off-white underparts. Bachman's Sparrow has a comparatively large bill and a long, rounded tail. Except when singing, at which times it selects a high open perch, the species often stays close to the ground.

ADULT ZAPATA SPARROW

Torreornis inexpectata

Zapata Sparrow

LENGTH 17cm (6½in)

WEIGHT 25g (7/8oz)

MIGRATION Non-migrant

HABITAT Forest and scrub, including extremely dry areas

RED LIST CATEGORY Endangered

Named after the shoe-shaped peninsula in southern Cuba where it was originally observed ("zapata" means "shoe" in Spanish), the Zapata Sparrow has a white throat, olive-grey upperparts, and yellow underparts, with short wings. In some areas, it feeds on water snails, eggs, and small lizards. Its call is a high-pitched trill.

Sicalis flaveola

Saffron Finch

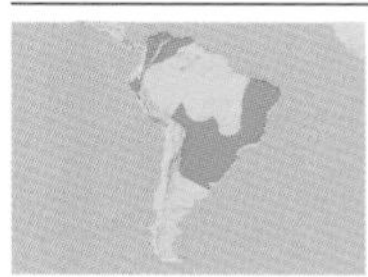

LENGTH 14cm (5½in)

WEIGHT 16–20g (9/16–11/16oz)

MIGRATION Non-migrant

HABITAT Open, weedy, and shrubby areas; secondary growth and parks

Almost entirely bright yellow, the male Saffron Finch has a striking orange forecrown. In contrast, the female and the juvenile have streaky greenish yellow plumage, relieved only by occasional yellow patches. The species mainly forages on the ground, frequently in large flocks, in which they sometimes join other seed-eating birds.

Sporophila corvina

Variable Seedeater

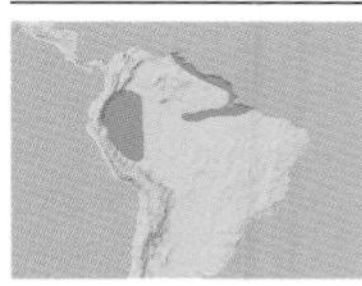

LENGTH 12cm (4½in)

WEIGHT 10g (3/8oz)

MIGRATION Non-migrant

HABITAT Grassy and shrubby areas, including in urban areas; woodland edges

The male Variable Seedeater is not difficult to identify, with its mainly black upperparts, white partial collar, black chest-band, and white to grey belly. The female is much more difficult to tell apart from other female seed-eaters, being essentially yellowish olive-brown above and paler below. The Variable Seedeater is a ground-loving bird, but if disturbed, it flies into nearby cover. It also clings to low grass-heads to feed on seeds. These birds are generally found in pairs or small groups, or in larger flocks outside the breeding season.

MALE VARIABLE SEEDEATER

Tiaris olivaceus

Yellow-faced Grassquit

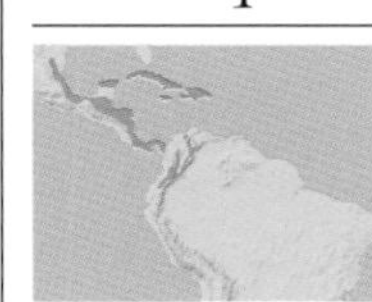

LENGTH 10cm (4in)

WEIGHT 9g (11/32oz)

MIGRATION Non-migrant

HABITAT Wooded areas, especially at edges; also bushy country

Both sexes of the small Yellow-faced Grassquit are olive-green with yellow on the face, but the male has a larger area of yellow on the throat, which is set off by black on the face and upper breast. It is a sociable sparrow-like bird that spends much time of its time feeding on the ground, searching for seeds and small fruit, but ascends to nearby trees to sing. The song is a high-pitched insect-like trill. It nests the year round, laying 2–4 eggs.

MALE YELLOW-FACED GRASSQUIT

WHITE-THROATED SPARROW
This sparrow usually breeds in Canada, but in winter it can be found across large parts of the eastern United States (this bird was photographed on Long Island).

ADULT LARGE GROUND FINCH

Geospiza magnirostris

Large Ground Finch

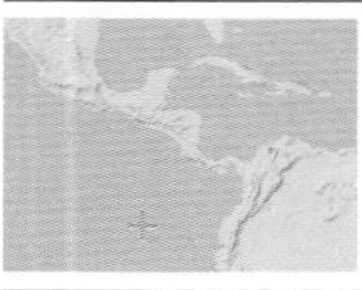

LENGTH 16cm (6½in)
WEIGHT 35g (1¼oz)
MIGRATION Non-migrant

HABITAT Arid zones, with deciduous, open dry forest and scrubland

Endemic to the Galapagos Islands, the Large Ground Finch has the deepest bill in its family, the depth at the base being the same length as the upper mandible, which it uses to crush seeds. Despite its name, this bird does not feed on the ground as often as the other ground finches.

Geospiza fuliginosa

Small Ground Finch

LENGTH 11cm (4½in)
WEIGHT 15g (9/16oz)
MIGRATION Non-migrant

HABITAT Arid, highland zones of Galapagos, in forest, scrub, and open areas

The Small Ground Finch is the smallest of the four species of ground finch. The male is black with white-tipped undertail feathers, while the female is brown with streaked underparts. Both have short, pointed bills. These finches have a symbiotic relationship with giant tortoises and iguanas, feeding on their skin parasites. After breeding, in the warm or wet season, they move up to the highlands.

ADULT SMALL GROUND FINCH

Camarhynchus pallidus

Woodpecker Finch

LENGTH 15cm (6in)
WEIGHT 25g (7/8oz)
MIGRATION Non-migrant

HABITAT Humid forest in highland zones of the Galapagos, also in dry forest in arid lowland

One of the few bird species in the world that uses a tool during foraging (see panel, below), the Woodpecker Finch probes under rocks, branches, or leaves to extract invertebrates, such as grubs, to eat, quite unlike the other Galapagos finches. The male and female are alike in plumage, which consists of plain olive or brown upperparts and yellow or off-white underparts, which are usually unmarked, although some birds show fine grey streaking on the upper breast. The bill is long and stout with the upper part markedly curved. The call of the Woodpecker Finch is a high-pitched whistle descending to a lower note.

ADULT WOODPECKER FINCH

USING TOOLS

The Woodpecker Finch is adept at holding tools, such as a twig or cactus spine, in its bill. It manipulates these tools to probe deep into cracks and crevices to prise out insects. The bird is one of the very few birds in the world to use tools to feed.

TOOLS AS COMPENSATION
With its short tongue, the Woodpecker Finch has to resort to using tools; in the dry season, it acquires half its prey in this way.

Pipilo maculatus

Spotted Towhee

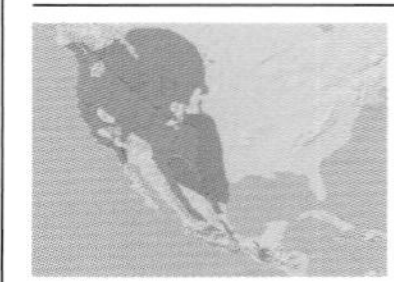

LENGTH 21cm (8½in)
WEIGHT 40g (17/16oz)
MIGRATION Partial migrant

HABITAT Brushy areas, sunny clearings, shrubland or undergrowth within open forest

Until recently, the Spotted Towhee was considered to be the same species as the Eastern Towhee (*P. erythrophthalmus*), but differences in their plumage and voice resulted in their separation into distinct species. However, the two species hybridize where their range overlaps. The male Spotted Towhee has a black head and breast, black upperparts, spotted white, black wings with two white wing-bars, a white-tipped black tail, red flanks, and a white belly. The female is duller, with a dark brown head, neck, breast, and upperparts and dark brown wings.

These birds forage on the ground by scratching in leaf litter, using their characteristic two-footed, backwards-scratching hop, to unearth insects, caterpillars, and seeds. They move in pairs or alone, but small family groups stay together after the nesting season.

MALE SPOTTED TOWHEE

Paroaria coronata

Red-crested Cardinal

LENGTH 19cm (7½in)
WEIGHT 40g (17/16oz)
MIGRATION Non-migrant

HABITAT Semi-open areas with shrubbery and scattered trees, particularly near water

A well-known and very distinctive inhabitant of the grasslands of southern South America, the Red-crested Cardinal has plumage that is striking in colour. The head, crest, throat, and central breast are bright red. The upperparts are grey, with blacker wings and tail, and the underparts are white. The juvenile is duller, with a shorter crest.

The species generally occurs in pairs or small groups, but larger flocks may form outside the breeding season. Red-crested Cardinals feed on open ground, foraging for seeds, fruit, and insects. In the nesting season, both parents feed the young when they are in the nest. As soon as they have fledged, however, the male takes sole responsibility for feeding and guarding the pair's offspring.

ADULT RED-CRESTED CARDINAL

TANAGERS

ORDER	Passeriformes
FAMILY	Thraupidae
SPECIES	202

PERHAPS THE MOST COLOURFUL of all the birds, the tanagers are native to the tropics of the Americas. This is reflected in their name, which is derived from "tangara," the name used by the Tupi native people of Brazil. The exact relationships of some birds long known as tanagers remains unclear, with some of the best known, such as the Scarlet Tanager and the euphonias, removed from the Tanager family by some authorities and placed in a limbo status between the tanagers and cardinals (see p.484).

BEHAVIOUR

Primarily fruit-eaters, tanagers will supplement their diet with insects and small spiders. Honeycreepers regularly feed on nectar. They are birds of the treetops and will move through the canopy in mixed-species flocks. Many species maintain their pair bond throughout the year; in these birds the males will occasionally feed the female, especially at the beginning of the breeding season. Nests are open and cup-shaped, placed in trees and small shrubs. Only the Swallow Tanager regularly nests on the ground.

SUMMER AND WINTER
The plumage of the male Scarlet Tanager changes from its bright red breeding coloration during the summer to dull yellow in the winter.

ANATOMY

Small to medium-sized forest birds, many tanagers exhibit combinations of brilliant yellows, reds, greens, and blues, with a few species even appearing metallic. Their bills are generally medium-sized and slightly pointed, although in some groups, such as the honeycreepers, they are thin and decurved. In the flowerpiercers, the bills are slightly up-turned and hooked at the tip. With the exception of the unique Giant Conebill, which looks remarkably like a nuthatch (see p.426) in both shape and posture, the overall body shape of tanagers is finchlike with a medium-sized tail. In most species there is no significant difference between males and females in either colour or size.

NESTING TANAGER
The Black-capped Tanager raises its young in a simple, open, cup-shaped nest.

Schistochlamys ruficapillus

Cinnamon Tanager

LENGTH	18cm (7in)
WEIGHT	30g (1 1/16oz)
MIGRATION	Non-migrant

HABITAT Semi-open grassy areas with scattered bushes and low trees, cerrado, and caatinga

An attractive denizen of the cerrado and caatinga (open grasslands) regions of east Brazil, the Cinnamon Tanager is fairly common in some areas but uncommon in others. Named because of the cinnamon colour of most of its head, throat, breast, upper belly and vent, the Cinnamon Tanager has a conspicuous black eye mask that offsets the cinnamon of its head. The belly is white and the flanks grey. The bill is blue, tipped black. Its upperparts are blue-grey with duskier wings and tail. In fact, the shade on the upperparts is reflected in the generic name of the species, which is derived from the Greek word for "slate cloak". Sexes are similarly plumaged.

The Cinnamon Tanager is usually seen singly or in pairs, perching in low shrubbery, often in the open. The species associates only infrequently with mixed flocks. The short song is a musical whistle, and is repeated several times in succession. It is usually given from a prominent perch. Although much of its habitat has been destroyed or degraded, the species is not considered a global conservation concern.

ADULT CINNAMON TANAGER

Cissopis leveriana

Magpie-tanager

LENGTH	25–29cm (10–11 1/2in)
WEIGHT	75g (2 5/8oz)
MIGRATION	Non-migrant

HABITAT Forest edges and shrubby clearings with scattered tall trees

A large and unmistakable tanager, the Magpie-tanager is called a "magpie" because of its superficial resemblance to the Black-billed (*P. hudsoni*) and Common Magpies (see p.392) of North America and Eurasia. It is mainly black and white in colour, with a black throat, mantle, and breast, extending to the upper back. It has piercing yellow eyes that stand out against its glossy black head. Its most distinctive feature, however, is its long, graduated, black and white tail, which it moves up and down as it perches or makes long hops from branch to branch. A noisy bird, it often calls from the tops of trees with loud, metallic squeaks, and is conspicuous as it flies, with its wings whistling, a trait unusual among tanagers and one that is produced by its modified flight feathers.

The Magpie-tanager rarely joins mixed flocks, preferring to move in pairs or small groups of up to 10 birds of its own kind. These groups search for food, usually seeds, fruit, and insects. In the breeding season, the Magpie-tanager builds a nest on a small tree or in dense vegetation, lining it with leaves, grass, or other plant material, and lays 2–5 eggs.

The form that occurs in Amazonia is smaller than that of eastern South America, and has a white back.

ADULT MAGPIE-TANAGER

FEMALE SILVER-BEAKED TANAGER

Ramphocelus carbo

Silver-beaked Tanager

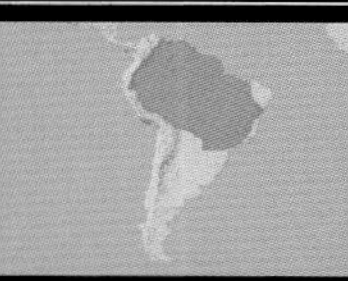

LENGTH 18cm (7in)

WEIGHT 30g (1 1/16oz)

MIGRATION Non-migrant

HABITAT Shrubby clearings, forest edges, and gardens, especially near water

Aptly named, the male Silver-beaked Tanager has a swollen lower mandible that gleams silver-white even in dim light. In bright light, the male's black upperparts take on a velvety-maroon sheen, highlighting its dark crimson throat and breast. The female is a duller red in colour. These social birds mainly eat fruit, but insects are also taken.

Anisognathus somptuosus

Blue-winged Mountain Tanager

LENGTH 18cm (7in)

WEIGHT 45g (1 5/8oz)

MIGRATION Non-migrant

HABITAT Humid forest and forest edges, mainly at altitudes of 1,500–2,500m (5,000–8,205ft)

One of a group of five strikingly patterned Andean tanagers, with either all-yellow or all-red underparts, the Blue-winged Mountain Tanager has cobalt blue patches on its wings, visible when the edges of its flight feathers close up together when it is at rest. It has stunning blue shoulders and upperparts, a yellow crown, broad black eye mask, and yellow underparts. The Blue-winged Mountain Tanager moves in flocks in the Andean forests.

ADULT BLUE-WINGED MOUNTAIN TANAGER

ADULT RED-NECKED TANAGER

Tangara cyanocephala

Red-necked Tanager

LENGTH 13cm (5in)

WEIGHT 18g (5/8oz)

MIGRATION Non-migrant

HABITAT Humid montane forest and forest edges

The prominent red neck band of the Red-necked Tanager helps to distinguish it from the other brightly coloured *Tangara* tanagers with which it usually flocks. The Red-necked Tanager's red collar is offset by a beautiful violet-blue crown, forehead, and chin, the rest of its plumage is basically a vivid green. Its eyes are circled in violet-blue and there is a small yellow-orange patch on its upper wing.

The Red-necked Tanager is common in its Atlantic forest range. The species feeds actively, usually gleaning insects in the canopy, but also descending lower to fruiting trees and to pick berries.

Tangara seledon

Green-headed Tanager

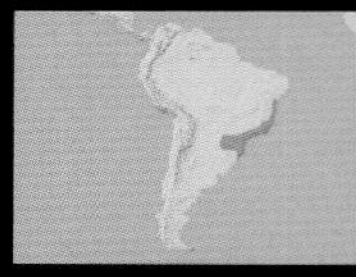

LENGTH 13cm (5in)

WEIGHT 19g (11/16oz)

MIGRATION Non-migrant

HABITAT Humid forest, forest edges, secondary woodland, and shrubby clearings

With its complex and colourful pattern, the Green-headed Tanager is easily recognizable in its Atlantic forest range. The male has a turquoise head and breast, yellow-green collar, black back and throat, and orange rump. Its wings, tail, and belly are green. The female is similar but duller in colour. The Green-headed Tanager occurs in groups of up to 10 vocal birds, which often form the centre of flocks feeding in the canopy.

ADULT MALE

Tersina viridis

Swallow Tanager

LENGTH 15cm (6in)

WEIGHT 30g (1 1/16 oz)

MIGRATION Partial migrant

HABITAT Humid forest edges and clearings with scattered trees and narrow strips of forest

Unusually among tanagers, the Swallow Tanager frequently flycatches for insects such as flying termites. At such times, with its partially forked tail, it may resemble a swallow. The male takes four years to develop the full adult plumage of turquoise, with a black throat. The female is bright green, with a grey mottled throat. This nomadic species moves in groups of up to 12 birds.

ADULT MALE WITH MATURE PLUMAGE

Cyanerpes cyaneus

Red-legged Honeycreeper

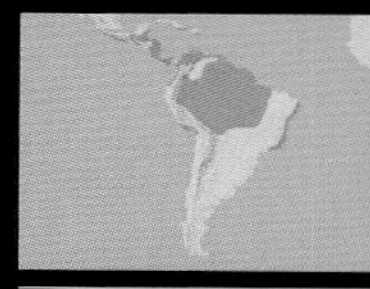

LENGTH 12cm (4 1/2in)

WEIGHT 14g (1/2oz)

MIGRATION Non-migrant

HABITAT Forest edges, woodland, clearings with scattered trees, and even residential areas

Almost alone among South American birds, the male Red-legged Honeycreeper moults into an "eclipse" plumage after the breeding season. For a few months, the male becomes dull green like the female, but with a black back, wings, and tail. The brilliance of its purplish blue plumage, with a contrasting pale turquoise crown, then returns. This splash of colour is offset by a black eye mask, nape, mantle, wings, and tail. The legs, as its common name indicates, are bright red. The female's legs, however, are red-brown. This bird uses its curved bill to suck nectar from flowers and to pick small insects as it forages in the forest.

MALE RED-LEGGED HONEYCREEPER

BLUISH GREEN MALE

Chlorophanes spiza

Green Honeycreeper

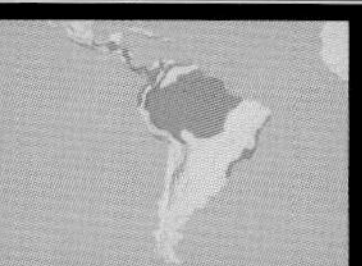

LENGTH 14cm (5½in)

WEIGHT 19g (11/16oz)

MIGRATION Non-migrant

HABITAT Humid tropical forest and secondary woodlands, including forest edges

As indicated by its name, green is the main colour of the plumage of both sexes of the Green Honeycreeper. The female is almost entirely bright "parakeet" green, darker on the wings and slightly paler below with a yellower throat and belly. The male is a shiny green or (in some races) bluish green, with duskier wings, and a contrasting black head.

The sole member of its genus, this bird is large and stocky, with a stout, slightly decurved yellow bill. It is a canopy fruit-eater, usually seen singly or in pairs (not in groups), although it often joins mixed flocks of tanagers.

Conirostrum cinereum

Cinereous Conebill

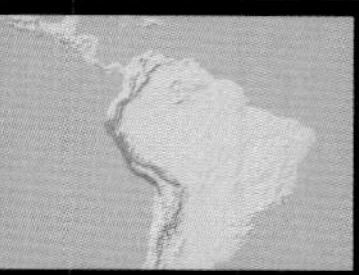

LENGTH 12cm (4½in)

WEIGHT 10g (3/8 oz)

MIGRATION Non-migrant

HABITAT Shrubby areas, woodland edges and areas with scattered trees and bushes, and even gardens

The Cinereous Conebill is the most common of the six Andean conebills (there are also four lowland members of the same genus). It is a small tanager, with a slender, sharply pointed bill. It has a white eyebrow, blue-grey upperparts that are darkest on the crown, and greyish white underparts, turning to buff on the vent. It has a distinctive L-shaped white patch on the wing, formed by white bases to the main flight feathers and white-tipped coverts.

Cinereous Conebills forage actively in foliage at all levels, usually in pairs or small groups, but may join mixed flocks.

ADULT CINEREOUS CONEBILL

Euphonia laniirostris

Thick-billed Euphonia

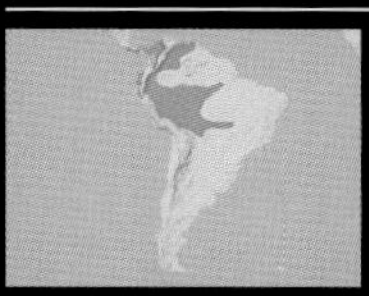

LENGTH 11cm (4½in)

WEIGHT 15g (9/16oz)

MIGRATION Non-migrant

HABITAT Forest edge, woodland, scrub, gardens, and agricultural areas with scattered trees

Typical of the euphonia species, the Thick-billed Euphonia is a small, short-tailed tanager with a stubby bill. The male is typically dark blue above, often with a yellow forehead, and yellow underparts. The female is dull olive and yellow, while the young male resembles the female but has a yellow forehead and a blue eye mask.

The Thick-billed Euphonia can be distinguished from all euphonias, except the Violaceous Euphonia (*E. violacea*), by its yellow throat; the two species do not overlap in range, so confusion is unlikely. While the Thick-billed Euphonia is well named, as it has the thickest bill of any euphonia, this characteristic is hard to determine in the field. It tends to forage for fruit in pairs or small groups, often with mixed tanager flocks, high up on trees. It builds its dome-shaped nest in a sheltered nook or cranny.

MALE IN FOREST CANOPY

Piranga olivacea

Scarlet Tanager

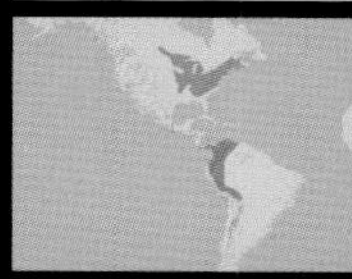

LENGTH 17cm (6½in)

WEIGHT 30g (11/16oz)

MIGRATION Migrant

HABITAT Deciduous forests; humid forest edges and secondary woodlands in winter

In breeding plumage, the male Scarlet Tanager is strikingly bicoloured with its black wings and tail offsetting its brilliant red plumage. In non-breeding plumage, it retains its black wings and tail, but otherwise resembles the female, being uniformly green above and greenish yellow below. The young male is dull orange-red, sometimes with faint pale wingbars.

After breeding in North America, virtually the entire population of Scarlet Tanagers migrates south in autumn, wintering in South America. In common with other members of its genus, but unlike other tanagers, the Scarlet Tanager feeds exclusively on insects and larvae, usually gleaned from the undersides of leaves.

MALE IN BREEDING PLUMAGE

Chlorophonia cyanea

Blue-naped Chlorophonia

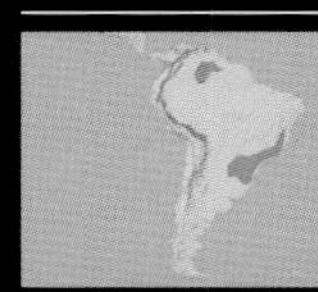

LENGTH 11cm (4½in)

WEIGHT 14g (½oz)

MIGRATION Non-migrant

HABITAT Humid forest edges and clearings with large trees

The head, throat, breast, wings, and tail of the Blue-naped Chlorophonia are bright green; its nape, mantle, and rump bright blue; and its belly and vent bright yellow. Despite this gaudy plumage, the Blue-naped Chlorophonia, like the other chlorophonias, can be inconspicuous, often remaining hidden in dense canopy foliage. These birds are fruit-eaters, favouring mistletoe berries, and unlike other tanagers, their nests are domed.

MALE BLUE-NAPED CHLOROPHONIA

CARDINALS AND GROSBEAKS

ORDER	Passeriformes
FAMILY	Cardinalidae
SPECIES	42

FOR SOME SPECIES of this heavy-billed, finchlike family of American birds, the name "grosbeak" is extremely apt. However, the English names of grosbeak and bunting that are used for some species in this family are also used for species in other families, such as finches (see p.464) and buntings and American sparrows (see p.474). The males are usually much more brightly coloured than the females, especially during the breeding season. Many species live in open woodland, which provides the seed-based diet, which they favour.

BEHAVIOUR

The males of most species of cardinals and grosbeaks are highly territorial. Many have loud, sweet, often repetitious songs, which they usually sing persistently from exposed perches during the breeding season. Birds of this family use their thick bills and powerful jaw muscles to crack open heavy seeds. They supplement their diet with berries, and will also feed on insects.

BREEDING RITUAL
As part of its elaborate courtship ritual, the bright red male Northern Cardinal feeds the much duller-coloured female when she assumes a begging posture.

SINGING MALE DICKCISSEL

Spiza americana

Dickcissel

LENGTH 15cm (6in)
WEIGHT 25g (7/8oz)
MIGRATION Migrant
HABITAT Grassy fallow fields, tall grass prairies, open country, and agricultural areas

The Dickcissel is a familiar bird in the farmlands in the Great Plains region of the USA. It is a stocky, sparrow-sized bird with a heavy bill and short tail. It has brown upperparts and a yellow breast. The distribution of this bird is obscured by its irregular movements. Birds may breed in large numbers at a site one year, only to be absent the next. During winter, these birds form huge flocks on the Venezuelan llanos, where they feed on rice and sorghum. Considered an agricultural pest, the roosts of this species – often in the millions – are targeted for poisoning.

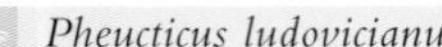

Pheucticus ludovicianus

Rose-breasted Grosbeak

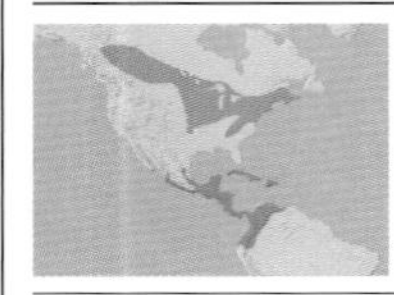

LENGTH 18.5cm (7½in)
WEIGHT 40g (1 7/16oz)
MIGRATION Migrant
HABITAT Mature, deciduous forest, forest edges, thick brush, semi-open country with scattered trees

A medium-sized stocky songbird, the male Rose-breasted Grosbeak is a striking creature, boldly patterned in black, white, and red. The drab female resembles a large sparrow or finch and is more of an identification challenge. However, it can be recognized by its large, thick, pale, cone-shaped bill, boldly striped head, and coarsely streaked breast. The juvenile resembles the female, although young males have an unstreaked orange breast.

PARENTAL CARE

The male Rose-breasted Grosbeak helps the female to incubate the eggs, and sings while on the nest. Incubation takes 14 days and fledging 9–12 days. Both parents care for the young. Juveniles remain under parental care for about three weeks.

MALE FEEDING JUVENILE
When two broods are produced in a season, the male feeds the fledged young, while the female builds the new nest.

Where their ranges overlap, the Rose-breasted Grosbeak hybridizes with the Black-headed Grosbeak (*P. melanocephalus*). Hybrids can look like either parent species, or show intermediate features. In areas of overlap, male Rose-breasted Grosbeaks respond equally to songs of either species. The song of this grosbeak resembles that of the American Robin (*Turdus migratorius*), but is longer, mellower, and more melodic.

The Rose-breasted Grosbeak provides an important economic service to farmers by eating large numbers of destructive insect pests such as potato beetles, grasshoppers, cankerworms, and moths. It also feeds on other insects, weed seeds, wild fruit, and buds. Females tend to forage higher in the tree canopy than males and hover-glean more frequently.

MALE ROSE-BREASTED GROSBEAK

Cardinalis cardinalis

Northern Cardinal

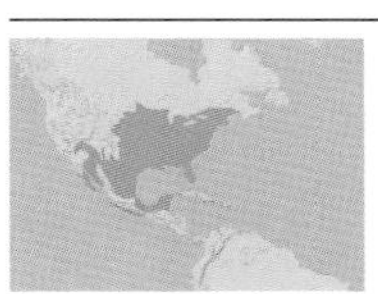

LENGTH 22cm (8½in)

WEIGHT 45g (1⅝oz)

MIGRATION Non-migrant

HABITAT Brushy habitat within or at edge of woodland, often in suburban areas

The Northern Cardinal is a popular bird in the USA, holding the title of state bird in no less than seven states. It is associated with Christmas and often appears on greetings cards. It is often seen at snow-covered bird-feeders throughout the east of the USA. Its name refers to the red-robed Roman Catholic cardinals and its crested head is also thought to resemble a bishop's mitre. The male's brilliant red plumage – which gives rise to its occasional moniker of Redbird – stands out majestically against snowy backdrops. A brighter red male holds territories with denser vegetation, feeds at higher rates, and has greater reproductive success than a duller male. The female is brown with a red crest, wings, and tail. The juvenile is also brown, with slightly orange underparts and a redder tail. Both sexes sing, the female often doing so from the nest, and its song is thought to inform the male that the chicks require food.

FEMALE NORTHERN CARDINAL
The female has a buff, golden-brown head, buff-olive upperparts, buff-brown underparts, and a red wash on the wings and tail.

ADULT MALE
The male is entirely brilliant red in colour, except for a thick black line around the bill.

Saltator maximus

Buff-throated Saltator

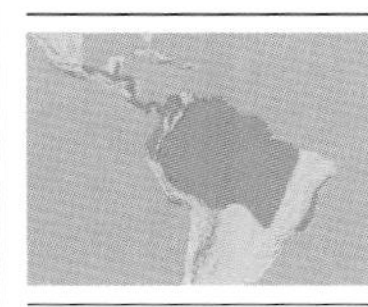

LENGTH 21cm (8½in)

WEIGHT 50g (1¾oz)

MIGRATION Non-migrant

HABITAT Shrubby clearings with scattered trees, forest borders, and secondary woodland

The *Saltator* genus is comprised of a dozen stout passerines with thick, convex bills, and the Buff-throated Saltator is one of its most widespread members. It has a slate-grey head with white eyebrows and a green crown. The upperparts are olive-green, the throat is buff-cinnamon, and the underparts grey to buff towards the central belly. Its song is a long series of short, melodious, phrases. This bird feeds on fruit, buds, and insects, and forages at low and mid-levels, sometimes with mixed-species flocks. It also eats army ants (rather than the insects that these ants flush out, a usual feeding tactic among birds).

ADULT BUFF-THROATED SALTATOR

Passerina caerulea

Blue Grosbeak

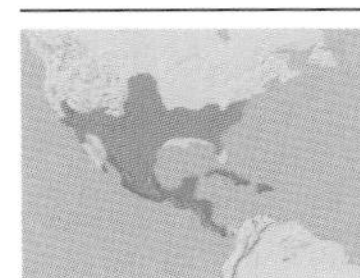

LENGTH 17cm (6½in)

WEIGHT 25g (⅞oz)

MIGRATION Migrant

HABITAT Open weedy fields with brushy patches, riparian woodland, forest edges, freshwater marshes

A beautiful blue bird with a silvery bill and chestnut wing-bars, the Blue Grosbeak was formerly placed in its own genus, *Guiraca*. Similarities with buntings in genetics, behaviour, moult, and plumage led to its inclusion in the bunting genus *Passerina*. Only the male is bright blue; the female and juveniles are chestnut-brown with chestnut wing-bars. The Blue Grosbeak forages by hovering and gleaning from weeds and bushes and by walking or hopping on the ground. The species' large bill allows for manipulation of large grains such as corn, and insects such as grasshoppers and mantids. It will also eat snails and fruit.

MALE BLUE GROSBEAK

MALE PAINTED BUNTING

Passerine ciris

Painted Bunting

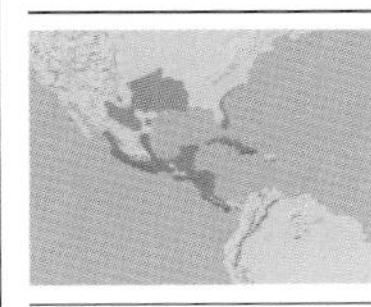

LENGTH 13.5cm (5¼in)

WEIGHT 16g (9/16oz)

MIGRATION Migrant

HABITAT Brushy lowland with tall trees, woodland borders, and overgrown fields

The male Painted Bunting's plumage – a vivid blue head and breast sides, bright green mantle, and red rump and underparts – made it a popular cage-bird until it came under federal protection. Despite its vibrant colours, it is difficult to spot as it skulks in dense thickets. This is particularly true of the female, which has green upperparts and olive-yellow underparts, and the uniform drab olive-grey juvenile.

NORTHERN CARDINAL
Male Northern Cardinals develop their intense red plumage progressively as they mature. They can be aggressive and often defend their territories fiercely.

GLOSSARY AND INDEX

GLOSSARY

A

adult A fully developed, mature bird that is able to breed. It is in its final plumage. See also *immature*.

aerofoil A bird's wing is based on an aerodynamic shape called an aerofoil. It is curved outwards along the entire upper surface, to produce an upward force known as lift.

air sac A thin-walled structure joined to the lungs of a bird, involved in respiration. There are usually nine air sacs, which may extend into some of a bird's hollow bones. Birds that plunge-dive into water, such as gannets and boobies, have modified air sacs beneath their skin to help cushion the impact.

alarm call A call made by a bird to signal danger. Alarm calls are often short and urgent in tone, and a few species use different calls to signify the precise nature of the threat. See also *call*.

albino An animal that lacks pigments. Albino birds have a white plumage, usually with red eyes and a pinkish bill and legs. See also *leucistic*.

allopreening Mutual preening between two birds, the main purpose of which is to reduce the instinctive aggression when birds come into close contact. In the breeding season, allopreening helps to strengthen the pair bond between the male and female. This behaviour is particularly common in parrots and estrildid finches. See also *preening*.

altricial Describes young birds that hatch naked or with a patchy covering of down, often with closed or non-functioning eyes. They are helpless and depend entirely on their parents. See also *precocial*.

alula A small group of two to six feathers projecting from a bird's "thumb", at the bend of its wing. When raised, the alula reduces turbulence, by enabling fine control of the airflow over the wing. It is also known as the bastard wing.

arboreal Living fully or mainly in trees.

altitudinal migrant see *vertical migrant*

anting A type of behaviour practised by some songbirds in which they allow ants to run through their plumage. Often the birds open their wings fully and lie on the ground to encourage the ants, sometimes even picking the ants up in their bills and rubbing them over their feathers. It is thought that this behaviour releases the ants' formic acid, which may help to kill parasites in the plumage or act as an insect repellant.

Australasia A biogeographical region that comprises Australia, New Guinea, New Zealand, and adjacent islands in the East Indies and Polynesia.

avian influenza A highly infectious disease carried by birds, especially waterfowl and domestic chickens and turkeys. It is caused by avian influenza viruses closely related to those that cause human influenza. The disease is popularly known as "bird flu".

axillary A term describing feathers at the base of the underwing. Axillary feathers often form small, distinct patches.

B

barb In most feathers, the central shaft (rachis) has thousands of barbs – tiny, closely spaced branches that project outwards to form a continuous, flat surface. Down feathers lack barbs. See also *down feather*.

barbule In a feather, a minuscule side branch that locks the barbs together, rather like a zip.

bastard wing see *alula*

beak see *bill*

bill A bird's jaws. A bill is made of bone, with a horn-like outer covering of keratin.

binocular vision Vision in which the two eyes have overlapping fields of view. This enables an animal to judge depth accurately. In birds, binocular vision is found mainly in predatory species, such as herons, gannets, boobies, birds of prey, and owls.

biome A characteristic grouping of living things, together with the setting in which they are found. On land, most biomes are defined mainly by their vegetation (for example, rainforest). The extent of any particular biome is determined by climatic conditions.

bird A warm-blooded, two-legged animal that has feathers, wings, and a bill, lays eggs, and can (in most cases) fly.

bird flu see *avian influenza*

bird of prey Any of the predatory birds in the orders Falconiformes (the eagles, hawks, falcons, kites, buzzards, ospreys, and vultures) and Strigiformes (the owls). They are typified by their acute eyesight, powerful legs, strongly hooked bill, and sharp talons. These birds, particularly the Falconiformes, are also known as raptors. See also *talon*.

body feather see *contour feather*

booming An unusual form of "song" produced by large species of bittern, the Kakapo (a New Zealand parrot), and a few other birds. The booming of male bitterns is a deep, resonant, hollow sound that carries for several kilometres.

brackish Containing a mixture of salt water and fresh water, for example, in a coastal lagoon.

breeding plumage A general term for the plumage worn by adult birds when they display and form breeding pairs. It is usually worn in the spring and summer, but this is not always the case; for example, in the northern hemisphere many species of duck are in their breeding plumage during the winter. See also *non-breeding plumage*.

brood (n.) The young birds produced from a single clutch of eggs and brooded together. See also *clutch*.

brood (vb) In birds, to sit on nestlings to keep them warm. Brooding is usually carried out mostly or entirely by the adult female, although in some species the male takes sole responsibility for this task. See also *incubate*.

brood parasite A bird that tricks another bird into raising its young. Some brood parasites, including cowbirds and many Old World cuckoos, always breed in this way, laying their eggs in the nests of different species. A variety of other birds, including waterfowl, gamebirds, and songbirds, are occasional brood parasites. They usually raise their young themselves, but sometimes dump their eggs in the nest of another member of the same species instead.

brood patch An area of bare skin on the belly of a parent bird that is richly supplied with blood vessels and thus helps to keep eggs warm during incubation. This area loses its feathers in readiness for the breeding season and is fully feathered at other times.

C

cage-bird A species of bird commonly kept in captivity. In general, the term refers to parrots and songbirds, which are kept for their colourful plumage or musical song. The trapping of wild birds to supply the international cage-bird trade is a major factor in the endangerment of many tropical species.

call A vocal sound produced by a bird to communicate a variety of messages. Calls are often highly characteristic of individual species and can be a major aid in locating and identifying birds in the field. Most bird calls are shorter and simpler than songs. See also *alarm call, contact call, song*.

canopy The highest layer of a forest or woodland, created by the overlapping branches of neighbouring trees.

carpal joint The outer joint of a bird's wing, equivalent to the human wrist.

carrion The remains of dead animals.

casque A bony extension on the head of an animal. Cassowaries and hornbills have a casque, typically larger in the male.

cere A leathery patch of bare skin that covers the base of a bird's bill. It is found only in a few groups, including birds of prey, pigeons, and parrots.

cerrado A type of South American savanna dotted with small, gnarled trees. Most cerrado is in Brazil. See also *savanna*.

chaparral A type of dry, scrub-like habitat dominated by evergreen shrubs, found only in southern California, USA.

churring An extremely long, far-carrying, repetitive trill produced at night by some species of nightjar, as a territorial song.

class A level used in classification. In the sequence of classification levels, a class forms part of a phylum, and is subdivided into one or more orders. The world's birds make up the class Aves.

clay lick A site, often a riverbank or exposed cliff, where animals regularly gather to eat clay, which contains useful salts and minerals. Among birds, parrots are the most frequent visitors to clay licks.

cloaca An opening towards the rear of a bird's body. It is present in both sexes and is used by the reproductive and excretory systems.

cloudforest A damp forest almost constantly under mist or clouds, especially in highland regions in the tropics. The tropical cloudforests of Central and South America support a wider variety of birds than any other habitat, except for lowland rainforest.

clutch The group of eggs in a single nest, usually laid by one female and incubated together. Clutch sizes vary from a single egg in some species, to as many as 28 eggs in the Northern Bobwhite of North America. The largest clutch recorded in a songbird is 19 eggs, laid by a European Blue Tit. See also *brood*.

cock A term sometimes used to describe the adult male in gamebirds and songbirds. See also *hen*.

collar The area around the middle of a bird's neck, which in some species is a prominent feature of the plumage.

colony In birds, a group of the same species nesting together in the same area. Colonial nesting is common among seabirds, herons and their relatives, swifts, bee-eaters, and weavers.

colour form One of two or more clearly defined plumage variations found in the same species. Also known as a colour morph or phase, a colour form may be restricted to a particular part of a species' range, or it may occur side by side with other colour forms throughout the entire range. Adults of different colour forms are able to interbreed, and these mixed pairings can produce young of either form.

comb A bare, fleshy growth on the top of the head in some birds.

contact call A call made by a bird to give its location as a means of staying in touch with others of the same species nearby. Contact calls are used by birds in flocks and by breeding pairs. See also *call*.

contour feather A general term for any feather that covers the outer surface of a bird, including its wings and tail. Contour feathers are also known as body feathers, and help to streamline the bird.

convergent evolution The independent evolution of similar characteristics in unrelated species. For example, the hummingbirds of the Americas and the sunbirds of Africa and Asia have independently evolved to lead a high-energy, nectar-eating lifestyle.

cooperative breeding A breeding system in which a pair of parent birds are helped in raising their young by several other birds, which are often related to them and may be the young birds from previous broods. A few hundred species worldwide reproduce in this way, including several well-studied species such as the Southern Ground Hornbill, Florida Scrub Jay, Groove-billed Ani, and Acorn Woodpecker.

courtship display Ritualized, showy behaviour used in courtship by the male and sometimes also by the female.

covert A small feather that covers the base of a bird's flight feather. Together, the coverts form a well-defined feather tract on the wing or at the base of the tail. See also *feather tract*.

crèche A group of young birds of about the same age, produced by different parents. One or more adults guards the entire crèche. This behaviour is found in penguins, flamingos, ostriches, and rheas.

crest A group of elongated feathers on the top of a bird's head, which may be raised during courtship or to indicate alarm. A crest is often a prominent plumage feature, but in some species it is not easily visible when lowered.

Critically Endangered (CR) A label used to describe a species that faces an extremely high risk of extinction in the wild in the immediate future. See also *IUCN*.

crop In birds, a muscular pouch below the throat, forming an extension to the oesophagus. Its purpose is to store undigested food, and it enables birds to feed quickly so that they can digest their meal later in safer surroundings.

crop milk A milk-like fluid rich in fat, protein, and vitamins, produced by adult pigeons and doves to feed their nestlings.

crown The area on top of a bird's head. It is often a prominent plumage feature.

cryptic coloration Coloration and markings that make an animal difficult to see against its background.

D

dabble To feed in shallow water by sieving water and food through comb-like filters in the bill. This behaviour is common in some ducks, giving rise to the name "dabbling duck".

Data Deficient (DD) A label used to describe a species about which there is insufficient up-to-date information to produce an estimate of its population, and therefore the level of threat that it faces. See also *IUCN*.

dawn chorus The intense, short-lived concentration of bird song around dawn. In temperate regions, it is usually restricted to the spring, when birds are establishing breeding territories and attracting mates.

decurved A term describing a bird's bill that curves downwards towards the tip.

dimorphism see *sexual dimorphism*

display see *courtship display*, *distraction display*, *threat display*

distraction display A special display in which a bird deliberately attempts to hold a predator's attention in order to lure it away from its nest and eggs. This behaviour is common in ground-nesting waders, which pretend to have an injured wing to tempt the predator to follow them, and in the fairywrens of Australia, which scurry along the ground in a zig-zag pattern while making a mouse-like noise.

diurnal Active during the day.

DNA-DNA hybridization A scientific technique used to determine how similar two different samples of DNA are. It is playing an increasingly important part in establishing the evolutionary relationships between different species and has resulted in various changes to bird classification.

down feather A soft, fluffy feather that provides good insulation. Young birds are covered by down feathers before they moult into their first juvenile plumage. Some adult birds, including waterfowl, have a layer of down feathers under their contour feathers. See also *contour feather*, *juvenile*.

drake An adult male duck. The adult female is known as the duck.

drumming An unusual form of non-vocal "song". In woodpeckers, drumming is a repetitive tapping noise made by vibrating the bill rapidly against a branch or tree-trunk. In snipes, it is a humming noise produced in mid-air by air rushing through specially modified outer tail feathers.

dusting A type of behaviour in which birds roll around in dry earth or sand, flicking their wings and ruffling their feathers to help spread the material evenly. This probably helps to keep their feathers clean by removing dry skin and getting rid of parasites such as lice, mites, and fleas. Dusting is also known as dust bathing.

dynamic soaring see *soaring*

E

ear tuft A distinct tuft of feathers on each side of a bird's forehead, with no connection to the true ears. Many owls have ear tufts.

echolocation A method of sensing nearby objects using pulses of high-frequency sound. Echoes bounce back from obstacles, enabling the sender to build up a "picture" of its surroundings. Echolocation is used by a small number of cave-dwelling birds, including the Oilbird and some cave swiftlets.

eclipse plumage An inconspicuous plumage worn in some birds by adult males for a short period after the breeding season is over. At this time, the males often resemble the females. The eclipse plumage helps to camouflage them during their moult.

egg tooth A small, horn-like growth on the bill of a nestling, with which it breaks out of its shell.

Endangered (EN) A label used to describe a species that faces a very high risk of extinction in the wild in the near future. See also *IUCN*.

endemic A species native to a particular geographic area, such an island, forest, mountain, state, or country, and which is found nowhere else.

escape An individual bird that has escaped from a zoo or other collection to live in the wild. Waterfowl and birds of prey are frequent escapes.

eyering A ring of colour around the eye of a bird.

eyestripe A stripe of colour running as a line through the eye of a bird.

eyrie The nest of a large bird of prey, usually on a cliff, or rocky promontory, often used by the same pair of adult birds in successive years.

F

family A level used in classification. In the sequence of classification levels, a family forms part of an order and is subdivided into one or more genera.

feather tract A distinct area on a bird's skin, covered by a particular type of feather.

fledge In young birds, to leave the nest or to acquire the first complete set of flight feathers. These birds are known as fledglings, and may remain dependent on their parents for some time after fledging. See also *flight feather*.

fledging period The average time taken by the young of a species to fledge, timed from the moment they hatch. In flying birds, fledging periods range from 11 days in some small songbirds to as long as 280 days in the Wandering Albatross.

fledgling see *fledge*

flight feather A collective term for a bird's wing and tail feathers, used in flight. More specifically, it also refers to the largest feathers on the outer part of the wing.

forewing The front section of a bird's spread wing. See also *hindwing*.

gallery forest A narrow strip of forest, often along a riverbank or beside a stream but also in savanna and other open country. Gallery forest may be an area's only forest for many miles.

gamebird A member of the order Galliformes, including species such as pheasants, quails, francolins, peafowl, turkeys, grouse, and the domestic chicken.

gape The mouth of a bird, or the angle at the base of its bill. Young birds, especially songbirds, often have brightly coloured orange or yellow gapes to stimulate their parents to push food into their mouths.

genus (pl. genera) A level used in classification. In the sequence of classification levels, a genus forms part of a family and is subdivided into one or more species. A genus that contains a single species is known as monotypic.

gizzard A muscular sac that forms the upper part of a bird's stomach. It plays an important part in grinding up food, especially in species that eat seeds and nuts, such as gamebirds, pigeons, doves, and parrots.

guano The accumulated droppings of seabirds at their nesting colony, sometimes harvested as a fertilizer.

gular sac Also known as a gular pouch, a large, fleshy, extendable sac just below the bill of some birds, especially fish-eaters such as pelicans and cormorants. It forms part of the throat.

habitat The area in which a particular kind of organism usually lives.

hawking A feeding technique in which a bird sits motionless on a perch and waits for a flying insect to come near, then suddenly flies out to catch it in mid-air. Hawking is used by flycatchers and bee-eaters in particular. See also *sally*.

hen A term sometimes used to describe the adult female in gamebirds and songbirds. See also *cock*.

hindwing The rear section of a bird's spread wing. See also *forewing*.

hybrid The offspring produced when two different species cross-breed. Hybrids are rare in the wild. Among birds, hybrids are most frequent in gamebirds and waterfowl, especially ducks.

I

immature In birds, an individual that is not yet fully mature or able to breed. Some birds, such as gulls, pass through a series of different immature plumages over a period of several years before finally adopting their first adult plumage. See also *adult, juvenile*.

incubate In birds, to sit on eggs to keep them warm, allowing them to develop. Incubation is often, but not always, carried out by the adult female. See also *brood*.

incubation period In birds, the period when a parent incubates its eggs. Incubation periods range from 11 days in some small songbirds to over two-and-a-half months in the Wandering Albatross.

Indomalayan A biogeographical region comprising southern and southeast Asia and associated islands. It is separated from the Palearctic region to the north by the Himalayas. See also *Palearctic*.

insectivorous An animal that feeds on insects and other invertebrates.

introduced species A species that humans have accidentally or deliberately brought into an area where it does not normally occur. Also known as an alien species.

iridescent plumage Plumage that shows brilliant, luminous colours that seem to sparkle and change when seen from different angles. It is found in a number of bird families, including kingfishers, hummingbirds, and starlings.

irruption A sporadic mass movement of animals outside their normal range. Irruptions are usually short-lived and occur in response to severe conditions, such as winter cold or lack of food.

IUCN The initials used to designate the World Conservation Union (formerly the International Union for the Conservation of Nature). This organization carries out conservation-related activities, including gathering and publishing information on the current status of threatened species.

JK

juvenile A term referring to the plumage worn by a young bird at the time it makes it first flight and until it begins its first moult. See also *adult, immature*.

keel In birds, a ridge-shaped enlargement of the breastbone that anchors the powerful muscles used in flight. It is sometimes known as the carina. See also *sternum*.

keratin A tough but lightweight structural protein, from which human fingernails and hair are made. In birds, keratin is found in the claws, feathers, and outer part of the bill.

kleptoparasite A bird that gets much of its food by stealing it from other birds. Skuas and frigatebirds all follow this piratic lifestyle.

L

lamellae Delicate, comb-like structures inside the bill of some birds – such as flamingos, ducks, and geese – used for filtering tiny food particles out of water.

leap-frog migration A pattern of migration in which some populations of a species travel much further than the other populations, by "leap-frogging" over the area where these sedentary (non-migratory) birds are found. For example, in some waders that breed in the northern hemisphere, the most northerly breeders fly furthest south to their wintering grounds, while the population that breeds further south stays in much the same area all year. See also *migration*.

Least Concern (LC) A label used to describe a species that is widespread or abundant or which is not likely to become threatened in the near future. See also *IUCN*.

lek A communal display area used by male birds during courtship. The same location is often revisited for many years. Species that display at leks include some gamebirds and waders and a variety of tropical forest birds, such as manakins, birds-of-paradise, and cotingas.

leucistic A term describing an animal that is lacking in some pigments. Leucistic birds appear very pale, often with abnormal patches of white plumage. See also *albino*.

lobed feet Feet with a series of loose, fleshy lobes on the toes, designed for swimming, as in the grebes and coots.

lore A small area between a bird's eye and the base of its upper bill.

M

mallee A dry, scrub-like habitat with scattered shrubs and small eucalyptus trees, found in parts of Australia.

mandible The upper or lower part of a bird's bill, known as the upper or lower mandible respectively.

mangrove swamp A forest-like habitat found in the tropics along muddy coasts and river mouths. It is formed by mangrove trees, which are adapted to grow with their roots immersed in saltwater. Mangrove swamps are an important habitat for nesting seabirds, herons, and egrets.

mantle The area on the upper surface of a bird between its wings.

melanistic A term describing an animal with more brown or black pigments than usual. Melanistic birds appear very dark.

migration A journey to a different region, following a well-defined route. Most birds that migrate regularly do so in step with the seasons, so that they can take advantage of good breeding conditions in one place, and good wintering ones in another. See also *leap-frog migration, partial migrant, reverse migration, sedentary, vertical migrant, visible migration*.

migrant A species that migrates. See also *partial migrant, sedentary*.

mimicry In birds, the act of copying the songs or calls of other species. The mimic often weaves these vocal fragments into its own usual song. Some birds, including parrots and mynas, can also copy mechanical sounds such as ringing telephones, machinery, and car alarms.

mobbing A type of defensive behaviour in which a group of birds gang up to harass a predator, such as a bird of prey or an owl, swooping repeatedly to drive it away.

monogamous Mating with a single partner, either in the course of a single breeding season or for life. See also *polygamous*.

morph see *colour form*

moult In birds, to shed old feathers so they can be replaced. Moulting enables birds to keep their plumage in good condition, change their level of insulation, and change their coloration or markings so that they are ready to breed.

N

nape The back of the neck.

Nearctic A biogeographical region that includes Greenland, Canada, most of the USA (except for the far south), and the highlands of northern Mexico. See also *Neotropics*.

Near Threatened (NT) A label used to describe a species that is not currently facing any serious risk of extinction in the wild, but which is considered likely to become threatened in the near future. See also *IUCN*.

Neotropics A biogeographical region that encompasses the tropical regions of the Americas, as well as the temperate region of southern South America. It includes the southern states of the USA, southern Mexico, Central America, the Caribbean, and South America. See also *Nearctic*.

nestling A young bird that is still in the nest.

New World The Americas, including the Caribbean and offshore islands in the Pacific and Atlantic oceans. See also *Old World*.

niche An animal's place and role in its habitat. Although two species may share the same habitat, they never share the same niche.

nictitating membrane A transparent or semi-opaque "third eyelid", which moves sideways across the eye. Water birds often use the membrane as an aid to vision when swimming underwater.

nidicolous A term describing young birds that need a period of parental care before they can leave the nest. Most birds are nidicolous, including all passerines.

nidifugous A term describing young birds that can leave the nest immediately or soon after hatching. Nidifugous birds include many gamebirds, rails, plovers, sandpipers, and ducks.

nomadic Being almost constantly on the move. Birds of deserts, grasslands, and the coniferous forests of the far north are commonly nomadic.

non-breeding plumage A general term referring to the plumage worn by adult birds outside the breeding season. In many species, particularly in temperate regions, it is also known as winter plumage. See also *breeding plumage*.

non-migrant see *sedentary*

non-passerine Any bird that is not a member of the order Passeriformes (or passerines). See also *passerine*.

Old World Europe, Asia, Africa, and Australasia. See also *New World*.

omnivorous An animal that eats both plant and animal food.

order A level used in classification. In the sequence of classification levels, an order forms part of a class and is subdivided into one or more families. The world's birds are separated into 29 orders.

oscine A term used to describe members of the suborder Passeri – the larger of the two main subdivisions of the order Passerifomes (or passerines). The oscines have a complex, highly specialized syrinx (voicebox), and as a result they can sing very intricate, often beautiful songs. These species are often known as the songbirds. See also *passerine, suboscine, syrinx*.

PQ

Palearctic A biogeographical region that comprises Europe, North Africa, the Middle East, and all but southern Asia. It is separated from the Indomalayan region, to the south, by the Himalayas. See also *Indomalayan*.

partial migrant A species in which some populations migrate while others are sedentary. This situation is common in birds with a wide distribution, because the different populations often experience very different climatic conditions. See also *migration, sedentary*.

passerine Any bird belonging to the vast order Passeriformes – the passerines. This group contains more species than all the other orders of birds combined, the members of which are known as non-passerines. An alternative name for the passerines is perching birds, because they have a unique type of foot that enables them to grip even the most slender branches or stems. See also *non-passerine, oscine, suboscine*.

pelagic Relating to the open ocean. Pelagic birds spend most of their life at sea and only come to land to nest. They include the albatrosses, petrels, shearwaters, tropicbirds, gannets, boobies, and skuas, as well as most auks and some penguins and terns.

phase see *colour form*

phylum (pl. phyla) A level used in classification. In the sequence of classification levels, a phylum forms part of a kingdom, and is subdivided into one or more classes.

polygamous Mating with two or more partners during the course of a single breeding season. See also *monogamous*.

precocial Describes young birds that are well developed at hatching, with down feathers and open, functioning eyes. Many precocial young are soon able to walk or swim and find food themselves. See also *altricial, down feather*.

preen gland A gland, found near the base of a bird's tail, that secretes oils that are spread over the feathers during preening. It is also known as the oil gland.

preening Essential routine behaviour by which birds keep their feathers in good condition. A bird grasps an individual feather at its base and then "nibbles" upwards towards the tip, and repeats the process over and over with different feathers. This helps to smooth and clean the plumage. Birds often also smear oil from their preen gland onto their feathers at the same time. See also *allopreening*.

primary feather One of the large outer wing feathers, growing from the digits of a bird's "hand". The primary feathers are often collectively referred to as primaries. See also *secondary feather*.

quill The lowest, exposed section of a feather's central shaft (rachis) – the part which grows from a bird's skin. See also *rachis*.

R

race see *species*

rachis The central, hollow shaft of a feather. See also *quill*.

rainforest A forest, usually in the tropics, with very high rainfall, high humidity, and high temperatures all year round. Undisturbed lowland tropical rainforest is home to the greatest variety of birds on Earth.

raptor see *bird of prey*

ratite A member of an ancient group of flightless birds called the ratites. Today, this group is quite small, comprising the ostriches, cassowaries, emus, rheas, and kiwis, but in the past it was larger and more diverse.

resident see *sedentary*

reverse migration A phenomenon that occurs when a young bird from a migratory species mistakenly travels in the opposite direction to normal, usually on a line that is approximately 180 degrees from its "correct" route. The reasons for this failure of orientation are not fully understood. Reverse migration causes birds to turn up in places far outside their normal range. See also *migration*.

rictal bristles Stiff, hair-like feathers that project from the base of the bill in many insect-eating birds. They provide protection against struggling prey, especially large stinging insects, and may help the birds to detect the movements of their victims.

rookery A nesting colony of Rooks (a species of Eurasian crow) or penguins.

roost A place where birds sleep, or the act of sleeping. The majority of birds roost at night. However, nocturnal species such as owls and nightjars roost by day, and many coastal species, particularly waders, roost at high tide when their feeding areas are flooded by the rising seawater.

rump The area between a bird's back and the base of its upper tail. It may be partly or wholly hidden when a bird is perched or on the ground with wings folded. In many species, the rump has a different colour from the rest of the plumage.

S

sally A short flight from a perch to catch an invertebrate, often in mid-air. See also *hawking.*

salt gland A gland located just above the eye of some birds, particularly seabirds. This enables them to extract the fluids they require from saltwater and then expel the excess salts through the nostrils.

salt marsh A habitat found on sheltered, flat, muddy coastlines. It consists of a wide, low-lying area colonized by salt-tolerant plants and is covered by high tides. Salt marsh is an important habitat for many waders and waterfowl.

savanna A general term for all tropical grasslands. Most savannas have a scattering of trees or scrub.

scrape A simple nest that consists of a shallow depression in the ground, which may be unlined or lined with soft material such as feathers and grasses. Birds that make nests of this type include terns, some gulls, waders, and gamebirds.

secondary feather One of the row of long, stiff feathers along the rear edge of a bird's wing, between the body and the primary feathers at the wingtip. The secondary feathers are often collectively referred to as secondaries. See also *primary feather.*

sedentary Having a settled lifestyle that involves relatively little movement. Sedentary birds remain in the same area throughout their life and are also said to be resident or non-migrants. See also *migration.*

sexual dimorphism The occurrence of physical differences between males and females. In birds, the most common type of sexual dimorphism is plumage variation. Other forms of sexual dimorphism include differences in bill length or body size; for example, in many birds of prey, the female is larger than the male.

shield In birds, a hard, shield-like structure on the forehead that joins the bill and often appears to be an extension of it. Coots are an example of a bird with a frontal shield.

soaring In birds, flight without flapping of the wings. A soaring bird stays at the same height or gains height. Many seabirds and large land birds soar; the smallest soaring birds are swifts. Slope soaring is a type of soaring in which a bird benefits from the rising currents of air that form at cliffs or along mountain ridges. Seabirds are expert at dynamic soaring, in which they repeatedly dive into the troughs between ocean waves and then use the rising air deflected off the waves to wheel back up into the air.

shorebird see *wader*

song A loud vocal performance by a bird, usually the adult male, to attract and impress a potential mate, advertise ownership of a territory, or drive away rival birds. Songs are often characteristic of individual species and can be a major aid in locating and identifying birds in the field. See also *call.*

songbird A general term popularly used to describe a member of the suborder Passeri (or oscines). This group includes the finest singers in the bird world. See also *oscine.*

song flight A special flight during which a bird performs its song. Song flights are particularly common in birds of open or treeless habitats, such as larks.

species A group of similar living things that are capable of interbreeding in the wild and of producing fertile offspring that resemble themselves. Species are the fundamental units used in biological classification. Some species have distinct populations that vary from each other. Where the differences are significant and the populations biologically isolated, these forms are classified as separate subspecies (or races). In situations where two individuals belonging to different subspecies meet and form a mixed pair, they are still capable of interbreeding successfully.

speculum A colourful patch on the wing of a duck, formed by the secondary feathers. See also *secondary feather.*

staging ground An area where migrant birds regularly pause while on migration, to rest and feed. Staging grounds are often used over many years by many different generations of birds, and their protection is an important part of bird conservation.

sternum The breastbone of a four-limbed vertebrate. The sternum of most birds is relatively large, with a prominent central ridge known as the keel. See also *keel.*

stoop A fast, near-vertical dive made by falcons and some other birds of prey when chasing aerial prey.

suboscine A term used to describe members of the suborder Tyranni – the smaller of the two main subdivisions of the order Passerifomes (or passerines). Their syrinx (voicebox) has a different structure to the rest of the passerines. The great majority of suboscine birds are found in the Americas, particularly South and Central America, but the tyrant flycatchers also occur in North America. Elsewhere, a few groups of suboscine birds are found in Africa, Asia, and Australia, including the broadbills, pittas, and asities. See also *oscine, passerine, syrinx.*

subspecies see *species*

syrinx A modified section of a bird's trachea (windpipe), equivalent to the voicebox in humans, that enables birds to call and sing. Membranes inside the syrinx vibrate and produce sound as air passes over them. Passerines, especially oscine birds, have the most complex syrinx. See also *oscine, passerine.*

T

talon The sharp, hooked claw of a bird of prey.

tarsus (pl. tarsi) A part of the leg. In birds, it is the longest, most exposed section of the leg, between the "ankle" joint and the "toes".

temperate The regions of the world that lie at mid-latitudes, between the polar regions and the tropics and subtropics.

territory An area defended by an animal, or group of animals, against other members of the same species. Territories often include useful resources, such as good breeding sites or feeding areas, which help a male to attract a mate. In birds, territories vary in size from just a few centimetres wide in colonial species, such as cliff-nesting seabirds, to many square kilometres in some large eagles.

thermal A rising bubble or column of warm air that soaring birds can make use of to gain height with little effort. Thermals only occur over land. See also *soaring.*

threat display A form of defence in which a bird adopts certain postures to drive away a rival or a potential predator. These postures are often designed to make the bird appear larger than it actually is. A threat display is sometimes accompanied by loud, agitated calls.

torpor A sleep-like state similar to hibernation, in which the heart rate and other body processes slow down below their normal rate. Animals normally become torpid to survive difficult conditions. This behaviour is relatively rare in birds: among the best known examples are swifts and hummingbirds, which become torpid at night to survive low temperatures, and the Common Poorwill, a nightjar from North America, which enters a state of torpor during cold weather or when its insect prey is scarce.

trachea A breathing tube in animals, also known as the windpipe.

twitcher A birdwatcher who travels specifically to see a rare or unusual bird that has already been discovered and whose location has been made public. See also *vagrant.*

tubenose A general term used informally to describe members of the order Procellariiformes, including albatrosses, petrels, and shearwaters. It refers to the distinctive tubular nostrils on their upper bill, which are not found in any other birds.

UV

underwing The underside of a bird's wing.

upperwing The upper surface of a bird's wing.

vagrant A bird that has strayed far from its normal range. Usually, vagrants are long-distance migrants that have been blown off course by storms while on migration, have overshot their intended destination due to strong winds, or have become disorientated. Intercontinental vagrants in particular are highly sought-after by keen birdwatchers. See also *twitcher.*

vane In most feathers, the flat surface on either side of the central shaft (rachis). The vane is largest in wing feathers.

vent The area of feathers between the base of a bird's tail and its legs.

vertical migrant A species that migrates up or down mountains, usually in response to changes in the weather or food supply. Many vertical migrants breed at higher altitudes and spend the winter lower down. See also *migration.*

visible migration Bird migration that can be observed overhead during the day, usually at certain favoured locations on the migration routes of many different species. See also *migration.*

Vulnerable (V) A label used to describe a species that faces a high risk of extinction in the wild in the medium-term future. See also *IUCN.*

W

wader Any member of several families in the order Charadriiformes, including plovers, sandpipers, godwits, snipes, avocets, stilts, oystercatchers, and curlews. Waders typically have a long bill and long legs. Many of them occur at the water's edge in wetlands or along coasts, but despite their name not all species actually wade in water and some live in quite dry habitats. An alternative name for waders is shorebirds, especially in the USA and Canada.

Wallace's Line An imaginary line in the Pacific region that passes between the Philippines and the Moluccas in the north, and between Lombok and Bali in the south. It separates the Indomalayan and Australasian biogeographical regions; the bird life either side of the line is quite different. This phenomenon is named after its discoverer, the naturalist Alfred Russel Wallace. See also *Australasian, Indomalayan.*

wattle A bare, fleshy growth that hangs loosely below the bill in some birds. It is often brightly coloured, and may play a part in courtship.

waterfowl A collective term for members of the family Anatidae, including ducks, geese, and swans.

wildfowl see *waterfowl*

wingbar A line or bar of colour across the upper surface of a bird's wing. Wingbars can often be seen when a bird is on the ground or perched and its wings are in the closed position, but they are normally much more obvious in flight. Wingbars may be single or in groups of two or more.

wing loading The ratio of a bird's body weight to its total wing area, usually measured in grams per square centimetre. Wing loading affects a bird's manoeuvrability and the energy it requires to fly. As the wing loading increases, so does the amount of work required for the bird to stay airborne.

wingspan The distance across a bird's outstretched wings and back, from one wingtip to the other.

wrist see *carpal joint*

Z

zygodactyl feet A specialized arrangement of the feet in which the toes are arranged in pairs, with the second and third toes facing forwards and the first and fourth toes facing backwards. This adaptation helps birds to climb and perch on tree-trunks and other vertical surfaces. Several groups of bird have zygodactyl feet, including the parrots, the cuckoos and turacos (Cuculiformes), the owls, the toucans, and the woodpeckers and their relatives (Piciformes).

INDEX

A

B

D

S

T

Z

ACKNOWLEDGMENTS

Dorling Kindersley would like to thank several people for their help in the preparation of this book. Sally Conyne, on behalf of Audubon, was unfailingly helpful and provided many valuable comments on the text, images, and maps. Joseph DiCostanzo provided text for some of the introductions to passerine families and also gave editorial advice. Adrian Long at Birdlife International and Sandy Pinto at Audubon were both extremely helpful and patient in their co-ordination of the project. Helen Hays provided additional validation of some of the images. Angeles Gavira Guerrero did editorial work on the book during its preparatory stages, Ina Stradins and Kenny Grant did initial design work, and Manisha Thakkar provided design assistance. With a small number of exceptions, the common names used in this book are taken from Birds of the World: Recommended English Names by Frank Gill and Minturn Wright. The map on page 63 is based on an original in Water birds on the Edge: the First Circumpolar Assessment of Climate Change Impact on Arctic Breeding Water Birds by Zöckler and Lysenko, 2000 (World Conservation Press, Cambridge, UK). Andy & Gill Swash of WorldWildlifeImages, Bryan Michie and Christine Fletcher for their assistance with picture research.

Schermuly Design Co. would like to thank Kim Bryan for editorial advice and Simon Peters for help with correction of the text.

PICTURE CREDITS

The publisher would like to thank the following for their kind permission to reproduce their photographs:

(Key: a-above; b-below/bottom; c-centre; f-far; l-left; r-right; t-top)

1 naturepl.com: John Waters (c). **1-489 Getty Images:** Geoff Brightling/Iconica (box background). **2-3 Corbis:** Bernhard, Tobias/zefa (c). **4 Getty Images:** John Downer (cra); Ernst Haas (clb). **5 Thomas Marent** (c) **Getty Images:** Joel Sartore (fcla). **6-7 Alamy Images:** Art Kowalsky (c). **8-9 Markus Varesvuo/Birdfoto.fi:** (c). **10-11 Jari Peltomäki/Birdfoto.fi:** (c). **12-13 Nigel Dennis:** (c). **14-15 Getty Images:** Timothy Laman (c). **16-17 naturepl.com:** Andy Sands (c). **18 Getty Images:** Joseph Van Os (c). **19 Jari Peltomäki/Birdfoto.fi:** (c). **20-21 Getty Images:** Tom Walker (c). **22-23 Getty Images:** John Downer (c). **24 Science Photo Library:** GILBERT S. GRANT (c); D. ROBERTS (bc). **24-25 FLPA:** ANDRE WIERINGA/FOTO NATURA/FLPA (c). **24-71 Getty Images:** Sami Sarkis (sidebar left and right). **25 Alamy Images:** David Hosking (tl); Dave Watts (bc). **26 Alamy Images:** Juniors Bildarchiv (br); Martin Harvey (bl). **naturepl.com:** Paul Hobson (cra). **OSF:** Mark Hamblin (cra/Oyster Catcher). **27 Alamy Images:** Arco Images (tl); Holger Ehlers (tr); Keith M Law (tc). **Corbis:** Fritz Polking (cla). **OSF:** John Downer (br); Tui De Roy (c). **Greg & Yvonne Dean/ WorldWildlifeImages.com:** (fbl). **28 Alamy Images:** Juniors Bildarchiv (cra). **Corbis:** Wolfgang Kaehler (bl). **DK Images:** Steve Gorton (br). **29 Ardea:** Piers Cavendish (br). **Corbis:** Eric and David Hosking (cb); Robert Essel NYC (cl); Darrell Gulin (ca); D. Robert & Lorri Franz (tr). **DK Images:** Kim Taylor (fcl). **30 Alamy Images:** blickwinkel (cr); David Tipling (cra). **OSF:** Daniel Cox (ca); Mark Hamblin (c). **George Reszeter:** (fbl). **30-31 Jari Peltomäki/Birdfoto.fi:** (bc). **31 Alamy Images:** Renee Morris (cla); Redmond Durrell (br). **Corbis:** Joe McDonald (tr). **FLPA:** Frants Hartmann (crb); Frans Lanting/Minden Pictures (ftl). **32 DK Images:** Kim Taylor (crb). **FLPA:** Mike Lane (tr). **OSF:** Tony Tilford (br). **32-33 DK Images:** Kim Taylor (c). **33 Ardea:** John Daniels (tr/Falcon). **DK Images:** Kim Taylor (cr). **FLPA:** Arthur Christiansen (tr). **OSF:** Michael Fogden (br). **34 Hanne & Jens Eriksen:** (clb). **FLPA:** Tom Vezo/Minden Pictures (bc). **OSF:** Mark Jones (cr). **35 Alamy Images:** Papilio (crb). **Ardea:** Eric Dragesco (tr). **Hanne & Jens Eriksen:** (ca). **FLPA:** Winfried Wisniewski (clb). **OSF:** Claude Steelman (br). **36 Alamy Images:** Images & Stories (clb); Renee Morris (cra). **Markus Varesvuo/Birdfoto.fi:** (br). **37 Alamy Images:** Danita Delimont (fcrb); Friedrich von Horsten (crb). **Getty Images:** GK Hart/Vikki Hart (tc). **38 Alamy Images:** Mike Hill (bc). **DK Images:** Peter Chadwick (cl). **Melvin Grey:** (ftr). **David Plummer:** (cra). **Cal Vornberger:** (ca). **39 Alamy Images:** Aguilar Patrice (cb/Eagle). **FLPA:** Tui de Roy/Minden Pictures (tr); Danny Ellinger/Foto Natura (cb). **Joe Fuhrman:** (br). **OSF:** Ifa-Bilderteam Gmbh (fbr). **40 Alamy Images:** ImageState (fclb); Scott Kemper (cl). **40-41 Jari Peltomäki/Birdfoto.fi:** (cla). **41 Alamy Images:** Philip Mugridge (cr); David J Slater (tl). **Ardea:** D. Parer & E. Parer-Cook (fbr). **Markus Varesvuo/Birdfoto.fi:** (tr). **OSF:** Werner Bollmann (crb/oystercatcher); Alain Christof (br). **42 Alamy Images:** David Chapman (clb); Simon Littlejohn (c). **Dudley Edmonson:** (cb). **naturepl.com:** John Cancalosi (fcla). **42-43 FLPA:** Fritz Polking (c). **43 Alamy Images:** Genevieve Vallee (tr). **Corbis:** Denis Balibouse (br). **FLPA:** John Holmes (fcr). **44 Alamy Images:** Keith M Law (br); Dave Watts (cra). **45 Alamy Images:** Arco Images (c); Juniors Bildarchiv (fcl); William Leaman (ftl). **FLPA:** Michael & Patricia Fogden (fcla); S & D & K Maslowski (cl). **naturepl.com:** Igor Shpilenok (fbr). **46 Alamy Images:** blickwinkel (cra). **46-47 FLPA:** Simon Litten (bc). **47 FLPA:** Frans Lanting/Minden Pictures (fcr). **Tomi Muukonen:** (tr). **48 Alamy Images:** Kevin Schafer (clb). **Josef Hlasek:** (tl). **48-49 FLPA:** Philip Perry (c). **49 Corbis:** Martin Harvey (cr). **Tomi Muukonen:** (tl). **naturepl.com:** Steven David Miller (clb). **OSF:** Mark Hamblin (br). **50 Jari Peltomäki/Birdfoto.fi:** (bc). **FLPA:** Frans Lanting/Minden Pictures (tr). **51 Alamy Images:** blickwinkel (clb) (fclb); Dave Watts (br). **FLPA:** Neil Bowman (cla); Rob Reijnen/Foto Natura (tr). **Barry Hughes:** (cr). **Tomi Muukonen:** (fcr). **52 Alamy Images:** Danita Delimont (tr). **Jari Peltomäki/Birdfoto.fi:** (bl). **FLPA:** Jurgen & Christine Sohns (cr). **53 Alamy Images:** blickwinkel (cr); Nick Haslam (cra). **Corbis:** Kevin Schafer (c). **DK Images:** Peter Chadwick (br/Osprey Egg) (br/American Robin egg) (br/Common Guillemot egg) (br/Magnificent Riflebird egg); Harry Taylor (br/Redshank egg). **FLPA:** David Hosking (tr). **54 Alamy Images:** Arco Images (bl). **DK Images:** (fcra). **Hanne & Jens Eriksen:** (clb). **OSF:** Owen Newman (br). **Cal Vornberger:** (cra). **55 Alamy Images:** Woodfall Wild Images (bc). **Ardea:** M. Watson (fcrb). **Corbis:** Dan Guravich (crb). **Cal Vornberger:** (ca). **56 Alamy Images:** America (tr). **Corbis:** George D. Lepp (cr). **Cal Vornberger:** (cl). **56-57 FLPA:** Richard Brooks (bc). **57 Jari Peltomäki/Birdfoto.fi:** (tr). **Corbis:** Eric and David Hosking (cl). **58 FLPA:** SA Team/Foto Natura (cl). **OSF:** Manfred Pfefferle (cla). **Photoshot/NHPA:** Hellio & Van Ingen (cb). **Cal Vornberger:** (cra). **58-59 Alamy Images:** Redmond Durrell (c). **59 Alamy Images:** Arco Images (cr); Chris Gomersall (br). **Ian Montgomery/Birdway.com.au:** (tr). **60 Alamy Images:** Michael McKee (bl); Dave Watts (br); Worldwide Picture Library (tr). **61 Alamy Images:** Arco Images (tr); Rick & Nora Bowers (tl); David Chapman (bl); David Tipling (cra). **FLPA:** Konrad Wothe (crb); Tom and Pam Gardner (br). **62 Alamy Images:** Arco Images (tl); Bruce Coleman Inc. (cl); Jaubert Bernard (cr). **Markus Varesvuo/Birdfoto.fi:** (c). **FLPA:** D Zingel Eichhorn (clb). **62-63 Alamy Images:** Ern Mainka (bc). **63 Alamy Images:** Juniors Bildarchiv (clb). **Corbis:** Bob Krist (tc). **FLPA:** Robin Chittenden (cra). **Clement Francis:** (cr). **64 Alamy Images:** Cameron Attree (cl). **Corbis:** Martin Harvey (bc). **FLPA:** Tom Vezo/Minden Pictures (cr); Yva Momatiuk/John Eastcott (cra). **65 Alamy Images:** Picture Contact (crb); Kevin Schafer (bl). **Corbis:** James L. Amos (tr); Terry W. Eggers (cr). **FLPA:** Jurgen & Christine Sohns (clb). **66 Hanne & Jens Eriksen:** (cr). **FLPA:** Michael Gore (bl); Minden Pictures (br). **The Natural History Museum, London:** (cra). **67 Alamy Images:** David Hosking (br). **Science Photo Library:** George Bernard (cr); Photo researchers (bl). **68-69 Getty Images:** Ernst Haas/Stone (c). **70 Alamy Images:** Keith M Law (cra). **FLPA:** Fritz Polking (tr); Terry Whittaker (bl). **71 Alamy Images:** ImageState (cl); Tom Uhlman (clb). **Corbis:** Joe McDonald (bc). **Ian Montgomery/Birdway.com.au:** (tr). **72 Alamy Images:** Andrew Harrington (cl); Arco Images (bl); Arthur Gebuys - Gebuys.com (c); Mike Lane (bc); Niall Benvie (tr); Pat Bennett (br). **72-97 Getty Images:** Richard Price/Taxi (fcr/sidebar left and right). **73 Alamy Images:** Pat Bennett (tr); Petr Svarc (crb); Steve Bloom Images (bl). **FLPA:** Mitsuaki Iwago (br); Richard Brooks (cr); Robert Chittenden (tl). **74 Alamy Images:** Arco Images (cla). **Jari Peltomäki/Birdfoto.fi:** (cra). **Markus Varesvuo/Birdfoto.fi:** (ca). **Corbis:** Macduff Everton (cb). **Josef Hlasek:** Lubomir Hlasek (bc). **Andy & Gill Swash/WorldWildlifeImages.com:** (fbr). **75 Alamy Images:** Richard Cooke (cb); Tim Graham (br). **Corbis:** Warwick Tarboton (cra). **FLPA:** Mitsuaki Iwago/Minden Pictures (cla). **Melvin Grey:** (fbl). **Andy & Gill Swash/WorldWildlifeImages.com:** (ca) (bc). **76 Alamy Images:** Martin Harvey (tc). **Corbis:** Eberhard Hummel/zefa (cr). **Hanne & Jens Eriksen:** (bc) (c) (ca) (cb). **77 Alamy Images:** Rick & Nora Bowers (ca). **Dudley Edmonson:** (bc). **FLPA:** Tom Vezo (tc). **Joe Fuhrman:** (cb). **Getty Images:** Tim Laman/National Geographic (cl). **Ian Montgomery/Birdway.com.au:** (br). **Peter S Weber:** (c). **78 FLPA:** Frans Lanting (cb); Pete Oxford (ca); Silvestris Fotoservice (bc); Jurgen & Christine Sohns (tc). **79 Alamy Images:** Petra Wegner (c). **Corbis:** Wayne Lawler (cl). **FLPA:** Frans Lanting (ca); David Hosking (bc); Mark Newman (br). **OSF:** Konrad Wothe (cb). **Photoshot/NHPA:** Daniel Heuclin (tc). **80 Markus Varesvuo/Birdfoto.fi:** (ca). **Corbis:** Benelux/zefa (cr); George McCarthy (tc). **Tomi Muukonen:** (c) (bc). **Cal Vornberger:** (cb). **81 Alamy Images:** Juniors Bildarchiv (ca). **Markus Varesvuo/Birdfoto.fi:** (cra). **Dudley Edmonson:** (fcra). **FLPA:** Frans Lanting (cl). **Melvin Grey:** (tr). **Ian Montgomery/Birdway.com.au:** (tc) (bc) (cb). **Tom Tarrant:** (c). **82 Alamy Images:** Danita Delimont (tc). **Jari Peltomäki/Birdfoto.fi:** (c). **Markus Varesvuo/Birdfoto.fi:** (bc) (ca) (cb). **82-83 Alamy Images:** Chad Ehlers (c). **83 Alamy Images:** Danita Delimont (ca). **Markus Varesvuo/Birdfoto.fi:** (bc) (cb) (tc). **FLPA:** Claus Meyer/Minden Pictures (br). **84 Alamy Images:** Mark Boulton (cr); Paul Carstairs (cb); Genevieve Vallee (ca). **Markus Varesvuo/Birdfoto.fi:** (tc). **Barry Hughes:** (bc). **85 Alamy Images:** Bill Coster (br). **Markus Varesvuo/Birdfoto.fi:** (tc). **Corbis:** Ashley Cooper (cl). **Hanne & Jens Eriksen:** (c). **Arto Juvonen/Birdfot.fi:** (bc). **Tomi Muukonen:** (ca). **OSF:** Roland Mayr (cb). **86 Corbis:** Joe McDonald (c); O. Alamany & E. Vicens (bc). **DK Images:** Frank Greenaway (tc). **FLPA:** Minden Pictures (cb). **86-87 Corbis:** Craig Tuttle (c). **87 Alamy Images:** Imagebroker (c). **Markus Varesvuo/Birdfoto.fi:** (cra). **Corbis:** Charles Mauzy (fcra); Tim Zurowski (ca). **Mike Read:** (bc). **Cal Vornberger:** (tc). **88 Alamy Images:** Arco Images (c); Elvele Images (ca); Renee Morris (bc); SBP (cb). **Corbis:** Dave G. Houser (r); Winfried Wisniewski/zefa (tc). **89 Alamy Images:** Arco Images (ca); Robert Fried (l); James Osmond (br); tbkmedia.de (tc). **OSF:** Ifa-Bilderteam Gmbh (bc). **90 Alamy Images:** Bob Gibbons (cb). **Jari Peltomäki/Birdfoto.fi:** (fcla) (cla). **Barry Hughes:** (br). **Tomi Muukonen:** (bc) (cra) (fcra). **91 Alamy Images:** Bruce Coleman inc (fbl). **Hanne & Jens Eriksen:** (br) (cla). **FLPA:** John Watkins (bl). **Getty Images:** Theo Allofs (cb). **Ian Montgomery/Birdway.com.au:** (tr). **Andy & Gill Swash/WorldWildlifeImages.com:** (ca). **92 Jari Peltomäki/Birdfoto.fi:** (cla) (ca). **Hanne & Jens Eriksen:** (bc) (bl). **Tomi Muukonen:** (br). **Cal Vornberger:** (cra). **92-93 Alamy Images:** David Robertson (cb). **93 Jari Peltomäki/Birdfoto.fi:** (ca) (bl). **Barry Hughes:** (bc). **Tomi Muukonen:** (cla) (br). **OSF:** Aldo Brando (cra). **94 Corbis:** George McCarthy (bc). **Getty Images:** Stone (r). **Ian Montgomery/Birdway.com.au:** (cb). **Tomi Muukonen:** (c). **95 Alamy Images:** Jon Arnold Images (l). **Hanne & Jens Eriksen:** (bc). **FLPA:** Mitsuaki Iwago/Minden Pictures (br) (c). **Ian Montgomery/Birdway.com.au:** (tc). **96 Corbis:** Richard Hamilton Smith (r). **Hanne & Jens Eriksen:** (cb) (tc). **Tomi Muukonen:** (ca). **Cal Vornberger:** (bc). **97 Alamy Images:** David Noble Photography (l). **Jari Peltomäki/Birdfoto.fi:** (tc). **Markus Varesvuo/Birdfoto.fi:** (cb). **Neil Fletcher:** (c). **Ian Montgomery/Birdway.com.au:** (ca). **Tomi Muukonen:** (br). **Cal Vornberger:** (bc). **100 Alamy Images:** fotolincs (br); William Leaman (cl); WoodyStock (br/Hooded Crow). **DK Images:** Philip Dowell (c). **100-485 Getty Images:** Siede Preis/photodisc (sidebar left and right). **101 Alamy Images:** Dave Watts (cl). **Roger & Liz Charlwood:** (clb/Tinamous) (ca/Parrot skull) (ca/Tawny Owl Skull). **DK Images:** Peter Chadwick (ca/Capercaillie skull) (cb/Kiwi); Dave King (cb/Ostrich); Jerry Young (cb/emu); Peter Cross (cb/Cassawary). **FLPA:** Martin B Withers (cb/Rhea). **Science Photo Library:** Hank Morgan (c). **102 Ardea:** Dennis Avon (cr). **Roger & Liz Charlwood:** (bc). **DK Images:** Harry Taylor (br). **FLPA:** Minden Pictures (tr). **Photoshot/NHPA:** Adrian Hepworth (cl). **103 Alamy Images:** Images of Africa Photobank (br). **OSF:** Peter Lillie (tr). **Photoshot/NHPA:** Nigel J. Dennis (cl). **Andy & Gill Swash/WorldWildlifeImages.com:** (bl). **104 naturepl.com:** Daniel Gomez (ca). **David Plummer:** (cl) (bl). **Andy & Gill Swash/WorldWildlifeImages.com:** (br). **105 Alamy Images:** Arco Images (cla); Henry Westheim Photography (crb); Robert Harding Picture Library Ltd (clb); Dave Watts (tr). **FLPA:** Neil Bowman (br). **Ian Montgomery/Birdway.com.au:** (bl) (fcla). **106 Alamy Images:** Jon Arnold Images (cla); Pat Bennett (tr); Westend 61 (bc). **FLPA:** Tui De Roy (br). **Photoshot/NHPA:** A.N.T Photo library (bl). **107 Alamy Images:** Images of Africa Photobank (br). **Markus Varesvuo/Birdfoto.fi:** (bl). **Josef Hlasek:** (ca) (fcrb). **Tomi Muukonen:** (cra). **108 Alamy Images:** David Hosking (clb). **Tomas Carlberg:** (bl). **Pete Morris:** (crb). **naturepl.com:** Jim Clare (br). **OSF:** Roger Brown (cla). **Tom Tarrant:** (tr). **109 Alamy Images:** Kevin Schafer (br). **FLPA:** R & M Van Nostrand (bl). **Joe Fuhrman:** (cr). **Mike Read:** (tl). **Andy & Gill Swash/WorldWildlifeImages.com:** (tr). **110 Alamy Images:** blickwinkel (cra). **Corbis:** Fridmar Damm/zefa (bc). **Joe Fuhrman:** (br). **justbirds.org:** (ca). **Mike Read:** (bl). **111 Dudley Edmonson:** (tr). **Melvin Grey:** (fcrb). **Barry Hughes:** (cra). **Mike Read:** (tl) (cb). **Peter S Weber:** (clb). **112 Jari Peltomäki/Birdfoto.fi:** (bl). **Dudley Edmonson:** (crb). **Joe Fuhrman:** (cla). **Barry Hughes:** (cl). **Tomi Muukonen:** (cra). **113 Markus Varesvuo/Birdfoto.fi:** (cb). **Barry Hughes:** (tr). **Mike Read:** (tl). **114 Alamy Images:** David Hosking (cla) (clb). **Hanne & Jens Eriksen:** (tr). **FLPA:** Gerard Lacz (br). **115 Alamy Images:** Arco Images (br). **FLPA:** Minden Pictures (cl). **Andy & Gill Swash/WorldWildlifeImages.com:** (tr) (crb). **116 FLPA:** Jurgen & Christine Sohns (tl). **Nigel Hicks:** (bl). **Sumit K Sen:** (tc). **116-117 Markus Varesvuo/Birdfoto.fi:** (cb). **117 James Eaton:** (cra). **Josef Hlasek:** (fcrb). **Sumit K Sen:** (tr). **Andy & Gill Swash/WorldWildlifeImages.com:** (tl). **118-119 Getty Images:** Johner (c). **120 Jari Peltomäki/Birdfoto.fi:** (br). **FLPA:** John Watkins (bc). **Josef Hlasek:** (tr). **Arto Juvonen/Birdfot.fi:** (bl). **120-121 Markus Varesvuo/Birdfoto.fi:** (c). **121 Markus Varesvuo/Birdfoto.fi:** (bl). **FLPA:** Tony Wharton (tr). **OSF:** Eric Woods (ca); Kemp Richard & Julia (cra). **122 Jari Peltomäki/Birdfoto.fi:** (br). **Melvin Grey:** (clb). **Barry Hughes:** (tr). **Greg & Yvonne Dean/ WorldWildlifeImages.com:** (fcla). **123 Dudley Edmonson:** (cb) (bc) (br). **Tomi Muukonen:** (tr). **Mike Read:** (tl). **124 Alamy Images:** Peter Fakler (bl). **Hanne & Jens Eriksen:** (fcla). **Ian Montgomery/ Birdway.com.au:** (fcl). **124-125 Corbis:** Theo Allofs (c). **126 Dudley Edmonson:** (tc). **Barry Hughes:** (cla) (crb). **Tomi Muukonen:** (bc). **George Reszeter:** (cra). **127 Jari Peltomäki/Birdfoto.fi:** (tc). **Markus Varesvuo/Birdfoto.fi:** (bl). **128 Hanne & Jens Eriksen:** (br). **Barry Hughes:** (tl) (c) (tr). **129 Alamy Images:** J. Schwanke (cr). **Melvin Grey:** (tr) (fcl). **Tom Tarrant:** (bl). **Andy & Gill Swash/ WorldWildlifeImages.com:** (br). **130 Dudley Edmonson:** (bl) (br). **Melvin Grey:** (cr). **Photoshot/ NHPA:** Joe Blossom (tr). **Cal Vornberger:** (fcla). **131 Markus Varesvuo/Birdfoto.fi:** (tc) (bl). **Joe Fuhrman:** (cra). **Barry Hughes:** (br). **132 Jari Peltomäki/ Birdfoto.fi:** (crb) (c). **Lars Carlsson:** (cla). **Melvin Grey:** (tl). **Mike Read:** (clb). **George Reszeter:** (bc). **Roni Väisänen:** (tr). **133 Jari Peltomäki/Birdfoto.fi:** (tc). **FLPA:** Chris Schenk (cr). **Cal Vornberger:** (br). **134 Jari Peltomäki/Birdfoto.fi:** (tr). **Markus Varesvuo/Birdfoto.fi:** (bl) (crb). **Barry Hughes:** (tl). **135 Jeff Higgott:** (br). **Barry Hughes:** (crb). **Arto Juvonen/Birdfot.fi:** (ca) (tr). **136 Alamy Images:** Martin Harvey (cr). **DK Images:** Frank Greenaway (tr). **136-137 OSF:** Colin Monteath (bl). **137 DK Images:** Frank Greenaway (tr). **Hanne & Jens Eriksen:** (br) (crb). **OSF:** Howard Hall (cl). **138 Melvin Grey:** Jonathan Grey (tl). **Barry Hughes:** (bl). **138-139 Barry Hughes:** (bc). **139 Hanne & Jens Eriksen:** (cl). **FLPA:** Minden Pictures (cla). **Barry Hughes:** (fcr) (br). **Per Smitterberg:** (cra). **140-141 Getty Images:** Tim Davis (c). **142 Alamy Images:** Ange (cra). **Barry Hughes:** (bl). **justbirds.org:** (tc). **Mike Read:** (br). **143 Alamy Images:** David Tipling (cra). **Jari Peltomäki/Birdfoto.fi:** (tl) (bl). **Dudley Edmonson:** (crb) (br). **144 Alamy Images:** David Hosking (cr); Steve Bloom Images (bl). **Hanne & Jens Eriksen:** (c) (tr). **145 Roger & Liz Charlwood:** (clb) (cra). **Hanne & Jens Eriksen:** (tc). **naturepl.com:** Peter Reese (br). **Anders Paulsrud:** (bl). **146 Alamy Images:** Dickie Duckett (cla); Kevin Schafer (clb). **Hanne & Jens Eriksen:** (fcl). **FLPA:** Frans Lanting (bl). **146-147 Corbis:** Momatiuk - Eastcott (c). **148 Hanne & Jens Eriksen:** (bl) (br). **FLPA:** Christiana Carvalho (crb). **Melvin Grey:** Jonathan Grey (fcla). **148-149 Mike Read:** (tc). **149 Hanne & Jens Eriksen:** (bl). **justbirds.org:** (tr). **Eric Preston:** (cr). **150 Hanne & Jens Eriksen:** (cl). **justbirds.org:** (tr). **Eric Preston:** (br). **150-151 George Reszeter:** (c). **151 Barry Hughes:** (tl). **Eric Preston:** (bc). **George Reszeter:** (tr). **152 Alamy Images:** Arco Images (tr). **Jari Peltomäki/Birdfoto.fi:** (ca). **Hanne & Jens Eriksen:** (bl). **Barry Hughes:** (crb). **Tom Tarrant:** (cb). **153 Jari Peltomäki/ Birdfoto.fi:** (ca). **Josef Hlasek:** Lubomir Hlasek (cb). **Barry Hughes:** (br). **justbirds.org:** (tl). **Peter S Weber:** (tr). **154 Corbis:** Bob Krist (bc). **Hanne & Jens Eriksen:** (bl) (br). **Neil Fletcher:** (c). **FLPA:** Minden Pictures (tr). **155 Alamy Images:** Visual&Written SL (cra). **Joe Fuhrman:** (ca). **156-157 OSF:** David W Breed (c). **157 Alamy Images:** blickwinkel (br); Danita Delimont (cra); Martin Creasser (crb). **Corbis:** Nigel J. Dennis (cr). **158 Alamy Images:** blickwinkel (tr); Dave Watts (br). **Corbis:** Mary Ann McDonald (crb). **Hanne & Jens Eriksen:** (cl). **159 DK Images:** Max Alexander (fbr). **Hanne & Jens Eriksen:** (tr). **Melvin Grey:** (cr). **Barry Hughes:** (br) (bc). **Peter S Weber:** (tl). **160 Lars Carlsson:** (clb). **Sujan Chatterjee:** (bl). **Barry Hughes:** (tr). **David Plummer:** (tl). **Andy & Gill Swash/ WorldWildlifeImages.com:** (br). **161 Alamy Images:** Byron Jorjorian (crb). **Dudley Edmonson:** (br). **Hanne & Jens Eriksen:** (bl). **Cal Vornberger:** (tr). **Andy & Gill Swash/WorldWildlifeImages.com:** (fcl). **162 Alamy Images:** Nature Photographers ltd (bl). **Hanne & Jens Eriksen:** (fcla) (fcl). **Sumit K Sen:** (fclb). **162-163 Corbis:** Roger Tidman (c). **164 Alamy Images:** David Tipling (clb). **Jari Peltomäki/Birdfoto.fi:** (cr).

Lars Carlsson: (cra). **165 Jari Peltomäki/Birdfoto.fi:** (br). **Hanne & Jens Eriksen:** (tl). **Joe Fuhrman:** (cr). **justbirds.org:** (tr). **Arto Juvonen/Birdfot.fi:** (bl). **166 Getty Images:** Angela Scott/Taxi (cra). **Melvin Grey:** (clb). **Barry Hughes:** (fcra). **OSF:** Brian Kenney (tl). **Mike Read:** (br). **167 Melvin Grey:** (tl). **Barry Hughes:** (clb). **OSF:** Brian Kenney (ca). **Cal Vornberger:** (br). **168–169 Melvin Grey:** (c). **170 Alamy Images:** blickwinkel (crb). **Corbis:** Annie Griffiths Belt (br). **Getty Images:** Daniele Pellegrini/The Image Bank (bl). **Ian Montgomery/Birdway.com.au:** (cla). **OSF:** Tobias Bernhard (tr). **171 justbirds.org:** (tc) (clb). **Ian Montgomery/Birdway.com.au:** (crb). **Photoshot/NHPA:** Martin Harvey (br). **172 FLPA:** Jurgen & Christine Sohns (cl). **Joe Fuhrman:** (bl). **Mike Read:** (tr). **172–173 Joe Fuhrman:** (bc). **173 Alamy Images:** Robert E. Barber (cra). **Joe Fuhrman:** (tc). **Ian Montgomery/Birdway.com.au:** (cla). **174–175 Photoshot/NHPA:** Mirko Stelzner (c). **175 Alamy Images:** blickwinkel (crb); David Tipling (cr); Simon Colmer and Abby Rex (cra). **Hanne & Jens Eriksen:** (fbr). **176 Alamy Images:** Juniors Bildarchiv (cl). **Hanne & Jens Eriksen:** (br). **Barry Hughes:** (tr). **Mike Read:** (bl) (cla). **177 Hanne & Jens Eriksen:** (clb). **Mike Read:** (tc) (br). **178 Hanne & Jens Eriksen:** (br). **FLPA:** Minden Pictures (cr). **Joe Fuhrman:** (cr). **Josef Hlasek:** Lubomir Hlasek (cla). **George Reszeter:** (bl). **179 Corbis:** George McCarthy (br). **Hanne & Jens Eriksen:** (tl). **Melvin Grey:** (cr). **Per Smitterberg:** (clb). **180 Hanne & Jens Eriksen:** (bc). **FLPA:** Pete Oxford/Minden Pictures (bl); Robert Canis (cl); Martin B Withers (cla). **OSF:** Mark Hamblin (clb). **180–181 Markus Varesvuo/Birdfoto.fi:** (c). **181 Alamy Images:** Malcolm Schuyl (c). **Corbis:** Galen Rowell (cr). **FLPA:** Paul Hobson (tr). **Josef Hlasek:** (br). **OSF:** Juniors Bildarchiv (ca). **182 Alamy Images:** blickwinkel (cra). **Dudley Edmonson:** (tl). **Josef Hlasek:** Lubomir Hlasek (bl). **Photoshot/NHPA:** Rich Kirchner (cla). **182–183 Josef Hlasek:** (c). **183 Joe Fuhrman:** (tr) (cr). **justbirds.org:** (br). **184 Alamy Images:** Mike Lane (bc). **Markus Varesvuo/Birdfoto.fi:** (fcr). **Joe Fuhrman:** (fclb). **Barry Hughes:** (tr) (br). **Peter S Weber:** (tl). **185 Markus Varesvuo/Birdfoto.fi:** (bl). **Dudley Edmonson:** (cr). **Josef Hlasek:** (cl). **186 Alamy Images:** Danita Delimont (bl). **Markus Varesvuo/Birdfoto.fi:** (cl). **Dudley Edmonson:** (tr). **Melvin Grey:** (tl). **187 Jari Peltomäki/Birdfoto.fi:** (tr). **Jeff Higgott:** (br). **Josef Hlasek:** (bl). **188 Ardea:** Jim Zipp (c). **Markus Varesvuo/Birdfoto.fi:** (tr). **Andy & Gill Swash/WorldWildlifeImages.com:** (cla). **188–189 Jari Peltomäki/Birdfoto.fi:** (bc). **189 Jari Peltomäki/Birdfoto.fi:** (crb). **Melvin Grey:** (cra). **justbirds.org:** (fcla). **Ian Montgomery/Birdway.com.au:** (tl). **190 Roger & Liz Charlwood:** (bl). **Dudley Edmonson:** (tl). **FLPA:** Minden Pictures (clb). **Melvin Grey:** (cra). **Josef Hlasek:** (br). **191 Hanne & Jens Eriksen:** (tl) (crb). **Clement Francis:** (tr). **Josef Hlasek:** (bc). **Barry Hughes:** (clb). **192–193 Melvin Grey:** (c). **194 Goran Ekstrom:** (tl). **Melvin Grey:** (br). **Barry Hughes:** (cla). **justbirds.org:** (bl). **194–195 Markus Varesvuo/Birdfoto.fi:** (tc). **195 Dudley Edmonson:** (tr). **Goran Ekstrom:** (bl). **Hanne & Jens Eriksen:** (br). **Josef Hlasek:** (cra). **Barry Hughes:** (bc). **Kogi Tagi:** (crb). **196 Hanne & Jens Eriksen:** (bl) (fcrb). **Barry Hughes:** (tl). **Arto Juvonen/Birdfot.fi:** (br). **Marijn Prins:** (clb). **Tom Tarrant:** (tr). **197 Jari Peltomäki/Birdfoto.fi:** (cr). **Melvin Grey:** (bl). **Cal Vornberger:** (tl). **Andy & Gill Swash/WorldWildlifeImages.com:** (br). **198 Dudley Edmonson:** (bl). **justbirds.org:** (tl). **David Plummer:** (tr). **198–199 David Plummer:** (cb). **199 Corbis:** Jonathan Blair (c). **Dudley Edmonson:** (fcr). **Joe Fuhrman:** (tc). **Mike Read:** (br). **200 Dudley Edmonson:** (bc). **Hanne & Jens Eriksen:** (cl). **Joe Fuhrman:** (br). **Melvin Grey:** (tr). **OSF:** David Boag (cra). **Cal Vornberger:** (tl). **201 Steve Berlin:** (tl). **Hanne & Jens Eriksen:** (cl) (bl). **OSF:** Patricio Robles Gil (cra). **202 Alamy Images:** Frank Blackburn (cr). **Jari Peltomäki/Birdfoto.fi:** (tc). **Hanne & Jens Eriksen:** (br). **Ian Montgomery/Birdway.com.au:** (bl). **203 Nigel Hicks:** (crb). **Barry Hughes:** (tl) (bl). **204–205 OSF:** (c). **205 Alamy Images:** Malcolm Schuyl (br); Shaun Levick (crb). **Corbis:** John Conrad (cra). **FLPA:** Jurgen & Christine Sohns (cr). **206 Alamy Images:** franzfoto.com (br); Martin Harvey (cra); Penny Boyd (cla). **Ardea:** M. Watson (bc). **207 Hanne & Jens Eriksen:** (bl). **Josef Hlasek:** (br); Lubomir Hlasek (tl) (fcl). **Barry Hughes:** (ca) (bc). **Ian Montgomery/Birdway.com.au:** (tr). **208 Ardea:** Jean Paul Ferrero (c). **Josef Hlasek:** (cr). **justbirds.org:** (bc). **Natural Visions:** Gregory Guida (cra). **Greg & Yvonne Dean/WorldWildlifeImages.com:** (tl). **209 Markus Varesvuo/Birdfoto.fi:** (tl). **Joe Fuhrman:** (br). **Barry Hughes:** (clb). **Pete Morris:** (tr). **Mike Read:** (crb). **210 Lars Carlsson:** (cl). **FLPA:** Minden Pictures (crb). **Joe Fuhrman:** (tr) (fcr). **Pete Morris:** (bc). **George Reszeter:** (tl). **211 Jari Peltomäki/Birdfoto.fi:** (ca) (br). **George Reszeter:** (bl). **212 Alamy Images:** Luke Peters (cra). **Melvin Grey:** (br). **Andy & Gill Swash/WorldWildlifeImages.com:** (tl). **Greg & Yvonne Dean/WorldWildlifeImages.com:** (clb). **213 Joe Fuhrman:** (cb) (cr). **Josef Hlasek:** (tc). **214 Roger & Liz Charlwood:** (cl). **Corbis:** Reuters (bl). **Hanne & Jens Eriksen:** (cr). **Barry Hughes:** (br). **justbirds.org:** (tr). **215 Markus Varesvuo/Birdfoto.fi:** (bl). **Dudley Edmonson:** (tr). **Barry Hughes:** (cr) (cla). **216–217 Nigel Dennis:** (c). **218 Alamy Images:** Albaimages (cr). **Jari Peltomäki/Birdfoto.fi:** (cra). **218–219 Jari Peltomäki/Birdfoto.fi:** (bl). **219 Alamy Images:** David Tipling (br); Paul David Drabble (cr). **Corbis:** Bryan Knox (ca); Peter Johnson (tr); Winfred Wisniewski (tl). **OSF:** Doug Allan (cb). **220 Hanne & Jens Eriksen:** (bl). **Barry Hughes:** (tr). **Tomi Muukonen:** (br). **Mike Read:** (cla). **Tom Tarrant:** (tl). **221 Corbis:** Klaus Honal (crb). **Hanne & Jens Eriksen:** (tl) (cb). **FLPA:** Paul Hobson/Holt (bl). **Joe Fuhrman:** (fcla). **Barry Hughes:** (cra). **Ian Montgomery/Birdway.com.au:** (br). **222–223 naturepl.com:** Steve Knell (c). **223 Alamy Images:** David Osborn (cra). **Jari Peltomäki/Birdfoto.fi:** (fbr). **Hanne & Jens Eriksen:** (fcr). **Arto Juvonen/Birdfot.fi:** (fclb). **224 Alamy Images:** Peter Fakler (cra). **Tomas Carlberg:** (clb) (br). **Hanne & Jens Eriksen:** (cla). **Mike Read:** (crb). **225 Barry Hughes:** (tc) (br) (cr). **George Reszeter:** (bl) (bc). **226 Joe Fuhrman:** (tl) (cla). **Barry Hughes:** (bl) (br). **Andy & Gill Swash/WorldWildlifeImages.com:** (cra). **227 Hanne & Jens Eriksen:** (tr). **Barry Hughes:** (cla). **Anders Paulsrud:** (bl). **Andy & Gill Swash/WorldWildlifeImages.com:** (br). **228 Dudley Edmonson:** (br). **Josef Hlasek:** (bl). **George Reszeter:** (tr). **Cal Vornberger:** (cl). **229 Jari Peltomäki/Birdfoto.fi:** (tr). **Dudley Edmonson:** (tl). **Hanne & Jens Eriksen:** (cra). **Joe Fuhrman:** (bl) (br). **230 Markus Varesvuo/Birdfoto.fi:** (br). **Hanne & Jens Eriksen:** (bc). **Joe Fuhrman:** (tl) (cra). **Mike Read:** (cla). **George Reszeter:** (bl). **231 Alamy Images:** Mike Lane (cb). **Hanne & Jens Eriksen:** (fcr). **Josef Hlasek:** Lubomir Hlasek (br). **Barry Hughes:** (tl). **Arto Juvonen/Birdfot.fi:** (bl). **234 Josef Hlasek:** Lubomir Hlasek (cl) (br). **Barry Hughes:** (cla) (cr) (tc). **235 Alamy Images:** The Photolibrary Wales (cr). **Jari Peltomäki/Birdfoto.fi:** (bc). **Barry Hughes:** (tr). **George Reszeter:** (tl). **236 Hanne & Jens Eriksen:** (bl). **justbirds.org:** (br). **Tomi Muukonen:** (tl). **Mike Read:** (cra). **George Reszeter:** (cla). **237 Barry Hughes:** (cra). **Tomi Muukonen:** (br). **George Reszeter:** (tl) (clb). **238 Dudley Edmonson:** (bl). **Hanne & Jens Eriksen:** (cra) (tr). **Barry Hughes:** (cb). **Mike Read:** (cla). **239 Joe Fuhrman:** (tl) (tr). **Barry Hughes:** (cla). **justbirds.org:** (br). **Cal Vornberger:** (bl). **240 Jari Peltomäki/Birdfoto.fi:** (tl) (bc). **Dudley Edmonson:** (clb). **Melvin Grey:** (tr). **Barry Hughes:** (crb). **241 Alamy Images:** Chris Gomersall (bl). **Tomi Muukonen:** (cr). **242 Alamy Images:** Sean O'Neill (crb). **Hanne & Jens Eriksen:** (cl). **Barry Hughes:** (tr) (bc) (bl). **Photoshot/NHPA:** Matt Bain (cra). **243 Alamy Images:** Juniors Bildarchiv (tr). **Hanne & Jens Eriksen:** (c) (crb). **Josef Hlasek:** Lubomir Hlasek (bl). **OSF:** Adrian Bailey (ftr). **Photoshot/NHPA:** Roger Tidman (cb). **244–245 FLPA:** Yva Momatiuk/John Eastcott (c). **245 Alamy Images:** Cornforth Images (cra) (cr); Oyvind Martinsen (br). **Cal Vornberger:** (fcrb). **246 Alamy Images:** David Hosking (crb); John Cancalosi (c). **FLPA:** Winfried Wisniewski (tr). **Barry Hughes:** (bl). **Greg & Yvonne Dean/WorldWildlifeImages.com:** (br). **247 Alamy Images:** A1E1P5 (ca). **Jari Peltomäki/Birdfoto.fi:** (tr). **DK Images:** Gary Ombler (clb); Getty Active (cla). **Neil Fletcher:** (fcl). **Ian Montgomery/Birdway.com.au:** (bl) (crb). **Tomi Muukonen:** (br). **248 Hanne & Jens Eriksen:** (cla). **Ian Montgomery/Birdway.com.au:** (tr). **Tom Tarrant:** (br). **249 Dudley Edmonson:** (cla). **Joe Fuhrman:** (fcl) (tl). **Barry Hughes:** (bl). **Pete Morris:** (br). **Greg & Yvonne Dean/WorldWildlifeImages.com:** (crb). **250 Nigel Hicks:** (cla) (bl) (cra). **Josef Hlasek:** (tc). **Ian Montgomery/Birdway.com.au:** (br). **Greg & Yvonne Dean/WorldWildlifeImages.com:** (clb). **251 Nigel Hicks:** (bl). **Ian Montgomery/Birdway.com.au:** (cla) (bc) (tc). **Greg & Yvonne Dean/WorldWildlifeImages.com:** (cra). **252 Alamy Images:** Dave Watts (br). **DK Images:** Cyril Laubscher (cl). **OSF:** Brian Kenney (tc); Nick Gordon (clb); Robin Bush (crb). **253 Alamy Images:** Ian Dagnall (cr). **FLPA:** Pete Oxford/Minden Pictures/FLPA (bl). **Andy & Gill Swash/WorldWildlifeImages.com:** (fcla). **254 A.N.T. Photo Library:** Cliff & Dawn Frith (clb). **Barry Hughes:** (tl). **justbirds.org:** (fcr). **Ian Montgomery/Birdway.com.au:** (br). **naturepl.com:** Tim Edwards (cra). **Photoshot/NHPA:** Gerald Cubitt (tr). **255 Barry Hughes:** (tr). **Ian Montgomery/Birdway.com.au:** (br). **Kogi Tagi:** (tl). **256 Corbis:** John Carnemolla/Australian Pic (cl). **Tom Tarrant:** (bl). **Andy & Gill Swash/WorldWildlifeImages.com:** (tc). **Greg & Yvonne Dean/WorldWildlifeImages.com:** (crb). **256–257 Ian Montgomery/Birdway.com.au:** (c). **257 Ardea:** Don Hadden (br). **Ian Montgomery/Birdway.com.au:** (tr). **Andy & Gill Swash/WorldWildlifeImages.com:** (crb). **258 Barry Hughes:** (tl). **Ian Montgomery/Birdway.com.au:** (br). **Tom Tarrant:** (bl). **Andy & Gill Swash/WorldWildlifeImages.com:** (fcl) (clb). **258–259 Alamy Images:** Danita Delimont (tc). **259 Alamy Images:** Juniors Bildarchiv (br); Gerry Pearce (tc). **Ian Montgomery/Birdway.com.au:** (cr). **Andy & Gill Swash/WorldWildlifeImages.com:** (bl). **260 FLPA:** Frank W Lane (cla). **Nigel Hicks:** (tr). **Ian Montgomery/Birdway.com.au:** (bl). **Tom Tarrant:** (cra). **260–261 Andy & Gill Swash/WorldWildlifeImages.com:** (bc). **261 Alamy Images:** Machteld Baljet & Marcel Hoevenaars (br). **Nigel Hicks:** (tl). **Andy & Gill Swash/WorldWildlifeImages.com:** (tr). **262 Markus Varesvuo/Birdfoto.fi:** (cra). **Sumit K Sen:** (cl). **Andy & Gill Swash/WorldWildlifeImages.com:** (crb). **Greg & Yvonne Dean/WorldWildlifeImages.com:** (br). **263 Alamy Images:** Images&Stories (fcra). **DK Images:** Cyril Laubscher (br). **justbirds.org:** (tl). **Ian Montgomery/Birdway.com.au:** (tc). **264 Alamy Images:** David Tipling (br). **FLPA:** Minden Pictures (tl). **Barry Hughes:** (tr). **justbirds.org:** (bl). **Greg & Yvonne Dean/WorldWildlifeImages.com:** (cr). **265 justbirds.org:** (br). **Pete Morris:** (cla). **Andy & Gill Swash/WorldWildlifeImages.com:** (bl) (cra) (tr). **266–267 Corbis:** Michael & Patricia Fogden (c). **267 Alamy Images:** Bill Coster (cb); Geraldine Buckley (cr); imagebroker (br). **FLPA:** Flip de Nooyer/Foto Natura (cra). **268 FLPA:** Minden Pictures (bl). **David Plummer:** (cr). **269 Alamy Images:** Krystyna Szulecka (tl). **FLPA:** Krystyna Szulecka (cla). **Photoshot/NHPA:** Haroldo Palo Jr (cra). **David Plummer:** (tr). **Andy & Gill Swash/WorldWildlifeImages.com:** (bl) (br) (fcrb). **270 justbirds.org:** (cl). **Andy & Gill Swash/WorldWildlifeImages.com:** (br). **Greg & Yvonne Dean/WorldWildlifeImages.com:** (tr). **271 Ardea:** Dennis Avon (cra). **FLPA:** Jurgen & Christine Sohns (tc). **Ian Montgomery/Birdway.com.au:** (bc). **272 Alamy Images:** Bowler, Mark Amazon-Images (clb); David Hosking (ca). **Barry Hughes:** (crb). **Renee Overbosch:** (tr). **Andy & Gill Swash/WorldWildlifeImages.com:** (bl). **273 Hanne & Jens Eriksen:** (cla). **Josef Hlasek:** Lubomir Hlasek (bl). **Pete Morris:** (cr). **Andy & Gill Swash/WorldWildlifeImages.com:** (tl). **274 Markus Varesvuo/Birdfoto.fi:** (cl). **Barry Hughes:** (tc). **Pete Morris:** (br). **Mike Read:** (crb). **275 Hanne & Jens Eriksen:** (br). **Ian Montgomery/Birdway.com.au:** (cl) (crb). **Tom Tarrant:** (tr). **276 Lars Carlsson:** (tl). **Barry Hughes:** (bl) (br). **justbirds.org:** (fcl). **Pete Morris:** (cr). **277 Joe Fuhrman:** (br). **Mike Read:** (cr). **Andy & Gill Swash/WorldWildlifeImages.com:** (cl). **278 Jari Peltomäki/Birdfoto.fi:** (ca) (br). **DK Images:** Peter Chadwick (cr). **Tomi Muukonen:** (bl). **279 Roger & Liz Charlwood:** (fcr). **Melvin Grey:** (clb) (br). **Mike Read:** (bl). **George Reszeter:** (cra). **Cal Vornberger:** (tr). **280 Hanne & Jens Eriksen:** (bl). **Joe Fuhrman:** (tl). **Josef Hlasek:** Lubomir Hlasek (bc). **Cal Vornberger:** (cla). **280–281 Cal Vornberger:** (tc). **281 Markus Varesvuo/Birdfoto.fi:** (bl). **Jari Peltomäki/Birdfoto.fi:** (br). **Pete Morris:** (cra). **282 Joe Fuhrman:** (bc). **Melvin Grey:** (tr). **Mike Read:** (bl). **Andy & Gill Swash/WorldWildlifeImages.com:** (fcr). **283 Dudley Edmonson:** (bl) (cla). **Joe Fuhrman:** (fcra). **Melvin Grey:** (br). **284 Alamy Images:** William Leaman (tc); Parker, Susan & Allan (bc). **Dudley Edmonson:** (clb) (cra). **Barry Hughes:** (tr). **Andy & Gill Swash/WorldWildlifeImages.com:** (br). **285 Markus Varesvuo/Birdfoto.fi:** (tr). **Jari Peltomäki/Birdfoto.fi:** (bc). **Melvin Grey:** (fcrb). **286–287 Getty Images:** Art Wolfe (c). **288 FLPA:** A (tr); Withers, Martin B (cra). **Barry Hughes:** (br) (bl). **289 Dudley Edmonson:** (cr). **Joe Fuhrman:** (tl) (br). **David Plummer:** (tr). **Andy & Gill Swash/WorldWildlifeImages.com:** (bl). **290 Joe Fuhrman:** (bl). **Vireo:** Bower, Rick & Nora (cr); Bowers, Rick & Nora (tr). **Andy & Gill Swash/WorldWildlifeImages.com:** (br). **291 FLPA:** Michael Gore (cl). **Melvin Grey:** (tl). **Barry Hughes:** (ca). **Andy & Gill Swash/WorldWildlifeImages.com:** (br). **292 Alamy Images:** Stock Connection Distribution (tr). **Markus Varesvuo/Birdfoto.fi:** (cla). **Corbis:** Ron Sanford (cr). **FLPA:** David Hosking (crb). **293 A.N.T. Photo Library:** Alan Gibb (tc); Dave Watts (tr). **FLPA:** Ron Austing (bl). **Melvin Grey:** (br). **Ian Montgomery/Birdway.com.au:** (tl). **George Reszeter:** (cl). **294 justbirds.org:** (clb). **Andy & Gill Swash/WorldWildlifeImages.com:** (bl). **Greg & Yvonne Dean/WorldWildlifeImages.com:** (ca) (cr). **295 Barry Hughes:** (cla). **Andy & Gill Swash/WorldWildlifeImages.com:** (tc). **Greg & Yvonne Dean/WorldWildlifeImages.com:** (bl) (cr). **296 Alamy Images:** Kevin Schafer (cb). **Roger & Liz Charlwood:** (tr). **FLPA:** Minden Pictures (bc). **Joe Fuhrman:** (cr). **Andy & Gill Swash/WorldWildlifeImages.com:** (cl). **Greg & Yvonne Dean/WorldWildlifeImages.com:** (tl) (br). **297 Alamy Images:** Oyvind Martinsen (crb). **Andy & Gill Swash/WorldWildlifeImages.com:** (tl). **Greg & Yvonne Dean/WorldWildlifeImages.com:** (tr) (cb). **298 Joe Fuhrman:** (bl). **justbirds.org:** (tr). **Pete Morris:** (crb). **299 Dudley Edmonson:** (ca). **Joe Fuhrman:** (br) (clb) (crb). **Cal Vornberger:** (tl). **300 Alamy Images:** fotolincs (crb). **Ardea:** Derrick England (bc). **FLPA:** Martin B Withers (tl). **Barry Hughes:** (tr). **Ian Montgomery/Birdway.com.au:** (bl). **301 Joe Fuhrman:** (bl). **Andy & Gill Swash/WorldWildlifeImages.com:** (cl). **302–303 Thomas Marent** (c). **303 Alamy Images:** Bruce Coleman Inc. (crb); Mike Lane (cra); Genevieve Vallee (cr). **FLPA:** Michael & Patricia Fogden/Minden Pictures (br). **304 Alamy Images:** blickwinkel (tr). **Corbis:** Karl Ammann (cl); Kevin Schafer (cr). **Melvin Grey:** (bc). **305 Markus Varesvuo/Birdfoto.fi:** (tl). **Lars Carlsson:** (br). **Ian Montgomery/Birdway.com.au:** (cra) (cr). **Tom Tarrant:** (cla). **Greg & Yvonne Dean/WorldWildlifeImages.com:** (clb) (bl). **306 Hanne & Jens Eriksen:** (bl) (fcra). **Nigel Hicks:** (crb). **Ian Montgomery/Birdway.com.au:** (br). **Sumit K Sen:** (tc). **307 Han Bouwmeester:** (br). **Corbis:** Polking, Fritz/Frank Lane Pict (bc). **Melvin Grey:** (tr). **Ian Montgomery/Birdway.com.au:** (tl). **308 FLPA:** Minden Pictures (cra). **Ian Montgomery/Birdway.com.au:** (tl). **David Plummer:** (bl) (br). **309 Hanne & Jens Eriksen:** (bl). **justbirds.org:** (clb). **Mike Read:** (br). **Cal Vornberger:** (tr). **Andy & Gill Swash/WorldWildlifeImages.com:** (cr). **310 OSF:** Carol Farneti Foster (bl); Konrad Wothe (cl). **Andy & Gill Swash/WorldWildlifeImages.com:** (tr) (crb). **311 Hanne & Jens Eriksen:** (tr). **Barry Hughes:** (tl). **Andy & Gill Swash/WorldWildlifeImages.com:** (cb). **312 Markus Varesvuo/Birdfoto.fi:** (tl). **FLPA:** John Hawkins (clb). **Andy & Gill Swash/WorldWildlifeImages.com:** (bl). **312–313 Melvin Grey:** (c). **313 Barry Hughes:** (cla). **Sumit K Sen:** (br). **Andy & Gill Swash/WorldWildlifeImages.com:** (clb). **314 Alamy Images:** Chris Fredriksson (cra). **Melvin Grey:** (br). **Barry Hughes:** (bl). **Sumit K Sen:** (tl). **Greg & Yvonne Dean/WorldWildlifeImages.com:** (tr). **315 Alamy Images:** Arco Images (c); Mike Hill (clb/Keel-billed Toucan). **Markus Varesvuo/Birdfoto.fi:** (tr). **Hanne & Jens Eriksen:** (fbr/Barbet). **FLPA:** Minden Pictures (br). **Greg & Yvonne Dean/WorldWildlifeImages.com:** (fcr/Jacamar). **316 justbirds.org:** (br). **David Plummer:** (tr). **Andy & Gill Swash/WorldWildlifeImages.com:** (crb). **Greg & Yvonne Dean/WorldWildlifeImages.com:** (bl). **317 Alamy Images:** Petra Wegner (tc). **Joe Fuhrman:** (br). **justbirds.org:** (tl). **Andy & Gill Swash/WorldWildlifeImages.com:** (cra) (clb). **318–319 Getty Images:** Art Wolfe (c). **320 Nigel Hicks:** (clb). **Sumit K Sen:** (tl). **Greg & Yvonne Dean/WorldWildlifeImages.com:** (cla) (bl). **321 Alamy Images:** FLPA (bc); HJB (br). **Hanne & Jens Eriksen:** (tr). **Melvin Grey:** (bl). **Greg & Yvonne Dean/WorldWildlifeImages.com:** (cla). **322 Markus Varesvuo/Birdfoto.fi:** (tr). **FLPA:** Wendy Dennis (cl). **Andy & Gill Swash/WorldWildlifeImages.com:** (bc). **323 Alamy Images:** William Leaman (c). **Joe Fuhrman:** (tr) (br). **Peter S Weber:** (tl). **Andy & Gill Swash/WorldWildlifeImages.com:** (bl). **324 Alamy Images:** FLPA (tc); Iain Davidson Photographic (br). **Joe Fuhrman:** (fcra). **Cal Vornberger:** (tl). **Andy & Gill Swash/WorldWildlifeImages.com:** (crb). **325 Ardea:** Peter Steyn (cl). **Jari Peltomäki/Birdfoto.fi:** (tr) (br). **Joe Fuhrman:** (tl). **Cal Vornberger:** (bl). **326 Rebecca Dean:** (bl). **Joe Fuhrman:** (cl). **David Plummer:** (cr) (br). **Andy & Gill Swash/WorldWildlifeImages.com:** (tc). **327 Markus Varesvuo/Birdfoto.fi:** (tl) (tc). **Sujan Chatterjee:** (cra). **Melvin Grey:** (br). **328 Ian Montgomery/Birdway.com.au:** (br). **Sumit K Sen:** (tl) (cl). **329 Ian Montgomery/Birdway.com.au:** (cr). **David Plummer:** (bl). **Andy & Gill Swash/WorldWildlifeImages.com:** (clb). **Greg & Yvonne Dean/WorldWildlifeImages.com:** (tl) (br). **330 Alamy Images:** © (clb); Michael J. Kronmal (ca); Stephen Hogan (bl). **330–331 Alamy Images:** Dave Watts (c). **331 Alamy Images:** Arco Images (crb/Sunbird). **Markus Varesvuo/Birdfoto.fi:** (tr). **Corbis:** Danny Lehman (bl). **FLPA:** G.F.J. Tik/Foto Natura (crb); John Hawkins (br); Martin Woike/Foto Natura (cr). **Tomi Muukonen:** (cra). **332 Alamy Images:** blickwinkel (tr) (cl) (clb); Nick Greaves (bc). **FLPA:** John Hawkins (br). **333 FLPA:** Michael Gore (ftr); S & D & K Maslowski (tr). **334 Corbis:** Roger Tidman (br). **FLPA:** (cr); Minden Pictures (bl); Geoff Moon (cra). **335 Ardea:** Alan Greensmith (cr). **Pete Morris:** (br). **Sumit K Sen:** (tc). **Greg & Yvonne Dean/WorldWildlifeImages.com:** (bl). **336 FLPA:** T S Zylva (tr). **Nigel Hicks:** (cla). **Ian Montgomery/Birdway.com.au:** (fcr). **Pete Morris:** (fclb). **Greg & Yvonne Dean/WorldWildlifeImages.com:** (crb) (bc). **337 FLPA:** Minden Pictures (tc). **David Plummer:** (fcr). **Andy & Gill Swash/WorldWildlifeImages.com:** (cla) (bl) (crb); John Dunning (bl). **338 Ardea:** John S. Dunning (cla); Pat Morris (tr). **Andy & Gill Swash/WorldWildlifeImages.com:** (cb). **Greg & Yvonne Dean/WorldWildlifeImages.com:** (br). **339 Ardea:** John Dunning (cla). **FLPA:** Frank W Lane (tr). **Ian Montgomery/Birdway.com.au:** (cb). **OSF:** Tui De Roy (clb). **340 FLPA:** R & M Van Nostrand (br). **Michael and Patricia Fogden:** Michael Fogden (tl). **Andy & Gill Swash/WorldWildlifeImages.com:** (tr) (bl). **341 Alamy Images:** Wendy Conway (cla). **FLPA:** Minden Pictures (tr). **justbirds.org:** (br). **Andy & Gill Swash/WorldWildlifeImages.com:** (clb). **342 Andy & Gill Swash/WorldWildlifeImages.com:** (ca) (bl) (br) (tr). **343 Joe Fuhrman:** (tl). **Andy & Gill Swash/WorldWildlifeImages.com:** (tr) (clb). **344–345 Cal Vornberger:** (c). **346 Dudley Edmonson:** (br). **Joe Fuhrman:** (tl) (clb). **George Reszeter:** (cra). **347 Andy & Gill Swash/WorldWildlifeImages.com:** (tl) (bl) (cra). **348 Barry Hughes:** (br). **justbirds.org:** (bl). **Andy & Gill Swash/WorldWildlifeImages.com:** (tl) (tr). **349 Dudley Edmonson:** (tr) (bl). **Goran Ekstrom:** (br). **350 Andy & Gill Swash/WorldWildlifeImages.com:** (bl). **Greg & Yvonne Dean/WorldWildlifeImages.com:** (crb) (bc). **351 Barry Hughes:** (tl) (cla). **Andy & Gill Swash/WorldWildlifeImages.com:** (tr). **Greg & Yvonne Dean/WorldWildlifeImages.com:** (bl) (crb). **352 Alamy Images:** Mike Lane (bl). **Joe Fuhrman:** (tl). **Vireo:** Doug Wechsler (cl) (cr). **Andy & Gill Swash/WorldWildlifeImages.com:** (br). **353 Alamy Images:** Robert Fried (bl). **Vireo:** Doug Wechsler (br) (tr). **Andy & Gill Swash/WorldWildlifeImages.com:** (cl). **354 Alamy Images:** Kevin Schafer (tr). **FLPA:** David Hosking (bc). **Ian Montgomery/Birdway.com.au:** (cr). **355 Alamy Images:** Juniors Bildarchiv (clb). **Hanne & Jens Eriksen:** (cra). **David Plummer:** (tl). **Andy & Gill Swash/WorldWildlifeImages.com:** (bl) (br) (crb). **356 Andy & Gill Swash/WorldWildlifeImages.com:** (bc) (cl) (cr) (cra) (tl). **357 David Plummer:** (br). **Andy & Gill Swash/WorldWildlifeImages.com:** (cla) (bl) (tr). **358 Alamy Images:** blickwinkel (c). **FLPA:** Michael Gore (bl); Minden Pictures (cr). **Ian Montgomery/Birdway.com.au:** (br). **Andy & Gill Swash/WorldWildlifeImages.com:** (tc). **359 Barry Hughes:**

(br). **Ian Montgomery/Birdway.com.au:** (tl) (bl) (cra). **Andy & Gill Swash/WorldWildlifeImages.com:** (cla). **Greg & Yvonne Dean/WorldWildlifeImages.com:** (bc). **360 A.N.T. Photo Library:** Keith Vagg (cl) (ca/Antwren). **Alamy Images:** Mike Lane (ca/Giant Antshrike). **FLPA:** Neil Bowman (bc). **Andy & Gill Swash/WorldWildlifeImages.com:** (cr). **361 Corbis:** Wolfgang Kaehler (c). **Andy & Gill Swash/WorldWildlifeImages.com:** (cla) (bc) (tc) (tr). **362 Ardea:** A.D. Trousson (clb). **Corbis:** Pam Gardner (cla). **FLPA:** Len Robinson (br). **Ian Montgomery/Birdway.com.au:** (tr). **naturepl.com:** Roger Powell (bl). **363 Roger & Liz Charlwood:** (tl). **Ian Montgomery/Birdway.com.au:** (tc) (bl) (crb). **364 Alamy Images:** Nic Cleave Photography (cra). **Ian Montgomery/Birdway.com.au:** (cl) (br). **365 Barry Hughes:** (cl) (tl). **Ian Montgomery/Birdway.com.au:** (cr) (bc) (bl) (br). **366 justbirds.org:** (bl). **Ian Montgomery/Birdway.com.au:** (cla) (br) (cr). **367 Ardea:** Don Hadden (clb). **Tom Tarrant:** (crb). **Andy & Gill Swash/WorldWildlifeImages.com:** (ca). **368 A.N.T. Photo Library:** Frank Park (tr). **Tomas Carlberg:** (bl). **Ian Montgomery/Birdway.com.au:** (cr). **369 Ardea:** Wilfred R. Taylor (tc). **Ian Montgomery/Birdway.com.au:** (tr) (bl) (br) (cb). **Tom Tarrant:** (cla). **370 A.N.T. Photo Library:** Cliff & Dawn Frith (bl). **Ian Montgomery/Birdway.com.au:** (tl) (crb). **Andy & Gill Swash/WorldWildlifeImages.com:** (tr). **371 A.N.T. Photo Library:** Cliff & Dawn Frith (tr). **Alamy Images:** Bruce Coleman Inc. (tl). **FLPA:** Gerry Ellis/Minden Pictures (cr). **Vireo:** W. Peckover (crb) (bl). **372 FLPA:** David Hosking (br); Minden Pictures (cl); Geoff Moon (tr). **373 FLPA:** Len Robinson (br). **Andy & Gill Swash/WorldWildlifeImages.com:** (cla). **Greg & Yvonne Dean/WorldWildlifeImages.com:** (tr). **374 Corbis:** FLPA/Gore, Michael (tc). **Andy & Gill Swash/WorldWildlifeImages.com:** (cl). **Greg & Yvonne Dean/WorldWildlifeImages.com:** (br). **375 Hanne & Jens Eriksen:** (cla) (br) (cra). **FLPA:** Michael Gore (tr). **Greg & Yvonne Dean/WorldWildlifeImages.com:** (bl). **376 A.N.T. Photo Library:** Cliff & Dawn Frith (cla); Ralph & Daphne Keller (tr). **Photoshot/NHPA:** Nick Garbutt (bl). **Greg & Yvonne Dean/WorldWildlifeImages.com:** (cr). **377 Photoshot/NHPA:** A.N.T Photo Library (c). **Tom Tarrant:** (bl) (br). **Greg & Yvonne Dean/WorldWildlifeImages.com:** (tl) (tr). **378 FLPA:** Neil Bowman (cla). **Sumit K Sen:** (br). **Vireo:** Vivak R. Sinha (clb). **Andy & Gill Swash/WorldWildlifeImages.com:** (tr). **379 Alamy Images:** Dave Watts (cl). **Ian Montgomery/Birdway.com.au:** (cra) (fcrb) (tc). **OSF:** Krupakar Senani (bl). **380 A.N.T. Photo Library:** Frank Park (bl). **justbirds.org:** (ca). **Ian Montgomery/Birdway.com.au:** (cla). **Sumit K Sen:** (tr). **Tom Tarrant:** (br). **381 A.N.T. Photo Library:** D. & M. Trounson (bl). **FLPA:** Len Robinson (cr). **Andy & Gill Swash/WorldWildlifeImages.com:** (tr) (crb). **382 Dudley Edmonson:** (bl). **Hanne & Jens Eriksen:** (tr). **Melvin Grey:** (br). **Barry Hughes:** (cb). **George Reszeter:** (ca). **383 Ron Austing:** (tc). **Dudley Edmonson:** (bl). **Joe Fuhrman:** (br). **Andy & Gill Swash/WorldWildlifeImages.com:** (cla). **384 Corbis:** Brendan Ryan; Gallo Images (tc). **Hanne & Jens Eriksen:** (cra) (cr). **Josef Hlasek:** Lubomir Hlasek (br). **Ian Montgomery/Birdway.com.au:** (cl). **385 A.N.T. Photo Library:** Cliff & Dawn Frith (bl). **Pete Morris:** (br). **Tom Tarrant:** (cra). **Andy & Gill Swash/WorldWildlifeImages.com:** (cla). **386 Alamy Images:** Genevieve Vallee (tr). **Ian Montgomery/Birdway.com.au:** (bl) (br). **Sumit K Sen:** (cla). **Andy & Gill Swash/WorldWildlifeImages.com:** (crb). **387 Alamy Images:** Hu Lan (tc). **Hanne & Jens Eriksen:** (bc). **OSF:** Densey Clyne (cra). **Sumit K Sen:** (clb) (br). **388 Alamy Images:** Douglas Peebles Photography (cla). **Ian Montgomery/Birdway.com.au:** (tr) (bl) (fcrb). **389 A.N.T. Photo Library:** Cyril Webster (clb). **Ian Montgomery/Birdway.com.au:** (tl) (bc) (cr). **390 Alamy Images:** blickwinkel (clb) (tr); Ashley Cooper (bc); Mike Lane (cla). **Jari Peltomäki/Birdfoto.fi:** (cr). **391 Markus Varesvuo/Birdfoto.fi:** (br). **Dudley Edmonson:** (cla) (fcr). **Joe Fuhrman:** (cra) (bl). **Nigel Hicks:** (tl). **392 Markus Varesvuo/Birdfoto.fi:** (br). **Melvin Grey:** (cl). **Mike Read:** (tr). **393 Alamy Images:** David Boag (br). **Markus Varesvuo/Birdfoto.fi:** (tr) (clb). **Joe Fuhrman:** (bl). **Barry Hughes:** (tl) (cra). **Arto Juvonen/Birdfot.fi:** (crb). **394 Alamy Images:** Juniors Bildarchiv (c). **Markus Varesvuo/Birdfoto.fi:** (bl). **Melvin Grey:** (tl). **Nigel Hicks:** (cr). **Andy & Gill Swash/WorldWildlifeImages.com:** (cra). **395 Barry Hughes:** (tr). **Ian Montgomery/Birdway.com.au:** (bl). **OSF:** Kathie Atkinson (cr). **Andy & Gill Swash/WorldWildlifeImages.com:** (br). **396 FLPA:** Minden Pictures (bc); Martin B Withers (tr). **397 Alamy Images:** blickwinkel (cr) (clb) (tr). **Corbis:** Pam Gardner/FLPA (cla); Michael S. Yamashita (crb). **FLPA:** Jurgen & Christine Sohns (br). **Greg & Yvonne Dean/WorldWildlifeImages.com:** (tl). **398 Roger & Liz Charlwood:** (br). **FLPA:** Len Robinson (tr). **Ian Montgomery/Birdway.com.au:** (cla) (bl) (crb). **399 Alamy Images:** Kevin Schafer (cra). **Markus Varesvuo/Birdfoto.fi:** (bl) (br). **Photoshot/NHPA:** Daniel Heuclin (cla). **400-401 Markus Varesvuo/Birdfoto.fi:** (c). **402 Markus Varesvuo/Birdfoto.fi:** (bl) (br). **Dudley Edmonson:** (c). **justbirds.org:** (tr). **403 Markus Varesvuo/Birdfoto.fi:** (tr). **Sujan Chatterjee:** (br). **Melvin Grey:** (cla). **Cal Vornberger:** (crb). **Greg & Yvonne Dean/WorldWildlifeImages.com:** (tl). **404 Alamy Images:** Worldwide Picture Library (cla). **Markus Varesvuo/Birdfoto.fi:** (cra) (crb). **Joe Fuhrman:** (br). **Arto Juvonen/Birdfot.fi:** (bl). **405 Alamy Images:** imagebroker (tr). **Jari Peltomäki/Birdfoto.fi:** (cra). **Barry Hughes:** (br). **Murray Lord:** (bl). **406 Dudley Edmonson:** (tr) (crb). **Joe Fuhrman:** (cl). **Andy & Gill Swash/WorldWildlifeImages.com:** (bl). **407 Jari Peltomäki/Birdfoto.fi:** (bl). **Markus Varesvuo/Birdfoto.fi:** (tr) (cr). **Barry Hughes:** (cl). **Mike Read:** (tl). **Andy & Gill Swash/WorldWildlifeImages.com:** (br). **408 Alamy Images:** FLPA (tr). **Jari Peltomäki/Birdfoto.fi:** (ca). **FLPA:** Minden Pictures (cla). **Barry Hughes:** (bl) (cr). **Andy & Gill Swash/WorldWildlifeImages.com:** (bc). **409 Alamy Images:** Clynt Garnham (bl). **Markus Varesvuo/Birdfoto.fi:** (cl) (crb). **Josef Hlasek:** Lubomir Hlasek (tl). **Barry Hughes:** (br). **Mike Read:** (cra). **410 Barry Hughes:** (cra). **Photolibrary:** Warwick Tarboton/Abpl (tr). **George Reszeter:** (bl). **Tom Tarrant:** (cla). **Andy & Gill Swash/WorldWildlifeImages.com:** (br). **411 Alamy Images:** mediacolor's (br). **FLPA:** Jurgen & Christine Sohns (cr). **Nigel Hicks:** (bc). **Josef Hlasek:** Lubomir Hlasek (tl). **Mike Read:** (fcrb). **Sumit K Sen:** (tr). **Greg & Yvonne Dean/WorldWildlifeImages.com:** (bl). **412 Hanne & Jens Eriksen:** (tl). **Nigel Hicks:** (cr). **Barry Hughes:** (bl). **Sumit K Sen:** (br). **413 Josef Hlasek:** (tl). **Ian Montgomery/Birdway.com.au:** (crb) (br). **Tomi Muukonen:** (cra). **Per Smitterberg:** (fcrb). **Andy & Gill Swash/WorldWildlifeImages.com:** (bl). **414 Markus Varesvuo/Birdfoto.fi:** (bl). **Barry Hughes:** (br). **Mike Read:** (tl). **Andy & Gill Swash/WorldWildlifeImages.com:** (tr). **415 Markus Varesvuo/Birdfoto.fi:** (br). **Hanne & Jens Eriksen:** (tr). **Barry Hughes:** (cr). **Tomi Muukonen:** (cl). **George Reszeter:** (cla). **416 Markus Varesvuo/Birdfoto.fi:** (tl) (bl). **Goran Ekstrom:** (br). **Pete Morris:** (cr/Ijima's). **Mike Read:** (tr). **417 Markus Varesvuo/Birdfoto.fi:** (cra). **Hanne & Jens Eriksen:** (bl). **Barry Hughes:** (tl). **Mike Read:** (cl) (br). **418 Alamy Images:** Dave and Sigrun Tollerton (tr). **Sumit K Sen:** (cla) (br). **419 FLPA:** John Holmes (crb). **Joe Fuhrman:** (tl). **Nigel Hicks:** (clb). **Sumit K Sen:** (cla) (bc). **Greg & Yvonne Dean/WorldWildlifeImages.com:** (cra). **420 Markus Varesvuo/Birdfoto.fi:** (c). **Nigel Hicks:** (tl) (bl) (tr). **justbirds.org:** (br). **421 Alamy Images:** Louise Heusinkveld (br); MM (fbr). **Hanne & Jens Eriksen:** (tc). **Nigel Hicks:** (cra). **Andy & Gill Swash/WorldWildlifeImages.com:** (cla). **422 Alamy Images:** Arco Images (clb); SPP Images (fcra). **Nigel Hicks:** (br). **Ian Montgomery/Birdway.com.au:** (tl). **423 Markus Varesvuo/Birdfoto.fi:** (bl). **Joe Fuhrman:** (cra). **Arto Juvonen/Birdfot.fi:** (tc). **424 Alamy Images:** Wendy Conway (tr). **Joe Fuhrman:** (br). **Barry Hughes:** (bl). **Arto Juvonen/Birdfot.fi:** (ca). **425 Markus Varesvuo/Birdfoto.fi:** (clb). **Dudley Edmonson:** (cla). **Hanne & Jens Eriksen:** (bl). **Joe Fuhrman:** (tl) (cra). **Mike Read:** (fcrb). **Cal Vornberger:** (tr). **Andy & Gill Swash/WorldWildlifeImages.com:** (bc). **426 FLPA:** S & D & K Maslowski (cla). **Photolibrary:** Andrew Anderson (bl). **Mike Read:** (br). **Cal Vornberger:** (tr). **427 Markus Varesvuo/Birdfoto.fi:** (bc). **FLPA:** Bill Baston (bl); Roger Tidman (tr). **Joe Fuhrman:** (tl). **Cal Vornberger:** (br). **428 Ardea:** Jim Zipp (cr). **FLPA:** Minden Pictures (tr). **Joe Fuhrman:** (br). **Cal Vornberger:** (cl). **429 Joe Fuhrman:** (cl). **Mike Read:** (br). **Cal Vornberger:** (tr). **Peter S Weber:** (cb). **430 Alamy Images:** Elvele Images (crb). **Markus Varesvuo/Birdfoto.fi:** (c). **Nigel Hicks:** (br). **431 Hanne & Jens Eriksen:** (fclb). **Nigel Hicks:** (tl) (bl) (tr). **Barry Hughes:** (br). **432 Markus Varesvuo/Birdfoto.fi:** (cl). **Barry Hughes:** (br). **432-433 Neil Fletcher:** (tc). **433 Alamy Images:** Danita Delimont (br). **Hanne & Jens Eriksen:** (bl). **Barry Hughes:** (crb). **Andy & Gill Swash/WorldWildlifeImages.com:** (tr). **434-435 naturepl.com:** John Waters (c). **436 Jari Peltomäki/Birdfoto.fi:** (bc). **Josef Hlasek:** (cra). **Cal Vornberger:** (tr) (cl). **437 Alamy Images:** Worldwide Picture Library (cra). **Dudley Edmonson:** (tl). **Joe Fuhrman:** (tr) (br). **Sumit K Sen:** (cl). **Greg & Yvonne Dean/WorldWildlifeImages.com:** (bc). **438 Lang Elliot:** (tl). **Neil Fletcher:** (c). **Photolibrary:** Oxford Scientific (crb). **Mike Read:** (tc) (bl) (br). **439 Markus Varesvuo/Birdfoto.fi:** (ca). **Hanne & Jens Eriksen:** (br). **Greg & Yvonne Dean/WorldWildlifeImages.com:** (bl). **440 Alamy Images:** FLPA (tr). **FLPA:** David Hosking (crb). **Nigel Hicks:** (ca). **Tomi Muukonen:** (cb). **Mike Read:** (tl). **441 Alamy Images:** Arco Images (br). **FLPA:** Jeremy Early (tr). **Huang How-Tang:** (bl). **Mike Read:** (ca). **442 Jari Peltomäki/Birdfoto.fi:** (cla). **Hanne & Jens Eriksen:** (tr) (clb). **Sumit K Sen:** (bc). **Greg & Yvonne Dean/WorldWildlifeImages.com:** (crb). **443 Alamy Images:** Arco Images (clb). **Markus Varesvuo/Birdfoto.fi:** (tl). **Melvin Grey:** (cra). **Nigel Hicks:** (br). **Sumit K Sen:** (bl). **444 Markus Varesvuo/Birdfoto.fi:** (clb). **Hanne & Jens Eriksen:** (br). **Nigel Hicks:** (tl). **Mike Read:** (tc) (crb). **Sumit K Sen:** (bl). **445 Jari Peltomäki/Birdfoto.fi:** (ca). **Markus Varesvuo/Birdfoto.fi:** (bl). **Nigel Hicks:** (bc). **Barry Hughes:** (tl). **Tomi Muukonen:** (cra). **Sumit K Sen:** (br). **446-447 Tomi Muukonen:** (c). **448 Alamy Images:** Arco Images (br). **Corbis:** David Hosking/FLPA (clb). **Joe Fuhrman:** (cra). **Photolibrary:** (bl); Oxford Scientific (cla). **Mike Read:** (tr). **449 FLPA:** John Holmes (bl) (tr). **Ian Montgomery/Birdway.com.au:** (cr) (br). **450 Alamy Images:** Hornbil Images (tr). **Hanne & Jens Eriksen:** (br). **justbirds.org:** (cl). **Sumit K Sen:** (cra) (cla/Malachite). **451 Hanne & Jens Eriksen:** (tl) (br). **Ian Montgomery/Birdway.com.au:** (tr). **Sumit K Sen:** (bc). **452 Alamy Images:** Arco Images (bl); John Henwood (cra). **Barry Hughes:** (tr). **Per Smitterberg:** (crb). **453 Markus Varesvuo/Birdfoto.fi:** (tr) (cla). **Barry Hughes:** (bc). **Mike Read:** (clb). **454 Alamy Images:** blickwinkel (cra); Jason Gallier (ca). **Barry Hughes:** (bl) (br). **naturepl.com:** Dietmar Nill (fcla). **Andy & Gill Swash/WorldWildlifeImages.com:** (clb). **455 Hanne & Jens Eriksen:** (c). **Barry Hughes:** (br). **justbirds.org:** (tr). **Mike Read:** (cl). **Andy & Gill Swash/WorldWildlifeImages.com:** (bc). **456-457 FLPA:** Jim Brandenburg/Minden Pictures (c). **458 DK Images:** Cyril Laubscher (cb). **FLPA:** Michael Gore (tr). **Still Pictures:** H. Schmidbauer (ca). **Andy & Gill Swash/WorldWildlifeImages.com:** (bl) (br). **459 Alamy Images:** Arco Images (br); David Hosking (tr). **Melvin Grey:** (clb). **Barry Hughes:** (cra). **David Smallshire:** (tl). **Andy & Gill Swash/WorldWildlifeImages.com:** (crb). **460 Ian Montgomery/Birdway.com.au:** (tl) (bl) (br) (tr). **461 Alamy Images:** mediacolor's (cl). **Melvin Grey:** (c). **Ian Montgomery/Birdway.com.au:** (br). **462 FLPA:** Jurgen & Christine Sohns (cla). **Melvin Grey:** (bl). **Barry Hughes:** (tr). **Tomi Muukonen:** (crb). **463 Hanne & Jens Eriksen:** (bc). **Melvin Grey:** (tl). **Barry Hughes:** (cra) (bl) (tr). **Mike Read:** (clb). **George Reszeter:** (cr). **464 Alamy Images:** Juniors Bildarchiv (crb). **FLPA:** John Hawkins (cla). **Getty Images:** Orion Press/Stone (cra). **Pete Morris:** (tr). **465 Markus Varesvuo/Birdfoto.fi:** (tl). **Jari Peltomäki/Birdfoto.fi:** (tc) (bl). **Dudley Edmonson:** (c). **Joe Fuhrman:** (cra). **Melvin Grey:** (br). **466 Jari Peltomäki/Birdfoto.fi:** (tl). **Hanne & Jens Eriksen:** (cra) (crb). **Kogi Tagi:** (br). **Andy & Gill Swash/WorldWildlifeImages.com:** (bl). **467 Markus Varesvuo/Birdfoto.fi:** (cra) (bc). **Corbis:** Tim Zurowski (tr). **Dudley Edmonson:** (tl). **Arto Juvonen/Birdfot.fi:** (clb). **468 Dudley Edmonson:** (ca). **FLPA:** Ron Austing (crb). **Nigel Hicks:** (tl). **Cal Vornberger:** (bl). **469 Alamy Images:** Ambient Images Inc. (crb). **Dudley Edmonson:** (tr) (br). **Joe Fuhrman:** (tl) (bl) (cl). **470 Dudley Edmonson:** (cla) (bl) (tr). **Cal Vornberger:** (tl). **Peter S Weber:** (br). **471 FLPA:** Minden Pictures (tr); Jurgen & Christine Sohns (bc). **Joe Fuhrman:** (cl). **Ian Montgomery/Birdway.com.au:** (br). **Peter S Weber:** (tl). **472 Alamy Images:** Rick & Nora Bowers (br). **Joe Fuhrman:** (tr) (bl) (cr). **Cal Vornberger:** (fcl) (tl). **473 Dudley Edmonson:** (fcla) (fcr) (tr). **Joe Fuhrman:** (br). **Ian Montgomery/Birdway.com.au:** (bl). **474 Alamy Images:** blickwinkel (cb). **FLPA:** Yuri Artukhin (cr). **Giovanni Visetti:** (tr). **475 Jari Peltomäki/Birdfoto.fi:** (tc) (bc). **Dudley Edmonson:** (cra) (br). **Hanne & Jens Eriksen:** (tl). **Tomi Muukonen:** (bl). **476 Dudley Edmonson:** (tl) (cr) (crb). **Joe Fuhrman:** (br). **Cal Vornberger:** (bl). **477 Joe Fuhrman:** (tl) (bl) (br) (tr). **Andy & Gill Swash/WorldWildlifeImages.com:** (cl). **478 Joe Fuhrman:** (tr). **David Plummer:** (br). **Andy & Gill Swash/WorldWildlifeImages.com:** (tl) (cla) (clb). **478-479 naturepl.com:** Tom Vezo (c). **480 FLPA:** Minden Pictures (bl). **481 Alamy Images:** Mike Lane (crb). **Photolibrary:** Patricio Robles Gil (cra) (fcla/winter). **Cal Vornberger:** (fcla/summer). **Andy & Gill Swash/WorldWildlifeImages.com:** (bl). **482 Joe Fuhrman:** (br). **Photoshot/NHPA:** Roger Tidman (tl). **Andy & Gill Swash/WorldWildlifeImages.com:** (cla) (clb) (cr) (tr). **483 Dudley Edmonson:** (tr). **Barry Hughes:** (tl). **David Plummer:** (br). **Andy & Gill Swash/WorldWildlifeImages.com:** (cla). **Greg & Yvonne Dean/WorldWildlifeImages.com:** (bl). **484 Alamy Images:** PhotoStockFile (tr); Don Vail (clb). **Dudley Edmonson:** (cla) (br). **485 Dudley Edmonson:** (cla). **Joe Fuhrman:** (cra) (bl) (br). **Peter S Weber:** (tc). **486-487 Getty Images:** Joseph Devenney/Photographer's Choice (c). **488-489 naturepl.com:** Solvin Zankl (c)

Jacket images: Front: **Werner Bollmann**. Back: **Alamy Images**: Kevin Schafer ftr; **Jari Peltomäki/Birdfoto.fi**: b; **Getty Images**: Leonardo Papini ftl; **naturepl.com**: Hanne Jens Eriksen tl; **RSPCA Photolibrary**: John Downer tr. Spine: **Werner Bollmann**: b, t; Front Endpapers: **naturepl.com**: Bernard Castelein; Back Endpapers: **naturepl.com** Bernard Castelein